# BEST 282
# BUSINESS SCHOOLS

# BEST 282 BUSINESS SCHOOLS

## 2007 EDITION

## Nedda Gilbert
## and the Staff
## of The Princeton Review

*Random House, Inc.*
New York
*www.PrincetonReview.com*

The Princeton Review, Inc.
2315 Broadway
New York, NY   10024
E-mail: bookeditor@review.com

ISBN: 0-375-76564-6

Editorial Director: Robert Franek
Production Editor: Christine LaRubio
Production Manager: Scott Harris
Account Manager: David Soto
Editors: Michael Palumbo, Adrinda Kelly

Manufactured in the United States of America.

9  8  7  6  5  4  3  2  1

2007 Edition

# ACKNOWLEDGMENTS

This book absolutely would not have been possible without the help of my husband, Paul. With each edition of this guide, his insights and support have been invaluable—this book continues to be as much his as it is mine. That said, I also need to thank my eleven-year-old daughter, Kaela, and her seven-year-old sister, Lexi, for enduring all the time I have spent immersed in this project.

A big thanks goes to Tom Meltzer and Anna Weinberg for their smart and savvy profile writing. The following people were also instrumental in the completion of this book: Scott Harris, Christine LaRubio, Michael Palumbo, Adrinda Kelly, David Soto, Ben Zelevansky, Steven Aglione, Sarah Kruchko, and Jeff Adams for putting all the pieces together; the sales staff at The Princeton Review, Josh Escott; Robert Franek and Young Shin, as well as Alicia Ernst and John Katzman, for giving me the chance to write this book; and to the folks at Random House, who helped this project reach fruition.

Thanks go to Kristin Hansen (Tuck '01) and Matt Camp (Tuck '02), and to Ramona Payne and all the folks at The Diversity Pipeline Alliance. I am also grateful for the unique insights provided by Cathy Crane-Moley, Stanford Graduate School of Business, Class of '92; Patricia Melnikoff and Chiara Perry, Harvard Business School, Class of '92; Caroline Grossman, University of Chicago Graduate School of Business, Class of '03; Sara Weiss, MIT Sloan School of Management, Class of '04; and Stephen Hazelton, MIT Sloan School of Management, Class of '05. Thanks are also due to the business school folks who went far out of their way to provide essential information. They continue to make this book relevant and vital.

Linda Baldwin, Director of Admissions, The Anderson School, UCLA

Derek Bolton, Assistant Dean and Director of Admissions, Stanford University School of Business

Eileen Chang, former Associate Director of Admissions, Harvard Business School

Allan Friedman, Director of Communications and Public Relations, University of Chicago

Wendy Hansen, Associate Director of Admissions, Stanford Business School

Stacey Kole, Deputy Dean for the full-time MBA Program and clinical professor of Economics, University of Chicago Graduate School of Business

Steven Lubrano, Assistant Dean and Director of the MBA Program, Tuck School of Business

Rose Martinelli, former Director of Admissions and Financial Aid, The Wharton School MBA Program

Jon McLaughlin, Assistant MBA Admissions Director, Sloan School of Management, MIT

Julia Min, Executive Director of MBA Admissions, UC—Berkeley, Haas School of Business

Jeanne Wilt, Assistant Dean of Admissions and Career Development, Michigan

Linda Meehan, Assistant Dean for Admissions, Columbia University

# CONTENTS

# INTRODUCTION

## A RETURN TO OUR ROOTS

Over the past 13 years, The Princeton Review has annually published a guide to business schools. For the early editions of the guide, we collected opinion surveys from thousands of students at a select group of graduate business schools as well as school statistics from school administrators that include enrollment and demographic figures, tuition, and the average GMAT scores of entering students. We used the students' opinions to craft descriptive narratives of the schools they attended and reported the statistics in the sidebars of those narrative profiles.

For the 2001–2004 editions of this guide, we discontinued collecting opinion surveys from students and writing narrative descriptions of the schools; instead we focused solely on collecting and reporting school statistics. While we were able to report statistics for many more business schools in the new format (the last [2000] edition of the guide with narrative descriptions profiled only 80 schools, and the first edition of the statistics-only guide profiled 372 schools), we learned over the next few years that readers are interested in more than just school-reported statistics. They want to read what the experts—current graduate business school students—have to say about the experiences of today's graduate business student. They want from-the-horse's-mouth accounts of what's great (*and* what's not) at each school.

So in 2005 we decided to reintroduce the student survey-driven descriptive narrative, offering students a more intimate look at the inner workings of each school, and we've continued with this approach ever since.

We also brought back several top 10 lists that rank the profiled schools according to various metrics (more on the rankings later). You'll find these rankings on page 67.

Taken together, we believe that these candid student opinions, school statistics, and rankings provide a unique and helpful resource to help you decide what business schools to apply to. But let us stress that we hope that this book will not be the *only* resource you turn to when making this expensive (both in terms of time and treasure) decision to enter a graduate business program. Do additional research on the Internet and in newspapers, magazines, and other periodicals. Talk to admissions officers and current students at the programs that interest you. If at all possible, visit the campuses you are seriously considering. But treat the advice of all these resources (including ours) as you would treat advice from anyone regarding any situation: as input that reflects the values and opinions of others as you *form your own opinion*.

## TWO TYPES OF ENTRIES

For each of the 451 business programs in this book, you will find one of two possible types of entries: a two-page profile with lots of descriptive text and statistics, or a straight statistical listing. Our descriptive profiles are driven primarily by 1) comments business students provide in response to open-ended questions on our student survey, and 2) our own statistical analysis of student responses to the many multiple-choice questions on the survey. While many business students complete a survey unsolicited by us at http://survey.review.com, in the vast majority of cases we rely on business school administrators to get the word out about our survey to their students. In the ideal scenario, the business school administration sends a Princeton Review-authored e-mail to all business students with an embedded link to our survey website (again, http://survey.review.com). If for some reason there are restrictions that prevent the administration from contacting the entire graduate business school student body on behalf of an outside party, they often help us find other ways to notify students of the fact that we are seeking their opinions, such as advertising in business student publications or posting on business student community websites. In almost all cases, when the administration is cooperative, we are able to collect opinions from a sufficient number of students to produce an accurate descriptive profile and ratings of its business school.

There is a group of business school administrators, however, that doesn't agree with us that current business school student opinions presented in descriptive profile and rankings formats are useful to prospective business school students. Administrators at the many AACSB-accredited business schools not appearing with two-page descriptive profiles are a part of this group. They either ignored our multiple attempts to contact them in order to request their assistance in notifying their students about our survey, or they simply refused to work with us at all. And while we would like to be able to write a descriptive profile each of these many schools anyway, we won't do so with minimal business student opinion.

So if you are a prospective business school student and would like to read current business student opinion about schools that do not appear with a two-page descriptive profile, contact the schools and communicate this desire to them. (We include contact information in each of the business school data listings.) If you are a current business student at one of the many AACSB-accredited business schools without a two-page descriptive profile, please don't send us angry letters; instead, go to http://survey.review.com, complete a survey about your school, and tell all of your fellow students to do the same.

You will find statistics for business schools whose administrators were willing to report their school statistics to us but unwilling to allow us to survey their students under the school's name in the section of the book entitled "Business School Data Listings."

One more thing to note about the different entries: The majority of our various rankings lists are based wholly or partly on student feedback to our survey. Only one top ten ranking, The Toughest to Get Into, is based on school-reported statistics alone. So while *any* of the 451 programs listed in the book may appear on that list, *only those schools with two-page descriptive profiles will appear on all other rankings lists.*

---

## BUT SOME THINGS NEVER CHANGE

Admission to the business school of your choice, especially if your choice is among the most selective programs, will require your absolute best shot. One way to improve your chances is to make sure you apply to schools that are a good fit—and the comments provided by students in our descriptive profiles will provide more insight into the personality of each school than does its glossy view book.

In addition, you'll find plenty of useful information in Part I of this book on how to get in to business school and what to expect once you arrive. You'll find out what criteria are used to evaluate applicants and who decides your fate. You will also hear directly from admissions officers on what dooms an application and how to ace the interview. We've even interviewed deans at several of the top schools to share with you their take on recent events, including trends in business, b-school applications, recruitment, and placement.

Again, it is our hope that you will consult our profiles as a resource when choosing a list of schools that suit your academic and social needs, and that our advice is helpful to you during the application process. Good luck!

# HOW WE PRODUCE THIS BOOK

In August 1999, we published *The Best 80 Business Schools, 2000 Edition*. By the time the 2001 edition of the guide was published, we had shifted our focus from student opinion-driven profiles of a select number of schools to more data-driven profiles of every graduate business school accredited by the AACSB. Although we continue to present readers with data from 451 accredited graduate b-school programs, we have reintroduced the student survey-based descriptive profile. In order to clarify our position, intent, and methodology, we've created a series of questions and answers regarding the collection of data and the production of our descriptive profiles.

**How do we choose which b-schools to survey and profile? And why do some competitive schools have only a data listing?**

Any business school that is AACSB-accredited and offers a Master of Business Administration degree may have a data listing included in the book, as long as that school provides us with a sufficient amount of school-specific data. In addition, this year we offered each of those accredited schools in which the primary language of instruction is English an opportunity to assist us in collecting online business student surveys.

Some schools were unable to solicit surveys from their students via e-mail due to restrictive privacy policies; others simply chose not to participate. Schools that declined to work with us to survey their students remain in the book, although they do not have a descriptive profile. A school with only a data listing does not suggest that the school is less competitive or compelling; we only separated these profile types into two sections for easier reference. If you're not sure where to find information on a school in which you're interested, you can refer to our alphabetical b-school listing in the back of the book.

There is no fee to be included in this book. If you're an administrator at an accredited business school and would like to have your school included, please send an e-mail to surveysupport@review.com.

**What's the AACSB, and by what standards are schools accredited?**

The AACSB stands for the Association to Advance Collegiate Schools of Business. In April 2003, the AACSB made some significant changes to its standards for accreditation. In fact, the actual number of standards went from 41 to 21. Some of the changes in accreditation included a shift from requiring a certain number of full-time faculty members with doctorates to a focus on teacher participation. Schools may employ more part-time faculty members if they are actively involved in the students' business education. The onus of both the development of a unique curriculum and the evaluation of the success of that curriculum will fall on each b-school, and schools will be reviewed by the association every five years instead of every ten. As a result of the changes in accreditation standards, a number of schools have been newly accredited or reaccredited.

**How were the student surveys collected?**

Back in Fall 2005, we contacted admissions officers at all accredited graduate b-schools and requested that they help us survey their students by distributing our Princeton Review-authored survey message to the student body via e-mail. The survey message explained the purpose of the survey and contained a link to our online business student survey. We had a phenomenal response from students—at least ten percent of full-time students responded at almost all institutions we surveyed; at many schools, we scored responses from as many as one-third or one-half of the student body—and nearly all students in a few cases.

The surveys are made up of 79 multiple-choice questions and 7 free-response questions, covering 5 sections: About Yourself, Students, Academics, Careers, and Quality of Life. Students may complete the secure online survey at any time and may save their survey responses, returning later, until the survey is complete and ready for submission. Students sign in to the online survey using their school-issued .edu e-mail address to ensure that their response is attributed to the correct school, and the respondent certifies before submission that he or she is indeed a current student enrolled in said program. In addition, an automated message is sent to this address once the student has submitted the survey, and they must click on a link in the e-mail message in order to validate their survey. We also offered a paper version of the survey to a few schools that were unable to e-mail their students regarding our online survey.

We use the resulting responses to craft descriptive profiles that are representative of the respondents' feelings toward the b-school they attend. Although well-written and/or humorous comments are especially appreciated, they would never be used unless they best stated what numerous students have told us.

Please note that several of the Southern schools featured in this book were affected by hurricanes during the past year. Loyola University of New Orleans, Tulane University, and the University of New Orleans were closed for either all or part of the fall 2005 semester. We did not resurvey or update the data listings for these schools during our most recent campaign, but each will be resurveyed in the upcoming year for the 2008 edition of the book. We advise prospective business school students considering schools in the South, particularly those in Louisiana and Eastern Texas, to contact each school regarding any changes in the business school experience that may have occurred as a result of the hurricanes.

### What about the ranking lists and ratings?

When we decided to bring the student opinion-driven resources back into the fold, we updated our online survey and reconsidered all ranking lists. You will find that only a few of the rankings in this year's book resemble our b-school rankings of yesteryear. We've done our best to include only those topics most vital to success in business school, and we have added a few brand new lists that you will find timely and relevant.

We offer several ranking lists on a variety of considerations, from academic experience to career expectations, to the atmosphere for women and minority students. It must be noted, however, that none of these lists purport to rank the business schools by their overall quality. Nor should any combination of the categories we've chosen be construed as representing the raw ingredients for such a ranking. We have made no attempt to gauge the "prestige" of these schools, and we wonder whether we could accurately do so even if we tried. What we have done, however, is presented a number of lists using information from two very large databases—one of statistical information collected from business schools and another of subjective data gathered via our survey of 11,000 business students at 282 AACSB-accredited business schools. We do believe that there is a right business school for you, and that our rankings, when used in conjunction with our profile of each school, will help you select the best schools to apply to.

Last year we added five ratings to the book: Admissions Selectivity, Academic Experience, Career, Professors Interesting, and Professors Accessible. The current edition will continue to incorporate these ratings, which are based on student survey responses and/or institutionally reported data. An Admissions Selectivity Rating has been assigned to each of the accredited institutions included herewith, but the other four ratings are assigned only to those schools that have a descriptive profile in the book; therefore, these four ratings should only be used to compare the institutions surveyed within this edition of the book. (We explain what factors are considered in each rating in the following section.)

### What do the schools have to say about all this?

Our contact at each school is kept abreast of the profile's status throughout the production process. After establishing a contact through whom we are able to reach online student respondents, we get to work writing our profiles and crunching the data. Once this information has been poured into profile pages, we send a copy of the school's profile to our contact via e-mail and "snail mail." We request that the administrator review the data and comments included in the profile, and we invite their corrections to any inaccurate data, or text that may be misrepresentative of overall student opinion. With their suggestions in hand, we revisit survey responses and investigate any such claims of inaccuracy.

We are aware that a general distaste for rankings permeates the business school community, and that top schools have recently backed down from providing the data necessary for such calculations. We agree that overall rankings that purport to decide the "best" overall school are not so helpful to students, and that they may be tainted by the agendas of school administrators hoping to advance their schools' reputations, without taking the necessary measures to actually improve the quality of the school. This is why the meat of our book is the schools' descriptive profiles, which are meant to showcase each school's unique personality. The ranking lists are simply used as reference tools for students looking for a particular attribute in a prospective b-school. We don't claim to be the final word on what school has the best MBA program in the country—that's nearly impossible to determine. We simply relay the messages that the students at each school are sending us, and we are clear about how our rankings are determined.

# HOW THIS BOOK IS ORGANIZED

This book is packed with information about business schools, and we want to make sure you know how to find what you're looking for. So here's a breakdown of how this book is organized.

Part I is comprised of several chapters that give you an idea of what to expect at business school and tell you how to put together a winning application.

Part II has our b-school ranking lists. Of the 12 lists, 7 are based entirely on student survey responses; 1 is based solely on institutionally-reported data; and 4 are based on a combination of survey responses and statistical information. Along with each list, you will find information about which survey questions or statistical factors were used to calculate the rankings.

Part III contains profiles of all AACSB-accredited graduate schools with MBA programs divided into two sections: those with descriptive profiles based on student surveys, and those with only a statistical listing.

Please see the sample descriptive profile below

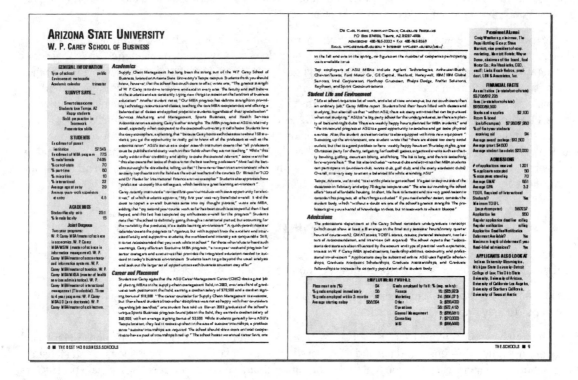

Each two-page spread is made up of eight major components. At the top of each page, you'll find the name of the business school, along with the name of an admissions contact and his or her address, phone number, fax number, if applicable, and e-mail address. This section also includes the b-school's website address. There are two sidebars (the narrow columns on the outer edge of each page) that contain information reported by the schools through the Business Data Set (BDS) and some student survey data as well. The Survey Says information reflects aspects of the school about which students feel the strongest; there are nine different possible results. We also offer an Employment Profile for each school, which is made up of statistical information from the BDS. The main body of the profile contains descriptive text discussing Academics, Placement and Recruiting, Student/Campus Life, and Admissions. Each description is based on student survey responses and may call upon statistical data where necessary.

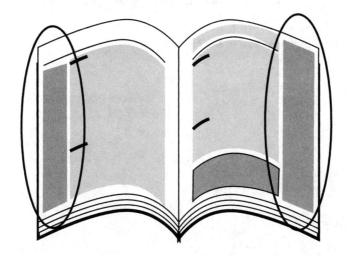

All information in the sidebars falls under the following categories: General Information, Academics, Financial Facts, and Admissions. Please note that not every category will appear for every school; in some cases the information is not reported or not applicable. These are the same data fields that are reported for those schools listed in Part III-B: Business School Data Listings, save for 4 of the 5 ratings, which appear only in the descriptive profiles.

Here is what each sidebar heading tells you.

## General Information

### Type of school

Public or private school

### Affiliation

Any religious order with which the school is affiliated

### Environment

Whether the campus is located in a metropolis, city, town, village, or rural setting

### Academic Calendar

Whether the school schedule runs according to trimesters, semesters, quarters, or another calendar type like a 4-1-4 (4 month semester - 1 month interim term - 4 month semester)

## Survey Says

Survey Says gives you an at-a-glance look at what students are most in agreement about at their school. You'll find up to six results per school. Three will reflect the top three subject areas as indicated by responses to the following question:

**How well has your school prepared you in the following areas:**

Marketing

Finance

Accounting

General management

Operations

Teamwork

Communication/Interpersonal skills

Presentation skills

Quantitative skills

Computer skills

Doing business in a global economy

Entrepreneurial studies

In addition, Survey Says may include (up to) three things from the following list that students were most in agreement about:

- Students like Hometown, State. Based on level of agreement with the statement, "I like the town where my school is located."

- Friendly students. Based on level of agreement with the statement, "Your business school classmates are friendly."

- Good social scene. Based on level of agreement with the statement, "Your business school classmates have active social lives."

- Good peer network. Based on level of agreement with the statement, "Your business school classmates are the type of people you want to network with after graduation."

- Cutting-edge classes. Based on responses to the question, "How well has your school integrated new business trends and practices into course offerings?"

- Helpful alumni. Based on responses to the question, "How helpful have alumni been in assisting you in your job search?"

- Happy students. Based on level of agreement with the statement, "Overall, I am happy here."

- Smart classrooms. Based on level of agreement with the statement, "Classroom facilities are equipped with computer/multimedia resources."

# Students

## Enrollment of parent institution

Total number of undergraduate and graduate students enrolled in parent institution program

## Enrollment of MBA program

Total number of students enrolled in MBA programs at the business school, including both full- and part-time programs

## "% male/female" through "% international"

Items based on demographic information about full-time b-school students as reported by the schools

## Average age at entry

The average age of incoming first-year MBA students

## Average years work experience at entry

The average years of work experience for incoming first-year MBA students

# Academics

## Academic Experience Rating

This rating measures the quality of the learning environment. Each school is given a score between 60 and 99. Factors taken into consideration include GMAT scores and undergraduate grades of enrolled students; percent accepted; percent enrolled; student/faculty ratio; and student survey questions pertaining to faculty, fellow students, and realization of academic expectations. This rating is intended to be used only to compare those schools within this edition of the book whose students completed our business student survey.

Please note that if a 60* Academic Experience Rating appears for any school, it means that the school didn't report all the rating's underlying data points by our deadline, so we were unable to calculate an accurate rating. In such cases, the reader is advised to follow up with the school about specific measures this rating takes into account.

Please also note that many foreign institutions use a grading system that is different from the standard U.S. GPA; as a result, we approximated their Admissions Selectivity and Academic Ratings, indicating this with a † following the rating.

## Student/Faculty Ratio

The ratio of full-time graduate instructional faculty members to all enrolled MBA students

## Professors Interesting Rating

Based on the answers given by students to the survey question, "Overall, how good are your professors as teachers?" Ratings fall between 60 and 99. This rating is intended to be used to compare those schools within this edition of the book whose students completed our business student survey.

## Professors Accessible Rating

Based on the answers given by students to the survey question, "How accessible are your professors outside of the classroom?" Ratings fall between 60 and 99. This rating is intended to be used to compare those schools within this edition of the book whose students completed our business student survey.

## % female faculty

Percent of graduate business faculty in the 2005–2006 academic year who were women

## % minority faculty

Percent of graduate business faculty in the 2005–2006 academic year who were members of minority groups

## Joint Degrees

A list of joint degrees offered by the business school. See Decoding Degrees on page 519 for the full name of each degree.

## Prominent Alumni

School administrators may submit the name, title, and company of up to five prominent alumni.

## Financial Facts

Please note that we rely on foreign institutions to convert financial figures into U.S. dollars. Please check with any foreign schools you are considering for up-to-date figures and conversion rates.

## "Tuition (in-state/out-of-state)" and "Fees (in-state/out-of-state)"

In-state and out-of-state tuition and fees per academic year. At state-supported public schools, in-state tuition and fees are likely to be significantly lower than out-of-state expenses.

## Books and supplies

Estimated cost of books and supplies for one academic year

## Room and board

Cost of room and board on campus per academic year, and estimate of off-campus living expenses for this time period

## "% of students receiving aid" through "% of students receiving grants"

Percent of students receiving aid, then specifically those receiving grants and loans. These numbers reflect the percentage of all enrolled MBA students that receive financial aid, regardless of whether or not they applied for financial aid or for specific aid types. Likewise, the second figure, "% of first year students receiving aid" takes into account all first-year MBA students, regardless of whether they applied for financial aid or specific aid types.

## Average award package

For students who received financial aid, this is the average award amount.

## Average grant

For students who received grants, this is the average amount of grant money awarded.

## Average student loan debt

The average dollar amount of outstanding educational MBA loans per graduate (class of 2004) at the time of graduation

# Admissions

## Admissions Selectivity Rating

This rating measures the competitiveness of the school's admissions. Factors taken into consideration include the average GMAT score and undergraduate GPA of the first-year class, the percent of students accepted, and the percent of applicants who are accepted and ultimately enroll. No student survey data is used in this calculation. Ratings fall between 60 and 99. This rating is intended to be used to compare all schools within this edition of the book, regardless of whether their students completed our business student survey.

Please note that if a 60* Admissions Selectivity Rating appears for any school, it means that the school did not report all of the rating's underlying data points by our deadline, so we were unable to calculate an accurate rating. In such cases, the reader is advised to follow up with the school about specific measures this rating takes into account.

Please also note that many foreign institutions use a grading system that is different from the standard U.S. GPA; as a result, we approximated their Admissions Selectivity and Academic Ratings, indicating this with a † next to the rating.

## # of applications received

The total number of applications received for any and all MBA programs at the school

## % applicants accepted

The percentage of applicants to which the school offered admission

## % acceptees attending

Of those accepted students, the percentage of those who enrolled

## Average GMAT

The average GMAT score for the first-year class

## Average GPA

The average undergraduate GPA of the first year class, reported on a 4-point scale

## TOEFL required of international applicants?

For those international students interested in applying, the b-school reports whether the Test of English as a Foreign Language (TOEFL) is required.

## Minimum TOEFL (paper/computer)

The minimum TOEFL score necessary for consideration. We list acceptable scores for both the paper and computer versions of the test.

## Application fee

The amount it costs to file an application with the school

**International Application Fee**

The amount it costs an international student to file an application with the school.

**"Regular application deadline" and "Regular notification"**

This regular application deadline reflects the date by which all materials must be postmarked; the notification date tells you when you can expect to hear back.

**"Early decision program?" and "ED deadline/notification"**

If a school offers an early decision option, we'll tell you when early decision apps are due to be postmarked, and when you'll be notified of the school's decision.

**"Deferment available?" and "Maximum length of deferment"**

Some schools allow accepted students to defer enrollment for a year or more, while others require students who postpone attendance to reapply.

**Transfer students accepted?**

Whether or not students are accepted from other MBA programs

**Transfer Application Policy**

Lets you know how transfer applications are reviewed and how many credits will be allowed to transfer from another program.

**Non-fall admissions?**

Some business schools may allow students to matriculate at the beginning of each semester, while for others, the invitation to attend stipulates that fall attendance is mandatory.

**Need-blind admissions?**

Whether or not the school considers applications without regard to the candidate's financial need

**Applicants also look at**

The school reports that students applying to their school are also known to apply to a short list of other schools.

## EMPLOYMENT PROFILE

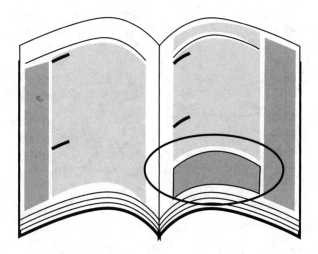

### Career Rating

Taking into account both student survey responses and statistical data, this rating measures the confidence students have in their school's ability to lead them to fruitful employment opportunities, as well as the school's own record of having done so. Factors taken into consideration include statistics on the average starting salary and percent of students employed at graduation from the Business Data Set and comments from the student survey, assessing the efforts of the placement office, the quality of recruiting companies, level of preparation, and opportunities for off-campus projects, internships, and mentorships. Ratings fall between 60 and 99. This rating is intended to be used to compare only those schools within this edition of the book whose students completed our business student survey.

* Please note that if a 60* Career Rating appears for any school, it means that the school did not report all of the rating's underlying data points by our deadline, so we were unable to calculate an accurate rating. In such cases, the reader is advised to follow up with the school about the specific attributes this rating takes into account.

### % grads employed within three months of graduation

This reflects the percentage of MBA grads who earned a job within three months of graduation.

### Average starting salary

Average starting salary of all 2005 graduates

### Grads employed by field %: avg. salary

Reflects the distribution of 2005 graduates across many different industries and the average starting salary for each field.

## Descriptive Profile

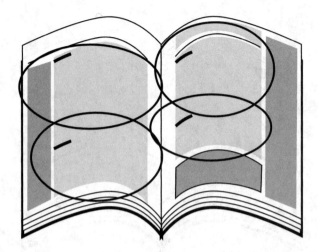

Each school's descriptive profile is made up of four sections which highlight those qualities that characterize the school as a unique institution. *Academics* covers students' opinions on the quality of professors, curriculum, special or noteworthy programs, the administration, and anything else academic in nature. *Career and Placement* deals with the school's efforts to secure internships and jobs for its current students and graduates; information about alumni assistance and popular recruiters of MBAs at the school may also be included. In *Student Life and Environment*, you'll find out how students balance work and play and whether they find it manageable to do so; often, you'll also find reviews of the school's facilities as well. Finally, the *Admissions* section describes what the admissions committee is looking for in potential students.

All quotes in these sections are taken from students' responses to our survey. We choose quotes that were consistent with the overall survey results.

## Part III-B: Business School Data Listings

This section contains all of the statistical info that is presented in the sidebars of the descriptive profile. Each school in this section will include an Admissions Selectivity rating but will not include the other 3 ratings, the Survey Says section, or a descriptive profile.

## Part IV: School Says

Part IV offers more detailed information about particular business schools authored by the schools themselves. The business schools included in this section pay a small fee for this space. These schools also have descriptive profiles or data listings in Part III.

## Everything Else

Following Part IV, we offer a small section of profiles of b-schools who may pay a small fee for inclusion. Next is a section entitled *Decoding Degrees* that will help you make sense of the myriad degree abbreviations you'll see listed in the book. You'll then find the indexes—alphabetical by school name, and then by location. Finally, you'll have an opportunity to learn more about our author, Nedda Gilbert.

Enjoy and good luck!

# PART I
# ALL ABOUT BUSINESS SCHOOL

# CHAPTER 1

## THIS ISN'T YOUR FATHER'S (OR MOTHER'S) B-SCHOOL ANYMORE

### THE NEW MBA CLASS: FEWER, YOUNGER, AND WORKING WHILE THEY LEARN

The MBA has always been seen as a golden passport, the trip ticket to romance and riches. The destination: career acceleration, power networks and recruiters, elite employers, and of course, generous paychecks.

But not everyone wants to make the trip. Several factors will always impact on the popularity of the MBA: 1) the state of the economy—interest in getting the MBA has generally waxed and waned with economic times; 2) trends and favorable or unfavorable press—in the 1980s, a rash of insider trading scandals in which MBAs were ensnared made the degree look smarmy and other graduate programs, notably law and medicine, look more appealing; 3) the immediacy of good professional opportunities—the collapse of the dot-com boom, followed by the severe retrenchment of traditional MBA destinations (such as investment banks and consulting firms) in a depressed economy, has left many current MBAs stranded; and 4) recruiter demand for newly minted MBAs—do employers see the skill sets of today's MBAs bringing measurable value to their companies?

### THE CONTINUING B-SCHOOL SLUMP: INTEREST AND APPLICATIONS SLIDE

It appears that more would-be managers are sticking it out and climbing the ladder in the workforce instead of turning to business schools to earn that resume-boosting MBA. According to the Graduate Management Admissions Council (GMAC), applications to business schools were slightly down in 2005, although the drop was not as steep as it was in 2004 when applications were down by 15-30 percent. This is the third year in a row for which a decline has been reported.

### A STRONGER ECONOMY + A HEFTY PRICE TAG = SCARING STUDENTS AWAY

The weak economy of the past few years has been behind the wheel in driving MBA unpopularity. Concerns about the lingering effects of the recession have made the once-golden MBA an unsure investment. In an already tight job market, fewer students wanted to take on the opportunity costs of leaving their current jobs, paying a hefty sum for tuition, and still having to scramble for a job after they graduate. The numbers do tell: B-school has lost its appeal as a safe haven from turbulent times, much less a straight-shot pathway to guaranteed riches.

Fortunately, the economy does appear to be recovering. But application numbers are still less than stellar and the hiring of new MBAs has not fully rebounded. One note of difference: at top-brand schools, the picture is much rosier. Placement rates are fast returning to pre-September 11 levels.

### YOUNGER MINDS

Although growing applicant pools may make admission seem more competitive, there are now some unrecognized opportunities for candidates with less than the traditional two to four years of work experience to make a strong case for admittance.

Interest in turning to b-school after September 11 reinforced a small but notable trend toward rethinking rigid admittance standards on work experience. Many schools had already begun to reassess their emphasis on work experience as the be-all and end-all.

Admissions officers at large benchmark schools such as Stanford say that this trend pre-dates the economic downturn. Derek Bolton, director of admissions at Stanford notes, "The pendulum has gone too far in one direction in terms of the number of younger candidates applying to b-school. It has not kept pace with the overall pace of applicants. We want more young applicants applying. The goal is to bring the average age down in the next couple of years."

"What's driving this is the willingness on the part of the b-schools to not be rigidly fixed on what's right for someone. We may not always be the best judge of when the best time is for a candidate to go to b-school," continues Bolton.

Wharton's former Director of Admissions Rose Martinelli observed "a shift in that we became more tuned in to when students are ready in their leadership, professional, and personal development. We see so many nontraditional students that we don't want to have rules on when they can apply. We don't want to miss out on fabulous applicants because they don't think they can get in."

"When the applicant pool continues to get older and older, then we're closing out younger applicants who are on a fast track." Martinelli continues, "Why should we wait? Why should they wait? We want to catch the human element in the application process."

Heading into the 2006 application filing period, this perspective continues to hold true. As University of Chicago's Stacey Kole sums up, "The pendulum had swung too far in terms of the type of student who should be admitted and when. Now schools are correcting that and experimenting, taking less experienced candidates. We believe that this experimentation is a good thing."

## THE DRAW OF THE PART-TIME PROGRAM

Ironically, even as the economy appears to be in an upswing, many young adults are choosing to brave a newly robust job market over immersing themselves in the uncertainty—not to mention the high costs—of a graduate program in business or even law. Because part-time and executive education programs have not suffered the decline that full-time programs have, pundits say that the future of b-school may lie in programs that offer more flexible part-time opportunities, allowing students to get the degree without making a full-time commitment. In fact, Stacey Kole, Deputy Dean for the full-time MBA Program and Clinical Professor of Economics, University of Chicago Graduate School of Business states, "There is this tendency to think of the MBA as a full-time-only product. But schools like Chicago offer MBA programs in the evening, on weekends, and in executive program formats. For us, whether the student matriculates in our part-time or full-time program, the process is exactly the same. Ours is the same degree, only delivered in full-time, part-time, and weekend formats with different scheduling options. Chicago GSB offers individuals interested in an MBA considerable flexibility in how they pursue their education."

Kole continues, "Part-time and executive programs are now providing more of the outside-the-classroom, extracurricular experience that did not exist 10 years ago. For example, they are offering student-led clubs, speakers, and recruiter events that historically were the exclusive domain of full-time programs. This is one explanation for why part-time programs are looking like better substitutes for a full-time program."

There may be more to the story, too. Because they may be less likely to be in committed relationships or have families, younger students are more active, generous alumni, and b-schools can't afford to ignore the market that these younger students represent. Despite the heightened competition, candidates with less experience are increasingly being deemed worthy of a coveted b-school acceptance.

## PAYBACK TIME

The MBA, particularly at the top schools, continues to pay out high dividends to grads. Even during these uncertain times, recent MBA graduates reported a surge in salary of over 35 percent. That's a hefty return on investment. But the degree doesn't come with any promises. The world of business requires some risk, as many MBA wannabes found out several years go: You can enter a business school program at the height of the economy only to graduate when things are dismal. But you can also enter b-school at low tide then watch as the job market swells and employers are fighting over the newest and brightest MBA grads, including you.

## FOREIGN MBA STUDENTS: THE NEW REALITY

Opportunities to study or work abroad during an MBA program are considered highly relevant. Likewise, international enrollment at U.S. business schools has always been a priority. At some schools, the percentage of foreign students has been sky-high, anywhere from 30 to 40 percent. Of course, that was before the new screening and tracking processes for international applicants went into effect.

Previously, our position was clear: International students represent a win-win proposition for both U.S. business schools and the foreign industries that send them here. American business schools prize the global perspective and diversity international students bring into the classroom and community; foreign businesses operating in a global economy desire expertise in U.S. business practices which are becoming the international standard.

Unfortunately, due to international security issues, this informal but critical partnership faces greater challenges. These have come primarily in the form of increased scrutiny. In fact, stricter U. S. visa restrictions are cited as the number-one reason for the decreased number of international applicants to U.S. MBA programs. According to GMAC, in 2004, this resulted in a significant decrease in foreign applications for over 70 percent of MBA programs. While the decline continued in 2005, it was much less steep than last year's drop.

Foreign students must slog through tougher rules and procedures for obtaining and maintaining a visa under the United States Citizenship and Immigration Services (USCIS). And many foreign students feel that even if they are successful in obtaining a student visa, they will face an even tougher battle after they graduate: trying to get a work visa. That puts them back at square one. Though armed with an American MBA, they often find themselves looking for work in their home country—a scenario from which they may originally have wanted a professional out.

## Foreign Students: Getting In

As of January 2003, U.S. institutions must comply with the Student and Exchange Visitor Information System, or SEVIS, which tracks foreign students and exchange visitors, as well as some foreign professors. While there is hope that SEVIS will prevent potential terrorists from slipping through the cracks, critics fear that the intensified scrutiny drives away many foreign applicants. The system causes major delays in obtaining a student visa and leaving or reentering the country. In addition, compliance with SEVIS requires the staff of international student offices to perform a great deal of data entry, detracting from the face-time advisors can spend with foreign students.

For the foreseeable future, students wishing to obtain a visa will not be able to escape the shadow of world events, but they should not be deterred. Most business schools stand firm on their commitment to foreign applicants throughout the entire process.

In fact, Don Martin, Director of Admissions at the University of Chicago notes that the number of international students enrolled at UChicago has remained constant. Martin says, "We have made no change in terms of our desire and commitment to enroll foreign students. This world will never go back to what it was before it became a global village. For the sake of diversity and the perspective international students bring to the table, or for understanding foreign business culture, we need to have people who represent that world in every sense of that word."

Martin does agree that for foreign MBA students intending to study on American soil, "The journey of enrolling them is going to be more challenging. A part of that is tied into the changes the U.S. government has imposed on getting visas. Some applicants will need to take another year for the paperwork." But most notably, he sees different forces at play in the shrinking foreign MBA market, namely, the competition U.S. schools are feeling from business schools abroad. Continues Martin, "The issue influencing more international business students away from U.S. business schools is the large amount of European, Australian, and Latin American business schools that heretofore I would not have thought would have had as much pull as they did. These business schools have become more visible and prominent. They are being ranked by the large news organizations and magazines. So I would say American business schools still want international students, but the ability to recruit and draw them here to us will be difficult against this new competition."

To those applying for a visa, Wharton's former Director of Admissions Rose Martinelli offers this advice: "Emphasize plans to return home, [not] plans to immigrate to the United States." If a visa is denied, many schools will defer admission and hold that student's spot until the visa is obtained. Sums up Martinelli: "It may take a little longer for students from some countries to get their visas. But decisions here are not made based on whether they got a visa or not. Decisions are made based on what they'll do at our school and on the contributions they'll make."

Of course, all this is subject to change, perhaps even by the time of this book's publication. Non-U.S. citizens should visit the USCIS website (http://uscis.gov) for the latest information on student visas.

## Foreign Students: Getting a Job

Just when a foreign student is ready to reap the rewards of his or her hard-won business degree, he or she hits another roadblock. And this one's a brick wall: an unforgiving and limited job market fueled not just by a new wartime security, but also a new nationalism.

Historically, foreign students have always had a tougher time than their American counterparts in trying to get that first job out of b-school. That's because of the hassle of sponsoring a foreigner on a visa, rigid immigration rules, and other cultural and relocation issues. Nonetheless, for grads of the top schools, there has always been a pot of gold waiting at the end of that long journey. That pot of gold has meant the opportunity to embark on an entirely new career and life—to be sponsored by a U.S. company, on U.S. soil, with post-MBA pay scales that supersede those of their home countries and launch them on a high-earnings career path.

Since September 11, the environment in the United States has changed, and the home-field advantage of American MBAs is even greater. Simply put, U.S. companies have been reluctant to offer a foreign MBA a plush job over an American MBA who is equally talented and qualified. The result is that foreign hires have been more limited to hard-to-fill positions, to employment in their locations abroad, or to positions in the student's home country. Many MBA recruiters won't even offer an international student an interview.

As for companies shrinking their foreign MBA hires down to bare bones, as we've said many times before, and Don Martin concurs, where you go to school matters. He explains, "Some companies have changed their hiring strategies. Fewer overall international students are being hired, but not at our school. Companies typically will drop down from their list of 10 schools they go to, to a much smaller number of programs. In a high percentage, we've remained on their lists. We are seeing 90 percent of our international students placed in internships and going on to full-time hires."

The result of the shrinking job market for most foreign students is that business schools have begun to cut back on the number of applicants admitted, and this has made it even tougher to get accepted. Many schools have begun to be upfront about the limited career opportunities on U.S. soil for foreigners. Indeed, this will soon be compounded by a reduction of more than 50 percent in the number of work visas the government issues annually to employees sponsored by their company.

But as the economy heats up and MBA hiring begins to rebound, it is possible that recruiters, particularly Wall Street and the top-flight consulting firms, will once again open their doors to whomever is most qualified, foreign or not. History, it should be remembered, shows us that the top jobs always go to the most capable applicants. This next cycle should be no different than the preceding cycles. Talent still rules.

In the meantime, buyers beware: an MBA is not the passport to riches it once was for foreign applicants. International students should think twice about the costs of pursuing a degree that may only deliver them back into the hands of their home countries saddled with the expense, but not the benefit, of an MBA education.

## THE CONTINUING RELEVANCE OF BUSINESS SCHOOL

The MBA is such an attractive option because it *does* confer huge value on the recipient. Business schools know how to keep pace with the rapidly changing face of business. After all, that's *their* business, so you're never really out of the game. In fact, if you look at the nation's top business programs, you'll find exciting innovations in curriculum that reflect all that's new and relevant. This includes unique opportunities for teamwork, internships, and laboratory simulations that replicate real-world, real-time business scenarios.

The integration of these real-world experiences into the basics produces better-trained, more well-rounded managers, as graduates are more adept at discerning the correlation between principle and reality. Even so, programs and students in search of business knowledge that is more widely applicable and more relevant long-term has caused a strong return to fundamentals.

### BACKPEDALING TO THE BASICS

Many top schools are reviving the old classics: it's back to basics. Both schools and students now have enough of a perspective to look back at the frenzy of the last business cycle and understand that enduring values are rooted in a solid foundation. Gone is the frothy demand for trendy courses on e-commerce and other hype-driven topics. Just three years ago, a class at Stanford on the principles of Internet marketing was oversubscribed. Last year, only a few people signed up for it.

So here's a sampler of the back-to-basics you'll get at b-school: an in-depth immersion in all of the key functional areas of an organization: marketing, management, sales, finance, operations, logistics, and so on. And you'll look at these areas across dozens of industries and organizational types, from start-ups to Fortune 500 companies.

But the renewed focus on basics doesn't mean that you'll find yourself shorted on current trends and events. Expect plenty of case study debate on corporate governance and the Enron debacle, and expect the themes of global perspective and technological competence to permeate many programs. You'll also find classes and seminars on leadership gaining popularity. "We're seeing a resurgence of leadership courses as students seek out professions and business models that are other-oriented," notes Stanford's Bolton. "This may be a new generation. But these are students who look at business as a positive force in the world, a more noble calling."

## SURVIVOR POWER

Once you have your MBA, you can expect to hit the ground running. You'll start off your post b-school career with a load of contacts that you will periodically leverage over your career. Many graduates use the degree to embark on entirely new career paths than those that brought them to the school; consultants become bankers, entrepreneurs become consultants, marketers become financiers, and so on. The MBA has and will continue to be a terrific opportunity to reinvent oneself.

"An MBA is unlike any other professional degree because the breadth of knowledge poises you for a multitude of career choices," says Julia Min, Director of MBA Admissions for NYU Stern School of Business. "You can be an investment banker, yet two years from that point, segue into nonprofit work. You can move from banking to corporate finance, to a venture-capital proposition, to ultimately having an entrepreneurial experience. So it's a credential that allows you the flexibility to explore different industries; it's a long-term investment that will give you the tools to transition if you want to."

"What's wonderful about the MBA is that it provides fundamental skills that you can use whenever and wherever you need them," champions Martinelli. "I'm a cheerleader for the nontraditional because I feel the MBA is such a fundamental tool. It offers an ability to enter the business world and link passion with functionality."

"For example, for folks who want to go into public service or nonprofit, even the arts industry, they're very narrow fields. You need the passion and vision to be successful in them. But often credibility is undermined when you don't understand the business world's perspective," states Martinelli.

"You've got to know that industry if you're going to make it viable for the future. But you have to be able to know how to talk to the business world in order to get those investments to make it happen. And that's one of the reasons why an MBA is so valuable. It bestows credibility in the marketplace and helps us maintain these organizations in a world that doesn't often respect passion over the bottom line," she continues.

The big question remains: Will your MBA get you the job you want when you graduate? Despite the recent economic downturn, hundreds of companies continue to visit and recruit from business school campuses, (though they may have reduced their hires). This is because recruiters exist in a symbiotic relationship with business schools. Companies that depend on business school talent can ill afford to bypass campus recruiting for fear that when their hiring needs increase again, the school or students will be less receptive to their offers. Employers need to maintain their strong presence. They need to know that they'll have top picks when the good times return. Thus, MBA programs remain one of the most effective means to get oneself in front of recruiters and senior managers from the most desirable companies. And while that may not grant you "immunity" from an economy characterized by up and downs, it will absolutely improve your survivor power.

## COMPETITION HAS EASED UP

With an economic recovery well underway, the chance to dive into any number of secure, well-paying jobs will lure a percentage of professionals away from the MBA. After years of struggling through economic hardship, a decent paycheck from the pocket of a much improved labor market may seem the best bet. And there's no doubt that risk-averse individuals would prefer the stability of a secure job to what might-be, could-be, or should-be two years down the road—even with an MBA in hand. This may keep the applicant pool smaller.

Additionally, the continued decrease in the number of foreign applicants, who at many schools comprised well over 20 percent of students, will keep applications down, too. Other factors include the fact that there are currently smaller percentages of people in the country who are in the typical age bracket of business school applicants. Lastly, the increased interest in part-time MBA programs may continue to drive the decline in full-time business school applications.

What does all of this mean? Basically this: If you have a handsome application and you plan on applying to the most competitive programs this year, you may find yourself met with welcoming arms.

## AS THE SONG GOES...MONEY, MONEY, MONEY, MONEY...

But don't go buying the flashy car to go with that flashy degree quite yet. It needs to be said that, after several years of a slump, there could actually be a surge in this upcoming applicant pool that would correspond with improvements in the economy. Recruiters are once again storming the top business schools as hiring slowly returns to healthy levels. At programs like Chicago, Harvard, and Stanford, six-figure salaries and signing bonuses of $10,000-plus are still the norm. That's why it's important to remember that the MBA from the right school can deliver an immediate and hefty return on investment. According to the Graduate Management Admission Council Global MBA Graduate Survey of 2005, respondents reported an annual (mean) salary of $59,635 before entering business school and a (mean) salary of $84,318 in their first job out. This number is expected to continue to rise for the class of 2006.

Another trend worth noting: Although applications are down overall at b-schools, that doesn't mean the quality of applicants has suffered. Notes Chicago's Kole, "Our applications are of high quality, and applicants appear to be quite focused with regard to why they seek an advanced degree. Whether they are career switchers or planning to resume their career path, those applicants who present a compelling story for why they want to be here leave a stronger impression with the admissions committee."

Top schools are always going to have people knocking at their doors. And the possibility that business school applications in general could once again rise means you'll still want to be competitive. The long application process starts with developing a solid application strategy and applying to a diverse portfolio of schools.

## LET US HELP YOU DECIDE

There are many factors to consider when deciding whether or not to pursue an MBA, and we'll help you make that decision in the following chapters. We'll also tell you a bit about each school in our profiles and prepare you to do further research on the schools on your list. We've worked hard to provide you with thorough information on every aspect of the MBA, but you don't have to take our word for it—see for yourself. Stanford's Bolton advises future applicants, "Start early. Visit as many schools as you can, because it's very hard to differentiate among programs from websites, books, and marketing materials. You need to get a feeling from walking down the halls."

After you decide to go, finding the right program can be extremely difficult. Bolton explains, "Applicants really have to dig beneath the programs they're looking at to determine what's going to make them happy. A lot of people wind up going to the wrong school. A lot of external factors contribute to that. People shouldn't worry about justifying the decision to others, but to themselves."

## MAKING THE DECISION TO GO

The next step for you may be b-school. Indeed, armed with an MBA you may journey far. But the success of your trip and the direction you take will depend on knowing exactly why you're going to b-school and just what you'll be getting out of it.

The most critical questions you need to ask yourself are the following: Do you really want a career in business? What do you want the MBA to do for you? Are you looking to gain credibility, accelerate your development, or move into a new job or industry? Perhaps you're looking to start your own business, in which case entrepreneurial study will be important.

Knowing what you want doesn't just affect your decision to go, it also affects your candidacy; admissions committees favor applicants who have clear goals and objectives. Moreover, once at school, students who know what they want make the most of their two years. If you're uncertain about your goals, opportunities for career development—such as networking, mentoring, student clubs, and recruiter events—are squandered.

You also need to find a school that fits your individual needs. Consider the personal and financial costs. This may be the single biggest investment of your life. How much salary will you forego by leaving the workforce? What will the tuition be? How will you pay for it? If you have a family, spouse, or significant other, how will getting your MBA affect them?

If you do have a spouse, you may choose a program that involves partners in campus life. If status is your top priority, you should simply choose the most prestigious school you can get into.

The MBA presents many opportunities but no guarantees. As with any opportunity, you must make the most of it. Whether you go to a first-tier school or to a part-time program close to home, you'll acquire the skills that can jump-start your career. But your success will have more to do with you than with the piece of paper your MBA is printed on.

# CHAPTER 2
## WHAT B-SCHOOL IS REALLY LIKE

### AN ACADEMIC PERSPECTIVE

The objective of all MBA programs is to prepare students for a professional career in business. One business school puts it this way:

Graduates should be all of the following:

1. Able to think and reason independently, creatively, and analytically

2. Skilled in the use of quantitative techniques

3. Literate in the use of software applications as management tools

4. Knowledgeable about the world's management issues and problems

5. Willing to work in and successfully cope with conditions of uncertainty, risk, and change

6. Astute decision makers

7. Ethically and socially responsible

8. Able to manage in an increasingly global environment

9. Proficient in utilizing technology as a mode of doing business

Sound like a tall order? Possibly. But this level of expectation is what business school is all about.

Nearly all MBA programs feature a core curriculum that focuses on the major disciplines of business: finance, management, accounting, marketing, manufacturing, decision sciences, economics, and organizational behavior. Unless your school allows you to place out of them, these courses are mandatory. Core courses provide broad functional knowledge in one discipline. To illustrate, a core marketing course covers pricing, segmentation, communications, product-line planning, and implementation. Electives provide a narrow focus that deepen the area of study. For example, a marketing elective might be entirely devoted to pricing.

Students sometimes question the need for such a comprehensive core program, but the functional areas of a real business are not parallel lines. All departments of a business affect each other every day. For example, an MBA in a manufacturing job might be asked by a financial controller why the company's product has become unprofitable to produce. Without an understanding of how product costs are accounted for, this MBA wouldn't know how to respond to a critical and legitimate request.

At most schools, the first term or year is devoted to a rigid core curriculum. Some schools allow first-years to take core courses side by side with electives. Still others have come up with an entirely new way of covering the basics, integrating the core courses into one cross-functional learning experience, which may also include sessions on topics such as globalization, ethics, and managing diversity. Half-year to year-long courses are team-taught by professors who will see you through all disciplines.

## TEACHING METHODOLOGY

Business schools employ two basic teaching methods: case study and lecture. Usually, they employ some combination of the two. The most popular is the case study approach. Students are presented with either real or hypothetical business scenarios and are asked to analyze them. This method provides concrete situations (rather than abstractions) that require mastery of a wide range of skills. Students often find case studies exciting because they can engage in spirited discussions about possible solutions to given business problems and because they get an opportunity to apply newly acquired business knowledge.

On the other hand, lecturing is a teaching method in which—you guessed it—the professor speaks to the class and the class listens. The efficacy of the lecture method depends entirely on the professor. If the professor is compelling, you'll probably get a lot out of the class. If the professor is boring, you probably won't listen, which isn't necessarily a big deal since many professors make their class notes available on computer disc or in the library.

## THE CLASSROOM EXPERIENCE

Professors teaching case methodology often begin class with a "cold call." A randomly selected student opens the class with an analysis of the case and makes recommendations for solutions. The cold call forces you to be prepared and to think on your feet.

No doubt, a cold call can be intimidating. But unlike law school, b-school professors don't use the Socratic Method to torture you, testing your thinking with a pounding cross-examination. They're training managers, not trial lawyers. At worst, particularly if you're unprepared, a professor will abruptly dismiss your contribution.

Alternatively, professors ask for a volunteer to open a case, particularly someone who has had real industry experience with the issues. After the opening, the discussion is broadened to include the whole class. Everyone tries to get in a good comment, particularly if class participation counts heavily toward the grade. "Chip shots"—unenlightened, just-say-anything-to-get-credit comments—are common. So are "air hogs," students who go on and on because they like nothing more than to hear themselves pontificate.

Depending on the school, class discussions can degenerate into wars of ego rather than ideas. But for the most part, debates are kept constructive and civilized. Students are competitive, but not offensively so, and learn to make their points succinctly and persuasively.

### A GLOSSARY OF INSIDER LINGO

B-school students, graduates, and professors—like most close-knit, somewhat solipsistic groups—seem to speak their own weird language. Here's a sampler of MBA jargon (with English translations):

**Admissions Mistake:** How each student perceives him or herself until getting first-year grades back from midterms.

**Air Hogs:** Students who monopolize classroom discussion and love to hear themselves speak.

**B2B:** "Business to Business"—a company that sells not to retail consumers, but to other enterprises. With the renewed focus on more traditional industries, this now stands for "Back to Basics."

**B2C:** "Business to Consumer"—a company that sells primarily to individual retail consumers. As with the above joke about B2B, business students occasionally say this really means "Back to Consulting."

**Back of the Envelope:** A quick analysis of numbers, as if scribbled on the back of an envelope.

**Benchmarking:** Comparing a company to others in the industry.

**Burn Rate:** Amount of cash a money-losing company consumes during a period of time.

**Case Study Method:** Popular teaching method that uses real-life business cases for analysis.

**Cold Call:** Unexpected, often dreaded request by the professor to open a case discussion.

**Chip Shot:** Vacant and often cheesy comments used not to truly benefit class discussion, but rather to get credit for participation.

**Cycle Time:** How fast you can turn something around.

**Deliverable:** Your end product.

**Four Ps:** Elements of a marketing strategy: Price, Promotion, Place, Product.

**Fume Date:** Date the company will run out of cash reserves.

**Functional Areas:** The basic disciplines of business (e.g., finance, marketing, R&D).

**HP12-C:** A calculator that works nothing like a regular one, used by finance types when they don't have Excel handy.

**Lingo Bingo:** A furtive game of Bingo whereby he who "wins" must work a decided upon, often trite phrase (see "chip shot") into the class discussion. For example: "I didn't actually read the case last night, but the protagonist is two beers short of a six-pack." The winner also earns a prize and the admiration of classmates.

**Low Hanging Fruit:** Tasks or goals that are most easy to achieve (consultant jargon).

**Monitize:** To turn an idea into a moneymaking scheme.

**Net Net:** End result.

**Power Nap:** Quick, intense, in-class recharge for the continually sleep-deprived.

**Power Tool:** Someone who does all the work and sits in the front row of the class with his or her hand up.

**Pre-enrollment Courses:** Commonly known as MBA summer camp—quantitative courses to get the numerically challenged up to speed.

**Pro Forma:** Financial presentation of hypothetical events, such as projected earnings.

**Quant Jock:** A numerical athlete who is happiest crunching numbers.

**Rule of Three:** You should not talk more than three times in any given class, but you should participate at least once over the course of three classes.

**Run the Numbers:** Analyze quantitatively.

**Shrimp Boy:** A student who comes to a corporate event just to scarf down the food.

**Skydeck:** Refers to the back row of the classroom, usually when it's amphitheater style.

**Slice and Dice:** Running all kinds of quantitative analysis on a set of numbers.

**Soft Skills:** Conflict resolution, teamwork, negotiation, oral and written communication.

**Take-aways:** The key points of a lecture or meeting that participants should remember.

**The Five Forces:** Michael Porter's model for analyzing the strategic attractiveness of an industry.

**Three Cs:** The primary forces considered in marketing: Customer, Competition, Company.

**Value-Based Decision Making:** Values and ethics as part of the practice of business.

---

## YOUR FIRST YEAR

The first six months of b-school can be daunting. You're unfamiliar with the subjects. There's a tremendous amount of work to do. And when you least have the skills to do so, there's pressure to stay with the pack. All of this produces anxiety and a tendency to overprepare. Eventually, students learn shortcuts and settle into a routine, but until then much of the first year is just plain tough. The programs usually pack more learning into the first term than they do into each of the remaining terms. For the schools to teach the core curriculum (which accounts for as much as 70 percent of learning) in a limited time, an intensive pace is considered necessary. Much of the second year will be spent on gaining proficiency in your area of expertise and on searching for a job.

The good news is that the schools recognize how tough the first year can be. During the early part of the program, they anchor students socially by placing them in small sections, sometimes called "cohorts." You take many or all of your classes with your section-mates. Sectioning encourages the formation of personal and working relationships and can help make a large program feel like a school within a school.

Because so much has to be accomplished in so little time, getting an MBA is like living in fast-forward. This is especially true of the job search. No sooner are you in the program than recruiters for summer jobs show up, which tends to divert students from their studies. First-years aggressively pursue summer positions, which are linked with the promise of a permanent job offer if the summer goes well. At some schools, the recruiting period begins as early as October, at others in January or February.

---

## A DAY IN THE LIFE

### MATT CAMP, FIRST YEAR
Tuck School of Business, Dartmouth College

**7:00 A.M.:** Get dressed. Out of the door by 7:45 A.M. to head to the campus dining hall for breakfast. If I have time, I'll grab the *Financial Times* and *The Wall Street Journal* and gloss over the front page. Today, I have an informal get-to-know-you-better meeting with a marketing professor over breakfast.

**8:30 A.M.:** Core class in Corporate Finance. Grab any seat in a tiered classroom set-up. I'm usually in the middle toward the side. If possible, the front row stays empty.

**10:00 A.M.:** Go to e-mail kiosk on campus and check messages. Hang out or do a quick run to the library to read more of the *Times*.

**10:30 A.M.:** Macroeconomics lecture/case study class. Again, no assigned seating. Expect cold calls on case. Cold calls are not terrifying. Professors are supportive, not out to embarrass you. Class discussion is lively, with a mix of people offering their views.

**Noon:** Back to the cafeteria. Tuck may be one of the few schools where everyone eats together at the same place. There isn't much in town, and you're tight on time, so it doesn't make sense to go back home or elsewhere. It's crowded, so I look for friends, but basically grab a seat anywhere at one of the large tables that seat six to seven. Professors, administrators, and students all eat at the same place. Food is above average.

**1:15 P.M.:** Classes are over for the day. From this point, I begin to start homework; there's a lot of work to do. I can go to a study room on campus, but they get booked up pretty quickly for groups, so I head to the library. The majority of the people are doing work for tomorrow. It's rare to have someone working on a project that's due the following week. It's pretty much day-to-day.

**4:00 P.M.:** I head off to one of the scheduled sports I've signed up for. Today it's soccer, played about one mile from campus. I drive; friends hitch a ride with me. This is a big international scene, mostly men, but there's a small group of women too. It's definitely a game we play hard, but in a very congenial way.

**6:00 P.M.:** Head back to campus. I'm hungry. It's off to the dining hall again. Most first-years live in dorms, so home cooking is not an option. Almost all second-years live off-campus, so they head back for a home-cooked meal. Cafeteria is not crowded; I may eat alone.

**7:00 P.M.:** Head home for a quick shower and change. The night is just beginning.

**7:30 P.M.:** Meet with study group at school to flesh out rest of work that needs to be done in preparation for tomorrow's classes.

**11:00 P.M.:** Students and their wives/husbands or partners head out to play ice hockey at one of the two rinks here. Wives/husbands and partners play. There are different games going on for different skill levels. It's a lot of fun.

**Midnight:** Time to go and celebrate either a hard game or a sore butt, but everyone goes to get some wings and a beer. There are only two bars on campus, and they close at 1:00 A.M. so we head to one of them.

**1:00 A.M.:** After the bar closes, people head home.

**1:15 A.M.:** Exhausted, I go to bed. No TV. I've forgotten what that is.

## Your Second Year

Relax, the second year is easier. By now, students know what's important and what's not. Second-years work more efficiently than first-years. Academic anxiety is no longer a factor. Having mastered the broad-based core curriculum, students now enjoy taking electives and developing an area of specialization.

Anxiety in the second year has more to do with the arduous task of finding a job. For some lucky students, a summer position has yielded a full-time offer. But even those students often go through the whole recruiting grind anyway because they don't want to cut off any opportunities prematurely.

Most MBAs leave school with a full-time offer. Sometimes it's their only offer. Sometimes it's not their dream job, which may be why most grads change jobs after just two years. One student summed up the whole two-year academic/recruiting process like this: "The first-year students collapse in the winter quarter because of on-campus recruiting. The second-years collapse academically in the first quarter of their second year because it's so competitive to get a good job. And when a second-year does get a job, he or she forgets about class entirely. That's why pass/fail was invented."

# A DAY IN THE LIFE

## Kristin Hansen, Second-Year
Tuck School of Business, Dartmouth College

**9:00 A.M.:** Wake-up (my first class is at 10:30 A.M.) and finish work for Monday classes.

**10:15 A.M.:** Ride my bike to campus for 10:30 A.M. class.

**10:30 A.M.:** Head to International Economics class, an elective. I have only three classes this semester, my last. Prior to this I had four and a half classes each term. I front-loaded so I would have a light last semester. Grab a yogurt and juice on way in. Eat in class. We discuss a currency crisis case.

**Noon:** Head to study room to plug my personal computer into one of the many networked connections on campus to check e-mail. Finish work for next class.

**1:00 P.M.:** Grab a quick lunch in the dining hall. Will bring it to eat during class.

**1:15 P.M.:** Managerial Decision Making class, another elective. Today is the very last class that second-years will have at Tuck; we're off to graduation! Our professor brings in strawberries and champagne to celebrate. We all hang out and toast each other. This obviously doesn't happen everyday, but this is just the kind of thing a Tuck professor would do.

**2:45 P.M.:** I'm one of four Tuck social chairpersons, so I use this time to send e-mails to my co-chairs about the upcoming chili cook-off and farm party. Then I send a message to the school regarding other social events for the weekend. I get an e-mail from the New York office of CS First Boston, with whom I've accepted a job offer, with a calendar of the dates for my private client-services training.

**3:00 P.M.:** Go for a run, swim, or bike ride.

**5:00 P.M.:** Head home to shower and change. Usually I'd make dinner at home and eat, but tonight, I'm heading out to a social event. So I relax a bit and do an hour of preparation for the next day. On Monday, Tuesday, and Wednesday nights, the workload is heavier.

**7:00 P.M.:** Off to a Turkey Fry Dinner. This is a meal that will be prepared by my two economics professors. They donated this "dinner" for the charity student auction. Friends of mine bid on it and won. Each of eight bidders gets to bring a guest, and I'm one of the guests. The professors are hosting this at one of their homes. Basically, they're taking three large turkeys and fry-o-lating them.

**8:30 P.M.:** We all head out to an open mic night, led by the same two economics professors that hosted the Turkey Fry. It's held at a local bar. Anyone in the audience can get onstage and perform. I'm a member of the Tuck band, so I get up on stage with my acoustic guitar and play various folk and bluegrass songs. This is a great warm-up for the Open Mic night at Tuck.

**10:45 P.M.:** We head out for Pub Night in downtown Hanover.

**1:00 A.M.:** The bar closes, so we head to "The End Zone," one of the second-year houses close to campus. All the second-year houses are named; these are names that have been passed down from generation to generation. On a typical Thursday night at Tuck, a small number of students will stay out until 3:00 A.M. I'm usually one of them.

**3:00 A.M.:** I walk home. My house, called "Girls in the Hood," is just a ten-minute stroll away. I may grab a 3:00 A.M. snack. Then, I quickly fall asleep, exhausted.

## Life Outside of Class

Business school is more than academics and a big-bucks job. A spirited community provides ample opportunity for social interaction, extracurricular activity, and career development.

Much of campus life revolves around student-run clubs. There are groups for just about every career interest and social need—from "MBAs for a Greener America" to the "Small Business Club." There's even a group for significant others on most campuses. The clubs are a great way to meet classmates with similar interests and to get in on the social scene. They might have a reputation for throwing the best black-tie balls, pizza-and-keg events, and professional mixers. During orientation week, these clubs aggressively market themselves to first-years.

Various socially responsible projects are also popular on campus. An emphasis on volunteer work is part of the overall trend toward good citizenship. Perhaps to counter the greed of the 1980s, "giving back" is the b-school style of the moment. There is usually a wide range of options—from tutoring in an inner-city school to working in a soup kitchen to renovating public buildings.

Still another way to get involved is to work on a school committee. Here you might serve on a task force designed to improve student quality of life. Or you might work in the admissions office and interview prospective students.

For those with more creative urges there are always the old standbys: extracurriculars such as the school paper, yearbook, or school play. At some schools, the latter is a dramatization of "b-school follies" and is a highlight of the year. Like the student clubs, these are a great way to get to know your fellow students.

Finally, you can play on intramural sports teams or attend the numerous informal get-togethers, dinner parties, and group trips. There are also plenty of regularly scheduled pub nights, just in case you thought your beer-guzzling days were over.

Most former MBA students say that going to b-school was the best decision they ever made. That's primarily because of nonacademic experiences. Make the most of your classes, but take the time to get involved and enjoy yourself.

# Chapter 3

## Blackberrys and Power Lunches: What Does an MBA Offer?

### NUTS-AND-BOLTS BUSINESS SKILLS

Graduate business schools teach the applied science of business. The best business schools combine the latest academic theories with pragmatic concepts, hands-on experience, and real-world solutions.

B-schools also teach the analytical skills used to make complicated business decisions. You learn how to define the critical issues, apply analytical techniques, develop the criteria for decisions, and make decisions after evaluating their impact on other variables.

After two years, you're ready to market a box of cereal. Or prepare a valuation of the cereal company's worth. You'll speak the language of business. You'll know the tools of the trade. Your expertise will extend to many areas and industries. In short, you will have acquired the skills that open doors.

### ACCESS TO RECRUITERS, ENTRÉE TO NEW FIELDS

Applicants tend to place great emphasis on "incoming" and "outgoing" statistics. First they ask, "Will I get in?" Then they ask, "Will I get a job?"

Obviously, the first is largely dependent on how selective the school is and the quality of your credentials. The latter question can almost assuredly be answered in the positive, "Yes, you will."

But the real question is: How many—and what kind—of offers will you receive? Again, that is dependent on the appeal of the school to recruiters (which is a readily available statistic you can get from each school) and the particular industry you elect to pursue. For example, investment banks and consulting firms are always going to come to the schools for formal recruiting periods, whereas more off-the-beaten-path choices will possibly require you to go off campus in search of opportunity.

#### It's Good to Be Wanted, It's Great to Be Paid

According to many top schools, recruiter appetite for new grads is up. The latest figures suggest a strong market for newly minted MBAs. This comes after several years of depressed interest in which the immediate economic value of the MBA was in question.

As we reported in Chapter 1, the average return on investment for business school grads in 2005 was an impressive 30 percent increase in annual salary. According to the Graduate Management Council, the before and after picture looks something like this: Average entering salary: roughly $59,635. Average first job out of school salary: $84,318. Presumably, starting salaries will continue to increase as the economy improves.

The majority of top grads receive a generous relocation package too. Indeed, if you were fortunate enough to have spent the summer between your first and second year at a consulting company, then you will, in all likelihood, also receive a "rebate" on your tuition. These companies often pick up a student's second-year tuition bill. The best package, however, goes to those MBA students who worked at the firm before b-school. These lucky capitalists often get their whole tuition paid for.

## GETTING THE MBA FOR THE LONG RUN

Although MBA hiring appears to be on an upswing, going to business school still requires you to take a bit of a gamble. Leaner years make business school a riskier proposition. The nation appears to be heading out of what has been a lingering recession, but economic factors are always unpredictable. Furthermore, the world has witnessed great political turmoil. All of these factors can quickly and negatively impact the job market for newly minted MBAs.

So as you make plans to go to b-school, you need to accept that there is some risk that the labor market won't greet you with open arms at graduation. Consider the plight of MBAs from just three years ago: when they entered b-school, the economy was roaring ahead. The immediate future looked exceptionally bright. Most MBAs probably thought that once they got in, they had it made, and they looked forward to generous starting salaries and bonuses. Few probably anticipated that tough times could hit so dramatically.

But that's just the point. Good times and bad times cycle in and out. Fortunately, it looks as though we are cycling into a good time. Many economic experts agree that the economy is looking up and the markets will continue to improve. This means traditional hirers of MBAs, such as the investment banks and consulting firms, may once again be wooing many a b-school grad. Still, it's hard to know when all of the recruiters who typically hire MBAs will feel comfortable again about bringing their hiring levels back up to what they were before the downturn.

The best way to consider the value of the degree is by focusing on its long-lasting benefits. "When people come here for their MBA, they talk about retooling for their life. They think about the long term and recognize that there are some short term hurdles," says Rose Martinelli, former director of admissions at the Wharton School. "Just out of business school, this is the very first job in a long career. This is really about building blocks and going for the long run. You may have to work harder to find a job now, but building your career is a lifelong process." The MBA gives you the tools, networking, and polish to meaningfully enhance your long-term prospects and earning potential.

"There is real opportunity here. The opportunity right now is to pursue your passion and perhaps not your wallet," continues Martinelli. "We're seeing more of an equalization in salary. Those high-paying jobs in finance, investment banking, and consulting are fewer and harder to find. So here you have an opportunity for a job with a true learning experience rather than one that just pays a lot. More people are going into nonprofit and government and making contributions back to the community."

## BRAND POWER COUNTS

Of course, there is great variability with placement rates and starting salaries among schools. The MBA does not swap your tuition bill for a guarantee that you'll get rich quick. As we've noted, it is at the best schools— those that have the greatest prestige and global recognition—where the strongest recovery is taking place. It's brand power at work. Even in an uncertain economy, top schools will continue to produce in-demand MBAs for the marketplace.

Branded schools tend to have an extensive history with big recruiting companies because the schools are a steady source of exceptional talent. As the economy stabilizes and hiring creeps up again, recruiters are naturally going to orient themselves at the top-brand schools.

At the University of Chicago, Deputy Dean Stacey Kole notes: "Recruiting activity is up, in the order of 20 percent. Hiring activity has really skyrocketed. I think that companies are feeling more comfortable that the economy is in good shape and are resuming their pre-September 11th hiring patterns. We had thousands of interviews available for our grads."

At less prominent schools, the picture may not be quite as optimistic. It is important to consider placement rates and the list of companies that typically recruit on campus at any school you are considering.

## GETTING A JOB

For most would-be MBAs, b-school represents a fresh beginning—either in their current profession or in an entirely different industry. Whatever promise the degree holds for you, it's wise to question what the return on your investment will be.

Several factors affect job placement and starting salary. School reputation and ties to industries and employers are important. At the top programs, the lists of recruiters read like a "Who's Who" of American companies. These schools not only attract the greatest volume of recruiters, but consistently get the attention of those companies considered to be "blue chip."

Not to be overlooked are lesser-known, regional schools that often have the strongest relationships with local employers and industries. Some b-schools (many of them state universities) are regarded by both academicians and employers as number one in their respective regions. In other words, as far as the local business community is concerned, these programs offer as much prestige and pull as a nationally ranked program.

Student clubs also play a big part in getting a job because they extend the recruiting efforts at many schools. They host a variety of events that allow you to meet leading business people, so that you can learn about their industries and their specific companies. Most important, these clubs are very effective at bringing in recruiters and other interested parties that do not recruit through traditional mainstream channels. For example, the high-tech, international, and entertainment student clubs provide career opportunities not available through the front door.

Your background and experiences also affect your success in securing a position. Important factors are academic specialization, academic standing, prior work experience, and intangibles such as your personal fit with the company. These days, what you did before b-school is particularly important; it helps establish credibility and gives you an edge in competing for a position in a specific field. For those using b-school to switch careers to a new industry, it's helpful if something on your resume ties your interest to the new profession. It's also smart to secure a summer job in the new area.

Finally, persistence and initiative are critical factors in the job search. Many fast tracks have been narrowed since the beginning of the decade. Increasingly, even at the best schools, finding a job requires off-campus recruiting efforts and ferreting out the hidden jobs.

## A RETURN ON YOUR INVESTMENT

Not everyone measures their return on investment from business school with a dollar amount. (See the interview at the end of this chapter as one example.) We've heard many b-school grads explain that the fundamental skills, the network of people, and the proper environment in which to formulate their long-term career path were the most valuable things they wanted to get back from their MBA programs—in doing so, they considered the experience a success, regardless of their starting salary at graduation.

But for those who are anxious to start paying back those school loans, it's important to note that the industry in which you are hired can strongly affect your job prospects. Traditionally heavy hirers such as investment banking and consulting companies continue to lead the salary pack. Historically these sectors have offered the highest starting salaries and sign-on bonuses, with recruiters gravitating to the name-brand schools. At Chicago, Kole notes, "We saw tremendous activity in consulting, investment banking, investment management, and in leadership development programs. We are up in all of these areas, but most significantly in management consulting."

Also impacting your placement outlook is the geographic location of the school. Regional powerhouses such as Rutgers University in New Jersey may hold great sway at nearby, national employers such as Johnson & Johnson and Warner Lambert/Pfizer, providing graduates of those programs a unique competitive advantage. Although these companies reach out far and wide to recruit everywhere, a homegrown MBA may catch their attention and hold greater appeal.

As always, prioritize your criteria for school selection. Research who the top hirers are at any school you are considering. If you know what field you are interested in, look at how strong a particular business school's track record is in finding jobs for their graduates in that industry. To cement the relationships between school and recruiter, companies often foster a partnership with the school that includes sponsoring academic projects and internships, and hosting school club functions and informational cocktail hour events.

You may indeed be accepted at one of the nation's most prestigious schools, but if they lack real access to the type of industry you desire to work in, you are better off elsewhere.

## FRIENDS WHO ARE GOING PLACES, ALUMNI WHO ARE ALREADY THERE

Most students say that the best part about b-school is meeting classmates with whom they share common goals and interests. Many students claim that the "single greatest resource is each other." Not surprisingly, with so many bright and ambitious people cocooned in one place, b-school can be the time of your life. It presents numerous professional and social opportunities. It can be where you find future customers, business partners, and mentors. It can also be where you establish lifelong friendships. After graduation, these classmates form an enduring network of contacts and professional resources.

Alumni are also an important part of the b-school experience. While professors teach business theory and practice, alumni provide insight into the real business world. When you're ready to interview, they can provide advice on how to get hired by the companies recruiting at your school. In some cases, they help you secure the interview and shepherd you through the hiring process.

B-schools love to boast about the influence of their alumni network. To be sure, some are very powerful. But this varies from institution to institution. At the very least, alumni will help you get your foot in the door. A resume sent to an alum at a given company, instead of to "Sir or Madam" in the personnel department, has a much better chance of being noticed and acted on.

After you graduate, the network continues to grow. Regional alumni clubs and alumni publications keep you plugged in to the network with class notes detailing who's doing what, where, and with whom.

Throughout your career, an active alumni relations department can give you continued support. Post-MBA executive education series, fund-raising events, and continued job placement efforts are all resources you can draw on for years to come.

In the interview below, you will see how a recent grad's professor is the source of the connections that will this student him start his own business overseas.

## STEPHEN HAZELTON, MIT SLOAN SCHOOL OF MANAGEMENT, CLASS OF 2005

Q: What made you decide to get the MBA and go to the MIT Sloan School of Business?

A: There are probably three different reasons why I went to school. First, there were skills I needed to learn. Examples of key courses I took include Entrepreneurial Finance, which will be very relevant for me in the coming months when I begin to negotiate with investors; Law for the Entrepreneur which was practical and relevant; Negotiations was another—whether it is for life in general or business—and Accounting—that's a very standard course, but it was an area in which I did not have much experience. So, the curriculum was a big draw for me.

The second draw was MIT Sloan's strong focus on entrepreneurship. If you look at the world of entrepreneurship on a map, the two hotspots are Silicon Valley and Route 128 (a highway in the Boston area where most start-ups and venture capital firms are located). I wanted to be in that community and understand and have access to it. Finally, I wanted to meet and learn from my classmates, given their diverse backgrounds.

Q: Now as you approach graduation, has the MBA performed for you in the way you thought it would?

A: I wanted to pursue entrepreneurship internationally. I have a background in Latin American markets, and for me the MBA has been highly relevant. The way I gauge that is how the MBA helped me with what I'm going to be doing after school, which is starting a business focused on financial services in Vietnam. A professor of mine went out of her way to put me in touch with a venture capitalist in Hanoi and things went on from there. This investor has a network in Vietnam and is going to support me both financially and otherwise; without this it would be a bit daunting to take a shot on my own.

Had I not gone to MIT Sloan and gotten to know this professor I'm not sure all this would have happened. So the MBA has been highly relevant because what I'm going to be doing is a direct result of my attending MIT Sloan.

Q: Specifically, how else did MIT Sloan provide you with real exposure and access?

A: Because of MIT's rich tradition in entrepreneurship, we get a lot of interest from that community. We have numerous opportunities to build business plans, receive feedback, pitch to investors, and learn from successful entrepreneurs that come to campus. It's a really special environment.

Another unique way is the popular course, Global Entrepreneurship Lab. Students in the course spend the month of January working with a start-up in emerging markets around the world. Companies host students and provide a view into how entrepreneurship is done in, for instance, Brazil or China.

Q: What were you doing before business school?

A: I was working for a nonprofit called Endeavor. Its mission is to promote entrepreneurship in emerging markets. They're in Africa and South America. My focus was on South America; I lived in Chile for a while and helped restart the local office there.

**Q: Does it matter where you go to school?**

A: In my case it definitely did.

**Q: What advice would you give to today's applicant?**

A: Make sure you understand why you want to go business school and what you want to get out of it. I would advise someone attending a program to use that two-year window to assess what they really are passionate about rather than pursue some of the fast-track careers by default.

**Q: What do you mean by "fast-track career by default?"**

A: Just because a company comes to campus to recruit doesn't mean it's necessarily right for you. I would consider those opportunities, but I think some people go into that track without considering other options. Consider other options based on your interests as well.

**Q: If you had to do it all over again would you do anything differently?**

A: I would apply to fewer schools. I applied to four. I would have applied to two b-schools because what I was looking for was at MIT Sloan and Stanford.

**Q; How do you measure return on investment?**

A: First off, I should say that I have a fellowship from Sloan that covers almost all of my tuition. I think that gives me a little bit of a different perspective. The flip side is I have the average debt that others do in my living expenses. So I invested a fair amount of my own money, although I will not have those huge tuition bills to pay off.

I think some people look at the MBA payoff based on what kind of job they will get that's well regarded or pays them better than what they were making before business school. I don't. I don't look at education as a financial thing. It's a lifelong thing. I feel very closely connected to MIT and will come back here for support for the rest of my career.

As for money, I will be making very little money starting my own business.

It's true, a business education costs a lot of money, but it should not be a financial decision.

I want to add that I'm an immigrant to this country. The MBA is a wonderful way for an immigrant to assimilate into the business world.

**Q: How would you describe your experience with your peers at Sloan?**

A: In going into any situation where there are relationships to be made, I'm a quality versus quantity type of person. So I've made some really great friends here—people I will keep in touch with for the rest of my life. It's what I expected and hoped for.

# CHAPTER 4

## ADMISSIONS

---

### PREPARING TO BE A SUCCESSFUL APPLICANT

#### GET GOOD GRADES

If you're still in school, concentrate on getting good grades. A high GPA says you've got not only brains, but also discipline. It shows the admissions committee you have what you need to make it through the program. If you're applying directly from college or have limited job experience, your grades will matter even more. The admissions committee will have little else on which to evaluate you.

It's especially important that you do well in courses such as economics, statistics, and calculus. Success in these courses is more meaningful than success in classes like "Monday Night at the Movies" film appreciation. Of course, English is also important; b-schools want students who communicate well.

#### STRENGTHEN MATH SKILLS

Number-crunching is an inescapable part of b-school. If your work experience has failed to develop your quantitative skills, take an accounting or statistics course for credit at a local college or b-school. If you have a liberal arts background and did poorly in math, or got a low GMAT Math score, this is especially important. Getting a decent grade will go a long way toward convincing the admissions committee you can manage the quantitative challenges of the program.

#### WORK FOR A FEW YEARS—BUT NOT TOO MANY

Business schools have traditionally favored applicants who have worked full-time for several years. There are three primary reasons for this: 1) With experience comes maturity; 2) You're more likely to know what you want out of the program; 3) Your experience enables you to bring real-work perspectives to the classroom. Because business school is designed for you to learn from your classmates, each student's contribution is important.

Until recently, b-schools preferred to admit only those students with two to five years of work experience. The rationale was that at two years you have worked enough to be able to make a solid contribution, while beyond four or five, you might be too advanced in your career to appreciate the program fully. However, as we noted earlier in this book, there is a new trend among top schools toward admitting "younger" applicants—that is, candidates with limited work experience as well as those straight from college.

Depending on the schools to which you're applying and the strength of your resume of accomplishments, you may not need full-time, professional work experience. Of course, there's a catch: The younger you are, the harder you'll have to work to supply supporting evidence for your case as a qualified applicant. Be prepared to convince admissions committees that you've already done some incredible things, especially if you're hailing straight from college.

If you've targeted top-flight schools like Wharton, Columbia, or Stanford, applying fresh out of college is still a long shot. While your chances of gaining admission with little work experience have improved, your best shot is still to err on the conservative side and get a year or two of some professional experience under your belt.

If you're not interested in the big league or you plan on attending a local program, the number of years you should work before applying may vary. Research the admissions requirements at your target school. There's no doubt the MBA will jumpstart your career and have long-lasting effects on your business (and perhaps personal) outlook. If you're not ready to face the real world after college, plenty of solid b-schools will welcome you to another two years of academia.

There is one caveat to this advice, however. If your grades are weak, consider working at least three years before applying. The more professional success you have, the greater the likelihood that admissions committees will overlook your GPA.

## LET YOUR JOB WORK FOR YOU

Many companies encourage employees to go to b-school. Some of these companies have close ties to a favored b-school and produce well-qualified applicants. If their employees are going to the kinds of schools you want to get into, these may be smart places to work.

Other companies, such as investment banks, feature training programs, at the end of which trainees go to b-school or leave the company. These programs hire undergraduates right out of school. They're known for producing solid, highly skilled applicants. Moreover, they're full of well-connected alumni who may write influential letters of recommendation.

Happily, the opposite tactic—working in an industry that generates few applicants—can be equally effective. Admissions officers look for students from underrepresented professions. Applicants from biotechnology, health care, not-for-profit, and even the Peace Corps are viewed favorably.

One way to set yourself apart is to have had two entirely different professional experiences before business school. For example, if you worked in finance, your next job might be in a different field, like marketing. Supplementing quantitative work with qualitative experiences demonstrates versatility.

Finally, what you do in your job is important. Seek out opportunities to distinguish yourself. Even if your responsibilities are limited, exceed the expectations of the position. B-schools are looking for leaders.

## MARCH FROM THE MILITARY

A surprising number of b-school students hail from the military (although the armed forces probably had commanders in mind, not CEOs, when they designed their regimen). Military officers know how to be managers because they've held command positions. And they know how to lead a team under the most difficult of circumstances.

Because most have traveled all over the world, they also know how to work with people from different cultures. As a result, they're ideally suited to learn alongside students with diverse backgrounds and perspectives. B-schools with a global focus are particularly attracted to such experience.

The decision to enlist in the military is a very personal one. However, if you've thought of joining those few good men and women, this may be as effective a means of preparing for b-school as more traditional avenues.

## CHECK OUT THOSE ESSAY QUESTIONS NOW

You're worried you don't have interesting stories to tell. Or you just don't know what to write. What do you do?

Ideally, several months before your application is due, you should read the essay questions and begin to think about your answers. Could you describe an ethical dilemma at work? Are you involved in anything outside the office (or classroom)? If not, now is the time to do something about it. While this may seem contrived, it's preferable to sitting down to write the application and finding you have to scrape for or, even worse, manufacture situations.

Use the essay questions as a framework for your personal and professional activities. Look back over your business calendar, and see if you can find some meaty experiences for the essays in your work life. Keep your eyes open for a situation that involves questionable ethics. And if all you do is work, work, work, get involved in activities that round out your background. In other words, get a life.

Get involved in community-based activities. Some possibilities are being a big brother/big sister, tutoring in a literacy program, or initiating a recycling project. Demonstrating a concern for others looks good to admissions committees, and hey, it's good for your soul, too.

It's also important to seek out leadership experiences. B-schools are looking for individuals who can manage groups. Volunteer to chair a professional committee or run for an office in a club. It's a wide-open world; you can pick from any number of activities. The bottom line is this: The extracurriculars you select can show that you are mature, multifaceted, and appealing.

We don't mean to sound cynical. Obviously, the best applications do nothing more than describe your true, heartfelt interests and show off your sparkling personality. We're not suggesting you try to guess which activity will win the hearts of admissions directors and then mold yourself accordingly. Instead, think of projects and activities you care about, that maybe you haven't gotten around to acting on, and act on them now!

## PICK YOUR RECOMMENDERS CAREFULLY

By the time you apply to business school, you shouldn't have to scramble for recommendations. Like the material for your essays, sources for recommendations should be considered long before the application is due.

How do you get great recommendations? Obviously, good work is a prerequisite. Whom you ask is equally important. Bosses who know you well will recommend you on both a personal and professional level. They can provide specific examples of your accomplishments, skills, and character. Additionally, they can convey a high level of interest in your candidacy.

There's also the issue of trust. B-school recommendations are made in confidence; you probably won't see exactly what's been written about you. Choose someone you can trust to deliver the kind of recommendation that will push you over the top. A casual acquaintance may fail you by writing an adequate, yet mostly humdrum letter.

Cultivate relationships that yield glowing recommendations. Former and current professors, employers, clients, and managers are all good choices. An equally impressive recommendation can come from someone who has observed you in a worthwhile extracurricular activity.

We said before you won't see *exactly* what's being written about you, but that doesn't mean you should just hand a blank piece of paper to your recommender. Left to their own devices, recommenders may create a portrait that leaves out your best features. You need to prep them on what to write. Remind them of those projects or activities in which you achieved some success. You might also discuss the total picture of yourself that you are trying to create. The recommendation should reinforce what you're saying about yourself in your essays.

About "Big Shot" recommendations: Don't bother. Getting some professional athlete who's a friend of your parent's to write you a recommendation will do you no good if he or she doesn't know you very well, even if he or she is "president of the universe." Don't try to fudge your application—let people who really know you and your work tell the honest, believable, and impressive truth.

## PREPARE FOR THE GRADUATE MANAGEMENT ADMISSION TEST (GMAT)

Most b-schools require you to take the GMAT. The GMAT is now a three-and-a-half-hour computer adaptive test (CAT) with multiple-choice Math and Verbal sections as well as an essay section. It's the kind of test you hate to take and schools love to require.

Why is the GMAT required? B-schools believe it measures your verbal and quantitative skills and predicts success in the MBA program. Some think this is a bunch of hooey, but most schools weigh your GMAT scores heavily in the admissions decision. If nothing else, it gives the school a quantitative tool to use to compare you with other applicants.

The test begins with the Analytical Writing Assessment (AWA) containing two essays questions. In the past, all questions that have appeared on the official GMAT have been drawn from a list of about 150 topics that appear in *The Official Guide to the GMAT* (published by the Educational Testing Service). Review that list and you'll have a pretty good idea of what to expect from the AWA. You will have 30 minutes to write each essay. By the way, you will be required to type your essay at the computer. Depending on how rusty your typing skills are, you may want to consider a bit of practice.

Next comes the multiple-choice section which has two parts: a seventy-five-minute Math section and a seventy-five-minute Verbal section. The Math section includes problem-solving questions (e.g., "Train A leaves Baltimore at 6:32 A.M. . . .") and data-sufficiency questions. Data-sufficiency questions require you to determine whether you have been given enough information to solve a particular math problem. The good news about these types of questions is that you don't actually have to solve the problem; the bad news is that these questions can be very tricky. The Verbal section tests reading skills (reading comprehension), grammar (sentence correction), and logic (critical reasoning).

For those unfamiliar with CAT exams, here's a brief overview of how they work: On multiple-choice sections, the computer starts by asking a question of medium difficulty. If you answer it correctly, the computer asks you a question that is slightly more difficult than the previous question. If you answer incorrectly, the computer asks a slightly easier question next. The test continues this way until you have answered enough questions that it can make an accurate (or so they say) assessment of your performance and assign you a score.

Most people feel they have no control over the GMAT. They dread it as the potential bomb in their application. But relax; you have more control than you think. You can take a test-preparation course to review the math and verbal material, learn test-taking strategies, and build your confidence. Test-prep courses can be highly effective. The Princeton Review offers what we think is the best GMAT course available. Even better, it offers two options for online preparation in addition to the traditional classroom course and one-on-one tutoring. Another option is to take a look at our book *Cracking the GMAT CAT*, which reviews all the subjects and covers all the tips you would learn in one of our courses.

How many times should you take the GMAT? More than once if you didn't ace it on the first try. But watch out: Multiple scores that fall in the same range make you look unprepared. Don't take the test more than once if you don't expect a decent increase, and don't even think of taking it the first time without serious preparation. Limiting your GMAT attempts to two is best. Three tries are okay if there were unusual circumstances or if you really need another shot at it. If you take it more than three times, the admissions committee will think you have an unhealthy obsession. A final note: If you submit more than one score, most schools will take the highest.

If you don't have math courses on your college transcript or numbers-oriented work experience, it's especially important to get a solid score on the quantitative section. There's a lot of math between you and the MBA.

## HOW THE ADMISSIONS CRITERIA ARE WEIGHTED

Although admissions requirements vary among business schools, most rely on the following criteria: GMAT score, college GPA, work experience, your essays, letters of recommendation (academic and/or professional), an interview with an admissions representative, and your extracurriculars. The first four are generally the most heavily weighted. The more competitive the school, the less room there is for weakness in any area. Any component out of sync, such as a weak GMAT score, is potentially harmful.

Happily, the admissions process at business school is one where great emphasis is placed on getting to know you as a person. The essay component is the element that allows the schools to do just that. Your essays can refute weaknesses, fill in gaps, and in general, charmingly persuade an admissions board you've got the right stuff. They are the single most important criteria in business school admissions.

But as we've just said, they're not the only criteria. All pieces of your application must come together to form a cohesive whole. It is the *entire application* that determines whether you win admission.

### ANTICIPATE AND COORDINATE

The application process is very time-consuming, so anticipating what you need to accomplish within the admissions time frame is critical. To make the best use of our advice, you should first contact each of the programs on your personal list of schools. Their standards and criteria for admission may vary, and you'll need to follow their specific guidelines. Please note that the less competitive a school is, the more easily you may be able to breeze through (or completely omit) the rigorous requirements we identify as crucial in the application process for the top programs.

In addition, business school applicants are often overwhelmed by how much they have to do to complete not only one, but several applications. Proper management of the process is essential, since there are so many factors to coordinate in each application.

You'll have to prep for the GMAT, then actually take the test, round up some writers for your recommendations, follow up with those chosen to write recommendations, make sure the recommendations are mailed in on time, have your college transcript sent, and finally, write the essays. Of course, some schools require an interview as well. What makes all of this particularly challenging is that many applicants have to do all of this while balancing the demands of a full-time job.

We know that it takes a supreme force of will to complete even one application. As grad school applications go, a top business school's is pretty daunting. So if you don't stay focused on the details and deadlines, you may drop the ball.

There are many common and incredibly embarrassing mistakes you can avoid with prudent early planning. These include allowing your recommenders to miss the deadline, submitting an application full of typos and grammatical errors, sending one school an essay intended for another, or forgetting to change the school name when using the same essay for several applications. Applicants who wind up cramming for the GMAT or squeezing their essay writing into several all-nighters end up seriously shortchanging themselves.

## APPLY EARLY

The best advice is to plan early and apply early. The former diminishes the likelihood of an accidental omission or a missed deadline. The latter increases your chances of acceptance.

The filing period ranges anywhere from six to eight months. The earlier you apply, the better your chances. There are a number of reasons for this:

First, there's plenty of space available early on. As the application deadline nears, spaces fill up. The majority of applicants don't apply until the later months because of procrastination or unavoidable delays. As the deadline draws close, the greatest number of applicants compete for the fewest number of spaces.

Second, in the beginning, admissions officers have little clue about how selective they can be. They haven't reviewed enough applications to determine the competitiveness of the pool. An early application may be judged more on its own merit than on how it stacks up against others. This is in your favor if the pool turns out to be unusually competitive. Above all, admissions officers like to lock their classes in early; they can't be certain they'll get their normal supply of applicants. Admissions decisions may be more generous at this time.

Third, by getting your application in early you're showing a strong interest. The admissions committee is likely to view you as someone keen on going to their school.

To be sure, some admissions officers report that the first batch of applications tend to be from candidates with strong qualifications, confident of acceptance. In this case, you might not be the very first one on line; but being closer to the front is still better than getting lost in the heap of last-minute hopefuls.

Of course, if applications are down that year at all b-schools or—thanks to a drop in its ranking—at the one to which you are applying, then filing later means you can benefit from admissions officers' desperate scramble to fill spaces. But this is risky business, especially since the rankings don't come out until the spring.

Conversely, if the school to which you are applying was recently ranked number one or two, applying early may make only a marginal difference. Swings in the rankings from year to year send school applications soaring and sagging. A newly crowned number-one or two school will be flooded with applications of a potential edge to be gained by filing earlier or later. Regardless from the beginning to the end of its filing period, do not put in your application until you are satisfied that it is the best you can make it. Once a school has passed on your application, it will not reconsider you until the following year.

## ROUNDS VS. ROLLING ADMISSIONS

Applications are processed in one of two ways: rounds or rolling admissions. Schools that use rounds divide the filing period into three or so timed cycles. Applications are batched into the round in which they are received and reviewed in competition with others in that round. A list of a b-school's round dates can be obtained by contacting its admissions office if it employs this method. Applications to schools with rolling admissions are reviewed on an ongoing basis as they are received.

## GMAT AND GPA

The GMAT and GPA are used in two ways. First, they're "success indicators" for the academic work you'll have to slog through if admitted—will you have the brainpower to succeed in the program? Second, they're used as benchmarks to compare each applicant to other applicants within the pool. At the more selective schools, you'll need a higher score and average to stay in the game.

Pearson VUE and the American College Testing Program (ACT) administer the GMAT. You'll need to register to take the exam by registering online at www.mba.com. Many applicants take the exam more than once to improve their scores. Test preparation is also an option for boosting your numbers—visit www.princetonreview.com for more information about The Princeton Review's GMAT courses.

Your college transcript is a major factor in the strength of your candidacy. Some schools focus more closely on the junior- and senior-year grades than the overall GPA, and most consider the reputation of your college and the difficulty of your course selections. A transcript loaded with offerings like "Environmental Appreciation" and "The Child in You" won't be valued as highly as one packed with calculus and history classes.

## THE ESSAYS

Admissions committees consider the essays the clincher, the swing vote on the "admit/deny" issue. Essays offer the most substantive information about who you really are. The GMAT and GPA reveal little about you, only that you won't crash and burn. Your work history provides a record of performance and justifies your stated desire to study business. But the essays tie all the pieces of the application together and create a summary of your experiences, skills, background, and beliefs.

The essays do more than give answers to questions. They create thumbnail psychological profiles. Depending on how you answer a question or what you present, you reveal yourself in any number of ways—creative, witty, open-minded, articulate, mature, to name a few. On the other hand, your essay can also reveal a negative side, such as arrogance, sloppiness, or an inability to think and write clearly.

For more in-depth information on writing b-school application essays, including samples from successful applicants, check out *Business School Essays That Made a Difference* at www.princetonreview.com/mba/bookstore.asp.

## LETTERS OF RECOMMENDATION

Letters of recommendation function as a reality check. Admissions committees expect them to support and reinforce what they're seeing in the rest of your application. When the information doesn't match up with the picture you've painted, it makes you look bad. Because you won't see the recommendation (it's sent in "blind"), you won't even know there's a problem. This can mean the end of your candidacy.

That's why you need to take extreme care in selecting your references.

Scan each application for guidelines on choosing your references—business schools typically request an academic and a professional reference. The academic reference should be someone who can evaluate your performance in an academic environment. It's better to ask an instructor, teacher's aide, or mentor who knew you well than a famous professor who barely knew your name.

The same holds true for your professional reference. Seek out individuals who can evaluate your performance on many levels. The reference will be far more credible. Finding the right person to write your professional reference, however, can be trickier. You may not wish to reveal to your boss early on that you plan on leaving, and if the dynamics of your relationship are not ideal (hey, it happens once in a while), he or she might not make an appropriate reference. If this is the case, seek out a boss at a former job or someone who was your supervisor at your current job but has since moved to another organization. Avoid friends, colleagues, and clients as references unless the school explicitly says its okay.

Advise your writers on themes and qualities you highlighted in your application. Suggest that they include real-life examples of your performance to illustrate their points. In other words, script the recommendation as best you can. Your boss, even if he or she is your biggest fan, may not know what your recommendation should include.

A great recommendation is rarely enough to save a weak application from doom. But it might push a borderline case over to the "admit" pile. Mediocre recommendations can be damaging; an application that is strong in all other areas now has a weakness, an inconsistency.

A final warning on this topic: Procrastination is common here. Micromanage your references so that each recommendation arrives on time! If need be, provide packaging for an overnight letter, have your reference seal it up, and then ship it out yourself.

## THE INTERVIEW

Not all business schools attach equal value to the interview. For some, it's an essential screening tool. For others, it's used to make a final decision on those caught somewhere between "admit" and "reject." Some schools may encourage, but not require, the interview. Others make it informative, with little connection to the admissions decision.

Like the letters of recommendation, an interview may serve as a reality check to reinforce the total picture. It may also be used to fill in the blanks, particularly in borderline cases.

If an interview is offered, take it. In person, you may be a more compelling candidate. You can use the interview to further address weaknesses or bring dull essays to life. Most importantly, you can display the kinds of qualities—enthusiasm, sense of humor, maturity—that can positively sway an admissions decision.

Act quickly to schedule your interview. Admissions departments often lack the time and staff to interview every candidate who walks through their doors. You don't want your application decision delayed by several months (and placed in a more competitive round or pool) because your interview was scheduled late in the filing period.

A great interview can tip the scale in the "admit" direction. How do you know if it was great? You were calm and focused. You expressed yourself and your ideas clearly. Your interviewer invited you to go rock climbing with him or her the following weekend. (Okay, let's just say you developed a solid personal rapport with the interviewer.)

A mediocre interview may not have much impact, unless your application is hanging on by a thread. In such a case, the person you're talking to (harsh as it may seem) is probably looking for a reason not to admit you, rather than a reason to let you in. If you feel your application may be in that hazy, marginal area, try to be extra-inspired in your interview.

Approach this meeting as you would a job interview. Dress and act the part of a professional. But at the same time, remember: You're being sized up as a person in all of your dimensions. Avoid acting stiff or like a stuffed shirt. Limit your use of business jargon. Be personable. Gear yourself up for an enjoyable conversation in which you may discuss your hobbies or recent cross-country trip. Talk about your passions or any areas in which you have achieved excellence—even something like gourmet cooking. Avoid stunt-like gimmicks (we don't advise you to pull out a platter of peppercorn pâté sautéed in anchovy sauce). The idea is to get the interviewer thinking of you as someone who will contribute greatly to the quality of campus life. Try to be your witty, charming, natural self.

# Chapter 5

## Quotas, Recruitment, and Diversity

B-schools don't have to operate under quotas—governmental or otherwise. However, they probably try harder than most corporations to recruit diverse groups of people. Just as the modern business world has become global and multicultural, so too have b-schools. They must not only teach diversity in the classroom but also make it a reality in their campus population and, if possible, faculty.

Schools that have a diverse student body tend to be proud of it. They tout their success in profiles that demographically slice and dice the previous year's class by gender, race, and geographic and international residency. Prospective students can review this data and compare the diversity of the schools they've applied to.

But such diversity doesn't come naturally from the demographics of the applicant pool. Admissions committees have to work hard at it. In some cases, enrollment is encouraged with generous financial aid packages and scholarships.

While they don't have quotas per se, they do target groups for admission, seeking a demographic balance in many areas. Have they admitted enough women, minorities, foreign students, marketing strategists, and liberal arts majors? Are different parts of the country represented?

As we've said before, the best b-schools tend to attract top talent, students, and recruiters to their campus. Women and minorities are the most sought-after groups targeted for admission. So it's no surprise that programs that report higher-than-average female and minority enrollments tend to be among the very best.

### AN INITIATIVE FOR MINORITIES

Some schools report higher minority enrollments than others, so our advice is consistent: you need to thoroughly research the program you've set your sights on. Consider your goals. Do you simply want to attend the most prestigious program? How will social factors impact your goals and experiences on campus?

Most business schools aspire to diversify their programs. It's the number of minorities applying to business school that has remained consistently low. An initiative of the Graduate Management Admissions Council called The Diversity Pipeline Alliance (www.diversitypipeline.org) was formed to reverse this trend and increase the number of underrepresented minorities pursuing a business career. Much like the initiative for women, this organization plans a powerful marketing campaign with a pro-business career message for minority students from middle school to graduate school. It offers information on current opportunities for mentorships, internships, and financial assistance and provides an impressive roster of member organizations, services, and educational opportunities.

Minority enrollment at business schools is still quite low, so in all likelihood, you will not experience the dramatic upward shift in b-school demographics in the near future that initiatives like the Diversity Pipeline Alliance hope to influence. However, by recognizing the disparity between the minority presence in the U.S. and minority involvement in business education and practice, we are working toward a solution.

As you make up your mind about where you want to go for b-school, know that the scenario is positive and that new infrastructures exist to support your business career.

# FEMALE APPEAL: BUSINESS SCHOOLS GET UP TO SPEED

If you've toured the campus and classrooms of a business school, you may have noticed something: On average, roughly 70 percent of any given MBA program's students are male. While this may make a nice pool of dating prospects for the women who are enrolled, it's not something business schools are happy with—far from it! In fact, it's something they are working to change as quickly as they can.

Top-flight schools typically see higher female enrollment, in part because of all they offer, but also because, like males, women want to benefit from the status of an elite school. Stanford, for example, had a 26 percent female enrollment 10 years ago; now, women make up 35 percent of the class of 2005. While 35 percent may not match the 50 percent male-to-female ratio of other graduate programs, closing the MBA gap is only a matter of time.

## School Initiatives

How can we be sure that female enrollment will continue to increase? One reason is that getting women enthused about a career in business is a sky-high priority at business schools across the country these days. To wit, many business schools have launched their own women-only outreach and recruiting events. Columbia University hosts an annual "Women in Business" conference that brings together more than 700 alumnae, business leaders, students and prospective students to network and share ideas on achieving success in the marketplace. Linda Meehan, Assistant Dean for Admissions at Columbia Business School, knows that this outreach is working because "applicants walk away wowed by the extraordinary experience of being surrounded by so many intelligent, passionate and successful women." Events like these aim to dispel myths, discuss the perceived lack of role models, and help women make informed decisions.

Stanford's events, says Wendy Hansen, Associate Director of Admissions at the Stanford Business School, "focus on the educational experience, but also on the unique types of issues women have, such as: how does getting the MBA fit in with having a family or having a spouse? How do I make this experience fit in with my life?" Julia Min, Executive Director of Admissions at UC Berkeley's Haas School of Business, says attendees often find comfort in numbers. "Seeing such a large presence of women is empowering. They realize they're not in this alone, that there are other women around like them."

If all this sounds like good public relations, it is. Schools want to get the word out: MBAs offer women viable opportunities. But if the business schools are talking the talk, they're also walking the walk. There's nothing superficial about this campaign. Bit by bit, the MBA landscape for women is changing.

Opportunities begin even before the first day of class. At Stanford, admitted women are treated to one-on-one admit-lunches with female alum. Once an admit gets to campus, they find MBA life is chock-full of student-run women and management programs, support groups, retreats, executive conferences, mentoring programs, and other dedicated resources for women-only.

For many years now, most business programs have had an on-campus Partners Club for spouses and significant others—a benefit to both female and male students. Newcomers to the business-school scene include groups like The Parents Club and Biz Kids where students can find family-oriented classmates and activities. Columbia University's Mother's Network is an initiative that provides a formal support network for new, current and future b-school moms. Perhaps the most symbolic gesture of the increasing influence of women in business school is Stanford's provision of a private nursing room for MBA-moms and their babies in its main classroom facility.

## More Flexibility and Making it Work

Of course, there's still room for improvement. A continuing problem at business schools is a lack of coursework and case study material featuring women leaders. Likewise, there is an absence of female professors on the academic front.

Apart from these lingering issues, business schools continue to tackle the particular challenges female students face. For many women, the late starting age can be a turn-off. But even here, there are new options and opportunities to consider.

If you are stressed out from trying to have it all and have written off getting an MBA, new early-initiative programs might make you pause and reconsider your decision. Harvard and Stanford have developed an early career track that aims to minimize the impact of the biological clock on a prospective applicant's decision to pursue an MBA. Other schools are likely to follow suit.

The early career track offers a solution that is as simple as it is practical: admit women (and men) to the MBA program either straight out of college or with just a few years of work experience. Business schools hope that the option to attain their MBA early on in their careers will prompt more women to apply to their programs. With a bigger window to accomplish their professional goals, more women will turn to the MBA as a viable option that won't require them to sacrifice their personal lives.

Beginning a business career earlier eliminates the immediate problem of timing. But what happens down the road? While it helps to remove one timing issue, it can't indefinitely postpone the balancing act that shadows many women's careers. It's hard to rationalize the opportunity costs of the MBA knowing that the investment might be forsaken when tough choices have to be made.

Business schools blame misconceptions about the utility of the MBA for women's reticence on this front. They feel that many women underestimate the broad reach of the degree. The MBA is not just for hard-core careers like banking and finance, but is also useful in not-for-profit work, less high-stress industries such as consumer goods, and leadership positions in a wide range of fields.

Further, says Hansen, "There is a tremendous amount of flexibility in a general management degree. The MBA positions you much more effectively to make an impact wherever you fall at different points in your life. It gives you the tools and framework to apply those skills at different levels and in different intensities. For example, women can rise to a partner level or a senior leadership position and then scale back to a different role within the organization. They can also scale back to part-time work." In other words, the investment doesn't have to be forsaken; it might instead be redirected.

There's no doubt the return on investment (that's ROI in business speak) for the MBA is high. Six-figure salaries and sign-on bonuses that pay you back for the cost of your MBA tuition are hard to beat (and unlike medical, veterinary, and law school grads, you won't have malpractice premiums eating into your take-home pay). If you've thought business school might be right for you, keep investigating—you might be right.

## WHERE ARE THE WOMEN IN MBA PROGRAMS?

Are you a professional woman in her mid-to-late twenties? Do you see graduate school in your future? During these tough times, you might envision yourself back on campus sooner rather than later. Downturns do tend to fuel grad school applications. After all, what better place to wait out the economy and avoid the gaping pit of joblessness?

Grad school can be a cure-all for many ills: It can jump-start or redirect a stubbornly off-track career; it can give you a place to hang out while you figure out what you want to be when you grow up (law school, a three-year degree, offers an even longer alternative); and it can transform your personal life as you vault into a new career. Even in uncertain times there is certainty in knowing that after two years in school you can emerge reborn as a professional with a spanking new identity, prescribed career track, and a solid alumni network.

Despite the huge appeal of graduate school, be it as an escape from bad times or as your true, chosen path, MBA programs have remained a problematic choice for many women. Female enrollment at law, medical, and veterinary schools now hovers at, or near, the 50 percent mark. So what's up with business schools? Why has female enrollment at business schools stagnated at around 30 percent?

Even during the best of times, business schools have struggled to attract women. Is this due to the unique challenges women face in building and sustaining their careers over a lifetime of choices, both professional and personal, or is there another reason? Clearly an MBA presents many opportunities, but, for women, will these opportunities upset their already delicate balancing acts?

## THINKING OF FAMILY

Let's start with biology—as in biological clocks. Since a prerequisite for admission to many business programs is prior work experience, first-year business school students are typically a bit older than their law or med school counterparts. In fact, the average age for entering full-time MBA students is 28. This means that by the time graduation rolls around, MBA students are heading into their thirties—a prime time for marriage and children. For some women, that timing couldn't be worse.

Newly minted MBAs in their early thirties are just starting to reap the rewards of their business school investments by scoring brand new, mid-to-senior level jobs. With these jobs come ever-greater demands and time pressures. But, for many, the pressure to have a personal life is just as great. Those kinds of competing priorities are the very headaches women hope to avoid. Making matters worse, MBA jobs at the senior level can vault women into a culture that may still be dominated by old-school thinking (translation: men) and a culture that may be less tolerant of efforts to balance work commitments with family.

But these dilemmas begin long before business school graduation. Again, because MBA students tend to be older, many women have to factor a partner or child into their graduate school decision, especially if it involves relinquishing a paycheck and/or relocation. And many of these women encounter a potential double standard: Husbands and boyfriends, especially those with careers, are often less willing to relocate on their female partner's behalf than vice versa.

## NO URGENT MATTER

Another reason business school enrollment for women may be low is that an MBA is not a barrier to entry nor is it a requirement for success in business. In addition, it isn't a rite of passage in many fields that appeal to high numbers of women: marketing, publishing, fashion, and teaching. By contrast, notes Eileen Chang, former Associate Director of Admissions at the Harvard Business School, "If your objective is to be a lawyer or doctor, you simply can't practice without the requisite degree. Business school is fundamentally different because the career path is one where the MBA can put you on any number of tracks—be it banking, accounting, or management—but doesn't require a credential." Between the lack of a required degree for entering business and the late starting age to enter a program, some women perceive a high opportunity cost for the MBA.

## FEAR OF MATH?

Why more women aren't pursuing an MBA is a question that business schools have been asking themselves for years. Some hard answers came in the form of a recent study by the University of Michigan's Business School Center for the Education of Women and the Catalyst Foundation. The following issues were identified as key deterrents to business school for women: the MBA is still seen as a male domain; there is a lack of support from employers; a lack of career opportunity and flexibility; a lack of access to powerful business networks and role models; and a perception that b-school is overloaded with math.

According to many schools, math fears are just that—fears. Harvard's Chang observes, "Maybe historically, math was considered a hurdle. But we see so many women who have strong skills coming from fields that are quantitative, such as banking and engineering, that I think the math fears are almost a myth. But this is a myth we want to work against. We want applicants to know they can handle the math."

Julia Min, Executive Director of Admissions at UC Berkeley's Haas School of Business, concurs, "The math phobia may be unfounded to a certain degree, and still it's a perception that has been long-lasting. Women [enter business school] and perform extremely well."

But if you're frightened by math, you need to know that a business school education does require a basic command of the subject. "You do need to be comfortable with numbers," advises Wendy Hansen, Associate Director of Admissions at the Stanford Business School. She continues, "The strongest MBA programs are going to be rigorous in math. Knowing how to influence and lead an organization requires understanding the language of business, which includes accounting and finance."

Still, prospective MBAs with a math phobia need not panic; most programs will work with students who lack the necessary math background. "At Stanford, we have a pre-term program of courses before classes begin to get students up to speed," says Hansen, "We also encourage people to take quantitative courses before they come to our school to develop their skills."

If your math fears are not so easily assuaged, concerns about a persistent Old Boys Network might be. As Hansen notes, "Women may say, I don't see the masses of female role models doing what I want to do. That is going to change slowly. But it is going to change. We have to reach a point where those in school reach a place where they are out in the world having an impact."

## OUR ADVICE

Look at the number of female MBA students attending your targeted school and evaluate whether you would feel comfortable there. Research the number and range of student organizations for women and speak with female MBAs about school life.

## WHERE ARE THEY NOW?

It takes a monumental leap of faith to go to business school—to take two years out of your professional life, go to zero income, and drop $60,000 or more on tuition. By contrast, making the decision to go to medical or law school is more straightforward. Of the three so-called primary professions—business, medicine, and law—business is the only one you can pursue without a degree. In fact, you can become highly successful (and may already be) without an MBA. So how do you decide if going to business school is the best option for you?

Perhaps the best way to assess the value of the MBA is to talk to the people who have already gone through the program and can reflect on the experience and the credential. Over the next several pages, you'll find a series of interviews with women who have graduated with an MBA. Their graduation dates range from 1992 to 2004, but their common thread lies in how valuable each of them found their advanced degree to be. Each of the women came from different backgrounds, went to different schools, were hoping for different things from their b-school experiences, and took different approaches to their career paths. Here, they share their choices, advice, and what they might change if they were to do it all again.

We begin with Cathy Crane-Moley, an outstanding MBA with the talent, passion, and drive that have made her one of America's most successful businesswomen. In fact, Entelos, Inc., which Cathy co-founded in 1996, was named one of the 13 coolest companies in the nation by *Fortune* magazine.

Ten years out, Crane-Moley is the co-founder and senior vice-president of strategy for Entelos, Inc., and former chief financial officer and head of corporate development.

## CATHY CRANE-MOLEY, STANFORD GRADUATE SCHOOL OF BUSINESS, CLASS OF '92

Q: Cathy, as a newly minted MBA, what were your thoughts on what the degree could do for you?

A: At that point in time, I didn't have a 10-plus-year horizon in my view. My thoughts were more about the immediate future of my career. I was a molecular biology major as an undergrad. I had worked in sales and in the field and had a big passion for health care. So that's really why I went to get an MBA, to follow through on my passion and vision for a business career in the health care sector.

Q: How did you target Stanford as the school that would deliver on that vision?

A: That's an interesting question. I lived in Virginia at the time and I did a lot of research on schools. I had a number of goals, some of which changed once I got to business school, but one of the goals was to go to a top school—which Stanford is. And I was really interested in somehow combining international business and entrepreneurship, so another goal was to find an environment that would support my exposure to that. So I applied to Stanford and Harvard and Wharton and all the types of schools that would have recruiters coming on campus from an international background. I chose Stanford as the best environment for my combined vision.

Q: What was it about Stanford that fit with your career aspirations in particular?

A: What I really wanted from the MBA was to have the credibility to go build a company in health care. I had an expectation that business school would help me be a better businessperson in science. My goal was to be able to tie together the business and science and pursue a business career in biotechnology health care.

When I went to Stanford I was pretty nervous because all these investment bankers and consultants were using intimidating terms like "run the numbers." When I got to business school I learned that it just meant 2 + 2. So for me it was really about learning a whole new language. Every domain has its own jargon and half the battle is learning the language. Business isn't rocket science. It has some very pragmatic, practical, and even intuitive components to it. So putting a language to it was a critical step for me.

Q: Did you use Stanford's formal on-campus recruiting to get your first job or did you have to do a one-of-a-kind type of job search?

A:   I did a little bit of both. The [formalized] on-campus recruiting I did was more for the sake of exposure. Mostly, I created my own job search, which touches on the MBA and [the] important[ance] [of] the school's networks. The Stanford community was pivotal to my getting the job. There is no question that if I hadn't come out of Stanford, I would not have had the job I had.

Q:  **Why?**

A:   A couple of things. Right out of school, I became an entrepreneur-in-residence at the Mayfield Fund, a venture firm on Sand Hill Road [one of the most nationally prominent addresses for ventures funding]. The combination of my background and MBA was a big plus, but mostly getting my foot in the door was the result of befriending a wonderful woman who was from Stanford's Class of '87. She became a really strong mentor and made endless introductions in the venture community for me. She is now a dear friend of mine and was instrumental in my soul-searching.

Until 1995, when we merged with a public company. Then I started my current company with my four co-founders in 1996, which is also in the biotechnology sector.

Q:  **It sounds as though the Stanford networks were invaluable to this first experience out. What about this next stage?**

A:   Absolutely invaluable. Not just because of the connections—that's one component—but in your own brainstorming about what you want to be in your life.

At business school, you are surrounded by people who have done everything. There were people in my environment who had been entrepreneurs, venture capitalists, investment bankers, and international marketers at pharmaceutical companies. There were incredibly helpful connected professors and alumni. It was all at your fingertips as you were solidifying your own vision.

Q:  **I'm guessing that you would advise students beginning their MBA studies to think hard about why they're there and to take advantage of all the opportunities?**

A:   Absolutely. What can happen is that it's easy to do it [pursue the opportunities], but it's also easy not to do it.

Stanford is a classic example. It's in such a beautiful location and people want to experience California; you can easily be distracted. But this is two years when anyone will return your call. You have heads of state, heads of corporations visiting, people in the nonprofit area showing up. And all you have to do is get on your bike and ride over there.

The other thing is, there are people who have come from a particular background, like investment banking and consulting, who know they intend to return to those careers after business school. But even if that is your goal, you still should use the two years to check everything out. You should use the two years to get more exposure and think about [your] long-term [goals].

Q:  **It's clear the networking opportunities were critical to your future career developments, but how important would you say actual content learning at school was?**

A:   It actually was. But you'll see differences depending on people's backgrounds. For my husband, who was an undergrad at Wharton (I met him at Stanford), he could do corporate finance with his eyes closed. But for me, a molecular biology major as an undergrad, I had never taken business classes, so the academic training was critical. Take corporate finance, for example. I cannot imagine anyone being in the business world without formal corporate finance. Our strategy classes, entrepreneurial classes, small business classes were all great for me. Anything like cost accounting or some of the options theory, I could have done without. But the pragmatic fundamentals gave me the tools to build two businesses from nothing.

**Q:   How was being a woman at Stanford?**

A:   It was wonderful. The quality of people, male and female, was superb. I believe we have a ratio of 33 percent female. We had strong women and we did great. I never noticed any sort of difference in abilities based on gender.

**Q:   Was the business school environment intimidating?**

A:   I didn't think so. I felt very inspired by the people around me.

**Q:   What advice do you have for someone thinking about going to business school now?**

A:   I think it comes back to the theme we've already touched on: make the most of the community that you can, way over and above what the classes offer. Business school is a very unique opportunity—live it while you are there.

## CHIARA PERRY, HARVARD BUSINESS SCHOOL, CLASS OF '92
## SENIOR PRICING ANALYST, A DIVISION OF UNITED TECHNOLOGIES

**Q:   In 1992 the nation was in a recession. Jobs, even for Harvard b-school grads, were scarce. What was your mindset coming out of the program?**

A:   Well, I was fortunate in that I had a job in place before graduating. And I was thinking about the opportunities and challenges I'd face in that position. The company that made me the offer was part of United Technologies, and they had come on campus looking for MBAs. I was really happy to already have the offer by graduation so I didn't have to worry about looking for some great job over the summer.

It's true that in 1992 the economy wasn't in great shape, so many people were heading into graduation without an offer yet. I had a lot of things going on in my life at that time: I got married and moved a thousand miles away from the East Coast to the middle of the Midwest [Indiana].

In terms of my expectations about the degree, I think [I expected] that it [would] put me into an elevated position and salary compared to the people I would be working with at my new job.

**Q:   Given your job offer, were you happy with what the MBA did for you?**

A:   Oh, absolutely. The company was excited to have hired me, and I was excited to work for them. I still work for the same company in the same location.

**Q:   To what do you attribute having stayed with the same company for so long?**

A:   I think it's several things. It's a great place to work. They treat their employees really well. And I don't like to play the sexist card, but it's a wonderful company to work for if you're a woman. My husband and I also really love Bloomington, Indiana. We have two children, and this is a great place to raise a family. So it's been several factors, including having children come into the equation. I only work three days a week now, but I have a professional position.

**Q:   Switching subjects, what kind of person is ideally suited for an MBA?**

A:   I think the type of person that benefits from the MBA is someone who wants to learn a lot, but also realizes that this isn't rocket science. Yes, there are challenging courses, and I learned a tremendous amount when I was at school. But I thought it was hard because of the overwhelming amount of work, the perceived competitiveness within the class, at least the first year. It wasn't necessarily hard academically. There was only one class I felt a bit overwhelmed by. Mostly, I pretty much felt, "Oh, I can do this."

So, back to your question. Someone who can go into a business school program with the attitude that this is a good thing to have, that you're going to challenge yourself and expand your expertise is going to benefit the most. It's great if you can do it full-time because you can really devote yourself to the program and figure out what you want to do with your life.

Q:   So how important is it to go to a really good school?

A:   I think it is important because people look at the school you've gone to and are impressed with you. And I have to be honest, that will make you feel good. People will say, "Oh my gosh, you went to Harvard!" In a social setting, when people ask me where I went to school, I almost hesitate, because I know there will be this big reaction, especially out here in the Midwest. Not very many people out here went to Harvard.

Right out of business school, I felt, you know, if this job doesn't work, I can go almost anywhere I want with this degree. I know that sounds kind of arrogant but I knew that with my business experience before I went to Harvard, and now with my MBA, I could take a risk. I could come out to this small town in the Midwest and if I needed to, I could leave and be okay.

Even ten years later, I think that's still true. A Harvard MBA certainly is helpful when you're trying to move to the next place or job. I don't think I can go anywhere I want now, because I've taken a little curve in my career track to be with my children. I've been working part-time for three years now, three days a week. But the MBA from Harvard is going to be very helpful if we decide to leave.

Q:   Do you ever anticipate reentering the workforce as a full-time person or leaving your job? And if so, how do you think the opportunities will be enhanced with the MBA?

A:   It's actually good you ask that question, because right now I'm grappling with that. Our factory is moving all of its manufacturing to Mexico. And so the question is, what will happen to the office staff? Will we go, have some role, or be laid off? That's an unanswered question right now.

Because we'd like to stay in the area, my husband and I have been thinking about different things I can do. So the MBA will be very beneficial as I face these issues.

Q:   What else did you get out of the two years you were at school?

A:   I met a lot of wonderfully diverse and interesting people. Many people were like Wall Street–Harvard–back to Wall Street, or consulting–Harvard–back to consulting. Or people were switching careers. There were people who had been in the Peace Corps, done public not-for-profit work, or come from the military. So from that perspective, it was just wonderful to meet all those incredible people.

And how many smart people can you put in a room? I mean students were just incredibly bright. It was impressive and added tremendously to the classes.

**Q:** As you have passed the ten-year mark, how do you feel about the value of your business school training?

**A:** I absolutely still utilize it. I still think back on cases and situations and examples that I use to resolve issues going on in work. For example, we are moving some aspect of the business to Mexico, and I can remember that I did a case on that. Plus, with this colleague of mine who is currently getting his MBA, we'll chat even more about some of those issues from class.

But looking back, I can still remember comments I made in class, and my teachers and the classes themselves. It was a very valuable, memorable time in my life. But it wasn't always pleasant . . . .

**Q:** Why wasn't it pleasant?

**A:** The first year class set-up and the overwhelming desire to make value-added comments was an immense amount of pressure on me. I mean, I'm probably obsessive, but I even think of comments now!

**Q:** Someone reading this book might not understand what this comment thing is all about.

**A:** Comments you made to contribute to classroom discussion which, depending on the class, counted toward your grade. Comments could almost define the class—coming up with comments to be brilliant, or prove yourself to the others. I remember I was always second-guessing what I said in class. I could have said it better, or I could have said it a different way, that kind of thing.

**Q:** Looking back, if you could do anything differently, what would it be?

**A:** Well, probably I would do a little better at networking and then keeping in touch with section mates, because I may need to call them at some point. I think if you have those networks in place, it's not really calling to ask for a job, it's talking about your situation, and then those people know what's going on and may be able to let you know about an opportunity.

Having been at the same job for more than ten years, and being out in the Midwest, I'm a little less connected to the pipeline of, "Hey, do you need someone like me at your company?" And that goes both ways. You know, time is a problem, and when kids come along, things change greatly. It's just hard to fit everything in.

**Q:** Summing up, what advice do you have for someone reading this book?

**A:** The MBA gives you an extra couple of years to go and figure out what you want to do. I liken it to what college does for you, but this is your second breath. And it's a very valuable one. I recommend you go full-time, so you can really focus.

## Patricia Melnikoff, Harvard Business School, Class of '92
## Vice President, Marketing and Business Development, Ariat International, a Manufacturer of Equestrian Footwear and Apparel

**Q:** Patty, what kind of opportunities were you looking for post-MBA?

**A:** I was looking for an opportunity with a consumer-oriented company that sold goods and services. I was seeking product management, marketing, or strategic planning opportunities.

I was interested in working for a large multinational company, so I interviewed with companies like Disney and Sara Lee Corporation.

Q: Did they come on campus?

A: Yes they did.

Q: So you relied heavily on on-campus recruiters?

A: Very heavily. My second year I attended quite a few corporate presentations from different sectors: technology, packaged goods, and so forth.

At that time, we had the opportunity to attend recruiting presentations and weekly Q&A sessions with well-known business leaders that are part of the second-year general management course. So by going to the more general presentations and learning about the companies or going to specific recruiting presentations, I actually came across quite a varied group of organizations.

Q: What was your summer position between your first and second year?

A: I participated in a fellowship in Eastern Europe. I worked with a group that was consulting with factories in Poland that were at risk of going out of business. It was 1991, so it was right after the fall of the communist system in Poland and there were a number of state-run factories and businesses that were in a state of collapse.

Q: How did you find your way to Poland?

A: I had worked previously with two of the founders of a consulting practice in Poland.

Q: You learned of this opportunity for a fellowship in Poland at Harvard? How did you unearth that?

A: Actually, it was a formalized program of doing nonprofit work. There were a number of HBS students who participated in the program.

I had to complete an application that explained the nature of the nonprofit work, and upon my return, I was required to write a summary report.

Q: Why did you seek out this particular opportunity in Europe for your summer job? A lot of MBAs expect that summer job to be the one that leads to a final job offer.

A: I'm always looking for interesting experiences in my life. I wanted to work overseas. I figured I probably wouldn't end up living my life in Eastern Europe, and so it was a unique opportunity at the time.

Q: How relevant were the things you learned at business school for your first job out?

A: I probably learned more basic analytical, communication, and process management skills from my experience at Bain & Co. My HBS education helped me to understand many of the big-picture issues facing the corporation.

Q: What did you learn at business school?

A: (Long pause) I can tell you more about how business school helps me today than how it helped me then. [Several people told me] that I would understand the true value of my MBA after 10 years. I would say that is mostly true.

In the short term however, I did find that the finance courses I took helped me in my first job. I chose to take several finance courses at HBS because I wanted to develop a more in-depth understanding of that area. I did not plan on working in finance post-HBS, and I didn't think I would ever have another opportunity to learn about it.

Ten years out, it's all about the leadership and people issues. For example, my company was facing a potential product recall recently. I found myself drawing upon the case we studied on the Tylenol recall at J&J. I asked myself, what were the big-picture decisions they had to make? How fast? How serious? What is the potential damage? What is the action plan and how will we communicate it? Being able to draw from that exposure to a crisis management situation was very helpful. Over a decade ago, I sat in a classroom and discussed for 90 minutes how to approach a crisis. Somehow that exercise of analyzing and debating potential scenarios left an impression on me that helped me years later.

Q:  If there were anything you could go back and do differently at business school what would it be?

A:  I would take more of those organizational behavior classes that I laughed at.

Q:  Because?

A:  Oh you know, power, "group norms," and other people issues. None of those issues seemed that important to me at the time. I was still focused on mastering my knowledge in academic disciplines.

Q:  Did you all laugh at them?

A:  I don't think we valued those courses as much as other courses in the curriculum. But now I see the value, having managed so many people. In the second year, I might have taken more leadership courses and those organizational behavior courses.

Q:  Do you think it was more intimidating for you to go to business school as a woman?

A:  No. But I think I had to work harder in certain ways earlier on to establish myself as a credible voice in the class. Somehow I felt that if a woman was perceived to be too harsh or too focused, there was a natural tendency not to like her. And so I do think that women have to work harder at finding their place and fitting in.

Q:  Overall would you say business school is an intimidating place?

A:  No. I enjoyed it. I made great friends at HBS. I think the first week is terrifying for everyone, but overall, no.

Q:  What would you say to someone who said, should I get my MBA today?

A:  I think it depends on their circumstances. If they're very successful in business already and they are financially secure, I'm not sure business school is necessary. I meet incredible business people all the time who don't have MBAs.

But I think if you're younger in your career, or you're trying to make a career change, or you've found yourself limited, then I think it's a wonderful opportunity to go for two years and get the MBA.

Q:  Do you think you went at the right time for the right reasons?

A: Absolutely. I was 25. It was perfect for a young woman with three years of business experience post-college, with my objectives, to go and get the MBA from the very best school I could.

## CAROLINE GROSSMAN, UNIVERSITY OF CHICAGO GRADUATE SCHOOL OF BUSINESS, CLASS OF 2003
## SENIOR ASSOCIATE BRAND MANAGER, KRAFT

**Q: Did you have a specific career path in mind, or an industry you wanted to gain entry to in deciding to get your MBA?**

A: My interests were fairly broad. I wanted to gain general management experience. So I was thinking about using the MBA to pursue either general management or consulting.

**Q: What did you do before business school?**

A: I worked as a teacher for three years, both abroad and in inner-city schools, and then worked in program management at an educational nonprofit. I had a liberal arts background.

**Q: So this was a big career change for you. What made you decide to switch gears?**

A: Although I liked the social service mission of the jobs I was doing, I wasn't fulfilled by the specific job functions in those positions. I wanted to go to business school to get to a place where I could be satisfied by and challenged by the actual work. When I thought about the kinds of work I liked most, I realized it was strategic thinking and project leadership. That pointed me toward business and the MBA.

**Q: So, how did you wind up at Kraft?**

A: I had an internship there in the summer between my first and second years. Now I'm working in a brand management position, and at Kraft, this offers me a perfect mix of marketing and general business management experiences. Brand Managers at Kraft have profit and loss responsibility in addition to setting the strategic vision for the business. Ultimately, they are responsible for achieving the business results on their brand. As my first job out of business school, it has very much met my needs.

**Q: What was your sense of the value of the degree around graduation, and now, one and a half years later?**

A: My MBA facilitated a major job transition. I had access to this specific opportunity through on-campus recruiting, and my coursework and extracurricular activities helped prepare me to do the job. I feel very pleased to have landed where I have, and I certainly needed the MBA to get started in this direction. I felt pretty confident that coming out of Chicago I would have the tool kit I needed for the job I was going to be doing.

**Q: In what ways is the MBA relevant and not relevant in today's world?**

A: The MBA opens a lot of doors. It allows a candidate access to companies to which one otherwise might not have access. The MBA is a ticket to a conversation with those organizations. Mind you, the ticket is only to a conversation—the job you have to get yourself. There are some companies who simply won't look at someone who does not have the MBA; it's a prerequisite.

I have to add that most of one's career is built in the workplace, not in the classroom. But school sets you up for success. You're creating a foundation of knowledge, as well as the strategic frameworks that you'll need to process all of the learning once you're in the workplace. For a very short time after business school, perhaps you could perform in my kind of job without the MBA. But over time, for strategy, decision-making, and being able to truly lead, the MBA will be highly relevant.

**Q: What advice would you give those considering leaving the workforce for an MBA?**

A: Be ready to hit the ground running because the job search process begins day one. Do some thinking about what you want to do with your career before you get to campus so you can focus your career exploration at school once you arrive.

**Q: How do you measure return on investment for the MBA?**

A: I was looking to make a major career switch, so my reasons for going to business school were very straightforward. Because I came from the teaching field, and am now in a position at a leading consumer goods company, I would have to say I am completely satisfied with the return on my investment.

But I think this will vary depending on the type of job you left behind. It will also depend on where you land after the MBA and the extent to which that new position meets your goal. The more introspection you have about what you are looking for, the greater your return on investment.

I also measure ROI (return on investment) in terms of long- and short-term returns. At Chicago, I learned a lot of frameworks for making business decisions, which will help me in the long run. And in the short run, I acquired the skills and knowledge I needed to hit the ground running at work.

**Q: How important is it where you go to school?**

A: I think it's very important. You should ask yourself what it is that you want to get out of the experience and then consider what the school offers and if it's a good fit.

In my case, I wanted a lens for looking at business challenges and problems. Because I had a liberal arts background, I was looking for quantitative rigor to balance that out, and wanted to be sure that I'd be somewhere I could master business fundamentals. Chicago gave me that. The economics courses, in particular, really helped frame my thinking, and it was in the Marketing course that I learned the basis of what I do every day at work.

You might also consider the regional location of the schools you're looking at. In certain industries, such as consulting and investment banking, firms interview at many business schools, then place hires in different offices nationally. But other companies tend to recruit in the geographic region in which they are based.

**Q: If you could go back in time, is there anything you would do differently with your time at Chicago?**

A: I'm not one for regrets. I had a balanced experience at Chicago. I had a leadership position in a student organization, and was a member of a couple of others, which helped me. I built a strong network, which facilitated the career transition I was looking for. I learned a lot, and I had a good time. What more could I ask for?

I think the key to achieving this level of satisfaction with business school is picking your mandatories (for me, a career transition) and balance. There is so much to do that you can't do everything to the fullest, so you have to either focus or do a little of everything. The latter approach was a good fit for me.

## Sara Weiss, MIT Sloan School of Management, Class of 2004

Q: What were your reasons for going to b-school?

A: I was looking for a career change. At the time, I wanted to become an energy trader. In fact, in my b-school essays I wrote about how I wanted to work for Enron. And then within three days of submitting my last application, Enron just imploded.

Q: Isn't that a little unusual, having a specific company to work for in mind?

A: Yes, it is. But Enron was unique in the role that they played in this field. That is why I had so specifically targeted the company. In the end, I wound up working in the financial market, which naturally is very different from the energy markets. But a lot of the attributes and experiences I was looking for in a job, I found in the financial markets.

Q: What were you doing before business school?

A: I was doing management consulting. I did process design and systems implementation for electric utilities. This is why I first got interested in energy-related fields.

Q: So how was the MBA going to advance your career? It sounds like you already had a strong career path and future.

A: I had a strong career path in consulting, but I didn't find myself fulfilled by that job. By the time I arrived at Sloan, I knew what I was looking for. It was something more dynamic and fast-paced. I wanted something where I had more control over my career path. I was looking for a job where I had immediately measurable results versus consulting, where you do these projects and you never really know if the project was successful until many years later.

It was really my Sloan classmates who helped me find my new focus. The community at Sloan is extremely supportive, and people are very willing to share their experiences and offer insight to each other. When I got to Sloan, I immediately knew that I had joined an incredible network. The students back each other up and help each other out. Without my peers, I would not have been able to find my focus so quickly or make such a successful transition.

Q: How did you feel about the value of the MBA as graduation approached?

A: I was able to look back and pinpoint several things I had gotten out of the MBA. First, I learned about finance, accounting, and other disciplines, which was the content I needed to start my new job. More importantly, I developed tremendously as a person. In a lot of ways, I became more level-headed in my decision-making and I fine-tuned my skills as a professional. I think I just came out as a better package. I looked back right after I graduated and thought, "Wow, this is a huge transformation I've undergone in these two years."

But probably the most important thing I got out of business school is a network of incredible friends. I really got to know my classmates well, because we spent so much time together doing a wide range of activities inside and outside the classroom. My Sloan friends are closer to me than my college friends. Not only are they valued friends, but they are also people I will turn to for career support for the rest of my life.

Q: How, if at all, has your perception of the value of the degree changed?

A:  I definitely feel the value. I absolutely use the finance content I learned directly in my job. Even the classes I thought were useless at the time, such as the organizational behavior classes, the touchy-feely classes, I have found those extraordinarily relevant.

Q:  **Why is that?**

A:  In my current job, I have many different layers of colleagues and clients. The dynamics of the teams I work with and am expected to perform with are complicated. So all of that stuff about how people interact with each other, require motivation, ownership, etc., I'm using all of that.

Q:  **Does it matter where you get your MBA?**

A:  Yes, of course. But it matters more what you decide to get out of it. A program is only as good as what you decide to invest in it and in turn what you take away from it.

Q:  **Do you notice a difference among graduates of different programs?**

A:  Yes, in their soft skills. For example, anyone can learn textbook accounting. Just about every business program has accounting courses and most schools will require you to take at least one. But not every school has a community that is team-oriented or is involved in projects with the local business community. Not every school provides students with presentation experience. Students in programs that support class participation learn to express themselves eloquently on the fly.

Q:  **In what ways is the MBA relevant and not relevant in today's world?**

A:  I think that everything you learn in business school can also be learned in the real world. I don't think there is anything new. You just learn it faster, better, and have more fun doing it in a full-time MBA program. That makes it ultimately relevant and yet completely unnecessary. Nobody ever needs an MBA, but it's a huge leg up. The MBA gives you a much more focused and concentrated experience. The magic of it is in the environment and the people.

Q:  **How do you measure return on investment?**

A:  Personally, I actually don't measure my experience in terms of return on investment. I believe very strongly that education is worth its cost, as long as you give it your all, so you don't just spend all this money and cut class. Some people I know look at it differently. They measure the opportunity cost in dollars and ensure for themselves that they will make back those dollars. I think those people are missing a big piece of what is most important about business school. The real value isn't measurable.

Q:  **What advice would you give to today's applicants?**

A:  Try to do as much thinking as you can (even if it's in abstract terms), before you do your applications. Think about what is important to you, what you're looking for, what's missing from your life today, and who you want to be in the future. You don't need to know specifically what your next steps are. But the more focused you are, the more you are prepared to take advantage of what business school has to offer.

Q:  **If you had to do b-school all over again, what would you do differently?**

A:  I would study less. I would stress less. I would join more extracurricular clubs unrelated to my chosen career path. I would definitely throw that cocktail party on my roof deck in Beacon Hill, something that I never got around to doing. And I would take a class at Harvard's Kennedy School. There. That's my list.

# CHAPTER 6

## MONEY MATTERS

---

## HOW MUCH WILL IT COST?

### THE TRUTH

To say that business school is an expensive endeavor is an understatement. In fact, to really gauge how expensive business school is, you need to look not only at your tuition costs and living expenses, but also at the opportunity cost of foregoing a salary for the length of your program. Think about it: You'll have a net outflow of money.

But keep in mind that, unlike law school or medical school, business school is just a two-year program. And once those two years are over, you can expect to reap the rewards of your increased market value. Unfortunately, business school differs from law school and medical school in a much less desirable way as well—there are serious limitations on the amount of money available through scholarships and grants. Most business school students will be limited to loans, and lots of them.

Try not to get too upset about borrowing the money for business school; think of it as an investment in yourself. But, like all investments, it should be carefully thought out and discussed with everyone (spouse, partner, etc.) concerned. This is especially important for those of you considering business school. You need a law degree to practice law, and a medical degree to practice medicine, but a business degree is not required to work in business. That said, certain professional opportunities may be tougher to pursue without an MBA on your resume.

### THE COST OF B-SCHOOL

So get out some paper, a pencil, and a calculator, and figure out how much it will cost you to attend school. What should you include? Your opportunity cost (lost income) and your cost of attending b-school (tuition and fees). One more thing: For a more accurate assessment of your investment, you should figure taxes into the equation by dividing tuition cost by .65 (this assumes taxes of about 35 percent). Why? Because in order to pay tuition of $25,000, you would have to make a pre-tax income of about $38,500. If you are lucky enough to have a source of aid that does not require repayment, such as a grant, scholarship, or wealthy benefactor, subtract that amount from the cost of attending b-school.

For example, if you currently make $50,000 and plan to attend a business school that costs $25,000 per year, your investment would be approximately $177,000.

$(50,000 \times 2) + [(25,000 \times 2)/.65] = 177,000$

Now say you receive an annual grant of $5,000. Your investment would now be approximately $161,500.

$(50,000 \times 2) + [(20,000 \times 2)/.65] = 161,500.$

---

## How Long Will It Take You to Recoup Your Investment?

To estimate this figure, you first need to estimate your expected salary increase post-MBA. Check out the average starting salaries for graduates of the programs you are looking at and adjust upward/downward based on the industry you plan to enter. Subtract your current salary from your expected salary and you'll get your expected salary increase.

Once you complete the step above, divide your investment (tuition and fees plus lost income) by your expected salary increase, and then add 2 (the length of a full-time MBA program). If you are contemplating a one-year MBA program, just add 1.

Going back to the example above, if your pre-MBA salary is $50,000 and you expect to make $75,000 when you graduate, your expected salary increase is $25,000 (a 50 percent increase). Let's assume you did not receive a grant and that your investment will be about $177,000.

$$(177,000/25,000) + 2 = 9.08$$

It will take you approximately nine years to earn back your investment.

Keep in mind, these are approximations and don't take into account annual raises, inflation, and so on. But it is interesting, isn't it?

While business school is an expensive proposition, the financial rewards of having your MBA can be immensely lucrative as we discussed before. You won't be forced into bankruptcy if you finance it correctly. There are tried-and-true ways to reduce your initial costs, finance the costs on the horizon, and manage the debt you'll leave school with—all without selling your soul to the highest bidder.

### Comparison Shopping

While cost shouldn't be the first thing on your mind when you are choosing a school, depending on your goals in getting an MBA, it might be fairly high on your list. Private schools aren't the only business schools. Many state schools have fantastic reputations. Regional schools may be more generous with financial aid. Tuition costs will vary widely between public and private schools, especially if you qualify as an in-state student. Keep in mind, however, that salary gains tend to be less dramatic at more regional schools.

## HOW DO I FUND MY MBA?

The short answer: loans. Unless your company is underwriting your MBA, or you're able to pay your way in cash, you'll be financing your two years of business school through a portfolio of loans. Loans typically come in one of two forms: federal and private. Only a few of you will be lucky enough to qualify for, and get, grants and scholarships.

Anyone with reasonably good credit, regardless of financial need, can borrow money for business school. If you have financial need, you will probably be eligible for some type of financial aid if you meet the following basic qualifications:

- You are a United States citizen or a permanent U.S. resident.

- You are registered for Selective Service if you are a male, or you have documentation to prove that you are exempt.

- You are not in default on student loans already.

- You don't have a horrendous credit history.

International applicants to business school should take note: Most U.S. business schools will require all international students to pay in full or show proof that they will be able to pay the entire cost of the MBA prior to beginning the MBA program.

## FEDERAL LOANS

The federal government funds federal loan programs. Federal loans are usually the "first resort" for borrowers because many are subsidized by the federal government and offer generous interest rates. Some do not begin charging you interest until after you complete your degree. Most federal loans are need-based, but some higher interest federal loans are available regardless of financial circumstances. Your business school's financial aid office will determine what your need is, if any.

## PRIVATE LOANS

Don't think private loans are available only from banks. There are programs that exist for the express purpose of lending money to business students. These loans are expensive and interest accumulates during your studies. You will also be responsible for many extra charges (guarantees and insurance fees).

## ALTERNATIVE SOURCES OF FUNDING

We've already mentioned these in one form or other, but they are worthy of a bit more attention.

The first alternative is sponsorship of your employer or educational reimbursement. Not all companies treat this the same way, but if you are able to get your employer to kick in a portion of the cost, you are better off than before. But beware, this benefit also comes with strings attached. Most companies that pay for your MBA will require a commitment of several years upon graduation. If you renege, you could be liable for the full cost of your education. Others will require that you attend business school part-time, which you may or may not want to do. Often, part-time students are ineligible to participate in on-campus recruiting efforts to the same extent as full-time students.

Educational reimbursement can come in another form as well. Some companies will provide sign-on bonuses to new MBAs that will cover the cost of a year's tuition. This is a fantastic development from the years of a robust economy, but it is by no means a guarantee during tougher times. Don't assume that you will have this option open to you just because it has been a common occurrence in past years.

The other "alternative" source of funding is a financial gift from family or another source. Either you have a resource that is willing and able to fund all or part of your MBA, or you don't. If you do, be thankful.

## APPLYING FOR FINANCIAL AID

In order to become eligible for financial aid of any kind, you will need to complete the Free Application for Federal Student Aid, also known as the FAFSA. You complete and submit this form after January 1 of the year in which you plan to enter business school. You should aim to complete and submit this form as soon as possible after the first of the year to avoid any potential delays. The FAFSA is available from a school's financial aid office. You can also download the form directly from the website of the U.S. Department of Education at www.fafsa.ed.gov. A third option is to use the FAFSA Express software (also downloadable from the website) and transmit the application electronically.

It is important to note that the form requires information from your federal income tax returns. Plan to file your taxes early that year.

In addition to the FAFSA form, most schools will have their own financial aid form that you will be required to complete and submit. These often have their own deadlines, so it is wise to keep careful track of all the forms you must complete and all their respective deadlines. Yes, it's a lot of paperwork, but get over it. You'll be much happier when the tuition bill arrives.

# LOAN SPECIFICS

## GUIDE TO FEDERAL LOANS
### Stafford Loans

Stafford loans require you to complete the FAFSA form in order to qualify. These are very desirable loans because they offer low-interest rates capped at 8.25 percent and are federally guaranteed. There is a limit to how much you can borrow in this program. The maximum amount per year you may borrow as a graduate student is $18,500; $10,000 of which must be unsubsidized loans. The maximum amount you may borrow in total is $138,500 (only $65,500 of this may be in subsidized loans). The aggregate amount includes any Stafford loans you may have from your undergraduate or other graduate studies.

Stafford loans come in two types: subsidized and unsubsidized. Subsidized loans are need-based as determined by your business school. They do not accrue interest while you are in school or in an authorized deferment period (such as the first six months after graduation). This cost is picked up by the government (hence the name "subsidized"). Repayment begins at that time. Unsubsidized loans are not need-based and do charge interest from the time of disbursement to the time of full repayment. You can pay the interest while you are in school or opt for capitalization, in which case the interest is added to the principal. You will pay more in the long run if you choose capitalization. Interest payments may be tax deductible, so be sure to check. The standard repayment period for both is ten years.

You will pay a small origination and guarantee fee for each loan, but this is not an out-of-pocket expense. It is simply deducted from the loan amount. Some schools will allow you to borrow the money under the Stafford program directly from them, while others will require you to borrow from a bank. For more information on federal loans, call the Federal Student Aid Information Center at 1-800-433-3243.

### Perkins Loans

Perkins loans are available to graduate students who demonstrate exceptional financial need. The financial aid office will determine your eligibility for a Perkins Loan. If you qualify for a Perkins Loan as part of your financial aid package, take it. The loans are made by the schools and are repaid to the schools, although the federal government provides a large portion of the funds. You can borrow up to $6,000 for each year of graduate study up to a total of $40,000 (this includes any money borrowed under this program during undergraduate study). The interest rates on this loan are low, usually 5 percent. There are no fees attached. The grace period is nine months upon graduation.

## PRIVATE/COMMERCIAL LOANS

This is expensive territory. Not only are interest rates high, but terms are also quite different from those found with federal loans. You may not be able to defer payment of interest or principal until after graduation. Origination and guarantee fees are also much higher since these loans are unsecured. After all, banks and other specialized lenders exist to loan money to folks like you, and unlike the federal government, want to make money doing it. If you go this route, shop around diligently. Think of it as good practice for your post-MBA executive career.

Below we list some of the more well-known and well-respected institutions that provide financial assistance for graduate and professional school. Keep in mind that most programs require the borrower to be attending an approved graduate program at least part-time. If you choose to investigate loans outside of the educational market, such as a personal line of credit, credit card, or a loan against an insurance plan, be aware that these can be quite costly.

The Access Group, Business Access Loan

>   Website: www.accessgroup.org

>   Phone: 1-800-282-1550

The Education Resources Institute (TERI) PEP Program

>   Website: www.teri.org

>   Phone: 1-800-255-TERI.

Citibank CitiAssist® Loan

>   Website:  http://studentloan.citibank.com

>   Phone: 1-800-967-2400

Nellie Mae EXCEL Grad Loan

>   Website: www.nelliemae.com

>   Phone: 1-800-FOR-TUITION

Sallie Mae MBA Loans

>   Website: www.salliemae.com

>   Phone: 1-888-2SALLIE (272-5543)

## SCHOLARSHIPS AND GRANTS

The usual sources for this type of funding are alumni groups and civic organizations. This funding is limited, and actual awards tend to be small. Even if you benefited from generous scholarship funding as an undergraduate, it would be unwise to assume you'll have the same experience as a graduate student. But do investigate. You never know what's out there. Schools will frequently list any scholarships and grants that are available at the back of their financial aid catalog.

> For more information about financing your business school education, check out *Paying for Graduate School Without Going Broke*, available in our online bookstore at www.princetonreview.com/mba/bookstore.asp.

# PART II
# SCHOOLS RANKED BY CATEGORY

On the following pages you will find eleven top ten lists of business schools ranked according to various metrics. As we noted earlier, none of these lists purports to rank the business schools by their overall quality. Nor should any combination of the categories we've chosen be construed as representing the raw ingredients for such a ranking. We have made no attempt to gauge the "prestige" of these schools, and we wonder whether we could accurately do so even if we tried. What we have done, however, is presented a number of lists using information from two very large databases—one of statistical information collected from business schools, and another of subjective data gathered via our survey of 16,000 business students at 282 business schools.

Ten of the ranking lists are based partly or wholly on opinions collected through our business student survey. The only schools that may appear in these lists are the 282 business schools from which we were able to collect a sufficient number of student surveys to accurately represent the student experience in our various ratings and descriptive profiles.

One of the rankings, Toughest to Get Into, incorporates *only* admissions statistics reported to us by the business schools. Therefore, any business school appearing in this edition of the guide, whether we collected student surveys from it or not, may appear on this list.

Under the title of each list is an explanation of what criteria the ranking is based on. For explanations of many of the individual rankings components, turn to the "How This Book is Organized" Section, on page 5.

It's worth repeating: there is no one best business school in America. There is a best business school for you. By using these rankings in conjunction with the descriptive profiles and data listings in subsequent sections of this book, we hope that you will begin to identify the attributes of a business school that are important to you, as well as those schools that can best help you to achieve your personal and professional goals.

Please note that in an effort to avoid comparing apples to oranges, we have not placed any international business schools on any of our rankings lists.

The top schools in each category appear in descending order.

## TOUGHEST TO GET INTO
*BASED ON THE ADMISSIONS SELECTIVITY RATING (SEE PAGE 10 FOR EXPLANATION)*

1. Harvard University
2. Stanford University
3. Columbia University
4. University of Pennsylvania
5. Massachusetts Institute of Technology
6. Northwestern University
7. University of California—Berkeley
8. Dartmouth College
9. New York University
10. University of Massachusetts—Amherst

## BEST CAREER PROSPECTS
*BASED ON THE CAREER RATING (SEE PAGE 12 FOR EXPLANATION)*

1. Stanford University
2. The University of Chicago
3. University of California—Berkeley
4. University of Michigan—Ann Arbor
5. Columbia University
6. University of Pennsylvania
7. New York University
8. Harvard University
9. University of California—Los Angeles
10. Northwestern University

## BEST OVERALL ACADEMIC EXPERIENCE
*BASED ON THE ACADEMIC EXPERIENCE RATING (SEE PAGE 8 FOR EXPLANATION)*

1. University of Pennsylvania
2. University of Massachusetts—Amherst
3. Massachusetts Institute of Technology
4. Dartmouth College
5. New York University
6. University of Florida
7. Northwestern University
8. Stanford University
9. Yale University
10. Harvard University

## BEST PROFESSORS
*BASED ON THE PROFESSORS INTERESTING AND PROFESSORS ACCESSIBLE RATINGS (SEE PAGE 9 FOR EXPLANATIONS)*

1. Indiana University—Bloomington
2. University of Virginia
3. Hardin-Simmons University, The Acton MBA in Entrepreneurship
4. University of Massachusetts—Amherst
5. University of Alabama—Tuscaloosa
6. The College of William and Mary
7. Washington University in Saint Louis (Olin)
8. Millsaps College
9. Harvard University
10. Duke University

## MOST COMPETITIVE STUDENTS

*Based on student assessment of how competitive classmates are, how heavy the workload is, and the perceived academic pressure*

1. Hardin-Simmons University,
   The Acton MBA in Entrepreneurship
2. University of Rochester
3. University of Mississippi
4. Rensselaer Polytechnic Institute
5. Howard University
6. Rice University
7. Purdue University
8. Bowling Green State University
9. Clarkson University
10. Texas A&M University—College Station

## BEST CAMPUS ENVIRONMENT

*Based on student assessment of the safety, attractiveness and location of the school*

1. Emory University
2. University of California—Los Angeles
3. Boston College
4. Stanford University
5. Dartmouth College
6. University of North Carolina at Chapel Hill
7. University of Utah
8. Pepperdine University
9. Loyola Marymount University
10. University of California—Berkeley

## MOST FAMILY FRIENDLY

*Based on student assessment of: how happy married students are, how many students have children, how helpful the business school is to students with children, and how much the school does for the spouses of students*

1. Brigham Young University
2. Stetson University
3. Dartmouth College
4. Stanford University
5. Duke University
6. Harvard University
7. Thunderbird
8. Cornell University
9. Naval Postgraduate School
10. Northwestern University

## BEST CAMPUS FACILITIES

*Based on student assessment of the quality of classroom, library and gym facilities*

1. Stetson University
2. University of Alabama—Tuscaloosa
3. Indiana University—Bloomington
4. University of Georgia
5. University of Virginia
6. University of Oregon
7. Harvard University
8. Texas A&M University—College Station
9. Texas Christian University (TCU)
10. University of Connecticut

## BEST ADMINISTERED

*Based on student assessment of how smoothly the school is run, and the ease with which students can get into required and popular courses*

1. Colorado State University

2. Elon University

3. Minnesota State University—Mankato

4. Washington University in Saint Louis (Olin)

5. Seattle Pacific University

6. Ithaca College

7. Miami University Ohio

8. Texas A&M University—College Station

9. University of Alabama—Tuscaloosa

10. West Virginia University

## GREATEST OPPORTUNITY FOR MINORITY STUDENTS

*Based on the percent of students from minorities, the percent of faculty from minorities, and student assessment of resources for minority students, how supportive the culture is of minority students, and whether fellow students are ethnically and racially diverse*

1. Howard University

2. University of Houston—Victoria

3. Texas A&M International University

4. Barry University

5. Montclair State University

6. Bowling Green State University

7. Thunderbird

8. San Francisco State University

9. University of Maryland—College Park

10. The University of Texas at San Antonio

## GREATEST OPPORTUNITY FOR WOMEN

*Based on the percent of students who are female, the percent of faculty who are female, and student assessment of: resources for female students, how supportive the culture is of female students, whether the business school offers coursework for women entrepreneurs, and whether case study materials for classes proportionately reflect women in business*

1. Babson College

2. University of Tennessee at Chattanooga

3. University of California—Berkeley

4. Cornell University

5. University of Massachusetts Amherst

6. New York University

7. University of Michigan—Ann Arbor

8. Worcester Polytechnic Institute

9. University of California—Davis

10. The George Washington University

# PART III-A
# BUSINESS SCHOOL
# DESCRIPTIVE PROFILES

# ALFRED UNIVERSITY
## COLLEGE OF BUSINESS

## Academics

If you're looking for an intimate MBA experience, you can hardly top the one offered at Alfred University: This program serves a population of 60 graduate students, only 15 of whom attend full-time. The result is a program with a "family atmosphere in which the school cares about the individual." As one student told us, "The greatest strength of Alfred University is its size. The classes are between 10 and 20 people, and the interaction is incredible. One really feels a part of the class discussions." The school is especially strong in entrepreneurial studies, an area abetted by the university's Center for Family Business and Entrepreneurial Leadership, a research center.

Professors at Alfred have the time to go the extra mile for students, and they do it by "making sure that the students are comprehending the course material [and] not just completing assignments. They are very personable with everyone and encourage one-on-one meetings." Students also appreciate that "professors here are very diverse and have experiences [in other countries] ranging from Japan to Tunisia."

With no crowd to fight, Alfred students have a better chance to shine. One student writes, "One professor liked a paper I wrote for his class. He offered to coauthor another paper with me and pursue getting it published. These opportunities are so valuable to me and something I would never have expected." Another student was able to land an assistantship in which she "helped plan an international business conference in Ecuador." She says, "Not only did I get great experience working on this project but I was also able to travel to Ecuador and participate in the conference. It was one of the best experiences I've ever had." One student sums up, "The personal relationship with faculty and administrators open a lot of doors that would normally slam shut in your face at other schools. It's these personal relationships that nurture change, improvement, and downright fantastic opportunities."

Of course, a small school can only offer students so much; many agree that "a larger variety of curriculum would bring a great deal of value to the students." Even so, they regard their MBA experience as extremely positive. They approve of the school's "active learning" strategies, which emphasize teamwork, case studies, simulations, and field experience (usually gained through an internship). They also love the administration's dedication to the program. "They are constantly striving to improve the program and the school. As a result, I have found the program challenging, rewarding, and enriching," explains one student.

## Career and Placement

All Alfred students receive career services through the Robert R. McComsey Career Development Center. The office provides one-on-one counseling sessions; workshops in interviewing, resume writing, and networking; a career library with online and conventional print resources; and annual job fairs. The school boasts a 100 percent placement rate for its MBAs. Students point out, however, that Alfred's remote location complicates their search for jobs and internships. One MBA candidate explains, "Outside internships and projects are more difficult to obtain due to the university's rural location. However, the administration is undertaking maneuvers to expand local, as well as international, opportunities with particular focus on MBA students."

Prominent employers of Alfred MBAs include Alstom, AOL Communications, Avantt Consulting, LLC, Met Life/New England Financial, General Electric, and Eli Lilly, A-Citynet, Corning Inc., Dresser Rand, Nestle Co., NYSEG, Toro Energy, Wal-Mart.

CATHLEEN JOHNSON, COORDINATOR OF GRADUATE ADMISSIONS
OFFICE OF GRADUATE ADMISSIONS, ALUMNI HALL, SAXON DRIVE, ALFRED, NY 14802 U.S.
PHONE: 800-541-9229 • FAX: 607-871-2198
E-MAIL: GRADINQUIRY@ALFRED.EDU • WEBSITE: WWW.BUSINESS.ALFRED.EDU/MBA.HTML

## Student Life and Environment

Alfred, New York, is a quiet, rural town with few distractions, and accordingly, student life centers on campus. The university is a community of about 2,500 students, including 250 business undergrads and 60 MBAs, making it large enough to support all manner of activity. One student explains, "Basically, if you can dream it up, you can do it at Alfred. I became an entrepreneur through all of Alfred's clubs and organizations long before I looked into a business degree. The MBA program has helped me hone my skills and expand my horizons by giving me valuable insight. I have become very empowered and am eager to take on a whole slew of projects and tasks to make a difference in the world—and if it helps me earn a living, too, all the better." One resident director adds, "I know that there are many activities on and around campus. It is up to the residents to take the initiative and join in."

Alfred's infrastructure includes "plenty of computers and good Internet bandwidth, [but] the recreational facilities aren't the best, and the library needs help. Fortunately, a large renovation and expansion project is slated to start very soon, which could be the largest project for the university within the last few decades. Renovations to both facilities will address shortcomings of the university, greatly enhance the campus, and benefit students." Alfred's sixteen Division III intercollegiate teams provide entertainment, as does the popular intramural sports program. The school's divisions of music, theater, and dance frequently hold performances. Alfred also has an active visual-arts community; it houses one of the best ceramic-arts programs in the country.

The village of Alfred has a year-round population of 1,000, and surrounding towns are not much larger. The city of Rochester is only 80 miles away, with Buffalo only a little farther down the road. Bring a four-wheel-drive vehicle with good snow tires.

## Admissions

Applicants must provide the school with official copies of undergraduate transcripts, GMAT scores, TOEFL scores (for international students whose first language is not English), a personal statement, and letters of recommendation (preferably from former employers or professors). Previous work experience is not required. An interview is optional.

### FINANCIAL FACTS

| | |
|---|---|
| Annual tuition | $28,450 |
| Fees | $810 |
| Books and supplies | $950 |
| Room & board | |
| (on/off-campus) | $9,590/$8,200 |
| % of students receiving aid | 70 |
| % of first-year students | |
| receiving aid | 100 |
| % of students receiving grants | 50 |
| Average award package | $18,500 |
| Average grant | $14,225 |

### ADMISSIONS

| | |
|---|---|
| Admissions Selectivity Rating | 82 |
| # of applications received | 33 |
| % applicants accepted | 36 |
| % acceptees attending | 50 |
| Average GMAT | 532 |
| Range of GMAT | 470–550 |
| Average GPA | 3.1 |
| TOEFL required of | |
| international students? | yes |
| Minimum TOEFL | |
| (paper/computer) | 590/243 |
| Application fee | $50 |
| International application fee | $50 |
| Deferment available? | yes |
| Maximum length | |
| of deferment | 2 years |
| Transfer students accepted? | yes |
| Transfer application policy | |
| Students may transfer a maximum of 6 credits from an AACSB-accredited institution. | |
| Non-fall admissions? | yes |
| Need-blind admissions? | yes |

### EMPLOYMENT PROFILE

| | |
|---|---|
| Career Rating | 71 |
| Average starting salary | $46,428 |

# AMERICAN UNIVERSITY
## KOGOD SCHOOL OF BUSINESS

## Academics

Founded in 1955, Kogod School of Business at American University was the first business school in Washington, DC. With only about 200 full-time students at a time, intimacy and friendliness is the name of the game. Students, for the most part, "have been impressed by almost every faculty member [they've] come into contact with. They are very open to questions and help outside of the classroom." Not only do professors aggressively push their "open door" policy, but administrators get top marks for helpfulness as well. As one student puts it, "It is a very good sign that most of the students have become personal friends with the administration staff." Students appreciate the responsiveness of the majority of the staff and say that, though "Kogod School of Business is still growing and expanding, [they appreciate that] students and professors are pushing the boundaries of what is possible."

Aside from the basic MBA, Kogod offers two dual degrees: an MBA/MA in international studies and a JD/MBA. They also offer an MS in taxation, an MS in accounting, an MS in information technology management, and an MS in management. According to students, "The academic strengths are corporate finance and international management, [and the school has] great professors in international business, finance, and IT." Most students greatly appreciate the emphasis the school places on "the use and impact of technology in business today and in the future."

More than half of the curriculum's credits are occupied by core courses: accounting concepts and applications, managerial economics, financial management, applied managerial statistics, organizational behavior and human resources management, and marketing management. The rest of the course load is taken up by "advanced breadth" electives in courses like manager in the international economy; applied production and operations management; business, ethics, and society; and business law. As one student says, "Kogod has done well to remain on the cutting edge of international business but still needs to clarify in which direction certain programs and projects will go."

## Career and Placement

Unlike many students of other schools, Kogod students seem more or less satisfied with the work done by their Graduate Career Services department. As one says, a great benefit of studying at Kogod is the "interaction with so many experienced businessmen from over 70 nations allows the students to build the communications skills and contacts needed for future success." Most students agree that the school would benefit if it would "involve more alumni [and work harder on] networking events with other schools and professionals." Despite this, most students point out that Kogod provides "a lot of different clubs and events that help the students to become involved and increase networking opportunities."

Companies like Accenture, Citibank, Ernst & Young, MCI Worldcom, NASDAQ, and World Bank (among many others) all have a recruiting presence on campus, and students generally place well out of the program. Marketing and sales jobs were the most common, with positions in finance and accounting coming in second place. The mean starting package (including bonus) was $71,117 for 2003, with those who chose to work in the nonprofit sector earning the highest average salary at $85,000.

SONDRA SMITH, DIRECTOR OF GRADUATE ADMISSIONS AND FINANCIAL AID
4400 MASSACHUSETTS AVENUE NORTHWEST, WASHINGTON, DC 20016-8044 UNITED STATES
PHONE: 202-885-1913 • FAX: 202-885-1078
E-MAIL: KOGODMBA@AMERICAN.EDU • WEBSITE: WWW.KOGOD.AMERICAN.EDU

## Student Life and Environment

Situated on 84 acres of land in one of DC's most attractive residential neighborhoods, Kogod School of Business earns rave reviews from its students for physical environs. They brag that Kogod's "biggest asset [is that] it is in Washington, DC. The opportunities are endless, being in such an international city. It's nice that the campus is in northern DC, though, because you feel like you're on a campus instead of in the heart of downtown." Others agree, adding, "The school has a very international flavor in both its studies and its social activities." Others praise the "great location [and] excellent technology." The Kogod building itself is both wireless and state-of-the-art. Students mostly appreciate the facilities, but some complain that the "size of the school building is too small to support a much larger student population."

The Graduate Business Association sponsors intramural sports (from soccer and golf to football and bicycling), and pickup games and informal competition are common on the wide green lawns of American University's quad. Students say that the university "has been good at providing a wide range of activities for students; however, amenities and study space is sparse and not a real priority." Other students say that, despite the heavy workload, "the full-time students have a very close and active social life. It is not uncommon for the majority of the class to head down to Adam's Morgan or Georgetown for the night."

American University provides a free shuttle bus from the campus to the DC Metro and runs a van service that runs to Capitol Hill, Dupont Circle, and Georgetown. The city bus also makes stops on campus. Though students are eager to point out that the campus caters to "many students from different countries," others counter that they would "like to see more racial diversity. There is already a lot of cultural diversity."

## Admissions

In the fall of 2005, the average undergraduate GPA at Kogod was 3.0, and the average GMAT was 580. Seventy-five different countries were represented in the student body, and 57 percent of the student body was male. The average number of years of work experience was five, and in total, there were 468 part- and full-time students enrolled. A minimum TOEFL score of 600 (paper-based) or 250 (computer-based) is required for acceptance.

## FINANCIAL FACTS

| | |
|---|---|
| Annual tuition | $25,852 |
| Fees | $380 |
| Books and supplies | $950 |
| Room & board (on/off-campus) | $10,210/$12,000 |
| % of students receiving grants | 25 |

## ADMISSIONS

| | |
|---|---|
| Admissions Selectivity Rating | 77 |
| # of applications received | 387 |
| % applicants accepted | 68 |
| % acceptees attending | 43 |
| Average GMAT | 580 |
| Range of GMAT | 540–600 |
| Average GPA | 3.02 |
| TOEFL required of international students? | yes |
| Minimum TOEFL (paper/computer) | 600/250 |
| Application fee | $75 |
| International application fee | $75 |
| Regular application deadline | rolling |
| Regular notification | rolling |
| Deferment available? | yes |
| Maximum length of deferment | 1 year |
| Transfer students accepted? | yes |
| Transfer application policy | |

Students must meet the same requirements as non-transfer students; 9 credits may be transferred from an AACSB-accredited MBA program.

| | |
|---|---|
| Non-fall admissions? | yes |
| Need-blind admissions? | yes |

### APPLICANTS ALSO LOOK AT

Georgetown University, The George Washington University, University of Maryland—College Park

| EMPLOYMENT PROFILE | | | |
|---|---|---|---|
| Career Rating | 79 | Grads employed by field: | % avg. salary: |
| Primary source of full-time job acceptances | | Finance | 33 $66,857 |
| | | Marketing | 15 $60,566 |
| School-facilitated activities | 39% | Operations | 4 NR |
| Graduate-facilitated activities | 62% | Consulting | 33 $71,555 |
| | | General Management | 11 NR |
| Average starting salary | $66,894 | Other | 4 NR |
| Percent employed | 61 | | |

# APPALACHIAN STATE UNIVERSITY
## WALKER COLLEGE OF BUSINESS

### GENERAL INFORMATION
| | |
|---|---|
| Type of school | public |
| Environment | rural |
| Academic calendar | semester |

### SURVEY SAYS...
Helpful alumni
Happy students
*Solid preparation in:*
Finance
Accounting

### STUDENTS
| | |
|---|---|
| Enrollment of parent institution | 14,000 |
| Enrollment of business school | 14 |
| % male/female | 70/30 |
| % out-of-state | 15 |
| % minorities | 15 |
| % international | 15 |
| Average age at entry | 27 |
| Average years work experience at entry | 5.2 |

### ACADEMICS
| | |
|---|---|
| **Academic Experience Rating** | **71** |
| Student/faculty ratio | 20:1 |
| Profs interesting rating | 71 |
| Profs accessible rating | 69 |
| % female faculty | 18 |

## Academics

The nascent graduate business program at Appalachian State University's Walker College of Business offers a select few students "what is probably the most reasonably priced graduate program in the state—incredible bargain." At present, fewer than 20 students are enrolled in the program, which offers a conventional MBA, an MS in accounting, and graduate certificate programs in finance, human-resource management, and information systems. Housed in the same hall as the university's mainframe computer, the MBA program puts computers to good use, employing computer simulations and computer analysis as well as computer-aided instruction in the classroom.

First-year studies at Walker commence with MBA Enrichment, a required program that includes "orientation sessions, workshops, a team-building outdoor experience, and social time for students to get acquainted." The freshman curriculum is entirely prescribed and is designed to "provide students with a broad foundation of knowledge." Students must complete an internship or international experience between their first and second years. Second-year studies consist of five required courses and five electives. Instruction at Walker incorporates case study, group discussion, role playing, guest-led seminars, field projects, team projects, and individual presentations. Students tell us that the Walker approach consists of "lots of work: You have to read and study a lot, [and] you get to learn! With so many assignments and reading, we are turning ourselves into sources of knowledge."

MBAs tell us that faculty members "are very well prepared; they have both the academic and professional experience that makes their teaching valuable. Academic quality is one of the greatest strengths of the school." They warn, however, that the program has a few kinks to iron out. One student warns, "Organization and overall program direction are currently being reassessed and will be better defined and articulated by next year. Once the restructuring has had time to develop, the MBA program will be one of the best buys in the state for the money."

## Career and Placement

ASU's MBA program is much too small to support its own Career Services Office; students must use the school's Career Development Center, which serves all ASU enrollees. The office offers a variety of career-prep classes in interviewing, resume writing, networking, cover letters, and job hunting. It also sponsors career fairs and provides online support including links to job boards and major-related resources.

Students recognize the limitations of their situation. They approvingly report, "The school has a good relationship with alumni and companies in nearby Charlotte, the second-largest financial mecca in the U.S.," but concede that that's not always enough. One student writes, "They need to do more to help students get internships and job positions. They do have departments and people that guide us and show us what steps we should take, but they should also have more agreements with some companies for sending students every year for internships." Companies most likely to hire Walker grads include Bank of America, BB&T, Duke Energy, IBM, Lowe's Companies, MDI, Murray Supply, North Carolina State University, Regeneron Pharmaceuticals, Rubbermaid Newell, Wachovia, and Wake Tech.

ANNA BASNIGHT, ADMISSIONS CONTACT
ASU BOX 32068, BOONE, NC 28608-2068 UNITED STATES
PHONE: 828-262-2130 • FAX: 828-262-2709
E-MAIL: BASNIGHTAL@APPSTATE.EDU • WEBSITE: WWW.BUSINESS.APPSTATE.EDU

## Student Life and Environment

Unlike most MBA programs, Walker does not support much of an extracurricular scene; with its tiny student body, it can barely populate one club, let alone several. Accordingly, "most people pursue their own personal hobbies during their spare time. Being near the Blue Ridge Parkway and several ski slopes, a lot of people are involved in outdoor activities." As one student puts it, "If you like nature, long winters, and small, close-knit groups of friends, then you should look into ASU. And if you like skiing, you're golden."

On the other hand, "when you want to have some nightlife, there is almost none." That's because "[hometown] Boone is a very small town. It has several movie theaters, including one that is $1.50," but not much else to offer. As one student explains it, "This is a beautiful place, meant for studying." Fortunately, the university community at large (which numbers over 15,000 students) offers up many forms of diversion, including ASU's 18 intercollegiate athletic teams. The university houses several museums and is host to numerous performing-arts series.

When students crave a more urban environment, they road-trip to either Asheville or Winston-Salem; each is just under a two-hour drive from campus. Lexington, NC, is also only two hours away. It's not a huge city, but it is home to arguably the best barbecue in the state (and thus, from a Tar Heel perspective, the best barbecue in the world).

## Admissions

Applications to the Walker MBA program are processed by the admissions office at the Cratis D. Williams Graduate School. Prospective students must submit GMAT scores, an undergraduate transcript, letters of recommendation, a resume (at least one year of work experience is required), and two essays. An interview is strongly recommended but not required. Applicants must have completed at least one undergraduate class in each of the following areas: calculus, microeconomics, and statistics (summer courses in these subjects are offered for applicants who do not meet this requirement). Students should arrive with a working knowledge of Microsoft Excel®, Word®, and PowerPoint®.

The school uses a formula to set minimum admissions requirements. The formula is (GPA x 200) + GMAT = admissions score; GPA is tallied based only on the final 60 hours of undergraduate course work. An admissions score of at least 1050 is required but does not guarantee admission. Application materials must arrive no later than 3/1; admission is for the fall term only.

### FINANCIAL FACTS

| | |
|---|---|
| Annual tuition (in-state/out-of-state) | $1,840/$5,888 |
| Fees | $744 |
| Books and supplies | $1,200 |
| Room & board (on-campus) | $4,082 |
| Average grant | $1,000 |

### ADMISSIONS

| | |
|---|---|
| Admissions Selectivity Rating | 69 |
| # of applications received | 27 |
| % applicants accepted | 81 |
| % acceptees attending | 59 |
| Average GMAT | 511 |
| Range of GMAT | 420–700 |
| Average GPA | 3.36 |
| TOEFL required of international students? | yes |
| Minimum TOEFL (paper/computer) | 550/233 |
| Application fee | $45 |
| International application fee | $45 |
| Regular application deadline | 3/1 |
| Regular notification | 3/31 |
| Deferment available? | yes |
| Maximum length of deferment | 1 year |
| Transfer students accepted? | yes |
| Transfer application policy | Up to six hours of graduate credit may be transferred for equivalent courses completed with at least grade of B. |
| Non-fall admissions? | yes |
| Need-blind admissions? | yes |

### APPLICANTS ALSO LOOK AT

North Carolina State University, University of North Carolina at Chapel Hill, University of North Carolina at Greensboro, Western Carolina University

# ARIZONA STATE UNIVERSITY
## W. P. CAREY SCHOOL OF BUSINESS

### GENERAL INFORMATION
| | |
|---|---|
| Type of school | public |
| Environment | city |
| Academic calendar | trimester |

### SURVEY SAYS...
Smart classrooms
*Solid preparation in:*
Teamwork
Communication/interpersonal skills
Presentation skills

### STUDENTS
| | |
|---|---|
| Enrollment of parent institution | 61,033 |
| Enrollment of business school | 515 |
| % male/female | 71/29 |
| % out-of-state | 67 |
| % part-time | 80 |
| % minorities | 13 |
| % international | 25 |
| Average age at entry | 31 |
| Average years work experience at entry | 6.8 |

### ACADEMICS
| | |
|---|---|
| **Academic Experience Rating** | **79** |
| Student/faculty ratio | 25:1 |
| Profs interesting rating | 77 |
| Profs accessible rating | 83 |
| % female faculty | 24 |
| % minority faculty | 22 |

### JOINT DEGREES
**Two-year programs:** MBA/MS in Economics; MBA/MS in Information Management; MBA/MAcct and Information Systems; MBA/Master of Taxation; MBA/Master of Health Services Sector Management; MBA/Master of International Management (Thunderbird)
**Three- to four-year programs:** MBA/JD; MBA/MArch

### PROMINENT ALUMNI
Craig Weatherup, Chair, The Pepsi Bottling Group; Steve Marriott, VP of Corp. Marketing, Marriott Hotels; Wayne Doran, Chair of the Board, Ford Motor Co.; George Schreiber, CEO, SEMCO ENERGY, Inc.; Jack Furst, Partner, Hicks, Muse, Tate & Furst, Inc.

## Academics

Supply Chain Management has long been the strong suit of the W. P. Carey School of Business, located on Arizona State University's Tempe campus. Students think you should know, however, that the school has much more to offer; one wrote, "The greatest strength of W. P. Carey is its drive to improve and excel in every area. The faculty and staff believe in the students and are constantly trying new things to remain on the forefront of business education." Another student notes, "Our MBA program has definite strengths in providing technology resources and classes, teaching the core MBA competencies, and offering a balanced set of classes and applied projects to students regardless of their specialization." Services marketing and management, sports business, and health services administration are among Carey's other strengths. The MBA program at ASU is relatively small, especially when compared with the mammoth university it calls home. Students love the cozy atmosphere, explaining that "because Carey limits each class size to about 150 students, you get the opportunity to really get to know all of the professors as well as the administration." ASU's status as a major research institution means that "all professors must be published and many work in their fields when they are not teaching." While "this really adds to their credibility and ability to make the material relevant," some warn that "this also means that some of them are not the best teaching professors." Most feel the benefits outweigh the drawbacks, telling us that "[they] have never been in an environment where so many top theorists in the field are the actual teachers of the courses. Dr. Ellram for TCO and Dr. Nadari for international finance are two examples." Students also appreciate how professors "treat [them] mostly like colleagues, which leads to a great learning environment."

Carey recently instituted a "revised first-year curriculum with more opportunity for electives," of which students approve. One student says, "My first year was very beneficial overall. It did the most to impart an overall business sense into my thought process. My second-year course work so far has been much less impactful than I had hoped, and this fact has tempered my enthusiasm overall for the program." Students note that "the school is definitely going through a transitional period, but accounting for the variability that produces, it's a stable learning environment." A quick-paced trimester calendar means the program is "rigorous, but with support from the excellent and interested faculty and supportive students, the workload and intensity are conquerable. Still, it is not recommended that you work while in school." For students who refuse to heed such warnings, Carey offers an executive MBA program, "a two-year weekend program for senior managers and executives that provides the integrated education needed to succeed in today's business environment. Students learn to go beyond the usual analysis and seek out the larger set of opportunities each business situation may offer."

## Career and Placement

Students at Carey agree that the W. P. Carey School Career Management Center (CMC) does a great job of placing MBAs in the supply-chain management field; in 2003, over one-third of graduates took positions in the field, earning a median salary of $70,500 and a median signing bonus of $10,000. "The career counselor for Supply Chain Management is awesome, but I have heard students from other disciplines were not as happy with their counselors regarding job searches," one student told us. Eleven 2003 graduates of the school's unique sports business program found jobs in the field; they earned a median salary of $60,000, with an average signing bonus of $3,500. While students generally love ASU's Tempe location, they feel it comes up short in the area of summer internships, a problem since "summer internships are required. The school should draw more on local companies to have a pool of internships lined up." The school hosts two annual career

DR. GERRY KEIM, ASSOCIATE DEAN, W. P. CAREY MBA
PO BOX 874906, TEMPE, AZ 85287-4906 UNITED STATES
PHONE: 480-965-3332 • FAX: 480-965-8569
E-MAIL: WPCAREYMBA@ASU.EDU • WEBSITE: HTTP://WPCAREY.ASU.EDU/MBA

fairs, one in the fall and one in the spring; no figures on the number of companies participating were available to us.

Top employers of W. P. Carey MBAs include Agilent Technologies, Anheuser-Busch, ChevronTexaco, Ford Motor Co., GE Capital, Hartford, Honeywell, IBM/IBM Global Services, Intel Corporation, Northrop Grumman, Phelps Dodge, ProNet Solutions, Raytheon, and Sprint Communications.

## Student Life and Environment

"Life at school requires a lot of work and a lot of time on campus, but not much more than an ordinary job," Carey MBAs report. Students find their hours filled with classes and studying but also tell us that "within ASU, there are many activities that can be pursued when not studying." ASU is "a big party school for the undergraduates, so there are plenty of bars and nightclubs. There are weekly happy hours planned for MBA students," and "the intramural program at ASU is a good opportunity to socialize and get some physical exercise. Also, the student recreation center is equipped with nice new equipment." Summing up the environment, one student wrote that "there are almost too many social outlets, but that is a good problem to have: weekly happy hours on Thursday nights, a great Christmas party for charity, tailgating for football games, organized events such as charity bowling, golfing, mountain biking, and hiking. The list is long, and there is something for everyone here." That list also includes "various clubs and activities that MBA students can participate in (outdoors club, tennis club, golf club, and the many academic clubs). Overall, it is very easy to attain a balanced life while attending ASU."

Tempe, Arizona, we're told, "is a terrific place to go to school. It's great to step outside of the classroom in February and enjoy 70-degree temperatures." The area surrounding the school offers "lots of affordable housing. In short, life here is fantastic and is a very good reason to consider this program, all other things excluded." If you need another reason, consider the student body, which "without a doubt are one of the school's greatest strengths. The professors give you a kernel of knowledge in class, but teamwork is where it blooms."

## Admissions

The admissions department at the Carey School considers undergraduate transcripts (which must show at least a B average in the final 60 semester-hours/90 quarter-hours of course work), GMAT scores, TOEFL scores, resume, personal statement, two letters of recommendation, and interview (all required). The school reports that "admission decisions are also influenced by the amount and type of practical work experience, interest in W. P. Carey MBA specializations, leadership abilities, community, and professional involvement." Applications may be submitted online. ASU uses PepsiCo scholarships, graduate academic scholarships, graduate assistantships, and graduate fellowships to increase the minority population of the student body.

### FINANCIAL FACTS

| | |
|---|---|
| Annual tuition (in-state/out-of-state) | $5,561/$15,825 |
| Fees | $9,500 |
| Books and supplies | $2,100 |
| Room & board (on/off-campus) | $7,960/$7,960 |
| % of students receiving aid | 86 |
| % of first-year students receiving aid | 86 |
| % of students receiving loans | 83 |
| % of students receiving grants | 13 |
| Average award package | $15,622 |
| Average grant | $8,052 |
| Average student loan debt | $31,245 |

### ADMISSIONS

| | |
|---|---|
| Admissions Selectivity Rating | 81 |
| # of applications received | 1,108 |
| % applicants accepted | 64 |
| % acceptees attending | 72 |
| Average GMAT | 588 |
| Range of GMAT | 540–640 |
| Average GPA | 3.08 |
| TOEFL required of international students? | yes |
| Minimum TOEFL (paper/computer) | 600/250 |
| Application fee | $50 |
| International application fee | $50 |
| Application deadline/notification | |
| Round 1: | 11/15 / 1/10 |
| Round 2: | 1/13 / 3/10 |
| Round 3: | 3/15 / 5/10 |
| Round 4: | 5/15 / 6/30 |
| Deferment available? | yes |
| Maximum length of deferment | 1 year |
| Non-fall admissions? | yes |
| Need-blind admissions? | yes |

### APPLICANTS ALSO LOOK AT

Indiana University—Bloomington, Michigan State University, The University of Texas at Austin, University of Arizona, University of California—Los Angeles, University of Maryland—College Park, University of Southern California

### EMPLOYMENT PROFILE

| Career Rating | 84 | Grads employed by field: | % | avg. salary: |
|---|---|---|---|---|
| Average starting salary | $70,843 | Finance | 25 | $76,529 |
| | | Marketing | 17 | $69,417 |
| | | MIS | 7 | $74,166 |
| | | Operations | 26 | $71,522 |
| | | Consulting | 11 | $63,556 |
| | | General Management | 9 | $58,820 |
| | | Other | 5 | $74,000 |

# AUBURN UNIVERSITY
## COLLEGE OF BUSINESS

## Academics

Students seeking an MBA from Auburn University can follow one of three curriculum models: the traditional on-campus model; the new, increasingly popular distance model, called the Outreach Program, which allows students to fulfill most of the obligations toward their degrees from the comfort of their own homes (students must attend one five-day case analysis during their final fall semester, but otherwise never need to visit campus); and the Executive MBA program (EMBA), which requires five one-week residencies over a two-year period, with the larger portion of instruction coming via Internet and CD technologies. The distance program offers concentrations in finance, health care administration, human resource development, management information systems, technology management, marketing, and production/operations management. The full-time program offers all of these, plus concentrations in agribusiness, economic development, and sports management. The EMBA offers specializations in technology management and health care administration.

Full-time students warn that "it can be too much of a course load in the first semester, an absolute killer!" However, they appreciate how "everything is organized" so that "students take the same classes, [meaning that] getting the right courses is not a problem," and also recognize other benefits of this curricular approach; one student explains, "This degree has taught me as much about life as it did business. You get to see the synergistic effect of these lessons when you reach the end of the curriculum." The workload and the design of the program "encourage us to work as a team, and participate in class. This provides us an opportunity to realize what we are strong at, and what we are not so strong at." One shortcoming of the program is that "the different course offerings at Auburn are limited. Currently, Auburn is working towards expanding the concentrations in which MBA students can focus."

Students tell us that "the atmosphere is the best aspect of Auburn. The academics are great and the faculty and administration are excellent, but that's just a part of . . . the MBA program at Auburn University. Auburn will prepare you inside and outside of the classroom to be successful. [It's] a choice that you'll never regret." Another student agrees, "The courses have been great, but the . . . extra training and development in things such as leadership and impression management have really made the program stand out." The program is challenging, but an administration that "is extremely helpful and always available to help with questions and problems" and professors who "treat us with respect and . . . as professionals" help students shoulder the load.

## Career and Placement

Auburn's Careers Services Office handles career counseling and recruitment services for MBAs. The office provides one-on-one counseling, seminars, workshops, and a career library; it also organizes career expos and on-campus recruiting events. Students approve, telling us that "over a hundred companies recruit on campus every semester" and touting "a huge alumni base with which to network. The alumni are a great strength of this school." Employers who often hire Auburn MBAs include AmSouth Bank, Colonial Bank, Home Depot, Total Systems, and Wal-Mart.

MR. J. DON FLOWERS, DIRECTOR MBA ADMISSIONS & OPERATIONS
415 WEST MAGNOLIA AVENUE, SUITE 503, LOWDER BUSINESS BUILDING, AUBURN, AL 36849 U.S.
PHONE: 334-844-4060 • FAX: 334-844-2964
E-MAIL: MBAINFO@AUBURN.EDU • WEBSITE: WWW.MBA.BUSINESS.AUBURN.EDU

## Student Life and Environment

"There is more to Auburn than an MBA program," students at this large, southern university remind us. "The school has quality sports teams and multitudes of other activities that allow you to really enjoy your time here." The town of Auburn itself is a source of pride and comfort for many MBAs; "There isn't a better college town in the country," writes a typical student, pointing out that "football season is always exciting and game days present a great tailgating atmosphere. The nightlife is good as well, with a good number of bars close to campus." With its "smaller-town atmosphere with plenty of things to do and people to meet," Auburn "can provide something to appeal to everybody," but especially to those who "like sweet tea, chicken fingers, and football."

Auburn's full-time MBA program "offers numerous opportunities for students to meet people and network. In addition to social events, the MBA program has an established mentor program that pairs first-year students with second-year students." Students note that "the way the program is structured, you can't help but know everyone in the on-campus MBA program, which creates a cohesive group that can be drawn on for help." Accordingly, MBA students note that they "all stick together and are willing to help each other out with studying and doing projects. Nobody is going to stab you in the back to get a better grade. We try to lift each other up."

Auburn MBAs evince "Southern hospitality in full force" by not only "tailgating, playing intramurals, and barhopping together" but also by "getting very involved in the community through volunteer organizations." It's "a very diverse group with different backgrounds. Some are married with children; some are international; some are businesspeople; some are engineering; some have years of work experience; some came straight from undergrad. Anyone of any age could fit in at Auburn because the students are so diverse."

## Admissions

All applicants to the Auburn MBA program must submit official transcripts for all post-secondary academic work, an official GMAT score report, three letters of recommendation, a completed application to the graduate school, and a completed application to the MBA program, including a signed copy of the MBA Code of Ethics and Responsibilities. Work experience and a personal interview are both encouraged, but neither is required. International students whose first language is not English must also submit TOEFL scores. Undergraduate-level competency in accounting, calculus, economics, finance, management, marketing, and statistics are all prerequisites to starting the Auburn MBA program. Students lacking appropriate undergraduate credentials may purchase the corresponding courses on CD, and must subsequently pass a competency exam in each course prior to commencing work on the MBA. In an effort to boost the population of underrepresented students, Auburn makes recruiting trips to minority campuses.

## FINANCIAL FACTS

| | |
|---|---|
| Annual tuition (in-state/out-of-state) | $4,800/$14,400 |
| Fees | $430 |
| Books and supplies | $900 |
| Room & board (on-campus) | $9,574 |
| % of students receiving aid | 95 |
| % of first-year students receiving aid | 89 |
| % of students receiving grants | 30 |
| Average award package | $6,115 |
| Average grant | $1,200 |
| Average student loan debt | $14,665 |

## ADMISSIONS

| | |
|---|---|
| Admissions Selectivity Rating | 84 |
| # of applications received | 94 |
| % applicants accepted | 63 |
| % acceptees attending | 44 |
| Average GMAT | 622 |
| Range of GMAT | 580–660 |
| Average GPA | 3.31 |
| TOEFL required of international students? | yes |
| Minimum TOEFL (paper/computer) | 550/213 |
| Application fee | $25 |
| International application fee | $50 |
| Regular application deadline | 3/1 |
| Deferment available? | yes |
| Maximum length of deferment | 1 year |
| Transfer students accepted? | yes |
| Transfer application policy | Students may transfer up to 12 elective credit hours from AACSB schools only; approval on a case-by-case basis. |
| Need-blind admissions? | yes |

## EMPLOYMENT PROFILE

| Career Rating | 66 | Grads employed by field: | % | avg. salary: |
|---|---|---|---|---|
| Average starting salary | $51,653 | Finance | 13 | $47,560 |
| Percent employed | 33 | Marketing | 32 | $50,850 |
| | | MIS | 10 | $51,500 |
| | | Operations | 16 | $46,800 |
| | | Consulting | 10 | $58,000 |
| | | General Management | 16 | $54,000 |
| | | Other | 3 | $70,000 |

# AUBURN UNIVERSITY—MONTGOMERY
## SCHOOL OF BUSINESS

## Academics

The AACSB-accredited MBA program at Auburn University—Montgomery is designed for part-time students; in fact, any student wishing to exceed a course load of nine hours per semester must first receive approval from the dean of the School of Business. Students in this program appreciate how "course offerings cater to students' work schedules" by meeting during convenient evening hours.

The MBA program at AUM is divided into three parts. The first is called the Basic Program, consisting of 11 half-term courses covering business concepts typically taught at the undergraduate level (accounting, management, marketing, business law, microeconomics, macroeconomics, operations management, statistics, MIS, and finance). Students who can demonstrate sufficient background in these areas may petition to be exempted from some or all of these requirements. The second part of the program is the Business Core, a 7-course set of classes covering such integrative concepts as managerial applications of accounting information and synergistic organizational strategy (the latter is a capstone course), as well as such essential functions as marketing, data analysis, and managing personnel. The program concludes with either three or four electives, depending on whether the student chooses a general MBA or a specialization. Specializations are offered in contract management, economics, finance, global business management, information systems, management of information technology, management, and marketing.

AUM MBAs brag that "the teachers are great and enjoy what they do," although some feel that some classes rely too heavily on lectures and that "professors could try to involve students more in the classroom and encourage more interaction." Many also agree that the program "would benefit from more offerings in high-tech and computer-related fields." Comprehensive exit exams are required of all students who complete the program with a GPA below 3.25. Comprehensive exams may be taken no more than three times.

## Career and Placement

The Career Development Center (CDC) at AUM serves all university students and alumni. The office maintains a library of career-related material, including documents tracking salary and hiring trends around the region, state, country, and world. Career counseling services are available, as are job fairs, seminars, and workshops in interviewing, job hunting, and resume and cover-letter writing. Students agree that the CDC's services are adequate, though on many students' wish lists are "better career advice and job placement" options. The office arranges internships and recruiting events for qualifying MBA students.

## Student Life and Environment

AUM MBAs are typically "commuters who attend mostly for education and do not contribute much to the university outside of classes." There are "lots of military" here as well as a large number of international students. Most students "are in their 20s or 30s and hold full-time jobs. Many have spouses and children" who take up what little free time they have. As a result, "social life isn't huge here, but that's great; there are no distractions!" notes one student. International students occasionally recreate through "a club called ISA (International Students Association), which helps new foreign students get together and socialize as well as share their culture with others, through banquets."

SHARON JONES, ADMISSION SPECIALIST
PO BOX 244023 MONTGOMERY, AL 36124 UNITED STATES
PHONE: 334-244-3623 • FAX: 334-244-3927
E-MAIL: VJONES1@MAIL.AUM.EDU • WEBSITE: WWW.AUM.EDU

Montgomery is a midsize southern city well known for its integral part in the civil rights movement. The population of the city is about evenly split between whites and blacks, with small Hispanic, Native American, and Asian populations accounting for a small minority. The city is home to the Alabama Shakespeare Festival, a year-round enterprise that mounts a dozen or more productions and draws over 300,000 visitors annually. Another major attraction is the minor-league baseball team, Montgomery Biscuits, the AA affiliate of the Tampa Bay Devil Rays. And no Montgomery summer is complete without City Stages, a three-day outdoor music festival that in recent years has attracted such headliners as Ralph Stanley, P-Funk, Al Green, Kid Rock, Jurassic 5, and Shelby Lynne. The all-day event closes a good portion of the downtown area to traffic.

## Admissions

Applicants to the AUM MBA program must submit official transcripts for all previous post-secondary academic work, official GMAT score reports, and a completed application form. The screening committee may request an interview, typically in the case of borderline candidates; otherwise, interviews are not required. The admissions committee applies an undisclosed mathematical formula to applicants' GPA and GMAT, using the formula results and other considerations in reaching its decision. International applicants must meet all of the above requirements and must also provide certified English translations of any academic transcripts not in English and a course-by-course evaluation of undergraduate work "by a recognized, expert service in the field of foreign credential evaluations and international admissions." Applicants whose first language is not English must submit TOEFL scores. Candidates may be admitted conditionally pending completion of prerequisite undergraduate-level classes in business.

## FINANCIAL FACTS

| | |
|---|---|
| Annual tuition (in-state/out-of-state) | $4,563/$13,689 |
| Books and supplies | $1,500 |
| % of students receiving aid | 60 |
| % of first-year students receiving aid | 65 |
| % of students receiving loans | 45 |
| % of students receiving grants | 15 |
| Average award package | $13,500 |
| Average grant | $3,000 |

## ADMISSIONS

| | |
|---|---|
| **Admissions Selectivity Rating** | **65** |
| # of applications received | 109 |
| % applicants accepted | 89 |
| % acceptees attending | 90 |
| Average GMAT | 500 |
| Average GPA | 2.9 |
| TOEFL required of international students? | yes |
| Minimum TOEFL (paper) | 500 |
| Application fee | $25 |
| Regular application deadline | rolling |
| Regular notification | rolling |
| Non-fall admissions? | yes |
| Need-blind admissions? | yes |

## EMPLOYMENT PROFILE

| | |
|---|---|
| **Career Rating** | **61** |
| Average starting salary | $37,000 |

# BABSON COLLEGE
## F. W. OLIN GRADUATE SCHOOL OF BUSINESS

### GENERAL INFORMATION

| | |
|---|---|
| Type of school | private |
| Environment | village |
| Academic calendar | semester |

### SURVEY SAYS...
*Solid preparation in:*
General management
Teamwork
Presentation skills
Entrepreneurial studies

### STUDENTS

| | |
|---|---|
| Enrollment of parent institution | 3,132 |
| Enrollment of business school | 1,435 |
| % male/female | 73/27 |
| % out-of-state | 27 |
| % part-time | 70 |
| % minorities | 12 |
| % international | 43 |
| Average age at entry | 28 |
| Average years work experience at entry | 5.3 |

### ACADEMICS

| | |
|---|---|
| **Academic Experience Rating** | **88** |
| Student/faculty ratio | 11:1 |
| Profs interesting rating | 95 |
| Profs accessible rating | 96 |
| % female faculty | 28 |
| % minority faculty | 13 |

### PROMINENT ALUMNI
Robert Davis, Founder, Lycos; Venture Partner, Highland Capital; Deborah Mclaughlin, CFO & COO, Slade's Ferry Bancorp; Win Priem, Retired President & CEO, Korn/Ferry International; Akio Toyoda, Managing Director Toyota Motor Group; Michael Smith, Chair and CEO, Hughes Electronics

## Academics

Babson's MBA program has many virtues to recommend it, and if you give students enough time, they'll get around to mentioning all of them. Invariably, however, the first two things they mention—usually one right after the other—are the school's excellent entrepreneurship program and its fully integrated first-year core curriculum. Nearly everyone we surveyed seemed to regard these two aspects of the program as the ones that make Babson a world-class business school.

Entrepreneurship has long been Babson's top discipline; one student writes, "It's the access to top-notch professorial talent that makes this program number one. Bob Rosenberg, the former CEO of Dunkin' Donuts, who grew the company from 13 stores to 3,000, is my franchising professor. And now he'll take my phone call for consultations and advice. How cool is that?" Babson's reputation in this field means the program attracts students who "seem to have the same type of personality, and they are all encouraged to look at things in a new, different light." One MBA explains, "Babson students don't go and generally become partners in huge companies, but they [start] companies and have good qualities of life." The school also boasts strong departments in marketing, finance (applied investments), high tech, and consulting.

Before students can specialize, however, they must first complete the demanding core curriculum. One student explains, "The first-year mod program is very integrated, and all the professors work very closely to provide cross-functional case work. Finance, marketing, accounting, entrepreneurship, ethics—all integrated each day." Another student adds, "Babson's integrative curriculum has been a highlight of my experience. We would have classes on current events such as Enron, taught by both accounting and ethics professors. It really gives a different perspective to the learning." First year also includes a year-long consulting project that "brings MBA students directly into contact with the 'real world,' instead of viewing reality from behind tempered glass, as is true of the case method. Also, you work with the same team for the entire year, so teamwork is very important." The core is so integral to the Babson experience that it is even integrated into the part-time evening program.

Students warn that Babson really piles on the work. "It's overwhelming," writes one student. "I realize that there just isn't enough time to cover a lot of materials within the limited time we have, but I sometimes question the strategy of the administration to overload us. We learn about so much that we usually have a hard time remembering what was learned last week." When the going gets rough, students can seek out their professors for help; they're "completely accessible, to the point of being willing to open their own Rolodexes to students."

## Career and Placement

Students in the past have expressed frustration over the Career Development Office. One MBA student mentioned last year that "the career services office could stand to be improved but I think it is an area of top priority right now. There is a struggle with maintaining the focus on entrepreneurship and recruiting big-name companies to campus. I don't think that it has to be mutually exclusive." Since we last surveyed Babson MBAs, the redesign of the Career Development Office has been completed, involving the creation of a new approach that centers on relationship management within the industry. The school reports that in 2005, both students and recruiters seem to be responding favorably to these recent improvements. Babson students benefit from an alumni network more than 10,000 strong. About 140 companies recruit on campus each year; about 80 come seeking summer interns.

JON KERBS, ACTING DIRECTOR OF GRADUATE ADMISSIONS
OLIN HALL BABSON PARK, WELLESLEY, MA 02457-0310 UNITED STATES
PHONE: 781-239-4317 • FAX: 781-239-4194
E-MAIL: MBAADMISSION@BABSON.EDU • WEBSITE: WWW.BABSON.EDU/MBA

Top employers of Babson MBAs include Adventis; A.T. Kearney; Bank of America; Bose Corporation; Boston Scientific Corporation; EMC Corporation; Fidelity Capital; Fidelity Investments; Genuity; The Hartford; IBM; International Data Corporation (IDC); Liberty Mutual; Merrill Lynch; Our Group; Philips Medical Systems; PricewaterhouseCoopers; Staples, Inc.; and Strategic Pricing Group, Inc.

## Student Life and Environment

For full-time, two-year students (the school also offers an accelerated one-year program, a hybrid learning program, and a part-time evening program), the Babson experience is actually two distinct experiences: an intensive, community-oriented first year, and a much-less-communal second year. The first-year workload and the emphasis on team-work means students are together nearly 24/7. The second year, on the other hand, "is all about taking the skills learned in the first, where we are trained as financial analysts and business consultants, and applying them to what you want to learn and develop."

Social opportunities are available, however. The school sponsors family events for married students. One such student reports, "My husband is welcome to partner's events, which are held frequently. My husband and I socialize with other couples (and single students) from the program. We celebrate each other's children's birthdays and celebrate one another's successes. This is a very close-knit, supportive, and caring community. I couldn't be happier." There's also "a regular Thursday night at Roger's Pub, and at least one or two other Boston social nights a week. With only 150 students per class, you get to know everyone in your class well." The fact that hometown Wellesley is a dry town actually helps matters, since it corrals students into Roger's (the campus bar). Wellesley, "a beautiful suburb, [is conveniently located to] allow easy access to Boston and all its resources for social activity."

## Admissions

A completed Babson application includes official copies of all undergraduate and graduate transcripts, GMAT scores, two letters of recommendation (from supervisors at current or former jobs), essays, TOEFL scores (non-native English speakers), and a resume or curriculum vitae. The admissions committee looks at all of these and notes that "admissions decisions are also influenced by the candidate's fit with Babson's team orientation, modular curriculum, entrepreneurial focus, and global mind-set." Interviews, while not required, are "an important part of the admission process."

### FINANCIAL FACTS

| | |
|---|---|
| Annual tuition | $31,544 |
| Books and supplies | $2,148 |
| Room & board (on-campus) | $17,110 |
| % of students receiving aid | 69 |
| % of first-year students receiving aid | 64 |
| % of students receiving loans | 51 |
| % of students receiving grants | 49 |
| Average award package | $19,380 |
| Average grant | $16,311 |
| Average student loan debt | $63,209 |

### ADMISSIONS

| | |
|---|---|
| Admissions Selectivity Rating | 81 |
| # of applications received | 551 |
| % applicants accepted | 83 |
| % acceptees attending | 47 |
| Average GMAT | 623 |
| Range of GMAT | 580–670 |
| Average GPA | 3.14 |
| TOEFL required of international students? | yes |
| Minimum TOEFL (paper/computer) | 600/250 |
| Application fee | $100 |
| Regular application deadline | 4/15 |
| Regular notification | 5/31 |
| Application deadline/notification | |
| Round 1: | 11/30 / 2/15 |
| Round 2: | 1/31 / 3/31 |
| Round 3: | 3/15 / 4/30 |
| Round 4: | 4/15 / 5/31 |
| Deferment available? | yes |
| Maximum length of deferment | 1 year |
| Transfer students accepted? | yes |
| Transfer application policy | |
| Students may transfer credits from an AACSB-accredited institution into the Evening MBA program. | |
| Non-fall admissions? | yes |
| Need-blind admissions? | yes |

### APPLICANTS ALSO LOOK AT

Boston College, Boston University, Dartmouth College, Harvard University, Massachusetts Institute of Technology, New York University, Northwestern University

### EMPLOYMENT PROFILE

| Career Rating | 85 | Grads employed by field: | % | avg. salary: |
|---|---|---|---|---|
| Average starting salary | $80,681 | Finance | 20 | $73,925 |
| Percent employed | 89 | Human Resources | 2 | $66,750 |
| | | Marketing | 24 | $78,590 |
| | | MIS | 1 | $61,000 |
| | | Operations | 1 | $90,000 |
| | | Consulting | 15 | $90,866 |
| | | Entrepreneurship | 10 | $87,300 |
| | | General Management | 15 | $75,933 |

# BARRY UNIVERSITY
## ANDREAS SCHOOL OF BUSINESS

## Academics

Besides offering all of the advantages of a small, private school, the Andreas School of Business at Barry University manages to offer a surprising number of custom-tailored options to meet the needs and goals of its student body. Part-timers, who make up about two-thirds of the student body here, can choose between evening classes (on both the main campus and the West Broward campus) or the Saturday MBA Program. Full-time students can complete their program of study at the main campus. All students can opt for dual degrees in Human Resource Development, Nursing, Podiatry, and Sports Management: The last is an especially popular option, cited by a number of MBAs as their primary reason for choosing Barry. Besides a general MBA, Andreas also offers a full complement of areas of specialization, with options including accounting, e-commerce, finance, health services administration, international business, management, MIS, and marketing. Besides the MBA, the School of Business also offers a Master of Science in Accounting (MSA) and a Master of Science in Management (MSM).

All told, Barry provides choices that are typically available only at larger universities. Yet this program is relatively pint-sized, to the great advantage of its MBAs. One such MBA explains, "Because the business school is small, you get the benefit of personalized attention. The administrators and class coordinators know your name, and professors can always make time for you to visit them." Another agrees, "No other school would give you such personal attention. Several of my classes have had fewer than 10 students, and the professor tailors the material to fit our schedules and individual ambitions. And because there's such close contact, it's easy to build relationships with professors. I even was able to collaborate with one professor on writing a business case that will appear in a textbook supplement."

Andreas classes "are designed to challenge students in several ways. One is the explanation of theories; others include the implementation of practical assignments or case studies." In keeping with the school's Catholic worldview, many courses "promote social responsibility." The school's religious affiliation also helps it attract international students, whose presence "truly prepares students for working with many different types of people in many different contexts."

## Career and Placement

The School of Business Career Resource & Alumni Relations Center maintains a close working relationship with local, state, and national companies. One student in the past indicated, "While job placement efforts could certainly be improved, I, like most Barry MBAs, have a job already, so I'm not really worried about the post-graduation job hunt, and that might be why Barry doesn't bring more companies to campus and be more aggressive in job placement. But for those students who do need to find work after school, Barry isn't equipped to be the kind of resource they really need." Additionally, international students are among those who feel most strongly that these services must be improved. However, since then, the school has reported that during the 2005 school year the center increased its placement by 27.6 percent along with an accompanying wage increase. The Career Resource Center has also partnered with the following organizations, firms, and companies: Burger King Corporation, Microsoft Latin America, Franklin Templeton, KPMG, FBI, JM Family Enterprises, Robert Half International, Northwestern Mutual, Morgan Stanley, and MTV Networks Latin America.

Jose J. Poza Jr., Marketing Director
11300 Northeast 2nd Avenue, Miami Shores, FL 33161 United States
Phone: 305-899-3535 • Fax: 305-892-6412
E-mail: jpoza@mail.barry.edu • Website: www.barry.edu/business

## Student Life and Environment

For MBA students, Barry is "mostly a commuter school, so most MBA students are on campus in the evenings or weekends. As a result, there is not much extracurricular life. Not that that's necessarily a bad thing; as one student observes, "Barry is tranquil and laid-back, the ideal place for a person who would get overwhelmed by a high-stress, backstabbing MBA program. The MBA school is also made for people already working full-time." The school offers "limited clubs" and didn't even have a graduate business association until students took the initiative to form one. Those who truly desire a higher level of involvement can find it here, though. One student explains, "I have made myself get involved. I am a former student-athlete, currently a residence assistant as well as a graduate assistant. So my life has been great here. There is potential for everyone if you look for it."

"There is a vast cultural diversity within the university" and the MBA program at Barry. "It is delightful to see the peace that exists among classmates." Students "are very willing to help one another. There are always study groups, and in every class all students have each others' phone numbers, e-mails, etc. so that we can discuss the class when we need to." One MBA notes, "Learning in a cohort group has been the number one reason my MBA experience at Barry has been so successful. We've bonded as classmates, collaborated on projects, and built friendships that will extend beyond our MBA studies. In general, Barry MBA students are culturally diverse, unfailingly nice, and, since most work full-time while going to school, eager to use their degree to move up the career ladder."

Barry is located in Miami Shores, a central location offering easy access to the entire Miami metropolitan area. The area surrounding the campus offers access to the beach, and plenty of shopping, dining, and housing.

## Admissions

The Admissions Committee at Barry University School of Business looks closely at the following components of the application: undergraduate GPA; GMAT scores (in lieu of the GMAT, we also accept the GRE, LSAT, or the MCAT); quality of undergraduate curriculum; personal essay; resume; two letters of reference supporting the resume; and TOEFL scores (for non-native English speakers). The GMAT requirement may be waived for applicants with substantial managerial experience. All of the following are prerequisites to MBA study: 6 credit hours of introductory accounting; 6 credit hours of macro and microeconomics; 3 credit hours of algebra or precalculus; 3 credit hours of statistics; 3 credit hours of introductory computer skills; 3 credit hours of operations management; and 3 credit hours of marketing. Students may demonstrate competency in any of these areas through undergraduate work or, in some cases, CLEP testing.

### FINANCIAL FACTS

| | |
|---|---|
| Annual tuition | $24,660 |
| Books and supplies | $1,500 |
| Room & board | |
| (on-campus) | $13,000 |
| % of students receiving aid | 76 |
| % of students receiving loans | 43 |
| % of students receiving grants | 61 |
| Average award package | $11,662 |
| Average grant | $1,782 |

### ADMISSIONS

| | |
|---|---|
| **Admissions Selectivity Rating** | **77** |
| # of applications received | 134 |
| % applicants accepted | 41 |
| % acceptees attending | 44 |
| Average GMAT | 496 |
| Range of GMAT | 400–710 |
| Average GPA | 3.09 |
| TOEFL required of | |
| international students? | yes |
| Minimum TOEFL | |
| (paper/computer) | 550/213 |
| Application fee | $30 |
| International application fee | $30 |
| Regular application deadline | rolling |
| Regular notification | rolling |
| Deferment available? | yes |
| Maximum length | |
| of deferment | 1 year |
| Transfer students accepted? | yes |
| Transfer application policy | |
| Students may transfer a maximum | |
| of 6 credits from an AACSB- | |
| accredited institution. | |
| Non-fall admissions? | yes |

### APPLICANTS ALSO LOOK AT

Florida Atlantic University, Florida International University, Nova Southeastern University, University of Miami

### EMPLOYMENT PROFILE

| | | | |
|---|---|---|---|
| **Career Rating** | **61** | **Grads employed by field:** | **% avg. salary:** |
| **Primary source of full-time** | | Accounting | 1 | $65,000 |
| **job acceptances** | | Finance | 1 | $48,000 |
| Unknown | 10 | Marketing | 2 | $58,000 |
| | | Consulting | 1 | $55,000 |
| Average starting salary | $55,000 | Entrepreneurship | 2 | NR |
| Percent employed | 10 | General Management | 2 | $50,000 |
| | | Global Management | 1 | $62,000 |

# BAYLOR UNIVERSITY
## HANKAMER SCHOOL OF BUSINESS

### GENERAL INFORMATION
| | |
|---|---|
| Type of school | private |
| Affiliation | Baptist |
| Environment | city |
| Academic calendar | semester |

### SURVEY SAYS...
Friendly students
Smart classrooms
*Solid preparation in:*
Teamwork
Communication/interpersonal skills

### STUDENTS
| | |
|---|---|
| Enrollment of parent institution | 13,975 |
| Enrollment of business school | 72 |
| % male/female | 74/26 |
| % minorities | 8 |
| % international | 36 |
| Average age at entry | 26 |
| Average years work experience at entry | 2.8 |

### ACADEMICS
| | |
|---|---|
| **Academic Experience Rating** | **84** |
| Student/faculty ratio | 14:1 |
| Profs interesting rating | 93 |
| Profs accessible rating | 96 |
| % female faculty | 20 |
| % minority faculty | 2 |

### JOINT DEGREES
MBA/JD, 4 years; MBA/MSIS, 2 years; MBA/Master of Engineering, 3 years; JD/MTax, 4 years

## Academics

A unique lockstep curriculum and an accelerated calendar (three semesters plus one summer semester constitutes the entire program, which can be completed in 16 months) distinguish the MBA program at Baylor University, a Baptist school south of Dallas. Students at Hankamer take all core courses as a single unit, a process that fosters camaraderie and teamwork; the approach also integrates the major disciplines (economics, accounting, marketing, finance, management, and quantitative business analysis) to foster an interdisciplinary approach to business problem-solving. MBAs love the "emphasis on understanding how each subject area fits with other subject areas," telling us that "the lockstep curriculum is a good way to remind me of the knowledge I learned in previous semesters and integrate everything in between the semesters."

Another distinctive feature of the Hankamer MBA is the Focus Firm Project, in which students work with executives of a chosen firm to address core problems at the company. According to the school, "The focus-firm approach to learning provides real-time delivery of theoretical applications, technological advances, global awareness, functional integration, and team-centered learning." In the spring of 2004, Baylor students worked with Chili's Too restaurants to help develop a brand strategy for the chain. MBAs tell us the program "positively separates Baylor from other MBA programs."

Baylor's program is small, meaning that "you have to come to every class prepared if you want to get good grades. Professors really know you." It also means lots of opportunities to show your stuff. One MBA reports, "In my first semester, I had over 30 presentations, most of which were in [a] team setting. Teamwork and presentation skills are really stressed here." Professors are "extremely accessible and willing to spend time with the students." And many students find them "very receptive to new ideas and differences of opinion." Although others temper this observation, pointing out that "Baylor is Baptist, and it affects the overall thinking of teachers [and] faculty. It is good when it comes to moral practice, which is so important in business, but it gets annoying sometimes, especially if you come from a different culture."

## Career and Placement

Baylor's MBA program offers career services through its central Baylor University Career Services Office. The office provides support in contacting alumni, career-development workshops, and access to the BearTRAK job database. The office also matches the resumes of current students and job-seeking alumni to positions posted through both BearTRAK and Monstertrak and contacts students when appropriate positions arise. Job fairs and similar events are organized for the university at large but not specifically for the MBA program. Students in the past have agreed that the Career Services Office "needs a lot of help. Currently they do not do much, but the administration has shown they are committed to building it." Fortunately, the school has taken this to heart and is making significant improvements to their career services efforts, reflected in their internships and placement statistics, which in May 2005 reached an all-time high.

Companies that most frequently hire Baylor MBAs include Accenture, Alltel, AT&T, Bank One, Cap Gemini, Conoco, Continental Airlines, Deloitte Touche Tomahtsu, Dynegy, ExxonMobil, HBK Investments, H.E.B. Grocery, IBM, Intecap, JP Morgan Chase, Lockheed Martin, Microsoft, Raytheon, SBC Communications, Shell, Southwest Airlines, Sprint, Tivoli, Tucker Alan, TXU, and VHA Inc. Two-thirds of Baylor grads remain in the Southwest Central region for work; about one in six find positions outside the country.

LAURIE WILSON, DIRECTOR, MBA ADMISSIONS
ONE BEAR PLACE #98013, 1311 SOUTH 5TH STREET, WACO, TX 76798-8013 UNITED STATES
PHONE: 254-710-3718 • FAX: 254-710-1066
E-MAIL: MBA_INFO@BAYLOR.EDU • WEBSITE: WWW.BAYLOR.EDU/MBA

## Location and Environment

Hankamer is located on Baylor's "huge, quite scenic campus [with] numerous resources, including an excellent gym/Student Life Center and a wide variety of intramurals." There's "a lot of construction going on here: new academic buildings, new dorms, garages, etc. It all makes you feel like you are a part of something really big and going forward." Much of that forward movement has already taken place at Hankamer, which occupies "one of the newest buildings on the Baylor campus." The facility "features wireless networking, seminar-style classrooms, a seventy-five-seat video-conferencing room, and the Graduate Center [to] maximize discussion and interaction between students and faculty." Students can use their laptops to hook into the wireless network anywhere on campus.

MBAs tell us that Baylor is "a great place to go to school. There are plenty of opportunities for social interaction with other students. Everyone is generally very friendly." The Graduate Business Association "does an excellent job of planning social and career events for students and faculty, [with] a doughnut hour every Wednesday, during which all the MBA students and faculty meet and talk, as well as mixer dinners and other activities several times per semester." A word of caution for those with families, though; "Life is geared towards the singles, with little emphasis for those who are married with children. Outside activities focus on sports, parties, and general fun. This works well for the majority of students who are single or just married." Also, extracurricular time at Baylor is limited by the demands of the curriculum. One student explains, "Life is very busy and fast paced due to five-week core courses. These courses are short and packed with action. You cannot afford to get behind even for a very short time."

Hometown Waco is in the proverbial heart of Texas. While it is within 150 miles of four major metropolitan areas (Dallas, Austin, San Antonio, and Houston), Waco itself "is a small town that does not have a good public transportation system, especially to and from Dallas. It would be good if the university could provide some transportation service between Baylor and Dallas."

## Admissions

Applicants to Baylor must provide the school GMAT (and TOEFL, when appropriate) scores, undergraduate transcripts, three essays (all examine aspects of whether the applicant is a good "fit" with Baylor's MBA program), letters of recommendation, and a current resume. An interview is optional. Evidence of leadership skills and community service is also considered. While applicants need not have majored in a business-related discipline as undergraduates, those who did not must complete the Integrated Management Seminar, "a unique one-semester seminar that satisfies all business prerequisites. It is offered for students without previous business training."

### FINANCIAL FACTS

| | |
|---|---|
| Annual tuition | $19,050 |
| Fees | $2,670 |
| Books and supplies | $8,000 |
| Room & board (on/off-campus) | $10,000/$10,000 |
| % of students receiving aid | 80 |
| % of first-year students receiving aid | 80 |
| Average grant | $17,425 |

### ADMISSIONS

| | |
|---|---|
| **Admissions Selectivity Rating** | **83** |
| # of applications received | 110 |
| % applicants accepted | 66 |
| % acceptees attending | 49 |
| Average GMAT | 605 |
| Range of GMAT | 540–640 |
| Average GPA | 3.38 |
| TOEFL required of international students? | yes |
| Minimum TOEFL (paper/computer) | 600/250 |
| Application fee | $50 |
| International application fee | $50 |
| Regular application deadline | 6/15 |
| Regular notification | rolling |
| Deferment available? | yes |
| Maximum length of deferment | 1 year |
| Transfer students accepted? | yes |
| Transfer application policy Students may transfer up to 6 credits from an AACSB-accredited institution. Students must submit a transcript that presents the student's active, satisfactory work toward the same degree. | |
| Non-fall admissions? | yes |
| Need-blind admissions? | yes |

### APPLICANTS ALSO LOOK AT
Babson College, Rice University, South Texas College of Law, Southern Methodist University, Texas Christian University (TCU), The University of Texas at Arlington, The University of Texas at Dallas

| EMPLOYMENT PROFILE | | | | |
|---|---|---|---|---|
| **Career Rating** | **74** | **Grads employed by field:** | **% avg.** | **salary:** |
| Average starting salary | $59,517 | Finance | 33 | $66,167 |
| | | Marketing | 5 | $42,000 |
| | | MIS | 6 | $40,000 |
| | | Operations | 6 | $42,000 |
| | | Consulting | 6 | $46,000 |
| | | General Management | 44 | $63,038 |

# BELMONT UNIVERSITY
## THE JACK C. MASSEY GRADUATE SCHOOL OF BUSINESS

## Academics

"Flexible scheduling combined with the real-world experiences of the students and professors really make Massey an excellent school for adults that work full-time," students at this Nashville business school tell us, tidily summarizing the key attractions of this predominantly part-time program. While Massey is home to a few full-timers, the MBA and MACC programs are designed to accommodate part-time students; all classes are held in long evening sessions.

Massey operates on an unusual five-term calendar. Both the fall and spring semesters are divided into one 10-week and one 5-week term; classes meet once a week during the 10-week term and twice a week during the 5-week term. A 10-week summer semester rounds out the school year. Both the short and long sessions pack a lot of information into a relatively short period. As a result, "the overall academic experience at Belmont is challenging, although not so challenging that it's intimidating." One student notes, "Class material is not watered-down in an attempt to make the MBA easy to obtain. The school expects a commitment and that is what it takes to complete the program." Easing the challenge is the fact that "Belmont offers a comfortable atmosphere where students are friendly with one another. Everyone wants to succeed, but I have never encountered the cutthroats that you hear about when MBA programs are mentioned."

Students especially appreciate that Massey's "practical curriculum places a strong emphasis on learning through practical applications, case studies, and teamwork." One student observes, "This approach mimics the real world quite well. I believe that because of this approach, I will be able to easily apply what I have learned. I am already seeing a change in my decision-making process at work." MBAs also tell us that "the school has a commitment not only to the development of business knowledge but also to the development of a business mentality and the nonacademic skills required for career success in our chosen field." Professors "prepare material beyond the textbook to increase students' overall experiences," which explains why students feel "the school's greatest strength is the faculty. Professors take pride in delivering their lectures so that students not only know but [also] understand the material being covered and can apply these business skills in their own careers." Students are especially sanguine about Massey's offerings in accountancy, entrepreneurship, and finance. The school also draws on its location in Music City to offer a number of electives focusing on the music biz.

## Career and Placement

Career Services at Belmont are provided by an office "solely dedicated to business students." Because most MBAs are part-time students with full-time jobs, this office naturally focuses most of its efforts on Belmont's undergraduates, causing one student to observe that "it would be nice to see a staff member who understands our needs help MBA students. Right now the undergraduate business and MBA programs share the same office and staff." The school reports that the office provides MBAs, MACCs, and alumni with "a wide range of resources to assist in conducting a job search or managing your current career. And this service is free and available to all Belmont MBAs—for life!" The school also claims a "powerful" alumni network that is over 1,000 strong. One student writes, "Out of all alumni, there are about 800 who work in the area. That is a large networking and recruiting base. The alumni are active participants in the school in testimonials at informationals and in recruiting students for employment."

TONYA HOLLIN, ADMISSIONS ASSISTANT
1900 BELMONT BOULEVARD, NASHVILLE, TN 37212 UNITED STATES
PHONE: 615-460-6480 • FAX: 615-460-6353
E-MAIL: MASSEYADMISSIONS@MAIL.BELMONT.EDU • WEBSITE: MASSEY.BELMONT.EDU

Top employers of Massey MBAs include Bridgestone/Firestone, Caterpillar Financial, Deloitte Touche Tohmatsu, Ernst & Young, and Hospital Corporation of America.

## Student Life and Environment

The MBA program at Belmont is populated by "students who primarily work full-time and go to classes at night. It's very difficult with that schedule and family responsibilities to get involved with social activities." Not that the school isn't trying; students report, "Currently, we are trying to involve students outside of classes. We are organizing community service activities and events after class. We have gotten good numbers at these events, so we will continue with more of them." Among these events are "various professional-development programs and lectures series. These, plus the personal attention you receive from professors and administrators, provide all students [with] the experience of a full-time MBA program."

The Massey program requires a good deal of teamwork; "most students try to work as efficiently and constructively as they can, especially in regard to group projects and presentations." One proud student comments that the "team-based environment tends to extend outside of the classroom. We are in a night program, but the friendships we have made definitely extend outside of the school walls. Our program is very time-consuming, but there is a strong sense of accomplishment amongst the students. The time definitely is worth it!" Off-campus opportunities are plentiful. One student explains, "Being in Nashville, an entertainment city, there is no shortage of things to do. It's not uncommon to go grab a drink or see a band after class. Everyone makes friends pretty fast."

## Admissions

Massey considers all of the following components of an application for both the MBA and MACC programs: undergraduate and (if applicable) graduate transcripts, GMAT scores, letters of recommendation, a personal statement, and a resume demonstrating a minimum of two years of post-baccalaureate professional experience. The school also looks for evidence of a student's "commitment to be involved and contribute to the learning experience of fellow students." Special programs to improve minority/disadvantaged recruitment include partnership programs with Fisk University and Meharry Medical College.

### FINANCIAL FACTS

| | |
|---|---|
| Annual tuition | $18,600 |
| Fees | $600 |
| Books and supplies | $750 |
| % of students receiving aid | 67 |
| % of first-year students receiving aid | 67 |
| % of students receiving loans | 54 |
| % of students receiving grants | 22 |
| Average award package | $15,173 |
| Average grant | $4,805 |

### ADMISSIONS

| | |
|---|---|
| Admissions Selectivity Rating | 71 |
| # of applications received | 55 |
| % applicants accepted | 80 |
| % acceptees attending | 77 |
| Average GMAT | 520 |
| Range of GMAT | 470–580 |
| Average GPA | 3.12 |
| TOEFL required of international students? | yes |
| Minimum TOEFL (paper/computer) | 550/213 |
| Application fee | $50 |
| International application fee | $50 |
| Regular application deadline | 7/1 |
| Regular notification | 7/1 |
| Deferment available? | yes |
| Maximum length of deferment | 1 year |
| Transfer students accepted? | yes |
| Transfer application policy | |

Application process is the same for all students. Students may transfer up to 6 credits from an AACSB-accredited institution.

| | |
|---|---|
| Non-fall admissions? | yes |
| Need-blind admissions? | yes |

### APPLICANTS ALSO LOOK AT
Middle Tennessee State University, University of Tennessee—Knoxville, Vanderbilt University

### EMPLOYMENT PROFILE

| Career Rating | 74 | Grads employed by field: | % | avg. salary: |
|---|---|---|---|---|
| Average starting salary | $52,500 | Accounting | 22 | NR |
| | | Finance | 11 | NR |
| | | Human Resources | 2 | NR |
| | | Marketing | 5 | NR |
| | | MIS | 2 | NR |
| | | Operations | 9 | NR |
| | | Consulting | 3 | NR |
| | | General Management | 5 | NR |
| | | Other | 17 | NR |

# BENTLEY COLLEGE
## THE ELKIN B. MCCALLUM GRADUATE SCHOOL OF BUSINESS

### GENERAL INFORMATION

| | |
|---|---|
| Type of school | private |
| Environment | city |
| Academic calendar | semester |

### SURVEY SAYS...

Cutting-edge classes
Smart classrooms
*Solid preparation in:*
Teamwork
Computer skills

### STUDENTS

| | |
|---|---|
| Enrollment of parent institution | 5,565 |
| Enrollment of business school | 591 |
| % male/female | 59/41 |
| % out-of-state | 8 |
| % part-time | 92 |
| % minorities | 4 |
| % international | 35 |
| Average age at entry | 29 |
| Average years work experience at entry | 2.8 |

### ACADEMICS

| | |
|---|---|
| **Academic Experience Rating** | **77** |
| Student/faculty ratio | 16:1 |
| Profs interesting rating | 79 |
| Profs accessible rating | 84 |
| % female faculty | 32 |
| % minority faculty | 13 |

### JOINT DEGREES

Dual degrees are available.

### PROMINENT ALUMNI

Joseph Antonellis, MBA 1982, CIO and Ex VP, State Street Corporation; Ullas Naik, MBA 1993, Managing Director, JAFCO Ventures; Thomas Venables, MBA 1985, Founder and CEO, Lighthousebank.com; Amy Hunter, MBA 1985, Exec. VP, Boston Private Bank and Trust; Anthony P. DiBona, MBA 1982, Exec. VP, PTC, Needham, MA

## Academics

"Bentley College's strengths are found in the integration of technology and business," business students tell us, confirming the school's reputation as one of the nation's most wired campuses. The school's state-of-the-art facilities, with "IT infrastructure second to none, [allow Bentley to pursue] work centered where business disciplines such as marketing, finance, and accounting intersect with technology." Coupled with the school's technology focus is its dedication to "constant reevaluation of curriculum [in order to adapt it to] our diverse business climate."

The curriculum, of course, lies at the heart of the Bentley experience, and students love it. "While all the bells and whistles that come with an MBA program are important (and Bentley has them all)," one student tells us, "the actual program itself is what we are all here for. More specifically, I am referring to the strong applicability of all of my classes to real-world issues and challenges, the breadth of business disciplines from which to choose, the strength of all of my fellow students, the highly engaging lectures, and the staggering level of IT infrastructure throughout our whole campus." While Bentley's reputation relies primarily on its finance programs, students tell us that other disciplines are equally strong, if not as widely celebrated. Students are particularly proud of the school's "tremendous Business Ethics Office and Center for Marketing Technology."

Students rave that Bentley professors "have real-world experience that they combine with cutting-edge curriculums to deliver a top-quality product." Most instructors "establish a very close relationship with the students, not only academically but personally, which helps in the development of the students throughout the program," another fact that students appreciate. One student writes, "I did my undergraduate degree at a large university, and the difference is striking. I find the faculty extremely supportive. I really get the feeling that they understand they must make larger investments in us to ensure our success, and they do it without hesitation. There are established lines of communication for the students to voice our opinions on class structure and curriculum, and the feedback/changes are immediate." Students say the administration "is also very involved in the graduate community and cares a lot about the students."

## Career and Placement

The Graduate Center for Career Services (GCCS) at Bentley recently introduced a new training program called the Career Management Series (CMS); this eight-module program is designed "to assist McCallum graduate students in developing skills that will allow them to compete more effectively in the marketplace." Modules are fine-tuned by degree program, meaning that students in marketing attend different sessions than do students in financial planning or accounting. GCCS' Career Development Workshop Series supplements the training, offering sessions on preparation for case consulting, interviewing, salary negotiation, creativity, and leadership.

Bentley hosts two career fairs, one each semester, and over the course of the school year approximately 250 recruiting opportunities are posted for graduate students. Students have access to a number of online resources, including MonsterTrak. Companies interviewing the greatest number of Bentley graduate students include Booz Allen; Deloitte Touche; EMC Corporation; FedEx; Fidelity; Gillette; IBM; Intel; Johnson & Johnson; KPMG; PricewaterhouseCoopers LLP; Raytheon; Staples, Inc.; State Street Corporation; Teradyne, Inc; and Verizon.

SHARON HILL, DIRECTOR OF GRADUATE ADMISSIONS
175 FOREST STREET, WALTHAM, MA 02452 UNITED STATES
PHONE: 781-891-2108 • FAX: 781-891-2464
E-MAIL: GRADADM@BENTLEY.EDU • WEBSITE: WWW.BENTLEY.EDU

## Student Life and Environment

Bentley students form a solid, supportive community that MBAs truly appreciate. "There are always people around working in teams, and there is a camaraderie that makes it easy to stop and talk," students tell us. One student writes, "We are all very interested in learning from each others' experiences, our current jobs, and even what we have recently read in publication. We work hard, and we help each other through open and honest feedback. We all agree to be here to learn about our strengths as well as our weaknesses, and these bitter pills are much better when administered by people who care about you." Students often meet for meals through the school's Lunch Connections and Dinner Connections series; each allows students to interact in a casual and convenient on-campus locale.

The student body's closeness is apparent in the "tons of student organizations and social activities" that Bentley students enjoy together. MBAs report, "The academic clubs are outstanding. They are student-run and continuously bring top-notch CEOs and senior management to campus for lectures, career panel sessions, etc. In addition, they plan such great events as trips to the New York Stock Exchange, investment trading contests, and alumni networking parties." Some groups are major-related (Graduate Finance Association, Graduate Marketing Organization, Graduate Information Systems Association), while others are professional groups (Society for the Advancement of Management, National Association of Black Accountants).

Students praise the "beautiful and peaceful campus" of Bentley and especially enjoy the facilities at the Dana Athletic Center. If you crave an urban environment, the "bustle of Boston" is only 10 miles east.

## Admissions

Bentley applicants must provide GMAT scores, an undergraduate transcript, two letters of recommendation, three essays (two required topics and a final essay answering one of three supplied questions), and a TOEFL score, when appropriate. Interviews are required for the daytime MBA only; they are recommended for all other programs. The admissions office reviews the entire application in an attempt to assess an applicant's academic potential, commitment to career, fit with the school and other admitted students, and the quality of prior work experience (a minimum of two years' work experience is strongly recommended).

### FINANCIAL FACTS

| | |
|---|---|
| Annual tuition | $21,864 |
| Fees | $204 |
| Books and supplies | $1,050 |
| Room & board (on/off-campus) | $11,940/$11,940 |
| % of students receiving aid | 35 |
| % of first-year students receiving aid | 52 |
| % of students receiving loans | 26 |
| % of students receiving grants | 15 |
| Average award package | $16,686 |
| Average grant | $11,846 |
| Average student loan debt | $32,307 |

### ADMISSIONS

| | |
|---|---|
| Admissions Selectivity Rating | 74 |
| # of applications received | 374 |
| % applicants accepted | 73 |
| % acceptees attending | 55 |
| Average GMAT | 544 |
| Range of GMAT | 490–590 |
| Average GPA | 3.52 |
| TOEFL required of international students? | yes |
| Minimum TOEFL (paper/computer) | 600/250 |
| Application fee | $50 |
| International application fee | $50 |
| Regular application deadline | 6/1 |
| Regular notification | rolling |
| Early decision program? | yes |
| ED Deadline/notification | 12/1, 1/15 |
| Deferment available? | yes |
| Maximum length of deferment | 1 year |
| Non-fall admissions? | yes |
| Need-blind admissions? | yes |

### APPLICANTS ALSO LOOK AT

Babson College, Boston College, Boston University, Northeastern University

### EMPLOYMENT PROFILE

| Career Rating | 94 | Grads employed by field: | % avg. salary: |
|---|---|---|---|
| Primary source of full-time job acceptances | | Accounting | 4 $52,500 |
| | | Finance | 4 $57,500 |
| School-facilitated activities | 3 (12%) | MIS | 11 $67,500 |
| Graduate-facilitated activities | 3 (11%) | Other | 81 $74,944 |
| Unknown | 20 (77%) | | |
| | | | |
| Average starting salary | $70,500 | | |
| Percent employed | 100 | | |

# Boston College
## Carroll School of Management

## Academics

For a first-year MBA student at the Carroll School, starting out "is one of the toughest experiences I have ever had, and it was just what I wanted out of a program. Long hours and challenging courses translated into a terrific learning experience." As one student says, "I've learned more in seven weeks than I did in four years of college."

Boston College strives for a "unique partnership between students and faculty with an innovative curriculum." In the first year of full-time enrollment, students take almost all core courses designed to enhance technical skills. But they also participate in the MBA Business Plan Competition, in which teams of first-years compete for the best plan for a new business venture. In the second year, however, there are only four required courses (Parts III and IV of management practice, "Strategic Management and Management Information Systems, and Social Issues in Management and Global Competitiveness"). The rest are electives chosen with specialization and career paths in mind.

The finance department is proudly touted as a great strength of the program, and most students agree, "Finance professors are some of the best in the country." The pride is justified, but that can sometimes come at a cost to other departments, especially when it comes to electives, which "could be more diverse." "The majority of them are focused around finance," complains one student, and many feel that "the excellence of the finance and accounting programs should be mirrored in the others."

Though the administration of late has been "somewhat in transition," they offer an executive lecture series "that includes such industry leaders as the president of Dell, CTO of Microsoft, and many other senior executives." Still, most students agree that the administration could stand to work on its communication with students.

## Career and Recruiting

The alumni network is acknowledged by most students as one of Carroll's greatest strengths. Because of the deep commitment to community-building while on campus, alumni often leave Boston College fiercely loyal to the school and especially the MBA program. The MBA student government sponsors tailgates for home football games, and it's not uncommon to see "alumni, faculty, and students alike mingle before and after the game." These are people who know the value of keeping in touch. "I'm working as well my second year, and my coworkers still are talking to my IT professor, networking," one student says.

If this loyalty has a downside, it's that career services might rely too heavily on it. Many students think that the Career Services Department could "always improve, especially in current times." Many complain that job opportunities are too often limited to the Northeast, where many alumni end up. "Boston College is too focused on the Northeast region and financial positions and sometimes neglects other opportunities for students."

Still, job placement is high. Students get ample opportunity to work with alumni, and a program during the first year has all first-year full-time MBAs consulting directly with a company through the MBA Consulting Project. Representatives from companies like Dell, GE, and Southwest Airlines have all been a presence on campus. Overall, most students agree that they've "never been so certain that [their] experience, academic and otherwise, would be relevant to [their] future success."

SHELLEY CONLEY, DIRECTOR OF GRADUATE MANAGEMENT ENROLLMENT
FULTON HALL 315, CHESTNUT HILL, MA 02467 UNITED STATES
PHONE: 617-552-3920 • FAX: 617-552-8078
E-MAIL: BCMBA@BC.EDU • WEBSITE: WWW.BC.EDU/MBA/

## Student Life and Environment

In order to survive in a small, rigorous environment, MBA students at Boston College tend to bond quickly. Rather than foster cutthroat competition, Carroll students have learned to pull together. All 100 students are "genuinely interested in learning and making sure that [their] peers are learning." People "emphasize the importance of working with each other and getting to know everybody." One student says, "In only a year and half, we've formed friendships that will last for our entire lives. We've seen our peers through weddings, the births of children, and the deaths and sicknesses of parents. It's rare to find a MBA program with a culture that supports a balance between competition/ambition and compassion."

With a campus just a T ride away from Boston center, the cultural life exceeds that of many institutions. City living is, as always, a plus for most of the MBA students at BC. "The other day," one student explains, "I sat and listened to a jazz band play the opening of an African American art exhibit. It was great. The night after, I met with almost my entire program at a local bar." For students of the Carroll School, social life is very much a part of academic life. With the newly revamped Fulton Hall serving as the social and academic center of the program, students have newer and better facilities in which to study and socialize, and they marvel at the "truly well-rounded nature of the community: extending from an incredible alumni network to vibrant art offerings to intense academic demands." Still, the tailgating parties, the winter social, spring formal, and "Thirsty Thursdays" (a weekly pub crawl) rate high on everyone's to-do list. "The emphasis is on excelling in all pursuits, none to the exclusion of the other (whether that means cutting loose at an Irish pub or contributing deep preparation to a class discussion or helping local kids do their biology homework)." Students "know how to balance the academic rigors with the right amount of social activity, whether that be going to the pub, intramurals, or other social events. The work gets done, but not at the expense of personal needs."

## Admissions

At Boston College, "the depth and breadth of academic, cultural, and professional experiences" are all considered when admitting new MBA students. The average GMAT score of an admitted MBA student was 643, and the average GPA was 3.3. Many incoming students had worked between three and five years before applying for the MBA, and the average class boasts a wide variety of undergraduate majors: humanities and social sciences are refreshingly well-represented. TOEFL scores are required of those students for whom English is not their first language, and the minimum score required for admission is 600 or an equivalent computer-based score of 250. Scholarships are awarded on the basis of academic merit.

### FINANCIAL FACTS

| | |
|---|---|
| Annual tuition | $31,620 |
| Fees | $150 |
| Books and supplies | $1,500 |
| Room & board | |
| (on/off-campus) | $19,620/$19,620 |
| % of students receiving aid | 75 |
| % of first-year students | |
| receiving aid | 34 |
| % of students receiving loans | 26 |
| % of students receiving grants | 58 |
| Average award package | $18,657 |
| Average grant | $17,191 |
| Average student loan debt | $28,355 |

### ADMISSIONS

| | |
|---|---|
| Admissions Selectivity Rating | 90 |
| # of applications received | 524 |
| % applicants accepted | 42 |
| % acceptees attending | 38 |
| Average GMAT | 643 |
| Range of GMAT | 593–690 |
| Average GPA | 3.3 |
| TOEFL required of | |
| international students? | yes |
| Minimum TOEFL | |
| (paper/computer) | 600/250 |
| Application fee | $100 |
| International application fee | $100 |
| Regular application deadline | 3/15 |
| Regular notification | 5/1 |
| Application deadline/notification | |
| Round 1: | 11/15 / 1/15 |
| Round 2: | 2/15 / 4/15 |
| Round 3: | 3/15 / 5/1 |
| Transfer students accepted? | yes |
| Transfer application policy | |
| Students may transfer up to 12 credits from an AACSB-accredited institution. | |
| Need-blind admissions? | yes |

### APPLICANTS ALSO LOOK AT

Babson College, Boston University, Georgetown University, Harvard University, Massachusetts Institute of Technology, New York University, Northeastern University

| EMPLOYMENT PROFILE | | | | |
|---|---|---|---|---|
| Career Rating | 89 | Grads employed by field: | % | avg. salary: |
| Primary source of full-time | | Finance | 31 | $82,579 |
| job acceptances | | Human Resources | 1 | NR |
| School-facilitated activities | 38 (54%) | Marketing | 29 | $72,333 |
| Graduate-facilitated activities | 33 (46%) | MIS | 1 | NR |
| | | Operations | 7 | $75,625 |
| Average starting salary | $79,139 | Consulting | 6 | $83,000 |
| Percent employed | 92 | General Management | 9 | $79,575 |
| | | Other | 10 | NR |
| | | nonprofit | 3 | $75,333 |

# BOSTON UNIVERSITY
## SCHOOL OF MANAGEMENT

## Academics

At Boston University School of Management, most students agree that the greatest strength is the faculty. Said to be "very accessible," professors often "go out to local bars with students." While research is a responsibility of all faculty members, "their focus is on teaching. Bad professors don't stay long." Teachers "pay due deference to the theoretical but place a strong emphasis on practical application of the knowledge they impart." The first year consists of mainly core courses, usually taught by department chairs who are "recognizable and well-respected leaders in their fields." The advantage of a pre-determined course schedule is that BU's administration can coordinate assignments and course materials in all of the classes. This means learning exactly "what you need to know from one class just in time to do the project in another class. It also results in a very choreographed, jam-packed schedule of projects." In addition to a strong core schedule, Boston University offers over 100 elective courses designed to focus studies on a specific kind of management or business. But occupying pride of place in Boston University's school of management is the joint MS/MBA program. It's the only program of its kind currently being offered in the world. The program, which can be completed in just 21 months, offers advanced degrees in both business management and information systems. According to BU's website, the program is designed to respond "to the digital revolution's impact on organizations, fusing a traditional management curriculum with expertise about the IT systems that have fundamentally changed business strategies and operations." And, according to one student, "Although the MS/MBA program has a technology focus, the learnings definitely have larger management and business strategy implications." Despite the strengths of the MS/MBA program, or *because* of them, some students feel that "the administration's focus on the MS/MBA program also seems to turn some students off. Other full-time MBAs feel left out of this 'signature' degree."

Each class of about 60, which the students call "cohorts," is divided into teams of five. Teams are carefully chosen and are meant to represent the same kind of diversity a student could expect to find in the workplace. Working with a mix of genders, cultures, experience, and age, the teams foster the development of communication and diplomacy. And it's a good thing: Each year teams prepare a case for a student-sponsored competition. Teams present their case analysis to a panel of judges made up of faculty members and professionals from the corporate world. One student says, "I usually hate working in a team. But I have learned a lot about how to work in one and efficiently complete projects." The only drawback of the team system, for some students, is that "the student population tends to be fragmented among cohort lines. Students within the same cohort are very likely to keep in contact after graduation. However, I cannot say for certain that intercohort relationships have the same level of depth." Others complain that "strict adherence to the cohort system reduces schedule flexibility and seems of little educational value. The same goals may be achieved, in my view, through group projects." Another much-lauded program is the Public and Nonprofit Management Program. Designed for students who hope to use business management skills to address humanitarian and governmental concerns, the program is "an incredible strength" of the school.

## Career and Placement

Although many students would like to see more businesses pursuing their employment —after all, "who can ever have enough companies coming to their school?"—recruiters from Akamai, Deloitte Touche Tohmatsu, Ernst & Young, Johnson & Johnson, JPMorgan Chase, and a number of other major companies all have a strong presence on campus. Despite some complaints that the career center is "still weak," 92 percent of the

Hayden Estrada, Assistant Dean for Graduate Admissions
595 Commonwealth Avenue, Boston, MA 02215 United States
Phone: 617-353-2670 • Fax: 617-353-7368
E-mail: mba@bu.edu • Website: www.management.bu.edu

graduate class of 2005 was employed within three months of their graduation. And with a significantly increased career-center staff, BU is "gradually beginning to attract companies that in the past only looked in Cambridge."

The public and nonprofit management program has its own director and a "strong alumni database." This is "very helpful in setting up internships and informational interviews." One of the major events sponsored by the public/nonprofit program, Link Day, in which students meet for one day with nonprofits, academics, and local professionals to analyze a specific problem facing a nonprofit organization, also offers valuable networking opportunities.

## Student Life and Environment

Located just around the corner from Fenway Park, Boston University's School of Management combines a "big-city feel" with many of the comforts of a small community. "Extremely convenient to public transportation and the city," the school offers countless cultural and social opportunities, and "a great Boston Harbor cruise and a fun spring gala every year. Social life is as diverse as the city." Other social events featured include an MBA soccer tournament and regular beers with professors. According to one student, "BU's second-greatest strength is the tight-knit community it develops. This leads to a strong alumni network, which is key to achieving career success." The downside of the big-city feel, for most students, is cost. Since housing in Boston (as in most urban areas) is dear, many would like to see more options for graduate student housing.

With about 30 percent of the class consisting of international students, many MBAs-to-be celebrate the diversity of the student population. "In every class we get such a broad perspective, and there are always students familiar with what (or which country) we are discussing." The Rafik B. Hariri Building for BU's School of Management is "beautiful and very high-tech—maybe the best business school campus in the country." With dataports from every seat, five computer labs, a lecture hall that seats 375, an in-house management library, and its own Starbucks, the Management School's building is "technologically at the forefront of the industry."

## Admissions

Often enrolling about 150 students a year, Boston University looks for students who can demonstrate "both academic and professional success." In 2005, about 80 percent of the GMAT scores fell between 620 and 720. The average undergraduate GPA was 3.29. Many incoming students had about five years of full-time, post-graduate work experience before they applied for the MBA. TOEFL scores are required of those students for whom English is not the first language, and the minimum required score is 250.

| EMPLOYMENT PROFILE | | | | |
|---|---|---|---|---|
| **Career Rating** | **87** | **Grads employed by field:** | **% avg. salary:** | |
| Average starting salary | $81,496 | Finance | 6 | $87,000 |
| Percent employed | 92 | Human Resources | 1 | $80,000 |
| | | Marketing | 12 | $81,017 |
| | | Consulting | 3 | $86,000 |
| | | General Management | 2 | $91,500 |
| | | Other | 3 | $76,667 |

### PROMINENT ALUMNI
Christine Poon, Chair, Pharmacy Group, Johnson & Johnson; Millard S. (Mickey) Drexler, Chair and CEO, J. Crew Group, Inc.; Edward J. Zander, Chair & CEO, Motorola; Thomas Jones, President /CEO of Citigroup, Global Investment; Dr. Suzanne Cutler, Executive VP/New York Federal.

### FINANCIAL FACTS
| | |
|---|---|
| Annual tuition | $30,530 |
| Fees | $386 |
| Books and supplies | $1,380 |
| Room & board | $10,782 |
| % of students receiving aid | 95 |
| Average award package | $24,508 |
| Average grant | $16,538 |

### ADMISSIONS
| | |
|---|---|
| **Admissions Selectivity Rating** | **92** |
| # of applications received | 811 |
| % applicants accepted | 45 |
| % acceptees attending | 39 |
| Average GMAT | 655 |
| Range of GMAT | 600–720 |
| Average GPA | 3.29 |
| TOEFL required of international students? | yes |
| Minimum TOEFL (paper/computer) | 600/250 |
| Application fee | $125 |
| Regular application deadline | 3/15 |
| Regular notification | 5/1 |
| Application deadline/notification | |
| Round 1: | 11/15 / 1/1 |
| Round 2: | 1/15 / 3/1 |
| Round 3: | 3/15 / 5/1 |
| Deferment available? | yes |
| Maximum length of deferment | 1 year |
| Transfer students accepted? | yes |
| Transfer application policy | |
| Students may transfer credits from an AACSB-accredited institution. | |
| Need-blind admissions? | yes |

### APPLICANTS ALSO LOOK AT
Babson College, Boston College, Case Western Reserve University, Duke University, Georgetown University, New York University

# BOWLING GREEN STATE UNIVERSITY
## COLLEGE OF BUSINESS ADMINISTRATION

## Academics

For students wishing to fast-track their business careers, the MBA program at the College of Business Administration at Bowling Green State University provides an excellent opportunity. BGSU's general MBA program can be completed in 14 months, even by students without an undergraduate degree in business; a specialization (currently available in accounting, finance, or management information systems) can be added with only an additional semester's work.

"Academics are intensive, as expected of an MBA program," students tell us. One student explains, "When I started BGSU, I thought it would be a piece of cake for me. But I soon realized that the professors were serious about their work and expectations and settled for nothing but the best. To my dismay, all the fun and frolic I thought I would experience went down the drain. I have to spend many, many hours studying and preparing for classes and tests." Despite the rigors of the curriculum, most students find the program manageable, including those with no previous business education. One such MBA student explains, "Having no business background, I found that professors' accessibility outside the classroom and readiness to assist in learning were of great importance to my success in BGSU MBA program."

BGSU professors are a mixed bag. One student notes, "Some are outstanding, while some are just okay. Few are terrible. Most are willing to help outside the classroom and encourage questions. The program is pretty well laid out for students." The curriculum puts a heavy emphasis on group projects and teamwork, creating an *esprit de corps* that permeates not only the student body but also the faculty and administration. One student writes, "Everyone here works together as a team! The professors, administrative staff, and students all want us to see our goal of graduating with MBAs."

The College of Business' full-time program features "a leadership assessment and development component consisting of a series of workshops. The workshops lead students through an ongoing process of reflection and self-discovery so that each obtains a better understanding of his or herself in relation to a desired management career." Students find the workshops helpful in their career development. They also appreciate "Professional Development Sessions on Fridays, where [they] meet with industry leaders and interact with them in a professional and mentorship atmosphere."

## Career and Placement

To assist BGSU students in their job searches, the College of Business offers "a series of co-curricular professional-development seminars, covering topics such as oral presentation and report writing, team facilitation, effective negotiations, career planning, and organizational politics." Career services are provided through the university's Career Center, which serves all undergraduates and graduates. The school's remote location and small student body dissuade many large companies from recruiting on campus, students tell us.

Top employers of BGSU MBAs in recent years include American Express, American Greetings, Ernst & Young, Marathon Ashland, National City Corporation, Nationwide Insurance, Owens Corning, Plante & Moran, Progressive Insurance, and State Farm Insurance. The school reports that over half its graduates find their first job outside the United States.

CARMEN CASTRO-RIVERA, DIRECTOR, GRADUATE STUDIES IN BUSINESS
369 BUSINESS ADMINISTRATION BUILDING, BOWLING GREEN, OH 43403 UNITED STATES
PHONE: 419-372-2488 • FAX: 419-372-2875
E-MAIL: MBA-INFO@CBA.BGSU.EDU • WEBSITE: WWW.BGSUMBA.COM

## Student Life and Environment

Students at BGSU tell us that "the graduate students' cohort is very internationally diverse, which gives the opportunity to enjoy different cultures and languages." This assertion is borne out by the statistics. About one-third of the MBAs are international students; they represent 16 countries. The school also notes that "across all programs, students range in age from 22 to 52, with an average of 29. The average work experience of full-time, part-time, and executive students is 3, 6, and 10 years, respectively, but work experience is not required of full-time or part-time students."

On a campus of roughly 20,000 students, the College of Business facility is home to "a smaller community of professors, business students, and equipment where it is extremely easy to locate resources. Classrooms and a computer lab are located on the main floor, and professors and more computer labs are located upstairs. At BGSU, time is not wasted locating resources." MBAs also appreciate how "BGSU provides numerous locations for dining, studying, relaxing, and socially interacting with other students. The Bowen-Thompson Student Union is a one-stop central place to do these things." They also tell us that "there are lots of extracurricular activities and opportunities available at the school," including plenty of clubs and organizations. The Business Club, for one, "has social activities ranging from guest speakers to having beers at the local bar. Sometimes we even invite our professors." Others are dedicated to the various international communities within the student body.

While no one would mistake Bowling Green for a megalopolis, students find the town charming. It's "a quiet town with not many distractions, so it's a good environment to study. The university is the city for the most part." Students extol the "low prices, very cheap places to live off campus, [and the fact that] more than anything, it's safe." BGSU's location provides "easy access to Chicago, Cleveland, Detroit, [and] Toledo, a large city, is only 15 to 20 [minutes] away." The chief drawback? "The weather may be a bit harsh during winter. If you don't mind the cold, it's a nice place to be."

## Admissions

The College of Business Administration notes on its website that "some schools require business experience for admission. BGSU does not. The full-time program is designed for students who will be new to their chosen fields." Prior work experience is a factor in the assignment of assistantships, however. Applicants must submit an official transcript from each college or university attended, GMAT scores, a current resume, two letters of recommendation, and a personal statement; interviews are optional and can be conducted in person or by telephone. International students must also provide the school with TOEFL scores if their native language is not English. BGSU undertakes Project Search to aid underrepresented and disadvantaged students; the program "recruits students for university graduate programs (primarily full-time) and then coordinates an array of services designed to lead these students from enrollment through graduation."

## FINANCIAL FACTS

| | |
|---|---|
| Annual tuition (in-state/out-of-state) | $10,808/$18,116 |
| Fees (in-state/out-of-state) | $1,256/$8,554 |
| Books and supplies | $1,000 |
| Room & board | $5,800 |
| % of students receiving aid | 100 |
| % of first-year students receiving aid | 100 |
| % of students receiving loans | 35 |
| % of students receiving grants | 100 |
| Average award package | $16,880 |
| Average grant | $13,015 |
| Average student loan debt | $16,310 |

## ADMISSIONS

| | |
|---|---|
| Admissions Selectivity Rating | 77 |
| # of applications received | 110 |
| % applicants accepted | 61 |
| % acceptees attending | 84 |
| Average GMAT | 524 |
| Range of GMAT | 400–650 |
| Average GPA | 3.22 |
| TOEFL required of international students? | yes |
| Minimum TOEFL (paper/computer) | 550/213 |
| Application fee | $30 |
| International application fee | $30 |
| Regular application deadline | rolling |
| Regular notification | rolling |
| Deferment available? | yes |
| Maximum length of deferment | 1 year |
| Transfer students accepted? | yes |
| Transfer application policy | Students may transfer 6 credits from an AACSB-accredited institution. Transfer credit may be applied to the foundation, core courses, and electives. See website for further details. |
| Non-fall admissions? | yes |
| Need-blind admissions? | yes |

# BRIGHAM YOUNG UNIVERSITY
## MARRIOTT SCHOOL OF MANAGEMENT

## GENERAL INFORMATION

| | |
|---|---|
| Type of school | private |
| Affiliation | Church of Jesus Christ |
| | of Latter-day Saints |
| Environment | city |
| Academic calendar | semester |

### SURVEY SAYS...
Friendly students
Good peer network
Happy students
*Solid preparation in:*
Accounting
Teamwork

### STUDENTS

| | |
|---|---|
| Enrollment of parent institution | 34,067 |
| Enrollment of business school | 247 |
| % male/female | 83/17 |
| % out-of-state | 50 |
| % minorities | 8 |
| % international | 11 |
| Average age at entry | 28 |
| Average years work experience at entry | 3.1 |

### ACADEMICS

| | |
|---|---|
| **Academic Experience Rating** | **94** |
| Student/faculty ratio | 8:1 |
| Profs interesting rating | 97 |
| Profs accessible rating | 82 |
| % female faculty | 15 |
| % minority faculty | 1 |

### JOINT DEGREES
MBA/JD, 4 years; MBA/MS, IPD Program with Engineering Dept., 3 years; MACC/JD, 4 years; MPA/JD, 4 years.

### PROMINENT ALUMNI
Kevin Rollins, President & CEO, Dell Computer Corp.; D. Fraser Bullock, Founder/Managing Director, Sorenson Capital; Robert Parsons, Executive VP, Exclusive Resorts; David W. Checketts, Chair, Sports Capital Partners; Bill P. Benac Sr., Chair, Crescent Equity, Inc.

## Academics

The MBA program at Brigham Young's Marriott School of Management "provides a success-oriented environment that also promotes students' finding an elusive work-life balance," report students at this full-time-only Utah institution. At Marriott, "the course work is intense but manageable, and professors are almost always available for private consultations with students who are experiencing difficulties or who simply want to discuss applications of concepts that go beyond the scope of the course."

Students love the finance and accounting tracks at Marriott, reporting that "many big companies come to recruit good accounting students." Organizational behavior/human resources is also "a well-developed track." Marriott is home to three career training centers: the Rollins Center for eBusiness, the Center for Entrepreneurship, and the Center for International Business Education and Research (CIBER), which offers an International Management Certificate. The school has also recently added the H. Taylor Peery Institute of Financial Services to enhance its already solid finance program.

Across the curriculum, students praise their "extremely impressive professors, nearly all of whom come from a top-five school." Professors here "push you to your edge, but are very willing to lend a hand when you're slipping." While "most of them have extensive real-world and consulting experience, not all professors are recognized experts in their academic fields. This is primarily a teaching university." For the most part, students are glad to receive "a practical education that might not be possible from a pure 'academic' professor," but some wonder whether "the school could benefit from recruiting and retaining more top-talent professors."

With a first year that requires the completion of 33 credits, students quickly learn "how to prioritize," a skill they acquire "by being overwhelmed with work." The second year is not quite as rigorous, as students are given much more freedom to pursue electives and fields of specialization (here termed "tracks"). Students appreciate the "academic rigor balanced by charity for the individual" as well as the "religious and ethical emphasis" of the curriculum. They also boast that "tuition is amazingly low." (Note that rates are slightly higher for non-LDS members.)

## Career and Placement

Career services at Marriott are provided by the Steven and Georgia White Business Career Center, which are described in school brochures as "the focal point for the school's placement, internship, and field study efforts." Facilities include a reference library, interview rooms, a large presentation room, and an eRecruiting system. School materials identify nearly 100 companies that recruit at the Marriott School.

Employers most likely to hire Marriott MBAs include American Express, Cigna, Daimler Chrysler, Dell, DOW Chemical, Ernst & Young, Ford Motor Company, Gap, Inc., General Electric, General Mills, Hewlett-Packard, Hollywood Entertainment, Honeywell, IBM, Intel, Nutraceutical, Payless Shoes, Partners Group, Procter & Gamble, Union Pacific, U.S. Department of Agriculture, and Yellow Freight.

## Student Life and Environment

The typical Marriott MBA student "is married, has at least one child, and has three years of work experience. He or she is very smart, competitive, socially active, team-oriented, and religious." (BYU is affiliated with the Church of Jesus Christ of Latter-day Saints, as are, in one student's estimate, 80 percent of students here.) They are also typically "a bit older than usual business school students, and they serve in the community more." It is

CAROL THORNTON, MBA ADMISSIONS COORDINATOR
635 TB, PROVO, UT 84602 UNITED STATES
PHONE: 801-422-3500 • FAX: 801-422-0513
E-MAIL: MBA@BYU.EDU • WEBSITE: HTTP://MARRIOTTSCHOOL.BYU.EDU/MBA

important to note that "the ethical standards at BYU are extremely high." Religious life imposes many restrictions that students outside the faith may find surprising. Indeed, "students have many lifestyle limitations." These include abstaining from consumption of alcohol and coffee.

For those comfortable in "such an undiverse place," students agree that "there is no better program in the world for students with families. The MBA spouses' association is the most active group on campus and provides unparalleled support" for family members of MBA students. In their leisure time, students enjoy "plenty of activities, many of them multicultural, including Asian, Polynesian, Latino-American festivals." There are also lots of opportunities for outdoor activities. Students boast of the school's proximity to "the Wasatch Front," a natural retreat that "offers an excellent opportunity to enjoy life outside the classroom." Students remind us, however, that "you won't see much of the 'beers on Friday after class' happening" here.

The Marriott MBA program is housed in the Tanner Building, "a great place to eat, socialize, get to know each other, and bond—but not a great place to do work. The study rooms ought to be quiet, well-lit, have an Internet jack (the wireless fails sometimes), and a power outlet. Power outlets come at a premium if you want one, so it's best to bring your own power strip to share." Students would like to see these problems remedied by the addition of new study areas.

## Admissions

A completed application to the Marriott MBA program includes an application form, personal essays, an official GMAT score report, official transcripts for all post-secondary academic work, three letters of recommendation (one academic, two professional), an honor code commitment form, and a personal statement of intent. An interview is required; the school contacts applicants who have cleared initial screening to set up an interview appointment. International students must submit all of the above and must also provide financial disclosure forms and, if appropriate, TOEFL scores. A minimum of two years of full-time, post-undergraduate professional experience is required, but management experience is strongly preferred. Personal attributes are also considered; the school "values applicants who exemplify a sense of directedness and a commitment to the principles of the restored gospel of Jesus Christ," according to the school's brochure.

### FINANCIAL FACTS

| | |
|---|---|
| Annual tuition | $7,450 |
| Fees | $60 |
| Books and supplies | $1,600 |
| Room & board (on/off-campus) | $7,280/$7,280 |
| % of students receiving aid | 76 |
| % of first-year students receiving aid | 82 |
| % of students receiving loans | 28 |
| % of students receiving grants | 68 |
| Average award package | $7,123 |
| Average grant | $5,242 |
| Average student loan debt | $19,317 |

### ADMISSIONS

| | |
|---|---|
| Admissions Selectivity Rating | 93 |
| # of applications received | 353 |
| % applicants accepted | 51 |
| % acceptees attending | 66 |
| Average GMAT | 660 |
| Range of GMAT | 630–690 |
| Average GPA | 3.51 |
| TOEFL required of international students? | yes |
| Minimum TOEFL (paper/computer) | 590/240 |
| Application fee | $50 |
| International application fee | $50 |
| Regular application deadline | 3/1 |
| Regular notification | rolling |
| Application deadline/notification | |
| Round 1: | 1/15 / 2/28 |
| Round 2: | 3/1 / 4/30 |
| Early decision program? | yes |
| ED deadline/notification | 1/15 / 2/28 |
| Deferment available? | yes |
| Maximum length of deferment | 2 years |
| Transfer students accepted? | yes |
| Transfer application policy | |
| Students may transfer 15 credits of approved graduate-level courses, no pass/fail grades, and a minimum grade of B. | |
| Need-blind admissions? | yes |

### APPLICANTS ALSO LOOK AT

Arizona State University, Harvard University, Stanford University, University of Utah, Utah State University, Weber State University

### EMPLOYMENT PROFILE

| | | Grads employed by field: | % | avg. salary: |
|---|---|---|---|---|
| Career Rating | 93 | Finance | 35 | $78,250 |
| Primary source of full-time job acceptances | | Human Resources | 11 | $72,364 |
| | | Marketing | 11 | $73,355 |
| School-facilitated activities | 77 (80%) | MIS | 1 | NR |
| Graduate-facilitated activities | 19 (20%) | Operations | 13 | $68,285 |
| | | Consulting | 3 | $73,333 |
| Average starting salary | $75,451 | General Management | 9 | $76,611 |
| Percent employed | 92 | Other | 1 | NR |

# BROCK UNIVERSITY
## FACULTY OF BUSINESS

## Academics

Ontario's Brock University is a newcomer to the MBA world; 2003–2004 marked the first academic year that the school accommodated more than a handful of business school students. Today the program is up and running, already enjoying "a good reputation for business and accounting" among students and area businesses. As one student puts it, "Overall, considering the fact that the MBA program is new, the administration has done a great job. They have accomplished AACSB accreditation within a few short years and are making excellent hiring decisions for professors."

Brock's chief asset, students tell us, is its small classes, which "help encourage a lot of discussion with teachers and students. The teachers here are eager to hear your insight on situations while still educating you on how to take your thinking to the next level." Students also love the "great facilities that provide easy wireless Internet access" and the "many computers on campus," and they appreciate the "great opportunities to become involved with the school. This school provides anyone interested in becoming an active and contributing member of university society the chance to get involved." Prospective students should note that the workload here can be quite heavy, as one student explains: "As I've always heard about MBA programs anywhere, it's not rocket science, but the volume [of work] may kill you!"

The Brock MBA includes a sequence of required courses and an option for specialization in one of four "streams": accounting, finance, human resource management, and marketing. Students may also opt for a general MBA. Students may choose to replace up to three of their specialization courses with independent research projects; such projects are subject to the approval of the dean and the MBA Committee.

## Career and Placement

The Faculty of Business at Brock University maintains a Business Center Development Office to serve all undergraduates and graduates enrolled at the faculty. The office manages the Graduate Recruitment Program for MBA students; through this program, students have access to employer information sessions and on-campus interviews. A Career Expo in the fall brings employers to campus for recruiting purposes. The office also offers resume review, interviewing and job search workshops, online job search tools, and assistance with international job placement. While Brock's website claims that the school boasts "the highest employment rate of any university in Ontario," students counter that "there are not a lot of companies recruiting from our program due to lack of knowledge about it." But students expect that career and placement issues will sort themselves out as the school sends more MBAs into the business world to "help other Brock students as they enter their careers."

## Student Life and Environment

Brock University is located in St. Catharines, a mere 12 miles from Niagara Falls and just 70 miles from Toronto. Students call the location "a great strength," pointing out that St. Catharines is "a great city that is near Toronto and the States. It is very safe and the rent is super cheap. There are tons of bars to party at and everyone in St. Catharines just wants to have a good time. That can really make a difference when you are stressed out from working too much and you need a break." "Great weather" and "a nice campus" that is "not too big so that it is comfortable for newcomers" complete the picture. Students accustomed to more cosmopolitan locales claim, however, that St. Catharines is "a small town with not a lot to offer in terms of extracurriculars."

SHARI LEITCH, DIRECTOR OF GRADUATE PROGRAMS, FACULTY OF BUSINESS
BROCK UNIVERSITY, 500 GLENRIDGE AVENUE, ST. CATHARINES, ON L2S 3A1 CANADA
PHONE: 905-688-5550 • FAX: 905-688-4286
WEBSITE: WWW.BUS.BROCKU.CA

Most of Brock's MBAs are younger full-time students with little professional experience. They "are interested in school but also enjoy hanging out together. There are lots of great people to get to know and you become close friends." As one student observes, "Due to the fact that this program has relatively younger students, participation in activities is very high. The students have to participate because if we don't do it, there is not a large student body behind us to carry us." Brock does its part to facilitate extracurricular life: "The school provides opportunities to get involved with athletics and clubs," notes one MBA. One such exciting opportunity is the Corporate Social Responsibility Center, which "will match students to projects in the nonprofit sector. This will help students with connecting to opportunities off campus."

## Admissions

Admission to the MBA program at Brock is based on five main criteria. The quality of one's undergraduate education is most important; Brock seeks students with at least a 3.0 undergraduate GPA. A minimum GMAT score of 550 is required, as are three letters of recommendation from professors and/or supervisors at work; a personal statement; and, as the Brock website states, a "resume detailing the applicant's education and career to date as well as a statement outlining career and learning objectives indicating how the MBA at Brock will help fulfill those objectives." Applications are assessed holistically; strength in one area may be sufficient to compensate for weaknesses elsewhere, according to the school's website. Professional experience, though preferred, is not required. Those whose first language is not English must demonstrate English proficiency through the TOEFL (minimum score 575, or 230 on the TOEFL (CBE), or 4.5 on the TWE).

## FINANCIAL FACTS

| | |
|---|---|
| Annual tuition (in-state/out-of-state) | $6,400/$15,100 |
| Fees (in-state/out-of-state) | $415/$415 |
| Books and supplies | $1,500 |
| Room & board (on/off-campus) | $8,800/$7,050 |

## ADMISSIONS

| | |
|---|---|
| Admissions Selectivity Rating | 79 |
| # of applications received | 81 |
| % applicants accepted | 67 |
| % acceptees attending | 57 |
| Average GMAT | 579 |
| Range of GMAT | 550–680 |
| Average GPA | 3.2 |
| TOEFL required of international students? | yes |
| Minimum TOEFL (paper/computer) | 620/260 |
| Application fee | $100 |
| International application fee | $100 |
| Deferment available? | yes |
| Maximum length of deferment | 1 year |
| Transfer students accepted? | yes |
| Transfer application policy | |
| Students may transfer up to 10 courses of advanced standing plus two courses from other AACSB-accredited schools. | |
| Non-fall admissions? | yes |
| Need-blind admissions? | yes |

## APPLICANTS ALSO LOOK AT

McMaster University, Wilfrid Laurier University (Canada)

## EMPLOYMENT PROFILE

| Career Rating | 77 | Grads employed by field: | % | avg. salary: |
|---|---|---|---|---|
| **Primary source of full-time job acceptances** | | Finance | 38 | NR |
| | | Marketing | 25 | NR |
| School-facilitated activities | 10 (37%) | Operations | 25 | NR |
| Graduate-facilitated activities | 4 (29%) | Other | 12 | NR |
| Unknown | 13 (34%) | | | |
| | | | | |
| Average starting salary | $59,000 | | | |
| Percent employed | 85 | | | |

# BUTLER UNIVERSITY
## COLLEGE OF BUSINESS ADMINISTRATION

### GENERAL INFORMATION
| | |
|---|---|
| Type of school | private |
| Environment | metropolis |
| Academic calendar | semester |

### SURVEY SAYS...
Students love Indianapolis, IN
Friendly students
Happy students

### STUDENTS
| | |
|---|---|
| Enrollment of parent institution | 4,384 |
| Enrollment of business school | 176 |
| % male/female | 50/50 |
| % part-time | 92 |
| % international | 36 |
| Average age at entry | 28 |
| Average years work experience at entry | 3 |

### ACADEMICS
| | |
|---|---|
| **Academic Experience Rating** | **78** |
| Student/faculty ratio | 20:1 |
| Profs interesting rating | 81 |
| Profs accessible rating | 80 |
| % female faculty | 32 |
| % minority faculty | 17 |

### JOINT DEGREES
PharmD/MBA, 6 years, full-time

## Academics

Butler's predominantly part-time MBA program provides students with a focus on relevant, real business experiences and projects. Students praise its "ability to cater to adult working professionals." They go on to tell us that "the program is very flexible, allowing students to choose their own schedules and take courses, for up to five years if necessary." In order to accommodate its overbooked MBAs, Butler's program eschews lockstep curricular organization; instead, it offers "a customized program in business administration [with] an individual path to graduation prepared for each incoming student based on his or her academic background." Because the program is tailored to each incoming student's needs and acquired experience, "the length of time it will take to get an MBA here depends on the total number of credit hours required in each student's individual path to graduation and how many courses are taken per semester." However, recent changes in the program allow most students to now finish in about two to two and a half years.

Butler offers concentration in four areas: finance, marketing, international business, and leadership. Students especially love the last, bragging that "the leadership concentration is awesome." They also praise the school's "focus on soft people skills. I don't think you get this in many MBA programs." One student commented that "the quality of technical courses such as accounting and finance could improve, [and] a better selection of classes overall" would help. Despite this, most of the students we surveyed would agree with one who wrote, "My overall experience at Butler has been tremendous. I will and do recommend Butler to anyone pursuing an MBA."

That's because MBAs at Butler are in near-universal agreement about the excellence of Butler's faculty. Professors "tie together theory and real-world practices [with] experience, intelligence, and wisdom, [offering] a good blend of academic and professional insight. Many of them serve as consultants for top firms." Perhaps most important to this crop of students is that the professors "are understanding about the pressures of working full-time and also going to graduate school, along with family responsibilities. They are willing to make time to meet with students and try to make class as fun as possible." Similarly, "the administration is always asking how well the program is preparing the students for the future. It continually evaluates the course offerings and considers changes while being sensitive to those who are midway through when changes occur." There's one final ingredient in the Butler mix: "the broad array of students' interests and work experiences. The background of the student population is a real asset. Most are out there working in the real world and can offer insightful thinking and examples."

## Career and Placement

Career services for Butler MBAs are handled through the Center of Career Planning and Development, which serves the university at large. The school does not hold an active role in seeking jobs for its students for the understandable reason that the vast majority of its students already have them. As one student told us, "There basically is no placement office for graduate programs."

Students who aren't Butler MBAs do have access to the university's career facilities, however. Butler's few full-timers can use the office to find internships. The office also offers counseling in interviewing, resume-building, and dining etiquette, as well as access to Internet-based job-search tools.

STEPHANIE JUDGE, DIRECTOR OF MARKETING
4600 SUNSET AVENUE, INDIANAPOLIS, IN 46208-3485 UNITED STATES
PHONE: 317-940-9221 • FAX: 317-940-9455
E-MAIL: MBA@BUTLER.EDU • WEBSITE: WWW.BUTLER.EDU/MBA

## Location and Environment

Butler's largely part-time student body spends little time on campus once schoolwork is done. As one student explains, "Since the overwhelming majority of students are in school part-time and employed full-time, most people have their lives outside of school and get together only for class, group projects, and study groups (which are very common)." Despite the dearth of social opportunities, students feel they know each other well enough to endorse their classmates. "They are very open and friendly, creating a pleasant environment," writes one MBA. Another notes, "The student body population is small enough to have smaller, more personal classes, which is beneficial in getting to know fellow classmates and creating an atmosphere of togetherness."

Although most students are too busy to take advantage of them, "many activities are offered to the students and faculty at Butler, [including] plenty of social activities and events aimed at improving the program." The school hosts "lots of business leaders as guest speakers, networking breakfasts, and an MBA Association [to help students] not only learn but also network with fellow classmates." Butler's men's basketball team is popular with some students, who find time in their busy schedules to attend home games.

The Butler campus is a homey environment, students tell us. One student writes, "After a long day of work and class, I enjoy walking out to my car and hearing the music students practicing through open windows in the building across the way. I also love the traditional campus environment. I can find a parking space right outside my building after work, and I feel safe walking to my car. Also, the buildings are well-equipped and clean." They also tell us that "the campus is beautiful [and that] Indianapolis is a wonderful city" offering both fine entertainment and exciting business opportunities.

## Admissions

The Butler admissions department "takes a very holistic approach when looking at applicants. [They] consider undergraduate record, GMAT score, work experience, and letters of recommendation. Admittance to the program is more personalized than a standardized minimum score on the GMAT." TOEFL scores are required of students whose native language is not English. The school accepts online applications, accessible at the school's website; the school waives the application fee for students who apply online.

### FINANCIAL FACTS

| | |
|---|---|
| Annual tuition | $10,000 |
| Books and supplies | $800 |

### ADMISSIONS

| | |
|---|---|
| **Admissions Selectivity Rating** | **78** |
| # of applications received | 67 |
| % applicants accepted | 70 |
| % acceptees attending | 83 |
| Average GMAT | 564 |
| Range of GMAT | 530–600 |
| Average GPA | 3.2 |
| TOEFL required of international students? | yes |
| Minimum TOEFL (paper/computer) | 550/213 |
| Regular application deadline | 7/15 |
| Regular notification | 8/10 |
| Deferment available? | yes |
| Maximum length of deferment | 1 year |
| Transfer students accepted? | yes |
| Transfer application policy Students may transfer 9 credits from an AACSB-accredited institution, pending approval. | |
| Non-fall admissions? | yes |

### APPLICANTS ALSO LOOK AT

Indiana University, Purdue University—Indianapolis, Indiana University—Bloomington

# CALIFORNIA STATE POLYTECHNIC UNIVERSITY—POMONA
## COLLEGE OF BUSINESS ADMINISTRATION

### GENERAL INFORMATION
| | |
|---|---|
| Type of school | public |
| Environment | city |
| Academic calendar | quarter |

### SURVEY SAYS...
Happy students
*Solid preparation in:*
Teamwork
Communication/interpersonal skills
Presentation skills
Quantitative skills

### STUDENTS
| | |
|---|---|
| Enrollment of parent institution | 19,800 |
| Enrollment of business school | 350 |
| % male/female | 55/45 |
| % minorities | 20 |
| % international | 18 |
| Average age at entry | 32 |
| Average years work experience at entry | 10 |

### ACADEMICS
| | |
|---|---|
| **Academic Experience Rating** | **84** |
| Student/faculty ratio | 15:1 |
| Profs interesting rating | 78 |
| Profs accessible rating | 69 |

## Academics

Cal Poly Pomona offers a number of intriguing MBA options to its predominantly part-time student body. Like nearly all business schools, Cal Poly Pomona offers a general MBA, but unlike many schools, Cal Poly Pomona offers required courses for the degree both on campus and "off campus at a variety of locations throughout Southern California," through its Professional MBA (PMBA) program. For students with precisely defined goals, Cal Poly Pomona offers the Career MBA, through which students may specialize in one of 11 predefined areas or design a custom emphasis of their own. Finally, Cal Poly Pomona offers the only MSBA in Information Systems Auditing in the United States.

Cal Poly Pomona stresses a "learn-by-doing teaching/learning style" that students appreciate. The approach "forces students to work in groups and deal with teamwork while polishing presentation skills. This is very valuable." Students also appreciate the fact that Cal Poly "has decent technology and wireless access. I like the fact the school can keep up with technology." Cal Poly Pomona's MBA program "offers a high-quality, well-structured education with challenging courses, and students definitely learn a lot." The faculty "brings real business experiences and problems to the table. They are still active in the business world—not a bunch of stuffy academics with outdated information and notes." As one student sums up, "The overall experience here has been exceptional, especially considering the fact that it is a state school! The administration bends over backwards for the students to fix any problems students or faculty may have. Professors are all top-quality and have a definite interest in seeing the students learn."

PMBA students at remote sites are particularly impressed with the level of service they receive. One PMBA student writes, "I live in a remote area, and the school provides instructors to teach not online but in person. The experience is perfect and quite rewarding." Faculty members "are very helpful and accessible despite the fact that classes are off campus."

## Career and Placement

Career services for MBAs here are provided by the Cal Poly Pomona Career Center (CPPCC), a central office serving all undergraduate and graduate students at the university. The CPPCC provides all standard counseling and placement services. Many students do not even use the service; they already have jobs that they hope to advance in by earning a graduate degree. Those who do visit the office wish that it would "focus on providing more internships, part-time jobs, and full-time job opportunities."

## Student Life and Environment

Cal Poly Pomona "is a commuter campus" for MBAs, who largely agree that "campus life is for undergrads who don't work. There is little time for working adults to enjoy campus life, but there is no shortage of clubs and organizations to join for those who want to." When students here get together outside of class, it is to complete required group projects, not to pound some brews or organize a lecture series. Cal Poly Pomona's MBAs appreciate the fact that "the campus is also continually improving its facilities and growing to become more modern and state-of-the-art every year."

Those who take classes at one of the school's satellite sites report that "classrooms are rented by the university at our site; thus, there are few student activities or resources here. There is no need for us to travel to the main campus, so we don't. The online services are excellent and that makes dealing with the university easy. And even though I am not at the main campus, I do have access to all main campus services and resources if I ever decide to travel there."

ADMINISTRATIVE COORDINATOR
3801 WEST TEMPLE AVENUE, POMONA, CA 91768 UNITED STATES
PHONE: 909-869-3210 • FAX: 909-869-4529 • E-MAIL: ADMISSIONS@CSUPOMONA.EDU
WEBSITE: WWW.CSUPOMONA.EDU/~MBA/

The MBA student body is "extremely diverse in terms of age, ethnicity, undergrad majors, and experience levels. Most are commuters who work full-time, come to class, and can't wait to get home after class is over. Most have very busy lives and do not network too strongly within this campus. It's a good group, but career- and family-minded, not socially minded." A substantial number are "enginerds" who "are broadening their intellect by going to b-school."

## Admissions

Cal Poly Pomona operates on a quarterly academic schedule; the school accepts MBA applications for each quarter. All of the following components of the application are carefully considered: complete postsecondary academic record as reflected in official transcripts; GMAT scores (must be no more than five years old); two letters of recommendation from current or former employers; and a resume. Applicants who attended an undergraduate institution at which English is not the primary language of instruction must provide official TOEFL scores. Applicants must meet the following criteria to be considered for admission: an overall undergraduate GPA of at least 3.0; a minimum GMAT score of 450; and, if required, TOEFL scores of at least 580 on the paper-and-pencil test or 237 on the computer-based test. Meeting minimum requirements does not guarantee admission to the program.

## FINANCIAL FACTS

| | |
|---|---|
| Annual tuition (in-state/out-of-state) | $4,420/$6,100 |
| Books and supplies | $3,000 |
| Room & board (on/off-campus) | $5,000/$8,000 |
| Average grant | $18,500 |
| Average student loan debt | $12,000 |

## ADMISSIONS

| | |
|---|---|
| **Admissions Selectivity Rating** | **87** |
| # of applications received | 163 |
| % applicants accepted | 30 |
| % acceptees attending | 59 |
| Average GMAT | 540 |
| Range of GMAT | 450–720 |
| Average GPA | 3.2 |
| TOEFL required of international students? | yes |
| Minimum TOEFL (paper/computer) | 580/237 |
| Application fee | $55 |
| International application fee | $55 |
| Regular application deadline | rolling |
| Regular notification | rolling |
| Deferment available? | yes |
| Maximum length of deferment | 1-2 quarters |
| Transfer students accepted? | yes |
| Transfer application policy Students may transfer up to 3 classes (13 units) from other AACSB-accredited schools. | |
| Non-fall admissions? | yes |
| Need-blind admissions? | yes |

## EMPLOYMENT PROFILE

| | |
|---|---|
| **Career Rating** | **70** |
| Average starting salary | $64,500 |

# CALIFORNIA STATE POLYTECHNIC UNIVERSITY AT SAN LUIS OBISPO
## ORFALEA COLLEGE OF BUSINESS

## Academics

"Learn by doing" is the educational philosophy of the Orfalea College of Business at California State Polytechnic at San Luis Obispo, and students tell us that it's a philosophy adhered to throughout the graduate business program. The program focuses strongly on the technological aspects of business. One student reports, "The learn-by-doing philosophy here is true. This school really teaches you to get into the nitty-gritty of how things work in the real world." Another student adds, "The learn-by-doing philosophy gives us a functional knowledge that will be essential in our jobs. We have a hands-on learning environment that includes great labs and really tough courses."

Cal Poly offers specializations in agribusiness, general management, and graphic communication; a master's of science in industrial and technical studies; and "blended programs" in architectural management and landscape architectural management. Also offered are dual-degree programs. Dual degrees are popular for those with an undergraduate degree in such areas as engineering, industrial technology, and agribusiness.

The Cal Poly MBA program is a 60–64 unit program that provides students who are willing to commit to a rigorous schedule of prescribed courses the option to complete the program in just over 10 months. A traditional MBA model for those not pursing this accelerated option and/or simultaneously pursuing dual degrees is also offered. Several specifically developed elective courses have been added to the curriculum, including "Commercial Development of Innovative Technologies, Effective Communication Skills for Managers" and a transformational two-and-a-half week "Doing Business in Asia" business study tour to the People's Republic of China.

While students love the curriculum, most feel that "Cal Poly's strongest asset is the professors. They are enthusiastic and very knowledgeable about their subjects." They also create a "casual atmosphere that is very conducive to learning and sharing ideas," which students appreciate; they attribute this atmosphere in part to "classes that are very small (some less then 10 people) so the interaction level is high. I feel I know all my professors very well. Lots of classroom participation, lots of group interaction." The administration, as at many large state schools, "is very disorganized in terms of records and paperwork. Administrative operations definitely need to improve."

## Career and Placement

The Career Services Office at Cal Poly SLO offers students assistance with job searches and career planning through workshops, counseling sessions, job fairs, and online databases and resume books. MBAs tell us, "Students generally find employment before graduation," in large part because the school feeds the region's tech-heavy businesses. Even so, some students feel the office could do a better job, and say the school "needs to create more connections with Bay Area companies." Approximately 300 companies recruit on campus during the year; about 25 travel to the school to recruit summer interns.

Companies most likely to recruit Orfalea MBAs include Agilent Technology; Amgen, Inc.; Deloitte Consulting; IBM; Lawrence Livermore Labs; Northrop Grumman; Pacific Gas & Electric; and Sun MicroSystems.

## Student Life and Environment

Students refer lovingly to the pace at Cal Poly San Luis Obispo as "the SLO life," describing it as "a good combination of hard work and fun. The vibe is quite casual." MBAs enjoy "a small-town atmosphere, which makes it easy to socialize on a regular basis.

CHRIS CARR, ASSOCIATE DEAN OF GRADUATE PROGRAMS
1 GRAND AVENUE, OCOB SAN LUIS, OBISPO, CA 93407 UNITED STATES
PHONE: 805-756-2637 • FAX: 805-756-0110
E-MAIL: MBA@CALPOLY.EDU • WEBSITE: HTTP://MBA.CALPOLY.EDU

Many of us have become good friends and spend most of our free time with each other." With "lots of social activities, [SLO is] a very comfortable, close-knit community. It's away from big cities; however, it is close enough for easy interviews and contacts." Students appreciate "the diversity of subcultures on campus (the university at large has substantial Asian and Hispanic populations), which provides a neat experience."

The town San Luis Obispo, MBAs brag, "is a beautiful, nearly idyllic place on the central coast of California. The climate is magnificent year-round." One student mentions that SLO "is near the beach and the mountains, so there is a lot of recreation available at all times throughout the year, and most people here enjoy the chance to relax outdoors often." The town also "has great character in its immediate surroundings, as well as traditions such as Thursday night Farmer's Market, which are a lot of fun. All of these enhance the entire education experience and make the town and college unique to other schools."

Orfalea MBAs enjoy "brand-new facilities including a great recreation center and performing-arts center." The school also has a "nice-size campus and a great gym, [as well as] beautiful surroundings [and] a friendly student body." No wonder students tell us that "Cal Poly is a wonderful school. It's a lot of work, but the MBA program does a lot to make sure you are still having fun."

## Admissions

Admissions at the Orfalea College of Business consider all of the following components of a student's application: GMAT score (minimum 530 required), TOEFL score (where applicable), undergraduate transcript (demonstrating at least a 2.5 GPA for the final two full years of undergraduate study), two letters of recommendation, and a supplemental application. Interviews are optional. While admission is "primarily based on GPA and GMAT achievement, some candidates who receive low scores may be evaluated based on additional factors such as work experience, statement of purpose, and letters of recommendation." The school also notes that work experience (three years) is desired, but not required.

### PROMINENT ALUMNI

Robert Rowell, President, Golden State Warriors; Linda Ozawa Olds, Founder, Jamba Juice; Bill Swanson, Chair & CEO, Raytheon Company; Burt Rutan, President, Scaled Composites, designer SpaceShipOne; Gary Bloom, CEO, Veritas

### FINANCIAL FACTS

| | |
|---|---|
| Annual tuition (in-state/out-of-state) | $3,102/$13,272 |
| Fees (in-state/out-of-state) | $1,725/$1,725 |
| Books and supplies | $1,260 |
| Room & board (on/off-campus) | $8,145/$8,145 |
| % of students receiving aid | 45 |
| % of first-year students receiving aid | 25 |
| % of students receiving loans | 45 |
| % of students receiving grants | 5 |
| Average award package | $11,634 |
| Average grant | $2,176 |

### ADMISSIONS

| | |
|---|---|
| Admissions Selectivity Rating | 89 |
| # of applications received | 126 |
| % applicants accepted | 50 |
| % acceptees attending | 79 |
| Average GMAT | 600 |
| Range of GMAT | 560–640 |
| Average GPA | 3.24 |
| TOEFL required of international students? | yes |
| Minimum TOEFL (paper/computer) | 550/213 |
| Application fee | $55 |
| International application fee | $55 |
| Regular application deadline | 6/1 |
| Regular notification | rolling |
| Transfer students accepted? | yes |
| Transfer application policy Students may transfer 8 credits from an AACSB-accredited institution, pending approval. | |
| Need-blind admissions? | yes |

### APPLICANTS ALSO LOOK AT

California State University—Sacramento, San Diego State University, San Francisco State University, San Jose State University, University of California—Davis, University of California—Los Angeles, University of California—Berkeley

### EMPLOYMENT PROFILE

| | |
|---|---|
| Career Rating | 82 |
| Average starting salary | $70,000 |

# CALIFORNIA STATE UNIVERSITY—CHICO
## COLLEGE OF BUSINESS

### GENERAL INFORMATION
Type of school                     public
Environment                        village
Academic calendar              semester

### SURVEY SAYS...
Friendly students
*Solid preparation in:*
Finance
Teamwork
Presentation skills
Computer skills

### STUDENTS
Enrollment of parent
  institution                          14,000
Enrollment of business school   65
% male/female                        65/35
% part-time                               30
% international                           43
Average age at entry                 27
Average years work experience
  at entry                                     3

### ACADEMICS
**Academic Experience Rating    65**
Student/faculty ratio                  35:1
Profs interesting rating                62
Profs accessible rating                 62
% female faculty                          20

### JOINT DEGREES
MBA with MIS emphasis, 2 years

### PROMINENT ALUMNI
Prabhakar Kalavacharla, Managing
Partner, KPMG; Ed Byers, Managing
Partner, Deloitte Touche Tohmatsu;
Masayuki Ishizaki, Managing
Partner, Accenture; Bill Bales, CFO,
Sierra Nevada Brewing Company

## Academics

Many students choose California State University—Chico for its "emphasis on cutting-edge information system knowledge and technologies," citing "their focus on IT, the future of business," as a primary reason for choosing to enroll in the program. Chico was the first school to participate in the SAP University Alliance Program, which trains students in software that manages and integrates information in a corporate business setting. College of Business students also publish an annual magazine, *Link*, dedicated to business and technology issues. Students tell us that they also enjoy excellent industry contacts through the teaching staff, internship office, and career services.

Chico stands out for its "outstanding achievement teaching MIS," though students report that the quality of instruction is generally very high. "Small classes mean good opportunity for individual attention from teachers," and applied learning is a foundation of the program. Course work emphasizes "tons of teamwork and presentation" and "most business professors choose the hands-on approach in teaching and are open-minded to suggestions and ideas." However, while students are highly satisfied with the instruction in modern topics such as e-commerce and technology, they warn that more traditional subjects do not always receive the attention they might at more conventional business schools. Students admit that "professors range from excellent to to-be-avoided," and that "instruction in finance is weak."

The College of Business at Chico "is geared toward MBA students who did not have business undergrad," and therefore the curriculum comprises a broad base of courses in accounting, finance, management, international business, technology, and e-commerce. For students with extensive professional experience or who pursued an undergraduate degree in business, the curriculum provides a worthy examination of these concepts, but such students tells us that "the workload is moderate" and easy to balance alongside full-time employment. In the words of a second-year student, "Coming from industry, the workload is not that difficult to manage." Those entering the program with a less intensive business background, however—particularly for those with less technology know-how—find the program rather challenging; writes one such student, "I was not prepared in computers for my accounting BS, so it's been a little overwhelming." As the curriculum is broad-based, with the exception of the technology focus, students at Chico may design a moderately focused business education. Chico does not offer concentrations in special areas of study, nor highly focused electives in certain industries or topics.

As part of the California State school system, Chico has been affected by the state's widely publicized budget cuts. As a result, the school is "sometimes a bit of a logistical nightmare." In addition, facilities and resources do not always meet student needs. For example, "the library is hardly ever open and closes early" and "the cash-strapped school needs updated computers for some labs."

## Career & Placement

Chico graduates tend to find work in a fairly wide range of industries. In an average year, students from the graduate and undergraduate programs find work in over 250 different companies. When interviewing for jobs, Chico students notice that "this school is appreciated by industry," especially in the high-tech sector. In particular, employers seek Chico grads for their strong knowledge of computers and technology, and students agree that "the unique curriculum helps a lot in job hunting."

SANDY JENSEN, ADVISER, BUSINESS GRADUATE PROGRAMS
CHICO 041, WEST 1ST & ORANGE STREET, CHICO, CA 95929 UNITED STATES
PHONE: 530-898-4425 • FAX: 530-898-5889
E-MAIL: SJENSEN@CSUCHICO.EDU • WEBSITE: WWW.COB.CSUCHICO.EDU

According to Chico's administration, 80 percent of recruiters rate the Chico State curriculum as outstanding or above average compared with other universities at which they recruit. In recent years, the following companies—among others—came to recruit at Chico State: Andersen Consulting, Anixter, Bank of America, Chevron, Deloitte Touche Tohmatsu, Ernst & Young, First Interstate Bank, Hewlett Packard, Intel, Paine Webber, PricewaterhouseCoopers, Sears, System Integrators, Tandem Computers, Wal-Mart, and Wallace Computer Services.

## Student Life & Environment

The undergraduate college at Chico is known throughout California as something of a "party school," and while "most graduate students are not socially active," they say the outgoing vibe definitely rubs off on the business-school community. At Chico, you won't see frowns, complaints, or negative competition. By all accounts, Chico is a "friendly environment with lots of happy students and professors." An MBA student writes, "The college environment—both people and campus—makes the experience here unforgettable." Drawing students from Northern California and across the world, the student body is very "culturally diverse," with a "vastly international student base." In general, the international students attend classes full-time, whereas the majority of California residents "are returning-to-school, working adults" who hold full or part-time jobs while pursuing their business degree.

Located in idyllic Northern California, hometown Chico is an excellent place to study, as it is "laid-back, small, safe, and affordable." In addition to its excellent atmosphere, Chico is well placed for anyone hoping to work in the greater Northern California region, drawing students from the local community, the San Francisco Bay Area, and Sacramento.

## Admissions

To apply to Chico's graduate program in business, you must submit a completed application, an application fee, a statement of purpose, three letters of recommendation, and GMAT scores. The minimum acceptable GMAT score is the 50th percentile. There is no minimum work requirement to apply to Chico State, and students are accepted from every undergraduate major.

### FINANCIAL FACTS

| | |
|---|---|
| Annual tuition (in-state/out-of-state) | $3,600/$9,600 |
| Books and supplies | $1,200 |
| Room & board (on/off-campus) | $9,500/$9,500 |
| % of students receiving aid | 65 |
| % of first-year students receiving aid | 50 |
| % of students receiving loans | 65 |
| % of students receiving grants | 10 |
| Average award package | $10,000 |
| Average grant | $1,000 |

### ADMISSIONS

| | |
|---|---|
| Admissions Selectivity Rating | 80 |
| # of applications received | 75 |
| % applicants accepted | 56 |
| % acceptees attending | 52 |
| Average GMAT | 560 |
| Range of GMAT | 540–710 |
| Average GPA | 3.3 |
| TOEFL required of international students? | yes |
| Minimum TOEFL (paper/computer) | 550/213 |
| Application fee | $55 |
| International application fee | $55 |
| Regular application deadline | rolling |
| Regular notification | rolling |
| Deferment available? | yes |
| Maximum length of deferment | 1 year |
| Transfer students accepted? | yes |
| Non-fall admissions? | yes |
| Need-blind admissions? | yes |

### APPLICANTS ALSO LOOK AT

California State University—Sacramento, San Francisco State University

### EMPLOYMENT PROFILE

| Career Rating | 73 | Grads employed by field: | % | avg. salary: |
|---|---|---|---|---|
| Average starting salary | $60,000 | Accounting | 10 | $58,000 |
| | | Finance | 2 | $55,000 |
| | | MIS | 70 | $60,000 |
| | | Consulting | 10 | $65,000 |
| | | General Management | 1 | $55,000 |
| | | Other | 5 | $55,000 |
| | | Internet/New Media | 2 | $55,000 |

# CALIFORNIA STATE UNIVERSITY—EAST BAY

## GENERAL INFORMATION
Type of school                    public
Environment                       city
Academic calendar                 quarter

## SURVEY SAYS...
Friendly students
*Solid preparation in:*
General management
Teamwork
Communication/interpersonal skills
Presentation skills

## STUDENTS
Enrollment of parent
  institution                     12,535
Enrollment of business school     663
% male/female                     40/60
% out-of-state                    47
% part-time                       57
% minorities                      21
% international                   47
Average age at entry              34
Average years work experience
  at entry                        3

## ACADEMICS
**Academic Experience Rating**    **63**
Student/faculty ratio             25:1
Profs interesting rating          68
Profs accessible rating           66

## PROMINENT ALUMNI
Jack Acosta, CFO/VP, Portal
Software; Louis Navellier, Pres/CEO,
Navellier & Assoc., Inc.; Georganne
Proctor, Former VP, CFO and Board
Member, Bechtel Corp.

## Academics

The MBA program at California State University—East Bay offers its busy student body an excellent assortment of specializations to choose from: 17 to be exact, including options in accounting, business economics, various computer-related areas, entrepreneurship, telecommunications, taxation, and supply chain management. Most classes here meet in the evenings, making them convenient for a student body comprised mainly of full-time workers.

The CSUEB MBA track includes foundation courses, which can be waived for students who earned undergraduate degrees in business; proficiency requirements in mathematics and statistics; 12 credits in core courses; four credits in international requirements, fulfilled by a course in international business or international economics; a five-credit capstone experience, consisting of either an entrepreneurship practicum or a seminar in strategic management; and course work sufficient to complete an MBA Option (what many schools call a "specialization" or "concentration"). All told, 45 quarter credits are required toward the MBA here.

CSUEB offers distance-learning options for students who cannot fit the campus evening classes into their schedules. Students love the convenience of this option but warn that "we can't really choose the subjects. There is very little flexibility in the program." In addition, the school offers a Transnational Executive MBA (TEMBA) program that emphasizes global business. TEMBA students attend 10 classes, each held once a month, and participate in three overseas trips and an international consulting project. As one participant explains, "The Transnational Executive MBA has a global strategy project that provides hands-on practice. The program is very flexible in that we only need to meet once a month for four days, and it is a short 13-month program."

In all programs, students appreciate the fact that "professors are very sympathetic to family and work issues." They report that "the professors are great in supply chain management," using "case studies that are oriented on real-life situations," and that "the accounting program is superb." Most of all, they love the low cost of attending. Some worry, however, that "the state is reducing its financial support of CSU, and that's caused a reduction in the number of classes offered. This is not a positive trend."

## Career and Placement

CSUEB MBAs receive career guidance from the university's Career Development Center (CDC). Individual counseling is available to help students develop a personalized career plan. The school maintains an online resume database, as well as a website with numerous helpful links for MBAs. "Proximity to Silicon Valley" is also a boon to students. Since "this MBA program is catered to working professionals," many students are already involved in a career track.

## Student Life and Environment

Those who get involved with campus life at CSUEB tell us that "life at school is dramatically enhanced when participating in campus organizations." Clubs such as the Operations Management Society, for example, "bring in speakers from top companies to address us, and good speakers from outside are sometimes invited to classes to talk about relevant topics." Few here, however, have the time or inclination to pursue such life-enhancing experiences. "This is a commuter school, and there's not too much life on campus," sums up one typical student.

DONNA WILEY, DIRECTOR OF CBE GRADUATE PROGRAMS
25800 CARLES BEE BOULEVARD, HAYWARD, CA 94542 UNITED STATES
PHONE: 510-885-2419 • FAX: 510-885-2176 • E-MAIL: DONNA.WILEY@CSUEASTBAY.EDU
WEBSITE: WWW.CBEGRAD.CSUHAYWARD.EDU

Business school facilities, students tell us, need improvement, but "a new building is coming up." For the time being, students appreciate the day-care facility and "a good library full of helpful librarians." "Nice weather and an outstanding view over the bay" also make difficult days a little less stressful.

Nearly half the MBA student population at CSUEB is international, the result of numerous partnerships between the school and overseas business schools. This creates a student body that is "not only from diverse employments, but also from diverse cultures, representing ideas and business methods from all over the world. Everyone shares experiences and everyone is very easy to talk to."

## Admissions

Applications to all graduate business programs at CSUEB are evaluated on the basis of academic transcripts for all undergraduate and post-undergraduate work, and GMAT scores. As the school's website states, "Admission is automatic for applicants with (1) a minimum 1050 'Index Score' and (2) minimum 20th percentile GMAT Verbal and Quantitative scores. [Index Score = (Upper Division GPA x 200) + Total GMAT]." Students failing to meet the above minimum criteria are assessed individually by the Graduate Admissions Committee, which considers work experience, community participation, letters of recommendation, and a personal statement in determining whether to admit. Some students may be admitted conditionally, pending the completion of nondegree foundation courses. Students must demonstrate writing proficiency prior to enrolling in graduate-level courses; this can be achieved with a score of at least 9 on the university's Writing Skills Test (WST) or a score of at least 4.5 on the GMAT essay. International students must prove proficiency in English in one of a few ways: by earning a TOEFL (Test of English as a Foreign Language) score of at least 550 (paper-based test) or 213 (computer-based test); by earning an IELTS (International English Language Testing System) score of at least 7.0; or by submitting an official transcript verifying receipt of a bachelor's degree from "a U.S. college or university or an international college or university where English is the principal language of instruction."

### FINANCIAL FACTS

| | |
|---|---|
| Annual tuition (in-state/out-of-state) | $4,664/$15,512 |
| Books and supplies | $10,000 |
| Room & board (on/off-campus) | $15,000/$17,400 |
| % of students receiving aid | 12 |
| % of first-year students receiving aid | 12 |
| % of students receiving loans | 8 |
| % of students receiving grants | 1 |
| Average award package | $12,943 |
| Average grant | $11,478 |
| Average student loan debt | $25,626 |

### ADMISSIONS

| | |
|---|---|
| Admissions Selectivity Rating | 71 |
| # of applications received | 354 |
| % applicants accepted | 77 |
| % acceptees attending | 66 |
| Average GMAT | 530 |
| Range of GMAT | 380–630 |
| Average GPA | 3.14 |
| TOEFL required of international students? | yes |
| Minimum TOEFL (paper/computer) | 550/213 |
| Application fee | $55 |
| International application fee | $55 |
| Regular application deadline | 6/1 |
| Regular notification | 6/21 |
| Deferment available? | yes |
| Maximum length of deferment | 1 quarter |
| Non-fall admissions? | yes |

### APPLICANTS ALSO LOOK AT

California State University—Sacramento, San Francisco State University, San Jose State University, University of California—Davis, University of California—Berkeley

# CALIFORNIA STATE UNIVERSITY—FRESNO
## CRAIG SCHOOL OF BUSINESS

### GENERAL INFORMATION
Type of school       public
Academic calendar      semester

### SURVEY SAYS...
*Solid preparation in:*
Teamwork
Communication/interpersonal skills
Presentation skills
Entrepreneurial studies

### STUDENTS
Enrollment of parent
   institution             21,000
Enrollment of business school   125
% male/female          55/45
% out-of-state            15
% part-time             64
% minorities            10
% international          65
Average age at entry      29
Average years work experience
   at entry                    5

### ACADEMICS
**Academic Experience Rating**   **80**
Student/faculty ratio       6:1
Profs interesting rating      78
Profs accessible rating      65
% female faculty         33

### PROMINENT ALUMNI
Ryan Turner, CEO, Chemicals,
Pacific Ethanol PEIX; Jeff Booey,
Plant Manager, Glass
Manufacturing, Guardian Ind.

## Academics

The MBA program at California State University—Fresno's Craig School of Business is designed with the working student in mind. All weekday classes here meet just once a week, from 6:00 P.M. to 8:45 P.M. Saturday morning classes (usually scheduled from 9:00 A.M. to 11:45 A.M.) are also available.

The Craig MBA consists of 11 classes and a final project. The curriculum commences with six core courses covering such fundamental areas as leadership, MIS, finance, accounting, marketing, and ethics. Students then complete three electives. Electives may be used to create a specialization in agribusiness, entrepreneurship, finance, human resource management, MIS, or marketing; or, students may choose to graduate with a General Management degree. The program concludes with a capstone class in Business Policy and Strategy and a culminating project or thesis.

Up to five introductory foundation courses that do not count toward the graduate degree may be required of some entering students. Students who have earned an undergraduate degree in business from an AACSB-accredited institution within the last seven years generally do not have to take these courses. Those not meeting these criteria may be able to place out of some or all of the introductory courses through examination.

Students identify entrepreneurship and courses dealing with globalization as the program's strengths. Those studying MIS, however, warn that "there currently are not enough professors to offer all of the courses, making it difficult to complete the degree." MBAs here appreciate the fact that the Craig School "has made a point to invest itself into the community for the sake of the community, as well as for the sake of the students. Fresno State feels like a hub of the community, and it's exciting to be affiliated with it." Professors here "are typically passionate about their subject matter, which leads to interesting classes, even when the material isn't what I'd like to be studying (accounting, for example)."

## Career and Placement

Career and placement services for Craig MBAs are limited. The school does not have a dedicated Career Services Office; rather, a single Career Services Office serves all undergraduate and graduate students at the university. The office provides a number of recruiting events and other support services, but few are designed to serve the unique needs of MBAs. An MBA Student Association offers additional services, organizing events that "connect MBA students with alumni, faculty, and local community, and business leaders" in order to "build a professional network and lay the foundation for friendships that will last a lifetime." Most Craig students are part-time students with full-time jobs (many attend at their employers' expense), and for them the dearth of career services is not a major drawback.

## Student Life and Environment

It's all business (pun intended!) on the Craig MBA campus, as one student expresses: "Extracurricular activities coincide with class times," making participation difficult. While "there are a number of activities available for undergraduate students, it's hard to make these available for graduate students who are busy with work throughout the day."

However, the Craig school is in the process of upgrading its facilities, and many here believe that the "facilities will be amazing in a few years." The library is being remodeled and the university has recently opened a 15,000-seat entertainment and sports center (Savemart Center), the largest of those facilities in California's Central Valley. This

DR. RAFAEL SOLIS, DIRECTOR OF GRADUATE PROGRAMS
5245 NORTH BACKER AVENUE, FRESNO, CA 93740 UNITED STATES
PHONE: 559-278-2107 • FAX: 559-278-2572 • E-MAIL: MBAINFO@CSUFRESNO.EDU
WEBSITE: WWW.CRAIG.CSUFRESNO.EDU/MBA

## FINANCIAL FACTS

| | |
|---|---|
| Books and supplies | $650 |
| Room & board | $10,700 |

## ADMISSIONS

| | |
|---|---|
| **Admissions Selectivity Rating** | **82** |
| # of applications received | 101 |
| % applicants accepted | 62 |
| % acceptees attending | 76 |
| Average GMAT | 566 |
| Range of GMAT | 530–580 |
| Average GPA | 3.4 |
| TOEFL required of international students? | yes |
| Minimum TOEFL (paper/computer) | 550/213 |
| Application fee | $55 |
| International application fee | $55 |
| Regular application deadline | 3/1 |
| Regular notification | rolling |
| Deferment available? | yes |
| Maximum length of deferment | 1 year |
| Transfer students accepted? | yes |
| Transfer application policy | |
| All foundation courses may be waived through prior course work. Up to 6 credits may be transferred into core and elective portion of program. Transfer credit granted on a case-by-case basis through syllabus review. | |
| Non-fall admissions? | yes |
| Need-blind admissions? | yes |

## APPLICANTS ALSO LOOK AT

Cal Poly State University—San Luis Obispo, Santa Clara University, University of California—Davis

venue is used for a variety of sports events ranging from basketball to ice hockey. It has also hosted musical, drama, and dance shows. Hopefully, this new recreation center will cater to graduate students' hectic schedules and provide them with multiple extracurricular options.

The Craig student body "represents a varied mix of industries, allowing for a 'cross-section' view of industries in general" during class discussions and group projects. Many foreign students attend, and "though there are times when language barriers exist, our lives are expanded by their presence." MBAs here report that "although we are so different in terms of age, ethnic background, and work experience, we are all here, going through the same courses and moaning about the same tough professors. There's a feeling of 'We're in this together.'"

## Admissions

Admission to the Craig MBA program is determined primarily by the applicant's undergraduate grade point average (GPA) during the final two years of undergraduate work, and GMAT scores. The average admitted student arrives with a GPA of 3.4 and a GMAT score of 566. The quality of undergraduate institution and curriculum pursued are considered when evaluating GPA. Work experience, personal statement, and two letters of recommendation (from employers, professors, or professional peers) also figure into the admissions decision. Because the GMAT score is a major factor in admissions, the admissions office strongly encourages all candidates to prepare for the exam for at least six to eight weeks. International students must have a minimum TOEFL score of 550 (paper-based test) or 213 (computer-based test) to be considered.

# CALIFORNIA STATE UNIVERSITY—FULLERTON
## GRADUATE SCHOOL OF BUSINESS

## Academics

The Graduate School of Business at California State University—Fullerton offers "one of only four accredited accounting programs in the state" as well as "a good selection of specializations [at] approximately one-fifth the cost of other MBA programs in the area (UCI, USC, UCLA, Pepperdine)." Students appreciate these assets, as well as the school's "flexible, nonlockstep" curriculum that allows the completely part-time student body to wedge an MBA program into their hectic lives.

CSUF offers three MBA options: the Generalist Plan, the Specialist Plan, and the International Business MBA. The Generalist Plan is designed for students with little or no undergraduate background in business. The program begins with a nine-course foundation sequence (up to three courses can be waived based on equivalent undergraduate work). Students then proceed through seven subject-specific advanced seminars (six prescribed, one elective), a comprehensive capstone course, and a concluding written project or oral examinations. Students with no business background are relieved to find that the program brings them up to speed. One student currently following the foundation sequence writes, "The professors are very helpful and knowledgeable, as well as approachable, which is truly appreciated." MBAs here warn, however, that "the program is long. It could take close to four years to complete on a part-time basis." They also note that "the program allows only elective course for Generalist program. I would prefer the option to have more."

CSFU's Specialist Plan allows students to develop a concentration in accounting, business economics, finance, e-commerce, entrepreneurship, management, management science/information systems, or marketing. The program commences with a 10-course foundation sequence (some or all courses can be waived based on equivalent undergraduate work), then proceeds to six advanced seminars. Students then choose four concentration-related electives before concluding the program with a comprehensive capstone course, and a concluding written project or oral examinations. Students praise this "well-structured program that allows flexibility yet covers all relevant topics," singling out the accounting and finance offerings as "outstanding."

The third option at CSFU is the International Business MBA, which consists of the 10-course foundation sequence (some or all courses can be waived based on equivalent undergraduate work), five advanced seminars, five concentration courses, the comprehensive capstone course, and the concluding written project or oral examinations.

Students in all programs agree that "the faculty consistently challenge us, but make sure we learn the material." Students go on to say that "the academic experience is very beneficial because there is a lot of interaction between students and professors." They also tell us that "the school could improve with some technology . . . like more wireless Internet access, which is limited to a few buildings on campus." For the convenience of those in the south Orange County region, CSUF offers slightly modified versions of the Generalist and Specialist MBA programs at a facility near the Irvine Spectrum.

## Career and Placement

The Cal State Fullerton Career Planning and Placement Center provides career services to MBAs at both the Fullerton and Irvine Spectrum locations. Services include walk-in counseling, interview tips, resume review, and job databases. Students may continue to utilize these facilities for up to one year after they graduate for a $25 fee.

## Student Life and Environment

Don't expect much hand-holding from the folks who run the CSUF MBA program. One student observes, "The school could do a better job in partnering and treating the graduate business students like the professionals that we are, and less like numbers. . . . Except for the milk and cookies that arriving MBA candidates get at the orientation, there are absolutely no mixers hosted by the school whatsoever. It's very clear from the beginning: You're on your own." Not that it matters much to most students, who "tend to work full-time and are not heavily involved in school life." One student explains, "I don't spend much time at school except when there is a group meeting and going to class." But the feeling is that "while I am there, I do enjoy the campus and the people." Students point out, "Some group-project efforts are challenging due to people's schedules and geographic locations. Overall, we always seem to work it out." Students respect each other's schedules and tell us, "These are great people that I love to hang out with."

The MBA program at Fullerton "has a diverse culture, which is great. The students and professors come from a wide variety of countries, backgrounds, and beliefs, which makes the experience even better." Additionally, "almost all MBA students have full-time careers—this is vital for the exchange of ideas." Overall, students tend to be on the youngish side. One student speculates, "Most are in their late twenties or early thirties." The "large international population [includes] a big percentage of Asian nationals."

## Admissions

Cal State Fullerton requires the following of all applicants to its MBA program: an "acceptable bachelor's degree from an appropriately accredited institution," with a minimum GPA of 2.5 for the final two years of undergraduate work; GMAT scores reflecting placement in the top 50 percent on the verbal, analytical, and quantitative sections of the exam; a completed background sheet that includes a summary of academic and professional experience and a personal essay; and demonstrated proficiency in calculus and introductory-level computer programming. International students whose first language is not English must score a minimum 570 on the TOEFL paper-and-pencil exam.

### FINANCIAL FACTS

| | |
|---|---|
| Annual tuition (in-state/out-of-state) | $0/$6,768 |
| Fees | $2,726 |
| Books and supplies | $810 |
| Room & board (on/off-campus) | $9,056/$10,810 |
| % of students receiving aid | 52 |
| % of first-year students receiving aid | 18 |
| % of students receiving loans | 37 |
| % of students receiving grants | 15 |
| Average award package | $6,738 |
| Average grant | $1,772 |
| Average student loan debt | $15,404 |

### ADMISSIONS

| | |
|---|---|
| **Admissions Selectivity Rating** | **83** |
| # of applications received | 528 |
| % applicants accepted | 34 |
| % acceptees attending | 46 |
| Average GMAT | 522 |
| Average GPA | 3.28 |
| TOEFL required of international students? | yes |
| Minimum TOEFL (paper/computer) | 570/230 |
| Application fee | $55 |
| International application fee | $55 |
| Regular application deadline | 5/6 |
| Regular notification | rolling |
| Transfer students accepted? | yes |
| Transfer application policy | |

Students must apply as a new student and courses will be evaluted. Students may transfer up to 9 units.

| | |
|---|---|
| Non-fall admissions? | yes |
| Need-blind admissions? | yes |

### EMPLOYMENT PROFILE

| | |
|---|---|
| **Career Rating** | **71** |
| Average starting salary | $62,666 |

# CALIFORNIA STATE UNIVERSITY—LONG BEACH
## COLLEGE OF BUSINESS ADMINISTRATION

### GENERAL INFORMATION
Type of school     public
Environment     city
Academic calendar     semester

### SURVEY SAYS...
Students love Long Beach, CA
Friendly students
Happy students
*Solid preparation in:*
Presentation skills

### STUDENTS
Enrollment of parent
  institution     33,000
Enrollment of business school   310
% male/female     58/42
% out-of-state     1
% part-time     70
% minorities     15
% international     30
Average age at entry     28
Average years work experience
  at entry     5

### ACADEMICS
**Academic Experience Rating**    **69**
Student/faculty ratio     25:1
Profs interesting rating     65
Profs accessible rating     77

## Academics

The College of Business Administration at California State University—Long Beach—the "best business school in the California State University system," according to some students here—offers five different MBA programs for the convenience of its students. Most popular among the different options is the Evening MBA, a self-paced program that can be pursued either full- or part-time. Evening classes meet during the week with a curriculum that includes prerequisite courses (which can be waived for students with undergraduate business degrees), core courses, electives (three in one area must be completed for an area of concentration), and a capstone course. Concentrations are offered in information systems, finance, human resources, marketing, general management, accounting, and health care.

Those looking for a more traditional, cohort-based MBA program in a part-time setting will appreciate the Fully Employed MBA (FEMBA) program, a 23-month sequence of four 10-week sessions per year, scheduled on Saturdays for the convenience of full-time workers. FEMBA combines the benefits of a lockstep curriculum and the team-based learning inherent in the cohort system with the expedience of weekend classes. All books and materials are included in the price of the FEMBA program—another plus for those who hate unpleasant surprises.

CSULB also offers three smaller, more specialized MBA programs: the Corporate MBA Program for Boeing, available only to qualified Boeing employees; the Fully Employed MBA Program for Municipal and Public Agency Managers, which focuses on business skills and concepts useful in government and education; and a one-year Accelerated MBA, a full-time program for students anxious to jump-start their business careers.

Students typically choose CSULB for its low tuition rates, which translate into an excellent return on investment. One student writes, "It was the best investment, when you take into account the tuition, the flexible schedule of classes, and the time it generally takes to complete the MBA program." Once admitted, students also enjoy "perfect class sizes that allow all students to contribute to discussions" and professors who "usually come from the private sector and teach more from 'real-world' experience than from theory." Professors here "take an interest in seeing you succeed." Some also describe "a light workload," which could be viewed as a plus or a minus, depending on what a particular student wants from the program.

## Career and Placement

CSULB's Career Development Center provides counseling and placement services for all students at the university. The office coordinates career fairs and manages online job postings through BeachLINK, a database accessible only to those with CSULB accounts and passwords. Students report that "the school has a great networking program through mentors in local business."

## Student Life and Environment

There are "many different countries represented, including Saudi Arabia and China" in CSULB's student body. One MBA observes, "I rarely have had access to such people before. It is great to meet them in an intellectual environment, which offers a contrast to information provided by the media." Students here are "friendly for the most part and very goal-oriented." In classes, "there seems to be a good mix of married and single students ranging from mid-20s to mid-40s. Some have children, but most don't. Most everyone works at least part-time, if not full-time [because] very few come from a privileged background." One student comments, "I am an older student (48), but found that my age didn't matter as much as I thought it would."

PAULA GLOECKNER, MBA EVALUATOR
1250 BELLFLOWER BOULEVARD, LONG BEACH, CA 90840-0119 UNITED STATES
PHONE: 562-985-7988 • FAX: 562-985-5590
E-MAIL: MBA@CSULB.EDU • WEBSITE: WWW.CSULB.EDU/~CBA/

The campus offers "plenty of places to eat" and "is very accommodating of wonderful group meetings and other opportunities to meet fellow students." On the downside, "because this is mostly a commuter campus, there is little or no after-school socializing." Students report that the campus itself "is beautiful and big enough to keep you in shape walking from place to place." Overall, students experience a "very laid-back atmosphere" on campus and point out that despite this, "everyone is still constantly focused on the tasks at hand."

## Admissions

Undergraduate GPA and GMAT score are the most important factors in admissions decisions at CSULB. The school requires a minimum GPA of 2.75 for the applicants' final two years' worth of undergraduate credits (either the final 60 semester credits or the final 90 quarter credits). In addition, applicants earn a minimum score of 490 on the GMAT, with a "good balance between the quantitative and verbal sections" and an analytical writing score of at least 3.0. Letters of recommendation, a personal essay, and a resume are also considered in the admissions process. The school notes that "work experience and computer experience are recommended" of all applicants.

### FINANCIAL FACTS

| | |
|---|---|
| Annual tuition (in-state/out-of-state) | $0/$7,896 |
| Fees (in-state/out-of-state) | $1,822/$3,164 |

### ADMISSIONS

| | |
|---|---|
| Admissions Selectivity Rating | 74 |
| # of applications received | 298 |
| % applicants accepted | 85 |
| % acceptees attending | 79 |
| Average GMAT | 560 |
| Range of GMAT | 480–710 |
| Average GPA | 3.3 |
| TOEFL required of international students? | yes |
| Minimum TOEFL (paper/computer) | 550/213 |
| Application fee | $55 |
| Regular application deadline | 3/30 |
| Regular notification | 5/1 |
| Deferment available? | yes |
| Maximum length of deferment | 1 semester |
| Transfer students accepted? | yes |
| Non-fall admissions? | yes |

### APPLICANTS ALSO LOOK AT

California State University—Fullerton, California State University—Los Angeles, Pepperdine University, University of California—Irvine

# CALIFORNIA STATE UNIVERSITY—SAN BERNARDINO
## COLLEGE OF BUSINESS AND PUBLIC ADMINISTRATION

## GENERAL INFORMATION
| | |
|---|---|
| Type of school | public |
| Environment | city |
| Academic calendar | quarter |

## SURVEY SAYS...
Friendly students
Happy students
Smart classrooms
*Solid preparation in:*
Presentation skills
Quantitative skills

## STUDENTS
| | |
|---|---|
| Enrollment of parent institution | 15,659 |
| Enrollment of business school | 324 |
| % male/female | 53/47 |
| % out-of-state | 1 |
| % part-time | 40 |
| % minorities | 15 |
| % international | 54 |
| Average age at entry | 30 |
| Average years work experience at entry | 5 |

## ACADEMICS
| | |
|---|---|
| **Academic Experience Rating** | **73** |
| Student/faculty ratio | 20:1 |
| Profs interesting rating | 89 |
| Profs accessible rating | 80 |
| % female faculty | 17 |
| % minority faculty | 6 |

## JOINT DEGREES
Claremont Graduate University (CGU) has an articulate PhD program in Information Science with CSUSB's MBA Program. As many as 54 CSUSB quarter units can be counted toward your PhD at CGU.

## Academics

The MBA program at California State University—San Bernardino is "designed for the working professional," with most classes meeting twice weekly in the evenings. Students appreciate the flexibility of the program and also love the way the school "beats the brush establishing student demand for a course. Courses are added when people respond in numbers that they need, and others are deleted based on this same criteria." Best of all, they love the "excellent return on investment" this low-priced program offers. CSUSB operates on a quarterly academic schedule. The MBA program requires 48 quarter units consisting of: seven core courses (accounting, financial theory, information management, organization theory, global corporate strategy, marketing, and operations); and five electives in one of seven concentrations (accounting, finance, entrepreneurship, information management, management, marketing management, and supply chain management). In addition, all students must create a portfolio of coursework, to be reviewed by faculty, and must complete either a comprehensive project or pass a comprehensive written examination in their area of concentration.

Students speak highly of CSUSB's program in supply chain management, where "students have competed against better-known schools and kick their butts. The small class size and attention to students serves CSUSB well." They also praise the finance and entrepreneurship programs. The latter is strengthened by the College of Business' Inland Empire Center for Entrepreneurship, a research center that promotes entrepreneurship in the surrounding area. Students report that faculty in all areas "seek to challenge the students, and they are more interested in learning rather than quantitative exam scores. They act as facilitators rather than dictators, and that is very motivating." Students also tell us that their "professors are real people who genuinely care about your academic and professional goals. Most professors have 'real-life' business experience and are not entrenched in academia."

CSUSB offers other strengths as well. The computer labs "are open extended hours and 99 percent of the stuff works." With more than 400 computer workstations in the business school facility, students generally have an easy time getting a workstation when they need one. The administration "does a satisfactory job considering the state financial mess." Finally, "the outside-of-class opportunities are very diverse." One student reports, "During my time at CSUSB I took an internship that allowed me face time with the CFO and vice president of a Fortune 500 company."

## Career and Placement

The Career Development Center at CSUSB serves all students at the university—undergraduate and graduate. Counselors there offer workshops in interviewing, resume writing, and job-search strategies. The office arranges on-campus interviews and alumni meet-and-greets, and also maintains a database of job listings. A few students feel that "there needs to be more interaction between the school and alumni and businesses in the area to develop more school programs and help students with job placement," but the school's newly formed Business Alliance group should help. Employers likely to hire CSUSB MBAs include Arrowhead Credit Union, GE Transportation, Enterprise Rent-A-Car, American Express Financial, ESRI, Arthur Anderson, FEMA, Wells Fargo, and almost all the regional accounting firms, banks, and credit unions.

## Student Life and Environment

The College of Business and Public Administration is located in the 10-year-old Jack H. Brown Hall, a modern facility that suits the needs of the program. Students describe the campus as "a little oasis in San Bernardino. You drive on a smog-filled freeway, and

DIRECTOR OF ADMISSIONS AND RECRUITMENT
5500 UNIVERSITY PARKWAY, SAN BERNARDINO, CA 92407 UNITED STATES
PHONE: 909-537-5703 • FAX: 909-537-7582
E-MAIL: MBA@CSUSB.EDU • WEBSITE: WWW.CSUSB.EDU

suddenly you see this open landscape in front of you. It is a pleasure walking around on a safe campus when the sun is shining, with the snow-covered mountains as the scenic backdrop." They also regard it as a "quiet, good place to do research because there are not a lot of recreation parks around."

Campus life is available for those with time to enjoy it. One student says, "There are many professional organizations open to MBA students. I belong to the Council of Logistics Management (CLM), Society for Human Resource Management (SHRM), and the American Production and Inventory Control Society (APICS). Our student organizations have visited operations such as Home Depot's cross-dock facility and Unilever's distribution center. The school even provided funding for all the student members of APICS who wished to attend the 2004 International Conference in San Diego." Most students, though, "do not live on or near campus. They are locally employed and attend school during the evenings." This group rarely has time for anything other than class, study, and group work.

CSUSB's student body "is split between a large contingent of foreign students and the rest, who are generally from the Inland Empire. Many students just continued their undergraduate studies and therefore lack any significant experience in the business work environment." The student body also includes "accomplished professionals returning to gain a competitive advantage over their peers due to changing market conditions." Students get along well, as one describes it: "My fellow students are an interesting, diverse group of people that have many experiences different from my own. They are what makes the environment relaxed yet professional all at the same time." Approximately "one-quarter to one-third of students live on campus or in apartments just off campus," with the rest commuting.

## Admissions

Applicants to the CSUSB MBA program must first apply for admission to the university, which requires a baccalaureate with a GPA of at least 2.5 for the final two years of undergraduate work. Students clearing this hurdle may then apply for admission to the MBA program. Applicants must submit two sets of official transcripts for all post-secondary academic work; an official GMAT score report; and a personal statement. Three letters of recommendation are recommended but are technically optional. International students must additionally provide an Affidavit of Financial Support and TOEFL scores. The minimum requirement for admission to the program is a formula score of 1050 under the formula [(undergraduate GPA 5 200) + GMAT score], with a minimum GMAT score of 470 and a minimum GPA of 2.5. No student may begin MBA work without having earned at least a C grade in the following undergraduate courses or their equivalent at another accredited institution: financial accounting I and II; microeconomics; macroeconomics; business finance; corporate finance; information management; business law; management and organization behavior; strategic management; marketing principles; business statistics; principles of supply chain management; and a grade of B or better in expository writing for administration.

| EMPLOYMENT PROFILE | |
| --- | --- |
| Career Rating | 74 |
| Average starting salary | $50,000 |

### FINANCIAL FACTS

| | |
| --- | --- |
| Annual tuition (in-state/out-of-state) | $0/$0 |
| Fees (in-state/out-of-state) | $3,500/$3,500 |
| Books and supplies | $1,500 |
| Room & board (on/off-campus) | $9,000/$12,000 |
| % of students receiving aid | 33 |
| % of first-year students receiving aid | 33 |
| % of students receiving loans | 33 |
| Average award package | $6,625 |

### ADMISSIONS

| | |
| --- | --- |
| Admissions Selectivity Rating | 72 |
| # of applications received | 225 |
| % applicants accepted | 74 |
| % acceptees attending | 57 |
| Average GMAT | 525 |
| Range of GMAT | 470–690 |
| Average GPA | 3.2 |
| TOEFL required of international students? | yes |
| Minimum TOEFL (paper/computer) | 550/213 |
| Application fee | $55 |
| International application fee | $55 |
| Regular application deadline | 7/1 |
| Regular notification | 9/1 |
| Early decision program? | yes |
| ED deadline/notification | 2/1 / 6/1 |
| Deferment available? | yes |
| Maximum length of deferment | 1 year |
| Transfer students accepted? | yes |
| Transfer application policy | |
| Students may transfer 9 credits from an AACSB-accredited institution, pending approval. | |
| Non-fall admissions? | yes |
| Need-blind admissions? | yes |

### APPLICANTS ALSO LOOK AT

California State Polytechnic University—Pomona, California State University—Fullerton, California State University—Los Angeles, University of California—Riverside

# CARNEGIE MELLON UNIVERSITY
## TEPPER SCHOOL OF BUSINESS

## Academics

Carnegie Mellon's Tepper School of Business prides itself on the lengths to which it goes "to fully integrate course curriculum throughout the campus community." The school's unique "cross-campus curriculum builds industry depth in tandem with business fundamentals," according to the school. The result is "a borderless b-school [that can quickly adapt to incorporate] emerging and high-growth industries." Students praise the approach, telling us it facilitates "opportunities to start technology-related companies with cross-campus collaboration."

Students caution that Carnegie Mellon's MBA program has a heavy quantitative emphasis, which translates into an often-burdensome workload. The upside is that it "leaves you with a skill set few other business schools can match." Students tell us that the curriculum is designed to "combine the deep quant. skills into practical understanding and intuition throughout all course work." It also means that the school has an unusually large population of engineers and computer scientists. Throughout the two-year program, "team and group work is stressed heavily, and there is a stress on effective communication." Also, "independent research projects are common."

By all accounts, the faculty at Tepper is stellar. The school touts its professors by reporting that they "are consistently represented among the highest-scoring ratings for Intellectual Capital reviews, attesting to their worldwide recognition for innovative research, peer-reviewed published papers, global consulting network as well as government and association appointments." MBAs agree, telling us, "The professors here are definitely leaders in their fields, such as Alan Meltzer in economics or Joel Stern in finance. They are all on the cutting edge of research, and they do a nice job of integrating their work into the classroom." Even better, they're "engaging and accessible outside of class." Students agree that "the academic side of this school is its real strength" and single out operations, IT, and finance as the best of the group.

About the only sore spot with students is the facility dedicated to their program. MBAs grouse, "We have too many students for too small a building. We need more study rooms for group study, more and bigger lockers, [and] more bathrooms. We need a dedicated lounge, not just an extension to the food court." Also, one student notes, "The building infrastructure has been allowed to fall apart."

## Career and Placement

Carnegie Mellon's Career Opportunities Center (COC) supplies a range of services to MBAs, including workshops on job-seeking skills and strategies, career panel presentations, counseling, mock interviews, resume review, career fairs, and alumni networking. The school maintains facilities to allow telerecruiting, which is important because "it's always a struggle to get employers to Pittsburgh. It's an unfortunate situation that is currently being approached in creative ways."

Top employers of Tepper MBAs include: Alcoa, Bank of America, Capital One, Deutsche Bank, Alex Brown, Goldman Sachs, Honeywell, IBM, McKinsey & Co., National City Corporation, PNC Bank, and Samsung Electronics. The school places 13 percent of its graduates outside the country; at least another 30 percent are placed with U.S. companies well outside Carnegie Mellon's geographic region.

LAURIE STEWART, EXECUTIVE DIRECTOR OF MASTERS ADMISSIONS
TEPPER SCHOOL OF BUSINESS, 5000 FORBES AVENUE, PITTSBURGH, PA 15213 UNITED STATES
PHONE: 412-268-2272 • FAX: 412-268-4209
E-MAIL: MBA-ADMISSIONS@ANDREW.CMU.EDU • WEBSITE: WWW.TEPPER.CMU.EDU

## Student Life and Environment

Carnegie Mellon MBAs "are always very busy" with course work, especially during their first two semesters, which are "very, very intense, with five core classes at a time." Second year "offers some more opportunities for socializing." All students try to find time for "the regular Thursday night bar crawl and free beer and food at school at 5 P.M. every Friday." Students tell us, "Social committee parties are also very well attended." Most events are open "not only to students of the MBA program but also to their friends, family, and spouses." Social life is made somewhat more manageable by the size of the school. As one student explains, "I enjoy very much being at a medium-sized school. You get to know most of the people, and you develop life-lasting friendships. Even though students work hard, you can always find someone to chat and relax [with]."

The program is also home to some 20-odd student clubs, ranging from professional and minority interest clubs to those with extracurricular foci, such as the golf club, the wine club, and the roadrunners club. Tepper MBAs somehow find time to publish a weekly newsletter, the whimsical *Robber Barons* (whose motto is "All the news that fits, we print").

Although its many assets are hardly a secret to residents, Pittsburgh often surprises out-of-towners who arrive expecting a decrepit steel town. MBAs tell us, "Pittsburgh is a better town than I ever expected. Full of culture and entertainment, it is not the steel town of old." The city has enjoyed a renaissance over the past decade and is now home to "great cultural [and] music opportunities for a midsized city. There's lots of interesting development being done around Pittsburgh." Students are especially partial to the "great local bars" where they often run into people just like themselves; "young professionals in Pittsburgh are a small, tight-knit group," students report.

## Admissions

Carnegie Mellon requires the following of MBA applicants: undergraduate transcripts (and graduate transcripts, if applicable), GMAT scores, TOEFL scores (for students whose native language is not English), two letters of recommendation, essays, and a resume/employment record. Post-undergraduate work experience is not required, although "candidates with post-undergraduate professional experience have, everything else equal, a better chance for admission." Most of those admitted to the program arrive with two to eight years of work experience. Minority recruiting is facilitated through Connections Weekend, a conference for prospective minority students (usually occurring in December) and through participation in the Consortium for Graduate Study and Management.

## FINANCIAL FACTS

| | |
|---|---|
| Annual tuition | $38,800 |
| Fees | $384 |
| Books and supplies | $3,325 |
| Room & board | $12,755 |
| % of students receiving aid | 85 |
| % of first-year students receiving aid | 81 |
| % of students receiving loans | 85 |
| % of students receiving grants | 61 |
| Average award package | $47,839 |
| Average grant | $6,974 |
| Average student loan debt | $59,346 |

## ADMISSIONS

| | |
|---|---|
| **Admissions Selectivity Rating** | **95** |
| # of applications received | 1,296 |
| % applicants accepted | 42 |
| % acceptees attending | 53 |
| Average GMAT | 692 |
| Range of GMAT | 660–720 |
| Average GPA | 3.38 |
| TOEFL required of international students? | yes |
| Minimum TOEFL (paper/computer) | 600/100 |
| Application fee | $100 |
| International application fee | $100 |
| Regular application deadline | |
| Regular notification | |
| Application deadline/notification | |
| Round 1: | 11/14 / 1/16 |
| Round 2: | 1/9 / 3/13 |
| Round 3: | 3/20 / 5/1 |
| Round 4: | 5/1 / 6/5 |
| Early decision program? | yes |
| ED deadline/notification | 11/14 / 1/16 |
| Need-blind admissions? | yes |

## APPLICANTS ALSO LOOK AT

Cornell University, Duke University, Massachusetts Institute of Technology, New York University, The University of Chicago, University of Michigan, University of Pennsylvania

| EMPLOYMENT PROFILE | | | | |
|---|---|---|---|---|
| **Career Rating** | **94** | **Grads employed by field:** | **% avg. salary:** | |
| **Primary source of full-time job acceptances** | | Finance | 44 | $83,621 |
| | | Marketing | 12 | $85,732 |
| School-facilitated activities | 109 (62%) | MIS | 3 | $84,083 |
| Graduate-facilitated activities | 60 (34%) | Operations | 7 | $82,000 |
| Unknown | 7 (4%) | Strategic Planning | 3 | $91,020 |
| | | Consulting | 23 | $99,468 |
| Average starting salary | $87,466 | General Management | 5 | $82,751 |
| Percent employed | 89 | Other | 3 | $59,246 |

# CASE WESTERN RESERVE UNIVERSITY
## WEATHERHEAD SCHOOL OF MANAGEMENT

## Academics

"The greatest strengths at Weatherhead," MBAs in Case Western Reserve's business school explain, "are innovation, commitment, and energy. This school is continuously looking for ways to stand out and be recognized, and they have done an excellent job." A "beautiful new building" with "great infrastructure—a wired building and multimedia classrooms, LAN, and wireless networks"—plays a role in Weatherhead's forward-thinking approach, but it's the curriculum and the professors who teach it that truly occupy center stage. A focus on organizational behavior, "a field in which Weatherhead is a world leader," helps define the Weatherhead way. One MBA explains, "All the current research has shown that effective organizations have resonant leaders. I believe Case's program is unique in that they incorporate this training into their management degree." However, this approach has its critics; one student complains, "The school's curriculum is dominated by organization behavior thought, often to the detriment of the more conventional business school courses. The school aims to be 'unique,' for better and for worse." But many of the MBAs approve enthusiastically. Students also speak highly of Weatherhead's offerings in finance and entrepreneurship.

Students are even more united in their praise of Weatherhead's faculty. One MBA writes, "Professors are the top in their field. The organizational behavior, entrepreneurship, and marketing faculty are all on the boards of *Fortune* 500 companies and bring a real-life experience to the table at each class. Many faculty have written 'the book' on their subject matters or contributed to another's book." Because "Weatherhead is smaller than many of the top business schools, [it] allows for a great deal of interaction. I see my professors around the building, and they are always very friendly and happy to chat." Administrators are also "wholly committed to the students. There is an energy that flows through the building, and it is contagious." Curriculum highlights include the Second Year Action Learning Project, "a great consulting opportunity for graduate business students to assist local companies with real issues." Teamwork and group projects are emphasized throughout the two-year program.

## Career and Placement

All on-campus interviews, information sessions, referrals, and resume books are processed through Weatherhead's e-Recruiting system (known as WeRS); students may check the WeRS website to keep abreast of all special events including club events and activities (career services are handled through the Career and Student Life Center). The school holds Career Expos in both the fall and spring terms. While some students feel that "the Career and Student Life Center is a great resource for everything from mock interviews, resume review, and job leads," others complain that "the career office has been largely unhelpful." One MBA notes, "In my experience, [they] focus too much on grooming the students and not enough on attracting quality companies to campus." Another MBA reconciles these disparate views by explaining that "the career services office is working hard to make improvements and be proactive in the face of a down economy. [However], they have a ways to go and need to focus on their ability to coordinate and stay on top of things."

Major employers of Case Western MBAs include American Greetings, Eaton Corporation, Emerson Electric, Honeywell, Johnson Controls, Johnson & Johnson, Progressive Corporation, and Samsung. Starting salaries range from just below $53,000 (marketing) to just below $80,000 (operations). About two-thirds of all graduates remain in the Midwest when they start their careers; a little over 10 percent head overseas.

AL DiFranco, Director of Admissions
160 Peter B. Lewis Building, 10900 Euclid Avenue, Cleveland, OH 44106-7235 U.S.
Phone: 216-368-2030 • Fax: 216-368-5548
E-mail: MBA.Admission@Weatherhead.cwru.edu • Website: www.weatherhead.cwru.edu

## Student Life and Environment

Weatherhead's home is "a new building designed by Frank Gehry. The libraries and resources are tremendous, and the classroom and study facilities are state-of-the-art." One part-time student writes, "The accessibility to the latest media and technology is incredible—in fact, it's better than my company's!" The school goes to great lengths to create homey touches, which students appreciate. One student reports, "On Wednesdays, they hire music students from the Cleveland Institute of Music to play chamber music in the open foyer, which is absolutely beautiful. Nothing can compare to the feeling I have when I enter this amazingly beautiful building, hear classical music echoing through the halls, and prepare for my classes!"

Wednesday isn't the only special day at Weatherhead. Thursdays bring an event called Business Casual, "which is a chance to get something to eat and relax. Once a month the Business Casuals take on an international flair and are hosted by a different ethnic group, such as the Latin American students, [who include] salsa dancing [at the event]." At other times, "there's beer and food provided. It's enjoyable because it give us a chance to relax and socialize with our peers." Students say that throughout the week, "life is very dynamic inside the school. There are a lot of events, group of interest meetings, snacks offered for late classes—a real city inside the city, except that you know everyone!" Most students are active in a number of clubs. One MBA explains, "Course work is heavy, but it would be completely manageable if so many people weren't involved with other campus activities like clubs, speakers, events, and projects." Weatherhead MBAs are proud of the diversity of their student body. "The fact that there are more than 25 states of the United States and more than 30 countries from across the world represented teaches you to work in a very diverse environment," one student writes. Another student adds, "I feel like I have to bring a passport when I go to class; we are truly an international school." Hometown Cleveland, we're assured, "is very underrated. There are tons [of things] to do here."

## Admissions

Prospective Weatherhead students must submit undergraduate transcripts, a GMAT score, two letters of recommendation, four essay responses to questions provided by the school, and a current resume. International students must also provide TOEFL scores and a statement of financial responsibility. Interviews are conducted only at the request of the Admission Committee. The committee pays close attention to "diversity of work and/or educational experience; demonstrated leadership abilities; and demonstrated community involvement." Minority recruitment is facilitated by "on-campus scholars weekends and networking with minority professional associations and Weatherhead alumni. [Also,] referrals from minority alumni are given an application-fee waiver." The school notes that applicants improve their chances of admission by applying during the early admission rounds.

### FINANCIAL FACTS

| | |
|---|---|
| Annual tuition | $30,500 |
| Fees | $910 |
| Books and supplies | $2,032 |
| Room & board | $14,474 |
| % of students receiving aid | 85 |
| % of first-year students receiving aid | 85 |
| % of students receiving loans | 55 |
| % of students receiving grants | 80 |
| Average award package | $32,577 |
| Average grant | $15,275 |
| Average student loan debt | $43,369 |

### ADMISSIONS

| | |
|---|---|
| Admissions Selectivity Rating | 74 |
| # of applications received | 388 |
| % applicants accepted | 76 |
| % acceptees attending | 57 |
| Average GMAT | 555 |
| Range of GMAT | 500–640 |
| Average GPA | 3.13 |
| TOEFL required of international students? | yes |
| Minimum TOEFL (paper/computer) | 600/250 |
| Application fee | $50 |
| International application fee | $50 |
| Regular application deadline | 3/1 |
| Regular notification | 4/15 |
| Application deadline/notification | |
| Round 1: | 12/1 / 1/31 |
| Round 2: | 1/15 / 3/1 |
| Round 3: | 3/1 / 4/15 |
| Round 4: | 3/1 / 6/1 |
| Transfer students accepted? | yes |
| Transfer application policy | |
| Students may transfer 6 credits from an AACSB-accredited institution, pending approval. | |
| Non-fall admissions? | yes |
| Need-blind admissions? | yes |

### APPLICANTS ALSO LOOK AT

The Ohio State University, University of Michigan, University of Notre Dame, University of Pittsburgh, University of Virginia, Vanderbilt University, Washington University

| EMPLOYMENT PROFILE | | | | |
|---|---|---|---|---|
| Career Rating | 85 | Grads employed by field: | % | avg. salary: |
| Primary source of full-time job acceptances | | Finance | 37 | $69,067 |
| | | Marketing | 39 | $65,895 |
| School-facilitated activities | 29 (51%) | Operations | 6 | $57,200 |
| Graduate-facilitated activities | 28 (49%) | Consulting | 11 | $85,500 |
| | | Other | 7 | $71,000 |
| Average starting salary | $68,662 | | | |
| Percent employed | 75 | | | |

# CATHOLIC UNIVERSITY OF LEUVEN & GHENT UNIVERSITY
## VLERICK LEUVEN GHENT MANAGEMENT SCHOOL

## Academics

Executive development programs are huge at Vlerick Leuven Ghent: The Belgian business school hosts over 3,000 managers in its open-enrollment seminars and company-specific programs, but the school is also home to a growing MBA program, one whose stature around the world is growing. The school currently offers a full-time English language MBA at its Leuven campus, a part-time Dutch language MBA at its Ghent campus, and a part-time English language MBA at both campuses. The full-time general MBA can be completed in one year, as can master's degrees in marketing and financial management; an MBA in financial services takes two years to complete. In total, about 250 students pursue MBAs at VLG.

Vlerick Leuven Ghent was founded in 1953 by Professor Andre Vlerick; over the years it has developed associations with Ghent University and the Katholieke Universiteit Leuven, and today it serves as the autonomous management school of these prestigious universities, the two largest in Belgium. Association with these two more established schools provides a solid research base; the school's autonomy allows it to "build strong ties with the business community" and "enables it to respond to the development needs of this community in an optimal way," according to the school's brochure. As one student observes, "The fact that the school is backed up by two recognized universities is apparent. It benefits greatly from its location and the support and research of its two parent universities."

MBA programs at Vlerick Leuven Ghent maintain "a strong international focus" derived not only from the curriculum but also from the student body. One student writes, "The basic strength of this program is the dual academic-practical approach. On the one hand, the academic orientation of the professors builds a solid knowledge foundation, while on the other, the experiences of the rest of the multicultural group enrich the whole educational experience." Students tell us that "professors and academics show a lot of respect for the audience, are extremely knowledgeable, and have in many cases extensive personal activity in the fields of management they are covering." MBAs here especially enjoy "the specialization seminars in entrepreneurship and doing business in Europe." Many students feel, however, that "the international MBA could use more international faculty. Most teachers are from Belgium." Students also report that "the workload is extremely heavy," but add that the benefits of the program—good value in a major economic center of the European Union—outweigh any shortfalls.

## Career and Placement

The Career Services Office (CSO) at Vlerick Leuven Ghent organizes regular career events on campus; the office also coordinates multi-campus events and online recruiting. In an effort to keep pace with the internationalization of the school's curriculum and student body, the CSO has spent the last few years developing business contacts throughout the world to supplement its already strong base of Belgian businesses. The CSO also offers counseling services and advice on resume-writing, interviewing, searching for jobs, and salary negotiation. According to the school's website, "The intention [of the CSO's efforts] is to develop a career management program that throughout the entire year will operate as an integral part of the various courses, with presentations, interactive workshops, and networking events." The office also plans to develop "a lifelong career guidance program, whereby alumni of Vlerick Leuven Ghent Management School will become even more deeply involved in activities organized by the CSO." Students tell us these efforts are working, praising the "great alumni network."

CHARLOTTE DE VOLDER, PROGRAMME COORDINATOR
VLAMINGENSTRAAT 83, 3000 LEUVEN, REEP 1, 9000 GHENT, VB 3000 BELGIUM
PHONE: 001-32-16-32-35-89 • FAX: 001-32-16-32-35-81
E-MAIL: MBA@VLERICK.BE • WEBSITE: WWW.VLERICK.COM

## Student Life and Environment

Full-time students at Vlerick Leuven Ghent experience a nonstop academic grind. One student reports, "Life in school starts every day (including exams period, studying for the exams, most of weekends) at 9:00 P.M. and ends at 12:00 A.M. After that, individual work at home is usually required. In this frame, the quality of life can't be good. But then again, this is a commitment well known before the enrollment, so its consistency is remarkable. I personally face time problems and issues with domestic tasks (laundry, house cleaning, nutrition). I skipped visiting my home country at Christmas to catch up with the material I needed to know . . . and this is the situation that I face [at] Easter." Some here manage to squeeze in some free time; they describe "an excellent lifestyle in the very small and safe student town of Leuven, with lots of social, sports, and cultural activities." One student notes, "Belgium is a beer-drinker's paradise. Need I say more?"

Students "represent every continent, which makes participating in the group a very interesting learning experience." They are "active social animals and real team players, and students are very much diversified in professional and academic experience and competencies."

## Admissions

Admission to the Vlerick Leuven Ghent Management School requires an undergraduate degree from an institution "recognized by the relevant authorities of the home country." Work experience "is beneficial but not required." Other admissions requirements depend on the method of application; students may choose the "distance procedure" or the "on-campus assessment procedure." Both require a completed application, a resume, a copy of one's passport, and official copies of all post-secondary transcripts and diplomas. The distance procedure requires, in addition, an official GMAT score report, an official TOEFL score report (students whose native language is English are exempted from this requirement), two letters of recommendation, and a personal statement. On-campus assessment "requires your attendance at one of [the school's] in-house admission tests, which consist of an analytical test, a written comprehension test, and two personal interviews (a motivation interview and a management potential/knowledge interview)."

### FINANCIAL FACTS

| | |
|---|---|
| Annual tuition | $18,000 |
| Fees | $18,000 |
| Room & board | |
| (on/off-campus) | $9,000/$11,000 |
| % of students receiving aid | 10 |
| % of first-year students receiving aid | 10 |
| % of students receiving grants | 10 |
| Average award package | $60,000 |
| Average grant | $6,000 |
| Average student loan debt | $5,000 |

### ADMISSIONS

| | |
|---|---|
| **Admissions Selectivity Rating** | **94** |
| # of applications received | 300 |
| % applicants accepted | 34 |
| % acceptees attending | 53 |
| Average GMAT | 636 |
| Range of GMAT | 600–650 |
| Average GPA | 3.5 |
| TOEFL required of international students? | yes |
| Minimum TOEFL (paper/computer) | NR/255 |
| Application fee | $50 |
| International application fee | $50 |
| Regular application deadline | 6/30 |
| Regular notification | 7/14 |
| Application deadline/notification | |
| Round 1: | 1/22 / 2/1 |
| Round 2: | 3/24 / 4/1 |
| Round 3: | 6/30 / 7/14 |
| Deferment available? | yes |
| Maximum length of deferment | 1 year |
| Need-blind admissions? | yes |

### APPLICANTS ALSO LOOK AT

Bocconi University, Cranfield University, ESADE, HEC School of Management—Paris, IMD (International Institute for Management Development), INSEAD, RSM Erasmus University

### EMPLOYMENT PROFILE

| Career Rating | 85 | Grads employed by field: | % | avg. salary: |
|---|---|---|---|---|
| **Primary source of full-time job acceptances** | | Accounting | 10 | $93,000 |
| | | Finance | 15 | $93,000 |
| School-facilitated activities | 25 (45%) | Marketing | 10 | $93,000 |
| Graduate-facilitated activities | 15 (30%) | Strategic Planning | 5 | $93,000 |
| Unknown | 14 (25%) | Consulting | 15 | $93,000 |
| | | Entrepreneurship | 20 | $93,000 |
| Average starting salary | $93,000 | General Management | 10 | $93,000 |
| Percent employed | 90 | Venture Capital | 5 | $93,000 |
| | | Internet/New Media | 5 | $93,000 |
| | | Nonprofit | 5 | $93,000 |

# CHAPMAN UNIVERSITY
## THE GEORGE L. ARGYROS SCHOOL OF BUSINESS AND ECONOMICS

## GENERAL INFORMATION

| | |
|---|---|
| Type of school | private |
| Affiliation | Disciples of Christ |
| Environment | metropolis |
| Academic calendar | semester |

### SURVEY SAYS...
Friendly students
Good peer network
Smart classrooms
*Solid preparation in:*
Accounting

### STUDENTS

| | |
|---|---|
| Enrollment of parent institution | 5,554 |
| Enrollment of business school | 135 |
| % male/female | 55/45 |
| % part-time | 65 |
| % minorities | 10 |
| % international | 11 |
| Average age at entry | 26 |
| Average years work experience at entry | 4 |

### ACADEMICS

| | |
|---|---|
| **Academic Experience Rating** | **76** |
| Student/faculty ratio | 22:1 |
| Profs interesting rating | 77 |
| Profs accessible rating | 71 |
| % female faculty | 28 |
| % minority faculty | 6 |

### JOINT DEGREES
MBA/JD, 4 years

### PROMINENT ALUMNI
The Honorable George L. Argyros, CEO, Arnel and Affiliates; The Honorable Loretta Sanchez, member of U.S. Congress; David Bonior, Former member of U.S. Congress; Steve Lavin, sports analyst; Michael Bell, Tony Award nominee

## Academics

"Chapman may be a small private university, but don't underestimate the quality here. Chapman is as good as, if not better than, many of the larger universities in the U.S.," MBAs in this Orange County program tell us. One student writes, "It was not a surprise to us to see Chapman listed among 'the hidden gems' in the *Washington Post*."

Chapman's MBA program—which can be completed on either a part-time or full-time basis—loads students up with core requirements. A whopping 33 of the 52 credits necessary for graduation are devoted to the core here. Students applaud the core's "strong foundation in concepts needed for today's business" and especially its "focus on business ethics as well as typical business topics." Some here, though, "wish the school allowed [them] to devote more time to majors and concentrations, as other business schools do." Students tell us that "the greatest strengths of [their] business school is in economics and international business." The school adds that the "four research centers represent the strength of the school: the Anderson Center for Economic Research, the Center for Real Estate, the Ralph Leatherby Center for Entrepreneurship and Ethics, and the Walter Schmid Center for International Business." Chapman also offers an Executive MBA program.

Chapman professors "are very accessible outside of class, and they help you to understand ideas or concepts not fully understood during class time. During projects they are helpful in steering you to the right path to get more justifiable solutions." Several students comment that they "would like to see more international faculty at Chapman." One writes, "The whole world is now heading towards globalization. To have international faculty come and teach at Chapman would open entirely new perspectives. This will strengthen Chapman's International Business program even more." Even those who see room for improvement, though, report satisfaction with the school. One MBA explains, "This program is as rigorous as top programs, but, unlike at other larger universities, you won't get lost here at Chapman. Not only do the faculty and staff know you by name but you'll also build a strong bond with the faculty, staff, and other students even after you have graduated, resulting in global networking."

## Career and Placement

Chapman's Career Development Center provides services—including job fairs, counseling, workshops, and online databases—to the entire student body of the university. Students wish there were "more activities geared toward MBA students. The only job fair I've heard of consisted of mail-order businesses and UPS. What if you don't want to work there? A professional career fair would be nice, or a job board/placement office dedicated solely to the business school." Students also bemoan the fact that "there is little communication with the school's alumni." Recognizing the need for improvement in this area, the school's administration is opening a new MBA Career Management Center in summer 2006. Additionally, the university is unveiling a state-of-the-art alumni database, which promises to significantly increase networking activity between students and alumni.

## Student Life and Environment

Chapman University has an enrollment of approximately 5,500, just under one-third of which represents graduate students. The business program is relatively small, with just under 140 MBAs, most attending part-time. The MBA population here is "a good mix, with some really smart and experienced students, and others who are book-smart, funny, nice, friendly, and helpful." Students' ages "run from early 20s to 40s. Ethnic back-

DEBRA GONDA, ASSOCIATE DIRECTOR
BECKMAN HALL, ONE UNIVERSITY DRIVE, ORANGE, CA 92866 UNITED STATES
PHONE: 877-CHAP-MBA • FAX: 714-997-6757
E-MAIL: MBA@CHAPMAN.EDU • WEBSITE: WWW.CHAPMAN.EDU/ARGYROS/

## FINANCIAL FACTS

| | |
|---|---|
| Annual tuition | $18,850 |
| Fees | $0 |
| Books and supplies | $1,650 |
| % of students receiving aid | 64 |
| % of students receiving grants | 25 |
| Average grant | $4,500 |

## ADMISSIONS

| | |
|---|---|
| Admissions Selectivity Rating | 78 |
| # of applications received | 108 |
| % applicants accepted | 57 |
| % acceptees attending | 85 |
| Average GMAT | 520 |
| Range of GMAT | 460–580 |
| Average GPA | 3.1 |
| TOEFL required of international students? | yes |
| Minimum TOEFL (paper/computer) | 550/216 |
| Application fee | $50 |
| International application fee | $50 |
| Regular application deadline | 7/1 |
| Regular notification | rolling |
| Deferment available? | yes |
| Maximum length of deferment | 1 year |
| Transfer students accepted? | yes |
| Transfer application policy Students may transfer 6 credits, pending approval. | |
| Non-fall admissions? | yes |
| Need-blind admissions? | yes |

## APPLICANTS ALSO LOOK AT

California State University—Fullerton, Pepperdine University, University of California—Irvine, University of Southern California

grounds and nationalities vary too, as well as types and degree of work experience. The gender mix is about 50–50." MBAs describe "a good, competitive yet friendly atmosphere with students. Everyone pushes fellow students to do better and go that extra mile, and not just to get a good grade but to understand the material."

Because "Chapman is a commuter school, most people don't relocate to take classes, and not many people are looking for additional friends. Between work, school, and the friends we already have, it doesn't leave much time for classmates." The school does plan occasional events for MBAs, though. One student writes, "The business school usually hosts a get-together event two to three times a semester, whether it's just an hour of eating pizza, sipping coffee, and chatting with the dean, associate deans, and faculty, or a soccer match between the faculty and the business students. Even though each of these events usually doesn't last longer than two hours, these types of activities have helped create a strong bond among the students, faculty, and staff." The school also hosts "a Distinguished Speaker series, where a CEO comes in and talks about their experiences and [students] get free dinner," as well as a dinner program in which students have the opportunity to share a meal and a conversation with highly respected members of Orange County and Southern California. Students appreciate that "the campus is located in a very nice area and has extremely good on-campus facilities, considering the small overall size of the school."

## Admissions

The Admissions Office factors "academic performance, leadership ability, work experience, and communication skills" into each of its decisions. The school requires a minimum GPA of 2.5 for the applicants' final two years' worth of undergraduate credits (either the final 60 semester credits or the final 90 quarter credits). All applications must include an official GMAT score report, sealed copies of official transcripts for all postsecondary academic work, two letters of recommendation "from individuals familiar with the applicant's academic or professional abilities," and a completed application with a personal statement "explaining why the applicant is interested in pursuing a graduate degree at Chapman." Two years of business-related work experience is preferred. International applicants must "submit a certified statement demonstrating financial ability to cover all education and living expenses for the full period of time for which the student is applying, [and] all international students, except those from countries where English is the primary language, must take the TOEFL examination and achieve a score of 550 or higher on the paper-based test (or 216 on the computerized version)." Admission to the Executive MBA program requires at least seven years of professional experience and a one-on-one on-campus interview.

# THE CHINESE UNIVERSITY OF HONG KONG
## FACULTY OF BUSINESS ADMINISTRATION

## Academics

China, it can be said without fear of contradiction, has one of the world's fastest-growing economies, and opportunities abound there for the savvy businessperson. The various MBA programs at the Chinese University of Hong Kong offer a foot in the door for students interested in those opportunities. As one of the region's older MBA programs, CUHK has a deep and loyal alumni network set to help newly minted MBAs make their mark in Asia. Even more to students' advantage, the school has a solid reputation in the region; *Asia Inc.* magazine has named the CUMBA program the best in the Asian Pacific for three consecutive years (2002–2004).

A broad range of options are available at CUHK. Besides its full-time and part-time MBA, the school offers more specific MBAs in finance and health care as well as its One MBA, Global Executive MBA Program, a truly international degree conferred jointly by the program's five participating programs (which are spread across four continents).

Students report that the CUMBA teaching method has "adopted quite a lot of the U.S. university systems. A large proportion of professors got their PhDs in the U.S., so their teaching styles are quite open-minded. Plus, they all know that lecturing is not their only function. They understand how to guide the students in their thinking and encourage class discussions." Instruction styles include "lots of case studies as well as in-class exercises and discussion. The faculty brings their experiences to the classroom, giving the material real-world application and making theories relevant to students." MBAs reap the best of American and local approaches; "Some professors coming from the U.S. have relatively more international business experiences, while local professors have extensive local business exposure," one MBA student explains. The international student body, we're told, "brings a scope of ideas to our study. Courses in HR, marketing, and global business wouldn't be nearly as interesting without such a range of viewpoints in the classroom. With professors facilitating discussion, the students really bring so much to the learning process."

CUHK administrators "are very interested in the quality of the education we are receiving," notes one student. "They are always interested in students' feedback about professors, classes, and courses we would like to see in the future." Students no doubt tell administrators how much they love the school's mentoring program. One happy student reports, "Through the mentorship program, I have the opportunity to get to know my 'big brother' (who works in a senior position of a top investment house) and learn from his wisdom and experience both personally and professionally."

## Career and Placement

Students give good marks to the Chinese University's Career Planning and Development Centre, which provides career services to CUMBAs. They save their highest praise, however, for the university's alumni network, explaining that "CUMBA has the longest history in HK as well as in Asia. That's why our large alumni network is a key strength of the school." Graduates who wish to remain in Hong Kong or China "will find a lot of support here," while students happily discover that "alumni act as mentors for students and give students an alternative to professors for feedback and help in locating jobs, networking with business professionals in the area, and giving guidance in making career choices. This is a great help to students, especially those from outside Hong Kong."

Major employers of CUMBAs include ABN AMRO Bank; The Boston Consulting Group; CalTEX Companies (Greater China), Ltd.; Citibank; Credit Suisse First Boston (HK), Ltd.; Dah Sing Bank; DBS Kwong On Bank; Deloitte Consulting; Goldman Sachs; Grey Advertising (HK); HKSAR Government; Hong Kong & China Gas Company, Ltd.;

| FINANCIAL FACTS | |
|---|---|
| Annual tuition | $26,654 |
| Books and supplies | $10,974 |
| Room & board | $3,000 |
| Average grant | $3,543 |

HSBC; JPMorgan Chase; KPMG; Mass Transit Railway Corporation; Merrill Lynch (Asia); Nestle (HK); and UBS Warburg.

## Student Life and Environment

The student body at CUHK comes from "a good mix of all types of backgrounds, including age, career, and country of origin." MBAs brag that they "are quite an international family. Through group projects and assignments, we have learned how to cooperate with classmates from different backgrounds and countries as well as how to allocate resources effectively through teamwork." Local students pitch in to help internationals adjust to life in Hong Kong. One helpful local student reports, "As we have a lot of nonlocal students (from countries such as the U.S., Canada, France, Japan, Korea, China, and India), we always organize activities outside campus such as camping, hiking, or eating Hong Kong–style food. As a local student, I like to bring the Hong Kong culture to [nonlocal students], and at the same time, I can learn their culture as well."

The CUHK curriculum places a heavy load on students, so students find themselves "spending quite a lot of time on team projects outside class." Extracurricular life also includes career-related activities such as "meeting local business leaders through executive talks." Students "also organize firm visits so that [they] have more connections to the business community." Despite their many school responsibilities, most MBAs still find time for occasional fun. Students report, "Sometimes the MBA Students Association will hold some extracurricular activities like a Halloween party, a boat cruise, football games, or karaoke." They also point out, however, that "with such a small program, student clubs and other activities are not so easy to organize."

CUHK's "beautiful campus [is] very spacious, with many trees and recreational infrastructure. This atmosphere is excellent for studying and living." Facilities are also top-notch; students tell us, "The learning infrastructure is excellent. We have wireless broadband network in every classroom, canteen, and building. We have numerous computer laboratories (30 to 50 computers in each room), four university libraries, and sufficient hostels for us." When students want to leave campus, they find that "transportation is excellent. We could take a bus/mini-bus/subway/train, and it's about 10 minutes to town."

## Admissions

The MBA program at the Chinese University of Hong Kong requires applicants to submit undergraduate transcripts (except in extraordinary circumstances, a minimum B average is required), GMAT scores, personal essays, and letters of recommendation. An interview, which can be conducted by telephone, is required. English proficiency (as demonstrated by TOEFL or IELTS test scores, for non-native English speakers) is also required. Applicants to the full-time MBA program are expected to have three years of post-qualification work experience; part-time applicants should have at least that.

### ADMISSIONS

| | |
|---|---|
| Admissions Selectivity Rating | 86 |
| # of applications received | 870 |
| % applicants accepted | 66 |
| % acceptees attending | 74 |
| Average GMAT | 623 |
| Average GPA | 3.3 |
| Application fee | $25 |
| International application fee | $25 |
| Regular application deadline | 2/28 |
| Regular notification | 4/30 |
| Early decision program? | yes |
| ED deadline/notification | 1/21 / 3/31 |
| Deferment available? | yes |
| Maximum length of deferment | 1 year |
| Need-blind admissions? | yes |

### EMPLOYMENT PROFILE

| Career Rating | 73 | Grads employed by field: | % | avg. salary: |
|---|---|---|---|---|
| Average starting salary | $42,307 | Accounting | 8 | NR |
| Percent employed | 80 | Finance | 21 | NR |
| | | Human Resources | 4 | NR |
| | | Marketing | 25 | NR |
| | | MIS | 4 | NR |
| | | Operations | 2 | NR |
| | | Consulting | 14 | NR |
| | | General Management | 4 | NR |
| | | Other | 18 | NR |

# THE CITADEL
## SCHOOL OF BUSINESS ADMINISTRATION

### GENERAL INFORMATION
| | |
|---|---|
| Type of school | public |
| Environment | city |
| Academic calendar | semester |

### SURVEY SAYS...
Students love Charleston, SC
Happy students
*Solid preparation in:*
Accounting
Communication/interpersonal skills
Presentation skills

### STUDENTS
| | |
|---|---|
| Enrollment of business school | 260 |
| % male/female | 50/50 |
| % part-time | 90 |
| % minorities | 10 |
| % international | 5 |
| Average age at entry | 27 |

### ACADEMICS
| | |
|---|---|
| **Academic Experience Rating** | **68** |
| Student/faculty ratio | 15:1 |
| Profs interesting rating | 91 |
| Profs accessible rating | 80 |
| % female faculty | 29 |

### JOINT DEGREES
PharmD/MBA Program, 4 years;
MBA with concentration in Health
Care Management, 2–6 years; MBA
concentration in Sports
Management; MD/MBA

## Academics

The Citadel offers "the only AACSB-accredited program in Charleston" as well as "a reasonably priced degree"—two features that attract the school's predominantly part-time student body.

The Citadel MBA is a 48-hour program consisting of 24 hours of basic required courses, 12 hours of advanced required courses, and 12 hours of electives. Students who have successfully completed equivalent courses at the undergraduate or graduate level may be permitted to waive some or all of the basic required courses. In order to qualify, students must have completed the work within the previous five years. Electives may be used to develop concentrations in health care administration, hospitality/tourism, or international business. The Citadel also offers two joint degrees: a PharmD/MBA and an MD/MBA.

Students report, "Citadel professors seem incredibly committed to their craft. Most have been at it for decades yet bring verve and enthusiasm to each class." Students appreciate that "professors understand that most of us work over 40 hours per week. They spread out the course load so we can manage it more easily." This spirit of accommodation permeates the entire school. One student writes, "I have found that at any point in my academic career in the Citadel's business school that I have been able to approach all administrators and faculty with ease. Overall, the business school has a family feel, and everyone is looking out for your best interest." In the realm of improvements, some students would like to see the school offer a wider range of electives, and some feel that the faculty needs to be broadened. One student explains, "Many of the core courses are taught by the same professor (i.e., one professor teaches all business law courses, another teaches all the marketing courses, etc.). For someone like me, who has no business background, it seems we receive a very narrow view of the business world."

## Career and Placement

The Citadel Career Center provides career services to all students on the Citadel campus. The office provides counseling services; workshops in interviewing, resume building, and job search strategies; career fairs; online job databases; and on-campus recruiting and interviewing. However, much of the office's work is geared toward serving the school's much-larger undergraduate population rather than MBAs and others enrolled in the College of Graduate and Professional Studies.

## Student Life and Environment

Citadel MBAs are typically "hardworking individuals juggling full-time jobs, a family, and classes at night." Even so, many try to make time to participate in the school's popular mentoring program, in which "interested students are paired with someone in the community who works or worked in the student's desired career field." The program capitalizes on the fact that "there are many successful retirees in the area who are interested in advising students," but also includes "many accomplished business professionals still working in the field. The program gives the student real insight into that profession rather than the candy-coated version that someone who has never worked in that profession may give."

Students here enjoy other extracurricular options as well. "As part of the Leadership Forum, guest speakers from all over the country come to the Citadel to share their experiences with students," we're told. Plus, "the MBA Association is instrumental in developing relationships among students and professors. It's a great organization to be a part

MARNA STILLEY, MBA ADMINISTRATOR
171 MOULTRIE STREET, CHARLESTON, SC 29409 UNITED STATES
PHONE: 843-953-5089 • FAX: 843-953-7630
E-MAIL: CGPS@CITADEL.EDU • WEBSITE: CITADEL.EDU/CSBA/

of." Students also find time in their busy schedules for "occasional social gatherings throughout the year. They range from beers at the local tavern to sit-down dinners in five-star restaurants."

Citadel MBAs "are extremely motivated and resourceful. Everyone greets each other with that wonderful Charleston charm." Commenting on the student body, one student notes that it is "ethnically diverse, in that 10 to 15 percent of my classmates are from other countries and cultures such as Africa, the Middle East, Europe, Asia, and South America." Students "attend classes during the evening either on campus or at a central-ized city location called the Low Country Graduate Center. Unlike most undergraduate classes, the students really want to be there and are always eager to participate in class discussions." As one student says, "I only go at night, but I really enjoy the beautiful, quiet campus that's full of diversity and a willingness to learn."

## Admissions

Students may apply for admission to the Citadel School of Business Administration for the fall, spring, or summer term. Applicants must submit all of the following materials: a completed application form with application fee; sealed copies of official transcripts for all post-secondary work (transcripts representing work completed outside the U.S. should be translated and evaluated by an academic credential evaluation organization recognized by the Citadel); a sealed official copy of the GMAT score report (a minimum score of 400 is required); two letters of reference from undergraduate professors, business associates, and/or supervisors in government or military service; a resume; and two short personal essays. International students whose first language is not English are required to submit official TOEFL score reports (a minimum score of 550 is required). The school may request an applicant to submit to an interview; otherwise, interviews are not required. The school offers provisional admission to some candidates; provisional status remains in effect until the student has completed all basic courses with a GPA of at least 3.0.

## ADMISSIONS

| | |
|---|---|
| **Admissions Selectivity Rating** | **60\*** |
| # of applications received | 71 |
| % applicants accepted | 89 |
| Average GMAT | 538 |
| TOEFL required of international students? | yes |
| Minimum TOEFL (paper/computer) | 550/NR |
| Application fee | $30 |
| Regular application deadline | 7/20 |
| Regular notification | 7/20 |
| Deferment available? | yes |
| Maximum length of deferment | 1 year |
| Transfer students accepted? | yes |

Transfer application policy
A maximum of six hours credit for graduate courses from an accredit-ed institution (including consortia and AACSB-accredited institutions) may be approved for transfer (except BADM 635), provided: (1) that those courses are determined to be equivalent to one of the advanced or elective courses at The Citadel, (2) that grades of "B" or better were received in the courses being considered for transfer credit, and (3) that credit for the courses was earned within the five years prior to admission into The Citadel MBA program.

| | |
|---|---|
| Non-fall admissions? | yes |
| Need-blind admissions? | yes |

# CITY UNIVERSITY OF NEW YORK—BARUCH COLLEGE

## ZICKLIN SCHOOL OF BUSINESS

## *Academics*

"Finance and accounting are known to be great subjects to study" at Baruch College's Zicklin School of Business, an MBA program that offers full-time study but caters primarily to the flex-time student. Baruch offers students three program options: a conventional full-time honors cohort-based MBA program (about 105 students), an Accelerated Part-Time Program (APT) that is less selective than the honors program but also a cohort program scheduled to allow graduation in just over two years (about 130 students), and a Flex-Time program that allows students to study toward the MBA degree at either a full- or part-time pace, switching back and forth as their work and study needs dictate (about 1,000 students).

Historically, Zicklin is known for its strengths in finance and accounting; study in finance, we're told, is enhanced by "an in-house financial trading floor with Bloomberg and Reuters" as well as the proximity of many finance bigwigs. ("There are a lot of top executives who have attended at least one [CUNY school], if not Baruch in particular," students explain, "and our administration and professors are always pulling in these types of people for guest lectures and panel discussions.") MBAs also love Baruch's "great fieldwork class, current topics in business, where each semester teams of students go on-site to a firm to solve a problem." Offerings in general management, operations, and entrepreneurship are also strong, if not as widely recognized. Professors are a mixed bag; one MBA writes, "The great teachers are committed to their students (no teaching assistants here), knowledgeable, always prepared with relevant new material, and an enthusiasm for the subject that is outstanding and contagious. The bad ones are set in their ways, not interested in the problems of the students, boring, and out-of-date." Some students happily report that the administration "is extremely concerned about quality of teaching, is taking drastic steps to improve the school's rating, and is proactively involved in all activities of the school."

Zicklin's facilities, "located in [midtown] Manhattan in a new, modern 14-story building, are equipped for multimedia integration." Undergraduates roam most of the building, but the top floor is reserved for MBAs, who love the new digs, praising the "ultracomfortable, interactive classrooms with great audiovisual capability" and the "high-tech wireless Internet connectivity" available to them. Their only complaint is that "space is at a premium, and at times a good place to study is hard to find, be that with a group using a whiteboard or just somewhere quiet to read." Most head across the street to Baruch's award-winning library to read and meet with study groups. A "good collection of online databases" helps students muddle through their case studies.

## *Career and Placement*

MBAs praise the "big efforts on career management for the students" at Zicklin; these efforts include a variety of workshops stressing the keys to successful interviewing, resume presentation, networking, and follow-up. Events held throughout the school year are designed to capitalize on alumni relations by bringing big-name grads back to campus; Baruch's Manhattan location looms large in this endeavor. The school maintains its own job-posting board; students can also access job postings at monstertrak.com.

Nearly half of Baruch's MBAs wind up in accounting and finance. Top employers include Citigroup, Colgate-Palmolive, Ernst & Young, Goldman Sachs, Lehman Brothers, and PricewaterhouseCoopers. Average starting salaries range from $53,275 (accounting) to

FRANCES MURPHY, DIRECTOR OF ADMISSIONS
ONE BERNARD BARUCH WAY, BOX H-0820, NEW YORK, NY 10010 UNITED STATES
PHONE: 646-312-1300 • FAX: 646-312-1301
E-MAIL: ZICKLINGRADADMISSIONS@BARUCH.CUNY.EDU • WEBSITE: WWW.ZICKLIN.BARUCH.CUNY.EDU

$75,000 (operations and production). The vast majority of grads remain in the Mid-Atlantic region, although some find employment overseas. MBAs note that "Baruch is historically an accounting school, and this is reflected in the companies that recruit here and what positions they recruit for."

## Student Life and Environment

"Since most students live scattered throughout New York City, the Bronx, Manhattan, Brooklyn, and Queens," students note that the Zicklin campus "lacks the typical college-campus feel. However, our school is located in the heart of New York City. There are many bars and great restaurants nearby. We have a standing Thursday night engagement at one of a few bars that are close by, and we get pretty good attendance." During the school day, MBAs keep "busy with classes, a lot of guest lectures, group assignments, and exams. Students gain the most from their school experience through working together, in formal groups and informal groups." The school's location, "in a neighborhood called Murray Hill, which has been locally renamed to 'Curry Hill' because of the plethora of amazingly great Indian restaurants nearby," places students just a few miles north of the city's famous Financial District.

Zicklin MBAs praise their fellow students as "one of the school's greatest strengths. The quality and diversity of students has been the best part of b-school. We have galvanized as a group and work hard for each other more so than for our professors' approval." They'd be even closer if they had the opportunity to live together, but unfortunately nearby housing is in very short supply. "I wish the school would look into providing housing/accommodation help," students complain.

## Admissions

Baruch requires applicants to submit the following: undergraduate and graduate transcripts, GMAT scores, letters of recommendation, a personal statement, and history of work experience. International students must submit TOEFL and TWE scores unless they have completed undergraduate work in the United States. The school stresses that "over 50 percent of Zicklin's full-time MBA and MS students are international, and the level of English proficiency of applicants whose native language is not English is an important admission criterion. [TOEFL/TWE] scores, along with the GMAT Verbal and Analytical Writing scores, are the primary indicators of English proficiency. They help determine not only who is offered admission but also whether or not admitted applicants are required to take advanced business English and other remedial English courses at Baruch before they begin their master's program." The school has no specific programs to promote minority recruitment, noting that "City University of New York affiliation and unusually low tuition rates make us well known to these groups."

## FINANCIAL FACTS

| | |
|---|---|
| Annual tuition (in-state/out-of-state) | $8,800/$17,100 |
| Fees | $238 |
| Books and supplies | $1,200 |
| Room & board (off campus only) | $20,000 |
| % of students receiving aid | 80 |
| % of first-year students receiving aid | 95 |
| % of students receiving loans | 19 |
| % of students receiving grants | 60 |
| Average award package | $9,200 |
| Average grant | $4,100 |
| Average student loan debt | $30,000 |

## ADMISSIONS

| | |
|---|---|
| Admissions Selectivity Rating | 79 |
| # of applications received | 1,029 |
| % applicants accepted | 68 |
| % acceptees attending | 57 |
| Average GMAT | 582 |
| Range of GMAT | 530–620 |
| Average GPA | 3.2 |
| TOEFL required of international students? | yes |
| Minimum TOEFL (paper/computer) | 590/243 |
| Application fee | $125 |
| International application fee | $125 |
| Regular application deadline | 4/30 |
| Regular notification | 6/15 |
| Deferment available? | yes |
| Maximum length of deferment | 1 year |
| Transfer students accepted? | yes |
| Transfer application policy | Same application process as all applicants; up to 12 credits from an AACSB-accredited institution may be transferred. |
| Non-fall admissions? | yes |
| Need-blind admissions? | yes |

## APPLICANTS ALSO LOOK AT

Columbia University, Fordham University, Hofstra University, New York University, Pace University, Rutgers—The State University of New Jersey, St. John's University

### EMPLOYMENT PROFILE

| Career Rating | 84 | Grads employed by field: | % | avg. salary: |
|---|---|---|---|---|
| Primary source of full-time job acceptances | | Accounting | 22 | $53,875 |
| | | Finance | 38 | $72,229 |
| School-facilitated activities | 24 (60%) | Marketing | 17 | $70,390 |
| Graduate-facilitated activities | 16 (40%) | MIS | 3 | $85,000 |
| | | Operations | 8 | $75,000 |
| Average starting salary | $68,599 | Consulting | 5 | $75,000 |
| Percent employed | 83 | Other | 7 | $70,000 |

# CLAREMONT GRADUATE UNIVERSITY
## THE PETER F. DRUCKER AND MASATOSHI ITO GRADUATE SCHOOL OF MANAGEMENT

## Academics

"The Drucker name and philosophy—that management is a liberal art—is the greatest strength" of the business school residing among the Claremont Consortium of Colleges in Claremont, California. Peter F. Drucker's groundbreaking insights into management have appeared in such prestigious publications as the *Harvard Business Review*, and they inform the entire curriculum at his namesake institution. As one MBA put it, "The greatest strength of the school is its orientation toward management rather than toward business. Management is a discipline taught at this school through the wisdom of Peter Drucker, perhaps the most prolific and perceptive observer of trends and management practices of the past century."

Consistent with Drucker's approach, "the school's academic strength is with the traditionally 'softer' skills. The classes in leadership, strategy, organizational behavior, morality and leadership, and Drucker-on-Management are outstanding." Drucker's global perspective necessitates an interdisciplinary approach; "accounting, organizational behavior, and strategy are connected to each other."

Drucker's relatively small size does pose some problems for students. One student explains, "Small schools have small-school problems. We need more classes and more professors to teach those classes." The school is too small to maintain full departments in all disciplines, necessitating the hiring of part-time or adjunct professors, who tend to be less accomplished and less popular with students. Permanent faculty, on the other hand, "are immediately accessible, and many are recognized leaders in venture finance, corporate governance, strategy, cost management, etc." Access to the Claremont Consortium means students "can take some classes in other departments, such as HRD, economics, psychology, biology, and education" and even develop their own dual degrees.

## Career and Placement

Drucker's career services are handled through the Claremont Graduate University Office of Career Management. According to the school's website, the office provides "structure and services, including counseling and specific workshops, to help students focus their search, to target appropriate employers, to implement their job-search strategies, and to build skills in self-marketing." While students don't like that the onus is on them to look for a job, and many feel that career services "needs a lot of improvement," Drucker grads are generally successful in landing positions soon after graduation; over half are employed before they even receive their sheepskin. Top hiring companies include Accenture, Boeing, Deloitte Touche Tohmatsu, Deutsche Bank, Jet Propulsion Laboratory, Johnson & Johnson, Marsh & MacLellan, Northop Grumman, PricewaterhouseCoopers, Rainbird, and Trust Company of the West. A robust 35 percent of Drucker MBAs gain employment outside the U.S.

## Location and Environment

"Life at Drucker is school, school, school, and a little playing on the side," students tell us, noting that theirs is not an especially cohesive student body. One MBA explains, "There are three groups of students at Drucker: (1) people who work part-time and spend little time at the school outside of class, (2) international students who keep to themselves largely, and (3) a small group of full-time students who spend large amounts of time at school. The three groups coexist, but do not interact too often outside of class, resulting in a school culture that lacks strong cohesion." Yet, despite this, students say their peers are "generally very friendly" and that here, "everyone knows your name."

MARIAESTELLA L. CUARA, RECRUITING & ADMISSIONS COORDINATOR
1021 NORTH DARTMOUTH AVENUE, CLAREMONT, CA 91711 UNITED STATES
PHONE: 909-607-7811 • FAX: 909-607-9104
E-MAIL: DRUCKER@CGU.EDU • WEBSITE: WWW.DRUCKER.CGU.EDU

The school's premium location helps make up for any lack of social life within the Drucker universe. Claremont is "one hour from the beach, 45 minutes from downtown Los Angeles, 40 minutes from skiing, and 20 minutes from great golf. Because there are so many activities around here, we can do many things during the two years." Claremont is also "very conducive to weekend getaways. Last semester I took weekend trips with fellow students to San Francisco, San Diego, Las Vegas, and Palm Springs. There is also something incredible about being within an hour of the beach, the mountains, or the desert." The location also allows for "network opportunities with other Southern California MBA programs (USC, UCLA, UCI, and Pepperdine)." The town of Claremont itself is "laid-back and mellow" and excellent for studying.

Claremont Graduate University is part of the Claremont Consortium, which includes five undergraduate colleges (Claremont McKenna, with its exceptional economics department; Harvey Mudd, an excellent engineering school; all-female Scripps College; Pomona College; and Pitzer) and the Keck Graduate Institute, "which is very popular and gaining industry recognition in leaps and bounds for its research and quality of students who are management-oriented scientists." MBAs tell us that "intellectually, there are a lot of opportunities here for stimulation between events offered at Drucker, events offered by the other colleges at CGU, and events offered by the other schools that comprise the Claremont Consortium."

## Admissions

Drucker's admissions committee "evaluates the whole individual rather than focusing on any single area." It considers GMAT scores, college transcript, three letters of recommendation, a personal statement (in 2005, the statement prompt asked students to identify what they would contribute to the school, and also to recount a previous ethical dilemma and their solution), and "leadership potential as indicated by experience (resume) and/or references." Interviews are required of all applicants by invitation. Minority recruitment is facilitated through "the Albrecht Endowed Fellowship, awarded to students who demonstrate academic and professional potential and financial need; other minority funding sources are available."

## FINANCIAL FACTS

| | |
|---|---|
| Annual tuition | $37,614 |
| Fees | $250 |
| Books and supplies | $1,500 |
| Room & board (on/off-campus) | $12,000/$13,000 |
| % of students receiving aid | 67 |
| % of first-year students receiving aid | 65 |
| Average award package | $15,000 |
| Average grant | $6,800 |
| Average student loan debt | $42,686 |

## ADMISSIONS

| | |
|---|---|
| **Admissions Selectivity Rating** | **84** |
| # of applications received | 199 |
| % applicants accepted | 57 |
| % acceptees attending | 50 |
| Average GMAT | 600 |
| Range of GMAT | 532–676 |
| Average GPA | 3.2 |
| TOEFL required of international students? | yes |
| Minimum TOEFL (paper/computer) | 600/250 |
| Application fee | $55 |
| International application fee | $55 |
| Regular application deadline | rolling |
| Regular notification | rolling |
| Deferment available? | yes |
| Maximum length of deferment | 2 semesters |
| Transfer students accepted? | yes |
| Transfer application policy Students may transfer 10 credits, pending approval. | |
| Non-fall admissions? | yes |
| Need-blind admissions? | yes |

## APPLICANTS ALSO LOOK AT

Pepperdine University, University of California—Irvine, University of California—Los Angeles, University of Southern California

| EMPLOYMENT PROFILE | | | | | |
|---|---|---|---|---|---|
| **Career Rating** | **74** | **Grads employed by field:** | **% avg. salary:** | |
| **Primary source of full-time** | | Finance | 21 | NR |
| **job acceptances** | | Human Resources | 2 | NR |
| Graduate-facilitated activities | 37 | Marketing | 17 | NR |
| Unknown | 63 | MIS | 3 | NR |
| | | Operations | 14 | NR |
| Average starting salary | $73,252 | Consulting | 21 | NR |
| Percent employed | 65 | Other | 18 | NR |
| | | Nonprofit | 4 | NR |

# CLARK UNIVERSITY
## GRADUATE SCHOOL OF MANAGEMENT

## Academics

A small MBA program with a strong finance department, Clark University's Graduate School of Management combines intimacy with the resources of a major university. Students approve, telling us that "the smaller size of the program is really a plus. As a student, you do not feel like a number or a dollar sign. Faculty actually know who you are and where your interests are." The small classes also mean that "students are able to initiate and put into action new ideas. Entrepreneurs and self-starters can really excel here."

Clark's professors "are wonderful. Their main focus is not lecturing and leaving once the class is over, but rather making sure everyone is understanding [the material]. They encourage questions to be asked throughout the class and will gladly provide outside classroom help for those who request it." The administration "is also quite helpful. They will go out of their way to help with questions or problems." Students approve of Clark's general philosophy regarding the academic grind, telling us that "Clark is a reality school. It's not a place where people expect the impossible just because it will be a learning experience or are unwilling to help you out for the same reason. The entire school is a team, working to prepare every graduate for excellence in the future. If you work hard and get things done as required and on time and are communicating with whomever is necessary, then people are willing to help you and problem-solve when you need it."

Of course, small programs also have their drawbacks, such as "too few elective courses" and relatively slow tech upgrades. Some students also feel "the business school is very isolated, and it would be better to integrate the other graduate schools on campus with our own." Despite these drawbacks, though, most students are satisfied; as one student puts it, "I am confident I will leave here with the tools necessary to succeed in my chosen field."

## Career and Placement

Clark University's Career Center trains MBAs in "the career development process of matching skills, interests, and values to career fields and occupations" and teaches students job-research skills, resume-writing techniques, and interviewing dos and don'ts through a series of seminars and mock interviews. Clark's website notes that the Graduate School of Management is "a small business school focused on individual students [that is] able to adapt to your career goals whether you are planning a mid-career change or are in the early stages of launching your professional life."

Companies that most often hire Clark MBAs include Anheuser-Busch; Bloomberg, L.P.; Deutsche Bank; EMC; Fallon Health Care System; the Federal Reserve Bank; KPMG; Lucent Technologies; Priceline.com; and the Worcester Art Museum. Many Clark MBAs go on to jobs outside the country, most likely due to the high number of full-time international MBAs.

## Student Life and Environment

With a huge international student population, Clark's Graduate School of Management offers students a useful "diversity of different cultures. The different perspectives on business and ethics are very valuable. I feel especially for American citizens that many good lessons are learned in and out of the classroom." As one student explains, "In times when globalization is one of the main features of modern business, the impact of the diverse student community on future business leaders cannot be overestimated." The school highlights its diversity by sponsoring a variety of international dinners throughout the school year.

PATRICIA TOLLO, DIRECTOR OF ADMISSION, GRADUATE SCHOOL OF MANAGEMENT
950 MAIN STREET, WORCESTER, MA 01610 UNITED STATES
PHONE: 508-793-7406 • FAX: 508-793-8822
E-MAIL: CLARKMBA@CLARKU.EDU • WEBSITE: WWW.CLARKU.EDU/GSOM

The dinners are just one of many activities that fill Clark MBAs' extracurricular schedules. The school "has a terrific student council that plans social activities for MBA students. The events are very popular" and quite numerous. One student recounts, "In the fall we went on two hiking trips, had a Halloween party, attended professional sports games, went to Six Flags amusement park, and went on ski trips, just to name a few. This spring already planned are whitewater rafting, a trip to Boston to see the Blue Man Group, a Harlem Globetrotters basketball game, a Red Sox game, an end-of-the-year banquet, and more hiking and skiing trips. There's a lot to do, if someone is willing to participate." As if that weren't enough, MBAs are "also having private parties and casual get-togethers on their own." As one MBA sums up, "This school [focuses on] more than just study. [It includes] students' lives, friendships, interesting work, and joy."

Business-related extracurriculars, however, are a little harder to come by; many MBAs complain that the school needs "more business clubs [and] more visits from business leaders who aren't alumni." Some MBAs see the student body as another shortcoming; while they appreciate the international influence, they think that many of their classmates lack the necessary experience to contribute in the classroom. "The school should consider admitting only students with a minimum of two years of work experience to enhance class quality," is how one MBA put it. Another MBA notes, "The students are quite immature. Many of them are fifth-year students [i.e., BA/MBA dual-degree students] who are earning a grad degree for free."

Clark's campus earns high marks. MBAs describe it as "attractive and well maintained. The classrooms are comfortable and conducive to learning." Worcester, on the other hand, "is not up to par, and social life is limited to our immediate neighborhood."

## Admissions

Clark offers applicants an unusual option: The school accepts either the GMAT or the GRE, to add diversity to the applicant pool. The program, Clark's website notes, benefits from "the fresh perspective that liberal arts and social science undergraduates bring to our classroom." All applicants must also submit an undergraduate transcript, a personal statement, two letters of recommendation, TOEFL scores (for international applicants), and a resume. Interviews are optional. The standardized-test requirement is automatically waived for any applicant holding a PhD, MD, or JD.

### FINANCIAL FACTS

| | |
|---|---|
| Annual tuition | $18,865 |
| Fees | $705 |
| Books and supplies | $800 |
| Room & board (on/off-campus) | $8,400/$9,500 |
| % of students receiving aid | 36 |
| % of first-year students receiving aid | 39 |
| % of students receiving grants | 34 |
| Average award package | $8,500 |
| Average grant | $7,500 |

### ADMISSIONS

| | |
|---|---|
| Admissions Selectivity Rating | 70 |
| # of applications received | 256 |
| % applicants accepted | 77 |
| % acceptees attending | 44 |
| Average GMAT | 530 |
| Range of GMAT | 500–550 |
| Average GPA | 3.23 |
| TOEFL required of international students? | yes |
| Minimum TOEFL (paper/computer) | 550/213 |
| Application fee | $50 |
| International application fee | $50 |
| Regular application deadline | 6/1 |
| Regular notification | rolling |
| Deferment available? | yes |
| Maximum length of deferment | 1 year |
| Transfer students accepted? | yes |
| Transfer application policy | Students may transfer 6 credits from an AACSB-accredited institution, pending approval. Additional courses taken on the graduate level may be applicable to course waivers. |
| Non-fall admissions? | yes |
| Need-blind admissions? | yes |

### APPLICANTS ALSO LOOK AT

Babson College, Bentley College, Boston University, Northeastern University, Rochester Institute of Technology, Suffolk University

## EMPLOYMENT PROFILE

| Career Rating | 71 | Grads employed by field: | % | avg. salary: |
|---|---|---|---|---|
| **Primary source of full-time job acceptances** | | Accounting | 12 | NR |
| | | Finance | 20 | NR |
| School-facilitated activities | 4 (27%) | Human Resources | 5 | NR |
| Graduate-facilitated activities | 6 (40%) | Marketing | 9 | NR |
| Unknown | 5 (33%) | MIS | 5 | NR |
| | | Strategic Planning | 5 | NR |
| Average starting salary | $58,333 | Consulting | 5 | NR |
| Percent employed | 71 | General Management | 6 | NR |
| | | Global Management | 5 | NR |
| | | Other | 23 | NR |
| | | Nonprofit | 5 | NR |

# CLARKSON UNIVERSITY
## SCHOOL OF BUSINESS

## Academics

Clarkson University is best known for its fine engineering programs, so it should come as no surprise that the focus at Clarkson University School of Business is on developing business acumen in engineers. Students recognize what makes their school special, telling us, "Clarkson's academic record is outstanding. It is a competitive engineering school with a growing business program." The curriculum stresses a creative approach to problem-solving typically associated with advanced engineers; as one student puts it, "The program's greatest strength is its emphasis on quality of work and its ability to get you to see beyond the surface of a particular subject or problem. Clarkson has made me a better strategic thinker." The school's "strong industry connections [and] good reputation in the technology world" are particularly valuable to those seeking to break into the business side of engineering.

Clarkson MBAs are anxious to get their degrees and move on, and the school's accelerated one-year program suits their needs perfectly. One MBA writes, "The one-year program is perfect in that it is economically sound and academically challenging." Another student adds, "The workload is intense, [with] a strong stress on the team-based experience." Students feel that "the group-work emphasis will help in future employment. And the fast pace and large workload proves [their] ability to work under pressure."

Two "Focus Weeks" shuffled into the academic calendar help slow the breakneck pace. In the fall semester, it's L.E.A.D Week, a leadership development program that uses videotaped simulations designed to help MBAs "develop meta-competencies in giving and receiving performance-related feedback." Springtime brings Perspectives Week, during which alumni return to campus to deliver speeches and provide networking opportunities. Student teams make presentations to panels of professors and alumni during this program.

Clarkson MBAs praise the faculty, reporting that "professors are incredibly concerned with student progress. They are very accessible outside the classroom and more than willing to start up conversations in the middle of a hallway with any student." However, "they will not tell you the way to succeed. All they will do is guide you in your search to find success." In this way, "the faculty at Clarkson treat their students as equals," which MBAs appreciate.

## Career and Placement

Clarkson MBAs receive career services from the university's Career Center, which serves all students at the university. The center schedules career fairs each semester (which draw between 80 and 90 recruiting companies), helps students contact Clarkson's alumni network, and provides students with access to the online job database MonsterTrak. MBAs give the office mixed reviews, telling us, "Clarkson gets many companies to the career fair; however, most are engineering firms. They could try to get more business-related type firms." Some students praise the "many helpful resources such as e-recruiting" provided.

Clarkson MBAs most frequently find work with Accenture, Cooper Industries, Frito-Lay, GE, Household International, IBM, Knowledge Systems and Research, Northwestern Mutual, Texas Instruments, and Whiting-Turner. About three-quarters remain in the region after graduation.

## Student Life and Environment

Clarkson's predominantly full-time student body tell us that there's a predictable rhythm to their school days. "In the MBA program, you are generally on campus from 8 A.M. until 6 or 7 P.M. There is a lot of work and a lot of meetings to attend with group members," explains one student. Students needn't brave the rugged Potsdam winters during the day because "all classes are taken in one single building." The business-school facility "is very businesslike. There are multiple computer labs as well as student lounges to relax. Multiple 'Learning Development Labs' are available for students to work quietly in throughout each day. It feels more like entering a business than classrooms. It helps one become more productive."

Potsdam, of course, is hardly a bustling metropolis. The closest large city is Ottawa, which lies approximately 90 miles and one international border to the north. Students warn that "it is cold for most of the year [and that] there are only about three bars in town, which are shared with a local SUNY school. Unless you skate or enjoy winter sports, there isn't much else in Potsdam to do." Another MBA puts it more bluntly: "The nightlife is terrible here in Potsdam, NY. There is really nothing to do here."

Some students, however, manage to see the glass as half-full instead of half-empty. One optimist reports that "a vast diversity of sports, intramurals, and clubs allow students to keep busy outside of class and to socialize with their peers. A vast majority of the students are involved in an activity of one sort or another." Fortunately for all, Clarkson's accelerated one-year program keeps most students too busy to worry about what type of fun they are, or are not, missing. Students work hard all week long and through much of the weekend as well. One MBA explains, "Weekends are spent doing work all day long. You go out with friends one night a week on the weekend; that's about it."

## Admissions

The admissions department at Clarkson University requires that applicants submit an undergraduate transcript, GMAT scores, TOEFL scores, and a Test of Spoken English (TSE) (for international students whose native language is not English; the TSE can be administered via telephone), a detailed resume, two one-page essays on assigned topics (both autobiographical), and three letters of reference. Awards of merit-based scholarships are determined during the admissions process; no separate application is required. Those requiring foundation course work prior to commencing their MBAs "may enroll in the courses at Clarkson before entering the advanced MBA program. For students doing graduate work at another university, they are allowed to transfer in nine credit hours of graduate work."

### FINANCIAL FACTS

| | |
|---|---|
| Annual tuition | $29,400 |
| Fees | $215 |
| Books and supplies | $2,000 |
| Room & board | $7,000 |
| % of students receiving aid | 85 |
| % of first-year students receiving aid | 85 |
| % of students receiving loans | 75 |
| % of students receiving grants | 85 |
| Average award package | $21,969 |
| Average grant | $5,500 |
| Average student loan debt | $29,920 |

### ADMISSIONS

| | |
|---|---|
| Admissions Selectivity Rating | 78 |
| # of applications received | 122 |
| % applicants accepted | 57 |
| % acceptees attending | 87 |
| Average GMAT | 520 |
| Range of GMAT | 440–640 |
| Average GPA | 3.24 |
| TOEFL required of international students? | yes |
| Minimum TOEFL (paper/computer) | 600/250 |
| Application fee | $25 |
| International application fee | $35 |
| Regular application deadline | rolling |
| Regular notification | rolling |
| Deferment available? | yes |
| Maximum length of deferment | 1 year |
| Transfer students accepted? | yes |

Transfer application policy
Graduate students who need to complete foundation course work may enroll in the courses at Clarkson before entering the advanced MBA program. For students doing graduate work at another university, they are allowed to transfer in up to 9 credit hours of graduate work.

| | |
|---|---|
| Non-fall admissions? | yes |
| Need-blind admissions? | yes |

### APPLICANTS ALSO LOOK AT

State University of New York at Binghamton, Rensselaer Polytechnic Institute, Rochester Institute of Technology, Syracuse University, University of Rochester

### EMPLOYMENT PROFILE

| Career Rating | 63 | Grads employed by field: | % | avg. salary: |
|---|---|---|---|---|
| Primary source of full-time job acceptances | | Accounting | 6 | $55,000 |
| | | Finance | 6 | $55,000 |
| School-facilitated activities | 40 (68%) | Human Resources | 13 | $51,000 |
| Graduate-facilitated activities | 14 (23%) | Marketing | 15 | $43,500 |
| Unknown | 5 (9%) | Operations | 13 | $56,000 |
| | | Consulting | 14 | $59,000 |
| Average starting salary | $59,400 | General Management | 15 | $44,000 |
| Percent employed | 28 | Other | 13 | $47,740 |
| | | Nonprofit | 5 | NR |

# CLEMSON UNIVERSITY
## GRADUATE SCHOOL OF BUSINESS AND BEHAVIORAL SCIENCE

### GENERAL INFORMATION

| | |
|---|---|
| Type of school | public |
| Environment | village |
| Academic calendar | Aug.–May |

### SURVEY SAYS...
Friendly students
Happy students
*Solid preparation in:*
Marketing
Communication/interpersonal skills

### STUDENTS

| | |
|---|---|
| Enrollment of parent institution | 17,200 |
| Enrollment of business school | 182 |
| % male/female | 76/24 |
| % out-of-state | 47 |
| % part-time | 66 |
| % minorities | 5 |
| % international | 15 |
| Average age at entry | 27 |
| Average years work experience at entry | 7 |

### ACADEMICS

| | |
|---|---|
| **Academic Experience Rating** | **77** |
| Student/faculty ratio | 9:1 |
| Profs interesting rating | 71 |
| Profs accessible rating | 71 |
| % female faculty | 22 |
| % minority faculty | 2 |

### JOINT DEGREES
Dual degrees are allowed on the master's level. Up to 1/6 of the total hours in both programs combined may be double counted. Dual degrees must be declared by the first semester of graduate school.

### PROMINENT ALUMNI
Jane Robelot, News Co-anchor, CBS; J. Strom Thurmond, U.S. Senator (died 2003); Robert H. Brooks, President, Naturally Fresh Foods; Kristie A. Kenney, U.S. Ambassador to Ecuador; Nancy Humphries O'Dell, Co-anchor, *Access Hollywood* and contributor to *Today* and *Dateline: NBC*

## Academics

Native South Carolinians seeking the MBA will have a hard time beating the ratio of value to quality that they'll find at Clemson University. Thanks to lower in-state tuition costs, Palmetto State residents can earn a highly regarded business degree for a small fraction of what their peers elsewhere in the country spend. Beautiful weather and first-rate intercollegiate football further sweeten the deal.

Approximately 30 full-time students enter Clemson's MBA program each year; full-timers make up a little less than half the student body. The program, students warn, "moves quickly. We complete 62 graduate-level credits in 21 months." One student explains, "I recommend the program to anyone who is confident that they can keep up with a heavy workload through effective time-management and teamwork skills." The first year is devoted entirely to foundation courses, some taught in a "highly intensive, highly rigorous seven-week format." The second year allows students to choose special-izations in one of two designated tracks (entrepreneurship or technology management), or to design their own specialization. Double degrees are not uncommon here; one stu-dent in our survey was earning an MBA in tandem with an MS in Parks, Recreation, and Tourism Management, while several others noted that "Clemson is strong in engineering and research, so it's a good place for engineers and scientists seeking business educa-tion." Students in all areas praise "the reputation of the professors and the school's rep-utation throughout the Southeast."

Part-time classes meet in the evening at Clemson; the program is open only to those with at least two years of work experience. The program consists of five core courses (some or all of which can be waived based on prior academic work or passing a proficiency exam), eight required advanced courses, and three electives. The program offers more flexibility than does the full-time program but also provides fewer opportunities for teamwork and group projects. Participants appreciate the fact that "classes only meet one night per week, which makes it easier on family life." They also tell us that "some professors are fantastic, and others are not so hot. Overall, though, the good outweighs the bad."

## Career and Placement

Clemson MBAs benefit from the Office of MBA Career Services and Alumni Relations, which "assists students and their career development." The office offers a range of self-assessment instruments, job-search counseling, interviewing and resume-writing workshops, seminars, and online job databases. Students praise the value of alumni con-nections but also feel that the office "needs help with national job-placement services. Clemson is very well connected within the state but not so much outside of the state."

Companies most likely to recruit Clemson MBAs include Accenture, Agfirst Farm Credit Bank, BB&T, Coca-Cola, Datastream Systems Inc., Deloitte Touche Tohmatsu, Duke Power Co., Hewlett-Packard, Hitachi, Lexmark International, Marriott Intl., Michelin North America, Milliken, Palmetto Farm Credit, Perrigo Co., PMSC, PricewaterhouseCoopers, Procter & Gamble, Reltec Corp., Schlumberger, Sherwin Williams, Solutia, Sonoco, Spring, Torrington, Trane Co., and Wachovia.

MBA Office - Admissions, Admissions Director, MBA Programs
124 Sirrine Hall, Box 341315, Clemson, SC 29634-1315 United States
Phone: 864-656-3975 • Fax: 864-656-0947
E-mail: mba@clemson.edu • Website: business.clemson.edu/mba/

## Student Life and Environment

"The greatest strength of Clemson University is the 'Clemson Family,'" and MBAs here agree. "The network of alumni and friends is outstanding. Every graduate is more than willing to lend a hand to a fellow Tiger." Community spirit runs especially high during football season, which "is very fun. Enthusiasm generated by the interest in football leads to better community involvement in . . . the university." The surrounding town of Clemson "is dedicated to the university. There is a small downtown area with plenty of bars/restaurants, nearby mountains/lakes, and plenty of other social activities for students to partake in." As one student sums up, "Clemson University is a special place. There are plenty of opportunities for intramural sports, nightlife, guest lectures and speeches, university events, and cultural events."

Clemson MBAs tend to be "laid-back people keeping very rigorous schedules. Small-town life helps because there aren't too many distractions." They are "very supportive of one another. We aid each other through study sessions, workshops, and other methods to ensure that everyone understands the material." One full-time MBA points out, "The other students are truly what make this program excellent. I have built so many friendships that I know I will take with me into the business world. We often take trips together, including spring break, study abroad, professional seminars, etc. Working so closely over the past few years in the classroom has really helped us to become tightly knit and great friends outside of the classroom."

## Admissions

Applicants to the MBA program at Clemson must submit a current resume (two years of work experience are required for the part-time evening program; work experience is preferred, but not required, for the full-time program); two official transcripts representing all undergraduate work (an overall GPA of at least 3.0 in a nonbusiness major is preferred); two letters of recommendation; a one- to two-page personal statement (required of applicants to the full-time program only); and an official GMAT score report (score of at least 580 preferred for applicants to the full-time program). Non-native English speakers applying to the full-time program must submit TOEFL scores.

### FINANCIAL FACTS

| | |
|---|---|
| Annual tuition (in-state/out-of-state) | $9,216/$18,440 |
| Books and supplies | $1,600 |
| Room & board (on/off-campus) | $9,300/$9,180 |
| % of students receiving aid | 53 |
| % of first-year students receiving aid | 35 |
| % of students receiving loans | 45 |

### ADMISSIONS

| | |
|---|---|
| **Admissions Selectivity Rating** | **85** |
| # of applications received | 176 |
| % applicants accepted | 61 |
| % acceptees attending | 63 |
| Average GMAT | 607 |
| Range of GMAT | 586–646 |
| Average GPA | 3.3 |
| TOEFL required of international students? | yes |
| Minimum TOEFL (paper/computer) | 580/237 |
| Application fee | $50 |
| International application fee | $50 |
| Regular application deadline | 4/15 |
| Regular notification | 4/30 |
| Deferment available? | yes |
| Maximum length of deferment | 1 year |
| Transfer students accepted? | yes |
| Transfer application policy Students may transfer up to 12 semester hours of acceptable course work from other AACSB-accredited schools. | |
| Need-blind admissions? | yes |

| EMPLOYMENT PROFILE | | | | |
|---|---|---|---|---|
| **Career Rating** | **72** | **Grads employed by field:** | **% avg. salary:** | |
| **Primary source of full-time job acceptances** | | Accounting | 8 | $52,300 |
| | | Finance | 36 | $60,000 |
| School-facilitated activities | 12 (39%) | Marketing | 28 | $55,000 |
| Graduate-facilitated activities | 16 (52%) | MIS | 8 | $54,500 |
| Unknown | 3 (9%) | Operations | 20 | $52,300 |
| Average starting salary | $56,000 | | | |
| Percent employed | 67 | | | |

# THE COLLEGE OF WILLIAM & MARY
## MASON SCHOOL OF BUSINESS

## Academics

In a small community like the College of William & Mary's Mason School of Business, it's no surprise that students consider their fellow scholars and faculty members their most valuable commodity. "The professors are class acts," says one MBA. "They know their subject matter and always make themselves available for further help." Another student adds, "Their energy is mind-boggling."

An already-intimate experience is made even more so through the teams into which first-year students are divided. Teams are designed to be diverse and aim to reflect varying strengths and the realities of today's workplace. As the school's website states, "As in today's corporate culture, your first-year team must work together to succeed." And cooperation begins with an outdoor obstacle course on the first day of orientation. Something's working, though, because throughout the two-year program, students tend to work with one another instead of against. "The environment is supportive and not as competitive as I assume other schools to be," says one student. "From the first day of class, we were told that we were not each other's competition—every other MBA from every other program was. I dig that." Another student says, "The atmosphere isn't set up for competition. I don't know who's at the top of my class, and frankly I don't care. Nor have I talked to anyone that does."

On one hand, electives aren't an option until the spring semester of the first year, at which point students select two six-week electives designed to prepare them for their summer internships. On the other hand, the key word for the second year is "focus." The Mason School of Business expects its students to choose targeted, advanced-level electives with a specific career in mind. Though in this year electives span seven major categories—accounting, finance and economics, marketing, information technology, operations and quantitative methods, organizational behavior and human resource management, and the environment of business—many students feel "the number of electives is a bit limited."

One oft-touted program at William & Mary is the Executive Partners mentoring program. One student says, "Williamsburg is a popular retirement location for senior executives, and many of them want to give back to the school. They mentor students, help with networking, and provide valuable input during projects." The retired executives work on a volunteer basis, and there are about 100 of them available to students at any given point.

As one student says, "William & Mary is very focused on providing its students with international business experience through short, intensive visits and exchange programs." In addition to hosting a student body that is about 35 percent international, William & Mary has an exchange program with Otto Beisheim Graduate School in Koblenz, Germany (for summer or semester-long programs) and a briefer program in Paris (summer only).

## Career and Placement

Unfortunately, career services appears to be the department that most students target as needing the most work. One student says, "There's not a big variety of companies recruiting on campus; it's hard to get internship placement due to the school's small-town location." New direction, however, may improve the quality, and several students

KATHY WILLIAMS PATTISON, DIRECTOR, MBA ADMISSIONS
PO BOX 8795, WILLIAMSBURG, VA 23187 UNITED STATES
PHONE: 757-221-2900 • FAX: 757-221-2958
E-MAIL: ADMISSIONS@BUSINESS.WM.EDU • WEBSITE: HTTP://MBA.WM.EDU

have high hopes. "I expect it will be much stronger next year," says one. In the past, however, students have compensated for the weakness of career services by getting involved in the Executive Partners mentoring program. Contact with retired executives has enabled many students to get jobs or internships at big-name firms.

## Student Life and Admissions

William & Mary has the unusual luck of being located in tiny historic Williamsburg, not far from the metropolitan area of Washington, DC. Students rave about the "breathtaking scenery" and the comforts of living in a small town. In such a town, students are "intimately involved in the community and feel accepted by most of the residents." Others agree, adding, "You do not feel like a number here." But even the quaint beauty of historic Williamsburg "can get old in a hurry. Clearly, there's a lack of places to hang out in this town." One of the most popular, however, is Green Leafe, a bar across the street from the business school, where students often meet on Thursday evenings to relax and kick off a three-day weekend of studying. Though some chafe at the small size of the town, most students agree, "This environment does have many benefits. It allows students to focus on their studies and also get to know their fellow classmates." In addition, with over 20 different countries represented on the business-administration school campus (ranging from Belarus to Thailand, from China to Peru), William & Mary isn't quite the provincial backwater some outsiders would claim.

One weakness on which the school is working is the facilities. Parking is limited, and "we don't have lockers, classrooms are packed, and we often are forced to drive to a satellite campus, which is 30 minutes away," one student reports. Still, the school is raising funds for a new business-school building, which will "provide better facilities for current students (i.e., more study rooms) and attract more applicants to the school."

## Admissions

At William & Mary, admissions look for students who can display a "wide range of academic fields and professional experiences [and] who demonstrate strong leadership skills and have clear professional goals." Only about 70 to 80 students meet these qualifications each year, and 43 percent of those are international students. The range of GMAT scores for accepted applicants in 2005 was 510 to 680, and the average was 592. Foreign students who have worked in the U.S. for two or more years (full-time) or who have received a degree at an English-speaking university are not required to submit TOEFL scores. For those who did take it, though, the average score for the computer-based test was 263 and 623 for the paper-based test.

### FINANCIAL FACTS

| | |
|---|---|
| Annual tuition (in-state/out-of-state) | $15,266/$27,938 |
| Books and supplies | $1,500 |
| Room & board | $14,481 |
| % of students receiving aid | 66 |
| % of first-year students receiving aid | 68 |
| % of students receiving loans | 51 |
| % of students receiving grants | 52 |
| Average award package | $23,896 |
| Average grant | $6,200 |
| Average student loan debt | $35,795 |

### ADMISSIONS

| | |
|---|---|
| **Admissions Selectivity Rating** | **71** |
| # of applications received | 184 |
| % applicants accepted | 76 |
| % acceptees attending | 47 |
| Average GMAT | 592 |
| Range of GMAT | 510–680 |
| TOEFL required of international students? | yes |
| Minimum TOEFL (paper/computer) | 600/250 |
| Application fee | $100 |
| International application fee | $100 |
| Application deadline/notification | |
| Round 1: | 11/15 / 1/15 |
| Round 2: | 1/15 / 3/15 |
| Round 3: | 3/15 / 5/15 |
| Round 4: | 5/15 / 6/15 |
| Need-blind admissions? | yes |

### APPLICANTS ALSO LOOK AT

University of Maryland—College Park, University of Virginia, Vanderbilt University, Wake Forest University, Washington University

### EMPLOYMENT PROFILE

| Career Rating | 82 | Grads employed by field: | % | avg. salary: |
|---|---|---|---|---|
| Average starting salary | $72,647 | Finance | 39 | $71,750 |
| Percent employed | 76 | Marketing | 26 | $68,100 |
| | | Operations | 7 | $65,000 |
| | | Consulting | 13 | $77,166 |
| | | General Management | 7 | $84,000 |
| | | Other | 8 | $78,500 |

# COLORADO STATE UNIVERSITY
## COLLEGE OF BUSINESS

## Academics

A distance-learning leader, Colorado State University has consistently endeavored to deliver one of the best distance-learning MBAs in the country. Its efforts seem to have paid off. Students in the program agree that "the CSU School of Business is an innovator in distance-learning techniques; it has worked the kinks out both academically and operationally." The school also offers a part-time evening MBA program. Both the evening and the distance-learning MBA are "comprehensive lockstep programs" that are identical in content.

Here's how the CSU MBA works: Part-time MBAs attend classes on campus two evenings for 21 months, and the distance MBA can be completed in the same period of time or extended for up to four years. Classes are taped, burned to DVD, and sent to students in the distance-learning program. Distance learners tell us that their program "seems less 'distancy' because of the recorded lectures on DVD and the fact that we have the identical pace and curriculum as the on-campus students." Students in both programs keep in touch with their professors and each other through Embanet, a communications software product that allows professors to post assignments and students to complete projects in a virtual meeting space. One student writes, "The program requires extensive use of work teams in a virtual environment, which is 100 percent what a graduate will likely experience in today's business world, because most coworkers will be located in another building, state, time zone, or country."

Whether they complete the program on campus or at home, students enjoy a curriculum that "is not just theory, but very heavy on application. What is taught has immediate applications at my job," comments one working student. CSU professors "are tough and require a heavy workload," but they are also "understanding of the demands on part-time students" and can be "flexible with emergencies." They "teach cutting-edge theory and practice" and are informed by their own experience in the business world. "All professors have worked or are currently working in the industry they are teaching us about. The adjunct professors are also well qualified and put a tremendous amount of time into the students." Accounting, economics, and finance are reportedly the faculty's strongest areas. Perhaps the greatest drawback of the program is that it offers only a general MBA. One student explains, "The school does not offer electives, only core courses." Nearly all students here agree that CSU's strengths far outweigh its weaknesses, however; sums up one MBA, "The school is very ambitious and works hard to create a program that really serves the business students. It is an outstanding program."

## Career and Placement

The part-time nature of CSU's MBA program is designed for working professionals, who comprise the vast majority of the student body. The school maintains a College of Business Career Liaison to coordinate activities between the College of Business and the university's Career Center, but the responsibilities of this office are primarily aimed at serving undergraduates. This doesn't have much of an impact on MBAs, however, since most CSU MBAs already have good jobs with such powerhouses as Agilent, Argen, Celestica, Colgate-Palmolive, ConAgra, FedEx, Hewlett-Packard, Honeywell, MCI WorldCom, National Textiles, the Parson Group, Siemens, Sun Microsystems, UPS, and Wells Fargo Bank.

RACHEL STOLL, GRADUATE ADMISSIONS COORDINATOR
160 ROCKWELL HALL, FORT COLLINS, CO 80523-1201 UNITED STATES
PHONE: 970-491-3704 • FAX: 970-491-3481
E-MAIL: RACHEL.STOLL@COLOSTATE.EDU • WEBSITE: WWW.BIZ.COLOSTATE.EDU

## FINANCIAL FACTS

| | |
|---|---|
| Annual tuition (in-state/out-of-state) | $9,000/$19,000 |
| Fees | $45 |
| Books and supplies | $2,100 |

## ADMISSIONS

| | |
|---|---|
| **Admissions Selectivity Rating** | **79** |
| # of applications received | 206 |
| % applicants accepted | 86 |
| % acceptees attending | 84 |
| Average GMAT | 620 |
| Average GPA | 3.2 |
| TOEFL required of international students? | yes |
| Minimum TOEFL (paper/computer) | 565/227 |
| Application fee | $50 |
| International application fee | $50 |
| Regular application deadline | 5/1 |
| Regular notification | 6/1 |
| Deferment available? | yes |
| Maximum length of deferment | 1 year |
| Non-fall admissions? | yes |
| Need-blind admissions? | yes |

## Student Life and Environment

Nestled in the foothills of the Rockies "with a beautiful view," Colorado State University "is a thriving, vibrant community" of 24,000 students, 1,550 faculty, and numerous administrators and employees. The school offers "great access to many academic and social venues, and a pleasant campus atmosphere that supports learning." Taking advantage of these proves "a little tough for older students. Within the MBA program, people are juggling so many balls that they hardly have time to partake." Those who can manage a few free moments enjoy and appreciate the "strong clubs and activities [and] plenty of intramural sports." Many distance students "never visit the campus at all," however.

Among the on-campus student body, "work experiences vary from vet students to engineers in high-tech companies to nurses and general mangers at *Fortune* 100 companies." One MBA writes, "There are even some students who work for not-for-profit firms, which adds yet another level of interest to class discussions and the overall quality of the program at Colorado State University." One student notes, however, that "the program does attract a lot of professional engineers. I wish there were more variety in terms of work experience." A solid mix of international MBAs includes "students from Asia, Latin America, and Canada." Distance learners come "from all types of backgrounds and from all over the place." The average age of students is around 35, and the typical CSU student has about 10 to 15 years of work experience.

## Admissions

CSU admits on-campus MBAs in the fall only; distance learners are admitted for either the fall or the spring semester. All applicants must submit a completed application form, a resume, a cover letter, an official GMAT score report, two copies of official transcripts for all post-secondary academic work, and three recommendations. Applicants whose native language is not English must also submit an official TOEFL score report. According to the school's website, CSU looks to "select a richly diverse set of students with various undergraduate degrees and professional experiences. Additional requirements include a minimum of four years post-undergraduate professional work experience, previous academic performance, GMAT scores, work experience, and recommendations are some of the factors considered. In addition, the applicant's personal cover letter should reflect carefully considered reasons for pursuing a business degree at the master's level." Applicants with GPAs below 3.0 must include a letter explaining the circumstances under which they received such grades.

# COLUMBIA UNIVERSITY
## COLUMBIA BUSINESS SCHOOL

## Academics

"No other school offers the same caliber of professors, students, varied curriculum, work-life balance, dedication to the local community, and connections and exposure to both the for-profit and nonprofit worlds" as does Columbia, graduate business students at this New York City stalwart tell us. A high-profile program in America's highest-profile city, Columbia offers the kind of MBA program where "it is an everyday occurrence to see a *New York Times* real estate article in which your professor is quoted, learn from a Nobel Prize-winning economist, and attend lectures given by CEOs from *Fortune* 100 companies."

Columbia "excels across academic programs," with solid offerings in finance, marketing, real estate, and management. Students are especially enthusiastic about the unique Social Enterprise program, which places social impact on equal footing with the bottom line; the program provides excellent training for those interested in government or the non-profit sector. Students also single out the Media program, another unusual offering; the program benefits heavily from the concentration of media outlets in and around New York City.

Columbia's core curriculum occupies most of a student's first year, accounting for 45 percent of credits required for the degree. Some students state that the core is the school's weakest aspect; while appreciating the integrated design of the core, they feel its execution could be better. One student writes, "With the core, the faculty are either extremely talented or extremely poor. There's little consistency and no middle ground. Core professors are generally not as good at teaching the 'soft courses.'" Things improve as students move on to electives, where "at least 80 percent of the professors fall into the 'fully committed' and 'engaging' categories." Through both years of the program, "students are amazingly respectful of each other in the classroom setting and offer real-world experience that enriches every lesson plan." Students also appreciate that "the administration is responsive and attentive to the needs of the student body and tremendously supportive of career and community-service activities."

## Career and Placement

The MBA Career Services Office (CSO) at Columbia benefits from a propitious location in the financial capital of the world. The office helps students coordinate internship and employment searches and also provides "a range of complementary resources . . . from intimate workshops on interviewing and presentation skills to a five-part course on different aspects of the job," according to the school's website. The CSO also draws from the region's many business leaders for lectures, seminars, and panel discussions. The school reports that "Hundreds of employers actively recruit at Columbia Business School each year, conducting thousands of on-campus interviews and numerous corporate presentations. Columbia also receives thousands of job postings for off-campus full-time and intern positions."

Nearly half the class of 2004 landed in the finance sector, and basically all graduates enjoyed handsome starting salaries. Top employers include: American Express; Bank of America; Booz Allen Hamilton; Citigroup; Deutsche Bank; Goldman Sachs, Inc.; McKinsey & Company; JPMorgan Chase; Lehman Brothers; and Morgan Stanley.

LINDA MEEHAN, ASSISTANT DEAN FOR ADMISSIONS
3022 BROADWAY, URIS HALL, ROOM 216, NEW YORK, NY 10027 UNITED STATES
PHONE: 212-854-1961 • FAX: 212-662-6754
E-MAIL: APPLY@CLAVEN.GSB.COLUMBIA.EDU • WEBSITE: WWW.GSB.COLUMBIA.EDU

## Student Life and Environment

Life at the Columbia Business School is busy, with "a diversity of clubs across all interest areas that, if anything, provide too many options." Then, of course, there's New York City, with its fabulous cultural outlets, world-class eateries, and endless selection of entertainment options. Observes one student, "Since a lot of students are coming from the city, they have lives outside of just the school social scene, which for me is good. We are in New York City so I think it is important to take advantage of that." Sums up another, "Columbia offers its students the greatest work-life balance. We work hard, party hard, volunteer our time in the community, explore New York City, and easily maintain groups of friends both within and outside the business school."

Columbia's campus is located in Morningside Heights, directly north of Manhattan's Upper West Side. The once run-down neighborhood has undergone quite a makeover in the last decade and is now a much more fashionable and expensive address. The enclosed campus runs eight city blocks, small by any standards other than New York's but absolutely expansive compared to, say, NYU. The business-school facilities "don't have enough space, but they're addressing that." Everyone agrees that Columbia's gym "is just terrible;" most prefer jogging in nearby Riverside Park to working out at the gym.

The student body here is "extremely diverse and interesting, international and helpful." The program's high degree of selectiveness ensures that all are accomplished, motivated, and talented. One MBA writes, "The students at Columbia are some of the most well-rounded, worldly, tolerant, intelligent, self-motivated, and fun people I've ever met. Beyond all of Columbia's amazing attributes, the students may be the biggest draw to the business school."

## Admissions

So you want to be a Columbia MBA? So do a lot of people, making Columbia one of the hardest graduate business schools to gain admission to. In selecting applicants for admission, the school reports that "by design, efforts are made to admit students who add different perspectives to the learning experience. In this way, students are continually learning from the diverse professional experiences and cultural/geographical backgrounds of their classmates. Columbia Business School has also maintained, through a concerted strategic effort, one of the highest enrollments of women and underrepresented minorities among top business schools. The Office of Admissions, in conjunction with the School's Black Business Students Association, Hispanic Business Association, and African American Alumni Association, sponsors information sessions and receptions for prospective students."

### FINANCIAL FACTS

| | |
|---|---|
| Annual tuition | $38,292 |
| Fees | $3,170 |
| Books and supplies | $1,170 |
| Room & board (on/off-campus) | $18,450/$18,450 |

### ADMISSIONS

| | |
|---|---|
| Admissions Selectivity Rating | 99 |
| # of applications received | 4,532 |
| % applicants accepted | 15 |
| % acceptees attending | 76 |
| Average GMAT | 706 |
| Range of GMAT | 660–750 |
| Average GPA | 3.4 |
| TOEFL required of international students? | yes |
| Application fee | $215 |
| International application fee | $215 |
| Regular application deadline | 4/20 |
| Regular notification | rolling |
| Early decision program? | yes |
| ED deadline/notification September entry; | 10/12 / 12/30 |
| Non-fall admissions? | yes |
| Need-blind admissions? | yes |

### APPLICANTS ALSO LOOK AT

Harvard University, Stanford University, University of Pennsylvania

### EMPLOYMENT PROFILE

| Career Rating | | 98 | Grads employed by field: | % | avg. salary: |
|---|---|---|---|---|---|
| **Primary source of full-time job acceptances** | | | Finance | 47 | $149,914 |
| | | | Human Resources | 1 | $100,000 |
| School-facilitated activities | 361 (67%) | | Marketing | 8 | $103,803 |
| Graduate-facilitated activities | 70 (13%) | | Strategic Planning | 2 | $116,028 |
| Unknown | 109 (20%) | | Consulting | 17 | $138,675 |
| | | | Entrepreneurship | 6 | $158,167 |
| Average starting salary | $138,064 | | General Management | 4 | $112,750 |
| Percent employed | 92 | | Venture Capital | 2 | $183,008 |
| | | | Other | 10 | $136,599 |
| | | | Internet/New Media | 1 | $105,625 |
| | | | Nonprofit | 1 | $86,750 |

# CONCORDIA UNIVERSITY
## JOHN MOLSON SCHOOL OF BUSINESS

## Academics

Students looking for "a family-like atmosphere with an emphasis on practice and real-world cases" should consider the MBA program at Concordia University's John Molson School of Business (JMSB). At JMSB, students receive a solid general education in business principles as well as the opportunity to specialize in accounting, investment finance, global business, supply chain management, corporate governance, entrepreneurship, marketing, decision sciences/MIS, and management. Private MBA programs such as global aviation and investment management are also offered. There is also an option of an Accelerated MBA or MBA Co-operative Education. The John Molson School of Business operates on a fast-paced, trimester academic calendar. Classes, given in English, are offered in both days and evenings on Mondays through Thursdays "to accommodate both the part-time and full-time student body." Summer classes are offered mainly in the evenings.

With approximately 250 MBAs (split nearly evenly among full-timers and part-timers), JMSB provides each student with the resources they need to maximize their education. One MBA notes, "The greatest strength of the school is its cooperative spirit in the administration, faculty, placement center, and fellow students. Whenever you are looking for something or trying to accomplish something, people here have a can-do attitude." Students agree that at JMSB "you are not just a number, but a person. Everything is more personal here."

One of the high points of the school's academic year is the John Molson MBA Case Competition, held on campus and billed as "the only truly global case competition in the world." JMSB students are extremely passionate about this event and bemoan only the fact that not everyone can participate. "The school should offer the incredible training that the case competition team gets to everyone," writes one student. "That boot-camp intense training is like putting your MBA skills into overdrive." The Concordia Small Business Consulting Bureau offers students another opportunity to flex their business muscles while helping local businesses fine-tune their business plans and reach new consumers.

JMSB MBAs praise the curricular mix of "practical and hands-on education with academics, rather than solely case studies or theories," and give their professors high marks, reporting that they "are keen and sharp with a sense of humor and realism about today's challenges. The professors are tough, and we'll do even better when we graduate because of it." Students are less sanguine about the facilities, which "are old and not very comfortable," but point out that "new facilities are under construction and should be ready by 2006–2007."

## Career and Placement

The Career Placement Centre at the John Molson School of Business serves both the undergraduates and graduates. "Graduate student-specific seminars" stand out as a Career Placement Center service in one MBA's opinion. The office provides the standard complement of career counseling, guest lectures, mock interviews, job postings, seminars in networking, resume writing, and salary negotiation. Students surveyed in the past generally agree that it was not enough, complaining about both the number and quality of positions available.

Employers who most frequently hire JMSB MBAs include Abbott Laboratories, Bombardier Aerospace, CIBC, Deloitte Consulting, Dynamic Mutual Funds, L'Oréal, National Bank of Canada, Pratt & Whitney, and RBC Financial Group.

LISSA MATYAS, ASSISTANT DIRECTOR
1455 DE MAISONNEUVE BOULEVARD WEST, GM 710 MONTREAL, QC H3G 1M8 CANADA
PHONE: 514-848-2717 • FAX: 514-848-2816
E-MAIL: MBA@JMSB.CONCORDIA.CA • WEBSITE: WWW.JOHNMOLSON.CONCORDIA.CA

## Student Life and Environment

JMSB MBAs have opportunities to get involved beyond the classroom, as "there is a minimum of one social activity a month (and up to three per month) for students to relax and have fun, such as a Halloween dance, pub night, an apple-picking trip, or wine-tasting. In addition, sports skills such as golf lessons or intro to scuba lessons and other sports are also offered." There are also "plenty of professional extracurricular activities to take part in, [such as] business leaders who are brought in from the community to share their experiences, past and present, [but] it seems like there is a core of 40 students who are active in everything (i.e., making the most out of their MBA) while the remainder only attend class."

The JMSB campus "is in downtown Montreal, an amazing city in which to live, and off-campus living is great." As a bonus, Montreal is a major player in international finance, pharmaceutical research, and aerospace development, providing lots of internship and placement opportunities for MBAs. The urban setting means that "the campus is not that attractive, but there are lots of possibilities to socialize outside of school. The student life is influenced by the Montreal lifestyle . . . it is not just work." Students complain that the campus "is lacking in open space where the students can sit down together, and the graduate lounge is often overcrowded," but they expect that the new business-school facility will remedy these problems.

"'Multicultural diversity' is the best way to describe what makes the difference in the Concordia MBA program," writes one student, alluding to the UN-style mix that constitutes the JMSB student body. About one-third of the students are Canadian and two-thirds are from around the world. American students typically make up about three percent of the student body. One MBA emphasizes, "The value of the program is greatly enhanced by the cumulative experiences of people coming from all parts of the world. Since people from Montreal are accustomed to this international environment, one feels really welcome here." Students tend to be "intellectually nimble, trustworthy, and respectful, with diverse professional experiences and a willingness to work cooperatively."

## Admissions

Concordia admissions officers seek students with "real-world work experience, strong academic backgrounds, clear career objectives, and a commitment to excellence." Applicants must meet the following minimum requirements: undergraduate GPA of 3.0; two years of full-time work experience; a GMAT score of 600; and, for international students, a TOEFL score of 600 (paper-and-pencil) or 250 (computer-based). Career/leadership potential, level of maturity, communication skills, and how closely the student's goals match the program's are also weighed. Complete applications include a personal essay, a resume, official undergraduate transcripts, at least two letters of recommendation, and test scores.

### FINANCIAL FACTS

| | |
|---|---|
| Annual tuition (in-state/out-of-state) | $1,668/$12,000 |
| Fees (in-state/out-of-state) | $945/$1,000 |
| Books and supplies | $3,992 |
| Room & board (on/off-campus) | $4,842/$10,688 |
| % of students receiving aid | 28 |
| % of first-year students receiving aid | 32 |
| Average award package | $9,000 |
| Average grant | $8,111 |

### ADMISSIONS

| | |
|---|---|
| Admissions Selectivity Rating | 89 |
| # of applications received | 458 |
| % applicants accepted | 43 |
| % acceptees attending | 55 |
| Average GMAT | 616 |
| Range of GMAT | 620–690 |
| Average GPA | 3.0 |
| TOEFL required of international students? | yes |
| Minimum TOEFL (paper/computer) | 600/250 |
| Application fee | $50 |
| International application fee | $50 |
| Regular application deadline | rolling |
| Regular notification | rolling |
| Early decision program? | yes |
| Deferment available? | yes |
| Maximum length of deferment | 1 year |
| Transfer students accepted? | yes |
| Transfer application policy Applicants may be eligible for advanced standing. | |
| Non-fall admissions? | yes |
| Need-blind admissions? | yes |

### APPLICANTS ALSO LOOK AT

HEC Montréal, McGill University, University of Toronto, York University

| EMPLOYMENT PROFILE | |
|---|---|
| Career Rating | 78 |
| Average starting salary | $68,118 |

# CORNELL UNIVERSITY
## JOHNSON GRADUATE SCHOOL OF MANAGEMENT

### GENERAL INFORMATION

| | |
|---|---|
| Type of school | private |
| Environment | town |
| Academic calendar | semester |

### SURVEY SAYS...
Friendly students
Good peer network
Happy students
Smart classrooms
*Solid preparation in:*
Finance
Teamwork

### STUDENTS

| | |
|---|---|
| Enrollment of parent institution | 20,000 |
| Enrollment of business school | 552 |
| % male/female | 71/29 |
| % minorities | 8 |
| % international | 26 |
| Average age at entry | 27 |
| Average years work experience at entry | 5 |

### ACADEMICS

| | |
|---|---|
| **Academic Experience Rating** | **97** |
| Student/faculty ratio | 6:1 |
| Profs interesting rating | 89 |
| Profs accessible rating | 99 |
| % female faculty | 24 |
| % minority faculty | 18 |

### JOINT DEGREES
MBA/MILR, 5 semesters;
MBA/MEng, 5 semesters; MBA/MA
Asian Studies, 6–7 semesters;
MBA/JD, 4 years; MBA/MPS-RE, 6
semesters; MD/MBA, 5 years (only
currently available to students at
Weill Medical College of Cornell
University)

### PROMINENT ALUMNI
Jim Morgan, 1963, Chair of Applied
Materials; Richard Marin, 1976,
Chair and CEO, Bear Stearns Asset
Management; H. Fisk Johnson,
1984, Chair, S.C. Johnson and Son;
Warren Staley, 1967, Chair and
CEO, Cargill Incorporated

## Academics

Students claim with justified pride that the Johnson School of Management at Cornell University is and always has been a student-focused school. The administration is quick to respond to student suggestions, and "the top five administrators (deans) attend the student-council meetings each week to listen to student feedback and take action items." Academics are "challenging but grounded in reality," and students agree that there is little of the backstabbing that may go on in other schools. "We are not cutthroat competitors trying to get the best grade we can. We are all successful people, coming together in this challenging and diverse environment to network, learn, and further ourselves as leaders for the business world." As one student points out, "All top business schools have great professors and great programs; this one provides an atmosphere of camaraderie and friendship. No other school could offer me that." Still, though the school's community values cooperation and teamwork, "in no way are Cornell MBAs pushovers—we can bring a competitive fight to anyone!"

Among the most unique features of the Johnson School are the voluntary immersion courses taken by students in the spring semester of their first year. According to the school's website, in these courses, "immersion-learning curriculum replaces lecture-and case-based training with integrated, experiential, reality-based learning." Students in immersion courses are asked to solve real business problems in real-world time and are then "evaluated as they would be on the job." The courses "provide a challenge in whatever field you're in, so that you will be well-equipped to handle the pressures of the summer internship." On one hand, immersion courses are among the most popular and do indeed often result in summer internships. "Some recruiters have said this is the primary reason they come to this school to recruit." On the other hand, "choosing an immersion forces you to pick your career rather quickly—perhaps too quickly if you don't know what you want to do just yet."

One benefit of being a part of such a large university is the access students have to other departments. Prospective MBAs brag about the "excellent contact [they have with] other Cornell schools—like the engineering and the hotel schools!" Working with other departments, students can often customize their immersion courses. One student says, "I was interested in real estate and was able to take courses from Cornell's Hotel School, City and Regional Planning Program, and program in real estate."

## Career and Placement

Some students feel that Cornell's somewhat remote location prevents companies from visiting, especially in the middle of an Ithaca winter—"cold!"—but the Career Management Center has tried its hardest to make up for that. In 2003 they hired "four corporate jets to fly recruiters from major cities to Ithaca for the day, which resulted in a significant number of summer internships and full-time jobs." Still, some students feel the center could be working harder. "The diversity of companies recruiting on campus could be improved, [and] more high-level speakers could be brought to campus to discuss timely business issues." Others point out that "while top companies from various industries come on campus to recruit, if a student wants to do something outside the norm, it is extremely difficult. A person looking to enter the investment-banking field will have no problem, but if you want investment management, the Career Services Department is lacking."

Nonetheless, the Career Management Center reported that, after graduation, "92 percent of the members of the Class of 2004 who were seeking full-time positions had received at least one offer." And 90 percent of the salaries for those graduates of the class of 2003

MR. RANDALL SAWYER, DIRECTOR, OFFICE OF ADMISSIONS AND FINANCIAL AID
111 SAGE HALL, ITHACA, NY 14853 UNITED STATES
PHONE: 607-255-4526 • FAX: 607-255-0065
E-MAIL: MBA@CORNELL.EDU • WEBSITE: WWW.JOHNSON.CORNELL.EDU

who were hired fell between $75,000 and $106,000.

Another boon to the program is the strong alumni network. According to most students, the alumni are "in many fields in high positions, and the school brings them back periodically to give inspiring talks. Cornell and Johnson School alumni are extremely helpful—they go out of their way to get involved in career planning and job search."

## Student Life and Environment

Located approximately three hours north of New York City, Cornell University is situated in beautiful Ithaca, New York, "a remote place, but a lovely one. The lake and trees provide for a beautiful backdrop in fall." A town of about 30,000, Ithaca is "a bit off the beaten path, but there is a surprisingly high number of outstanding restaurants (thanks to the hotel school)." The small size and the distance from major cities is a drawback for some, but most students, particularly those who've come with families, agree that, though "we might not have as many social options as students in major cities, we definitely have as much fun—we just create it ourselves!" Clubs and teams abound on a campus of about 20,000: "We have a club for everything," students say, "from health care to operations management and from hockey to singing," and there's a happy hour every Thursday.

Unfortunately, what they lack in size, they sometimes also lack in diversity: "Our location and size require that we put forth a more formal effort than schools in large cities, and we should probably do even more to attract candidates from underrepresented groups." On the other hand, their Office of Diversity and Inclusion is largely agreed to be "outstanding in their ability to nurture and support minorities and women in the program, as well as prospective students."

Sage Hall, the main building for the school, is the envy of other departments on campus. Over 100 years old, the building was completely gutted in 1996 and rebuilt "with the latest and greatest technology (wireless in whole building and stadium seating/wireless/LAN connections in classrooms)," while still retaining the beauty of the original structure.

## Admissions

According to its admissions office, students admitted to the Johnson School are "not only intelligent and highly professional but can bring a fresh perspective and energy to their interactions with faculty and peers. In addition to a clear record of academic and professional achievement, we value independent thinking, teamwork, and interpersonal skills." All applicants are required to take the GMAT, and those for whom English is not their native language are required to take the TOEFL exam. Prior work experience is strongly recommended.

### FINANCIAL FACTS

| | |
|---|---|
| Annual tuition | $36,350 |
| Fees | $62 |
| Books and supplies | $1,100 |
| Room & board (on/off-campus) | $9,500/$9,500 |
| % of students receiving aid | 79 |
| % of first-year students receiving aid | 80 |
| % of students receiving loans | 72 |
| % of students receiving grants | 36 |
| Average award package | $42,000 |
| Average grant | $26,000 |
| Average student loan debt | $73,000 |

### ADMISSIONS

| | |
|---|---|
| Admissions Selectivity Rating | 94 |
| # of applications received | 1,940 |
| % applicants accepted | 34 |
| % acceptees attending | 43 |
| Average GMAT | 660 |
| Range of GMAT | 620–700 |
| Average GPA | 3.31 |
| TOEFL required of international students? | yes |
| Minimum TOEFL (paper/computer) | 600/250 |
| Application fee | $180 |
| International application fee | $180 |
| Application deadline/notification | |
| Round 1: | 10/3 / 11/30 |
| Round 2: | 11/7 / 1/25 |
| Round 3: | 12/5 / 4/12 |
| Round 4: | 1/4 / 3/21 |
| Non-fall admissions? | yes |
| Need-blind admissions? | yes |

### APPLICANTS ALSO LOOK AT

Columbia University, Dartmouth College, Harvard University, University of Michigan, University of Pennsylvania

### EMPLOYMENT PROFILE

| Career Rating | 95 | Grads employed by field: | % | avg. salary: |
|---|---|---|---|---|
| Primary source of full-time job acceptances | | Finance | 51 | $83,015 |
| | | Marketing | 21 | $85,426 |
| School-facilitated activities | 123 (57%) | Operations | 1 | $89,000 |
| Graduate-facilitated activities | 100 (43%) | Consulting | 11 | $98,224 |
| | | General Management | 12 | $88,259 |
| Average starting salary | $89,290 | Other | 4 | $91,375 |
| Percent employed | 88 | | | |

# CRANFIELD UNIVERSITY
## CRANFIELD SCHOOL OF MANAGEMENT

## Academics

The Cranfield approach to business education, MBAs at the school tell us, stresses "application rather than pure theory and teamwork rather than individual reward." This intensive program "is very demanding due to the condensed nature of the course (it covers a traditional U.S. two-year syllabus in 11 months)." It cuts right to the heart of the matter by "focusing on the personal and professional skills that business leaders need. Teamwork, communication, and presentation skills are crucial to the Cranfield experience." As one MBA puts it, "The academic experience at Cranfield is so much more than just a series of business classes. It is a lifestyle and leadership-development course."

Students heap praise on practically every discipline offered at Cranfield, from accounting to finance to supply-chain management. They love that all areas "focus on practical and applied learning, with teaching provided by leading consultants in their field." Professors, "almost all of whom are great teachers with industry experience, which brings real meaning to the case studies and the learning," push students to their limits. As one MBA explains, "We are actively encouraged to do things and to get out of our comfort zone, and I believe that our personal communication and networking skills will be superior as a result."

Cranfield MBAs often work in "learning teams," attacking case studies in three-day cycles; teams start preparing Wednesday's cases on Monday or Thursday's cases on Tuesday, for example. Teams must produce group reports, which earn a single grade for each member; therefore, individuals must work through their differences to present a report that satisfies everyone in the group. This "team approach to assignments teaches us to respect diversity," students tell us. One student explains, "The emphasis on teamwork means that you have to develop good interpersonal skills very quickly." Students also note that "the fact that students have significant work experience (more than seven years on average) helps."

Because of the curriculum's breakneck pace, "the main issue is being able to humanly process all the material!" The reward for all the hard work is "knowing you will be prepared for life after Cranfield." One student analogizes, "Being at Cranfield is like skydiving. It's risky, expensive, and scares the living hell out of you just before you make the leap. But once you have jumped, it's an exhilarating roller coaster of a ride, and I have the feeling that it will all be over too soon and that I will want to do it again."

## Career and Placement

Cranfield's Careers Office supports its MBAs with a variety of services, including a yearbook (distributed to hundreds of recruiters, the book contains all graduates' short resumes), on-campus recruiting events, and career-preparatory workshops. Students can use the Careers Office to access employer databases, self-assessment instruments, and alumni. This last is considered most valuable by the MBAs we spoke with. One typical survey respondent lauded the "incredible alumni help," reporting, "I contacted several in jobs with a high level of responsibility and mostly received answers within 24 hours!" Students are not entirely sold on the office's efficacy; however, many wish for "a greater diversity of recruiting companies on campus." One student writes, "We need more proactive support by the career center in order to compete with other famous schools located in big cities, especially because this school is not located in a big city." Companies recruiting on the Cranfield campus include Accenture, American Express, Atkins, Bank of Luxembourg, Booz Allen Hamilton, Eli Lilly and Company, General Motors, KPMG, Marconi, Pfizer, Pharmacia, Sir Robert McAlpine Ltd., and Tesco.

## Student Life and Environment

Cranfield University "is located in a quiet village, creating a close community where most students live in houses and flats." This isolated locale—"it takes 20 minutes to drive

EILEEN FISHER, ADMISSIONS EXECUTIVE
CRANFIELD SCHOOL OF MANAGEMENT, CRANFIELD, BEDFORD, MK43 0AL ENGLAND
PHONE: 011-440-1234 754431 • FAX: 011-440-1234 752439
E-MAIL: MBAADMISSIONS@CRANFIELD.AC.UK • WEBSITE: WWW.CRANFIELDMBA.INFO

to the nearest supermarket"—means that students must rely on one another for entertainment. Fortunately, "there is no dearth of social events, which more than makes up for the school being in a bit of wilderness." Students tell us, "There are many social activities and opportunities to network with other business schools, such as Oxford, London Business School, Cambridge, and others [as well as tons of] clubs for different sports activities like badminton, basketball, cricket, football, motor sports, scuba diving, sailing, or rugby and others for dancing, jujitsu, or yoga."

Students especially appreciate Cranfield's family-friendly atmosphere, telling us that extracurricular activities "are inclusive of the diverse student population, partners, and families." One MBA notes, "My wife enjoys socializing with other partners, attending the dancing club, and other sports activities such as touch rugby and badminton. My two kids enjoy playing in the safe school playground. They also enjoy [the] various activities arranged by school or student clubs."

There are drawbacks to Cranfield's remote location, of course. Students warn, "You need a car, as public transport in rural England is not great." They also complain that "there are very few options to eat on campus and very little access to options off-campus. Restaurants on campus are closed by 7:30 P.M., further reducing the options for hardworking students."

Cranfield's diverse student body is "a real eye-opener that helps us understand different viewpoints," MBAs tell us, as well as an excellent source of food and entertainment. One student reports, "We recently had international week, with presentations and food given by students from over 10 countries. Our Diwali festival celebration was attended by over 350 people—and there are only 136 students on the course!" Students interact constantly due to the curricular emphasis on teamwork; every term, students "are split into teams consisting of six or seven persons, all mostly of different nationalities."

## Admissions

Applicants to Cranfield are required to submit the following to the school's admissions department: undergraduate transcript, GMAT scores, TOEFL scores (for ESL students), a resume demonstrating a minimum of three years' full-time work experience, letters of recommendation, personal essays, and an interview. The school notes that it is possible for applicants lacking undergraduate degrees to gain entrance to the MBA program; such students, however, "all have considerably more than the minimum requirement of three years' work experience" and are required to "prove to the Admissions Board that [they] can cope with the academic side of the work by achieving a GMAT score of 600 or more."

## FINANCIAL FACTS

| | |
|---|---|
| Annual tuition (in-state/out-of-state) | $47,320/$47,320 |
| Books and supplies | $100 |
| Room & board (on-campus) | $7,000 |
| % of first-year students receiving aid | 45 |
| Average grant | $16,000 |

## ADMISSIONS

| | |
|---|---|
| Admissions Selectivity Rating | 85 |
| # of applications received | 261 |
| % applicants accepted | 56 |
| % acceptees attending | 45 |
| Average GMAT | 654 |
| Range of GMAT | 620–690 |
| TOEFL required of international students? | yes |
| Minimum TOEFL (paper/computer) | 600/250 |
| Application fee | $130 |
| International application fee | $130 |
| Regular application deadline | rolling |
| Regular notification | rolling |
| Deferment available? | yes |
| Maximum length of deferment | 2 years |

## APPLICANTS ALSO LOOK AT

INSEAD, University of Cambridge, University of London, University of Manchester, University of Oxford, University of Warwick

### EMPLOYMENT PROFILE

| Career Rating | 89 | Grads employed by field: | % | avg. salary: |
|---|---|---|---|---|
| Primary source of full-time job acceptances | | Finance | 8 | $113,444 |
| | | Human Resources | 2 | $129,146 |
| School-facilitated activities | 23 (27%) | Marketing | 8 | $89,006 |
| Graduate-facilitated activities | 54 (64%) | MIS | 1 | $99,583 |
| Unknown | 8 (9%) | Operations | 8 | $95,987 |
| | | Strategic Planning | 9 | $99,477 |
| Average starting salary | $98,826 | Consulting | 24 | $92,500 |
| Percent employed | 72 | Entrepreneurship | 2 | |
| | | NR | | |
| | | General Management | 16 | $109,953 |
| | | Other | 22 | $71,553 |

# DARTMOUTH COLLEGE
## TUCK SCHOOL OF BUSINESS

## Academics

Founded in 1900, Tuck School of Business at Dartmouth was the first graduate school of business in the country. And today, in the New England town of Hanover, New Hampshire, the school honors its tradition of excellence and continues to attract the very best to its campus. Students brag that they "have the opportunity to have lunch, dinner, and office hours with top executives on a daily basis." In addition, "faculty who come to Tuck are here to teach, which really differentiates Tuck from other top schools where visiting executives or adjunct faculty are primarily doing the instruction."

The first year is comprised of core courses, one elective, and projects, and at the beginning of each year, the class is divided into study groups of four or five. The school selects the groups for "diversity of experience," and students are "wowed" by the cooperation that they feel "fosters a culture of excellence without being competitive, overbearing, or arrogant." Other students agree, and add that "teamwork is important at Tuck, which is fantastic." The new curriculum also offers the Leadership Forum with specific training and coaching on building leadership skills.

The second year at Tuck consists of electives. In this year, students are offered the opportunity to develop courses of independent studies and are encouraged to pursue field studies. General management is Tuck's forte, and students recognize and applaud this: "Specialization is not Tuck's focus. General management is—and that is what the school excels at." Other students point out that with general management as its focus, the school becomes a "consulting and banking feeder school, with great connections to the top firms."

For students hoping to work on a joint degree, while escaping the busy city atmosphere, Tuck has partnered with the Fletcher School of Law and Diplomacy at Tufts University, the Kennedy School of Government at Harvard University, Paul H. Nitz School of Advanced International Studies at Johns Hopkins University, Thayer School of Engineering at Dartmouth College, Dartmouth Medical School, and Vermont Law School. Tuck has recently expanded international business opportunities, as well as increased recognition outside of the United States; international exchange programs are also offered with schools in Japan, Germany, England, Spain, and Chile. The curriculum also includes specific training and coaching on leadership skills.

A common complaint in the past years has been the rapid increase in the number of students and the relatively static status of the school's faculty and facilities. "The school is currently growing enrollment," one student complained, "but I do not see a commensurate increase in resources such as housing and teaching." Fortunately, the school seems to be addressing this by pointing out that it added faculty and it is not planning to grow enrollment any further.

## Career and Placement

Alumni cooperation amazes most students at Tuck, who have reported exceptional cooperation from alumni at every level of the business sector. "Admission to the school," one student says, "is a lifelong pass to a 'secret society' that starts the day you matriculate." According to the school, annual alumni giving is as high as 64 percent—higher than any business school in the country. For the Tuckies, though, they easily explain, "There's a reason why Tuck alums are known to be so loyal and helpful: They loved their time here."

The administration has worked hard to bring executives and recruiters to campus, and once they arrive they tend to spend at least a full day with students. In addition, most students feel that the "geographical diversity" of companies that recruit on campus is insufficient: Another student says, "The career office is East Coast-focused and apparently is unaware that large sections of the United States exist, let alone the rest of the world." In order to combat the potential isolation of the location, "administrators put forth great efforts to bring CEOs and business leaders to campus."

If there's anything that the career office has not been slow to recognize, however, it is the value of preparation. Several students report that they "started reviewing resumes and preparing for [their] internship search during orientation—before classes even started."

## Student Life and Environment

Students at Tuck describe the student body as "a unique group of urban sophisticates in a rural setting." Lest you're thinking *Green Acres*, know that most students agree that in Hanover, life is "idyllic," not dull. "Unlike the schools in big cities, I can leave my laptop anywhere," one student says. "It sounds trivial, but it's been important to feel that I am in a safe environment, both among my peers and in the community." Students agree and add that "half [of] the first-years live on-campus, so there is a very tight feeling of community." Students will also find natural beauty and resources abound.

Those students enrolled at Tuck describe a "real family feel," and this may be due to the fact that of the approximately 240 full-time MBA students per class, almost half are married. Luckily, most students agree that "Tuck does a great job integrating spouses into the mix." Spouses and partners are welcome at all events and even some classes, and the program has even made room for "Tiny Tuckies" (children of students).

Some find the male-to-female ratio discouraging—in 2003, only about 25 percent of MBAs were female, but Tuck has been working on outreach efforts to female student perspectives and 31 percent of the Class of 2007 is female. Students also complain about insufficient on-campus housing. However, the close-knit community atmosphere at Tuck receives high praise, as one student explains, "The 'TPs' (Tuck Partners), 'Tiny Tuckies' (children) and 'TCs' (Tuck Canines) are fully part of the community. Family members are invited to every nonacademic event and some TPs have been allowed to sit in on classes." Still, in the end, most Tuckies agree that "if you want a city or variety, go somewhere else. If you want intense learning and a somewhat conformist camaraderie, go to Tuck."

## Admissions

The average GMAT score of an admitted Tuck MBA student was 699, and the average GPA was 3.3. All incoming students had worked full-time prior to applying for the MBA, and the average class boasts a wide variety of undergraduate majors. TOEFL scores are required of those students for whom English is not the first language. Both need-based and merit scholarships are awarded.

### PROMINENT ALUMNI

Glenn A. Britt, Chair and CEO, Time Warner Cable; Peter R. Dolan, CEO, Bristol-Meyers Squibb Company; Alexander M. Cutler, Chair and CEO, Eaton Corporation; Christina L. Shea, President, General Mills Fndtn., Sr. VP, General Mills; Peter F. Volanakis, COO, Corning Inc.

### FINANCIAL FACTS

| | |
|---|---|
| Annual tuition | $38,400 |
| Fees | $240 |
| Books and supplies | $2,910 |
| Room & board (on/off-campus) | $9,525/$10,310 |
| % of students receiving aid | 80 |
| % of first-year students receiving aid | 81 |
| % of students receiving loans | 73 |
| % of students receiving grants | 38 |
| Average award package | $46,816 |
| Average grant | $14,370 |
| Average student loan debt | $76,373 |

### ADMISSIONS

| | |
|---|---|
| Admissions Selectivity Rating | 97 |
| # of applications received | 1,757 |
| % applicants accepted | 24 |
| % acceptees attending | 59 |
| Average GMAT | 699 |
| Range of GMAT | 670–730 |
| Average GPA | 3.3 |
| TOEFL required of international students? | yes |
| Application fee | $220 |
| International application fee | $220 |
| Regular application deadline | 4/10 |
| Regular notification | 5/15 |
| Application deadline/notification | |
| Round 1: | 10/17 / 12/16 |
| Round 2: | 12/1 / 2/1 |
| Round 3: | 1/12 / 3/24 |
| Round 4: | 4/10 / 5/15 |
| Early decision program? | yes |
| ED deadline/notification | 10/17 / 12/16 |
| Deferment available? | yes |
| Maximum length of deferment | case-by-case basis |
| Need-blind admissions? | yes |

### APPLICANTS ALSO LOOK AT

Columbia University, Harvard University, Northwestern University, Stanford University, University of Pennsylvania

| EMPLOYMENT PROFILE | | | | |
|---|---|---|---|---|
| Career Rating | 97 | Grads employed by field: | % | avg. salary: |
| Average starting salary | $100,000 | Finance | 40 | $109,600 |
| Percent employed | 93 | Marketing | 10 | $85,900 |
| | | Consulting | 32 | $100,400 |
| | | General Management | 15 | $90,200 |
| | | Other | 3 | $86,100 |

# DREXEL UNIVERSITY
## BENNETT S. LeBOW COLLEGE OF BUSINESS

## GENERAL INFORMATION
| | |
|---|---|
| Type of school | private |
| Academic calendar | July- Jun |

### SURVEY SAYS...
Smart classrooms
*Solid preparation in:*
Teamwork
Presentation skills

## STUDENTS
| | |
|---|---|
| Enrollment of parent institution | 18,466 |
| Enrollment of business school | 174 |
| % male/female | 79/21 |
| % out-of-state | 60 |
| % part-time | 68 |
| % minorities | 17 |
| % international | 50 |
| Average age at entry | 30 |
| Average years work experience at entry | 7.5 |

## ACADEMICS
| | |
|---|---|
| **Academic Experience Rating** | **83** |
| Student/faculty ratio | 16:1 |
| Profs interesting rating | 75 |
| Profs accessible rating | 73 |
| % female faculty | 26 |
| % minority faculty | 29 |

## JOINT DEGREES
MBA/MAcct; MBA/MS in Finance; MD/MBA; MBA/MS; MBA/JD

## PROMINENT ALUMNI
Raj Gupta, Chair & CEO, Rohm & Haas; Walker C. Tompkins, Jr., President & CEO, American Express; Barry C. Burkholder, Retiring President & CEO, Washington Mutual; Elaine M. Garzarelli, Former Exec. VP, Lehman Brothers, President Garzarel; Dominic J. Frederico, Deputy Chair, President and CEO, Assured Guaran.

## Academics

Drexel University's LeBow College of Business offers a variety of MBA options, all designed to maximize the time students devote to their studies. At the top of the list are two full-time options: the one-year MBA, an intensive full-time program that offers an MBA degree in half the usual time, and a traditional two-year program. Then there's the professional MBA for busy professionals seeking a part-time degree; two types of program MBAs are offered—one traditional; the other an accelerated program (LEAD) offered at either the Center City campus or at Great Valley. For students with at least five years of professional experience, Drexel offers an Executive MBA program. The MBA curriculum integrates leadership and ethics, industry perspectives, and technology management.

Drexel has long been known as a fine tech and engineering school, so it should come as no surprise that the LeBow curriculum "stresses technology at every level, from class lectures to student presentations to learning modes. We are even required to take a class on technology's effect in the business world," says one student. As a result of this focus, "the majority of the faculty is up on all of the latest information and communications technologies, which is a rarity at more traditional, nontech-focused MBA programs." The school really flashes its tech chops with its "flexible and high-quality Techno MBA Online program, which enables me to take classes from anywhere I wish, even when traveling on business for my job," says one busy MBA.

The LeBow faculty offers an "excellent mix of experienced academia with entrepreneurial professors." Students tell us, "The quality of the professors, particularly in the areas of quantitative studies (finance, statistics, decision sciences) is very high" and point out that "Wharton is across the street, and some of their professors also teach at Drexel." Students who attend the majority of their classes on campus note, "Most professors are very accessible and truly care about their students. You get a very high degree of personal attention at Drexel, particularly in the one-year MBA program." They also appreciate that "the technology is great. It's a WiFi campus, with great audio/visual in classrooms and work areas."

Other LeBow assets include the school's Laurence A. Baiada Center for Entrepreneurship in Technology, which "provides workshops facilitated by professionals with real-world experience. They show how the concepts taught in class are applied to real-world experiences." Students praise the availability of online classes at LeBow, although they wish the school would make the classes available to all students; they are currently available primarily to students in the online MBA programs.

## Career and Placement

The Office of MBA Career Services is a new office at LeBow since 2003. The staff provides students with "extensive career counseling and customized job-search resources through a series of workshops, self-assessment counseling, and formal employer networking activities." Students agree that the office meets these obligations, but they also feel that "Career Services looks at the job-search process from a very high level and takes a 'one-size-fits-all' approach. Career Services at Drexel is very good for students with little or no experience. For those of us with significant experience (5 or 10-plus) years, it isn't much help." Many also feel that the school could do a better job of attracting on-campus recruiters. "We need to improve Career Services so that students have a chance with top companies," says one student.

## Student Life and Environment

Drexel "is primarily a 'commuter' school located in the city of Philadelphia. Most MBA students live off campus and commute at least a half an hour to school." "I was looking

ANNA SEREFEAS, GRADUATE ADMISSIONS AND RECRUITMENT
3141 CHESTNUT STREET, 105 MATHESON HALL, PHILADELPHIA, PA 19104-2875 UNITED STATES
PHONE: 215-895-0592 • FAX: 215-895-1012
E-MAIL: AS326@DREXEL.EDU • WEBSITE: WWW.LEBOW.DREXEL.EDU/

for a quality education in a compressed time frame," one MBA says. Most students are only interested in squeezing their MBAs into already-hectic schedules. Even most of those who visit the campus "really only attend classes. We use the library when we have to meet with other students but do not spend much time on the campus." Those who study online or who attend satellite classrooms have even less interaction with one another.

In an effort to foster some sense of community, LeBow students recently formed an MBA Association. "It tries, but it's still new," students tell us, adding that it's worth the effort to join clubs and make connections with fellow classmates. One MBA writes, "Life is all about the people you meet and making the effort. The people in the program are generally great—you just need to make an effort to meet them. You can usually meet people at the New Deck Tavern, just off campus. Join the MBA Association and be active. It really helps you meet new people and provides networking opportunities."

Fortunately, for those with the time and inclination for a social life, Drexel is located in one of America's great cities, Philadelphia. Students agree, "One of Drexel's strong points is its location. Philly is between New York and Washington, DC, and there are many companies within this area, which makes networking much easier. This also allows students to have a wider variety of companies to choose from for internships (they can still take classes part-time and work)." The school itself is "located in a very social area (with bars, restaurants, [and] entertainment)."

## Admissions

According to the admissions committee at LeBow, "Successful applicants possess intellectual curiosity, strong analytical ability, effective communication skills, and well-defined areas of academic interest that are connected to their future career goals." Full-time post-baccalaureate professional experience is not required for admission, although it is "strongly recommended." Applicants must provide the admissions committee with official copies of all college and university transcripts, GMAT scores, TOEFL scores (where applicable), letters of recommendation, a personal statement, and a resume. An interview is optional.

### FINANCIAL FACTS

| | |
|---|---|
| Annual tuition | $45,600 |
| Books and supplies | $1,200 |
| Room & board | $9,000 |
| Average grant | $15,500 |

### ADMISSIONS

| | |
|---|---|
| **Admissions Selectivity Rating** | **89** |
| # of applications received | 796 |
| % applicants accepted | 38 |
| % acceptees attending | 58 |
| Average GMAT | 577 |
| Range of GMAT | 540–610 |
| Average GPA | 3.24 |
| TOEFL required of international students? | yes |
| Minimum TOEFL (paper/computer) | 600/250 |
| Application fee | $50 |
| International application fee | $50 |
| Regular application deadline | 8/24 |
| Regular notification | rolling |
| Early decision program? | yes |
| ED deadline/notification | Summer: 10/1 and 12/1 / 1/1 |
| Deferment available? | yes |
| Maximum length of deferment | 1 year |
| Transfer students accepted? | yes |
| Transfer application policy | Completed application and all supporting materials will be reviewed by Admissions Committee. |
| Non-fall admissions? | yes |
| Need-blind admissions? | yes |

### APPLICANTS ALSO LOOK AT

Temple University, University of Pennsylvania, Villanova University

## EMPLOYMENT PROFILE

| Career Rating | 77 | Grads employed by field: | % | avg. salary: |
|---|---|---|---|---|
| Average starting salary | $60,060 | Accounting | 29 | $52,243 |
| Percent employed | 75 | Finance | 14 | $63,857 |
| | | Marketing | 23 | $59,583 |
| | | MIS | 6 | $67,666 |
| | | Operations | 10 | $69,285 |
| | | Consulting | 12 | $66,142 |
| | | General Management | 6 | $66,500 |

# DUKE UNIVERSITY
## FUQUA SCHOOL OF BUSINESS

## Academics

Student involvement—not just in academics, but in all facets of extracurricular life—is a hallmark of the MBA program at Duke's Fuqua School of Business. Students here use the term "Team Fuqua" to sum up the collaborative spirit that binds MBAs, professors, and administration. "A strong focus on leadership" is fostered by the school's Center on Leadership and Ethics and "Coach K [Duke basketball coach Mike Krzyzewski, to the uninitiated] takes an active role in this organization and provides an excellent link to real-world leadership."

Fuqua terms are "rapid-paced," lasting only six weeks (classes meet in two two-hour sessions weekly). The curriculum "emphasizes leadership and communication skills," with outstanding offerings in marketing, finance, and health management. Students describe the program as "well-balanced, with strengths in many areas," and boast that it "allows [them] to explore many different options." One MBA student says that the professors are "leaders in their fields. They are engaged in the class, and they are highly passionate about their subjects. It's hard to imagine a professor making basic accounting enjoyable, but my professor has me loving the class because of his energy and passion."

Students and administrators are also on the same team at Duke. "Fuqua is exceptionally responsive to student feedback, and any issue is resolved quickly." For example, "Duke University has made a specific point in the last two years to get its top professors back into teaching core courses after some weakness two years ago in student reviews of core classes. They have been successful, and it has made the core course offerings very strong." Duke MBAs are deeply involved in nearly all aspects of managing the program, which they describe as "almost completely student-run. Almost any event you attend—whether career, speaker, social, or otherwise—is devised, organized, and marketed by students."

Duke also offers three Executive MBA options: an MBA Weekend Program that meets alternate weekends in Durham; an MBA Global Program that combines distance learning and international in-classroom residencies; and the MBA Cross Continent Program that combines week-long international residencies and distance learning. The Global Program requires a minimum of 10 years of professional experience; the Cross Continent Program is designed for less experienced managers.

## Career and Placement

Students agree that Fuqua's Career Management Center "has recently taken a huge step forward." The hiring of a new director and additional staff has resulted in improved services and enhanced communication between the CMC and students. "Career counselors are extremely dedicated and have even been known to come in on the weekends to help students/clubs," students tell us. The CMC also boasts "a new online tool that makes the job application and research process a lot simpler and more user-friendly." As a bonus, alumni are "phenomenally loyal. Alums bend over backward to help students find jobs and offer career wisdom."

Employers most likely to hire Fuqua MBAs include Johnson & Johnson, IBM, American Express, McKinsey & Company, Kraft Foods, Citigroup, Deloitte Consulting, Bank of America, Bear Sterns, DuPont, and Eli Lilly & Company.

Liz M. Riley, Assistant Dean and Director of Admissions
1 Towerview Drive, Durham, NC 27708-0104 United States
Phone: 919-660-7705 • Fax: 919-681-8026
E-mail: ADMISSIONS-INFO@FUQUA.DUKE.EDU • Website: WWW.FUQUA.DUKE.EDU

## Student Life and Environment

Duke offers "excellent health care and leadership resources." The Team Fuqua spirit pervades all aspects of life at Duke, including extracurricular activities. On Fuqua Fridays, the school "provides free food, beer, and wine to all Fuqua students, faculty, and their families." One happy student writes, "It's great to see everyone outside of the classroom, and to meet people's wives, husbands, and kids." MBAs also enjoy "regular cultural events," such as "two International Food Festivals each year, International Week, Asian Festival, Latin American/South American events, and events with European business leaders." Students "arrange an annual MBA Games event at which many top-tier business schools compete." The school uses the "monies raised to help the North Carolina Special Olympics athletes to compete." Despite their busy schedules, students also find time to collaborate on FuquaVision, an *SNL*-like parody of life at Fuqua produced "at least once per term. The films are a riot and really show the initiative of students here."

Basketball fanatics could hardly find a happier home, nor could golf enthusiasts; the Duke course is the best of many excellent local facilities available to Duke students. Students point out that "the weather here is great, and the area is outstanding for families." Hometown Durham, although small, "has tons of great restaurants and more to do than most people think." It also offers easy access to Raleigh and Chapel Hill; together the three cities form North Carolina's Triangle region, which offers a decent (if sprawling) approximation of urban amenities. One student sums up, "With 800 like-minded classmates around, a great climate, awesome natural resources, and (Chapel Hill's) Franklin Street only a short drive away, there is plenty to do. The culture and people are great, and school will suck up any ounce of time you give it."

## Admissions

Applicants to the Fuqua MBA Program must provide the Admissions Department with a one-page business resume, three essays (describe your work experience; describe your career goals; explain what you will contribute to the Fuqua Program), official GMAT scores, official transcripts for all post-secondary academic work, and two recommendations. An interview, though not required, is "strongly encouraged." International students must also provide official TOEFL scores if English is not their first language. To promote recruitment of underrepresented students, Duke conducts MBA Workshops for Minority Applicants, participates in "aggressive minority scholarship programs with partners, including the Toigo Foundation," and hosts the Leadership Education and Development (LEAD) Summer Business Institute. The Weekend Executive MBA prefers at least five years of professional experience; the Global Executive MBA requires a minimum of 10 years' professional experience; the Cross Continent Executive MBA requires three to nine years' experience.

### FINANCIAL FACTS

| | |
|---|---|
| Annual tuition | $37,500 |
| Fees | $1,794 |
| Books and supplies | $1,600 |
| Room & board | $13,300 |
| % of students receiving aid | 79 |
| % of first-year students receiving aid | 77 |
| % of students receiving loans | 70 |
| % of students receiving grants | 38 |
| Average award package | $44,180 |
| Average grant | $13,098 |
| Average student loan debt | $81,677 |

### ADMISSIONS

**Admissions Selectivity Rating 60\***

| | |
|---|---|
| # of applications received | 2,163 |
| Average GMAT | 700 |
| Range of GMAT | 645–750 |
| Average GPA | 3.39 |
| TOEFL required of international students? | yes |
| Application fee | $175 |
| International application fee | $175 |
| Application deadline/notification | |
| Round 1: | 10/27 / 12/16 |
| Round 2: | 1/10 / 3/7 |
| Round 3: | 3/21 / 5/9 |
| Deferment available? | yes |
| Maximum length of deferment | 1 year |
| Need-blind admissions? | yes |

### EMPLOYMENT PROFILE

| | | | | |
|---|---|---|---|---|
| Career Rating | 97 | **Grads employed by field:** | **%** | **avg. salary:** |
| **Primary source of full-time job acceptances** | | Finance | 32 | $89,569 |
| | | Marketing | 25 | $86,525 |
| School-facilitated activities | 227 (72%) | MIS | 1 | $94,000 |
| Graduate-facilitated activities | 87 (28%) | Operations | 1 | $85,000 |
| | | Consulting | 17 | $100,728 |
| Average starting salary | $90,241 | General Management | 15 | $89,246 |
| Percent employed | 90 | Other | 7 | $83,523 |

# DUQUESNE UNIVERSITY
## JOHN F. DONAHUE GRADUATE SCHOOL OF BUSINESS

## Academics

"Duquesne is very up-to-date with current business practices, research, and ethics," students at the John F. Donahue Graduate School of Business tell us. Among the distinctive curricular features at this prestigious Pittsburgh university is the "great emphasis on understanding the value chain of a company and how all functions interact within the entire enterprise value chain." Donahue even requires a course in the subject: understanding the value chain is designed to give MBAs unique insight into "how business disciplines work together as a process to create value for customers, employees, and shareholders," according to the school catalog.

The concept that business is a process requiring interdisciplinary analysis is stressed repeatedly throughout the MBA program, which consists of nine core courses and five electives. Students lacking sufficient undergraduate coursework in business are typically required to take some or all of an additional nine-course complement of pre-MBA knowledge and skills-related classes. The Donahue School offers a whopping 13 areas of concentration: accounting, business ethics, electronic business, entrepreneurship, environmental management, finance, health care management, human resource management, information systems management, international business, marketing, supply chain management, and taxation. Students may also opt for a general MBA without specialization. Students in our survey singled out offerings in accounting, business ethics, and finance for praise.

Duquesne faculty members "are easily approachable and always available for students outside of class," not only at the downtown campus but also at satellite locations. One student explains, "I am attending school part-time at a satellite campus, yet still we have full, tenured, and even department-heading professors who drive out of their way to instruct us." Professors are also "very professional and knowledgeable about their fields." One student writes, "Most professors are able to provide real-life examples, experiences, and issues. It is not just 'academic perspectives' that only exist in the classroom. Most topics we cover are solutions that could be implemented in a practical setting."

## Career and Placement

Duquesne's Career Services Office provides placement and counseling services to all of the university's undergraduate and graduate students. Yet students are "disappointed with the career services program," which they complain "does not do a good job of recruiting potential employers outside of the Pittsburgh region." Some feel the school's top priority should be "to better integrate the students in social/networking situations, and to involve its alumni to assist students as career mentors." Others think the focus should be on marketing. One student comments, "This is a great school, and I think we should take the time to submit the paperwork that needs to get done to rank us as one of the top business schools in the country by those 'Top B-Schools' lists. With greater visibility, more companies would recruit at Duquesne, which would improve our postgraduate job-placement rates, which don't seem to be very strong."

Employers most likely to hire Donohue MBAs include the Mellon Financial Corporation, Management Science Associates, PNC Corporation, U.S. Steel Corporation, Mine Safety Appliance Corporation, Alcoa, Deloitte Touche Tohmatsu, Federal Express Ground, and the H. J. Heinz Corporation.

PATRICIA MOORE, ASSISTANT DIRECTOR
600 FORBES AVENUE, PITTSBURGH, PA 15282 UNITED STATES
PHONE: 412-396-6276 • FAX: 412-396-1726
E-MAIL: GRAD-BUS@DUQ.EDU • WEBSITE: WWW.BUS.DUQ.EDU/GRAD/

## Student Life and Environment

"The MBA program at Duquesne is really a part-time program," students here explain, with "most of the classes held at night. As a result, you are removed from the rest of the campus." MBAs point out, "Student social clubs do exist, but participation is low due to most students' part-time status. Full-time students do integrate during the day." These full-timers, who make up about 20 percent of the student body, participate in the "many clubs and activities available," which include "MBA happy hours, pizza sessions with speakers, and a Halloween party with a bus trip." The faculty "is very willing to help students establish and advise student organizations."

Students here also enjoy the campus's "modern and well-constructed gym facilities, [the] nice coffee shops and food on campus, [and] the overall safe environment." Because the school is located downtown, students are "not far from professional sports activities. You can walk to Penguins hockey games in five minutes and to Pirates and Steelers games in just a little more." Pittsburgh, most here agree, "is a great city for universities. There is a wealth of knowledge in the area." One student challenges, "For those people who have never been to Pittsburgh, I think they would be surprised as to how great a city it is. It has grown beyond its dark, Steel City image." Students from warmer climes should take note that winters in Pittsburgh are long, cold, and snowy.

"The age range of students is very mixed" at Duquesne. Students observe that "some have just earned their undergraduate degrees, some took a few years off to work, and others are married with kids and coming back to school after many years in the workforce." Quite a few are "middle to upper managers with backgrounds in engineering and manufacturing." Because of "a great international program, [there are] many international students, mostly from Latin America, Eastern Europe, China, and Africa. The diversity adds a lot to classes, as does hearing about the experiences of international classmates."

## Admissions

All applicants to the Donahue MBA program must submit official transcripts for all post-secondary academic work, an official GMAT score report, two letters of recommendation, and an autobiographical statement. International students must also submit official TOEFL scores. Work experience is not a prerequisite to entering the program.

### FINANCIAL FACTS

| | |
|---|---|
| Annual tuition | $16,767 |
| Fees | $1,593 |
| Books and supplies | $2,500 |
| Room & board (on-campus) | $7,170 |
| % of students receiving aid | 70 |
| % of first-year students receiving aid | 70 |
| % of students receiving grants | 27 |
| Average grant | $16,767 |

### ADMISSIONS

| | |
|---|---|
| Admissions Selectivity Rating | 70 |
| # of applications received | 201 |
| % applicants accepted | 76 |
| % acceptees attending | 64 |
| Average GMAT | 510 |
| Average GPA | 3.1 |
| TOEFL required of international students? | yes |
| Minimum TOEFL (paper/computer) | 550/213 |
| Application fee | $50 |
| International application fee | $50 |
| Regular application deadline | 6/1 |
| Regular notification | 7/1 |
| Deferment available? | yes |
| Maximum length of deferment | 1 year |
| Transfer students accepted? | yes |
| Transfer application policy Students may transfer up to 15 credits from an accredited college or university. | |
| Non-fall admissions? | yes |
| Need-blind admissions? | yes |

### APPLICANTS ALSO LOOK AT

Carnegie Mellon, University of Pittsburgh

### EMPLOYMENT PROFILE

| | |
|---|---|
| Career Rating | 69 |
| Average starting salary | $55,000 |

# EAST CAROLINA UNIVERSITY
## COLLEGE OF BUSINESS

**GENERAL INFORMATION**

| | |
|---|---|
| Type of school | public |
| Environment | town |
| Academic calendar | semester |

**SURVEY SAYS...**

Smart classrooms
*Solid preparation in:*
Accounting
Teamwork
Communication/interpersonal skills
Computer skills

**STUDENTS**

| | |
|---|---|
| Enrollment of parent institution | 22,767 |
| Enrollment of business school | 465 |
| % male/female | 57/43 |
| Average age at entry | 29 |
| Average years work experience at entry | 3 |

**ACADEMICS**

| | |
|---|---|
| **Academic Experience Rating** | **62** |
| Student/faculty ratio | 20:1 |
| Profs interesting rating | 76 |
| Profs accessible rating | 69 |
| % female faculty | 24 |
| % minority faculty | 5 |

**JOINT DEGREES**

MD/MBA

## Academics

"The greatest strengths of East Carolina University are the many excellent programs that are available, and the fact that most of them are nationally accredited programs," explain students at this state university about 90 miles east of Raleigh. Students also appreciate the availability of online classes that are "better than [they] would have imagined. The professors are computer savvy so you notice little difference between online and a classroom setting."

The ECU MBA is designed to meet the needs of both business and nonbusiness undergraduates. It can also accommodate those without professional experience as well as those who have worked in business, though the school "strongly encourages" those without professional experience "to obtain career-related experience while earning their MBA." Depending on the student's background, the MBA program requires between 10 and 20 courses. For a quick return on investment, the curriculum can be completed in as little as one year by a full-time student with a strong undergraduate background in business.

ECU's MBA program starts with 10 core courses covering material traditionally covered in undergraduate business programs. Some or all of these classes may be waived. Waiver decisions are made on a student-by-student and course-by-course basis. In order for a waiver to be granted, the university requires a minimum grade of B in equivalent undergraduate courses. The core makes up the first half of the program; the second half consists of 10 business breadth courses, seven required and three electives. Elective choices are limited; only 15 are offered at any given time, with elective selection rotating on an annual basis. Those seeking a concentration must take four courses in their chosen area of specialization. ECU offers concentrations in development and environmental planning, finance, health care management, international management, MIS, school business management, and security studies. Most students devote their three breadth electives to their specialization, and therefore need complete only one additional course. Approximately 20 percent of ECU MBAs choose a specialization.

Students here applaud "the helpfulness of the instructors," whom they regard as "demanding and, at the same time, willing to do anything for everyone in order to do excellently." One student notes, "Our instructors may not currently be industry leaders, but they have amazing and successful (i.e., enviable) past careers and seem to be here as volunteers to help the future." Another says, "I took away something important from each of them." ECU administrators "do a great job of improving the quality of resources and courses to stay current with business trends."

## Career and Placement

Career services are provided to ECU MBAs by the in-house Career Office. The office provides recruiting resources, sponsors on-campus job fairs, organizes seminars and classroom presentations on job-search skills, and offers one-on-one counseling and other advising resources, in addition to internship programs.

LEN RHODES, ASSISTANT DEAN FOR GRADUATE PROGRAMS
3203 BATE BUILDING, GREENVILLE, NC 27858-4353 UNITED STATES
PHONE: 252-328-6970 • FAX: 252-328-2106
E-MAIL: GRADBUS@MAIL.ECU.EDU • WEBSITE: WWW.BUSINESS.ECU.EDU/GRAD

## Student Life and Environment

Many MBAs at ECU describe a collegiate atmosphere both on campus and within their program, lauding the "school spirit," "good parties, [and] excellent sports teams, especially the football team, which receives a lot of support from students." Students also keep busy with more diverse pursuits. One student explains, "We're active in business projects to help local businesses, which is a great way to find local opportunities and learn along the way. Many MBA students are involved with something else at the school, like film, international house, physics, hospital, etc. Many MBAs also volunteer building websites, analysis, and at the hospital." Students also recommend the campus's Ledonia Wright Culture Center, which "holds interesting events that are fun to go to."

Hometown Greenville is conveniently located less than two hours from both Raleigh and the North Carolina shore. There's not a lot of big business in the immediate area, however, and students warn that the crime rate here is relatively high.

Students in the MBA program describe themselves as "very open and friendly, and always willing to help you try to understand something or explain a problem you might have in a particular subject." There are "many international students from Asian countries and Africa," with most of the domestic students originating from the eastern part of the state. One-third of the students here are freshly minted college grads, meaning that they don't bring a whole lot in the way of real-world experience to their graduate business classes.

## Admissions

To be considered for admission to the MBA program at ECU, applicants must score at least 950 under the formula [(undergraduate GPA 5 200) + GMAT score], with a minimum GMAT score of 400. Students who received their undergraduate degrees less than a year before their projected starting date for the MBA program must achieve a score of 950 with a minimum GMAT score of 450. However, if their undergraduate GPA was at least 3.5, they must score at least 400 on the GMAT. Applicants must submit official copies of all postsecondary academic transcripts and official GMAT score reports. International students must exceed the formula-score requirements indicated above by 50 points and must also provide official TOEFL score reports.

### FINANCIAL FACTS
| | |
|---|---|
| Annual tuition (in-state/out-of-state) | $5,088/$15,404 |
| Books and supplies | $500 |

### ADMISSIONS
| | |
|---|---|
| **Admissions Selectivity Rating** | **67** |
| # of applications received | 190 |
| % applicants accepted | 83 |
| % acceptees attending | 77 |
| Average GMAT | 503 |
| Average GPA | 3.12 |
| TOEFL required of international students? | yes |
| Minimum TOEFL (paper/computer) | 550/213 |
| Application fee | $50 |
| International application fee | $50 |
| Regular application deadline | rolling |
| Regular notification | rolling |
| Deferment available? | yes |
| Maximum length of deferment | 1 year |
| Transfer students accepted? | yes |
| Transfer application policy Students may transfer a maximum of 9 semester credits from an AACSB-accredited institution. | |
| Non-fall admissions? | yes |
| Need-blind admissions? | yes |

# EAST TENNESSEE STATE UNIVERSITY
## COLLEGE OF BUSINESS AND TECHNOLOGY

## Academics

There aren't many choices at the College of Business and Technology at East Tennessee State University—the small program maintains only three business and four technology departments (accounting, economics/finance—urban studies, management/marketing)—but for those who are interested in a general-purpose business degree, ETSU delivers. In addition to the traditional MBA, the school also offers an MAcc (master's of accounting), an MPA (master's of public administration), and a graduate certificate in business administration for "those who seek a basic understanding of business administration but who may not be able to make the commitment of time, effort, and money required to seek a master's degree."

MBAs at ETSU feel that "the administration and faculty here are very student-oriented. Most have set times when they are available outside of class; others excel and really go the extra mile both in class presentation and in their availability to those students that require extra instruction." Professors are regarded as "very knowledgeable in their fields, and many of them are widely recognized as great scholars." One student writes, "Most of them have a work background that can lead to some very good discussions in class, and [the professors present] the applications of the concepts in the real world through their stories." Faculty members are also "easy to work with and understanding about personal matters that can arise."

Some students feel that the program could raise its standards. One MBA mentions that "it teaches to a very low level. Many of the courses are easier than AP-level high-school courses. It seems as if the school is afraid to challenge its students for fear of decreased enrollment. In multiple classes we have touched on a subject that is 'too complex for this program.'" Others see the situation somewhat differently, telling us, "They do a very good job of getting the student prepared with the knowledge that is needed in the workplace, but there is just so much that can be taught in the classroom setting, and the true learning from the classroom is applied to the jobs that are obtained after school." Part of the problem lies in the student body; most have full-time jobs in addition to school responsibilities, leaving them overextended. One student warns, "Group work here is a big problem. In 10 out of 13 classes, I have been required to be in a group. Most likely you have one or two people who do not participate in the group, leaving the workload for the other two or three people. Those individuals who do not participate always get the same grade." On a positive note, students love that "the school is large enough to offer remote-learning facilities, and classes are generally available at convenient times for working adults."

## Career and Placement

The Career Placement and Internship Services Office at East Tennessee University serves the school's entire undergraduate and graduate student body. The office hosts recruitment visits from various companies, sponsors and participates in career fairs, maintains online job boards and resume books, and offers counseling in interview skills, job search, career match, and resume writing. In the spring of 2004, on-campus recruiters included New York Life, Norfolk Southern, Wachovia, and Wells Fargo. Students are aware that "Johnson City is a small town, which limits the amount of recruiting that is done on campus." Even so, many "believe that [the] school could improve by really showing students what is available out there and helping them find jobs when they get done. It is there right now [at the Career Placement and Internship Services Office], but a student really has to push to find it."

## Student Life and Environment

East Tennessee State University is located in Johnson City, a small Appalachian city close to both the North Carolina and Virginia borders. The surrounding area, dubbed the

DRIVE MARTHA POINTER, DIRECTOR OF GRADUATE STUDIES
PO BOX 70699 JOHNSON CITY, TN 37614 UNITED STATES
PHONE: 423-439-5314 • FAX: 423-439-5274
E-MAIL: BUSINESS@BUSINESS.ETSU.EDU • WEBSITE: WWW.ETSU.EDU/GRADSTUD/INDEX.HTM

Tri-Cities region, also includes Bristol and Kingsport; the charming town of Abingdon, Virginia, is also not too far afield. The area is an outdoor enthusiast's paradise, offering plenty of opportunities for hiking, climbing, skiing, and nature walks. The Tri-Cities area is a rising force in the health care industry, with a developing biotech industry that could bring big players to the region.

With 11,000 students (about 2,000 of whom are graduate students), the ETSU campus has the population to support a busy social scene. MBAs report, "There is a very good social scene, with Thursday nights being the night that most students go out to the clubs. There are not a lot of clubs in the area, but there are many places that one can go and have a beer if they so choose." Students try to find time to support their men's basketball team, the ETSU Bucs, which in the 2003–2004 year won its second consecutive trip to "the Big Dance" (that's the NCAA Tournament to the uninitiated).

ETSU has expanded in recent years, adding several new buildings, including a fitness center (students love the "new, fully equipped athletic facility"). Not all MBAs take the time to enjoy the ETSU campus, however; they note that "the school is a high commuter school. This leads to a low participation level in on-campus clubs" and other activities. Those who do participate recommend the school's several national honor societies. One student touts "the university organization called 'President's Pride.' Through this organization, I am able to socialize with other students, faculty, administrators, and [members of the] community by volunteering for university/community functions."

Through its Adult, Commuter, and Transfer Services (ACTS) Office, ETSU assists its many nontraditional students in adapting to student life. ACTS staff advise students on the nuts and bolts of registration, direct them to the campus's various tutoring services, and help parents find child-care services. This last one can be a problem for MBAs, who typically attend evening classes. One such student comments, "I have a 15-month-old, and I have tried to get some type of care for my child so I can study or attend group meetings, and I have had no luck. This has been the most frustrating part of my school experience."

## Admissions

Applications to the College of Business and Technology at East Tennessee State University are considered on a rolling basis. Applicants must submit the following to the Graduate Admissions Office: official copies of transcripts for all undergraduate and graduate work, standardized test scores (GMAT for the MBA or MAcc, GRE for the MPA), TOEFL scores (where applicable; minimum score 550), a personal statement, letters of recommendation, and a resume. Applicants to the MPA program must have a minimum undergraduate GPA of 3.0. All applicants are presumed to be competent with computers and math literate through calculus.

## FINANCIAL FACTS

| | |
|---|---|
| Annual tuition (in-state/out-of-state) | $4,936/$13,000 |
| Fees | $750 |
| Books and supplies | $1,000 |
| Room & board | |
| (on/off-campus) | $3,500/$7,000 |
| % of students receiving aid | 25 |
| % of first-year students | |
| receiving aid | 25 |
| % of students receiving grants | 25 |
| Average award package | $6,000 |
| Average grant | $6,000 |
| Average student loan debt | $5,000 |

## ADMISSIONS

| | |
|---|---|
| **Admissions Selectivity Rating** | **75** |
| # of applications received | 70 |
| % applicants accepted | 77 |
| % acceptees attending | 85 |
| Average GMAT | 535 |
| Range of GMAT | 450–700 |
| Average GPA | 3.25 |
| TOEFL required of | |
| international students? | yes |
| Minimum TOEFL | |
| (paper/computer) | 550/213 |
| Application fee | $25 |
| International application fee | $35 |
| Regular application deadline | 6/4 |
| Regular notification | rolling |
| Deferment available? | yes |
| Maximum length | |
| of deferment | 1 year |
| Transfer students accepted? | yes |
| Transfer application policy | |
| Students may transfer a maximum | |
| of 9 semester credits from an | |
| AACSB-accredited institution, | |
| pending approval. | |
| Non-fall admissions? | yes |

## APPLICANTS ALSO LOOK AT

University of Tennessee—Knoxville, Virginia Tech

| EMPLOYMENT PROFILE | | | | |
|---|---|---|---|---|
| **Career Rating** | 61 | **Grads employed by field:** | **% avg.** | **salary:** |
| Average starting salary | $38,000 | Accounting | 20 | $40,000 |
| | | Human Resources | 10 | $30,000 |
| | | Marketing | 10 | $38,000 |
| | | Entrepreneurship | 10 | $35,000 |
| | | General Management | 50 | $30,000 |

# EASTERN MICHIGAN UNIVERSITY
## COLLEGE OF BUSINESS

### GENERAL INFORMATION
Type of school                      public
Environment                           city
Academic calendar          4 semesters

### SURVEY SAYS...
Happy students
*Solid preparation in:*
General management
Teamwork
Communication/interpersonal skills
Presentation skills

### STUDENTS
Enrollment of parent
  institution                      23,486
Enrollment of business school       279
% male/female                      76/24
% part-time                           64
% minorities                          24
% international                       20
Average age at entry                  30
Average years work experience
  at entry                             4

### ACADEMICS
**Academic Experience Rating**        **71**
Student/faculty ratio               21:1
Profs interesting rating              72
Profs accessible rating               65
% female faculty                      28
% minority faculty                    18

### JOINT DEGREES
Accounting, 150-hour program;
BS/MS, 5 years.

### PROMINENT ALUMNI
Raymond Lombardi, CEO, Deloitte
Touche Tohmatsu; James Webb,
Aon Risk Services; Joseph
Chrzanowski, Executive Director,
GM; Laurie Bohlen, VP, Field
Marketing, Dominos Pizza; Michael
Procida, Executive Director, HR Ford

## Academics

With its "ability to pull professionals from the different industries located in the southeastern Michigan area [and] an excellent location for jobs," the College of Business at Eastern Michigan University offers "an awesome MBA" to aspiring area businesspeople. The program is designed to fast-track students to their desired degrees; students with undergraduate degrees in business can conceivably complete the program with as few as 36 semester hours (others will require 57 to 63 semester hours). The program is offered during weekday evenings at the Ypsilanti campus and on Saturdays in Livonia, in order to accommodate students with full-time jobs.

The EMU curriculum, the school states, offers "a broad understanding of business functions, including the relationship of business to society as a whole and the impact of legal forces on business" in the following areas: computer information systems, e-business, entrepreneurship, enterprise business intelligence, finance, human-resource management, international business, nonprofit management, and supply-chain management. The school offers specialized degrees in all these areas and a general MBA, as well as further specialized graduate certificates in accounting, human resources, information systems, and organizational development. Throughout the program "an international perspective is provided."

Students praise a wide range of EMU offerings, touting the "excellent entrepreneur services, [the] very demanding but great management professors," and the faculty in finance, computer information, and supply-chain management. Students warn that instructors can occasionally plow through material at breakneck pace. Students say the professors sometimes "need to know that students are not as good as [the professors] are, and they need to come down to the student level to teach." All MBAs are impressed with the fact that "the professors are approachable and easy to talk to. They help as much as they can," even going the extra mile to meet with students whose jobs and family obligations make get-togethers difficult.

## Career and Placement

The Career Services Center of Eastern Michigan University assists all EMU students, graduate and undergraduate, in their efforts to "plan a career, develop job-search skills, obtain student employment while attending college, and secure a job upon graduation. Most services are also available to EMU alumni." The office offers walk-in advising, a candidate-referral service, and several job fairs over the course of the school year.

All told, about 40 companies visit campus to recruit EMU MBAs every year. Major employers of EMU MBAs include American Sun Roof, Bank One, Com Share, Compuware, Creative Solutions, Deloitte Touche Tohmatsu, Ford Motor, General Motors, Johnson Controls, Masco Corp, Pfizer Inc., Visteon Corporation, and Yakaki. Average starting salaries of EMU grads range from $32,000 (nonprofit sector) to $61,500 (marketing), with most categories falling into the high $40K to low $50K range.

## Student Life and Environment

EMU works hard to serve its varied student body. Residents and singles find much to do within the MBA community. One student writes, "Beside my classes, I attend weekly meetings of various student groups and participate in events organized by these groups. I spend time at our library, where I do my research using the excellent computer labs, books, and journals. Students often come together outside of the campus and spend quality time together." MBAs agree that "there are a number of organizations/clubs and activities that anyone can join. There are postings for many activities all year long." The

DAWN MALONE, ASSISTANT DEAN, GRADUATE PROGRAMS
4004 OWEN, YPSILANTI, MI 48197 UNITED STATES
PHONE: 734-487-4444 • FAX: 734-483-1316
E-MAIL: COB.GRADUATE@EMICH.EDU • WEBSITE: WWW.COB.EMICH.EDU/GR/

school's many part-timers and students with families find amenities tailored to their needs as well. Another student writes, "There is child-care service and early childhood programs for students with children. Family housing is available for those who need it. Overall, everything at this school is excellent." The Department of Safety provides a "SEEUS" walking- and mobile-escort service for extra on-campus security after dark.

That's good, since Ypsilanti is an urban environment with a traditionally high crime rate. Students report that "the crime in the city has improved, but there are still occasional incidents near campus," but hasten to add that SEEUS and other campus security measures ensure a "safe and friendly environment" on campus. A sizable part of the university's population (approximately 24,000) lives "on or near the immediate campus [in] typical lower-income student housing off-campus or typical student dorms/apartments on-campus." MBA students, however, are primarily commuters; as one student writes, "It is more or less a commuter campus, and the students spend a lot more time off campus than on." MBAs appreciate the school's proximity to Ann Arbor and Detroit; both cities are seen as major assets in their search for work.

Students praise EMU's capacity to attract "a nontraditional student body with a wealth of real-life business experience." The MBA program draws a large international population, representing 32 countries in all.

## Admissions

EMU's admissions office requires applicants to earn a degree from a regionally accredited college and submit transcripts from undergraduate institutions, GMAT scores, TOEFL scores (when appropriate), essays, and a resume. To gain admission, students must demonstrate an undergraduate GPA of at least 2.5 or a GPA of at least 2.75 for the final two years of undergraduate course work and a GMAT score of at least 450, as well as letters of recommendation; an interview is optional. Conditional admission may be granted to students whose undergraduate GPA or GMAT score is lower than the graduate business school normally considers acceptable, but shows promise of success in the program by other means. Applicants lacking the "required common body of knowledge that each student must complete before enrolling" must take EMU's 500-level foundation courses.

### FINANCIAL FACTS

| | |
|---|---|
| Annual tuition (in-state/out-of-state) | $5,226/$10,514 |
| Fees | $1,520 |
| Books and supplies | $1,000 |
| Room & board (on-campus) | $6,356 |
| % of students receiving aid | 30 |
| % of first-year students receiving aid | 38 |
| % of students receiving loans | 24 |
| % of students receiving grants | 4 |
| Average award package | $7,974 |
| Average grant | $3,181 |

### ADMISSIONS

| | |
|---|---|
| Admissions Selectivity Rating | 72 |
| # of applications received | 192 |
| % applicants accepted | 59 |
| Average GMAT | 470 |
| Range of GMAT | 390–750 |
| Average GPA | 3.6 |
| TOEFL required of international students? | yes |
| Minimum TOEFL (paper/computer) | 500/213 |
| Application fee | $35 |
| International application fee | $35 |
| Regular application deadline | 5/15 |
| Regular notification | 6/15 |
| Application deadline | |
| Round 1: | 5/15 |
| Round 2: | 10/15 |
| Round 3: | 3/15 |
| Round 4: | 4/15 |
| Deferment available? | yes |
| Maximum length of deferment | 1 year |
| Transfer students accepted? | yes |
| Transfer application policy | |
| Students may transfer a maximum of 6 credits toward core classes and 6 credits toward electives from an AACSB-accredited institution, pending approval. | |
| Non-fall admissions? | yes |
| Need-blind admissions? | yes |

### APPLICANTS ALSO LOOK AT

Central Michigan University, Michigan State University, Oakland University, University of Michigan, University of Michigan—Dearborn, Wayne State University, Western Michigan University

### EMPLOYMENT PROFILE

| Career Rating | 60* | Grads employed by field: | % | avg. salary: |
|---|---|---|---|---|
| | | Accounting | 10 | $48,000 |
| | | Finance | 9 | $44,500 |
| | | Human Resources | 8 | $40,400 |
| | | Marketing | 15 | $61,500 |
| | | MIS | 8 | $44,500 |
| | | Operations | 16 | $52,600 |
| | | Consulting | 7 | $49,600 |
| | | General Management | 18 | $57,500 |
| | | Global Management | 5 | $50,500 |
| | | Other | 1 | $50,000 |
| | | Nonprofit | 3 | $32,000 |

# EASTERN WASHINGTON UNIVERSITY
## COLLEGE OF BUSINESS AND PUBLIC ADMINISTRATION

### GENERAL INFORMATION

| | |
|---|---|
| Type of school | public |
| Environment | town |
| Academic calendar | quarter |

### SURVEY SAYS...

Friendly students
Happy students
*Solid preparation in:*
Teamwork

### STUDENTS

| | |
|---|---|
| Enrollment of parent institution | 9,700 |
| Enrollment of business school | 63 |
| % male/female | 41/59 |
| % out-of-state | 27 |
| % part-time | 57 |
| % minorities | 5 |
| % international | 22 |
| Average age at entry | 28 |
| Average years work experience at entry | 5 |

### ACADEMICS

| | |
|---|---|
| **Academic Experience Rating** | **69** |
| Student/faculty ratio | 25:1 |
| Profs interesting rating | 64 |
| Profs accessible rating | 69 |
| % female faculty | 46 |
| % minority faculty | 2 |

### JOINT DEGREES

MBA/MPA, 69 credits, 2 years

## Academics

Eastern Washington University offers an MBA that's "cheaper than that offered by other local schools" (namely Gonzaga University) and can be completed in just one year by the extremely diligent. Thanks to the school's active Center for Entrepreneurial Studies, entrepreneurship is among the standout disciplines here. Students praise the school's offerings in health care administration as well, lauding the "great certificate program to accompany the MBA that gives great versatility and unprecedented access in seminar format to professionals active in our community's health care industry."

EWU's MBA program is one of the few anywhere "taught by faculty from more than one department." Instructors here are drawn not only from the Department of Management but also from the Departments of Accounting and Information Systems, ensuring students the opportunity to develop "a unique and interdisciplinary business expertise." Because the business facility also houses the school's Public Administration Program, EWU students have the option to combine an MBA with an MPA.

The EWU MBA consists of 49 credit hours. Core courses constitute 33 hours of required work; electives take up the remaining 16 hours. Foundation courses can add up to an additional 32 hours of required coursework, and many or all of these courses can be waived for students with relatively recent undergraduate business degrees. Because EWU operates on a quarterly academic calendar, students who place out of foundation courses may complete the program in one year by taking 10+ credits per semester. Some here feel that "quarters are too short to learn anything" and that "classes spanning two quarters (i.e., with a part I and part II) would be beneficial." Others would like to see "a greater variety of electives offered" as well as "concentrations in areas such as marketing, project management, leadership management, finance, and technology." It should be noted, both of these problem areas are typical of smaller programs. In the asset column, students love "the great evening schedule with convenient hours for working professionals" and praise the "excellent group of well-rounded professionals staff[ing] the program. They are welcoming when you drop by their offices to ask for assistance or guidance."

## Career and Placement

The Office of Career Services provides counseling and placement services for the entire EWU student body. The office organizes occasional career fairs and posts notices for other career fairs held in the area. In addition, the office hosts on-campus interviews and other recruitment events and maintains an online placement files service, which provides students' resumes, letters of recommendation, and other documents to prospective employers. Most of Career Services' efforts are directed at the school's substantial undergraduate population. MBAs feel that the school "could definitely improve career services and offer students more opportunities to interact with potential employers."

CYNTHIA PARKER, SECRETARY SENIOR
668 NORTH RIVERPOINT BLVD., SUITE A, SPOKANE, WA 99202-1660
PHONE: 509-359-2285 • FAX: 509-358-2267
E-MAIL: CPARKER@MAIL.EWU.EDU • WEBSITE: WWW.EWU.EDU/X1032.XML

## Student Life and Environment

The smallish, predominantly part-time MBA program at EWU consists of "many working professionals and/or students with adequate business experience, [with] a number of younger, less experienced students from Asia" thrown into the mix. The size and part-time nature of the program is not conducive to a cohesive student community. Further exacerbating the situation is the fact that "there's really no organized method of creating social networks with fellow students available. Some students do go out after class to discuss politics, school, etc. all the same, but it's not under the auspices of the school." Students don't even get to tap into the culture of EWU's main campus, since the MBA program "is located on a satellite campus in downtown Spokane, 20 miles from the main campus." While the location can inhibit extracurricular life, it does have the advantage of convenience for those students who work in the downtown area.

Classes convene at the Riverpoint Higher Education Park, located on the banks of the Spokane River. The facility is home to EWU's College of Business and Public Administration, a boon to those seeking a dual degree in those two fields. Riverpoint houses a 200-seat auditorium and a number of state-of-the-art classrooms.

## Admissions

Eastern Washington University requires all the following materials from applicants to its MBA program: two copies of the completed application for admission to a graduate program; two copies of official transcripts for all post-secondary academic work; and an official GMAT score report no more than five years old. The MBA program director reserves the right to require additional information. International applicants must provide all of the above materials as well as an official TOEFL score report (if their first language is not English; students must score 580 for admission to the MBA program, 525 to be considered for pre-MBA foundation course work). EWU requires a minimum undergraduate GPA of 3.0 in the last 90 graded quarter credits. The school's website notes, "All students who graduate from the MBA program should have some practical work experience. The majority of students who are accepted into the program are working professionals and meet this requirement. For those students who enter the program lacking professional work experience, an internship should be part of the student's MBA program. Up to four credits earned while in an internship may be used for MBA elective credit."

### FINANCIAL FACTS

| | |
|---|---|
| Annual tuition (in-state/out-of-state) | $7,696/$15,800 |
| Fees | $75 |
| Books and supplies | $1,500 |
| Room & board (on/off-campus) | $6,900/$12,000 |

### ADMISSIONS

| | |
|---|---|
| Admissions Selectivity Rating | 79 |
| # of applications received | 115 |
| % applicants accepted | 62 |
| % acceptees attending | 94 |
| Average GMAT | 533 |
| Range of GMAT | 445–610 |
| Average GPA | 3.37 |
| TOEFL required of international students? | yes |
| Minimum TOEFL (paper/computer) | 580/237 |
| Application fee | $100 |
| International application fee | $100 |
| Regular application deadline | 1/1 |
| Regular notification | 1/1 |
| Deferment available? | yes |
| Maximum length of deferment | 1 year |
| Transfer students accepted? | yes |
| Transfer application policy Students may transfer a maximum of 12 credits from an AACSB-accredited institution, pending approval. | |
| Non-fall admissions? | yes |
| Need-blind admissions? | yes |

# ELON UNIVERSITY
## MARTHA AND SPENCER LOVE SCHOOL OF BUSINESS

## Academics

Flexible scheduling, an affordable degree, and a "focus on leadership and soft-skill development" earn the praises of MBA students at Elon, a premier regional university in North Carolina's Triad region. Nearly all the part-timers here work full-time in addition to fulfilling their academic responsibilities, so students understandably demand convenience in their program. Elon delivers, scheduling all classes once a week in the evenings (6 P.M. to 8:50 P.M., Monday through Thursday) during the spring and fall semesters; classes during the accelerated January and summer terms meet twice a week. Since the school doesn't have lockstep sequencing, "students can choose the courses they feel fit with their current schedules and timetables." As a result, many finish the program in as brief a period as 21 months—on average, students take approximately two years to complete the program.

Elon MBAs can also earn their degrees without putting a significant dent in their bank accounts. One student explains, "What binds most students is the desire to have a strong, valued-added education at a reasonable expense." Many here feel that "the marginal benefits received at schools with higher tuitions aren't worth the extra costs." For the 2004–2005 academic year, courses cost $1,113 each, and students were able to complete their degrees for just under $15,000.

MBAs here praise the "alternative teaching styles and small class sizes." The curriculum "stresses community and teamwork. We do many projects together. The school does not curve the grades in a way such that a portion of the class makes an F; therefore, we all try to work together and not fight for the top position." True to its historic connection to the United Church of Christ, "Elon is as much concerned with producing ethical, trustworthy, and successful leaders as it is with developing students' academic performance." Professors here "are very accessible and actively engage students to improve both the learning experience and the program overall. There is a tremendous opportunity to tailor class projects to individual interests, which enhances the level of enthusiasm and discussion."

## Career and Placement

Career-placement services are provided by Elon's Career Development Office, which serves all students in the university. Services offered specifically for MBAs include a battery of self-assessment tools, faculty advising, and seminars with area business leaders. (Through the Legends of Business program, students have met with and learned from Knight Kiplinger, editor-in-chief of the *Kiplinger Letter*; J. Richard Munro, Former Chairman and CEO of Time Warner; and Edward N. Ney, former ambassador to Canada and former Chairman, President and CEO of Young and Rubicam, Inc.) The Love School Board of Advisors meets regularly to work with the administration and faculty to ensure that the program is relevant to the needs of organizations.

Elon MBAs work for some of the area's top employers, including AstraZeneca Pharmaceuticals, Blue Cross & Blue Shield of North Carolina, Cisco Systems, Duke Energy, GE Capital, GlaxoSmithKline, IBM, LabCorp, Lucent Technologies, Procter & Gamble, UNC Hospitals, Wachovia, and Wake Med.

ARTHUR W. FADDE, DIRECTOR OF GRADUATE ADMISSIONS
100 CAMPUS DRIVE, 2750 CAMPUS BOX, ELON, NC 27244 UNITED STATES
PHONE: 800-334-8448 EXT. 3 • FAX: 336-278-7699
E-MAIL: GRADADM@ELON.EDU • WEBSITE: WWW.ELON.EDU/MBA

## Student Life and Environment

While students do "study together and occasionally socialize outside of class, most of [them] are older, working, and have active lives apart from the school." Because "the school draws from a large geographic area, it's somewhat hard to mingle with classmates outside of class."

Despite the lack of a "life at school," Elon students sing the praises of their classmates, whom they regard as "an extended family. Students accept each other for who they are and are more than willing to help each other grow and develop in the program." One MBA notes, "I've worked in groups with many strong opinions stemming from a depth of experience and awareness of current events and trends. Many personalities lean towards leadership, and there is a good diversity in both culture and professional background." The student body spans "a wide range of ages, with experienced students helping to educate the less experienced, and the less experienced often assisting the older ones with new perspectives."

Facilities at Elon are undergoing a major upgrade with construction on the Ernest A. Koury Sr. Business Center. The facility, which will house both the undergraduate and graduate business programs, will include the Read Finance Center, computer and research labs, a digital theater, and a variety of classroom designs to suit Elon's nationally recognized style of engaged learning.

Elon's central North Carolina location makes it well situated to serve the Triad region, which includes the Greensboro, High Point, and the Winston–Salem metropolitan areas. As a destination, Elon is notable mostly for its proximity to fine dining in Durham, Chapel Hill, and Greensboro; great barbecue in Lexington; the state's best zoo in Asheboro; and some of the finest golf courses in the nation.

## Admissions

The Elon MBA requires a minimum of two years' professional experience for all applicants. A completed application must include three letters of recommendation (two from work supervisors), official transcripts from all postsecondary schools attended, and GMAT scores. Students whose native language is not English must also submit TOEFL scores (minimum 550 written, 213 computer). Applicants must exceed a score of 1000 under the formula [(undergraduate GPA 5 200) + GMAT score], and must also have a minimum GMAT score of 470. Undergraduate classes in financial accounting, management, microeconomics, and statistics are required foundation courses in the MBA program. Students may begin in August or January; applications are assessed on a rolling basis.

### FINANCIAL FACTS

| | |
|---|---|
| Average grant | $30,000 |

### ADMISSIONS

| | |
|---|---|
| Admissions Selectivity Rating | 71 |
| # of applications received | 69 |
| % applicants accepted | 81 |
| % acceptees attending | 84 |
| Average GMAT | 524 |
| Range of GMAT | 480–560 |
| Average GPA | 3.2 |
| Minimum TOEFL (paper/computer) | 550/213 |
| Application fee | $50 |
| International application fee | $50 |
| Regular application deadline | rolling |
| Regular notification | rolling |
| Deferment available? | yes |
| Maximum length of deferment | 1 year |
| Transfer students accepted? | yes |
| Transfer application policy | Students may transfer a maximum of 9 credits from an AACSB-accredited institution, pending approval. |
| Non-fall admissions? | yes |
| Need-blind admissions? | yes |

### APPLICANTS ALSO LOOK AT

North Carolina State University, University of North Carolina at Greensboro, Wake Forest University—Winston-Salem

### EMPLOYMENT PROFILE

| Career Rating | 60* | Grads employed by field: | % | avg. salary: |
|---|---|---|---|---|
| | | Accounting | 12 | NR |
| | | Finance | 9 | NR |
| | | Human Resources | 3 | NR |
| | | Marketing | 9 | NR |
| | | MIS | 9 | NR |
| | | Operations | 22 | NR |
| | | General Management | 9 | NR |
| | | Other | 18 | NR |
| | | Nonprofit | 9 | NR |

# EMORY UNIVERSITY
## GOIZUETA BUSINESS SCHOOL

## Academics

Named after the one-time CEO of the Coca-Cola Company, the Goizueta (pronounced "goy-SWET-uh") Business School at Emory University shares its namesake's penchant for innovative change. Students report favorably that their school "is constantly striving to improve Goizueta. Administrators often ask for our feedback. If we want something to change, we provide our suggestions and a plan to change it, and it's changed. They want to give us the best experience possible." Another MBA adds, "On numerous occasions, projects or proposals generated by students have been adopted by the MBA program. Specifically, several courses have been created by students (they designed the curriculum and interviewed candidates to teach it). If a student is willing to take on the responsibility of addressing a need and taking the solution from paper to fruition, he or she finds the administration to be an excellent partner in the process."

Students appreciate Goizueta's customer-friendly approach, but that's hardly the school's only asset. Goizueta MBAs also benefit from the school's Atlanta locale, which puts them in the neighborhood of many of the nation's largest companies. The strength of Atlanta's business community feeds the faculty and the guest-speaker roster; as one student puts it, "Professors do a great job of bringing business leaders into the classroom. They take full advantage of Atlanta's business connections." Students love Goizueta's finance program; marketing, strategy/entrepreneurship, and consulting are also reportedly strong. Goizueta offers students a fair amount of flexibility, allowing two-year MBAs eleven electives to supplement core courses and other requirements. Core courses "are extremely rigorous and challenging, [some students feel that] there could be more electives to choose from," but the courses that are available are largely excellent. Professors earn high marks for accessibility. One student reports, "I met one-on-one with every one of my professors first semester, and they were all so supportive and willing to give me extra help. Last semester, I had met with my managerial accounting professor a few times throughout the semester and had spent a few hours with her before the final. She came up to me in the middle of the final to see how I was doing and to boost my confidence by reminding me that I was extremely prepared for the test and that I would do great!" Students also love the "fantastic facilities," telling us that "the wireless network in the building makes it easy to be connected."

## Career and Placement

The Career Management Center (CMC) at Goizueta "has made tremendous strides over the past three years, but there is still room for improvement. The staff is focused on bringing companies to campus, but could perhaps focus more on cultivating stronger relationships with businesses in the Atlanta community." Many students feel that the office's shortcomings result more from a weak economy than from any lack of effort or expertise on its part. Recruitment efforts are enhanced by the fact that over 700 of the U.S.'s *Fortune* 1000 companies have headquarters in Atlanta. Employers who most frequently hire Goizueta MBAs include Bright House, CHEP International, Citigroup, Delta Air Lines, Earthlink, Eastman Kodak, GE Capital, Honeywell, IBM, ING, Kimberly Clark, NCR, PricewaterhouseCoopers, Procter & Gamble, The Gallup Organization, The Home Depot, Trammell Crow, Turner Broadcasting, and Wachovia. About three-fifths of Goizueta MBAs remain in the South Atlantic region; approximately 1 in 10 finds work outside the United States.

## Student Life and Environment

Students love the tight community formed within the Goizueta MBA program. As one student explains, "Life at Goizueta is terrific. I know all of the 160+ members of my two-year MBA class and approximately half of the first-year and one-year MBA students via

JULIE R. BAREFOOT, ASSOCIATE DEAN AND DIRECTOR OF MBA ADMISSIONS
1300 CLIFTON ROAD, ATLANTA, GA 30322 UNITED STATES
PHONE: 404-727-6311 • FAX: 404-727-4612
E-MAIL: ADMISSIONS@BUS.EMORY.EDU • WEBSITE: WWW.GOIZUETA.EMORY.EDU

the Finance Club and other activities. I believe that this is the reason there exists such a pleasant atmosphere at school; without sounding too corny, it really becomes like an extended family." Another student agrees, "We have such a tight network that most people know everybody. You can walk through our common areas and always see people working together on a project, someone helping someone with his resume, someone helping someone with her finance homework. Even when we are not working on assigned team projects, we are always working in teams for something—to help someone with a resume, a cover letter, or an interview. Whatever it is, we work as a team." Students tell us, "The familial atmosphere among students is facilitated to a large degree by the administration. Activities such as student orientation (ropes course, skydiving), three-week international business modules in January, and frequent student get-togethers provide a wealth of opportunities for the students to socialize with one another." Regular program-wide rendezvous include kegs in the courtyard every Thursday ("since there are no classes on Fridays," and bagels every Monday and Wednesday morning. There are "constant gatherings in people's homes, including a weekly poker game, [and, at the end of the fall semester,] a school-wide, *Family Feud*–style event. It gives a great break prior to final exams." All contribute to the especially strong sense of community at Goizueta.

Because it is a relatively small program, Goizueta "offers a large number of leadership positions in the school, particularly in proportion to the number of students. If you want to get involved, you can. There's something for everyone." MBAs tell us that they are "extremely busy. While a fair portion of this can be attributed to classwork, there are also a tremendous number of activities that are run by students. These activities range from case competitions to speaker panels to charity events to intramural sports; everyone is involved in something." Then, of course, there's Atlanta, which offers "great restaurants and concerts, as well as major league baseball, hockey, football, and basketball games."

## Admissions

Applicants to the Goizueta MBA program must submit undergraduate transcripts (course work should demonstrate solid analytical and/or quantitative skills; one semester of college-level statistics is required), GMAT scores, TOEFL scores (international students), a resume (applicants are required to have "several years of full-time work experience"), two letters of recommendation, and essays. An interview is strongly recommended but is not required. Minority recruitment efforts include participation in the Consortium of Graduate Study in Management, Management for Tomorrow (MLT), and the Forte Foundation. Additionally, the school reports that it hosts "Inside Goizueta: A Conference for Prospective Minority Students" and attends the National Black MBA and National Society for Hispanic MBA conferences.

## FINANCIAL FACTS

| | |
|---|---|
| Annual tuition | $32,096 |
| Fees | $422 |
| Books and supplies | $1,900 |
| Room & board | $15,000 |
| % of students receiving aid | 82 |
| % of first-year students receiving aid | 74 |
| % of students receiving loans | 57 |
| % of students receiving grants | 60 |
| Average award package | $31,542 |
| Average grant | $17,815 |
| Average student loan debt | $54,404 |

## ADMISSIONS

| | |
|---|---|
| Admissions Selectivity Rating | 95 |
| # of applications received | 1,080 |
| % applicants accepted | 37 |
| % acceptees attending | 39 |
| Average GMAT | 680 |
| Range of GMAT | 650–710 |
| Average GPA | 3.4 |
| TOEFL required of international students? | yes |
| Minimum TOEFL (paper/computer) | 600/250 |
| Application fee | $140 |
| International application fee | $140 |
| Regular application deadline | 3/15 |
| Regular notification | rolling |
| Deferment available? | yes |
| Maximum length of deferment | 1 year |
| Need-blind admissions? | yes |

## APPLICANTS ALSO LOOK AT
Duke University, New York University, Northwestern University, University of Michigan, University of North Carolina at Chapel Hill, University of Pennsylvania, University of Virginia

## EMPLOYMENT PROFILE

| Career Rating | 96 | Grads employed by field: | % | avg. salary: |
|---|---|---|---|---|
| Average starting salary | $85,734 | Finance | 33 | $78,248 |
| | | Marketing | 24 | $76,109 |
| | | Operations | 4 | $76,000 |
| | | Consulting | 21 | $89,252 |
| | | General Management | 4 | $74,938 |
| | | Other | 14 | $81,497 |

# ESADE BUSINESS SCHOOL

## Academics

Students at the prestigious ESADE Business School in Barcelona have two full-time MBA options: an 18-month program geared toward students seeking an international dual degree as well as students with nonbusiness backgrounds; and a one-year program designed for highly experienced students seeking a career boost or a fresh start as international entrepreneurs. Both are bilingual programs (but courses in the one-year program are conducted primarily in English). ESADE also offers a part-time program, taught primarily in Spanish, to local students.

Students report that "ESADE places emphasis on teamwork and collaborative learning." They go on to say, "The workload is significant, but always manageable." The teamwork focus means "half of the learning is done among students through interactions, arguments, and negotiations. These are the skills you will never learn by simply sitting in the classroom, even with the greatest professors teaching you the greatest classes ever." Leadership is also stressed in the "cutting-edge" LEAD (Leadership Assessment and Development) program, in which student groups undertake a challenging business simulation, then review a videotape of their work to analyze which roles were taken by each group member and how successfully each member utilized leadership skills in performing his or her role.

Professors at ESADE sometimes make courses too "heavily lecture-oriented," and some "don't speak good English," but generally professors earn praise for "knowing exactly the material and subjects of the other courses" and for being "accessible after class." Furthermore, students say, "Since class size is small, you can approach professors very casually, and they are friendly and helpful." Students are especially impressed with the marketing program, and they also tell us, "ESADE has one of the best language programs in Europe, which is very important in an International MBA." The administration is very responsive to student input. One MBA writes," It is not uncommon for student suggestions or proposals to change school policy. In this sense, students feel very respected and important at ESADE."

ESADE offers a dual-degree MBA in conjunction with four prestigious U.S. MBA-granting institutions and four equally prestigious Latin American schools; those who complete the program receive degrees from both ESADE and the participating American school.

## Career and Placement

ESADE's Career Services office "has only gotten properly started the last couple of years and is not up to par by standards of U.S. schools," observes one American exchange student. However, MBAs report that "the department has made strong improvements in the last few years. There is still room to grow, especially in the connection between employers and students, but they are on their way. They are improving, and this effort must be recognized." Although the school claims contact with more than 1,500 employers, a few students still feel that "ESADE could improve recruiting efforts to companies based in the U.S." and "abroad." The office hosts on-campus forums, recruiting events, corporate presentations, networking and alumni events, workshops, and seminars. It also maintains a Career Resources Center with hard-copy and electronic databases and other reference materials.

Employers most likely to hire ESADE MBAs include Novartis, Citigroup, Bayer, PWC, L'Oreal, General Electric, BBVA, Accenture, Nike, Deloitte Touche Tohmatsu, Intel, Danone, Dupont, and KPMG.

NURIA GUILERA, MBA MARKETING AND ADMISSIONS DIRECTOR
AVENUE D'ESPLUGUES, 92-96 BARCELONA, 08034 SPAIN
PHONE: 011-34-934-952-088 • FAX: 011-34-934-953-828
E-MAIL: MBA@ESADE.EDU • WEBSITE: WWW.ESADE.EDU

## Student Life and Environment

"ESADE is a well-balanced school," and it features "individual activities as well as team-work opportunities." While the workload can be demanding, "there is always time to go and have a beer with your friends." Many students enjoy spending each morning "with a cup of café con leche on the sunny terrace of the school overlooking Barcelona." Whether working or playing, ESADE MBAs enjoy a convivial atmosphere. One student comments, "People are very friendly. Even though we may work a lot, social life is very important. I don't see ESADE as an MBA factory like many other business schools, but more like a place to live a once-in-a-lifetime experience."

ESADE "doesn't provide accommodations for students, but the school has an agency that will find you the living space you want. This city is unbeatable and very, very safe." Barcelona, which students call "a very attractive city that has a great social and cultural life," is home to world-renowned art galleries and museums, concert halls, theaters, and international athletic events—not to mention the trippy architectural masterpieces by Antonio Gaudí. It's also a port city and one of the great economic centers of southern Europe.

ESADE's student body is "very diverse, interactive, friendly, creative, and dynamic." One student reports, "My academic team of seven students (which works together the entire first year) has people from Greece, Spain, Puerto Rico, France, Canada, the U.S., and Japan. In terms of business background: corporate finance in a blue-chip company, stock trading in a brokerage, marketing in IT, marketing in biotech, managing a theme park, operations/logistics in the automobile industry, and operations/logistics in meat production. It's a very diverse group." Students go on to say this school "is a very team-oriented and supportive culture and people form very personal and strong relationships."

## Admissions

Applicants to the 18-month full-time MBA program must have a minimum of two years' full-time work experience. Applicants to the one-year full-time MBA program must have at least five years of full-time work experience and an undergraduate degree in business or economics (candidates with engineering or mathematics degrees are evaluated in the light of their business experience). Completed applications must include: official transcripts for all undergraduate work, official GMAT and English proficiency scores (ESADE offers its own English proficiency exam), two letters of recommendation, and an application form. Interviews are conducted at the school's request only; all admitted students are interviewed prior to admission. According to the school's website, "Aspects taken into account during the admission process include: the candidate's intellectual abilities; professional potential; maturity; motivation; and ability to work as part of a team."

### FINANCIAL FACTS

| | |
|---|---|
| Annual tuition | $29,575 |
| Books and supplies | $200 |
| Room & board | $10,660 |
| % of first-year students receiving aid | 40 |
| Average grant | $18,474 |

### ADMISSIONS

| | |
|---|---|
| **Admissions Selectivity Rating** | **86** |
| # of applications received | 281 |
| % applicants accepted | 63 |
| % acceptees attending | 45 |
| Average GMAT | 630 |
| Range of GMAT | 600–700 |
| Average GPA | 3.5 |
| TOEFL required of international students? | yes |
| Minimum TOEFL (paper/computer) | 600/250 |
| Application fee | $100 |
| International application fee | $100 |
| Regular application deadline | 6/30 |
| Regular notification | rolling |
| Deferment available? | yes |
| Maximum length of deferment | 1 year |
| Non-fall admissions? | yes |
| Need-blind admissions? | yes |

### EMPLOYMENT PROFILE

| Career Rating | 84 | Grads employed by field: | % | avg. salary: |
|---|---|---|---|---|
| Average starting salary | $72,093 | Finance | 16 | NR |
| | | Marketing | 23 | NR |
| | | Consulting | 23 | NR |
| | | General Management | 34 | NR |
| | | Other | 3 | NR |
| | | Nonprofit | 1 | NR |

# ESSEC BUSINESS SCHOOL
## THE ESSEC MBA PROGRAM

## Academics

ESSEC advertises its program as a "flexible, integrative MBA," and students confirm that this French business school adheres to truth-in-advertising principles. As per flexibility, "students choose all the courses they attempt. It's the first school in France that decided to follow a process like that. It's great because you don't spend your time in courses that don't interest you." The integrative aspect comes through 18 months of required internships (which can be waived for students with equivalent post-baccalaureate professional experience) and optional apprenticeships.

ESSEC MBAs "are allowed to choose their own classes and professional experiences. Each student is tutored by a resident teacher who provides advice and insights; by alternating periods in school and interning with companies, ESSEC students gain much maturity and understanding of the stakes of their future careers." One student explains, "Everything is flexible, as long as we stay within the criteria needed to graduate, from the number of courses per day, per week, per quarter, per semester, the lengths of each internship and other professional experience, to the choice of courses or the way to fulfill our required international content." ESSEC MBAs can meet this requirement through study abroad at an ESSEC partner school, a dual degree at one of six international schools, or an internship or humanitarian mission abroad.

The ESSEC curriculum is broad, offering over 200 electives each term, so "you can be a generalist or become really specialized in a particular domain." Students report that "for a business school, ESSEC is really aware of new concerns like ethics and sustainable development, and it tries to make the students aware of what happens in the world economy nowadays." MBAs warn, "You have to be responsible and define your own goals, and the course attribution system is somehow complicated, but the administration is outstanding: They make this complex system work smoothly, deal with the high flexibility, answer your questions, and always try to improve our school, making it the most innovative in France." All students work with a mentor "who follows you and helps you throughout your scholarly half of the program."

ESSEC professors are often "top executives in French companies and are thus experts of the evolutions of the techniques used in the fields in which they teach." Others are well-known in research circles. ESSEC's strengths include such uncommon areas as international hospitality management, luxury brand management, agrifood and agribusiness management, sports marketing, and ethics and biotechnology.

## Career and Placement

The Office of Corporate/Student Relations at ESSEC Business School keeps busy by handling the 8,000+ internship offers that pour into the school each year. In addition, the office provides one-on-one counseling; organizes on-campus recruitment, company visits, and job fairs; and manages the school's large apprenticeship program (under which students work for an area company for two years while simultaneously continuing their studies at ESSEC). Each year 220 employers visit the campus to recruit MBAs for full-time work; another 700 offer internship positions.

Employers who most frequently hire ESSEC graduates include Accenture, BNP Paribas, Danone, Deloitte Touche Tohmatsu, Deutsche Bank, EDF-GDF, L'Oréal, Michelin, Pfizer, Pinault Printemps Redoute, PricewaterhouseCoopers, Procter & Gamble, Renault, Societe Generale, and 3 Suisses International.

Mr. Philippe Regimbart, Director of Admissions
Avenue Bernard Hirsch, B.P. 50105 Cergy-Pontoise, 95021 France
Phone: 011-33-1-3443-3095 • Fax: 011-33-1-3443-3111
E-mail: merizio@essec.fr • Website: www.essec.edu

## Student Life and Environment

ESSEC "has a very good feeling of *appartenance* (belonging), [forged in part by the] many school clubs which easily bring people together." One MBA notes, "The number of associations in this business school enables you to do any activities you ever dreamed of, from skydiving to bartending, or any others. The associations and clubs are really numerous and different, encompassing sports (sailing, football, basketball, tennis, golf), culture (theater, poetry, cinema, photography), and economics and politics. Any student can create a new association, and the administration helps us."

"Students note that the campus is relatively large by French standards," and that "new amenities have been built to modernize the old-looking main buildings from the 1970s!" While some complain that "the location is unfortunately outside the capital," others like their hometown of Cergy Pontoise, "a suburb in the northwest of Paris. Cergy is 30 minutes away by tube from the center of Paris, and the train station is near the school. Cergy Pontoise is quite a big city (150,000 people) with all facilities (supermarkets, many different shops for all types of shopping). So you do not have to go into Paris all the time if you do not want to. Last but not least, living in Cergy Pontoise is very nice because you can have quite a cheap flat, and you are at the same time very close to the center of Paris with a straight tube line. It is perfect!"

The ESSEC student body represents 63 countries; nearly half its students are women. Most MBAs are young. According to one student, "There are very few students who are married or have children because the average age is 22 to 23."

## Admissions

ESSEC requires the following of international applicants to its MBA program: official copies of all undergraduate and graduate transcripts; TOEFL, GMAT or TAGE/MAGE (the French equivalent of the GMAT) scores; letters of recommendation; a personal statement; and a resume. According to the school's website, "A minimum of 18 months of validated professional experience is required, but students with insufficient experience may enroll if admitted and carry out this work requirement during their ESSEC MBA program in periods of internship. In such cases, the program will be prolonged and may last longer than two years."

### FINANCIAL FACTS

| | |
|---|---|
| Annual tuition | $20,200 |
| Books and supplies | $565 |
| Room & board | |
| (on/off-campus) | $7,500/$11,260 |
| % of students receiving aid | 36 |
| % of first-year students | |
| receiving aid | 33 |
| % of students receiving grants | 12 |
| Average award package | $5,822 |
| Average grant | $4,225 |
| Average student loan debt | $25,422 |

### ADMISSIONS

| | |
|---|---|
| **Admissions Selectivity Rating** | **97** |
| # of applications received | 4,007 |
| % applicants accepted | 23 |
| % acceptees attending | 65 |
| Average GMAT | 670 |
| Range of GMAT | 600–780 |
| TOEFL required of | |
| international students? | yes |
| Minimum TOEFL | |
| (paper/computer) | 600/230 |
| Application fee | $195 |
| International application fee | $195 |
| Application deadline/notification | |
| Round 1: | 10/14 / 12/1 |
| Round 2: | 1/6 / 3/2 |
| Round 3: | 2/24 / 4/13 |
| Round 4: | 5/5 / 6/15 |
| Deferment available? | yes |
| Maximum length | |
| of deferment | 1 year |
| Need-blind admissions? | yes |

### APPLICANTS ALSO LOOK AT
E.M. LYON, ESCP-EAP European School of Management, HEC School of Management—Paris

### EMPLOYMENT PROFILE

| Career Rating | 83 | Grads employed by field: | % | avg. salary: |
|---|---|---|---|---|
| Average starting salary | $52,273 | Accounting | 4 | NR |
| Percent employed | 80 | Finance | 11 | NR |
| | | Human Resources | 2 | NR |
| | | Marketing | 27 | NR |
| | | MIS | 8 | NR |
| | | Operations | 1 | NR |
| | | Consulting | 30 | NR |
| | | Communications | 1 | NR |
| | | Entrepreneurship | 4 | NR |
| | | General Management | 2 | NR |
| | | Other | 9 | NR |
| | | Nonprofit | 1 | NR |

# FAIRFIELD UNIVERSITY
## CHARLES F. DOLAN SCHOOL OF BUSINESS

## Academics

"Jesuit tenets" guide instruction at the Dolan School of Business, a small, mostly part-time program at Fairfield University that boasts "a fine finance program." Dolan offers graduates an MBA (part-time and full-time), an MS in finance, and a one-year MBA in accounting. Qualified professionals may enroll in certificate programs for advanced study in accounting, finance, human resource management, information systems and operations management, international business, marketing, and taxation.

The Dolan MBA curriculum is divided into three components: core courses, breadth courses, and elective specialization or concentration courses. Core classes count toward the graduate degree; they are meant to be functional areas of deficiency in students' academic business backgrounds, and some or all can be waived for students who successfully completed undergraduate courses in the areas these classes cover. Breadth courses account for 18 credits toward the degree and cover important concepts in accounting, finance, information systems, management, business ethics, and marketing. The remainder of the curriculum consists of 12 credits of concentration courses (concentrations are available in accounting, finance, human resource management, information systems and operations, general management, international business, marketing, and taxation), an additional three elective credits, and a three-credit capstone course in global competitive strategy.

The One-Year MBA in accounting is open to undergraduates in accounting from all undergraduate institutions. Pursued full-time, this program "leads to the MBA and fulfills requirements to sit for the uniform CPA examination" in 12 to 15 months.

Dolan students praise their "very accessible and helpful faculty," telling us that "professors' enthusiasm contributes a lot to the learning experience. The course work is current and interesting." Courses are held between 7:00 and 10 P.M. on weekday evenings for the convenience of employed students; a limited number of weekend courses are also available.

## Career and Placement

The Dolan MBA program is a small, predominantly part-time program in which most students already have careers; a number of students actually attend at their employers' expense. This situation creates a relatively small demand for career services within the program; students seeking such services must use the Career Planning Center, which serves the entire student body of the university. The Dolan Graduate Business Association, run by students, is probably the most aggressive advocate for career services within the program. Professors and alumni are also regarded as valuable resources for those seeking internships or careers.

Employers most likely to hire Dolan MBAs include American Skandia, Bayer Corporation, Cendant Corporation, The Common Fund, Gartner, General Electric, People's Bank, Pitney Bowes, Pfizer, UBS Warburg, Unilever, and United Technologies.

Dr. Dana A. Wilkie, Assistant Dean/Director of Graduate Programs
1073 North Benson Road, Fairfield, CT 06824 United States
Phone: 203-254-4000 • Fax: 203-254-4029
E-mail: dlauria@mail.fairfield.edu • Website: www.fairfield.edu/mba

## Student Life and Environment

The Dolan School of Business is housed in a 70,000-square-foot facility that includes a 150-seat amphitheater, a wireless computer network, two high-tech computer labs, eight breakout rooms for meetings and projects, and numerous classrooms and offices. Classrooms are equipped to accommodate all up-to-date teaching technologies. Students here praise the "informal, relaxed atmosphere" and "safe campus" that make the "heavy workload" a little easier to handle. Most agree that extracurricular life is minimal, and that there's "not much for MBAs to do here on campus except go to class."

Dolan students benefit from the school's location near New York City. Nearly 50 *Fortune* 500 companies are headquartered within 50 miles of the school; a little farther afield (in New York City itself and lower Westchester County, all within an hour from campus) approximately 100 *Fortune* 500 companies maintain significant presences. Fairfield County is home to the greatest concentration of U.S. headquarters for foreign multinationals; many of these firms work with the university to provide experiential learning opportunities.

## Admissions

Applications may be submitted to Dolan via mail or the Internet. Applications are processed on a rolling basis, and students may commence the program in any term. The Admissions Committee considers applicants' post-secondary academic records, GMAT scores, two letters of recommendation, and resume or other self-evaluation of work experience. International students from non-English-speaking countries must submit TOEFL scores (a minimum score of 550 is required). Applicants to the one-year MBA program in accounting and taxation must meet all the above criteria and must also provide a statement of certification from his/her accounting department faculty and a letter of recommendation from either a former employer or a faculty member outside the discipline of accounting. This program is open only to students who hold, or are in the process of earning, an undergraduate degree in accounting. All entering students in all programs must demonstrate proficiency in microeconomics, macroeconomics, calculus, and statistics. Successful completion of undergraduate work in these areas is the most common way of demonstrating proficiency.

### FINANCIAL FACTS

| | |
|---|---|
| Annual tuition | $22,000 |
| Fees | $100 |
| Books and supplies | $1,000 |

### ADMISSIONS

| | |
|---|---|
| **Admissions Selectivity Rating** | **81** |
| # of applications received | 120 |
| % applicants accepted | 62 |
| % acceptees attending | 100 |
| Average GMAT | 550 |
| Range of GMAT | 490–650 |
| Average GPA | 3.2 |
| TOEFL required of international students? | yes |
| Minimum TOEFL (paper/computer) | 550/213 |
| Application fee | $55 |
| International application fee | $55 |
| Regular application deadline | rolling |
| Regular notification | rolling |
| Deferment available? | yes |
| Maximum length of deferment | 1 year |
| Transfer students accepted? | yes |
| Transfer application policy 6 credits or Jesuit University Transfer Program | |
| Non-fall admissions? | yes |

### APPLICANTS ALSO LOOK AT

Pace University, Quinnipiac University, University of Connecticut

# FAIRLEIGH DICKINSON UNIVERSITY
## SILBERMAN COLLEGE OF BUSINESS

## Academics

Most of the MBA offerings from Fairleigh Dickinson University are available at both of the school's campuses: the College at Florham campus, located in Madison, and the Metropolitan campus, located in Teaneck. A few specialized programs are available at the Metropolitan campus only; these include the full-time one-year Global Business Management MBA program.

Students appreciate the convenience of the two campuses—although students must enroll at one campus, they are free to take classes at either—and the "flexibility of the program to accommodate working schedules," an important factor for the schools' 550-plus part-time students, most of whom work full-time. Students also appreciate the fact that FDU offers a "well-rounded program" with a "breadth of concentrations." The school offers concentrations in entrepreneurship, finance, information systems, international business, marketing, management, and pharmaceutical management studies at both campuses; corporate communications management and human resources management at the Florham campus only; and health systems management at the Metropolitan campus only. Those in a hurry to finish their degrees especially appreciate the five-week-long Saturday classes. One student explains, "The workload is heavy given the short time period, but without taking some of these classes, I would probably only take one class per semester, and it would have taken me a lot longer to complete the program."

FDU MBAs tell us that "classwork here is fine and moderately challenging." Students enjoy a "good rapport among students" and great professors, especially "the adjuncts who bring a great deal of real-life experience to the classroom." One first-year student says, "I have taken five courses so far. Out of these classes, three of the professors I would rate as top-shelf. I was challenged intellectually and gained a lot from these classes. The other two were introductory classes, yet the professors were always accessible and passionate about their subject. There are definitely some hidden treasures in the faculty." The administration is not so universally admired; students complain that "convoluted processes and unhelpful individuals" mar their dealings with the school. Some also feel that "the school needs to upgrade some of the classrooms."

## Career and Placement

Each of FDU's campuses maintains its own Career Development Center. Both offices offer self-assessment tools, one-on-one counseling, libraries, resume critiquing, interview and job-search seminars, job listings, on-campus recruitment interviews, co-op and internship services, and career fairs. Past on-campus recruiters have included Advanced Technology Group, Ameriphrise Financial, AXA Advisors, the Drug Enforcement Agency, First Investors, Northwest Mutual, ProFinance, Wachovia, and the World Savings Bank.

## Student Life and Environment

Most of FDU's full-time MBAs (as well as many part-time students) attend the Metropolitan campus in Teaneck, not far from the George Washington Bridge, thus providing easy access to New York City. The program is housed in Dickinson Hall, which offers three microcomputer laboratories, an auditorium, classrooms, and office space. The wooded campus straddles the Hackensack River.

FDU's College at Florham campus in Madison attracts mostly part-time students. The campus was landscaped by famed architect Frederick Law Olmstead; unfortunately for most MBAs, it's often dark here when they arrive and leave, making it more difficult to appreciate the surrounding beauty. Not that students would have much time to take in

THOMAS M. SHEA, UNIVERSITY DIRECTOR OF INTERNATIONAL & GRADUATE ADMISSIONS
1000 RIVER ROAD, T-KB1-01, TEANECK, NJ 07666 UNITED STATES
PHONE: 201-692-2554 • FAX: 201-692-2560 • E-MAIL: GRAD@FDU.EDU
WEBSITE: WWW.FDU.EDU

their environs anyway, since "most of the MBA students also work full-time. They don't have time for involvement with the school outside the classroom."

At both sites, FDU attracts "a very mixed conglomerate of people" that includes "lots of foreign students." These "intelligent, hardworking, and dedicated" MBAs don't socialize much, but "you meet a lot of people anyway because there are a lot of group assignments." Students are "competitive, but in a friendly way." A considerable number are just starting out in their careers; writes one student who isn't, "I am a mid-career manager and am older than most of the students. However, I do not feel out of place. All of my classes have been great, and the diversity of experiences has resulted in great learning sessions."

## Admissions

Applicants to the FDU MBA program must apply to a specific campus; after being admitted, students are allowed to attend classes on either campus. Applications are generally processed on a rolling basis, with the exception of a couple of specialized programs. All applications must include official copies of transcripts for all academic work completed after high school, an official GMAT score report, and a completed application form. Certain programs also require interviews and letters of recommendation; check with the school to learn whether your desired program is included. Students who have not completed all prerequisite courses for the MBA may be admitted conditionally; they may enroll in undergraduate business classes on a nondegree basis in order to qualify for the MBA program. International students whose native language is not English and who have not completed undergraduate degrees in an English-language institution must take the TOEFL and achieve a satisfactory score.

### FINANCIAL FACTS

| | |
|---|---|
| Fees | $244 |
| Books and supplies | $1,000 |
| Room & board (on-campus) | $6,500 |
| % of students receiving aid | 63 |
| % of students receiving loans | 31 |
| % of students receiving grants | 39 |
| Average award package | $3,038 |
| Average grant | $3,000 |

### ADMISSIONS

| | |
|---|---|
| **Admissions Selectivity Rating** | **75** |
| # of applications received | 550 |
| % applicants accepted | 68 |
| % acceptees attending | 57 |
| Average GMAT | 525 |
| Average GPA | 3.5 |
| TOEFL required of international students? | yes |
| Minimum TOEFL (paper/computer) | 550/213 |
| Application fee | $40 |
| International application fee | $40 |
| Regular application deadline | rolling |
| Deferment available? | yes |
| Maximum length of deferment | NA |
| Transfer students accepted? | yes |
| Transfer application policy All core courses can be waived by meeting FDU waiver policy. Nine credits can be transferred. | |
| Non-fall admissions? | yes |
| Need-blind admissions? | yes |

# FLORIDA ATLANTIC UNIVERSITY
## COLLEGE OF BUSINESS

### GENERAL INFORMATION
| | |
|---|---|
| Type of school | public |
| Environment | city |
| Academic calendar | semesters |

### SURVEY SAYS...
*Solid preparation in:*
Teamwork
Communication/interpersonal skills
Presentation skills

### STUDENTS
| | |
|---|---|
| Enrollment of parent institution | 25,994 |
| Enrollment of business school | 505 |
| % male/female | 54/46 |
| % out-of-state | 17 |
| % part-time | 65 |
| % minorities | 16 |
| % international | 13 |
| Average age at entry | 31 |
| Average years work experience at entry | 6.5 |

### ACADEMICS
| | |
|---|---|
| **Academic Experience Rating** | **80** |
| Student/faculty ratio | 14:1 |
| Profs interesting rating | 89 |
| Profs accessible rating | 81 |
| % female faculty | 30 |

## Academics

A wide variety of programs and an equally wide variety of class sites distinguish the MBA programs at Florida Atlantic University's College of Business. Local students are drawn here by the price and convenience; those from farther away come for such distinctive programs as the MBA in Sports Management, which is "one of a handful of such programs in the country that is AACSB accredited," or the Masters of Forensic Accounting—"the oldest program in the nation and one of the few available online. Others come for the MBA in Accounting, "whose students rank among the top ten in CPA Exam passage rates," or the MS in International Business program through which "many students go to Spain and Brazil."

FAU offers MBA classes online as well as on its campuses in Boca Raton, Jupiter, Port Saint Lucie, and two sites in Fort Lauderdale. While students appreciate that "the multiple campuses allow the school to draw students from a wide geographic area," some complain that "the school does not offer a full curriculum at any single location, so you frequently have to drive between campuses that range from 20 to 60 miles apart. Also, courses aren't always offered in the same order as the curriculum requires they are taken." MBAs' praise for the distance-learning program is more unequivocal; they love its convenience and describe it as "a good value." One participant writes, "For those of us in distance learning, the professors are very accommodating and available. I am very pleased with distance delivery."

Students here tell us that FAU professors "are recognized leaders in industry." Several "do consulting, expert-witness, or law-enforcement work outside of the classroom," while others "are solid professors from northern schools that have come to retire in South Florida." One student reports, "Many of my professors have outstanding multidisciplinary knowledge and easiness in sharing it with the students." But another explains, "I come from a top-20 undergraduate school, so I've been disappointed in the ambition of some of the students, but the professors make up for that." Students also tell us that "classes are challenging and involved, and the cases are from real-world scenarios." As at many state schools, the administration "is a nightmare—not at all user-friendly."

## Career and Placement

FAU's College of Business houses the Career Resources and Alumni Relations Center to provide undergraduates and graduate business students with "invaluable guidance with interviewing skills, resume preparation, locating employment opportunities, and locating internships." The office also compiles student resumes on a CD-ROM to be distributed to South Florida businesses. Graduate students have exclusive access to the Job Connection, an Internet-based notification system that alerts them to job postings that match their qualifications. FAU participates in a statewide job fair held in the autumn.

## Student Life and Environment

FAU attracts students from "a variety of different backgrounds both in business and culture," with "many coming from fields other than business, such as health care, law, and government." There are also a number of freshly minted undergrads in the program. This "diversity of the student body gives students a chance to share different job experiences and look at the business world from many perspectives." International students appreciate that "colleagues are friendly and helpful, which is extremely important for those of us who are separated from family and friends. During my MBA program I have made many friends and I am sure that even after graduation I will be able to maintain good relationships with many of my colleagues."

FREDRICK TAYLOR, GRADUATE ADVISOR
MASTERS STUDIES, FW 101, 777 GLADES ROAD, BOCA RATON, FL 33431 UNITED STATES
PHONE: 561-297-3650 • FAX: 561-297-1315
E-MAIL: MBA@FAU.EDU • WEBSITE: WWW.BUSINESS.FAU.EDU

Because so many MBAs are part-time students with full-time jobs, "there is virtually no social activity on campus. It is a great school for students who are married, have children, or are already pursuing a career." One student explains, "The students are focused on getting home after class, since most have been working all day before class. The interaction is limited to what is necessary to get the work done, mostly. People are generally nice, but not very sociable unless they are part of some special group, like sports management or the like." Full-time students enjoy more opportunities to participate in the university community, and they take advantage of them. One writes, "The university gives all students a chance to participate in sport events, concerts, charity actions, religious organizations, and minority clubs. FAU also offers free access to self-defense classes, fitness classes, a gym, and a swimming pool."

## Admissions

Admission to a FAU MBA program requires: an undergraduate degree with a GPA of at least 3.0 (on a four-point scale) for the final 60 semester hours of undergraduate course work from an accredited institution. In addition, international students whose first language is not English must also submit official score reports indicating a score of at least 600 on the TOEFL and at least 250 on the Test of Spoken English (TSE). All international applicants must submit Certification of Financial Responsibility and must provide translation and accredited evaluation of their undergraduate transcripts (the latter is necessary only if a grading system other than the American system was used at the degree-granting institution). For all applicants, letters of recommendation, a resume, an interview, and a personal statement are all optional. After undergraduate record and standardized test scores, work history is the most important factor in admissions decisions.

### FINANCIAL FACTS
| | |
|---|---|
| Annual tuition (in-state/out-of-state) | $5,860/$21,921 |
| Books and supplies | $1,200 |

### ADMISSIONS
| | |
|---|---|
| Admissions Selectivity Rating | 79 |
| # of applications received | 612 |
| % applicants accepted | 52 |
| % acceptees attending | 69 |
| Average GMAT | 519 |
| Range of GMAT | 470–560 |
| Average GPA | 3.3 |
| TOEFL required of international students? | yes |
| Minimum TOEFL (paper/computer) | 600/250 |
| Application fee | $30 |
| International application fee | $30 |
| Regular application deadline | 7/1 |
| Regular notification | rolling |
| Deferment available? | yes |
| Maximum length of deferment | 1 year |
| Non-fall admissions? | yes |
| Need-blind admissions? | yes |

### APPLICANTS ALSO LOOK AT
Florida International University, Florida State University, Miami University, University of Central Florida, University of Florida, University of South Florida

### EMPLOYMENT PROFILE
| | |
|---|---|
| Career Rating | 67 |
| Average starting salary | $39,000 |

# FLORIDA GULF COAST UNIVERSITY
## COLLEGE OF BUSINESS

### GENERAL INFORMATION
| | |
|---|---|
| Type of school | public |
| Academic calendar | semester |

### SURVEY SAYS...
Friendly students
Happy students
*Solid preparation in:*
Teamwork
Doing business in a global economy

### STUDENTS
| | |
|---|---|
| Enrollment of parent institution | 7,254 |
| Enrollment of business school | 143 |
| % male/female | 85/15 |
| % out-of-state | 10 |
| % part-time | 86 |
| % minorities | 25 |
| % international | 10 |
| Average age at entry | 27 |
| Average years work experience at entry | 5 |

### ACADEMICS
| | |
|---|---|
| **Academic Experience Rating** | **75** |
| Student/faculty ratio | 4:1 |
| Profs interesting rating | 88 |
| Profs accessible rating | 85 |
| % female faculty | 28 |
| % minority faculty | 11 |

## Academics

Pragmatic concerns—location, affordability, convenience, and the ability to earn a degree quickly—motivate most who select the MBA program at Florida Gulf Coast University, a relatively new institution located two hours' south of Tampa Bay. This predominantly part-time program, which pursues "a clear mission to incorporate the global, national, and local business environment into the curriculum of our specific classes," represents a real bargain for native Floridians who, thanks to a well-developed distance-learning program, can benefit no matter where they live in the state.

FGCU was established in 1997, which means that "the school has new facilities with technology in most classrooms," a major plus in today's tech-driven business world. One student writes, "Technological savvy is important, and we maximize and leverage our position as a new school with new equipment to aid learning, communication, and feedback." The school has quickly developed a reputation among Sunshine State natives. As one put it, "I chose this school because I know that FGCU is going to be the next big university in Florida, and I want to be part of it."

The FGCU MBA "emphasizes the application of analytical, technical, and behavioral tools to solve organizational problems," with "a focus on teamwork and team building so students frequently work closely together." The program consists of 24 hours of foundation courses, 21 hours of core courses, and 9 hours of concentration courses. Students with solid business backgrounds or college transcripts deep in business courses may have some or all of their foundation courses waived. Concentrations are available in finance, general management, marketing, or information systems. There is also an Executive MBA option, which is a two-year lockstep program with a concentration available in real estate development. Or, students may choose to design their own interdisciplinary concentration.

MBAs praise the faculty at FGCU, telling us that professors "are very helpful. They bring a lot of experience and tips with them to the class." One MBA observes, "The generally small size of the program makes the professors very available." Students also appreciate that "FGCU has made a big commitment to online access, not only in distance learning but in having nearly all services online—registration, submitting homework (even for traditional classroom classes), the bookstore, class chat rooms, class-specific e-mail, etc." Although there are still a few bugs in the system, "time should help all of the programs and the campus to become more well-rounded. For being such a new school, FGCU should be commended for where they are now."

## Career and Placement

All career services at Florida Gulf Coast University are provided by the school's Career Development Services Office, which assists undergraduates and graduate students in all areas. The office sponsors a variety of events throughout the year, including workshops, seminars, on-campus recruiting visits, and a career fair.

Because the school is relatively new—FGCU welcomed its first students in 1997—its alumni network is in the early stages of development with a major campaign under way to network alum. One student writes, "Over time I hope the university gets more national recognition to reward the staff for their efforts. As alumni become distributed through the national workforce, I hope for more national corporations to recruit from our student ranks."

ANA HILL, ADMISSIONS-REGISTRAR OFFICER-GRADUATE ADMISSIONS
10501 FGCU BOULEVARD SOUTH, FORT MYERS, FL 33965 UNITED STATES
PHONE: 888-889-1095 • FAX: 239-590-7894
E-MAIL: GRADUATE@FGCU.EDU • WEBSITE: WWW.FGCU.EDU

## Student Life and Environment

FGCU's location, "fifteen minutes from the Gulf of Mexico (Bonita Springs or Fort Myers Beach) in the center of a cypress swamp filled with wildlife," is regarded as one of the school's greatest assets. Students say, "You can't beat the quality of life in southwest Florida. It's still a fairly small town in a beautiful part of the country where it's warm and green all year with great beaches." Better still, the region is "a major growth area, with exciting opportunities for employment in the near future."

FGCU is growing right along with its surroundings. "During the past four years the student population has doubled at FGCU. There have been a number of buildings added," students report. While FGCU "is too young to have a major college sports presence, [the] student athletics program has excellent student athletes who are also great in academics." Greek life "is beginning to become established," and those who live on campus enjoy dorms "located on a lake with water sports (sailing, kayaking, and canoeing). There are always activities available either to the general population or through clubs."

Most students here, however, don't have much time for such diversions. Those who actually attend classes on campus—the school also serves a sizable distance-learning population—generally work full-time. Many have family obligations too, leaving little (make that zero) time for extracurriculars. One MBA explains, "Other than being in class, there really is no campus life for MBA students, as we all have regular full-time jobs, families, and we live scattered around the area in our own homes. Additionally, many of the classes are offered online, so sometimes your 'classmates' might be located in other countries. As for on-campus classes, the students are friendly and laid-back (this is southwest Florida after all!). But we all go our separate ways to our 'real' lives, home, and our families when class is over." FGCU MBAs "range from students who have just graduated from an undergraduate program to those who have been in the workforce for over 20 years." The types of professions in which these students work range from accounting and real estate to law and the service industry.

## Admissions

Admission to the MBA program at FGCU is based on a combination of undergraduate GPA and GMAT scores. To be considered, applicants must have either (1) a minimum GPA of 3.0 for their final 60 credit hours of undergraduate work; or (2) a minimum GMAT score of 500; plus (3) a formula score of at least 1050 under the formula [(undergraduate GPA + 200) + GMAT score], with a minimum GMAT score of at least 400. International students must also submit TOEFL scores (minimum 550 written, 213 computerized). Students may apply for admission to either the Fall or Spring semester. Students may complete a maximum of nine credit hours of graduate-level courses before gaining official admission to the program.

### FINANCIAL FACTS
| | |
|---|---|
| Annual tuition (in-state/out-of-state) | $13,565/$50,633 |
| Fees | $1,796 |
| Room & board (on-campus) | $7,460 |
| % of students receiving aid | 36 |
| % of first-year students receiving aid | 18 |
| % of students receiving loans | 32 |
| % of students receiving grants | 8 |
| Average award package | $11,080 |
| Average grant | $7,696 |
| Average student loan debt | $22,203 |

### ADMISSIONS
| | |
|---|---|
| Admissions Selectivity Rating | 68 |
| # of applications received | 95 |
| % applicants accepted | 74 |
| % acceptees attending | 61 |
| Average GMAT | 490 |
| Range of GMAT | 470–490 |
| Average GPA | 3.03 |
| TOEFL required of international students? | yes |
| Minimum TOEFL (paper/computer) | 550/213 |
| Application fee | $30 |
| International application fee | $30 |
| Regular application deadline | 6/1 |
| Regular notification | 7/1 |
| Deferment available? | yes |
| Maximum length of deferment | 1 semester |
| Transfer students accepted? | yes |
| Transfer application policy | Students may transfer 6 credits of approved graduate-level course work from a regionally accredited institution. |
| Non-fall admissions? | yes |
| Need-blind admissions? | yes |

# FLORIDA STATE UNIVERSITY
## COLLEGE OF BUSINESS

### GENERAL INFORMATION
Type of school                public
Environment                   city
Academic calendar             semesters

### SURVEY SAYS...
Smart classrooms
*Solid preparation in:*
Presentation skills
Computer skills

### STUDENTS
Enrollment of parent
  institution                 38,000
Enrollment of business school  274
% male/female                 61/39
% part-time                   80
% minorities                  18
% international               9
Average age at entry          25
Average years work experience
  at entry                    3.25

### ACADEMICS
**Academic Experience Rating**   **81**
Student/faculty ratio            30:1
Profs interesting rating         89
Profs accessible rating          88
% female faculty                 13
% minority faculty               3

### JOINT DEGREES
MBA/JD, 113 credits, 4 years

### PROMINENT ALUMNI
Gary Rogers, President & CEO, GE
Plastics; Craig Wardlaw, Executive
VP & CIO, Bank of America; Craig
Ramsey, Partner, Accenture; Chuck
Hardwick, Senior VP, Pfizer

## Academics

"Florida State University's MBA program is comparatively small," which students tell us "has many advantages." One student reports, "Every person within the admissions and administrative offices knows each student's name and a little about each person. We say 'hello' in the halls and their doors are never closed. They assist each student not only with academic affairs and support but also with personal issues if needed." The small size of the program also means that "professors are easily accessible to help with any questions or concerns that may arise. The size of the program also allows them to act on their concern for the progress of the students." On the downside, "as a smaller program, they don't receive much national recognition."

For most of the school's current students, national recognition is not their main concern anyway. They are mostly local and predominantly part-time, looking to advance in jobs they already hold or make an upward move within the local job market. What students here generally want most is affordability, convenience, and a solid reputation within the state. FSU scores big on all three counts. A low, in-state tuition suits most MBAs' budgets, while a selection of part-time and full-time options presents an unusually wide range of choices for a program of this size. This all adds up to make an "MBA program that is a hidden treasure waiting to be discovered." Both the full-time program and the part-time program on the main campus in Tallahassee offer concentrations in finance and marketing and supply-chain management. Part-time programs at branch campuses, "though completely served by the faculty of the main campus, offer only general MBAs. There is no real area of concentration offered because electives are inconsistent." The school also offers an online MBA that students can complete "from anywhere in the world." The online program allows for a general MBA, as well as concentrations in hospitality administration and real estate finance and analysis.

## Career and Placement

Even though FSU's MBA program is small and largely part-time, the school maintains a separate career services office for graduate students in business. It also sponsors a mentoring program that "connects protégés with mentors who can share their experience and wisdom concerning general business leadership skills, professional success factors, management skills, team building, and communication skills," according to the school's website.

Employers most likely to hire FSU MBAs include Raytheon, Harris, and BB&T. The school reports that 33 percent of its graduates find work in operations (average salary $70,000), 25 percent find work in finance ($42,500), and 17 percent in marketing ($51,250).

## Student Life and Environment

Students love FSU's "amazing, beautiful campus" with its "enthusiastic students and diligent professors." They also love hometown Tallahassee, which they describe as "a small town, but big enough to have malls and good restaurants. It's also close to the beach, which is great." Those interested in government careers should find plenty to interest them here, as "Tallahassee is a very political city with thousands of state employees, providing a unique opportunity to take advantage of many state employment positions."

RONALD G. MOTTER, COORDINATOR, MASTERS PROGRAMS ADMISSIONS
GRADUATE OFFICE, COLLEGE OF BUSINESS, FSU, TALLAHASSEE, FL 32306-1110 UNITED STATES
PHONE: 850-644-6458 • FAX: 850-644-0588
E-MAIL: GRADPROG@COB.FSU.EDU • WEBSITE: WWW.COB.FSU.EDU

The mostly part-time students here "usually attend evening classes twice a week and meet with small groups outside of class whenever we can. That's about it for campus involvement." Full-timers get more involved in the life of the university, which of course includes "outstanding athletics programs. The FSU football and baseball teams are constantly in the national championship race, so it makes for a very exciting sports atmosphere." One student writes, "The best time is during football season when students can get to know each other at tailgates and other events." Another claims that for students here, "the nightlife is second to none. There's nothing like going to Bullwinkle's after a tough exam!"

FSU MBAs tell us the school runs "a smooth operation" all around. They enjoy "a friendly atmosphere that allows for positive group cohesiveness during teamwork exercises." Students benefit from each others' "diverse backgrounds. We have people who have just graduated from undergraduate programs, people returning to school after a few years of work experience, and people with previous experience in the military. Overall, we have a very tight-knit group of students." Students speculate that their classmates have, "on average, about five years of work experience."

## Admissions

The Admissions Office at Florida State University requires all of the following from applicants to its MBA program: official copies of transcripts for all post-secondary academic work; an official GMAT score report; three letters of recommendation from former professors and/or employers; a resume; and a personal statement. Students must have proficiency working with PCs. International students whose first language is not English must also submit an official score report for the TOEFL (minimum score of 600 paper-based test or 250 computer-based test required). All test scores must be no more than five years old. The school lists the following programs designed to increase recruitment of underrepresented and disadvantaged students: the FAMU Feeder Program, FAMU Graduate & Professional Days, GradQuest, MBA Advantage, Minority Student Orientation Program, Leslie Wilson Assistantships, the Delores Auzenne Minority Fellowship, and the University Fellowship.

## FINANCIAL FACTS

| | |
|---|---|
| Annual tuition (in-state/out-of-state) | $9,600/$36,153 |
| Books and supplies | $5,750 |
| Room & board (on/off-campus) | $13,000/$15,000 |
| % of students receiving aid | 32 |
| % of first-year students receiving aid | 32 |
| % of students receiving grants | 28 |
| Average award package | $10,000 |
| Average grant | $2,500 |

## ADMISSIONS

| | |
|---|---|
| Admissions Selectivity Rating | 81 |
| # of applications received | 116 |
| % applicants accepted | 62 |
| % acceptees attending | 74 |
| Average GMAT | 560 |
| Range of GMAT | 500–600 |
| Average GPA | 3.43 |
| TOEFL required of international students? | yes |
| Minimum TOEFL (paper/computer) | 600/250 |
| Application fee | $30 |
| International application fee | $30 |
| Regular application deadline | 2/1 |
| Regular notification | rolling |
| Deferment available? | yes |
| Maximum length of deferment | 1 year |
| Transfer students accepted? | yes |
| Transfer application policy Transfer applicants must complete the same application process as all other applicants. | |
| Non-fall admissions? | yes |
| Need-blind admissions? | yes |

## APPLICANTS ALSO LOOK AT

University of Florida, University of North Florida, University of South Florida

## EMPLOYMENT PROFILE

| | | | | |
|---|---|---|---|---|
| Career Rating | 69 | Grads employed by field: | % | avg. salary: |
| Primary source of full-time job acceptances | | Finance | 38 | $60,625 |
| | | Human Resources | 6 | NR |
| School-facilitated activities | 10 (56%) | Marketing | 17 | NR |
| Graduate-facilitated activities | 8 (44%) | MIS | 11 | NR |
| | | Operations | 6 | NR |
| Average starting salary | $63,455 | Consulting | 16 | $67,333 |
| Percent employed | 33 | Other | 6 | NR |

# FORDHAM UNIVERSITY
## GRADUATE SCHOOL OF BUSINESS ADMINISTRATION

## Academics

With top-dog competitors like Columbia University and NYU just a short subway ride away from its Manhattan campus, Fordham's Graduate School of Business Administration has quite a crowd to elbow its way through in order to get the attention it deserves. The school faces a "catch-22": Located anywhere else in the country, Fordham's program would be much better known and much more highly regarded. But at the same time, if it were located anywhere else it couldn't piggyback on the world's business center or the faculties of its competitors, from which it sometimes draws adjunct professors.

Students at Fordham recognize that they have a good thing going, and they have faith that the rest of the world will soon catch on. The school already has a solid reputation in accounting and tax. Its finance department enjoys "a strong reputation on Wall Street," and for good reason: "Professors in Finance are like the drill sergeants in the Marines. They make you work, and they make you think. It is all very practical. They touch on theory here and there, but mostly help you to understand why you need to know this, and then you learn it inside and out. They are also very open to questions. They never force you to just accept that this is the way it is done." Fordham also boasts "the only communications and media management concentration in New York City," a program that sets students up for careers with the city's many broadcast giants.

Fordham caters to part-time students with a "great, flexible schedule" that "allows students to switch between full- and part-time attendance just by taking more or fewer classes. Other schools require you to withdraw and reapply; you don't have to go through that process here." Students who live or work in Westchester County may wish to take advantage of the program's satellite campus in Tarrytown, at which all required courses and select electives are offered. The many full-time employed students here appreciate these conveniences. As one student explains, "The greatest strength of the school is the flexibility it offers. It has core courses and a minimum number of credits to be taken, but you can choose which core courses you want to start with and with what professors. You can also take some elective courses in the first year. It allows you to do internships outside of the summer months because you can regulate your class hours yourself, and there are many evening classes."

## Career and Placement

The Fordham MBA Career Services Office provides placement and counseling to the school's business graduate students. The office benefits greatly from the school's location in a world finance center; one student observes, "Although not a Top 10 school—yet—Fordham still attracts some of the top 200 businesses located in the New York metro area to recruit for employment." Even so, students are aware that their student body is at best the third choice of most big recruiters in New York. One MBA writes, "Honestly, campus recruitment is difficult. Top companies do not invest enough money in recruiting the very talented, best, and brightest students at Fordham." The perception that "career services and a larger, better-equipped staff for career services are needed" does not help matters. On a positive note, "the school is currently getting more involved with the alumni," which should improve networking opportunities. Full-timers also benefit from their interactions with part-time students, "most of whom work for prestigious companies in New York City. Networking with the part-time students can lead to jobs and internships."

FRANK FLETCHER, DIRECTOR
33 WEST 60TH STREET, 4TH FLOOR, NEW YORK, NY 10023 UNITED STATES
PHONE: 212-636-6200 • FAX: 212-636-7076 • E-MAIL: ADMISSIONSGB@FORDHAM.EDU
WEBSITE: WWW.BNET.FORDHAM.EDU

## Student Life and Environment

Life in Fordham's MBA program "is very social, with Thursday happy hours every week where you can meet full-time and part-time students and network. There are also many opportunities to join clubs and actively participate in the many activities arranged by the different clubs. You don't have time to do everything!" The school's Lincoln Center location means that fine dining and upscale shopping are just outside the school's doors. One student notes, "We're in the heart of New York City, just off of Central Park at Lincoln Center. It's a great place to enjoy the spring and summer weather. Catching up in Central Park on a Wi-Fi-enabled computer is definitely one of the perks."

About the only criticism of Fordham's facilities is that MBAs feel a little crowded out by other students. One MBA observes, "They need to separate the graduate business school from the other graduate schools located on the campus. The law school feels separate, but the business school shares many resources with both undergraduate and other graduate programs. A graduate business lounge and special study areas within the library that facilitate discussion groups would really help."

## Admissions

Admission to the Fordham MBA program is competitive. Applicants must submit all of the following materials: a completed application, either hard copy or online; copies of all postsecondary transcripts; an official GMAT score report; two letters of recommendation, preferably from current supervisors, managers, clients, and/or coworkers; a personal statement of length 500 to 1,000 words; and a current resume. International applicants whose first language is not English must also submit an official TOEFL score report. Interviews are not required, but can be granted at the applicant's request. Interview availability is limited; those wishing to interview are encouraged to make their request early in the admissions process. The median GMAT score among admitted students is 600 in the full-time program, 575 in the part-time program.

### FINANCIAL FACTS

| | |
|---|---|
| Annual tuition | $26,565 |
| Fees | $387 |
| Books and supplies | $1,600 |
| Average grant | $3,000 |

### ADMISSIONS

| | |
|---|---|
| Admissions Selectivity Rating | 85 |
| # of applications received | 1,054 |
| % applicants accepted | 55 |
| % acceptees attending | 69 |
| Average GMAT | 590 |
| Range of GMAT | 530–660 |
| Average GPA | 3.12 |
| TOEFL required of international students? | yes |
| Minimum TOEFL (paper/computer) | 600/250 |
| Application fee | $65 |
| International application fee | $65 |
| Regular application deadline | 6/1 |
| Regular notification | rolling |
| Deferment available? | yes |
| Maximum length of deferment | 1 year |
| Transfer students accepted? | yes |
| Transfer application policy Prerequisites and core courses may be waived based on course work taken at other ACCSB-accredited institutions. | |
| Non-fall admissions? | yes |
| Need-blind admissions? | yes |

### APPLICANTS ALSO LOOK AT

Boston University, City University of New York—Baruch College, Columbia University, New York University, Pace University, Rutgers—The State University of New Jersey, St. John's University

### EMPLOYMENT PROFILE

| Career Rating | 84 | Grads employed by field: | % | avg. salary: |
|---|---|---|---|---|
| Average starting salary | $76,236 | Accounting | 12 | $57,000 |
| Percent employed | 80 | Finance | 32 | $83,333 |
| | | Human Resources | 2 | $58,500 |
| | | Marketing | 27 | $86,600 |
| | | MIS | 4 | $86,125 |
| | | Operations | 3 | $90,533 |
| | | Strategic Planning | 2 | $103,000 |
| | | Consulting | 4 | $85,000 |
| | | Communications | 6 | $75,000 |
| | | General Management | 7 | $82,928 |
| | | Nonprofit | 1 | $72,000 |

# FRANCIS MARION UNIVERSITY
## SCHOOL OF BUSINESS

## GENERAL INFORMATION

| | |
|---|---|
| Type of school | public |
| Environment | rural |
| Academic calendar | semester |

### SURVEY SAYS...
Friendly students
*Solid preparation in:*
Presentation skills
Quantitative skills
Computer skills

### STUDENTS

| | |
|---|---|
| Enrollment of parent institution | 3,947 |
| Enrollment of business school | 61 |
| % male/female | 49/51 |
| % part-time | 95 |
| % minorities | 20 |
| % international | 7 |
| Average age at entry | 29 |

### ACADEMICS

| | |
|---|---|
| **Academic Experience Rating** | **63** |
| Student/faculty ratio | 3:1 |
| Profs interesting rating | 71 |
| Profs accessible rating | 64 |

## Academics

The School of Business at South Carolina's Francis Marion University offers a "convenient" MBA program "scheduled in the evening to accommodate working students." Since FMU is a state school, it does so at a price that doesn't break the bank.

This small school—one of the smallest state universities to earn AACSB accreditation, according to the university view book—affords "plenty of good one-on-one time with teachers" to its almost exclusively part-time student body. FMU offers both a general MBA and an MBA with a concentration in Health Management. The former is designed to serve the general business population of the Pee Dee region and beyond; the latter is directed toward individuals currently employed in the health care field and/or those with backgrounds in health care. The Health Management Degree is delivered to FMU students through online classes and resources.

All FMU MBAs must complete courses in accounting for management control, managerial economics, financial theory and applications, management science and statistics, marketing, and finance. Students in the general MBA program must also complete classes in financial accounting, information systems, international business, production management, entrepreneurship, and strategic management. Students pursuing a health concentration must also complete classes in health policy, health economics, health care delivery systems, financial management for health care organizations, and health law and risk management. Students in health management may also take three hours of elective course work. At the conclusion of the program, students must pass comprehensive final examinations covering 10 of 12 functions.

MBAs tell us that the program meets their needs, although some feel that "there is too much busywork" and others complain that "some classes are too easy, more suitable to undergraduates than MBAs." One student suggests, "Tailor the program to the real jobs graduates will get." Many also feel that "the school needs to offer more and a wider variety of MBA classes." Most, however, tell us that the convenience and cost of the degree are strong positives.

## Career and Placement

FMU's MBA program is too small to support career services dedicated exclusively to its students. MBAs receive career assistance from the university's Office of Career Development, which serves undergraduates and graduates in all divisions. Students here also benefit from an active Alumni Association, whose newest chapter is the MBA Alumni Chapter.

BEN KYER, DIRECTOR
BOX 100547 FLORENCE, SC 29501-0547 UNITED STATES
PHONE: 843-661-1436 • FAX: 843-661-1432
E-MAIL: ALPHA1@FMARION.EDU • WEBSITE: HTTP://ALPHA1.FMARION.EDU/~MBA/

## Student Life and Environment

Life in the FMU MBA program "can be hectic," especially toward the end of the semester. "It seems like all projects and exams are due at the same time," writes one student. Most students are "intelligent and hardworking . . . professional adults trying to obtain a common goal" while juggling careers and family obligations along with their academic responsibilities. As a result, few participate in extracurricular activities.

To enhance campus life, FMU hosts regular artists and lecture series. The school also houses an art gallery that displays student and faculty work as well as traveling exhibitions, film series, a planetarium and observatory, concerts, and festivals. FMU's Patriots compete in Division II of the NCAA. Popular spectator sports include basketball, soccer, men's baseball, women's softball, and women's volleyball.

FMU is located just outside of Florence, SC, a city of 33,000 that offers movie theaters, malls, restaurants, a symphony orchestra, and professional hockey (the Pee Dee Pride skate in the East Coast Hockey League). The city is located at the intersections of I-95 and I-20, making travel in all four cardinal directions a snap. Columbia, Charleston, Myrtle Beach, and Fayetteville, NC, are all within 100 miles.

## Admissions

Applicants to the FMU MBA program must submit a completed application; official transcripts for all post-secondary academic work, in a sealed envelope addressed to the applicant from the awarding school; official GMAT scores; two letters of recommendation; and a personal statement of purpose. All materials must be delivered to the school in a single envelope or package. In addition, international applicants must submit official TOEFL scores and a Confidential Financial Statement form demonstrating their ability to pay all expenses related to an FMU MBA. All successful applicants meet the following minimum guidelines: a score greater than 950 under the formula [(undergraduate GPA 5 200) + GMAT score] or a score greater than 1000 under the formula [(GPA for final 60 hours of undergraduates work 5 200) + GMAT score]. Applicants with nonbusiness undergraduate degrees are generally required to complete the business foundation sequence prior to beginning work on their MBA. The sequence is an 18-hour, 8-course curriculum covering the basics of accounting, economics, statistics, business law, management, information systems, finance, and marketing. Students with undergraduate business degrees typically have this requirement waived.

### FINANCIAL FACTS

| | |
|---|---|
| Annual tuition (in-state/out-of-state) | $3,460/$6,920 |
| Fees | $60 |
| Books and supplies | $600 |
| % of students receiving aid | 8 |
| Average grant | $1,000 |

### ADMISSIONS

| | |
|---|---|
| Admissions Selectivity Rating | 62 |
| # of applications received | 33 |
| % applicants accepted | 85 |
| % acceptees attending | 93 |
| Average GMAT | 400 |
| Average GPA | 3 |
| TOEFL required of international students? | yes |
| Minimum TOEFL (paper/computer) | 550/213 |
| Application fee | $25 |
| Regular application deadline | rolling |
| Regular notification | rolling |
| Deferment available? | yes |

# THE GEORGE WASHINGTON UNIVERSITY
## SCHOOL OF BUSINESS

## GENERAL INFORMATION
| | |
|---|---|
| Type of school | private |
| Environment | metropolis |
| Academic calendar | semester |

### SURVEY SAYS...
Students love Washington, DC
*Solid preparation in:*
Teamwork
Communication/interpersonal skills
Presentation skills

## STUDENTS
| | |
|---|---|
| Enrollment of parent institution | 24,092 |
| Enrollment of business school | 719 |
| % male/female | 60/40 |
| % out-of-state | 82 |
| % part-time | 80 |
| % minorities | 17 |
| % international | 31 |
| Average age at entry | 29 |
| Average years work experience at entry | 5.54 |

## ACADEMICS
| | |
|---|---|
| **Academic Experience Rating** | **85** |
| Student/faculty ratio | 25:1 |
| Profs interesting rating | 86 |
| Profs accessible rating | 89 |
| % female faculty | 23 |
| % minority faculty | 5 |

## JOINT DEGREES
MBA/JD, 4 years; MBA/MA in
International Affairs, 30 months;
MBA/MS in Finance, 27 months

## PROMINENT ALUMNI
Colin Powell, MBA, Former U.S.
Secretary of State; Henry Duques,
BBA & MBA, Former President &
CEO, First Data Corp.; Edward M.
Liddy, MBA, Chair & CEO, Allstate
Insurance; Michael Enzi, BBA, U.S.
Senator; Clarence B. Rogers Jr.,
MBA, Chair, President & CEO,
Equifax, Inc.

## Academics

It would be difficult to overestimate the impact George Washington's DC address has on the university's School of Business. It influences everything from the curriculum (especially strong in international business) to the extraordinary quality of the faculty to the "incredible speakers who 'stop by' while they're in town" (recent visitors included Colin Powell, Warren Buffett, and Sumner Redstone). It allows the school to forge "a strong relationship with the government and nonprofit organizations [and to] allow access to DC VIPs and great internships," all of which help students mold their future careers while still in the program. As one student put it, "One of the greatest strengths of GW is its location in downtown DC. It allows you to network with numerous employers without practically having to leave the campus. It allowed me also to combine my second-year full-time studies with working at the World Bank (it was just a five-minute commute from school to work)."

Of course, the School of Business is much more than just a fashionable address. The school boasts a broad variety of excellent tracks; besides the aforementioned international business, operational management, accounting, entrepreneurship, and management science offerings are all considered first-rate. Students proudly note, "There are several unique concentrations that are excellent, such as tourism, environmental policy, and public policy." The school encourages students to explore and even create these off-the-beaten-path disciplines. One MBA explains, "I am in a unique concentration (environmental policy and management), and instead of viewing me as 'the strange one,' the faculty and students embrace this nontraditional business pursuit." Throughout the curriculum, there is a "strong emphasis on teamwork [that] makes learning much more efficient, effective, and enjoyable." One student writes, "We learn how to work in teams and how to make teams function and perform toward our goals. That's a really great asset because now when I am working I feel that I can have any project done regardless of the deadline pressure and diversity of team composition." Team projects also help students get through the "very heavy [workload, which is so demanding that] it's a matter of figuring out the 'need to get done' versus the 'nice to get done.'" One student explains, "Some of the professors give us [a] really hard time in class, but at the end we could not believe how much we have learned." GW's faculty is "very internationally oriented, originates from various parts of the world, participates in think tanks, committees, [and] sometimes act as consultants."

## Career and Placement

GW is well-connected throughout our nation's capital and does an excellent job of bringing DC-area recruiters to campus. This suits many students perfectly; some, however, complain that "the school definitely needs to do a better job of bringing in firms who are looking to recruit outside of the DC area. Many of the students are looking to work outside of DC, and there is almost no chance to get a job outside of DC through the school."

GW's F. David Fowler Graduate Career Center does provide students with the tools they need to search for jobs on their own, including access to various e-recruiting databases and alumni contacts. While most graduates remain in the DC area after graduation, about one in five finds work overseas. Top employers of GW grads include BB&T Corporation, Bearing Point, Corporate Executive Board, Cushman & Wakefield, General Services Administration, Johnson & Johnson, KPMG, Science Applications International Corporation, and World Bank Group.

## Student Life and Environment

"The greatest strength of the George Washington full-time MBA program is its size," students tell us, pointing out that "the classes are small and intimate and by the end of the

TRACY WIDMAN, DIRECTOR, DATA AND ENROLLMENT MANAGEMENT
710 21ST STREET, NORTHWEST, SUITE 206, WASHINGTON, DC 20052 UNITED STATES
PHONE: 202-994-5536 • FAX: 202-994-2286
E-MAIL: MBAFT@GWU.EDU • WEBSITE: WWW.BUSINESS.GWU.EDU/

first semester, you know everyone! No one gets lost in the shuffle like in larger programs." First-year students form an especially tight group because "the first year is all done in cohorts. You are assigned to a group of five students that you perform all work with in all classes your first year. This was a great experience, and I learned a lot from working with my group. These groups facilitate teamwork and communication. As an added bonus, "there is not a high level of cutthroat competition" notes one MBA. During the second year, "there is no fixed study team anymore; however, most professors include one assignment (project, case, presentation) to be done with other students."

Students also get together for various social and extracurricular functions. The program "has happy hours once every week that are a good time for students to meet each other and have fun." The MBA Association "is very involved in getting everyone involved in different types of events, [including] date parties, formals, and informal events like dinner parties, cocktail parties, and movies. Professors often join us at social events," students say. To keep students up-to-date, "the MBA Association sends out 'Monday Mail' weekly; it gives an overview of activities during the week (sports, cultural, community), and IPO (Informal Public Outing), which takes place each Thursday in a different bar in the area." The school as a whole strives "to make sure that people are not always study-oriented, but also social-oriented and community-oriented."

Even without a heavy workload and a crammed-full extracurricular schedule, students could busy themselves by enjoying the major metropolis GW calls home. The school "has an excellent location in the heart of Washington, DC. It has a lot of connections with the business community, which also plays a part in class activities." Students note that the "extremely accessible public transportation [makes it easy for them to attend cultural events and] a variety of seminars all over the city." The school is building a "new, state-of-the-art facility" for the business school, which should open in the spring of 2006. Students say it will be "a wonderful improvement." The student body is "a diverse mix of international students and a fair amount of women. The students are interested in international and global business issues, and a significant number of students may pursue careers in nonprofit and government. Most of the students are young."

## Admissions

The admissions office at the School of Business requires applicants to submit undergraduate transcripts, GMAT scores, TOEFL scores (for non-native English speakers), two recommendations, an interview, a resume, and three essays (for the 2005–2006 year, the prompt asked students to describe their goals in pursuing an MBA). In its quest to ensure diversity in its student body, the GWU admissions office takes country of origin into account when making its decisions.

### FINANCIAL FACTS

| | |
|---|---|
| Annual tuition | $23,652 |
| Books and supplies | $2,480 |
| Room & board | $14,598 |
| % of students receiving aid | 75 |
| % of first-year students receiving aid | 75 |
| % of students receiving loans | 50 |
| % of students receiving grants | 40 |
| Average award package | $25,000 |
| Average grant | $10,000 |
| Average student loan debt | $42,254 |

### ADMISSIONS

| | |
|---|---|
| Admissions Selectivity Rating | 84 |
| # of applications received | 777 |
| % applicants accepted | 71 |
| % acceptees attending | 49 |
| Average GMAT | 630 |
| Range of GMAT | 550–710 |
| Average GPA | 3.6 |
| TOEFL required of international students? | yes |
| Minimum TOEFL (paper/computer) | 600/250 |
| Application fee | $60 |
| International application fee | $60 |
| Regular application deadline | 4/1 |
| Regular notification | rolling |
| Transfer students accepted? | yes |
| Transfer application policy Standard application procedures | |
| Non-fall admissions? | yes |
| Need-blind admissions? | yes |

### APPLICANTS ALSO LOOK AT

Boston College, Boston University, Georgetown University, New York University, Thunderbird, University of Maryland—College Park, Vanderbilt University

| EMPLOYMENT PROFILE | | | | |
|---|---|---|---|---|
| Career Rating | 83 | Grads employed by field: | % | avg. salary: |
| Average starting salary | $67,966 | Finance | 29 | $60,556 |
| | | Marketing | 24 | $58,640 |
| | | Operations | 7 | $77,500 |
| | | Consulting | 22 | $59,625 |
| | | General Management | 11 | $68,750 |
| | | Nonprofit | 7 | $46,000 |

# GEORGETOWN UNIVERSITY
## MCDONOUGH SCHOOL OF BUSINESS

## Academics

The fact that the McDonough School of Business at Georgetown University is a young program is a point of considerable pride with most of its MBA students. With "only 20 years as a program, [it has] experienced many growing pains," but students note, "We are a top-30 business school!" Despite its youth, the school lays claim to "truly remarkable, distinguished professors that make time to be sociable after class" and a friendly, helpful bunch of students who make time to help study and party. According to students, this is thanks to an extremely responsive administration and "a great program that is never satisfied with the status quo."

McDonough's MBA program is a two-year, full-time program. Students don't take majors or concentrations, as the program is designed for general management. As a general-management program, an MBA from McDonough is ideal for students with backgrounds in the liberal arts, science, or with technical undergraduate degrees. All courses in the fall of the first semester are core requirements, but in the second semester, students are invited to take three electives. The program runs in a module system that breaks the semesters up. Students say it's "great for cramming many subjects into a short amount of time. The problem is that we have midterms or finals every three weeks." Others say that modules, combined with the "heavy core course load, leaves very little time for lively current topic debate."

Just as in the undergraduate program, a major strength of Georgetown's MBA program is the international focus of the education. Students proudly boast of their school's "international presence with a great mix of cultures." Students agree, "The large percentage of international students and internationally focused classes help prepare students for working in a global economy." International students, of course, also bring in valuable and "diverse perspectives and opinions." In the second year of the program, students are required to participate in a one-week project in a country with emerging business markets. "Also," says one student, "the link to Georgetown University's School of Foreign Service and the location in Washington, DC, means that there are always interesting things going on linked to international business." In addition, the school's prime location means that students experience "many visits by important statesmen and opportunities to meet them."

With the department's approval, MBA students are welcome to take elective courses outside of the business department. Students at McDonough often opt to take electives in the School of Foreign Service, the Government Department, and the Public Policy Program—all strong programs in their own right. Students appreciate it and say that "access to Georgetown's other schools is one of its key strengths."

McDonough also offers joint degrees with the Graduate Public Policy Program (MBA/MPP), the Law Center (JD/MBA), the School of Foreign Service (MBA/MSFS), the Medical School (MD/MBA), and the Graduate School (MBA/MA Physics, MBA/PhD Physics).

MONICA GRAY, DIRECTOR OF ADMISSIONS
BOX 571148, WASHINGTON, DC 20057-1148 UNITED STATES
PHONE: 202-687-4200 • FAX: 202-687-7809
E-MAIL: MBA@GEORGETOWN.EDU • WEBSITE: WWW.MBA.GEORGETOWN.EDU

## FINANCIAL FACTS

| | |
|---|---|
| Annual tuition | $33,960 |
| Fees | $2,592 |
| Books and supplies | $2,088 |
| Room & board | $12,750 |
| % of students receiving aid | 76 |
| % of first-year students receiving aid | 38 |
| % of students receiving loans | 80 |
| % of students receiving grants | 26 |
| Average award package | $45,000 |
| Average grant | $12,000 |
| Average student loan debt | $58,000 |

## ADMISSIONS

| | |
|---|---|
| Admissions Selectivity Rating | 90 |
| # of applications received | 1,314 |
| % applicants accepted | 47 |
| % acceptees attending | 39 |
| Average GMAT | 658 |
| Range of GMAT | 600–710 |
| Average GPA | 3.2 |
| TOEFL required of international students? | yes |
| Minimum TOEFL (paper/computer) | 600/250 |
| Application fee | $125 |
| International application fee | $125 |
| Regular application deadline | 2/10 |
| Regular notification | 3/30 |
| Application deadline/notification | |
| Round 1: | 12/2 / 1/26 |
| Round 2: | 2/10 / 3/30 |
| Round 3: | 4/21 / 5/25 |
| Need-blind admissions? | yes |

## Career and Placement

Most students agree that McDonough's Career Management Center could step up its efforts a little, but then "career management is always an issue with students [at many campuses]." On the other hand, the alumni network is outstanding. Graduates of the McDonough program seem to be able to rely not just on fellow MBA alums but anyone who went to Georgetown. As one student says, "Alumni of the school are very loyal to the school." Being Georgetown, of course, there's also a very "strong international alumni network" in place, and the projects and competitions in which students participate internationally have led to numerous internships and employment offers.

## Student Life and Environment

Most McDonough students agree that you can't beat the nation's capital for location. "DC is a great city with its finger on the pulse of the nation." And Georgetown, located slightly outside of the bustling metropolis's center, is situated on "one of the most beautiful campuses [students have] ever seen." Life in the city, obviously, offers students a variety of options for social and cultural life. In addition, "the university offers a variety of speakers, guest lecturers, and events. The most difficult task is managing your time appropriately so that you can take advantage of all Georgetown has to offer."

Because 35 percent of all students entering the McDonough School are international students, diversity is something students come to expect and enjoy. Indeed, students claim to be able to "go out for drinks with a half-dozen students and realize that six different countries are represented in [their] party." Countries represented range from Trinidad/Tobago to Switzerland.

Though most students agree that McDonough's facilities leave something to be desired, the program is working feverishly to remedy that and have just broken ground for a new, high-tech facility, which they aim to complete in 2008.

## Admissions

The average GMAT score of an admitted MBA student at McDonough was 658, and the average GPA was 3.2. Most incoming students had worked between three and five years before applying for the MBA, and at least two years of full-time work experience is generally recommended. TOEFL scores are required of those students for whom English is not their first language, unless they've obtained a degree from an English-speaking institution of higher education. The minimum required TOEFL score is 600 for the written test and 250 for the computer-based test. Merit-based scholarships are awarded, and the school considers every student admitted to the program for scholarships.

### EMPLOYMENT PROFILE

| Career Rating | 93 | Grads employed by field: | % | avg. salary: |
|---|---|---|---|---|
| Primary source of full-time job acceptances | | Finance | 41 | $90,388 |
| | | Marketing | 22 | $81,586 |
| School-facilitated activities | 86 (39%) | Consulting | 26 | $90,313 |
| Graduate-facilitated activities | 62 (28%) | General Management | 5 | $83,571 |
| Unknown | 75 (34%) | Other | 4 | $86,642 |
| | | Nonprofit | 2 | $77,666 |
| Average starting salary | $87,816 | | | |
| Percent employed | 88 | | | |

# GEORGIA INSTITUTE OF TECHNOLOGY
## COLLEGE OF MANAGEMENT

## Academics

"There is no better business-school deal in the country than Georgia Tech," MBA students at the College of Management tell us, an assertion that's true especially for Georgia residents; their total two-year bill amounts to a small fraction of what they're likely to earn after graduation. Despite the College of Management's low tuition and fees, Georgia Tech hardly skimps on its offerings. The school's new home, Technology Square, is a $53 million multipurpose facility that, according to the school, "brings the College of Management together in the same location with Georgia Tech's programmatic centers for improving the economy of the state of Georgia, nurturing high-tech business ventures, and spreading knowledge all over the world via distance learning." Making a good deal even better is the fact that "at least half of the students have assistantships where they work within the business school or at Georgia Tech, receiving a full scholarship plus $6,000-a-year stipend."

As one would expect at a tech school, the College of Management maintains a "sharp technical focus." One student notes, "The student body is heavily weighted towards engineers, so there is a strong quantitative bias. Poets will find it challenging, but not impossible, to keep up with all the math." About half the student body majored in engineering or computer science in undergraduate school; a little less than one-third earned baccalaureate degrees in business.

In part because of the emphasis on quantitative analysis, "the workload is heavy, but fair." One MBA explains, "Georgia Tech as a whole cultivates a tough academic image, and the business school in general does its best to uphold that tradition. Final grades are distributed as you would expect in an MBA program, but there is a lot of sweating until the curve is applied." Those seeking an extra challenge can pursue a dual degree, combining the MBA with any master's or PhD degree offered at the university.

Professors defy the tech-school stereotype of the incomprehensible, research-driven geek; on the contrary, they are "excellent and extremely accessible outside of class, [offering] lots of personal attention." Students say, "They care about how we are doing and seem open to our feedback." Similarly, administrators are "student-friendly and open to feedback, and [they're] forever looking for ways to improve." About the only complaint students register concerns the school's national reputation. A typical MBA writes, "This program is absolutely wonderful, but too few people know about it at all. [The College of Management] needs to do a much, much better job of getting the word out."

## Career and Placement

Unique among the various schools that comprise Georgia Tech, the College of Management maintains its own distinct Career Development Office. A two-day career fair, held each fall, is among the major annual on-campus recruiting events, drawing more than 300 companies to visit the campus. Four smaller career fairs are scattered across the calendar. The school also participates in a 15-member MBA consortium that organizes events in Atlanta, New York, and on the West Coast; the consortium helps attract companies that might not visit the Georgia Tech campus due to the relatively small size of the MBA program. Students give the Career Development Office high marks, telling us, "The career center has been incredibly active in making sure every student is able to find internships or jobs in the coming summer."

Tech grads often head overseas for their first jobs; one in five is employed outside the U.S. after graduation. Approximately 60 percent remain in the Southeast. Top employers include Assurant Group, BellSouth, Caterpillar, Coca-Cola Company, Dell, Disney,

Earthlink, Ernst & Young, GE Supply, Georgia Pacific Corporation, McKesson, NASD, Philip Morris, Southern Company, and United Parcel Service.

## Student Life and Environment

The College of Management's new digs are in a "great new location on campus, right in the middle of an area of town on the rise." The "brand-new incredible facility [features not only the requisite] plasma screens, video-conferencing, and computers [but also] a Starbucks and Barnes & Noble just downstairs, so there's no falling asleep or staying out of touch with the rest of the world." The school's Atlanta location is unquestionably an asset. Students tell us, "Atlanta is a great city to live in," as it offers great internship and job opportunities. "I have been working on several real-life projects for world-class companies based in Atlanta," notes an MBA. The city also "contributes a great deal to the social life here. There's always a bunch of activities going on."

The Georgia Tech campus is almost as hopping as the city surrounding it. Students report, "There are great opportunities to get more involved with the school and help shape the direction of the program during your two years here and beyond. The staff regularly conducts town halls and lunch meetings to make sure the students are getting their needs met." Students also say, "Study groups, classes, social meets, guest speakers, and presentations and research [help fill the days, as do] intramurals and intercollegiate athletics [and] mixers with surrounding schools (Emory and GSU) and lots of clubs; everyone is involved in a club."

MBA students "really enjoy the diversity of the student body, with its high percentage of international students." Many opine, "The student body is a bit more experienced and mature than other campuses, which was one of the reasons I chose to come here."

## Admissions

Georgia Tech reviews all application materials carefully; those materials must include undergraduate transcripts, GMAT scores, TOEFL scores (when required), letters of recommendation, personal essays, and work history. Applicants must have completed study in calculus prior to enrollment. The school "strongly recommends [that applicants] have a familiarity with probability concepts prior to beginning the MBA program." It also points out that "full-time work experience greatly enhances your application and the quality of learning you receive in the MBA program. More than 95 percent of [the school's] most recent class had worked full-time prior to admission." Georgia Tech's MBA program is full-time, and admission is for the fall semester only. Minority recruitment is enhanced through "FOCUS programs on campus, information sessions, Regent's Opportunity Scholarships, and minority-student outreach."

## FINANCIAL FACTS

| | |
|---|---|
| Annual tuition (in-state/out-of-state) | $5,950/$23,804 |
| Fees | $505 |
| Books and supplies | $1,400 |
| Room & board (on/off-campus) | $12,000/$12,000 |
| % of students receiving grants | 30 |
| Average grant | $6,000 |
| Average student loan debt | $16,000 |

## ADMISSIONS

| | |
|---|---|
| Admissions Selectivity Rating | 95 |
| # of applications received | 276 |
| % applicants accepted | 38 |
| % acceptees attending | 61 |
| Average GMAT | 657 |
| Range of GMAT | 620–690 |
| Average GPA | 3.32 |
| TOEFL required of international students? | yes |
| Minimum TOEFL (paper/computer) | 600/250 |
| Application fee | $50 |
| International application fee | $50 |
| Regular application deadline | 3/15 |
| Regular notification | rolling |
| Deferment available? | yes |
| Maximum length of deferment | 1 year |
| Need-blind admissions? | yes |

## APPLICANTS ALSO LOOK AT

Emory University, Indiana University—Bloomington, Purdue University, University of Georgia, University of Maryland—College Park, University of North Carolina at Chapel Hill, Vanderbilt University

## EMPLOYMENT PROFILE

| Career Rating | 87 | Grads employed by field: | % | avg. salary: |
|---|---|---|---|---|
| Primary source of full-time job acceptances | | Finance | 25 | $64,318 |
| | | Human Resources | 3 | $85,000 |
| School-facilitated activities | 58% | Marketing | 18 | $84,400 |
| Graduate-facilitated activities | 27% | MIS | 6 | $76,750 |
| Unknown | 15% | Operations | 18 | $69,833 |
| | | Consulting | 21 | $78,154 |
| Average starting salary | $75,029 | Other | 8 | $78,375 |
| Percent employed | 94 | | | |

# GEORGIA SOUTHERN UNIVERSITY
## COLLEGE OF BUSINESS ADMINISTRATION

## Academics

The College of Business Administration at Georgia Southern University serves a predominately local student population with a general MBA, as well as MBAs with concentrations in accounting, health services administration, information systems, and international business. A Master of Accounting Degree is also available, and students in our survey speak especially highly of the accountancy programs.

Less than half of Georgia Southern's MBAs are full-time students; others attend part-time, usually on top of a full-time work schedule. Well aware of this noble act, the school works hard to accommodate the varied lifestyles of its students. One part-timer writes, "The administration at Georgia Southern has been very helpful. My schedule has been hectic, but they have worked with me to graduate in a timely manner." Many of the full-timers are students who "got their BAs here and just stuck around." One such student explains, "I completed my undergraduate degree at Georgia Southern, and when the MBA program started a concentration in Information Systems, I took the opportunity to continue my education in a field that I am very interested in."

Convenience, cost, and comfort are the three main reasons so many undergraduates choose to remain on at GSU. One student writes, "I love the faculty here. Because Georgia Southern is a teaching institution, the professors are very accessible and willing to help. They have time to work with students and to teach classes." Another notes, "There's no academic Darwinism here, no weed-out courses. Unlike other schools, GSU professors support and assist students, and seem genuinely interested in their success." Students also appreciate "that the quality of the courses offered is equivalent to those at larger business schools, but there is no 'big school mind-set.'" One drawback students point out is that "there are sometimes difficulties getting into classes. This is due to a sudden boom in business-school students. Currently, the student/professor ratio is fairly high."

Full-time students attend classes at GSU's Statesboro campuses. Part-timers may attend classes in Statesboro or Savannah, or they may participate in the distance-learning program by attending classes in Brunswick. A Web-exclusive collaborative MBA is offered in conjunction with five other schools in the University of Georgia system.

## Career and Placement

Georgia Southern's small MBA program is served by a satellite office of the university's central Career Services Office. Many career-oriented events, such as workshops and recruitment events, serve the university at large rather than business students exclusively. According to the school's website, the COBA Satellite Office houses "literature on academic majors, career information . . . handouts and other resources to help prepare you for professional employment and graduate school."

Nearly 100 employers visit the Georgia Southern campus each year. Top employers of graduating MBAs include: Gulfstream Aerospace, Inc.; Memorial Medical Hospital; Great Dane Trucking, Inc.; and Sun Trust Bank.

## Student Life and Environment

GSU's MBA program boasts "a highly diverse" student body. Students tell us that they "vary widely in terms of race, sex, and culture. Most are working in a related business field, but there are also students who have recently completed their undergraduate degrees and have no related experience to contribute. They range in ages between 23 and 53." More than 10 percent of the student body is international.

Dr. Michael McDonald, Graduate Program Director
PO Box 8154, Statesboro, GA 30460-8154 United States
Phone: 912-681-5767 • Fax: 912-681-0740
E-mail: gradschool@georgiasouthern.edu • Website: coba.georgiasouthern.edu/mba

With a small student body (and an even smaller full-time population), GSU lacks the makings of an active extracurricular scene. Even so, one student reports that "there are many different functions and activities to attend. For example, this year I attended an evening dinner that was directed at teaching students how to maintain etiquette in a professional setting. There were different companies that sponsored tables and either one or two representatives would also participate at each table." The school also hosts major-related organizations. Students tell us they feel "a lot of pressure from the faculty to achieve and to remain active in school-sponsored events. There are incentives (positive and negative) that encourage participation."

Hometown Statesboro "is a small town in southeast Georgia where the college and Wal-Mart are pretty much all that's going on. Because GSU is the attraction in Statesboro, life here is all about studying and working. Most people go to Savannah or Atlanta on weekends." At least it's good to know that "the area surrounding the campus is primarily geared toward serving the needs of students, producing a 'college town' atmosphere. The facilities provided (gyms, computer labs, student center, etc.) are of a quality usually only seen at much larger schools."

## Admissions

Admission to the Georgia Southern MBA program is determined through the application of the formula [(undergraduate GPA 5 200) + GMAT score]. A score of at least 1000 ensures admission. Applicants may receive provisional admission with a score between 950 and 1000, with an undergraduate GPA of at least 2.80, or with a GMAT score of at least 470.

An alternate formula applies to students who do not qualify under the formula above but who excelled during their final two years of undergraduate work. This formula, called the upper-level formula, is [(undergraduate GPA for final 60 semester hours 5 200) + GMAT score]. A score of at least 1050 qualifies. Students who have not taken the GMAT may also gain admission if their undergraduate GPA is at least 3.25, or their GPA for their final 60 semester hours is at least 3.5. Students in this category must submit an acceptable GMAT score by the time they complete their second graduate-level course.

## FINANCIAL FACTS

| | |
|---|---|
| Annual tuition (in-state/out-of-state) | $2,926/$11,704 |
| Fees | $1,024 |
| Books and supplies | $1,000 |
| Room & board (on/off-campus) | $6,300/$2,600 |
| % of students receiving aid | 85 |
| % of first-year students receiving aid | 86 |
| % of students receiving loans | 56 |
| % of students receiving grants | 56 |
| Average award package | $9,956 |
| Average grant | $4,870 |
| Average student loan debt | $27,392 |

## ADMISSIONS

| | |
|---|---|
| Admissions Selectivity Rating | 70 |
| # of applications received | 127 |
| % applicants accepted | 77 |
| % acceptees attending | 67 |
| Average GMAT | 510 |
| Range of GMAT | 440–540 |
| Average GPA | 3.15 |
| TOEFL required of international students? | yes |
| Minimum TOEFL (paper/computer) | 530/213 |
| Application fee | $50 |
| International application fee | $50 |
| Regular application deadline | 6/1 |
| Regular notification | 7/1 |
| Deferment available? | yes |
| Maximum length of deferment | 1 year |
| Transfer students accepted? | yes |
| Transfer application policy | Students may transfer up to 6 credits; only grades of B or higher will be accepted for transfer. |
| Non-fall admissions? | yes |
| Need-blind admissions? | yes |

## APPLICANTS ALSO LOOK AT

Georgia State University, Kennesaw State University, University of Georgia

# GEORGIA STATE UNIVERSITY
## J. MACK ROBINSON COLLEGE OF BUSINESS

## GENERAL INFORMATION
Type of school                public
Environment               metropolis
Academic calendar           semester

### SURVEY SAYS...
Happy students
Smart classrooms

### STUDENTS
Enrollment of business
  school                       1,735
Average years work experience
  at entry                         6

### ACADEMICS
**Academic Experience Rating   80**
Student/faculty ratio         23:1
Profs interesting rating        88
Profs accessible rating         85
% female faculty                30
% minority faculty               6

### JOINT DEGREES
MBA/JD, 63 credits; MBA/MHA,
51–63 credits

### PROMINENT ALUMNI
James E. Copeland, Deloitte Touche
Tohmatsu; A.W. Bill Dahlberg, Chair,
Mirant; Kenneth Lewis, Chair &
CEO, Bank of America; Richard H.
Lenny, Chair, Hershey Foods;
Mackey McDonald, Chair, President
& CEO, VF Corp.

## Academics

Georgia State University offers four types of MBAs through its J. Mack Robinson College of Business: the Flexible MBA, a full-time or part-time program that allows students to begin during any semester and to schedule classes around other obligations; the Global Partners MBA, a full-time, 14-month program that includes six-week residencies in Paris and Rio, a two-week residency in China, three days in Washington, DC, and the remaining time in Atlanta and at an internship or field-experiment site; the Professional MBA, a 24-month, lockstep Thursday-and-Saturday program based on the Flexible MBA curriculum, for high-potential professionals with at least three years of management experience; and the Executive MBA, an 18-month, lockstep, Friday-and-Saturday program focusing on international business and leadership. The Executive MBA program is open only to applicants with at least seven years of work experience and a minimum of five years at the management level.

In all programs, students report that "professors at GSU are highly qualified. Many of them either work or have worked outside academia, giving them a much fuller understanding of business and the pressures students face. Additionally, the professors seem to be enthusiastic about teaching. They seem to genuinely enjoy class and stimulate class discussions." One student notes, "The top-quality instructors have enabled me to quickly turn business theory into real-world results for my employer." Students are especially high on the finance program, which they tell us is "super hard, but super good!" Programs in accounting and actuarial science also receive MBAs' praise. In all disciplines, students report that "the workload is challenging, but it all is very relevant," although a few students complain that "some of the case studies seem a little dated." In the best classes, professors "really focus on drawing course work right out of the *Wall Street Journal*. The professor never even touched the textbook. It was great, but I understand why everyone doesn't do it; it's a lot of additional work for the professor."

## Career and Placement

The Office of Graduate Career Management (GCM) at GSU offers a full range of services, including career advising, career workshops, the career leader self-assessment service, assistance with internships, resume review, resume referral, alumni contacts, a career library, recruitment events, on-campus interviews, and online job databases. While students "would like to see some bigger names recruiting on campus, especially in banking," most agree that the GCM does a solid job serving a large clientele.

In 2004, the top 10 recruiters of GSU MBAs were: BB&T; Chick-fil-A; ChoicePoint; Cox Communications; GE Power Systems; KPMG, LLP; PricewaterhouseCoopers; Radiant Systems; Reznick, Fedder & Silverman; and Wachovia. Three-tenths of recent graduates found work in accounting (average starting salary $58,000). About one in four found work in finance ($55,000); one in six was employed in marketing ($51,500).

## Student Life and Environment

The MBAs at Georgia State are "mostly older students with more work experience. Many have families. All are very intelligent and hardworking." Most attend part-time while working full-time jobs and are "very willing to share job experiences that relate to classroom material. They talk a lot in class, which is helpful." "Many are international students," all of them full-timers. Because most students have substantial obligations outside school, "there is no real sense of a student body here. It's every wo/man for

NAOMI LEADER, ASSISTANT TO THE DIRECTOR
PO BOX 3988, ATLANTA, GA 30302-3988 UNITED STATES
PHONE: 404-463-4568 • FAX: 404-651-2721
E-MAIL: MASTERSADMISSIONS@GSU.EDU • WEBSITE: ROBINSON.GSU.EDU

her/himself." One student writes, "I wish there is something that we could do to make life more communal, but given that so many attendees work, this is difficult. This is one of the drawbacks from going to part-time school. If I could do it over, I may have quit work and gone to school full-time. But on the other hand, I have continually been able to apply, in real-time, the things that I learn in school to my work. In retrospect, [this experience] has probably reinforced this work more than anything."

Students love hometown Atlanta, which "offers great resources" both for career opportunities and for fine living. The city is home to a number of *Fortune* 500 companies, including Coca-Cola, Home Depot, and Delta Airlines. On campus, GSU's MBA Centers "are immaculate and well thought out in terms of their design to facilitate class discussion and student/teacher interaction."

## Admissions

Applicants to GSU MBA programs must submit all of the following materials to the Office of Admissions: official copies of transcripts for all post-secondary academic work; an official GMAT score report; a resume (at least two years of full-time professional experience is preferred); and two personal essays. Letters of recommendation are not required but are considered for those candidates who submit them. International students must submit, in addition to the above materials, evidence of sufficient financial resources to fund their MBA studies; an independent evaluation of all academic transcripts for work completed abroad; and, for students whose first language is not English, an official score report for the TOEFL. International students are required to carry a full-time course load.

### FINANCIAL FACTS

| | |
|---|---|
| Annual tuition (in-state/out-of-state) | $5,698/$20,306 |
| Fees | $826 |
| Books and supplies | $1,000 |
| Room & board (on/off-campus) | $8,976/$8,876 |
| % of students receiving aid | 15 |
| % of first-year students receiving aid | 15 |
| % of students receiving loans | 11 |
| % of students receiving grants | 2 |
| Average award package | $16,889 |
| Average grant | $4,500 |
| Average student loan debt | $35,667 |

### ADMISSIONS

| | |
|---|---|
| Admissions Selectivity Rating | 84 |
| # of applications received | 561 |
| % applicants accepted | 70 |
| % acceptees attending | 76 |
| Average GMAT | 610 |
| Range of GMAT | 560–640 |
| Average GPA | 3.36 |
| TOEFL required of international students? | yes |
| Minimum TOEFL (paper/computer) | 610/255 |
| Application fee | $50 |
| International application fee | $50 |
| Regular application deadline | 5/1 |
| Regular notification | 6/15 |
| Deferment available? | yes |
| Maximum length of deferment | 2 semesters |
| Non-fall admissions? | yes |
| Need-blind admissions? | yes |

### APPLICANTS ALSO LOOK AT

City University of New York—Baruch College, Clark Atlanta University, Emory University, Georgia Institute of Technology, Kennesaw State University, University of Florida, University of Georgia

### EMPLOYMENT PROFILE

| Career Rating | 76 | Grads employed by field: | % | avg. salary: |
|---|---|---|---|---|
| Primary source of full-time job acceptances | | Accounting | 36 | $46,071 |
| | | Marketing | 16 | $43,166 |
| School-facilitated activities | 8 (42%) | MIS | 16 | $54,000 |
| Graduate-facilitated activities | 11 (57%) | Consulting | 26 | $62,700 |
| | | Other | 5 | NR |
| Average starting salary | $52,069 | | | |

# GONZAGA UNIVERSITY
## GRADUATE SCHOOL OF BUSINESS

### GENERAL INFORMATION
| | |
|---|---|
| Type of school | private |
| Affiliation | Roman Catholic/Jesuit |
| Environment | city |
| Academic calendar | semester |

### SURVEY SAYS...
Friendly students
Good peer network
Happy students
Smart classrooms

### STUDENTS
| | |
|---|---|
| Enrollment of parent institution | 6,500 |
| Enrollment of business school | 219 |
| % male/female | 62/38 |
| % out-of-state | 40 |
| % part-time | 60 |
| % minorities | 21 |
| % international | 11 |
| Average age at entry | 29 |
| Average years work experience at entry | 4 |

### ACADEMICS
| | |
|---|---|
| **Academic Experience Rating** | **77** |
| Student/faculty ratio | 10:1 |
| Profs interesting rating | 87 |
| Profs accessible rating | 93 |
| % female faculty | 26 |
| % minority faculty | 21 |

### JOINT DEGREES
MBA/MAcc, 1–2 years; MBA/JD and MAcc/JD, 3 to 3.5 years

### PROMINENT ALUMNI
Michael R. Coleman, VP, IBM; Jerome Conlon, Retired VP, NBC, Current VP, Brand Alchemy; Stuart McKee, National Technology Officer, Microsoft

## Academics

With its "Jesuit tradition in which ethics are strongly emphasized," Gonzaga University serves up a solid AACSB-accredited MBA to its predominantly part-time working professional student body. Accounting is among the school's strongest areas, as "Gonzaga has an excellent reputation for preparing students to take the CPA exam, of which the pass rate among Gonzaga students is high." Number-crunchers here may opt for an MAcc, an MBA with a concentration in accounting, or a combined MBA/MAcc. Gonzaga offers concentrations in finance, management information systems, and marketing. In Fall 2005, concentrations in entrepreneurship, ethics, sports management and supply-chain management were added. Students may also opt to design an individualized concentration.

Gonzaga's MBA curriculum consists of 22 credits in core courses (11 two-credit classes) and 11 credits in electives, through which students may develop a concentration if they so desire. Students who did not major in business as undergraduates are typically required to complete a series of foundation requirements prior to beginning work on their MBA. Overall, students appreciate the program's "very integrated approach [and the] accessible teachers who are friendly and intelligent and have created a great learning environment." For the most part, students report that they find the professors and administration members "wonderful to work with." Some, however, complain about a "heavy emphasis on examination-based measurement. It can be too much like the under-graduate experience. There is little emphasis on writing papers and research, and thus little opportunity for creativity."

In the past, the MBA respondents to our survey saw improvements on the horizon, however, referring to some of the problems they encountered as mere "growing pains." Gonzaga's Graduate School of Business has experienced a dramatic increase in enroll-ment from 166 students in 2000 to 229 students in 2004. To ensure that quality was not sacrificed as a result of this growth, Gonzaga embarked on a major expansion to Jepson Center, added nine new professors, and expanded the curriculum to include eight areas of concentration. Class sizes remain small, and the program has maintained its reputa-tion for high quality and flexibility. One MBA elaborates: "The administration of the university and the business school are both very forward-thinking. Both have been expanding and upgrading the programs at the school. I know that I am at a school that is continuing to grow and gain in national prominence."

## Career and Placement

The Gonzaga Career Center and the School of Business Administration staff and faculty provide career counseling and placement services to MBAs here, including 301 seminars covering self-assessment, career planning, resume writing, and conducting a successful job search; mock interviews and interview critiques; on-campus recruiting and inter-viewing; a career resources library; alumni events; and internship placement assistance. Some would like to see "more internship" opportunities, but students have few com-plaints.

Employers of Gonzaga business graduates include Accenture, Bank of America, Boeing, Empire Health, Ernst & Young, Itron, KPMG, Nordstrom Corporate, Merrill Lynch, Microsoft, Nike, Pitney Bowes, Potlatch, Washington Trust, and Wells Fargo.

STACEY CHATMAN, GRADUATE PROGRAMS SPECIALIST FOR ADMISSIONS
502 EAST BOONE AVENUE, SPOKANE, WA 99528-0009 UNITED STATES
PHONE: 509-324-4622 • FAX: 509-323-5811
E-MAIL: CHATMAN@JEPSON.GONZAGA.EDU • WEBSITE: WWW.JEPSON.GONZAGA.EDU/GRADUATE

## Student Life and Environment

MBAs mention that there are two types of students in the Graduate School of Business: There are "those who graduated from GU as an undergrad; most of these students are straight out of the undergrad program. There are also those who are new to the university; most of them have work experience and are a few years older than the students who have their undergrad degree from GU." In general, "Students here are friendly and intelligent." There are a fair number of international MBAs, including "students from places like Nepal, China, the Ukraine, the UK, India, Lebanon, and Latin America." Women make up just under 40 percent of the student body. (One female respondent would like to see the school place a "greater emphasis on women in business.") Students call their fellow MBAs "warm, intelligent, [and] hardworking" and are quick to sing the praises of the "friendly" atmosphere at GU.

Life at GU is great for those who spend time around campus (though part-timers generally don't, as many work full-time). "There are all sorts of activities and club sports for students to participate in (including Young Republicans and Young Democrats clubs, philosophy clubs, business clubs, and sports teams in hockey, lacrosse, and much more)." Gonzaga's nationally ranked men's basketball team is the source of much GU student pride. One MBA writes, "Going to the games is fun, and it builds camaraderie within the student body." While "the curriculum is challenging, there is still plenty of free time to work or enjoy life outside of school," a fact of GU life that students appreciate. While a few report that they opted to pursue their degrees at GU because of the "Jesuit educator emphasis," most don't comment at all on the school's religious affiliation.

## Admissions

Applicants to the MBA program at Gonzaga must submit two official copies of all post-secondary academic transcripts, official GMAT scores, two letters of recommendation, a professional resume, three short essays, and a completed application. International students must also submit official TOEFL scores (if English is not their first language) and a financial declaration form. Work experience is not required, "although the majority of students who enter the program have 4 or 5 years prior work experience." A minimum GMAT score of 500 is strongly preferred by the Admissions Committee.

## FINANCIAL FACTS

| | |
|---|---|
| Annual tuition | $10,620 |
| Fees | $150 |
| Books and supplies | $600 |
| Room & board | $8,250 |
| % of students receiving aid | 90 |
| % of first-year students receiving aid | 90 |
| % of students receiving loans | 30 |
| % of students receiving grants | 70 |
| Average grant | $7,000 |
| Average student loan debt | $10,404 |

## ADMISSIONS

| | |
|---|---|
| Admissions Selectivity Rating | 76 |
| # of applications received | 143 |
| % applicants accepted | 87 |
| % acceptees attending | 85 |
| Average GMAT | 570 |
| Range of GMAT | 500–610 |
| Average GPA | 3.4 |
| TOEFL required of international students? | yes |
| Minimum TOEFL (paper/computer) | 570/230 |
| Application fee | $45 |
| International application fee | $45 |
| Regular application deadline | rolling |
| Regular notification | rolling |
| Deferment available? | yes |
| Maximum length of deferment | 4 years |
| Transfer students accepted? | yes |
| Transfer application policy | |
| Transcripts are evaluated to ensure that desired learning objectives have been fulfilled. Up to 6 credits may be transferred in. | |
| Non-fall admissions? | yes |

## APPLICANTS ALSO LOOK AT

Montana State University, Seattle Pacific University, Seattle University, University of Montana—Missoula, University of Portland, Washington State University, Willamette University

### EMPLOYMENT PROFILE

| Career Rating | 74 | Grads employed by field: | % avg. salary: | |
|---|---|---|---|---|
| Average starting salary | $55,000 | Accounting | 10 | NR |
| | | Finance | 20 | NR |
| | | Human Resources | 10 | NR |
| | | Marketing | 10 | NR |
| | | MIS | 5 | NR |
| | | Strategic Planning | 5 | NR |
| | | Consulting | 5 | NR |
| | | Entrepreneurship | 5 | NR |
| | | General Management | 10 | NR |
| | | Venture Capital | 10 | NR |
| | | Other | 5 | NR |
| | | Nonprofit | 5 | NR |

# GRADUATE COLLEGE OF UNION UNIVERSITY
## SCHOOL OF MANAGEMENT

## Academics

The School of Management at the Graduate College of Union University offers both a conventional MBA and a unique MBA in Health Care Management. The former focuses on all areas of general management with an emphasis on global business; the latter "prepares graduates for management positions in health-service-delivery organizations (for example, hospitals, managed-care organizations, group practices, long-term care) and in related organizations (for example, consulting, government, corporate benefits)," according to the school's website.

MBA students at the Graduate College benefit from small classes (the average class size is 17). Classes meet in the evening to accommodate part-time students, who make up roughly half the student population. A conventional MBA consists of 10 core courses and 10 advanced. The core includes a capstone course and standard surveys of core business skills (including accounting, statistics, and finance) as well as such unique classes as "Managing Ethically in a Global Environment" and "Managing People and Teams in organizations." Students choose courses from any of the following elective areas to establish a concentration: finance, economics, marketing, operations/management science, and international business. The program typically takes a full-time student two years to complete; part-timers generally complete it in four years.

The Graduate College's MBA in Healthcare Management emphasizes both theory and practice; that's why the academic curriculum is supplemented with a mandatory internship, typically completed between the first and second years of the program. Because of the specialized nature of the degree, only two electives are allowed in this program; the other 18 courses are required. The 10 required courses mirror the conventional MBA core. The other 8, which include such subjects as "Health Systems Marketing and Planning," "Structural Dynamics in Health Systems," and "Legal Aspects of Health Care," are specific to the health administration program.

Graduate College MBAs can pursue joint degrees in law or pharmacy; a five-year BA/MBA option is quite popular because it allows students to pursue an MBA without first accumulating several years of experience. Students appreciate that "teachers are all very enthusiastic and interested in our learning program" and "are, for the most part, always available to talk, whether it be class-related or not." The administration is reportedly "outstandingly friendly and service-oriented," and "tuition is reasonable."

## Career and Placement

MBA Career Services operates in conjunction with Union's Becker Career Center to provide internship opportunities, mentoring programs, and job-search guidance. Approximately 25 companies visit the college to recruit graduating MBAs; about 30 companies recruit summer interns. Students say that the career center is "great for internships but not for careers."

Top employers of the Graduate College MBAs include General Electric, IBM, KPMG, Lehman Brothers, and PricewaterhouseCoopers. Nearly all MBAs remain in and around the New York State area after graduation.

RHONDA SHEEHAN, DIRECTOR OF GRADUATE ADMISSIONS AND REGISTRAR
LAMONT HOUSE, 807 UNION STREET, SCHENECTADY, NY 12308 UNITED STATES
PHONE: 518-388-6238 • FAX: 518-388-6686
E-MAIL: GCUU@UNION.EDU • WEBSITE: WWW.GCUU.EDU

## Student Life and Environment

The Graduate College's student body is "diverse in age, race, citizenship, occupation, and career goals. Students are friendly and team-oriented." The MBA program is an unusual mix of the very young and the much older; there are "lots of five-year under-grads, and nontraditional students generally return after a long time in the workforce. There aren't a whole lot of young professionals here." Students report that, unlike many MBA programs, "minority and female students are very common and thus are very well supported." There are roughly one in five students that are international students.

The Graduate College is located near Albany, New York, in the town of Schenectady. Sperling's Best Places recently ranked the Albany-Schenectady area the least stressful city among America's top-100 metropolitan areas. The area is home to many schools that together bring a total of 55,000 students to the region every school year. The Graduate College is located on the Union College campus, which covers 100 acres and houses a substantial library, several new classroom and laboratory facilities, an arts center, and a student center with a 3,000-seat hockey arena and rink.

## Admissions

In evaluating MBA applications, the Graduate College of Union University reviews aca-demic records, stated career goals, letters of recommendation, and standardized test scores (GMAT for all applicants, plus TOEFL for international students). Admissions offi-cers also use the application to assess applicants' stated career goals and their fit with both the program and the university community. The Graduate College generally requires an undergraduate GPA of 3.0; the average full-time student typically enters with a higher undergraduate GPA. Applications are assessed on a rolling basis with admis-sions decisions delivered within two weeks of receipt of the completed application.

### FINANCIAL FACTS

| | |
|---|---|
| Annual tuition | $20,750 |
| Fees | $150 |
| Books and supplies | $1,200 |
| Room & board | $8,800 |
| % of students receiving aid | 35 |
| % of first-year students receiving aid | 61 |
| % of students receiving loans | 22 |
| % of students receiving grants | 20 |
| Average award package | $16,847 |
| Average grant | $6,665 |
| Average student loan debt | $19,008 |

### ADMISSIONS

| | |
|---|---|
| Admissions Selectivity Rating | 72 |
| # of applications received | 87 |
| % applicants accepted | 90 |
| % acceptees attending | 86 |
| Average GMAT | 545 |
| Range of GMAT | 470–610 |
| Average GPA | 3.32 |
| TOEFL required of international students? | yes |
| Minimum TOEFL (paper/computer) | 550/213 |
| Application fee | $60 |
| International application fee | $60 |
| Regular application deadline | |
| Regular notification | |
| Deferment available? | yes |
| Maximum length of deferment | 1 yr |
| Transfer students accepted? | yes |
| Transfer application policy Students may transfer up to 8 courses (20 required). See website for details. | |
| Non-fall admissions? | yes |
| Need-blind admissions? | yes |

### APPLICANTS ALSO LOOK AT

Albany Law School, Rensselaer Polytechnic Institute

### EMPLOYMENT PROFILE

| Career Rating | 76 | Grads employed by field: | % | avg. salary: |
|---|---|---|---|---|
| Average starting salary | $51,932 | Finance | 43 | $51,769 |
| Percent employed | 97 | Human Resources | 3 | NR |
| | | Marketing | 15 | $50,500 |
| | | Operations | 6 | $42,000 |
| | | Strategic Planning | 12 | NR |
| | | Consulting | 12 | $48,833 |
| | | General Management | 6 | $50,000 |
| | | Other | 3 | NR |

# GRAND VALLEY STATE UNIVERSITY
## SEIDMAN COLLEGE OF BUSINESS

**GENERAL INFORMATION**

| | |
|---|---|
| Type of school | public |
| Environment | metropolis |
| Academic calendar | semester |

**SURVEY SAYS...**

Students love Grand Rapids, MI
Happy students
Smart classrooms

**STUDENTS**

| | |
|---|---|
| Enrollment of parent institution | 22,565 |
| Enrollment of business school | 272 |
| % male/female | 66/34 |
| % part-time | 87 |
| % minorities | 5 |
| % international | 27 |
| Average age at entry | 31 |
| Average years work experience at entry | 9 |

**ACADEMICS**

| | |
|---|---|
| **Academic Experience Rating** | **78** |
| Student/faculty ratio | 25:1 |
| Profs interesting rating | 86 |
| Profs accessible rating | 86 |
| % female faculty | 9 |
| % minority faculty | 6 |

**JOINT DEGREES**

MSN/MBA, 4 years

## Academics

With a newly renovated campus, state-of-the-art facilities, and a solid regional reputation, the Grand Valley State University MBA program has quite a lot to offer its working-professional student body. MBAs here appreciate what they have, bragging that "technologically, the campus has no equal when it comes to wireless Internet access and computer resource availability." They also praise the "affordability" and "flexibility" of the program as well as the "quality of instruction."

Most students are part-timers, and thus take advantage of the aforementioned flexible scheduling options, which include evening and weekend courses delivered in seven- or 14-week modules. Students wishing to fast-track can complete the program in as few as 16 months. Most students here are from the area, and as a result, many are familiar with the local business leaders who "work with the school and take interest in the curriculum being offered. Their input also lends real-world examples to classroom material and theory." Students' work experiences similarly enrich the classroom experience.

Seidman professors "are often active in the business world, maintaining the edge to pass on to the students." Their involvement with more than 400 local and national companies generates opportunities for students to work on projects in area organizations under the supervision of the faculty and establish "connections with the West Michigan business community." One MBA reports, "I have had accounting instructors who were former Securities and Exchange Commission executives. My global competitiveness class was taught by a former director of the World Bank. My auditing professor was an adjunct professor who also happened to be a Partner at BDO Seidman. Overall, of the 11 classes taken to earn my MBA, nine were taught by PhDs and two of those PhDs were also CPAs." Many students single out faculty in finance and accounting for praise; of the latter, they note, "The Seidman School of Business has always had a very high pass rate on the CPA exam. I was able to pass in two attempts after having been out of school for a number of years and then brushing up through the Becker Review. The accounting courses definitely gave me a good background to draw from."

## Career and Placement

Career placement and counseling services are provided through the university's Career Services Office, which offers a variety of online resources, seminars and workshops, individual counseling services, and recruitment events. "The Business School office has been incredible in supporting student goals," and someone is "always available."

## Student Life and Environment

The Seidman MBA program is housed in the DeVos Center on GVSU's downtown Grand Rapids campus, which students tell us is "nearly new and maintained with incredible focus and attention." Assets include "beautiful courtyards and facilities to accommodate a person who wants to relax, [and a] great new high-tech library." Although a few express past parking woes, some also praise the "new parking garage with lots of spots." The DeVos Center also features "many open gathering spaces, which increase the experiences of interacting with other students inside and outside of the business school," as well as "great technology, with free wireless Internet for laptops and PDAs." Students report that "classrooms are all up-to-date with equipment and lighting," and mention that they "are invited to use the technology for presentations and lectures during many activities."

CLAUDIA BAJEMA, GRADUATE BUSINESS PROGRAMS DIRECTOR
401 WEST FULTON, GRAND RAPIDS, MI 49504 UNITED STATES
PHONE: 616-331-7400 • FAX: 616-331-7389
E-MAIL: GO2GVMBA@GVSU.EDU • WEBSITE: WWW.GVSU.EDU/BUSINESS

MBAs enjoy "strong ties with the balance of the university to keep students in touch with the rest of college life." Students tell us, "Strong athletic programs also serve as an avenue to bring students together for a common, energetic experience" Even so, most students here spend little extracurricular time on campus. One explains, "The MBA program is pretty nonsocial, as most people are working full-time. The undergrad campus has a more active life." Some would like to see more of "a community for graduate students," while others are happy with the status quo.

"GVSU pulls from a fairly wide geographic area for business graduate students, and many commute 40 minutes to an hour for classes and library use. With strong family commitments, many students return home after class, but there is networking between students that live in similar areas, which is very helpful." The post-work environment can be very comforting as "occasionally a portion of the class will gather at a local establishment following class or an exam." Students represent "a diverse base coming from various sectors, including teaching, accounting, health sciences, engineering, and law. The students have strong ties, ranging from local, small businesses to international conglomerates, located here in the area." They are "career-oriented, driven, experienced people who are often balancing an active family, social, and business life."

## Admissions

Completed applications to the Grand Valley State MBA program include official transcripts for all previous post-secondary academic work, an essay describing the applicant's goals and objectives, GMAT scores, and, for non-native English speakers, TOEFL scores. Students who have previously completed graduate programs may apply for a waiver of the GMAT requirement. Students who have not previously completed course work in core business disciplines may be admitted to the program conditionally, pending completion of foundation courses in financial and managerial accounting, data analysis, finance, business law, macro- and micro-economics, marketing, and operations. Students can place out of foundation courses through school-administered examinations. In its efforts to attract underrepresented students, GVSU offers scholarships for African American and Hispanic students.

## FINANCIAL FACTS

| | |
|---|---|
| Annual tuition (in-state/out-of-state) | $5,364/$10,800 |
| Fees | $90 |
| Books and supplies | $1,500 |
| Room & board (on/off-campus) | $6,500/$5,000 |
| % of students receiving aid | 26 |
| Average grant | $4,360 |

## ADMISSIONS

| | |
|---|---|
| **Admissions Selectivity Rating** | **76** |
| # of applications received | 165 |
| % applicants accepted | 80 |
| % acceptees attending | 86 |
| Average GMAT | 562 |
| Range of GMAT | 520–680 |
| Average GPA | 3.3 |
| TOEFL required of international students? | yes |
| Minimum TOEFL (paper/computer) | 550/213 |
| Application fee | $30 |
| International application fee | $30 |
| Regular application deadline | 8/1 |
| Regular notification | rolling |
| Deferment available? | yes |
| Maximum length of deferment | 1 year |
| Transfer students accepted? | yes |
| Transfer application policy Students may transfer up to 9 credits with B or better at discretion of program director. | |
| Non-fall admissions? | yes |
| Need-blind admissions? | yes |

## APPLICANTS ALSO LOOK AT

Western Michigan University

## EMPLOYMENT PROFILE

| Career Rating | 60* | Grads employed by field: | % | avg. salary: |
|---|---|---|---|---|
| | | Accounting | 13 | NR |
| | | Finance | 13 | NR |
| | | Human Resources | 3 | NR |
| | | Marketing | 10 | NR |
| | | Operations | 10 | NR |
| | | Strategic Planning | 10 | NR |
| | | Consulting | 10 | NR |
| | | Entrepreneurship | 10 | NR |
| | | General Management | 10 | NR |
| | | Global Management | 10 | NR |
| | | Quantitative | 1 | NR |

# HARDIN SIMMONS UNIVERSITY
## THE ACTON MBA IN ENTREPRENEURSHIP

**GENERAL INFORMATION**

| | |
|---|---|
| Type of school | private |
| Affiliation | American Baptist |
| Academic calendar | Aug.–Apr. |

**SURVEY SAYS...**

*Solid preparation in:*
Operations
Entrepreneurial studies

**STUDENTS**

| | |
|---|---|
| Enrollment of parent institution | 2,200 |
| Enrollment of business school | 18 |
| % male/female | 78/22 |
| % out-of-state | 5 |
| % minorities | 22 |
| % international | 5 |
| Average age at entry | 28 |
| Average years work experience at entry | 5 |

**ACADEMICS**

| | |
|---|---|
| **Academic Experience Rating** | **95** |
| Student/faculty ratio | 1:1 |
| Profs interesting rating | 99 |
| Profs accessible rating | 87 |
| % female faculty | 9 |

## Academics

An MBA from Acton stands out in many ways, but primarily in experience in entrepreneurship that it offers. Students are pushed, pulled, bullied, and coddled in an extremely intense nine-month program, but at the end, most of them feel they come out with the skills they need to launch their own businesses or to help others launch theirs. As one student puts it, "The 80 to 90 hours per week that are described are real. It requires that much time. If you want clubs and day care and society, go to UT. If you want a cut-and-dry, no-nonsense business education, go with an Acton MBA."

Acton professors are "highly successful entrepreneurs who teach the keys to business success [by] using the Socratic methods and expecting a high workload to be accomplished every week." Because Acton recognizes that every student is also a customer, feedback on teacher performance is relied upon heavily. One student reports, "We have no tenured faculty. The professor(s) who are ranked at the bottom by the students must take a semester off to audit other professors. If they fail to improve when they come back, they're asked to leave." For the most part, however, "they work hard and [students] must work even harder to keep pace and push [them]selves to learn the lessons that are not commonly taught in most business schools in America today."

Students move through the program in a cohort of "highly talented students that have been handpicked by [the] admissions committee; students will come to rely upon each other in a profound way." During the first semester, students take five case-based courses. Three of these are the sales, operations, and accounting courses, which are also known as the tools courses. During the second semester, students take four classes that "dig more deeply into the four phases of the life cycle of a business covered in the entrepreneurial process." These courses are opportunity analysis, gathering resources and launch, growth and harvest. One class that some consider the most important of all is "Life of Meaning," in which students learn how to think about their business careers in broader and longer terms—about the impact a job will have on their lives, not just their income.

What students find most exciting about the curriculum, however, is how case-focused it is. During their time in the program, students are confronted with more than 300 "challenging case dilemmas." Students boast that "the case-based style of learning is the nearly exclusive approach used in this program, which [they] find exceptional. The real-world experience of the professors has also been vital to [their] experience." And others call Acton's program an "intense learning experience for those who like the complete immersion technique."

*Nota bene:* At the time we were going to print, Acton was in talks about, but had not yet applied for, accreditation from the Association to Advance Collegiate Schools of Business (AACSB).

TRACY BALBOA, DIRECTOR OF ENROLLMENT
515 CONGRESS AVENUE, SUITE 1875, AUSTIN, TX 78701 UNITED STATES
PHONE: 512-703-1232 • FAX: 512-495-9480
E-MAIL: TBALBOA@ACTONMBA.ORG • WEBSITE: WWW.ACTONMBA.ORG

## Career and Placement

Unlike many business schools, Acton's career resource center doesn't send out millions of resumes each year. Instead, students are encouraged to focus on specific jobs at specific companies that could help them achieve their long-term goals. According to the school's website, "once a professor is convinced that a student has made a considered choice, the professor will call that employer to make a personal introduction."

Companies who have accepted Acton students in the past include 3M, American Airlines, AT&T, BP, Goldman Sacks, Merrill Lynch, Microsoft, Newgistics, and Salion.

## Student Life and Environment

Some students go out of their way to emphasize that "while this is the most fun [they've] ever had, the only thing [students] will be doing is case prep and analysis, individually and with your classmates. There is no time for *anything* else. [Students] will not be able to shop, socialize, etc. This is 100 percent immersion." Still, one part of becoming a successful entrepreneur is learning "how to manage our time for studies, health, and family." And most students agree that there is no better place to learn this than Acton. "This program is focused on learning how to start and operate businesses, and the goal is to put you under enough pressure to give you that experience while managing your schedule."

## Admissions

Most students will agree that "if you are not willing to give all you can for nine months solid, then please, don't apply." Overall, Acton students have an average GMAT score of 620 and an average undergraduate GPA of 3.2. Approximately 25 percent of the students have 10 years or more of full-time work experience, and 33 percent had less than three years of work experience. Students who studied at a college level in a language other than English are required to take the TOEFL. A minimum score of 550 is required on that exam.

### FINANCIAL FACTS

| | |
|---|---|
| Annual tuition | $32,000 |
| % of students receiving aid | 43 |
| % of first-year students receiving aid | 43 |
| % of students receiving loans | 43 |

### ADMISSIONS

| | |
|---|---|
| Admissions Selectivity Rating | 85 |
| # of applications received | 28 |
| % applicants accepted | 71 |
| % acceptees attending | 90 |
| Average GMAT | 620 |
| Range of GMAT | 590–700 |
| Average GPA | 3.2 |
| TOEFL required of international students? | yes |
| Minimum TOEFL (paper/computer) | 550/260 |
| Application fee | $50 |
| International application fee | $50 |
| Regular application deadline | 3/15 |
| Regular notification | rolling |
| Application deadline/notification | |
| Round 1: | 11/15 / 12/15 |
| Round 2: | 3/15 / 4/15 |
| Round 3: | 5/15 / 6/15 |

### APPLICANTS ALSO LOOK AT

The University of Texas at Austin

| EMPLOYMENT PROFILE | | | | |
|---|---|---|---|---|
| Career Rating | 75 | Grads employed by field: | % | avg. salary: |
| Primary source of full-time job acceptances | | Finance | 20 | $70,000 |
| | | Marketing | 10 | $60,000 |
| School-facilitated activities | 2 (16%) | Consulting | 20 | $50,000 |
| Graduate-facilitated activities | 8 (62%) | Entrepreneurship | 20 | $90,000 |
| Unknown | 3 (22%) | Other | 30 | $70,000 |
| | | | | |
| Average starting salary | $80,000 | | | |
| Percent employed | 54 | | | |

# HARVARD UNIVERSITY
## HARVARD BUSINESS SCHOOL

## GENERAL INFORMATION

| | |
|---|---|
| Type of school | private |
| Environment | city |
| Academic calendar | Sept.–May |

### SURVEY SAYS...
Good social scene
Good peer network
*Solid preparation in:*
General management
Entrepreneurial studies

### STUDENTS

| | |
|---|---|
| Enrollment of business school | 1,770 |
| % male/female | 66/34 |
| % minorities | 21 |
| % international | 32 |
| Average age at entry | 27 |
| Average years work experience at entry | 4 |

### ACADEMICS

| | |
|---|---|
| **Academic Experience Rating** | **97** |
| Profs interesting rating | 98 |
| Profs accessible rating | 94 |
| % female faculty | 23 |

### JOINT DEGREES
MBA/JD, 4 years

## Academics

A "tried-and-true General Management focus with no concentrations or majors and no published GPAs," a "pedagogical approach that relies strongly on the case method," and most of all "a reputation as the best business program in the country" make Harvard Business School one of the top prizes in the MBA admissions sweepstakes. Applicants lucky enough to gain admission here rarely decide to go elsewhere.

The school's full-time-only program is relatively large; approximately 900 students enter the program each year. Students tell us, "Despite its large size, the school feels surprisingly small" thanks to a combination of factors. First is an administration that "could be a role model for any enterprise. This place is very well run." Second is the subdivision of classes into smaller sections of 90 students, who together attack approximately 500 case studies during their two years here. Finally, there's a faculty that "is obviously committed to excelling at teaching and developing relationships with the students. Each faculty member loves being here, regardless of whether they are a superstar or not, and that makes a difference. Faculty guide discussion well and enliven the classroom."

The case method predominates at Harvard; explains one student, "I sit in my section of 90 students every day and debate business topics. My section mates come from all walks of life and all of them are incredibly successful. I prepare my 13 cases per week so that I can contribute to this environment." Students love the approach, although they point out that "the case method is not as great for quantitative courses such as finance." Numerous field-study classes supplement the program, especially during the second year, which is devoted to elective study. School-wide initiatives—combinations of interdisciplinary classes, field study, contests, and club work—encourage research and provide added focus in the areas of social enterprise, entrepreneurship, global issues, and leadership.

Ultimately, though, HBS' strength resides in the quality of its instructors. One student notes, "HBS is one of the few schools where a large part of the professor's evaluation is based on classroom teaching. The professors at HBS are wonderful teachers and take great interest in their students." As one first-year puts it, "If first semester is representative of the whole experience, I'll be a happy grad. My accounting professor managed to make accounting my favorite class (seems unimaginable!), and I'll definitely take whatever he teaches during the second year of elective courses."

## Career and Placement

Harvard Business School hardly needs a Career Development Center, any more than Rolls Royce needs salesmen to move its cars. The school maintains a robust career services office all the same, providing a full range of counseling and internship- and career-placement services. Over 800 companies pay recruiting visits to the HBS campus each year in search of full-time hires; another 400 come looking for summer interns. Nearly half of all MBAs remain on the East Coast after graduation, about half of whom take jobs in New York City. Twenty percent find international placements; half work in Europe and about a quarter work in Asia.

## Student Life and Environment

Life at HBS "is as hectic as you want it to be." One student writes, "My life is pretty much moving along at breakneck speed. I wouldn't want it any other way because the school offers an incredible amount and array of activities, from volunteer consulting to running conferences." Because Harvard University is a magnet for innovative and prestigious thinkers in all disciplines, "This place is like a candy store for a five-year-old; you want

## FINANCIAL FACTS

| | |
|---|---|
| Annual tuition | $37,500 |
| Room & board | $22,432 |
| % of students receiving aid | 66 |

## ADMISSIONS

| | |
|---|---|
| **Admissions Selectivity Rating** | **99** |
| # of applications received | 7,130 |
| % applicants accepted | 13 |
| % acceptees attending | 87 |
| Average GMAT | 708 |
| Average GPA | 3.6 |
| TOEFL required of international students? | yes |
| Minimum TOEFL (paper/computer) | 610/253 |
| Application fee | $200 |
| Application deadline/notification | |
| Round 1: | 10/16 / 1/21 |
| Round 2: | 1/8 / 3/31 |
| Round 3: | 3/11 / 5/12 |
| Need-blind admissions? | yes |

to eat a lot more than what's good for you. You can spend all your time on studies, lectures from academics/politicians from all over the world, visiting business leaders, conferences, sports, or the nightlife. A 60-hour day would be appropriate."

Students generally manage to find the time to enjoy "a very social and outgoing environment" at HBS. One married student writes, "Most weekends my husband and I have a choice: the 'college scene' where we can hit up the Harvard or Central Square bars with the singles, or the 'married scene' where we have dinner, play goofy board games, and drink with our 'couple friends.' Either can be a great escape from the other, and both are always a lot of fun!" Close relationships are easy to forge here, as "the section system means you have 89 close friends in the program, which makes learning and being here fun. It also means in the business world there will always be 89 incredibly smart, connected people who will go to bat for me no matter what."

The population of this program is, unsurprisingly, exceptional. As one MBA explains, "The quality of people here is unlike anything I've experienced. For the first time in my adult life, I'm surrounded by people whose interests and abilities fascinate and inspire me. All religions, nationalities, cultures, and sexual orientations exist here, happily, and together. I think Boston cultivates this kind of 'meshing of all thoughts' in such a way that everyone is comfortable, and everyone learns. The city and the school are both comfortable in their own skins, and the students take on that characteristic here."

## Admissions

Applicants to Harvard Business School must submit a "complete HBS application portfolio, including personal essays, academics transcripts, and three letters of recommendation." In addition, students must provide scores from the GMAT, and applicants from non-English-speaking countries must submit scores for either the TOEFL or the IELTS (scores must be no more than two years old). Applications must be submitted online. Academic ability, leadership experience, and unique personal characteristics all figure prominently into the admissions decision. The school's viewbook notes that "because our MBA curriculum is fast-paced and rigorously analytical, we strongly encourage all applicants to complete introductory courses in quantitative subjects such as accounting, finance, and economics before coming to HBS. For some candidates, we may make admission contingent upon their completing such courses before they enroll." Good luck!

## EMPLOYMENT PROFILE

| Career Rating | 98 | Grads employed by field: | % | avg. salary: |
|---|---|---|---|---|
| Average starting salary | $100,000 | Finance | 37 | $100,000 |
| Percent employed | 94 | Marketing | 20 | $94,750 |
| | | Consulting | 29 | $110,000 |
| | | General Management | 11 | $96,000 |
| | | Other | 3 | $85,000 |

# HEC MONTREAL
## MBA PROGRAM

## Academics

HEC Montreal, the "little school that could," has truly ascended the ranks of international MBA programs in recent years. A relatively obscure school until the 1990s, HEC Montreal launched a curriculum overhaul midway through the decade that yielded dramatic results: Within a decade, the school had become the first North American institution to earn accreditation from EQUIS (the European Foundation for Management Development), AMBA (the Association of MBAs of the United Kingdom), and AACSB International.

HEC Montreal offers both a full-time and a part-time MBA program. International students are eligible for the full-time program only; this program, aptly named 'the Intensive MBA,' "is really a full two-year program condensed into 53 weeks. If you are motivated and disciplined, then you will succeed in this environment." Students warn that "it is very intensive and there is a solid workload throughout the program, with very few breaks in between." Cohort-based education and an emphasis on team projects helps students develop an esprit de corps to weather the program's challenges; explains one MBA, "We, all 180 students, take all the same classes for the first six months, which makes for great understanding amongst ourselves. We all know what the others are going through regarding workload and projects." While most here praise the full-time program, a few complain that "sometimes the pace is a bit too fast and we don't have time to sit back and reflect on what we've learned. Also, the pace does not allow much time for extracurricular seminars." Students may choose between French-only instruction and English-only instruction; roughly 60 percent of students opt for the English-only program.

The part-time program at HEC Montreal, called the MBA in Action, takes three years to complete. The curricula for the full-time and part-time programs are virtually identical; the major difference is that part-time students are exempted from the requirement to complete a field project. Part-timers warn that "occasionally we get professors who are low-level outsiders rather than the mostly experienced professors who teach the entire full-time program, and some of them are not such great teachers." They also point out that the program's team-learning format is hampered by the fact that "lots of students drop out or don't show up for meetings because of work obligations. Not enough effort is put into restoring team spirit when that happens." Students in both programs agree that the school "makes good use of classroom technology" and that "teaching methods tend to be very participative and pragmatic."

## Career and Placement

The HEC Montreal Career Centre provides career and placement services to undergraduates, graduates, and alumni. According to the school viewbook, "The Centre is well known for its personalized approach, and provides constant support for students as well as recent and past graduates: helping them prepare for interviews and draw up their résumés, providing information on the labor market, job-search strategies, conducting psychometric assessments (academic guidance and skills profiling), and career planning, assessment and redirection."

Companies that recruit on campus include Bank of Canada, Bombardier Inc., Canadian National, CDP Caisse de dépôt et placement du Québec, L'Oréal, Deloitte Consulting, Johnson & Johnson, KPMG, McKinsey, Merrill Lynch, National Bank, Procter & Gamble, Scotiabank, and the Toronto Stock Exchange.

IVANA.BONADUCE@HEC.CA, STUDENT ADVISOR
3000 CHEMIN DE LA COTE STE-CATHERINE, MONTREAL, QC H3T 2A7 CANADA
PHONE: 514-340-6957 • FAX: 514-340-5640
E-MAIL: MBA@HEC.CA • WEBSITE: WWW.HEC.CA

## Student Life and Environment

The MBA program at HEC Montreal is "very well located in Montreal, near the subway with access to all the Université de Montreal complex for other classes, if wanted." Facilities include "a new building that is aesthetically very nice, with lots of services for students," and "the biggest business library on campus." Students appreciate that the school is situated on "a nice, open space and that everything you need—food, lodging, subway, sports—is available on site." The gym facilities, students tell us, "are considered to be the best in Montreal."

For both full-time and part-time students, "the compressed six-week course terms (including exam period) makes the work pace fast and heavy," so "there is not necessarily a lot of time for social activities. However, the student association does try very hard to coordinate activities for" students, including "cinq à sept happy hours, a Quebec tradition that is alive and well at HEC Montreal. Every other Thursday, the student association takes over the campus lounge and we blow off a little steam! The parties are so much fun that the undergraduates try to sneak in, no doubt attracted by the dancing on the bars!" One student observes, "Our MBA association aims to involve all students in deciding what types of activities are provided. They concentrate on providing social activities that encourage the integration of English- and French-speaking students, as well as the international student community of HEC Montreal. Events such as the Magic of the Lanterns in the Botanical Gardens and an International Potluck dinner are perfect ways of opening up cultural barriers and introducing a broader, more international environment, where students are encouraged to share experiences and learn from each other."

## Admissions

Applicants to HEC Montreal must hold a baccalaureate earned "with a satisfactory average." Students must also demonstrate "at least two years of relevant full-time work experience" subsequent to completing undergraduate study. Applications must also include an official score report for the GMAT and two letters of recommendation (at least one from an employer). Non-native English speakers applying to the English-only program must pass the HECTOPE business English test (administered by HEC Montreal) or submit scores for either the TOEFL or IELTS. Non-native French speakers applying to the French-only program must complete the Test de français international (an ETS-administered exam). Applicants who are not citizens of Canada must obtain a certificat d'acceptation du Québec (C.A.Q.) and a document attesting to their right to reside in Canada (Student Authorization or Ministerial Permit). The school recommends that accepted students apply for these documents as soon as they receive confirmation of their admission to the program.

### FINANCIAL FACTS

| | |
|---|---|
| Annual tuition (in-state/out-of-state) | $3,750/$17,500 |
| Books and supplies | $1,700 |
| Room & board | $15,000 |
| % of first-year students receiving aid | 42 |
| % of students receiving grants | 42 |
| Average grant | $4,780 |

### ADMISSIONS

| | |
|---|---|
| Admissions Selectivity Rating | 79 |
| # of applications received | 426 |
| % applicants accepted | 62 |
| % acceptees attending | 59 |
| Average GMAT | 605 |
| TOEFL required of international students? | yes |
| Minimum TOEFL (paper/computer) | 600/250 |
| Application fee | $50 |
| International application fee | $50 |
| Regular application deadline | 2/1 |
| Regular notification | 4/1 |
| Deferment available? | yes |
| Maximum length of deferment | 1 year |
| Need-blind admissions? | yes |

### EMPLOYMENT PROFILE

| | | | | |
|---|---|---|---|---|
| Career Rating | 83 | | | |
| Primary source of full-time job acceptances | | Grads employed by field: | % | avg. salary: |
| School-facilitated activities | 30% | Finance | 16 | $59,750 |
| Graduate-facilitated activities | 50% | Marketing | 32 | $56,300 |
| Unknown | 20% | Operations | 15 | $55,500 |
| | | Consulting | 19 | $81,460 |
| | | General Management | 10 | $75,800 |
| Average starting salary | $61,200 | Other | 8 | $56,600 |
| Percent employed | 81 | | | |

# HEC School of Management—Paris
## HEC MBA Program

## Academics

"The sense of community [and] the focus on creating international managers [are] amazing" at the HEC School of Management, whose full-time, 16-month MBA program is offered in both an English-only and bilingual format. Because of its generalist approach, the HEC MBA "enables students to understand and participate in all functions of a business." Students tell us that "there is heavy emphasis on general skills as well as the human, personal interactions that are necessary in order to be successful in business, particularly in a multicultural and multilingual environment." Arithmophobes, take note: "Because it focuses on creating general management skills, the school does not focus on developing in-depth quantitative skills."

At HEC, "teamwork is stressed among the students, faculty, and administration to build a memorable MBA family, [especially] during the early phases of the program. The latter part of the course is more individual." The classroom atmosphere, students agree, is convivial. Students report, "The academic workload and class schedule are challenging but workable" and appreciate the duration of the program, which "is neither too short nor too long."

HEC instructors are "a diversified group of professors, with differing talents and competencies. The differentiation in styles and backgrounds is as apparent in the faculty as in the student body, which adds to the international experience of adapting to new cultures and environments." Students note, "Open communication and willingness to cooperate is a strong forte among all faculty, [and] professors' contacts in the business community make the classroom interactive." HEC's name carries considerable weight in Europe, allowing the school to "attract excellent speakers." One student writes, "During my 15 months of class, HEC had the pleasure of welcoming the prime minister, some of his team of ministers, and CEOs of global and French companies (Airbus, Nissan, Renault, Dassault)."

Of course, the school's location also means that the school has "a French public-service-type administration," which catches more than a few foreign students off-guard. American students, in particular, have little patience for the "completely rigid, bureaucratic, and inefficient structure [that] needs to be completely overhauled." Some, however, see a silver lining to this dark cloud: "The advantage is that you get a much better understanding of French society than you would if there was a non-French-style administration."

## Career and Placement

The Career Development Office at HEC provides counseling services, workshops, and seminars in job-search skills and interview techniques, access to online self-assessment instruments, contact to the school's 25,000-plus alumni worldwide, four major job fairs per year, and "privileged access to firms actively supporting HEC." The office sponsors regular corporate presentations and recruitment programs that bring over 200 employers to campus each year. Thirty-eight percent of all non-European members of the class of 2004 found employment in Europe; 88 percent found positions "of international scope." Nearly half used their degree to change both the sector and function of their careers.

Students see both strengths and weaknesses in the career office. One writes, "If you want to work in France, the name of HEC will help you for life. This is a fantastic networking opportunity in France, and it is growing on the international scale." However, many feel that career services are "currently too focused on French companies or French divisions

ADMISSIONS ADVISOR
JOUY-EN-JOSAS, CEDEX, 78351 FRANCE
PHONE: 011-33-0-139-67-71-67 • FAX: 011-33-0-139-67-74-65
E-MAIL: ADMISSIONMBA@HEC.FR • WEBSITE: WWW.MBA.HEC.EDU

of international companies. Efforts need to be made to improve the relationship with other international companies." Employers most likely to hire HEC MBAs include Barclays Capital; BT Retail; Hilti; Johnson & Johnson; L'Oréal; Michelin; Nestlé; and Société Générale.

## Student Life and Environment

The first term at HEC is grueling, students tell us, and during that initial period, "life centers around the campus and the MBA building. Students are getting involved in one or two extracurriculars that are important to them, but it is difficult to get involved in much more because of the workload." Things ease up afterwards, allowing students a little more time to enjoy all that the campus and Paris have to offer. Throughout the school year, "there are never two days without an event organized by one of the clubs, either a professional club or sports club." Every Wednesday night brings "Happy Hour at the Piano Bar, a chilled-out bar with wood floors, glass walls that overlook campus, candles, and good beer." Beer? Not for everyone. Many here "love kicking back after a hard day's work and enjoying a glass of Bordeaux."

HEC "offers the advantage of being part of a larger institution and as such is not insulated within its own self-absorbed environment," which students appreciate. They also praise the campus, which is "located in a beautiful forest, not far from Versailles and Paris." The 250-acre campus provides plenty of space to kick the soccer ball (i.e., football) around. The campus also features tennis courts, basketball courts, a climbing wall, and a nine-hole golf course. The proximity to Paris "adds a cultural and artistic flavor to the experience."

HEC's student body is 80 percent international, representing over 40 countries. The setting is "incredibly international [and] intellectually stimulating. Everyone has unique and insightful insights into not just business, but politics, society, and culture."

## Admissions

HEC requires the following of applicants: an electronically filed application form; official undergraduate transcripts, transcripts for all graduate work; GMAT scores (and TOEFL scores, where appropriate); two letters of recommendation; four passport-size photos and a copy of one's passport or birth certificate; and the application fee. An interview is required as its results are given serious consideration in the admissions decision. The school's literature states, "The admissions process for the HEC MBA Program is a rigorous one. The MBA experience is an interactive one, and each participant is called upon to contribute to the learning process through his or her personal and professional experience." As a result, past academic, professional, and personal experience are all important factors. The ability to perform well in teamwork situations is also considered essential.

### FINANCIAL FACTS

| | |
|---|---|
| Annual tuition | $46,000 |
| Books and supplies | $1,100 |
| Room & board | |
| (on/off-campus) | $15,000/$20,000 |
| % of students receiving aid | 70 |
| % of students receiving loans | 60 |
| % of students receiving grants | 33 |
| Average grant | $9,000 |

### ADMISSIONS

| | |
|---|---|
| Admissions Selectivity Rating | 98 |
| # of applications received | 888 |
| % applicants accepted | 21 |
| % acceptees attending | 58 |
| Average GMAT | 660 |
| Range of GMAT | 590–750 |
| Average GPA | 3.65 |
| TOEFL required of | |
| international students? | yes |
| Minimum TOEFL | |
| (paper/computer) | 600/250 |
| Application fee | $100 |
| International application fee | $100 |
| Regular application deadline | 4/29 |
| Regular notification | 6/3 |
| Deferment available? | yes |
| Maximum length | |
| of deferment | 1 year |
| Non-fall admissions? | yes |
| Need-blind admissions? | yes |

### APPLICANTS ALSO LOOK AT
INSEAD, University of London

### EMPLOYMENT PROFILE

| Career Rating | | 90 | Grads employed by field: | % | avg. salary: |
|---|---|---|---|---|---|
| Average starting salary | | $100,568 | Finance | 24 | $94,850 |
| | | | Marketing | 18 | $90,203 |
| | | | MIS | 1 | NR |
| | | | Operations | 4 | NR |
| | | | Consulting | 9 | $100,450 |
| | | | General Management | 18 | $102,314 |
| | | | Global Management | 20 | $96,660 |
| | | | Other | 4 | NR |

# HHL—Leipzig Graduate School of Management

## GENERAL INFORMATION

| | |
|---|---|
| Type of school | private |
| Academic calendar | term |

### SURVEY SAYS...
Friendly students
Happy students
*Solid preparation in:*
Teamwork

### STUDENTS

| | |
|---|---|
| Enrollment of business school | 66 |
| % male/female | 75/25 |
| % part-time | 27 |
| % international | 60 |
| Average age at entry | 31 |
| Average years work experience at entry | 6 |

### ACADEMICS

| | |
|---|---|
| **Academic Experience Rating** | **91** |
| Student/faculty ratio | 5:1 |
| Profs interesting rating | 80 |
| Profs accessible rating | 92 |
| % female faculty | 25 |

### PROMINENT ALUMNI
Jack Artman, M&A Manager; Bodo Marr, M&A Manager; Thomas Ludwig, Investment Banking Professional

## Academics

HHL—the Leipzig Graduate School of Management offers German and international business students an appealing mix of a well-established name and modern innovation. Founded in 1898, HHL is the oldest business school in Germany, and its students benefit from its deserved reputation as a solid training ground for European managers. The MBA program, however, is relatively new, having only graduated its first class in 2001. Because the program is still in its nascent stages, students tell us, "It is striving to achieve more in the global ranking, so they really make an effort, as opposed to many established schools that expect their reputation to work for them." Since the program runs its course in a scant 15 months, it also appeals to the cost-conscious and to those in a hurry to climb the corporate ladder of success.

The HHL curriculum is divided into three categories. Core courses cover the basics in management; this segment of the program is particularly well-suited to the German students "whose prior academic training was not focused on business but rather was in the natural sciences, humanities, or social sciences" and whom the Admissions Office targets. Specialization courses in accounting, finance, marketing, business organization, and strategy allow students to hone a particular skill set. Students tell us that specializations in finance, marketing, and strategy "are the tops, especially finance and marketing with very well-known professors who publish a lot in their field and are on boards of corporations." Application courses in such areas as entrepreneurship, innovation management, and corporate-government relations keep students abreast of contemporary issues in the business world.

HHL professors "can be contacted almost 24 hours a day," and "those who are comfortable with English can even be fun in classes." Internships, study abroad, and independent study options are all available. A high-quality education at a reasonable price is cited by students as one of the main reasons they chose the school.

## Career and Placement

HHL MBAs report with satisfaction that "one of the big strengths of this program is its excellent contact to companies. Almost all top companies in consulting, banking, and industry come for presentation and recruiting. Companies react surprisingly positively when saying that you are from our school." One student comments, "Concerning placement, there is a huge database of direct contact people. Rather than applying over a 'website' one can contact people or alumni. This helps to stay away from the crowd that applies over recruiting websites of companies."

According to HHL, the school "has a record of placing graduates with prominent international firms—including Arthur Andersen, BASF, Bayer, BGG, Bertelsmann, BDO, Booz Allen & Hamilton, Boston Consulting Group, Daimler-Chrysler, Deutsche Bank, E.ON, Ernst & Young, Ford, Henkel, Kirch-Gruppe, KPMG, McKinsey, Nestlé, PricewaterhouseCoopers, Procter & Gamble, Siemens, Tui, and Volkswagen—as well as with many German 'Mittelstand' companies." Other companies that recruit on campus include A.T. Kearney, Accenture, Allianz AG, BMW, Citibank, FairAd, Goldman Sachs, Horváth & Partner, Lufthansa Cargo, OnVista, Porsche, Sachsen LB, and Wellington.

PETRA SPANKA, EXECUTIVE DIRECTOR
JAHNALLEE 59, LEIPZIG, 04109 GERMANY
PHONE: 01149341-9851-734 • FAX: 01149341-9851-731
E-MAIL: PETRA.SPANKA@HHL.DE • WEBSITE: WWW.HHL.DE

## Student Life and Environment

An accelerated academic schedule at HHL means that "life is somewhat focused on the courses. There is a lot of pre-work and post-work to do for almost all courses. Most courses integrate a high amount of applied case studies and group work. In some weeks/months the balance of studying and doing other things is bad (i.e., a lot of studying)." One student notes, "Classes in finance are especially tough, but teach a lot that you need later in respective jobs." Even so, there is some time leftover to socialize. One MBA writes, "The school organizes a lot of parties and integrates in social-life staff (i.e., professors) and students. The professors and students are almost on a friendship level and they help the students where they can."

Many students were attracted to the school because it represents "a somewhat wild mixture of nations, ages, and backgrounds," with about one third hailing from Germany and the rest "from different countries in Asia, South and North America, Europe, etc. Also, they have different working experiences; some of them are businessmen, some are engineers. Some worked for law firms, some served in the Navy as IT engineers." What they all share in common is that they "are ready to help, ready to work, and ready to party." As one student observes, "They are very interesting and challenging to work with. I can't imagine better fellow students!"

Leipzig is "a great town [with] a long academic record [and] many sports facilities," students tell us. Bach and Schumann put this ancient trade center on the musical map, and their traditions are carried on today in the city's many concert halls, theaters, cafés and cabarets, jazz clubs, and discos. The city is conveniently located for travel to and from Berlin, Dresden, and Weimar, as well as to major Czech and Polish cities.

## Admissions

All applicants to HHL's MBA program must submit GMAT scores (according to the school, students with scores of at least 650 "are more likely to be offered admission than applicants with lower scores"), proof of undergraduate degree and transcripts, two recommendations, a resume, and a completed application. Non-native English speakers must also submit proof of English proficiency. HHL accepts TOEFL scores to fulfill this requirement. The admissions committee convenes once a month to consider all completed applications, at which point it decides either to accept, reject, or wait-list each candidate.

## FINANCIAL FACTS

| | |
|---|---|
| Annual tuition | $27,477 |
| Books and supplies | $300 |
| Room & board | $7,500 |
| % of students receiving aid | 15 |
| % of first-year students receiving aid | 10 |
| Average grant | $100,000 |

## ADMISSIONS

| | |
|---|---|
| Admissions Selectivity Rating | 93 |
| # of applications received | 120 |
| % applicants accepted | 38 |
| % acceptees attending | 87 |
| Average GMAT | 600 |
| Range of GMAT | 550–780 |
| Average GPA | 3.5 |
| TOEFL required of international students? | yes |
| Minimum TOEFL (paper/computer) | 600/250 |
| Application fee | $0 |
| International application fee | $0 |
| Regular application deadline | 6/1 |
| Regular notification | 7/1 |
| Application deadline/notification | |
| Round 1: | 4/1 / 5/1 |
| Round 2: | 5/1 / 6/1 |
| Round 3: | 6/1 / 7/1 |
| Deferment available? | yes |
| Maximum length of deferment | 1 year |
| Transfer students accepted? | yes |
| Transfer application policy | |
| Course work and examinations in an economic degree program at another university or college of equal status. | |
| Need-blind admissions? | yes |

## EMPLOYMENT PROFILE

| Career Rating | 84 | Grads employed by field: | % | avg. salary: |
|---|---|---|---|---|
| **Primary source of full-time job acceptances** | | Accounting | 3 | NR |
| | | Finance | 3 | NR |
| School-facilitated activities | 12 (30%) | Human Resources | 5 | NR |
| Graduate-facilitated activities | 10 | Marketing | 12 | NR |
| Unknown | 17 | MIS | 5 | NR |
| | | Operations | 12 | NR |
| Average starting salary | $55,000 | Consulting | 12 | NR |
| Percent employed | 85 | Communications | 7 | NR |
| | | Entrepreneurship | 5 | NR |
| | | General Management | 12 | NR |
| | | Global Management | 5 | NR |
| | | Other | 5 | NR |
| | | Internet/New Media | 12 | NR |

# HOFSTRA UNIVERSITY
## FRANK G. ZARB SCHOOL OF BUSINESS

## GENERAL INFORMATION
Type of school                private
Environment                   city
Academic calendar             4-1-4

### SURVEY SAYS...
Smart classrooms
*Solid preparation in:*
Teamwork
Presentation skills
Computer skills

### STUDENTS
Enrollment of parent
  institution                 12,890
Enrollment of business school  452
% male/female                 61/39
% out-of-state                6
% part-time                   65
% minorities                  32
% international               21
Average age at entry          32
Average years work experience
  at entry                    2.5

### ACADEMICS
**Academic Experience Rating**  **67**
Student/faculty ratio         8:1
Profs interesting rating      63
Profs accessible rating       70
% female faculty              18
% minority faculty            21

### JOINT DEGREES
MBA/JD, 4 years; BBA/MBA, 5
years; BBA/MS, 5 years

### PROMINENT ALUMNI
Frank G. Zarb, Senior Advisor &
Managing Dir., Hellman & Friedman;
Salvatore F. Sodano, Former Chair &
CEO, American Stock Exchange;
James Campbell, President & CEO,
GE Consumer & Industrial
Americas; Patrick J. Purcell,
President & Publisher, Herald
Media; Donna Iucolano, CEO North
America, International Masters
Publisher

## Academics

Business grad students come to Hofstra seeking "a state-of-the-art education at an accessible price," and most leave feeling they've accomplished their goal. The Zarb School, students report, "is on the cutting edge of technology—almost all classrooms have a computer at every desk." A world of research awaits students, as the library "provides off-campus access to 34 business-specific databases, including Lexis/Nexis services."

Zarb students may choose from a variety of degree options: an MBA, an MS, a four-year combined JD/MBA program, and an executive MBA (EMBA) for those already deeply immersed in the working world. Students tell us, "If you hope to have managerial position, you should go for an MBA because you will learn from each field of business," but those interested in marketing should consider the MS "since you have to take a lot of marketing classes, many more than MBA students even if their concentration is marketing. You will learn a lot about this specific field."

Hofstra's finance program earns the highest praise from students. They tell us, "Finance professors are cutting edge, often pulling together a curriculum not found in textbooks, incorporating tools developed and used in the field." Throughout all disciplines, instructors "are, to a person, accomplished and well-recognized leaders in the business realm. The body of instructors is truly unparalleled in terms of experience and ability." They are also readily accessible; "many of them have open-door policies," one MBA reports.

Perhaps Hofstra's greatest asset, however, is its location. As one student put it, "Although the school is not as well-known as Harvard, the great strength of Hofstra is the location. Because we have New York City very close to us, we can benefit a lot from it. There are so many more job opportunities here than any other cities, and Hofstra is pretty well-known for people in New York. Also we can benefit a lot socially being here. Since networking is a very important factor, if you are an ambitious business student, you might happen to bump into someone at a restaurant and end up networking with him or her—and who knows? You might get a job!"

## Career and Placement

Hofstra maintains an MBA career center separate from the university career center, which provides advisement, networking, and career development plans. Fortunately, Hofstra's proximity to New York City—and to numerous businesses headquartered on Long Island—makes students' search for employment easier than at many business schools. Over 300 employers pay recruiting visits to the Hofstra campus each year; about half as many come to Hofstra seeking summer interns. Top employers include Arrow Electronics, Inc.; Citibank; Computer Associates; Deloitte Touche Tohmatsu; Deutsche Bank; Ernst & Young; JP Morgan Chase; Pall Corporation; PricewaterhouseCoopers; North Shore, LIJ Health Systems; Hain Celestial; KPMG; Integrated Business Systems; Quest Diagnostics; and Henry Schein.

Marketing and finance claim the majority of Hofstra MBAs. Average starting salaries range from $53,667 (accounting) to over $100,000 (consulting). In 2004, the average starting salary in finance was $66,800; in marketing, the average starting salary was $68,692. Over 90 percent find work in the Northeast region.

CAROL DRUMMER, DEAN FOR GRADUATE ADMISSIONS
126 HOFSTRA UNIVERSITY, 105 MEMORIAL HALL, HEMPSTEAD, NY 11549 UNITED STATES
PHONE: 866-472-3463 • FAX: 516-463-4664
E-MAIL: GRADSTUDENT@HOFSTRA.EDU • WEBSITE: WWW.HOFSTRA.EDU/ACADEMICS/BUSINESS

## Student Life and Environment

Hofstra's "safe, friendly, [and] gorgeous [campus boasts] great facilities, including a wonderful library, laboratories, and gym." The campus is home to "a lot of social events, and the school offers transportation to the Nassau Veterans Memorial Coliseum," home to the New York Islanders, concerts, and major trade shows. Students are less excited about the school's hometown of Hempstead but consider the school's location a plus overall. One MBA explains, "Although the school is located [in] not-too-nice [of a] neighborhood, we can easily go to Manhattan (New York City) by taking the Long Island Railroad. We can go there on weekends and have fun, which is a very good way of removing stress and forgetting about school for just a little while. I truly believe that New York City is one of the most exciting cities in the world, and having it very close to the school is the biggest advantage of students of Hofstra, both socially and academically." The location also "offers students the opportunity to live among the suburbs of New York City, [placing them in] the hub of the business world" without having to endure big-city crowds and expenses.

Most graduate students "are very friendly, helpful, and driven, as well as pretty active in student associations, of which there are plenty." Clubs and organizations include the International MBA/MS Association, Graduate Women in Business, the Hofstra Investment Banking Association, and the Hofstra Business Consulting Group. If there's a knock on the student body, it is that it's "overwhelmingly part-time, comprising working professionals. Students tend not to engage themselves in thorough discussion and analysis of presented material. It is understandably difficult to work a full day and then contribute to a class at night, but if one desires a quality education, then it is a necessity."

## Admissions

Applicants to Hofstra's graduate business programs must submit an official undergraduate transcript, GMAT scores, letters of recommendation, a personal statement, and a resume; students whose first language is not English must submit TOEFL scores. Admissions decisions are "also influenced by evidence of leadership, communication skills, [and performance on the] analytical writing assessment of GMAT," the school tells us. The admissions department also reports that "special consideration in the application process is given to minority students from disadvantaged backgrounds." Hofstra makes no undergraduate curricular requirements of its MBA students, no major precludes admission to the school, and no specific courses are required prior to admission. Applicants to the MS program in accounting or taxation must hold an undergraduate degree in accounting. Applicants to the EMBA program must document a minimum of seven years' work experience.

### FINANCIAL FACTS

| | |
|---|---|
| Annual tuition | $17,280 |
| Fees | $930 |
| Books and supplies | $3,210 |
| Room & board | |
| (on/off-campus) | $9,290/$12,725 |
| % of students receiving aid | 45 |
| % of first-year students | |
| receiving aid | 56 |
| % of students receiving loans | 33 |
| % of students receiving grants | 14 |
| Average award package | $14,564 |
| Average grant | $10,493 |
| Average student loan debt | $32,891 |

### ADMISSIONS

| | |
|---|---|
| Admissions Selectivity Rating | 71 |
| # of applications received | 339 |
| % applicants accepted | 74 |
| % acceptees attending | 51 |
| Average GMAT | 527 |
| Range of GMAT | 490–570 |
| Average GPA | 3.2 |
| TOEFL required of | |
| international students? | yes |
| Application fee | $60 |
| International application fee | $60 |
| Regular application deadline | rolling |
| Regular notification | rolling |
| Deferment available? | yes |
| Maximum length | |
| of deferment | 1 year |
| Transfer students accepted? | yes |
| Transfer application policy | |
| Number of transferable credits is | |
| limited to a maximum of 9 credits. | |
| Non-fall admissions? | yes |
| Need-blind admissions? | yes |

### APPLICANTS ALSO LOOK AT

City University of New York—Baruch College, New York University, Pace University, St. John's University

| EMPLOYMENT PROFILE | | | | |
|---|---|---|---|---|
| Career Rating | 76 | Grads employed by field: | % | avg. salary: |
| Primary source of full-time | | Accounting | 33 | $54,429 |
| job acceptances | | Finance | 18 | $55,000 |
| School-facilitated activities | 9 (38%) | Human Resources | 4 | $55,000 |
| Graduate-facilitated activities | 10 (42%) | Marketing | 8 | $50,000 |
| Unknown | 5 (20%) | MIS | 8 | $52,000 |
| | | Operations | 13 | $76,000 |
| Average starting salary | $57,947 | Consulting | 4 | NR |
| Percent employed | 80 | General Management | 4 | NR |
| | | Other | 8 | $63,000 |

# HONG KONG U. OF SCIENCE AND TECHNOLOGY
## HKUST BUSINESS SCHOOL

### GENERAL INFORMATION
Type of school                     public
Academic calendar               semester

### SURVEY SAYS...
*Solid preparation in:*
Finance
Accounting
Teamwork

### STUDENTS
Enrollment of parent
  institution                       8,823
Enrollment of business school   194
% male/female                      48/52
% part-time                           71
% international                       80
Average age at entry                28
Average years work experience
  at entry                             5

### ACADEMICS
**Academic Experience Rating   62**
Profs interesting rating            83
Profs accessible rating             71
% female faculty                     15

### JOINT DEGREES
MBA/MS in Financial Analysis, 3
years; MBA/MS in Investment
Management, 3 years; MBA/MS in
Information Systems Management,
3 years

### PROMINENT ALUMNI
Edmond Ho, Director, Citigroup
Global Markets Asia; Rebecca Chan,
Partner, PricewaterhouseCoopers;
Marco Elli, President and CEO,
Pirello Japan KK; Jackson Ng, CFO
& Director, Modern Terminals Ltd;
SC Liu, Chair, Evergreen Real Estate
Consultant

## Academics

"You can't learn about a region from a distance. You need to experience it personally." So say the international students drawn to the MBA program at the Hong Kong University of Science and Technology; they come here looking for "easy access to the Chinese culture for Western students," and they know that this is the place to get it. One MBA writes, "There is no way a school in Europe or the U.S. could teach you about this region as well as HKUST can. There is no other school in Asia that can touch it in that respect." Another agrees, "HKUST has the best Chinese faculty in the world catering to business in China."

Full-time students can choose from two curricular options at HKUST: a 12-month option that minimizes the student's time away from work, and a 16-month option that allows for participation in exchange programs with one of 51 overseas business schools. The school also offers a part-time MBA. Students tell us that "the finance faculty is top-notch, as it needs to be for a financial center of the world like Hong Kong," and that "the school is also excellent in accounting and IT." Consulting, strategy, and marketing reportedly "could be stronger." The faculty has strong credentials. One MBA reports, "It's a very strong research faculty who present their findings at the international level. They are also, for the most part, very capable of imparting with their insights in a compelling and engaging manner."

MBAs also praise the program's "emphasis on teamwork, [the] good balance of practical case-based teaching and theory" in the classroom, and a curricular structure that ensures students are prepared to participate in class. "There are compulsory assignments to hand in before class, which is good to force students to prepare for class and also arrive on time. The professors also count participation towards the grade, so students are encouraged to raise questions."

HKUST is also home to a part-time MBA program, which takes two years to complete. Part-time students complete the same required courses as do full-timers but have fewer elective options; the school admits about 120 part-timers each year, dividing them into two cohorts of 60. The program is scheduled "to meet the special needs of working professionals and managers."

## Career and Placement

HKUST maintains a dedicated MBA Career Development Office for its graduate students in business. The office offers career counseling, a variety of self-assessment tools, workshops in job-search and interview skills, recruiting events, internships, resume books, and job listings. Students feel that they "need closer relationships or partnerships with companies, especially large companies in mainland China and other important countries or cities outside Hong Kong." MBAs also tell us that "this is still a young program," which they see as both an impediment and an asset. "Our alumni network is still relatively small; however, there is no doubt that the people we are studying with are the future of China and this region. So it's a small network, but a very useful one indeed," writes one student.

Employers who most frequently hire HKUST MBAs include UBS, Morgan Stanley, FedEx, Citibank, HSBC, and Emerson Electric Co. Just under half od HKUST grads wind up in the finance sector.

## Student Life and Environment

Full-time students at HKUST constitute "a small group with around 60 students, yet with diversity in cultural, background, and working experience. We are friendly, helpful, active, and full of creative ideas!" Students come here from all around the world; as one student reports, "The range of nationalities present spans from Thai, Korean, Israeli, Indian, and Filipino to New Zealander, Swiss, Irish, French, and Canadian." There are a lot of students from mainland China here; international students appreciate how "their background provides invaluable input into the program."

The HKUST campus "on a hill overlooking the ocean [is] an oasis that is only 20 minutes by MTR from the heart of the central business district." Students enjoy "numerous activities after class. Every Friday noon, students, faculty, and some staff of MBA office will have a self-service lunch together. It is a small family atmosphere, and we chat with each other casually. After the lunch, there will be a country presentation by one or a group of students from a certain country." Students spend leisure time together too, "hiking the trails beside the sea, boating, enjoying nightlife on the famous bar street of Hong Kong, attending concerts, [or] shopping." One MBA writes, "School life cycles between periods of intense work and pure fun."

Students love Hong Kong, "a very international city" of seven million. As one MBA puts it, "Hong Kong is Asia's world city. If you don't have a life here, you just don't have a life." The "nightlife, food, entertainment are all world-class," the city is "super-safe," and the "public transportation is excellent." The school's location "is convenient to visit the Hong Kong stock exchange or other big companies. You are even able to do some field study in mainland China."

## Admissions

HKUST expects all applicants to hold "a good bachelor degree from a recognized university" and to have strong GMAT scores, full-time work experience (at least three years for the part-time program, at least one year for the full-time program), and to be proficient in English. All applicants must provide two letters of reference along with official copies of their transcripts and GMAT score reports. Students whose first language is not English must also provide TOEFL scores. An interview, scheduled at the school's behest, is required prior to admission; it can be conducted by telephone if a face-to-face interview is impractical. The online application is "strongly advised" by the school "for data accuracy and convenience of data update."

### FINANCIAL FACTS

| | |
|---|---|
| Annual tuition | $32,000 |
| Books and supplies | $1,000 |
| Room & board | |
| (on/off-campus) | $3,100/$6,200 |
| Average grant | $7,400 |

### ADMISSIONS

**Admissions Selectivity Rating  60***

| | |
|---|---|
| Range of GMAT | 560–660 |
| Minimum TOEFL | |
| (paper/computer) | 600/250 |
| Application fee | $64 |
| International application fee | $64 |
| Regular application deadline | 3/31 |
| Regular notification | 6/15 |
| Application deadline/notification | |
| Round 1: | 12/15 / 2/28 |
| Round 2: | 3/31 / 6/15 |
| Deferment available? | yes |
| Maximum length | |
| of deferment | 1 year |

| EMPLOYMENT PROFILE | | | | |
|---|---|---|---|---|
| **Career Rating** | 70 | **Grads employed by field:** | **%** | **avg. salary:** |
| Average starting salary | $58,000 | Accounting | 3 | NR |
| | | Finance | 33 | NR |
| | | Marketing | 13 | NR |
| | | Operations | 3 | NR |
| | | Strategic Planning | 5 | NR |
| | | Consulting | 15 | NR |
| | | Entrepreneurship | 5 | NR |
| | | General Management | 8 | NR |
| | | Other | 7 | NR |
| | | Nonprofit | 8 | NR |

# HOWARD UNIVERSITY
## SCHOOL OF BUSINESS

## Academics

One of the few primarily African American universities in the country, Howard University also boasts the oldest fully accredited business school in the Washington, DC, area. And pride in the legacy of both the university and their business-school program really pulls the community together. As one student puts it, "What is lovely about Howard University is the easy access to professors and the close relations the students have with their professors. They not only impart their knowledge but also treat the students like family." Students find a sense of cooperative spirit in their classmates as well, despite the rigors of academic life. According to one student, "My classmates are the best. You [can] always borrow someone's notes or text to catch up on if you're falling behind. That, to me, is the ultimate MBA experience: having a group of people you enjoy working with and who are willing to work with you." Another student points out that, with such a small, friendly group of people, Howard's greatest strength is its "ability to personalize the education and tend to the individual needs of a smaller student body."

Along with huge amounts of time spent on studying, Howard students also attend case competitions and conferences all over the country and are often particularly involved in the National Black MBA Association, which provides scholarships, funding, and counseling to prospective MBAs. Howard students are regularly awarded scholarships—often at a higher rate than other institutions—and greatly benefit from these networking opportunities. As one student says, "Throughout my tenure at Howard, I have been involved in more than 10 case competitions. The cases cover a broad spectrum of topics. From these experiences, I have acquired valuable research skills that I have used later both in my courses at school and in my internships in corporate America."

In 2000, in response to current business trends and needs, Howard added a supply-chain management concentration to their basic MBA program, and it has quickly become one of the program's greatest strengths. Students point out Howard's "very strong supply chain and finance concentrations, [these departments often draw] prominent individuals to Howard to teach. If one is fortunate enough, he or she may get into the respective class. It is good to know that some people still see the potential at the school." Still, some are disappointed that these two departments seem to stand alone. "The finance department seems to be the only department that has involvement from the graduate level. All other organizations and activities are centered around undergraduates."

## Career and Placement

Like so many students, Howard University's prospective MBAs place "exposure to *Fortune* 500 companies and executives of those companies" high at the top of their wish list and would like to see the career-resource center doing more to facilitate those meetings. In fact, complaints about job placement are fairly frequent. Still, among the top recruiters at Howard were Ariba, Citigroup, Dell, Eaton, IBM, Intel, K + MG, PWC, Tyco, and UTC. Other students do claim that the school's "great relationship with major employers results in very high job placement." And in 2004, the mean base salary for graduating MBAs was $72,786, not including bonuses and other compensation.

Students would also like to see a "stronger alumni network" and think that "administration and recruitment efforts" could be kicked up a notch. Students would also like to see more "alumni involvement and endowments" and think the school has a long way to go to make that happen.

VERNA K. SUPEL, ASSOCIATE DIRECTOR
2600 SIXTH STREET NORTHWEST, SUITE 236, WASHINGTON, DC 20059 UNITED STATES
PHONE: 202-806-1725 • FAX: 202-986-4435 • E-MAIL: MBA_BSCHOOL@HOWARD.EDU
WEBSITE: WWW.BSCHOOL.HOWARD.EDU/PROGRAMS/MBA/INDEX.HTML

## Student Life and Environment

Though Howard benefits from its Washington, DC, location and lovely historic campus, most students say that, with their schoolwork, they have little time to enjoy the world around them. As one student puts it, "Life at my school does not extend very much beyond academics, and even if it did, "by the time I finish all my schoolwork, all I want to do is sleep. I have no extra energy left over for much of a social life," relates another MBA.

Despite the rigorous schedule, students agree that Howard "definitely exudes a sense of family." Many graduate students live on-campus and point out that "the university administration does a good job in ensuring the security of both the students and their property. A nonresident cannot get into the dorms unless signed in by a resident who is held responsible for any visitors in his or her name." Others, however, complain that "campus housing is just as expensive as off-campus housing, which leads many people to move farther away and commute. Howard really needs to provide more housing at lower costs."

## Admissions

At Howard University's School of Business, the entering class of 2005 had a mean GPA of 3.1, and the mean GMAT score was 500; 82 percent of the incoming students were African American, and 18 percent were African and Caribbean. In addition, 56 percent of the incoming full-time students were female, 29 percent were international, 87.5 percent of the incoming students had some postgraduate work, and the average amount of post-graduate work was 3.7 years. Students with an undergraduate degree in business equaled 52.5 percent.

### FINANCIAL FACTS

| | |
|---|---|
| Annual tuition | $14,065 |
| Fees | $805 |
| Books and supplies | $2,500 |
| Room & board (on/off-campus) | $12,000/$17,000 |
| % of students receiving aid | 98 |
| % of first-year students receiving aid | 98 |
| % of students receiving loans | 65 |
| % of students receiving grants | 73 |
| Average award package | $23,499 |
| Average grant | $14,343 |
| Average student loan debt | $38,142 |

### ADMISSIONS

| | |
|---|---|
| Admissions Selectivity Rating | 81 |
| # of applications received | 215 |
| % applicants accepted | 36 |
| % acceptees attending | 62 |
| Average GMAT | 500 |
| Range of GMAT | 420–550 |
| Average GPA | 3.1 |
| TOEFL required of international students? | yes |
| Minimum TOEFL (paper/computer) | 550/213 |
| Application fee | $65 |
| International application fee | $65 |
| Regular application deadline | 4/1 |
| Regular notification | 5/1 |
| Application deadline/notification | |
| Round 1: | 11/15 / 1/1 |
| Round 2: | 2/1 / 3/1 |
| Round 3: | 4/1 / 5/1 |
| Round 4: | 5/15 / 6/1 |
| Early decision program? | yes |
| ED deadline/notification | Fall 11/15 / 1/1 |
| Deferment available? | yes |
| Maximum length of deferment | 2 semesters |
| Transfer students accepted? | yes |
| Transfer application policy Must meet Howard's MBA Program Admission Criteria; can only transfer a maximum of 6.0 credit hours from an AACSB-accredited graduate business program. | |
| Non-fall admissions? | yes |
| Need-blind admissions? | yes |

### APPLICANTS ALSO LOOK AT
American U., Clark Atlanta U., George Mason U., Georgetown U., The George Washington U., U. of Maryland—College Park

### EMPLOYMENT PROFILE

| | | Grads employed by field: | % | avg. salary: |
|---|---|---|---|---|
| Career Rating | 70 | Finance | 18 | $78,750 |
| Primary source of full-time job acceptances | | Human Resources | 8 | $77,500 |
| School-facilitated activities | 17 (68%) | Marketing | 5 | $90,000 |
| Graduate-facilitated activities | 8 (32%) | Operations | 32 | $73,900 |
| | | Consulting | 32 | $72,833 |
| Average starting salary | $75,770 | General Management | 5 | $75,000 |
| Percent employed | 89 | | | |

# IAE Universidad Austral
## Management and Business School

### GENERAL INFORMATION
| | |
|---|---|
| Type of school | private |

### SURVEY SAYS...
Happy students
*Solid preparation in:*
Marketing
Finance
General management

### STUDENTS
| | |
|---|---|
| Enrollment of business school | 48 |
| % male/female | 69/31 |
| % minorities | 15 |
| % international | 35 |
| Average age at entry | 28 |
| Average years work experience at entry | 5 |

### ACADEMICS
| | |
|---|---|
| **Academic Experience Rating** | **85** |
| Profs interesting rating | 89 |
| Profs accessible rating | 89 |
| % female faculty | 9 |
| % minority faculty | 16 |

## Academics

Future MBAs choose IAE Universidad Austral's intensive one-year program because of the school's "excellent reputation in Argentina and throughout Latin America" as well as for the speed with which it delivers results. The bilingual program (classes are taught in Spanish and English), which runs from January to December, has been honed over time to provide a quality education to its students. As the school's website states, the one-year MBA program "is the result of the 25-year experience IAE has acquired in providing part-time Executive MBA programs and the contributions of many years of delivering full-time programs supplied by the Harvard Business School and the IESE of Barcelona."

IAE's "intensive" program is "a one-year hardworking MBA. The schedule runs from 9:00 A.M. to 6:00 P.M., with only a two-hour break in the middle of the day (from 12:30 P.M. to 2.30 P.M.) for sports and eating." The program begins with a month-long "leveling course," during which students are reacquainted with fundamental quantitative skills in statistics, mathematics, and accounting. The second module of the program consists of an extensive core curriculum that focuses on three areas: "technical skills in marketing, finance, etc.; critical thinking skills that teach you new ways to approach both professional problems and personal problems; and teamwork skills." During the third module, students choose from a selection of electives. The fourth and fifth modules of the program are devoted to interdisciplinary analysis of business problems, fieldwork, networking, and developing management skills.

Students speak highly of the program, reporting that "professors are all very good. Most of them have PhDs, and they have a lot of patience. They always are able to help you inside and outside the class." The program runs smoothly, and this ease is especially important given the amount of work piled on students; no one here has time to wade through bureaucratic red tape. As one MBA notes, "The administration provides exceptional service. It is well prepared for the needs of its classmates: Everything we need is available for us." And perhaps most important, "IAE has very good contacts with businesses in Latin America, and a very important aspect is that it provides us with internal and external mentors."

## Career and Placement

The Career Services Department at IAE works with students and companies to facilitate recruitment and placement. Students report, however, that "the department is underdeveloped, especially in the international job market." The alumni network, on the other hand, "is unbelievable," according to students; one reports, "I could speak to many important executives from the best companies of my country because they were alumni." Employers who have worked with IAE include Alto Parana SA, Arthur D. Little, Banco Galicia, Belise & Asociados, Bodegas Lagarde, CCBA SA, Citibank NA, Fiat Argentina, Ford Argentina, GE Capital Cia, Global Praxis, Hart Casares, Johnson & Johnson Medical SA, KPMG Consultores, Kraft Food Argentina, McKinsey & Company, Nestlé Argentina SA, Novartis Argentina SA, Sade Skanska Ingeniería y Construcciones SA, and Walt Disney Company.

Casilla de Correo Nº49 - Mariano Acosta
s/nº y Ruta Nac. 8 Pilar - Bs.As., 1629 Argentina
Phone: 011-54-2322-48-1000 • Fax: 011-54-2322-48-050 • E-mail: ffragueiro@iae.edu.ar
Website: www.iae.edu.ar/web2005_eng/home/home.html

| ADMISSIONS | |
| --- | --- |
| Admissions Selectivity Rating | 85 |
| # of applications received | 111 |
| % applicants accepted | 57 |
| % acceptees attending | 76 |
| Average GMAT | 618 |
| TOEFL required of international students? | yes |
| Minimum TOEFL (computer) | 230 |

## Student Life and Environment

IAE's campus "is located in Pilar, 50 kilometers from the capital" of Argentina, in a beautiful setting "with a lot of trees, grass, and greenery everywhere." Despite the bucolic setting, "you can find everything near the campus: a mall, restaurants, supermarkets, movies, gas stations, etc." Campus facilities include areas where students "can play soccer, tennis, and rugby during the two-hour lunch break." Big-city life isn't too far off, as "the campus is one hour away from Buenos Aires." Students note, however, that "since IAE's program is a one-year MBA, the workload is so heavy that there is very little time to do activities outside the classroom." Classes convene from 9:00 A.M. to 6:00 P.M.; most students "study until 9:00 P.M., then have some dinner with friends," and then call it a day.

About 70 percent of IAE's students are Argentine; the remaining students come from other parts of Latin America, Europe, and the United States. Students are drawn from all sectors: marketing, banking, consulting, engineering, services, and even agriculture are represented here. About half the students consider themselves "young entrepreneurs," and nearly as many see themselves as "young, socially oriented professionals." Students generally "have great senses of humor, don't hesitate to help one another, and enjoy hanging out, drinking beer and wine, and watching movies."

## Admissions

Applicants to the full-time MBA program at IAE must have at least three years of post-undergraduate work experience. The admissions department requires all of the following materials: official transcripts for all postsecondary academic work; an official GMAT score report (minimum acceptable score 550; IAE also offers its own skills exam which can be taken in lieu of the GMAT); a resume; personal essays; letters of recommendation; a completed application form; and, for students whose first language is not English, a minimum TOEFL score of 570 (paper-based test) or 230 (computer-based test). The admissions committee uses the above materials to screen candidates. Those deemed possible candidates for the program must undergo an admissions interview with an IAE professor and members of both the admissions and career management departments.

| EMPLOYMENT PROFILE | | | |
| --- | --- | --- | --- |
| Career Rating | 64 | Grads employed by field: | % avg. salary: |
| | | Accounting | 2 | NR |
| | | Finance | 4 | NR |
| | | Human Resources | 4 | NR |
| | | Marketing | 13 | NR |
| | | Operations | 6 | NR |
| | | Consulting | 11 | NR |
| | | Communications | 2 | NR |
| | | Entrepreneurship | 2 | NR |
| | | Nonprofit | 6 | NR |

# ILLINOIS INSTITUTE OF TECHNOLOGY
## STUART GRADUATE SCHOOL OF BUSINESS

## Academics

The Stuart Graduate School of Business at Chicago's Illinois Institute of Technology recognizes the diverse needs of its student body and works hard to accommodate them all. Those looking to expedite their MBAs, for example, can enroll in the school's full-time program; about one-third of the students here do just that. Those who want to pursue their degrees contemporaneously with their careers have a number of part-time options, including the lockstep "two-year part-time fast-track MBA" (offered at the school's Rice Campus in Wheaton) and the "customizable world-class MBA." Classes are scheduled during weekdays, evenings, and weekends for the convenience of all of Stuart's constituencies. All MBA programs consist of a minimum of 16 classes; specialization is available in all but the fast-track program and requires an additional four classes.

IIT is a world-class research institution, and, not surprisingly, Stuart MBAs benefit from the presence of the high-powered academics here. Three research centers—the Center for Financial Markets, the Chicago Geospatial Exchange, and the Center for Sustainable Enterprise—offer unique options to adventurous MBAs. There is even an optional specialization in sustainable enterprise that trains students "to identify, develop, communicate, and help implement practical and equitable business strategies that advance the ecological sustainability of the Chicago area while fostering current and future economic viability." Stuart was recently ranked among the world's leaders in incorporating environmental management.

Many here, however, prefer more traditional fare. Stuart MBAs laud the school's entrepreneurship program as well as offerings in finance and marketing. Some extol the advantages conferred by the presence of a health care concentration, and quite a few full-timers take advantage of dual-degree programs in law or public administration. Throughout the curriculum, students praise "the use of technology and real-life examples, and the application of business problems." Stuart professors "are always willing to help and provide out-of-the-classroom tutorials and further explanations," plus "their experience and techniques are outstanding." Similarly, administrators "are extremely helpful and go out of their way to get to know each student personally and help anyone." With IIT's small cohorts, "there is no crowding in the libraries, computer labs, etc. And, we get to learn a lot from group discussions." For many, though, "the school's greatest strength is its strategic location. It is because of its location that we are able to get internships and other opportunities to work." About the only weakness here, students tell us, is that "the school's image needs to be improved. The rankings need improvement and people need to know about IIT a lot more."

## Career and Placement

The Office of Career Services at the Stuart MBA program provides students with one-on-one career counseling, workshops in interviewing and resume preparation, and research on companies and opportunities appropriate to each student's goals. A self-assessment, conducted as students enter the program, helps the office tailor its services to the individual needs of each MBA. The university at large conducts career fairs through its Career Development Center.

Employers who most frequently hire Stuart MBAs include Bank One, Northern Trust, Bank of America, ABN-Amro, Lucent Technologies, JP Morgan, Navistar, Johnson & Johnson, Capitol One, Vankampen, US EPA, Reuters, Cantor Fitzgerald, McLagan Partners, Motorola, Inc., and Akamal Trading. About half of all Stuart MBAs remain in the Midwest after graduation; most of the rest head to one of the two coasts.

AMANDA SCHONFELD, ASSOCIATE DIRECTOR OF ADMISSIONS
565 WEST ADAMS STREET, CHICAGO, IL 60661 UNITED STATES
PHONE: 312-906-6521 • FAX: 312-906-6549
E-MAIL: ADMISSIONS@STUART.IIT.EDU • WEBSITE: WWW.STUART.IIT.EDU

## Student Life and Environment

IIT's main MBA programs are located "in a separate building in downtown Chicago. That building houses law and business school students only, so there isn't much activity there really, just serious-looking students walking to and fro. The main campus has more life, and there is a free shuttle to transport you between campuses. I appreciate the peace and quiet of our building, though. It's very easy to find a nook to study in without constant interference," remarks one student. MBAs participate in "lots of study groups. We also have socials every Wednesday, and students often go out into town in small groups." Despite these opportunities, many here feel that they "need more organizations, activities, a bigger career center, and more seminars and activities with others outside the school (i.e. businesses, other universities, etc.)."

The student body includes many who have considerable work experience, as well as "a lot of diversity in terms of nationality and occupation." One student observes, "The diverse population aids in creating a learning experience unlike any other. Students learn as much (if not more) outside the classroom than in the classroom, just by interacting with everyone around them." When they can find the time, students love to take advantage of "the world's biggest financial city," which also offers plenty in the way of culture, entertainment, fine dining, and nightlife. Again, it comes back to location. "Stuart is located near the Chicago loop in the midst of big-name business companies, allowing for excellent networking and job opportunities. It's also very close to public transportation."

## Admissions

The IIT Stuart Graduate School of Business requires applicants to submit GMAT scores, official undergraduate transcripts for all schools attended, two letters of recommendation from people "who can attest to your academic or professional qualifications," two required essays (personal statement and career goals) with the option to submit additional essays (describe a difficult challenge you have faced, describe your ideal company), and a resume. International students must also submit TOEFL scores no more than two years old. Undergraduate transcripts in languages other than English must be accompanied by an English translation.

## FINANCIAL FACTS

| | |
|---|---|
| Annual tuition | $24,333 |
| Fees | $1,030 |
| Books and supplies | $1,000 |
| Room & board | |
| (on/off-campus) | $10,600/$14,000 |
| % of students receiving aid | 47 |
| % of first-year students receiving aid | 27 |
| % of students receiving loans | 43 |
| % of students receiving grants | 47 |
| Average award package | $6,249 |
| Average grant | $6,249 |
| Average student loan debt | $40,000 |

## ADMISSIONS

| | |
|---|---|
| Admissions Selectivity Rating | 80 |
| # of applications received | 202 |
| % applicants accepted | 58 |
| % acceptees attending | 22 |
| Average GMAT | 604 |
| Range of GMAT | 500–650 |
| Average GPA | 3.0 |
| TOEFL required of international students? | yes |
| Minimum TOEFL (paper/computer) | 600/250 |
| Application fee | $75 |
| International application fee | $75 |
| Regular application deadline | 8/15 |
| Regular notification | rolling |
| Deferment available? | yes |
| Maximum length of deferment | 1 year |
| Transfer students accepted? | yes |
| Transfer application policy | |
| With advisor approval may transfer up to 4 core courses and 2 elective courses. | |
| Non-fall admissions? | yes |
| Need-blind admissions? | yes |

### EMPLOYMENT PROFILE

| | | | | |
|---|---|---|---|---|
| Career Rating | 79 | Grads employed by field: | % | avg. salary: |
| Primary source of full-time | | Finance | 8 | $68,000 |
| job acceptances | | Marketing | 38 | $83,000 |
| School-facilitated activities | 3 (13%) | MIS | 8 | NR |
| Graduate-facilitated activities | 5 (21%) | Operations | 17 | $51,500 |
| Unknown | 16 (66%) | Consulting | 8 | $55,000 |
| | | General Management | 8 | $80,000 |
| Average starting salary | $71,000 | Other | 13 | $50,750 |

# ILLINOIS STATE UNIVERSITY
## COLLEGE OF BUSINESS

### GENERAL INFORMATION
Type of school     public
Environment     village
Academic calendar     semester

### SURVEY SAYS...
Smart classrooms
*Solid preparation in:*
Teamwork
Communication/interpersonal skills

### STUDENTS
Enrollment of parent
  institution     20,757
Enrollment of business school   199
% male/female     67/33
% out-of-state     29
% part-time     77
% minorities     4
% international     31
Average age at entry     26
Average years work experience
  at entry     6

### ACADEMICS
**Academic Experience Rating**    **78**
Student/faculty ratio     3:1
Profs interesting rating     82
Profs accessible rating     83
% female faculty     22
% minority faculty     16

### JOINT DEGREES
MBA/Master of Professional
Accountancy, 30 hours beyond the
undergraduate degree in accounting

### PROMINENT ALUMNI
Ann Baughan, Assistant VP, State
Farm Insurance; Phil Maughan, VP,
The Northern Trust Company; Karl
Heien, VP, Smith Barney Inc.; James
C. Tyree, Chair and CEO, Mesirow
Financial Group; Marty Lyons, VP,
Archer Daniels Midland Company

## *Academics*

With a new $30 million College of Business building that students describe as "state-of-the-art" and "absolutely amazing," the College of Business at Illinois State University is clearly making a big investment in the future of undergraduate and graduate business studies. The school's MBA program is tailored toward the needs of part-time students: Classes convene once a week, always starting at 6:00 P.M. About one-quarter of the student body attends full-time, typically taking three classes per semester. Part-time students usually enroll in one or two classes per semester.

With a total of 200 students, the MBA program at ISU is small enough to allow "individualized attention from professors." Students praise the "big university resources with a small classroom focus" here. One MBA writes, "Although the atmosphere is challenging, the professors are available to assist students outside of class periods, and I believe they are personally vested in the success of their students. I believe I am getting the quality of education one would only expect to find at nationally known private colleges." The size of the program has its drawbacks as well: Several students in our survey complained that "electives are few and far between. Almost all electives are only offered every two years." To clarify, of the 23 MBA electives offerings, 8 are offered every year and 15 are offered every other year.

The ISU curriculum is divided into three segments: foundation work, core courses, and electives. Seven foundation courses cover the material typically covered in an undergraduate business program; students with undergraduate business degrees typically are allowed to forego all of these classes. Nine core courses and three electives must be completed by all MBAs. Students may use their electives to develop an area of concentration in accounting, finance, international business, management, marketing, or fine arts administration. The arts program is relatively unique, helping the school draw students from outside the immediate region.

## *Career and Placement*

Illinois State University's career services include resume and job posting through eRecruiting. Other services are provided by the Career Center, which serves the entire undergraduate and graduate population of the university. Students report that the university's "affiliation with such local companies as State Farm, Caterpillar, Mitsubishi, and Country Companies" translates into "great internship opportunities." Students also feel that "getting more diversity in corporate recruiters from different areas of business other than finance and insurance to appeal to a broader MBA group" should be a major priority of the MBA program. The school reports that 94 percent of its MBAs are employed at the time of their graduation.

LEE A. GRAF, MBA PROGRAM DIRECTOR
CAMPUS BOX 5570 / MBA PROGRAM, NORMAL, IL 61790-5570 UNITED STATES
PHONE: 309-438-8388 • FAX: 309-438-7255 • E-MAIL: ISUMBA@EXCHANGE.COB.ILSTU.EDU
WEBSITE: WWW.MBA.ILSTU.EDU/

## Student Life and Environment

"You are able to become as involved as you would like" in the MBA program at ISU. Students report that "various activities take place on campus, and it is up to each student to get involved. Clubs, events, sports, and plays are just a few of the options that students have to choose from." Students enjoy "a great social network with the MBAs. We all have a lot of classes together as it is a relatively small group. We build homecoming floats and meet for drinks regularly. There seems to be a very good balance between learning, getting our work done, and sharing our experience."

Not everyone gets involved, of course. Many of the students here are part-time students with full-time jobs, and many just want to fulfill their academic obligations and get home. One student explains: "School life is spent with three-hour classes per week for each course. Group meetings for projects, research, case studies, and homework assignments: This is very much the pattern for 90 percent of the courses." While "the workload can be tough," most here agree that "the homework load is fair, and expectations are fair. The culture is typically Midwestern, with values of accountability for oneself and helping out others. This starts with the professors and is imparted to the students."

While the school reports that the average work experience of full-time MBA students is 2.59 years, some of our survey respondents find their full-time peers' lack of work experience troubling. As one puts it, "I have noticed a tremendous difference between those students [with little work experience] and the ones with careers. It can be very frustrating to work with full-time students because they do not exert as much effort or have strong time-management or leadership skills." They also "cannot speak from experience or relate real-life stories to the class." Large local companies such as State Farm, Country Companies, and Mitsubishi contribute many students to the part-time program.

## Admissions

Applicants to the ISU MBA program must submit applications to both the graduate college of the university and the MBA program. To receive priority in the admissions process, applications should be received February 1; applications for spring entry are due by September 1. All applications must include two official copies of transcripts for all academic work completed beyond high school; GMAT scores; a resume; two personal essays; and two letters of reference. GPA for the final 60 credit hours of undergraduate work and GMAT scores are the primary determining factors in the admissions decision. In recent years, successful applicants have posted an average GPA of 3.4 and an average GMAT score of 545. International students whose first language is not English must submit TOEFL scores. A minimum score of 600 on the paper-and-pencil test or 250 on the computer-based test is required. Work experience is considered "beneficial" and is "strongly encouraged," but is not required.

### FINANCIAL FACTS

| | |
|---|---|
| Annual tuition (in-state/out-of-state) | $2,610/$5,454 |
| Fees | $778 |
| Books and supplies | $825 |
| Room & board (on/off-campus) | $5,576/$5,834 |
| % of students receiving aid | 94 |
| % of first-year students receiving aid | 89 |
| % of students receiving loans | 53 |
| % of students receiving grants | 95 |
| Average award package | $14,110 |
| Average grant | $6,889 |
| Average student loan debt | $20,439 |

### ADMISSIONS

| | |
|---|---|
| Admissions Selectivity Rating | 72 |
| # of applications received | 50 |
| % applicants accepted | 86 |
| % acceptees attending | 67 |
| Average GMAT | 545 |
| Range of GMAT | 500–580 |
| Average GPA | 3.46 |
| TOEFL required of international students? | yes |
| Minimum TOEFL (paper/computer) | 600/250 |
| Application fee | $30 |
| International application fee | $30 |
| Regular application deadline | 8/1 |
| Regular notification | 8/15 |
| Early decision program? | yes |
| ED deadline/notification | 2/1 / 2/15 |
| Deferment available? | yes |
| Maximum length of deferment | 1 year |
| Transfer students accepted? | yes |
| Transfer application policy | Students must be in good academic standing and complete all regular application requirements, maximum 9 hours transfer credit accepted. |
| Non-fall admissions? | yes |
| Need-blind admissions? | yes |

# IMD INTERNATIONAL
## INTERNATIONAL INSTITUTE FOR MANAGEMENT DEVELOPMENT

## *Academics*

A highly selective one-year MBA program with a strong focus on leadership skills, the IMD MBA is an "intense" but "worthwhile" program in which "the development of leadership and team skills in a demanding environment gets everyone ready for the real world beyond the MBA program." Students appreciate the "real-world, real-learning" focus at IMD, where "classes feel more practical than academic, which is suitable for the average student, who is 31 years old with seven years of work experience."

IMD starts its program in January with a five-month sequence called Building Blocks, combined with start-up projects. It is the toughest part of the program, students tell us, in which "14-hour days are the norm [and] just about everything is done in teams that work under high time pressure. This brings out all the colors of team members very quickly, so you learn much about people and teamwork, even those of us already experienced with it." MBAs warn that the "class and teams are expected to self-manage their priorities and meet all program goals." The school does a good job of selecting students who can handle these responsibilities; as one MBA explains, "We receive a ton of information in a short period of time, and it works because the students and faculty are both up for the challenge to be the best."

The second portion of the MBA program commences in June, when students prepare for a field-learning experience in Argentina, a country facing a difficult business environment. After a summer break, students return to undertake long-term (two months) international consulting projects, then return to school for electives and a weeklong leadership program. With so many strands to coordinate, it's fortunate that "this school is run in the traditional Swiss way; in other words, like clockwork. Everything is very structured and it works, (although it can, at times, be perceived as inflexible)."

IMD professors "bring many real-life situations into the classroom and share with us the latest thinking." Students report approvingly that "there is no tenure for the faculty, which makes people listen to the feedback from the MBA class. This is taken very seriously." Students only wish the school were better known in the U.S.; one student remarks, "We are not very well known outside of Europe, and there needs to be work done to raise the awareness of IMD."

## *Career and Placement*

Career Development Services at IMD are provided by the school's career services team, faculty members, a corporate development team that "works closely with IMD clients to solve their corporate development needs through IMD public and in-company programs," a "learning network" of 150 affiliated international companies, and alumni. Self-assessment, individual counseling, workshops, and on-campus recruiting are all available to IMD MBAs. Employers most likely to hire IMD graduates include Dupont, Medtronic, Philip Morris, GE Capital, Shell International, Novartis International AG, McKinsey & Company, Indesit Company, and the Samsung Global Strategy Group.

## *Student Life and Environment*

IMD's MBA program is intensive. One student warns, "The first six months are like bootcamp: classes eight hours a day, 5 and a half days a week, and group work another six hours a day minimum. Everything is closed when we are free, so there is very little interaction with the city during the first semester of work." Fortunately, "that first semester is not just all about working hard. The bonds and friendships you develop here last a lifetime, and the alumni networks are a great testament to that." Also, "it gets a bit better the last five months, [when] life changes dramatically" and travel becomes an integral part of the program. Students first take a one-week Discovery Expedition to Argentina, then "become consultants to international companies for two months. This involves extensive traveling for most and exciting exposure."

Because of the nature of the program, students see precious little of hometown Lausanne, but when they can get out they find a small, lovely European city that provides ready access to Lac Léman and the mountains. Geneva is close by to provide big-city diversions and access to international banks and corporations, government agencies, and NGOs.

The "small group of 90 students [at IMD] enables MBAs to really get to know each and every one of the participants in the program very well. Also, the student environment promotes a real sense of shared purpose and makes people actively contribute not only to courses but also in extracurricular activities." Students are competitive, but in a healthy way— "competition is between teams, not individuals"—and appreciate that "you will never find arrogant know-alls in this program, despite the high level of experience students have. You will find brilliant people with an exceptional sense of curiosity to learn from your experiences. The strict selection convinces everyone that each student is here for a reason." Over 35 nationalities are represented within the student body, bringing a "wide diversity of student backgrounds from a cultural and nationality point of view as well as work experiences, which bring great value during discussions."

## Admissions

"The admission process is probably the longest and toughest among all the top business schools," students at IMD tell us, and they may well be right. The first stage of the application process is pretty standard: applicants send in an application, 10 short essays, official transcripts, GMAT scores, three letters of recommendation, and a resume (showing a minimum three years' professional experience that includes "some international exposure"). The next stage, though, is unusually rigorous; it's a by-invitation-only interview day that includes not only a personal interview with an admissions committee member but also an impromptu presentation and a case-study discussion with a group of other interviewees. The school uses this multistage review process to cull from its applicant pool a group of 90 students who are not only bright, accomplished, and innovative but who also demonstrate both leadership potential and strong interpersonal skills.

### FINANCIAL FACTS

| | |
|---|---|
| Annual tuition | $42,000 |
| Fees | $15,000 |
| Room & board | $10,000 |
| % of students receiving aid | 30 |
| % of students receiving loans | 22 |
| % of students receiving grants | 16 |
| Average award package | $33,216 |
| Average grant | $19,000 |

### ADMISSIONS

| | |
|---|---|
| **Admissions Selectivity Rating** | **97** |
| # of applications received | 371 |
| % applicants accepted | 29 |
| % acceptees attending | 84 |
| Average GMAT | 680 |
| Range of GMAT | 640–710 |
| Application fee | $230 |
| International application fee | $230 |
| Regular application deadline | 9/1 |
| Regular notification | rolling |
| Application deadline/notification | |
| Round 1: | 4/1 / rolling |
| Round 2: | 6/1 / rolling |
| Round 3: | 8/1 / rolling |
| Round 4: | 9/1 / rolling |
| Non-fall admissions? | yes |
| Need-blind admissions? | yes |

### APPLICANTS ALSO LOOK AT

Columbia University, Harvard University, IESE Business School, INSEAD, Stanford University, University of London, University of Pennsylvania

---

### EMPLOYMENT PROFILE

| Career Rating | 95 | Grads employed by field: | % | avg. salary: |
|---|---|---|---|---|
| Average starting salary | $113,000 | Finance | 12 | $108,000 |
| Percent employed | 94 | Consulting | 12 | $103,000 |
| | | Other | 76 | $115,000 |

# INDIANA STATE UNIVERSITY
## COLLEGE OF BUSINESS

## Academics

Mainly geared toward students early in their business careers, the MBA program at Indiana State University offers graduate-level preparation to aspiring managers and business professionals. "You get a lot of value for the money" at ISU, where small class sizes and public-school tuition combine to deliver plenty of bang for your buck. With fewer than 100 students in the MBA program, the school offers a friendly and caring environment in which to study. Students repeatedly report that the "faculty is very knowledgeable," but also "very friendly, always willing to help, and very supportive." The school's administration also earns praise for its accessibility. The result is a school community in which "everyone works together to achieve a common goal: allowing us to get our MBA in an excellent environment. The whole school—including the dean—recognizes the MBAs and appreciates what they do for the school."

The Indiana State MBA consists of 33 semester units (plus foundational course work for students who did not study business as an undergraduate), which can be completed in one year and four months of full-time study. Students wishing to continue to work while they earn their MBAs may also choose to study part-time. Part-time students tell us that the school's small and intimate environment is particularly beneficial for them, as "the small size of the university and of the MBA program is advantageous in getting to know fellow students, even if one works full-time." Through core course work and electives, the program emphasizes strategic thinking, problem-solving skills, organizational change, international business, and group dynamics.

The program's emphasis on critical thinking means that "students come out of school without the idea that they already know everything. Students are more than willing to learn and can think outside the box." But students also have plenty of access to hands-on projects: Business students have the opportunity to assist faculty in real-world research projects through programs such as the Small Business Development Center (SBDC), which provides business planning assistance to start-up companies, and through consulting services to existing small businesses. In addition, the school offers excellent Graduate Assistantship programs, which cover the cost of tuition and give participants the opportunity to "work with faculty on a daily basis."

## Career and Placement

In 2004, the College of Business opened the Career Experience Center (CEC), where students can research positions using the Sycamore CareerLink electronic database, attend career-building workshops, and prepare for interviews. A premier institution in the tri-state area, students at Indiana State University say their school "provides opportunities in the region which otherwise would not exist;" however, they also point out that the school could provide more internship and job fairs to improve the career development opportunities available to students.

DALE VARBLE, DIRECTOR, MBA PROGRAM
INDIANA STATE UNIVERSITY TERRE HAUTE, IN 47809 UNITED STATES
PHONE: 812-237-2002 • FAX: 812-237-8720 • E-MAIL: MBA@INDSTATE.EDU
WEBSITE: WWW.WEB.INDSTATE.EDU/SCHBUS/MBA.HTML

## Student Life and Environment

Like many business schools, ISU tends to attract two types of students: recent graduates and older, returning students, "many of whom are part-time." Not surprisingly, part-time students tend to limit their campus activities to class and have little interest in extracurricular socializing. The full-time students tend to be more social. As many have recently graduated from college, they share a general camaraderie and sense of campus culture. In fact, many of the full-time students "live in the same housing, so they have gotten to know each other well." Moreover, the faculty and staff help to promote unity and spirit amongst the MBA population: For example, a second-year student tells us, "I am VP of our MBA Association and try to plan social events in which the faculty participates. We have had decent turnout considering the fact that professors do have lives outside of ISU." Campus culture in general is welcoming, and "students are generally very friendly with one another and accepting of new students from varied backgrounds."

For those looking for a typically collegiate experience, the ISU campus is home to over 10,000 students. The active college community provides a wide variety of clubs, organizations, and activities for interested students, so "there is plenty to do as long as students make an attempt to get involved in student organizations such as fraternities, sororities, or any other social club." The school's "many international students" provide the student body with a diversity of backgrounds and experiences. The school's location in downtown Terre Haute, Indiana, also provides students with plenty of off-campus opportunities to amuse themselves.

## Admissions

In considering applicants for the MBA program, Indiana State University considers the following criteria: acceptance to the School of Graduate Studies; successful completion of undergraduate degree; GPA of at least 2.5; basic computing skills; GMAT scores; and prerequisite competency. Prerequisite course work for the program includes micro- and macroeconomics, financial and managerial accounting, finance, principles of marketing, principles of management, management science, and statistics. Potential students must display a GMAT-GPA admissions index of 1050 or higher (the admissions index numbers are calculated by multiplying GPA by 200 and adding GMAT scores). However, the school states that "applicants with an index between 950 and 1050, or whose grade point average is less than 2.5 on a 4-point scale, will be considered on a case-by-case basis."

### FINANCIAL FACTS

| | |
|---|---|
| Annual tuition (in-state/out-of-state) | $2,720/$5,920 |
| Fees (in-state/out-of-state) | $25/$25 |
| Books and supplies | $900 |
| Room & board (on/off-campus) | $7,800/$7,800 |
| % of students receiving aid | 30 |
| % of first-year students receiving aid | 30 |
| % of students receiving grants | 30 |
| Average award package | $12,210 |
| Average grant | $6,210 |

### ADMISSIONS

| | |
|---|---|
| Admissions Selectivity Rating | 71 |
| # of applications received | 137 |
| % applicants accepted | 64 |
| Average GMAT | 504 |
| Range of GMAT | 400–750 |
| Average GPA | 3.1 |
| TOEFL required of international students? | yes |
| Minimum TOEFL (paper/computer) | 550/213 |
| Application fee | $35 |
| International application fee | $35 |
| Regular application deadline | rolling |
| Regular notification | rolling |
| Deferment available? | yes |
| Maximum length of deferment | 2 years |
| Transfer students accepted? | yes |
| Transfer application policy Will only accept 6 credit hours from AACSB-accredited universities. | |
| Non-fall admissions? | yes |

### APPLICANTS ALSO LOOK AT

Ball State University, Illinois State University, Indiana University—Kokomo, Indiana University—Indianapolis, McMaster University, Purdue University, The University of Texas at Austin

| EMPLOYMENT PROFILE | | | |
|---|---|---|---|
| Career Rating | 60* | | |
| | | Grads employed by field: | % avg. salary: |
| | | Accounting | 40 | NR |
| | | Human Resources | 10 | NR |
| | | Marketing | 10 | NR |
| | | MIS | 10 | NR |
| | | General Management | 30 | NR |

# INDIANA UNIVERSITY—BLOOMINGTON
## KELLEY SCHOOL OF BUSINESS

## Academics

Blue-chip offerings in marketing, finance, and general management distinguish the Kelley School of Business at Indiana University—Bloomington, a highly regarded MBA program boasting a stellar faculty, a first-class facility, and an innovative integrated core curriculum. Of the last, students tell us, "The integrated core curriculum is seamless. A mix of 8 professors come in and out of class during the 15-week core, and the timing is perfect. For example, soon after we learn about regressions in quant, we apply those skills in finance to forecast betas and in marketing research. Everything is like that." One MBA writes, "I can't imagine the amount of time that goes into organizing that many professors and their related subjects into one smooth 15-week class that covers the core business competencies." It's a heady sequence, students warn. One student who has been through the core explains, "Initially, it can be overwhelming, but the beauty of it is that it all comes together at the end."

Kelley professors are a distinguished lot. As one student observes, "The first thing that I noticed was that all of my first-year professors had written top-selling books for their academic field. Soon after attending classes I realized that these were the best professors I had ever had." Another student notes, "Most have served on multiple boards and advised companies like Microsoft, Owens, the Dallas Mavericks, and the Pentagon, [and better still,] they're our friends. They get to know us outside the classroom and really want to help us reach our personal goals. They care about us as people too." Students love how "the faculty and administration take an active role outside the classroom, advising student clubs and organizations, participating in charitable events, and contributing to students' professional endeavors by taking the time to review resumes, conduct mock interviews, and actively networking with their professional contacts to help students succeed in their lives after graduation."

Kelley is housed in a "brand-new, state-of-the-art facility [that is] simply amazing. Every classroom has projectors, document cameras, an audio/video system, wireless and hard-wire connections, teleprompters, and video cameras to tape class for online replay." MBAs have access to "approximately 30 breakout rooms for team meetings, a trading room with many Bloomberg terminals, a student lounge with a big-screen TV, vending machines, and places to reheat meals. All students have lockers and access to changing rooms for interviews." Students especially appreciate that "the classrooms are available to the students 24 hours a day." No wonder MBAs agree that "the Kelley School of Business building is fabulous."

Students also love Kelley's academies, "an integral feature of the Kelley MBA program [that blends] advanced course work, sector-focused experiences, special projects, field trips, industry speakers, and direct involvement with the senior practitioners on their advisory boards." One student tells us, "The dedication by a professor to focus on a specific set of students that are actively interested in a specific area is unusual and extremely effective."

## Career and Placement

IU's Graduate Career Services Office does a good job of bringing both regional and national companies to campus, but students feel that "not enough effort is made to bring new companies to campus. The office heavily focuses in brand management and corporate finance." Students pursuing a career in other fields suggest conducting an independent off-campus job search to supplement Career Services efforts. Some students optimistically note, "Career services is improving by moving from focusing mostly on a

James Holmen, Director of Admissions and Financial Aid
1275 East Tenth Street, Suite 2010, Bloomington, IN 47405-1703 United States
Phone: 812-855-8006 • Fax: 812-855-9039
E-mail: mbaoffice@indiana.edu • Website: www.kelley.indiana.edu/mba

stable of on-campus recruiters to more progressive career development methods," such as e-recruiting. Students are also helped by the fact that "the faculty actively works with the students to find jobs/internships."

In 2003, companies most likely to hire Kelley MBAs (in descending order of number of hires) were Lilly, Bristol Meyers Squibb, Mead Johnson, Procter & Gamble, Brown and Williamson Tobacco, Kraft Foods, Whirlpool Corporation, Johnson & Johnson, Ethicon, DePuy, Bank of America Securities, and Intel. Nearly two-thirds of all graduates found work in the manufacturing sector; about one in five was employed in the financial services sector. The average hiring bonus for all 2003 MBAs was slightly over $12,000.

## Student Life and Environment

Life in Bloomington, MBAs report, "is wonderful. It is a small, safe town and community where you have the opportunity to see peers and professors/administrators at local restaurants and grocery stores." Bloomington offers "a surprising number of great ethnic restaurants: Afghan, Chinese, Thai, Indian, Korean, and Japanese [as well as] many sports bars that offer half-priced martini nights."

Kelley students benefit greatly from the greater Indiana University. One student reports, "The School of Music and School of Theatre and Arts give outstanding performances. Many Broadway and high-profile performers come to the school. There is no shortage of things to do." Many MBAs attend IU basketball games religiously, and we're told that athletic events and intramural sports in general are very popular. While students appreciate all that IU offers, they are also pleased that they "have [their] own separate building away from undergrads. This is important for a Big Ten school," where at least some of the undergrads are more interested in a good time than in getting work done.

Kelley's student body demonstrates "ethnic and professional diversity, which really enhances your view of both the business and cultural world. Students are very concerned with the well-being of their classmates and the program. This is illustrated by the deep commitment students make beyond their academic pursuits to lead professional clubs and extracurricular activities that enrich not only their fellow classmates but the community as well."

## Admissions

IU evaluates potential MBAs on the basis of their previous academic record, GMAT scores, work experience (most successful applicants have at least two years of relevant work experience), record of leadership, two letters of reference, and essays. Applicants are expected to be familiar with algebra, statistics, and the functions of a spreadsheet. "For some majors, a working knowledge of calculus is important," the school notes. IU is a member of the Consortium for Graduate Study in Management, "which offers substantial support to underrepresented minority students."

### FINANCIAL FACTS

| | |
|---|---|
| Annual tuition (in-state/out-of-state) | $13,402/$27,320 |
| Fees | $1,221 |
| Books and supplies | $1,900 |
| Room & board | |
| (on/off-campus) | $8,750/$8,750 |
| % of students receiving aid | 95 |
| % of first-year students receiving aid | 95 |
| % of students receiving loans | 90 |
| % of students receiving grants | 60 |
| Average award package | $32,000 |
| Average grant | $14,000 |
| Average student loan debt | $35,000 |

### ADMISSIONS

| | |
|---|---|
| Admissions Selectivity Rating | 93 |
| # of applications received | 1,004 |
| % applicants accepted | 40 |
| % acceptees attending | 48 |
| Average GMAT | 646 |
| Range of GMAT | 610–690 |
| Average GPA | 3.33 |
| TOEFL required of international students? | yes |
| Minimum TOEFL (paper/computer) | 600/250 |
| Application fee | $75 |
| International application fee | $75 |
| Regular application deadline | 3/1 |
| Regular notification | 4/30 |
| Application deadline/notification | |
| Round 1: | 11/15 / NR |
| Round 2: | 1/15 / NR |
| Round 3: | 3/1 / NR |
| Round 4: | 4/15 / NR |
| Deferment available? | yes |
| Maximum length of deferment | 1 year |
| Need-blind admissions? | yes |

### APPLICANTS ALSO LOOK AT

Purdue University, University of Michigan, University of North Carolina at Chapel Hill, Vanderbilt University, Washington University

### EMPLOYMENT PROFILE

| Career Rating | 87 | Grads employed by field: | % | avg. salary: |
|---|---|---|---|---|
| Primary source of full-time job acceptances | | Finance | 44 | $81,294 |
| | | Human Resources | 2 | $76,800 |
| School-facilitated activities | 137 (72%) | Marketing | 37 | $81,460 |
| Graduate-facilitated activities | 52 (27%) | Operations | 2 | $81,000 |
| | | Consulting | 11 | $89,412 |
| Average starting salary | $82,487 | General Management | 2 | $101,600 |
| Percent employed | 82 | | | |

# INDIANA UNIVERSITY—KOKOMO
## SCHOOL OF BUSINESS

### GENERAL INFORMATION

| | |
|---|---|
| Type of school | public |
| Environment | village |
| Academic calendar | semester |

### SURVEY SAYS...
Happy students
*Solid preparation in:*
Marketing
Operations

### STUDENTS

| | |
|---|---|
| Enrollment of parent institution | 2,895 |
| Enrollment of business school | 107 |
| % male/female | 57/43 |
| % part-time | 98 |
| % minorities | 17 |
| % international | 10 |
| Average years work experience at entry | 8 |

### ACADEMICS

| | |
|---|---|
| **Academic Experience Rating** | **72** |
| Student/faculty ratio | 15:1 |
| Profs interesting rating | 81 |
| Profs accessible rating | 99 |
| % female faculty | 36 |
| % minority faculty | 20 |

## Academics

The predominantly part-time, local student body of the MBA program at Indiana University—Kokomo love the convenience, the affordability, and the prestige of their graduate business program. A public school that is one of only a dozen AACSB-accredited MBA programs in the state of Indiana, Kokomo represents the best option for businesspeople seeking an affordable career advancement opportunity in and around this city of 50,000.

IU Kokomo's program is "attuned to the regional industry base" of north-central Indiana but is also flexible enough to "foster effective management of resources in diverse organizational units and settings." Students tell us that the program is well designed "to meet the overall aspirations of the employees of the local companies," which they appreciate. Because nearly all its students work full-time, the program offers flexible scheduling. All required classes are held during the week in the evening hours; electives are offered either during the day or in the evenings. Classes are alternately offered in 8- and 16-week formats, accommodating both those in a hurry to complete course work and those who wish to learn at a (somewhat) less frantic pace. In either format, "MBA classes emphasize frequent presentations and assignments, so the pace of classes is hectic and challenging." Except for a capstone course, classes may be taken in any order, another accommodation to the convenience of IU's busy students. Part-time students generally complete the 30-credit program in four years.

Students love the IU faculty, which is comprised of many "active researchers published in peer-review journals," some of whom also happen to be "excellent instructors with teaching awards." One MBA writes, "We have an excellent group of professionals who constantly strive to improve themselves and their students by seeking new challenges." Most professors "are extremely knowledgeable and very eager to help students and offer advice or guidance, [and they] are understanding of working students, especially when work requires us to travel." MBAs also appreciate how Kokomo's smaller campus "offers an intimate learning environment."

There are also drawbacks to a small program on a small campus, MBAs note. Many feel that they "need more diverse business classes. The school needs to offer more electives and concentration areas." One MBA opines, "More major choices like finance and accounting and IT in the MBA would be welcome. Also, the school needs to offer electives on entrepreneurship. Right now it's only available as an independent study." Also on students' wish list remain "opportunities to work with local companies and industries and participate on projects with them."

NIRANJAN PATI, DEAN OF THE SCHOOL OF BUSINESS
PO BOX 9003, KOKOMO, IN 46904-9003 UNITED STATES
PHONE: 765-455-9465 • FAX: 765-455-9348 • E-MAIL: MBADIRECTOR@IUK.EDU
WEBSITE: WWW.IUK.EDU/ACADEMIC_PROGRAM/BUSINESS/INDEX.HTML

## Career and Placement

IU Kokomo does not aggressively promote its career services for MBA students. Because most students in the program "are employed full-time in positions of responsibility," few actually require placement services or career counseling, and those who do generally rely on the assistance of their professors. MBAs may take advantage of the university's Office of Career Services, which maintains job boards, a Career Library and Resource Center, and online career-related databases. Those actively seeking work complain that "the quality of on-campus recruiting employers, the placement facilities, and the connections to alumni and businesses in the community all need improvement."

Kokomo MBAs are "a very diverse group with a wide range of industry backgrounds." Their employers include DaimlerChrysler, Delphi Delco, First National Bank, First Source Bank, Star Financial Bank, General Motors, Haynes International, Howard Community Hospital, St. Joseph Hospital, Subaru-Isuzu, and other smaller local businesses. Students regard their peers as "friendly, and more importantly, they submit assignments [on] time and are well prepared for tests. They value teamwork."

## Student Life and Environment

"There's not much to do on campus" at IU Kokomo, which provides "a good learning environment [but] no social aspects." The situation doesn't bother most MBAs, who barely have time for their classes and study groups, much less extracurricular activity. The school offers child care services, which students greatly appreciate. Additionally, it is worth highlighting the efforts of the MBA Student Association (MBASA), which organizes social events for those students who do spend time on campus.

## Admissions

Admission to the MBA program at IU Kokomo requires a bachelor's degree from an accredited college or university (business major not required); a completed application to the program; a personal statement; and official transcripts for all post-secondary academic work. Most applicants must also submit GMAT scores; those already holding graduate degrees from accredited institutions, however, are exempted from this requirement. An admission index (AI) of at least 1000 under the formula [(undergraduate GPA 5 200) + GMAT score] is required of all applicants who submit GMAT scores. Successful completion of undergraduate-level courses in calculus, statistics and composition, and a background in microcomputer applications are prerequisites to beginning the MBA program; however, these courses can be completed after admission to the program. International applicants must meet the aforementioned requirements and must also submit TOEFL scores. The school reports that "admission decisions are based on an overall assessment of the applicant's academic capability, professional achievement, and potential. The MBA program admits students for Fall, Spring, and Summer semesters."

## FINANCIAL FACTS

| | |
|---|---|
| Annual tuition (in-state/out-of-state) | $6,765/$15,203 |
| Fees (in-state/out-of-state) | $432/$432 |
| Books and supplies | $850 |

## ADMISSIONS

| | |
|---|---|
| **Admissions Selectivity Rating** | **71** |
| # of applications received | 29 |
| % applicants accepted | 90 |
| % acceptees attending | 100 |
| Average GMAT | 516 |
| Average GPA | 3.45 |
| TOEFL required of international students? | yes |
| Minimum TOEFL (paper/computer) | 550/213 |
| Application fee | $40 |
| International application fee | $60 |
| Regular application deadline | 8/1 |
| Regular notification | rolling |
| Deferment available? | yes |
| Maximum length of deferment | NR |
| Transfer students accepted? | yes |
| Transfer application policy Students may transfer up to 9 credits from AACSB-accredited schools. | |
| Non-fall admissions? | yes |
| Need-blind admissions? | yes |

## APPLICANTS ALSO LOOK AT

Indiana University—Bloomington, Purdue University

# INDIANA UNIVERSITY OF PENNSYLVANIA
## EBERLY COLLEGE OF BUSINESS AND INFORMATION TECHNOLOGY

## GENERAL INFORMATION
Type of school                public
Academic calendar             semester

## SURVEY SAYS...
Good social scene
Helpful alumni
Smart classrooms
*Solid preparation in:*
Communication/interpersonal skills
Computer skills

## STUDENTS
Enrollment of parent
  institution                 14,081
Enrollment of business school  159
% male/female                  51/49
% out-of-state                    72
% part-time                       13
% minorities                       5
% international                   67
Average age at entry              26
Average years work experience
  at entry                        2.2

## ACADEMICS
**Academic Experience Rating**    **74**
Student/faculty ratio            11:1
Profs interesting rating           64
Profs accessible rating            74
% female faculty                   23
% minority faculty                 33

## PROMINENT ALUMNI
Richard B. Clark, 1980, President &
CEO, Brookfield Financial Properties
LP; Terry L. Dunlap, 1981,
President, Allegheny Ludlum;
Regina Dressel Stover, 1975, Senior
VP, Mellon Financial Corporation;
Timothy W. Wallace, 1979, CEO,
FullTilt Solutions; Jeffrey R.
DeMarco, 1981, Director of Human
Resources, KPMG Peat Marwick

## Academics

Eberly College of Business at Indiana University of Pennsylvania features a fully AACSB-accredited general MBA that lays a strong foundation in basic management skills. There are several areas of concentration available, including accounting, finance, international business management, management information systems, and marketing. Though it is not a large program, students appreciate that "Eberly College of Business [is not only] nice and modern [but] the class sizes are just right and the professors, for the most part, are great." Another student adds, "The smaller classrooms are my favorite part. You can get to know the professor on a name-to-name basis."

There are only twelve required courses for the MBA: managerial economics, managerial accounting, marketing management, organizational analysis, management information systems, financial management, quantitative methods, business law, business communications, international business, operations management, and business policy. In addition, concentrations can be selected from any of the following areas: marketing, management, business statistics, management information systems, international business, accounting, management, or finance. Students are also permitted to count an internship toward their elective credit. Graduate-level courses outside of the business-school curriculum are also permitted, and in the past, students have opted to study in such diverse areas as labor relations, economics, and public affairs. Some students argue that Eberly's "greatest strength is its marketing department."

According to students, one of the school's greatest strengths is its faculty. As one student puts it, "Our professors are very passionate about their careers, and this passion is displayed in the classroom. I think this passion is absorbed by us and transferred into maybe a slight interest in the subject." Students appreciate how "the university tries to facilitate a relationship between students with diverse backgrounds."

## Career and Placement

Eberly students are mostly enthusiastic about the efforts of their career center. According to one, "There are actually conventions in school where marketing companies come and talk to the graduating students. Many companies choose IUP graduates. This is a great way to network and get a job interview." Others point out numerous networking opportunities. One student mentions, "IUP holds Business Day every year where you can network with current and past students. There are numerous job fairs we can attend. We have a business-networking event every year at homecoming and then again for the business days." In a small town with few distractions, most students learn the value of bonding with their classmates as well, forging future networking opportunities, and feel confident that these bonds and their education will serve them well once they graduate.

## Student Life and Environment

Though the name is confusing, Eberly is not, in fact, a dual-state school. Nestled in the Allegheny foothills, Eberly is located in Indiana, Pennsylvania, a small town about an hour northeast of Pittsburgh. Because of the size of the town (about 30,000), the campus of Indiana University is ranked among the five safest campuses in the United States (for campuses housing 5,000 students or more). Despite the small size, Eberly promises that students don't lack entertainment. According to their website, "You'll be able to attend any of more than 200 cultural and entertainment events each year; choose from some 200 recognized clubs, activities, and organizations (including one of the country's finest marching bands); and enjoy the fun and the excitement of successful varsity, intramural, and club sports programs." And students, though somewhat grudgingly, admit that

KRISH KRISHNAN, DIRECTOR OF ADMISSIONS
101 STRIGHT HALL, 210 SOUTH 10TH STREET, INDIANA, PA 15705-1081 UNITED STATES
PHONE: 724-357-2222 • FAX: 724-357-4862
E-MAIL: GRADUATE_ADMISSIONS@IUP.EDU • WEBSITE: WWW.EBERLY.IUP.EDU

there are perks to living in a small town. One MBA lists the vast amount of things to do: "There are movies at the downtown theater for $4, and that includes admission, popcorn, and drinks. We have lots of places to eat; a few nice places to shop. We are within an hour of Pittsburgh, and a group on campus sells tickets for bus tours to NYC and DC. There are plenty of other activities to keep yourself busy." In addition, "IUP also has a co-op recreational park that people can go to for free and throw a Frisbee in the acres and acres of ground, hike on trails, go sledding or tubing on the hills, rent sleds, or sit in the lodge. It's fun here!" remarks another student. And in spite of the location of the school, "We get a wide range of students from many cities. Diversity is not bad, [even though] we could become a more diverse school."

Being somewhat isolated, students have to make their own fun. Sororities and fraternities abound, and, according to some students, Indiana University is "well-known as a party school." According to most MBAs, "The social aspect of this school is great. Once the kids get out into the real world and get a job, their social skills will be really good for working in groups." The $10 million Eberly College of Business complex has been around since 1996, but students aren't complaining and seem to agree with the school's claim that the building houses "teaching-intensive, state-of-the-art technology, [and is] designed with students in mind." The building "features a 500-seat auditorium, two 24-hour computer labs, large-screen television monitors, and a fiber-optics network throughout the complex." As one student puts it, "The student union is a few years new, and the exercise facility is superb. It's a great place to blow off steam before a huge test."

The only thing to watch out for, it seems, is the weather. One somewhat diplomatic student points out that "the weather in this part of the state isn't the best. We have a lot of cold, cloudy, and rainy/snowy days. An umbrella is your best friend."

## Admissions

Eberly's student body is 67 percent international, 35 percent of the students have some prior work experience in business, and 25 percent are still working full-time while pursuing their MBA. Though Eberly has no minimum GMAT or TOEFL scores, they do prefer that applicants score above 500 on the GMATs and above 550 on the TOEFL exam. TOEFL scores are required of those students for whom English is not their native language. There is no minimum GPA: Applicants who have a GPA lower than 2.6 who have still scored above 500 on the GMAT will be considered by Eberly's Board of Admissions.

### FINANCIAL FACTS

| | |
|---|---|
| Annual tuition (in-state/out-of-state) | $5,888/$9,422 |
| Fees (in-state/out-of-state) | $1,038/$1,038 |
| Books and supplies | $900 |
| Room & board (on/off-campus) | $3,891/$3,891 |
| % of students receiving aid | 36 |
| % of first-year students receiving aid | 22 |
| % of students receiving loans | 72 |
| % of students receiving grants | 5 |
| Average award package | $8,100 |
| Average grant | $8,100 |

### ADMISSIONS

| | |
|---|---|
| **Admissions Selectivity Rating** | **77** |
| # of applications received | 208 |
| % applicants accepted | 59 |
| % acceptees attending | 76 |
| Average GMAT | 532 |
| Range of GMAT | 450–620 |
| Average GPA | 3.17 |
| TOEFL required of international students? | yes |
| Minimum TOEFL (paper/computer) | 550/213 |
| Application fee | $30 |
| International application fee | $30 |
| Regular application deadline | 7/30 |
| Regular notification | rolling |
| Deferment available? | yes |
| Maximum length of deferment | 1 year |
| Transfer students accepted? | yes |
| Transfer application policy Written request for transfer required of transfer applicants. Maximum of 6 credits transfer. | |
| Non-fall admissions? | yes |
| Need-blind admissions? | yes |

### APPLICANTS ALSO LOOK AT

Duquesne University, University of Pittsburgh, West Virginia University

| EMPLOYMENT PROFILE | |
|---|---|
| **Career Rating** | **67** |
| Average starting salary | $40,896 |
| Percent employed | 62 |

# INDIANA UNIVERSITY—SOUTH BEND
## SCHOOL OF BUSINESS AND ECONOMICS

**GENERAL INFORMATION**

| | |
|---|---|
| Type of school | public |
| Environment | city |
| Academic calendar | semester |

**SURVEY SAYS...**
Friendly students
Happy students
Smart classrooms

**STUDENTS**
Enrollment of business school   198

**ACADEMICS**

| | |
|---|---|
| **Academic Experience Rating** | **61** |
| Student/faculty ratio | 17:1 |
| Profs interesting rating | 65 |
| Profs accessible rating | 64 |
| % female faculty | 7 |
| % minority faculty | 5 |

## Academics

The School of Business and Economics at Indiana University—South Bend gears its MBA program toward the needs of the part-time student. Here, "classes meet once a week in the evening, making it easy to attend school and work full-time." Most classes begin at 7:00 P.M., accommodating students who have to travel some distance after work in order to get to class. MBA students here typically take two classes in each of the fall and spring semesters and one class during each summer session; this allows most students who hold business undergraduate degrees to complete the program in just two years.

Phase I of the IUSB MBA covers skills prerequisite to advanced business study. Classes in economics, financial accounting, financial management, marketing, mathematics, organizational behavior, and statistics cover material typically covered in undergraduate business programs. Students with undergraduate business degrees typically place out of these courses; other students may place out by passing a competency examination in each field. Phase II consists of seven core courses in buyer behavior, international business, legal and ethical issues in business, managerial information systems, managerial price theory, production management, and strategic financial management. Phase III covers advanced subjects and allows for students to take two electives. Phase IV consists entirely of a capstone course. Students must pass a final comprehensive exam in order to receive their degrees.

Students here praise the "excellent MIS/MIT offerings" and the "small classes with friendly, approachable professors" who "have a wealth of experiences in the business world. The whole experience is very student-centered here." A "great library and facilities" and "strength in the high-technology area" help students handle the heavy burden of the program, and international students enjoy "strong support in housing, counseling, etc." Many here, however, feel that "the program needs to allow for specialization" and wish that "the school could offer more choices for specific strategic business classes and project management classes."

## Career and Placement

The Career Services Office at IUSB serves the entire student and alumni population of the school. The office is primarily dedicated to undergraduates, although its services are also available to MBAs. The office provides the standard complement of job-search services, skills seminars, personal assessments, and one-on-one counseling. The following is a partial list of employers who attended IUSB's spring job fair in 2006: First Source Bank, AM General, Ave Maria Press, Bankers Life and Casualty Company, Becker Professional Review, Cintas, Citigroup, Craighead, Lange and Hough, Crowe Chizek and Company, Fastenal, Fastsigns, JPMorgan Chase, John Hancock Financial Network, Lippert Components Inc., Menards, Northwestern Mutual Finance Network, Peoplelink Staffing Solutions, Productivity Management, Inc., SCORE, Spyglass Search, and the Teachers Credit Union.

SHARON PETERSON, GRADUATE BUSINESS RECORDS REPRESENTATIVE
1700 MISHAWAKA AVENUE, SOUTH BEND, IN 46634-7111 UNITED STATES
PHONE: 574-520-4138 • FAX: 574-520-4866 • E-MAIL: GRADBUS@IUSB.EDU
WEBSITE: WWW.IUSB.EDU/~BUSE/GRAD

## Student Life and Environment

The IUSB MBA program caters to part-time students, the majority of whom are "full-time employed, mostly with children, working to improve their situation." Full-time students "tend to be foreign exchange students" representing "a wide mix of nationalities from Africa, Asia, the Americas, etc." This "mostly friendly and helpful" population includes individuals from "a wide range of ages, from the 20s to the 50s." Students note that "all the diversity in the student body helps us see things from different perspectives."

Don't expect to pal around with your classmates here, though, as "going to class at night and working all day leaves little time for socializing during the week." IUSB MBA students "have mostly a commuter attitude. They only spend time on campus to attend class."

IUSB is a midsize state university with an undergraduate population of approximately 6,400 and a graduate population of about 1,100. South Bend is a substantial city, with a population of over 100,000. Major employers in the metropolitan area include IUSB, the University of Notre Dame, ADP, AG Edwards, Bosch, Coachman Industries, FedEx, Honeywell, Liberty Mutual, and State Farm. The advertising, aviation, biotechnology, engineering, finance, and nonprofit sectors all have a strong presence in the region. South Bend's location offers relatively easy access to Indianapolis and Chicago.

## Admissions

The MBA program at Indiana University—South Bend requires applicants to submit all of the following: a completed application and data sheet, available online; official transcripts for all postsecondary academic work; two letters of recommendation (recommendation form available online); a personal statement describing one's background, outlining one's goals in the program, and recounting an experience that led to personal growth; and an official score report for the GMAT. International students whose native language is not English must submit all of the above as well as an official score report for the TOEFL; minimum required score for consideration is 550 (paper-based test) or 213 (computer-based test). Applications are accepted for admission commencing with the Fall, Spring, or Summer semesters. IUSB admits students at two levels: Full Admission and Probationary Admission. Full Admission requires a minimum GMAT score of 450 and an undergraduate business degree from an AACSB-accredited school with a minimum GPA of 2.75. Probationary Admission is granted to applicants "whose GPA does not quite meet minimum standards." Such students must maintain an in-program GPA of at least 2.75 in order to remain in the program.

### FINANCIAL FACTS

| | |
|---|---|
| Annual tuition (in-state/out-of-state) | $3,316/$7,918 |
| Fees | $390 |
| Books and supplies | $700 |
| Room & board | |
| (on/off-campus) | $5,000/$8,000 |

### ADMISSIONS

| | |
|---|---|
| **Admissions Selectivity Rating** | **60*** |
| # of applications received | 49 |
| % applicants accepted | 100 |
| % acceptees attending | 69 |
| Range of GMAT | 430–690 |
| TOEFL required of | |
| international students? | yes |
| Minimum TOEFL | |
| (paper/computer) | 550/213 |
| Application fee | $45 |
| International application fee | $55 |
| Regular application deadline | 7/1 |
| Regular notification | rolling |
| Deferment available? | yes |
| Maximum length | |
| of deferment | 1 year |
| Non-fall admissions? | yes |

### APPLICANTS ALSO LOOK AT

University of Notre Dame, Western Michigan University

# INDIANA UNIVERSITY—SOUTHEAST
## SCHOOL OF BUSINESS

### GENERAL INFORMATION
| | |
|---|---|
| Type of school | public |
| Environment | village |
| Academic calendar | semester |

### SURVEY SAYS...
Cutting-edge classes
Happy students
*Solid preparation in:*
Operations
Computer skills

### STUDENTS
| | |
|---|---|
| Enrollment of parent institution | 6,164 |
| Enrollment of business school | 230 |
| % male/female | 64/36 |
| % part-time | 98 |
| % minorities | 10 |

### ACADEMICS
| | |
|---|---|
| **Academic Experience Rating** | **69** |
| Student/faculty ratio | 15:1 |
| Profs interesting rating | 83 |
| Profs accessible rating | 76 |
| % female faculty | 22 |
| % minority faculty | 16 |

### JOINT DEGREES
MBA/MSSF, 3–4 years (plus foundation course work)

## Academics

The MBA program at Indiana University—Southeast is designed to be a part-time program; students must petition the MBA Policies Committee to take more than the normal course load of six credit hours per semester and three credit hours per each of two summer sessions. That suits most students here fine. They're largely a full-time working, part-time degree-seeking group ready to put in at least two years' work to earn their degrees.

IUS's MBA curriculum is divided into four phases. The first "emphasizes the development and mastery of the fundamental tools of decision-making," while the second focuses on communication skills, ethical issues, and functioning within the business environment. The third phase consists of advanced courses as well as an integrative class in decision-making; the fourth includes a strategic management class and two electives. Students with nonbusiness undergraduate degrees typically must complete up to eight foundation classes before beginning their MBA work. Some students tell us that "course work doesn't seem to 'build' and there are no academic concentrations, which is a major disappointment." Most, however, focus on the positives, which include "good technology integration into curriculum, . . . small classes that can be very attractive to someone wanting more one-on-one interaction with their professor, [and the] challenging workload."

A community service requirement of 20 hours "in projects such as volunteering for Big Brothers/Big Sisters, providing tax assistance to the elderly or disadvantaged, or participating in a United Way agency" is a unique aspect of this program. "Services such as directing or participating in a community cleanup sponsored by the Rotary Club or chairing a church clothing drive for the needy are acceptable projects because they serve a need of the greater community." Once students have completed their service, they must submit a one- to two-page summary of their role in the experience to the MBA director.

## Career and Placement

The Office of Career Services and Placement at IUS serves all undergraduate and graduate students at the school. It offers all the standard services: "opportunities for career exploration, clarification, and professional growth, thereby increasing career awareness, instilling personal confidence, providing enhanced employment opportunities, and encouraging [students and alumni] to achieve their personal and professional career-related goals"—in other words, counseling, job fairs, workshops, and online job boards. MBAs here would like to see "better networking and job-search opportunities. Because nearly every student already has a job, there is not much in the way of recruitment or networking through the school."

## Student Life and Environment

IUS "is a commuter campus," so "students come to class and leave." Classes are also offered at an off-campus site in Jeffersonville, IN, at the IU Southeast Graduate Center; this is very convenient for students who are coming in from nearby Louisville, KY. A typical student writes, "I tend to go straight to my class, which meets once a week, am engaged in it for three hours, then go right home. I have a family at home, and it is my preference to not participate in the limited school activities." Those limited activities include "various meetings to help students network with other students, teaching staff, and other business professionals." Some here feel "more clubs and/or activities geared specifically toward MBA students would be nice."

JAY WHITE, DIRECTOR OF GRADUATE BUSINESS PROGRAMS
HILLSIDE HALL 117, 4201 GRANT LINE ROAD, NEW ALBANY, IN 47150 UNITED STATES
PHONE: 812-941-2364 • FAX: 812-941-2581
E-MAIL: IUSMBA@IUS.EDU • WEBSITE: WWW.IUS.EDU/MBA/

| ADMISSIONS | |
|---|---|
| **Admissions Selectivity Rating** | **68** |
| # of applications received | 99 |
| % applicants accepted | 93 |
| % acceptees attending | 82 |
| Average GMAT | 525 |
| Average GPA | 3.2 |
| TOEFL required of international students? | yes |
| Minimum TOEFL (paper/computer) | 550/213 |
| Application fee | $35 |
| International application fee | $55 |
| Regular application deadline | rolling |
| Regular notification | rolling |
| Deferment available? | yes |
| Maximum length of deferment | indefinite |
| Transfer students accepted? | yes |
| Transfer application policy Students may transfer a maximum of 6 credits (with a grade of B or better) from another AACSB-accredited program, pending approval. | |
| Non-fall admissions? | yes |
| Need-blind admissions? | yes |

The IUS curriculum requires some teamwork, and fortunately "there are many locations available to meet with groups or teams." The school also boasts "a brand-new, state-of-the-art library that is almost completed, which will offer many more meeting rooms and high-tech equipment available for student use."

MBAs at IUS are a "diverse group. Some students are younger and the MBA program represents an extension of their undergraduate degree, while others have been in the workforce for at least ten years prior to returning to the classroom." One MBA writes, "The diversity (minority, work experience, life experience) in the student population is what contributes so much to the academic excellence at the school. Students learn from each other." The preponderance of professionals here means students are "generally more cooperative, as the vast majority hold full-time jobs and competition is really a non-factor."

## Admissions

Completed applications to the IUS MBA program must include an official GMAT score report, official copies of all undergraduate transcripts, and a resume. The school uses the following formula to evaluate candidates: [(undergraduate GPA 5 200) + GMAT score]. IUS looks for candidates with a formula score of at least 1050, with GMAT scores of at least 470. Students with undergraduate degrees in business are likely to place out of some or all of the school's eight foundation courses in business; all other admitted students must complete these foundation courses before beginning work on the actual MBA.

# INSEAD

## Academics

To some INSEAD MBAs, their school is "the only truly international MBA" available. With two campuses located halfway around the globe from each other—one in Singapore, the other outside Paris—and the option to study at both during the "very accelerated" one-year program offered here, INSEAD truly has an advantage over other pretenders to the title. A student body "from all over the world, with no nationality represented by more than 10 percent of the intake" in any give term, further bolsters INSEAD's claim to primacy. Students may apply to either INSEAD campus; more than half choose to take their core requirements in one location, and then travel to the other for at least one of the curriculum's three elective segments. Exchange with Wharton is also available during the fourth and fifth segments of the curriculum. The program begins with two two-month core sequences covering basic business principles and functional skills. The final three two-month segments include courses in global and IT management issues plus 10 electives, chosen from a portfolio of 80. Students tell us that the program "is really well designed. It is probably the most dynamic and innovative school in the world." While some say "it's too intensive, with not enough time to digest sufficiently before graduation," others tell us "it suits [our] ambitions perfectly. We learn fast and there is never a lull, but the workload is manageable and [we]'ve learned a great deal that I think [we] can apply directly." INSEAD professors are "a mix of stars and some clouds of dust. The stars can make a lecture blow your mind, while the clouds of dust can leave you stranded in a boring space. Fortunately there are more stars." An exchange student from Wharton reports, "INSEAD professors are much better prepared for classes—evident in the depth of material covered in the allotted time—than professors I had at Wharton." Students identify consulting, finance, and entrepreneurship as the faculty's strongest areas. INSEAD's administration is a tale of two campuses—or, more accurately, a tale of two countries. One student explains, "In France, the day-to-day administration is poor, as is the IT. The country is not efficient, nor particularly friendly." In Singapore, on the other hand, "The administration is extremely efficient. Everyone knows your name—the food servers, the office personnel, sometimes even the receptionist. The campus has about 100 students and it is very intimate." Basically, "the Singapore campus runs like a Ferrari while the Fontainebleau campus runs like a Peugeot."

## Career and Placement

INSEAD maintains Career Services offices on both its European and Asia campuses. The offices promote students to employers around the globe while providing MBAs with one-on-one counseling and coaching, job-search strategies, and on-campus recruiting events. Students generally feel that "Career Services could improve. The school has a great record of top companies coming on campus, and the alumni network is very efficient, but sometimes INSEAD Career Services could be more proactive in connecting students with companies who are not on-campus recruiters." Students in Asia complain that "the Career Services is not yet connected to all major Asian companies here in Singapore," but they also point out that "additional resources recently allotted to Career Services here is a good start." An "alumni network so huge you find them wherever you go [is] extremely accessible and supportive." Employers most likely to hire INSEAD MBAs include McKinsey & Company; American Express; Booz Allen Hamilton; General Electric; the Boston Consulting Group; Johnson & Johnson; Bain & Company; A.T. Kearney; Honeywell; and Royal Dutch Shell.

## Student Life and Environment

Dealing with "a one-year program that leaves everyone fully focused on school life" means "life at school is very hectic" for students on both INSEAD campuses. The school mandates some fun time by declaring about 15 "National Weeks" per school year, during which "each

## FINANCIAL FACTS

| | |
|---|---|
| Annual tuition | $57,000 |
| Books and supplies | $30,000 |
| % of first-year students receiving aid | 50 |
| Average grant | $15,000 |

## ADMISSIONS

**Admissions Selectivity Rating 60\***

| | |
|---|---|
| Average GMAT | 702 |
| Range of GMAT | 650–750 |
| Average GPA | 4 |
| TOEFL required of international students? | yes |
| Minimum TOEFL (paper/computer) | 620/260 |
| Application fee | $250 |
| Regular application deadline | 3/23 |
| Regular notification | 6/24 |
| Application deadline/notification | |
| Round 1: | 3/23 / 6/24 |
| Round 2: | 5/18 / 9/9 |
| Round 3: | 6/29 / 10/14 |
| Non-fall admissions? | yes |
| Need-blind admissions? | yes |

country 'owns' a specific week and activities are organized around a country theme. Students are given specific names related to the country and the professors use them, which make interactions really funny. One of my friends was called Albert Einstein all through German Week." Students also participate in "twenty or so different clubs. The school is MBA-only, so clubs are all with MBAs. This puts pressure on MBAs to organize clubs in an already hectic year, but it also means that the networking with your classmates is that much better." When they can find time, students in Fontainebleau organize small group dinners or "blowout parties in elegant French country chateaus with professional DJs, dancers, and always an open bar." Students experience "good French cuisine, good wine, enjoyable social activities, a great forest, and the pleasure of living in a nice and typical French town." Coming along with the territory is a "bureaucracy and inefficiency impossible to experience elsewhere." Students organize "fewer activities in Singapore but more group travel and barbecues. Indeed, most participants tend to stay in the same two buildings near the campus," which is "fabulous" with its "modern facilities," and is contrasted by escapes to Bali or Thailand. INSEAD students "are definitely the greatest asset at the school," according to their peers. One explains, "You will not find a more international group at any school in the world. I've been to other schools that boast an 'international' student body. That usually means the occasional token Asian. Here you have equal numbers of Chinese, Indians, French, Brits, Americans, etc. To top it off, every one of those people is from the top of their respective classes before coming here." Even though "students are graded on a forced z-curve, so there are people who will fail a class," INSEAD MBAs "are helpful to each other and most tend to do fine." One student says, "This year has been truly unforgettable—I would recommend the program to anyone who wants to meet talented, fantastic people from literally every corner of the world."

## Admissions

INSEAD has two intake points, in September and January. Students may apply to begin the program at either time; application is online only. All applicants must provide a personal profile, resume, five personal essays, two recommendations attesting to leadership potential and management capacity, a photograph, an official GMAT score report, and official transcripts for all post-secondary academic work. In addition, all students must enter the program with proficiency in English and a second language. Non-native English speakers may submit results from the TOEFL, TOEIC, CPE, or IELTS. English speakers must provide certification of a second language. A third commercially useful language (sorry, no Latin!) is required to graduate. While language instruction is available through INSEAD, the intensity of the MBA program is such that the school recommends students get a start on their third language before the program begins. While most admitted students have "several years of meaningful professional experience and demonstrate clear management potential," work experience is not a hard-and-fast prerequisite to admission. The applicant's choice of campus is not taken into account in the admission decision; however, placement at one's campus of choice is not fully guaranteed.

### EMPLOYMENT PROFILE

| Career Rating | 94 | Grads employed by field: | % | avg. salary: |
|---|---|---|---|---|
| Average starting salary | $106,043 | Finance | 21 | NR |
| Percent employed | 88 | Marketing | 12 | NR |
| | | Operations | 4 | NR |
| | | Strategic Planning | 10 | NR |
| | | Consulting | 38 | NR |
| | | General Management | 10 | NR |
| | | Other | 5 | NR |

# IONA COLLEGE
## HAGAN SCHOOL OF BUSINESS

## Academics

Flexibility and convenience are among the top selling points of the Hagan School of Business MBA at Iona College. Hagan's student body is drawn largely from the ranks of full-time professionals seeking a career boost. The school delivers what students seek through concentrated classes (usually meeting one evening per week, for three hours), a trimester schedule that allows students to receive their degrees more quickly, and a limited number of distance-learning courses per trimester (usually six or seven). Students enjoy the accelerated academic calendar, saying, "It keeps us involved in school all year long. Since many of the students are working, it makes sense not to have a long winter break. We can continue to progress in the MBA program and not waste six or eight weeks around the holidays."

For its full-timers, Hagan also offers a nice campus in a location convenient to job seekers. AT&T, Bell Atlantic, IBM, Kraft Foods, Inc., Lederle Laboratories, MasterCard, PepsiCo, and a number of large banks, brokerage houses, and insurance firms all make their homes in surrounding Westchester and Rockland counties. Students approvingly report, "The school has a good relationship with several large companies. They just moved their Pearl River campus into a professional building, which I feel helps make it more attractive to professional students." One student points out that "Wyeth Pharmaceutical has a relationship with Hagan School of Business in which professors teach MBA-level courses on-site. This creates a great atmosphere, as all of the students taking classes on-site at Wyeth are Wyeth employees, with common interests."

Hagan takes a practical approach to business education; classes "deal with many real-world situations, and through my course work I feel better prepared to handle them. Many of the situations covered in class have been discussed through the eyes of my fellow classmates, and it is great to get their perspectives since they have lived through these situations," one student says. Professors also bring a lot of professional experience to the table as they "are not professors from the 'ivory tower' but professional, successful businesspeople who are sharing their knowledge. It is wonderful to be able to apply theoretical concepts to real-life examples with their help." One student points out many positive aspects, saying, "[Hagan] puts great emphasis on presentation and teamwork skills, and I believe by repetition, one can become better in these crucial areas of everyday business. I know it has definitely helped me in my managerial position."

Hagan offers concentrations in management, human-resource management, financial management, marketing, and information and decision-technology management.

## Career and Placement

The Career Services Office at Iona College serves MBAs with counseling services, job listings, Internet-based job databases and resume books, resume and cover letter workshops and critiques, mock interviews, and tests to assess students' interests and strengths. Forty-two businesses and organizations attended Iona's 2003 Fall Career and Internships Expo; they included the American Red Cross, Country Bank, Fleet Boston, New York Life, Northwestern Mutual, and PepsiCo. Over the course of the year, approximately 100 recruiters visit the Iona campus. Career Services are important to only some of Iona's MBAs; many are part-time students with full-time employers that pay part or all of their tuition.

VERONICA JAREK-PRINZ, DIRECTOR OF MBA ADMISSIONS
715 NORTH AVENUE, NEW ROCHELLE, NY 10801 UNITED STATES
PHONE: 914-633-2288 • FAX: 914-637-7720
E-MAIL: HAGAN@IONA.EDU • WEBSITE: WWW.IONA.EDU/HAGAN

## Student Life and Environment

"The majority of students at Hagan work full-time jobs along with taking classes," students tell us, meaning that "between work and classes, there isn't much time for [much] else." Many take classes at one of Iona's satellite campuses, where they see even less of one another than do MBAs on the main campus. One student observes, "[They] show up for class and go home. There isn't much of a student life involved. That is not a criticism of the school, it's just the way it is for a part-time graduate program at a campus that is removed from the college scene of their main campus in New Rochelle."

Hagan's student body features "a good mix of the ages of students. The experience levels of students greatly differ, but that makes the classes more interesting." Some students feel that Iona needs to be a bit more selective in its admissions. One such MBA writes, "I think most students are there for the right reasons and work hard, but I believe by interviewing prospects, they could weed out many of the unmotivated students. Some seem to come back immediately after graduating from undergraduate school only because they have nothing better to do, and I think an interview would help to eliminate these students."

The full-timers on Iona's New Rochelle campus tell us that they enjoy "a very friendly atmosphere. There are always students on or around campus. There are activities and social events coordinated by the school to help people meet each other." They also appreciate that "school facilities and resources are easily accessible to students. There is a welcoming and warm feeling on campus." However, "the school doesn't offer many clubs at the graduate level. They should also host or refer people to more networking events." One MBA agrees, "There could be more networking and social events for students in the MBA program. I would like to be able to meet more students outside of class in a social setting, but it is difficult with students who do not live on or close to campus. More networking events for MBA students would bring classmates together who have never met one another."

## Admissions

Applications to Hagan must include official transcripts from each undergraduate and graduate institution attended, a GMAT score report, two letters of recommendation, a personal statement, and a resume. International students must also provide TOEFL scores, WES, and a cash-support affidavit. Interviews are optional; work experience is not required, although "many students do have considerable work experience." Applications are processed and admissions decisions made on a rolling basis. Applications remain valid for one year.

### FINANCIAL FACTS

| | |
|---|---|
| Annual tuition | $16,767 |
| Fees | $195 |
| Books and supplies | $700 |
| % of students receiving aid | 72 |
| % of first-year students receiving aid | 73 |
| % of students receiving loans | 48 |
| % of students receiving grants | 41 |
| Average award package | $12,086 |
| Average grant | $3,233 |
| Average student loan debt | $21,688 |

### ADMISSIONS

| | |
|---|---|
| **Admissions Selectivity Rating** | **75** |
| # of applications received | 75 |
| % applicants accepted | 64 |
| % acceptees attending | 96 |
| Average GMAT | 494 |
| Range of GMAT | 440–600 |
| Average GPA | 3.2 |
| TOEFL required of international students? | yes |
| Minimum TOEFL (paper/computer) | 550/213 |
| Application fee | $50 |
| International application fee | $50 |
| Regular application deadline | rolling |
| Regular notification | rolling |
| Deferment available? | yes |
| Maximum length of deferment | 1 year |
| Transfer students accepted? | yes |
| Transfer application policy Max of 6 upper-level credits accepted; 30-credit minimum required to earn a degree at Iona. | |
| Non-fall admissions? | yes |
| Need-blind admissions? | yes |

### APPLICANTS ALSO LOOK AT

Fordham University, Pace University

# ITHACA COLLEGE
## SCHOOL OF BUSINESS

### GENERAL INFORMATION
Type of school        private
Academic calendar     semesters

### SURVEY SAYS...
Helpful alumni
Happy students
*Solid preparation in:*
Teamwork Operations

### STUDENTS
Enrollment of parent
   institution            6,412
Enrollment of business school   17
% male/female         59/41
% out-of-state           29
% part-time             42
% international            6
Average age at entry      24
Average years work experience
   at entry                  1

### ACADEMICS
**Academic Experience Rating**   **79**
Student/faculty ratio        1:1
Profs interesting rating      91
Profs accessible rating       87
% female faculty          27
% minority faculty         14

### JOINT DEGREES
Master of Business Administration,
10-month full-time program;
MBA of Professional Accountancy,
10-month full-time program

## Academics

MBA students in Ithaca College's small graduate program may choose between two programs: an MBA in business administration and an MBA in professional accountancy. Both degrees require 35 credit hours and can be completed by full-time students in 12 months.

The curriculum for Ithaca's Business Administration MBA starts with function-level analysis of firms. Once students have mastered the workings of an individual business, the curricular focus grows wider, encompassing entire industries. The program concludes with a culminating project in which students analyze an industry of their choice and assess individual firms within that industry. Classes emphasize "a balance between building technical and interpersonal skills," students tell us. Students also praise professors for their "hands-on teaching philosophy" and for "going above and beyond to do all that is necessary to assure our success in the program as well as in our careers." As one student notes, "The small size of the program is a real asset. We get plenty of personal attention from our professors."

Ithaca's Professional Accountancy MBA primarily functions as the culmination of a five-year undergraduate/graduate program for students in the college's undergraduate accounting program, although candidates from other schools can gain admission. The curriculum includes a thorough review of principles of business administration as well as advanced instruction in financial accounting and reporting, managerial and cost accounting, auditing, taxation, and principles of business law.

Students in both programs are full of praise for the school. One writes, "Tuition is high, but you can definitely see where the money went. Everything from the smart boards in the classrooms—which help make articulating difficult accounting concepts much easier—to the trading room is state-of-the-art." Students note that the one-year duration of the program helps offset the relatively high cost of attending. They also appreciate the fact that the business-school administration "welcome(s) comments and suggestions from the grad students on what could help better the program. If you have any problems, they do their best to help you solve the issues." The future here looks bright: As one student points out, "When the new business building is constructed (which should be soon), the program will get bigger and become better known."

## Career and Placement

The Ithaca College Career Services Office provides self-assessment inventories, eRecruiting tools, one-on-one advisement, mock interviews, workshops, a library, and on-campus recruiting. The school hosts a graduate school job fair and other special recruiting events. Employers who recruit on the Ithaca campus include Accredited Home Lenders, Allegis Group, Carolinas Healthcare System, CIGNA, Commerce One Financial, Cowan Financial Group, Ernst & Young, Katz Media Group, McCann Erickson, Merrill Lynch, Mutual of Omaha Companies, New York Life Insurance, Procter & Gamble, and Sun Life Financial.

OFFICE OF GRADUATE STUDIES, ITHACA COLLEGE, 101 TERRACE CONCOURSE,
ITHACA, NY 14850-7020 UNITED STATES
PHONE: 607-274-3527 • FAX: 607-274-1263 • E-MAIL: MBA@ITHACA.EDU
WEBSITE: WWW.ITHACA.EDU/BUSINESS/MBA

## Student Life and Environment

MBA students at Ithaca College enjoy "a great community atmosphere" at a school that "is just the right size, so that you can go anywhere and know somebody, and meet somebody new." One student writes, "The one-year intensive program creates an environment in which students quickly form strong bonds with one another for support. Since the same students are together for a full year, the atmosphere emulates an elementary-school feeling of closeness. It's a very strong community. We laugh together, complain together, go out and party together. It's a great experience and I've made friends for life." The demands of the program keep MBA students "pretty detached from the rest of the campus. You never deal with grad students from any of the other programs (unless they happen to take a business elective)."

Ithaca MBAs tend to be on the youngish side, with many transitioning straight from undergraduate programs. A 29-year-old student notes that "[my] classmates, while nearly all younger than myself, are highly motivated and add to the challenge of the program."

## Admissions

Applicants to Ithaca's MBA program must have completed one of the following: a bachelor's program in business or accounting, or a bachelor's program in any field and Ithaca's Pre-MBA Modules. Post-undergraduate work experience is not required; in fact, many students enter the program immediately after completing work on their bachelor's degree. Successful applicants typically have an undergraduate GPA of at least 3.0 and GMAT scores "that indicate future success in their chosen MBA program." All applications must include official undergraduate transcripts, official GMAT scores, and two letters of recommendation.

## FINANCIAL FACTS

| | |
|---|---|
| Annual tuition | $21,875 |
| % of students receiving aid | 32 |
| % of first-year students receiving aid | 44 |
| % of students receiving grants | 32 |
| Average grant | $5,500 |

## ADMISSIONS

| | |
|---|---|
| Admissions Selectivity Rating | 69 |
| # of applications received | 22 |
| % applicants accepted | 82 |
| % acceptees attending | 83 |
| Average GMAT | 500 |
| Range of GMAT | 460–540 |
| Average GPA | 3.17 |
| TOEFL required of international students? | yes |
| Minimum TOEFL (paper/computer) | 550/213 |
| Application fee | $40 |
| International application fee | $40 |
| Regular application deadline | 8/1 |
| Regular notification | 8/15 |
| Deferment available? | yes |
| Maximum length of deferment | NR |
| Transfer students accepted? | yes |
| Transfer application policy Transfer credits from AACSB-accredited insitutions accepted on case-by-case basis. | |
| Non-fall admissions? | yes |
| Need-blind admissions? | yes |

## EMPLOYMENT PROFILE

| | | Grads employed by field: | % | avg. salary: |
|---|---|---|---|---|
| Career Rating | 92 | Accounting | 14 | NR |
| Primary source of full-time job acceptances | | Finance | 19 | NR |
| | | Human Resources | 10 | NR |
| Unknown | 21 (100%) | Marketing | 10 | NR |
| Percent employed | 91 | MIS | 14 | NR |
| | | Operations | 10 | NR |
| | | General Management | 4 | NR |
| | | Other | 19 | NR |

# JACKSONVILLE STATE UNIVERSITY
## COLLEGE OF COMMERCE AND BUSINESS ADMINISTRATION

## Academics

The College of Commerce and Business Administration at Jacksonville State University offers a small, predominantly part-time AACSB-accredited MBA program that students praise for its convenience, affordability, and "personalized attention." The school serves the city of Jacksonville and the eastern Alabama region.

JSU offers both full-time and part-time MBA tracks. JSU's undergraduate program generally provides the majority of full-time students, as most continue directly from their bachelor's degree on to earn their master's. The part-time program is the almost-exclusive domain of area residents "who are working full-time and trying to get ahead in their careers by getting an MBA."

A sequence of foundation courses makes the JSU MBA available to everyone, even students with no previous academic experience in business. The eight-course foundation track covers business organization and administration; statistics; principles of financial accounting; macroeconomics; business; finance; business law and ethics; operations and technology; and marketing. Students with undergraduate coursework in these areas may place out of the courses and begin immediately on degree-related coursework, which consists of 10 courses: seven required courses, one organization class chosen from a group of three, one international business class chosen from a group of three, and an elective. Students may choose to pursue a concentration in accounting, which requires an additional six hours of course work.

All candidates for a master's degree at JSU must pass comprehensive oral examinations at the end of their program, which some here find stressful and unnecessary. "I do not agree with the oral exams policy. If instructors believe that a student knows the material and that student makes the grade on exams and projects, that should be sufficient," writes one student. Otherwise, students generally express satisfaction with the program, praising the school's administration ("It has a good vision and is focused") and the "well-read, detail-oriented, and dedicated" professors who "have good experience in the fields in which they teach." While most here applaud the school's efforts to provide distance-education options, they also anxiously await the day when the school works the bugs out of the system. One MBA warns, "The school often puts too many students in the distance-learning classes. Also, we lose 20 minutes on average per class due to technical difficulties."

## Career and Placement

JSU's Office of Career Placement Services is oriented primarily toward serving the school's undergraduate programs, although it also offers services to graduate students and alumni. The office coordinates career fairs, referrals, on-campus job interviews, and job listings. It also maintains a reference room, conducts mock interviews, and offers workshops in resume writing. Students can sign up for an e-mail service that notifies them whenever new jobs are posted with the school. Individual career counseling is offered through the Office of Counseling and Career Services.

DRIVE JEAN PUGLIESE, ASSOCIATE DEAN
700 PELHAM ROAD NORTH, JACKSONVILLE, AL 36265 UNITED STATES
PHONE: 256-782-5329 • FAX: 256-782-5321
E-MAIL: PUGLIESE@JSUCC.JSU.EDU • WEBSITE: WWW.JSU.EDU

## FINANCIAL FACTS

| | |
|---|---|
| Annual tuition (in-state/out-of-state) | |
| | $2,940/$5,880 |
| Books and supplies | $1,500 |
| Average grant | $1,000 |

## ADMISSIONS

| | |
|---|---|
| **Admissions Selectivity Rating** | **63** |
| # of applications received | 40 |
| % applicants accepted | 90 |
| % acceptees attending | 83 |
| Average GMAT | 450 |
| Range of GMAT | 320–570 |
| Average GPA | 3.0 |
| TOEFL required of | |
| international students? | yes |
| Minimum TOEFL | |
| (paper/computer) | 500/173 |
| Application fee | $20 |
| International application fee | $20 |
| Transfer students accepted? | yes |
| Transfer application policy | |
| Students may transfer up to 6 | |
| credits of approved courses with | |
| grade of B or better. | |
| Non-fall admissions? | yes |
| Need-blind admissions? | yes |

## *Student Life and Environment*

Students describe their peers as "academically curious, energized, competitive, and sociable." While "there are a lot of activities from student organizations Monday to Thursday" available to MBAs on the FSU campus, most students are "way too busy balancing personal lives (jobs, spouses, kids, volunteer work, church) and school to worry about clubs!" Once Friday rolls around, "most residents go home, and the campus is a ghost town on weekends." The school could "improve school spirit and attendance at school activities" but so many students only have time to be on campus for class that the point might be moot.

JSU is the largest employer in Jacksonville, an eastern Alabama town of approximately 8,000. Other major employers in the area include the Anniston Army Depot, the Regional Medical Center, and a number of manufacturing and distribution concerns. Jacksonville is less than 100 miles from Atlanta and Birmingham.

## *Admissions*

Applicants to the JSU MBA program must meet one of the following minimum requirements to be considered for unconditional admission: a score of at least 950 under the formula [(undergraduate GPA 5 200) + GMAT score]; or a score of at least 1000 under the formula [(undergraduate GPA for final 64 hours of course work taken toward undergraduate degree 5 200) + GMAT score]. Scores of 850 (entire undergraduate GPA) or 900 (final 64 hours) are sufficient to qualify students for conditional admission. Students admitted conditionally must earn a GPA of at least 3.0 for their first 12 hours of graduate course work and must complete the course work within a time frame established by the Graduate Committee. All applicants must first seek admission to the College of Graduate Studies; only after gaining admission to the college are they admitted to a particular program. Applicants must then provide the college of Graduate Studies with official copies of all post-secondary academic transcripts and three Graduate Reference forms completed by people who can assess the applicant's potential for success in the MBA program. Applicants whose native language is not English must provide an official TOEFL score report.

# JOHN CARROLL UNIVERSITY
## THE BOLER SCHOOL OF BUSINESS

### GENERAL INFORMATION

| | |
|---|---|
| Type of school | private |
| Affiliation | Roman Catholic/Jesuit |
| Environment | metropolis |
| Academic calendar | semesters |

### SURVEY SAYS...

Students love University Heights, OH
Friendly students
Helpful alumni
Happy students
*Solid preparation in:*
Communication/interpersonal skills

### STUDENTS

| | |
|---|---|
| Enrollment of parent institution | 3,830 |
| Enrollment of business school | 187 |
| % male/female | 60/40 |
| % part-time | 86 |
| % minorities | 2 |
| Average age at entry | 27 |
| Average years work experience at entry | 3 |

### ACADEMICS

| | |
|---|---|
| **Academic Experience Rating** | **78** |
| Student/faculty ratio | 17:1 |
| Profs interesting rating | 78 |
| Profs accessible rating | 83 |
| % female faculty | 25 |
| % minority faculty | 1 |

### JOINT DEGREES

MBA/Communications
Management, 33 credits, 2–3 years

## Academics

Accountancy is the strongest area at the Boler School of Business at John Carroll University, a Jesuit institution on the outskirts of Cleveland. One JCU student reports, "The people in this program are predominantly accounting students. The emphasis in many of the classes, even non-accounting classes, has a strong focus on accounting." Through the Accountancy Department, students can receive either an MBA with a concentration in accountancy or an MSAcc. Beyond this specialization, Boler also offers MBA concentrations in finance, marketing, human resource management, and international business.

Designed to meet the needs of part-time students, the Boler MBA offers a great degree of "flexibility of scheduling." Students may proceed through the program at their own pace, taking as few as one or as many as four courses per term (the latter option allows students with undergraduate business degrees to graduate in one year). Boler's membership in the 23-school Jesuit MBA network also affords students who relocate mid-program the opportunity to transfer all their credits to a Jesuit MBA program in or near their new hometown.

The Boler MBA is divided into four blocks. The first block consists of eight foundation courses, some or all of which can be waived on the basis of undergraduate academic achievement. Required courses covering fundamental business functions constitute the second block. The third block consists of three electives, one of which must be among a group of international business classes. The final block consists of two integrative courses covering business ethics and corporate strategic management. The school's Jesuit foundations ensure that ethics are stressed throughout the curriculum.

MBAs at Boler report that "the greatest strength of JCU is its culture. The students, faculty, staff, and administrators are all friendly and helpful. The focus is always on developing the whole person though academics and ethics discussions." Instructor access is the subject of much praise. One student writes, "I didn't think I would be able to meet and speak with my professors with the same frequency as my undergraduate experiences, but every time I've requested to meet or speak with one of my professors, it has always been a smooth process." Professors "are able to bring experience as well as theory to their classes [and] are very well known in their fields—in many cases considered experts." Some MBAs here feel that the school "needs to develop more concentrations and focus the program toward those concentrations" in order "to become more competitive with leading business schools." Campus technology also needs an upgrade, students report.

## Career and Placement

Boler MBAs seeking career guidance and placement services may use the Center for Career Services, which attends to the needs of the entire university population. Services provided include online job and resume posting, counseling, and interview scheduling. The office also functions as a clearinghouse for alumni network contacts and employer inquiries. An annual business-related job fair, open to both graduates and undergraduates in the business school, draws more than 100 recruiters to the campus.

GAYLE BRUNO-GANNON, ASSISTANT TO THE DEAN, ADMISSIONS AND RECRUITING
20700 NORTH PARK BOULEVARD, UNIVERSITY HEIGHTS, OH 44118-4581 UNITED STATES
PHONE: 216-397-1970 • FAX: 216-397-1728
E-MAIL: GGANNON@JCU.EDU • WEBSITE: HTTP://BSOB.JCU.EDU/GRADBUSINESS

## Student Life and Environment

Because "about half the MBA students have jobs and are extremely busy; a good portion are married; [and] most students here attend part-time and only come to campus for class once a week, it is more difficult to bond here than it would be in a full-time program, and most people are mainly focused on their lives/jobs outside of school." School thus functions as "a complement to that life." Some wish the school offered "more graduate-student activities, clubs, and more opportunities for career planning, mentoring, and meeting with successful alumni." They see the formation of a Graduate Student Association, which "is working on developing a graduate-student life and addressing graduate-student issues," as a step in the right direction.

The "hardworking, busy professionals" who populate most of the part-time ranks stand in stark contrast to the majority of full-timers, who "have just completed their undergraduate degrees and have no relevant real-world work experience." Some feel that "the school caters to these students a great deal; the classes are more like advanced undergraduate classes rather than graduate classes for working professionals." Others approve of both the pacing and the classroom mix, telling us that their peers "come from a variety of academic and work backgrounds. Many are entry-level and midlevel management. The program is somewhat competitive, but not a cutthroat environment."

## Admissions

Applicants to John Carroll University's MBA program must provide the school's admissions department with a completed graduate school application form, an official GMAT score report, official transcripts for all post-secondary academic work, at least one letter of recommendation, a resume, and a statement of purpose essay titled, "Graduate business education: Enabling me to achieve my personal goals and become a leader." International students must also provide TOEFL scores, appropriate financial documentation, and, when applicable, an English translation of all documents submitted in a language other than English. Academic record and GMAT scores are the most important factors in the admissions decision; letters of recommendation, the essay, and work experience are also considered important. According to the school's website, previous work experience "is not required, but having professional experience provides a frame of reference for classroom discussion, and is therefore encouraged."

### FINANCIAL FACTS

| | |
|---|---|
| Annual tuition | $14,274 |
| Books and supplies | $800 |
| % of students receiving aid | 46 |
| % of first-year students receiving aid | 21 |
| % of students receiving loans | 61 |
| % of students receiving grants | 23 |
| Average award package | $5,300 |
| Average grant | $5,300 |

### ADMISSIONS

| | |
|---|---|
| **Admissions Selectivity Rating** | **82** |
| # of applications received | 126 |
| % applicants accepted | 54 |
| % acceptees attending | 93 |
| Average GMAT | 540 |
| Range of GMAT | 450–640 |
| Average GPA | 3.2 |
| TOEFL required of international students? | yes |
| Minimum TOEFL (paper/computer) | 550/215 |
| Application fee | $25 |
| International application fee | $35 |
| Regular application deadline | rolling |
| Regular notification | rolling |
| Deferment available? | yes |
| Maximum length of deferment | 1 year |
| Transfer students accepted? | yes |
| Transfer application policy Applicants from members of the Network of MBA Programs at Jesuit Universities and Colleges will have all credits transferred. Otherwise, applications are reviewed on a case-by-case basis. | |
| Non-fall admissions? | yes |
| Need-blind admissions? | yes |

### APPLICANTS ALSO LOOK AT

Case Western Reserve University,
Cleveland State University

# KENNESAW STATE UNIVERSITY
## MICHAEL J. COLES COLLEGE OF BUSINESS

## Academics

Prospective MBAs at the Michael J. Coles College of Business at Kennesaw State University may choose from three program options: the Career Growth MBA, a traditional on-campus MBA program scheduled for the convenience of its predominantly part-time student body; a WebMBA, which allows more experienced students to complete the degree in 18 months with only a single visit to campus (the rest of the program can be completed from home); and an MBA for Experienced Professionals, an 18-month Executive MBA program in which classes meet one weekend per month. Coles also offers a Master of Accounting (MAcc) degree.

Students in the Career Growth MBA program, the most popular of the options, appreciate the "flexibility it gives students who work full-time" and the "excellent curriculum that lets you choose from courses that are actually applicable to your career." Professors here "are knowledgeable and supportive [and] have extensive experience in their fields. They usually have more than one graduate degree and are very involved in the business community in Atlanta." One MBA tells us, "Never have I experienced such a committed group of individuals." Some students complain that "there are many excellent classes in the catalog. However, most are rarely offered." But most focus on positive aspects of the program. One student sums up, "The challenge of this program has shown me what I'm truly made of! I've done things that I never would have dreamed of doing. As a result, I have a tremendous amount of confidence in my personal ability. This experience has and will open hundreds of doors, not just in the workplace, but most importantly, in my mind."

## Career and Placement

KSU's Career Services Center coordinates a number of events and provides a range of services to the school's graduate business students. Events and services include career fairs, internship fairs, a statewide job fair, and ongoing on-campus interviews, as well as OwlTRAK, an online job- and resume-posting database. The CSC regularly updates its website to keep students informed of upcoming events.

In addition, KSU has contracted Advanced Career Development, Inc. (ACDI) to provide students with assessments and counseling services, access to exclusive databases, and resume, cover letter, and career-planning counseling. (Call it outsourcing if you like.) Students give the service good marks, and especially like the fact that the services are provided at no additional cost to them.

## Student Life and Environment

With over 18,000 students, Kennesaw State is the third-largest school in the University System of Georgia. Located just 20 miles northwest of downtown Atlanta, KSU is conveniently located to benefit from the wealth of the big city. The school draws faculty and guest lecturers from the metropolitan area and full-time students find it easier to secure meaningful internships because of the city's many opportunities.

The Coles school is located in the Burruss Building, a modern business facility complete with tiered and traditional classrooms, seminar rooms, meeting areas, and networked computer labs. All classrooms are equipped to accommodate modern presentation technology. Burruss is also the site of the Tetley Lectures, an endowed series that regularly brings business leaders to campus to lecture and interact with Coles students.

STEVEN KING, ASSISTANT DIRECTOR
1000 CHASTAIN ROAD, #0132, KENNESAW, GA 30144 UNITED STATES
PHONE: 770-420-4377 • FAX: 770-420-4435
E-MAIL: KSUGRAD@KENNESAW.EDU • WEBSITE: HTTP://COLES.KENNESAW.EDU/GBO

Most Coles MBAs are part-time students with jobs and families, and accordingly, most "show up, do [their] work, discuss some issues with classmates, and head home." To accommodate these students, "classes are mainly at night. The people here are friendly; it is not a competitive program at all since people are usually already employed." A "significant number of foreign students adds to [the] diverse mix," though students detect "a couple of distinct groups of students. There is one group of people who have plenty of work experience and are building upon this. The other group has little work experience and doesn't add as much to group activities. The first group seems to be taking harder classes and harder professors to learn more from this experience. The second group targets less challenging professors just to get out." Full-time students report "a diverse environment that is set up to promote interaction between students. There are many activities designed to bring the school together. The athletics give the school the national recognition that they deserve."

## Admissions

Applicants to all graduate business programs at Kennesaw State must submit the following to the Office of Graduate Admissions: a completed application (hard copy or online); one official transcript for each school attended, including the school that awarded the baccalaureate (a minimum undergraduate GPA of 2.8 is required for admission); and an official report of GMAT score. In addition, international applicants must also provide TOEFL scores (if their native language is not English); a sponsor letter; a bank letter certifying sufficient support funds; a copy of a valid passport; an evaluation of all transcripts for academic work completed outside the U.S.; and proof of immigrant status. The Graduate Business Office reserves the right to request, in addition, a resume, statement of objectives, and two letters of recommendation from all candidates. At least two years of full-time professional business experience is strongly preferred for candidates to all programs.

### FINANCIAL FACTS

| | |
|---|---|
| Annual tuition (in-state/out-of-state) | $1,393/$5,573 |
| Fees | $676 |
| Books and supplies | $1,050 |
| Room & board (on-campus) | $0 |

### ADMISSIONS

| | |
|---|---|
| Admissions Selectivity Rating | 75 |
| # of applications received | 193 |
| % applicants accepted | 65 |
| % acceptees attending | 74 |
| Average GMAT | 510 |
| Range of GMAT | 480–550 |
| Average GPA | 3.2 |
| TOEFL required of international students? | yes |
| Minimum TOEFL (paper/computer) | 550/213 |
| Application fee | $30 |
| International application fee | $30 |
| Regular application deadline | rolling |
| Regular notification | rolling |
| Deferment available? | yes |
| Maximum length of deferment | 1 year |
| Transfer students accepted? | yes |
| Transfer application policy | |
| Transfer credit from AACSB International–accredited universities is possible, pending approval. | |
| Non-fall admissions? | yes |
| Need-blind admissions? | yes |

### APPLICANTS ALSO LOOK AT

Georgia State University

# KENT STATE UNIVERSITY

## COLLEGE OF BUSINESS ADMINISTRATION & GRADUATE SCHOOL OF MANAGEMENT

## Academics

The Graduate School of Management at Kent State University offers both a full-time MBA and a part-time Professional MBA, with the ratio of part-time students to full-time students being roughly two to one. The school also offers three dual-degree options (in conjunction with the Nursing Program, the Library Science Program, and the Architecture Program), as well as opportunities to study abroad. Finally, the Kent State GSM offers an Executive MBA to candidates with the prerequisite amount of work experience and the support of their employers.

A Kent State MBA requires between 39 and 54 hours of course work. It can be completed by a full-time student in 15 months, though many students take two years to finish. The number of required credits depends upon the student's undergraduate work in business. A core course can be waived, for example, for students who have previously taken two undergraduate courses or one graduate course in the core subject and earned a grade of B or better. The entire core curriculum consists of 30 credit hours of classwork; the remainder of the program is made up of executive modules, integrative management courses, and electives. The school offers concentrations in accounting, finance, human resource management, information systems, international business, and marketing.

Students here tell us that the majority of professors "are very passionate about their fields." Most have deep real-world experience. They are "also lawyers and businesspeople and everything else, so they know what it's like to have a heavy workload, and they demand excellence without letting the class get so stuffy that you don't want to be there." Some excel at "incorporating new computer-based learning tools and keeping up with technology," although they can be stymied in their efforts by the resources of the university. "Many of the classrooms are not equipped with multimedia connections, and some professors still rely on overheads instead of PowerPoint presentations," one student warns. Students here do appreciate that the "tutoring possibilities are fabulous."

## Career and Placement

The Kent State Career Services Center provides "comprehensive employment search services" for the GSM graduate students, as well as workshops in interviewing, resume writing, and job-search strategies. The CSC posts employment opportunities and coordinates on-campus interviews, and the office reports that approximately 500 employers visit the campus to hire for business and government positions each year.

Employers most likely to hire Kent State MBAs include Ernst and Young, Progressive Insurance, Key Bank, Little Tikes, Jo-Ann Stores Inc., Summa Health System, FedEx Systems, The Timken Company, and Diebold Inc.

LOUISE DITCHEY, DIRECTOR, MASTER'S PROGRAMS
PO BOX 5190, KENT, OH 44242-0001 UNITED STATES
PHONE: 330-672-2282 • FAX: 330-672-7303
E-MAIL: GRADBUS@BSA3.KENT.EDU • WEBSITE: WWW.BUSINESS.KENT.EDU/GRAD

## Student Life and Environment

Kent State is a large university where "there is always something going on, whether it is a sports event or a speaker on campus. Kent gives its students many opportunities to get out of their rooms and meet people." Many agree that the school is "very large but very friendly." Full-time students here tend to be either international students or recent undergraduates. In either case, they are typically closer in age to undergraduates than to the older part-time students in their program, and they are more likely to enjoy collegiate recreation. Many work out regularly, taking advantage of "the 52,000-square-foot student recreation center, which houses an enormous weightlifting facility and cardio machines. There is a three-story rock wall, a one-sixth-mile indoor track, racquetball courts, basketball courts, volleyball courts, and badminton courts. It is the best part of campus."

Students report that Kent has "a beautiful campus" with "nice dorms" but that its "classrooms are older and not aesthetically pleasing or comfortable. The rooms are too hot in the winter and cold in the summer. The chairs are connected to the tables and when you move yours, you may move your neighbor as well." Commuters appreciate that "if you have a night class, you have the opportunity to have a member of campus security walk you to your class. Also, the bus system here is very helpful."

Kent's part-time students are typically "blue-collar managers or individuals working in small- to medium-size manufacturing and financial institutions. Most are married with children." It is "harder for those students to make time for the group projects that teachers frequently assign," we're told, which sometimes creates tension between the "older, nontraditional students" and the younger ones with fewer outside commitments. But, for the most part, full-time and part-time students get along well here. International students "are from so many different countries and walks of life, it gives an extremely diverse learning environment. Everyone learns from one another's experiences."

## Admissions

Applicants to the MBA program at Kent State must provide the school with official transcripts from all post-secondary institutions attended; an official GMAT score report; a resume; letters of recommendation (three for the full-time program, two for the Professional MBA program); and a personal statement. International students must additionally provide TOEFL scores (if English is not their native language) and must complete an International Student Application to the school.

### FINANCIAL FACTS

| | |
|---|---|
| Annual tuition (in-state/out-of-state) | $8,460/$15,472 |
| Books and supplies | $1,100 |
| Room & board (on/off-campus) | $7,040/$6,500 |
| % of students receiving aid | 32 |
| % of first-year students receiving aid | 24 |
| Average award package | $14,960 |

### ADMISSIONS

| | |
|---|---|
| Admissions Selectivity Rating | 73 |
| # of applications received | 114 |
| % applicants accepted | 74 |
| % acceptees attending | 61 |
| Average GMAT | 526 |
| Range of GMAT | 480–560 |
| Average GPA | 3.4 |
| TOEFL required of international students? | yes |
| Minimum TOEFL (paper/computer) | 550/213 |
| Application fee | $30 |
| International application fee | $30 |
| Regular application deadline | 4/1 |
| Regular notification | 4/15 |
| Deferment available? | yes |
| Maximum length of deferment | 1 year |
| Transfer students accepted? | yes |
| Transfer application policy | |

Students may transfer up to 12 credits from an AASCB-accredited program, pending approval; credits must be less than 6 years old.

| | |
|---|---|
| Non-fall admissions? | yes |
| Need-blind admissions? | yes |

### APPLICANTS ALSO LOOK AT

Case Western Reserve University, Cleveland State University, John Carroll University, The Ohio State University, The University of Akron, Youngstown State University

# Lamar University
## College of Business

### GENERAL INFORMATION

| | |
|---|---|
| Type of school | public |
| Environment | village |
| Academic calendar | semester |

### SURVEY SAYS...

Good social scene
Happy students
*Solid preparation in:*
Communication/interpersonal skills
Presentation skills
Computer skills

### STUDENTS

| | |
|---|---|
| Enrollment of parent institution | 10,595 |
| Enrollment of business school | 87 |
| % male/female | 45/55 |
| % out-of-state | 31 |
| % part-time | 37 |
| % minorities | 7 |
| % international | 29 |
| Average age at entry | 26 |
| Average years work experience at entry | 3 |

### ACADEMICS

| | |
|---|---|
| **Academic Experience Rating** | **62** |
| Student/faculty ratio | 14:1 |
| Profs interesting rating | 72 |
| Profs accessible rating | 66 |
| % female faculty | 30 |
| % minority faculty | 30 |

### JOINT DEGREES

MBA/MSN in Administration, 42 credits

## Academics

Texans seeking an affordable MBA in a cozy atmosphere would do well to consider the College of Business at Lamar University, a public institution in Beaumont (about 90 miles east of Houston). This program of fewer than 100 students "has made great improvements in recent years," students tell us. One student reports, "I've only seen things get better since I arrived. The quality of a business degree here is improving rapidly as compared with other schools, and Lamar is becoming a true leader in a business education." The size of the program translates into "a student-teacher ratio that is somewhat smaller than it is at other colleges. The quality of our education is competitive despite the size, and we are at a distinct advantage of having one-on-one assistance with professors."

Students can receive a Lamar MBA in short order. Those with undergraduate business degrees, for example, can place out of some or all first-year courses, allowing them to procure their degrees in a year's time. Those without a business degree can complete 18 hours of prerequisites in less than two semesters. In addition, "there are mini-sessions and summer sessions, which allow students to pick up extra classes in a short amount of time. These sessions are very beneficial." Management and marketing offers the largest number of courses at Lamar; the school also offers courses in economics and finance, information systems and analysis, and accounting and business law. Lamar is home to the Institute for Entrepreneurial Studies and the Small Business Development Center.

Lamar professors are well-loved by the MBAs, who tell us that "for the most part, all the professors are wonderful. They are all educated and have work experience in the field in which they are teaching, [and] the majority are willing to take extra time to help you with your questions." Professors' willingness to work with both individuals and groups of students, MBAs tell us, "reflects the prioritization the faculty gives students and teaching." Advisors are similarly "very nice and helpful." The pace of the curriculum can be slow at times, due in part to some students' lack of background in business studies. One student complains, "The school seriously needs to raise the admission standards. My school's relaxed admission policy lowers my overall learning experience."

## Career and Placement

All career services for Lamar MBAs are provided by the university's Career Center; apart from contacts provided by professors, there are few career services offered at Lamar that specifically serve MBAs. The office conducts school-wide job fairs (including recruitment events geared specifically toward minorities), interviewing and resume-building workshops, one-on-one counseling, and online job databases.

Students warn that "the Career Center has limited resources. There aren't many companies that come to the Lamar campus to recruit students, and job-placement programs for business undergrads and grad students need to be improved." A February 2004 report in *The Beaumont Enterprise* confirms this assessment, pointing out that the number of companies attending Lamar's Spring Career Expo has declined by two-thirds in the past five years. Students can, however, access a wide range of companies by attending the Houston Area Consortium of Career Centers Texas Job Fair, held annually at the University of Houston.

SANDY DRANE, GRADUATE ADMISSIONS OFFICE
PO BOX L0078 BEAUMONT, TX 77710 UNITED STATES
PHONE: 409-880-8356 • FAX: 409-880-8414
E-MAIL: DRANESL@HAL.LAMAR.EDU • WEBSITE: WWW.LAMAR.EDU

## Student Life and Environment

With fewer than 100 students and a largely part-time population, Lamar's MBA program is "fairly small. Also, unlike most schools, Lamar University is mostly composed of students that commute to and from school. Even though a large living facility has been set up for students, most students live off campus. The overall mood of the university is distant." Most students agree, "There is not much life on campus besides the occasional party."

The neighborhood surrounding the school offers little help, as "Lamar University is in a somewhat run-down area of town. Fortunately, the campus police department and City of Beaumont P.D. do a very good job of providing a secure environment for students, staff, and visitors." It is not, however, an area that encourages students to hang out in their free time. As one student puts it, "The area around the campus does not reflect the growing university population. There's not much for students."

That's not to say one can't get involved at Lamar; it just requires more than the usual amount of effort. One go-getter explains, "I've been involved on campus in some of the clubs as well as attending classes. There are all sorts of opportunities. I've participated in the choir and gone to all types of extracurricular events: deaf events, art shows, literary events, musical concerts, and performances."

Students feel that Lamar is making efforts to upgrade campus life by "providing the opportunity of a social life through student organizations and activities, newly constructed living quarters, and exceptional eating facilities." Furthermore, "Lamar University is currently making great strides to improve not only the physical appearance of the campus but also bring the classrooms up to modern standards with new multimedia equipment."

## Admissions

Lamar University requires all applicants to provide GMAT scores, undergraduate transcripts, and TOEFL scores (for students whose native language is not English). An interview, letters of recommendation, personal statement, resume, and evidence of computer experience are all recommended but not required; all are taken into account in rendering an admissions decision. The school applies two formulae combining GPA and GMAT scores to set minimum admissions standards; see the school's website for details. In all instances, a minimum GMAT score of 450 is required for unconditional admission; students with scores between 400 and 450 qualify for conditional admission, pending completion of nine hours of course work with at least a 3.0 GPA.

### FINANCIAL FACTS

| | |
|---|---|
| Annual tuition (in-state/out-of-state) | $2,790/$8,310 |
| Fees | $974 |
| Books and supplies | $1,000 |
| Room & board (on/off-campus) | $5,140/$4,000 |
| % of students receiving aid | 55 |
| % of first-year students receiving aid | 52 |
| % of students receiving loans | 26 |
| % of students receiving grants | 49 |
| Average award package | $1,955 |
| Average grant | $1,007 |

### ADMISSIONS

| | |
|---|---|
| Admissions Selectivity Rating | 70 |
| # of applications received | 52 |
| % applicants accepted | 73 |
| % acceptees attending | 71 |
| Average GMAT | 485 |
| Range of GMAT | 440–560 |
| Average GPA | 3.2 |
| TOEFL required of international students? | yes |
| Minimum TOEFL (paper/computer) | 525/200 |
| Application fee | $25 |
| International application fee | $75 |
| Regular application deadline | 5/1 |
| Regular notification | rolling |
| Deferment available? | yes |
| Maximum length of deferment | 1 year |
| Transfer students accepted? | yes |
| Transfer application policy Students may transfer up to 6 credits from another AACSB-accredited program, pending approval. | |
| Non-fall admissions? | yes |
| Need-blind admissions? | yes |

| EMPLOYMENT PROFILE | |
|---|---|
| Career Rating | 72 |
| Primary source of full-time job acceptances | |
| School-facilitated activities | 40% |
| Graduate-facilitated activities | 60% |
| | |
| Average starting salary | $45,000 |
| Percent employed | 95 |

# LONG ISLAND UNIVERSITY—CW POST CAMPUS
## COLLEGE OF MANAGEMENT

## Academics

One of only two AACSB-accredited MBA programs on Long Island (the other is Hofstra, located in nearby Hempstead), the College of Management at Long Island University—CW Post Campus serves the area's sizable population by providing a prestigious graduate degree accessible to full-timers and part-timers alike.

The vast majority of graduate students here are part-timers, attending classes in the evenings and/or on Saturdays. The college offers two part-time programs to satisfy these students' needs: the Campus MBA, with classes that meet weekly Monday through Thursday (there are two time slots for classes each night: 6:40 to 8:30 P.M., and 8:40 to 10:30 P.M.); and the Saturday MBA, which features intensive five-week classes (meeting from 9:00 A.M. to 3:30 P.M.) to allow students with the requisite undergraduate background in business to earn their degrees in 15 to 23 months. Students in the Campus MBA program may supplement their curricula with Saturday classes.

Full-time students may also enroll in the Campus MBA, or they may opt for the Accelerated International MBA. The latter, a 36-credit program "particularly suited for students who have majored in business administration at the undergraduate level," sends students to London for one semester and to Paris for a summer term; the entire program is completed in one year (students spend the fall semester on the CW Post campus).

Students here extol the "excellent academic experience" and "professors who understand and are willing to accommodate students." Students complain that "the school should offer a wider range of elective courses" and wish that it would "allow independent study to better accommodate students' interests and their graduation time frames." All students here may supplement their degrees by combining four 700-level electives to earn an advanced certificate in any of the following areas: accounting and taxation, finance, international business, management, management information systems, and marketing.

## Career and Placement

The Office of Professional Experience & Career Planning at CW Post handles counseling and placement responsibilities for all students. The office provides self-assessment diagnostics, career counseling, resume and job-search advisement, mock interviews, job fairs, recruiting events, and online databases. An MBA Association supplements these services by "helping students network with each other and exchange ideas and information helpful for career advancement in our competitive business world," according to the College's *MBA Bulletin*.

BETH CARSON, DIRECTOR OF GRADUATE AND INTERNATIONAL ADMISSIONS
720 NORTHERN BOULEVARD, BROOKVILLE, NY 11548 UNITED STATES
PHONE: 516-299-3952 • FAX: 516-299-2418
E-MAIL: BETH.CARSON@LIU.EDU • WEBSITE: WWW.LIU.EDU/POSTMBA

## Student Life and Environment

Unlike most New York area schools, the Post campus of LIU boasts a "beautiful campus" spread out across 300+ acres of prime real estate. Twenty acres of the campus are devoted to an arboretum; the entire campus is heavily wooded, with over 4,000 trees that include some of the largest trees on Long Island. Students love the campus but warn that "it's hard to find many buildings the first few times on campus because it's so big" and that "there is definitely a parking problem around the most heavily used buildings."

College of Management facilities include "an excellent library and computer labs." Students appreciate that the school "is willing to spend the money necessary to upgrade facilities and classrooms, which, as a result, tend to be in great shape." Unfortunately, "the resources are not geared toward returning adult students, so things like the bookstore hours and campus facilities are not open when we're usually here." The part-timers who make up the majority of the student body note that "this is a commuter school, so there are very few clubs or activities geared toward graduate students, especially those of us who work. There is the occasional function during business hours, but many of us can't make it to them."

Post's "extremely friendly and helpful" MBA students include many students hit by the nation's recent economic woes; "There are a number of students who are here because they were not able to get a job after graduation," explains one student. Others "are working toward getting another job." Overall, "there is a range of experience levels, from significant work experience to none at all."

## Admissions

Prerequisites to admission to the Post MBA include competence in business communications, mathematics, and computers, as demonstrated through undergraduate work, successful completion of a related workshop, or successful completion of a waiver exam. All applicants must submit a completed application form, an official GMAT score report, two copies of official transcripts for all post-secondary academic work, a resume, a personal essay explaining one's purpose in pursuing an MBA, and two letters of recommendation. Students whose first language is not English must also submit official results for the TOEFL (minimum score of 527 on the paper-based test, 197 on the computer-based test); students who completed undergraduate degrees from institutions that teach primarily in English are exempted from this requirement.

### FINANCIAL FACTS

| | |
|---|---|
| Annual tuition | $13,446 |
| Fees | $950 |
| Books and supplies | $1,650 |
| Room & board | |
| (on/off-campus) | $9,000/$6,200 |
| % of students receiving aid | 80 |
| % of students receiving loans | 80 |
| % of students receiving grants | 2 |
| Average award package | $8,500 |
| Average grant | $3,000 |

### ADMISSIONS

| | |
|---|---|
| **Admissions Selectivity Rating** | **76** |
| # of applications received | 305 |
| % applicants accepted | 51 |
| % acceptees attending | 71 |
| Average GMAT | 490 |
| Range of GMAT | 420–690 |
| Average GPA | 3.0 |
| TOEFL required of | |
| international students? | yes |
| Minimum TOEFL | |
| (paper/computer) | 527/197 |
| Application fee | $30 |
| International application fee | $30 |
| Regular application deadline | 8/6 |
| Regular notification | 7/6 |
| Deferment available? | yes |
| Maximum length | |
| of deferment | 1 year |
| Transfer students accepted? | yes |
| Transfer application policy | |
| Students may transfer up to 6 | |
| credits with a grade of B or better | |
| from another AACSB-accredited | |
| program, pending approval. | |
| Non-fall admissions? | yes |
| Need-blind admissions? | yes |

### APPLICANTS ALSO LOOK AT

Hofstra University, St. John's University

# LOUISIANA STATE UNIVERSITY
## E.J. OURSO COLLEGE OF BUSINESS

## Academics

A "world-renowned internal audit program, very intense and real-world driven," and a great football team are two of the main attractions of the Flores MBA Program at the E.J. Ourso College of Business—and not necessarily in that order. Sure, students here take their schoolwork and careers very seriously, but there's something about the school's location in Baton Rouge that reminds MBAs there's more to life than case studies and presentations. They get the job done here, and they do it well, but they also remember to save time to enjoy the gorgeous campus, the accommodating hometown, the darn good food, and their convivial classmates.

Although the marquee feature at Ourso is the internal audit program—its graduates have won the International CIA Student High Achievement Award on the Certified Internal Auditor Examination 15 times in the last 18 years—the school is hardly a one-trick pony. Other standouts include the entrepreneurship program ("consistently one of the top in the nation") and a solid concentration in finance. All students here must complete "a strong core curriculum" that provides "a good academic foundation, but without the cutthroat competition that I think could be harmful to the learning environment," writes one MBA. Another notes, "The combination of case studies and current-event discussions that have been integrated into the course work provide the chance to see exactly how the lessons from lectures and text are implemented in today's fluid business environment."

Professors "really try to connect in-class concepts with real-world application. Also, students are exposed to professional panels, presentations by industry leaders, and in-state trips to prominent businesses. And trips to foreign countries are offered for international business classes." Students also love the administration, praising it as "second to none. They provide students with a place to go if they need to resolve a problem or just have someone to speak to." "The only drawback here is the brick-and-mortar facilities, [which] are old and deteriorating."

## Career and Placement

Flores MBAs are served in their career pursuits by a number of offices and programs, including the LSU Career Services Center, the MBA Placement Program, the Center for Internal Audit Placement Services, and the school's MBA specialization advisers.

Of 68 graduating members of the class of 2003, 41 had full-time employment at commencement. Eighteen MBAs found work at *Fortune* 500 companies (Altria Group, Inc; Chevron; Eli Lilly; Entergy Corporation; ExxonMobil; FedEx; Hartford Financial Services; IBM; International Paper; Lockheed Martin; Schering-Plough;The Shaw Group; and Wal-Mart). Employers that most consistently hire the greatest number of Flores MBAs include Accenture, Chevron, Deloitte Touche Tohmatsu, Entergy Corporation, ExxonMobil, Ernst & Young, Eli Lilly, FedEx, IBM, KPMG Peat Marwick, Lockheed Martin, LSU, PricewaterhouseCoopers, and Shell. Nearly 350 companies recruit for full-time employees each year on the LSU campus; just over 100 seek summer interns here.

## Student Life and Environment

You'd be hard pressed to find an MBA student here who will badmouth the quality of life at LSU. Students praise the "great social scene," the campus ("one of the most attractive available"), and the "many clubs and organizations that one can join, so that there is always some type of activity going on for the general school public." One student reports, "The MBA Association is always having a gathering or some service activity. The

KATHLEEN BOSWORTH, ASSOCIATE DIRECTOR, FLORES MBA PROGRAMS
3170 CEBA BUILDING, BATON ROUGE, LA 70803 UNITED STATES
PHONE: 225-578-8867 • FAX: 225-578-2421
E-MAIL: BUSMBA@LSU.EDU • WEBSITE: WWW.BUS.LSU.EDU/MBA

students are always getting together for trips to the bar after a particularly tough day at school." Extracurricular life peaks during the fall, when football dominates the entire campus. One MBA explains, "No matter where you're at on campus or what's going on in your classes or life, you can't ignore the electricity of what's happening each Saturday night. You have to fight the RV's to park for class . . . on Thursday! Anticipating the Golden Band from Tigerland marching through campus, watching the games at Death Valley . . . there's nothing like it."

Students also love hometown Baton Rouge, where "there are lots of places to go out, from the Chimes, with a beer menu of over 120 [varieties], to multiple dance clubs around town. The downtown area is beginning to see more life brought to it, which adds more flavor to the mix." Even the pigskin-averse can't resist the allure of "walking through campus amongst the newly bloomed azaleas, under the stately oaks that have adorned the banks of the Mississippi for over 200 years. Friends and professors alike stroll down Highland Road, just a few miles from plantations as old as sugar, all the while getting an education that anyone would be proud of."

The "true Southern ladies and gentlemen" who attend LSU "take advantage of the opportunity to socialize during and after class. This small class size has ultimately allowed us to become a close-knit class," notes one MBA. The class includes "quite a few highly technical engineers, because of the proximity to large oil refineries" and some other professionals. However, "the majority do not have work experience, and this means there are strong differences between the objectives that everyone has. Married students and older students with more work experience tend to have better focus toward their career objectives."

## Admissions

All applicants to Flores must submit a complete set of undergraduate transcripts (minimum 3.0 GPA required), GMAT scores, letter of recommendation, a personal statement, and a professional resume. An interview is required but previous work experience, while preferred, is not. Admissions officers study the application for evidence of "community work, demonstrated leadership potential, career direction and purpose, personal qualities and interpersonal skills, and academic performance and promise." International applicants must also submit the TOEFL (minimum score: 550 written, 213 computer-based).

### FINANCIAL FACTS

| | |
|---|---|
| Annual tuition | $4,272 |
| Fees (in-state/out-of-state) | $4,153/$12,453 |
| Books and supplies | $1,500 |
| Room & board | $5,800 |

### ADMISSIONS

| | |
|---|---|
| **Admissions Selectivity Rating** | **86** |
| # of applications received | 154 |
| % applicants accepted | 60 |
| % acceptees attending | 73 |
| Average GMAT | 600 |
| Range of GMAT | 520–690 |
| Average GPA | 3.42 |
| TOEFL required of international students? | yes |
| Minimum TOEFL (paper/computer) | 550/213 |
| Application fee | $25 |
| International application fee | $25 |
| Transfer students accepted? | yes |
| Transfer application policy Applicants must have attended an AACSB-accredited school and meet the entrance requirements for the Flores MBA Program. | |
| Need-blind admissions? | yes |

### APPLICANTS ALSO LOOK AT

Loyola University—New Orleans, Mississippi State University, The University of Texas at Austin, Tulane University, University of Alabama, University of Georgia, University of New Orleans

### EMPLOYMENT PROFILE

| | | Grads employed by field: | % | avg. salary: |
|---|---|---|---|---|
| **Career Rating** | **86** | Accounting | 55 | $54,050 |
| **Primary source of full-time** | | Finance | 16 | $60,944 |
| **job acceptances** | | Marketing | 5 | $45,000 |
| School-facilitated activities | 46 (84%) | MIS | 5 | $50,167 |
| Graduate-facilitated activities | 9 (16%) | General Management | 1 | $35,000 |
| Average starting salary | $54,147 | | | |
| Percent employed | 100 | | | |

# Loyola College in Maryland

## Sellinger School of Business and Management

## Academics

Students at the Sellinger School of Business and Management at Loyola College in Maryland love the school's "solid reputation in the Baltimore/Washington DC area" as well as the program's "great flexibility for part-time MBAs." Sellinger's self-paced curriculum suits the lifestyles of its busy students, allowing them to schedule classes around their other commitments. Sellinger's two campuses (Timonium and Columbia) that "offer most of the same courses," further augment students' options.

Loyola's MBA program requires between 33 and 53 credits, depending on one's undergraduate background in business. Those eligible to waive pre-program competencies and foundation courses can complete the program in as little as 12 months. The Sellinger curriculum is organized around five integrated areas of study: leadership and teamwork, social responsibility and ethics, IT, global markets, and learning through reflection. MBAs here appreciate the "strong focus on ethics throughout the curriculum." They also tell us that international business studies here are greatly enhanced by "mini-mester courses that involve traveling to a foreign country. There is a two-week trip to Europe and a one-week trip to Chile. It's a nice bonus, and a great way to pick up credits between semesters." Concentrations are offered in accounting, finance, general business, international business, management, MIS, and marketing. Loyola also has an Executive MBA Program.

Students give the academics here an "A+" and report that Sellinger "uses people who are well-established in business to teach the core courses. This means there is no gap between what is taught in the classroom and what the 'real world' is doing. The businesspeople who teach these classes greatly enjoy teaching, and it shows." Classes are interactive, too. One MBA candidate explains, "We don't just read the text and do the homework from the book. We read the text, relate it to our business and personal lives, and apply models to help us comprehend what we just learned." When things get rough, "there are tutors available, with the ability to focus on individual needs." Advisors, on the other hand, "are very hands-off. If you want to find out about resources such as programs, you might not be aware these things exist unless you dig for them yourself."

## Career and Placement

Loyola students tell us that "because this is a part-time program, almost all students have full-time jobs, and the school does not offer a lot of resources in career counseling and placement." One student writes, "I only know about the career counseling program because I went to this school for my undergraduate degree. Most graduates are probably not aware we have one." Those who are aware of the service would like to see it beefed up. "Yes, we have jobs. However, this does not mean students are not looking for a job change upon graduation," points out one student. A "strong local alumni network" is Loyola's greatest asset in this area.

SCOTT GREATOREX, GRADUATE ADMISSIONS DIRECTOR
4501 NORTH CHARLES STREET, BALTIMORE, MD 21210 UNITED STATES
PHONE: 410-617-5020 • FAX: 410-617-2002
E-MAIL: GRADUATE@LOYOLA.EDU/MBA@LOYOLA.EDU • WEBSITE: HTTP://SELLINGER.LOYOLA.EDU

## Student Life and Environment

The Sellinger MBA program is entirely part-time, which students say "creates an atmosphere similar to a community college. There is really no life at school," which actually suits students just fine. Students explain, "Obtaining an MBA is an extremely hard thing to do when working full-time, and the students are very respectful of each other and the teacher because of that. We are all here to strengthen our educational background and move up in the world. School life in a part-time MBA program centers around academics." Fortunately, "the administration and faculty are sensitive to student work/school balance issues. They work to strike a balance between maintaining a top-quality curriculum and providing some flexibility when needed by students."

Occasional extracurricular events do occur here, and students make the most of them. For example, "the school sponsors an alumni night every semester where current students and alumni can network in a relaxed atmosphere. It also sponsors a student appreciation night every semester with refreshments before class." Students socialize on a more casual basis as well. "During evening classes, students are able to meet for a cup of coffee at Starbucks, relax in the lounge and read a book, or catch a show on one of its many flat-screen televisions," explains one student.

The Sellinger student body "is a vibrant population of many young professionals, many with type-A personalities." There is "an intense, yet friendly and productive, sense of competition at Loyola," with students generally "more concerned with learning and networking than being the best at the expense of other classmates." Some here observe that "due to the recent economic environment, there is a noticeable percentage of students right out of undergrad, who decided to get more education before jumping into the market." Overall, though, there is "definitely a diverse group here. There are younger students and older students; married students and single students; students completing the MBA program to move up at their current job; and students completing the MBA program to move to a different company."

## Admissions

A complete application to the Loyola College MBA program includes: a completed application form; a personal statement; a resume; an official GMAT score report; official transcripts for all degree work and for any post-secondary academic work completed within five years of application; as well as international documents, where appropriate. Applicants with a 3.25 undergraduate GPA and five years of work experience may waive the GMAT requirement, as may students with an advanced degree in any other discipline (e.g., a master's, a PhD, a JD, etc.). Interviews and letters of recommendation are optional.

### FINANCIAL FACTS

| | |
|---|---|
| Annual tuition | $9,450 |
| Fees | $50 |
| Books and supplies | $630 |
| Room & board | $13,365 |
| % of students receiving aid | 38 |
| % of first-year students receiving aid | 62 |
| % of students receiving loans | 33 |
| % of students receiving grants | 12 |
| Average award package | $16,120 |
| Average grant | $10,920 |
| Average student loan debt | $26,550 |

### ADMISSIONS

| | |
|---|---|
| **Admissions Selectivity Rating** | **74** |
| # of applications received | 558 |
| % applicants accepted | 81 |
| % acceptees attending | 85 |
| Average GMAT | 536 |
| Range of GMAT | 440–680 |
| Average GPA | 3.34 |
| TOEFL required of international students? | yes |
| Minimum TOEFL (paper/computer) | 550/215 |
| Application fee | $50 |
| International application fee | $50 |
| Regular application deadline | rolling |
| Regular notification | rolling |
| Deferment available? | yes |
| Maximum length of deferment | 1 year |
| Transfer students accepted? | yes |
| Transfer application policy Only classes from another AACSB-accredited school will be counted. | |
| Non-fall admissions? | yes |
| Need-blind admissions? | yes |

# LOYOLA MARYMOUNT UNIVERSITY
## COLLEGE OF BUSINESS ADMINISTRATION

### GENERAL INFORMATION
| | |
|---|---|
| Type of school | private |
| Affiliation | Roman Catholic/Jesuit |
| Environment | metropolis |
| Academic calendar | semester |

### SURVEY SAYS...
Students love Los Angeles, CA
Happy students
Smart classrooms
*Solid preparation in:*
Teamwork

### STUDENTS
| | |
|---|---|
| Enrollment of parent institution | 8,582 |
| Enrollment of business school | 298 |
| % male/female | 60/40 |
| % part-time | 70 |
| % minorities | 30 |
| % international | 37 |
| Average age at entry | 26 |
| Average years work experience at entry | 4 |

### ACADEMICS
| | |
|---|---|
| **Academic Experience Rating** | **79** |
| Student/faculty ratio | 22:1 |
| Profs interesting rating | 90 |
| Profs accessible rating | 87 |
| % female faculty | 20 |
| % minority faculty | 21 |

### JOINT DEGREES
MBA/JD, 4 years; MBA/SELP, 4 years

## Academics

Loyola Marymount University capably serves its largely part-time student body with an extremely accommodating program that allows students to enter in either the Fall or Spring semester, take as many classes as they can handle, and choose from "a cafeteria-style of elective courses in which a variety of subjects are offered."

Students love LMU's "unbelievable" entrepreneurship program taught by "renowned professors." They also love the international business program and the unique Comparative Management Systems (CMS) option, "where you research issues in foreign countries and then travel to those countries to do hands-on research and interview. CMS is a great alternative to a traditional thesis." Dual-degree options such as the Systems Engineering Leadership Program (MBA and MS in Systems Engineering) and the JD/MBA program also earn praise.

Students love the "teamwork-oriented and friendly" vibe, with "none of that backstabbing you hear about on other campuses. It's like *The Apprentice* for the winning team, not the losing team." Classwork involves "going to class and participating, not just sitting there and listening to the professor lecture. There is a lot of group work, so you really get to know your peers through large projects and presentations." MBAs also appreciate the Jesuit influence on the curriculum, which translates to "a lot of emphasis on ethics." Professors, we're told, are the school's "greatest strength. They challenge us and push our ideas and we get our money's worth for our education." They also "do a great job of applying real-world situations to theory [and] are a great networking resource."

## Career and Placement

LMU serves two distinct student bodies: a majority of part-timers who already have full-time jobs, and a minority who attend full-time and will be looking for job placement post-MBA. The MBA Career Services Office (CSO) doesn't see much of the former, whose employers frequently foot the bill for their MBAs. The latter benefit from resume and cover-letter seminars; interview and salary-negotiation workshops; and career counseling. An MBA Mentor program pairs students with area execs, while the annual Meet the Firms event brings employers to campus to meet with prospective employees and interns.

The CSO also offers the CareerLeader assessment tool and access to Vault.com and Monstertrak.com. The office maintains an online bulletin board for job postings. Students feel that "the school could improve in its ability to attract top-notch companies to the career fair. This would allow LMU grads to compete on a more level playing field with the likes of USC and UCLA." They also "would like to see LMU's alumni association have the power and prestige of a USC."

## Student Life and Environment

All students, full-time and part-time, attend classes together at LMU. Classes begin at 4:25 P.M. and continue through the evening. MBAs appreciate that the "beautiful campus" is "very safe," that "faculty and staff are usually available from 9:00 A.M. to 7:00 P.M.," and that "the business building remains open after classes end at 10:00 P.M., allowing students to work." They warn, however, that parking is extremely difficult.

MARIA McGILL, MBA PROGRAM COORDINATOR
ONE LMU DRIVE, MS 8387, LOS ANGELES, CA 90045-2659 UNITED STATES
PHONE: 310-338-2848 • FAX: 310-338-2899
E-MAIL: MBAPC@LMU.EDU • WEBSITE: HTTP://MBA.LMU.EDU

## FINANCIAL FACTS

| | |
|---|---|
| Annual tuition | $24,165 |
| Fees | $400 |
| Books and supplies | $1,300 |

## ADMISSIONS

| | |
|---|---|
| **Admissions Selectivity Rating** | **78** |
| # of applications received | 260 |
| % applicants accepted | 66 |
| % acceptees attending | 61 |
| Average GMAT | 562 |
| Average GPA | 3.29 |
| TOEFL required of international students? | yes |
| Minimum TOEFL (paper/computer) | 600/250 |
| Application fee | $50 |
| International application fee | $50 |
| Regular application deadline | rolling |
| Regular notification | rolling |
| Deferment available? | yes |
| Maximum length of deferment | 1 year |
| Transfer students accepted? | yes |

Transfer application policy
Students from other Jesuit MBA Programs may transfer core and electives through the Jesuit Transfer Network. Students who attend an AACSB-accredited MBA Program (not Jesuit) with equivalent course work of B or better may ONLY transfer in 6 units of upper-division course credit but may be eligible for core course waivers.

| | |
|---|---|
| Non-fall admissions? | yes |
| Need-blind admissions? | yes |

### APPLICANTS ALSO LOOK AT
Pepperdine University, University of California—Los Angeles, University of Southern California

LMU offers "many organized social and networking activities" to its business students, but many are too busy with work, class assignments, and family obligations to take advantage. Those who do speak highly of the opportunities; as one reports, "The school provides weekday and weekend activities that encourage students, faculty, and alumni to mingle. From yacht cruises to a day at the horse-races, LMU has a great social culture." Students add, "We have multiple Food 'n' Schmooze nights each semester, which give us the opportunity to get to know our fellow students before and after class over dinner. We also do First Fridays by meeting at different bars on the first Friday of every month." Even so, this "is an evening program, so I don't think we have the same intensity of community as full-time MBA programs might have," concedes one MBA. Another explains, "Because the program is geared towards working adults, most students are part-time and thus come to class and leave immediately afterwards. It's almost like a commuter school in that sense. I wish the program would offer day courses and not just evening courses."

The typical LMU professional is "an aerospace or entertainment industry professional who is very smart and highly motivated." In recent years, an increasing proportion of the student body has arrived with little or no professional experience. One student explains, "The student body is changing in that many students used to come from local engineering companies, but they have cut tuition subsidies so students are now younger." Another observes, "About 25 percent of students are recent college grads. They don't participate much in class discussions. About 75 percent are over 24. This group is the most vocal in class, participate more, and are engaging."

## Admissions

LMU implements a relatively lenient admissions policy. Work experience, for example, is not required; while most students have worked post-baccalaureate an average of four years, some students arrive here with little or no professional experience. The school enforces no minimum undergraduate GPA or GMAT score, although the average GPA of 3.29 among admitted students bespeaks an academically accomplished student body. No prerequisite courses are required of enrollees; however, students must show evidence of college-level math proficiency (i.e., business math or intermediate algebra) before enrolling in quantitative courses. Applicants may be admitted for Fall or Spring semester. Applications are processed on a rolling basis.

# LOYOLA UNIVERSITY—CHICAGO
## GRADUATE SCHOOL OF BUSINESS

## Academics

"Loyola University—Chicago is the ideal MBA program for students who work full-time and take classes part-time," students report; about four-fifths of the school's MBAs fall into the "part-time student, full-time worker" category. The program suits these students in part because "it is very flexible; [students] can take one to four courses each quarter." The system even suits those without jobs, since it "makes it easy to be full-time in one quarter and in another to easily take an opportunity for a good internship at the same time we are studying," says one such student. LUC operates on a quarterly academic calendar, which "allows students to finish quickly if they load up on classes. This flexibility is often not found in many MBA programs."

Full-timers and part-timers agree that "one of Loyola's main strengths is its value. It offers a Northwestern or University of Chicago education at affordable prices. Many of the professors have their degrees from these other two schools." Students rate the faculty highly, telling us that professors "are all very eager to develop students' skills. I believe they consider the success of a student a personal success. It provides for a better learning environment because the professors are not so focused on their research that they can't spend time discussing their findings with students." Another student adds, "The classes are great; professors are usually up-to-date. We discuss current strategic marketing events or global challenges/opportunities in classes, which is useful and fun! We prepare real-life cases with brand managers from top-notch multinational companies and have great guest speakers in classes who proved themselves to be leaders in their business."

LUC offers specializations in 13 areas, including such unique disciplines as business ethics, derivative markets, and health care management. One marketing student reports that Loyola "is a great place to learn about integrated marketing communications. Real-life cases and great in-class materials and discussions helped me stay in contact with the business atmosphere." Students also praise the school's research in information systems and operations management. They also cite the "great opportunities to study abroad."

LUC's large part-time population is not without its drawbacks. The LUC curriculum "requires a team project in nearly every class, [and] the nature of our student body makes this twice as difficult to schedule because you have to meet with your team outside of class. Most students are simply too busy with work or other commitments." Further complicating the situation is the fact that some students are too busy with work to prepare adequately for every class, thus unfairly increasing the workload of their teammates.

## Career and Placement

Loyola's Business Career Center is dedicated exclusively to School of Business students and alumni; this is usually a strong indicator of a solid career office. Loyola students, however, find much to fault with the BCC. Many complain that "the office is understaffed, so services are limited. Loyola GSB has great alumni, especially in the Chicago area and Midwest, but unfortunately, the BCC does not utilize these connections well." Some detect a recent trend toward improvement; one full-time student writes, "This year has been better than the last year, but still we need more co-op positions that school arranges with companies, like other schools do."

Employers who recently hired Loyola MBA students for internships and full-time jobs

OLIVIA HEATH, ENROLLMENT ADVISOR
1 EAST PEARSON, CHICAGO, IL 60611 UNITED STATES
PHONE: 312-915-6124 • FAX: 312-915-7207
E-MAIL: GSB@LUC.EDU • WEBSITE: WWW.GSB.LUC.EDU

include Abbott Laboratories, Alcoa, Allstate, Bank One, Citigroup, Classified Ventures, Emmaus Ministries, the Federal Reserve Bank of Chicago, Graco Inc., IIT, Johnson & Johnson, Merck, Northern Trust, PricewaterhouseCoopers, Richland Mortgage, and Walgreens.

## Student Life and Environment

LUC's MBA program "is well designed for part-time students. Almost all MBA classes are offered between 6:00 P.M. and 9:00 P.M. downtown at the Water Tower campus." This location "makes it easy for those that work in the city [as well as commuters, as the site] provides easy access for students who travel from the suburbs and other parts of Chicago. There are buses and trains within a few blocks of the school itself."

While many of the part-timers "arrive just in time for class and leave right afterward, [others] get together after classes fairly often. Many [students] go to Flapjaws, the bar across the street, after class. After midterms, a bunch of people got together to go skating to celebrate." LUC offers "plenty of great student-run organizations such as the Loyola Strategic Consulting Group, [and] the school sponsors a number of events, from International Night to Christmas parties. Each of these events allows the students to network to build friendships and potential business contacts."

The "international and cultural diversity [of LUC's student body] brings together an incredibly diverse body of work experience, helping to expand career choices and networks." On the downside, "Loyola has a fairly open admission policy. The school has a lot of good students. However, sometimes a poorer student is admitted. These students fail to contribute as well in classroom discussion and on group projects." Group projects abound, boosting class cohesion. One MBA explains, "The teamwork allows us to get to know each other. We ask about family and share in new babies and weddings and love to head across the street to the pub for beers after class to catch up. We're kind of like an extended family."

## Admissions

According to the GSB Admissions Office, "Applicants are evaluated on the basis of academic GPA, GMAT score, professional work experience, personal statements/essays, letters of recommendation, and their written responses to the questions on our application." Two letters of recommendation from "current or past employers, academic references, or professional colleague," are required. Interviews are not required. Although work experience is not required, nearly all Loyola students—98 percent of them, to be precise—have it; about 80 percent work while attending school part-time. Admissions decisions are made on a rolling basis, usually within 10 days of receiving all application materials.

## FINANCIAL FACTS

| | |
|---|---|
| Annual tuition | $24,408 |
| Fees | $300 |
| Books and supplies | $800 |
| Room & board | |
| (on/off-campus) | $10,000/$12,000 |
| Average grant | $8,016 |

## ADMISSIONS

| | |
|---|---|
| Admissions Selectivity Rating | 75 |
| # of applications received | 755 |
| % applicants accepted | 73 |
| % acceptees attending | 60 |
| Average GMAT | 550 |
| Range of GMAT | 500–620 |
| Average GPA | 3.2 |
| TOEFL required of | |
| international students? | yes |
| Minimum TOEFL | |
| (paper/computer) | 550/213 |
| Application fee | $40 |
| International application fee | $40 |
| Regular application deadline | 8/1 |
| Regular notification | rolling |
| Deferment available? | yes |
| Maximum length | |
| of deferment | 1 year |
| Transfer students accepted? | yes |
| Transfer application policy | |
| Up to 9 hours of B or better course work can transfer from AACSB-accredited institutions. | |
| Non-fall admissions? | yes |
| Need-blind admissions? | yes |

## APPLICANTS ALSO LOOK AT

DePaul University, Illinois Institute of Technology, Northern Illinois University, College of Business, Northwestern University, The University of Chicago, University of Illinois at Chicago, University of Illinois at Urbana-Champaign

## EMPLOYMENT PROFILE

| Career Rating | 71 | Grads employed by field: | % | avg. salary: |
|---|---|---|---|---|
| Primary source of full-time job acceptances | | Accounting | 3 | $54,000 |
| | | Finance | 13 | $70,025 |
| School-facilitated activities | 14 (19%) | Marketing | 10 | $65,000 |
| Graduate-facilitated activities | 47 (65%) | MIS | 1 | $70,000 |
| Unknown | 11 (15%) | Consulting | 1 | $81,000 |
| | | Other | 69 | $61,900 |
| Average starting salary | $56,000 | Nonprofit | 3 | $48,000 |

# LOYOLA UNIVERSITY—NEW ORLEANS
## JOSEPH A. BUTT, S. J., COLLEGE OF BUSINESS ADMINISTRATION

### GENERAL INFORMATION
| | |
|---|---|
| Type of school | private |
| Affiliation | Roman Catholic/Jesuit |
| Environment | metropolis |
| Academic calendar | semester |

### SURVEY SAYS...
Friendly students
Good social scene
Smart classrooms

### STUDENTS
| | |
|---|---|
| Enrollment of parent institution | 5,423 |
| Enrollment of business school | 77 |
| % male/female | 64/36 |
| % out-of-state | 33 |
| % part-time | 50 |
| % minorities | 31 |
| % international | 33 |
| Average age at entry | 26 |
| Average years work experience at entry | 3.5 |

### ACADEMICS
| | |
|---|---|
| **Academic Experience Rating** | **79** |
| Student/faculty ratio | 14:1 |
| Profs interesting rating | 77 |
| Profs accessible rating | 89 |
| % female faculty | 33 |
| % minority faculty | 3 |

### JOINT DEGREES
MBA/JD, 4 years

## Academics

MBA students who crave small classes and tons of personal attention should consider the MBA program at Loyola University—New Orleans. With a combined full-time/part-time student body of under 100, Loyola can offer "small classes of 10 to 20 students, which allows for many class discussions and sharing [and] professors who are always available to interact with students." And because the MBA program piggybacks on a much larger undergraduate program (about 20 percent of Loyola's undergrads major in business disciplines), it can offer a relatively wide range of options along with all these boutique-style amenities.

Of course, like any program, this one has areas of relative strength and weakness. Students are especially enthusiastic about the "very informative classes in operations management, e-commerce, and management and organization, [and love the] emphasis on international business." On the downside, they feel that offerings in finance and marketing could stand to improve. In all areas, the MBA program remains true to its Jesuit tradition by "focusing on critical reasoning, discernment, business ethics, leadership, entrepreneurship, and international business." Students tell us the program does a solid job of developing general business acumen. One student reports, "As the lead revenue coordinator for my current company, I feel the depth and breadth of the Loyola MBA program has further developed the skill sets needed to compete in the current corporate environment."

"Like any school, you have a mix of good and bad professors," at Loyola, although students add that "a large percentage of them are very knowledgeable and actually fun to learn from. There's only a small number that make you ask, 'Why am I here?'" MBAs appreciate the "open-door policy maintained by most professors who are willing to assist students, even if one calls them at their home during weekends, [and are satisfied that] the administrative staff as well as the professors and students know the name of each person in the business school. It is just amazing to be known by your name from everyone! That's the real network you should expect for the future." MBAs agree, Loyola's library "is outstanding from a resource and technology standpoint, [and the business building] has excellent technology. All classrooms and conference rooms are equipped with the latest multimedia technology ([like] wireless LAN connectivity [and] computer labs), and class material is also available through Blackboard."

## Career and Placement

A program as small as Loyola's obviously cannot dedicate a career office exclusively to MBA students. Instead, MBA students receive career guidance from the university's Counseling and Career Center, which, according to the school's website, "offers personal counseling (individual and group) and informational workshops and prevention programs. The center's staff is sensitive to the stresses and concerns of the students. Additionally, staff members provide resume assistance, job fairs, internships, employer research, and job-search support."

JAN MOPPERT, COORDINATOR OF GRADUATE AND EXTERNAL PROGRAMS
6363 ST. CHARLES AVENUE, CAMPUS BOX 15, NEW ORLEANS, LA 70118 UNITED STATES
PHONE: 504-864-7965 • FAX: 504-864-7970
E-MAIL: JAMOPPER@LOYNO.EDU • WEBSITE: CBA.LOYNO.EDU/MBA

## Student Life and Environment

In most programs that convene classes only in the evening, students typically tell us that they spend relatively little time on campus and/or with classmates off campus. Most programs are not in New Orleans, however. Students report that "since it is a night program, students don't just go to class and go home. We usually go out to dinner or to a bar. We really get to know each other on a more personal level." That is, of course, unless you aren't partial to the New Orleans lifestyle. One student observes, "If you like to get drunk, this is the city (and the school) to be in. I don't drink, so the one thing I dislike about it is that all planned off-campus social activities focus on alcohol. I wish there were more activities planned that were family-oriented or just not all about drinking. I have missed out on getting to know some fellow students better because I do not enjoy those environments." The school's location carries another drawback; as one student notes, "Louisiana ranks either last or next-to-last in the U.S. in job growth, opportunities, and most other positive attributes of acceptable living."

MBAs are "a close-knit community and group of friends." One student explains, "Because the MBA program at Loyola is relatively small, I have had the opportunity to interact with most students. As I do my research assistantship at school, I have had the opportunity to interact and develop closer relationships with some faculty and other students." This "noncompetitive, supportive [population includes] many Latinos who bring the Latin culture into every classroom and open global knowledge." The main student group is the MBA Association, which provides leadership opportunities to interested students; it also coordinates community-service projects and schedules special events such as guest speakers from the New Orleans and Louisiana business communities.

## Admissions

Loyola requires the following of applicants to its MBA program: Official transcripts for all past academic work, GMAT scores, two letters of recommendation, a personal statement of purpose, and a resume. International students whose first language is not English must also submit TOEFL scores. The school's website states, "Applicants are in competition with one another initially on the basis of undergraduate grade-point average and professional work experience." Work experience, though not required, is strongly recommended. Interviews are optional.

### FINANCIAL FACTS

| | |
|---|---|
| Annual tuition | $24,800 |
| Fees | $1,056 |
| Books and supplies | $1,500 |
| Room & board | $8,000 |
| Average grant | $5,000 |

### ADMISSIONS

| | |
|---|---|
| **Admissions Selectivity Rating** | **79** |
| # of applications received | 85 |
| % applicants accepted | 59 |
| % acceptees attending | 62 |
| Average GMAT | 545 |
| Average GPA | 3.28 |
| TOEFL required of international students? | yes |
| Minimum TOEFL (paper/computer) | 580/237 |
| Application fee | $50 |
| International application fee | $50 |
| Regular application deadline | 6/15 |
| Regular notification | rolling |
| Deferment available? | yes |
| Maximum length of deferment | 1 academic year |
| Transfer students accepted? | yes |
| Transfer application policy | |

If an applicant comes from an AACSB-accredited program, the foundation work may apply to the Loyola program. Also, a maximum of 6 credit hours may be applied to the advanced level. Only B's or better are accepted.

| | |
|---|---|
| Non-fall admissions? | yes |
| Need-blind admissions? | yes |

### APPLICANTS ALSO LOOK AT

Louisiana State University, Tulane University, University of Lousiana at Lafayette, University of New Orleans

| EMPLOYMENT PROFILE | |
|---|---|
| **Career Rating** | **72** |
| Average starting salary | $52,000 |

# MARIST COLLEGE

## Academics

Many business schools offer students some online options these days, but Marist goes the extra mile; its students can complete their entire degree and barely ever set foot on campus. One student reports, "I am one class away from obtaining my MBA, having taken all required classes online at Marist." Nearly everyone we spoke with at Marist praises the school's "excellent online program, which allows students to go to school anytime, anywhere. Marist is definitely technologically advanced." As one student put it, "The combination of online and classroom-based offerings makes for a very good program that can fit around a wide variety of schedules."

Whether you take courses online, on campus, or pursue both options in combination, Marist serves up a "solidly designed degree that provides a broad-based coverage of business to a student body that has a wide range of backgrounds and levels of managerial experience." This "complete academic experience benefits from the support among faculty members to integrate the different courses to one combined excellent education. Classes are taught by well-established professors who are always available for extra help." Although in the past there has been confusion with the differing duration of classroom and online classes, starting in the Fall of 2006, all classes will last for 15 weeks.

The Marist faculty earn students' accolades. MBAs tell us, "The majority of the professors are solid instructors with real-world experience to help them take theory and convert it into applied tools. They are all generally open to new ideas and are usually happy to talk and interact with the students." Their ranks include "a good mix of full-time professors and professionals who hold high-level positions in organizations. This helps to diversify the education. [It's] a good mix of academia and current professionals." One student points out, "There are several assisting professors who are recent Marist MBA grads, people I knew in courses I took who now are assisting professors in classes I'm taking now. It makes it more intimate, and it shows that those who work hard in the program are recognized by the faculty as being good students who can add to the flavor of the classes by teaching them too."

## Career and Placement

All career services at Marist College are provided by the Center for Career Services. Over 95 percent of Marist's MBAs are full-time professionals; relatively few seek the help of the center. Those who do find that the office maintains resume books; offers resume critiques; holds workshops in interviewing, resume writing, and job seeking; organizes job expos and coordinates joint job-fair ventures with regional and national organizations; and provides access to self-assessment tools such as DISCOVER. Marist has forged a partnership with IBM to "offer students and faculty opportunities to collaborate with these world-renowned leaders in business, history, and ecology."

ANU R. AILAWADHI, DIRECTOR OF GRADUATE ADMISSIONS
3399 NORTH ROAD, POUGHKEEPSIE, NY 12601 UNITED STATES
PHONE: 845-575-3800 • FAX: 845-575-3166
E-MAIL: GRADUATE@MARIST.EDU • WEBSITE: WWW.MARIST.EDU/MANAGEMENT/MBA

## Student Life and Environment

Students tell us that Marist "is primarily an undergraduate institution at this point, and don't really see a need for them to build a culture or 'life' for grad students. Almost none of the grad students live on campus." They also point out that Marist's MBA program "is centered around part-time students who are completing their degrees over a period of several years. Given that, there is not a lot of focus on the grad students in terms of building or catering to a student community. In all fairness, most of the MBA students aren't looking for that from the school, so it is hard to say it is a true weakness. It's more of a factor that might limit the long-term growth of the program." For many, "life at Marist as a grad student is on the Internet, so outside of pure academics, there is no 'life.' The academic environment is great, though."

Those who attend classes on campus tell us, "Our graduate programs offer flexibility for demanding schedules, which is a good thing. While the schedules get hectic with the start of semester, we usually get enough time to do some extracurricular activities if we are so inclined." The school is home to numerous clubs and organizations; the Student Governing Council brings lectures, performing arts, comedy, and musical acts to campus on a regular basis. Marist's athletic teams, the Red Foxes, compete in the Metro Atlantic Athletic Conference. In 2004, the women's basketball team earned its first-ever trip to the NCAA Tournament by winning its conference.

Marist is located in the city of Poughkeepsie, New York, about a 90-minute drive from both New York City and Albany. It's a small city of 30,000 that covers just under five square miles, but it packs a lot into a little space, including a dozen parks, a public boat launch, an 18-hole golf course, and numerous other recreational facilities. The city is also home to the Bardavon 1869 Opera House, which frequently hosts touring productions of Broadway shows. Top employers in Poughkeepsie include IBM, Vassar Brothers Hospital, the county government, the Department of Transportation, Central Hudson Gas and Electric, and various local schools.

## Admissions

Applicants to Marist's conventional and online programs follow the same procedure. All must provide the college with official copies of undergraduate and graduate transcripts, GMAT scores, a resume, a response to essay questions, and letters of recommendation. The school welcomes all students, even those without undergraduate experience in business. Students lacking the requisite academic background must complete seven foundation courses prior to commencing work on the MBA. Students may place out of one or more of these courses through testing.

### FINANCIAL FACTS
| | |
|---|---|
| Annual tuition | $10,800 |
| Fees | $60 |
| Books and supplies | $1,298 |
| % of students receiving aid | 23 |
| % of first-year students receiving aid | 33 |
| % of students receiving loans | 21 |
| % of students receiving grants | 15 |
| Average award package | $13,139 |
| Average grant | $1,438 |

### ADMISSIONS
| | |
|---|---|
| Admissions Selectivity Rating | 65 |
| # of applications received | 83 |
| % applicants accepted | 93 |
| % acceptees attending | 60 |
| Average GMAT | 515 |
| Range of GMAT | 430–550 |
| Average GPA | 3.2 |
| TOEFL required of international students? | yes |
| Minimum TOEFL (paper/computer) | 560/220 |
| Application fee | $50 |
| International application fee | $50 |
| Regular application deadline | 8/1 |
| Regular notification | 8/15 |
| Deferment available? | yes |
| Maximum length of deferment | 1 year |
| Transfer students accepted? | yes |
| Transfer application policy | No more than 6 credit hours of core courses accepted from AACSB-accredited programs. |
| Non-fall admissions? | yes |
| Need-blind admissions? | yes |

### APPLICANTS ALSO LOOK AT
Fairfield University, Pace University, University of Connecticut

### EMPLOYMENT PROFILE
| Career Rating | 78 | Grads employed by field: | % | avg. salary: |
|---|---|---|---|---|
| Average starting salary | $65,000 | General Management | 92 | $65,000 |
| Percent employed | 92 | | | |

# MARQUETTE UNIVERSITY
## COLLEGE OF BUSINESS ADMINISTRATION

## Academics

A strong reputation like "the best business school in the area," a "superior faculty," and "a strong international focus in the curriculum" all appeal to the MBA students at Marquette University's College of Business Administration, a nationally known Jesuit-run school in Milwaukee. Marquette belongs to the Network of MBA Programs at Jesuit Colleges and Universities. This means all credits here transfer to any other participating Jesuit MBA program, a significant convenience in today's fluid employment environment. Jesuit sponsorship also ensures a strong curricular focus on ethics.

Marquette offers a part-time and full-time MBA, an Executive MBA, and MS degrees in accounting, applied economics, engineering management, and human resources. The MBA is offered in three locations: Downtown, Waukesha, and Kohler. Programs operate on a semester calendar, which makes for a demanding academic load. But part-time students here—who constitute the majority of the student body—report, "Professors understand the challenges that a working professional faces when going back to school. They are friendly and supportive and really help the transition back into school." Similarly, the administration "offers an impressive level of assistance. They know that most of us have busy lives so they make registering for class simple. If there is a problem, you call and it is taken care of. And they know your name, which is remarkable for a school our size."

MBAs at Marquette may specialize in e-business, economics, finance, human resources, international business, management information systems, marketing, or total quality management. Offerings are especially broad in human resources. Across the curriculum, students commend Marquette professors for "keeping up with new technological trends." MBAs also appreciate "Marquette's focus on teaching. You can tell that, for the most part, professors are here because they like to teach. They like students, people, and helping out. They want to challenge you and make sure that you've learned something along the way. It's a nice balance." Instructors also incorporate "a good balance of text, case work, and projects" to give students a wide range of learning experiences.

## Career and Placement

The Career Services Center at Marquette provides counseling and placement services to all undergraduates and graduate students at the university. The office organizes workshops, one-on-one counseling sessions, on-site recruiting events, and job databases. In addition, the College of Business offers career-management services. Students are happy to report that the MBA program provides "a number of opportunities to interview with the Big Four firms as well as a number of local and regional firms," and also praise the "strong alumni and business connections in Milwaukee/southern Wisconsin."

## Student Life and Environment

Most MBA students at Marquette are part-time students with full-time jobs. They generally "go to class and go home. That's it." One MBA explains, "I feel about as connected to Marquette as one does to, say, a parking garage at work: You're there all the time and it's very useful, but you wouldn't notice any difference if you had to park somewhere else one day, and you wouldn't miss it." There are also about 90 full-time students here, however, who involve themselves in the life of the university. One reports, "Marquette offers about 80 clubs and organizations—everything from athletics to cultural groups to arts to academic organizations and honor societies. Athletics (especially basketball) is strongly supported. In addition, the College of Business/MBA program hosts events. There is a strong sense of identity and belonging to a great, dynamic group." The program "tries to include the family when possible," which students appreciate.

Dr. Jeanne Simmons, Assistant Dean
PO Box 1881, Milwaukee, WI 53201-1881 United States
Phone: 414-288-7145 • Fax: 414-288-1660
E-mail: mba@marquette.edu • Website: www.marquette.edu/business

Students at Marquette see Milwaukee as another asset, one that provides "many activities, connections, and opportunities that come from being near a large city." Some worry about safety on the downtown campus, although others report that "the campus is becoming more enclosed," reducing safety issues. Chicago is less than a two-hour drive to the south.

Marquette's student body consists "mostly of career people who are working toward their MBA part-time. They are friendly and enthusiastic, are good in group work situations, [and] provide a collegial attitude to the program." Because "they come from many different large corporations in the Milwaukee area," they offer "good insight into the economic environment of Milwaukee." Some, though, "are not from business backgrounds. They come from engineering, health care, public service, or not-for-profits. The problem with this mix is that these students do not have the ability to offer many strategic business insights because they are just learning the concepts." For many at this Jesuit institution, "spiritual life takes a priority, which is a healthy change from state institutions."

## Admissions

Applicants to the Marquette MBA program must provide the Admissions Office official transcripts for all previous post-secondary academic work, an official GMAT score report, a personal essay, and a resume. International students are additionally required to submit three letters of recommendation and an official score report for the TOEFL or another acceptable English proficiency exam. Marquette encourages applicants to apply for full admission but also offers a temporary-admission option for noninternational applicants, good for one semester only. Students applying to campuses other than the downtown campus must remember to specify their campus of choice on their application.

### FINANCIAL FACTS

| | |
|---|---|
| Annual tuition | $12,600 |
| Books and supplies | $750 |

### ADMISSIONS

| | |
|---|---|
| **Admissions Selectivity Rating** | **77** |
| # of applications received | 249 |
| % applicants accepted | 81 |
| % acceptees attending | 80 |
| Average GMAT | 575 |
| Average GPA | 3.24 |
| TOEFL required of international students? | yes |
| Minimum TOEFL (paper/computer) | 550/NR |
| Application fee | $40 |
| International application fee | $40 |
| Regular application deadline | rolling |
| Regular notification | rolling |
| Deferment available? | yes |
| Maximum length of deferment | usually one year |
| Transfer students accepted? | yes |
| Transfer application policy | We accept transfers from other Jesuit Schools (JEBNET agreement—see www.JEBNET.org). We will also accept up to 6 approved credits from AACSB-accredited schools. |
| Non-fall admissions? | yes |

### APPLICANTS ALSO LOOK AT

Loyola University—Chicago, University of Wisconsin, University of Wisconsin—Milwaukee

# MASSACHUSETTS INSTITUTE OF TECHNOLOGY
## SLOAN SCHOOL OF MANAGEMENT

## Academics

Students tell us that MIT Sloan "is the very best school for innovation in business," pointing to "the absolute best operations research people in the world;" the fact that "today's leaders in finance and economics were all either educated at Sloan or teach here;" and the university's role as one of the nation's leading engineering, tech, and science research centers. They also cite the Sloan Innovation Period, a week wedged in the middle of each semester during which "students learn from faculty about their current research interests."

Sloan's quant-intensive, two-year, full-time program commences with a rigorous core that involves a large measure of "friendly, team-based learning" as well as "a combination of videos, cases, group exercises, etc. The classes are extremely engaging, and I expect to retain a lot more due to the variation in styles of learning," says one student. Requirements can largely be dispensed with during the first semester here, after which "the design of students' MIT Sloan education is mostly in their own hands, provided they acquire appropriate credits in leadership, research, and practice," according to the school's website.

Students speak highly of MIT's Entrepreneurial Program, noting that it benefits greatly from the research taking place throughout the university. One writes, "Sloan students visit various MIT labs, assessing the marketability of technology projects. They also write business plans and help start-up ventures emerging from MIT's labs, and are heavily involved in supporting new businesses—both locally and globally—through the entrepreneurial department." Another adds, "The environment is very entrepreneurial and with the opportunities students have to take initiative to shape the extracurricular and academic life here, Sloan is a fantastic place to develop your leadership skills."

Other special programs singled out for praise include the Leaders for Manufacturing Program: "The best of its kind, it tailors the MBA experience toward people interested in working for a manufacturing company in the future." Another is the MIT Sloan Fellows Program in Innovation and Global Leadership, "clearly the best program for a mid-career executive due to the intensity of the one-year program." The Cambridge address means "students have many opportunities to network with the school and beyond by cross-registering with other MIT schools or Harvard."

## Career and Placement

Sloan's Career Development Office provides MBAs with a range of career management resources, including seminars, self-assessment tools, library materials, and online databases. The CDO hosts on-campus recruiting events throughout the school year to much success. The school reports that approximately 60 percent of students seeking a career change achieve their goal through such events, with the remainder finding new jobs through alumni connections, faculty recommendations, job postings, and other similar methods. Students tell us that the CDO is supportive but could stand to improve in some areas; "Career placement services are nonexistent for special programs, like the Biomedical Enterprise Program," writes one student. To make up for it, the "supportive nature of the student body" means "people try to use their network to help other students find jobs."

Employers most likely to hire Sloan MBAs include McKinsey and Co., Merrill Lynch, Boston Consulting Group, Citigroup, Bain and Company, IBM Corporation, Lehman Brothers, Unilever, Goldman Sachs, and United Technologies Corporation.

## Student Life and Environment

"The tough part of MIT Sloan is balancing your time to take advantage of all that the school and community offer," students tell us. This is especially true during the first semester core, which students describe as "intense." One first-semester MBA writes,

Rod Garcia, Admissions Director
50 Memorial Drive, E52-118, Cambridge, MA 02139 United States
Phone: 617-258-5434 • Fax: 617-253-6405
E-mail: mbaadmissions@sloan.mit.edu • Website: mitsloan.mit.edu

"People work real hard, and at the same time, companies are coming to campus and there are a lot of clubs. This semester is an exercise in prioritization and balancing tasks." One confesses, "There is so much work that you have to make choices as to which review sessions you can attend." Fortunately, "although there is a lot of work, very little of it is useless or busy work." The MBA continues, "When it's all over, I'll be very happy that I was made to do this much at the beginning of my busines-school experience." Students tell us that "after first semester, the pressure is off and life consists of an even mix of schoolwork, socializing, career exploration, and personal time."

MIT offers "a plethora of social activity options. A large portion of students play in various intramural sports, [and] there are actually routine options for each weeknight: 'Muddy Mondays' at the on-campus pub, 'Thirst Quenchers' moves the happy hour location each Tuesday, each Wednesday Sloan students gather at the BHP (Beacon Hill Pub), and have 'Consumption Functions' each Thursday night." Clubs "are all student-driven, and there are quite a number of them." There are also "lots of trips, both school-sponsored (company networking) and among the students." One student sums up, "I end every night complaining to myself, 'Why does the day have only 24 hours?' The amount of activities, projects, presentations, and friendships are so abundant and high quality that I'd love if the days were much longer."

Sloan MIT students are "very diverse and extremely impressive with respect to what they did before business school. Many were entrepreneurs who had their own companies." One writes, "What really impresses me is how humble they are. Though most have made remarkable and sometimes extraordinary accomplishments, they rarely speak of them." Although "students are, by nature, competitive and put a lot of effort into winning intramural athletic events, [they are] very collaborative and helpful" in the classroom. "Teams work together to learn yet complete work efficiently, leaving time for the other opportunities in graduate school," explains one Sloan MBA.

## Admissions

Completed applications to the Sloan MBA program include two letters of recommendation, post-secondary transcripts (self-reported prior to interview; if called for an interview, applicants must provide official transcripts), a resume, four personal essays, supplemental information (hobbies, interests, leadership experience), and GMAT scores. The school requires additional materials from applicants to the Leaders for Manufacturing Program and the Biomedical Enterprise Program. Sloan is extremely competitive; the school's website points out that "nearly all the applicants to the MIT Sloan School of Management have noteworthy academic records, competitive GMAT scores, and an average of five-plus years of professional experience." The nature of the program favors candidates with strong quantitative and analytical skills, as well as those with well-demonstrated leadership potential and a clear vision of their career goals.

### FINANCIAL FACTS

| | |
|---|---|
| Annual tuition | $39,844 |
| Fees | $200 |
| Books and supplies | $4,000 |
| Room & board | $27,190 |
| % of students receiving aid | 75 |
| % of first-year students receiving aid | 69 |
| % of students receiving loans | 70 |
| % of students receiving grants | 22 |
| Average award package | $51,126 |
| Average grant | $17,588 |
| Average student loan debt | $56,389 |

### ADMISSIONS

| | |
|---|---|
| Admissions Selectivity Rating | 98 |
| # of applications received | 2,622 |
| % applicants accepted | 22 |
| % acceptees attending | 65 |
| Average GMAT | 710 |
| Range of GMAT | 610–740 |
| Average GPA | 3.5 |
| Minimum TOEFL (paper/computer) | 600/NR |
| Application fee | $230 |
| International application fee | $230 |
| Regular application deadline | 11/2 |
| Regular notification | 1/31 |
| Application deadline/notification | |
| Round 1: | 11/2 / 1/31 |
| Round 2: | 1/11 / 4/3 |
| Need-blind admissions? | yes |

### EMPLOYMENT PROFILE

| Career Rating | 96 | Grads employed by field: | % | avg. salary: |
|---|---|---|---|---|
| Average starting salary | $88,217 | Finance | 30 | $86,170 |
| | | Marketing | 11 | $85,095 |
| | | MIS | 2 | $90,250 |
| | | Operations | 10 | $86,736 |
| | | Consulting | 25 | $91,085 |
| | | General Management | 14 | $91,844 |
| | | Other | 8 | $86,417 |

# MERCER UNIVERSITY—ATLANTA
## EUGENE W. STETSON SCHOOL OF BUSINESS AND ECONOMICS

## GENERAL INFORMATION
| | |
|---|---|
| Type of school | private |
| Affiliation | Baptist |
| Academic calendar | 2–8 wk./sem. |

### SURVEY SAYS...
Students love Atlanta, GA
Friendly students
Good peer network
Cutting-edge classes
Happy students
Smart classrooms

### STUDENTS
| | |
|---|---|
| Enrollment of parent institution | 7,188 |
| Enrollment of business school | 329 |
| % male/female | 54/46 |
| % out-of-state | 8 |
| % part-time | 44 |
| % minorities | 38 |
| % international | 12 |
| Average age at entry | 30 |
| Average years work experience at entry | 6 |

### ACADEMICS
| | |
|---|---|
| **Academic Experience Rating** | **79** |
| Student/faculty ratio | 20:1 |
| Profs interesting rating | 82 |
| Profs accessible rating | 70 |
| % female faculty | 38 |
| % minority faculty | 19 |

### JOINT DEGREES
MBA/PharmD, 4 years; MBA/MDiv, 3 years

### PROMINENT ALUMNI
Karen Romaine Thomas, VP, CFO, Schwan's Bakery, Inc.; John F. Hough, DrPH, MPH, MBA, Health Scientist Administrator, NIH; William Astary, Sr. Vice Pres. of Sales, Acuity Brand Lighting; Paul Gianneschi, Managing Prin. & Founder, Hatch Medical, LLC; Joann Herold, VP Marketing, Honey Baked Ham Company

## Academics

Designed for the convenience of its predominantly professional student body, Mercer University in Atlanta offers a number of accommodations to suit busy MBAs. Classes here meet only once a week, on weekday evenings or on Saturday. Eight-week sessions help students proceed through the program at a steady pace, while five separate admissions entry points mean students can begin the program at virtually any time of the year. As the school's website asserts, "The program is tailored to meet the needs of individuals already employed as managers," as well as those "preparing for advancement into middle-management and administrative levels."

Mercer is a Baptist university with its main campus an hour south of Atlanta, in Macon, Georgia, and a graduate and professional campus in Atlanta. The school draws on its roots to provide a program that "focuses on ethical leadership and problem-solving skills" in order to give students a "competitive edge" in today's business world. This goal is further achieved through "the establishment of a real-world experience base by maintaining continuous interaction with community organizations, profit and non-profit, through seminars and special programs for practicing managers and administrators." The school's location in a major metropolis is a great asset in achieving this goal.

The heart of the Mercer MBA in Atlanta is a core curriculum covering managerial economics, managerial accounting, marketing, management information systems, corporation finance, operations management science, and ethics. A concluding simulation student seminar and electives are also part of the program. Prior to beginning core coursework, incoming Mercer students may be required to complete a sequence of four non-graduate-level foundation courses covering micro- and macro-economics, accounting and finance, management and marketing, and business law. Equivalent courses previously completed at the undergraduate level may allow students to place out of these requirements.

Mercer MBAs appreciate their "professional" and "personable" professors who are "helpful outside the class, open to feedback, [and] truly care that the students are learning." One respondent exclaims, "They push you!" Students also love "the timeliness of the program" and the "state-of-the-art equipment in the lecture rooms," but wish that "more class options were available throughout the school year."

## Career and Placement

The Office of Career Services at Mercer "provides support to students and alumni in the areas of decision-making and networking," according to the school catalog, which also notes that "students and alumni can view and be informed of ongoing full-time, part-time, and internship opportunities by registering online with SUCCESSTRAK. Annual career days, an academic majors fair, a senior kick-off event, and presentations on resume design and other job-search topics" are all offered here. Students here tell us that "recruiting and corporate partnerships" all could use improvement.

KAREN M. GOSS, ASSISTANT VICE PRESIDENT FOR ADMISSIONS
MERCER UNIVERSITY, 3001 MERCER UNIVERSITY DRIVE, ATLANTA, GA 30341-4155 UNITED STATES
PHONE: 678-547-6417 • FAX: 678-547-6367
E-MAIL: ATLBUSADM@MERCER.EDU • WEBSITE: WWW.MERCER.EDU/BUSINESS

## Student Life and Environment

Mercer's Atlanta campus is "primarily a commuter campus" where classes "are held in the evenings to accommodate working individuals." Although most students spend very little time on campus, a few would like to see a stronger MBA community and call for "more graduate associations, especially for minorities and women."

Mercer MBAs are "mostly full-time workers in the professional world" who "generally have substantial real-world experiences to contribute." This mélange of professionals makes for "good networking because there's lots of different people in different fields." Students also appreciate the "diverse mix of cultural ethnicities" drawn to Mercer's Atlanta campus.

Hometown Atlanta is one of the great cities of the Southeast, a corporate and cultural mecca that is home to Coca-Cola, Home Depot, Delta, and a slew of other business giants. The city is awash in restaurants, clubs, live music venues, theaters, culture of every shape and form, and great professional athletics. Top that off with the fact that the weather's fantastic.

## Admissions

Applicants to the Stetson MBA program at Mercer must provide the school with a completed application form, two sets of official transcripts from each post-secondary academic institution attended, a resume, and an official GMAT score report showing test results no more than five years old. In addition, international applicants whose first language is not English must demonstrate English proficiency through TOEFL scores. All students who received undergraduate degrees abroad must, at their own expense, provide an independent evaluation (and, where appropriate, a translation) of their undergraduate records. International students must additionally demonstrate the ability to finance their education at Mercer.

### FINANCIAL FACTS

| | |
|---|---|
| Annual tuition | $12,900 |
| Books and supplies | $1,000 |
| Room & board | $9,450 |
| % of students receiving aid | 60 |
| % of first-year students receiving aid | 60 |
| % of students receiving loans | 60 |
| % of students receiving grants | 1 |
| Average award package | $12,666 |
| Average grant | $1,140 |
| Average student loan debt | $20,000 |

### ADMISSIONS

| | |
|---|---|
| Admissions Selectivity Rating | 81 |
| # of applications received | 193 |
| % applicants accepted | 38 |
| % acceptees attending | 81 |
| Average GMAT | 503 |
| Range of GMAT | 450–610 |
| Average GPA | 3 |
| TOEFL required of international students? | yes |
| Minimum TOEFL (paper/computer) | 550/213 |
| Application fee | $50 |
| International application fee | $100 |
| Regular application deadline | 8/1 |
| Regular notification | rolling |
| Deferment available? | yes |
| Maximum length of deferment | 5 years past GMAT |
| Transfer students accepted? | yes |
| Transfer application policy Will consider up to 2 courses (6 semester hours) in transfer within past five years. | |
| Non-fall admissions? | yes |
| Need-blind admissions? | yes |

### APPLICANTS ALSO LOOK AT

Georgia State University, Kennesaw State University, University of Georgia

### EMPLOYMENT PROFILE

| Career Rating | 81 | Grads employed by field: | % | avg. salary: |
|---|---|---|---|---|
| Average starting salary | $73,100 | Accounting | 10 | $59,908 |
| Percent employed | 86 | Finance | 11 | $69,000 |
| | | Human Resources | 2 | $83,000 |
| | | Marketing | 21 | $79,781 |
| | | MIS | 5 | $76,833 |
| | | Operations | 12 | $80,281 |
| | | Consulting | 2 | $112,000 |
| | | General Management | 10 | $69,528 |
| | | Other | 27 | $69,953 |

# MERCER UNIVERSITY—MACON
## EUGENE W. STETSON SCHOOL OF BUSINESS AND ECONOMICS

### GENERAL INFORMATION
| | |
|---|---|
| Type of school | private |
| Affiliation | Baptist |

### SURVEY SAYS...
Friendly students
Happy students
Smart classrooms
*Solid preparation in:*
Finance

### STUDENTS
| | |
|---|---|
| Enrollment of parent institution | 51 |
| Enrollment of business school | 51 |
| % part-time | 100 |
| Average age at entry | 28 |
| Average years work experience at entry | 10 |

### ACADEMICS
| | |
|---|---|
| **Academic Experience Rating** | **63** |
| Student/faculty ratio | 20:1 |
| Profs interesting rating | 71 |
| Profs accessible rating | 68 |
| % female faculty | 33 |
| % minority faculty | 15 |

### JOINT DEGREES
JD/MBA, 4 years

## Academics

Baptist-affiliated Mercer University provides its MBAs a program that "focuses on ethical leadership and problem-solving skills" in order to give students a "competitive edge" in today's business world. Nearly all the students in this program attend part-time while working full-time. According to the school, "The program is tailored to meet the needs of individuals already employed as managers," as well as those "preparing for advancement into middle-management and administrative levels."

Incoming Mercer students should have at least 18 hours of undergraduate work in business with a grade of C or better; those lacking these credentials will need to complete an additional nine hours of graduate electives. All students must demonstrate mastery in statistics, microeconomics, and principles of finance, either through examination or successfully completed undergraduate work. Students lacking these credentials are required to take the appropriate foundation classes before beginning work on their MBA.

The heart of the Mercer MBA is a 12-course core curriculum covering financial reporting, operations management, applied microeconomic analysis, global macroeconomic environment, management and business law, corporate finance, accounting, leadership, and ethics. A seminar in strategic management, an integrative capstone class, and electives (available in accounting, economics, general business, management, MIS, and marketing) are also part of the program.

Students praise the MBA program for providing "lots of individual attention," an outcome of the school's choice to "keep class sizes small." The "solid faculty make themselves available," which is helpful since "some of the course work is hard for people who work full-time to get done." A surprising number of students here warn that class times are too often inconvenient for full-time workers, and some suggest class time could be used more wisely ("Lectures are too long!" says one). They also point out that "it would be nice to have a wider selection of classes," although they recognize that "at so small a school, it would be hard to offer more without increasing costs."

## Career and Placement

The Office of Career Services at Mercer "provides support to students and alumni in the areas of decision-making and networking," according to the school catalog, which also notes that "students and alumni can view and be informed of ongoing full-time, part-time, and internship opportunities by registering on-line with SUCCESSTRAK. Annual career days, an academic majors fair, a senior kick-off event, and presentations on resume design and other job-search topics" are all offered here. Students in the MBA program would like to see the services improved.

ROBERT HOLLAND, DIRECTOR OF UNDERGRADUATE ADMINISTRATION
STETSON SCHOOL OF BUSINESS AND ECONOMICS, MERCER UNIVERSITY, MACON, GA 31207 U.S.
PHONE: 478-301-2835 • FAX: 478-301-2635
E-MAIL: HOLLAND_R@MERCER.EDU • WEBSITE: WWW.MERCER.EDU

| FINANCIAL FACTS | |
| --- | --- |
| Annual tuition | $17,000 |
| Fees | $483 |
| Books and supplies | $2,000 |
| Room & board | $7,000 |

| ADMISSIONS | |
| --- | --- |
| **Admissions Selectivity Rating** | **68** |
| # of applications received | 15 |
| % applicants accepted | 100 |
| % acceptees attending | 100 |
| Average GMAT | 520 |
| Range of GMAT | 450–600 |
| Average GPA | 3.5 |
| TOEFL required of international students? | yes |
| Minimum TOEFL (paper/computer) | 550/213 |
| Application fee | $50 |
| International application fee | $50 |
| Regular application deadline | rolling |
| Regular notification | rolling |
| Non-fall admissions? | yes |
| Need-blind admissions? | yes |

## Student Life and Environment

"Most people in the MBA program work," so "there is limited outside contact" among Mercer MBAs, "but everyone is very close in class." The pace of life here is always a little frantic because most students are juggling full-time jobs and school obligations, but "it is especially frantic around finals and midterms, in part due to the number of classes each professor teaches."

Mercer students include "a mix of people from off campus who have full-time jobs and graduate assistants, as well as other Mercer employees." They "contribute a vast array of experience that enriches the program," students tell us. The school's Baptist affiliation tends to help the school attract minorities.

Hometown Macon, a city of about 125,000, is home to three other colleges and universities, making it a serious college town. The city offers all the typical school-town prerequisites, including clubs, bowling alleys, bars, cheap eats, and plenty of shopping. Medicine is big business here, as is education; insurance is another major player, as both GEICO and the Georgia Farm Bureau Federation maintain major operations in Macon.

## Admissions

Applicants to the Stetson MBA program at Mercer must provide the school with a completed application form, two sets of official transcripts from each post-secondary academic institution attended, a resume, and an official GMAT score report showing test results no more than five years old. In addition, international applicants whose first language is not English must demonstrate English proficiency both through TOEFL scores and, upon arrival at the school, a test administered by the English Language Institute of Mercer University. All students who received undergraduate degrees abroad must, at their own expense, provide an independent evaluation (and, where appropriate, a translation) of their undergraduate records. International students must additionally demonstrate the ability to finance their education at Mercer.

# MIAMI UNIVERSITY OHIO
## RICHARD T. FARMER SCHOOL OF BUSINESS

## Academics

The Richard T. Farmer School of Business at Miami University has completely revamped its MBA program over the last few years, and it finally rolled out its new-and-improved program for the 2005–2006 academic year. The new Farmer MBA is an accelerated 14-month full-time-only program (the school will introduce its new part-time program in 2006–2007) that emphasizes practical experience: All participants complete a nine-month extended internship and a capstone international field study. Early reviews are extremely positive. In one student's opinion, "This has to be one of the most progressive and relevant program designs available."

Miami's MBA program kicks off with a four-month "Summer Boot Camp," an intensive survey of graduate-level material in accounting, economics, information systems, marketing, organizational behavior, and statistics. Boot Camp lays the groundwork for the "highly integrated" classes of the Fall and Spring semesters. Fall semester focuses on internal enterprise by "investigating processes and functions within the business itself," according to the school's website. External enterprise, "those relationships or factors which affect the business but which are not found within the company itself, such as supply-chain management, vendor partnerships, and capital acquisition," is the focus of Spring classes. Throughout both semesters, students participate in an extended internship that sends them off-campus one day per week.

Students here brag that "our administration is of the highest quality—comprised of seasoned businesspeople who understand what the market's needs are for skills and qualities of tomorrow's MBA." They also appreciate the fact that "the program utilizes a group of consulting business partners (some of the most seasoned and recognized business leaders in their fields) who advise on the program design and career opportunities for its students. The program offers a unique opportunity for all of its students to mentor under these respectable business leaders, where a rapport can be built and subsequent networks can be expanded." Instructors also earn high praise for "always being willing to help. They are enthusiastic and passionate about their subjects, whether customer acquisition or strategy or new product development and integration."

## Career and Placement

Miami's Office of Career Services "does an exceptional job bringing a diverse group of *Fortune* 500 companies in for recruiting," students report, observing that "the setup of the interviewing schedule allows each student a fair opportunity to interview for any position with any company on campus, but also requires responsibility, research, and awareness on the student's part." The office provides a number of other standard career-placement services, but students tell us that their careers receive their greatest push from the internships and mentoring relationships incorporated into the MBA program itself. One writes, "The exposure to top executives (Jeff Immelt, Brad Alford, John Faraci), the Mentorship program, and the integrated internship—it's all great. No other school places you with a Fortune 25 company for a whole year, but that's what this school did for me."

JUDY BARILLE, MBA DIRECTOR
LAWS HALL, OXFORD, OH 45056 UNITED STATES
PHONE: 513-529-6643 • FAX: 513-529-2487
E-MAIL: MIAMIMBA@MUOHIO.EDU • WEBSITE: WWW.MBA.MUOHIO.EDU

## Student Life and Environment

Miami has upgraded its MBA program in recent years. It hasn't upgraded its facility yet, but it is in the process of doing just that. The school breaks ground on the $30 million Farmer Hall in the summer of 2006 and expects to have the new business center open for the Fall semester of 2008.

Students love the Miami campus, which one describes as "among the nicest I've seen." Hometown Oxford "is pretty nice. It is a college town so something is always going on, but the town is still very laid-back and residents are quite friendly. The atmosphere is light, young, vibrant, and active." The city is "also only 45 minutes away from Cincinnati, and with so many people commuting, the city is very accessible."

The Miami MBA student body "seems to be split. Half are very involved in the program, half are here to get their degree." Regardless of their level of commitment, everyone here "grows really close because of the small size of the class. We get along very well and know what to expect from one another."

## Admissions

Admission to the MBA program at Miami University requires a minimum undergraduate GPA of 2.75, with a minimum GPA of 3.00 for the final two full years (i.e., four semesters) of undergraduate study; applicants must provide two official transcripts of all postsecondary academic work. GMAT scores are also required. Miami admissions officers also consider work experience (a minimum of three years post-undergraduate professional experience is typically required) and personal qualities as reflected in the essays, two letters of recommendation, and an interview. International students must meet all of the above requirements and must, in addition, demonstrate English competency through the TOEFL and the Test of Written English (TWE). Transcripts in languages other than English must be translated and must bear the official seal of the issuing institution.

### FINANCIAL FACTS

| | |
|---|---|
| Annual tuition (in-state/out-of-state) | $15,755/$34,050 |
| Fees | $1,382 |
| Books and supplies | $1,000 |
| Room & board | $6,000 |
| % of students receiving aid | 25 |
| % of first-year students receiving aid | 80 |
| Average grant | $2,000 |

### ADMISSIONS

| | |
|---|---|
| Admissions Selectivity Rating | 86 |
| # of applications received | 102 |
| % applicants accepted | 41 |
| % acceptees attending | 74 |
| Average GMAT | 552 |
| Range of GMAT | 520–580 |
| Average GPA | 3.2 |
| TOEFL required of international students? | yes |
| Minimum TOEFL (paper/computer) | 550/220 |
| Application fee | $35 |
| International application fee | $35 |
| Regular application deadline | 2/1 |
| Regular notification | rolling |
| Deferment available? | yes |
| Maximum length of deferment | 2 years |
| Non-fall admissions? | yes |

### APPLICANTS ALSO LOOK AT

Bowling Green State University, Indiana University—Bloomington, The Ohio State University, University of Cincinnati, University of Dayton

### EMPLOYMENT PROFILE

| Career Rating | 85 | Grads employed by field: | % | avg. salary: |
|---|---|---|---|---|
| Average starting salary | $55,167 | Finance | 42 | $45,000 |
| | | Marketing | 42 | $61,670 |
| | | MIS | 16 | $52,333 |

# MICHIGAN STATE UNIVERSITY
## ELI BROAD GRADUATE SCHOOL OF MANAGEMENT

## Academics

At the Broad School, which rhymes with "road," students can expect a collaborative, well-structured environment and one of the top supply-chain management programs in the country. Students praise their fellow MBAs as "friendly and cooperative." Students add, "Our professors work with us outside of class on job searching and with case competitions as advisors."

All first-year students are required to complete the same program of core courses. Students are divided into cohorts—groups of no more than 40—and follow the same class schedule during their first semester. Cohorts switch around and re-form in the second semester to ensure that all students get a chance to work with one another and gain additional perspectives. Students enjoy working with their classmates within this system. Many students agree, "The teamwork dynamic is very good. We even have a class dedicated to it in the first five weeks of our first semester." With this focus in mind, students say that professors do "a great job helping the students realize how important it is to work well together, figure out what to do when things go south, and how to persevere and overcome difficulties working with other people."

In the first year, students build a foundation with core business courses and courses in their selected concentrations (finance, human resource management, marketing, or supply-chain management). Students also can take a second concentration in one of the other three primary areas, or select from one of the secondary concentrations. In the second year, students have flexibility as they take only two required courses (strategy and ethics) with the rest consisting of their concentration electives. Students feel that Broad has "a definite presence in supply-chain management." One student says, "In this field, I find the material and professors to be top-tier and highly respected. Most [professors] teach from their own textbooks or teaching modules." All students are required to take at least one class with an international perspective along with one noncredit seminar in professional development. Many students also manage to create a customized course of study in topics like business information systems, corporate accounting, international business, and leadership and change management.

There are two joint-degree options: international business and JD/MBA. The international business degree is acquired through cooperation with Thunderbird—the American Graduate School of International Management in Glendale, Arizona. Students enrolled in this joint-degree program receive the master's of international management from Thunderbird and the master of business administration from Michigan State University. Students say that because international management isn't a strength of their school, "the dual-degree relationship with Thunderbird is a plus." The JD/MBA is offered in conjunction with MSU's College of Law.

Many students believe that "availability of courses" is a problem, especially outside of the supply-chain management program. They would also like to see more electives added to the curriculum. However, most students feel that overall "the growth potential of the school is great. We already have a great supply-chain program, are building up the finance program, and our HR folks always land great jobs."

## Career and Placement

Broad's total alumni network is currently about 70,000, and their careers are varied—a helpful factor for any job seeker. Alumni live and work in all 50 states and 88 other countries besides the United States. One student says, "Networking is a large part of school here at MSU. The contacts I have made so far will greatly aid in finding the position I want when I graduate."

For the most part, the efforts of the Career Services Center are appreciated, but some students feel they cater too much to the school's acknowledged strength—supply-chain management. One student complains, "As for the students who are interested in entrepreneurship, forget it! The MBA Career Services Center doesn't even acknowledge that they exist." Another student says that though the office of Career Services tries, "most of my job hunting has been self-directed."

## Student Life and Environment

Charming East Lansing surrounds Michigan State University and offers all of the amenities of a good college town. It is filled with bookstores, coffeehouses, cinemas, and hosts annual art and music fairs. A river winds through campus, and the school boasts about a major performing arts center and two museums. Detroit is only a 90-minute drive away, and Chicago and Toronto are both within a five-hour drive. The cost of living is relatively low, and students enjoy the town's laid-back atmosphere.

According to students, the university is not lacking in social opportunities. As one student says, "Whether it's coffee in the MBA lounge, a social hour at a local restaurant/bar, an alumni reception, a tailgate, [or] whatever, there is always something going on." Broad, like most good business schools, understands that the contacts students make in school can be the most important contacts of their careers and the school has a very strong MBA Association that organizes social activities for students. One student explains, "[The coordinators] send out weekly e-mails to all students letting us know what's happening that week. Some typical fall activities are canoe rides, hayrides, and bonfires."

## Admissions

The Broad Admissions Committee evaluates students from many different backgrounds using the following criteria: their ability to work in teams, the quality of their work experience, leadership potential, and a very high level of motivation. This results in a very diverse program in regard to professional experiences, gender, national origin, and ethnicity. The average GMAT score of a student entering in 2005 was 637, and the average undergraduate GPA was 3.5. The average length of work experience is five years. All international students are required to submit a TOEFL score. (If the student has graduated from an English-speaking school, a waiver request is acceptable.) The minimum score required is a 600 on the paper-based test and a score of 250 on the computer-based test.

### FINANCIAL FACTS

| | |
|---|---|
| Annual tuition (in-state/out-of-state) | $17,000/$23,800 |
| Fees | $31 |
| Books and supplies | $1,550 |
| Room & board | $7,314 |
| % of students receiving aid | 94 |
| % of first-year students receiving aid | 88 |
| % of students receiving loans | 56 |
| % of students receiving grants | 58 |
| Average award package | $21,700 |
| Average grant | $6,015 |
| Average student loan debt | $17,302 |

### ADMISSIONS

| | |
|---|---|
| Admissions Selectivity Rating | 94 |
| # of applications received | 530 |
| % applicants accepted | 32 |
| % acceptees attending | 47 |
| Average GMAT | 637 |
| Range of GMAT | 590–680 |
| Average GPA | 3.3 |
| TOEFL required of international students? | yes |
| Minimum TOEFL (paper/computer) | 600/250 |
| Application fee | $85 |
| International application fee | $85 |
| Application deadline/notification | |
| Round 1: | 11/1 / 12/16 |
| Round 2: | 1/10 / 3/3 |
| Round 3: | 3/7 / 4/28 |
| Round 4: | 5/2 / 6/2 |
| Need-blind admissions? | yes |

### APPLICANTS ALSO LOOK AT

Arizona State University, Indiana University—Bloomington, Purdue University, The Ohio State University, The Pennsylvania State University, University of Michigan, University of North Carolina at Chapel Hill

### EMPLOYMENT PROFILE

| Career Rating | 89 | Grads employed by field: | % | avg. salary: |
|---|---|---|---|---|
| Primary source of full-time job acceptances | | Finance | 34 | $79,993 |
| | | Human Resources | 5 | $76,375 |
| School-facilitated activities | 50 (81%) | Marketing | 18 | $79,509 |
| Graduate-facilitated activities | 14 (19%) | MIS | 1 | NR |
| | | Operations | 31 | $79,538 |
| Average starting salary | $79,576 | Consulting | 7 | $73,750 |
| Percent employed | 95 | General Management | 1 | NR |
| | | Other | 3 | NR |

# MILLSAPS COLLEGE
## CHARLES W. ELSE AND ELOISE T. ELSE SCHOOL OF MANAGEMENT

## Academics

Reflecting the spirit and friendliness of the Millsaps undergraduate institution, the Else School of Management at Millsaps College offers a rigorous MBA program in a refreshingly intimate atmosphere. The student/faculty ratio at Millsaps is very low, with many classes taught in teams by two or more professors. In fact, "in class sizes of less than 20, we often have 2 PhDs or 1 PhD and a JD." These numbers allow for an engaging and productive classroom experience: "Classes focus on participation and discussion," and "students are eager to learn as well as participate in class."

While professors at Millsaps actively engage in research and professional activities, they "really love teaching and their students," and "are available outside of class through e-mail or meetings. They give students the one-on-one attention that you'd expect at a small school." For students who are struggling with course work or wish to solicit professional advice, professors "always have an open-door policy and are very open to questions, comments, or suggestions." No matter what subjects they teach, "all the professors know a lot about their fields, but they also know about other fields so they help us relate all aspects of business together." According to one student, "they prepare us for the real world, not just the academics."

While the academic atmosphere at Millsaps is friendly and supportive, students make it clear that "the course work is challenging." Overall, students value the preparation this workload gives them; in particular, students appreciate the fact that "the program really focuses on effective oral and written communications skills." In fact, "several weekend communications seminars are part of the core curriculum." A current student tells us that applicants should "expect to write, write, and then write some more!"

Working students say that Millsaps is particularly suited to their unique needs: "The classes are conveniently scheduled and the school's proximity to the downtown central business district makes it very easy to get to classes easily and on time." In fact, 90 percent of the MBA classes at the Else School are offered in the evening to accommodate work or internships. The library is also "open at all hours to facilitate all schedules." "Professors understand that working students have obligations other than school and exert every effort to help students who have missed class."

## Career and Placement

"Millsaps has an excellent academic reputation within the state and certainly within the local community," making it a great choice for students who wish to launch or promote their careers in the Jackson region. One second-year student explains, "I chose this school based on three factors: its reputation, the kind of students that it produces, and the respect that a degree from Millsaps garners." Many students who attend Millsaps are already working in Jackson and have chosen to pursue an MBA at Millsaps to increase their opportunities at their current companies. For recent college grads who want to build their professional experience, Millsaps offers academic credit for internship experiences in a professional environment. Students may receive additional assistance through the Millsaps College Career Center, which offers resume and interview counseling, career-development services, and internship placement. The school also organizes a variety of career-development opportunities, community-service activities, and professional development seminars.

BILL BRISTER, DIRECTOR OF GRADUATE BUSINESS ADMISSIONS
1701 NORTH STATE STREET, JACKSON, MS 39210 UNITED STATES
PHONE: 601-974-1253 • FAX: 601-974-1224
E-MAIL: MBAMACC@MILLSAPS.EDU • WEBSITE: WWW.MILLSAPS.EDU/ESOM

## FINANCIAL FACTS

| | |
|---|---|
| Annual tuition | $23,520 |
| Books and supplies | $550 |
| % of students receiving aid | 85 |
| % of first-year students receiving aid | 100 |
| % of students receiving grants | 90 |

## ADMISSIONS

| | |
|---|---|
| **Admissions Selectivity Rating** | **73** |
| # of applications received | 69 |
| % applicants accepted | 80 |
| % acceptees attending | 71 |
| Average GMAT | 540 |
| Range of GMAT | 510–640 |
| Average GPA | 3.39 |
| TOEFL required of international students? | yes |
| Minimum TOEFL (paper/computer) | 550/230 |
| Application fee | $25 |
| International application fee | $25 |
| Deferment available? | yes |
| Maximum length of deferment | 1 year |
| Transfer students accepted? | yes |
| Transfer application policy | Students may transfer up to 6 hours from a non-AACSB program; 12 hours from an AACSB-accredited program. |
| Non-fall admissions? | yes |
| Need-blind admissions? | yes |

## Student Life and Environment

A "friendly, very Southern atmosphere" permeates the Else School campus, whose location in Jackson makes for plenty of social and cultural opportunities. While most students hail from the state of Mississippi, the student body is nevertheless "a diverse bunch that has the utmost respect for individuals from various backgrounds." Given the school's flexible evening schedule and supportive academic environment, it's not surprising that many Millsaps students are older professionals; however, there is also a decent population of younger students, of whom "quite a few are actually right out of undergraduate [programs]."

There are several business honoraries chartered at Millsaps College, including Beta Gamma Sigma, Beta Alpha Psi, and the Financial Management Association. For those looking for a little fun, the Else School hosts several annual events for MBAs: "The dean attempts to pull the MBA students into the school activities; for example, we had a tailgating party for homecoming." However, since the program is largely part-time, students admit that "working full-time and being in school part-time doesn't leave much time for social activities." In general, "most of the students go to class and then go home to their families." A second-year student admits, "Besides group work and the occasional holiday party or community-service activity, there is not as much social interaction as I would like."

## Admissions

Admission to Millsaps is rolling. To apply, prospective students must submit an application form, GMAT scores, two letters of recommendation, and official transcripts from all previously attended graduate and undergraduate institutions. Along with their application materials, students must submit an essay detailing their reasons for pursuing an MBA. The Else School also requires a personal interview for all applicants. Prospective students do not need to have studied business as an undergraduate, but students with no background in accounting may be required to take undergraduate courses to catch up. There is no minimum GMAT score requirement for admission to the MBA program, although a score of 500 or better is preferred.

## EMPLOYMENT PROFILE

| Career Rating | 64 | Grads employed by field: | % | avg. salary: |
|---|---|---|---|---|
| Percent employed | 8 | Finance | 2 | NR |
| | | Marketing | 2 | NR |
| | | MIS | 2 | NR |
| | | Global Management | 1 | NR |
| | | nonprofit | 1 | NR |

# MINNESOTA STATE UNIVERSITY—MANKATO
## COLLEGE OF BUSINESS

## Academics

The MBA program at Minnesota State University—Mankato's College of Business employs an unusual calendar. Each semester here is divided into two eight-week modules, during which students complete two-credit courses that meet once a week. The school's goal in creating this system is to afford maximum flexibility to the school's busy students. MBAs here can take one or two classes per module, and they can skip a module entirely when necessary without losing too much ground. A student who takes the maximum number of classes per module can complete the program in about two years. One student writes, "The most attractive part of this program was the class schedule. I am a working individual, so classes from 6:00 to 9:00 P.M. are a great option for me, because I don't have to take off from work to attend classes!"

MSU Mankato's MBA program allows students to concentrate in international business (international study opportunities are available) or leadership and organizational change. Students may also fashion their own concentrations in consultation with a faculty advisor. An executive lecture series and executive seminars give students the chance "to learn from, as well as interact with, top executives." Students appreciate that the curriculum "places more emphasis on real life. Theories are great, but theories won't get you through life. Tying current business trends to course work makes the material applicable to life today and allows business students to use course information in their current jobs." They also approve of the school's "attempts to teach course-work fundamentals as well as up-to-date problems, situations, and changes that are currently affecting businesses today."

Mankato MBAs report that "most classes have moderate reading, and many use case studies. The class formats are split between lecture and interactive learning. The class sizes are just great, and the level of feedback from the professors and from the other students' insights really makes a difference." The financial burden of attending is lessened by the "many great opportunities for graduate assistantships, which pay for tuition while giving you work experience."

## Career and Placement

MSU Mankato's Career Development Center serves all undergraduate students, graduate students, and alumni of the school. MBA students tell us, however, that "the job-placement office could improve. There are a lot of interviews on and off campus, but there seems to be a lack of opportunities for the MBA students." However, the MBA program is relatively new, with its first graduating class being Spring 2006 so there is still plenty of room for growth. Students here should consider mining another valuable resource: the faculty. One student explains, "I am sure not every student takes advantage of this, but I have talked with many professors regarding career path, industry insight, corporate contacts, etc., and they all have been extremely useful developing postgraduate career prospects. I have about five months left in the program and have secured numerous interviews and a few job offers."

Liz Olmanson, Department Assistant
MSU MBA Program, 150 Morris Hall, Mankato, MN 56001 United States
Phone: 507-389-2967 • Fax: 507-389-5497
E-mail: mba@mnsu.edu • Website: www.cob.mnsu.edu

## Student Life and Environment

Mankato, students tell us, is "a great college town with a warm and friendly community, and a growing university with a vast support system from local businesses and leaders." The town of 45,000 is located about 65 miles southwest of Minneapolis. The surrounding region is "the health care, commercial, and cultural center of south-central Minnesota," according to the school's website. Residents have easy access to parks and ski facilities; outdoor activities are very popular here. MSU's athletic teams, which compete in the North Central Conference, enjoy strong support from area residents. The Twin Cities can be reached in less than one and a half hours by automobile.

MSU Mankato's MBAs generally work full-time in addition to attending school, so they "don't have any time to enjoy campus life. Most of us try to spend as little time on campus as possible." Some students complain that "there are few programs outside of class to provide learning and application experiences. Groups, clubs, or other opportunities focused toward the graduate student body would enrich the graduate experience." Most, however, acknowledge that they wouldn't take advantage of such opportunities because they lack the time to do so.

## Admissions

Applicants to the MBA program at MSU Mankato's College of Business must submit all of the following materials to the College of Graduate Studies: a completed application form; two official transcripts from one's degree-granting institution(s); and official score reports for the GMAT and, if applicable, the TOEFL. International applicants must also complete a Financial Statement Form demonstrating that they have sufficient funds to pay for the program. Most international applicants are required to have their undergraduate transcripts evaluated by a well-regarded credential evaluation service. All applicants must also submit a separate MBA program application form, a resume, and two letters of reference to the College of Business. Admission to the MBA program is competitive. Applicants are assessed holistically. Relevant factors include test scores (a score of at least 500 on the GMAT and 550 on the paper version of the TOEFL are recommended), undergraduate GPA, work experience, and quality of letters of reference.

### FINANCIAL FACTS

| | |
|---|---|
| Annual tuition (in-state/out-of-state) | $7,088/$9,600 |
| Fees | $478 |
| Books and supplies | $550 |
| Room & board | $8,600 |
| % of students receiving aid | 8 |
| Average award package | $15,000 |

### ADMISSIONS

| | |
|---|---|
| Admissions Selectivity Rating | 71 |
| # of applications received | 13 |
| % applicants accepted | 85 |
| % acceptees attending | 100 |
| Average GMAT | 511 |
| Range of GMAT | 460–590 |
| Average GPA | 3.36 |
| TOEFL required of international students? | yes |
| Minimum TOEFL (paper/computer) | 550/210 |
| Application fee | $40 |
| International application fee | $40 |
| Regular application deadline | 6/1 |
| Regular notification | 7/15 |
| Deferment available? | yes |
| Maximum length of deferment | 1 year |
| Transfer students accepted? | yes |
| Transfer application policy Students may transfer up to 6 credits from a regionally accredited institution. | |
| Non-fall admissions? | yes |
| Need-blind admissions? | yes |

Note: Since the first graduation class from the Minnesota State University—Mankato, College of Business' revised MBA program graduates in Spring 2006, no current data is available.

# MISSISSIPPI STATE UNIVERSITY
## COLLEGE OF BUSINESS AND INDUSTRY

### GENERAL INFORMATION
Type of school              public
Environment                 town
Academic calendar           semester

### SURVEY SAYS...
Friendly students
Happy students
Smart classrooms
*Solid preparation in:*
Teamwork
Communication/interpersonal skills

### STUDENTS
Enrollment of parent
  institution               16,101
Enrollment of business school   88
% male/female               52/48
% out-of-state              21
% part-time                 19
% minorities                6
% international             7
Average age at entry        28

### ACADEMICS
**Academic Experience Rating    82**
Student/faculty ratio       2:1
Profs interesting rating    79
Profs accessible rating     84
% female faculty            27
% minority faculty          10

### JOINT DEGREES
MBA in Project Management, 1–2 years

### PROMINENT ALUMNI
John Grisham, Best-selling author; Bailey Howell, Hall of Fame basketball player; Hartley Peavey, Founder, Peavey Electronics; Turner Catledge, Former Executive Editor, the *New York Times*; Pat Spainhour, Retired Chair & CEO, Ann Taylor Stores

## Academics

The MBA program at Mississippi State's College of Business and Industry takes a broad approach to graduate business education, stressing general principles and deemphasizing details. The idea is to expose students to a broad range of business theories and practices, a methodology students appreciate; as one put it, "The greatest strengths that I have encountered here lie in the fact that the MBA program allows students to experience and learn all aspects of business that will affect them in the future." Another student agrees, "The well-rounded design of the program is very strong. Courses are offered in every aspect of managing a business." Only a few students complain that "more in-depth material could be covered instead of the basics."

MSU's MBA program is small, resulting in "an excellent learning atmosphere in each class [and] lots of personal attention." One MBA notes, "Every professor I have had knows who I am, where I'm from, and what I want to do with my life. It's comforting to know that someone cares whether or not I am in class." Another student adds, "All of the professors are willing to help each student in class and outside of class. Many will take away from their own time and go out of their way to help a student. I know that I have become more competent and more prepared for the business world because of my experience here at Mississippi State."

MSU's program is flexible enough to accommodate both full-timers and part-time students with full-time jobs. In fact, Mississippi State's Internet-based distance-learning program allows students to complete the entire MBA and MBA Project Management degrees from anywhere. The school offers a wide range of business degrees, including the MBA, an MS in business administration, a master's in professional accountancy, a master's in taxation, an MS in information systems, and several PhDs. The most popular fields of specialization include finance, general management, and operations.

## Career and Placement

Placement services for Mississippi State business grads are handled by the university's Career Center. The office provides all the standard career services: career counseling, job fairs, seminars, workshops, interview books, career days, and access to online job databases. But because it serves 15,000 students, it doesn't have much time to tailor services specifically to the school's more than 300 business grad students. One MBA notes, "The biggest improvement this school could make would be to get a better career-placement office. The current office is more geared toward engineering than business." Another student offers, "The school could improve in the areas of possible internships for students within the course of the program." On the plus side, the Career Center can put students in contact with MSU's considerable alumni network.

Companies that most frequently employ MSU MBAs include Amsouth Bank, BellSouth, Cintas, Exxon Mobil, International Paper, JCPenny, Shell Oil, and the U.S. General Accounting Office.

## Student Life and Environment

Mississippi State University provides MBAs with a "very intimate setting, since the school makes up the majority of the town." Students love the "small-town setting and college atmosphere," telling us that "the southern charm and friendliness that surround you are the greatest strengths of MSU." Like many other southern schools, MSU has "a great sense of tradition that is upheld very well" by students, faculty, and administrators alike; also like its peer institutions, it is crazy for intercollegiate athletics, particularly football. One MBA explains, "For the sports lover, we have plenty of activities like

Dr. Barbara Spencer, Director of Graduate Studies in Business
PO Drawer 5288, Mississippi State, MS 39762 United States
Phone: 662-325-1891 • Fax: 662-325-8161
E-mail: gsb@cobilan.msstate.edu • Website: www.cbi.msstate.edu/gsb

tailgating at football games. There are activities for many sporting events here." Another student adds, "You just can't match the atmosphere of the 'Left-Field Lounge' for college baseball."

Within the College of Business, the MBA Association is the most active force in extracurricular life. It "organizes intramural football, basketball, and softball teams and usually organizes an MBA Social every few weeks. The socials are usually held at local bars and restaurants, and they really give students an opportunity to get to know each other." Students also have access to "more clubs and other organizations than you can count, outdoor sports and recreation, and a very supportive local community." They love the "beautiful campus [and MSU's] state-of-the-art fitness facility that houses a weight room, eight basketball courts, a walking track, climbing wall, pool, and about 10 racquetball courts."

Most of all, though, they love the tight community formed by this small MBA program. One student describes the relationship dynamic: "You form such bonds with your classmates that you spend your outside time with them as well. It is a very tight-knit group. You spend a lot of time at the MBA lab working on projects, but it is well worth it." Another student relates an atmosphere that "is very much like a family. Classmates in general are supportive. I love the people that I am in class with. The school is very laid-back and a fun place to be."

## Admissions

Admission to Mississippi State University's graduate business program, the school notes, is "based primarily on results of the Graduate Management Admission Test (GMAT), GPA over the last 60 semester hours of baccalaureate work, and past work experience." The school employs a formula to establish minimum criteria for applicants; that formula is (200 5 GPA for final 60 undergraduate credit hours) + GMAT score. All applicants need a score of at least 1110. The school's website states, "Some exceptions to these standards may be granted based on the strength of other materials contained in the student's application." Mitigating factors may include the required letters of recommendation and personal statement. MSU visits a number of minority schools in its efforts to recruit underrepresented minority students.

## FINANCIAL FACTS

| | |
|---|---|
| Annual tuition (in-state/out-of-state) | $6,468/$14,658 |
| Books and supplies | $900 |
| Room & board | $7,580 |
| % of students receiving aid | 65 |
| % of first-year students receiving aid | 67 |
| % of students receiving loans | 38 |
| % of students receiving grants | 41 |
| Average award package | $14,615 |
| Average grant | $2,634 |

## ADMISSIONS

| | |
|---|---|
| Admissions Selectivity Rating | 76 |
| # of applications received | 92 |
| % applicants accepted | 61 |
| % acceptees attending | 71 |
| Average GMAT | 508 |
| Range of GMAT | 460–560 |
| Average GPA | 3.48 |
| TOEFL required of international students? | yes |
| Minimum TOEFL (paper/computer) | 575/232 |
| Application fee | $30 |
| International application fee | $30 |
| Regular application deadline | 7/1 |
| Regular notification | rolling |
| Deferment available? | yes |
| Maximum length of deferment | 1 year |
| Transfer students accepted? | yes |
| Transfer application policy 6 hours of transfer credit from accredited institutions. | |
| Non-fall admissions? | yes |
| Need-blind admissions? | yes |

## EMPLOYMENT PROFILE

| Career Rating | 60* | Grads employed by field: | % | avg. salary: |
|---|---|---|---|---|
| Primary source of full-time job acceptances | | Accounting | 20 | NR |
| | | Finance | 20 | NR |
| School-facilitated activities | 5 | MIS | 20 | NR |
| Graduate-facilitated activities | 19 | Operations | 30 | NR |
| Unknown | 7 | Other | 10 | NR |

# MISSOURI STATE UNIVERSITY (FORMERLY SW MISSOURI STATE U.)
## COLLEGE OF BUSINESS ADMINISTRATION

## GENERAL INFORMATION
Type of school                  public
Environment                     city

## SURVEY SAYS...
Happy students
Smart classrooms
*Solid preparation in:*
Teamwork
Presentation skills
Computer skills

## STUDENTS
Enrollment of parent
  institution                   21,000
Enrollment of business school   343
% male/female                   39/61
% out-of-state                  5
% part-time                     53
% minorities                    4
% international                 29
Average age at entry            28
Average years work experience
  at entry                      2

## ACADEMICS
**Academic Experience Rating**  **70**
Student/faculty ratio           20:1
Profs interesting rating        79
Profs accessible rating         76
% female faculty                32
% minority faculty              4

## PROMINENT ALUMNI
David Glass, former CEO of Wal-
Mart and CEO of KC Royals; Todd
Tiahrt, 4-Term Congressman;
Richard McClure, President, Uni
Group, Inc.; Jim Smith, President,
American Banking Association,
2001–02; Terry Thompson, Former
President, Jack Henry

## Academics

With a solid reputation in its home state and a growing reputation throughout the country, the College of Business Administration (COBA) at Missouri State University provides a "highly affordable" MBA to a diverse mix of local and international students. Students agree the college is "consistently recognized as a strong business school, especially in technology management." They also love the management and accounting departments at MSU.

Through an arrangement with both the International School of Management Studies in Chennai (Madras), Indian students can complete their "foundation" courses in India, and then complete the remainder of the program (33 credit hours) in Missouri. One of the many Indian students attending MSU writes, "The arrangement allowed me to do my prerequisite courses in India and the regular MBA in the U.S." About one third of the full-time MBA student body is international.

The college offers "true diversity among the faculty. There are conservatives as well as liberals here." Professors earn high marks for "always being willing to take extra time to help a student understand a difficult concept. They expect a lot of preparation and in turn will work their hardest to help you succeed." Most here feel that "this school is definitely headed in the right direction. Class selection is expanding, and the student population is becoming increasingly diverse. The school keeps fairly up-to-date on technology as well."

## Career and Placement

MSU hosts "many career fairs, with many companies from the surrounding states recruiting here." Respondents to our survey are satisfied with the school's career center, praising its "commitment to helping students find internship opportunities during school and permanent employment after school." Nearly 400 companies visit the campus looking for full-time hires each year; a little over 100 recruit summer interns on campus. These figures apply to the entire university; the figure for how many of these companies specifically recruit MBAs is unknown.

A little more than half of MSU's MBAs remain in the region after graduation. About a third find work overseas, an unsurprising figure given the large international population. Top employers of MSU MBAs include Wal-Mart, Payless, Hallmark, Samson, FedEx, Anheuser Busch, DataTronics, Edward Jones, State Farm, Caterpillar, Occidental, Petroleum Renaissance Financial, John Hancock, Boeing, State Street, Gateway Financial, the Federal Reserve Bank, Cerner, Target, Toys R Us, Federated Insurance, Enterprise, Archer Daniels Midland, KPMG, Baird Kurtz & Dobson, Deloitte Touche Tohmatsu, Kirkpatrick, Phillips & Miller, CPAs, Sherwin Williams, AG Edwards, and Koch Industries.

## Student Life and Environment

MBAs love the "nice and quiet city" of Springfield, with its "unique 'small town' atmosphere with all the amenities of a major city. You get the best of both worlds!" The city boasts "outdoor recreation that is second to none, with several area lakes [and state and national parks], two regional medical centers, a regional shopping mall, and minor league baseball, football, and hockey teams, and even a professional tennis team." Other amenities include "over 300 different churches to attend, plenty of nightlife in the Jordan Valley Park area, [and] several golf and racquet clubs, as well as one of the largest

TOBIN BUSHMAN, GRADUATE COLLEGE COORDINATOR
901 SOUTH NATIONAL AVENUE, SPRINGFIELD, MO 65804 UNITED STATES
PHONE: 417-836-5335 • FAX: 417-836-6888
E-MAIL: GRADUATECOLLEGE@MISSOURISTATE.EDU • WEBSITE: WWW.COBA.MISSOURISTATE.EDU

equestrian communities in this region of the country." With "plenty of low-cost housing available [and] Branson, one of the entertainment capitals of the world, only 45 minutes away," what's not to love about Springfield?

Best of all, students needn't even leave school grounds to find something to do because "the campus is always brimming with activity." Student organizations "regularly conduct events to keep students involved." Students advise, "Whether you get involved or not is completely up to you. You are accepted if you want to be, and never shunned." Either way you'll feel secure on this "very well-lit and safe campus. A number of safety features are offered throughout [the] campus, including a service where the Safety & Transportation officials will walk you back to your car or residence hall at night." No wonder MBA students agree that "this university is really student-oriented. Everything is done here to create good atmosphere for learning and having fun at the same time."

The rhythm of life in the COBA is such that "life goes on smoothly, and with lots of fun." There is "lots of reading and preparing for classes during the week. Every class has a group project and individual assignments. The midterm times are silent with the libraries full of studies." The weekends, on the other hand, "are crowded with students playing and cheering up." The student body here is drawn "from all different countries, which offers a vast knowledge of other cultures on top of the knowledge of business." Many come from India, where MSU participates in a twinning program to facilitate exchange students. Everyone here enjoys "a very friendly atmosphere where everyone is very helpful towards each other."

## Admissions

The admissions office at MSU makes the following minimum requirements of applicants: a GPA of at least 2.75 for the final two years (60 semester hours) of undergraduate work; a minimum GMAT score of 400, with at least a 20-percentile ranking in both verbal and written portions of the test; and a minimum GPA–GMAT score of 1000 based on this formula: (undergraduate GPA in last 60 hours of undergraduate work 5 200) + GMAT score. International students who do not initially meet the verbal or written requirements may be admitted conditionally and subsequently required to demonstrate English proficiency through additional testing and/or course work. For these students, a minimum score of 550 on the paper-based TOEFL is also generally required.

### FINANCIAL FACTS

| | |
|---|---|
| Annual tuition (in-state/out-of-state) | $4,536/$9,072 |
| Fees | $508 |
| Books and supplies | $875 |
| Room & board (on/off-campus) | $4,860/$5,200 |
| % of students receiving aid | 55 |
| % of students receiving loans | 53 |
| % of students receiving grants | 34 |
| Average award package | $8,909 |
| Average grant | $3,112 |
| Average student loan debt | $16,500 |

### ADMISSIONS

| | |
|---|---|
| Admissions Selectivity Rating | 67 |
| # of applications received | 160 |
| % applicants accepted | 98 |
| % acceptees attending | 98 |
| Average GMAT | 510 |
| Range of GMAT | 440–570 |
| Average GPA | 3.4 |
| TOEFL required of international students? | yes |
| Minimum TOEFL (paper/computer) | 550/213 |
| Application fee | $30 |
| International application fee | $30 |
| Regular application deadline | rolling |
| Regular notification | rolling |
| Deferment available? | yes |
| Maximum length of deferment | 1 semester |
| Transfer students accepted? | yes |
| Transfer application policy With advisor permission | |
| Non-fall admissions? | yes |

### APPLICANTS ALSO LOOK AT

Arkansas State University, Central Missouri State University, Southeast Missouri State University, University of Arkansas at Little Rock, University of Missouri—Kansas City, University of Missouri—St. Louis, University of Missouri—Columbia

### EMPLOYMENT PROFILE

| Career Rating | 75 | Grads employed by field: | % | avg. salary: |
|---|---|---|---|---|
| Primary source of full-time job acceptances | | Accounting | 10 | $47,265 |
| | | Finance | 9 | $41,875 |
| School-facilitated activities | 30% | Human Resources | 3 | $33,456 |
| Graduate-facilitated activities | 20% | Marketing | 12 | $43,667 |
| Unknown | 50% | MIS | 12 | $48,920 |
| | | Operations | 10 | $41,000 |
| | | Consulting | 12 | $39,810 |
| Average starting salary | $56,000 | General Management | 20 | $40,988 |
| | | Other | 12 | $43,210 |

# MONMOUTH UNIVERSITY
## SCHOOL OF BUSINESS ADMINISTRATION

## Academics

"The administration and professors at Monmouth University are always looking out for students' best interests," MBAs at this private institution an hour south of New York City tell us. One student observes, "Monmouth keeps up with the changing business world. For example, it added a health care program, and it is constantly updating its courses with new practices and techniques." Monmouth may not be the school for everyone—students warn that "the breadth of the subject matter offered is narrow, as there are only two concentrations, real estate and health care administration"—but for those looking for a general degree or with interest in those specific areas, Monmouth may well fit the bill. Monmouth also offers an MBA track in accounting. The program is designed to fulfill New Jersey's requirement of 150 credit hours prior to sitting for the CPA exam.

Monmouth's general MBA requires a minimum of 30 credit hours. Note, however, that students with deficiencies in their undergraduate business educations may be required to take core courses that can increase the requirement to up to 48 hours. The accounting track requires a minimum of 33 credit hours, as does the concentration in real estate. The health care concentration requires 36 credit hours. All tracks conclude with an integrative capstone course. Students report that required courses for all MBAs provide "a good foundation in the history and evolution of a business concept." They warn that elective options are scant. One writes, "Of the many nonrequired courses listed in the catalog, very few are offered each semester. For example, there are only two finance courses offered for the Spring 2005 term!" Even more worrisome is that "required courses fill up quickly, and are packed full with 30 students. Sometimes a new section is added, and sometimes it isn't."

On a positive note, "professors at Monmouth have a vast amount of business experience related to the courses they teach." One student offers, "I feel confident I am learning about how things work in the real business world along the prevalent academic thinking on a given subject." Teachers also "seem to always be available for consultation before class and many other hours as well. It's nice being able to talk to the professors about concepts you may be trying to relate to the current working world, as well as concepts with which you may struggle." Students inform us that "the library is very good, with many valuable resources, both print and electronic." One MBA remarks, "The computer labs are good too. Wi-fi service is a plus; I hope they continue adding more coverage."

## Career and Placement

Career services are provided to Monmouth MBAs by the Life and Career Advising Center, which serves the entire university. The office administers aptitude tests and career inventories, and provides a contact point between students and alumni and businesses. One-on-one counseling services are also available.

## Student Life and Environment

Monmouth has "an absolutely beautiful campus with lovely historical buildings of import" located "one mile from the beach," a location that provides "a lot of places to go and things to do outside the classroom." Those who stick around campus long enough to socialize report, "Life at Monmouth is very active. While the school is very quiet on weekends, the weekdays are filled with fun, educational activities. There is great school spirit" fostered by "university sporting events, which the majority of students attend." Between classes, students often head for "the Java Coffee Cafe at the student center." These same students get the most out of "a wide range of clubs and a very helpful Career Advising Center staff."

KEVIN ROANE, DIRECTOR, GRADUATE ADMISSION
400 CEDAR AVENUE, WEST LONG BRANCH, NJ 07764-1898 UNITED STATES
PHONE: 732-571-3452 • FAX: 732-263-5123
E-MAIL: GRADADM@MONMOUTH.EDU • WEBSITE: WWW.MONMOUTH.EDU

For the many part-time MBA students here with major commitments outside of school, participation in extracurriculars is a rarity. One such student explains, "In part-time MBA programs, students don't really get to socialize much with their classmates. Most graduate students come to school, put their time in for classes, and then go home to their work and families. We rarely see each other outside of class. It's not the same as a full-time experience." Part-time or full-time, "the majority of graduate students at Monmouth are very friendly and are always looking to share experiences and network with new students."

Campus amenities include "plenty of study areas on campus. Recently the school added two 24-hour computer labs." Monmouth has begun to admit larger MBA classes of late. One student observes, "While the buildings are relatively new, Monmouth has expanded so much that they are already outgrowing their facilities!" Students' wish lists include more classrooms and some on-campus housing for graduate students.

## Admissions

Minimum requirements for admission to the Monmouth MBA program include: a GMAT score of at least 450; a formula score of at least 1000 under the formula [(undergraduate GPA × 200) + GMAT score]; and an overall undergraduate GPA of at least 2.75. Regular admission generally requires a minimum GMAT score of 500. For those whose undergraduate degree is more than eight years old, a GMAT score of 450 is acceptable, provided the applicant has sufficient managerial experience and produces two letters of recommendation and a detailed resume. Students who hold graduate degrees in other areas (PhD, EdD, MD, JD, CPA) may be exempted from the above admissions requirements. International students whose native language is not English must submit official TOEFL score reports in addition to all required documents listed above. Foreign language documents and transcripts must be notarized and translated (Monmouth recommends World Education Service in New York). International students must demonstrate sufficient funds to support at least their first year of study at Monmouth University and sufficient additional resources to fund completion of their degree.

## FINANCIAL FACTS

| | |
|---|---|
| Annual tuition | $12,114 |
| Fees | $620 |
| Books and supplies | $900 |
| % of students receiving aid | 83 |
| % of first-year students receiving aid | 94 |
| % of students receiving loans | 43 |
| % of students receiving grants | 66 |
| Average award package | $12,118 |
| Average grant | $2,263 |

## ADMISSIONS

| | |
|---|---|
| Admissions Selectivity Rating | 63 |
| # of applications received | 133 |
| % applicants accepted | 95 |
| % acceptees attending | 57 |
| Average GMAT | 500 |
| Range of GMAT | 470–530 |
| Average GPA | 3.15 |
| TOEFL required of international students? | yes |
| Minimum TOEFL (paper/computer) | 550/225 |
| Application fee | $35 |
| International application fee | $35 |
| Regular application deadline | 7/15 |
| Regular notification | rolling |
| Deferment available? | yes |
| Maximum length of deferment | 1 year |
| Transfer students accepted? | yes |
| Transfer application policy | must complete at least 30 credits at Monmouth; transfer credits must be within 7 years and with acceptable grade. |
| Non-fall admissions? | yes |
| Need-blind admissions? | yes |

# MONTCLAIR STATE UNIVERSITY
## SCHOOL OF BUSINESS

### GENERAL INFORMATION
| | |
|---|---|
| Type of school | public |
| Environment | village |
| Academic calendar | year-round |

### SURVEY SAYS...
Students love Montclair, NJ
Friendly students
Good peer network
Helpful alumni

### STUDENTS
| | |
|---|---|
| Enrollment of parent institution | 15,000 |
| Enrollment of business school | 372 |
| % male/female | 52/48 |
| % out-of-state | 10 |
| % part-time | 76 |
| % minorities | 51 |
| % international | 34 |
| Average age at entry | 26 |
| Average years work experience at entry | 4 |

### ACADEMICS
| | |
|---|---|
| Academic Experience Rating | 67 |
| Student/faculty ratio | 25:1 |
| Profs interesting rating | 62 |
| Profs accessible rating | 61 |
| % female faculty | 25 |
| % minority faculty | 40 |

### JOINT DEGREES
MS in Chemistry/MBA, 68 credits

## Academics

Affordability, "proximity to New York City," and "a program that caters to part-time students" are the main attractions at the MBA Program at Montclair State University. The school offers a full-time program, with classes in the evenings and Saturdays; a part-time evening program; and an accelerated part-time Saturday program. Approximately one-quarter of the student body attends full-time.

The Montclair MBA is a 48-credit sequence including nine credits of introductory management classes, a 15-credit functional core (covering accounting, finance, marketing, and information management), 9 credits of advanced business courses, 21 credits of electives (some of which may be used to create an area of concentration), and a three-credit capstone course in advanced strategic management. Up to 21 hours of these classes can be waived based on prior academic work or through challenge examinations. Concentrations are available in accounting, economics, finance, international business, management, marketing, and MIS.

Montclair professors "have a good amount of practical knowledge and integrate current topics well, without going into overkill mode. The program design offers a good balance of individual and group assignments, papers, exams, and presentations." Instructors earn praise for being "understanding of students' other obligations, but without being pushovers," and for "bringing great real-world experience to [the] classroom." Administrators earn praise for soliciting Student evaluations of their professors, and for actually listening to these comments: Students claim that "some professors have actually been removed from the program upon student request." Administrators are also very approachable; one student states, they "hold lunches that are a great environment for conversation. They're really good at listening to students."

## Career and Placement

The MSU Career Development Center serves all undergraduates and graduates at the school. MBAs are not impressed; one writes, "We need to establish an alumni club or organization and a career/campus recruiting office." Another agrees, "It would be nice to have a career services center active for MBAs. In all my years attending I have yet to have anyone from the MBA office or career office offer a meeting, discussion, or follow-up on my studies." Living near New York City, "the greatest free market in the world," makes it a little easier for students to find internships and jobs on their own. Most MSU MBAs attend while pursuing full-time careers; their employers include Abbott Laboratories, ADP, AT&T Wireless Services, Bank of New York, Con Edison, Deloitte Touche Consulting, Goldman Sachs, Gucci, Kodak, the *New York Times*, the Office of the New Jersey Attorney General, PricewaterhouseCoopers, Prudential Financial, Sodexho USA, Thomson Financial, United Parcel Service, and Wyeth-Ayerst Research.

## Student Life and Environment

Montclair is "mostly a commuter campus," with "about 75 percent of the students attending part-time and working full-time." As a result, "Most people don't get involved in activities because there are higher priorities (work, family, the rest of life)." The part-time student body arrives with "an interesting array of backgrounds and work experiences," we're told. The large number of part-time commuters means "group work can be difficult because we all have different schedules, but we figure out how to work together."

Ms. Michelle Eckman, MBA Coordinator
Partridge Hall 210, Montclair, NJ 07043 United States
Phone: 973-655-4306 • Fax: 973-655-3449 • E-mail: mba@mail.montclair.edu
Website: www.montclair.edu/mba

The town of Montclair has several major parks and lots of quiet streets. It boasts four movie theaters, an art museum and several art galleries, lots of artisan shops, two off-Broadway theater companies, a host of funky restaurants, and an abundance of coffee shops. Students remark that they often see no need to venture into New York City proper, as they are able to partake in a range of cultural activities without ever leaving the Montclair vicinity. Cross-town public transportation is also pretty good, and access to and from NYC is frequent, easy, and cheap.

Those MBAs who live on campus and attend full-time "tend to be the international students." They tell us that "overall, campus life is good. We have many graduate- and undergraduate-level clubs and organizations to choose from. There is something for everyone at MSU." Full-timers and commuters alike appreciate the fact that "there is a diner on campus, proof that this is a Jersey school."

## Admissions

Applicants to the MSU/MBA program "must have at least earned a bachelor's degree from a regionally accredited college or university (or the foreign equivalent)" and must submit two official copies of transcripts for all academic work completed after high school; an official score report for the GMAT (applicants holding a terminal degree—a PhD, MD, or JD, for example—are exempt from the GMAT requirement); a personal statement of professional goals; two letters of recommendation from "persons qualified to evaluate the applicant's promise of academic achievement and potential for professional growth;" and a completed application form. International students whose first language is not English must submit an official score report for the TOEFL. Of these elements, the undergraduate GPA and the GMAT score are among the most important factors that the Admissions Department considers. The average GMAT score of the 2005 entering class was 500, and the average GPA was 3.24. Prior work experience is "strongly recommended" but is not required.

## FINANCIAL FACTS

Annual tuition (in-state/out-of-state)
$11,269/$15,077
Books and supplies $1,200
Room & board (on-campus) $8,250

## ADMISSIONS

| | |
|---|---|
| Admissions Selectivity Rating | **73** |
| # of applications received | 163 |
| % applicants accepted | 64 |
| % acceptees attending | 66 |
| Average GMAT | 500 |
| Range of GMAT | 450–600 |
| Average GPA | 3.24 |
| TOEFL required of international students? | yes |
| Minimum TOEFL (paper/computer) | 550/213 |
| Application fee | $60 |
| International application fee | $60 |
| Regular application deadline | rolling |
| Regular notification | rolling |
| Deferment available? | yes |
| Maximum length of deferment | 1 year |
| Transfer students accepted? | yes |
| Transfer application policy Students may transfer 6 credits (semester hours) of graduate course work. | |
| Non-fall admissions? | yes |
| Need-blind admissions? | yes |

### APPLICANTS ALSO LOOK AT

Fairleigh Dickinson University, Rutgers—The State University of New Jersey, Seton Hall University

# MONTEREY INSTITUTE OF INTERNATIONAL STUDIES
## FISHER GRADUATE SCHOOL OF INTERNATIONAL BUSINESS

## GENERAL INFORMATION
| | |
|---|---|
| Type of school | private |
| Environment | town |
| Academic calendar | semester |

### SURVEY SAYS...
Friendly students
*Solid preparation in:*
Teamwork
Communication/interpersonal skills
Doing business in a global economy

### STUDENTS
| | |
|---|---|
| Enrollment of parent institution | 750 |
| Enrollment of business school | 80 |
| % male/female | 38/62 |
| % part-time | 4 |
| % minorities | 21 |
| % international | 36 |
| Average age at entry | 28 |
| Average years work experience at entry | 5 |

### ACADEMICS
| | |
|---|---|
| **Academic Experience Rating** | **68** |
| Student/faculty ratio | 6:1 |
| Profs interesting rating | 66 |
| Profs accessible rating | 81 |
| % female faculty | 14 |
| % minority faculty | 18 |

### JOINT DEGREES
MBA/MA International Policy
Studies, 3 years; MBA/MA
International Environmental Policy
Studies, 3 years; MBA/MA
International Trade Policy Studies, 3
years; MBA/MPA Nonprofit
Management, 3 years; MBA/MA
Translation, 3 years

### PROMINENT ALUMNI
Fumio Matsushima, Head of Private
Banking, HSBC Japan; J. R.
Williams, VP, Prudential Securities;
Elizabeth Powell, VP, Customer
Service, Motorola; Naoko
Yanaghara, VP, AT&T Japan;
Venkatesh Baggubati, Actor

## Academics

With its "truly international focus," the Fisher Graduate School of International Business at the Monterey Institute of International Studies prepares students for "an exciting future [in] a world of business that is going global." At MIIS, "every course places emphasis on international aspects, from case studies to projects, and everyone speaks at least two languages." MBAs appreciate that "everyone here, from faculty to students, has international experience." Nearly half the student body is international.

The school's Monterey, CA, location is a huge advantage, allowing it to "play upon the wealth of business in the San Francisco Bay area. Many top executives and CEOs frequently visit as guest speakers and offer mentorship to students." It also allows the school to "pull professors from Stanford and Berkeley for once-weekly classes and weekend-long seminars." And lastly (it almost goes without saying) Monterey provides an idyllic setting in which students can relax and devote themselves to study.

"The workload is very heavy here," MBAs report, with "lots of simulation, oftentimes in other languages so you don't always understand what is going on—much like in the real world. In these instances we have to rely on each other for translations and try alternative ways of contributing to teamwork." In addition to the curriculum, one student notes the benefits from "a great workshop series [that runs] 15 hours over one weekend, exploring a specific topic in-depth with acknowledged leaders. I love the workshops. Plus, the school lets you audit them if your workload doesn't permit you to take the class for a grade." The workshops are frequently led by "visiting professors who are great resources for future career contacts and have a wealth of knowledge in their chosen field of expertise." MIIS's full-time faculty receives similarly high praise. Students say, "We are all on a first-name basis. Not only are the professors very experienced in instruction, but they are also still heavily involved in outside, real-world consulting and/or professions. They are very eager to help, but unwilling to spoon-feed."

## Career and Placement

The Career Management Center (CMC) for the Fisher MBA program offers "a customized approach to each individual's goals, skill set, and educational and personal background," according to the school. The office "acts as an 'executive search firm'" to help students "target potential employers and enhance their added value" through online career assessments, one-on-one consultations, and workshops in interviewing skills, salary negotiation, internships, and networking.

Many of the students in our survey tell us, however, that they would like to see "more active company involvement in recruiting at the school." They concede that the CMC faces a tough challenge: The school is too small to attract many on-campus recruiters and too new to have much in the way of an alumni network. Most recruiters, we're told, are drawn from within a 30-mile radius, and big international players are unfortunately absent. (The exceptions are NGOs and U.S. government agencies, which do recruit here.) About one-third of Monterey's MBAs move on to jobs in the nonprofit sector. Consulting gobbles up another 20 percent. About half remain on the Pacific coast, while one in five finds work outside the United States.

## Student Life and Environment

"The Business School at Monterey is very small," students point out, noting that "the entire institute has only about a thousand students at the most." Full-time MBAs number less than 100, so "students tend to be fairly tight and there is a lot of interaction

JILL STOFFERS, ENROLLMENT MANAGER
460 PIERCE STREET, MONTEREY, CA 93940 UNITED STATES
PHONE: 831-647-4123 • FAX: 831-647-6405
E-MAIL: ADMIT@MIIS.EDU • WEBSITE: WWW.MIIS.EDU

between cohorts." MBAs also mix with graduate students in other programs. An MBA reports, "We have institute-wide happy hours every other Friday. There are always opportunities to socialize with fellow students, but no pressure to do things you don't feel comfortable with." Most do feel comfortable, though. As one MBA put it, "It's such a great way to get to know classmates and students in other schools, even the book-worms find a way to make it. It is a good time!"

As you might expect at a school this size, social and extracurricular life isn't exactly buzzing. However, MBAs here point out, "for graduate students wanting to study and focus, that can be a plus." Also in the plus column, "Monterey is a beautiful place to go to school." [Monterey] provides excellent additional resources, as there are two military academic institutions with libraries and research utilities that are accessible to students. Home not only to MIIS but also to the Defense Language Institute, the Navy Postgraduate School, three post-secondary schools, and Language Line Services (a provider of telephone-based interpretation), Monterey has earned its nickname of "the language capital of the world." The benefit is that this combination of schools and busi-nesses "brings an incredible mix of people to the peninsula."

Many of those people can be found on the MIIS campus, where "about half the students are international while the Americans have all spent significant amounts of time abroad and are competent in another language." This makes it "very easy to find a conversation partner to foster an interest in many languages, including Korean, Mandarin Chinese, Arabic, French, Spanish, Italian, Japanese, and many more." Students describe the setting as "a very accu-rate representation of the future of the global business village. You can be exposed to and appreciate the cultures and behaviors of businesspeople from all over the world—you're interacting with them, not just reading about it in a book." Students "tend to be more col-laborative than competitive, more socially responsible than purely financially motivated." The drawback: They're "inexperienced overall in business, [and] lack practical experience."

## Admissions

MIIS will consider any applicant with at least a 3.0 undergraduate GPA, provided the applicant speaks English and at least one other language at an advanced (i.e., third-year undergraduate) level. Applicants must also submit GMAT scores, letters of recommen-dation, and a personal statement. A resume and an interview, while not required, are strongly recommended.

### FINANCIAL FACTS

| | |
|---|---|
| Annual tuition | $25,500 |
| Fees | $200 |
| Books and supplies | $900 |
| Room & board | $7,400 |
| % of students receiving aid | 85 |
| % of first-year students receiving aid | 89 |
| % of students receiving loans | 65 |
| % of students receiving grants | 78 |
| Average award package | $24,931 |
| Average grant | $6,329 |
| Average student loan debt | $25,690 |

### ADMISSIONS

| | |
|---|---|
| Admissions Selectivity Rating | 70 |
| # of applications received | 107 |
| % applicants accepted | 88 |
| % acceptees attending | 48 |
| Average GMAT | 549 |
| Range of GMAT | 500–610 |
| Average GPA | 3.3 |
| TOEFL required of international students? | yes |
| Minimum TOEFL (paper/computer) | 550/213 |
| Application fee | $50 |
| International application fee | $50 |
| Regular application deadline | 3/15 |
| Regular notification | 5/1 |
| Transfer students accepted? | yes |
| Transfer application policy | |
| Credits must be from an AACSB-accredited college or university, and must be with a B or better. Possible to transfer up to 25% of total program. Dean makes final determination. | |
| Non-fall admissions? | yes |
| Need-blind admissions? | yes |

### APPLICANTS ALSO LOOK AT

Pepperdine University, Thunderbird, University of California—San Diego, University of South Carolina

### EMPLOYMENT PROFILE

| Career Rating | 71 | Grads employed by field: | % | avg. salary: |
|---|---|---|---|---|
| Primary source of full-time job acceptances | | Finance | 4 | $63,000 |
| | | Marketing | 13 | $64,583 |
| School-facilitated activities | 12 (22%) | MIS | 2 | NR |
| Graduate-facilitated activities | 7 (13%) | Operations | 8 | $54,666 |
| Unknown | 35 (65%) | Strategic Planning | 2 | $70,000 |
| | | Consulting | 11 | $59,500 |
| Average starting salary | $65,339 | Communications | 8 | $63,666 |
| Percent employed | 73 | Entrepreneurship | 4 | $87,500 |
| | | General Management | 8 | $65,000 |
| | | Global Management | 8 | $68,500 |
| | | Other | 15 | $55,000 |
| | | Internet/New Media | 4 | $70,000 |
| | | Nonprofit | 13 | $81,666 |

# NATIONAL UNIVERSITY OF SINGAPORE
## NUS BUSINESS SCHOOL

## Academics

By delivering a "strong curriculum with an Asian focus," the National University of Singapore Business School has developed a solid reputation in the Asian Pacific. So solid, in fact, that *Asia Inc.* magazine has rated the program among the region's top three MBA programs every year since 1999 and recently ranked the school among the top 15 programs in all of Asia. The magazine cited curriculum, joint programs with such solid institutions as Peking University and UCLA, and the school's reputation among administrators at other MBA programs as the main reasons for its high ranking.

NUS offers both a full-time and part-time MBA. The full-time program is truly international, drawing students from as many as 30 countries around the globe. Both programs consist of 10 core modules and 7 elective modules, with electives available in finance and banking, international business, management and organization, management of technology, marketing, strategic management, human resource management, and decision sciences. Students speak most highly of the finance and marketing courses. Some feel that "the fact that students are required to take 10 core courses leaves them with less time to delve into a specific concentration. Also, courses in communication are conspicuously absent."

In all areas, MBAs agree, the "faculty is the biggest strength. Most of the professors are experienced lecturers from renowned universities in the United States, Canada, and Europe, and they are mostly very knowledgeable in their respective fields." Professors are also "concerned about the student's progress and are always willing to help," which students appreciate. To supplement instruction, "the business school brings in lecturers with working experiences. Such moves allow the lecturers to give insight on how theoretical models could be applied in the actual business world." NUS MBAs warn that "the academic work is a killer, with a heavy workload that lacks time for personal development, generally. Still, it's manageable," in part because of the "easily accessible resources through well-established IT infrastructure, IVLE tools, and wireless Internet connection throughout the campus."

## Career and Placement

The MBA Career Services Office at NUS offers the following services: job postings, recruitment talks by employers, career workshops and panel discussions, and on-campus interviews for internships and full-time jobs. The school reports that 60 to 80 employers recruit graduating students each year; 30 to 40 employers recruit summer interns. Students have mixed feelings about the office; some praise both it and the "strong alumni network," while others complain that "career services is nonexistent for most part of the year, though it does organize at least 40 events per semester."

Top employers of NUS MBAs include Accenture, British Petroleum, Citigroup, CSPB, Deutsche Securities, Emerson Network Power, Frost & Sullivan, Goodyear Tires, HSBC, JPMorgan, KPMG, Lehman Brothers, McKinsey, Reuters, and Standard Chartered Bank. In the school's most recent employment survey, all students who responded were employed in the region.

Ms. Tan Hwee Har, MBA Programs Office
BIZ 2 Building, 1 Business Link, Level 5, Singapore, 117592 Singapore
Phone: 011-065-6516-2068 • Fax: 011-065-6872-4423
E-mail: MBA@NUS.EDU.SG • Website: WWW.BSCHOOL.NUS.EDU.SG

## Student Life and Environment

Due to the heavy workload, students tell us that life in the NUS MBA program "revolves around classwork, case studies, [and] projects. Time for external community activities is limited." One MBA explains, "Student life has never been a breeze, especially when there are tests and project deadlines. You'll feel like cursing yourself and asking why on earth you're putting yourself through all this in the middle of the night when you're trying to rush out that finance project by 9:00 A.M. the next day. But when it's all over, you'll feel really happy that you've had the chance to go through all that, sweating it out and learning invaluable knowledge while doing the project." When students can break away from their studies, they "try to use it well." Students note that "extracurricular activities in the form of clubs are limited for the school, although there is every opportunity available with a number of activities [and] clubs available for post-graduate students for the university overall."

The NUS student body is "very diverse, with students from different nationalities and different industries. The mixture of part-time students and full-time students enables students to share working experiences and even work on projects from the part-timers' companies." Getting up to speed on life in Singapore is a breeze because "the local students help the foreigners adapt to Singapore life quickly." Women in the program warn that "there are relatively few women, and there is a very slight undercurrent of sexism among the student body." On the positive side, NUS is "a safe environment [where] a lady can jog on campus even at three o'clock in the morning without feeling unsafe."

## Admissions

Applicants to NUS School of Business must provide the admissions office with transcripts for all undergraduate and graduate work, GMAT scores, TOEFL scores (for non-native English speakers), a personal statement, letters of recommendation, and a resume demonstrating at least two years of post-baccalaureate professional experience. The admissions committee also reviews the application for evidence of "the attitude and aptitude of applicant, leadership skills, entrepreneurial quality, and value to alumni." The school's website notes that an "acceptable" GMAT score is one above 600. Scholarships are available.

### FINANCIAL FACTS

| | |
|---|---|
| Annual tuition | $8,750 |
| Books and supplies | $600 |
| Room & board | |
| (on/off-campus) | $8,625/$5,625 |
| % of students receiving grants | 16 |
| Average grant | $17,000 |

### ADMISSIONS

| | |
|---|---|
| **Admissions Selectivity Rating** | **88** |
| # of applications received | 258 |
| % applicants accepted | 49 |
| % acceptees attending | 50 |
| Average GMAT | 647 |
| Range of GMAT | 620–680 |
| TOEFL required of | |
| international students? | yes |
| Minimum TOEFL | |
| (paper/computer) | 620/260 |
| Application fee | $35 |
| International application fee | $20 |
| Regular application deadline | 3/31 |
| Regular notification | 5/31 |
| Application deadline/notification | |
| Round 1: | 12/31 / 1/31 |
| Round 2: | 3/31 / 5/31 |
| Deferment available? | yes |
| Maximum length | |
| of deferment | 1 year |

### APPLICANTS ALSO LOOK AT
Nanyang Technological University
(Singapore)

### EMPLOYMENT PROFILE

| | | | | |
|---|---|---|---|---|
| Career Rating | 73 | **Grads employed by field:** | **%** | **avg. salary:** |
| **Primary source of full-time** | | Finance | 15 | NR |
| **job acceptances** | | Marketing | 24 | NR |
| School-facilitated activities | 10% | MIS | 8 | NR |
| Graduate-facilitated activities | 33% | Operations | 3 | NR |
| Unknown | 24% | Consulting | 16 | NR |
| | | General Management | 11 | NR |
| Average starting salary | $49,700 | Other | 23 | NR |
| Percent employed | 86 | | | |

# NAVAL POSTGRADUATE SCHOOL
## THE GRADUATE SCHOOL OF BUSINESS AND PUBLIC POLICY

## Academics

At the Graduate School of Business and Public Policy at the Naval Postgraduate School, the MBA that you receive is uniquely defense-focused. Designed to educate officers in the armed forces as well as civilian employees of the Department of Defense (DoD), the school focuses its education exclusively on the current management practices that will be useful in a defense-related position. This does not by any means indicate that the education is below the standards of other schools. As one student puts it, an MBA from the Naval Postgraduate School means a "quality education for no charge from exceptional personnel. The majority of students are navy, but a growing amount of them are from other services and governmental agencies." Still, keep in mind that ordinary civilians—those who are not affiliated with the DoD or armed services—need not apply. This is a shame; as one student says, "The school is great! It's too bad civilians can't attend."

The Naval Postgraduate School is in the unique position to offer, in its own words, an "interdisciplinary approach to problem-solving and policy analysis by applying quantitative, financial, economics, information technology, and other state-of-the-art management techniques and concepts to military management and policy issues." And a graduate of the Naval Postgraduate School's MBA program is guaranteed to "know the latest management theory and practices, embracing leadership, communication, organization design, and planning within large public and private-sector organizations, as well as military subunits and activities."

To satisfy the unique objectives of the program, an MBA from the Naval Postgraduate School takes 18 months. There's the 33 business core (33 credit hours), the 18 mission-related core (18 credit hours), and the master's application project or thesis. For the most part, students are enthusiastic about their classes. As one puts it, "the professors are experts in their field but respect us as military officers, so the rapport is very good. They are extremely accessible and many will keep in touch even after graduation." Still, many feel overly taxed by the intense concentration of education in such a short period of time. As one says, "the course load is very heavy, and we are made to finish in a very short time period (much less than civilians who choose [what] school they go to). They should either lighten the load or make the length of schooling longer." In addition, "being a military school, joint professional/military education is also a requirement. All said, there is little room left over for anything but school." Still, students are enthusiastic and claim with pride that they attend a "great defense/public-policy-oriented program."

## Career and Placement

Placement and recruiting are less of an issue at the Naval Postgraduate School, since most of the students are already employed by the United States military and are working toward a degree that will more or less ensure them a job with the Department of Defense. As one student puts it, "This school is geared for people involved in government service of some type. Therefore, it is unnecessary to have employment recruiters or job fairs on campus." And another points out that "the school's contacts with Department of Defense and contractors provide some pretty amazing research possibilities to include sponsoring of students to work on real-world issues."

## Student Life and Environment

Although, like all students, Naval Postgraduate MBAs complain about the workload, the beauty of their natural surroundings (the Monterey Peninsula in Northern California) leaves little room for complaints. As one student puts it, "I can't think of a more gorgeous place to go to school. There is plenty to do outside of school. Whether you're a golfer,

### FINANCIAL FACTS

| | |
|---|---|
| % of students receiving aid | 100 |
| % of first-year students receiving aid | 100 |
| % of students receiving grants | 100 |

### ADMISSIONS

**Admissions Selectivity Rating 60\***

| | |
|---|---|
| TOEFL required of international students? | yes |
| Minimum TOEFL (computer) | 207 |
| Application fee | $0 |
| International application fee | $0 |
| Deferment available? | yes |
| Maximum length of deferment | 6 months |
| Non-fall admissions? | yes |

kayaker, biker, scuba diver, or you just like to take pleasant oceanfront walks, you'll find something you'll love to do here." Because the school itself was built on the grounds of an aging luxury resort, "the campus preserves the sense of being on a resort. The administration building is located in the old main building of the hotel and is absolutely gorgeous. The gardens are still well tended and it is not uncommon to see peacocks and geese strutting about campus." Another adds, "Monterey is a beautiful location with plenty to do. Beach parties, skiing trips, whale watching, professional sports, and trips to national parks are usually ongoing for students to participate in." The only problem, it seems, is finding the time to enjoy it all. One student complains, "I thought I'd have a lot more time for golf. But I guess it beats being on a boat!"

Despite the grandeur of the physical surroundings, some students feel compelled to point out that "the biggest issue with the Naval Postgraduate School is the cost of living. This is something the school cannot do anything about. It is located in a beautiful luxury vacation area that requires a hefty wallet to support it." Others add, "The housing we live in is substandard—way too small and 50 years old with no improvements been done on them. The navy does not pay enough of a housing allowance to live in the community, so it is prohibitively expensive."

## Admissions

Requirements for admission to the Graduate School of Business and Public Policy at the Naval Postgraduate School are a little different from most MBA programs. For one thing, civilians—that is, those not enlisted in a branch of the military or in government work—are not admitted at all. The school points out, however, that quality is not affected by limiting the applicant pool. To be considered, "a baccalaureate degree with above-average grades is required." In addition, an APC score of 345 is required. The admissions board says that, at the Naval Postgraduate School, "officers from the U.S. services and DoD employees may start the program with widely varied academic backgrounds. Each student's prior academic work and related military and civilian experiences are evaluated for courses previously completed and applicable to the student's concentration area for possible validation examination to satisfy some required core courses."

| EMPLOYMENT PROFILE | | | | |
|---|---|---|---|---|
| **Career Rating** | 92 | **Grads employed by field:** | **% avg. salary:** | |
| **Primary source of full-time job acceptances** | | Other | 100 | NR |
| School-facilitated activities | 165 (100%) | | | |
| Average starting salary | $90,000 | | | |

# NEW JERSEY INSTITUTE OF TECHNOLOGY
## SCHOOL OF MANAGEMENT

### GENERAL INFORMATION
| | |
|---|---|
| Type of school | public |
| Environment | metropolis |
| Academic calendar | semester |

### SURVEY SAYS...
Friendly students
Happy students
*Solid preparation in:*
General management
Teamwork
Presentation skills
Quantitative skills
Computer skills
Doing business in a global economy

### STUDENTS
| | |
|---|---|
| Enrollment of parent institution | 8,249 |
| Enrollment of business school | 191 |
| % male/female | 62/38 |
| % out-of-state | 10 |
| % part-time | 66 |
| % minorities | 9 |
| % international | 38 |
| Average age at entry | 31 |
| Average years work experience at entry | 5 |

### ACADEMICS
| | |
|---|---|
| **Academic Experience Rating** | **76** |
| Student/faculty ratio | 13:1 |
| Profs interesting rating | 72 |
| Profs accessible rating | 62 |

## Academics

The New Jersey Institute of Technology MBA program "offers a technology-focused curriculum" that "is best suited for future managers/leaders in the technical/IT field." Students enrolled in this "affordable, convenient" program tell us that an "interesting curriculum focused on practical knowledge" "provides a very good blend of business and technology management" supplemented by "first-rate facilities." The school offers a 48-credit MBA that can be completed in two years by full-timers or four years by part-timers. An 18-month accelerated Executive MBA is open to managers and professionals; the program meets on alternate Saturdays. The availability of "both in-class and online course options makes the school very flexible."

NJIT's curriculum focuses on the development and interrelation of four themes: the transition toward a knowledge-based economy, the emergence of the digital firm, the increasing globalization of business, and the primacy of innovation in gaining a competitive advantage in the modern business world. All students here complete a 27-credit core curriculum, followed by a six-credit module in knowledge and information management, a six-credit module in technology and innovation, and nine credits to be applied toward a concentration. Concentrations are available in e-commerce, finance, infrastructure management, marketing, MIS, operations management, and transportation and logistics. The school also offers "appealing independent study opportunities."

Students report that the faculty is mixed in quality. As one of them notes, "Most professors I've encountered are decent to good. Some professors are outstanding. The overall academic experience has been very solid so far." Another explains, "There are professors who have demanding workloads that keep you up all night trying to meet deadlines and grade incredibly hard and there are those that give moderate workloads and demand far less." Many agree that "the only area that the graduate degree program can improve in is the diversification of classes. Many classes in the later modules are not available for various reasons. Most of these reasons are very valid, but when you want to take one class and it won't be offered until two semesters from now, it can leave you scrambling for another class that can take its place." EMBA students tell us that their program "is well administered and continues to get better. The program is extremely aggressive in its schedule and scope and the professors and administrators are cognizant of the fragile balance between work, family, and school."

## Career and Placement

NJIT maintains a Career Resources Center to serve all undergraduates and graduates at the university. The center includes a library, self-assessment exams, and online job postings. Counseling services are also available. Some of the companies recruiting MBAs on the NJIT campus in 2005 included ASCO Power Technologies, BAE Systems CNIR, IBM, Keyence Corporation of America, Lucent Technologies, Peri Software Solutions Inc., Schindler Elevator Corporation, Sensor Products, Sozoh Technologies, Inc, Stryker Orthopaedics, Telcordia Technologies, and Vonage.

## Student Life and Environment

Students who take their classes on the NJIT campus tell us that "academic life here consists of a strong learning culture. The supporting facilities are excellent. There is less emphasis on extracurricular activities." One MBA adds, "Commuters will find themselves driving to school and home with the lack of fun things to do after hours. Living on campus is another story. You can find things to do almost all the time. However, most grad students don't live on campus."

NJIT is located in Newark, NJ, meaning that it is not much more than a stone's throw from downtown New York City. Thus, students have access not only to endless entertainment opportunities but also to an equally robust supply of business resources.

NJIT's student body consists of "an ethnically diverse group of working professionals ranging in age from 30 to 45. Most are married with children and have extremely active lives. The range of professional business experience varies greatly. The majority of the students have low to middle-management positions. However . . . the class is committed to learning and to the overall objective of career development through the program. In general, students are friendly and helpful. The classroom dynamic is robust and healthy and as a result lends itself to thoughtful discussion."

## Admissions

All applications to the NJIT MBA program must, at minimum, include complete transcripts for all work done at the undergraduate level and an official score report for the GMAT (although applicants who already hold a master's or doctoral degree from an accredited university are exempt from the GMAT requirement). Students entering the program must also demonstrate competency in economics, finance, information systems, and quantitative methods; these requirements may be met with undergraduate work or through completion of pre-degree foundation courses. International students whose first language is not English are required to submit scores for the TOEFL exam. All students may provide supplemental application materials, including up to three letters of recommendation, a personal statement, and a description of work experience or a resume, if they wish.

### FINANCIAL FACTS

| | |
|---|---|
| Annual tuition (in-state/out-of-state) | $10,390/$14,624 |
| Fees | $1,236 |
| Books and supplies | $1,200 |
| Room & board (on/off-campus) | $8,242/$10,300 |
| Average grant | $12,000 |

### ADMISSIONS

| | |
|---|---|
| **Admissions Selectivity Rating** | **79** |
| # of applications received | 178 |
| % applicants accepted | 60 |
| % acceptees attending | 46 |
| Average GPA | 3.5 |
| TOEFL required of international students? | yes |
| Minimum TOEFL (paper/computer) | 525/213 |
| Application fee | $60 |
| International application fee | $60 |
| Regular application deadline | rolling |
| Regular notification | rolling |
| Non-fall admissions? | yes |

# NEW MEXICO STATE UNIVERSITY
## COLLEGE OF BUSINESS ADMINISTRATION AND ECONOMICS

## Academics

"Of all strengths" exhibited by the College of Business Administration and Economics at New Mexico State University, "the administration/faculty/staff are the greatest components of the business college," students agree. NMSU, which offers a general MBA with the opportunity to forge an area of specialization in agribusiness, international business, or information systems, has a faculty that is "very helpful and friendly, approachable, encouraging, and respectful of our contributions. Some of them are the greatest teachers." Students have their pet theories about how NMSU attracts its teachers, especially the more experienced ones: "A big reason senior faculty are so prevalent at NMSU is because of the wonderful climate," explained one MBA.

The NMSU curriculum consists of thirty hours of required courses, including a capstone course that culminates in a term paper, which must be defended in an oral examination. The school's website states that "while there are no elective courses required in the MBA degree program, students are encouraged to take any additional course work that fits their interests. Careful scheduling may enable interested students to complete the requirements of a minor or specialization during their courses of study." Students love the curriculum's focus on in-class discussion, telling us that "the class discussion always gives a lot of benefits to students. Because of the superfriendly people here, the student always enjoys being in school." However, they wish that the curriculum would reduce the number of lecture courses and incorporate more case studies and hands-on lessons.

The program is among the nation's more affordable, especially for in-state students. One student observes, "Considering the cost of tuition and the value of education at NMSU, there is no other program in the region that can compete. Most would say the business college is a 'diamond in the rough.'" The bargain-basement price occasionally impacts school policy, as when professors have to teach courses outside their fields of expertise; one MBA notes, "The professors are knowledgeable in their fields, but when the university has some [of them] teach other courses outside of their field, that makes it difficult. They struggle with structuring the class instruction to the needs of the students. My overall experience here at NMSU has been great otherwise."

Unlike most state schools, NMSU's MBA program is well run. Students tell us that "NMSU's administration does an admirable job keeping things running smoothly," and that "the business administration is very organized and helpful to students." They also appreciate how the school is "moving into the future by utilizing technology for registering and tuition payments" (among other areas).

## Career and Placement

NMSU's Placement and Career Services office provides university students with on-campus employment, internship listings, career listings, workshops, advising, job fairs, and online research tools. The annual Career Expo is the main on-campus recruiting event; because it serves the entire school, only some of the hundreds of companies who visit during the Expo are seeking MBA students. Top employers in the Las Cruces area include Border Foods, the City of Las Cruces, Excell Agent Services, Memorial Medical Center, NASA, New Mexico State University, Wal-Mart, and White Sands Missile Range.

Dr. R. Wayne Headrick, Director, MBA Program
114 Guthrie Hall, MSC 3GSP, Las Cruces, NM 88003-8001 United States
Phone: 505-646-8003 • Fax: 505-646-7977
E-mail: mba@nmsu.edu • Website: http://mba.nmsu.edu

## Student Life and Environment

MBAs enjoy a "very mellow and enjoyable life on campus, with a true Southwest climate." The "laid-back atmosphere" is enhanced by "helpful and friendly people, a great education at a low cost, a nice campus, and a climate that is also a great bonus." A confluence of white, Chicano, and Mexican populations (as well as smaller Black and Indian populations) contributes to this "culturally rich area in and around Las Cruces." The student body reflects the region's diversity; MBAs boast that "this is a very multicultural school, no question. The fact that we are a Land Grant institution and highly rated by the Carnegie Foundation helps." Students also love the "pristine location" in this agricultural area bordered on the east by the Organ Mountains.

NMSU works students hard, but not too hard. One MBA explains that "life at school is at a comfortable pace. Professors are willing to push you as far as you are willing. You are not held to any outrageous standards. In fact, you really have an opportunity to discover your own limits and capabilities." Most students work at least part-time, which they can do since classes are held at night. Some students find time for extracurricular activities, such as Delta Sigma Pi, the Professional Business Fraternity; Sigma Iota Epsilon, the Professional Management Fraternity; and numerous professional associations, cultural-heritage groups, and national honor societies.

## Admissions

New Mexico State University requires applicants to provide official copies of all transcripts for graduate and undergraduate work, as well as GMAT scores. International applicants must also submit TOEFL scores. NMSU uses the formula GPA x GMAT to eliminate candidates; successful applicants must score at least a 1400 under the formula. All students must demonstrate proficiency in financial accounting, macroeconomics, statistics and calculus, as well as some familiarity with the program's core areas of analysis and markets, domestic and global economic environments of organizations, financial reporting, human behavior in organizations, and the creation and distribution of goods and services.

### FINANCIAL FACTS

| | |
|---|---|
| Annual tuition (in-state/out-of-state) | $3,624/$11,550 |
| Books and supplies | $1,000 |
| Room & board | |
| (on/off-campus) | $5,200/$7,000 |
| % of students receiving aid | 95 |
| % of first-year students receiving aid | 19 |
| % of students receiving grants | 23 |

### ADMISSIONS

| | |
|---|---|
| **Admissions Selectivity Rating** | **75** |
| # of applications received | 73 |
| % applicants accepted | 60 |
| % acceptees attending | 59 |
| Average GMAT | 491 |
| Range of GMAT | 440–550 |
| Average GPA | 3.7 |
| TOEFL required of international students? | yes |
| Minimum TOEFL (paper/computer) | 530/197 |
| Application fee | $30 |
| International application fee | $50 |
| Regular application deadline | 7/1 |
| Regular notification | 8/4 |
| Deferment available? | yes |
| Maximum length of deferment | 1 year |
| Transfer students accepted? | yes |
| Transfer application policy A maximum of 12 semesters credits from AACSB-accredited schools. | |
| Non-fall admissions? | yes |
| Need-blind admissions? | yes |

| EMPLOYMENT PROFILE | | | |
|---|---|---|---|
| **Career Rating** | **62** | **Grads employed by field:** | **% avg. salary:** |
| Average starting salary | $40,000 | Accounting | 7 | NR |
| | | Finance | 2 | NR |
| | | Marketing | 5 | NR |
| | | Operations | 2 | NR |
| | | Consulting | 2 | NR |
| | | General Management | 7 | NR |
| | | Quantitative | 2 | NR |

# NEW YORK UNIVERSITY
## LEONARD N. STERN SCHOOL OF BUSINESS

### GENERAL INFORMATION

| | |
|---|---|
| Type of school | private |
| Environment | metropolis |
| Academic calendar | semester |

### SURVEY SAYS...
Good social scene
*Solid preparation in:*
Finance
Quantitative skills

### STUDENTS

| | |
|---|---|
| Enrollment of parent institution | 55,128 |
| Enrollment of business school | 2,550 |
| % male/female | 67/33 |
| % part-time | 70 |
| % minorities | 11 |
| % international | 28 |
| Average age at entry | 27 |
| Average years work experience at entry | 4.9 |

### ACADEMICS

| | |
|---|---|
| **Academic Experience Rating** | **98** |
| Student/faculty ratio | 4:1 |
| Profs interesting rating | 90 |
| Profs accessible rating | 97 |
| % female faculty | 21 |

### JOINT DEGREES
JD/MBA, with the School of Law, 4 years; MA/MBA, with the Institute of French Studies (GSAS), 3 years; MA/MBA, with the Department of Politics (GSAS), 3 years; MPA/MBA, with the School of Public Administration, 3 years

### PROMINENT ALUMNI
Richard Fuld, Chair and CEO, Lehman Brothers Holdings, Inc.; Thomas E. Freston III, Chief Executive, Viacom; Kathryn B. Swinter, Head, Leveraged Finance, N. America, BNP Bank; Robert Greifeld, President and Chief Executive Officer, the Nasda; Kathleen Corbet, President, Standard & Poor's

## Academics

Students at NYU's Leonard N. Stern School of Business are quick to point out that "business schools need to keep pace with the business environment" and even quicker to point out that there may be no better place in the world to do that than New York City. Stern students celebrate the fact that their prime location makes it "well-connected with the large financial institutions [and boast that] there are countless internships offered throughout the school year and opportunities to supplement course work with practical experience." In addition, Stern's location allows it to attract top businesspeople as adjunct faculty. From them, students get practical training and valuable connections. "I've been taught by many 'celebrity'-level professors," says one student. "How many schools have Nobel Prize winners teaching economics?"

Still, celebrity won't mean lack of access, according to most Sternies: "One professor finally had to declare the men's room off-limits to get a little peace. That's the only limit I've ever heard a teacher set on accessibility." And almost everyone agrees that the faculty "teaches concepts in a clear and concise manner and demonstrates how they operate in a real-world context. I could not ask for a more rewarding and challenging academic experience."

With the rapid changes taking place in business today, Stern has made a conscious effort to adapt and change. According to the school, "an international perspective has been formally incorporated into the core program." The core program is covered in the first two semesters with a capstone core course in the second year. There is flexibility to waive, by undergraduate degree or proficiency exams, certain of the 8 core courses. This allows students to take more elective courses in their program. Summer internships between the first and second years are a critical part of the students' overall MBA experience.

All students graduate with an MBA and can choose as many as three specializations or decide to pursue only a general management degree. And many students believe that, though "some areas such as management lag behind the school's core strength in finance, [Stern is] making a genuine attempt to steer the image from being just a finance school to a general-management school."

Special programs and initiatives abound at Stern. They claim to be able to use New York City as a "learning laboratory," and it shows. In the integrated development program, select first-year students receive a year of in-depth mentoring from alumni and recent graduates working in the students' field of interest. In the Stern Consulting Corps, students work at nonprofits and small businesses all around the city. Student exchange programs send potential MBAs overseas for long- or short-term programs (to Germany, Denmark, and Argentina, most recently). In the Stern Speakers Lunch program, select students wine and dine some of today's best-known business leaders. With all that's going on, it is no wonder most students claim to feel "a strong sense of momentum and energy at the school that is completely revitalizing."

## Career and Placement

Being between Wall Street and Midtown definitely has its perks for Stern's Office of Career Development. Recruiters such as American Express, Bank of New York, Bear Stearns & Company Inc., Citigroup, Deloitte Touche Tohmatsu, Goldman Sachs, and JPMorgan Chase all have a strong presence at the school. As one student says, "There is

DINA DOMMETT, ASSISTANT DEAN, MBA ADMISSIONS
44 WEST 4TH STREET, SUITE 6-70, NEW YORK, NY 10012 UNITED STATES
PHONE: 212-998-0600 • FAX: 212-995-4231
E-MAIL: STERNMBA@STERN.NYU.EDU • WEBSITE: WWW.STERN.NYU.EDU

a huge emphasis on career here. It's overwhelming at first, and then you realize how great it is. After all, that is why you are here. Everything is right here—anyone you want to meet with, anything you want to do." If there is a downside to this, it is that Stern tends to rely rather heavily on employers within New York City's limits. "Since the school is in New York, having access to many investment banks is not as spectacular an accomplishment on the part of the school as it is a facet of the New York City location. The Office of Career Development needs to focus much more on establishing relationships outside of the core New York City recruiters." According to the school, "while students do accept positions nationally and internationally, by and large students that come to Stern for a 2-year educational experience wind up falling in love with New York and staying. Moreover, its location is a mecca for several key industries and provides Stern students with a broad range of opportunities that meet their career objectives."

Though students report good relations with alumni, particularly those who participate in the Integrated Development Program, others gripe that Stern has only "recently established a formal alumni relations office, and so it is slightly behind other schools in that respect."

## Student Life and Environment

For students at Stern, the consensus seems to be that life in the city is fabulous. "We're in the middle of New York City! How could life be any less than fantastic?" one MBA asks. From free music in Washington Square to museums, from fashion shows to ferry rides, Stern's campus boasts all of the advantages of New York City. "Stern is a city school. There's a lot going on outside the campus, and people take advantage. Also, lots of Stern students lived in NYC before school, so they already have social lives that exist outside school. That said, I think there's still a decent amount of social activity around the school." Of course Stern also offers some of the disadvantages of New York City. Some students not native to the city feel that "it is harder to make friends with people in a school in New York City as many people have established their own lives." Overall, though, students seem to enjoy the life. One student relates, "From Thursday night Beer Blasts to a 13-day trip to South Africa where I went cage-diving with white sharks, I've enjoyed every moment of bonding with my classmates and made great friends from the start."

## Admissions

Stern enrolls somewhere between 350 to 400 students each year. The average GMAT score of an admitted MBA student is 699, and the average GPA is 3.4. Almost all the undergraduate degrees of admitted students are in business, math, science and engineering, or economics. Very few were in arts and humanities. Though mastery of English is required for all applicants to Stern, they do not have a minimum TOEFL score requirement.

### FINANCIAL FACTS

| | |
|---|---|
| Annual tuition | $35,900 |
| Fees | $1,800 |
| Books and supplies | $1,350 |
| Room & board | $18,040 |
| % of students receiving aid | 74 |
| % of first-year students receiving aid | 73 |
| % of students receiving loans | 63 |
| % of students receiving grants | 48 |
| Average award package | $45,600 |
| Average grant | $13,950 |
| Average student loan debt | $66,271 |

### ADMISSIONS

| | |
|---|---|
| **Admissions Selectivity Rating** | **97** |
| # of applications received | 3,231 |
| % applicants accepted | 25 |
| % acceptees attending | 45 |
| Average GMAT | 699 |
| Range of GMAT | 650–750 |
| Average GPA | 3.4 |
| TOEFL required of international students? | yes |
| Application fee | $175 |
| International application fee | $175 |
| Application deadline/notification | |
| Round 1: | 12/1 / 2/15 |
| Round 2: | 1/15 / 4/1 |
| Round 3: | 3/15 / 6/1 |
| Non-fall admissions? | yes |
| Need-blind admissions? | yes |

### EMPLOYMENT PROFILE

| Career Rating | 98 | Grads employed by field: | % | avg. salary: |
|---|---|---|---|---|
| **Primary source of full-time job acceptances** | | Finance | 62 | $143,208 |
| | | Marketing | 19 | $118,120 |
| School-facilitated activities | 216 (69%) | MIS | 2 | $124,667 |
| Graduate-facilitated activities | 69 (22%) | Operations | 2 | $108,333 |
| Unknown | 3 (9%) | Consulting | 13 | $139,724 |
| | | General Management | 1 | $104,927 |
| Average starting salary | $90,766 | Venture Capital | 1 | $144,750 |
| Percent employed | 92 | | | |

# NORTH CAROLINA STATE UNIVERSITY
## COLLEGE OF MANAGEMENT

### GENERAL INFORMATION
| | |
|---|---|
| Type of school | public |
| Environment | metropolis |
| Academic calendar | semester |

### SURVEY SAYS...
Cutting-edge classes
Smart classrooms
*Solid preparation in:*
Teamwork
Communication/interpersonal skills
Presentation skills

### STUDENTS
| | |
|---|---|
| Enrollment of parent institution | 29,957 |
| Enrollment of business school | 319 |
| % male/female | 67/33 |
| % out-of-state | 12 |
| % part-time | 76 |
| % minorities | 8 |
| % international | 43 |
| Average age at entry | 27 |
| Average years work experience at entry | 3.6 |

### ACADEMICS
| | |
|---|---|
| **Academic Experience Rating** | **88** |
| Student/faculty ratio | 10:1 |
| Profs interesting rating | 86 |
| Profs accessible rating | 84 |
| % female faculty | 19 |
| % minority faculty | 12 |

### JOINT DEGREES
Joint Masters of Microbial Biotechnology and MBA, 3-year program; Joint Degree in Doctor of Veterinary Medicine (DVM) and MBA, 5-year program

### PROMINENT ALUMNI
Tony O'Driscoll, Senior Learning Strategist, IBM; John McCarley, CIO, VP for IT, Bowe/Bell & Howell; Eric Gregg, Publisher, Triangle Tech Journal; John Silvestri, VP Operations, Cantor Fitzgerald; Sam Matheny, DTV-VP & General Manager, Capital Broadcasting Group

## Academics

"The greatest strength of the MBA program at North Carolina State is its focus on technology," many students at this small, new graduate business program in Raleigh tell us. NCSU's program is tailor-made to fit the needs of businesses in nearby Research Triangle Park, where communications, technology, and pharmaceutical firms are always looking to hire "the engineers and scientists to whom this program caters."

NCSU's focus on technology and engineering allows it to offer some unique areas of concentration. The school is "very strong in the integration of marketing and technical knowledge" thanks to its "unique Product Innovation Management program," for example. A biotechnology and pharmaceutical program is another standout; both the faculty and student body benefit from the school's proximity to GlaxoSmithKline, Novartis, and other big regional pharmaceutical players. Students here also boast about the "outstanding supply-chain management program, which carries a great reputation in the region."

Students describe NCSU professors as "hit and miss," but with more hits than misses. They're generally "very energetic about the subjects they teach," "have a wealth of experience from the real world that they use to help teach," and "are easy to contact outside of class and quick to return phone calls." Students appreciate a pedagogical approach across the curriculum that is "focused more on practical team projects and less on business case study." "Strong emphases on communications and presentations skills" and "cross-functional insight into business" are also highly valued. On the downside, "being at a state-funded school [means] budget crunches have hit hard and cut back a lot of nice extras" here.

About two-thirds of all students attend part-time. Full-timers find internships between their first and second year. As one second-year full-time student observes, "Having done an internship this past summer and continued it part-time into the school year, I can definitely say that school is much tougher than real life. I don't know what other scale I can use, other than to say that school appears to be preparing me for difficult situations I may face in the future."

## Career and Placement

The program at NCSU "has some very strong industry connections, so students have very well-known companies to choose from for employment," MBAs tell us. In 2005, internship placements included positions with CAT, Chevron Texaco, Cree, Delphi, Duke Energy, Heard & Associates, IBM, Halliburton, the Hoop Group, Last Mile, MCNBC, MTS Sensors, Murphy Family SAS, Ventures, Northrop Grumman, Progress Energy, Red Hat, Starquest Dance, Talecris, and VF Corporation. Graduating MBAs found work with BB&T, Bechtel, Boston Scientific, Capital One, Chevron Texaco, Cisco, Credit Suisse, Duke Energy, First Boston, IBM, John Deere, Last Mile, Nortel, RBC Centura, Red Hat, SAS, Sigmon, Team Pharma, Tech Engage, Teleflex, and Withers.

PAM BOSTIC, MBA PROGRAM DIRECTOR
MBA PROGRAM OFFICE /CAMPUS BOX 7229, RALEIGH, NC 27695-7229 UNITED STATES
PHONE: 919-515-5584 • FAX: 919-515-5073
E-MAIL: MBA@NCSU.EDU • WEBSITE: WWW.MBA.NCSU.EDU

## Student Life and Environment

The majority of NCSU's MBAs are part-time students, most of whom work in addition to attending school. One such student explains, "We don't have a lot of free time. We enjoy the experience of being in school, but work, classes, and the constant group meetings for classes limit the amount of free time." Full-time students "generally do not work at the same time" and so "usually have more free time to concentrate on things outside of school." As one of these students explains, "Our academic work and social life is well balanced. Almost every fortnight the entire class has a party. All the students in the class are constantly working on group projects and we have formed good study groups, which help us a lot by dividing the work among ourselves and thus making us able to accomplish everything."

Full-timers and part-timers alike agree that "Raleigh, NC, is a great city. The weather here is outstanding. And there are plenty of available activities, such as attending NC State football and basketball games." Located in central North Carolina, Raleigh allows for easy escapes to the beach (about two hours away by car) or the mountains (about three hours away, in the other direction). Raleigh is part of a greater metropolitan area known as the Triangle that is also home to University of North Carolina, Duke University, and numerous other smaller colleges and universities.

The MBA program at NCSU draws a "friendly, professional, mature, experienced, and extremely helpful" student body. A "strong sense of sharing our experience and supporting each other as we face many challenges" helps students survive the sometimes intense demands of the program. China, Belarus, India, Turkey, Romania, Bulgaria, and Jamaica are among the nations represented in the student body here.

## Admissions

Admission to NCSU's MBA program is "highly competitive." Successful candidates typically have strong undergraduate academic records and solid GMAT scores, work experience "demonstrating management potential, leadership skills, creativity," the ability to work in teams, and a genuine interest in technology as it relates to management issues. Requirements include preparatory classes in accounting, statistics, finance and economics, which are taken online by all students. Interviews are required prior to admission; the school contacts applicants who are deemed potential candidates for the program.

### FINANCIAL FACTS

| | |
|---|---|
| Annual tuition (in-state/out-of-state) | $10,338/$22,261 |
| Fees | $1,174 |
| Books and supplies | $1,000 |
| Room & board (on/off-campus) | $6,000/$8,574 |
| % of first-year students receiving aid | 97 |
| Average grant | $9,220 |
| Average student loan debt | $40,473 |

### ADMISSIONS

| | |
|---|---|
| Admissions Selectivity Rating | 85 |
| # of applications received | 107 |
| % applicants accepted | 60 |
| % acceptees attending | 64 |
| Average GMAT | 602 |
| Range of GMAT | 570–640 |
| Average GPA | 3.3 |
| TOEFL required of international students? | yes |
| Minimum TOEFL (paper/computer) | 600/250 |
| Application fee | $55 |
| International application fee | $65 |
| Regular application deadline | 3/1 |
| Regular notification | 4/1 |
| Application deadline | |
| Round 1: | 10/13 |
| Round 2: | 1/4 |
| Round 3: | 3/1 |
| Early decision program? | yes |
| ED deadline/notification | 10/13 / 11/13 |
| Deferment available? | yes |
| Maximum length of deferment | 1 year |
| Transfer students accepted? | yes |
| Transfer application policy Students may transfer up to 12 credits from another AACSB-accredited MBA program. | |
| Need-blind admissions? | yes |

### APPLICANTS ALSO LOOK AT

University of Maryland, University of North Carolina at Chapel Hill, University of North Carolina at Charlotte, University of South Carolina, Wake Forest University—Babcock

### EMPLOYMENT PROFILE

| Career Rating | 86 | Grads employed by field: | % | avg. salary: |
|---|---|---|---|---|
| Average starting salary | $70,973 | Accounting | 7 | $66,000 |
| Percent employed | 82 | Finance | 8 | $66,000 |
| | | Marketing | 13 | $59,000 |
| | | Operations | 50 | $71,000 |
| | | Consulting | 15 | $73,000 |
| | | General Management | 5 | $64,000 |
| | | Other | 2 | $80,000 |

# NORTHEASTERN UNIVERSITY
## COLLEGE OF BUSINESS ADMINISTRATION

## Academics

Northeastern University has long been known as a leader in the field of cooperative education, and full-time MBAs here benefit from the school's expertise through a six-month corporate residency program that "puts students with brand-name corporations. The program provides a venue for students to apply and prove themselves in the industry they desire." Students love both the idea and the execution of co-op—it is the number one reason cited by full-time students for choosing Northeastern. They report that "the six-month corporate residency opportunity allows students to graduate with measurable real-world experience, unlike schools that offer six-week internships. NEU has strong relationships with a lot of Boston's biggest companies. Especially if you are looking to gain experience in a new field, this program is great." As an added bonus, it "pays pretty well, too!"

Approximately one-third of MBAs at NEU enroll in the full-time Co-op MBA Program, which can typically be completed in 20 to 24 months. The curriculum consists of foundation courses, in a career management course, a globalization requirement, elective work (concentrations are available in finance, marketing, and supply-chain management), and a corporate residency (optional, but most students opt in). Students report that "the required full-time courses tend to be more challenging than the electives (which are offered in the evenings to accommodate both the full- and part-time students)" and praise their professors, telling us that they are "very well-regarded in their field." One student notes, "Several professors have produced highly influential research studies, and many are accomplished professionals in the private/public sectors." Another mentions, "All of my professors have been Ivy-League educated, and have taught at many of the leading business schools around the country. The administrators are very accessible as well, and all of my concerns have been addressed promptly."

Northeastern also offers a part-time MBA consisting of 12 core courses and nine electives. Part-time students typically take between two and seven years to finish the degree, taking one or two classes per semester in once-a-week evening and/or Saturday sessions. Other degree options at Northeastern include a High-Tech MBA (for tech experts seeking business acumen), an Executive MBA, master's programs in accounting, finance, and taxation, and certificate programs in advanced study of business administration, supply-chain management, and taxation.

## Career and Placement

Northeastern's full-time program necessitates that the school forge strong connections to Boston-area businesses, and these relationships pay dividends for the efforts of the school's Career Center. "Our Career Center's corporate residency placement efforts and relationships with companies for that purpose are outstanding," explains one student. Employers in 2004 included Bayer, Blue Cross Blue Shield, Fidelity Investments, Manulife Financial, Masterfoods, Neutrogena, Sun Microsystems, and Terrapin Capital. NEU students agree the corporate residency program definitely provides students with a leg up when it comes time for their corporate residency companies to hire new full-timers.

All told, more than 50 companies typically recruit MBAs on campus each year; another 80 come looking for summer interns and corporate residency employees. Employers most likely to hire Northeastern MBAs after graduation include TJX Corporation, Raytheon Company, Masterfoods, Maersk Logistics, WR Grace, Texas Instruments, Mellon Financial Corporation, and the State Street Corporation.

EVELYN TATE, DIRECTOR, RECRUITMENT AND ADMISSIONS
350 DODGE HALL, 360 HUNTINGTON AVENUE, BOSTON, MA 02115 UNITED STATES
PHONE: 617-373-5992 • FAX: 617-373-8564
E-MAIL: GSBA@NEU.EDU • WEBSITE: WWW.CBA.NEU.EDU/GRADUATE

## Student Life and Environment

Full-time students in Northeastern's MBA program describe a "very close-knit group" of students who "go out with each other every week and often have get-togethers outside of school. The business school also sets up weekly events that we all go to." The program helps, as "classes stress group work, and students have a chance to bond and form life-time friendships" through group work. So too does life in Boston, a city that "is good fun. You can live, shop, and go to school in the best parts of Boston. Newbury, Commonwealth, and Marlborough Streets are all only a couple of blocks away." Part-time students, on the other hand, are generally too busy with work and family commit-ments to participate regularly in extracurricular life.

The Northeastern student body "is very diverse with students from all areas. Aside from U.S. students, there are international students from Asia, Africa, Europe, Central/South America, and the Caribbean represented. This gives students a global business perspec-tive and a chance to share different ideas." MBAs observe that "the student body is a happy medium of older students who are more career-focused and younger students who want to enjoy the grad-school lifestyle."

## Admissions

All applicants to the Northeastern MBA program must provide the Admissions Office with the following: a completed application (preferably online); sealed copies of official transcripts for all post-secondary schools attended; a current resume; three essays; two professional letters of recommendation; and an official GMAT score report. In addition, international students whose first language is not English must submit TOEFL results. All international students must submit transcripts that have been translated with U.S. grade equivalents assigned for work completed, as well as a certified Declaration and Certification of Finances Statement. Successful candidates will have a minimum of two years' work experience (postgraduate), demonstrated leadership ability or potential, and a strong undergraduate academic preparation.

### FINANCIAL FACTS

| | |
|---|---|
| Annual tuition | $29,770 |
| Fees | $1,843 |
| Books and supplies | $1,400 |
| Room & board | $18,900 |
| % of first-year students receiving aid | 94 |
| Average award package | $28,480 |
| Average grant | $15,135 |
| Average student loan debt | $50,427 |

### ADMISSIONS

| | |
|---|---|
| Admissions Selectivity Rating | 77 |
| # of applications received | 241 |
| % applicants accepted | 53 |
| % acceptees attending | 37 |
| Average GMAT | 537 |
| Range of GMAT | 480–590 |
| Average GPA | 3.07 |
| TOEFL required of international students? | yes |
| Minimum TOEFL (paper/computer) | 600/250 |
| Application fee | $100 |
| International application fee | $100 |
| Regular application deadline | 4/1 |
| Regular notification | 5/1 |
| Deferment available? | yes |
| Maximum length of deferment | 1 year |
| Transfer students accepted? | yes |
| Transfer application policy Transfer credit awarded for MBA courses taken at AACSB-accredited institutions. | |
| Need-blind admissions? | yes |

### APPLICANTS ALSO LOOK AT

Babson College, Boston College, Boston University, University of Massachusetts—Amherst

### EMPLOYMENT PROFILE

| Career Rating | 82 | Grads employed by field: | % | avg. salary: |
|---|---|---|---|---|
| **Primary source of full-time job acceptances** | | Accounting | 21 | $57,938 |
| | | Finance | 22 | $57,938 |
| School-facilitated activities | 44 (73%) | Human Resources | 3 | $75,000 |
| Graduate-facilitated activities | 13 (22%) | Marketing | 29 | $59,182 |
| Unknown | 3 (5%) | MIS | 3 | $85,000 |
| | | Operations | 3 | $75,000 |
| Average starting salary | $60,027 | Consulting | 16 | $60,833 |
| Percent employed | 88 | Other | 3 | $80,000 |

# NORTHERN ARIZONA UNIVERSITY
## COLLEGE OF BUSINESS ADMINISTRATION

### GENERAL INFORMATION
| | |
|---|---|
| Type of school | public |
| Environment | town |
| Academic calendar | July–May |

### SURVEY SAYS...
Cutting-edge classes
*Solid preparation in:*
General management
Teamwork
Communication/interpersonal skills
Presentation skills

### STUDENTS
| | |
|---|---|
| Enrollment of parent institution | 19,147 |
| Enrollment of business school | 12 |
| % male/female | 70/30 |
| % out-of-state | 38 |
| % minorities | 8 |
| Average age at entry | 28 |
| Average years work experience at entry | 5.3 |

### ACADEMICS
| | |
|---|---|
| **Academic Experience Rating** | **78** |
| Student/faculty ratio | 12:1 |
| Profs interesting rating | 74 |
| Profs accessible rating | 80 |
| % female faculty | 20 |
| % minority faculty | 10 |

## Academics

Students who are in a hurry to get their MBAs might want to consider the program at Northern Arizona University, whose "big strength is the fact that the program is compressed into 10 months. While it is hell completing those 10 months, we all know we won't have to spend another year in school, and we'll be able to start our careers earlier than if we had chosen a different MBA program." Those who love beautiful surroundings are in for an added bonus; NAU's Flagstaff campus is surrounded by the world's largest ponderosa pine forest, which in turn is bordered by the San Francisco Peaks. The campus setting is simply gorgeous.

Because of the intensive curriculum, however, students rarely have time to take in the stunning scenery. Course work begins with a five-week summer session that starts in early July; the summer session covers PC and communication skills for professionals, system orientation, and a survey of human-asset issues. Three core courses and two electives make up the Fall semester, which "focuses on organizational processes that provide customer value." The Spring semester, which consists of two core courses and two electives, centers on analytical approaches to managerial decision-making. Students may use their electives to forge a concentration in one of three areas of new emphasis: accounting, finance, or general management. In the summer of 2006, three new career tracks will be introduced: Marketing Analysis & Distribution Management, Environmental Management, and Geographic Information Systems. The last two will be in partnership with the renowned programs in GIS and Environmental Sciences at Northern Arizona University.

Students tell us that the entire curriculum stresses "a teamwork environment, integrated studies, topical issues, and plenty of case studies." They appreciate this approach, explaining, "the collaborative environment and emphasis on team projects help [them] learn to work well with others and show [them] that the output is better and [they] learn more." The school website reinforces this point, stating that "the goal of the core curriculum is to develop an integrated systems perspective that facilitates management of functional areas as a related unit. This integrative approach to curriculum is essential to quality systems approaches that increasingly focus on continuous improvement to enhance customer value." NAU MBAs give the faculty a thumbs-up, noting that "we have some excellent professors who are well known in the academic world."

## Career and Placement

NAU MBAs receive personalized career development advising from the MBA Director. In addition, students take a 1-credit-hour course in Career Management during both the Fall and Spring semesters. Throughout the year, employers participate in workshops, mock interviews, and company presentations. Students feel that "the placement office could do a better job of bringing recruiters up to meet [them]," but concede that "it's difficult for a small public school high up in the mountains" to attract such traffic. Between 40 and 50 companies pay recruiting visits to the campus each year.

Top employers of NAU MBAs include Intel, Pulte Homes, and General Dynamics. About one in five graduates finds a first job outside the United States.

TED BOURAS, DIRECTOR, MBA PROGRAM
PO BOX 15066, FLAGSTAFF, AZ 86011-5066 UNITED STATES
PHONE: 928-523-7342 • FAX: 928-523-7996
E-MAIL: MBA@NAU.EDU • WEBSITE: WWW.CBA.NAU.EDU/MBA

## Student Life and Environment

Full-timers at NAU finish their MBAs in less than a year's time, which makes for an extremely accelerated academic pace. One explains, "since the NAU MBA is less than one year in length, it is very intense. There is little time to spend on anything other than school. Although school is demanding, the workload is manageable." Another adds, "when not studying (which is rare), time is usually spent downtown at the bars or at small parties held by other MBA students." Flagstaff's bars "are numerous," we're told, and students in the program "enjoy getting together, especially on Thursday nights. We hit the bars to decompress."

While Flagstaff is hardly a booming economic center, it does have its benefits, especially for students in an intensive program like NAU's. One student explains, "The pace of life in Flagstaff is slower and less stressful than other places. It's laid-back, and there really is time to smell the roses (or pine trees) when we're not in class, which isn't often." The region offers plenty of opportunities to blow off steam in a healthy way; many "enjoy the outdoors (rock climbing [or] mountain biking) and they love the environment to do those activities. It's beautiful here, and doing outdoor activities is a must when living in Flagstaff." The mountain location means that things never get too hot in the summer (the average high temperature is 81 degrees F) and that skiing is readily available in the winter. The campus is not too far from Sedona and the Grand Canyon.

Students currently enjoy "modern resources such as multimedia presentation facilities, three computer-equipped classrooms, two state-of-the-art student computer laboratories, and classrooms, offices, and labs that all have access to the Internet." Future MBAs will enjoy a whole lot more; construction began on a new College of Business Administration facility in May 2004. The 110,000-square-foot facility, complete with 8 breakout rooms, 20 team-meeting rooms, and a number of network-ready public space, will be ready for occupancy in January 2006.

## Admissions

The admissions committee at NAU requires applicants to submit official copies of all undergraduate and graduate transcripts, GMAT scores, two required essays, two letters of recommendation, and a resume. MBA students are required to possess a common body of knowledge (CBK), covered at NAU in its CBK classes. All CBK course work must be completed successfully before a student can register for a 600-level class (these are core courses that are offered during summer session II).

### FINANCIAL FACTS

| | |
|---|---|
| Annual tuition (in-state/out-of-state) | $5,865/$14,514 |
| Fees | $3,500 |
| Books and supplies | $1,295 |
| Room & board | $7,520 |
| % of students receiving aid | 80 |

### ADMISSIONS

| | |
|---|---|
| **Admissions Selectivity Rating** | **84** |
| # of applications received | 57 |
| % applicants accepted | 37 |
| % acceptees attending | 57 |
| Average GMAT | 532 |
| Range of GMAT | 510–560 |
| Average GPA | 3.27 |
| TOEFL required of international students? | yes |
| Minimum TOEFL (paper/computer) | 600/250 |
| Application fee | $50 |
| International application fee | $50 |
| Regular application deadline | 5/1 |
| Regular notification | 6/1 |
| Early decision program? | yes |
| ED deadline/notification | 11/1 / 12/1 |
| Deferment available? | yes |
| Maximum length of deferment | 1 year |
| Transfer students accepted? | yes |
| Transfer application policy 9 hours towards electives only | |
| Non-fall admissions? | yes |
| Need-blind admissions? | yes |

| EMPLOYMENT PROFILE | | | | |
|---|---|---|---|---|
| Career Rating | 61 | Grads employed by field: | % | avg. salary: |
| **Primary source of full-time job acceptances** | | Accounting | 22 | NR |
| | | Finance | 22 | NR |
| School-facilitated activities | 7 (41%) | Human Resources | 6 | NR |
| Graduate-facilitated activities | 10 (59%) | Marketing | 17 | NR |
| | | General Management | 22 | NR |
| Average starting salary | $48,657 | Other | 11 | NR |
| Percent employed | 35 | | | |

# NORTHWESTERN UNIVERSITY
## KELLOGG SCHOOL OF MANAGEMENT

## GENERAL INFORMATION
| | |
|---|---|
| Type of school | private |
| Environment | town |
| Academic calendar | quarter |

### SURVEY SAYS...
Friendly students
Good social scene
Good peer network
Happy students
*Solid preparation in:*
Teamwork

### STUDENTS
| | |
|---|---|
| Enrollment of parent institution | 14,000 |
| Enrollment of business school | 2,400 |
| % male/female | 69/31 |
| % part-time | 56 |
| % minorities | 13 |
| % international | 26 |
| Average age at entry | 28 |
| Average years work experience at entry | 5.2 |

### ACADEMICS
| | |
|---|---|
| **Academic Experience Rating** | **98** |
| Student/faculty ratio | 10:1 |
| Profs interesting rating | 95 |
| Profs accessible rating | 91 |
| % female faculty | 15 |
| % minority faculty | 5 |

### JOINT DEGREES
MBA/MD, 5 years; MBA/JD, 3 years; MEM/MBA, 2 years

### PROMINENT ALUMNI
Craig Donahue, CEO, The Chicago Mercantile Exchange; Greg Josefowicz, Chair and CEO, Borders Group; Somkid Jatusripitak, Deputy Prime Minister of Thailand; Bob Eckert, CEO, Mattel; Phil Marineau, CEO, Levi Strauss & Co.

## Academics

At the Kellogg School of Management at Northwestern University, you can almost feel the cooperation in the air. Students are besieged with constant surveys and reviews, their input is always sought, and their voices and desires have a huge impact on the course the school takes both academically and socially. According to one student, "Kellogg almost doesn't have a formal administration. Students run everything." Other students agree that "it's not always the most efficient approach, but it is the best way to train tomorrow's business leaders." It also lends the school "a certain energy around the campus that brings excitement to each and every day." In the past nine years, over fifty new courses have been added to the school's curriculum, often as a result of student initiative. The continual curricular development, along with the constant initiation of new clubs and ventures, ensure that classes keep up with the cutting edge of business management. One facet of the cooperative spirit is that both professors and students receive regular evaluations. Students review the performance of the professors both at mid- and end-of-quarter. According to some students, another incentive for professors to stay at the top of their game is that "[their] year-end bonuses are based on their ratings from students." Students aren't exempt from the scrutiny of their peers, either. Through a Web-based program called TeamNet, Kellogg students are able to receive "confidential, detailed, and honest feedback on how they work in teams" from fellow students, faculty, and staff. According to the school, this produces an unparalleled ability to "respond to and give confidential peer feedback, something excellent managers do well."

Kellogg also features a unique one year program, in which students attend classes during the fall, winter, and spring programs. Students in the full-time, two-year program have the opportunity to complete an internship in the summer after their first year. The core-curriculum classes consist of nine courses in the "fundamental areas of accounting, management and organizations, marketing, finance, decision sciences, and management and strategy."

The four-quarter program also allows students to earn their MBAs in just 12 months. "Kellogg's one-year program is one-of-a-kind," one enthusiastic MBA says. "It's the best return on investment and offers great flexibility combined with small classes and highest-quality students." The school's other unique program is the Master of Management and Manufacturing (MMM), which is designed to aid students who wish to pursue "management roles in product-driven companies." This program is shared with Northwestern's McCormick School of Engineering.

Kellogg offers a lengthy list of majors in which students can specialize, from biotechnology to technology industry management. However, students often feel that "application of technology is a little slow compared to other schools." Most students who have had contact with the finance department say it's "outstanding." However, even though they have been "as well trained or better trained than peers at other top finance-business schools," Kellogg has not really developed a reputation as a premier finance school; yet, students feel that "Kellogg deserves it." One student says, "For some reason, people think Kellogg grads are not quant heavy, but [one-]third of my class are finance majors."

## Career and Placement

Major recruiters with a presence at Kellogg include McKinsey and Company, Merrill Lynch, and Bain and Company, Inc.; most students are confident that their school has a "sterling reputation among corporate recruiters." One student says, "Kellogg is not a tech school; nor is it particularly well-connected on Wall Street. I personally don't care, but some people might." Many students would also like to see "more recruiting in fields other than

BETH FLYE, ASSISTANT DEAN AND DIRECTOR OF ADMISSIONS AND FINANCIAL AID
2001 SHERIDAN ROAD, 2ND FLOOR, EVANSTON, IL 60208 UNITED STATES
PHONE: 847-491-3308 • FAX: 847-491-4960
E-MAIL: MBAADMISSIONS@KELLOGG.NORTHWESTERN.EDU
WEBSITE: WWW.KELLOGG.NORTHWESTERN.EDU

## FINANCIAL FACTS

| | |
|---|---|
| Annual tuition | $38,844 |
| Room & board | $13,515 |
| % of students receiving aid | 72 |
| Average award package | $45,900 |
| Average grant | $12,000 |
| Average student loan debt | $71,000 |

## ADMISSIONS

| | |
|---|---|
| **Admissions Selectivity Rating** | **98** |
| # of applications received | 3,918 |
| % applicants accepted | 24 |
| % acceptees attending | 56 |
| Average GMAT | 700 |
| Average GPA | 3.45 |
| TOEFL required of international students? | yes |
| Application fee | $210 |
| International application fee | $210 |
| Regular application deadline | 1/6 |
| Regular notification | 3/20 |
| Application deadline/notification | |
| Round 1: | 10/21 / 1/16 |
| Round 2: | 1/6 / 3/20 |
| Round 3: | 3/10 / 5/1 |
| Deferment available? | yes |
| Maximum length of deferment | case by case |
| Non-fall admissions? | yes |
| Need-blind admissions? | yes |

marketing, finance, and consulting." While students agree that the team-focused environment ensures that "networking at Kellogg is tremendous," many would like to see the career center focus more on locating smaller job opportunities. Some students worry that the center "is not focused enough on helping out international students get jobs—either in the U.S. or internationally."

## Student Life and Environment

Kellogg is situated in Evanston, Illinois along the shores of Lake Michigan. It is just a short commute on the El (elevated train) into downtown Chicago. According to some students, because there aren't "a lot of activities in the city of Evanston," most students appreciate the proximity to all that Chicago has to offer. However, for those who choose not to make the 30-minute commute, "there is a lot going on [at] school." There are regular social hours on Tuesdays and Fridays, and there are no classes on Wednesdays. Students say that because "a large group of students go out together regularly, you can feel confident about going out alone and meeting at least a few friends at whatever bar you choose." As one student says, "When it's time to study, we study, and [we] study hard. When it's time to play, we play well."

Many students feel that for a school whose classes hover somewhere around 700 students, "Kellogg could stand to work on its diversity—both ethnically and in terms of people from industries other than consulting."

Though the school has done multiple renovations to its facilities, which now features "17 new classrooms wired for network access, 50 group study rooms, several quiet study rooms, a 20-terminal computer training facility, an expanded computer lab, free-standing computer terminals for checking e-mail and accessing the Web, a student lounge, lockers, and a sky-lit atrium," many students would like to see more care taken with their physical environment. According to some students, "[The] buildings are getting long in the tooth."

## Admissions

Admissions officers at Kellogg have the unenviable job of having to reduce a pile of approximately 4,000 applications down to an admitted class of about 500. During this process, they look for work experience, academic excellence, and personality. The school's admissions board conducts thousands of interviews each fall. The average GMAT score is 700. Of the applicants who scored above 700 (about 3,000 in all), 21 percent were offered admission. Over 15 percent of applicants who scored within the 650 to 690 range were also accepted for admission. All Kellogg's incoming students had some full-time work experience, and the average amount of employment time was about five years. Almost 26 percent of Kellogg students hail from outside of the United States, and for those applicants, TOEFL scores are required. The average TOEFL score for enrolled students is 650.

## EMPLOYMENT PROFILE

| | |
|---|---|
| **Career Rating** | **97** |
| **Primary source of full-time job acceptances** | |
| School-facilitated activities | 285 (60%) |
| Graduate-facilitated activities | 151 (32%) |
| Unknown | 40 (8%) |
| | |
| Average starting salary | $96,690 |
| Percent employed | 92 |

# THE OHIO STATE UNIVERSITY
## FISHER COLLEGE OF BUSINESS

## Academics

"If you want a challenge and you don't want a school where you can hide in the back row or behind a laptop, consider the Fisher College of Business at Ohio State University," where "there's ample opportunity to access incredible minds and develop your own personal style to problem solving." As "a small school with intimate classes complemented by the resources of a large university," Fisher is small enough to hear students' suggestions and big enough to find quick solutions to problems. As one student explains, "The administration is very responsive to students' requests for changes to the program. The orientation for first-year students, for example, was far better this year after comments from my class." A fast-moving program (Fisher is on a quarterly academic calendar), the Fisher College MBA stresses teamwork to manage the heavy workload. One student explains, "one of the primary strengths of the program is the team concept created in the first year. You are provided with a group of four to five fellow classmates who become your team (or cohort) for the year. This concept allows students the opportunity to develop immediate connections with fellow students and teaches you the importance of team values. It also helps to ease some of the competitive pressures associated with business schools."

Fisher MBAs tout courses in supply chain, finance, operations, and "various technical specialties of business." The marketing program "needs more options," and some wish the school "would dedicate more resources for those going into nonbusiness fields after graduation (i.e., government and public service)." Fisher has "excellent international programs" whose offerings are enhanced by the university's Center for International Business and Research (CIBER). One MBA reports, "I did a course involving emerging-market field studies in Hungary and the Czech Republic in my first year and am studying abroad in Australia in my second year. Great stuff." Fisher professors are "all extremely knowledgeable about the latest trends in their fields and publish heavily in very reputed journals," but one students says, "their quality as teachers vary. I have a professor who murmurs in class and nobody can hear her clearly. Another professor is a research leader in his field but does a horrible job teaching." Students happily take the bad with the good, noting that "while their teaching styles vary, they know their material (and expect us to know it too!)" and that "they are more than willing to help anyone who requests it of them and encourage informal conversation." Some students complain that "there are too many night classes. This is one of the disadvantages of being small. We need the part-timers to create sufficient interest in some classes; hence, the evening classes."

## Career and Placement

Most Fisher MBAs agree that "the Career Services Office is good, but tends to be limited to local companies. The school's reputation is very strong in Ohio and the Midwest, but needs to continue marketing the Fisher brand so that graduates have more opportunity on the coasts and abroad." For those students who do secure employment outside of the Midwest (40 percent), a travel fund has been established to help offset the student costs associated with school-sponsored trips to a variety of job fairs and alumni events in numerous cities. Many students feel that "there is tremendous potential to leverage the alumni better, both of Fisher and OSU in general," in the past. In response, an Internet-based alumni database was established at Fisher in 2004 that contains contact information for alumni who have volunteered to assist current MBA students with their job search and internship searches. Starting in August 2004, a full-time career consultant was hired to work exclusively with international students in securing employment opportunities. Gripes aside, most concede that the office does good work; as one student observes, "despite the downturn, only 15 students from last year's class [were] still hunting for jobs" at the start of the Fall quarter. Major employers of OSU MBAs include Accenture; American Electric Power; AT Kearney; Deloitte; Eaton; Ford Motor Company;

ADMISSIONS DIRECTOR, GRADUATE PROGRAMS OFFICE
100 GERLACH HALL, 2108 NEIL AVENUE, COLUMBUS, OH 43210 UNITED STATES
PHONE: 614-688-5443 • FAX: 614-292-9006
E-MAIL: FISHERGRAD@COB.OSU.EDU • WEBSITE: WWW.FISHER.OSU.EDU/MBA

General Electric; Kimberly-Clark; IBM; Lexmark; Limited Brands; Nationwide; National City; Nestle; PricewaterhouseCooper; Ross/Abbott Labs; Procter & Gamble, and The Scotts Company. Over 200 companies make recruiting trips to the OSU campus each year. One in five students finds work outside the U.S. following graduation.

## Student Life and Environment

Extracurricular life at Fisher is driven by the program's many student-run organizations. The MBA Association, for one, "organizes several activities every week. Thursdays we have Event of the Week, which is often cosponsored by another MBA organization. They also organize tailgates for the football games and publicize events/concerts where our classmates are performing." Each of the many function- and interest-specific MBA organizations sponsor events as well, "including festival hops, industry-related networking trips, golf tournaments—the list seems endless!" There's even a group dedicated to community service. Students join as many organizations as they can handle; one MBA writes, "I am involved with three clubs and will probably be involved with more as the year goes on."

Ohio State football is practically a religion among MBAs; they report that "the football tailgating is incredible. You not only create a solid network of associates for the future, but you also create a solid network of friends, which will last a lifetime." Hometown Columbus "is a fun and growing city. There's lots to do here for all interests," including Columbus Clippers baseball (AAA level), ski trips, whitewater rafting, and lots of great local restaurants. Students warn that it is "not a city for people with seasonal mood disorder. Columbus can be miserable in winter. Take it as a hint: There are tunnels underneath the business-school complex to walk to class." Fisher is housed in a six-building complex. Students love it, describing it as "phenomenal. The classrooms are great and are well-equipped with all of the technology we need." One architect pursuing his MBA writes, "The facilities are the best of any school I have visited or seen. They are designed for the student and not for show like many other schools."

## Admissions

The admissions office at Fisher requires applicants to provide two official copies of transcripts for all undergraduate and graduate institutions attended, GMAT scores, TOEFL scores (for students whose first language is not English), three letters of recommendation, essays, and a resume of work experience (three or more years preferred), extracurricular activities, and community service. The admissions office carefully considers "the caliber of undergraduate institution and major, the quality of work experience, evidence of leadership and teamwork, and communication skills." Minority outreach programs include Graduate and Professional Schools Visitation Day, the Graduate Enrichment Fellowship Program, the Targeted Minority Recruitment Initiative, and Minority Student Visitation Weekend.

## FINANCIAL FACTS

| | |
|---|---|
| Annual tuition (in-state/out-of-state) | $17,181/$29,778 |
| Fees | $675 |
| Books and supplies | $1,956 |
| Room & board (on/off-campus) | $6,486/$6,372 |
| % of students receiving aid | 74 |
| % of first-year students receiving aid | 84 |
| % of students receiving loans | 57 |
| % of students receiving grants | 61 |
| Average award package | $26,409 |
| Average grant | $17,609 |

## ADMISSIONS

| | |
|---|---|
| Admissions Selectivity Rating | 91 |
| # of applications received | 591 |
| % applicants accepted | 50 |
| % acceptees attending | 41 |
| Average GMAT | 662 |
| Range of GMAT | 630–700 |
| Average GPA | 3.44 |
| TOEFL required of international students? | yes |
| Minimum TOEFL (paper/computer) | 600/250 |
| Application fee | $40 |
| International application fee | $50 |
| Regular application deadline | rolling |
| Regular notification | rolling |
| Deferment available? | yes |
| Maximum length of deferment | 1 year |
| Need-blind admissions? | yes |

## APPLICANTS ALSO LOOK AT

Indiana University—Bloomington, Purdue University, University of Michigan, University of North Carolina at Chapel Hill

## EMPLOYMENT PROFILE

| Career Rating | 94 | Grads employed by field: | % | avg. salary: |
|---|---|---|---|---|
| Primary source of full-time job acceptances | | Accounting | 1 | $69,000 |
| | | Finance | 27 | $78,529 |
| School-facilitated activities | 65 (73%) | Marketing | 18 | $81,568 |
| Graduate-facilitated activities | 24 (27%) | Operations | 25 | $75,211 |
| | | Strategic Planning | 4 | $100,000 |
| Average starting salary | $80,081 | Consulting | 14 | $88,767 |
| Percent employed | 95 | General Management | 8 | $78,524 |
| | | Global Management | 2 | $97,500 |
| | | Internet/New Media | 1 | $75,000 |

# OLD DOMINION UNIVERSITY
## COLLEGE OF BUSINESS AND PUBLIC ADMINISTRATION

### GENERAL INFORMATION
| | |
|---|---|
| Type of school | public |
| Environment | metropolis |

### SURVEY SAYS...
Happy students
Smart classrooms
*Solid preparation in:*
General management
Operations

### STUDENTS
| | |
|---|---|
| Enrollment of parent institution | 21,000 |
| Enrollment of business school | 374 |
| % male/female | 61/39 |
| % part-time | 68 |
| % minorities | 17 |
| % international | 18 |
| Average age at entry | 28 |
| Average years work experience at entry | 7 |

### ACADEMICS
| | |
|---|---|
| **Academic Experience Rating** | **65** |
| Student/faculty ratio | 14:1 |
| Profs interesting rating | 63 |
| % female faculty | 63 |
| % minority faculty | 7 |

### PROMINENT ALUMNI
Elizabeth Duke, Chair & EVP; Linda Middleton, Senior VP; John Sanderson, President; Larry Kittelberger, Senior VP & CIO; Lloyd, CFO

## Academics

Asked to list the strengths of the MBA program at Old Dominion University's College of Business and Public Administration, one student responded thus: "(1) affordability; (2) value for the price; (3) facilities; (4) laid-back atmosphere." And most other students agree. One student says, "I truly enjoy the atmosphere and the way all of my classes have been taught," while another student exclaims, "I have been surprisingly pleased with the school, what I am learning, and the value I am receiving for my dollar." A third student adds, "I am thrilled with the course curriculum and how well the business school is operated. My professors are wonderful, and I have learned more in my first year of business school at ODU than my entire undergraduate career, where I majored in business."

The MBA program at Old Dominion University (ODU) is, according to the school, designed to "present broad but thorough insights into issues relevant to all effective managers. Our focus is on quality." Students agree; as one puts it, "my professors were knowledgeable in their fields. They include an operational expert and MSCE for e-commerce, a former Wall Street investment banker for finance, a senior VP of Carlson Company for accounting, a former university dean for marketing, and other elite academicians as instructors who are stewards of business and operational knowledge."

But perhaps "excellence with flexibility" would be a better motto. With programs around the state, and ample opportunity for distance learning, prospective MBAs are faced with a wide array of choices. Students can choose to specialize in any of the following areas: decision science, assurance services, information technology, international business management, management accounting, business and economics forecasting, finance, maritime and port management, marketing, public administration, or they can choose a general MBA. Students are extremely excited about "the Maritime Institute. This is the only school in the country that offers an MBA with a concentration in maritime management/port management." Many students, however, say that they're "disappointed with the school's marketing emphasis but all other areas are good" and one complains that "a structured entrepreneurial class would be beneficial."

ODU offers several other masters-level programs in addition to the MBA, including a master of science in accounting, master of arts in economics, master of science in computer science, master of urban studies, and master of public administration degree. Although most students seem to truly enjoy their work, some lament the dearth of big-name professors in the school's program. As one student says, "We need more outstanding professors in business courses." Another adds that although students would "like to have more teachers that are recognized leaders in their field," most "teachers overall are committed to the material and care about the student's learning experience." And others point out that although "the curriculum is demanding, it's not to the point of all-nighters."

## Career and Placement

Although the school proudly claims "active support for faculty and students from its alumni, more than half of whom reside within a 100-mile radius of the campus," most students wish that ODU would exert more energy in utilizing its alumni network—and in placing students in jobs. Students complain that they definitely need to "have more opportunities to meet with people in the business community." And while some point out that "there is an MBA association that offers a social outlet and some job search assistance," most regret that the "on-campus recruiting is far from helpful."

MRS. RHYANNE HENLEY, MBA PROGRAM MANAGER
CONSTANT HALL 1026, NORFOLK, VA 23529 UNITED STATES
PHONE: 757-683-3585 • FAX: 757-683-5750
E-MAIL: MBAINFO@ODU.EDU • WEBSITE: WWW.ODU-MBA.ORG

## Student Life and Environment

Located in historic Norfolk, Virginia, Old Dominion University is blessed with lovely weather, happy students, proximity to major business centers, and a brand-new Business School building—Constant Hall—which boasts state-of-the-art facilities. As one student puts it, "the actual building in Norfolk is brand new and equipped with all technology aides for training." Because the building opened so recently, students are still excited about the "media-equipped classrooms," although other aspects of the school's facilities could be improved, according to most. As one student says, "it is a nightmare to park, even in the evening," and others claim that something needs to be done to prevent the undergrads from driving like crazy people.

Still, "there are many activities organized by the school's associations and organizations. However, it doesn't seem to be heavily advertised. Many services are offered to students ([such as] health, off-campus housing, [and] banks), which makes life on campus easier." Despite all these activities, many students would like to see a greater effort on ODU's part to "build a substantial school culture." As one student says, "until 2004, the social scene at Old Dominion was virtually nonexistent outside of the classroom. Hopefully this year will be different with the formation of a strong MBA association and a social club called The Loop. Only time will tell."

## Admissions

Anyone applying to be one of the 120-odd full-time MBA students at ODU should have a GMAT score around the average (541) and a competitive GPA. Those students applying from countries in which English is not the native language should be prepared to take the TOEFL exam. The minimum required score is 550 paper-based and 213 computer-based. The program currently hosts about 250 part-time students on-campus and around 50 part-timers working through the distance program. There are 20-odd PhD candidates, and about 1,500 undergraduates in the business school. Graduate assistantship positions are highly coveted and competitive; approximately 60 percent of students applying for a teaching or research assistantship are awarded one.

## FINANCIAL FACTS

| | |
|---|---|
| Annual tuition (in-state/out-of-state) | $6,312/$15,864 |
| Fees | $168 |
| Books and supplies | $1,000 |
| Room & board (on/off-campus) | $5,900/$6,500 |
| Average grant | $14,500 |

## ADMISSIONS

| | |
|---|---|
| **Admissions Selectivity Rating** | **76** |
| # of applications received | 212 |
| % applicants accepted | 68 |
| % acceptees attending | 81 |
| Average GMAT | 541 |
| Average GPA | 3.2 |
| TOEFL required of international students? | yes |
| Minimum TOEFL (paper/computer) | 550/213 |
| Application fee | $40 |
| International application fee | $40 |
| Regular application deadline | 6/1 |
| Regular notification | rolling |
| Application deadline/notification | |
| Round 1: | 11/1 / 12/1 |
| Round 2: | 3/1 / 4/1 |
| Round 3: | 6/1 / 7/1 |
| Deferment available? | yes |
| Maximum length of deferment | 1 year |
| Transfer students accepted? | yes |
| Transfer application policy Credits accepted from AACSB-accredited schools only. | |
| Non-fall admissions? | yes |
| Need-blind admissions? | yes |

# PENNSYLVANIA STATE UNIVERSITY
## SMEAL COLLEGE OF BUSINESS

### GENERAL INFORMATION
| | |
|---|---|
| Type of school | public |
| Environment | town |
| Academic calendar | 7-1-7 mods |

### SURVEY SAYS...
*Solid preparation in:*
Communication/interpersonal skills
Presentation skills

### STUDENTS
| | |
|---|---|
| Enrollment of parent institution | 41,289 |
| Enrollment of business school | 139 |
| % male/female | 75/25 |
| % out-of-state | 62 |
| % minorities | 16 |
| % international | 33 |
| Average age at entry | 28 |
| Average years work experience at entry | 5 |

### ACADEMICS
| | |
|---|---|
| **Academic Experience Rating** | **96** |
| Student/faculty ratio | 2:1 |
| Profs interesting rating | 87 |
| Profs accessible rating | 84 |
| % female faculty | 15 |
| % minority faculty | 20 |

### JOINT DEGREES
Science BS/MBA, 5 years; Quality and Manufacturing Management, 2–3 years depending upon portfolio selection; MHA/MBA, 3 years; JD/MBA, 5 years

### PROMINENT ALUMNI
John Arnold, MBA, Chair and CEO, Petroleum Products Corporation; J. David Rogers, MBA, Chair and CEO, JD Capital Management; James R. Stengel, MBA, CMO, Procter & Gamble Corporation

## Academics

Even at a large institution like Pennsylvania State University, Smeal maintains a strong feeling of intimacy and comfort. With only about 100 students in each entering class, "the size of the class gives it a personal touch." The faculty members are always available to students. Students say, "The dean is accessible and so is the program director. In fact, we've all been to their homes!" The program is filled with "collaborative, not competitive students, [and] second-years invest so much time in helping first-years." Even alumni are willing to do anything they can to help current students. Students are "energetic and eager to get involved" and are heartened by the fact that, even with a small program, huge investments are made. One student comments, "The school is putting great effort and money into becoming one of the top programs in the United States, and that shows in the quality of faculty, career services, and the new business building being constructed that is scheduled to open in Fall 2006."

Smeal's academic calendar is divided into an unusual module program referred to as the "7-1-7" system. Each semester of the first year is divided into two learning modules, separated by an immersion program. In the first seven-week module, for example, students study communications, introduction to managerial accounting, management, and teams, and then break midway through for a one-week immersion program in negotiations. After the immersion program, they go on to their second seven-week module, which teaches analysis for managerial decision-making, communication, economics for managers, financial accounting, and a second immersion experience where every student experiences an international culture. It isn't until the fourth module (in the second half of the spring semester) that students start taking electives for their chosen portfolios.

Despite the rigor of this system, students feel comfortable and capable. Students say, "We spent an entire year becoming completely comfortable in public-speaking situations, based on a rigorous methodology that incorporates oral, written, and graphic communication. It will undoubtedly differentiate us from [our] peers at other schools." Other students add, "this is tops in the b-school community."

There are six academic departments from which Smeal students can choose to specialize: corporate, finance, investment banking, strategic consulting, entrepreneurship, marketing, and supply chain and information systems. Students say that "finance, accounting, entrepreneurship, and communications [programs] are top-notch." The school also offers three joint degrees: an MBA/JD, a MBA/MHA, and a MBA/MMM.

Diversity remains something of a problem for some students. Many students agree that they would like to see Smeal "create activities or clubs to cater to nontraditional students and also admit more of these nontraditional students instead of so many engineers."

## Career and Placement

A strong alumni network is one of Smeal's biggest strengths. One student says, "There are so many successful alumni that stay very actively involved—it is overwhelming. I have several VP- and officer-level contacts already that I can contact personally if I wish, and I've only been here three months!"

In terms of career services—which are "being revamped"—many students believe that "the finance area for jobs needs improvement." Students agree that "not many firms travel [to the university] from New York City," but yet more students end up in finance/accounting than in any other field. By the September following the completion of their degree, 74 percent of the 2003 class had one or more job offers. A few years ago, IBM was the top recruiter,

Ms. Carrie Marcinkevage, Director, MBA Admissions
220 Business Building, University Park, PA 16802-3000 United States
Phone: 814-863-0474 • Fax: 814-863-8072
E-mail: smealmba@psu.edu • Website: www.smeal.psu.edu/mba

but now Andersen, Bear Stearns, Merrill Lynch, Sony Electronics, and Wyeth Pharmaceuticals (among many others) all maintain a presence on campus. Still, students would like to see a little more action from the office itself. According to some students, "Smeal is a place where you have to be somewhat creative and show a great deal of personal commitment to get a great job." One student adds, "But that's a good thing in my opinion."

## Student Life and Environment

"Although we're in a small town, there's plenty to do," one student says. "Dinners hosted by the International Students Association are big hits, and intramural sports are a popular way to blow off some steam." Students add, "We have our nightly happy-hour spots. A great number of students live in one building downtown, so there are 'apartment crawls' and lots of opportunities to study in groups." The school, situated right in the middle of Pennsylvania, is equidistant from "major nerve centers of the Northeast, Mid-Atlantic, and Midwest," which means Baltimore; Cleveland; Detroit; New York City; Philadelphia; Pittsburgh; Washington, DC; and many other places are accessible by trains, planes, and automobiles. The area's unofficial name is "Happy Valley." *Psychology Today* ranked State College (yes, that's the name of the town) as one of the least stressful places to live in the nation. Students say the town has an "active downtown area, but little beyond restaurants and bars." For them, life is more about "tailgates, tailgates, tailgates." Another student says, "Football games are a big part of the weekend relief at Smeal. It is an opportunity to network with alumni, and all the festivities are coordinated by our MBA Association, a student-run group."

As for actual campus life, one student says, "The Smeal MBA Program is a very small program in a very large school. So it allows students to feel a part of community within the program." Being a part of a huge university, "there are amazing resources for literally anything you could want: sports facilities, international student clubs, investment and finance clubs, great intercollegiate sports teams, [and] good classrooms." In an effort to make the campus still more attractive to students, Smeal completed a new 210,000-sq. ft. building, which is entirely technology-enabled and the largest academic facility at Penn State.

## Admissions

With only about 100 students admitted each year, Smeal's goal is to "recruit, admit, and enroll candidates who will be successful in the MBA program and as Smeal alumni." In order to be considered for admission, students must be computer literate, demonstrate competency in mathematics (including linear algebra), knowledge of statistics, and some knowledge of micro and macroeconomics. International students are required to submit TOEFL scores. Students admitted in the program have an average of five years work experience; 25 percent of them are female, and 16 percent are part of a minority group. The mid-80 percent range for their GMAT scores was 580 to 720, and the mid-80 percent range for undergraduate GPA was 2.7 to 3.8.

### FINANCIAL FACTS

| | |
|---|---|
| Annual tuition (in-state/out-of-state) | $15,356/$26,080 |
| Fees | $484 |
| Books and supplies | $1,500 |
| Room & board | $12,650 |
| % of students receiving aid | 89 |
| % of first-year students receiving aid | 88 |
| % of students receiving loans | 34 |
| % of students receiving grants | 84 |
| Average award package | $15,033 |
| Average grant | $9,365 |
| Average student loan debt | $29,997 |

### ADMISSIONS

| | |
|---|---|
| Admissions Selectivity Rating | 94 |
| # of applications received | 394 |
| % applicants accepted | 37 |
| % acceptees attending | 47 |
| Average GMAT | 652 |
| Range of GMAT | 530–740 |
| Average GPA | 3.33 |
| TOEFL required of international students? | yes |
| Minimum TOEFL (paper/computer) | 600/250 |
| Application fee | $60 |
| International application fee | $60 |
| Regular application deadline | 4/15 |
| Regular notification | 5/30 |
| Early decision program? | yes |
| ED deadline/notification | 12/1 / 1/31 |
| Deferment available? | yes |
| Maximum length of deferment | 1 year |
| Need-blind admissions? | yes |

### APPLICANTS ALSO LOOK AT

Indiana University—Bloomington, Michigan State University, Purdue University, The Ohio State University, University of Illinois at Urbana-Champaign, University of Maryland—College Park

## EMPLOYMENT PROFILE

| Career Rating | 89 | Grads employed by field: | % | avg. salary: |
|---|---|---|---|---|
| Primary source of full-time job acceptances | | Finance | 33 | $76,167 |
| | | Human Resources | 1 | NR |
| School-facilitated activities | 60 (80%) | Marketing | 14 | $83,853 |
| Graduate-facilitated activities | 15 (20%) | Operations | 29 | $75,399 |
| | | Consulting | 13 | $85,753 |
| Average starting salary | $78,100 | General Management | 10 | $64,250 |
| Percent employed | 88 | | | |

# PENNSYLVANIA STATE UNIVERSITY—ERIE, THE BEHREND COLLEGE
## SAM AND IRENE BLACK SCHOOL OF BUSINESS

## GENERAL INFORMATION

| | |
|---|---|
| Type of school | public |
| Environment | village |
| Academic calendar | semester |

### SURVEY SAYS...
Friendly students
Happy students
Smart classrooms
*Solid preparation in:*
Accounting
General management
Teamwork

### STUDENTS

| | |
|---|---|
| Enrollment of parent institution | 3,539 |
| Enrollment of business school | 157 |
| % male/female | 69/31 |
| % out-of-state | 12 |
| % part-time | 68 |
| % minorities | 12 |
| % international | 2 |
| Average age at entry | 26 |
| Average years work experience at entry | 4 |

### ACADEMICS

| | |
|---|---|
| **Academic Experience Rating** | **73** |
| Student/faculty ratio | 6:1 |
| Profs interesting rating | 81 |
| Profs accessible rating | 79 |
| % female faculty | 22 |
| % minority faculty | 22 |

## Academics

At the Sam and Irene Black School of Business at Penn State Erie—The Behrend College, the MBA program primarily serves students who are already fully employed. The MBA degree stresses integration of business knowledge across disciplines, and emphasizes the development of "planning and problem-solving skills crucial in middle and upper management." Because so many of the prospective MBAs are "mature students with significant work experience," many students "juggle their work, family, and school responsibilities and have little free time." However, students point out that "the average age of the typical MBA student is decreasing due to an influx of recent business under-graduates who are staying in school for their MBA because of a poor job market." Still, quality of instruction remains the same. As one student says, "Professors are good at relating today's business trends into classroom activities and discussions;" another adds, "I feel very lucky to have found a great school."

Although the amount of time it takes to complete an MBA at the Sam and Irene Black School of Business varies depending on students' needs, all students are required to complete between 30 and 48 credits (depending on their undergraduate degree). The curriculum consists of 18 credits of foundation-core course work, 15 credits of advanced-required course work, and 15 credits of electives designed to allow students to pursue their areas of special interest. To accommodate the differing schedules of its students, courses are taught in the mornings and evenings. Students say that "professors are good people and their command of the material is good."

## Career and Placement

Each fall, the career-development center sponsors a business fair, which is well attended by both MBA students and recruiters. According to the school's website, "a growing number of local, regional, national, and international companies participate in the fair each year, and many return to campus in the spring to recruit our graduates for jobs."

Still, because many of the students at the Black School are already employed and are being educated on their company's dime, postgraduation employment is less of an issue in Behrend's MBA program as it is at others.

## Student Life and Environment

Erie is, according to most students at Behrend's b-school, an overlooked gem. Students cite the "beautiful location" of their school as one very good reason to attend. The Black School's facilities themselves are located in the campus' historic center, and Turnbull Hall, the center, is graced with a special management information science computer lab with more than forty PCs, which provides constant access to "the latest in business-application software." A new location is in the works as well, and the school's administrators feel confident that "students and faculty will benefit greatly when the School of Business relocates into the $30 million Research and Economic Development Center, which opens in the Fall of 2006 and contains information science labs, state-of-the-art classrooms, and a funding floor." As one student says, "most of its campus facilities are relatively new, and the campus itself is visually appealing."

ANN M. BURBULES, GRADUATE ADMISSIONS COUNSELOR
5091 STATION ROAD, ERIE, PA 16563 UNITED STATES
PHONE: 814-898-7255 • FAX: 814-898-6044
E-MAIL: PSBEHRENDMBA@PSU.EDU • WEBSITE: WWW.PSERIE.PSU.EDU

The social life for MBAs at Behrend leaves a little something to be desired, according to many. Although student activities programming is open to all students, one student observes that "approximately 80 percent of MBA students are working professionals, attending school during the evening on a part-time basis. Activities are very strongly skewed toward the undergraduate student enrollment. Undergrads have lots of things to keep them busy." Another explains the dearth of social activity saying, "Students in the MBA program have little time to spend socializing with other students as most work full-time jobs." And because "most are married with children," students often feel they lack a cohesive community. "Everyone tends to come to class and that's the only time you interact with them."

But in fact, the community is not that homogenous. According to one student, "A lot of students are from GE or Erie Insurance where the company pays for their education. They are friendly and everyone is diverse in background." Because of the economy, many students who recently completed undergraduate degrees "enrolled in the MBA program to finish in one year," which means that all ages and experience levels are welcomed.

## Admissions

The admissions process at the Sam and Irene Black School of Business is in some ways more forgiving than at other schools. Although they, like almost everyone, require GMAT scores, the minimum GMAT total score is 400. All applicants must score a 4.0 or better on the Analytical Writing Assessment section of the GMAT exam, in addition to that. A GPA of no lower than 3.0 is preferred, but the school will allow students with a GPA lower than that to apply, as long as their GMAT score is higher in proportion. In other words, they use the following formula to determine admissibility: Grade Point Average x 200 - 1000 = GMAT score required to be admissible to the MBA program. Students for whom English is not the first language are also required to take the TOEFL exam and are expected to score no lower than 550 (paper-based exam) or 213 (computer-based exam).

## FINANCIAL FACTS

| | |
|---|---|
| Annual tuition (in-state/out-of-state) | $10,836/$16,866 |
| Fees | $478 |
| Books and supplies | $1,075 |
| Room & board (off-campus) | $8,262 |
| % of students receiving aid | 50 |
| % of first-year students receiving aid | 68 |
| % of students receiving loans | 58 |
| % of students receiving grants | 4 |
| Average award package | $15,565 |
| Average grant | $1,800 |

## ADMISSIONS

| | |
|---|---|
| Admissions Selectivity Rating | 73 |
| # of applications received | 84 |
| % applicants accepted | 71 |
| % acceptees attending | 88 |
| Average GMAT | 511 |
| Range of GMAT | 440–560 |
| Average GPA | 3.16 |
| TOEFL required of international students? | yes |
| Minimum TOEFL (paper/computer) | 550/213 |
| Application fee | $45 |
| International application fee | $45 |
| Regular application deadline | 7/4 |
| Regular notification | rolling |
| Deferment available? | yes |
| Maximum length of deferment | 2 years |
| Transfer students accepted? | yes |
| Transfer application policy | |

Up to 10 credits of relevant graduate work completed at any accredited institution may be applied toward the Penn State—Erie MBA. Credits earned to complete a previous graduate degree may not be used to fulfill MBA degree requirements. Transferred graduate work must have been completed no more than five years before the student is fully admitted as a degree candidate at Penn State—Erie. Course work must be of at least a B quality and appear on the graduate transcript of a regionally accredited institution. Pass/Fail grades are not transferable.

| | |
|---|---|
| Non-fall admissions? | yes |
| Need-blind admissions? | yes |

## EMPLOYMENT PROFILE

| Career Rating | 66 | Grads employed by field: | % | avg. salary: |
|---|---|---|---|---|
| Average starting salary | $52,222 | Finance | 11 | NR |
| | | MIS | 11 | NR |
| | | Operations | 11 | NR |
| | | Consulting | 11 | NR |
| | | General Management | 11 | NR |
| | | Other | 44 | $49,375 |

# PEPPERDINE UNIVERSITY
## THE GRAZIADIO SCHOOL OF BUSINESS AND MANAGEMENT

## GENERAL INFORMATION

| | |
|---|---|
| Type of school | private |
| Affiliation | United Church of Christ |
| Environment | village |
| Academic calendar | trimester |

### SURVEY SAYS...
Smart classrooms
*Solid preparation in:*
Teamwork
Communication/interpersonal skills
Presentation skills

## STUDENTS

| | |
|---|---|
| Enrollment of parent institution | 8,000 |
| Enrollment of business school | 1,575 |
| % male/female | 60/40 |
| % out-of-state | 25 |
| % part-time | 73 |
| % minorities | 34 |
| % international | 28 |
| Average age at entry | 27 |
| Average years work experience at entry | 4 |

## ACADEMICS

| | |
|---|---|
| **Academic Experience Rating** | **77** |
| Student/faculty ratio | 20:1 |
| Profs interesting rating | 76 |
| Profs accessible rating | 78 |
| % female faculty | 24 |
| % minority faculty | 7 |

## JOINT DEGREES
JD/MBA, 4 years; MBA/MPP
(Master of Public Policy), 3 years

## PROMINENT ALUMNI
Victor Tsao, Founder, Linksys, 2004
*Inc. Magazine* Entrepreneur; Shirley
Choi, Executive Director and CEO,
Seapower Group; David T. Mount,
Former Chair and CEO, Warner
Elektra Atlantic; Jose Collazo, CEO,
BT Infonet; Matt Fong, Former State
Treasurer

## Academics

Los Angeles now boasts the eleventh largest economy in the world, and the Graziadio School, located just 30 minutes away in Malibu, is poised to take advantage of that. In the past few years, the school has built an entirely new graduate campus along the Pacific Coast, increased the size of their student body by several hundred students, and revamped their administration. With "a brand-new campus and a new administration with full support from full-time faculty, [most students] imagine that the school can only move forward from here." Not to say the transition has happened without any troubles—many students have had considerable difficulty adjusting—most agree however, that the administration "seems to be on the right track now."

Students have already seen improvements in the campus and say that the administration has attempted to be responsive to their input. For the most part, students are positive about their interactions with professors. One MBA observes, "The teachers are usually current consultants or former top executives with PhDs, and they bring real-life cases in their classes, a source of knowledge very precious for managers who want practical solutions to current business issues they are likely to face once out of school." For the most part, students applaud the practical application of knowledge that their professors are able to demonstrate, although some students feel that "some departments seem to be stuck in the world of academia rather than the business world."

Pepperdine's tradition as a religious school has an effect on the business school, though students say that "the label 'Church of Christ' is much less influential in the graduate campus than it is in the undergrad campus." But students do attribute one of the Graziadio program's greatest strengths to a religious background. "Ethics, ethics, ethics. It is a moral place to learn where gray areas are explored and analyzed and the current environment of business is studied and reviewed." According to students, most of the classes focus on ethical choices and practices, and "this focus challenges the students to give thought to their personal ethics so that we will be more likely to make the right choices when faced with ethical dilemmas."

Core requirements make up 30 to 40 units of study out of 54 to 60 total, and the first year is almost all core classes. Students have freedom in their second year to take electives, though they'd like to see more options. In accounting and finance, students rate their courses as "outstanding." One student adds, "However, some classes, such as organization behavior or information technology need to be more practical. As I was a manager, I don't think I learned efficient tools to turn into practice. I need less theory and more practical tools."

## Career and Placement

Like many students at business schools in today's economy, students would like to see their Career Services Office working harder. Students say, "Relations with the business community in Southern California could be stronger. People don't have negative perceptions about the school. The problem is they don't have any perceptions of the school, as everything in LA is focused on the two big schools." In an attempt to better leverage its relationship with the business community, Graziadio recently merged its Career Services and Alumni Offices.

DARRELL ERIKSEN, DIRECTOR OF ADMISSIONS
6100 CENTER DRIVE, LOS ANGELES, CA 90045 UNITED STATES
PHONE: 310-568-5535 • FAX: 310-568-5779
E-MAIL: GSBM@PEPPERDINE.EDU • WEBSITE: WWW.BSCHOOL.PEPPERDINE.EDU

Many major companies have found their employees at Graziadio, including American Express Financial Advisors, Arthur Andersen LLP, the City of Los Angeles, Deloitte Touche Tohmatsu, The Disney Channel, Gap, Herbalife International, Kaiser Permanente, Morgan Stanley Dean Witter, Salomon Smith Barney, and Wells Fargo. Still, some students feel "on-campus recruiting is weak."

## Student Life and Environment

In terms of natural beauty, there are few campuses that can rival Graziadio's. Students call it the "most beautiful campus in the country." Nestled in the Santa Monica mountains and facing the winding coast of the Pacific Ocean, "the weather and campus beauty are great forms of therapy. Stepping outside for five minutes for a break from an intensive econometrics class or a tense group meeting is amazing." "B-school in Malibu—there's not much more to say. Classes are great, and the views are gorgeous. You haven't lived until you hit the bar after classes end on Thursday and chatted with colleagues while the surf crashes against the beach."

With a school so close to a major metropolitan area, students are "out of LA enough to have a more relaxed feel but close enough to tap into the job resources." Being in Southern California, "the overall atmosphere is laid-back and friendly, but it is obvious that everyone is hard-working and ambitious."

Students do lament one thing about the social scene. "We are a dry campus," reports one student. "The campus social scene is somewhat limited by the complete prohibition of alcohol." Still, students take advantage of "big house parties once a month or so and occasional trips to the beach after class." Because Malibu is an extremely expensive area and many students opt not to live on campus, "study groups and other networking takes place almost exclusively on campus since everyone is spread out so far."

## Admissions

Each admitted class is only about 130 students, and Graziadio's board of admissions looks carefully at the applications, searching for "highly motivated self-starters who thrive on challenge. We carefully select each new class to represent diverse academic, cultural, and professional backgrounds." For the 2005 entering class, the average GMAT score for MBA students was 627. Many incoming students had about four years of full-time postgraduate work experience before they applied for the MBA. TOEFL scores are required of those students for whom English is not the first language, and the minimum score required for admission is a 600. The school awards merit-based scholarships.

### FINANCIAL FACTS

| | |
|---|---|
| Annual tuition | $30,784 |
| Fees | $585 |
| Books and supplies | $1,000 |
| Room & board | $15,000 |
| % of students receiving aid | 64 |
| % of students receiving loans | 41 |
| % of students receiving grants | 39 |
| Average award package | $31,783 |
| Average grant | $15,704 |
| Average student loan debt | $72,739 |

### ADMISSIONS

| | |
|---|---|
| Admissions Selectivity Rating | 84 |
| # of applications received | 427 |
| % applicants accepted | 62 |
| % acceptees attending | 38 |
| Average GMAT | 627 |
| Range of GMAT | 580–650 |
| Average GPA | 3.31 |
| TOEFL required of international students? | yes |
| Minimum TOEFL (paper/computer) | 600/250 |
| Application fee | $50 |
| International application fee | $50 |
| Regular application deadline | 5/1 |
| Regular notification | rolling |
| Early decision program? | yes |
| ED deadline/notification | 12/15 / 1/15 |
| Deferment available? | yes |
| Maximum length of deferment | 1 year |
| Transfer students accepted? | yes |
| Transfer application policy No more than 2 courses may be transferred, contingent upon approval of policy committee. | |
| Need-blind admissions? | yes |

### EMPLOYMENT PROFILE

| Career Rating | 72 | Grads employed by field: | % | avg. salary: |
|---|---|---|---|---|
| Average starting salary | $63,485 | Finance | 46 | $63,750 |
| | | Marketing | 39 | $61,000 |
| | | Consulting | 8 | $62,500 |
| | | Other | 7 | $57,375 |

# PITTSBURG STATE UNIVERSITY
## GLADYS A. KELCE COLLEGE OF BUSINESS

### GENERAL INFORMATION
| | |
|---|---|
| Type of school | public |
| Environment | village |
| Academic calendar | semester |

### SURVEY SAYS...
Smart classrooms
*Solid preparation in:*
Marketing
Presentation skills

### STUDENTS
| | |
|---|---|
| Enrollment of parent institution | 6,500 |
| Enrollment of business school | 136 |
| % male/female | 55/45 |
| % out-of-state | 53 |
| % part-time | 27 |
| % international | 43 |
| Average age at entry | 25 |
| Average years work experience at entry | 1 |

### ACADEMICS
| | |
|---|---|
| **Academic Experience Rating** | **73** |
| Student/faculty ratio | 25:1 |
| Profs interesting rating | 80 |
| Profs accessible rating | 85 |
| % female faculty | 15 |
| % minority faculty | 10 |

### PROMINENT ALUMNI
Lee Scott, President & CEO, Wal-mart; John Lampe, President & CEO, Firestone/Bridgestone; John Lowe, Executive VP, ConocoPhillips; Orvil Bicknell, CEO, NPC International; Richard Colliver, Executive VP, American Honda

## Academics

Students choose the MBA program at Pittsburg State University because "it's reasonably priced, convenient to home, [and perhaps most importantly,] because it is one of the best in the state of Kansas." In fact, the school's reputation is such that—despite its relatively remote location—PSU's MBA program attracts a substantial international student population on a consistent basis. This "strong international student community" contributes significantly to classroom instruction here.

Students may attend PSU on either a full-time or part-time basis; part-time classes are offered in Kansas City as well as on the Pittsburg campus. Either program requires a minimum of 34 course hours beyond foundation courses; some or all of the 30 hours of foundation courses may be waived for students with undergraduate degrees in business. A waiver of all 30 hours of foundation classes makes it possible to receive an MBA in 12 months. The part-time program requires a minimum of two and a half years to complete.

PSU's professors are "accessible and approachable [and] dedicated to making you work hard and learn, but doing it in a caring and fun way." One student writes, "A high ratio of PhDs teach the core courses." Like the students, "Professors come from a variety of different countries." Classes at PSU "are relatively small, allowing for good interaction between instructors and the class," which students appreciate. They also appreciate how "the administration is very supportive of the MBA program and interested in the views of the students."

PSU MBAs may earn concentrations in accounting and general administration. Although no concentration is offered in marketing, students single the discipline out for praise, telling us the school is "famous for its marketing section."

## Career and Placement

According to PSU's website, the university's relationship with area businesses and its reputation for applying high admissions standards result in "an excellent record of placement of [the school's] MBA candidates." Students confirm this assertion; one writes, "I chose PSU because of its reputation for being a great business school and because of the many job opportunities that are available through PSU's career service after you graduate."

Career services are provided through the university's Career Services Office. Employers who most frequently hire PSU MBAs include Deloitte, PricewaterhouseCoopers, Payless ShoeSource, Core-Mark, Sprint, Hallmark, Cessna, Koch Industries, Inc., Wal-Mart, and Allstate.

## Student Life and Environment

"Located in a peaceful small town," Pittsburg State offers students a lifestyle that "is pretty laid back." The university at large "not only offers excellent academic programs but also excellent entertainment programs, such as outdoor movies [and] comedians." Besides "various clubs and organizations to join for nearly any student's taste or major" and a recently remodeled student center, the school offers events such as "recitals at the music school building. There are also plays at the theater department to attend, and there are about five art exhibits, both student and traveling, per school year."

The majority of Pittsburg MBAs attend full-time, although there is also a sizeable part-time population here. One student notes a distinction between the two groups: "The majority of the full-time students at my school are international students, and they tend to stick together in their own groups. Most of the American students work during the day and go to class at night." Students are typically "hardworking, goal-oriented, [and]

MARVENE DARRAUGH, ADMINISTRATIVE OFFICER—GRADUATE STUDIES
1701 SOUTH BROADWAY, PITTSBURG, KS 66762-7540 UNITED STATES
PHONE: 620-235-4222 • FAX: 620-235-4219
E-MAIL: GRAD@PITTSTATE.EDU • WEBSITE: WWW.PITTSTATE.EDU/KELCE/

very friendly." With just over 100 MBAs in the entire program, "students know virtually everyone in the MBA program, which is nice." An MBA Association promotes the goals of MBA students and helps organize recruiting events.

Pittsburg is a town of just under 20,000. It is situated in the southeast corner of Kansas, 120 miles to the south of Kansas City. The region's rolling prairies attract outdoor enthusiasts; hunters, fishers, and hikers are all welcome. The university occupies a central role in the life of the community, providing entertainment as well as employment to the town's citizens. PSU's athletic teams, the Gorillas, receive enthusiastic support from sports fans throughout the area.

## Admissions

Applicants to Pittsburg's MBA program must provide the admissions department with official copies of transcripts for all postsecondary academic work, official GMAT score reports, and a completed application to the Graduate School of PSU. International students whose first language is not English must also submit TOEFL scores. All applicants must achieve a minimum GMAT score of 400 and must receive a formula score of at least 1,050 under the formula [(undergraduate GPA 5 200) + GMAT score]. Students with undergraduate degrees in non-business areas are typically required to complete foundation courses in statistics; organizational theory; marketing; business law; production management; financial and managerial accounting; MIS; business finance; and micro and macro economics prior to beginning the MBA program. Such applicants may be admitted to the program conditionally, pending successful completion of these courses.

### FINANCIAL FACTS

| | |
|---|---|
| Annual tuition (in-state/out-of-state) | $3,728/$9,652 |
| Books and supplies | $1,200 |
| Room & board (on/off-campus) | $4,570/$6,000 |
| % of students receiving aid | 50 |
| % of first-year students receiving aid | 25 |
| % of students receiving loans | 25 |
| % of students receiving grants | 15 |
| Average award package | $8,500 |
| Average grant | $3,500 |

### ADMISSIONS

| | |
|---|---|
| Admissions Selectivity Rating | 72 |
| # of applications received | 270 |
| % applicants accepted | 76 |
| % acceptees attending | 67 |
| Average GMAT | 510 |
| Range of GMAT | 400–710 |
| Average GPA | 3.5 |
| TOEFL required of international students? | yes |
| Minimum TOEFL (paper/computer) | 550/213 |
| Application fee | $30 |
| Regular application deadline | 7/15 |
| Regular notification | 8/1 |
| Deferment available? | yes |
| Maximum length of deferment | 1 year |
| Transfer students accepted? | yes |
| Transfer application policy Up to 9 semester hours may be transferred from another accredited program. | |
| Non-fall admissions? | yes |
| Need-blind admissions? | yes |

| EMPLOYMENT PROFILE | | | | |
|---|---|---|---|---|
| Career Rating | 66 | Grads employed by field: | % | avg. salary: |
| Average starting salary | $46,000 | Accounting | 30 | $48,000 |
| | | Marketing | 17 | $44,000 |
| | | MIS | 15 | $45,000 |
| | | General Management | 38 | $45,000 |

# PORTLAND STATE UNIVERSITY
## SCHOOL OF BUSINESS ADMINISTRATION

### GENERAL INFORMATION
Type of school      public
Academic calendar      year-round

### SURVEY SAYS...
Students love Portland, OR
Friendly students
Happy students
*Solid preparation in:*
Teamwork
Presentation skills

### STUDENTS
Enrollment of parent
  institution      23,486
Enrollment of business school   354
% male/female      56/44
% out-of-state      20
% part-time      82
% minorities      14
% international      16
Average age at entry      30
Average years work experience
  at entry      5

### ACADEMICS
**Academic Experience Rating**    **73**
Student/faculty ratio      35:1
Profs interesting rating      82
Profs accessible rating      86
% female faculty      35
% minority faculty      6

### PROMINENT ALUMNI
Gary Ames, former President/CEO,
U.S. West; Gerry Cameron, retired
Chair of the Board, U.S. Bancorp;
Scott Davis, CFO, UPS; Ray
Guenther, Northwest Operations
Director, Intel; Darrell Webb,
President, Fred Meyer/Kroger

## Academics

The Portland State University School of Business Administration's "strong ties to the business community" are what appeal most to the school's MBA students. "Thanks to the efforts of the deans and faculty, Portland State is extremely well-connected with the Portland business community," one student writes, adding that "this program has provided exceptional opportunities to meet and learn from top business leaders." The school notes that "[they] consider ourselves partners with area businesses and continually seek joint opportunities to further enrich the livability and economic well-being of the region. Resources available to business are many, ranging from faculty research expertise and professional development courses to small business consulting and the MBA Business Project."

Although small, PSU offers some unique, off-the-beaten-path areas for students to investigate. "The Food Industry Leadership Center deserves special recognition for its exceptional work on behalf of students," MBAs brag; also noteworthy is the school's A-Center for Technology, Entrepreneurship, and Law (in cooperation with the Northwestern School of Law at Lewis and Clark College). Among more conventional fare, students tell us that "stand-out courses include financial accounting, financial management and theory, and business strategy and policy. These courses have really delivered." Some feel the school "should incorporate more quantitative material both in existing classes and [by] adding more quantitative classes," and that "a greater emphasis on small, entrepreneurial business issues would be welcome, as would an opportunity to focus on sustainable, socially-responsible operations."

Throughout the curriculum, "the PSU MBA program puts strong emphasis on teamwork and interpersonal communication and conflict-management skills. Many of the PSU instructors are able to successfully incorporate their career experiences into meaningful class discussion." The faculty offers "a good balance between tenured professors to teach the more academic subjects and adjunct professors for topics where business experience is critical to teaching the subject." The majority, students agree, "are very enthusiastic, animated, and passionate about their areas of expertise. Class discussions are generally very lively and quite often humorous." On the downside, the school "needs more funding to have better technology, though a 2005 remodeling should help improve things."

## Career and Placement

The School of Business Administration Career Services Office exclusively serves graduate b-students at PSU. The office provides a number of counseling services, workshops, and online job-search tools to students ("the school has great networking events and always keeps the students informed of what job opportunities are available with online graduate Job and Internship Boards," MBAs tell us). On-campus recruiting is minimal; "due to the school's small size, big companies are not interested in recruiting here," one student explains. Part-timers gripe that they get "zero placement help. The career coach says 'Well, part-timers never come to my seminars.' But that's because we're at work! The school needs to integrate all of the career-management components directly into the curriculum for part-timers."

Companies that most frequently hire PSU MBAs include Adidas, AT&T, Coca-Cola, Freightliner, IBM, Intel, KPMG, Lufthansa, Nike, OHSU, Planar, The Standard, U.S. Bancorp, U.S. Bank, Wells Fargo Bank, and Xerox. Approximately one in five full-time PSU MBAs finds work outside the United States; most of the rest remain in the Portland area.

Pam Mitchell, Graduate Programs Advisor
631 Southwest Harrison Street, Portland, OR 97201 United States
Phone: 503-725-8001 • Fax: 503-725-5740
E-mail: mbainfo@pdx.edu • Website: www.mba.pdx.edu

## Student Life and Environment

The majority of PSU's MBAs are part-time students, meaning they typically have jobs, families, and lots of other responsibilities to go along with their schoolwork. That cuts back on campus life. Even so, students see their demographic as a plus, telling us that "the part-time program brings together a more mature and experienced group. You learn a lot more from other students when they actually have some real-world experience to share." Part-timers generally "grind it out every Tuesday and Thursday nights from 5:40 to 9:20 P.M., and then usually have group team meetings on most weekends."

The school is also home to about 70 full-time MBAs, for whom a typical day consists of "meeting with study groups and go[ing] to your classes. In between you relax in the student lounge, [and] meet lots of international students. Discussions range from current presidents to recipes for Swedish food. You end your day with a pint from one of the numerous microbreweries." Students become especially close with those in their cohort; they tell us that "the school pools together a great team of students for each cohorts. I think that the types of people that you are taking intense classes with can make or break a program, and PSU brings together excellent people for a great school experience." The program offers MBAs access to "organizations for any interest or hobby. Meetings can be a problem, however, with people living in various parts of the city."

Hometown Portland "is a great place, and nearly all of the students want to stay here" when they graduate. Students love that "PSU is an urban campus, adjacent to downtown Portland, on the trolley line. Most students live off campus but are active socially. Portland is a friendly community, and the campus reflects the city. Portland has an active, urban, lifestyle with a [lot of] respect for diverse interests."

## Admissions

Admission to the MBA program is competitive based on GMAT scores, undergraduate GPA, and letters of reference. Applicants must achieve at least a 470 on the GMAT, with both verbal and quantitative scores exceeding the 35th percentile. Their undergraduate GPA must be above 2.75; those with lower GPAs may be asked to complete at least 12 hours of graduate work with a minimum GPA of 3.0 before gaining admission to the MBA program. Applicants must also provide two letters of recommendation and a one-page personal statement. Some international students are required to take the TOEFL. Students need a working knowledge of introductory calculus and basic computer functions. The school prefers applicants with a minimum of two years of business work experience.

### FINANCIAL FACTS

| | |
|---|---|
| Annual tuition (in-state/out-of-state) | $9,467/$15,695 |
| Fees | $1,050 |
| Books and supplies | $1,300 |
| Room & board | $15,324 |
| % of first-year students receiving aid | 68 |
| Average grant | $11,120 |

### ADMISSIONS

| | |
|---|---|
| Admissions Selectivity Rating | 76 |
| # of applications received | 226 |
| % applicants accepted | 84 |
| % acceptees attending | 73 |
| Average GMAT | 594 |
| Range of GMAT | 550–640 |
| Average GPA | 3.25 |
| TOEFL required of international students? | yes |
| Minimum TOEFL (paper/computer) | 550/213 |
| Application fee | $50 |
| International application fee | $50 |
| Regular application deadline | 4/1 |
| Regular notification | 6/30 |
| Early decision program? | yes |
| ED deadline/notification | 1/1 / 4/1 |
| Transfer students accepted? | yes |
| Transfer application policy Maximum of one third of the total number of PSU credits may transfer from a U.S. accredited university. | |
| Need-blind admissions? | yes |

### APPLICANTS ALSO LOOK AT

Oregon State University, University of Oregon, University of Portland, Willamette University

### EMPLOYMENT PROFILE

| Career Rating | 83 | Grads employed by field: | % |
|---|---|---|---|
| Average starting salary | $51,500 | Finance | 17 |
| Percent employed | 86 | Marketing | 17 |
| | | Operations | 8 |
| | | Consulting | 17 |
| | | General Management | 33 |
| | | Other | 8 |

# PURDUE UNIVERSITY
## KRANNERT SCHOOL OF MANAGEMENT

### GENERAL INFORMATION

| | |
|---|---|
| Type of school | public |
| Environment | town |
| Academic calendar | semester |

### SURVEY SAYS...

Smart classrooms
*Solid preparation in:*
Teamwork
Quantitative skills

### STUDENTS

| | |
|---|---|
| Enrollment of parent institution | 38,653 |
| Enrollment of business school | 281 |
| % male/female | 80/20 |
| % out-of-state | 86 |
| % minorities | 6 |
| % international | 38 |
| Average age at entry | 28 |
| Average years work experience at entry | 4 |

### ACADEMICS

| | |
|---|---|
| **Academic Experience Rating** | **93** |
| Student/faculty ratio | 2:1 |
| Profs interesting rating | 85 |
| Profs accessible rating | 89 |
| % female faculty | 17 |
| % minority faculty | 10 |

### JOINT DEGREES

BS Management/MBA 3+2 Program, 5 years; Pharm D/MSIA, 6 years; BS Industrial Engineering/MBA, 5 years; BS Mechanical Engineering/MBA, 5 years

### PROMINENT ALUMNI

Joseph Forehand, Chair, CEO, Accenture; Marshall Larsen, President, COO, Goodrich; Marjorie Magner, Chair, CEO, Global Consumer Group, Citigroup; Albert Nahmad, Chair, CEO, Watsco, Inc.; Jerry Rawls, CEO, Finisar.

## Academics

Students who enroll in Krannert's School of Management at Purdue University can expect to receive a "no-nonsense MBA." According to most students, "the workload is extremely high, but the results include the ability to tackle any type of business problem." This is in part due to the faculty. Students say, "Professors range from very good to outstanding." Aside from being experts in their fields, they're "extremely accessible and are very open to students, even when the students are no longer in the professor's classes, [and know how to] seamlessly blend detailed academic understanding into real-world applications that create an enjoyable learning experience." And it's not just the faculty that is committed to the success of Krannert students. "The general administration faculty are outstanding. They go out of their way to make you feel at home and let you know they are always there if you need them." The student body, which is (internationally speaking, at least) very diverse, is also counted among Krannert's greatest strengths. "I believe we have the largest international population of any business school. This diverse group of people help enrich the learning experience here."

Krannert offers three full-time master's programs: a master's of business administration (MBA), a master's of science in human resource management (MSHRM), and a master's of science in industrial administration (MSIA). The MBA program is a two-year, 60-credit course of study, with 35 credits of required core courses. Students may choose to specialize in any of the following areas: accounting, finance, marketing, strategic management, operations management, information systems, e-business, and human-resource management. They may also select from three interdisciplinary options: general management, international management, and manufacturing management.

The MSHRM, also two years, requires 61 credits, divided into 24 credits for human-resource management and organizational behavior, 25 for general management with an analytical core, and 12 for a wide range of electives. The MSIA, however, is a one-year program and is considered the equivalent of an accelerated MBA. MSIAs aren't required to select a formal concentration but have the option of specializing during their spring and summer courses. According to Krannert's website, the MSIA program is "intended for highly ambitious students who are prepared for complete immersion into a very demanding and rewarding professional business-management curriculum."

For the most part, students appreciate the quant-oriented appeal of the program, especially because professors are skilled at teaching through case study. According to one student, "Only Harvard uses more cases to teach than Krannert. Case analysis takes a long time to complete, but I am refreshed to see that there is an emphasis placed on actual business-related scenarios instead of made-up examples." Students say courses in strategy, operations, quantitative skills, and finance are "top-notch," but many of them would like to see "more soft skills like negotiations and communication," and others think the school would benefit from more marketing electives.

Overall, most students say Krannert "boasts a warm, friendly environment, a solid curriculum, excellent placement assistance, and talented students. The burden truly is upon the student to take advantage of the wonderful resources available." Another student says, "Purdue's strength is its commitment to excellence and its challenging atmosphere. Even the best student would learn a lot."

## Career and Placement

From the moment students arrive on campus, they're prepped for their eventual job search. According to one student, "Placement is a big focus here. They provide all the resources we need to find the perfect placement for our desires and needs." Students complain, however, that "the companies recruiting here are often small divisions or groups with a few Purdue MBA alumni. We are not on many of the corporations' official recruiting stops. If companies don't come, you need to search through databases, write cover letters, and practically jump through hoops in order to try and get an interview!" Others wish that career services would "increase its efforts in attracting companies interested in recruiting international students to campus." Indeed, Purdue has recognized these issues and is continuing to work on attracting and retaining employers to recruit students; 2004–2005 recruiting was up 21 percent from the previous year.

Despite their gripes, numbers show that most students manage to find employment pretty quickly. By the August after they'd completed their degree, 80 percent of the class of 2003 had at least one offer of employment, and 75 percent had accepted an offer. Almost 75 percent of students ended up in the industry of manufacturing, but marketing/sales was the job function more popular than any other.

## Student Life and Environment

Krannert is only home to about 375 students at any one time, so it makes sense that people talk about the school's "family atmosphere." Located in West Lafayette, Indiana, students say that while "most of the cultural life is found in Chicago, two hours away, or Indianapolis, a one-hour drive away," Krannert life is quite simple. "Of course," says one MBA, "West Lafayette does not provide any distractions that would make life complicated." Still, students say that on-campus activities comprise "almost anything anyone would want with nightlife, plays, entertainment, varsity sports, Greek life, and other activities." Students congregate at Harry's Chocolate Shop—a converted speakeasy—every Thursday night for drinks and networking, and there are "many, many clubs, both academic (i.e., finance club) and social (i.e., sushi club) for everyone to participate in."

West Lafayette's low cost of living is also a large draw, and the family feel ensures that "people say 'hi' to each other in the halls, and faculty have more time to give to individual students." In addition, an "incredible" new state-of-the-art building was recently completed, and the school continues to work on the building that houses the Morgan Center for Entrepreneurship.

## Admissions

Of the thousands of applications Krannert receives each year, the ones that often stand out to admissions officers are those that "have substantial industry or military work experience." The mean GMAT score is 657, while the median is 670. The mean undergraduate GPA is 3.3, and 88 percent of the students had some full-time postgraduate work experience; 38 percent were international students, 6 percent were minority students, and 20 percent were female students in 2005.

### FINANCIAL FACTS

| | |
|---|---|
| Annual tuition (in-state/out-of-state) | $14,174/$28,076 |
| Fees | $500 |
| Books and supplies | $1,900 |
| Room & board | $7,500 |
| % of students receiving aid | 73 |
| % of first-year students receiving aid | 64 |
| Average award package | $17,931 |
| Average grant | $5,288 |
| Average student loan debt | $32,530 |

### ADMISSIONS

| | |
|---|---|
| Admissions Selectivity Rating | 91 |
| # of applications received | 828 |
| % applicants accepted | 44 |
| % acceptees attending | 33 |
| Average GMAT | 657 |
| Range of GMAT | 640–710 |
| Average GPA | 3.3 |
| TOEFL required of international students? | yes |
| Minimum TOEFL (paper/computer) | 575/230 |
| Application fee | $55 |
| International application fee | $55 |
| Regular application deadline | 3/1 |
| Regular notification | 4/15 |
| Application deadline/notification | |
| Round 1: | 11/1 / 12/15 |
| Round 2: | 1/1 / 3/1 |
| Round 3: | 3/1 / 4/15 |
| Round 4: | 5/1 / 6/15 |
| Early decision program? | yes |
| ED deadline/notification | 11/1 / 12/15 |
| Deferment available? | yes |
| Maximum length of deferment | 2 years |
| Need-blind admissions? | yes |

### APPLICANTS ALSO LOOK AT

Indiana University—Bloomington, The Ohio State University, The University of Chicago, The University of Texas at Austin, University of Michigan, University of North Carolina at Chapel Hill, University of Southern California

### EMPLOYMENT PROFILE

| Career Rating | 87 | Grads employed by field: | % avg. salary: | |
|---|---|---|---|---|
| Average starting salary | $80,621 | Finance | 22 | $82,092 |
| Percent employed | 91 | Marketing | 26 | $78,599 |
| | | MIS | 4 | $82,367 |
| | | Operations | 17 | $84,387 |
| | | Consulting | 9 | $77,333 |
| | | General Management | 15 | $79,027 |
| | | Other | 7 | NR |

# QUEEN'S UNIVERSITY
## QUEEN'S MBA FOR SCIENCE AND TECHNOLOGY

## GENERAL INFORMATION

| | |
|---|---|
| Type of school | public |
| Environment | city |
| Academic calendar | 12 months |

### SURVEY SAYS...
Smart classrooms
*Solid preparation in:*
Teamwork
Communication/interpersonal skills
Quantitative skills
Entrepreneurial studies

### ACADEMICS

| | |
|---|---|
| **Academic Experience Rating** | **78** |
| Student/faculty ratio | 3:1 |
| Profs interesting rating | 89 |
| Profs accessible rating | 95 |

### JOINT DEGREES
Queen's-Cornell Executive MBA
(dual degree), 17 months part-time

### PROMINENT ALUMNI
Mel Goodes, Retired Chair & CEO,
Warner-Lambert Co.; Don Carty,
Former President & CEO, AMR
Corp. & American Airlines; Donald
Sobey, Chairman, Empire
Corporation; Cathy Williams, CFO,
Shell Canada; Gord Nixon, President
and CEO, RBC Financial Group

## Academics

Queen's University quickly burst onto many prospective MBAs' radars in 2004, when *Business Week* magazine named it the number one international MBA program. The school was no secret to Canadian and international employers, though; in fact, their high regard for Queen's MBAs contributed substantially to the lofty BW ranking.

Queen's has taken a unique route to the top: specialization. The Queen's MBA is officially called the "Queen's MBA for Science and Technology," a designation that accurately indicates the program's focus. Although the curriculum looks like that of a standard MBA program, all students and professors here have considerable backgrounds in science, mathematics, technology, and/or engineering. Their backgrounds inform every aspect of instruction and class discussion here. "The analytical strength in the class is unbelievable," students agree.

Queen's offers a great return on investment, thanks to a 12-month calendar that allows students "to return to the work force faster." Like most one-year MBAs, the Queen's MBA "is very intense and the course load is pretty heavy." A "very strong team-based learning" approach permeates all classes. All students here are assigned to a single team for the duration of the program, and "a significant portion of a student's overall marks is derived from group work." The idea is to model the team atmosphere in which students will work throughout their careers.

With between 60 and 80 students each year, Queen's runs "a very small program" that "allows the administration and students to get to know each other very well." The result is a happy student body: MBAs tell us that the "amazing administration couldn't be more helpful. It is amazingly receptive to any requests." Likewise, professors are regarded as "warm-hearted, committed, responsible, open-minded, and talented." Most of all, students appreciate the school's "excellent reputation, which is on the upswing across the world."

## Career and Placement

Career and placement services to MBA students at Queen's University are provided by personal career managers, who offer "one-on-one coaching to help you explore your career options and chart your career path." Career managers assist students with practice interviews, resume counseling, and self-assessment instruments. Numerous online job postings are available through the Student Career Services Office, which also coordinates student-alumni contacts. Students appreciate the office's hard work but feel that "on-campus recruitment companies lack variety and this needs to improve." Some note that "Kingston is a small town, and that may be why we have fewer connections with companies compared with schools in big cities."

Typically, about one-fourth of Queen's MBAs find their first post-degree jobs in finance. The same number take positions with high tech and telecommunications firms. Around 16 percent go into management consulting, and just under 10 percent find work in manufacturing and bio-pharmaceuticals. About half the graduating class typically has a position by graduation day.

## Student Life and Environment

Queen's one-year curriculum means "a hectic academic schedule" that leaves little free time. As one student notes, "Despite efforts to balance our lifestyles as students, our lives are school. Since the program is only one year long, our friends and families are very accepting of this fact." Life here generally consists of "classes followed by preparation assignments, exams, projects, and presentations."

There are opportunities to blow off steam, however: "the school organizes numerous social events such as a cruise and hockey games," for example. Most popular of all is the "Point Four" club, a "tradition that has the whole class going out for drinks every Thursday night. This tradition is continued in numerous cities in Canada after graduation." The origin of the club's name, incidentally, is the notion that "going out one day a week will only reduce your grade by 0.4 percent."

MBAs in this high-caliber program are "very bright and intelligent" and the community "friendly and close-knit," qualities that are assets to the team-oriented approach to learning. While some feel that "the science and technology background sometimes hinders the very technical ones who cannot think out of the box," few would argue with the assertion that everyone here is "very strong analytically and mathematically." The international nature of the student body means that "people can talk about issues in North America as easily as issues in Africa or Asia."

## Admissions

Minimum requirements for admission to the Queen's MBA for Science and Technology program include: a four-year undergraduate degree in an engineering, technology, or science discipline, plus two years of relevant work experience; or, a four-year undergraduate degree in some other discipline, plus two years work experience in a science- or technology-related area. Most admitted students have an undergraduate grade point average (GPA) of at least 3.3 and a GMAT score of at least 600. Students whose first language is not English must submit a score for the TOEFL, IELTS, or MELAB. A cover letter and resume, three letters of reference, and three short-answer essays—all of which can be completed online—are also required. Applicants from the USA must obtain a student visa from the Canadian government in order to attend the school; the school warns that this process can take up to three months.

## FINANCIAL FACTS

| | |
|---|---|
| Annual tuition | $47,850 |
| Fees (in-state/out-of-state) | $736/$746 |
| Room & board | $17,340 |
| % of students receiving aid | 15 |
| % of students receiving grants | 70 |
| Average grant | $10,000 |

## ADMISSIONS

| | |
|---|---|
| Admissions Selectivity Rating | 60* |
| Average GMAT | 660 |
| Range of GMAT | 560–770 |
| TOEFL required of international students? | yes |
| Minimum TOEFL (paper/computer) | 600/250 |
| Application deadline | |
| Round 1: | 11/30 |
| Round 2: | 1/15 |
| Round 3: | 2/28 |
| Deferment available? | yes |
| Maximum length of deferment | 1 year |
| Non-fall admissions? | yes |
| Need-blind admissions? | yes |

## APPLICANTS ALSO LOOK AT

Harvard University, IMD (International Institute for Management Development), INSEAD, Massachusetts Institute of Technology, University of Toronto, University of Western Ontario— Richard Ivey School of Business, York University

| EMPLOYMENT PROFILE | | | | |
|---|---|---|---|---|
| Career Rating | 88 | Grads employed by field: | % | avg. salary: |
| Primary source of full-time job acceptances | | Finance | 35 | $64,158 |
| | | Consulting | 26 | $80,630 |
| School-facilitated activities | 48% | Other | 39 | $61,557 |
| Graduate-facilitated activities | 52% | | | |
| Average starting salary | $71,094 | | | |
| Percent employed | 87 | | | |

# QUINNIPIAC UNIVERSITY
## LENDER SCHOOL OF BUSINESS

## Academics

The School of Business at Quinnipiac University capably serves both a part-time and a full-time MBA population. Part-time students make up about three-quarters of the MBA program and are primarily full-time working professionals, while one-quarter of the program is comprised of full-time students. The School of Business offers "extraordinary resources [and] small classes with ample instructor attention" to its MBAs.

Full-time students can complete the Quinnipiac MBA—which can be taken with either a thesis or non-thesis option—in as little as 15 months. Students who opt for the six-credit thesis research project must complete a thesis paper over the course of two semesters, under the supervision of a faculty member. Thesis topics must be approved by the department head and the director of the MBA program; theses are reviewed by the student's thesis advisor and a second faculty member. Students choosing the thesis option complete two additional electives to reach the required 12 credits of electives.

Quinnipiac offers concentrations in accounting, computer information systems, economics, finance, health administration, international business, management and marketing, as well as a new MBA Chartered Financial Analyst track and an MBA in Health Care Management. While most are "more than pleased with the learning environment and the pro-student attitude from the faculty and administrative personnel, some complain that the program is "much easier and less time consuming" than they expected, and wish for a "more competitive/demanding program." Students tell us that the faculty across departments is "very well rounded. Every teacher at the MBA level has a PhD from a top business school and business experience in the given course." They are "generally accessible and great teachers," leading to "a good all-around experience."

## Career and Placement

Quinnipiac maintains a central Office of Career Services, which serves both undergraduates and graduate students at the university. Many of Quinnipiac's part-time students are concurrently employed by such prominent area concerns as AT&T, Anthem Blue Cross/Blue Shield, Yale New Haven Hospital, the Hospital of St. Raphael, Bayer, and United Technologies.

## Student Life and Environment

Quinnipiac's MBA program makes its home in the Lender School of Business Center, whose assortment of classroom styles (tiered, semicircular, and conventional) accommodates a wide range of teaching and presentation styles. The facility also includes six breakout rooms for small meetings, two LAN rooms equipped with 24 workstations, wireless Internet access, and television monitors continually broadcasting CNBC and CNN. The school's network makes business databases available to students both on campus and at home, via the Internet. Quinnipiac's 47,000-square-foot Arnold Bernhard Library boasts a high-tech infrastructure that allows for access to numerous digital archives and online business resources. The newest resource to grace the campus is The Terry W. Goodwin 1967 Financial Technology Center. Dedicated in February 2005, it is a 1,500 square foot simulated financial trading room with 31 dual-monitor computer workstations. This state-of-the-art facility allows students to access real-time financial data, practice analytical finance methods, conduct trading simulations, analyze economic databases, and develop financial models.

LOUISE HOWE, ASSOCIATE DIRECTOR OF GRADUATE ADMISSIONS
275 MOUNT CARMEL AVENUE, AB-GRD, HAMDEN, CT 06518-1940 UNITED STATES
PHONE: 203-582-8672 • FAX: 203-582-3443
E-MAIL: GRADUATE@QUINNIPIAC.EDU • WEBSITE: WWW.QUINNIPIAC.EDU

Working students make up most of the part-time program; one student writes, "Each group has a different approach to course work. Those students who I have been involved with on group projects rely heavily on the more experienced students, in part because their course load is too heavy." They also rely on more experienced students because "they are young and inexperienced, and they are in graduate-level courses which require business experience to participate. They are unprepared." Fortunately, "everyone seems to support each other within the framework of a healthy competitive environment. There is diversity, respect, and always something enriching to the learning experience." Part-timers note that "there is very little social activity offered for graduate students, especially those of us who attend part-time. The school life is really focused on the undergraduate campus community." Hopefully, the relatively new Graduate Student Council will continue remedying this dearth of events

The Quinnipiac campus, set amid 400 wooded acres on the periphery of Sleeping Giant State Park, "is very beautiful. The setting of the state park sells itself; it creates a beautiful atmosphere." The bucolic location is very convenient to New Haven, which is eight miles away. New York City is one and a half hours away by train or by automobile. Boston is about two hours to the Northeast.

## Admissions

Quinnipiac processes MBA applications on a rolling basis. A complete application includes official transcripts for all postsecondary academic work, a recent resume, an official GMAT score report, two letters of recommendation, and a completed application form. The Admissions Office screens applicants using the formula [(undergraduate GPA 5 200) + GMAT score], with a minimum acceptable score of 1,100, a minimum undergraduate GPA of 2.7, and a minimum GMAT score of 500 generally required. Not all applicants who meet these criteria are admitted to the program. The school notes that "work experience and recommendations also are strongly considered in the process." Many Quinnipiac MBAs enter through the BS/MBA program, which is open to Quinnipiac undergraduates only; the school expects such students to have a minimum undergraduate GPA of 3.0 with at least a 3.25 GPA in their major. BS/MBA applicants with a cumulative GPA less than 3.0 are required to submit GMAT scores. International applicants must provide an official statement of sufficient financial support and, if their native language is not English, TOEFL scores.

### FINANCIAL FACTS

| | |
|---|---|
| Annual tuition | $10,260 |
| Fees | $540 |
| Books and supplies | $1,000 |
| Room & board | $9,408 |
| % of students receiving aid | 55 |
| % of first-year students receiving aid | 65 |
| % of students receiving loans | 41 |
| Average award package | $13,789 |
| Average student loan debt | $13,074 |

### ADMISSIONS

| | |
|---|---|
| Admissions Selectivity Rating | 74 |
| # of applications received | 107 |
| % applicants accepted | 65 |
| % acceptees attending | 79 |
| Average GMAT | 502 |
| Range of GMAT | 460–563 |
| Average GPA | 3.19 |
| TOEFL required of international students? | yes |
| Minimum TOEFL (paper/computer) | 575/233 |
| Application fee | $45 |
| International application fee | $45 |
| Regular application deadline | rolling |
| Regular notification | rolling |
| Deferment available? | yes |
| Maximum length of deferment | 1 year |
| Transfer students accepted? | yes |
| Transfer application policy Nine transfer credits allowed with equivalent courses. | |
| Non-fall admissions? | yes |
| Need-blind admissions? | yes |

### APPLICANTS ALSO LOOK AT

Fairfield University, University of Connecticut, University of Hartford

# RADFORD UNIVERSITY
## COLLEGE OF BUSINESS AND ECONOMICS

## Academics

The College of Business and Economics at Radford University is home to a large undergraduate population; nearly one in four RU undergrads majors in a business-related area. The much smaller MBA program capitalizes on the resources and strengths of the school's undergraduate program to provide a solid generalist graduate degree. As one student assessed the program says, "the school is affordable, and it is good for someone who does not plan on conquering the world, but rather [someone who] wants to stay in their community and better themselves."

Because of the size of the program, MBAs at Radford enjoy "small classes with plenty of personal attention." One student notes, "after only one semester, I am already convinced going to this school was the right decision for future endeavors. Professors are easily accessible and responsive to students' needs, and the administration is very attentive." Radford's curriculum focuses on "the presentation experience" and a large dose of writing; "there are lots of challenging papers assigned," students warn. Because of the predominantly part-time nature of the program (classes are held almost exclusively in the evening), the program tends to be a little more lecture-based and academic than others. Some feel that "they need more opportunities to work with outside companies and more real-life examples of local companies and speakers" in order to gain more practical experience within the program.

What Radford isn't is a place to forge a high degree of expertise in one area. That's because "it is a basic MBA program that does not allow for specialization." Some students see this as a drawback; one writes, "I would like more marketing courses because I would like to go into the marketing field upon graduation. This program only offers one marketing course." Others feel they are best served by the program's broad approach; one student explains, "My analytical business-diagnosing skills and presentation skills have been greatly enhanced by this MBA program." Radford's curriculum consists of eight required courses and two electives; the greatest number of electives are available in economics, finance, and management. Aggressive students can complete the degree in as little as 12 months, although most students work full-time and accordingly attend the program on a part-time basis. MBA courses are offered in two locations: the main campus in Radford, Virginia, and the Roanoke Higher Education Center in Roanoke, Virginia.

Radford's "tough but fair" professors "are excellent and even inspiring. Students find that they want to do their best work for all of them." They also "have a good sense of humor," which comes in handy during those long three-hour classes following a full work day.

## Career and Placement

The Center for Experiential Learning and Career Development at Radford University offers a variety of resources to undergraduates, graduates, and alumni. These include a virtual resume, internship, and job database "where students and employers come together to post and view resumes and position openings," as well as workshops in resume and portfolio development, career fairs, and career-assessment tools. In the spring of 2004, on-campus recruiters included DMG Securities, Ferguson Enterprises, Northwestern Mutual, State Farm, Wachovia Securities, and the federal government.

DR. DUNCAN HERRINGTON, DIRECTOR, MBA PROGRAM
MBA OFFICE, BOX 6956, RADFORD, VA 24142 UNITED STATES
PHONE: 540-831-5258 • FAX: 540-831-6655
E-MAIL: RUMBA@RADFORD.EDU. • WEBSITE: WWW.RADFORD.EDU/~COBE-WEB/

## Student Life and Environment

Radford's MBA program serves two identifiable populations. The larger of the two consists of full-time workers who live in the area or in nearby Roanoke. The second, which is also substantial, is made up of "students fresh from Radford undergraduate programs. Many of these are relatively immature in behavior and in life knowledge." Wrote one of the professional students of his younger peers, "some of their writing skills have not been up to graduate-level quality, which can be a real problem in team situations. All of these issues should be taken care of through the admissions process."

The Radford campus "has many formally organized activities," but most students are too busy to participate. The campus is small and pretty, attributes appreciated by the school's MBAs. Those who attend classes at the Roanoke Higher Education Center tell us that "the RHEC is a newly remodeled, high tech, and comfortable facility more suited to providing an appropriate atmosphere for educating older MBA students." Students at both campuses praise the school's "excellent website, telecommunications equipment, [and] library."

Hometown Radford is a small town in the Blue Ridge Mountains; Roanoke is about a half-hour away. The area is most amenable to outdoor enthusiasts, as it provides easy access to the Appalachian Trail, the New River, and Clayton Lake. Shopping, restaurants, nightlife, and such are not in great supply, students warn, although the proximity of Roanoke helps to make up for this deficiency. Charleston, Virginia, and Greensboro, North Carolina, are also within a reasonable driving distance.

## Admissions

Admission to Radford's MBA program requires successful completion of an undergraduate degree with a minimum GPA of 2.75. Applicants must also submit an official report of GMAT scores, TOEFL scores (international students), two letters of recommendation, a resume of work experience, a personal statement of purpose, and "evidence of creativity and leadership." Also, "applicants must also have taken accredited collegiate preparation in the following foundation areas (or equivalents): fundamentals of financial accounting, fundamentals of managerial accounting, principles of economics I and II, organizational behavior, essentials of marketing, introduction to business finance, business statistics, and business calculus." Students can earn credit for some of these prerequisites through CLEP testing. Competency with computers is also a prerequisite.

### FINANCIAL FACTS

| | |
|---|---|
| Annual tuition (in-state/out-of-state) | $7,140/$13,140 |
| Books and supplies | $800 |
| Room & board | $6,040 |

### ADMISSIONS

| | |
|---|---|
| **Admissions Selectivity Rating** | **74** |
| # of applications received | 60 |
| % applicants accepted | 67 |
| % acceptees attending | 82 |
| Average GMAT | 514 |
| Range of GMAT | 410–590 |
| Average GPA | 3.1 |
| TOEFL required of international students? | yes |
| Minimum TOEFL (paper/computer) | 550/213 |
| Application fee | $40 |
| International application fee | $40 |
| Regular application deadline | rolling |
| Regular notification | rolling |
| Deferment available? | yes |
| Maximum length of deferment | 1 year |
| Transfer students accepted? | yes |
| Transfer application policy Maximum of 6 credit hours. | |
| Non-fall admissions? | yes |
| Need-blind admissions? | yes |

### APPLICANTS ALSO LOOK AT

Virginia Tech

# RENSSELEAR POLYTECHNIC INSTITUTE
## LALLY SCHOOL OF MANAGEMENT AND TECHNOLOGY

## GENERAL INFORMATION

| | |
|---|---|
| Type of school | private |
| Environment | city |
| Academic calendar | semester |

### SURVEY SAYS...
Cutting-edge classes
*Solid preparation in:*
Teamwork
Entrepreneurial studies

### STUDENTS

| | |
|---|---|
| Enrollment of parent institution | 7,241 |
| Enrollment of business school | 265 |
| % male/female | 68/32 |
| % out-of-state | 70 |
| % part-time | 74 |
| % minorities | 12 |
| % international | 47 |
| Average age at entry | 28 |
| Average years work experience at entry | 4.5 |

### ACADEMICS

| | |
|---|---|
| **Academic Experience Rating** | **85** |
| Student/faculty ratio | 15:1 |
| Profs interesting rating | 88 |
| Profs accessible rating | 87 |
| % female faculty | 14 |
| % minority faculty | 7 |

### PROMINENT ALUMNI
George M. Low, NASA administrator who headed the Apollo program; James Q. Crowe, Founder and Builder of telecom industry companies; Denis Tito, Founder of Wilshire Associates; Ray Tomlinson, Inventor of e-mail in 1971

## Academics

The Lally School is located in Troy, New York, a historic town along the Hudson river that's over 200 years old. Once a major center of the Industrial Revolution (during the 1800s), Troy now finds itself at the center of a technological revolution. Rensselear's sterling reputation as a technical school has influenced Lally's direction. They have created an MBA program that combines technological innovation and a focus on entrepreneurship in a faculty team-taught curriculum that cuts across all business functions.

Lally's students, only about 70, find themselves in a place feverishly dedicated to the creation of entrepreneurial energy. Rensselear has state-of-the-art technical facilities, including a Center for Entrepreneurship, Business Incubator Program and the RPI tech-park, so it's no surprise that the Lally School's strength is in technological entrepreneurship. As the school says, "Technology creation and commercialization do not occur in an ivory tower; they happen in a competitive, increasingly global marketplace. Our students and faculty have a passion for taking ideas and turning them into real-world products." The students concur that "everybody at Rensselaer thinks about initiating a company." One student adds, "This makes it one of the best schools in providing a technology-driven MBA."

This year, Lally introduced a dynamic new MBA curriculum that identifies five critical areas for advancing business through innovation and mimics real-world decision-making. The curriculum is based on "streams of knowledge" modeled after their signature course, "Developing Innovative Products and Services", in which student teams develop a new product or service, write a business and marketing plan, and learn how to market and sell it. Students love this program, arguing that it "prepares future business leaders and strategic thinkers. Most courses incorporate projects that are applied to real businesses in the community." Some of the groups have even taken their products to compete in the "Tech Valley Collegiate Business Plan Competition" sponsored by the school's own Severino Center for Technological Entrepreneurship. There, teams compete for the money to make their theoretical venture a reality. Some groups from these classes have "actually now established themselves as startups!" Some students point out that "even if you don't have a desire to start your own company, the experiences you gain can be used in established tech companies."

However, none of this means that traditional business school material is lacking. The school has a strict core curriculum, which takes up the entire first year of the MBA program and a summer internship is encouraged. In the second year, there are only three required classes; that year is primarily dedicated to specialization. A summer internship between the two years is strongly recommended, but is not a degree requirement. Throughout the academic program, students say that "professors are exceptional and expect high technical standards from students." Still, students would like to be allowed "more freedom to take electives" and would like to see "more seminars and more of a focus on financial-market topics."

Another specialized aspect of the Lally School is the strong connection it has with international businesses—particularly business education in Asia. An international management exchange program is offered, in which students can elect to spend a semester abroad at one of several universities in Europe and Asia. This creates a "diverse composition of student body" that students appreciate. In short, at a school described as "very techie and wired," there are plenty of opportunities to learn from the "cutting-edge research going on across campus."

FRANK J. MENDELSON, DIRECTOR OF GRADUATE ADMISSIONS, MBA/MS PROGRAMS
110 EIGHTH STREET, PITTSBURGH BUILDING, TROY, NY 12180-3590 UNITED STATES
PHONE: 518-276-6565 • FAX: 518-276-2665
E-MAIL: MENDEF@RPI.EDU • WEBSITE: WWW.LALLYSCHOOL.RPI.EDU

## Career and Placement

Though the emphasis at Lally is so much about creating jobs rather than looking for them, Career Services reports that they've managed to place plenty of their students. The average salary for their MBA graduates in 2002 was around $75,000; 70 percent of those who completed the MBA were employed in the Northeast region of the United States, but 17 percent (the next-largest group) were employed internationally. Companies like GE Power Systems, Kaiser Permanente, and PricewaterhouseCoopers all recruit on campus, and about 30 percent of Lally graduates in 2002 ended up in project management. According to some students, the weakest link in the employment chain is Lally's "circle of alumni," who are not as involved as most current students would like to see.

## Student Life and Environment

Troy is home to just about 55,000 people and once boasted such illustrious citizens as Samuel Wilson—that's Uncle Sam to you. Though it's a relatively small city, Troy—and students who make Troy their home—benefit from its proximity to Albany, which, despite what New York City likes to believe, is still the capital of the state. And students who manage to make time in their hectic academic schedule point out that there are "tons of cultural opportunities like readings, speakers, and music on campus and in town. We have a brewpub in town making great beer. There is a good live music scene." The school, along with student-run groups, tries to facilitate student interaction as well. "We have regular social functions that get both classes together and try to involve faculty as well. Since it's a smaller program, it's pretty close-knit and a lot of students organize social activities and invite the entire class."

Despite the assurances of most students that all the whole Rensselear campus boasts top-of-the-line technology, some students would like to see Lally "upgrade some of its classrooms." Another common complaint is that recent changes in administration have led to breakdowns in communication. Though the administration overall scores a high rating, most students wish the school could better communicate its goals to its students.

## Admissions

Though the majority of Lally's admitted students come from some sort of technical background, 29 percent have some background in liberal arts or business. The average age for an admitted student at Lally is 28, but ages range from 21 to 39. The average work experience is about five years, the average GMAT is 635, and the average undergraduate GPA is 3.16.

### FINANCIAL FACTS

| | |
|---|---|
| Annual tuition | $31,000 |
| Fees | $1,548 |
| Books and supplies | $1,631 |
| Room & board | $9,000 |

### ADMISSIONS

| | |
|---|---|
| Admissions Selectivity Rating | 81 |
| # of applications received | 164 |
| % applicants accepted | 81 |
| % acceptees attending | 70 |
| Average GMAT | 635 |
| Average GPA | 3.16 |
| TOEFL required of international students? | yes |
| Minimum TOEFL (paper/computer) | 600/250 |
| Application fee | $75 |
| International application fee | $75 |
| Regular application deadline | rolling |
| Regular notification | rolling |
| Early decision program? | yes |
| ED deadline/notification | Fall semester, 1/15 / 2/15 |
| Deferment available? | yes |
| Maximum length of deferment | 1 year |
| Need-blind admissions? | yes |

### APPLICANTS ALSO LOOK AT

Babson College, Boston University, Carnegie Mellon, Case Western Reserve University, Cornell University, Georgia Institute of Technology, Massachusetts Institute of Technology

| EMPLOYMENT PROFILE | | | |
|---|---|---|---|
| **Career Rating** | 84 | **Grads employed by field:** | **% avg. salary:** |
| Average starting salary | $65,033 | Finance | 34 | $55,830 |
| Percent employed | 85 | Marketing | 24 | $81,670 |
| | | Operations | 18 | $72,670 |
| | | Consulting | 12 | $77,500 |
| | | General Management | 6 | NR |
| | | Other | 6 | $60,000 |

# RICE UNIVERSITY
## JESSE H. JONES GRADUATE SCHOOL OF MANAGEMENT

## GENERAL INFORMATION
| | |
|---|---|
| Type of school | private |
| Environment | metropolis |
| Academic calendar | semester |

## SURVEY SAYS...
Smart classrooms
*Solid preparation in:*
Finance
Accounting
Communication/interpersonal skills
Presentation skills

## STUDENTS
| | |
|---|---|
| Enrollment of parent institution | 4,855 |
| Enrollment of business school | 468 |
| % male/female | 69/31 |
| % out-of-state | 54 |
| % minorities | 18 |
| % international | 32 |
| Average age at entry | 28 |
| Average years work experience at entry | 5 |

## ACADEMICS
| | |
|---|---|
| **Academic Experience Rating** | **85** |
| Student/faculty ratio | 9:1 |
| Profs interesting rating | 86 |
| Profs accessible rating | 92 |
| % female faculty | 27 |
| % minority faculty | 13 |

## JOINT DEGREES
MBA/Master of Electrical Engineering, 22 months; MBA/Master of Computer Science; MBA/Master of Chemical Engineering; MBA/Master of Civil Engineering; MBA/Master of Environmental Engineering; MBA/Master of Science in Mechanical Engineering; MBA; MBA/MD with Baylor College of Medicine

## Academics

Because business schools contribute so heavily to the workforce of their local communities, the synergy between school and location can be an especially important factor in an MBA program. Rice—which would be a world-class university even if it were located in the middle of the tundra—benefits greatly from its location in Houston, a city second only to New York in the number of *Fortune* 500 companies hosted. A demanding curriculum with a number of standout features contributes equally to the high regard given Rice's Jones Graduate School of Management.

Rice piles on the work in the first-year core, doled out in 5- and 10-week modules to "allow for more flexibility and the opportunity to be exposed to a wider array of topics." The core includes courses in Rice's three strongest areas: finance, communications, and entrepreneurship. The highlight of first year is the action learning project, a 10-week undertaking that has students "working in teams on real-world problems on behalf of a wide variety of significant companies, such as Continental Airlines, ConocoPhillips, ExxonMobil, and Deloitte Touche Tohmatsu, as well as smaller start-ups and nonprofits." At least one student feels, "The Action Learning Project offered at Rice has helped me become an attractive candidate to employers," an added benefit of the project. Overall, students feel that "the course load is a bit too heavy for first years," noting that "the school offers fabulous enrichment experiences (such as guest speakers, seminars, and training programs), but we are too busy with schoolwork to enjoy all of them." Even so, they also praise the curriculum as "well-structured to impart the basics of the business experience while simultaneously enhancing writing, presentation, and communication skills so as to be prepared for internships and other outside business-related projects hosted by the school."

Second-year course work includes five more five-week core courses (including unique offerings in business-government relations, business ethics, and globalization); the rest of the year is given over to electives. Older MBAs observe that "the full-time program is very much geared towards very young, relatively inexperienced people. This includes the career-placement center. Students with more than eight years of experience should definitely enroll in the EMBA program or go to another school."

## Career and Placement

Most MBAs agree that "Rice has a very good career center, which brings top recruiters to the school and helps immensely with finding employment/internship positions for MBA students." They also praise the "close-knit alumni network;" one student notes, "Every Rice alumni I have contacted has offered to help with job opportunities, which I found really impressive." Asked where the service could improve, students suggested that "the office should pay greater attention to recruiting a wider variety of companies, such as marketing and real estate companies. There is perhaps too much focus on finance, oil, and gas, to the detriment of other areas."

Top employers of Rice MBAs include BP, CapRock, Deloitte Touche Tohmatsu, Deutsche Bank, ExxonMobil, FMC Technologies, Goldman Sachs, Hewlett-Packard, JPMorgan Chase, Lehman Brothers, the Methodist Hospital, Noble Drilling, Sabre, Stewart & Stevenson, and UBS Warburg. About three-quarters of all Rice MBAs remain in the Texas region, with many of them remaining in Houston.

LISA W. ANDERSON, DIRECTOR OF ADMISSIONS
6100 MAIN STREET , MS 531, JONES SCHOOL SUITE 109, PO BOX 2932, HOUSTON, TX 77005-1892 U.S.
PHONE: 888-844-4773 • FAX: 713-348-6147
E-MAIL: RICEMBA@RICE.EDU • WEBSITE: WWW.JONESGSM.RICE.EDU

## Student Life and Environment

Life at Rice "is balanced between personal studies and numerous team projects," an equation most students find agreeable. The academic week ends on Thursday, students report, "and is typically capped with a first-year and second-year joint party on the patio—or as we say, 'partio'—at which time pizza is sponsored either by the student association or an outside firm that may want to mingle and informally meet with students." Other program-wide events include "alumni receptions and golf tourneys twice a year to network with alumni." In addition, there are "twice-a-week coffee colloquiums for students and faculty to mingle, and weekends frequently consist of groups of students planning social outings at area night establishments."

The Jones MBA program is housed in an "incredible state-of-the-art building" with "lots of team rooms, cutting-edge technology in all classrooms (incredible audiovisual tools)," and "comfortable classrooms with seats that can be changed to fit your comfort." Wireless connectivity "is everywhere." In sum, students agree that "the building and facilities are second to none. They really facilitate a learning environment where your options are almost unlimited."

They're just as enthusiastic about the Rice campus and hometown Houston. A typical MBA writes, "The campus is absolutely beautiful; the weather is great most of the time. Rice is located inside of Houston, so it gives you both the cozy campus life and the opportunity to venture into the city for more diverse entertainment. In Houston, there are more restaurants per capita than in any other city in the United States. Houston is a very international city with a great deal of diversity in terms of its people, its restaurants, and its entertainment."

## Admissions

Applicants to Jones must provide the admissions committee with official copies of all undergraduate and graduate transcripts, GMAT scores, two letters of recommendation, three personal essays, and a resume. An interview is also required. "Meaningful post-undergraduate leadership and professional experience" is "strongly encouraged" but not required. The admissions committee considers an applicant's "leadership experience and team-based experiences, as well as the unique qualities that the candidate will contribute to the program." The school reports that "an independent organization, RICE-TMS, offers merit-based scholarships for underrepresented minority students completing an MBA at Rice."

### PROMINENT ALUMNI

James S. Turley, Chair, Ernst & Young LLP, Worldwide; Abby Rodgers, VP of Innovation, Coca-Cola; Keith Anderson, Founding Partner, BlackRock, Inc.; Doug Foshee, Chair, President & CEO, El Paso Energy Company; Caroline Caskey, Founder and CEO, Identigene

### FINANCIAL FACTS

| | |
|---|---|
| Annual tuition | $32,150 |
| Fees | $1,920 |
| Books and supplies | $1,300 |
| Room & board (on/off-campus) | $7,500/$10,500 |
| % of students receiving aid | 81 |
| % of students receiving loans | 63 |
| % of students receiving grants | 62 |
| Average award package | $39,105 |
| Average grant | $8,800 |
| Average student loan debt | $38,444 |

### ADMISSIONS

| | |
|---|---|
| Admissions Selectivity Rating | 82 |
| # of applications received | 468 |
| % applicants accepted | 62 |
| % acceptees attending | 47 |
| Average GMAT | 602 |
| Range of GMAT | 550–650 |
| Average GPA | 3.24 |
| TOEFL required of international students? | yes |
| Minimum TOEFL (paper/computer) | 600/250 |
| Application fee | $100 |
| International application fee | $100 |
| Regular application deadline | 4/10 |
| Regular notification | 5/31 |
| Application deadline/notification | |
| Round 1: | 10/17 / 11/23 |
| Round 2: | 12/5 / 2/1 |
| Round 3: | 2/6 / 3/31 |
| Round 4: | 4/10 / 5/31 |
| Deferment available? | yes |
| Maximum length of deferment | 1 year |
| Need-blind admissions? | yes |

### APPLICANTS ALSO LOOK AT

Babson College, Georgetown University, Indiana University—Bloomington, Purdue University, Southern Methodist University, The University of Texas at Austin, Vanderbilt University

| EMPLOYMENT PROFILE | | | | |
|---|---|---|---|---|
| Career Rating | 90 | Grads employed by field: | % avg. | salary: |
| Primary source of full-time job acceptances | | Finance | 54 | $81,687 |
| | | Marketing | 11 | $79,000 |
| School-facilitated activities | 68 (50%) | Operations | 4 | $77,000 |
| Graduate-facilitated activities | 66 (49%) | Consulting | 11 | $91,964 |
| Unknown | 2 (1%) | General Management | 10 | $87,275 |
| | | Other | 10 | $82,500 |
| Average starting salary | $83,000 | | | |
| Percent employed | 93 | | | |

# ROLLINS COLLEGE
## CRUMMER GRADUATE SCHOOL OF BUSINESS

## Academics

Rollins College's Crummer Graduate School of Business offers students an MBA program "geared for general managers, not specialists" that "truly prepares students for general management and big-picture issues." For convenience's sake, Crummer, which has "a great regional reputation," serves the program up in five different varieties: full-time students can choose either a one-year or two-year program, while part-timers have the option of attending either the professional MBA program (part-time evening program) the Saturday MBA Program (classes are held on Saturdays), or the executive MBA program (alternating Fridays/Saturdays for students with extensive professional experience). All five programs include core courses, electives, and integrative capstone course work; the full-time programs also include an international study trip. Crummer tells us that its "experienced faculty has developed an international reputation for teaching through a hands-on method of applying business concepts." Students approve, telling us that "the faculty and administration at Crummer are completely committed to making the student experience as successful as possible. I believe that the professors take pride in the art of teaching." Noted one MBA, "I was really surprised by the teachers I got for my classes. Not only are they leaders in their field of work, but also they convey their knowledge in an understandable manner. Excellent teacher selection!" Administrators, we're told, "are constantly initiating innovative programming to enhance the student experience." Students also appreciate the curriculum's "strong focus on working in teams, giving presentations, class participation, and use of technology" and the "small class size, which helps us greatly." The program "has less of a focus on quantitative than expected, yet with very intensive use of Excel spreadsheets."

Top concentrations at Crummer include management, finance, e-commerce, and international business. MBAs observe that "[twenty percent] of our students are international, and a focus on international business issues are woven into most classes." Crummer "has an excellent mentor program and is very active in the community;" all students must fulfill a ten-hour service requirement to a not-for-profit organization.

## Career and Placement

The Crummer Career Management Center offers skill-development workshops, online self-assessment tools, job listings, and online job databases and resume books. Crummer depends on participation in consortia for recruiting to offset the trend that fewer companies are scheduling on-campus interviewing sessions. Students feel that "a much greater emphasis needs to be put on bringing more companies to campus for recruiting. The office also needs to put more pressure on the MBA Consortium it is a member of to include only MBA-caliber jobs at its career events." Many feel that "the office is understaffed to properly serve the needs of all five MBA programs, although the center just increased the staff this year."

Major employers of Rollins MBAs include Anderson Consulting, AT&T, CIA, Citigroup, CNL, Darden Restaurant Group, Dyntech, FedEx, General Mills, Harris Corporation, Bank of America, The Marriott Corporation, Dell, Seimens Westinghouse, SunTrust Bank, Tupperware, Universal Studios, and Walt Disney. About 1 in 10 Rollins MBAs finds a first post-degree job outside the United States.

## Student Life and Environment

Crummer MBAs agree that Rollins and hometown Winter Park offer an extraordinary quality of life. As one student put it, "Central Florida is paradise, so what more needs be said? When we're not involved in schoolwork, the area offers anything you could ever want to do, from beaches to amusement parks to lively entertainment districts. The warm climate allows me to participate year-round in outdoor activities such as biking, golf, and soccer." Another writes, "Winter Park is very upscale, so there is a wide variety

STEPHEN GAUTHIER, ASSOCIATE DEAN
1000 HOLT AVEENUE, 2722, WINTER PARK, FL 32789-4499 UNITED STATES
PHONE: 407-646-2405 • FAX: 407-646-1550
E-MAIL: CRUMMER@ROLLINS.EDU • WEBSITE: WWW.CRUMMER.ROLLINS.EDU

## FINANCIAL FACTS

| | |
|---|---|
| Annual tuition | $25,680 |
| Fees | $60 |
| Books and supplies | $2,000 |
| Room & board | $15,000 |
| % of students receiving aid | 50 |
| % of first-year students receiving aid | 47 |
| % of students receiving grants | 50 |
| Average award package | $15,154 |
| Average grant | $15,154 |
| Average student loan debt | $28,900 |

## ADMISSIONS

| | |
|---|---|
| **Admissions Selectivity Rating** | **81** |
| # of applications received | 201 |
| % applicants accepted | 58 |
| % acceptees attending | 59 |
| Average GMAT | 565 |
| Range of GMAT | 510–650 |
| Average GPA | 3.2 |
| TOEFL required of international students? | yes |
| Application fee | $50 |
| International application fee | $50 |
| Regular application deadline | rolling |
| Regular notification | rolling |
| Deferment available? | yes |
| Maximum length of deferment | 1 year |
| Transfer students accepted? | yes |
| Transfer application policy | |
| The school accepts up to 6 credits transferred from an MBA program that is accredited by the AACSB. | |
| Non-fall admissions? | yes |
| Need-blind admissions? | yes |

## APPLICANTS ALSO LOOK AT

Florida State University, Stetson University, University of Central Florida, University of Florida, University of Miami, Vanderbilt University, Wake Forest University

of top restaurants and bars in town and some more reasonably priced sports bars. Orlando is close by, so there are clubs and bars." Students in the full-time Early Advantage MBA programs are a tight-knit group of "mostly young people (with little business experience and with strong academic backgrounds), so there are regular bar outings for those who party." One full-timer writes, "Whether it be happy hour at the local Irish pub, dinner at one of the bistros on Park Avenue, paintball, a bowling competition, or a casino cruise, this school knows how to offer students a good break from the grueling world of case studies and marketing plans." The pace of life has quickened of late; students report that the "2003 to 2004 has been the year of student activities. Existing clubs were reinvigorated and new clubs have been created, such as the Entrepreneurship Club." One student gleefully claims that "students here are more alive than ever."

Crummer has a large international population, with "students from the U.K., India, Belgium, China, Romania, and many more. There's a real international focus; last summer the entire class went on a trip to London and Dublin. (This is included in tuition.) This trip focused on visiting businesses and academic institutions. It was also a great chance to party together and see some sights."

The Rollins campus "is beautiful in both appearance and people," and because "there are only four main classrooms, students tend to see a lot of each other. The student lounge just got a face lift and looks better, but it still needs some work." Also in need of an upgrade are nuts-and-bolts tech facilities; one MBA explains, "There is high-speed Internet, but some of the connections work while others do not. True, there is state-of-the-art technology, videoconferencing, and speaker phones for group interviews. Nevertheless, it is the little things that count, and in this arena, the school really needs to make sure all the Ethernet ports work, without question." Agreed another student, "The b-school study area could use an upgrade in technology. Our copier, printing capabilities, and wireless system always seem to be having problems, forcing us to run across to the Kinko's or the UPS store." However, the school has reacted by replacing some of the older printers and is in the process of upgrading the campus-wide Internet system.

## Admissions

"Previous academic records, score on the Graduate Management Admission Test (GMAT), prior work experience, and evidence of maturity and motivation" all factor into the Rollins admissions decision. Admission to the school's five MBA programs is competitive. Applicants are required to submit official transcripts for all undergraduate and graduate work, GMAT scores, personal essays, two letters of recommendation, and a resume. A personal interview is required phone or teleconference interviews can be arranged for candidates who cannot visit the campus. Rollins offers scholarships and graduate assistantships to attract minority students and students from disadvantaged backgrounds.

| EMPLOYMENT PROFILE | | | | |
|---|---|---|---|---|
| **Career Rating** | 75 | **Grads employed by field:** | **%** | **avg. salary:** |
| **Primary source of full-time job acceptances** | | Finance | 18 | $44,000 |
| | | Marketing | 6 | $42,000 |
| Graduate-facilitated activities | 25 (67%) | Operations | 1 | $51,000 |
| Unknown | 5 (13%) | Consulting | 2 | $48,500 |
| | | General Management | 4 | $56,000 |
| Average starting salary | $46,000 | Other | 6 | $47,500 |
| Percent employed | 95 | | | |

# ROWAN UNIVERSITY
## COLLEGE OF BUSINESS

## GENERAL INFORMATION
Type of school      public
Academic calendar      semester

## SURVEY SAYS...
Helpful alumni
Happy students
*Solid preparation in:*
Teamwork
Communication/interpersonal skills
Presentation skills

## STUDENTS
Enrollment of parent
  institution      9,762
Enrollment of business school    85
% male/female      50/50
% part-time      88
% minorities      25
% international      13
Average age at entry      29

## ACADEMICS
**Academic Experience Rating**    **73**
Student/faculty ratio      19:1
Profs interesting rating      87
Profs accessible rating      75
% female faculty      32
% minority faculty      29

## Academics

Rowan University's MBA program, the school tells us, "is especially suited for full-time employees working in the tri-state area" encompassing Pennsylvania, New Jersey, and Delaware. "As working adults, we have been treated like valued customers," one student notes, pointing out that the once-a-week, three-hour classes (mostly weeknights, with some classes held on Saturday mornings) best fits her busy work schedule. Because most students attend part-time, a Rowan degree usually takes between three and six years to complete; the school's few full-time students can conceivably complete the program in a single year.

The Rowan MBA curriculum commences with 27 hours of required core courses covering fundamental general-management skills and concludes with an integrative capstone seminar. The curriculum also leaves room for nine hours of electives; students may choose to take a variety of courses that match their career needs or may use these courses to specialize in finance, accounting, or entrepreneurship. MBAs tell us that "every class involves group work, which teaches students to work well with each other and share work. This skill set has helped in the workforce as well." They also wish the school would expand its selection of electives; one student observes, "Rowan could offer specializations in some different tracks, such as human resources and marketing. This would help the program grow."

The program has been growing in recent years, a fact that students acknowledge and appreciate. The school recently earned AACSB accreditation, placing it among the nation's top programs. Students tell us that "there has been an increase in the quality of the program, and [they] were delighted when the Rowan program was accredited in 2003. Enrollment has increased, and [they] see a great future for Rowan's MBA program." One graduating BA/MBA student told us that "although the program started at a low level, it is now getting tougher and tougher to get into." The increased standards, we're told, have paid dividends in more challenging classes and more illuminating in-class discussions.

Rowan MBAs love that "we are able to access the library's databases from our home computers. It's great to be able to look up material 24/7. Also, online and tele-registrations have reduced the hassle of registering to zero." Technology remains in the spotlight in the classroom; "Rowan teaches computer skills that have proven invaluable in the workforce," students tell us, although they also complain that "the audiovisual capabilities are terrible in all but one classroom. It is a very limiting feature when trying to receive information or do presentations." Overall, students feel that Rowan "is a great regional school whose current programs and commitment to expansion of the program will continue to take great strides in drawing students from outside this region."

## Career and Placement

Rowan maintains a Career and Academic Planning Center "to provide developmental advising" to all students in their pursuit of academic and professional goals. The CAPC serves the entire school; there is no office dedicated specifically to MBAs or to business students on the undergraduate and graduate levels. CAPC Services include one-on-one counseling, workshops, online self-assessment and job databases (CampusRecruiter, Career Key), career publications, and employer directories. Services are available to alumni as well as to current students. It should be noted that most current students are full-time workers looking to advance within their current places of work; relatively few students seeking MBAs are actively searching for new jobs.

## Student Life and Environment

Because Rowan serves part-time students almost exclusively, its student body is more "a collection of people that get together in the evening for three hours" than a coherent and cohesive community. That's not to say the opportunities to socialize and network aren't there; as one BA/MBA student explains, "As an undergraduate, I found many activities that were available to students who lived on and off campus. I enjoyed my four years living on campus. Rowan had activities for everyone, including day and evening events, student government, community-service efforts, fraternities, and campus-wide events. As a graduate student, however, I am a working professional, so I do not have any time to participate in the activities available."

Rowan's suburban New Jersey home town of Glassboro is a mere half-hour's drive from Philadelphia; the Jersey shore is less than an hour to the east, and Atlantic City is only 50 miles away. New York; Washington, DC; and the Chesapeake are all within easy travel distances. The Rowan campus is in the middle of an ambitious expansion program, with makeovers planned for most facilities and several new buildings going up. Students praise the new athletic center and enjoy watching Rowan's Division III excellent men's and women's basketball teams.

## Admissions

Rowan's graduate b-students are required to complete seven foundation courses, or their undergraduate equivalents, prior to enrolling in the MBA program; those courses are foundations of accounting, statistics I, principles of finance, principles of marketing, calculus, operations management, and global perspective on economics. Those lacking the required course work must enroll in the pre-MBA program; admission to the pre-MBA program does not ensure admission to the MBA program. Applicants to the MBA program must submit official transcripts for all undergraduate work (with a minimum GPA of 2.5. overall or 2.8 for final 60 semester hours), GMAT scores, two letters of recommendation, a personal statement of career objectives, evidence of computer proficiency, and a resume. International students whose first language is not English must also provide TOEFL scores.

### FINANCIAL FACTS
| | |
|---|---|
| Annual tuition (in-state/out-of-state) | $4,943/$7,917 |
| Fees | $944 |
| Books and supplies | $700 |
| Room & board | $5,600 |

### ADMISSIONS
| | |
|---|---|
| **Admissions Selectivity Rating** | **70** |
| # of applications received | 47 |
| % applicants accepted | 77 |
| % acceptees attending | 78 |
| Average GMAT | 503 |
| Range of GMAT | 460–540 |
| Average GPA | 3.21 |
| TOEFL required of international students? | yes |
| Minimum TOEFL (paper/computer) | 550/213 |
| Application fee | $50 |
| International application fee | $50 |
| Regular application deadline | rolling |
| Regular notification | rolling |
| Deferment available? | yes |
| Maximum length of deferment | 1 year |
| Transfer students accepted? | yes |
| Transfer application policy Student may transfer up to 9 credit hours. | |
| Non-fall admissions? | yes |
| Need-blind admissions? | yes |

### APPLICANTS ALSO LOOK AT
Rutgers, The State University of New Jersey

# RSM Erasmus University

## GENERAL INFORMATION
Type of school                private
Academic calendar            semester

## SURVEY SAYS...
Friendly students
Good peer network
*Solid preparation in:*
Marketing
Teamwork
Doing business in a global economy

## STUDENTS
Enrollment of parent
  institution                16,000
Enrollment of business school  292
% male/female                  69/31
% part-time                        28
% international                    95
Average age at entry               30
Average years work experience
  at entry                          6

## ACADEMICS
**Academic Experience Rating**      **89**
Student/faculty ratio              3:1
Profs interesting rating            70
Profs accessible rating             77

## PROMINENT ALUMNI
Durk Jager, ex-CEO, Procter &
Gamble; Bert van den Bergh,
President, Neuroscience Products,
Eli Lilly; Hans Ten Cate, Member
Executive Board, Rabobank
International; Johan Andresen, CEO,
Ferd AS, Norway; Cees de Jong,
Managing Director, Gist Brocades

## Academics

An international curriculum well-suited to an international student body—that's the formula at RSM Erasmus University, and it's one students endorse. In a typical year, aspiring MBAs representing more than 40 countries attend the school; the faculty has a similarly international aspect. Course materials, case studies, and class discussion all focus steadily on global business issues. With nearly 30 exchange partner schools available to students, MBAs can even take their business studies abroad to any continent (well, except Antarctica).

RSM Erasmus University's full-time MBA is a 15-month intensive program divided into four terms. The first term covers core competencies and career- and professional-development skills; the second investigates business disciplines and continues career-development work; the third consists of core career concentration courses, followed by an internship and a research project on the company sponsoring the internship; and the fourth term allows students to pursue electives. Students praise the curriculum's "recognition of environmental and sustainability issues in business" and rate the accounting and marketing faculty very highly. They are less enthusiastic about economics and statistics professors. "Overall, this is a great program for general management studies," sums up one MBA, adding that "the visiting professors are generally better than the resident professors."

Throughout the RSM Erasmus University curriculum, "an important part of the learning process is working on assignments in groups. Group members not only come from different cultures but also from different backgrounds. This diversity results in sharing both knowledge and experiences and, of course, learning how to cope with such cultural diversity. Not easy during tough times!" Students also appreciate how "the small class size ensures that everybody gets individual attention. The sessions are highly interactive, making our classes very interesting."

## Career and Placement

The Career Management Centre at RSM Erasmus University, according to the school, "is dedicated to helping students make sound career choices. They provide guidance, training, and support to help you. The CMC also supports, coordinates, and facilitates company presentations and other recruitment events for many top international firms to provide you with the opportunity to meet as many companies as possible on campus." Students tell us that the office does a good job of attracting recruiters from consultancies and banks but is less adept with other sectors.

Major employers of MBAs include ABN Amro, AT Kearney, Bain and Company, Barclays Capital, Benson, Bertelsmann, Boston Consulting Group, Citibank, Citigroup, Eli Lilly, Ford Motor Company, General Electric, Hilti, Johnson & Johnson, Lehman Brothers, McKinsey, Novartis, Roland Berger Strategy Consultants, and Royal Dutch Shell. About one in four graduates finds work in the Netherlands; another 40 percent take jobs in Western Europe, and 14 percent of all graduates find jobs in the Americas.

VERVOORN, MARKETING & ADMISSIONS MANAGER
BURGEMEESTER OUDLAAN 50—J BUILDING, 3062 PA ROTTERDAM, NETHERLANDS
PHONE: 011-31-10-4082222 • FAX: 011-31-10-4082222
E-MAIL: MBA.INFO@RSM.NL • WEBSITE: WWW.RSM.NL

## Student Life and Environment

The 15-month curriculum condenses a lot of information into a relatively short period, placing a substantial academic burden on students. MBAs observe, "It is crucial to find a balance between hard work and social life. As a first-class European MBA program, the school puts significant pressure with lots of readings and work, either in groups or class preparation. On the other hand, it does give you time to enjoy other activities (i.e., social events like the Chinese celebration of New Year, where many students had a beautiful dinner together) and help you understand what your career should really look like."

A collegial student body helps MBAs manage the workload, which "is so intense that you are constantly running to and from lectures or group meetings. Fortunately, people are very helpful and friendly, and everyone looks out for each other regardless of nationality." Students are "an extremely diverse and international group. It is amazing to talk with people from different backgrounds." Many convene in program-related clubs serving many different professional and extracurricular interests.

Rotterdam, a large port city of 600,000, is located just 45 miles from Amsterdam. It lacks the many tourist attractions common to large European cities, primarily because the city was nearly destroyed during World War II. The city harbor, considered by many the world's largest, brings in trade from around the world and makes Rotterdam a truly international city. Shopping areas and restaurants are plentiful, although students warn that "prices in the Netherlands are high."

## Admissions

Admission to the RSM Erasmus University MBA program is contingent on all the following factors: professional achievements and goals, as reflected in one's resume/curriculum vitae; academic achievement, as reflected in one's academic transcripts and GMAT scores; leadership qualities; English-language proficiency; personality; and ability to contribute to an international atmosphere. Two letters of recommendation and a personal interview are required. The school estimates that the entire review process takes about 6 weeks from the time the admissions office receives all application materials.

### FINANCIAL FACTS

| | |
|---|---|
| Annual tuition | $41,088 |
| Books and supplies | $23,800 |

### ADMISSIONS

| | |
|---|---|
| Admissions Selectivity Rating | 87 |
| # of applications received | 340 |
| % applicants accepted | 59 |
| % acceptees attending | 53 |
| Average GMAT | 620 |
| Range of GMAT | 550–720 |
| Average GPA | 3.5 |
| Minimum TOEFL (paper/computer) | 600/250 |
| Application fee | $100 |
| International application fee | $100 |
| Regular application deadline | 7/15 |
| Regular notification | rolling |
| Need-blind admissions? | yes |

### EMPLOYMENT PROFILE

| Career Rating | 81 | Grads employed by field: | % | avg. salary: |
|---|---|---|---|---|
| Average starting salary | $72,500 | Finance | 21 | NR |
| Percent employed | 79 | Human Resources | 1 | NR |
| | | Marketing | 25 | NR |
| | | Operations | 7 | NR |
| | | Consulting | 30 | NR |
| | | General Management | 12 | NR |
| | | Other | 4 | NR |

# RUTGERS, THE STATE UNIVERSITY OF NEW JERSEY—CAMDEN
## SCHOOL OF BUSINESS MBA PROGRAM

### GENERAL INFORMATION
| | |
|---|---|
| Type of school | public |
| Academic calendar | semester |

### SURVEY SAYS...
Friendly students
Happy students
*Solid preparation in:*
Marketing
Teamwork
Communication/interpersonal skills
Presentation skills

### STUDENTS
| | |
|---|---|
| Enrollment of parent institution | 5,052 |
| Enrollment of business school | 247 |
| % part-time | 85 |
| Average age at entry | 27 |
| Average years work experience at entry | 2.8 |

### ACADEMICS
| | |
|---|---|
| **Academic Experience Rating** | **81** |
| Student/faculty ratio | 9:1 |
| Profs interesting rating | 88 |
| Profs accessible rating | 86 |
| % female faculty | 25 |
| % minority faculty | 6 |

### JOINT DEGREES
MBA/JD, 3-5 years; MBA/MD, 5-6 years

## Academics

Located just across the Benjamin Franklin Bridge from Philadelphia, the School of Business MBA Program at Rutgers—Camden offers a convenient and affordable graduate degree option for both Garden State and City of Brotherly Love residents. This small program consists almost entirely of part-time students pursuing degrees while simultaneously engaging in careers and, quite often, starting families.

Fortunately for these busy students, "professors and administrators bend over backwards for the students to ensure they are achieving their educational goals" by "making themselves very accessible. Their main priority is ensuring that we understand everything gone over in class and can apply it to the real world." Students here also appreciate that "classes are well organized and there are many opportunities to enroll in unique courses that include exposure to industry professionals." On the downside, some here feel that "expectations for student performance are too low in general and the amount of material covered is not enough to feel really comfortable in a number of areas."

The Rutgers MBA consists of 60 credits, 36 devoted to the core curriculum and 24 to electives. The school website notes, "Some course requirements may be waived based upon prior knowledge gained at the undergraduate level." Students may combine four electives to create a concentration in one of the following disciplines: accounting, e-commerce technology, finance, international business, healthcare management, management, or marketing. Concentrations in international business and healthcare management piggyback on other divisions of the university, allowing students to gain exposure to the School of Law and the Department of Public Policy and Administration. Students are not required to concentrate in an area; they may opt instead for a general MBA. Thanks to "institutional relationships with universities and companies in Namibia and South Africa," Rutgers MBAs have the opportunity to study abroad and "experience firsthand the issues facing emerging global markets." Study in Europe is also an option. The business school also offers classes in Voorhees and Atlantic City.

## Career and Placement

The Career Center at Rutgers University/Camden handles counseling and placement services for all undergraduate and graduate students. The office provides all the following services: assessment inventories, career counseling, a career library, job fairs, on-campus recruiting events, resume critique, skills seminars, and Web-based resume posting. More than one hundred recruiters visit the Camden campus each year. Top recruiters include: Bally's Park Place Casino and Resort, Bristol-Myers Squibb, Campbell Soup Company, PHH Mortgage, Commerce Bank, Galaxy Scientific, J&J Snack Foods, Lockheed Martin, Merck, Mobil, Okidata, PaineWebber, PSE&G, Rohm and Haas, and the U.S. Air Force.

## Student Life and Environment

Most Rutgers-Camden MBAs "are married with children and work full-time. In spite of this, they show up to class regularly, have their work done on time, and participate a lot in class. We do a lot of group work, and most people are easy to work with." One student observes, "Everyone is really nice and willing to help you out with knowledge from other classes they may have taken already. Throughout the semester you get real close with your classmates. The business school is really like a family here." Rutgers' on-the-go grads appreciate how "the campus is specifically geared toward the busy professional who wants to jump start his or her career. The library is open late during the regular semesters, although it closes early in the summer and winter intermission sessions."

Dr. Barbara Bickart, MBA Program Director
MBA Program, Camden, NJ 08102-1401 United States
Phone: 856-225-6452 • Fax: 856-225-6231
E-mail: mba@camden-sba.rutgers.edu • Website: www.camden-sbc.rutgers.edu

Those who seek opportunities on this campus usually find them. One MBA explains, "The business school has connected me with a lot of great employers and I have been doing a lot of interviews. The campus offers a lot of activities and events that are open to all students regardless of what school they are in." Students love the convenience of Camden, which can be easily accessed via public transportation (the PATCO Hi-Speed train line) or automobile. They warn that "there's not a lot to do in Camden," but with Philadelphia so close by (and Atlantic City an easy drive or bus ride away), there's always plenty to do within a reasonable travel distance.

## Admissions

Applicants to the School of Business MBA Program at Rutgers—Camden must submit the following materials: an online application form, an official score report for the GMAT (the average score is approximately 588), two official copies of transcripts for all postsecondary academic work (minimum undergraduate GPA of 2.5 required), three letters of recommendation, a personal statement, and a resume. International students must also submit appropriate financial documentation, those whose first language is not English must submit official score reports for the TOEFL (minimum acceptable score of 550 paper-based test or 230 computer-based test) or IELTS (minimum acceptable score of Band 7).

### FINANCIAL FACTS

| | |
|---|---|
| Annual tuition (in-state/out-of-state) | $14,472/$21,879 |
| Fees | $1,318 |
| Room & board | $4,200 |

### ADMISSIONS

| | |
|---|---|
| **Admissions Selectivity Rating** | **85** |
| # of applications received | 177 |
| % applicants accepted | 51 |
| % acceptees attending | 52 |
| Average GMAT | 588 |
| Average GPA | 3.2 |
| TOEFL required of international students? | yes |
| Minimum TOEFL (paper/computer) | 550/230 |
| Application fee | $50 |
| Regular application deadline | 8/1 |
| Regular notification | 11/1 |
| Deferment available? | yes |
| Maximum length of deferment | 1 semester |
| Transfer students accepted? | yes |
| Transfer application policy Students must complete at least 36 credits in our program. We will transfer courses from AACSB-accredited schools with a grade of B or better. | |
| Non-fall admissions? | yes |
| Need-blind admissions? | yes |

### EMPLOYMENT PROFILE

| | |
|---|---|
| **Career Rating** | **79** |
| Average starting salary | $76,000 |

# RUTGERS, THE STATE UNIVERSITY OF NEW JERSEY—NEWARK
## RUTGERS BUSINESS SCHOOL

## Academics

A "renowned international business program," "marketing professors who are well-known in their respective fields," and perhaps most of all "a top-rated pharmaceutical MBA program" draw a strong applicant pool to the MBA program at Rutgers Business School. The school's location "in a metropolitan area with easy access to New York City and Philadelphia" is another one of Rutgers' prized assets. But for many New Jersey natives, the low in-state tuition is the greatest attraction; coupled with the quality of the program, the cost of attending RBS allows Garden Staters to realize a substantial return on investment here.

A full-time Rutgers MBA requires a minimum of 60 class-hour credits. The curriculum includes 30 core credits (delivered in one or more five week modules over the course of the first year), 2 required integrative courses, a second-year inter-functional team consulting project, and up to 24 class-hour credits in electives. The part-time curriculum varies slightly from the full-time curriculum but follows the same general approach. Concentrations are available in six primary disciplines, including finance, management and global business, information technology and e-commerce, marketing, pharmaceutical management and supply chain management.

Students love the fact that Rutgers offers "terrific professors who know real-life situations and bring that experience to the classroom," and "an administration that is constantly active and involved." "Proximity to New York City" and "connections within the pharmaceutical industry" translate into plenty of job opportunities for graduates. The school's website boasts that the region "has the highest concentration of corporate headquarters for U.S. metro areas of comparable size." Part-time students appreciate that "the workload is perfect—not too overwhelming, but still substantial. We learn a lot and I feel that we will be well prepared when we graduate."

## Career and Placement

The Office of Career Management provides counseling and placement services to Rutgers' full-time and part-time MBAs as well as to alumni of the program. Students report that the office provides "great career forums that network students with alumni" but also point out that "the office caters to the full-time students and not the part-time students. The office is not open past 5:00 P.M., and there are very few seminars or companies available at night." In 2005, students completing their first year in the program found summer internships in the following industries: pharmaceutical, 50 percent; finance and health care, 10 percent each; manufacturing, technology, and telecommunications, 6 percent each; consumer goods, government, nonprofit, and real estate, 3 percent each. Recent employers of Rutgers MBAs include Aeneas Capital, Amerisource, Becton, Dickinson and Company, Bristol-Myers Squibb Company, Deloitte Touche Tohmatsu, Envision Consulting Group, Hoffmann-La Roche Inc., Iberica USA, IBM Corporation, IDT Corporation, Johnson & Johnson, Kaufman Bros., Mercedes-Benz USA, Merck, NetPixel, Novartis, Organon Pharmaceuticals USA, Pfizer, and Siemens AG.

RITA GALEN, DIRECTOR OF ADMISSIONS
190 UNIVERSITY AVENUE, NEWARK, NJ 07102-1813 UNITED STATES
PHONE: 973-353-1234 • FAX: 973-353-1592 • E-MAIL: ADMIT@BUSINESS.RUTGERS.EDU
WEBSITE: WWW.BUSINESS.RUTGERS.EDU

## FINANCIAL FACTS

| | |
|---|---|
| Annual tuition (in-state/out-of-state) | $17,202/$28,624 |
| Fees | $1,308 |
| Books and supplies | $3,000 |

## ADMISSIONS

| | |
|---|---|
| **Admissions Selectivity Rating** | **88** |
| # of applications received | 259 |
| % applicants accepted | 53 |
| % acceptees attending | 51 |
| Average GMAT | 629 |
| Range of GMAT | 600–680 |
| Average GPA | 3.2 |
| TOEFL required of international students? | yes |
| Minimum TOEFL (paper/computer) | 600/250 |
| Application fee | $50 |
| International application fee | $50 |
| Regular application deadline | 5/1 |
| Regular notification | rolling |
| Deferment available? | yes |
| Maximum length of deferment | 1 year |
| Transfer students accepted? | yes |
| Transfer application policy | |

Students may transfer a maximum of 18 applicable credits earned in an MBA program at an AACSB-accredited school with a B or better.

| | |
|---|---|
| Non-fall admissions? | yes |
| Need-blind admissions? | yes |

## APPLICANTS ALSO LOOK AT

Baruch College—City University of New York, Columbia University, Fordham University, New York University, Seton Hall University

## *Student Life and Environment*

Rutgers Business School boasts an extremely diverse student body. Women constitute nearly half the population here—an unusually high proportion for an American MBA program. The international population is substantial: 40 countries are represented among the graduate business student population. Students tell us that their peers "come from greatly diverse backgrounds, both culturally and professionally" and that "although they are competitive, they are always willing to help one another." Approximately 25 percent of the student body attends full-time. The majority part-timers tell us that "social contact is limited, as people are tired after work and want to go home. We are very busy juggling work, school, and family (those of us who have one). Involvement outside of class is usually limited to one study group per class per week."

Full-time classes are offered at Rutgers' Newark and New Brunswick campuses; part-time classes are available at these two main campuses and also at satellite sites in Jersey City, Morristown, and Princeton. New Brunswick is among the nation's premier health care centers, providing an optimal setting for the school's health-related programs. Newark is a large city located about a half hour away from central Manhattan by train. New Jersey Transit makes travel to and from New York City relatively easy, convenient, and affordable. It certainly beats driving in the area.

## *Admissions*

The admissions committee serving the Rutgers MBA program gives primary consideration to evidence of academic promise. Undergraduate transcripts and transcripts for any graduate work are scrutinized both for the student's performance in class and for the quality and rigor of the program pursued. GMAT scores also figure into the committee's assessment of a candidate's readiness. Admissions officers also consider applicants' professional history, recommendations from professional peers and supervisors, evidence of leadership and civic involvement, and the personal essay. The school "seeks a diverse student body to bring to the classroom varying experiences and backgrounds;" appraisal of students' personal histories allows it to achieve this goal. Applicants must submit a completed application form, official transcripts for all postsecondary academic work, an official GMAT score report, two letters of professional reference, and a personal essay. International applicants must meet all of the above requirements and must submit an official score report for the TOEFL, professional translations of all transcripts not in English, and appropriate financial documentation.

## EMPLOYMENT PROFILE

| Career Rating | 68 | Grads employed by field: | % | avg. salary: |
|---|---|---|---|---|
| **Primary source of full-time job acceptances** | | Finance | 41 | $69,382 |
| | | Marketing | 15 | $67,000 |
| School-facilitated activities | 25 (34%) | Operations | 15 | $63,833 |
| Graduate-facilitated activities | 14 (61%) | Consulting | 17 | $71,057 |
| Unknown | 2 (5%) | General Management | 12 | $65,500 |
| Average starting salary | $68,034 | | | |

# SAGINAW VALLEY STATE UNIVERSITY
## COLLEGE OF BUSINESS AND MANAGEMENT

## Academics

Students cite convenience, affordability, and AACSB accreditation as their main reasons for choosing the MBA program at Saginaw Valley State. Most students attend the school part-time while holding down full-time jobs. That's why they appreciate the flexibility of the program, which allows them to complete their degree at their own pace. Full-timers here are typically international students or accounting undergraduates participating in the 3/2 BBA/MBA degree program.

The MBA program at SVSU begins with a nine-course business and management foundation sequence covering the basic principles of accounting, economics, statistics, finance, business law, organization, operations, MIS, and marketing. Students with related undergraduate course work are generally allowed to waive these courses and proceed directly to the business core, a nine-course curriculum of required courses. The business core courses focus on global business, business ethics, managerial accounting, macroeconomics, managerial finance, organizational behavior and leadership, business process design, integrated marketing management, and management of global corporations. Students must also complete three elective courses. The school offers an international business concentration.

Students at SVSU say, "Most of the professors have taught us through real-life experiences of their own, which is a definite plus." (Though some students remark that several professors could "use even more real life experience to teach from.") Another plus is that "professors make themselves available more than I would have imagined. Sometimes e-mail is most convenient, and they seem to be quick at getting back with me," one student notes. Students also praise the school's "relatively new equipment and facilities," the "small class size," and "the option to take a class as an independent study for some classes." Their complaints generally derive from the size of the program, which limits options. One student writes, "There are limited electives every term and it's hard to wait until one is offered that looks interesting, so sometimes you have to take one just because it is the only class available for you during the term."

## Career and Placement

Though Saginaw Valley State's Career Planning and Placement Office primarily serves undergraduates, MBA students also receive assistance and counseling in the areas of online databases, counseling, mock interviews, and coordination between students and alumni. For MBAs, professors are generally more helpful; many are, or recently were, active in the area business community and can provide contacts and recommendations to students. A recent SVSU internal survey showed that 93 percent of its MBA holders were employed full-time; 83 percent were employed in fields related to their major. Of the many students who attended SVSU while working full-time, 61 percent received a promotion from their employer after completing the degree.

JILL WETMORE, ASSISTANT DEAN, COLLEGE OF BUSINESS AND MANAGEMENT
7400 BAY ROAD, 320 CURTIS HALL, UNIVERSITY CENTER, MI 48710 UNITED STATES
PHONE: 989-964-4064 • FAX: 989-964-7497
E-MAIL: CBMDEAN@SVSU.EDU • WEBSITE: WWW.SVSU.EDU/CBM

## Student Life and Environment

SVSU's 782-acre campus is located in east central Michigan's tri-city area and serves the communities of Bay City, Midland, and Saginaw. The MBA program makes its home in Curtis Hall, a facility that also houses the University Conference and Events Center. As a result, students needn't leave the building to attend plays, conferences, and lectures.

Most SVSU MBA students have full-time commitments beyond school—work, family, community, often all three—and thus have time to visit campus only for classes, study, group meetings, and meetings with professors. Students are relieved to find that "the environment has worked out well" to meet their busy schedules, noting that "professors are very accommodating." One student writes, "Most of the group projects have team members who are willing to meet to get the project done and they are flexible in meeting times."

Although they don't spend as much time with each other as do their peers in predominantly full-time programs, SVSU MBAs manage to bond through classes and projects. One explains, "Classes encourage interaction and we get to know most of our fellow students because the average class size is relatively small." They tell us that their classmates "tend to be here because of a desire to be more competitive in the professional world, but do not tend to be overly competitive with each other." SVSU "seems to attract a large percentage of its students from the professional world, and a fair number of students internationally. The number of international students is surprising because SVSU is a smaller school in a smaller community."

## Admissions

The admissions department applies a formula to establish a floor for all applicants. To be considered for admission, students must score above 1,050 under the formula [(undergraduate GPA for final two years of four-year undergraduate program 5 200) + GMAT score], and must have a GMAT score of at least 450. Applicants must also submit a current resume, a one-page personal essay (statement of goals), two letters of reference, and official copies of all undergraduate and graduate transcripts. International students also need to demonstrate sufficient finances to support themselves while studying in the United States; additional documents are also required of them. Applicants whose first language is not English must submit official TOEFL scores. Undergraduates in the SVSU Accounting Program may opt for a 3/2 option at the end of their junior year—successful completion of which results in a BBA and MBA at the end of five years' study.

### FINANCIAL FACTS

| | |
|---|---|
| Annual tuition (in-state/out-of-state) | $5,122/$9,882 |
| Fees | $243 |
| Books and supplies | $800 |
| Room & board | $6,475 |
| % of students receiving aid | 39 |
| % of first-year students receiving aid | 39 |
| % of students receiving loans | 20 |
| % of students receiving grants | 11 |
| Average award package | $6,397 |
| Average grant | $1,802 |
| Average student loan debt | $4,065 |

### ADMISSIONS

| | |
|---|---|
| **Admissions Selectivity Rating** | **66** |
| # of applications received | 36 |
| % applicants accepted | 94 |
| % acceptees attending | 56 |
| Average GMAT | 538 |
| Range of GMAT | 450–610 |
| Average GPA | 3.26 |
| TOEFL required of international students? | yes |
| Minimum TOEFL (paper/computer) | 525/197 |
| Application fee | $25 |
| International application fee | $25 |
| Regular application deadline | rolling |
| Regular notification | rolling |
| Deferment available? | yes |
| Maximum length of deferment | 7 semesters |
| Transfer students accepted? | yes |
| Transfer application policy May transfer 6 credits | |
| Non-fall admissions? | yes |
| Need-blind admissions? | yes |

### APPLICANTS ALSO LOOK AT

Central Michigan University,
Michigan State University,
Northwood University, University of
Michigan—Flint

| EMPLOYMENT PROFILE | |
|---|---|
| **Career Rating** | **73** |
| Average starting salary | $73,600 |

# SAINT JOSEPH'S UNIVERSITY
## ERIVAN K. HAUB SCHOOL OF BUSINESS

**GENERAL INFORMATION**

| | |
|---|---|
| Type of school | private |
| Affiliation | Jesuit |
| Environment | metropolis |
| Academic calendar | semesters |

**SURVEY SAYS...**
*Solid preparation in:*
Teamwork
Communication/interpersonal skills
Presentation skills

**STUDENTS**

| | |
|---|---|
| Enrollment of parent institution | 7,700 |
| Enrollment of business school | 561 |
| % male/female | 56/44 |
| % part-time | 90 |
| % minorities | 10 |
| % international | 51 |
| Average age at entry | 29 |
| Average years work experience at entry | 4.5 |

**ACADEMICS**

| | |
|---|---|
| **Academic Experience Rating** | **74** |
| Student/faculty ratio | 20:1 |
| Profs interesting rating | 81 |
| Profs accessible rating | 78 |
| % female faculty | 20 |
| % minority faculty | 10 |

**JOINT DEGREES**
DO/MBA Program with Philadelphia College of Osteopathic Medicine (2 years for MBA component)

## Academics

The Erivan K. Haub School of Business at Saint Joseph's University has about 60 full-time students, but the vast majority of MBAs here attend part-time, and the program is designed for their convenience. One part-timer explains, "The academic experience appeals to those who work full-time, offering night classes for the MBA program, which opens the doors to many other people in professional careers." Saint Joseph's recognizes that not all its potential students can finish work and make it into Philadelphia by class time; therefore, they offer classes at Ursinus College in Collegeville (about 30 miles northwest of downtown Philly) as well as on its main campus.

The Haub MBA program is distinguished in part by "a constant focus on ethics. Given the number of scandals in the news today, ethics has become increasingly important. This continues to be a core competency for Saint Joseph's, as it has been since 1978." That's not to suggest that the Haub curriculum is written in stone; on the contrary, the administration here is not afraid to adapt the program to meet the ever-changing needs of the business world. Students admire how "the administration is constantly looking for ways to improve the MBA program, whether it is by offering courses relevant to hot topics in industry or hosting lectures from industry leaders." They also appreciate the "great use of technology and state-of-the-art equipment in the classrooms."

The Haub faculty "offers a nice combination of full-time professors, who bring academic knowledge to the classroom, and adjunct professors, who bring real-world experience, which actually enhances the learning experience in a business school. The caliber of students here is also high," MBAs report. One student writes, "There are some awesome professors here, and the intellectual abilities of my classmates make classes even more challenging and intriguing." Students also tell us that "if one gets to know faculty members, they can be a great asset when it comes to finding a job. Almost all of the best employment opportunities presented to me came from faculty members and people they knew."

Haub offers a wide selection of areas of concentration, but students wish the school would "give more choices of elective courses within each concentration." The curriculum allows students only six credits worth of electives—that's only two courses—which helps explain the relative lack of selection.

## Career and Placement

The Career Services Office at Saint Joseph's University "is currently working to help MBA students find new jobs through a resume network and online support," according to the school's website. The university encourages MBAs to take advantage of MBAFutureStep, a free online service introduced by the Graduate Management Admissions Council (the same folks who bring you the GMAT). Some of the students feel that the CSO focuses too little on graduate students. One student explains, "Almost everything encountered in the Career Services Office is tailored toward undergraduate placement." Another student adds, "They need to improve the Career Services. The same types of companies recruit here all the time and most are for just marketers and accountants. If you are in finance and do not want to do financial services, you are basically out on your own. Also, forget about [companies] out of the Philly area."

In 2003 the average graduating Haub MBA earned a salary of $71,600 with an average signing bonus of $9,000. Companies and organizations that recruit graduate students on Saint Joseph's campus include Bryn Mawr Trust, Citigroup, SEI Investments, Wachovia Securities, and Wilmington Trust.

SUSAN KASSAB, DIRECTOR
5600 CITY AVENUE, PHILADELPHIA, PA 19131 UNITED STATES
PHONE: 610-660-1101 • FAX: 610-660-1224
E-MAIL: GRADSTAFF@SJU.EDU • WEBSITE: WWW.SJU.EDU

## Student Life and Environment

Haub's full-time student body is small but active. Even so, they concede that their extracurricular life "is not as rich as it could be"; since most students attend class after work, out-of-class networking opportunities get short shrift. One student says, "If Saint Joe's can improve and develop the social aspect of the program, there is no reason why our school cannot be competitive with top-tier schools given its proven and strong academic curriculum."

Saint Joseph's University is home to "a great basketball team" and "really makes [students] feel at home on the campus," as well as being "a good place to hang out, with good weekend entertainment." The campus is located 20 minutes outside the downtown area in the pleasant, quiet northwest corner of the city. Philadelphia's extensive SEPTA system of buses and trains connects the campus to the heart of America's fifth-largest city. The campus is only a half-mile walk from the closest commuter train station.

## Admissions

Haub admits MBA candidates for all three academic semesters (Fall, Spring, and Summer). A completed application to the program includes copies of official transcripts for all undergraduate and graduate academic work, an official GMAT score report (results no more than seven years old), two letters of recommendation, a personal statement, and a resume reflecting professional experiences. The TOEFL is required of international students, as is a WES (World Education Services) evaluation of transcripts and proof of financial support. The Haub curriculum includes seven foundation courses. Completion of equivalent undergraduate courses (equivalency determined by the admissions committee) can also earn students a waiver on up to 18 credits or foundations.

### FINANCIAL FACTS

| | |
|---|---|
| Annual tuition | $14,400 |
| Books and supplies | $800 |
| Average award package | $14,900 |
| Average student loan debt | $14,900 |

### ADMISSIONS

| | |
|---|---|
| **Admissions Selectivity Rating** | **72** |
| # of applications received | 311 |
| % applicants accepted | 74 |
| % acceptees attending | 69 |
| Average GMAT | 519 |
| Average GPA | 3.2 |
| TOEFL required of international students? | yes |
| Minimum TOEFL (paper/computer) | 550/213 |
| Application fee | $35 |
| International application fee | $35 |
| Regular application deadline | rolling |
| Regular notification | rolling |
| Deferment available? | yes |
| Maximum length of deferment | 1 year |
| Transfer students accepted? | yes |
| Transfer application policy They must provide a completed application, including original test scores. | |
| Non-fall admissions? | yes |
| Need-blind admissions? | yes |

### APPLICANTS ALSO LOOK AT

Drexel University, La Salle University, Penn State University—Great Valley Campus, Temple University, Villanova University

# SAINT LOUIS UNIVERSITY
## JOHN COOK SCHOOL OF BUSINESS

## Academics

The John Cook School of Business at Saint Louis University offers both a full-time and a part-time Professional MBA (PMBA) program. A substantial majority of the students here attend the part-time program, usually while working full-time jobs in the St. Louis area.

The "enhanced, flexible" curriculum of the PMBA program, which was first introduced in the fall of 2004, is designed to allow working professionals to take as many or as few courses as they want, when they want. The sequence of 11 to 15 courses (four foundation courses may be waived, depending on the student's undergraduate and professional qualifications) can be completed in as little as two years. All classes are offered in the evenings, typically once a week from 6 P.M. to 9 P.M. Besides the foundation courses, the PMBA curriculum includes five breadth courses; a capstone course; three mini-courses (together constituting one full course) covering business law, business ethics, and career management; and four electives.

The SLU full-time MBA is also a relatively recent arrival, with its first classes convening in 1999. The two-year program covers the same fundamental business functions covered in the PMBA program, but also "emphasizes oral and written communications, teamwork skills, and other leadership competencies, linked with a practical, working knowledge of business ethics and a global perspective," according to the school's website. The 45-credit curriculum, offered primarily during the day, includes five electives, allowing students to specialize in accounting, economics, entrepreneurship, finance, international business, management, marketing, MIS, or operations and supply chain management.

"Because of the relatively small class size" in both MBA programs, "professors are able to interact with students easily and frequently" at SLU. One student explains, "The school is like a tight-knit community where faculty, staff, and administration make students the first priority. This is obvious in every aspect of campus interaction." Students praise offerings in finance and international business, telling us that the latter benefits from "excellent study-abroad opportunities." A few here complain that "some professors lack the necessary real-world experience to teach graduate students" and feel that "the school could upgrade the technology in the classroom. Lectures should be taped and made available online."

## Career and Placement

The Career Resources Center at the John Cook School of Business provides Career Services and counseling for all MBAs. The center offers self-assessments, personal advising, resume assistance, mock interviews, and access to multiple online and hard-copy databases and reference sources. Students tell us that the school's regional reputation and alumni network are its most effective career-enhancing assets. One writes, "I chose the school for its regional name recognition and the quality associated with the education given here. In the St. Louis area, this school opens many doors in the business field. The school is also well-networked in the community." Another adds, "The variety and reputations of the companies at which SLU alums and faculty currently work or have worked at in the past are impressive. I know that when I am close to graduating, I will have no trouble finding a great job."

## Student Life and Environment

SLU's "beautiful campus" is a park-like setting peppered with sculptures, fountains, archways, and verdant open spaces. Because the Jesuit tradition seeks to educate the whole person, SLU brings numerous cultural events to campus. Through the campus

JANELL KIEL NELSON, ASSOCIATE DIRECTOR
3674 LINDELL BOULEVARD, SUITE 132, ST. LOUIS, MO 63108 UNITED STATES
PHONE: 314-977-6221 • FAX: 314-977-1416
E-MAIL: MBA@SLU.EDU • WEBSITE: WWW.MBA.SLU.EDU

ministry, opportunities for service and spiritual growth are readily available. SLU competes in 16 NCAA Division I sports; the men's basketball and soccer teams both draw hefty crowds. The school's midtown location provides students easy access to the Fox Theatre, the Sheldon Concert Hall, the Grandel Square Theatre, and the Powell Symphony Hall.

"On-campus activities are readily available and student-driven," MBAs report, although many part-timers have difficulty making time to take advantage of them. One first semester, part-timer writes, "I plan to join various business clubs eventually, such as the Marketing Club and/or MIS Club, after I have chosen a concentration in the program." The student body here includes "new college graduates and seasoned professionals. Some are single while others have kids and are married. Some have business backgrounds while others have engineering and other backgrounds. It is a fairly diverse cross-section of people." Students are "competitive, friendly, smart, anxious to learn," yet "always willing to help each other out."

## Admissions

Saint Louis University accepts both online and paper-and-pencil applications; an Adobe Acrobat file of the application can be downloaded at the school's website. All applications must include a completed application form, personal essays, two letters of recommendation (at least one professional), official transcripts for all postsecondary academic work, and an official GMAT score report. International applicants must provide all of the above plus certification of financial support and, for non-native English speakers, an official TOEFL score report. According to the school, "Work experience plays a large role [in the admissions decision]. For applicants with limited or no work experience, the GMAT and GPA become very important. Interviews are recommended for all applicants, but are required for applicants with no work experience."

### FINANCIAL FACTS

| | |
|---|---|
| Annual tuition | $46,800 |
| Fees | $190 |
| Books and supplies | $1,250 |
| Room & board (off-campus) | $11,000 |
| % of students receiving aid | 75 |
| % of first-year students receiving aid | 85 |
| % of students receiving grants | 84 |
| Average grant | $9,000 |

### ADMISSIONS

| | |
|---|---|
| Admissions Selectivity Rating | 75 |
| # of applications received | 52 |
| % applicants accepted | 71 |
| % acceptees attending | 65 |
| Average GMAT | 549 |
| Range of GMAT | 492–607 |
| Average GPA | 3.12 |
| TOEFL required of international students? | yes |
| Minimum TOEFL (paper/computer) | 600/250 |
| Application fee | $90 |
| International application fee | $90 |
| Deferment available? | yes |
| Maximum length of deferment | 1 year |
| Transfer students accepted? | yes |
| Transfer application policy Six credit hours only from another AACSB-accredited school. | |
| Non-fall admissions? | yes |
| Need-blind admissions? | yes |

### APPLICANTS ALSO LOOK AT
Washington University

### EMPLOYMENT PROFILE

| Career Rating | 73 | Grads employed by field: | % | avg. salary: |
|---|---|---|---|---|
| Primary source of full-time job acceptances | | Finance | 23 | $42,500 |
| | | Marketing | 31 | $57,100 |
| Unknown | 21 (100%) | Consulting | 23 | $63,000 |
| | | Global Management | 8 | $70,000 |
| Average starting salary | $57,867 | Nonprofit | 15 | $48,000 |
| Percent employed | 65 | | | |

# SAN DIEGO STATE UNIVERSITY
## GRADUATE SCHOOL OF BUSINESS

## GENERAL INFORMATION
| | |
|---|---|
| Type of school | public |
| Environment | city |
| Academic calendar | semester |

### SURVEY SAYS...
Students love San Diego, CA
Cutting-edge classes
Happy students

### STUDENTS
| | |
|---|---|
| Enrollment of parent institution | 32,693 |
| Enrollment of business school | 640 |
| % male/female | 57/43 |
| % out-of-state | 12 |
| % part-time | 50 |
| % minorities | 12 |
| % international | 20 |
| Average age at entry | 28 |
| Average years work experience at entry | 5 |

### ACADEMICS
| | |
|---|---|
| **Academic Experience Rating** | **82** |
| Student/faculty ratio | 35:1 |
| Profs interesting rating | 76 |
| Profs accessible rating | 79 |
| % female faculty | 14 |
| % minority faculty | 3 |

### JOINT DEGREES
Master of Business Administration/Master of Arts in Latin American Studies (MBA/MA), 3-4 years; MBA/JD, 4 years to complete

## Academics

A solid return on investment—especially for California natives—and a "great reputation in international business and entrepreneurship" are among the major attractions at San Diego State University's Graduate School of Business. Entrepreneurship is a particular strength, with the prestigious Entrepreneurial Management Center helping SDSU earn a "high ranking among all entrepreneurship programs." A sports business MBA program "that partners with Major League Baseball, National Football League, and National Basketball Association teams" is another big draw.

Potential SDSU business grads have a number of choices to consider. The conventional MBA program here presupposes that students did not study business as undergraduates. Thus, it includes 19 foundation credits that cannot be waived (because the program is cohort-based). Students who studied business as undergraduates, however, are more suitable candidates for the MSBA program. Students "really like the way it is set up. It allows you to finish in one year and specialize in an area." The Sports Business Management MBA has its own separate program. SDSU also offers an MS in accounting ("one of the few accredited accounting programs in the state," one student writes) and an Executive MBA program.

Students praise SDSU as an "efficient school" where "the faculty is very attuned with latest trends in the business world, and professors can offer very practical experience in the classroom based on their consulting work." Faculty instruction is supplemented by "guest lecturers who are well-respected and powerful." Throughout the curriculum, students here "do a lot of group work, which facilitates good student relationships and teamwork." Students appreciate that "classes are taught in an open and participatory environment" that fortunately is "not overly competitive. Quality of life is important to the people attending and working in the community, and they aim to balance academic achievement with living well." The school's city of San Diego location also means that a steady supply of local business leaders are always on hand, whether as mentors or potential employers.

## Career and Placement

Career and placement services for SDSU MBAs are handled through the Career Services Office of the university; there is no dedicated Career Services Office for the MBA program. Supplemental services are provided through the MBA Association and the Entrepreneurial Management Center. Students see Career Services here as a weak area, with comments that "on-campus recruiting needs to be improved." As far as the effectiveness of the alumni network goes, students are split. Some see it as a strength, while others feel the school should work harder to "foster better communication between the students and alumni for employment purposes."

S. Scott or S. Temores-Valdez, Associate Director of the MBA and MS Programs
5500 Campanile Drive, San Diego, CA 92182-8228 United States
Phone: 619-594-8073 • Fax: 619-594-1863 • E-mail: sdsumba@mail.sdsu.edu
Website: www.sdsu.edu/business

## Student Life and Environment

SDSU "provides an interesting, active environment, allowing students to be as involved or as isolated as they choose." Business students at this school are presented with "an incredible array of options to create the ultimate experience." Most important to business students, "There are many clubs to join that are great networking, social and career opportunities." In addition to these "great clubs" are "large events and a variety of cultural activities to participate in" while enjoying a "nice campus. . .that seems always to be striving for continual improvement."

The city of San Diego brings a lot to the table as well. It's "an outstanding place to live" with plenty of opportunity for those who wish to stick around after they graduate. Biotechnology, software development, and wireless communications industries all thrive here. The city is widely regarded as a leading laboratory for entrepreneurial development, and the U.S. military has a huge presence.

SDSU attracts "a great mix of enthusiastic people who are excited about furthering their education." This "intelligent, multi-cultural, driven, diverse" population includes "some who have many years of work experience and others who have only recently finished their undergraduate degrees." True to the Californian character, "Many here don't appear to be very competitive, which makes the atmosphere pretty relaxed and easy going. Still, the students are often the quietly successful type, so you never know what they are capable of until you ask them."

## Admissions

Nearly 700 potential MBAs apply to SDSU's "highly competitive" program every year. The Admissions Committee considers a number of factors, including GMAT score (minimum score of 540 is required; the average score of an admitted student is 609); GPA for the final sixty course hours of undergraduate academic work (minimum 2.85 for American students, 3.0 for international students (for their entire four year degree); average GPA for admitted students was 3.3); letters of recommendation, resume (work experience is preferred but not required); and personal statement. None of the final three is required, but each "can enhance an application," according to the school's website. International students whose first language is not English must also submit official TOEFL scores; a minimum paper-and-pencil test score of 550 or an Internet-based test score of 79 is required. Applications are accepted for both the Fall and Spring terms. They are processed on a rolling basis, so it's best to apply as early as possible.

### FINANCIAL FACTS

| | |
|---|---|
| Annual tuition (in-state/out-of-state) | $3,704/$11,840 |
| Books and supplies | $1,260 |
| Room & board | $9,391 |

### ADMISSIONS

| | |
|---|---|
| **Admissions Selectivity Rating** | **88** |
| # of applications received | 649 |
| % applicants accepted | 52 |
| % acceptees attending | 61 |
| Average GMAT | 609 |
| Range of GMAT | 560–620 |
| Average GPA | 3.3 |
| TOEFL required of international students? | yes |
| Minimum TOEFL (paper/computer) | 550/213 |
| Application fee | $55 |
| International application fee | $55 |
| Regular application deadline | 4/15 |
| Regular notification | 5/15 |
| Transfer students accepted? | yes |
| Transfer application policy Normal admissions process; credits will transfer at the school's discretion. | |
| Non-fall admissions? | yes |
| Need-blind admissions? | yes |

### APPLICANTS ALSO LOOK AT

University of California—San Diego, University of San Diego

# SAN FRANCISCO STATE UNIVERSITY
## COLLEGE OF BUSINESS

### GENERAL INFORMATION
Type of school                public
Environment               metropolis

### SURVEY SAYS...
Students love San Francisco, CA
Friendly students
Happy students
*Solid preparation in:*
Computer skills

### STUDENTS
Enrollment of parent
  institution                29,000
Enrollment of business school 594
% male/female                49/51
% out-of-state                   1
% part-time                     65
% minorities                    25
% international                 35
Average age at entry            29
Average years work experience
  at entry                       3

### ACADEMICS
**Academic Experience Rating   73**
Student/faculty ratio         24:1
Profs interesting rating        69
Profs accessible rating         63
% female faculty                36
% minority faculty              40

### PROMINENT ALUMNI
Mohan Gyani, CEP & President, AT
& T Wireless Group; Gordon Hoff,
VP of International Deposit Services
Bank of America; Jo Malins, VP of
International Conformance, Citibank

## Academics

The College of Business at San Francisco State University offers a range of MBA options to satisfy the needs of every student. A conventional MBA, the most popular of the school's choices, is offered on both a full-time and part-time basis and includes a thorough complement of foundation courses for those with little undergraduate or practical business experience (such courses may be waived for students with a deeper academic background in business). Two part-time MBA programs are available off campus: the Executive MBA, a fixed-curriculum cohort program that ensures a degree in 23 months (students attend class for seven hours a week), and the Alliance MBA, a flexible, intensive program delivered via audio-video teleconferencing technology (and occasional on-site visits by professors) to students' workplaces. SFSU also offers a master's in business, the MSBA, for students seeking a personalized curriculum that allows for in-depth specialization in one or more areas, such as accounting, finance and information systems.

Students at SFSU appreciate "the flexibility of the program" and praise its "strong accounting department, [the] great faculty in the secision sciences department, [and the] access to great professors, contacts, and networking in the field of marketing." San Francisco itself is seen as a tremendous asset. One student explains, "Many top-quality professors want to live in the San Francisco Bay area, but there are only so many jobs at Stanford and Berkeley, so SFSU benefits from the overflow of top-quality professors. Overall, I feel that I'm getting Stanford-level instruction at community college-level prices. The professors and the program structure are excellent. It's like getting a Porsche at Hyundai prices." Another student agrees, "This could be the best value MBA program in the country, and it's in a great city with a great professional environment, including Silicon Valley and the San Francisco financial district nearby."

Like many state-run schools, SFSU is sometimes a little deficient in administrative functions. Students tell us that the program "needs to provide more advising time, especially for new students, at the beginning of the semester. We also need clearer guidelines in terms of classes that the students need to take." The administration itself, reports one student, "has been in almost constant turnover since I began the program. The staff is very knowledgeable, yet they can provide different answers to the same questions, which causes confusion among the students."

## Career and Placement

SFSU maintains a Business Relationship Center dedicated exclusively to its College of Business. This office provides career counseling services, organizes job fairs, conducts career skills seminars, and assists students in their search for internships. Online services include job databases and an alumni networking site. Students are unimpressed, "career placement is non-existent here. Students are on their own when it comes to the job/internship search. Although students ask for job-placement assistance, the school provides no valuable help at all," writes one student. Another MBA observes, "In exchange for the low tuition, one cedes the network that would have come from attending a UC or private school."

## Student Life and Environment

The MBA program at SFSU is in the process of relocating from the school's main campus to a new downtown campus. Many part-timers applaud the move, telling us that "the development of the downtown campus will make the program extremely convenient for those of us who work in the financial district." A few opponents ask, "What about the

Victor V. Cordell, PhD, Director
1600 Holloway Avenue, San Francisco, CA 94132 United States
Phone: 415-338-1279 • Fax: 415-405-0495
E-mail: mba@sfsu.edu • Website: http://cob.sfsu.edu/mba

people who don't work downtown? There is no parking and I don't want to take public transportation home after a night class. The current location is excellent. People working downtown can easily hop on the M streetcar to arrive at the front door of the school in 20 minutes." Regardless of how they feel about the move, nearly everyone here agrees that "the school's greatest strength is that it's located in San Francisco, where there are lots of opportunities around."

Because SFSU "is a commuter school," MBAs "come on campus only to go to their classes or meet with other students to work on group projects." Students feel that "more social functions to connect fellow MBA students with each other would be a plus." One student writes, "There is not a lot of time for social interaction. The group work assignments help compensate for this deficiency and is something I have, eventually, learned to appreciate, despite the added onus of making time." Students also love such high-tech campus amenities as "wi-fi throughout the building and great online research possibilities through the library."

SFSU draws a large international population, "especially from Asia and Europe, although I also know people from Georgia (former USSR), Turkey, Egypt, Venezuela, Chile, [and] Brazil," observes one student. Another notes, "Having received my undergraduate degree from a small private college that touted its 'diversity,' I was unsure what to expect from a larger state school. But the diversity of the students in my classes is amazing. This is what my private undergrad college was trying to accomplish. We have all types, colors, background—married, unmarried, old, young, you name it. It makes for a very interesting and stimulating learning environment." Many students here "have worked for high-tech companies in Silicon Valley," although the general impression is that most international students arrive with little work experience.

## Admissions

The admissions office at SFSU requires all of the following materials of applicants: a completed application (pencil-and-paper or computer-based); two sealed copies of official transcripts from all post-secondary programs attended; a sealed official GMAT score report; and a letter of intent (i.e., personal statement of purpose). Letters of recommendation are optional. International students whose first language is not English must submit sealed official TOEFL score reports. All international students must submit a financial statement demonstrating that the student has at least $20,000 to cover the cost of the program, and a signed form indicating agreement to purchase medical health insurance. The minimum GMAT score for all applicants is 500; a minimum rank of 25th percentile on the verbal, math, and writing sections is also required.

### FINANCIAL FACTS

| | |
|---|---|
| Annual tuition (in-state/out-of-state) | $3,366/$11,502 |
| Books and supplies | $2,000 |
| Room & board | $10,000 |

### ADMISSIONS

| | |
|---|---|
| Admissions Selectivity Rating | 85 |
| # of applications received | 521 |
| % applicants accepted | 45 |
| % acceptees attending | 51 |
| Average GMAT | 559 |
| Range of GMAT | 500–600 |
| Average GPA | 3.45 |
| TOEFL required of international students? | yes |
| Minimum TOEFL (paper/computer) | 570/230 |
| Application fee | $55 |
| International application fee | $55 |
| Regular application deadline | 5/1 |
| Regular notification | 5/15 |
| Transfer students accepted? | yes |
| Transfer application policy Applicants need to apply to the program and waive out our foundation requirements. | |
| Non-fall admissions? | yes |

### APPLICANTS ALSO LOOK AT

California State University—East Bay, San Jose State University

### EMPLOYMENT PROFILE

| | |
|---|---|
| Career Rating | 79 |
| Average starting salary | $75,000 |
| Percent employed | 90 |

# SAN JOSE STATE UNIVERSITY
## LUCAS GRADUATE SCHOOL OF BUSINESS

## GENERAL INFORMATION
| | |
|---|---|
| Type of school | public |
| Environment | metropolis |
| Academic calendar | semester |

### SURVEY SAYS...
Friendly students
Happy students
*Solid preparation in:*
Teamwork
Communication/interpersonal skills

### STUDENTS
| | |
|---|---|
| Enrollment of parent institution | 28,400 |
| Enrollment of business school | 554 |
| % male/female | 56/44 |
| % out-of-state | 29 |
| % part-time | 70 |
| % minorities | 56 |
| % international | 25 |
| Average age at entry | 31 |
| Average years work experience at entry | 8 |

### ACADEMICS
| | |
|---|---|
| **Academic Experience Rating** | **78** |
| Student/faculty ratio | 28:1 |
| Profs interesting rating | 66 |
| Profs accessible rating | 61 |
| % female faculty | 29 |
| % minority faculty | 26 |

### JOINT DEGREES
MBA/MSE, 32 months

## Academics

San Jose State University serves the MBA needs of the Silicon Valley with a variety of convenient options. SJSU's intensive MBA-One program gets students in and out of the program in one year. For those working full-time, the school offers several part-time options, including an off-campus program located conveniently in the Rose Orchard Technology Center (near the Cisco campus). The Lucas Graduate School of Business also offers an MS in transportation management, an MS in taxation, an MS in accountancy, and a double-degree MBA/MS Engineering.

SJSU's MBA-One is "for nonworking individuals who prefer an intensive, cohort style of learning." The 16-course curriculum is entirely lockstep (no electives), taught in six terms of eight weeks. The final term of the curriculum includes a comprehensive project. Students tell us that the MBA-One is "very well coordinated" but caution that it is "intense and rigorous. Basically, you can kiss your social life good-bye for one year. On the plus side, you cover a complete two-year curriculum in a single year." Students love the cohort system, as it allows them to share work and to get to know one another well.

Two part-time options are available at SJSU. The on-campus MBA offers students a wider variety of courses than the off-campus option but is, of course, less convenient to the many students who work on the north end of the city. The on-campus calendar consists of two 16-week semesters and a 6-week summer session. Off-campus classes run year-round in three 16-week trimesters, broken down into two eight-week sessions offered each term. Students in the off-campus program generally complete their MBAs in less time than those on campus. Students in both part-time programs praise their convenience and affordability. They also speak highly of their professors, who "know how to relate course material to real-life situations and how to help us understand complicated material." Students warn, however, that their classmates' busy work and home schedules sometimes negatively impact classroom instruction.

Although both part-time programs include elective courses, areas of concentration are not part of the MBA program. Students tell us that elective choices include "great entrepreneurship classes" but that "marketing and general-management instruction should be improved."

## Career and Placement

The school tells us that its career center "offers a range of resources to help students and recent graduates meet with success in the search for employment. Services include career advising and assistance with resume preparation and interview skills. The center maintains a resource library, a career lab with workstations and career-guidance software, and a job bank. On-campus recruiting and job fairs are organized by the center, putting students and recent graduates in touch with potential employers," but many full-time students are unimpressed. With a population of nearly one million, San Jose is one of California's major cities. Even after the dot-com bust, it has remained a major hub of U.S. tech industry. Major employers include Adobe Systems, BEA Systems, Cisco, eBay, Hewlett-Packard, IBM, Lockheed Martin, and MicroSystems.

ADMISSIONS COORDINATOR
ONE WASHINGTON SQUARE, SAN JOSE, CA 95192-0162 UNITED STATES
PHONE: 408-924-3420 • FAX: 408-924-3426
E-MAIL: MBA@COB.SJSU.EDU • WEBSITE: WWW.COB.SJSU.EDU/GRADUATE

## Student Life and Environment

SJSU attracts "awesome and open students" with "good industry experience." The student population is "very diverse in terms of international students. We lack African American and Hispanic students, though." Part-timers are generally "too busy to be sociable" and "not very network-oriented outside of class." Students in the MBA-One program "spend a lot of time together and are a very tight-knit group, even though [they] are mainly a commuter community." They count on one other's help to complete the curriculum, since "the MBA-One program is quite demanding and [they] are quite involved in schoolwork. On weekends, [they] still need to study."

The main SJSU campus is located in downtown San Jose. Business classes meet in the recently renovated Boccardo Business Education Center. All classrooms are wired for Internet access, and many are equipped for multimedia instruction. Off-campus classes are held at the Rose Orchard Technology Center "in the heart of the Silicon Valley high tech corridor, making it convenient to many working adults."

## Admissions

Priority is given to applicants with: a four-year undergraduate degree with a GPA of at least 3.0 for the final 60 semester hours of course work; a GMAT score of at least 500, with a minimum; and, for any student whose main language is not English, a TOEFL score of at least 550 (paper-based) or 213 (computer-based). A personal statement of purpose is also required with the application.

### FINANCIAL FACTS
Annual tuition (in-state/out-of-state) $5,140/$13,620
Books and supplies $1,200

### ADMISSIONS
Admissions Selectivity Rating 89
# of applications received 473
% applicants accepted 38
% acceptees attending 56
Average GMAT 580
Range of GMAT 540–610
Average GPA 3.37
TOEFL required of international students? yes
Minimum TOEFL (paper/computer) 550/213
Application fee $55
International application fee $55
Regular application deadline 5/1
Regular notification 7/1
Transfer students accepted? yes
Transfer application policy
Applicant must meet admission requirements. Up to 20 percent of units can be transferred from AACSB-accredited institution.
Non-fall admissions? yes

### APPLICANTS ALSO LOOK AT
California State University—East Bay, San Francisco State University, Santa Clara University, University of California—Berkeley

### EMPLOYMENT PROFILE
Career Rating 63
Average starting salary $60,188

# SANTA CLARA UNIVERSITY
## LEAVEY SCHOOL OF BUSINESS

## GENERAL INFORMATION
Type of school                 private
Affiliation      Roman Catholic/Jesuit
Environment                       city
Academic calendar            quarters

## SURVEY SAYS...
Students love Santa Clara, CA
Friendly students
Good peer network
Happy students
*Solid preparation in:*
General management
Teamwork

## STUDENTS
Enrollment of parent
  institution                   8,213
Enrollment of
  business school               1,064
% male/female                   66/34
% part-time                        82
% minorities                       15
% international                    22
Average age at entry               29
Average years work experience
  at entry                          7

## ACADEMICS
**Academic Experience Rating    76**
Student/faculty ratio            34:1
Profs interesting rating           84
Profs accessible rating            78
% female faculty                   16
% minority faculty                 13

## JOINT DEGREES
JD/MBA, 4 years

## Academics

The Leavey School of Business at Santa Clara University combines "Jesuit values, primarily in the quality of education and the emphasis on high integrity," with a Silicon Valley location that draws "the cream of the crop to the faculty, such as the former 3Com CEO." The result is a unique MBA program that "caters to part-time students" but also has plenty to offer full-timers.

Customer service is the name of the game at Leavey, where "the dean runs the school as if it was a company in itself. He provides quarterly reports of the progress of school and reviews student evaluations as a measure of the progress." Administrators "do everything they can to keep up with the changing trends in business and business schools. For example, this year, they introduced international exposure for the student. Every summer, one or two student groups visit another country to meet with business leaders and financial institutions to understand how business is done in that country. This year, the group went to China. Next year, one group will go to China and another, to Germany." Professors take a similar student-first approach; they are "eager to help students in the classroom and to introduce them to colleagues for future employment opportunities. They are always available for personal/professional consultation."

Leavey's curriculum employs "a great case-study approach" that "is structured to maximize teamwork abilities." Students find this pedagogical approach immediately applicable to their professional lives. MBAs also "love the 'experimental' classes that students can choose as electives, such as Spirituality and Leadership, which really gets you to focus on your inner self and become a better, less stressed person." Students tell us the school excels in accounting, general management, and marketing. Asked where the school should improve, one student comments, "For some reason, the school is not so well recognized as other schools in the area, namely Stanford and Berkeley. But I have been quite impressed with SCU so far. The campus is good and the academic standards are excellent. I think the school will stand to gain if marketed better."

## Career and Placement

Students appreciate the "great Bay Area network" connected to SCU; MBAs here benefit from "a terrific level of interaction with leaders and innovators in Silicon Valley." The Graduate Business Career Services Office capitalizes on these connections to help students procure internships ("The quarter system allows for some interesting internship opportunities in the area because local employers know some students can be available part-time or full-time for a quarter or two," explains one student) and post-graduation jobs. Even so, students feel the service isn't all it could be. As one observes, "Since most students are working, there are limited resources devoted to the internship/career placement program. Also, SCU also does not do enough promotion of the program out in the business community. Its reputation is only good regionally, despite its high ranking as a part-time business program."

The top ten employers of graduates of the class of 2004 were Applied Materials, Inc.; Cisco Systems, Inc.; eBay; Hewlett-Packard; KLA-Tencor Corporation; Silicon Valley Bank; Sun Microsystems; VERITAS Software; Wells Fargo Bank; and Xilinx.

Julie Krugman, Director, Graduate Business Admissions
223 Kenna Hall, 500 El Camino Real, Santa Clara, CA 95053-0001 United States
Phone: 408-554-4539 • Fax: 408-544-4571
E-mail: mbaadmissions@scu.edu • Website: www.scu.edu/business

## Student Life and Environment

MBAs report that SCU "provides a safe, clean, study environment coupled with a very caring and personal staff. The school really treats students as 'customers' and caters to their needs, offering extended library hours during exams. The staff wants the students to succeed." Part-timers also appreciate that "the schedule is really terrific [and] works for working folks as well as commuters." A new facility is in the works, we're told, which is a good thing; students agree that "the current facility is old and cramped."

SCU's "gorgeous and safe campus" offers a number of top amenities, including "a state-of-the-art gym and pool, great recreation areas, and a late-night venue called The Bronco with a pool table and a large television and several couches," as well as "campus-wide wireless access, [and] a peaceful rose garden and a church for when you need serenity." Although most students are part-timers with numerous other commitments outside school, MBAs here do occasionally socialize. One writes, "There are quarter-end bar nights which are great for relaxing after your last final with current classmates, catching up with past classmates, and meeting new people." Another student points out that "life at school can be great for those who do the work to get involved. It can be a commuter school if that is all a student wants to get out of it. [But] there is always something social to do on the weekends, either sponsored by the school or just going out with other MBA students."

"Many students here have jobs," which "provides the best opportunity for networking and recruiting after graduation, as you have gained so many resources at numerous organizations," students here tell us. MBAs range from the mid 20s to the mid 40s. Their "backgrounds are extremely diverse; they come from such areas as financial services, banking, semiconductors, software, technology management, finance, and human resources, to name a few." Engineers from the Silicon Valley are the single most visible contingent.

## Admissions

Applicants to Leavey MBA programs at SCU must provide the Admissions Office with all of the following: official transcripts for all post-secondary academic work; official GMAT score reports reflecting scores no more than five years old; a completed application and a copy of same; two letters of recommendation; and personal essays. A third essay is optional. Candidates whose first language is not English must also submit official score reports for the TOEFL (minimum required score: 600 paper-based test, 250 computer-based test). Work experience is not a prerequisite to admission, although a minimum of two years of experience is recommended; on average, admitted students have between five and seven years of post-undergraduate professional experience. All applicants must demonstrate competency in four areas: college algebra, calculus, and oral communications. SCU uses targeted advertising and recruiting events to enhance its minority and disadvantaged populations.

### FINANCIAL FACTS

| | |
|---|---|
| Annual tuition | $17,496 |
| Fees | $120 |
| Books and supplies | $700 |
| Room & board | $13,000 |

### ADMISSIONS

| | |
|---|---|
| Admissions Selectivity Rating | 78 |
| # of applications received | 377 |
| % applicants accepted | 86 |
| % acceptees attending | 73 |
| Average GMAT | 619 |
| Range of GMAT | 530–710 |
| Average GPA | 3.19 |
| TOEFL required of international students? | yes |
| Minimum TOEFL (paper/computer) | 600/250 |
| Application fee | $75 |
| International application fee | $100 |
| Regular application deadline | 6/1 |
| Regular notification | rolling |
| Early decision program? | yes |
| ED Deadline/notification | 3/1 Fall only / 4/15 |
| Deferment available? | yes |
| Maximum length of deferment | 2 quarters |
| Transfer students accepted? | yes |
| Transfer application policy Apply as all others | |
| Non-fall admissions? | yes |
| Need-blind admissions? | yes |

### APPLICANTS ALSO LOOK AT

San Jose State University,
University of California—Berkeley,
University of California—Davis,
University of San Francisco

### EMPLOYMENT PROFILE

| | |
|---|---|
| Career Rating | 89 |
| Average starting salary | $88,680 |

# SEATTLE PACIFIC UNIVERSITY
## SCHOOL OF BUSINESS AND ECONOMICS

## Academics

The School of Business and Economics at Seattle Pacific University is distinguished by its dedication to mission and vision. Students say, "The school does a good job of staying close to its Christian vision and integrating it into their studies." Both the MBA and the MSISM (master's of science in information systems management) programs "maintain a commitment to competence, character, and ethical decision-making from a Christian perspective." According to the school, "[The programs] teach students to provide values-based leadership in organizations from a general-management perspective."

Students are drawn by the school's ethical focus, as well as by its caring atmosphere and adaptability to the needs of its part-time student body. Professors and administrators "care a lot about the students, and they are understanding about other influences (like work and family) and try to be as accommodating as possible." Classes are generally offered once a week, for 11 weeks, in three-hour evening or weekend sessions; this arrangement allows most part-timers to complete an MBA in three years or an MSISM in two years.

The SPU MBA program commences with nine core courses; these courses cover basic principles of business and can be waived for those who have completed equivalent undergraduate courses within the previous seven years. Ten advanced courses and five electives round out the curriculum. Students can use their electives to develop a specialization in any of the following areas: e-business, human-resource management, information-systems management, finance, and management of business processes. The MSISM is a shorter program consisting of two core courses, twelve required courses, and three electives. Both curricula "approach instruction with an eye to the practical" and a "stress on applied learning." Students note that the program also places "a continuing emphasis on teamwork and team achievement."

Most of all, students love the atmosphere at SPU, which emanates from "warm professors and staff who make the experience very enjoyable." They also appreciate the school's desire to improve and to act on student feedback. Students who say "some professors are outstanding while others are only okay," also point out that students are able to evaluate professors at the end of each quarter. Students note, "The dean of the school meets with professors who receive less-than-satisfactory feedback, and improvements in instruction occur because of this feedback." As an added bonus, SPU's location allows the school to offer "great business-world networking with companies like Boeing, Microsoft, and Starbucks."

## Career and Placement

The Career Development Center at SPU handles career services for all students at the school. These services include on-site job listings, workshops, a career library, one-on-one career counseling, and access to online job databases. In addition, the School of Business and Economics maintains the Center for Applied Learning, which helps students develop "mentorship contacts, internship training, entrepreneurial ingenuity, and service appreciation" through projects in the business and nonprofit communities. The school also notes, "SPU's strong ties to the business community offer further networking and learning opportunities. Business leaders are welcomed into the classroom as guest speakers, sources for team projects, and informal advisors. The MBA and MS/ISM programs, along with the Center for Integrity in Business, also sponsor quarterly events such as the Faith and the Marketplace Speaker Series, where executives share their career experiences and commitment to Christian faith."

Companies most frequently employing SPU MBAs include Boeing, Microsoft, Safeco, and Starbucks. Approximately one in twelve MBAs finds their first post-degree job outside the United States.

DEBBIE WYSOMIERSKI, ASSOCIATE GRADUATE DIRECTOR
3307 THIRD AVENUE WEST, SUITE 201, SEATTLE, WA 98119-1950 UNITED STATES
PHONE: 206-281-2753 • FAX: 206-281-2733
E-MAIL: MBA@SPU.EDU • WEBSITE: WWW.SPU.EDU/SBE

## Student Life and Environment

The average SPU business graduate student is 31 years old and has been in the professional workforce for seven years. Most attend part-time while working full-time at such companies as Adobe Systems, Cingular Wireless, Boeing, Eldec, Microsoft, Safeco, Starbucks, Virginia Mason Medical Center, and Washington Mutual. Despite the fact that most students come in at night, take a class, and then leave, MBAs tell us that "SPU has a true sense of community that they enjoy." One student writes, "Everyone is friendly, and the values and mission of the school serve it and its students and faculty well. There is always something going on and interesting things to do and see." Extracurricular events include lectures at the school's Center for Integrity in Business.

The university is located on the north slope of Queen Anne Hill, less than 10 minutes from downtown Seattle. Students agree that "[it's] a pretty campus with an intimate feel" that's "easily accessible." McKenna Hall, home to the School of Business and Economics, is also "well-wired with technology." Students love the setting, but they complain that "many facilities are closed when [they] take classes in the evening."

Hometown Seattle offers aspiring business mavens many benefits. The city is a gateway to international trade, home to a number of major corporations and organizations, and offers plenty of great dining, entertainment, arts, sports, and shopping. The cherry on the sundae is the area surrounding Seattle: The Pacific Northwest is an outdoor lover's paradise, offering (besides plenty of rain) opportunities ranging from skiing and hiking to fishing, kayaking, and scuba diving.

## Admissions

Applicants to SPU must submit an official undergraduate transcript demonstrating a 3.0 grade point average (overall or final three semesters, whichever is higher), GMAT scores (MBA program) or GRE scores (MS/ISM program), two letters of recommendation, TOEFL scores (international students), a three- to four-page personal statement, and a resume demonstrating at least one year of full-time, substantive professional experience. Additional work experience is preferred; work experience is a significant factor in the admissions decision process.

### FINANCIAL FACTS

| | |
|---|---|
| Annual tuition | $16,254 |
| Books and supplies | $1,107 |
| Room & board | $7,158 |
| % of students receiving aid | 41 |
| % of first-year students receiving aid | 35 |
| % of students receiving loans | 27 |
| % of students receiving grants | 3 |
| Average award package | $14,982 |
| Average grant | $7,077 |
| Average student loan debt | $33,482 |

### ADMISSIONS

| | |
|---|---|
| **Admissions Selectivity Rating** | **72** |
| # of applications received | 221 |
| % applicants accepted | 75 |
| % acceptees attending | 64 |
| Average GMAT | 551 |
| Range of GMAT | 500–610 |
| Average GPA | 3.33 |
| TOEFL required of international students? | yes |
| Minimum TOEFL (paper/computer) | 580/237 |
| Application fee | $55 |
| International application fee | $55 |
| Regular application deadline | 8/20 |
| Deferment available? | yes |
| Maximum length of deferment | 1 year |
| Transfer students accepted? | yes |

Transfer application policy
Applicants must meet standard admission requirements. University will accept 9 quarter credits from AACSB-accredited schools. Students transferring from an accredited Jesuit MB program (JEBNET) may transfer up to 50% of credits.

| | |
|---|---|
| Non-fall admissions? | yes |
| Need-blind admissions? | yes |

### APPLICANTS ALSO LOOK AT

Pacific Lutheran University, San Francisco State University, Seattle Pacific University, University of Washington, Washington State University, Western Washington University

| EMPLOYMENT PROFILE | |
|---|---|
| **Career Rating** | **60*** |
| Average starting salary | $64,390 |
| Percent employed | 80 |

# SEATTLE UNIVERSITY
## ALBERS SCHOOL OF BUSINESS AND ECONOMICS

## Academics

Students praise the convenient flexibility of the Albers MBA program at Seattle University, telling us that "both in scheduling classes for each term and in the order that you take your classes, the curriculum is very open. Thus, people who are going to school in addition to a job and family can manage their time effectively." Students say, "There are both full-time and part-time options with most classes being offered during the evenings on Monday to Thursday, which gives us the time to work for a living during the day and be with our families on the weekends." This is, in short, "a good-quality program for those who can't quit working for two years to go to school."

Ethics are featured prominently in the Albers curriculum because "Seattle University is a private Jesuit organization that reflects Christian principles." Students agree that "it has a very friendly atmosphere." The school also places a premium on the teaching ability of its faculty; as one MBA explains, "The professors at Seattle University are rated by the school on three areas: Research and publications, service to the university community, and on the quality of teaching (as rated by student evaluations)—with teaching quality being the most heavily emphasized metric. Because of this, Seattle University is a place where professors come to teach and enjoy the quality of life in the Pacific Northwest." MBAs praise the "willingness of professors to engage with students in class and outside of class." One student writes, "The professors here are great. It is wonderful to be at a school where the professors care about the students and want to see them succeed."

Professorial instruction here is supplemented by "CEOs from Wells Fargo to Boeing to Starbucks to Safeco coming to [speak in] class," a windfall of the school's location in a major corporate city. Students tell us that the program is "really strong in finance, accounting, entrepreneurship, and ethics. It's also a very good program for building teamwork and leadership skills." In addition, one student says, "The administration is outstanding, giving quick and professional responses and help every time I need to contact someone, and [they provide] constant updates on ongoing events." Several students note, "No wonder students love this program, [but] they would love it even more if the tuition weren't so high." One MBA sums up, "The academics here are comparable to traditional programs in the region, but the program is as flexible as those of nontraditional programs. [This] flexibility helps students complete their degree while still working. That is a huge strength!"

## Career and Placement

The Albers Placement Center serves both undergraduates and graduate students in business at Seattle University. The office sponsors a mentoring program that pairs MBAs with area senior executives and provides a standard roster of career-related services including counseling and job posting. The office organizes a career fair: employers attending the 2005 fair included Boeing, Costco, Russell Investment, Smith Barney, Washington Mutual, and Wells Fargo Financial. Approximately 30 employers visit campus each year for the purpose of recruiting MBAs.

Employers most likely to hire Albers MBAs include Boeing, Paccar, Deloitte Touche Tohmatsu, Alaska Airlines, Amazon, PricewaterhouseCoopers, Washington Mutual Bank, and Weyerhaeuser. At least 10 percent of Albers MBAs find a post-degree job outside the United States.

## Student Life and Environment

Albers does "a really good job of making life easy for its many part-time students." It has extended bookstore hours during the beginning of quarters and an espresso stand is

Janet Shandley, Director, Graduate Admissions
901 12th Avenue, PO Box 222000, Seattle, WA 98122-1090 United States
Phone: 206-296-2000 • Fax: 206-296-5656
E-mail: grad-admissions@seattleu.edu • Website: www.seattle.edu/asbe

open throughout evening class hours in the b-school building. There are also two campuses with duplicate sections for almost all of the initial courses, allowing students to choose the one that is more convenient for their schedule and location in the area. Some students comment that the only problem with the East Side campus in Bellevue is that it "has no sense of community; it's simply a drab office park in which students spend as little time as possible." The downtown campus, located near Capitol Hill is "very beautiful, and the buildings are new. There is wireless Internet all over the campus for student use."

Students say that "because our [program] is an evening program, it's very difficult to participate in school activities. But the school recognizes this factor and provides events specifically targeting the evening programs such as the pizza get-togethers after class to meet and [talk] with professors and students." Students also bond during the required leadership and teambuilding course. Students say, "[The course] is an excellent networking class that allows roundtable discussions about solutions to the real pitfalls in the business world."

The student body at Albers has "a lot of age diversity." MBAs say, "We have students in their early 20s fresh in the work force, and we have students with 10, 20, and even more years of experience. Many students run their own companies or manage departments for local corporations. The breadth of experience within the student body surpasses every other MBA program in the region." There's also "a nice mix of international students, and a very good travel-abroad program where course credit can be obtained while studying aspects of business in another country (like France, Italy, or China)."

## Admissions

Applicants to Seattle University must provide the admissions committee with official transcripts from all schools attended, GMAT scores, TOEFL scores (for applicants whose native language is other than English), and a resume. The school's website notes that "most successful applicants have a 3.0 undergraduate GPA, score a minimum of 500 on the GMAT, and have at least one year full-time of work experience." Applicants must meet the math and computer proficiency requirement; the former requires an understanding of calculus, while the latter requires the ability to use e-mail, web browsing, word processing, and spreadsheet applications.

### FINANCIAL FACTS

| | |
|---|---|
| Annual tuition | $13,584 |
| Books and supplies | $1,200 |
| Room & board | $10,829 |
| Average grant | $1,200 |

### ADMISSIONS

| | |
|---|---|
| **Admissions Selectivity Rating** | **75** |
| # of applications received | 41 |
| % applicants accepted | 76 |
| % acceptees attending | 61 |
| Average GMAT | 527 |
| Range of GMAT | 460–610 |
| Average GPA | 3.38 |
| TOEFL required of international students? | yes |
| Minimum TOEFL (paper/computer) | 565/225 |
| Application fee | $50 |
| International application fee | $50 |
| Regular application deadline | 8/1 |
| Regular notification | 8/31 |
| Deferment available? | yes |
| Maximum length of deferment | 2 quarters |
| Transfer students accepted? | yes |
| Transfer application policy Regular Admission Process | |
| Non-fall admissions? | yes |
| Need-blind admissions? | yes |

### APPLICANTS ALSO LOOK AT

Seattle University, University of Washington

---

### EMPLOYMENT PROFILE

| | |
|---|---|
| **Career Rating** | **80** |

# SHIPPENSBURG UNIVERSITY
## THE JOHN L. GROVE COLLEGE OF BUSINESS

## Academics

The MBA program at the Shippensburg University's John L. Grove College of Business exploits twenty-first century technology to the great convenience of its busy student body. Two-thirds of each course in the program is taught in an electronic classroom; videoconferencing technology allows the classes to be broadcast to remote sites so that students and professors in different locations can interact. Area employers may even have their electronic conference rooms added to the school's roster of videoconferencing sites, thus allowing employees to complete the program from their workplaces. The other third of the course content is presented via the Internet, which permits students to complete the work at their own pace. For added convenience, all classes are recorded on digital video and uploaded to the program's website so that students may later stream the classes online.

The Shippensburg MBA consists of 30 credits, meaning "you can do the whole program in one year," which is exactly what some students here are after. Most students attend part-time though, taking two or more years to earn the degree. Students whose undergraduate degree was in an area other than business typically must take up to six prerequisite under-graduate-level courses (in accounting, economics, finance, operations, organizational behavior, and marketing) prior to beginning course work on the MBA proper. The MBA curriculum consists of eight required classes (managerial accounting, global manage-ment finance, entrepreneurship, international business, organizational leadership, information management, supply chain, and strategic management) and two electives.

Students tell us that Shippensburg professors "tend to be very friendly and like to see success. They bond well with successful students who show that they are interested in doing well and learning the material." Some concede that "It takes money to keep really, really good professors here and we do not have it!" but quickly add that "The professors that we do have are very good and dedicated." The online component of the program stresses independent learning, which many students appreciate; as one student explains, "Because we have to teach ourselves, we end up learning a lot." Students also love the convenience of taking classes in remote locations; many attend a learning center in Harrisburg near their places of employment. Students also note approvingly that "because this is a new program, the administration takes suggestions seriously. And the technology is great, when it works."

## Career and Placement

The Career Development Center (CDC) of Shippensburg University serves current stu-dents and alumni of the university. The office offers counseling services, organizes job search programs, provides seminars in job-search skills, and publishes a bi-weekly newsletter announcing upcoming on-campus interviews. Employers who have recruited on the Shippensburg campus in the past include Advantica, Allegis Group, CACI International, Capital Blue Cross, Citibank, Edward Jones Investments, Ernst & Young, Federated Mutual Insurance, Fulton Bank, G E Fanuc Automation, Highmark, Inc., IBM, Integrated Management Solutions, KPMG, LLP, Lockheed Martin, Nationwide Insurance, Northwestern Mutual Financial Network, the Pennsylvania Department of Revenue, PricewaterhouseCoopers, Raytheon, The Vanguard Group, Vectron International, and Wells Fargo.

## Student Life and Environment

Shippensburg is a public university that is home to over 6,500 undergraduate students and about 1,000 graduate students. The campus, spread over 200 acres, is located 40 miles southwest of Harrisburg, not far from the Pennsylvania Turnpike. The school is accredited by the AACSB. Many MBA students attend the Dixon University Center in Harrisburg, where they participate in Shippensburg-based classes via teleconferencing technology.

Most students in the MBA program attend part-time and have little time for extracurricular involvement. While some feel "the department needs to have more clubs and social events for the students to join," most are happy to restrict their involvement to class-related activities. The majority of students here are "older, married adults who are employed full-time." They share the common bond of "all working toward the same goal" and "don't feel in competition with each other in the least." In fact, there's a "definite sense of community within the school." Some here tell us that "the students who take classes on campus at Ship tend to be more immature than those at Harrisburg. The Harrisburg people tend to be working professionals, whereas Shippensburg has more students who came straight from undergrad to the MBA program."

## Admissions

The Admissions Office at Shippensburg University requires applicants to submit official copies of transcripts for all undergraduate work and a current resume. GMAT scores are required only for applicants whose undergraduate GPA is below 3.0; students required to take the GMAT must submit an official GMAT score report. In addition, applicants must either have work experience or undergraduate credits in computer usage, oral and written communication, and quantitative analysis. A personal statement and letters of recommendation are both optional. International applicants must not only meet all of the above requirements, but must also submit an international student application, an evaluation of their transcripts by a professional evaluating service (either Educational Credential Evaluators (ECE) or World Education Services (WES)); an official score report for the TOEFL; and an affidavit of support accompanied by a current bank statement. Applicants who do not meet Shippensburg's admissions requirements may seek special consideration. Some such students do receive provisional admissions status, which allows them to enter the program and continue contingent upon success in their initial MBA course work.

### FINANCIAL FACTS

Annual tuition (in-state/out-of-state)
$5,888/$9,422

Fees
(in-state/out-of-state) $979/$1,042

### ADMISSIONS

| Admissions Selectivity Rating | 60* |
|---|---|
| # of applications received | 45 |
| % applicants accepted | 88 |
| Average GMAT | 515 |
| Application fee | $30 |
| Regular application deadline | rolling |
| Regular notification | rolling |

# SOUTHEAST MISSOURI STATE UNIVERSITY
## DONALD L. HARRISON COLLEGE OF BUSINESS

## GENERAL INFORMATION

| | |
|---|---|
| Type of school | public |
| Environment | town |
| Academic calendar | semester |

### SURVEY SAYS...
Smart classrooms
*Solid preparation in:*
Teamwork
Communication/interpersonal skills
Presentation skills
Computer skills

## STUDENTS

| | |
|---|---|
| Enrollment of parent institution | 10,000 |
| Enrollment of business school | 88 |
| % male/female | 55/45 |
| % out-of-state | 16 |
| % part-time | 35 |
| % minorities | 5 |
| % international | 15 |
| Average age at entry | 26 |
| Average years work experience at entry | 2 |

## ACADEMICS

| | |
|---|---|
| **Academic Experience Rating** | **68** |
| Student/faculty ratio | 20:1 |
| Profs interesting rating | 73 |
| Profs accessible rating | 82 |
| % female faculty | 40 |
| % minority faculty | 10 |

## Academics

The Donald L. Harrison College of Business at Southeast Missouri State University (SEMO) offers students plenty of "bang for their buck." In 2003, *U.S. News & World Report* reported that the school produces some of the "least indebted students" in the nation. As one MBA student says, "It's not Kellogg, but it's as good as you'll find for the money. I was an MBA at another university for a semester and transferred because the education there was not up to par with the tuition charged. SEMO, which charges much less, has provided a much better value." Harrison MBAs can choose from seven different degree options: accounting, environmental management, finance, general management, industrial management, international business, and a recently added concentration in health administration. MBAs praise "the variety of available disciplines of study, given the size of the institution," although they also warn that "there should be a wider variety of courses offered each semester." One student adds, "Sometimes you may be very limited to what [courses] you will be able to take. For instance, I can't take any summer courses because the courses that will be offered are ones that I have already taken." Internships play an integral role in the Harrison MBA—at least for its younger full-timers. The school notes, "Students have the opportunity to participate in internship assignments (and receive full credit as an elective course) that bring our graduate students into contact with the managerial practice of business. Our students have benefited from internships with American Express Financial, Coca-Cola, KPMG, Merrill Lynch, [and] Northwestern Mutual Life, to name just a few." Many Harrison MBAs have jobs (they attend evening classes), and so, do not participate in the internship program. Students love Harrison's small classes and the focus on in-class discussion. One older MBA student writes, "As a nontraditional student with over 30 years [of] business experience, my reflections and experiences were sometimes sought [after] and discussed as another means to broaden the overall picture of the real work place. I felt valued as a contributor by most professors and younger students. Diversity and variety seemed to be positive influences in most of my classes. Students were supportive of each others' efforts." However, some other students feel that "some professors do not demand enough from students, especially in the area of presentation and revision of work. Overall, this school's MBA program should be more challenging."

## Career and Placement

Harrison placement services are provided by SEMO's Career Services Office, which serves all undergraduates and graduate students at the university. In conjunction with the Alumni Affairs office, Career Services has established the Southeast Career Alumni Network to facilitate job searches. The office also offers the standard array of services including counseling, workshops, and online support. Students are unimpressed; they feel that "the biggest area the MBA administration must improve on is the career center. The business school doesn't have a career center. We must use the undergraduate career center that focuses on attracting jobs for undergraduates. Obtaining a job through the career center at Southeast is nearly impossible. All work must be self-initiated and completed." Harrison MBAs who seek new jobs after graduation most often find themselves working for Accenture, Bausch and Lomb, Dow Jones, PricewaterhouseCoopers, TG Missouri, and Texas Instruments. About one in ten students finds a job outside the United States.

## Student Life and Environment

"Life at school is good!" one Harrison MBAs reports. The student body is tight and the surrounding town of Cape Girardeau is pleasant and quiet. Another student explains, "Cape Girardeau is a fairly small town, so there are some limitations on recreational activity. In

DR. KENNETH HEISCHMIDT, DIRECTOR, MBA PROGRAM
MBA OFFICE CAPE GIRARDEAU, MO 63701 UNITED STATES
PHONE: 573-651-5116 • FAX: 573-651-5032
E-MAIL: MBA@SEMO.EDU • WEBSITE: WWW.SEMO.EDU

warm months, there are many lakes, parks, and trails nearby to enjoy. The people in the community are friendly overall." One MBA student says, "Even though Cape Girardeau is a relatively small town, there is actually quite a lot to do, and it is close to Memphis and St. Louis for people who want to get to a city every once in a while." Campus life centers on the MBA Association, which "has holiday parties, happy-hour gatherings, intramural sports teams, [and] sponsors speakers." One student says, "I must give credit to the MBA Association because they work hard to create a positive social atmosphere for students." However, other MBAs believe that is pretty much the only school-related extracurricular. One student writes, "It seems the only student organization that MBA students are a part of is the MBA Association. This may be because MBA students have busy schedules." Other students feel that "the administration needs to work at creating more community. Although the student-run MBA Association does well, the administration does little to make new students feel welcomed." Students agree that "[SEMO's campus] is nice and fairly attractive [with] good facilities on-campus for student recreation, exercise, leisure, activities, and so on. The library resources are adequate and [continue to] improve—considering the budget crisis of the past couple years. The surrounding community is fairly supportive of the university and recognizes the impact it plays on its economy." Although one student comments, "For those who work during the day and study at night, some of the facilities are not open (for example, the bookstore). Sometimes the working student just simply cannot get to campus before it closes and has to take time off work to get necessary books for class." Students agree, "[The Harrison student body] comes from a wide array of backgrounds: rural, urban, suburban, international, and so on. The mix of such a diversity of students offers a relatively interesting student population." The school notes, "Approximately 16 percent of our MBA students and half of our alumni are international students. Since Southeast Missouri State University launched its MBA program in fall 1996, students from more than 25 countries have studied in the program. Currently, students from more than eight countries represent their nations and bring the world to the classroom."

## Admissions

Harrison admissions officers use a formula to establish a floor for all MBA applicants: (200 5 GPA [on a four-point scale] + GMAT score). Applicants must score at least 1,000 to be considered for admission. In addition, applicants must score at least 400 on the GMAT and must have earned at least a C in all required foundation courses for the GMAT program. These foundation courses are applied calculus, financial management, introductory statistics, management and organizational behavior, management information systems, principles of financial accounting, principles of macroeconomics, principles of managerial accounting, principles of marketing, and principles of microeconomics. Students without the requisite undergraduate work may place out of foundation courses through local and/or CLEP exams.

## FINANCIAL FACTS

| | |
|---|---|
| Annual tuition (in-state/out-of-state) | $4,320/$7,752 |
| Books and supplies | $500 |
| Room & board | $4,500 |
| % of students receiving aid | 38 |
| Average award package | $11,200 |
| Average grant | $11,200 |

## ADMISSIONS

| | |
|---|---|
| Admissions Selectivity Rating | 66 |
| # of applications received | 51 |
| % applicants accepted | 96 |
| % acceptees attending | 94 |
| Average GMAT | 510 |
| Range of GMAT | 460–560 |
| Average GPA | 3.2 |
| TOEFL required of international students? | yes |
| Minimum TOEFL (paper/computer) | 550/213 |
| Application fee | $20 |
| International application fee | $100 |
| Regular application deadline | rolling |
| Regular notification | rolling |
| Deferment available? | yes |
| Maximum length of deferment | 1 year |
| Transfer students accepted? | yes |
| Transfer application policy May transfer 9 hours authorized by the director of MBA program | |
| Non-fall admissions? | yes |
| Need-blind admissions? | yes |

## APPLICANTS ALSO LOOK AT

Missouri State University (Formerly SW MSU), Saint Louis University, Southern Illinois University—Carbondale, University of Missouri—St. Louis, University of Missouri—Columbia

## EMPLOYMENT PROFILE

| Career Rating | 78 | Grads employed by field: | % | avg. salary: |
|---|---|---|---|---|
| Average starting salary | $50,000 | Accounting | 15 | $45,000 |
| Percent employed | 95 | Finance | 20 | $45,000 |
| | | MIS | 15 | $55,000 |
| | | Consulting | 10 | $55,000 |
| | | General Management | 40 | $40,000 |

# SOUTHERN ILLINOIS UNIVERSITY—CARBONDALE
## COLLEGE OF BUSINESS AND ADMINISTRATION

## Academics

The College of Business and Administration at Southern Illinois University—Carbondale offers both a traditional MBA and off-campus EMBA options in Hong Kong, Singapore, and Taiwan. All programs are AACSB-accredited. About half the graduate students at SIUC attend full-time. While part-time students can manage the program as well, the mixed schedule of daytime and nighttime classes limits their options somewhat.

SIUC MBAs report that "the school is famous for its finance department" and that it offers "good courses in the Management of Information Systems." Classes here "are very interactive, with only 20 to 30 students in a class," and "professors work to extend the understanding of the discipline in all classes. Also, most professors seek to design classes in an unorthodox manner to develop skills needed for business." Many students cite the low cost of attending as their primary reason for choosing SIUC; relatively low tuition rates are made effectively lower by the availability of "a lot of assistantships for students." SIUC maintains a relationship with ESC-Grenoble, which allows SIUC MBAs to study for a Masters of International Business (MIB) in France.

Entering students who lack the required knowledge base for an MBA program are required to complete up to 37 hours of foundation courses prior to beginning work on their MBA. It helps that students with degrees outside business may receive credit for any equivalent undergraduate business classes in which they earned a grade of C or better. Such students must present both a transcript and a course syllabus for each course in order to be considered for the exemption. Students with undergraduate degrees in business generally are exempt from all foundation course work.

Full-time students who arrive with undergraduate business degrees under their belt can finish the 33-semester hour MBA program in 12 months. The MBA curriculum includes seven core courses and four electives. Students may also pursue electives in finance, marketing, international business, management information systems, and organizational behavior. Those who wish to concentrate in a particular area can opt to take all of their electives in one discipline.

## Career and Placement

Southern Illinois University maintains a separate Business Placement Center to serve the College of Business and Administration. The office serves undergraduates, graduates, and alumni of the school. The office coordinates an annual job fair, maintains e-recruiting resources, and provides career counseling to students. Some here feel that "The career center could use a more hands-on effort with graduates. The only contact I had was through e-mail notices of career center activities." On-campus recruiters include 7-Eleven, Aldi, Archer Daniels Midland (ADM), CBIZ Business Solutions, Deloitte Touche Tohmatsu, Disney, Ernst & Young, Federated Insurance, KPMG, MB Financial, MMP&W, PricewaterhouseCoopers, Regions Financial Corporation, State Farm Insurance, Swink, Fiehler & Company, Watkins Uiberall, and Woodbury Financial.

Dr. Don Gribbin, MBA Program Director

Rehn Hall 133, 1025 Lincoln Drive, Mail Code 4625 Carbondale, IL 62901 United States

Phone: 618-453-3030 • Fax: 618-453-7961 • E-mail: mbagp@cba.siu.edu

Website: www.cba.siu.edu

## Student Life and Environment

An overall student population of more than 20,000 keeps the SIUC campus hopping. As one MBA student explains, "There are lots of things to do here, such as [hearing] guest speakers and seminars to attend. The school often has forums for students to express their opinions on politics. They also offer fun events like concerts, and many students are avid sports fans, so sporting events are social gatherings." The campus recreation center "is very good, with basketball courts, swimming pools, racquetball courts, etc. There are also weight rooms and many cardiovascular fitness machines, and the staff that works at the Rec Center is very helpful." As if all that weren't enough, "The Student Center is an excellent facility for throwing pots, woodworking, and metal smithing." Even the surrounding campus "is beautiful, with forests all around where you can go hiking if the weather allows."

The city of Carbondale has a population of about 26,000, and the surrounding county is home to nearly 60,000 Illinoisans. St. Louis is the closest big city; it's less than 100 miles to the west. Both Chicago and Kansas City are just over 300 miles away. Major employers in the area include Nascote Industries, West Teleservices, Southern Illinois Healthcare, and the Maytag Corporation.

SIUC MBAs include "many international students. There are more young students than in many MBA programs, but not at the expense of competence." To some "it seems that almost every other student in the MBA program is a recent graduate of SIUC. Although they come from varied backgrounds...they are very similar," especially in that "few seem to have undergraduate degrees in business."

## Admissions

All applicants to the MBA program at SIUC must provide the admissions department with a completed application to the university's graduate school; a separate application to the College of Business; official transcripts for all postsecondary academic work; an official score report for the GMAT; and three letters of recommendation. International applicants must also provide an official score report for the TOEFL (minimum score: 550 paper, 213 computer), a financial statement for graduate international students, and a photocopy of their passport. Work experience is not required; however, students with work experience do receive special consideration. All applications are assessed individually and holistically. Admission to the program requires a minimum undergraduate GPA of 2.7 (on a four-point scale) over the applicant's most recent 60 semester hours.

### FINANCIAL FACTS

| | |
|---|---|
| Annual tuition (in-state/out-of-state) | $5,760/$11,520 |
| Fees | $1,414 |
| Books and supplies | $840 |

### ADMISSIONS

| | |
|---|---|
| **Admissions Selectivity Rating** | **73** |
| # of applications received | 78 |
| % applicants accepted | 69 |
| % acceptees attending | 63 |
| Average GMAT | 507 |
| Range of GMAT | 440–570 |
| Average GPA | 3.39 |
| TOEFL required of international students? | yes |
| Minimum TOEFL (paper/computer) | 550/213 |
| Application fee | $35 |
| International application fee | $35 |
| Regular application deadline | 3/15 |
| Regular notification | 6/1 |
| Deferment available? | yes |
| Maximum length of deferment | 1 year |
| Transfer students accepted? | yes |
| Transfer application policy Maximum number of transfer credits accepted for core curriculum is 6. | |
| Non-fall admissions? | yes |

### APPLICANTS ALSO LOOK AT

Eastern Illinois University, University of Illinois at Urbana-Champaign, University of Missouri—Columbia, Western Illinois University

# SOUTHERN ILLINOIS UNIVERSITY—EDWARDSVILLE
## SCHOOL OF BUSINESS

### GENERAL INFORMATION
| | |
|---|---|
| Type of school | public |
| Environment | village |
| Academic calendar | 10 weeks |

### SURVEY SAYS...
Happy students
*Solid preparation in:*
General management
Computer skills

### STUDENTS
| | |
|---|---|
| Enrollment of parent institution | 13,460 |
| Enrollment of business school | 196 |
| % male/female | 100/0 |
| % part-time | 100 |
| Average age at entry | 27 |
| Average years work experience at entry | 5 |

### ACADEMICS
| | |
|---|---|
| **Academic Experience Rating** | **71** |
| Student/faculty ratio | 9:1 |
| Profs interesting rating | 78 |
| Profs accessible rating | 75 |
| % female faculty | 24 |
| % minority faculty | 16 |

### PROMINENT ALUMNI
Fernando G. Aguirre, President & CEO of Chiquita Brands International; John Shimkus, U.S. Representative (IL) 19th District; Ralph Korte, President, Korte Construction Company; Ann Ficken, General Partner, Edward Jones; Matthew P. Kulig, President & CEO of Global Velocity, Inc.

## Academics

Students are drawn to the business programs at Southern Illinois University—Edwardsville by "the cheapest tuition in the St. Louis metro area," the convenience of "a lot of night and weekend classes," and "the good reputation" of the program, bolstered by its AACSB accreditation. SIUE offers a general MBA as well as specialized master's programs in accountancy, marketing research, economics, finance, and computer management and information systems.

SIUE's MBA program commences with a sequence of seven foundation courses covering basic principles of business and management. Students with undergraduate degrees in business generally place out of all these courses, provided they earned a grade of at least C in the corresponding undergraduate course. Nonbusiness majors who completed related undergraduate courses may place out of individual foundation courses. Foundation courses are not credited toward the MBA.

Credit-bearing MBA coursework consists of 30 semester hours, half devoted to required courses and half to electives. Electives are available in accounting, economics, finance, international business, management, computer management and information systems, marketing, and production. A student may elect to write an independent thesis in order to fulfill some of the elective requirements. All students must complete a comprehensive examination.

MBA students at SIUE tell us that "professors are very knowledgeable and well-prepared for classes." Overall, they "are very interested in providing an excellent learning environment." While "the administration of the School of Business is first-rate," the "administration of the university as a whole is not as impressive." Students warn that "There is far too much red tape and far too many walls built into the system." Some here also feel that "the physical classroom environment needs an overhaul for the MBA student. We need something much different than the kindergarten desks-in-a-row. Some professors have made efforts to improve this, but for the most part it is very poor, not conducive for most adults who work all day at a desk." Students also would like to see the program incorporate online classes.

## Career and Placement

Business students at SIUE are served by the university's Career Development Center, which provides career counseling and placement services for all students and alumni. Services include individual counseling, resume referral, on-campus interview sessions, workshops on various career-related skills, and a Career Resources Center with both online and hard-copy materials. SIUE holds two annual career fairs, one in the fall and one in the spring.

SCHOOL OF BUSINESS STUDENT SERVICES, ADMISSIONS OFFICER
CAMPUS BOX 1186, EDWARDSVILLE, IL 62026 UNITED STATES
PHONE: 618-650-3840 • FAX: 618-650-3979 • E-MAIL: MBA@SIUE.EDU
WEBSITE: WWW.SIUE.EDU/BUSINESS

## Student Life and Environment

SIUE is located in Edwardsville, a city of 22,000 strong that's just twenty miles northeast of St. Louis, Missouri. St. Louis provides copious opportunities for work, shopping, and entertainment. The school's location in a major metropolitan area also means that it serves a potential market of nearly three million people. Major employers in the area include the Bank of Edwardsville, Keller Companies, Richards Brick, and SIUE.

The university is home to more than 13,000 students and sits on a meandering campus that features woodlands, lakes, and rolling hills. Students note that "the campus is very nice and has all the amenities you could need." Most business students "don't spend a lot of time on campus," though, as "we commute and attend evening and weekend classes. This is very helpful to those of us in the working world" but it dampens student partic-ipation in the school community at large.

SIUE business students "come from impressively diverse backgrounds," are "pleasant to work with," and "have a great deal of real-world knowledge to share." Most "have chil-dren and full-time jobs, yet they have decided to come back to school and finish their degrees. Their commitments outside the classroom force them to be creative with their time-management skills and this, in turn, becomes a valuable tool that they can use in the business world." The student body includes "people from various cultures, which makes class interesting. They are also very easy to talk to!"

## Admissions

Applicants to the MBA program at SIUE must apply for admission to the Graduate School. Applications are processed in two stages: During the first, admissions officers consider only the applicant's undergraduate GPA (as indicated by official copies of tran-scripts for all postsecondary academic work) and GMAT score. Applicants who meet one of the following minimum requirements are admitted to the program: an admission score of at least 950 under the formula [(undergraduate GPA $\times$ 200) + GMAT score], or a GMAT score of at least 400 with a minimum raw score of at least 20 on both the verbal and quantitative portions of the exam and an analytical writing score of at least 4.0. The average admitted student greatly exceeds both of these minimum criteria, boasting an undergraduate GPA of 3.28 and a GMAT score of approximately 518. In the second review stage, candidates who fail to meet the minimum requirements are reviewed indi-vidually by a faculty committee, which considers the quality of the applicant's under-graduate curriculum and program, evidence of business skills, work experience, and writing sample. The faculty committee admits those who, in its estimation, demonstrate the promise to succeed in the program. International applicants must submit official TOEFL score reports and provide proof of financial means to support themselves while enrolled in the program.

### FINANCIAL FACTS

| | |
|---|---|
| Annual tuition (in-state/out-of-state) | $2,400/$4,800 |
| Fees | $629 |
| Books and supplies | $1,000 |
| Room & board (on-campus) | $7,000 |
| % of students receiving aid | 34 |
| % of first-year students receiving aid | 4 |
| % of students receiving loans | 20 |
| % of students receiving grants | 6 |
| Average award package | $9,062 |
| Average grant | $3,694 |
| Average student loan debt | $18,793 |

### ADMISSIONS

| | |
|---|---|
| Admissions Selectivity Rating | 75 |
| # of applications received | 210 |
| % applicants accepted | 68 |
| % acceptees attending | 77 |
| Average GMAT | 518 |
| Range of GMAT | 440–570 |
| Average GPA | 3.28 |
| TOEFL required of international students? | yes |
| Minimum TOEFL (paper/computer) | 550/213 |
| Application fee | $30 |
| Regular application deadline | rolling |
| Regular notification | rolling |
| Deferment available? | yes |
| Maximum length of deferment | 1 year |
| Transfer students accepted? | yes |
| Transfer application policy Students must transfer from an accredited school; up to 9 credit hours transferable. | |
| Non-fall admissions? | yes |
| Need-blind admissions? | yes |

### APPLICANTS ALSO LOOK AT

Saint Louis University, University of Missouri—St. Louis, Washington University in St. Louis

# SOUTHERN METHODIST UNIVERSITY
## COX SCHOOL OF BUSINESS

### GENERAL INFORMATION
| | |
|---|---|
| Type of school | private |
| Environment | town |
| Academic calendar | mod/semester |

### SURVEY SAYS...
Students love Dallas, TX
*Solid preparation in:*
Communication/interpersonal skills
Presentation skills

### STUDENTS
| | |
|---|---|
| Enrollment of parent institution | 11,000 |
| % male/female | 64/36 |
| % out-of-state | 49 |
| % minorities | 18 |
| % international | 37 |
| Average age at entry | 28 |
| Average years work experience at entry | 4.2 |

### ACADEMICS
| | |
|---|---|
| **Academic Experience Rating** | **92** |
| Student/faculty ratio | 12:1 |
| Profs interesting rating | 96 |
| Profs accessible rating | 98 |
| % female faculty | 19 |
| % minority faculty | 10 |

### JOINT DEGREES
JD/MBA, 4 years; MBA/MA in Arts
Administration, 2 years

### PROMINENT ALUMNI
Thomas W. Horton, EVP Finance
and Planning and CFO, AMR
Corporation; Thaddeus F. Arroyo,
CIO, Cingular Wireless; Ruth Ann
Marshall, President of the Americas,
MasterCard Intl.; James
MacNaughton, Managing Director,
Rothschild, Inc.; C. Fred Ball, Chair
& CEO, Bank of Texas

## Academics

For students looking for a prime school education combined with more than a dash of southern hospitality, there may be no better place than the Edwin L. Cox School of Business at Southern Methodist University. Located in the Dallas/Fort Worth area, the school certainly benefits from Dallas's reputation as one of the "Best Cities for Business" (according to *Fortune* magazine). Though it's a businessperson's paradise, students say Cox is not as straight-laced as you might expect. Students describe their school as "friendly, laid-back, and enjoyable." And, they add, "Environment is emphasized more than the academics, so its students don't have sharp elbows like at other large schools." The administration is "outstanding. Everyone in the admissions department is very accessible. They basically carry you through the entire process. The dean has an open-door policy as well."

Each term of the two years is divided into two modules (called A and B). Each of these consists of an eight-week-long, two-hour-credit course. Students appreciate the module system for the amount of information that's crammed in and the "greater flexibility to customize an MBA experience." However, students confess to sometimes being a bit "overwhelmed." As in most b-schools, the first year is comprised almost entirely of general knowledge style classes like accounting, economics, statistics, finance, marketing, organization behavior, operations, and team-interaction skills. The second year, however, is designed to allow students to really focus on their own professional goals. To that end, a wide range of electives is offered. But it's neither the core courses nor the range of electives that sets Cox apart. Though students say that "Cox made its name with finance, but the marketing faculty is rock-solid in everything from research and analytics to marketing communications," it's the international focus of the program that garners the most attention. In partnership with American Airlines, Cox developed a Global Leadership Program in 2000 in which all students participate. In this program, students begin their first semester with a "comprehensive study of the culture, politics, and business of [their] region of choice." Cox is also notable for its mentoring program, in which every student is paired with a mentor—"business leaders representing every major industry and many of the most prominent companies in the Dallas/Fort Worth metroplex"—each of whom provides students with "the business contacts, career advice, and industry insight that only experienced professionals can offer." For a school located so close to the "telecom corridor," however, Cox seems to be somewhat lacking in technology. Students "wish the school had more emphasis on high tech." Others point out that "if Cox concentrated a little more on building better [high tech] connections, starting salaries would improve significantly."

## Career and Placement

As is the case with so many b-school programs, recruiting and placement can often be focused on the region in which the school resides. Cox is no exception. Luckily for students at SMU, Dallas's economy is strong, and top businesses abound. Students say the "alumni network is the greatest advantage—especially if you want to work in Dallas. The school does a tremendous job of putting us in front of alumni." In addition, "prestigious business leaders serve on the Cox board and are very willing to help students." For most students, this is a plus. Some, however, would like to see the "geographic diversity of the companies that recruit on-campus" increase. Others point out that for those with interests in nontraditional business fields, career placement can be difficult. One student seeking a change comments, "Our career center is mostly devoted to the traditional Dallas economy drivers (oil, banks, real estate, Frito-Lay). I would like to see some companies that stray outside these fields onto more unconventional ground."

PATTI CUDNEY, DIRECTOR, MBA ADMISSIONS
PO BOX 750333, DALLAS, TX 75275 UNITED STATES
PHONE: 214-768-1214 • FAX: 214-768-3956
E-MAIL: MBAINFO@MAIL.COX.SMU.EDU • WEBSITE: WWW.COXMBA.COM

Students say that although "career management is still building itself up from two very slow years, the new office of corporate relations has done an amazing job of pulling in new companies this year to recruit." Among the many companies that recruit on the Cox campus are AT&T, Citigroup/CitiFinancial, Coca-Cola, the ExxonMobil Corporation, Morgan Stanley, American Airlines, Sabre Holdings, and Wells Fargo.

## Student Life and Environment

With such an emphasis on international business, it's no surprise that on any given day, students at Cox might encounter students who speak Bengali, Japanese, Italian, Spanish, Hebrew, Punjabi, Bulgarian, Russian, French, Tagalog, or Urdu, just to name a few. Add this international feel to the fact that Cox School of Business is located in "a residential area" between Dallas's downtown and the North Texas telecom corridor, and it is obvious that cultural opportunities abound. With dozens of museums, theaters, shopping centers, and sports venues at their fingertips, Cox students are rarely bored (not that they'd have time to be). One student says, "The school is a very vibrant place to be. There are more opportunities than time available to take advantage of them. Some event is always taking place on the arts and culture front." And like most schools, students have the opportunity to socialize and network at weekly happy hours. "We're a little crazy with the intramural sports, too. Rugby, soccer, volleyball—there's always a turn-out. And the SMU football games are marked with campus-wide festivities that crowd the grass areas. (Our dean provides free beer, which has made him very popular.)"

Facilities are somewhat lacking, as the MBAs still find themselves cheek-by-jowl with undergraduates, but, for the most part, students can expect a "very social atmosphere, [in an exciting area, and a] close-knit community of full-time students."

## Admissions

Cox admissions officers seek to create a qualified and diverse student body. In doing this, they put together a class that is 37 percent international students, 36 percent female, and 18 percent minority students. The average GMAT is 644, and the average GPA is 3.25. Average work experience was around five years, and the undergraduate degrees were mostly in business and engineering, but also included a surprisingly large number of social sciences. Cox is committed to making private education affordable, and for that reason, 75 percent of the most recent group of MBAs received some form of a scholarship. Scholarships range from as little as 10 percent of tuition to as much as 100 percent, but it's best to apply early to snatch these opportunities up.

## FINANCIAL FACTS

| | |
|---|---|
| Annual tuition | $30,255 |
| Fees | $3,034 |
| Books and supplies | $2,000 |
| Room & board | $10,000 |
| % of students receiving grants | 73 |
| Average grant | $18,000 |

## ADMISSIONS

| | |
|---|---|
| Admissions Selectivity Rating | 87 |
| # of applications received | 318 |
| % applicants accepted | 57 |
| % acceptees attending | 42 |
| Average GMAT | 644 |
| Range of GMAT | 570–720 |
| Average GPA | 3.25 |
| TOEFL required of international students? | yes |
| Minimum TOEFL (paper/computer) | 600/250 |
| Application fee | $75 |
| International application fee | $75 |
| Regular application deadline | 4/30 |
| Regular notification | 6/15 |
| Application deadline/notification | |
| Round 1: | 11/30 / 1/30 |
| Round 2: | 1/30 / 3/30 |
| Round 3: | 3/15 / 5/15 |
| Round 4: | 4/30 / 6/15 |
| Early decision program? | yes |
| ED Deadline/notification | 11/30 / 1/30 |
| Deferment available? | yes |
| Maximum length of deferment | 1 year |
| Need-blind admissions? | yes |

## APPLICANTS ALSO LOOK AT

Arizona State University, Rice University, Texas Christian University (TCU), The University of Texas at Austin, University of Arizona, Vanderbilt University, Washington University

## EMPLOYMENT PROFILE

| Career Rating | 91 | Grads employed by field: | % | avg. salary: |
|---|---|---|---|---|
| Primary source of full-time job acceptances | | Finance | 52 | $76,500 |
| | | Human Resources | 2 | NR |
| School-facilitated activities | 39 (61%) | Marketing | 22 | $77,028 |
| Graduate-facilitated activities | 25 (39%) | MIS | 2 | NR |
| | | Operations | 5 | $71,166 |
| Average starting salary | $77,979 | Consulting | 8 | $97,000 |
| Percent employed | 90 | General Management | 6 | $78,333 |
| | | Other | 3 | NR |

# ST. JOHN'S UNIVERSITY
## PETER J. TOBIN COLLEGE OF BUSINESS

## Academics

"New York City is the financial capital of the world," one MBA student at St. John's Tobin College of Business correctly observes, "and SJU's proximity to the city is one of its greatest strengths." Indeed, Tobin offers three location options to students seeking an MBA at New York, the university's main campus in Jamaica, Queens; a small campus in the financial district of Manhattan (the focus here is primarily on risk management, insurance, and financial services); and another small campus on Staten Island (most courses here are in accounting-related fields). A fourth campus gives students yet another fabulously urban option: Rome, Italy, where international business and finance are in the spotlight.

Access to New York means access to great faculty, and MBAs at Tobin tell us that St. John's has recruited a solid core of teachers. "Most of my accounting/tax professors have graduated from prestigious law schools and have had successful careers. Learning from them has been a huge benefit," writes one accounting student. Students also praise the faculty in insurance and marketing. MBAs here appreciate the fact that "New York City is known throughout the world as a financial hub. This can provide many opportunities for employment, or even education experiences for students."

Students love how Tobin "is currently updating curriculum, constantly improving teaching methods, implementing new technology, and hiring new professors educated in the academic and professional fields. The result is a positive and worthwhile experience." The program "places a lot of emphasis on team-building and presentation skills," which students find useful. One writes, "Most classes are presented, in full or in part, as seminars, requiring students to work in groups and presenting to the class. These activities are helpful in developing needed skills." Students also approve of "the strong emphasis the school places on ethics in business practice." The administration scores high marks in the helpfulness department. Asked where SJU needs an upgrade, students suggest that Tobin "could further improve by continuing the technology program currently being undertaken to encompass the entire campus, with emphasis on including wireless capabilities in lecture halls and on laptop computers in standard course procedures for the MBA program." Some even feel that "the emphasis on technology within the program will allow SJU to propel the MBA program years ahead of other comparable universities."

## Career and Placement

The Career Center at St. John's University provides placement and counseling services for Tobin MBAs as well as for all other students of the university. Students remind us that St. John's location is a great boon to their career searches. Being in New York provides "great networking opportunities with companies long before you start working through clubs and departmental events."

Employers most likely to hire Tobin MBAs include Accenture, American Express, Citi Group, City of New York, JPMorgan Chase, Merrill Lynch, and Revlon.

SHEILA RUSSELL, ASSISTANT DIRECTOR OF MBA ADMISSIONS
8000 UTOPIA PARKWAY, 111 BENT HALL, QUEENS, NY 11439 UNITED STATES
PHONE: 718-990-1345 • FAX: 718-990-5242
E-MAIL: MBAADMISSIONS@STJOHNS.EDU • WEBSITE: WWW.STJOHNS.EDU / TOBINCOLLEGE

## Student Life and Environment

The Tobin MBA program "is mostly designed for those who work during the day, so classes are only offered at night." One full-time student writes, "The schedule took some getting used to, but once I got used to it, I began to appreciate it, as I can spend my days studying and doing research for my graduate assistant program." Full-timers are otherwise "very active and very proactive on campus. Within the past year, many students have combined their efforts to implement clubs and activities that provide networking opportunities, academic opportunities, and social gatherings." Even the campus itself "is an active one. Due to the NYC area and the fast-paced environment, the campus is always fluttering with excitement, from sports events to guest lectures by individuals such as Spike Lee and Cornell West." The majority of MBA students, however, experience little of this excitement; they're here as part-timers who come to campus for class, then leave. One MBA Explains, "Unfortunately, my work and school schedule do not provide me with many opportunities to participate in campus activities. I attend St. John's on a part-time basis while working full-time."

One look at the student body here tells you that Tobin is "a real New Yorker school" with "type-A MBA students in abundance,"—and they wouldn't have it any other way. "Their aims are clear, their motivations are apparent, their goals are attainable, and their willingness to increase the level of competition in the program produces professionals uniquely qualified and highly valued in their particular professional fields," explains one student. With its main campus in Queens, Tobin needn't look far to attract an international student body; one of the world's most international populations lives within a 10-mile radius of the school. Students "come from different countries and bring their business experience to the table." One student comments, "It has also been a pleasure meeting such a diverse group of students and having the opportunity to study and prepare group projects with them while surrounded by the energetic city of New York."

## Admissions

Tobin requires all applicants to provide the admissions with: official transcripts for all undergraduate, graduate, and professional school academic work attempted; an official GMAT score report for an exam taken within the last five years; letters of recommendation; a personal statement; and a resume. Students whose native language is not English must also submit an official TOEFL score report. Work experience is not required for admission to the program, although it is preferred. Informal on-campus interviews are available for prospective students but are not required, except in special cases.

### FINANCIAL FACTS

| | |
|---|---|
| Annual tuition | $20,750 |
| Fees | $250 |
| Books and supplies | $3,000 |
| Room & board (on/off-campus) | $12,000/$15,000 |
| % of students receiving aid | 30 |
| % of first-year students receiving aid | 14 |
| Average award package | $14,914 |
| Average grant | $1,812 |

### ADMISSIONS

| | |
|---|---|
| Admissions Selectivity Rating | 74 |
| # of applications received | 604 |
| % applicants accepted | 69 |
| % acceptees attending | 61 |
| Average GMAT | 530 |
| Range of GMAT | 440–630 |
| Average GPA | 3.2 |
| TOEFL required of international students? | yes |
| Minimum TOEFL (paper/computer) | 580/NR |
| Application fee | $40 |
| International application fee | $40 |
| Regular application deadline | 6/1 |
| Regular notification | rolling |
| Deferment available? | yes |
| Maximum length of deferment | 1 year |
| Transfer students accepted? | yes |
| Transfer application policy Must use regular application. Individual review of transfer credits. | |
| Non-fall admissions? | yes |
| Need-blind admissions? | yes |

### APPLICANTS ALSO LOOK AT

Baruch College/City University of New York, Fordham University, Hofstra University, New York University, Pace University

### EMPLOYMENT PROFILE

| | |
|---|---|
| Career Rating | 86 |
| Average starting salary | $68,000 |

# ST. MARY'S UNIVERSITY
## BILL GREEHEY SCHOOL OF BUSINESS

## GENERAL INFORMATION

| | |
|---|---|
| Type of school | private |
| Affiliation | Roman Catholic |
| Environment | metropolis |
| Academic calendar | semester |

### SURVEY SAYS...
Students love San Antonio, TX
Friendly students
Happy students
*Solid preparation in:*
Teamwork

### STUDENTS

| | |
|---|---|
| Enrollment of parent institution | 3,925 |
| Enrollment of business school | 121 |
| % part-time | 100 |
| Average age at entry | 29 |
| Average years work experience at entry | 3 |

### ACADEMICS

| | |
|---|---|
| **Academic Experience Rating** | **70** |
| Student/faculty ratio | 10:1 |
| Profs interesting rating | 79 |
| Profs accessible rating | 74 |
| % female faculty | 36 |
| % minority faculty | 4 |

### JOINT DEGREES
JD/MBA, 108 hours

### PROMINENT ALUMNI
Bill Greehey, CEO, Valero Energy

## Academics

There are big days ahead for the MBA program at St. Mary's University. Thanks to a $25 million donation from Valero Energy chairman Bill Greehey, the university has planned major upgrades to the faculty, curriculum, and student scholarship support in the business school. The school of business—renamed in Greehey's honor in March of 2006—is one of the major beneficiary of the local philanthropist's largesse. Whatever improvements are made will only add to some already commendable assets here, including "a unique international entrepreneurship program" a "solid financial planning curriculum," and a professional accounting curriculum.

Prerequisites to MBA study at Greehey begin with the completion of six undergraduate-level fundamentals courses. Students arriving with undergraduate degrees in business can place out of these courses, as can students who demonstrate proficiency through CLEP and DANTES examinations. After completing or placing out of these fundamentals courses, students must complete a 30 semester-hour program that includes five core courses (in human resources, accounting/finance, international business, informational technology, and marketing). Tracks are offered in financial planning, professional accountancy and general management as well as a joint JD/MBA. (Note that the financial planning concentration requires two additional classes, meaning that students who choose this option must complete 36 semester hours to graduate.) All students must pass a written examination at the end of the program.

MBAs here praise the faculty for "focusing on teaching and understanding" and "providing real-life experience. They bring a lot of outside experience to the classroom." St. Mary's has always been known for its personal touches, and students confirm that "classes are small and the program as a whole is small. This allows for a lot of individual attention from professors and administrators." Students here appreciate this "laid back program with not too much pressure" but wish that the administration was sometimes a little less laid back. They tell us that administrators "are very disorganized. They lose papers way too often."

## Career and Placement

The Career Services Center at St. Mary's University serves all undergraduate students, graduate students, and alumni of the school. The office provides one-on-one advisement with career counselors, a library of career-related materials including hard-copy and online job search databases, special events (Resume Drive, Business Etiquette Dinner, Mock Interview Day), a career fair, and connections to an alumni mentoring program. Students tell us that "the strong alumni network" is one of the biggest attractions of a St. Mary's degree. Employers interviewing on the St. Mary's campus in the spring of 2006 included BNSF Railway; Fisher, Herbst, & Kemble; USAA; Valero Energy; and Walgreens.

Dr. Richard Menger, MBA Program Director
One Camino Santa Maria, San Antonio, TX 78228-8507 United States
Phone: 210-436-3101 • Fax: 210-431-2220 • E-mail: LBAGLEY@STMARYTX.EDU
Website: WWW.STMARYTX.EDU/BUSINESS

## Student Life and Environment

St. Mary's student body includes "many Hispanic women working toward improving their careers." The school has traditionally served the Hispanic community well; over half of all undergraduates here are Hispanic. On the whole, students "are diverse in age and cultures, all striving toward a common goal." Many "have careers and a family." Their classmates describe them as "team-oriented, hard-working, and friendly."

With over one million residents within city limits and almost as many living in the metropolitan area, San Antonio is the third-largest city in Texas and one of the larger cities in the country. The military and the petroleum industry both have major presences here. With nearly 20 million visitors every year, San Antonio is also a major player in the nation's tourism trade. Students speak highly of the city, although they warn that "the school is located in a very rough part of town."

## Admissions

Applicants to the MBA program at St. Mary's must apply to the graduate school for admission. Applications are reviewed by the MBA program director, who makes recommendations to the Graduate Council. The council is then responsible for the final admissions decisions. Candidates must submit all of the following materials to the graduate admissions office: a completed application form; an official score report for the GMAT; two sets of official transcripts for all postsecondary academic work; two letters of recommendation "from individuals well acquainted with your academic/professional ability" (graduates of St. Mary's University are exempt from this requirement); and a completed health form (required by Texas State Law). An interview may also be required; candidates for whom an interview is required will be notified by the school. International applicants must provide all of the above materials as well as a signed financial statement; and, an official score report for the TOEFL (minimum acceptable score: 570 paper-based, 230 computer-based, 67 internet; students with lower TOEFL scores may be allowed to attend the English Language School in order to meet minimum language proficiency requirements). Admitted students may receive regular admission, which is unconditional. Students may also receive conditional admission, which allows them to enroll in no more than nine hours of classes, after which their admission status is reappraised; or they may receive special admission as a nondegree seeking student. They may also receive auditor status, which is a noncredit option for students who are not working toward a graduate business degree.

### FINANCIAL FACTS

| | |
|---|---|
| Room & board | |
| (on/off-campus) | $6,000/$7,500 |

### ADMISSIONS

| | |
|---|---|
| **Admissions Selectivity Rating** | **74** |
| # of applications received | 62 |
| % applicants accepted | 61 |
| % acceptees attending | 95 |
| Average GMAT | 481 |
| Range of GMAT | 390–672 |
| Average GPA | 3.1 |
| TOEFL required of | |
| international students? | yes |
| Minimum TOEFL | |
| (paper/computer) | 570/230 |
| Application fee | $30 |
| International application fee | $30 |
| Regular application deadline | rolling |
| Regular notification | rolling |
| Deferment available? | yes |
| Maximum length | |
| of deferment | 1 year |
| Transfer students accepted? | yes |
| Transfer application policy | |
| On recommendation of the graduate program director, school may accept a maximum of 6 semester hours from AACSB-accredited programs. | |
| Non-fall admissions? | yes |
| Need-blind admissions? | yes |

### APPLICANTS ALSO LOOK AT

The University of Texas at San Antonio

| EMPLOYMENT PROFILE | |
|---|---|
| **Career Rating** | **69** |
| Average starting salary | $55,767 |

# STANFORD UNIVERSITY
## STANFORD GRADUATE SCHOOL OF BUSINESS

## Academics

It's the company you'll keep at Stanford Graduate School of Business (GSB) that ultimately distinguishes a Stanford MBA from all but a few other elite programs. First there's the faculty, who "are brilliant. Most are world leaders in their fields." One student notes, "I am amazed at how accomplished my professors are in the non-academic world. For example, my entrepreneurship professor this quarter founded a large cable company and now owns the Boston Celtics! Other professors hold similar experiences; better still, all hold a true zest for teaching." Then there are the visiting lecturers, who include "frequent luminaries such as top CEOs. Three winners of the Nobel Prize for economics gave separate guest lectures in the same week not too long ago." Finally, there are your classmates, whom students describe as "amazingly accomplished." One MBA observes, "The admissions office takes great care to bring in the right students, not just the students with the highest test scores and grades—the director said he didn't accept one 800 GMAT for the Class of 2005."

Students tell us that Stanford excels in large part because of its location. One student explains, "While the school itself is phenomenal, I don't think it would be possible if it were in any other place. The location in the Silicon Valley gives us instant access to an amazing group of entrepreneurs, so our school is consequently very entrepreneurial. There are always some great ideas floating around here." Among top programs, Stanford is relatively small, which students describe as "both a strength and a weakness." One student writes, "I'm sure that Harvard Business School or Wharton are better-run academic machines, but Stanford does have a small-school feel that is quite nice. You do get the sense that if everyone wasn't pulling an oar, the school would break down." Another student adds, "The class offering is not as deep as some other schools (I was a Wharton undergrad, so I have some basis for comparison), but the classes that are taught are excellent."

That's because a "relentless pursuit of best teaching methods and material" and a "level of subject matter that is both intellectually challenging and strong enough for practical application when we leave" ensure that students are constantly testing their limits. One MBA reports, "The emphasis here is on learning, not grades. We are encouraged to take risks, even at the risk of failure—because this is when the deepest learning occurs." In order to encourage risk-taking, Stanford neither posts grades publicly nor includes class rank in students' transcripts. Students add, "Our collaborative culture frees you from focusing on grades and enables you to take academic risks and broaden your general management skills."

## Career and Placement

The Career Management Center at Stanford doesn't have to do a whole lot; companies come looking for Stanford MBAs without much prompting. According to students, the office does a fine job of providing the standard complement of career services including personal counseling, self-assessment exercises, workshops, seminars, networking events, lectures and presentation, online job posting, and alumni events. Students agree that Stanford has "a strong alumni network where you can get help when needed."

Major employers of Stanford MBAs include Bain and Company; McKinsey & Co.; The Boston Consulting Group; Lehman Brothers; Yahoo!; Gap Inc.; Morgan Stanley; Google; Amazon; Eli Lilly; General Mills; Goldman Sachs. Last year, Stanford MBAs dispersed across the globe to take their first post-degree jobs; half remained on the Pacific coast, one in five headed to the Northeast, and one in seven found work outside the United States.

DERRICK BOLTON, DIRECTOR OF MBA ADMISSIONS
518 MEMORIAL WAY, STANFORD, CA 94305-5015 UNITED STATES
PHONE: 650-723-2766 • FAX: 650-725-7831
E-MAIL: WWW.GSB.STANDFORD.EDU/MBA/CONTACT/ASK.QUESTION.HTML • WEBSITE: WWW.GSB.STANFORD.EDU

## Student Life and Environment

"There is an amazing balance of hard work and enjoyment" at Stanford, whose idyllic setting is praised by one and all. With "an amazingly beautiful campus, one of the best golf courses in the country, [and] a sunny climate that definitely makes people happier than gray skies, [Stanford] in many ways feels like a country club, but without the negative connotation. People play hard here, but they also work hard." Stanford is also a "great environment for families with children. You can rollerblade with your family every Sunday morning, bike to school everyday, have lunch at the Stanford museum. It's simply amazing!"

The Stanford campus is constantly abuzz with activity; students report that "there's tons of stuff going on all the time. We are often hard-pressed to choose between talks, visits, trips, and other academic and social events. It is not uncommon for me to have to choose between three different brown-bag lunch events every day or every other day." One MBA explains, "The GSB is more than simply a business school; it is an experience. There are no boundaries between classroom and everyday, real-life learning. The most difficult thing I find here is choosing amongst so many extraordinary opportunities and focusing on only a few. It is easy to overextend yourself, when learning to achieve life balance and prioritize one's time is a critical centerpiece of living a high-impact, successful life."

Hometown Palo Alto "can be somewhat boring, [but] the small-town atmosphere makes people bond more, especially since it is such a small class." Students note, "We're just 30 minutes from San Francisco and 20 minutes from San Jose, so we get the best of both areas. The Bay Area has so much to offer that you will never be bored."

## Admissions

Admissions are highly competitive at Stanford GSB. The admissions office sets no minimum standards for work experience, GMAT score, or GPA, but don't let that fool you; only exceptional candidates receive the precious invite to attend. The school reports that it is most interested in "a unique combination of high leadership potential, academic excellence, and individual background and interests." The school also seeks students who "contribute to a diverse community, because we believe that all students learn invaluable lessons from sharing experiences and perspectives with classmates from many different backgrounds." Applicants must provide the school with GMAT scores, TOEFL scores (if applicable), undergraduate and graduate transcripts, letters of reference, two essays, and a resume.

### FINANCIAL FACTS

| | |
|---|---|
| Annual tuition | $43,380 |
| Average student loan debt | $72,535 |

### ADMISSIONS

| | |
|---|---|
| Admissions Selectivity Rating | 99 |
| # of applications received | 4,582 |
| % applicants accepted | 11 |
| % acceptees attending | 76 |
| Average GMAT | 712 |
| Average GPA | 3.56 |
| TOEFL required of international students? | yes |
| Minimum TOEFL (paper/computer) | 600/250 |
| Application fee | $235 |
| International application fee | $235 |
| Deferment available? | yes |
| Maximum length of deferment | very limited |
| Need-blind admissions? | yes |

### APPLICANTS ALSO LOOK AT

Harvard University

### EMPLOYMENT PROFILE

| Career Rating | 99 | Grads employed by field: | % | avg. salary: |
|---|---|---|---|---|
| Average starting salary | $104,917 | Finance | 31 | $115,269 |
| | | Marketing | 28 | $96,193 |
| | | Operations | 3 | $79,444 |
| | | Strategic Planning | 4 | $106,300 |
| | | Consulting | 20 | $108,263 |
| | | General Management | 10 | $102,947 |
| | | Venture Capital | 2 | $134,000 |
| | | Other | 2 | $102,000 |

# STATE UNIVERSITY OF NEW YORK AT ALBANY
## SCHOOL OF BUSINESS

## Academics

Students in the MBA programs at State University of New York at Albany School of Business love that the school "constantly updates the curriculum to mirror current business trends." In its full-time and various part-time programs, Albany uses "a combination of classroom instruction and applied experience" to prepare students for the business world of tomorrow.

About one in four MBA students at Albany attend the program full-time. This number includes the majority of international students, who account for approximately 20 percent of the student body. The full-time program takes two years to complete. The first year is dedicated to core competencies; students undertake in-depth study in accounting, economics, finance, human resources, information systems, and marketing. Case studies play a central role in classroom study, as do reading assignments and classes that divide time between lectures and discussions. Group projects supplement the curriculum and offer students opportunities to develop important teamwork skills. The first year culminates in a five-week integrative course that addresses social, legal, and political issues in international business. According to students, the first-year curriculum "is heavily weighted toward global business and the changing economy."

The second year of the full-time program—which also allows students to develop an area of specialization—focuses on technology, an area in which Albany excels. Students praise the school's "cutting-edge use of technology and IT knowledge" and note that "everyone learns IT here." Students' work in this area reaches its high point in an information systems-based field project during which students provide consulting services to such organizations as the Albany Medical Center, Dupont, GE, KeyCorp, PepsiCo, Tiffany & Co., Towers Perrin, and a variety of regional nonprofits. The field project consumes one-third of the second-year curriculum; the second year concludes with a capstone integrative course.

Albany also offers several part-time options. In the Evening MBA Program, classes convene once a week in three-hour sessions. The program is "extremely flexible" and allows students to enter during the Fall, Spring, or Summer semester. Evening MBA program students may use elective classes to develop a specialization in management information systems, management, marketing, finance, new venture development, or tax. A Weekend MBA Program is also available; its classes meet every other weekend, with classes held on Friday afternoons and all day Saturday. It now also includes a one-week international business experience. This program meets off campus at a satellite facility in Saratoga. Students may enter the program in the fall only, and enrollment is limited to 24 students per year.

## Career and Placement

Albany's School of Business maintains its own Career Services Office, whose work is supplemented by the school's Career Development Center, which serves the entire university. The Career Services Office provides workshops on cover letter writing, resume writing, interviewing, developing job-search skills, and honing business-related social skills. MBAs who graduate from Albany receive job offers from many small and medium-sized businesses as well as from such business giants as Accenture, Bear Stearns, Deloitte, Deutsche Bank, Ernst and Young, Goldman Sachs, IBM, KPMG, Merrill Lynch, and PricewaterhouseCoopers. Results from a recent survey indicate that MBAs typically receive initial offers in the $60,000 range.

ZINA LAWRENCE, DIRECTOR, GRADUATE STUDENT SERVICES
1400 WASHINGTON AVENUE, BA 361 ALBANY, NY 12222 UNITED STATES
PHONE: 518-442-4961 • FAX: 518-442-4975 • E-MAIL: BUSWEB@ALBANY.EDU
WEBSITE: WWW.ALBANY.EDU / BUSINESS

## Student Life and Environment

Most students in the Albany MBA program attend part-time; they have little time to devote to extracurricular life because of their commitments to coursework, careers, and family. The program attracts "many area IT professionals and their coworkers," but the student body is fairly diverse, with participants "from many different fields, industries, career levels, and cultural backgrounds." Students tell us that "it is a wonderful experience to be in a classroom with people that have very diversified backgrounds."

Nearly 17,000 students are enrolled in the nine degree-granting schools and colleges at the State University of New York at Albany. Like all large state universities, it pursues the mission of offering an affordable education to state residents while also providing the state and country with cutting-edge research. The university was founded in 1844; undergraduate business study was not added to the curriculum until 1970. Graduate business programs began a few years later. Facilities include classrooms and computer labs equipped with the latest high-tech accoutrements; these serve the program's focus on technology well. Students appreciate the facilities but note that "the campus buildings should be spruced up a bit. The buildings are old and unattractive."

## Admissions

Applicants to the MBA program at the State University of New York at Albany School of Business must provide the graduate admissions department with all of the following: official copies of transcripts for all postsecondary academic work, an official score report for the GMAT, a resume, three letters of recommendation, and a personal statement of purpose. International applicants must provide all of the above plus an official score report for the TOEFL (minimum acceptable score: 600 paper-based; 250 computer-based); and a financial affidavit accompanied by appropriate supporting documentation to demonstrate the applicant's "ability to meet all educational and living expenses for the entire period of intended study." Furthermore, international academic transcripts in languages other than English must be accompanied by a certified English translation.

## FINANCIAL FACTS

| | |
|---|---|
| Annual tuition (in-state/out-of-state) | $7,100/$11,340 |
| Fees | $1,028 |
| Books and supplies | $1,000 |
| Room & board (on/off-campus) | $9,000/$7,500 |
| % of students receiving aid | 60 |
| % of first-year students receiving aid | 50 |
| % of students receiving loans | 75 |
| % of students receiving grants | 10 |
| Average award package | $14,200 |
| Average grant | $15,000 |
| Average student loan debt | $20,000 |

## ADMISSIONS

| | |
|---|---|
| Admissions Selectivity Rating | 80 |
| # of applications received | 282 |
| % applicants accepted | 56 |
| % acceptees attending | 73 |
| Average GMAT | 542 |
| Range of GMAT | 450-640 |
| Average GPA | 3.24 |
| TOEFL required of international students? | yes |
| Minimum TOEFL (paper/computer) | 600/250 |
| Application fee | $60 |
| International application fee | $60 |
| Regular application deadline | 4/6 |
| Regular notification | 6/6 |
| Deferment available? | yes |
| Maximum length of deferment | 1 year |
| Transfer students accepted? | yes |
| Transfer application policy Students may transfer up to 6 credits. | |
| Need-blind admissions? | yes |

## APPLICANTS ALSO LOOK AT

State University of New York at Binghamton

## EMPLOYMENT PROFILE

| Career Rating | 74 | Grads employed by field: | % | avg. salary: |
|---|---|---|---|---|
| Primary source of full-time job acceptances | | Finance | 4 | $40,000 |
| | | Human Resources | 26 | $56,500 |
| School-facilitated activities | 70% | MIS | 27 | $52,600 |
| Graduate-facilitated activities | 20% | Consulting | 41 | $63,000 |
| Unknown | 10% | Nonprofit | 2 | $42,000 |
| | | | | |
| Average starting salary | $54,200 | | | |
| Percent employed | 87 | | | |

# STATE UNIVERSITY OF NEW YORK AT BINGHAMTON
## SCHOOL OF MANAGEMENT

## Academics

The School of Management at SUNY Binghamton (Binghamton University to the locals) piggybacks on the university's "world-renowned Center for Leadership Studies" to offer a highly regarded concentration in HRM/consulting and leadership. Finance is another strong area at SOM; the *Journal of Finance* recently ranked the faculty twenty-third out of 330 finance departments in terms of research productivity per faculty member. MBAs here also speak highly of Binghamton's accounting program.

That's not a bad trifecta for a program as small as this one (fewer than 130 MBAs attend, most full-time); the presence of a large research university with a big undergraduate business program certainly helps a lot here. Despite their high profile as research heavy-weights, professors earn praise for being "very approachable. Many prefer to be on a first-name basis with students [and] are available for hours each day and very willing to work with students. They can be flexible with workload if there is a week with an inordinate amount of projects due and/or tests." As at many research-intensive institutions, not all are great teachers. "Most present their ideas clearly, some less so diplomatically," offers one MBA.

Students especially appreciate that "the SOM is constantly trying to improve. That means administrators are open to student suggestions and they support students as much as they can in academics and job searching." One MBA observes, "Everyone, including the Dean and Associate Dean, has an open-door policy." MBAs are less enthusiastic about the pervasiveness of team-based study throughout the curriculum. One student laments, "So many of my international colleagues are dependent on my assistance for understanding the basic information being presented in class that it greatly hampers my ability to learn as an individual."

Despite this drawback, most here feel that this same "diversity (of interests and backgrounds) among students and faculty" is actually one of Binghamton's strengths. Best of all, it's an MBA that can be acquired for the proverbial song. As one student explains, "Considering the price of an MBA here, you get a great education for your money!"

## Career and Placement

Like most small programs, Binghamton lacks a powerhouse Career Development Center; it's simply too hard to attract lots of recruiters to a campus this remote to interview so few MBAs. The office does what it can, offering counseling services, career workshops, resume-development services, resume-referral services, a career-resource library, and access to the alumni network.

Top employers of Binghamton MBAs include Ernst & Young, Estée Lauder, Wal-Mart, Canon, American Express, BAE Systems, State Street Corp., KPMG, and First Capital. About two-thirds of all graduates remain in the Mid-Atlantic states or New England. Approximately one in eight lands a job overseas.

## Student Life and Environment

Binghamton MBAs "focus heavily on academics. One MBA says, "Many of us are teaching as well as pursuing our own degree. For many of us, there is little time for clubs or other activities." Which works out just fine, since there aren't many, anyway. The program is simply too small to sustain much in the way of MBA-specific extracurricular clubs. The university at large, however, is another matter. It's home to "many undergraduate-organized clubs (over 250) that accept any student as a member." One MBA explains, "Because Binghamton has such a large undergraduate population, there are

ALESIA WHEELER-WADE, ASST. DIRECTOR MBA/MS PROGRAM
SCHOOL OF MANAGEMENT, BINGHAMTON, NY 13902 UNITED STATES
PHONE: 607-777-2317 • FAX: 607-777-4872
E-MAIL: SOMADVIS@BINGHAMTON.EDU • WEBSITE: SOM.BINGHAMTON.EDU

clubs for many activities, sports, intellectual interests, and nationalities. If you're out-doorsy, this is a great place to be." So long as you own a raincoat, that is. As one MBA warns, "The weather is very overcast and it rains a lot," making "the town seem worn-down and lethargic."

Indeed, students agree that hometown Binghamton "doesn't have much going on, but it's a quiet, inexpensive place to concentrate on studies. And the graduate student population is large and diverse, providing opportunities to meet people." On another positive note, "The areas surrounding campus are very safe" and the downtown area has "a number of college bars." There's also an "excellent transportation system run by students (grad and undergrad) that specifically targets the off-campus locations where most students live. It also provides jobs for students." For those so inclined, "the athletic facilities on campus are very nice, and very usable to every student."

Binghamton's "enthusiastic, outgoing, very diverse" student body includes a sizable aggregation of international students who "share what they have learned through life experience." Most here "are very studious and competitive," which "fosters an intellectually stimulating environment." They're not cutthroat, however. They "enjoy commiserating with each other over [their] workloads" and when it comes down to it are "more cooperative than competitive, which helps create a friendly learning environment for everyone."

## Admissions

Applicants to the Binghamton MBA program must submit two copies of official undergraduate transcripts for all college work, two letters of recommendation, a personal statement, and GMAT scores. Work experience, while preferred, is not required. Additionally, international students must submit a certified statement of financial responsibility and TOEFL scores (minimum acceptable paper-and-pencil score is 580).

To attract minority applicants, the School of Management offers the Clifford D. Clark Graduate Fellowship Program for Underrepresented Minority Students. According to the school, "These fellowships are granted to students entering both master's and doctoral degree programs and carry stipends of between $6,800 and $12,750 (depending on discipline) for the academic year plus a full-tuition scholarship. Renewals or graduate assistantships may be awarded in subsequent years, depending upon availability of funds.

## FINANCIAL FACTS

| | |
|---|---|
| Annual tuition (in-state/out-of-state) | $7,100/$11,340 |
| Fees (in-state/out-of-state) | $917/$917 |
| Books and supplies | $1,500 |
| Room & board (on/off-campus) | $0/$6,800 |
| % of students receiving aid | 50 |
| % of first-year students receiving aid | 40 |
| % of students receiving loans | 17 |
| % of students receiving grants | 31 |
| Average award package | $8,275 |
| Average grant | $8,275 |
| Average student loan debt | $25,653 |

## ADMISSIONS

| | |
|---|---|
| Admissions Selectivity Rating | 83 |
| # of applications received | 245 |
| % applicants accepted | 58 |
| % acceptees attending | 42 |
| Average GMAT | 602 |
| Range of GMAT | 580–640 |
| Average GPA | 3.28 |
| TOEFL required of international students? | yes |
| Minimum TOEFL (paper/computer) | 580/237 |
| Application fee | $55 |
| International application fee | $55 |
| Regular application deadline | 3/15 |
| Regular notification | rolling |
| Deferment available? | yes |
| Maximum length of deferment | 1 year |
| Need-blind admissions? | yes |

## APPLICANTS ALSO LOOK AT

Albany Law School, City University of New York—Baruch College, Syracuse University

## EMPLOYMENT PROFILE

| Career Rating | 79 | Grads employed by field: | % | avg. salary: |
|---|---|---|---|---|
| Primary source of full-time job acceptances | | Finance | 24 | $55,000 |
| | | Marketing | 24 | $45,000 |
| School-facilitated activities | 6 (32%) | Operations | 24 | $54,102 |
| Graduate-facilitated activities | 13 (63%) | Consulting | 24 | $53,600 |
| | | General Management | 4 | $55,000 |
| Average starting salary | $53,000 | | | |
| Percent employed | 92 | | | |

# STATE UNIVERSITY OF NEW YORK—OSWEGO
## SCHOOL OF BUSINESS

### GENERAL INFORMATION
Type of school                        public
Academic calendar                   semester

### SURVEY SAYS...
Smart classrooms
*Solid preparation in:*
General management
Teamwork Operations
Presentation skills
Computer skills
Doing business in a global economy

### STUDENTS
Enrollment of parent
  institution                          8,282
Enrollment of business school          80
% male/female                          53/47
% part-time                            41
% minorities                           11
% international                        21
Average age at entry                   26
Average years work experience
  at entry                              5

### ACADEMICS
**Academic Experience Rating**         **71**
Student/faculty ratio                  6:1
Profs interesting rating               79
Profs accessible rating                73
% female faculty                       32

## Academics

Students who enroll in the School of Business at SUNY Oswego can expect several things: excellent value for their money, intimate classes, knowledgeable professors, state-of-the-art facilities, and an excellent hockey team. As one student puts it, "in most areas, the school of business is at the top of its class. The classes are challenging and worth-while. Most professors are really good at their areas. They are also widely available to help students both inside and out of class." According to most of the students, the "very small classes promote learning and student-professor interaction."

Designed as a degree in general management, an MBA from SUNY Oswego provides a solid grounding in the basics of modern business organization. The school says that "this program is intended to be equally applicable to private, public, and governmental sectors of management." The core subjects required of students include management, accounting, marketing, organization, law, and finance. In addition, students can choose to specialize in a specific field such as international management, manufacturing management, organizational leadership, or financial services. Core requirements include management information systems, managerial finance, marketing management, management science I, international business, global perspectives on organizational management, and management policy. A wide range of electives is also available to students at SUNY Oswego, including management economics, database development, collective bargaining, industrial and organizational psychology, industrial sociology, principles of forecasting, business research, futures and options markets, database development, project management, public-sector accounting, and advanced auditing.

Students find their course work both rigorous and exciting. As one puts it, "the professors are excellent and the classes are fun and challenging." Another says, "the course load is challenging, requiring solid communication and organization skills. Many professors are conducting research on global trade, accounting, and management science. My academic experience has been very positive. I would suggest Oswego to all prospective business students (undergraduate or graduate)."

## Career and Placement

Although Oswego has a lot to offer—lovely campus, low cost, quality education, intimate program—most students wish it would go further in strengthening its Career Services department. There is little aid specifically for prospective MBAs, and the job search is often directed almost entirely by the student. As one puts it, "Connecting with employers is a difficult task. Linking up with quality employers looking for graduates with postgraduate degrees needs to be addressed."

## Student Life and Environment

Students at SUNY Oswego rave about their "beautiful campus," which, they proudly point out, is also extremely "technologically advanced and mostly wireless." The typical MBA's social life is strong, and there are "plenty of bars around for an active nightlife." As one student says, "At Oswego, I had the opportunity to make new friends from all over the world. The social life is active and I consider myself lucky." For the most part, students claim to be "very active on campus. There is a multitude of clubs and organizations to choose from." Students enjoy their "great gyms to work out in or play a game of racquetball." Plus—as is typical in upstate New York—the school's athletic life centers on their "excellent hockey team, instead of football." As one student puts it, "what's excellent about living on campus here is that there is every resource that you could possibly need available on campus. There are new buildings and renovations, from a new student center to the newly renovated freshman residence hall and new business center with technology classrooms."

## Admissions

To be considered for admission to the small MBA program at the School of Business at SUNY Oswego, a candidate must have a minimum GPA of 2.6 out of 4.0. The minimum required score for the GMAT is 450, unless the applicant's native language is not English, in which case the minimum score is 400. Taking the TOEFL test is also required for students whose native language is not English.

### FINANCIAL FACTS

| | |
|---|---|
| Annual tuition (in-state/out-of-state) | $7,100/$11,340 |
| Fees | $696 |
| Books and supplies | $800 |
| Room & board | $8,340 |
| % of students receiving aid | 62 |
| % of first-year students receiving aid | 65 |
| % of students receiving loans | 62 |
| % of students receiving grants | 26 |
| Average award package | $16,091 |
| Average grant | $302 |
| Average student loan debt | $26,869 |

### ADMISSIONS

| | |
|---|---|
| Admissions Selectivity Rating | 65 |
| # of applications received | 72 |
| % applicants accepted | 86 |
| % acceptees attending | 58 |
| Average GMAT | 500 |
| Range of GMAT | 350–650 |
| Average GPA | 3.28 |
| TOEFL required of international students? | yes |
| Minimum TOEFL (paper/computer) | 550/213 |
| Application fee | $50 |
| Regular application deadline | 4/1 |
| Regular notification | 6/1 |
| Deferment available? | yes |
| Maximum length of deferment | 1 year |
| Transfer students accepted? | yes |
| Transfer application policy 2 classes may be transferred into the program. | |
| Non-fall admissions? | yes |
| Need-blind admissions? | yes |

### APPLICANTS ALSO LOOK AT

Albany Law School, TEST, The State University of New York

### EMPLOYMENT PROFILE

| Career Rating | 65 | Grads employed by field: | % | avg. salary: |
|---|---|---|---|---|
| Average starting salary | $38,000 | Accounting | 50 | $39,000 |
| | | Finance | 10 | $38,000 |
| | | Human Resources | 5 | NR |
| | | MIS | 5 | NR |
| | | Operations | 10 | NR |
| | | General Management | 5 | NR |
| | | Quantitative | 5 | NR |
| | | Nonprofit | 10 | NR |

# STATE UNIVERSITY OF NEW YORK—UNIVERSITY AT BUFFALO
## SCHOOL OF MANAGEMENT

## GENERAL INFORMATION
| | |
|---|---|
| Type of school | public |
| Environment | metropolis |
| Academic calendar | semester |

## SURVEY SAYS...
Friendly students
Smart classrooms
*Solid preparation in:*
Teamwork
Communication/interpersonal skills
Computer skills

## STUDENTS
| | |
|---|---|
| Enrollment of parent institution | 27,200 |
| Enrollment of business school | 443 |
| % male/female | 65/35 |
| % out-of-state | 45 |
| % part-time | 37 |
| % minorities | 8 |
| % international | 35 |
| Average age at entry | 25 |
| Average years work experience at entry | 2.4 |

## ACADEMICS
| | |
|---|---|
| **Academic Experience Rating** | **78** |
| Student/faculty ratio | 9:1 |
| Profs interesting rating | 64 |
| Profs accessible rating | 72 |
| % female faculty | 20 |
| % minority faculty | 30 |

## JOINT DEGREES
JD/MBA; MD/MBA;
Architecture/MBA; Pharmacy/MBA;
Geography/MBA; BS/MBA Business
or Engineering; MBA/MSW;
AuD/MBA; MBA/MPH

## PROMINENT ALUMNI
Harold Kutner, VP of Worldwide
Purchasing, GM; Jeremy Jacobs Sr.,
CEO, Delaware North Cos.; Robert
Rich Sr., Chair & Founder, Rich
Products; David Gasiewicz, General
Manager, Microsoft

## Academics

Students look at the bottom line and like what they see at University of Buffalo School of Management. As one student explains, "The sheer cost of an MBA today can be overwhelming, but UB combines affordability and a great academic reputation to make it one of the best returns on an investment in graduate education that anyone can get." ROI is boosted by the school's excellent reputation with recruiters; according to the *Wall Street Journal*, the full-time MBA program has ranked among the world's top programs for the past five years.

UB offers a full-time MBA, a professional MBA (part-time), an executive MBA, and an international MBA with programs in Beijing and Singapore. (UB's focus on international business affords students study-abroad opportunities in 20 countries around the world as well as numerous international internships. Even when they're in Buffalo, students are exposed to international perspectives; more than one third of the student body is international.) The school also offers MS degrees in accounting, management information systems, and supply chains and operations management. UB offers formal concentrations in accounting, biotechnology management, finance, information systems and e-business, international management, management consulting, marketing management, and supply chain and operations management. Students often pursue dual concentrations.

In all programs, students praise the "small, well-connected atmosphere where all classmates help each other out and network well together." The use of "study teams" in many courses helps students develop "team skills, including things such as oral and written communication, managing diversity and conflict, making meetings work, and leadership. In addition, students can work together to minimize weaknesses and maximize strengths." Students tell us that their professors cover "a wide range [of material] in quality, with some of the best teachers and also some of the worst. On average, they are very good." Overall, students describe study at UB as "an excellent experience. Most professors are very available, and the administration has done everything possible to make our experience meaningful."

## Career and Placement

The School of Management Career Resource Center offers a wide range of services to MBAs including participation in a major MBA consortium, the alumni Telementor Program (through which students receive guidance from alumni and other mentors via e-mail and telephone contact), recruiting events, workshops and seminars, online job databases, and on-campus recruiting sessions. State-of-the-art facilities allow for videoconference interviews and the maintenance of a student information system database that is "used to complement traditional methods of on-campus and off-campus recruiting."

Employers most likely to hire Buffalo MBAs include Advantage Energy, Aldi Foods, Citigroup, Deloitte, Delphi, Dopkins and Co. CPA, Eli Lilly, Ernst and Young, Fisher Price, General Dynamics, International Monetary Fund, Itochu/USA, Johnson & Johnson, Medical, Kalieda Health, Lockheed Martin, M&T Bank, Mentholatum, Morgan Stanley, National Fuel, Praxair, PricewaterhouseCoopers, Rich Products, Samsung Capital, Turner Construction, Washington Mutual, Bearing Point, Eastman Kodak, HSBC Bank, IBM, and Unifrax Corp.

JAIMIE TAYLOR, ASSOCIATE DIRECTOR OF MBA RECRUITING & ADMISSIONS
203 ALFIERO CENTER, BUFFALO, NY 14260 UNITED STATES
PHONE: 716-645-3204 • FAX: 716-645-2341
E-MAIL: SOM-MBA@BUFFALO.EDU • WEBSITE: HTTP://MGT.BUFFALO.EDU

## Student Life and Environment

UB's international business program translates into a student body that is "extremely diversified, with fellow students hailing from Japan, China, India, Bulgaria, Sweden, Brazil, Taiwan, Egypt, and the United States, to name a few. This mix provides a culturally rich environment and an excellent opportunity to learn about other cultures." Students overcome cultural and, in some cases, language barriers to work and play together. One MBA student reports, "The culture is upbeat around the school. Most of the students seem to have developed a bond in and out of class. There is great opportunity to learn about different cultures from international students."

Extracurriculars are largely the function of the Graduate Management Association, which "organizes happy hours, sometimes with other schools such as the law school, at least once a month." One student says, "The GMA also provides School of Management grad students with an opportunity to assume leadership roles as well as contribute to graduate life in terms of organizing social and community functions by way of participating on committees. In addition, there are clubs that cater to just about every interest imaginable, and if there isn't one that covers your particular interest, I understand clubs are fairly easy to form." The recently-added Alfiero Center provides team breakout rooms, office space for student clubs, as well as lecture halls, and carrer academic advisement offices.

The university community and the city of Buffalo both contribute to "a fun social atmosphere" within the MBA program. As the state's "largest and most comprehensive public university," UB can support thriving social, artistic, and athletic scenes that literally offer something to just about everyone (the exception: people who hate cold weather). The city of Buffalo, known as "the City of Good Neighbors," offers students plenty of entertainment outlets as well as "a wide range of living situations to accommodate any income level. In addition, a comprehensive public transportation system precludes the need for private transportation."

## Admissions

According to the school's website, admissions decisions at the School of Management "are based on quantitative and qualitative factors within the scope of the enrollment and academic goals of the program. GMAT, GPA, TOEFL (for international applicants), undergraduate degree field, undergraduate institution, work experience, recommendations, and essays all factor into a decision." The school reports that it "offers competitive fellowships and assistantships to highly qualified minority applicants." Post-baccalaureate professional experience is recommended but not required. Entering students are required to have a functional understanding of calculus.

### FINANCIAL FACTS
Annual tuition (in-state/out-of-state) $7,100/$11,340
Fees (in-state/out-of-state) $1,131/$1,224
Books and supplies $1,025
Room & board $9,300
% of students receiving aid 15
% of first-year students receiving aid 12
% of students receiving grants 15
Average grant $5,000

### ADMISSIONS
Admissions Selectivity Rating 84
# of applications received 489
% applicants accepted 57
% acceptees attending 51
Average GMAT 597
Range of GMAT 550–640
Average GPA 3.22
TOEFL required of international students? yes
Minimum TOEFL (paper/computer) 573/230
Application fee $50
International application fee $50
Regular application deadline 6/1
Regular notification rolling
Need-blind admissions? yes

### APPLICANTS ALSO LOOK AT
Albany Law School, Baruch College—City University of New York, Binghamton University, Syracuse University, The University of Texas at Dallas, University of Illinois at Urbana-Champaign, University of Rochester

### EMPLOYMENT PROFILE
| Career Rating | 76 | Grads employed by field: | % | avg. salary: |
|---|---|---|---|---|
| Primary source of full-time job acceptances | | Accounting | 24 | $53,000 |
| | | Finance | 25 | $52,500 |
| School-facilitated activities | 60 (66%) | Marketing | 19 | $48,350 |
| Graduate-facilitated activities | 30 (34%) | MIS | 6 | $58,250 |
| | | Operations | 6 | $48,633 |
| Average starting salary | $50,157 | Consulting | 4 | $55,667 |
| Percent employed | 58 | General Management | 12 | $43,375 |
| | | Other | 4 | $36,000 |

# STETSON UNIVERSITY
## SCHOOL OF BUSINESS ADMINISTRATION

## GENERAL INFORMATION
| | |
|---|---|
| Type of school | private |
| Environment | town |
| Academic calendar | semesters |

### SURVEY SAYS...
Smart classrooms
*Solid preparation in:*
Finance
Accounting
Teamwork Operations
Communication/interpersonal skills

### STUDENTS
| | |
|---|---|
| Enrollment of parent institution | 2,700 |
| Enrollment of business school | 185 |
| % male/female | 68/32 |
| % out-of-state | 2 |
| % part-time | 65 |
| % minorities | 9 |
| % international | 15 |
| Average age at entry | 26 |
| Average years work experience at entry | 2 |

### ACADEMICS
| | |
|---|---|
| **Academic Experience Rating** | **78** |
| Student/faculty ratio | 15:1 |
| Profs interesting rating | 88 |
| Profs accessible rating | 82 |
| % female faculty | 25 |
| % minority faculty | 4 |

### JOINT DEGREES
MBA/JD 3 years

## Academics

One of the advantages of small programs like the Stetson University School of Business Administration—which sometimes hosts fewer than 20 students—is that you really get a chance to get to know everyone. As one student says, "The faculty and administration at Stetson are easily accessible and extremely supportive. Everyone is on a first-name basis, and the individual attention makes me feel as if my money was well-spent." Other students are enthusiastic about the "low ratio of students to faculty," and many claim that the "nicest thing is that the school is small and class sizes are small." One student says, "Each and every professor I have taken a class with at Stetson has been excellent! I would recommend this school to any and everyone!"

The school, which is located on campuses throughout central Florida, "offers classes in three locations to serve the needs of not just the full-time student but also the working student. The locations are geographically located throughout central Florida, including Orlando and Tampa, two of the largest metropolitan areas in Florida and two major job markets," one student says. Other students also point out that "the proximity of the school to major job markets like Orlando, Tampa, and Jacksonville is a major strength of the program and helps to draw a diverse mixture of students including international, female, and minority students."

Stetson's MBA offers a general business-management degree, though students can choose to specialize in a number of different areas. According to the school, "[The] programs are designed not to make you a technical specialist, but rather to provide you with a range of knowledge needed by the professional manager." The MBA program is divided into two parts: the business foundation and the advanced level courses. Foundation-level courses include business statistics, information system, law or legal environment and ethics, macro and microeconomics, principles of management, and principles of marketing. Advanced-level courses include an advanced accounting seminar, electronic commerce, international business and finance, and a variety of business electives. Students appreciate the focus of the program and say that "professors are very concerned with students learning and integrate their professional experience into the curriculum." Others have been extremely impressed by "the professional experience that the faculty brings from their diverse backgrounds" and the "camaraderie among the students and faculty at [the] school."

Stetson also offers several special programs for its business students including the Family Business Center, the Joseph C. Prince Entrepreneurial Program, and the Roland George Investments Program. Stetson also has a summer school abroad program in Innsbruck, Austria, that is open to students in all majors and concentrations. Still, many students would like to see a stronger focus on "an entrepreneurship program for students interested in that field." Another complaint is the uneven distribution of classes among the campuses. Though DeLand houses the main campus, many students complain that "the course offerings at the Celebration campus in Orlando and the Law School campus in Gulfport are not as plentiful as in DeLand."

## Career and Placement

Stetson's Career Management Office offers a variety of services to its MBA students including "individual career counseling, career planning and development in the classroom, resume referrals, internship development, full-time placement, on-campus recruiting, mock interviews, and the Business and Industry Speaker Series presentations." Their

Dr. Frank A. DeZoort, Director, Graduate Business Programs
421 North Woodland Boulevard, Unit 8398, DeLand, FL 32723 United States
Phone: 386-822-7410 • Fax: 386-822-7413
E-mail: jbosco@stetson.edu • Website: www.business.stetson.edu

new, more aggressive approach to marketing their students also seems to be paying off. Industry and employer presence was up 75 percent from four years ago, and on-campus recruiting had increased 85 percent. In 2002 and 2003, every student seeking an internship was able to get one, and, though jobs in the private sector have been rare, the center proudly points out that even in a depressed economy there has "been more activity in government jobs, health care, sales positions, and education."

## Student Life and Environment

With campuses in DeLand (20 minutes north of Orlando), Celebration (located in Orlando, right near Disney World), and Gulfport, Stetson University has the advantages of pleasant weather, active campus life, vital student athletics, and an extremely friendly student body. As a "values-centered, comprehensive, private liberal-arts university," Stetson promises on its website that all of its students will be "challenged by [the] academic programs in more than 40 disciplines. Just as importantly, [students] will learn about life and all the opportunities it holds." As one student says, "Overall, the life at Stetson has been incredible. The school is continuously improving and staying on top of technology. Our campus is outstanding as well as our library, computer labs, and tutorial sessions." Another student adds, "It is not uncommon for large groups of students to go out to dinner after class or meet on the weekends for extracurricular activities. There are many activities and clubs to choose from, and all serve to enrich the Stetson experience."

Besides the fact that "the student body feels like a small community where most people know each other," students are impressed that they've "met so many wonderful people while going to Stetson." Because it's a b-school, students need time to decompress as well as study and bond with their peers, which is why having campuses so close to beaches, and Disney World is a major plus for the prospective MBAs. As one student says, "It is also conveniently located less than 30 minutes from Daytona, which offers students wonderful, inexpensive nightlife and vacation spots."

## Admissions

In order to be eligible for admission to Stetson's MBA program, all applicants must have received a BA from an accredited college or university. Stetson is quick to point out that "the undergraduate degree need not be in business administration. The course of study is specifically designed to accommodate the nonbusiness as well as the business degree holder. Combining the MBA with a nonbusiness undergraduate degree is considered outstanding career preparation in many fields." Applicants must submit an acceptable GMAT score, recommendation forms, and a recent photograph of themselves in order to be considered.

### FINANCIAL FACTS

| | |
|---|---|
| Annual tuition | $11,400 |
| Books and supplies | $1,400 |

### ADMISSIONS

| | |
|---|---|
| **Admissions Selectivity Rating** | **73** |
| # of applications received | 240 |
| % applicants accepted | 85 |
| % acceptees attending | 90 |
| Average GMAT | 531 |
| Range of GMAT | 425–690 |
| Average GPA | 3.5 |
| TOEFL required of international students? | yes |
| Minimum TOEFL (paper/computer) | 550/213 |
| Application fee | $25 |
| Regular application deadline | 1/1 |
| Regular notification | 1/11 |
| Application deadline/notification | |
| Round 1: | 1/1 / 1/11 |
| Round 2: | 3/1 / 3/15 |
| Round 3: | 5/1 / 5/15 |
| Round 4: | 8/1 / 8/12 |
| Early decision program? | yes |
| ED Deadline/notification | Fall 8/1, Spring 10/15, Summer 4/15 / 6/15 |
| Deferment available? | yes |
| Maximum length of deferment | 1 year |
| Transfer students accepted? | yes |
| Transfer application policy Maximum 6 credit hours from an AACSB accredited school | |
| Non-fall admissions? | yes |
| Need-blind admissions? | yes |

| EMPLOYMENT PROFILE | |
|---|---|
| **Career Rating** | **75** |
| Average starting salary | $44,670 |

# SUFFOLK UNIVERSITY
## SAWYER SCHOOL OF MANAGEMENT

## Academics

With five MBA options and four campuses in Massachusetts, the Sawyer School of Management at Suffolk University is the model of flexibility. Add to that "the diversity of students from different careers and from different countries," and professors "representing all corners of the Earth," and the options at Sawyer seem almost too broad. Luckily, students are saved by the administration from drowning in choices. "[The administration] works very closely with the students and is incredibly approachable." Overall, most students agree that "the academic experience seems to be the conventional combination of sweat and idealism, but the interactivity of this program is what puts it over the top." Another adds, "the school's administration provides events that bring distinguished Boston business leaders in (many of whom are Suffolk alumni), which have been very resourceful. I have yet to be unimpressed. My overall academic experience has been more than I could have ever imagined."

The five MBA options include the full-time MBA, the part-time MBA, the global MBA, executive MBA, and the online MBA. The program that garners the most enthusiasm from our survey respondents is the global MBA. One student reports "The focus is very international and very cutting edge." Another warns that the program is "condensed and very intense. Nine classes per semester doesn't leave for much outside school." Of all departments, professors in accounting receive particular praise.

In the full-time and part-time MBA, eight elective courses allow students to specialize their education in accounting, finance, organizational behavior, business law, health administration, marketing, entrepreneurship, taxation, nonprofit, international business, or corporate financial executive skills.

The school also offers a number of overseas seminars and study options. According to the school's website, students who take one of these routes "make corporate site visits, meet government officials to discuss business policies, and attend lectures in English at a leading international university. Suffolk MBAs have recently studied in Belgium, China, France, Ireland, Italy, and Turkey." This outright focus on the global isn't lost on students, either; an international student echoes the sentiments of many of his classmates and says, "Cultural diversity is the main strength of Suffolk. It is easy to have a truly multinational network [at this school]."

## Career and Placement

Although students recognize the strengths of their program, many wish there were a better way to make more companies recognize them, too. One student says that the school could be better "in creating on-campus meetings with top recruiters more frequently to show them the great quality of our education, which they can use to add value to their companies." Still other students complain that there simply isn't enough "help for the students who are looking for jobs."

Despite these complaints, students from the Sawyer School have been recruited at companies as various as the Associated Press, *The Boston Globe*, Fidelity Investments, Fleet Financial, the Peace Corps, and PricewaterhouseCoopers.

JUDITH L. REYNOLDS, DIRECTOR OF GRADUATE ADMISSIONS
8 ASHBURTON PLACE, BOSTON, MA 02108 UNITED STATES
PHONE: 617-573-8302 • FAX: 617-305-1733
E-MAIL: GRAD.ADMISSION@SUFFOLK.EDU • WEBSITE: WWW.SUFFOLK.EDU/BUSINESS

## Student Life and Environment

Although many students take advantage of the online and off-site options that the school offers, those who opt to attend regular classes at the main Boston campus have little to complain about. Students rave about "downtown Boston and Boston's life" and say it is "very usual to go for a drink after class. People are outgoing and very active around the city. I see classmates in all sorts of happenings." According to one student, "From my point of view Boston is one of the most beautiful cities...with a lot of cultural activities and entertainment." The school itself ranks community building high on its list of priorities, and students say Suffolk offers "several cultural activities, like ski trips, Latin events, [and] food festivals." Besides this, one students raves that "the small feel of the school is great. Everyone knows who I am, and they know my story. You really feel connected to the administration, and we are treated as clients whom they want to succeed."

Despite the wealth of activities available and the cultural variety of Boston, some students complain that they barely get a chance to enjoy them. "Life at our school is basically the classroom and tons of meetings on a daily basis. Socializing, clubs, or activities are definitely not one of the strengths of our school," one typical student offers.

## Admissions

To be considered for admission to the Sawyer School, students' undergraduate GPAs should be a solid B, which is the average for most of Sawyer's programs. The average GMAT is 490. Applicants who are not native speakers of English must take the TOEFL and score a minimum of 550 (paper-based) and 213 (computer-based) on the exam.

### PROMINENT ALUMNI

Robert Mudge, New England Region President, Verizon; Arthur Driscoll II, President, Sunsweet Growers, Inc.; Edward J. Boudreau, Chmn, John Hancock Advisers, Inc; Peter Gicheru, Finance Controller, Coca-Cola South Africa

### FINANCIAL FACTS

| | |
|---|---|
| Annual tuition | $25,800 |
| Fees | $140 |
| Books and supplies | $1,000 |
| Room & board | $10,651 |
| % of students receiving aid | 30 |
| % of first-year students receiving aid | 37 |
| % of students receiving loans | 18 |
| % of students receiving grants | 10 |
| Average award package | $20,171 |
| Average grant | $2,000 |

### ADMISSIONS

| | |
|---|---|
| **Admissions Selectivity Rating** | **66** |
| # of applications received | 424 |
| % applicants accepted | 77 |
| % acceptees attending | 54 |
| Average GMAT | 490 |
| Range of GMAT | 430–550 |
| Average GPA | 3.14 |
| TOEFL required of international students? | yes |
| Minimum TOEFL (paper/computer) | 550/213 |
| Application fee | $50 |
| International application fee | $50 |
| Regular application deadline | 6/15 |
| Regular notification | rolling |
| Deferment available? | yes |
| Maximum length of deferment | 1 year |
| Transfer students accepted? | yes |
| Transfer application policy | |
| Same as for regular applicants | |
| Non-fall admissions? | yes |
| Need-blind admissions? | yes |

### APPLICANTS ALSO LOOK AT

Babson College, Bentley College, Boston College, Boston University, Northeastern University

| EMPLOYMENT PROFILE | | | |
|---|---|---|---|
| **Career Rating** | **82** | **Grads employed by field:** | **% avg. salary:** |
| Average starting salary | $67,800 | Accounting | 15 | $47,500 |
| | | Finance | 17 | $67,300 |
| | | Marketing | 17 | $68,400 |
| | | MIS | 6 | $77,300 |
| | | Operations | 2 | $62,000 |
| | | Consulting | 6 | $95,000 |
| | | Entrepreneurship | 2 | $85,000 |
| | | General Management | 17 | $63,500 |
| | | Global Management | 2 | $40,000 |
| | | Internet/New Media | 4 | $58,000 |
| | | Nonprofit | 2 | $70,000 |
| | | Other | 9 | $64,800 |

# SYRACUSE UNIVERSITY
## MARTIN J. WHITMAN SCHOOL OF MANAGEMENT

## Academics

The Martin J. Whitman School of Management at Syracuse University is among the oldest business schools in the nation, but this is not a program content to rest on its considerable laurels. On the contrary, Whitman's administration continually retools its MBA to meet the ever-changing needs of the modern business world. In its search to offer areas of study that are both unique and valuable, Whitman has developed concentrations and specialty tracks in such areas as innovation management; entrepreneurship, innovation, and global leadership; management of technology; and supply-chain management. These complement more traditional offerings in accounting, finance, general management, and marketing management.

A Whitman MBA consists of 18 courses, 10 of which are required core courses; the remaining courses are electives. Full-time, two-year MBAs complete an internship during the summer between their first and second years; a number of international internships are available, as are some six-month internships. (Students who choose this option increase their second-year spring course load in order to graduate on time.) An accelerated MBA is available to students who enter with highly developed business skills and knowledge. Students may also choose to pursue an iMBA that relies heavily on Internet-based distance learning. MBAs tell us, "The academics are tough but not impossible. You just need to have time-management skills. Professors are aware of other courses and their assignments, and [they] work with each other to make sure [the] workload is equally balanced."

Students at Whitman say, "[We appreciate the] vast number of resources available at our disposal at this school including computer clusters, libraries, tutors, [and] the resources of top schools in other areas, such as the Maxwell School for Public Administration and Newhouse School for Communication." Students agree that "[the faculty members] are very approachable outside of the classroom and give valuable insight," although "their effectiveness as teachers ranges widely. More emphasis needs to be placed on professors that have consistently shown poor performance in communicating effectively." Students comment that when professors are "on their game, the overall experience is very good. The discussion (rather than lecture) format is popular and seems to be more beneficial for overall understanding of topics. Also, casework is a popular technique and has been very effective."

## Career and Placement

Whitman's Career Center provides a full range of services to all business undergraduates and graduate students including access to Internet job databases, in-office job postings, and an alumni database. The office maintains an online and traditional library of career resources, conducts workshops, seminars, mock interviews, and they also organize on-campus recruiting sessions. Students feel the office needs to do more, and they agree that "there are not enough valuable events for networking and career service." Students add, "We need to improve alumni connections. Those that are available are very helpful, but not many alumni are available, and [the] system for keeping track of them is poor."

In the spring of 2004, employers seeking Whitman MBAs included CallStreet LLC, Forest Laboratories, Johns Hopkins Health System, the Noel Group, and Xerox. One in five MBAs found work outside of the United States; nearly as many took jobs on the Pacific coast.

CAROL J. SWANBERG, DIRECTOR OF ADMISSIONS AND FINANCIAL AID
900 SOUTH CROUSE AVENUE, SUITE 100, SYRACUSE, NY 13244-2130 UNITED STATES
PHONE: 315-443-9214 • FAX: 315-443-9517
E-MAIL: MBAINFO@SOM.SYR.EDU • WEBSITE: WWW.WHITMAN.SYR.EDU

## FINANCIAL FACTS

| | |
|---|---|
| Annual tuition | $24,180 |
| Fees | $850 |
| Books and supplies | $1,325 |
| Room & board | $12,000 |
| % of students receiving aid | 60 |
| % of first-year students receiving aid | 70 |
| % of students receiving grants | 49 |
| Average award package | $13,000 |
| Average grant | $10,000 |
| Average student loan debt | $16,000 |

## ADMISSIONS

| | |
|---|---|
| Admissions Selectivity Rating | 76 |
| # of applications received | 291 |
| % applicants accepted | 65 |
| % acceptees attending | 37 |
| Average GMAT | 568 |
| Range of GMAT | 530–620 |
| Average GPA | 3.17 |
| TOEFL required of international students? | yes |
| Minimum TOEFL (paper/computer) | 600/250 |
| Application fee | $65 |
| International application fee | $65 |
| Regular application deadline | 3/1 |
| Regular notification | 4/1 |
| Application deadline/notification | |
| Round 1: | 1/15 / 2/15 |
| Round 2: | 3/1 / 4/1 |
| Round 3: | 5/1 / 6/1 |
| Deferment available? | yes |
| Maximum length of deferment | 1 year |
| Need-blind admissions? | yes |

## APPLICANTS ALSO LOOK AT

Boston University, Cornell University, New York University, Penn State University—Great Valley Campus, University of Illinois at Urbana-Champaign, University of Rochester, University of Wisconsin

## Student Life and Environment

Like many small MBA programs on big campuses, Whitman fosters a community unto itself, one in which, "students are all pretty close. The MBA Student Association organizes functions like happy hours, parties, and trips to the movies." One student elaborates, "Despite the normal gripes of student life, there is a familial atmosphere here at Syracuse that's hard to explain. For example, we recently appointed a new chancellor, and everyone—grad students, undergrad students, and faculty—seemed to view this as a very personal act. [It was] as if we were inducting a new patriarch (actually, a matriarch in our case) of sorts. I think it's a sign of the personal level of involvement that accompanies enrollment in the School of Management."

Students also enjoy the assets of the university at large, especially the intercollegiate athletics. One MBA explains, "Sports are big here. Many students go to the football and basketball games." Students also brag that "the campus itself is beautiful and is well maintained." As a major research university, Syracuse attracts a number of prominent speakers every semester.

The city of Syracuse has "a good local bar scene" that includes the famous Dinosaur, a blues club that serves some of the best and most authentic barbecue north of the Carolinas. Unfortunately, according to students, that's about all it has. Students say, "The city of Syracuse is not a very nice city. It is generally very filthy and in very poor economic condition. Crime is a problem." Also, winter arrives early here and really digs in its heels. Other students see a positive side of the situation; one student explains "The weather's so bad, you have no choice but to put in extra time studying."

## Admissions

Applicants to the Whitman MBA program must submit official copies of all undergraduate and graduate transcripts, GMAT scores, TOEFL scores (international students), three short essays, two letters of recommendation, and a personal history detailing work and academic achievement. The school tells us that the admissions committee looks at "the quality of full-time work experience, the student's appropriateness for Syracuse's program, and evidence of leadership potential, motivation, teamwork ability, and perseverance." An admissions interview is strongly encouraged but not required.

### EMPLOYMENT PROFILE

| Career Rating | 70 | Grads employed by field: | % | avg. salary: |
|---|---|---|---|---|
| Average starting salary | $60,500 | Accounting | 20 | $55,375 |
| | | Finance | 26 | $64,000 |
| | | Marketing | 25 | $53,125 |
| | | Operations | 17 | $68,500 |
| | | Consulting | 12 | NR |

# TEMPLE UNIVERSITY
## THE FOX SCHOOL OF BUSINESS AND MANAGEMENT

## Academics

Flexibility is a key selling point of Temple's Fox School of Management, which offers 11 areas of concentration to a good mix of both full-time and part-time students. With programs in accounting, business administration, economics, finance, general and strategic management, health-care management, human resource administration, international business administration, international business (tri-continent), management-information systems, and risk management and insurance, Temple gives graduate students an unusually wide array of choices, especially given the relatively intimate size of their program. The school also offers a variety of master's of science degrees, a master's of arts in economics, and a solid assortment of joint degrees.

"The health care and IMBA groups are the strongest of all the majors [at Fox]," according to students. The former, the first accredited program of its kind in the United States, benefits from its relatively long history as well as the presence of five medical schools and 30 teaching hospitals in the Philadelphia area. The latter is a natural outgrowth of Temple's "huge international student body," which has helped drive the focus of the curriculum toward globalization. Students also praise Temple's "great strategic management and MIS professors" as well as its "excellent consulting practicum" and "first-rate faculty in finance."

Temple recently revamped the MBA curriculum; it currently consists of six foundation courses, a seven-course sequence in advanced managerial perspectives, electives (leading to an area of concentration), and a capstone course. Students appreciate the administration's "willingness to take student assessment into consideration and re-evaluate current offerings (for the next class of students)." In general, students are happy with the program, but they would like to see more in-class practical application of the material. As one student says, "Theory is great and all, but practical experience in consulting, systems analysis, financial analysis, [or] project management is what matters. [The] extensive client-based project work with professors as mentors is by far the best teaching method applied here. Those that teach solely out of a textbook seem to be missing the big picture. The school is moving toward this type of learning, but it hasn't completely embraced it yet."

## Career and Placement

Fox MBAs receive Career Services from the Fox School of Business Graduate Career Management Center (GCMC). "[It] provides [students with] assistance in focusing and preparing for both summer internships and post-MBA careers and provides opportunities for networking, meeting, and interviewing with top employers." Services include seminars, networking events, online job databases, and recruiting events. Students say, In the past, students have expressed concern over the quality of MBA recruitment efforts. However, in the three years following the creation of the GCMC, both international and American students have experienced a significant increase in employment by top firms within three months of graduation. Job searches benefit from "a strong alumni network and heavy presence in the Philadelphia/New Jersey/New York region, as well as strong connections with regional executives and industry experts."

Among the companies that most frequently hire Fox MBAs are Cigna, Eli Lilly, First Union, GlaxoSmithKline, IBM, Independence Blue Cross, JPMorgan, Mass Mutual, McNeil, Merck, Subaru of America, Unisys, Vanguard, William M. Mercer, and Wyeth.

STEPHEN BORO, ASSOCIATE DIRECTOR, RECRUITING AND ADMISSIONS
1810 NORTH 13TH STREET, SPEAKMAN HALL, ROOM 5, PHILADELPHIA, PA 19122 UNITED STATES
PHONE: 215-204-5890 • FAX: 215-204-1632
E-MAIL: FOXINFO@TEMPLE.EDU • WEBSITE: WWW.FOX.TEMPLE.EDU/MBAMS

## Student Life and Environment

Temple delivers its full-time MBA program entirely at the smaller downtown campus in Center City, while the part-time MBA program is conducted at both Center City and the Fort Washington Campus. Classes at Center City are held during the day and in the evening, while only evening classes are offered in Fort Washington. Features of both MBA campuses include a dedicated graduate business center, high tech classrooms and exceptional meeting and event facilities. In addition, many co-curricular activities take place in both locations including networking events, executive lectures and professional development workshops. MBAs appreciate that "shuttle buses provide handy service" between the two campuses. One student writes, "I love the classes at Fort Washington where the MBA crowd has much more job experience, and the place itself is so scenic during the spring season."

Full-time MBAs at Temple enjoy "active student organizations that organize networking events. There's also very active involvement in seminars by internationally recognized social, economic, and political leaders." Students add that fortunately "before we become exhausted from all the schoolwork and such, the MBA Association provides happy hours, networking events, club parties, and a lot of [enjoyable] things." Students also blow off steam by attending the games of the school's popular men's basketball team. Part-timers are less connected; one student explains, "Everyone at my school is very busy attempting to balance schoolwork, family, and a social life. It becomes very stressful. But everyone seems to work together to achieve a common goal: graduating."

Students love hometown Philadelphia, the second-largest metropolitan area in the eastern United States. The city not only provides innumerable business opportunities, but also lays out an impressive spread of restaurants, clubs, museums, parks, galleries, tourist attractions, professional sporting events, and shopping venues. One student notes that public transportation makes "traversing Philly a snap."

## Admissions

Fox admissions officers review all undergraduate and graduate transcripts, GMAT scores, TOEFL scores (international students), and letters of recommendation for all candidates. In addition, the committee seriously considers "work experience and the applicant's statement of goals. Prospective students should have a statement of goals that expresses the direction [in which] they wish to move their career and how an MBA will serve that goal." Interviews are required of all students. To enhance recruitment of under-represented minority students and students with disadvantaged backgrounds, Temple "participates in annual state-wide and national conferences for minority candidates looking to further their education and participates with KPMG in their diversity recruiting."

### FINANCIAL FACTS

| | |
|---|---|
| Annual tuition (in-state/out-of-state) | $13,608/$19,980 |
| Fees | $1,170 |
| Books and supplies | $1,200 |
| Room & board | $15,000 |
| % of students receiving aid | 63 |
| % of first-year students receiving aid | 58 |
| % of students receiving loans | 82 |
| % of students receiving grants | 41 |
| Average award package | $450,000 |
| Average grant | $5,000 |
| Average student loan debt | $36,000 |

### ADMISSIONS

| | |
|---|---|
| Admissions Selectivity Rating | 92 |
| # of applications received | 294 |
| % applicants accepted | 44 |
| % acceptees attending | 52 |
| Average GMAT | 651 |
| Range of GMAT | 600–710 |
| Average GPA | 3.31 |
| TOEFL required of international students? | yes |
| Minimum TOEFL (paper/computer) | 575/230 |
| Application fee | $50 |
| International application fee | $50 |
| Regular application deadline | 6/1 |
| Regular notification | rolling |
| Deferment available? | yes |
| Maximum length of deferment | 1 year |
| Transfer students accepted? | yes |
| Transfer application policy May apply to transfer up to 6 credits toward concentration requirements. Transferred classes cannot be part of a previously awarded degree. | |
| Non-fall admissions? | yes |
| Need-blind admissions? | yes |

### APPLICANTS ALSO LOOK AT

DUPE - Drexel University—Professional MBA, La Salle University, Rutgers, The State University of New Jersey, Saint Joseph's University, The Pennsylvania State University, University of Pennsylvania, Villanova University

### EMPLOYMENT PROFILE

| | | Grads employed by field: | % | avg. salary: |
|---|---|---|---|---|
| Career Rating | 81 | Finance | 37 | $64,800 |
| Primary source of full-time job acceptances | | Marketing | 12 | $70,600 |
| School-facilitated activities | 38 (76%) | Operations | 5 | $42,000 |
| Graduate-facilitated activities | 12 (24%) | Consulting | 29 | $88,000 |
| | | Other | 17 | $56,500 |
| Average starting salary | $69,256 | | | |
| Percent employed | 84 | | | |

# TENNESSEE TECHNOLOGICAL UNIVERSITY
## TENNESSEE TECH MBA PROGRAM

## Academics

Accessibility and convenience are the most frequently cited attributes of the MBA program at Tennessee Tech, a midsize state university located halfway between Nashville and Knoxville. Students here may take classes on campus or at home through the school's distance-learning option. The program actually allows students to exercise both options simultaneously, so it's not either/or. In fact, MBAs are encouraged to find the ideal combination of on- and off-campus classes to suit their personal schedules. Students may attend part-time or full-time (more than half are part-timers), and may enter the program in the fall, spring, or summer. The program is also accessible to most students' budgets, especially those who reside in the state of Tennessee.

Enrollees love the distance program. One MBA writes, "The DMBA (Distance MBA) is a big strength of TTU. It allows students to get their MBA without ever stepping foot on campus. This is very valuable to out-of-state students and to those of us who work full-time." Despite the novelty of the program, most report that it runs smoothly. One student writes, "My graduating class is the first class of the Distance MBA program, and we have had an excellent experience. Our professors are very flexible and the staff is top-notch. The coursework is the same for the on-campus program, so we are fully prepared to succeed in today's business environment." Lectures are delivered on a set of CD ROMs, providing students with a rare and valuable permanent record. Class interaction is facilitated through WebCT; students log on to a site that provides access to e-mail, a course calendar, bulletin boards, quizzes and exams, and chat rooms, as well as downloadable PowerPoint presentations.

Even the campus-based courses incorporate "some online components," which students appreciate, noting the school's "total commitment to staying current with technological trends, which ensures Tech students have the latest tools for use in their jobs." Professors here represent "a good mix. Some are more traditional, others very technological. Some are really laid back and may have a class meeting at a downtown restaurant during happy hour. Some bring things to life by presenting research in an understandable form. For example, did you know that just the smell of fresh-baked cookies can increase productivity? There's a little bit of everything to keep it interesting." Administrators are "very approachable. They are always willing to go the extra mile to help the students. They truly care about giving us a quality education, and they do it with a smile."

TTU offers concentrations in accounting and MIS. The MBA program, which consists of seven, three-hour core courses and nine hours of electives, can be completed in one year by a full-time student.

## Career and Placement

Career Services at Tennessee Tech are of interest primarily to the school's full-time MBAs, since most of the part-timers and distance-learning enrollees are currently employed. Placement services are handled through the university's Career Services Office; there is no career office dedicated solely to the MBA program or to the College of Business. The MBA office does provide some supplemental career counseling and placement assistance. The school's website states that "the key to placement is flexibility. We generally place all MBAs who are seriously looking for a position."

Nearly all graduates remain in the Tennessee region following graduation. A few find work in the Southern Atlantic states, while a few others relocate to the Southwest. On average, 85 employers recruit each year on the Tennessee Tech campus.

BOB WOOD, DIRECTOR OF MBA STUDIES
BOX 5023 TTU, 1108 NORTH PEACHTREE, COOKEVILLE, TN 38505 UNITED STATES
PHONE: 931-372-3600 • FAX: 931-372-6544
E-MAIL: MBASTUDIES@TNTECH.EDU • WEBSITE: WWW.TNTECH.EDU/MBA/

## Student Life and Environment

The MBA Program at Tennessee Tech provides a "small school environment within a larger university" for the cadre of students who attend classes on campus. Full-timers tell us that "life at Tech is thoroughly enjoyable. There is enough diversity to offer something for everyone as well as being small enough that you don't get lost in the crowd." Students "can join the MBA society and get involved in the panel discussions" to fill out their extracurricular schedules. Part-timers, on the other hand, "do not get very involved with the student activities that are offered" but they can still "enjoy going to Tech because," as one says, "I can go to on-campus courses as opposed to taking them online."

Many Tech MBAs do take the courses online, however, and for them "there is not any face-to-face contact with classmates." Even so, one distance learner reports that "the WebCT experience has been more enriching for me than my on campus classes. I do miss the amenities found on campus, such as the library, help desk, and fitness center, though." In the plus column, distance learners needn't cope with a parking situation that "will give you a headache."

Hometown "Cookeville and the surrounding area provide many outdoor activities. With major cities like Nashville and Knoxville within 100 miles, many students leave for the weekend." The student body is a mix of people who "just graduated from Tech as undergrads and are somewhat insular" and professionals "with strengths in various fields: some financial, some technology, some creative." One student writes, "I can't count the times I've leaned on my fellow classmates for support and vice versa. The morale here is wonderful." Full-timers form a tight group, saying they "study together, get our work done, and then go out and have a couple of drinks. Even though we're in the heart of the 'Bible Belt,' we know how to have a good time."

## Admissions

Successful applicants to the Tennessee Tech MBA Program must have a minimum undergraduate GPA of 2.5, a minimum GMAT score of 450, and a minimum formula score of 1,000 using the formula [(undergraduate GPA 5 200) + GMAT score] or 1050 using the formula [(undergraduate GPA for final 60 semester hours × 200) + GMAT score]. Applicants must also provide a statement of computer proficiency attesting to aptitude in word processing, spreadsheet, and presentation software. Students whose native language is not English must provide TOEFL scores (minimum 550 paper-and-pencil, 213 computer-based). Entering students who have not completed an undergraduate business core are required to complete pre-MBA foundation modules in accounting, business law, economics, finance, management, marketing, and business statistics/quantitative methods. Special minority fellowships and graduate assistantships are offered to attract students from underrepresented populations.

### FINANCIAL FACTS
| | |
|---|---|
| Annual tuition (in-state/out-of-state) | $0/$9,996 |
| Fees | $6,550 |
| Books and supplies | $1,500 |
| Room & board (on/off-campus) | $4,380/$5,500 |
| % of students receiving aid | 50 |
| % of first-year students receiving aid | 16 |
| % of students receiving grants | 24 |
| Average award package | $8,426 |
| Average grant | $1,336 |
| Average student loan debt | $5,000 |

### ADMISSIONS
| | |
|---|---|
| Admissions Selectivity Rating | 67 |
| # of applications received | 94 |
| % applicants accepted | 93 |
| % acceptees attending | 63 |
| Average GMAT | 538 |
| Range of GMAT | 450–760 |
| Average GPA | 3.2 |
| TOEFL required of international students? | yes |
| Minimum TOEFL (paper/computer) | 550/213 |
| Application fee | $25 |
| International application fee | $30 |
| Regular application deadline | rolling |
| Regular notification | rolling |
| Deferment available? | yes |
| Maximum length of deferment | 1 year |
| Transfer students accepted? | yes |
| Transfer application policy | |
| TTU will transfer 9 hours or less from an AACSB-accredited school. | |
| Non-fall admissions? | yes |
| Need-blind admissions? | yes |

### EMPLOYMENT PROFILE
| Career Rating | 64 | Grads employed by field: | % | avg. salary: |
|---|---|---|---|---|
| Average starting salary | $41,800 | Accounting | 17 | NR |
| | | Finance | 8 | NR |
| | | Marketing | 3 | NR |
| | | MIS | 8 | NR |
| | | Strategic Planning | 3 | NR |
| | | Consulting | 8 | NR |
| | | Entrepreneurship | 3 | NR |
| | | General Management | 14 | NR |
| | | Other | 33 | NR |
| | | Internet/New Media | 3 | NR |

# TEXAS A&M INTERNATIONAL UNIVERSITY
## COLLEGE OF BUSINESS ADMINISTRATION

## Academics

The College of Business Administration at Texas A&M International University "is dedicated to the delivery of a high quality professional and internationalized education to a graduate student population that is drawn from a wide variety of countries and cultures," according to the college's website, which also points out that "these programs [are intended to] contribute to the students' success in leadership positions in both domestic and international settings." This AACSB-accredited school offers a general MBA, an MBA in international banking (MBA-IBK), an MBA in international trade (MBA-IT), and a PhD in International Business Administration.

All MBA programs at TAMIU require mastery of eight foundation areas: accounting, information systems, quantitative methods, economics, finance, management, marketing, and operations. Students may fulfill these requirements by completing corresponding undergraduate courses at TAMIU, by showing evidence of equivalent coursework at another undergraduate institution, or by having earned an undergraduate business degree from an AACSB-accredited program. Waivers are only granted for coursework completed within the previous seven years.

TAMIU's general MBA is taught in both English and Spanish. The 30-hour program allows students to concentrate in one of the following areas: accounting, information systems, international business, international finance, international trade economics, logistics, and management marketing. The strong international focus of the program "gives students the opportunity to immerse themselves in an international environment in which we can analyze situations of different countries. The diversity of the student body helps." Students also praise the "extremely optimistic" professors who "honestly care about their students and are always willing to offer a helping hand." One student writes, "Teachers are very good and highly cooperative, with great academic ability. They have the knowledge to impart, help the students and, offer their valuable suggestions to guide their further course of action."

Students also point out that "the small size of the program is a great strength. The student population is not big, so there is enough opportunity to interact with your professors and get to know everyone in your college." MBAs here appreciate how "professors acknowledge that the majority of the class works full-time and also goes to school, so they make the assignments challenging, but not impossible." In addition to the abovementioned degrees, TAMIU also offers a master of professional accountancy (MPAcc), a master of science in international logistics (MS/IL), a master of science in information systems (MS/IS), and a doctorate in international business administration (PhD/BA).

## Career and Placement

The Texas A&M International Career Services Office provides counseling and placement services to the entire undergraduate and graduate student body. The office organizes on-campus recruiting events, career expos, and job fairs. It also offers one-on-one counseling, workshops, library services, and resume review.

## Student Life and Environment

Around 40 percent of TAMIU's MBA students attend full-time, providing a sizeable base for clubs, organizations, and extracurricular activity. Students tell us that "campus life offers a diverse field of organizations. New clubs and sports are always developing." They also report that "seminars provided by the school are good. Many important speakers visit the campus to deliver inspirational speeches on important current topics, including politics, finance, economics, and health." Part-timers generally "don't get to spend much time on campus, but rather just get here for class at night and leave once classes are done." They "visit the computer labs and library to do research and work," but otherwise spend little extra time socializing.

Hometown Laredo "is poised at the gateway to Mexico," placing it "at an enviable crossroads of international business and life." 156 miles south of San Antonio and 153 miles north of Monterrey, Mexico, this city of over 150,000 is the fastest growing in the state of Texas. The area's growth has been spurred by Laredo's increasing role as a center for international manufacturing and trade. Top employers in the area, outside of education and government, include the Laredo Medical Center, the H-E-B Grocery Company, Doctor's Hospital, Laredo Candle, and area banks.

TAMIU's "friendly, frank, cheerful and helpful" students "enjoy the challenge of studying in a foreign country and expect the experience to give them a better professional future." More than half the MBAs here are international students; most of whom are Mexican and Latin American. Almost twenty percent of the international student body comes from Asia.

## Admissions

Applying to the TAMIU MBA program is a two-step process, as applicants must be admitted to both the university at large and the College of Business in order to enroll in the MBA program. Applicants must submit the following materials to the Office of Graduate Admission: a completed application; an official copy of transcripts for all post-secondary academic work undertaken; and an official score report for the GMAT. Applicants must also provide a statement of purpose, a resume, and two letters of recommendation. The TOEFL is required of all students who completed undergraduate study in a country where English is not the language of instruction; a minimum score of 550 paper-based or 213 computer-based is required. International students must also submit documentation demonstrating the ability to support themselves financially while studying at TAMIU.

### FINANCIAL FACTS

| | |
|---|---|
| Annual tuition (in-state/out-of-state) | $900/$5,868 |
| Fees | $1,959 |
| Books and supplies | $2,096 |
| Room & board (on/off-campus) | $6,566/$5,633 |
| % of students receiving aid | 40 |
| % of first-year students receiving aid | 15 |
| % of students receiving loans | 20 |
| % of students receiving grants | 25 |
| Average award package | $3,900 |
| Average grant | $1,000 |

### ADMISSIONS

| | |
|---|---|
| Admissions Selectivity Rating | 63 |
| # of applications received | 69 |
| % applicants accepted | 99 |
| % acceptees attending | 71 |
| Average GMAT | 480 |
| Range of GMAT | 440–570 |
| Average GPA | 3.29 |
| TOEFL required of international students? | yes |
| Minimum TOEFL (paper/computer) | 550/213 |
| Application fee | $25 |
| International application fee | $25 |
| Regular application deadline | 7/1 |
| Regular notification | 7/30 |
| Deferment available? | yes |
| Maximum length of deferment | 1 year |
| Transfer students accepted? | yes |
| Transfer application policy | |

In terms of the application process, this remains the same as first-time applicants. However, for F1 applicants, it is critical these applicants be in-status at their current institutuion.

| | |
|---|---|
| Non-fall admissions? | yes |
| Need-blind admissions? | yes |

### APPLICANTS ALSO LOOK AT

Texas A&M University—Corpus Christi, Texas A&M University—Commerce, The University of Texas—Pan American

---

**EMPLOYMENT PROFILE**

| | |
|---|---|
| **Career Rating** | **65** |
| Average starting salary | $65,000 |

# TEXAS A&M UNIVERSITY—COLLEGE STATION
## MAYS BUSINESS SCHOOL

## Academics

The top-ranked Mays Business School at Texas A&M University—College Station combines a one-size-fits-all approach with specialization options to provide its small student body a cost-effective and streamlined, yet flexible, MBA degree. This inexpensive public school offers one of the 10 quickest returns on investment, according to *Business Week*. *Financial Times* ranked it the fourth best value in U.S. graduate business education. One MBA agrees, "The education you receive is top notch for the cost."

All Mays students complete a 49-credit core sequence over a 16-month period. This core covers accounting, business communication, finance, global management, information and operations management, marketing, negotiations, and management, all with "an emphasis on character and ethics, a very appealing aspect of the program." This mandatory curriculum that combines "business competencies, communications, international issues, teamwork, and ethics" means all Mays MBAs "are prepared to be strategic thinkers, effective communicators, and accountable team members and leaders in today's global marketplace," according to the school.

Those seeking specialization are welcome to remain at Mays for an additional semester, participate in study abroad, or undertake other enrichment opportunities. The school offers specialization in 11 predefined areas (students speak most highly of accounting, marketing, management, and real estate). MBAs may also design specializations of their own. Other unique aspects of the program include the Technology Transfer Challenge, in which MBAs compete to develop commercial applications for promising new technologies. The school writes, "The Challenge's design is based on state-of-the-art knowledge management theory, demonstrating how knowledge management principles can be used to help evaluate the potential of patents and other raw technologies. It demands a level of creativity not possible with traditional case competitions."

Students here love the "low cost and excellent financial aid," as well as the school's vision. One MBA exclaims, "The school continues to replace weak faculty in an effort to improve. And the program is definitely improving, with great faculty leading the way." They also appreciate that it's a "conservative, strong program with high starting salaries and great recruiting companies." Naturally, though, a few see its small size as a drawback. One such student opines, "The Mays MBA Class of 2006 is only 70 students strong. If the school is ever to be mentioned amongst Harvard, Texas, and Michigan, then it will have to expand to upwards of 500 students."

## Career and Placement

A&M's legendary alumni network works its magic for MBAs. Students exploit this valuable asset through publications, a website, newsletters, and on- and off-campus events. The Mays Graduate Business Career Services (GBCS) Office also provides one-on-one counseling, online assessment tools, and frequent workshops on crafting resumes and cover letters, networking, interviewing, and negotiating your salary.

Hundreds of companies recruit on the College Station campus each year—just how many come for the purpose of interviewing MBAs is less clear. What counts is that the results are pretty impressive. Employers of Mays MBAs include BP, CattleSoft, ChevronPhillips, China National Petroleum Corp, CIA, Citibank, Citigroup, DuPont, Eagle Pass Winery, the Federal Reserve Bank, First Houston Mortgage, Ford, Hewlett Packard, Johnson-Lancaster & Associates, Procter & Gamble, Smith Barney, Solutions Inc., Sovico Trading Ltd., USAA, Wal-Mart, and World Savings. In 2004, the mean starting salary of a Mays MBA was $77,153. One student sums up, "One of the greatest facets of a Texas A&M education is the high salary upon graduation with relatively low tuition costs."

WENDY FLYNN, ASSOCIATE DIRECTOR, MAYS MBA
4117 TAMU COLLEGE STATION, TX 77843-4117 UNITED STATES
PHONE: 979-845-4714 • FAX: 979-862-2393
E-MAIL: MAYSMBA@TAMU.EDU • WEBSITE: MBA.TAMU.EDU

## Student Life and Environment

Although "school requires much of a student's time" at A&M, "the lifestyle in College Station is still very enjoyable." Furthermore, "those who wish to participate in social activities will not be disappointed," MBAs write, since "there are weekly events organized, as well as plenty of hot spots to frequent." It will come as no surprise to anyone who knows anything at all about the school that "football is the major activity" and that A&M is "big into traditions, and it really enhances the life here." Lesser-known but popular diversions also include "rollerblading, volleyball, tennis, and other sports." Overall, MBAs here agree that "Texas A&M is very conservative and an excellent environment to learn quality business practices."

With a substantial international population, Mays' student body is "very diverse in ethnicity, education, and experience," although not so much in gender. MBAs tend to be "boisterous in class, friendly and intelligent, [and] proactive in regards to career advancement and networking." All "have some special skills which make them unique. If one is good in math, another is very good in communications." One MBA observes, "Fellow students are like good coworkers at the office: During class and study time they work hard, but after class, they know how to have fun."

## Admissions

With a limited number of slots available, the Mays MBA program can keep admissions very competitive. Successful applicants typically have at least two years of post-college, full-time work experience, good GMAT scores ("quant and verbal sections must have scores at least at the 50th percentile for consideration," notes the Admissions Office), and evidence of leadership and professional skill. All applicants must submit a current resume, three letters of recommendation from professional sources, and application essays. International students must provide TOEFL scores (minimum 600 on the paper-and-pencil test, 250 on the computerized test for admission). A&M "aggressively seeks to enhance diversity on all levels in the program, and has programs in place to recruit all students who will bring diversity to our program."

### FINANCIAL FACTS

| | |
|---|---|
| Annual tuition (in-state/out-of-state) | $7,045/$18,745 |
| Fees | $7,903 |
| Books and supplies | $1,428 |
| Room & board | $9,679 |
| % of students receiving aid | 75 |
| % of first-year students receiving aid | 75 |
| % of students receiving loans | 65 |
| % of students receiving grants | 75 |
| Average award package | $17,281 |
| Average grant | $4,968 |
| Average student loan debt | $26,300 |

### ADMISSIONS

| | |
|---|---|
| Admissions Selectivity Rating | 92 |
| # of applications received | 304 |
| % applicants accepted | 43 |
| % acceptees attending | 62 |
| Average GMAT | 635 |
| Range of GMAT | 600–670 |
| Average GPA | 3.44 |
| TOEFL required of international students? | yes |
| Minimum TOEFL (paper/computer) | 600/250 |
| Application fee | $50 |
| International application fee | $75 |
| Regular application deadline | 5/31 |
| Deferment available? | yes |
| Maximum length of deferment | 1 year |
| Need-blind admissions? | yes |

### APPLICANTS ALSO LOOK AT

Arizona State University, Brigham Young University, Rice University, The University of Texas at Austin, University of Maryland, College Park, University of Notre Dame, Vanderbilt University

### EMPLOYMENT PROFILE

| | | | | |
|---|---|---|---|---|
| Career Rating | 91 | Grads employed by field: | % | avg. salary: |
| Primary source of full-time | | Finance | 36 | $72,765 |
| job acceptances | | Human Resources | 3 | $76,500 |
| School-facilitated activities | 43% | Marketing | 18 | $81,000 |
| Graduate-facilitated activities | 57% | MIS | 2 | $68,500 |
| | | Operations | 7 | $87,750 |
| Average starting salary | $77,087 | Consulting | 18 | $71,190 |
| Percent employed | 97 | General Management | 16 | $87,429 |

# TEXAS A&M UNIVERSITY—COMMERCE
## COLLEGE OF BUSINESS AND TECHNOLOGY

### GENERAL INFORMATION
Type of school                 public
Academic calendar            semester

### SURVEY SAYS...
Friendly students
Happy students
*Solid preparation in:*
Marketing
Finance
General management

### STUDENTS
Enrollment of parent
  institution                    4,170
Enrollment of business school  195
% male/female                  49/51
% out-of-state                    25
% part-time                       57
% minorities                      25
% international                   23
Average age at entry              29

### ACADEMICS
**Academic Experience Rating   66**
Student/faculty ratio           27:1
Profs interesting rating          62
Profs accessible rating           61
% female faculty                  10
% minority faculty                10

### JOINT DEGREES
BPA/MBA in Accounting, 4 years +
1 year

### PROMINENT ALUMNI
Sam Rayburn, Speaker of the
House; Sheryl Leach, Creator of
Barney; Durwood Merril, Baseball
Umpire- Texas Baseball Hall of
Fame; Duane Allen, Oak Ridge
Boys- Lead Singer

## Academics

With classes offered in five locations, the College of Business and Technology at Texas A&M Commerce has made convenience one of its chief selling points. The approach seems to be working; the program is now one of the biggest MBA programs in the Dallas/Fort Worth region, according to the *Dallas Business Journal*. The school uses only its regular, full-time graduate faculty to teach MBA classes in Commerce, Mesquite, McKinney, Dallas, and Waco. (The Waco program, which began in the spring of 2004, is cohort-based.) According to a survey, easy-to-reach locations, affordability, and connections to area industry are the reasons most students choose to pursue a Commerce MBA.

Students can choose not only from a wide range of sites, but also from a variety of program options. The Fast Track MBA offers a general management degree consisting of 10 courses. This program, which can be finished in one year, is favored by the school's five-year BA/MBA students. The Comprehensive MBA can also be completed in a year, although most students take longer due to required foundation courses (which can be waived for students with mastery in foundation areas). The school also offers MBAs a minor that is available in accounting, economics, finance, human-resources management, international business, management-information systems, marketing, and management of technology. In addition, students at Commerce can pursue a British study option, study in China through the China University of Geosciences Partnership, and MS degrees in e-commerce, economics, finance, management, and marketing. The MS in management can be completed entirely online; there are select MBA classes also available over the Internet.

Big things are ahead for Texas A&M Commerce. The school introduced an online MBA program in the fall of 2004 and will soon offer an A&M MBA in Beijing, China. "If they cannot come here to Commerce, we will take the MBA program to them," explains university President Keith McFarland, alluding to the difficulty foreign students have receiving United States visas in the post-9/11 world. "They will receive the same high quality education we are known for." That means Chinese students will soon benefit from "very experienced faculty [and] a low student-teacher ratio that shows the school really cares about the students and tries to get to know them."

## Career and Placement

The university maintains a career-services office on its main campus in Commerce. The office includes a library of job-related materials and a bulletin board of job postings; its staff offers one-on-one counseling to students searching for jobs. The school is one of 44 members of the Metroplex Area Consortium of Career Centers (MAC3), "organized for the purpose of 'uniting students, employers, educators, and the community to form a better workplace.'" MAC3 maintains an online job database and holds regular career fairs.

Tammi Thompson, Admissions Advisor
PO Box 3011, Commerce, TX 75429 United States
Phone: 903-886-5167 • Fax: 903-886-5165
E-mail: graduate_school@tamu-commerce.edu
Website: www.tamu-commerce.edu/graduateprograms

## Student Life and Environment

The cooperative students in Commerce's various programs constitute "a melting pot of many ethnic backgrounds; [there are] both male and female students [with] fairly large variances in age and work experience." The population includes "a large proportion of international students from East Asia and India." MBAs say, "Students are either really involved in extracurricular life or not at all," and that their ranks contain "many commuters who don't participate in on-campus activities."

The Commerce campus includes "a brand-new, multimillion-dollar recreation center. The students love it." MBAs comment that "even though it is a small campus, there is plenty to do." Nationally touring performers, lecturers, festivals, and parties fill the extracurricular calendar here. The school's athletic programs are hit-and-miss; the women's soccer team is quite competitive, while the men's football and basketball teams are dolorous endeavors.

Commerce, Texas is a quaint town sixty miles east of Dallas. Its population totals around 7,500 permanent residents; when school is in session, the population doubles. Major employers in the area include Bank One, Ben E. Keith Foods, Tyco, and the university. MBAs warn that "the town is a very low-income town, which results in a low-income lifestyle at the school."

## Admissions

Applicants to the MBA program at the College of Business must send the Admissions Office copies of all undergraduate and graduate transcripts, GMAT or GRE scores, three letters of recommendation (from present or past employers and/or from professors), a personal statement describing one's goals in pursuing a graduate degree, and a current resume. A minimum undergraduate GPA of 2.75 and a GMAT score of at least 400 are both required to qualify for full admission; students not meeting these requirements may still enter under probationary status, or they may enter with nondegree status. Applicants to MS programs may take the GRE or GMAT. To gain entrance into the 33-hour program, students must have successfully completed introductory undergraduate classes in accounting, finance, macroeconomics, management, marketing, microeconomics, operations, and statistics.

### FINANCIAL FACTS
Annual tuition (in-state/out-of-state) $3,274/$8,242
Books and supplies $900
Room & board (on/off-campus) $5,740/$2,170

### ADMISSIONS
Admissions Selectivity Rating 81
# of applications received 600
% applicants accepted 30
% acceptees attending 95
Average GMAT 460
Range of GMAT 380–620
Average GPA 3
TOEFL required of international students? yes
Minimum TOEFL (paper/computer) 500/173
Application fee $35
International application fee $50
Regular application deadline 6/1
Regular notification rolling
Deferment available? yes
Maximum length of deferment 2 semesters
Transfer students accepted? yes
Transfer application policy
Students can transfer up to 12 semester hours in the 36-48 HR program and 9 semester hours for the 30-33 HR.
Non-fall admissions? yes

### APPLICANTS ALSO LOOK AT
Southern Methodist University, Texas Christian University (TCU), The University of Texas at Arlington, University of Dallas, University of North Texas, University of Phoenix Online

### EMPLOYMENT PROFILE
Career Rating 61
Average starting salary $62,000

# Texas Christian University (TCU)
## The M. J. Neeley School of Business

## Academics

The greatest strengths of the M. J. Neeley School of Business, the boutique-size MBA program at Texas Christian University, "all have to do with its size," students say. "Because it is small, students' needs are recognized and addressed quickly, professors give students a lot of attention, and the students are all very close. It all makes for good learning environment and good networking." Neeley excels in a variety of areas; finance and investments, supply-chain management, and the entrepreneurs program all received plaudits from our survey respondents, who happily added that the school is not content to rest on its laurels. "They want to break into the top-50 business schools and stay there, and they push us accordingly," MBAs tell us. "The recent additions of several prominent and recognizable faculty" represent just one stage of TCU's efforts in this area.

Not that the faculty has never been a group of slouches. According to one second-year student, "The professors are great teachers and are available at all times. Some outstanding teachers were Vassil Mihov, Steve Lim, Bill Cron, Chuck Williams, Rob Rhodes, Larry Lockwood, and In-mu Haw. All of these men have great minds and are great teachers." They also "go the extra mile to ensure that we learn and feel prepared for exams or for our future careers." Instruction is often integrated; "course material overlaps, and we are looking at similar issues from different perspectives in different classes." While "professors do lecture, students must be prepared to discuss the reading materials in class." The workload can be heavy, but rarely is it overly quant-heavy. One student explains, "The professors design classes to help bring nonbusiness majors quickly up to speed. This is a good school to attend if you have a liberal-arts background."

TCU offers students a number of user-friendly options, including "the ability to take classes with other graduate-program students," which as one student notes is "very helpful." The school's location, near the Dallas/Forth Worth area, offers "networking opportunities and close ties to companies in the area." An Executive MBA program is "open to qualified candidates with eight or more years of work experience, five of which must be managerial in nature."

## Career and Placement

Neeley offers its MBAs free access to a number of premium online career services, including CareerLeader, CareerSearch, WetFeet, Vault and H1 Base. The school also offers a series of workshops throughout students' tenure to teach them everything from how to prepare a great resume to which fork to use during the salad course. In 2005, 95 percent of the class of 2006 sought summer internships; 100 percent received and accepted offers. Students report approvingly, "Since we are a relatively small program, we get a lot of personal attention from the faculty and staff."

Employers who most frequently hire Neeley graduates include Accenture, Alcon Labs, American Airlines, Auto Zone, Bell Helicopter Textron, Buxton, Countrywide, Citigroup, Wachovia, Key Bank, Wells Fargo, Celanese, CBiz, First Command Financial Planning, Handango, IBM China, Whitley Penn, Bernstein, Conklin and Balcomb, PepsiCo, Sabre Holdings, 7-Eleven, Southwest Securities, CSFB, Deloitte Touche Tohmastu, Mary Kay, Staubach, Q Investments, and AT&T. More than 80 percent of Neeley graduates secure positions in Texas. Five percent find employment overseas.

## Student Life and Environment

Neeley recently relocated to a "great new building with a number of team rooms." Students tell us, "Having so many available rooms keeps many students on campus the entire day and evening. The rooms are very conducive to getting to know each other. Not

OLIVIA WILLIAMS, ASSISTANT DIRECTOR OF MBA ADMISSIONS
PO BOX 298540, FORT WORTH, TX 76129 UNITED STATES
PHONE: 817-257-7531 • FAX: 817-257-6431
E-MAIL: MBAINFO@TCU.EDU • WEBSITE: WWW.MBA.TCU.EDU

only do we all study together and help each other, we also get to know each other well. We have everything we need in the new building [like] study rooms, a sandwich shop, [and a] lounge." MBAs describe an unusually congenial atmosphere at their school; it's the kind of place where students stay in touch year-round. One student reports, "During the summer, most of us had internships here in the area, so we would meet for happy hour on Friday to discuss our work for the week and just keep in touch."

A typical day at Neeley is "busy, but good. The workload is manageable but challenging. There is always some project to be working on, a case to read, or a problem set to complete." When school is done, "there's always something going on, whether it's an employer-appreciation reception, industry speaker or presentation, mentor dinner, community-service project, or tailgate party." Tailgates are central to the TCU experience; "the MBA student association has sponsored a tailgate at each home football game." Students also "often go out together on Thursday nights, first-years and second-years. Happy hours are also very common on Fridays. The MBA Association is making more of an effort to include the professional MBA students in the activities."

Students praise TCU's efforts to diversify its student body but report that it still has some ground to cover. One student writes about the diversity, "While women, Hispanic students, and international students are well represented, there [are only a few] African American students found in either of the full-time classes," although efforts are underway to attract a more diverse group of students. Students love TCU's location "in the Dallas/Fort Worth area because it gives the school several connections within the metroplex, which makes us very accessible to local employers." TCU, we're told, enjoys "a great relationship with both the city and the businesses [in Dallas/Fort Worth]."

## Admissions

Applicants to the Neeley MBA program must submit undergraduate transcripts, GMAT scores, letters of recommendation, a personal statement, and a resume. An interview, while not required, is "strongly encouraged"; interviews can be conducted via telephone for applicants unable to visit the campus. At least two years of work experience is recommended. The school reports that "a holistic admissions approach is used to assess the applicant's fit with the program. In addition to academic ability, applicants must demonstrate the desire and ability to perform in a highly interactive, team-based environment." To attract minority students, the school awards "scholarships to recognize the achievements of Henry B. Gonzalez and Martin Luther King, Jr., made available to TCU MBA students by the PepsiCo Foundation." The school also offers National Hispanic MBA and National Black MBA scholarships.

### FINANCIAL FACTS

| | |
|---|---|
| Annual tuition | $22,200 |
| Fees | $2,200 |
| Books and supplies | $1,600 |
| Room & board | $10,000 |
| % of students receiving aid | 86 |
| % of first-year students receiving aid | 100 |
| % of students receiving loans | 60 |
| % of students receiving grants | 83 |
| Average award package | $28,753 |
| Average grant | $18,577 |
| Average student loan debt | $35,000 |

### ADMISSIONS

| | |
|---|---|
| **Admissions Selectivity Rating** | **83** |
| # of applications received | 109 |
| % applicants accepted | 64 |
| % acceptees attending | 61 |
| Average GMAT | 604 |
| Range of GMAT | 550–650 |
| Average GPA | 3.2 |
| TOEFL required of international students? | yes |
| Minimum TOEFL (paper/computer) | 550/213 |
| Application fee | $50 |
| International application fee | $50 |
| Regular application deadline | 4/30 |
| Regular notification | rolling |
| Early decision program? | yes |
| ED Deadline/notification | Completed application by 1/31 / 2/15 |
| Deferment available? | yes |
| Maximum length of deferment | 1 year |
| Transfer students accepted? | yes |
| Transfer application policy | |
| Maximum transferable credits are 6 semester hours from an AACSB-accredited institution. | |
| Non-fall admissions? | yes |
| Need-blind admissions? | yes |

### APPLICANTS ALSO LOOK AT

Baylor University, Rice University, South Texas College of Law, Southern Methodist University, The University of Texas at Austin, Tulane University

## EMPLOYMENT PROFILE

| Career Rating | 88 | Grads employed by field: | % | avg. salary: |
|---|---|---|---|---|
| **Primary source of full-time job acceptances** | | Finance | 42 | $64,461 |
| | | Marketing | 19 | $83,900 |
| School-facilitated activities | 20 (77%) | Operations | 16 | $64,250 |
| Graduate-facilitated activities | 6 (23%) | Consulting | 3 | NR |
| | | General Management | 7 | NR |
| Average starting salary | $67,732 | Other | 13 | $57,334 |
| Percent employed | 84 | | | |

# TEXAS TECH UNIVERSITY

## JERRY S. RAWLS COLLEGE OF BUSINESS ADMINISTRATION

### GENERAL INFORMATION
| | |
|---|---|
| Type of school | public |
| Environment | city |
| Academic calendar | rolling |

### SURVEY SAYS...
Friendly students
*Solid preparation in:*
Teamwork
Communication/interpersonal skills
Presentation skills

### STUDENTS
| | |
|---|---|
| Enrollment of parent institution | 28,001 |
| Enrollment of business school | 367 |
| % male/female | 75/25 |
| % out-of-state | 9 |
| % part-time | 82 |
| % minorities | 6 |
| % international | 17 |
| Average age at entry | 25 |
| Average years work experience at entry | 4 |

### ACADEMICS
| | |
|---|---|
| **Academic Experience Rating** | **71** |
| Student/faculty ratio | 8:1 |
| Profs interesting rating | 74 |
| Profs accessible rating | 84 |
| % female faculty | 11 |
| % minority faculty | 1 |

### JOINT DEGREES
MD/MBA 4 years; JD/MBA 3 years;
MA foreign language/MBA 2 years;
MA Architecture/MBA 2 1/2 years;
Dual MBA programs with:
Universidad Anahuac/Mexico 2
years; Sup de Co Montpellier 2
years

### PROMINENT ALUMNI
Jerry V. Smith, President/J. V. Smith
Professional Corporation-CPA;
Robert C. Brown, Director, Wayne &
Gladys Valley Foundation; James C.
Wetherbe, PhD, TTU-Bobby G.
Stevenson Chair in Information
Technology

## Academics

"Excellent cost-benefit" is the fare of the day at Texas Tech University's Rawls College of Business Administration, where "[students] can get an inexpensive MBA in a year-and-a-half program." Students love the price tag, but they also appreciate Texas Tech's regional reputation; according to students, "It's a big school known for its research activities and is considered among the best schools in Texas." The program also accommodates part-time students by offering all required MBA courses in the evening each academic year.

The Rawls MBA curriculum consists of 27 hours of required general business courses, 6 hours of credited out-of-class experience (internship, international study, directed experience), a 3-hour capstone course, and 12 hours of electives. Students can earn a concentration by dedicating all 12 elective hours to a single subject; Rawls offers concentrations in agribusiness, energy commerce, entrepreneurship, finance, health-organization management, international business, management-information systems, and marketing. Rawls also offers a more specialized MS in business administration, an IMBA (international MBA), and an MSA (master of science in accounting).

MBAs note that "[the professors] are world leaders in research and consulting and yet remain easily accessible to all of their students." Students add, "[We] really like the professors' attitudes here—they teach as well and as much as they can. [They] want their students to know everything they do, instead of concealing some things to retain their status and power." One student comments, "Our professors are constantly trying to incorporate the demands of the working world into our courses, which I think makes us very prepared. Our courses are constantly being updated and changed to fit the current climate of the business world." They are also good contacts and mentors. One MBA reports, "Several [professors] have offered to help me as I begin my job search, and most know me by my first name."

The wish lists of many students include the addition of "leveling courses for nonbusiness majors." (Texas Tech welcomes students with little previous business education or experience.) One student notes, "I'm completely lost in half of my classes because we just jumped right in, and starting intermediate accounting after majoring in journalism was a bit of a shock." Some students would also "like to see Texas Tech get involved with the city of Lubbock [and] get companies to set up shop in the city. A commonality of top MBA programs seems to be their proximity to large cities, and the opportunities that are created with companies located there. It would be in the interest of Tech to have companies as liaisons." One student says, "I believe the school should be more active in participating with Lubbock in creating beneficial opportunities."

## Career and Placement

According to students, "Rawl's Business School [built] its own career center about a year ago." Students add, "It's doing very well for only being there almost a year. However, the opportunities that it brings in for MBA students is very much lacking. Most of the opportunities are for undergrad degrees." Students also feel that the center needs to "improve counseling for career opportunities for students, especially international students" and "provide one-to-one counseling to help students decide their courses, internships, jobs, and finally to choose career paths." They also see great potential in the new office, though, and have high hopes for its future.

CINDY BARNES, DIRECTOR, GRADUATE SERVICES CENTER
RAWLS COLLEGE OF BUSINESS, GRADUATE SERVICES CENTER LUBBOCK, TX 79409-2101 U.S.
PHONE: 806-742-3184 • FAX: 806-742-3958
E-MAIL: MBA@BA.TTU.EDU • WEBSITE: WWW.GRAD.BA.TTU.EDU

Companies that most frequently employ Rawls MBAs include Accenture; Andersen; Cap Gemini; CINTAS; Comerica; Covenant Health Systems; Dell; Deloitte Touche Tohmatsu; DePuy Orthopaedics, Inc.; First Investors Corporation; Kellogg's; KPMG; National Instruments; NHK International; PNB Financial; PricewaterhouseCoopers; Ryan and Company; SBC; Walgreens; Wells Fargo Financial; and Yvew Socher. About 10 percent of Rawls graduates find their first post-graduation jobs outside of the United States.

## Student Life and Environment

Texas Tech MBAs praise their hometown of Lubbock, where "good old West Texas friendliness" is always the rule. Students say, "Life in Lubbock is relaxed. There is plenty of shopping, a good selection of housing, and diversified activities available." Located in the midst of a rich agricultural area, this city of approximately 200,000 has developed into a regional commercial, financial, cultural, educational, and medical center (the school even offers a concentration in health-facility management). The cost of living is reasonable, and the city is hospitable to entrepreneurial enterprise. The area also has a rapidly growing—and surprisingly well-regarded—wine industry.

Texas Tech is home to a huge undergraduate population (approximately 22,000), and according to students, "Texas Tech has a good nightlife. Lots of students go Greek and there are tons of clubs for undergrad and grads alike." MBAs note, "If you're doing your schoolwork right, you stay busy, but there is still time to enjoy yourself." Nearly all students enjoy Texas Tech's "excellent football team" and the tailgating parties preceding home games; the school also has a well-loved women's basketball team. Texas Tech's campus has "an excellent recreation center with lots of other opportunities for physical activities, a theater that shows movies, a sprawling campus with greenery, a great bookstore, and a coffee place in the university center. There is always something happening on campus," according to students.

## Admissions

In considering candidates for its MBA program, the admissions department at Texas Tech reviews "work experience, awards, leadership positions held in college and/or industry, likelihood of bringing a unique perspective to the program, civic and volunteer activities, motivation, past success, and letters of recommendation." The school requires students to submit official transcripts of all undergraduate and graduate work and GMAT scores; international students whose first language is not English must also provide TOEFL scores. To increase minority interest in the school, Texas Tech advertises in minority magazines, recruits in minority colleges in New Mexico and Texas, and attends and recruits at minority forums and conferences, such as the National Black Graduate Student Conference.

### FINANCIAL FACTS

| | |
|---|---|
| Annual tuition (in-state/out-of-state) | $4,296/$10,920 |
| Fees | $3,542 |
| Books and supplies | $1,500 |
| Room & board | $6,000 |
| % of students receiving grants | 18 |
| Average grant | $1,000 |
| Average student loan debt | $10,333 |

### ADMISSIONS

| | |
|---|---|
| Admissions Selectivity Rating | 74 |
| # of applications received | 394 |
| % applicants accepted | 81 |
| % acceptees attending | 68 |
| Average GMAT | 545 |
| Range of GMAT | 500–590 |
| Average GPA | 3.45 |
| TOEFL required of international students? | yes |
| Minimum TOEFL (paper/computer) | 550/213 |
| Application fee | $50 |
| International application fee | $60 |
| Regular application deadline | rolling |
| Regular notification | rolling |
| Deferment available? | yes |
| Maximum length of deferment | 1 year |
| Transfer students accepted? | yes |
| Transfer application policy | Up to 6 hours may be transfered. |
| Non-fall admissions? | yes |

### APPLICANTS ALSO LOOK AT

South Texas College of Law, The University of Texas at Austin

| EMPLOYMENT PROFILE | | | | |
|---|---|---|---|---|
| Career Rating | 68 | Grads employed by field: | % | avg. salary: |
| Average starting salary | $45,362 | Accounting | 9 | $42,400 |
| Percent employed | 70 | Finance | 31 | $48,571 |
| | | Human Resources | 4 | $40,000 |
| | | Marketing | 17 | $38,625 |
| | | Operations | 4 | $51,733 |
| | | Consulting | 9 | $64,400 |
| | | General Management | 13 | $45,000 |
| | | Other | 13 | $36,16 |

# THUNDERBIRD
## THE GARVIN SCHOOL OF INTERNATIONAL MANAGEMENT

## Academics

"Thunderbird has an international focus and curriculum that others try to emulate," students say, explaining why their school often turns up atop lists of the best international-business programs in the United States. MBAs here love that certain tracks have a "very flexible program that allows students to complete their MBA in one year or two years;" it's a "tripartite curriculum focusing in global business, international studies, and modern languages." However, students warn that "the overall academic rigor is unbelievably challenging. It gets more and more difficult each module (we have two modules per trimester). The program is condensed and very fast-paced, so it is very demanding." Number-crunching is a must; according to "[one] nonquant person, the learning curve through the first two-thirds of the program was vertical. I have worked harder in this program, for a longer period of time, than I have ever worked at anything in my life (including 10 years of business experience and past participation in a Big Ten major sports program); and, despite the painful moments, I've probably enjoyed it more than any prior experience as well." Casework is also critical; one MBA explains, "Thunderbird does a good job of using casework to reinforce the concepts learned in class. It also does a good job promoting team and project work."

Students say that there are "down-to-earth [professors]" who "are all high achievers in their field, erudite (knowledgeable outside of their field), interesting, fun, and from diverse backgrounds." This includes a number of professors who "are truly top-shelf. They are not afraid to challenge you, and many demand (and usually get) more from you than you may think you have." Students also appreciate such technical perks as wireless Internet and "a powerful Intranet community; we communicate by 'My Thunderbird' (MTB). It is a way of life bringing information to our fingertips and maximizing interaction. At Thunderbird, class is always in session." Students also praise the library, Thunderbird International Business Information Center (TBIC) describing it as "second to none."

## Career and Placement

Thunderbird's website lists over 200 companies that "have visited the Thunderbird campus to interview students and/or have hired recent graduates in the past year." The school's biggest on-site recruiting activity is the fall Career Fair, which drew at least 56 companies last year. Off-campus events in which Thunderbird participates include the International MBA Conference, the National MBA Consortium, the National Black MBA Association, the National Society of Hispanic MBAs, and Winterim programs in Washington, DC; Wall Street; Cuba; South Africa; Chile; Peru; Argentina; Prague; Singapore; India; and Switzerland. The Career Fair, designed to procure summer work for first-year students, drew 49 companies this year. Students generally agree that "the Career Management Center is very good, but not excellent." One MBA student opines, "The school needs to market itself more to the United States. Thunderbird is recognized around the world and in the United States as the best MBA international-business program around. However, its brand management needs to improve with all companies and with undergraduate schools so that it can recruit the best companies and students to its campus." The school has addressed this by intensifying its marketing efforts in the U.S. and abroad with a new web marketing/lead generation program, a worldwide branding campaign and is currently in the process of upgrading its corporate website to reflect the new "Truly Global" brand and provide increased accessibility for prospective students.

Companies looking at Thunderbird graduates include Abbott Japan, AIG, American Express, Citigroup, Daimler Chrysler, Dell Computer Corporation, Deloitte Touche Tohmatsue, Echo Star, GE, Honeywell, IBM, Intel, Johnson & Johnson, LG Electronics,

JUDY JOHNSON, DEAN OF ADMISSIONS
15249 NORTH 59TH AVENUE, GLENDALE, AZ 85306-6000 UNITED STATES
PHONE: 602-978-7100 • FAX: 602-439-5432
E-MAIL: ADMISSIONS@THUNDERBIRD.EDU • WEBSITE: WWW.THUNDERBIRD.EDU

L'Oréal, Lufthansa, Microsoft, Novartis, Post World Net, Samsung Electronics, and UBS Warburg. Average starting salary for 2005 graduates was $72,395. Average signing bonus was $10,760.

## Student Life and Environment

Students at Thunderbird agree that there is a "good mix of social life and school life." Sometimes both come rolled up in the same activity; one MBA notes, "There are a million clubs for all ethnicities, for business interests, and for personal/social interests. We attract a lot of ambassadors and former princes or presidents to speak, and the quality of speakers is excellent. The clubs on campus are also very active in putting together topical panels and networking events." Another adds, "We have fantastic cultural nights that allow a group of international students to present their customs and cuisine. There are always great events and good excuses to sample a seemingly endless variety of regional alcoholic delights." MBAs also appreciate the presence of "a very nice pub on campus. It's a great place to network on the weekends. It's like a small family reunion every weekend." These get-togethers are unusually festive because Thunderbird students genuinely appear to like each other a lot; they regard each other as "the school's greatest strength. I can (and do) sit down at lunch every day with students from any number of countries. The cultural mix here is fantastic. I can have conversations every day with people from Finland to Fiji; everyone speaks two, three, even four or more languages. There are also many more 'nonstandard' business types here than you might find at traditional b-schools; that is, people bring perspectives from all walks of personal and professional experience. I know I could pick out almost anyone on campus for a dinner out and have a great conversation about something besides net present value or statistical anomalies," according to one student. Students agree that the benefits of the school's social life extend beyond graduation, as MBAs "all know that the Thunderbird Network is one of the most valuable aspects of this school. Wherever we are in the world after we graduate, either for business or leisure, a Thunderbird graduate is not far away." What more could you ask for in a student body? How about "the best rugby team of all the United States b-schools?" You got it.

## Admissions

Thunderbird considers all of the following in evaluating its MBA program applicants: GMAT scores, personal essays, TOEFL scores (if required), letters of reference (preferably from a supervisor or professional peer), college transcripts, and a resume. Applicants must demonstrate at least two years of work experience; international or cross-cultural experience is recommended. Applications are considered on a rolling basis; offers of admission are term-specific and are valid only until all spaces in a particular term's class have been filled. Applications may be submitted online at www.PrincetonReview.com.

## PROMINENT ALUMNI

Frances Sevilla-Sacasa, President, US Trust Corporation; Luis Moreno, President, Inter-American Development Bank; Mark Emkes, Chair and CEO, Bridgestone Americas Holding; Lewis Lucke, Ambassador, Kingdom of Swaziland; Bill Burrus, President and CEO, Accion USA

## FINANCIAL FACTS

| | |
|---|---|
| Annual tuition | $32,100 |
| Fees | $1,038 |
| Books and supplies | $1,420 |
| Room & board (on/off-campus) | $3,900/$7,200 |
| % of students receiving aid | 71 |
| % of first-year students receiving aid | 69 |
| % of students receiving loans | 47 |
| % of students receiving grants | 36 |
| Average award package | $27,387 |
| Average grant | $16,613 |
| Average student loan debt | $24,993 |

## ADMISSIONS

| | |
|---|---|
| Admissions Selectivity Rating | 80 |
| # of applications received | 612 |
| % applicants accepted | 72 |
| % acceptees attending | 57 |
| Average GMAT | 603 |
| Range of GMAT | 530–640 |
| Average GPA | 3.3 |
| TOEFL required of international students? | yes |
| Minimum TOEFL (paper/computer) | 600/250 |
| Application fee | $125 |
| International application fee | $125 |
| Regular application deadline | 8/11 |
| Regular notification | rolling |
| Non-fall admissions? | yes |
| Need-blind admissions? | yes |

## APPLICANTS ALSO LOOK AT

Babson College, Southern Methodist University, University of Notre Dame, University of South Carolina, University of Southern California

| EMPLOYMENT PROFILE | | | | |
|---|---|---|---|---|
| **Career Rating** | **75** | **Grads employed by field:** | **%** | **avg. salary:** |
| **Primary source of full-time** | | Finance | 23 | $72,465 |
| **job acceptances** | | Human Resources | 1 | $75,000 |
| School-facilitated activities | 107 (37%) | Marketing | 34 | $67,653 |
| Graduate-facilitated activities | 394 (63%) | MIS | 1 | $79,234 |
| | | Operations | 10 | $70,073 |
| Average starting salary | $72,395 | Consulting | 12 | $74,000 |
| Percent employed | 47 | General Management | 12 | $83,394 |
| | | Other | 7 | $74,722 |

# TULANE UNIVERSITY
## FREEMAN SCHOOL OF BUSINESS

## Academics

"Class size is one of the strong points at the Freeman School of Business, [the MBA program at Tulane University, where] MBA classes are limited to around 100, which places a personal touch on classroom lectures." All small schools must perform a balancing act; of course, it is difficult to cover all areas unless your customer base is large enough to support them all, but Tulane manages well. "Course offerings are numerous for a small student body. The academic experience can be tailored many different ways," students tell us. Of course, all business schools have standout departments; at Freeman, it's finance. One MBA tells us, "Tulane is very heavy on the finance area, with the majority of my classmates undertaking at least a supporting concentration in finance." While other areas receive sufficient coverage, we're told, they do not receive the five-star handling that Tulane lavishes on its finance department.

Freeman's size is designed to maximize contact between students and professors, and in that area the school also succeeds. MBAs tell us that the "knowledgeable, outgoing, and sometimes brilliantly innovative [professors] are always approachable either face-to-face or via e-mail." Students especially appreciate that "some top-notch professors teach core courses. The recent additions to the faculty are first-rate, reflecting the school's commitment to improving quality." Students can "get very involved, with professors acting as their teachers' assistants or research assistants due to small class size." That is, if they can find the time. Freeman's intensive seven-week academic terms mean that heavy course work starts on day one and doesn't let up until exam day. "I haven't been able to spend as much time on Bourbon Street as I had planned," is how one student put it.

How long Tulane intends to maintain its little-school charm is open to question. Enrollment has grown 57 percent in the past six years in anticipation of the school's new home, Goldring/Woldenberg Hall II; the new business-school facility opened in November of 2003. Students feel that "with the new building opening and bigger MBA class enrollment, it will be very possible in the next couple of years for the administration to improve practices and invite more leading professors." One thing that probably will not change is Freeman's overriding philosophy, which "is very concerned with providing the skills that will be directly applicable to your career. I think they've got the recipe for professional success right," notes one student.

## Career and Placement

Career prep begins as soon as students arrive at the Freeman School; orientation includes training in the use of e-recruiting, Tulane's online student information-management system. Subsequent training in interviewing, resume building, internship hunting, and salary negotiation follows and is offered throughout the program. Tulane also maintains a database (called the Career Consultants Network) of Freeman alumni willing to counsel current students. Job fairs and other recruiting events pepper Freeman's academic calendar.

The school's best efforts notwithstanding, students are less than 100 percent satisfied with their career office. One MBA complains, "We only had less than 10 *Fortune* 500 companies visiting last year. You do the math." Most students concede that "perhaps the biggest disadvantage with the school is the limited employment opportunities around New Orleans; [the] tough economy" hasn't helped either. Things are looking up, however, as "the Career Development Center just hired a new director from one of the leading business schools who is making a lot of great changes."

BILL D. SANDEFER, DIRECTOR OF GRADUATE ADMISSIONS AND FINANCIAL AID
7 MCALISTER DRIVE, SUITE 401, NEW ORLEANS, LA 70118 UNITED STATES
PHONE: 504-865-5410 • FAX: 504-865-6770
E-MAIL: FREEMAN.ADMISSIONS@TULANE.EDU • WEBSITE: WWW.FREEMAN.TULANE.EDU

Companies most likely to hire Freeman MBAs include Bank of America, Citibank, Credit Suisse First Boston, D&T Management Solutions, Entergy, FedEx, First Union Securities, Jackson & Rhodes, JPMorgan Chase, PA Consulting, Reliant Energy, Towers Perrin, and TXU. One-fifth of Freeman graduates find their first jobs outside the U.S.; about 60 percent wind up working somewhere in the South.

## Student Life and Environment

With the November 2003 completion of the Goldring/Woldenberg Hall II, the A.B. Freeman Business school has "finished its expansion and now it can host more students and faculties." The facility earns top marks from all students, who tell us that the "attractive and technologically advanced [business-school home is] amazing. It boasts the latest and greatest technology, including a trading floor, digital media theater, 60-inch plasma TVs, all the latest technology, [and] a number of breakout rooms for students to use for group work."

The new facility also has plenty of room to host speakers, club meetings, and social functions. "We have several school-sponsored events that are usually well-organized, though in New Orleans style," MBAs report. They add, "Social functions are extremely fun and occur quite often. We usually have a great turnout for each and every one, which makes for great friendships and networking opportunities within the MBA program." Students enjoy a "very broad choice of clubs to join depending on interests." One student approvingly notes, "Student organizations also invite speakers, do community consulting and other helpful jobs for the communities in New Orleans."

New Orleans, as you probably already know, "is a great place to live; [its legendary party scenes makes it] ideal for honing or exploiting social skills." One MBA explains, "Life in New Orleans is pretty terrific for all ages. There is always something fun to do for everyone; the weather is great almost year-round; the city is beautiful; and the people are friendly." Tulane's student body has a global flavor, as "more than 40 percent of the students are international." Those seeking employment in the East, take note: "Tulane also has over 1,000 alumni in Asia."

## Admissions

Freeman reviews applications to its graduate programs in three separate rounds; the school encourages students to apply as early as possible to maximize their chances of gaining admission. All of the following are required components of the application: undergraduate transcript, GMAT scores, TOEFL scores, letters of recommendation, work resume, personal statement, and interview. Minority recruitment efforts include Destination MBA, the National Black MBA Association Career Fair, targeted GMASS searches, and minority fellowships.

### FINANCIAL FACTS

| | |
|---|---|
| Annual tuition | $33,750 |
| Fees | $1,600 |
| Books and supplies | $1,600 |
| Room & board | $11,000 |
| % of students receiving aid | 80 |
| % of first-year students receiving aid | 74 |
| % of students receiving loans | 42 |
| % of students receiving grants | 47 |
| Average award package | $41,055 |
| Average grant | $9,350 |
| Average student loan debt | $67,010 |

### ADMISSIONS

| | |
|---|---|
| Admissions Selectivity Rating | 88 |
| # of applications received | 360 |
| % applicants accepted | 58 |
| % acceptees attending | 43 |
| Average GMAT | 654 |
| Range of GMAT | 600–710 |
| Average GPA | 3.34 |
| TOEFL required of international students? | yes |
| Minimum TOEFL (paper/computer) | 600/250 |
| Application fee | $125 |
| International application fee | $125 |
| Regular application deadline | 5/1 |
| Regular notification | 6/1 |
| Application deadline/notification | |
| Round 1: | 11/15 / 12/15 |
| Round 2: | 1/15 / 2/15 |
| Round 3: | 3/15 / 4/15 |
| Round 4: | 5/1 / 6/1 |
| Need-blind admissions? | yes |

### APPLICANTS ALSO LOOK AT

Emory University, Rice University, Southern Methodist University, The University of Texas at Austin, University of North Carolina—Chapel Hill, Vanderbilt University, Washington University

### EMPLOYMENT PROFILE

| Career Rating | 78 | Grads employed by field: | % | avg. salary: |
|---|---|---|---|---|
| Average starting salary | $72,961 | Finance | 64 | $76,273 |
| | | Marketing | 15 | $67,417 |
| | | Consulting | 8 | $71,000 |
| | | General Management | 13 | $66,333 |

# THE UNIVERSITY OF AKRON
## COLLEGE OF BUSINESS ADMINISTRATION

**GENERAL INFORMATION**

| | |
|---|---|
| Type of school | public |
| Environment | city |
| Academic calendar | fall |

**SURVEY SAYS...**
Friendly students
Helpful alumni
Happy students
Smart classrooms
*Solid preparation in:*
Communication/interpersonal skills
Computer skills
Doing business in a global economy

**STUDENTS**

| | |
|---|---|
| Enrollment of parent institution | 23,240 |
| Enrollment of business school | 235 |
| % male/female | 59/41 |
| % out-of-state | 5 |
| % part-time | 58 |
| % minorities | 5 |
| % international | 49 |
| Average age at entry | 28 |
| Average years work experience at entry | 4 |

**ACADEMICS**

| | |
|---|---|
| **Academic Experience Rating** | **64** |
| Student/faculty ratio | 22:1 |
| Profs interesting rating | 69 |
| Profs accessible rating | 77 |
| % female faculty | 15 |
| % minority faculty | 20 |

**JOINT DEGREES**
MBA/JD; MTax/JD; MSM in Human Resources/JD

**PROMINENT ALUMNI**
Ernest Pouttu, VP of Finance & CFO, Harwick Standard Distribution; James McCready, Chair of Cypress Companies; John Piecuch, Retired President & CEO of LaFarge Coppee; Joanne Rohrer, Secretary/Treasurer, Rohrer Corporation

## Academics

Full-time students in the University of Akron's MBA program have a number of options available to them. They can choose to pursue the conventional two-year program, or—if they have the requisite undergraduate course work to place out of all foundation courses—they can complete the degree more quickly via the accelerated 12-month program. The College of Business Administration (CBA) also offers a part-time MBA, an International Executive MBA, a masters of science (MS) in accountancy, an MS in management, and a master of taxation degree.

Akron's MBA program is large enough to offer a wide range of concentrations. Students here may specialize in accounting, e-business, finance, global sales management, health care management, international business, international finance, management, management of technology and innovation, marketing, and supply-chain management. Students appreciate the way the curriculum "emphasizes real cases to study" and "always tries to bring the latest technology to students." Most agree that "the greatest strength of the College of Business at the University of Akron is the professors. They take the initiative to make sure the students are exposed to the topics by giving real-world problems to the students." One part-time student notes, "I have found with my own background in operation, the examples used in class are very similar to what really happens on the job." Students also report that "the professors are friendly and approachable and are very willing to help by any means they can."

Specialized education is enhanced by the many institutes and research centers at the university; these include the Fisher Institute for Professional Selling (a sales-simulation and skills-practice facility), the Institute for Global Business (which provides "plenty of opportunities to study abroad"), the Center for Information Technology and e-Business, the Center for Organizational Development, and the Fitzgerald Institute for Entrepreneurial Studies. *Entrepreneur* magazine recognized the last of these in 2003 when it ranked the University of Akron among the top-25 schools offering a program in entrepreneurial studies. Students are proud that "the school is very focused on the latest trends in business; it is one of the few business schools with an e-business concentration for the MBA program. Also, the facilities are very modern have the latest technology."

## Career and Placement

The University of Akron's Center for Career Management provides career services for all undergraduates, graduate students, and alumni; the school does not maintain a separate career office for graduate students or business students. The office provides assistance in career planning, procuring a summer internship, developing job-search, interviewing, and resume-writing skills, and locating potential employers. Opinions about the office are widely mixed; some praise its work, while others feel that services for graduate students are minimal.

A paucity of on-campus recruiters led one student to state that "the career fairs are a waste of time. It is the same employers year after year. I stopped going because of this." Some of the employers who frequently hire Akron MBAs include Sogistics Corporation, Rhein Chemie Corporation, Lockheed Martin, Computer Sciences Corporation, and the Greater Cleveland Regional Transit Authority.

MYRA WEAKLAND, ASSISTANT DIRECTOR
THE UNIVERSITY OF AKRON, 259 SOUTH BROADWAY, ROOM 412, AKRON, OH 44325-4805 U.S.
PHONE: 330-972-7043 • FAX: 330-972-6588
E-MAIL: GRADCBA@UAKRON.EDU • WEBSITE: WWW.UAKRON.EDU/CBA/GRAD

## Student Life and Environment

CBA students are a varied group, with "friendly and intelligent international students" and a mix of people who "either have full-time jobs or have recently graduated from undergrad. There is a good diversity of age, experience, gender, and race here." One student happily notes, "I have met lots of really nice people and have study groups for almost all of my classes, which in my opinion is essential to being successful in grad school." Students convene in clubs—"there is one for every concentration"—and "parties hosted by students outside of school." Most agree, however, that this is not an especially social program; students generally spend their free time away from the program, not with classmates.

The University of Akron is a large school, with more than 24,000 undergraduates and graduate students. It is widely heralded for its science and engineering programs; these programs are outgrowths of the city of Akron's historical role as "the Rubber Capital of the World," which has spurred polymer research and development for well over a century. Students appreciate that "the business school is very accessible off the interstate. Most business classes are in one of two buildings that are connected by a parking deck."

Akron itself "is very small and there is not much to do except go to the movies or go see a play sometimes," students tell us. The historic downtown region is currently undergoing a revitalization program; it's too early into the process to judge the results. Cleveland is only an hour to the north, and it offers many of the cosmopolitan amenities currently absent from Akron.

## Admissions

The admissions committee at the University of Akron considers all of the following components of a business graduate student's application: undergraduate GPA, GMAT scores, TOEFL scores (international applicants), two letters of recommendation, a letter of purpose, resume, previous graduate and post-baccalaureate performance, and professional-association and student-organization memberships. The Graduate School of the University of Akron sponsors a diversity program to enhance minority recruitment within the MBA program.

## FINANCIAL FACTS

| | |
|---|---|
| Annual tuition (in-state/out-of-state) | $13,690/$22,006 |
| Fees | $777 |
| Books and supplies | $1,200 |
| Room & board | $10,000 |
| % of students receiving aid | 43 |
| % of first-year students receiving aid | 36 |
| Average award package | $25,235 |
| Average grant | $2,500 |

## ADMISSIONS

| | |
|---|---|
| Admissions Selectivity Rating | 70 |
| # of applications received | 112 |
| % applicants accepted | 88 |
| % acceptees attending | 49 |
| Average GMAT | 547 |
| Range of GMAT | 450–630 |
| Average GPA | 3.3 |
| TOEFL required of international students? | yes |
| Minimum TOEFL (paper/computer) | 550/213 |
| Application fee | $30 |
| International application fee | $40 |
| Regular application deadline | 8/1 |
| Regular notification | 8/15 |
| Deferment available? | yes |
| Maximum length of deferment | 2 years |
| Transfer students accepted? | yes |
| Transfer application policy | |

Up to 24 credits of foundation courses may be waived. Nine credits of the core may transfer from AACSB-accredited schools if approved by the director.

| | |
|---|---|
| Non-fall admissions? | yes |
| Need-blind admissions? | yes |

## APPLICANTS ALSO LOOK AT

Case Western Reserve University, Cleveland State University, John Carroll University, Kent State University, The Ohio State University, University of Cincinnati, Youngstown State University

## EMPLOYMENT PROFILE

| Career Rating | 62 | Grads employed by field: | % | avg. salary: |
|---|---|---|---|---|
| Primary source of full-time job acceptances | | Accounting | 21 | $55,360 |
| | | Finance | 17 | $52,000 |
| School-facilitated activities | 5 (13%) | Marketing | 8 | $43,500 |
| Graduate-facilitated activities | 1 (2%) | General Management | 33 | $46,500 |
| Unknown | 34 (85%) | Other | 21 | $49,600 |
| | | | | |
| Average starting salary | $49,658 | | | |
| Percent employed | 53 | | | |

# UNIVERSITY OF ALABAMA—BIRMINGHAM
## SCHOOL OF BUSINESS

## GENERAL INFORMATION
| | |
|---|---|
| Type of school | public |
| Environment | metropolis |
| Academic calendar | semester |

### SURVEY SAYS...
Happy students
Smart classrooms
*Solid preparation in:*
Teamwork

## STUDENTS
| | |
|---|---|
| Enrollment of parent institution | 16,000 |
| Enrollment of business school | 334 |
| % part-time | 97 |
| Average age at entry | 27 |
| Average years work experience at entry | 4 |

## ACADEMICS
| | |
|---|---|
| **Academic Experience Rating** | **72** |
| Student/faculty ratio | 30:1 |
| Profs interesting rating | 81 |
| Profs accessible rating | 77 |
| % female faculty | 16 |
| % minority faculty | 12 |

## JOINT DEGREES
MBA/MPH, 2-3 years; MBA/MSHA, 2-3 years; MBA/MSN, 2-3 years

## PROMINENT ALUMNI
John Bakane, CEO, Mills; Daryl Byrd, CEO and President, Iberia Bank; Susan Story, CEO and President, Gulf Power Company; James Woodward, Chancellor, UNC; Stephen Zelnak, CEO and President, Martin Marietta Materials.

## Academics

The School of Business MBA program at the University of Alabama—Birmingham is a part-time, evening program designed for students who are working full-time. Cost and convenience are the main reasons they choose this affordable program. Once MBAs arrive at UAB, they discover one of the university's lesser-known assets: a faculty of "inspiring, truly top-notch lecturers and researchers." Students say, "[The faculty] are always willing to offer real-world advice and assist us in reaching our goals once we are finished with the program." One student adds, "The faculty are very knowledgeable, and they all have great life experiences to use as valuable teaching tools. I have learned more about the real world through their experiences than I would have any other way. I feel that I am well prepared for life in the business world."

UAB has other assets as well. The administration here "has been working hard to increase the value of the program through class changes and student contact. The overall experience has been smooth and extremely educational." Students also love the classroom experience, which is "very informative and open to discussion." Students say, "Most of the faculty know us on a first-name basis. The classes are not excessively large, and the overall environment is conducive toward the learning process." Courses are offered at convenient times; students explain that "the class scheduling works well around the working students, which [includes] the majority of graduate students at UAB."

As at most state schools, UAB has problems stemming from a lack of funding. Some students grumble about "limited class offerings in the summer" and would like to see "more class offerings and concentrations during the year." In addition, while all classrooms have computer based multi-media systems and Internet access, at present the MBA program offers "video conferencing classes." But, despite this drawback, most students are extremely happy with the MBA at UAB. When students take the entire package into view, they conclude that "the MBA program here at UAB is outstanding, and it could benefit all students even more if the business school were given more funds to work with."

## Career and Placement

UAB maintains a branch office of its Career Services in the business wing of the Business-Engineering Complex to serve business undergraduates, graduates, and alumni. While a considerable 44 percent of current MBA students plan to stay with their current employer after graduation, the center works with the remaining students looking for assistance with job searches. The staff there "offers career counseling, coaching, and consultation, provide up-to-date information about the job market, career options, salary, and graduate school." Several students, however, feel that the school needs to create "more networking opportunities with large and prominent employers in Birmingham and surrounding areas."

Many students love Birmingham and feel that the city location "benefits the school because of the large business community it surrounds. It also allows the school to recruit professors with exceptional work experience." The manufacturing and service sectors supply most of the jobs; the city has steadily moved away from its past reliance on iron and steel.

Top employers in Birmingham include the university; the state and city governments; Alabama Power; AmSouth Bank; Baptist Health System; BellSouth; Blue Cross/Blue Shield; Bruno's, Inc.; and Wal-Mart.

GLENN KINSTLER, MBA PROGRAM COORDINATOR
1530 3RD AVENUE SOUTH, BEC 219, BIRMINGHAM, AL 35294-4460 UNITED STATES
PHONE: 205-934-8815 • FAX: 205-934-9200
E-MAIL: GKINSTLER@BUSINESS.UAB.EDU • WEBSITE: WWW.BUSINESS.UAB.EDU

## Student Life and Environment

Some students say that because "UAB is a commuter college," the school has "no campus identity; therefore, no real affiliation or bond is ever solidified between students and the school."; however, since students were last surveyed, UAB has reported an active MBA alumni association that has sponsored an annual scholarship for MBA students, golf tournaments, lunch and learn events as well as tailgating at UAB sports events. Other MBAs with busy schedules ask, "Who has time to be involved in student life? It is extremely tough to balance full-time work while being a full-time student." Even so, some would like to feel more like part of a community and would welcome more "opportunities for students to become involved."

With a metropolitan-area population of nearly one million, Birmingham is the biggest city in Alabama and one of the bigger cities in the South. Sports fans will appreciate that the area is home to competitive college football teams, arena football, an AA baseball team, and tons of excellent golf courses. Outdoor lovers will enjoy the easy access to fishing, hunting, boating, and hiking areas.

## Admissions

Admission to UAB's MBA program is based on evaluation of official transcripts, GMAT scores, and TOEFL scores (and work experience). A minimum score of 480 on the GMAT is required, as is a minimum score of 1,050 when the formula (200 5 undergraduate GPA) + GMAT score) is applied. A minimum TOEFL score of 550 (paper-based; 213 computer based) is also required of international students. UAB has a calculus prerequisite that students can waive by passing a proficiency exam or short review offered by the school.

### ADMISSIONS

| | |
|---|---|
| Admissions Selectivity Rating | 75 |
| # of applications received | 275 |
| % applicants accepted | 77 |
| % acceptees attending | 79 |
| Average GMAT | 553 |
| Range of GMAT | 510–600 |
| Average GPA | 3.2 |
| TOEFL required of international students? | yes |
| Minimum TOEFL (paper/computer) | 550/213 |
| Application fee | $50 |
| International application fee | $75 |
| Regular application deadline | 7/1 |
| Regular notification | 8/1 |
| Deferment available? | yes |
| Maximum length of deferment | 1 year |
| Transfer students accepted? | yes |

Transfer application policy
Must meet UAB MBA admission requirements, transfer courses must be from an AACSB-accredited program and equivalent to our required courses. We will accept up to 25 percent of the degree program in transfer work with a minimum "B" grade.

| | |
|---|---|
| Non-fall admissions? | yes |
| Need-blind admissions? | yes |

**APPLICANTS ALSO LOOK AT**
Samford University

### EMPLOYMENT PROFILE

| | |
|---|---|
| Career Rating | 73 |
| Average starting salary | $59,400 |

# UNIVERSITY OF ALABAMA—TUSCALOOSA
## MANDERSON GRADUATE SCHOOL OF BUSINESS

### GENERAL INFORMATION
| | |
|---|---|
| Type of school | public |
| Environment | city |
| Academic calendar | semester |

### SURVEY SAYS...
Happy students
Smart classrooms
*Solid preparation in:*
Marketing
Teamwork
Communication/interpersonal skills

### STUDENTS
| | |
|---|---|
| Enrollment of parent institution | 22,000 |
| Enrollment of business school | 105 |
| % male/female | 72/28 |
| % out-of-state | 37 |
| % minorities | 14 |
| % international | 10 |
| Average age at entry | 25 |
| Average years work experience at entry | 2.1 |

### ACADEMICS
| | |
|---|---|
| **Academic Experience Rating** | **97** |
| Student/faculty ratio | 12:1 |
| Profs interesting rating | 97 |
| Profs accessible rating | 98 |
| % female faculty | 13 |
| % minority faculty | 10 |

### JOINT DEGREES
MBA/JD, 4 years; MBA/MA in Modern Languages, 3 years; MBA/MSN, 3 years; MBA/MS in Engineering

### PROMINENT ALUMNI
Thomas Cross, Managing partner, PricewaterhouseCoopers; Samuel D. DiPiazza, Vice Chair, PricewaterhouseCoopers; Marvin Mann, Founding CEO, Lexmark

## Academics

With fewer than 55 full-time students per class, University of Alabama's Manderson Graduate School of Business truly offers its MBAs "the ability to develop personal relationships with all of [the] professors." It does so at a "very affordable" tuition rate, thanks to both the state sponsorship and to the assistantships that most students receive; many students at U of A feel that the university offers one of the best returns on investment available anywhere.

Students love U of A's "cutting-edge technology, which is a huge strength of [the] program. There are multimedia podiums in every classroom, and students have access to numerous computer labs. The business school has invested in wireless routers to allow students to access the Internet from laptops and PDAs. The classrooms and library have all the relevant technology," according to students. They also appreciate the "great atmosphere and the sense of tradition and pride at the University of Alabama." One MBA reports, "The campus is beautiful, and the architecture is superb. There are a few buildings that date back to before the Civil War. The grounds and facilities are well-maintained."

Manderson brags about the flexibility of its program, which allows students to create their own "niche of interest." MBAs concur and explain that "the flexibility of the program allows students to take on more than just a general degree but allows study abroad and dual concentrations." This flexibility arrives in the second year of the program, as the first year is given over to "a prescribed program of courses and cross-discipline work that blends an introduction to the analytical tools of management and the functional areas of business into a general management perspective." Throughout the curriculum, "teamwork is a focus of the program and students get a lot of practice in it," and "lectures, case studies, and current-event publications create an interactive learning experience." Students also add that "the class atmosphere encourages participation, and the instructors do an excellent job of letting class discussion lead the direction of the course, while still providing all the necessary tools to be a contributor in the business world."

Students explain that the professors at Manderson "are all recognized leaders in their perspective fields, and they are very compassionate. Our professors truly care about us and work with us." Students are particularly enthusiastic about the MIS faculty. Other students add that "more widespread project-management hands-on training would help the school."

## Career and Placement

Career Services are provided to Manderson MBAs through the university's Career Center and the College of Commerce and Business Administration Satellite Center. The office provides counseling services, workshops, online job databases, and biannual job fairs, which students say "assist [them] in the job hunt. Excellent companies are brought in for recruitment specifically from the MBA program." However, many feel that "the school could improve its recruitment of companies outside of the Southeast to come to campus for recruiting."

Top recruiters at the University of Alabama include Accenture, AmSouth Bank, Cap Gemini, Ernst & Young, Compass Bank, Eli Lilly, FedEx, Lithonia Lighting, Procter & Gamble, Southern Company, and Tait Advisory Services.

## Student Life and Environment

Despite the school's laid-back Southern setting, "life at the University of Alabama is fast-paced." Students describe a typical day: "Generally, each MBA class meets twice a week for an hour and 15 minutes. Each class has a heavy amount of team-based cases. Our

Ms. Burch Barger, Coordinator of Admission & Recruiting
PO Box 870223, Tuscaloosa, AL 35487-0223 United States
Phone: 205-348-9122 • Fax: 205-348-4504
E-mail: mba@cba.ua.edu • Website: www.cba.ua.edu/mba

entire class is divided into four- or five-member teams, which typically meet twice a week for an hour to discuss projects and divide responsibilities. In addition to the academic course load, the majority of our students are employed through student assistantships on campus or extended internships in the Tuscaloosa business community. Students' work schedules vary; however, the hour requirements range from 10 to 20 hours per week."

On top of their school and work responsibilities, "the majority of MBA students are active in the recruitment process. First-year students serve as MBA Hosts by giving tours to prospective students and corporate recruiters. Second-year students volunteer as Interview Fellows and actually interview all prospective students." These commitments leave some MBAs too busy to enjoy all the Tuscaloosa area has to offer. One student writes, "I wish I had more time for fishing in one of the area's many beautiful lakes, rivers, or nearby Gulf coast. There is some world-class golf nearby as well. Instead, I pretty much wake up, go to class, work as a grad assistant, study, and go to sleep."

Most students, however, manage to find time for social life. One student explains, "Everyone is voluntarily involved in the MBA Association. This provides many social activities and philanthropic opportunities for students. We also have events that bring us together as a class and help with networking opportunities, including hosting a golf tournament each year. My classmates also often hold impromptu parties to watch the latest sporting event or have a 'themed' dinner party, from Thai to a traditional Christmas dinner." Active organizations include: "Toastmaster's International, Women in Business, Finance Association, and the Dinner Club. Leadership positions are available for both first- and second-year students." Students also report that "weekends are filled with relaxation, social time, and great bands. During football season, two words: 'Roll Tide!'"

## Admissions

Applicants to Manderson must provide the admissions department with official copies of all undergraduate and graduate transcripts, GMAT scores, TOEFL scores (for applicants whose native language is not English), professional recommendations, and a resume. An interview is typically required of candidates. According to the school's catalog, "applicants must show evidence of career interest in management, and relevant employment experience is considered in the admissions decision." An understanding of introductory calculus and facility with basic computer functions (word processing, spreadsheets, databases) is expected.

### FINANCIAL FACTS

| | |
|---|---|
| Annual tuition (in-state/out-of-state) | $4,630/$12,664 |
| Fees | $1,600 |
| Books and supplies | $800 |
| Room & board | $8,800 |
| % of students receiving aid | 70 |
| % of first-year students receiving aid | 100 |
| % of students receiving loans | 25 |
| % of students receiving grants | 65 |
| Average award package | $14,522 |
| Average grant | $7,956 |
| Average student loan debt | $13,424 |

### ADMISSIONS

| | |
|---|---|
| **Admissions Selectivity Rating** | **96** |
| # of applications received | 248 |
| % applicants accepted | 32 |
| % acceptees attending | 62 |
| Average GMAT | 641 |
| Range of GMAT | 600–690 |
| Average GPA | 3.4 |
| TOEFL required of international students? | yes |
| Minimum TOEFL (paper/computer) | 550/213 |
| Application fee | $25 |
| International application fee | $25 |
| Regular application deadline | 4/15 |
| Regular notification | rolling |
| Application deadline/notification | |
| Round 1: | 1/5 / 1/20 |
| Round 2: | 2/15 / 3/1 |
| Round 3: | 4/15 / 5/1 |
| Round 4: | 7/1 / 7/15 |
| Early decision program? | yes |
| ED Deadline/notification | Fall |
| (rolling up to Jan. 5) / 1/20 | |
| Deferment available? | yes |
| Maximum length of deferment | 1-year renewable |
| Transfer students accepted? | yes |
| Transfer application policy | |
| Up to 12 credit hours accepted for transfer from an AACSB-accredited programs subject to committee approval. | |
| Need-blind admissions? | yes |

### APPLICANTS ALSO LOOK AT

Auburn University, The University of Mississippi, University of Florida, University of Georgia, University of South Carolina, University of Tennessee—Knoxville, Wake Forest University

### EMPLOYMENT PROFILE

| Career Rating | 79 | Grads employed by field: | % | avg. salary: |
|---|---|---|---|---|
| Average starting salary | $58,404 | Finance | 17 | $51,500 |
| | | Marketing | 17 | $51,000 |
| | | MIS | 21 | $53,625 |
| | | Operations | 8 | $67,500 |
| | | Consulting | 12 | $51,667 |
| | | General Management | 8 | $71,000 |
| | | Other | 17 | $73,500 |

# UNIVERSITY OF ALBERTA
## SCHOOL OF BUSINESS

### GENERAL INFORMATION
Type of school                     public
Environment                          city
Academic calendar          Sept. start

### SURVEY SAYS...
Friendly students
Happy students
Smart classrooms

### STUDENTS
Enrollment of parent
  institution                      35,666
Enrollment of business school   271
% male/female                    64/36
% part-time                          57
% international                      44
Average age at entry                 30
Average years work experience
  at entry                            7

### ACADEMICS
Academic Experience Rating       91
Student/faculty ratio              4:1
Profs interesting rating            89
Profs accessible rating             89
% female faculty                    22

### JOINT DEGREES
MBA/LLB, 4 years; MBA/MEng, 2
years; MBA/MAg, 2 years; MBA/MF,
2 years

### PROMINENT ALUMNI
Guy Kerr, President & CEO; Gay
Mitchell, Executive Vice-President-
Ontario; Guy Turcotte, Chair; Eric
Morgan, President; Michael Lang,
Chair

## Academics

Why trek up to the Northland of Edmonton for an MBA, you may ask yourself? Well, you may be the type who wants a program with "a great reputation and excellent research in a broad array of fields." Or you may be the cost-conscious type who values "a reasonably affordable education that returns excellent education value per dollar." Maybe you want to pursue an unusual specialization, such as natural resources and energy, technology commercialization, or leisure and sport management. All are good reasons to choose the Alberta School of Business, but the best of all might well be the quality of the faculty. As students here justifiably brag, "The professors at the U of A School of Business have won more 3M Teaching Fellowships (which recognize excellence in teaching and educational leadership) than any other school in Canada, and it shows in the lectures. The lectures are as real-world as possible."

Only a chosen few can enjoy this embarrassment of riches, unfortunately, as "only 50 full-time MBAs are accepted each Fall." Students love how "this keeps classes small. You take almost all of your courses together and this becomes a very tight-knit group. The small class size means that professors know your name and recognize you in the hallways." They also love the curriculum; another student says that "[the courses] provide core business fundamentals without the hype of other schools. Also, U of A has just the right mix of lecture and case learning. In recent years, schools have shifted to mainly case learning, which in my opinion does a poor job in communicating fundamentals. [U of A's] method of learning is the right one for me."

Those interested in research are well-served by 12 separate research centers in diverse areas such as social entrepreneurship, cultural industries, and professional service firm management. Those with an eye toward international markets will happily observe that "the program is very sensitive to ethnic and cultural differences, and it shows in the lectures. All professors are very aware of cultural differences and will take the time to explain examples, which may be lost on international students because of cultural differences." And those just looking for a solid MBA will be pleased to hear that "overall, academically, the program is challenging, but with good reason. The students here want to be as prepared as possible for their chosen career paths, and the faculty here assists with that by presenting us with a very high level of learning paired with incredible extracurricular activities. It's a program and culture well worth engaging in," according to students.

## Career and Placement

U of A's MBA Career Management Services does a solid job of serving students and alumni of the School of Business. Students explain that "one of the greatest strengths of the university is the connection to the local job market and the MBA program's adaptation using the specialization programs to better serve that market." MBAs also note that "there is less representation from other job markets than maybe there could be."

Employers most likely to hire Alberta MBAs include Alberta Energy; Alberta Environment; Alberta Sustainable Resources; ATB Financial; Lilydale Foods; Maple Leaf Foods; PepsiCo; Petro-Geotech RBC Financial; Sask Power; SCIMED; Stantec, Inc.; Vogel Publishing; and the University of Alberta.

## Student Life and Environment

"The culture is unique at the U of A; it is incredibly social, friendly, and collaborative." Students say, "There are always several different activities going on consecutively or at once, ranging from TGIFs to international potluck dinners, to guest-speaker lectures and

JOAN WHITE, EXECUTIVE DIRECTOR, MBA PROGRAMS
2-30 BUSINESS BUILDING, EDMONTON, AB T6G 2R6 CANADA
PHONE: 780-492-3946 • FAX: 780-492-7825
E-MAIL: MBA.PROGRAMS@UALBERTA.CA • WEBSITE: MBA.BUS.UALBERTA.CA

recruiting events. Everyone is invited and welcome to participate, and almost everybody does." The result of all this activity is "a tight-knit group that studies and plays hard together." As one student notes, "We placed third at the annual MBA games this year, which was pretty good. However, the real bonus for me was all the relationships and teamwork that was developed to make it there."

Because admission is so competitive, the student body is an exceptional lot. "A high percentage of international students from both Europe and Asia are both competent in the English language and willing to integrate and socialize with the other students." This enhances classroom and social interaction, while the "true team spirit" of the student body contributes to the "very cooperative, rather than overly competitive atmosphere. If someone has an undergrad in, say, economics, that person will lead study groups to bring those without an economic background up to speed before exams. Quants are happy to help out nonquants on their stats, [and] nonquants [assist in] proofreading quant papers," according to students.

Alberta MBAs enjoy "state-of-the-art facilities in classrooms, which have considerably enhanced the learning environment." One student comments, "We have access to our own computer lab, and many locations on campus have wireless connections (including our MBA classrooms). Our professors have excellent websites where we can access lecture notes in advance." Students concede that their Edmonton address "allows some of the great aspects of the school to come through, but also causes some difficulties. Given the living costs of the location, students can get a much higher standard of living for a lower cost than larger cities. However, this can be a negative for placement opportunities." Other assets of the locale include a campus boasting "many beautiful historic and modern buildings. It's situated adjacent to the beautiful River Valley and several large parks. U of A is certainly a beautiful campus."

## Admissions

Applicants to the Alberta MBA program must provide the school with all academic transcripts; GMAT scores; TOEFL, IELTS, or MELAB scores (non-native English speakers); three letters of reference; a personal statement of educational and professional goals; and a resume. Applicants should have a GPA of at least 3.0, a GMAT score of at least 550, and at least two years of post-baccalaureate employment experience in the business world. At the U of A website, the school notes that "admission into the MBA program is competitive and only a small number of applicants are admitted. We receive more applications from qualified individuals than we can admit."

### FINANCIAL FACTS

| | |
|---|---|
| Annual tuition (in-state/out-of-state) | $8,900/$17,900 |
| Fees | $650 |
| Books and supplies | $1,300 |
| Room & board (on/off-campus) | $6,700/$9,300 |
| % of students receiving aid | 35 |
| % of first-year students receiving aid | 50 |
| % of students receiving grants | 25 |
| Average grant | $3,100 |

### ADMISSIONS

| | |
|---|---|
| Admissions Selectivity Rating | 86 |
| # of applications received | 152 |
| % applicants accepted | 55 |
| % acceptees attending | 51 |
| Average GMAT | 610 |
| Range of GMAT | 550–640 |
| Average GPA | 3.3 |
| TOEFL required of international students? | yes |
| Minimum TOEFL (paper/computer) | 600/250 |
| Application fee | $88 |
| International application fee | $88 |
| Regular application deadline | 4/30 |
| Regular notification | rolling |
| Deferment available? | yes |
| Maximum length of deferment | 1 year |
| Need-blind admissions? | yes |

### APPLICANTS ALSO LOOK AT

McGill University, The University of British Columbia, University of Calgary, University of Toronto, University of Western Ontario Richard Ivey School of Business, York University

### EMPLOYMENT PROFILE

| Career Rating | 81 | Grads employed by field: | % | avg. salary: |
|---|---|---|---|---|
| Primary source of full-time job acceptances | | Finance | 30 | $61,559 |
| | | Consulting | 5 | $52,889 |
| School-facilitated activities | 9 (17%) | General Management | 27 | $55,492 |
| Graduate-facilitated activities | 32 (63%) | Quantitative | 11 | $50,400 |
| Unknown | 10 (20%) | Other | 27 | $55,492 |
| | | | | |
| Average starting salary | $52,100 | | | |
| Percent employed | 87 | | | |

# UNIVERSITY OF ARIZONA
## ELLER COLLEGE OF MANAGEMENT

## Academics

"The Eller MBA is highly quantitative, reasonably priced, and close-knit," one student writes about the University of Arizona's MBA program, neatly summarizing many of it's greatest strengths. Eller students especially appreciate the intimate size of the program. One student explains, "Because of its small size, it's more responsive when changes are effected, and the administration has the ability to work with a student to create a custom solution for the student." Another student notes, "The program has a lot of potential, and administrators spend time with students to empower them to improve the program."

Eller's heavy focus on quantitative skills feeds its strongest disciplines, MIS and finance. It also means a deluge of challenging work in the first semester of the program, especially for students with little quant or business experience. "Students with little or no business background struggle mightily with the course load," one student writes.

According to the school, Eller's core courses for the year-one schedule "build the analytic skills in economics, statistics, accounting, finance, and communication that form the basis of managerial decision-making. [These courses also] develop the viewpoint of the general manager, introducing MBAs to the functional areas of the firm and the tools for integrating technological and human resources to achieve organizational goals." Year two consists primarily of electives, though students may choose to develop a concentration or "construct a plan of study suited to [their] unique career goals." Dual degree programs also boost the rigor of the program.

Along with MIS and finance, entrepreneurship is one of Eller's major focal points. Its McGuire Entrepreneurship Program was named a NASDAQ Center for Entrepreneurial Excellence in 2002. The program's success has resulted in the integration of entrepreneurship into the core and has created opportunities for students to participate in business-plan competitions across the country. The program also helps students find internships with area startup companies during the summer between the first and second year.

## Career and Placement

The Eller MBA Office of Career Development (OCD) works with students to conduct an effective job search. OCD provides services such as career counseling, interview preparation, resume preparation and review, professional development workshops, executive mentoring, on-campus interviews and information regarding career fairs.

Eller MBAs most frequently find jobs with the following employers: U.S. Airways, Advanced Micro Devices, Burlington Northern, Santa Fe Railway, Ernst and Young, Intel Corporation, MBA Enterprise Corporation, Raytheon and PricewaterhouseCooper. Slightly more than half of graduates find work in the Southwest or on the Pacific coast; one in five finds a job outside the United States, a statistic that reflects Eller's large international population.

Simone L. Pollard, Associate Director of MBA Programs
McClelland Hall 210, Building 108, 1130 E Helen Street, PO Box 210108
Tucson, AZ 85721-0108 United States
Phone: 520-621-4008 • Fax: 520-621-2606
E-mail: mba_admissions@eller.arizona.edu • Website: www.ellermba.arizona.edu/

## Student Life and Environment

The University of Arizona offers a comfortable, casual setting that allows students to pursue MBA. The school states that "MBA spaces at Eller blur the distinctions between in and out, work and play. Classrooms, meeting spaces, study centers, and technical labs all reflect the casual comfort and relaxed living of Southwest style." There's nothing casual or laid-back about the program itself; however, MBAs caution that "most students spend a significant amount of time studying. It's a lot of work."

Fortunately, students have plenty of opportunities to unwind. One student reports, "Happy hour on Thursdays (which is the last day of the school week for us) and tailgates, when applicable on Saturday, are just a couple of the regular social activities on campus. The mix of social and academic life is pretty good and has helped the student body become more integrated." Students note that "much of the work is group work," with "social breaks occurring with study buddies frequently before, after, or during study sessions." The schoolwork itself brings students closer together, as they "all work together to help each other achieve a higher level [of learning]. There is certainly competition, but it's not cutthroat."

Hometown Tucson is a growing city with a population of about 870,000. The city's architecture retains elements of the city's past with a mixture of frontier, Hispanic, and Native American styles. Winter barely glances the city (from November to March, the average daily temperature range is from 38 to 65 degrees Fahrenheit), and the desert setting means that humidity is rarely a concern; this is a dry place that heats up considerably in the summer. The university and defense-related industries are among the city's top employers. The Grand Canyon, Mexico, San Diego, and Phoenix, are all within reasonable driving distance.

## Admissions

Major factors in the decision process of Eller's admissions committee include undergraduate GPA (at least 3.0 preferred); evidence of a rigorous undergraduate curriculum (the committee has no preference for particular majors; nonbusiness majors are welcome); GMAT score; and a minimum of two years work experience postdating undergraduate schooling (this requirement cannot be waived, according to the school). The school warns that the program is "highly quantitative," and accordingly the admissions committee looks for "evidence of your capacity to successfully handle the analytic parts of the program in undergraduate coursework, the quantitative portions of GMAT scores, and work experience." Applications must include an essay, letters of recommendation, and a resume. Interviews are required and by invitation only.

### FINANCIAL FACTS

| | |
|---|---|
| Annual tuition (in-state/out-of-state) | $14,451/$23,431 |
| Fees | $96 |
| Books and supplies | $2,500 |
| Room & board (on/off-campus) | $12,000/$14,000 |
| % of students receiving grants | 75 |
| Average grant | $13,337 |

### ADMISSIONS

| | |
|---|---|
| Admissions Selectivity Rating | 87 |
| # of applications received | 238 |
| % applicants accepted | 58 |
| % acceptees attending | 46 |
| Average GMAT | 641 |
| Range of GMAT | 570–720 |
| Average GPA | 3.3 |
| TOEFL required of international students? | yes |
| Minimum TOEFL (paper/computer) | 600/250 |
| Application fee | $50 |
| International application fee | $50 |
| Regular application deadline | 4/15 |
| Regular notification | 5/15 |
| Application deadline/notification | |
| Round 1: | 11/15 / 12/15 |
| Round 2: | 2/15 / 3/15 |
| Round 3: | 4/15 / 5/15 |
| Early decision program? | yes |
| ED Deadline/notification | 11/15 / 12/15 |
| Deferment available? | yes |
| Maximum length of deferment | 1 year |
| Need-blind admissions? | yes |

### APPLICANTS ALSO LOOK AT

Arizona State University, Babson College, The University of Texas at Austin, Thunderbird, University of California—Irvine, University of Colorado, Wake Forest University

| EMPLOYMENT PROFILE | | | | |
|---|---|---|---|---|
| Career Rating | 68 | Grads employed by field: | % | avg. salary: |
| Primary source of full-time job acceptances | | Finance | 31 | $57,500 |
| | | Human Resources | 3 | NR |
| School-facilitated activities | 17 (43%) | Marketing | 13 | $54,480 |
| Graduate-facilitated activities | 23 (57%) | MIS | 10 | $78,250 |
| | | Operations | 5 | NR |
| Average starting salary | $58,343 | Consulting | 23 | $57,822 |
| Percent employed | 80 | General Management | 10 | $40,645 |
| | | Other | 5 | NR |

# UNIVERSITY OF ARKANSAS—FAYETTEVILLE
## SAM M. WALTON COLLEGE OF BUSINESS

## GENERAL INFORMATION
| | |
|---|---|
| Type of school | public |
| Environment | town |
| Academic calendar | Jan. start |

### SURVEY SAYS...
Friendly students
Smart classrooms
*Solid preparation in:*
Presentation skills

## STUDENTS
| | |
|---|---|
| Enrollment of parent institution | 17,269 |
| Enrollment of business school | 150 |
| % male/female | 70/30 |
| % out-of-state | 18 |
| % part-time | 63 |
| % minorities | 13 |
| % international | 14 |
| Average age at entry | 24 |
| Average years work experience at entry | 1.5 |

## ACADEMICS
| | |
|---|---|
| **Academic Experience Rating** | **83** |
| Student/faculty ratio | 24:1 |
| Profs interesting rating | 72 |
| Profs accessible rating | 86 |
| % female faculty | 20 |
| % minority faculty | 4 |

## JOINT DEGREES
MBA/JD, 4 years

## PROMINENT ALUMNI
S. Robson Walton, Chair, Wal-Mart Stores Inc.; William Dillards Sr., Chair, Dillards Inc.; Frank Fletcher, Entrepreneur; Jack Stephens, Stephens Inc.; Thomas F. McLarty, Former U.S. Presidential Advisor

## Academics

From the name above the door to the endowment that funds its high tech facilities to the employer who hires many of its MBAs, it's difficult to avoid the influence of Wal-Mart at University of Arkansas' Sam M. Walton College of Business. Students can't resist drawing comparisons to their megacorporate neighbor and benefactor; one student writes, "The school offers good quality at low cost. It's the Wal-Mart of schools." And Wal-Mart money, students brag, has made Walton College "the most technologically advanced of any school in the U of A system. The classrooms and facilities are second to none."

In order to maximize return on students' investment, Walton offers a one-year accelerated MBA program. It begins with a set of optional one-week "short courses" in basic management and number-crunching skills. Mandatory foundations courses, which cover intermediate skills and concepts, run from late June through early August. The core is covered in two 8-week integrated modules in the fall; the spring starts with a five-week strategic management course followed by an 11-week consulting project, during which, students apply classroom lessons to the real-world problems of local companies (many of which are *Fortune* 500 companies drawn to the area by Wal-Mart; students describe this phenomenon as "the Wal-Mart effect"). Students take electives concurrently with the consulting project and then wind up the program with two more electives in a summer session.

MBAs report that "this program is intense and requires you to manage your time." They love the school's "local reputation and contacts, especially if you want to get involved in the retail/Wal-Mart vendor industry." However, most students agree that "the faculty is what makes this program great. Most of the classes are very interactive, and a top-notch faculty applies and teaches the most current tools to solve today's business problems. They really do challenge us to think outside the box." Students also appreciate how "the administration tries their hardest to accommodate [them] despite all the red tape and bureaucracy that come with a large university." They also have high hopes for the program's future; as one student comments, "I know the school is looking to the future. With a $50 million gift to the business school and a $300 million gift to the entire university, I am aware of many new things the school is planning, including a new graduate building and a quad devoted just to business students."

## Career and Placement

The Career Development Center at Walton offers students a number of job fairs each year, some aimed specifically at a particular function (supply-chain management, engineering, IT), and others that are open to the entire campus. The office promises "personalized career planning and placement" with lots of "one-to-one attention; it employs four full-time staffers to serve the university's business students. Over 200 employers use the school's interview rooms each year; roughly a quarter of those employers are looking specifically for MBAs."

Top employers of Walton MBAs include J.B. Hunt, Masterfoods, Tyson Foods, Unilever, and, of course, Wal-Mart Stores, Inc. About three in five graduates remain in the area; approximately 10 percent find jobs outside of the United States.

MICHELE HALSELL, MANAGING DIRECTOR, GRADUATE SCHOOL OF BUSINESS
475 BUSINESS BUILDING, FAYETTEVILLE, AR 72701 UNITED STATES
PHONE: 479-575-2851 • FAX: 479-575-8721
E-MAIL: GSB@WALTON.UARK.EDU • WEBSITE: WWW.GSB.UARK.EDU

## Student Life and Environment

The old real-estate cliché holds true; it's all about "location, location, location." In Fayetteville, students enjoy "close proximity to Wal-Mart headquarters and 'Vendorville' (all Wal-Mart suppliers, including Newell-Rubbermaid, Procter & Gamble, and Unilever, have offices here) in the fastest-growing region in the country (according to the Milken Institute). It creates great opportunities for newly minted MBAs." In addition, students agree, "Fayetteville is a great town to be in. There is plenty to do socially after hours. Dixon Street, Fayetteville's version of Bourbon Street in New Orleans, is a common place for our networking activities." Although a city of just under 60,000, Fayetteville is home to a symphony orchestra, an arts center, and a film society. It is an understatement to say that college athletics are huge here.

According to students, MBAs form a tight-knit community at the university. The rigors of the accelerated academic program also help forge an esprit de corps, but there's more to it than that. One student explains, "The students in the Walton College of Business have formed a collegial and cohesive group. The small size of the program and efforts of the MBA program administration have fostered a supportive and team-oriented approach to our business education." Another students adds, "I went to undergrad at a small liberal arts college, so the large university is somewhat overwhelming and not really my cup of tea. However, the MBA program is small and caters to us, so it still has that small-school feel."

## Admissions

The Walton admissions committee reports that successful applicants typically have high undergraduate GPAs (at least 3.4), score at least 580 on the GMAT, have at least two years of work experience (or substantial extracurricular involvement in their undergraduate programs), produce three strong letters of recommendation, and write a compelling personal statement. Although work experience is not required, applicants with at least two years of experience are given preference for admission. The school tells us that "underrepresented minorities are encouraged to apply, and special financial assistance is available to minority students."

### FINANCIAL FACTS

| | |
|---|---|
| Annual tuition (in-state/out-of-state) | $12,672/$28,110 |
| Fees | $1,690 |
| Books and supplies | $1,000 |
| Room & board (off-campus) | $11,700 |
| % of students receiving aid | 87 |
| % of first-year students receiving aid | 87 |
| % of students receiving loans | 33 |
| % of students receiving grants | 10 |
| Average award package | $22,162 |
| Average grant | $12,672 |
| Average student loan debt | $21,475 |

### ADMISSIONS

| | |
|---|---|
| Admissions Selectivity Rating | 86 |
| # of applications received | 215 |
| % applicants accepted | 61 |
| % acceptees attending | 79 |
| Average GMAT | 603 |
| Range of GMAT | 560–640 |
| Average GPA | 3.47 |
| TOEFL required of international students? | yes |
| Minimum TOEFL (paper/computer) | 550/213 |
| Application fee | $40 |
| International application fee | $50 |
| Regular application deadline | 4/15 |
| Regular notification | 5/15 |
| Deferment available? | yes |
| Maximum length of deferment | 1 year |
| Transfer students accepted? | yes |
| Transfer application policy | Max 6 hours, electives from an AACSB-accredited school, A or B grades |
| Non-fall admissions? | yes |
| Need-blind admissions? | yes |

### APPLICANTS ALSO LOOK AT

Oklahoma State University, South Texas College of Law, The University of Mississippi, The University of Texas at Austin, University of Georgia, University of Oklahoma, University of Tennessee—Knoxville

### EMPLOYMENT PROFILE

| | | Grads employed by field: | % | avg. salary: |
|---|---|---|---|---|
| Career Rating | 77 | Finance | 30 | $57,587 |
| Primary source of full-time job acceptances | | Marketing | 23 | $60,180 |
| School-facilitated activities | 18 (45%) | MIS | 9 | $48,750 |
| Graduate-facilitated activities | 18 (45%) | Operations | 17 | $61,250 |
| Unknown | 4 (10%) | Consulting | 4 | $55,000 |
| | | Other | 17 | $61,250 |
| Average starting salary | $57,500 | | | |
| Percent employed | 78 | | | |

# UNIVERSITY OF BRITISH COLUMBIA
## SAUDER SCHOOL OF BUSINESS

### GENERAL INFORMATION
Type of school                          public
Academic calendar                       unique

### SURVEY SAYS...
Students love Vancouver, BC
Happy students
Smart classrooms

### STUDENTS
Enrollment of parent
  institution                           40,000
Enrollment of business school           144
% male/female                           67/33
% part-time                             35
% minorities                            60
% international                         62
Average age at entry                    30
Average years work experience
  at entry                              6

### ACADEMICS
Academic Experience Rating              88
Student/faculty ratio                   20:1
Profs interesting rating                91
Profs accessible rating                 96
% female faculty                        17

### JOINT DEGREES
MBA/LLB, 4 years; MBA/MAPPS
(Master of Arts, Asia Pacific Policy
Studies), 2 years; Combined
MBA/CMA, 2 years

## Academics

Students in this prestigious 15-month, full-time MBA program at Vancouver's University of British Columbia report that "Sauder professors look for an integrated approach that develops every student's overall understanding of each facet of business, using relevant materials and current events. This results in ensuring that Sauder students are ready for the challenges of today's business world without burdening them with outdated business concepts." Through "a mix of theory and concepts, case studies, real-project analysis, and internships," students agree, "this program provides [them] with very good opportunities [to develop] practical, useful management practices."

"The most valuable part of the Sauder MBA program is the integrative core," students report. The core, an intensive 13-week sequence, is taught as a single course rather than as a set of discrete disciplines, an approach befitting Sauder's focus. Because of both the sheer quantity of work and the level of complex thinking required, the core is extremely challenging. One student explains, "I feel I'm going through the business equivalent of Navy Seal training. Surviving the core is the toughest thing I've ever done...but I can honestly say I've never laughed this hard nor had so much fun." Students happily note that "after solving so many cases, analyzing so many businesses, and critically tearing apart complex business theories, you come out of the core thinking you can do almost anything. It really is inspiring." Another benefit of the workload is that "it prepares students to cope with demanding deadlines and timelines in their chosen careers." But such preparation results from rigorous training, including "twenty-four hours a week of class lectures, case studies and presentations, assignment submissions, course readings to catch up on, and multiple submissions due on some days."

The remainder of the program post-core is devoted primarily to specialization and professional development. Students tell us that finance is "by far" the school's strongest area, although supply chain management, entrepreneurship, and international business also earn praise. Administrators here "do their job and more. They are service-oriented and very focused in addressing students' needs." When students find spare time to put down the business books, they "can learn about the interesting research happening in other faculties, because the school has so much interesting research-oriented stuff happening all the time."

## Career and Placement

UBC's Business Career Centre offers both personal consultation as well as a structured program to help students identify goals and then develop strategies to meet those goals. Its services include self-assessment assistance, coaching sessions, skills training programs (in resume writing, interviewing, and networking), recruiting events (which bring "corporate recruiters from prominent companies" to interview job candidates), and job postings. Students wish the office could do more to attract companies from the east coast, and many emphasize that "UBC needs to continue to build its alumni network, and its Business Career Centre needs more resources to attract recruiters and companies to come to UBC to find qualified MBA grads in all areas, not just finance," the school's strongest discipline.

Employers likely to hire UBC MBAs include Accenture, Bank of Montreal, Bombardier, Citibank, General Motors of Canada, Genome BC, Ledcor Industries, MacDonald Dettwiler & Associates, the Ministry of Energy & Mines, the PepsiCo, Procter & Gamble, Westport Innovations, and Xantrex Technology.

MBA Programs Office
#160 - 2053 Main Mall, Vancouver, BC V6T 1Z2 Canada
Phone: 604-822-8422 • Fax: 604-822-9030
E-mail: mba@sauder.ubc.ca • Website: www.sauder.ubc.ca/mba

## Student Life and Environment

It's impossible to separate the quality of life at UBC from its hometown of Vancouver, which students unanimously proclaim "one of the best places on earth." This "vibrant city [is] a great place to live. It's very safe, and there's always so much to do. Whistler Mountain is on your doorstep, so lots of ski trips are planned, with hiking in the Rockies during the summer. The wineries aren't too far away, either!" Vancouver's "strategic location—facing directly into the Asian market"—provides excellent internship and career opportunities for UBC MBAs. Non-Canadian students happily report that "our spouses can work here legally for the duration of our courses! In the U.S., my wife would have had to do nothing for two years." About the only downside is that "because Vancouver is a great place to live, people are willing to take lower wages. There are a lot of excellent-quality people looking for jobs in Vancouver too, so the competition is tough. It is difficult to get a really high-paid job in Vancouver, but your quality of life makes [taking a lower-paying job] worth it!"

UBC's "park-like campus" is located "on a peninsula with vistas of mountains and oceans." The facilities are "excellent. The commerce building is wireless-enabled, the MBA lounge is a great place to hang out, and there are adequate restaurants for all tastes." Furthermore, "the facilities include pools and gyms, and a movie theater located in the university. There's also a graduate bar on campus that provides a beautiful view of Vancouver, and the school has a great 18-hole golf course." Students can participate in "tons of different clubs" that help them network while developing business-related or recreational skills. "There is a good balance between the workload and time for yourself," with "plenty and diverse social and development events."

## Admissions

Admission to the Sauder MBA program is extremely competitive. All applicants must submit official transcripts for undergraduate work (students who attended schools where English was not the primary language must arrange for a literal translation of their transcripts to be delivered to UBC), official GMAT score reports, evidence of English proficiency (TOEFL scores for students whose first language is not English), a resume, and three letters of reference. Interviews are by invitation only; the school interviews roughly half of its applicant pool. The school's viewbook notes that "only under exceptional circumstances will applicants with less than two years of full-time work experience be admitted to this program." On average, students enter the program with between six and eight years' full-time professional experience. Applications are processed on a rolling basis; admitted students may not defer admission.

### FINANCIAL FACTS

| | |
|---|---|
| Annual tuition | $21,500 |
| Books and supplies | $1,200 |
| Average grant | $5,000 |

### ADMISSIONS

| | |
|---|---|
| Admissions Selectivity Rating | 83 |
| # of applications received | 381 |
| % applicants accepted | 69 |
| % acceptees attending | 55 |
| Average GMAT | 620 |
| Range of GMAT | 590–680 |
| Average GPA | 3.3 |
| TOEFL required of international students? | yes |
| Minimum TOEFL (paper/computer) | 600/250 |
| Application fee | $125 |
| International application fee | $125 |
| Regular application deadline | 4/30 |
| Regular notification | rolling |
| Need-blind admissions? | yes |

### EMPLOYMENT PROFILE

| Career Rating | 83 | Grads employed by field: | % | avg. salary: |
|---|---|---|---|---|
| **Primary source of full-time job acceptances** | | Finance | 18 | $66,000 |
| | | Human Resources | 3 | NR |
| School-facilitated activities | 28 (31%) | Marketing | 21 | $58,000 |
| Graduate-facilitated activities | 49 (54%) | Operations | 12 | $57,000 |
| Unknown | 14 (15%) | Consulting | 15 | $77,000 |
| | | General Management | 22 | $67,000 |
| Average starting salary | $65,000 | Other | 9 | $66,000 |
| Percent employed | 92 | | | |

# UNIVERSITY OF CALGARY
## HASKAYNE SCHOOL OF BUSINESS

## GENERAL INFORMATION

| | |
|---|---|
| Type of school | public |
| Academic calendar | semester |

### SURVEY SAYS...

Students love Calgary, AB
Friendly students
Happy students
Smart classrooms
*Solid preparation in:*
Teamwork

### STUDENTS

| | |
|---|---|
| Enrollment of parent institution | 27,928 |
| Enrollment of business school | 330 |
| % male/female | 61/39 |
| % part-time | 73 |
| % international | 36 |
| Average age at entry | 30 |
| Average years work experience at entry | 6 |

### ACADEMICS

| | |
|---|---|
| **Academic Experience Rating** | **75** |
| Student/faculty ratio | 3:1 |
| Profs interesting rating | 62 |
| Profs accessible rating | 74 |
| % female faculty | 30 |

### JOINT DEGREES

MBA/LLB, 4 years; MBA/MSW, 2 years; MBA/MD, 5 years; MBA/MBT, 2 full years

### PROMINENT ALUMNI

Al Duerr, CEO, Emergo Projects International; Charlie Fisher, President and CEO, Nexen; Hal Kvisle, President & CEO, Trans Canada; Brett Wilson, Managing Director, First Energy Capital; Byron Osing, Chair, Launchworks Inc.

## Academics

Because Calgary is "the center of Canada's energy markets, [it] is the perfect location for a program like the one offered by the Haskayne School of Business" at the University of Calgary. One MBA explains, "I think Haskayne's strength lies in the potential of alliances and joint ventures with the large business sector for such a small community. With so many head offices located in our community, I think Haskayne has the ability to capitalize on this available resource." Indeed, it already does, by offering "such unique features as its global energy and sustainable development program."

Haskayne MBAs may pursue their degrees during the day as a full-time student or part-time in the evening. This course-based track requires up to 20 courses; 12 required and 8 electives. (Some foundation courses can be waived for students with demonstrable knowledge in the subject matter covered.) Specializations—completed by taking four electives in a single area—are available in entrepreneurship and innovation, finance, global energy and sustainable development, and marketing. A select few students (all with relatively deep academic and professional backgrounds in business) are admitted to a thesis-based MBA program, which consists of eight half-courses and a research paper that is completed under the supervision of a faculty sponsor.

Students give the Haskayne faculty mixed reviews and one MBA elaborates, "There's a vast difference between having a PhD professor, who may have submitted umpteen research papers for publication, but can't teach and someone with a master's degree who can. Recently, the school has responded by bringing in faculty from around the world, and their marks are improving. MBAs are firmly behind the administration and say that "[the university] has been excellent in planning. Contingency situations are handled with ease." One student notes, "Administrators are very helpful when questions need to be answered, timely at getting new information out to us, and generally courteous."

Haskayne draws on its geographical advantage to offer students mentorship opportunities. According to the school, "Senior business leaders from a diverse range of industries with an economic and operational impact locally, regionally, and internationally provide professional development opportunities for full-time MBA students." Overall, students feel that "the program provides students with the basic skills necessary to begin a career in management." One student says, "I believe that the learning environment is very positive and allows students to develop their communication and social skills."

## Career and Placement

Students either seem to have mixed feelings about the Haskayne Career Center. Its champions tell us that "the Career Center is second to none with respect to the services offered. The center tries to promote networking opportunities." One international student notes, "The Career Center in this school provides us with amazing experience. For example, they provide business etiquette courses which encourage international students to attend local business events and behave correctly." The bottom line, however, is how effective the office is in facilitating the job search. After many past complaints, the school's new beefed-up Career Center has seen 95 percent placement within three months of graduation.

PENNY O'HEARN, ADMISSIONS OFFICER
2500 UNIVERSITY DRIVE, NW, CALGARY, AB T2N 1N4 CANADA
PHONE: 403-220-3808 • FAX: 403-282-0095 • E-MAIL: MBAREQUEST@MGMT.UCALGARY.CA
WEBSITE: WWW.HASKAYNE.UCALGARY.CA/MBA

Employers of Haskayne MBAs include Calgary Catholic School Board; Canadian Natural Resources Limited; Cap Gemini; Ernst & Young; CIBC; Coral Energy; Deloitte Touche Tohmatsu; Dustsoft Technologies; Encryption Systems; ENMAX; Gibson Petroleum; Merak; Opportunity Capital Corporation; PanCanadian Petroleum Limited; Rainbow Contractors; RLG International; SagaTech Electronic; SAP Canada; and TELUS Communications.

## Student Life and Environment

Life within the Haskayne program "is comfortable and safe. Students can study right into midnight without worrying about personal or property security. There are security officers wandering on the building regularly, and school security office offers 24-hour accompany services to all students who stay late or need accompaniment to the parking lot." Students say, "The school puts real efforts to make our study experience convenient, secure, and enjoyable." Haskayne's facility boasts "state-of-the-art technology utilization for studies (like online access to teaching staff and on-campus wireless access)."

The MBA program also offers "excellent opportunities for participation in extracurricular activities. Students can practice skills through involvement in MBA Society activities like hosting business conferences or participating in MBA games. There are excellent opportunities for networking, career counseling, and the MBA student business case competition." While "people are very involved in their studies and work together, any outside social activities are segmented into cliques." In part because many students attend part-time, Haskayne is not an especially social program.

Hometown Calgary is "a good business city" with a population approaching one million. Proximity to the Rocky Mountains means that "students can go skiing and camping in marvelous surroundings." Calgary is an international city, and this is reflected in the student population. Students explain that "the focus on a diverse mix of students in the MBA class provides a global perspective to [the] learning process."

## Admissions

Minimum admission requirements to the Haskayne MBA program include a four-year undergraduate degree completed with at least a 3.0 GPA over the final two years of study, a GMAT score of 550, a personal statement of career and academic goals; three letters of reference, and a resume. Non-English speaking applicants must submit TOEFL scores (minimum 600). A minimum of three years of appropriate employment are required. Applicants to the thesis-based program must have a minimum GPA of 3.3 and a minimum GMAT score of 600.

## FINANCIAL FACTS

| | |
|---|---|
| Annual tuition (in-state/out-of-state) | $10,32/$21,033 |
| Fees | $713 |
| Books and supplies | $1,700 |
| Room & board (on/off-campus) | $4,300/$12,900 |
| % of students receiving grants | 67 |
| Average grant | $4,300 |

## ADMISSIONS

| | |
|---|---|
| Admissions Selectivity Rating | 80 |
| # of applications received | 206 |
| % applicants accepted | 73 |
| % acceptees attending | 54 |
| Average GMAT | 621 |
| Range of GMAT | 550–680 |
| Average GPA | 3.22 |
| TOEFL required of international students? | yes |
| Minimum TOEFL (paper/computer) | 600/250 |
| Application fee | $100 |
| International application fee | $130 |
| Regular application deadline | 5/1 |
| Regular notification | rolling |
| Application deadline/notification | |
| Round 1: | 11/15 / 1/15 |
| Round 2: | 1/15 / 3/1 |
| Round 3: | 3/1 / 5/1 |
| Round 4: | 5/1 / 6/15 |
| Deferment available? | yes |
| Maximum length of deferment | 1 year |
| Transfer students accepted? | yes |
| Transfer application policy Up to 9 courses accepted. | |
| Need-blind admissions? | yes |

## APPLICANTS ALSO LOOK AT

Queen's University, The University of British Columbia, University of Alberta, University of Western Ontario, York University

## EMPLOYMENT PROFILE

| Career Rating | 87 | Grads employed by field: | % | avg. salary: |
|---|---|---|---|---|
| Primary source of full-time job acceptances | | Finance | 26 | NR |
| | | Human Resources | 1 | NR |
| School-facilitated activities | 46% | Marketing | 2 | NR |
| Graduate-facilitated activities | 53% | MIS | 15 | NR |
| | | Operations | 19 | NR |
| Average starting salary | $79,705 | Consulting | 8 | NR |
| Percent employed | 95 | Other | 24 | NR |

# UNIVERSITY OF CALIFORNIA—BERKELEY
## HAAS SCHOOL OF BUSINESS

### GENERAL INFORMATION
Type of school                    public
Environment                       city
Academic calendar              semester

### SURVEY SAYS...
Good peer network
Happy students

### STUDENTS
Enrollment of parent
  institution                     32,714
Enrollment
  of business school             1,312
% male/female                     68/32
% out-of-state                       61
% minorities                          2
% international                      29
Average age at entry                 29
Average years work experience
  at entry                          5.5

### ACADEMICS
Academic Experience Rating         97
Student/faculty ratio            10:1
Profs interesting rating           84
Profs accessible rating            94
% female faculty                   20
% minority faculty                  3

### JOINT DEGREES
MBA/MPH in Public Health, 5
semesters; MBA/JD, 6 semesters (3
academic years)

### PROMINENT ALUMNI
Arun Sarin, CEO, Vodafone; Rodrigo
Rato, Managing Director,
International Monetary Fund;
Barbara Desoer, Exec VP, Bank of
America; Paul Otellini, CEO of Intel;
Jorge Montoya, President, Procter
& Gamble Latin America.

## Academics

The Haas School of Business at the University of California—Berkeley offers students "a truly interactive environment," one in which "professors learn from the students as well as the other way around" thanks to students' substantial input into the program. The full-time program in particular is designed to provide students with an unusual degree of autonomy; explains one student, "Student initiative comes into play in every aspect of the program, from scheduling speakers to career search." Students here also design and run, with faculty oversight, a number of electives every semester. The result of all this freedom is that "students are forced to become entrepreneurs as part of their education." The small size of the program (only 250 full-time students and about as many part-timers) contributes to the experience by "forcing a collaborative environment where competition is put aside in order to help one another."

Haas backs up its unique approach to graduate business education with a strong curriculum and a solid faculty. The school excels in social entrepreneurship, corporate social responsibility, general management, and technology; this last area capitalizes on Berkeley's location "across the bay from San Francisco and just one hour from Silicon Valley." The faculty includes a number of stars; boasts one MBA, "Our finance professor is serving as the president of the San Francisco Federal Reserve. Our dean is on leave as [Governor] Arnold Schwarzenegger's Finance Director. They don't get better than this." Better still, "not only are the professors outstanding in their fields, but they are also highly approachable and willing to make changes to the class to meet the students' needs." Semesters move along quickly here; "The academic pace is very fast," students observe, "but the workload is not overwhelming." While the core "is solid," most here prefer the "awesome electives that give you some great opportunities outside the classroom."

## Career and Placement

When it comes time to find a career, Haas MBAs benefit from their program's high profile and sound reputation. As is often the case at such schools, the Haas Career Center provides a broad range of excellent services. Students here benefit from one-on-one advisement, access to numerous online job databases, industry clubs, workshops, seminars, and a mentoring program in which second-year students counsel first years in their search for internships.

Employers most likely to hire Haas MBAs include Bank of America; the Clorox Company; Deloitte; Gap, Inc.; Johnson & Johnson; LeapFrog Enterprises, Inc.; McKinsey & Company; Microsoft Corporation; Samsung Group; and Wells Fargo Bank.

## Student Life and Environment

For full-time students, "student clubs are at the heart of the school" because they help organize student input to the program. Explains one MBA, "Nothing happens at Haas without student involvement. Just about every full-time student is heavily involved in all aspects of the school. From student government to admissions to industry clubs to sports and wine clubs, everyone is able to express their interests and tap their fellow students for more information or just someone to share a good meal." The administration "fully supports club activities and has our needs on their minds continuously. It is only with their aid that we have been able to accomplish so much in our short time here."

PETER JOHNSON, DIRECTOR OF INTERNATIONAL ADMISSIONS, FULL-TIME MBA PROGRAM
430 STUDENT SERVICES BUILDING #1902, BERKELEY, CA 94720-1902 UNITED STATES
PHONE: 510-642-1405 • FAX: 510-643-6659
E-MAIL: MBAADMS@HAAS.BERKELEY.EDU • WEBSITE: WWW.HAAS.BERKELEY.EDU

Between classes, clubs, and other extracurricular options, "live is very busy" for full-time students at Haas. There are "groups constantly getting together to go to arts festivals, AIDS walks, golfing, cycling, surfing, skiing, attending seminars, hearing guest lecturers, and hiking, to name just a few activities. The opportunities are endless and everyone loves being here." Thursday nights "are a tradition at Haas. We have BoW (Bar of the Week) in Berkeley and San Francisco, so there are always fun places to check out as you get to know the area." Students also appreciate their "access to the Bay Area's business, culture, natural beauty, and geographic diversity. Networking opportunities abound because so many business and thought leaders either live in the area or pass through here."

The "great, resourceful, creative, and mellow" students of Haas are "warm, but with a competitive edge—in the best sense of the word." Students speculate that "Haas' long-standing 'no grade-disclosure' policy" results in "students who are extremely helpful to each other, making certain that learning is truly a collaborative process." Indeed, our survey respondents all agree that "students at Haas are extremely team-oriented. They very much work together to get things done. The Berkeley MBA attracts top-notch students from all over the world and we mutually benefit from one another's experiences." Adds one student, "Given how diverse the work experiences are here, I find myself learning from those around me every day. These are truly the type of people I want to work with and for after graduation."

## Admissions

Applicants to Haas graduate programs must submit all the following materials to the admissions department: official copies of transcripts for all postsecondary academic work, an official GMAT score report, letters of recommendation, a personal statement, and a resume. Interviews are optional. In addition to the above materials, international applicants whose first language is not English must also submit official score reports for the TOEFL (minimum score of 570 for the paper-based test, 230 for the computer-based test). The school considers all of the following in determining admissions status: "demonstration of quantitative ability; quality of work experience, including depth and breadth of responsibilities; opportunities to demonstrate leadership, etc.; strength of letters of recommendation; depth and breadth of extracurricular and community involvement; and strength of short answer and essays, including articulation of clear focus and goals."

## FINANCIAL FACTS

| | |
|---|---|
| Annual tuition | $12,245 |
| Fees (in-state/out-of-state) | $27,024/$25,847 |
| Books and supplies | $2,500 |
| Room & board (on/off-campus) | $17,846 |
| % of students receiving aid | 67 |
| % of first-year students receiving aid | 66 |
| % of students receiving loans | 52 |
| % of students receiving grants | 26 |
| Average award package | $31,160 |
| Average grant | $19,140 |
| Average student loan debt | $39,780 |

## ADMISSIONS

| | |
|---|---|
| **Admissions Selectivity Rating** | **98** |
| # of applications received | 2,170 |
| % applicants accepted | 23 |
| % acceptees attending | 49 |
| Average GMAT | 702 |
| Range of GMAT | 680–720 |
| Average GPA | 3.49 |
| TOEFL required of international students? | yes |
| Minimum TOEFL (paper/computer) | 570/230 |
| Application fee | $175 |
| International application fee | $175 |
| Regular application deadline | 3/10 |
| Regular notification | 5/22 |
| Application deadline/notification | |
| Round 1: | 11/4 / 1/30 |
| Round 2: | 12/12 / 3/20 |
| Round 3: | 1/20 / 4/24 |
| Round 4: | 3/10 / 5/22 |
| Need-blind admissions? | yes |

## APPLICANTS ALSO LOOK AT

Columbia University, Harvard University, New York University, Northwestern University, Stanford University, University of California—Los Angeles, University of Pennsylvania

| EMPLOYMENT PROFILE | |
|---|---|
| **Career Rating** | **99** |
| **Primary source of full-time job acceptances** | |
| School-facilitated activities | 130 (58%) |
| Graduate-facilitated activities | 78 (25%) |
| Unknown | 16 (7%) |
| | |
| Average starting salary | $95,519 |
| Percent employed | 94 |

# UNIVERSITY OF CALIFORNIA—DAVIS
## GRADUATE SCHOOL OF MANAGEMENT

## GENERAL INFORMATION
Type of school                public
Environment                   town
Academic calendar             quarters

### SURVEY SAYS...
Friendly students
Good peer network
Happy students
*Solid preparation in:*
Teamwork

### STUDENTS
Enrollment of parent
  institution                 30,065
Enrollment of business school 117
% male/female                 68/32
% minorities                  25
% international               15
Average age at entry          28
Average years work experience
  at entry                    5

### ACADEMICS
**Academic Experience Rating   94**
Student/faculty ratio          8:1
Profs interesting rating       82
Profs accessible rating        97
% female faculty               20
% minority faculty             25

### JOINT DEGREES
JD/MBA, 4 years; MD/MBA, 6 years;
Engineering/MBA, 2 years; Ag
Econ/MBA, 2 years.

### PROMINENT ALUMNI
David H. Russ, Chief Investment
Officer, Dartmouth College;
Christine Smith, Entrepreneur,
Researcher and Venture Capitalist;
Gordon C. Hunt, Jr., M.D., Senior
VP and Chief Medical Officer; Eric
Robison, Owner & President,
IdeaTrek, Inc.; Steve Spadarotto, VP,
Diageo Chateau & Estate Wines

## Academics

UC Davis' Graduate School of Management still has the glow of youth about it. Its proud students state confidently, "We're only 20 years old, and we're doing great!" That youthful energy carries into most aspects of the program and influences the teaching styles of the professors, the attitudes of the administrators, and the caliber of the students. One student says, "The GSM provides student reviews to all faculty at midterm. Every one of my teachers (even tenured ones) has embraced this feedback and tried to improve their classes." Others say, "Because the school is young, we do have some green professors. The positive aspect of these new professors is that they are totally committed to learning how to best teach us, and they bring fresh ideas into the classroom."

Another part of being a young program is flexibility. There are only six core courses, all of which must be taken in the first year. Core courses are "designed to provide students with a foundation in the functional areas of business—accounting, economics, finance, marketing, organizational behavior, and statistics." Most disciplines are taught through the use of case studies, lectures, and the study of real companies and the problems they face. Along with the core classes in the first year, students have to select three "breadth" classes, which "prepare them for in-depth study in their concentration." Breadth classes "are designed to bring into focus the initial required topics of study and apply them to each student's chosen concentration." This gives GSM students much earlier access to electives than they would have at many schools.

Students are encouraged to design their own concentrations. As one student says, "If we want something done, the administration will find a way to do it." The school also has four joint-degree program options. Students can choose between an MBA/JD, an MBA/master's of engineering, an MBA/master's of agricultural economics, and an MBA/MD. In addition, there is one interdisciplinary degree program, a master's of agriculture and management.

While students would still like to see better technology on campus and more classes that cater to the nonprofit concentration, for the most part, they agree that their experience has "more than exceeded expectations." Davis also seems to have applied the management skills they teach to the work they do. "The staff and administration are incredible. The amount of resources at the student's disposal is almost overwhelming. The dean invites us to 'just drop in,'" one student says. In the end, it seems, administration and faculty "consider the students the product of the school and make every effort to turn out a top-notch product."

## Career and Placement

UC Davis students are in the relatively rare position of being able to praise their Career Services Center, which is "really the cream of the crop." Students say, "The career counselors are absolutely stellar in helping students identify their career goals as well as helping them find an internship or job." Students admire the center's "efforts to get the school name more recognition among the recruiting landscape. We can continue to do better in this regard." Some students, however, would like to see a "stronger conduit between UC Davis and the Bay Area for additional career-placement opportunities." Companies that recruit on campus include Genentech, Inc.; Accenture; Hewlett-Packard Company; IBM; Calama Wines; Packard Bell; Deloitte Touche Tohmatsu; E & J Gallo Winery; UBS PaineWebber; and many more.

Students point out that Davis's "small size is a great advantage in some respects, but a bit of a disadvantage when it comes to recruiters and the size of the alumni database. Luckily,

JAMES STEVENS, ASSISTANT DEAN, STUDENT AFFAIRS
ONE SHIELDS AVENUE, DAVIS, CA 95616 UNITED STATES
PHONE: 530-752-7658 • FAX: 530-754-9355
E-MAIL: ADMISSIONS@GSM.UCDAVIS.EDU • WEBSITE: WWW.GSM.UCDAVIS.EDU

this is made up for by a very helpful and friendly alumni group." The size certainly has not stopped the students from finding employment—97 percent of the class of 2000 had been placed in a position just three months after graduation. As for where they end up, "the majority of Graduate School of Management students find positions in the high tech industries, in corporate finance, or in consulting," according to the school's website.

## Student Life and Environment

Half of Davis's population of 50,000 is made up of students at the university, which makes it, according to students, "the perfect small college town." As one says, "It allows you to immerse yourself in your schoolwork, but still have enough distractions to keep you busy during those much needed 'study breaks.'" Since the GSM student population is so small, the feeling is pretty intimate, and "students get to know each other well and become almost a surrogate family." Most are confident that their "relationships will continue long after school ends, especially since so many classmates will likely stay in beautiful Northern California!" Despite being a small town, Davis is "near beaches, mountains, rivers, lakes, cities, and just about everything else that California has to offer." For most students, "weekends are filled with trips to San Francisco, Lake Tahoe, Yosemite, and Las Vegas. There's never a dull moment, especially when you organize a group skydiving trip to Lodi." UC Davis prides itself on its environmental and ecological awareness, and the graceful campus shows that care. Davis boasts multiple greenbelts and 18 landscaped parks. Miles of bike paths and jogging paths link the campus to the town. Students appreciate the emphasis on the natural and say "a school that doesn't allow private vehicles on campus is really cool. It isn't often that you can own the street with an old clunker bike." Students say the current facilities leave much to be desired, but the school is diligently at work on a new, state-of-the-art building, which should be completed in late 2005/early 2006. Students often find housing in Davis prohibitively expensive and advise prospective students to "get housing early! It's expensive and difficult to come by."

## Admissions

Only one out of three applicants is admitted to Davis' GSM. Admissions looks for "applicants whose academic background, intellectual capability, work experience, demonstrated leadership, and communication skills meet the demands of the MBA program and a managerial career." Davis' GSM doesn't have a minimum GMAT or GPA, but the average GMAT was 673, and scores ranged between 620 and 720. The average GPA was 3.3, with a range of 2.5 to 4.0. Unless they've earned a degree at a college or university within the United States or their undergraduate education was conducted in English, all international students must take the TOEFL exam. The minimum score requirements are 600 (paper-based) and 250 (computer-based). More than 70 percent of the GSM students who apply for financial assistance receive some type of support, either from the GSM program or from the university itself.

### FINANCIAL FACTS

| | |
|---|---|
| Fees (in-state/out-of-state) | $21,759/$34,004 |
| Books and supplies | $1,665 |
| Room & board | $9,555 |
| % of students receiving aid | 83 |
| % of first-year students receiving aid | 89 |
| % of students receiving loans | 63 |
| % of students receiving grants | 91 |
| Average award package | $21,448 |
| Average grant | $11,928 |
| Average student loan debt | $34,600 |

### ADMISSIONS

| | |
|---|---|
| Admissions Selectivity Rating | 96 |
| # of applications received | 273 |
| % applicants accepted | 30 |
| % acceptees attending | 64 |
| Average GMAT | 673 |
| Range of GMAT | 620–720 |
| Average GPA | 3.3 |
| TOEFL required of international students? | yes |
| Minimum TOEFL (paper/computer) | 600/250 |
| Application fee | $100 |
| International application fee | $100 |
| Application deadline/notification | |
| Round 1: | 11/16 / 1/26 |
| Round 2: | 1/18 / 3/31 |
| Round 3: | 3/15 / 5/31 |
| Round 4: | 5/17 / 6/30 |
| Early decision program? | yes |
| ED Deadline/notification | 11/16 / 1/26 |
| Deferment available? | yes |
| Maximum length of deferment | 1 year |
| Need-blind admissions? | yes |

### APPLICANTS ALSO LOOK AT

Stanford University, The University of Texas at Austin, University of California—Irvine, University of California—Los Angeles, University of California—Berkeley, University of Southern California, University of Washington

### EMPLOYMENT PROFILE

| | | | | |
|---|---|---|---|---|
| Career Rating | 88 | Grads employed by field: | % | avg. salary: |
| Primary source of full-time job acceptances | | Accounting | 10 | $75,417 |
| | | Finance | 22 | $75,417 |
| School-facilitated activities | 20 (53%) | Marketing | 19 | $70,914 |
| Graduate-facilitated activities | 18 (47%) | Operations | 10 | $87,190 |
| | | Consulting | 18 | $89,286 |
| Average starting salary | $76,920 | General Management | 13 | $70,760 |
| Percent employed | 85 | Other | 8 | $70,500 |

# UNIVERSITY OF CALIFORNIA—IRVINE
## PAUL MERAGE SCHOOL OF BUSINESS

### GENERAL INFORMATION
| | |
|---|---|
| Type of school | public |
| Environment | city |
| Academic calendar | Sept.-June |

### SURVEY SAYS...
Friendly students
Smart classrooms
*Solid preparation in:*
Teamwork
Computer skills

### STUDENTS
| | |
|---|---|
| Enrollment of parent institution | 21,550 |
| Enrollment of business school | 820 |
| % male/female | 68/32 |
| % out-of-state | 6 |
| % part-time | 74 |
| % minorities | 5 |
| % international | 28 |
| Average age at entry | 28 |
| Average years work experience at entry | 4.8 |

### ACADEMICS
| | |
|---|---|
| **Academic Experience Rating** | **88** |
| Student/faculty ratio | 7:1 |
| Profs interesting rating | 70 |
| Profs accessible rating | 75 |
| % female faculty | 32 |
| % minority faculty | 13 |

### JOINT DEGREES
MD/MBA: 5 or 6 years program

### PROMINENT ALUMNI
Lisa Locklear, VP, Ingram Micro; Darcy Kopcho, Executive VP, Capital Group Companies; George Kessinger, President and CEO, Goodwill Industries International; Norman Witt, VP, Community Development, The Irvine Co.

## Academics

Students praise the "great IT focus" at UC—Irvine's Paul Merage School of Business; as one student points out, "IT management, which is the major focus of the school, is something every manager must understand and be able to do successfully in the current economy. The UC Irvine MBA stresses the appropriate use of technology to improve business processes." Research plays a major role in this aspect of the program; the school explains, "[It is] our distinguished faculty conduct [and] leading-edge research that brings the very latest thinking on management practices to classrooms and corporations. Their work has an international impact on management knowledge, deepening our understanding of how technological innovations are transforming the way business is done. As a full-time MBA, you can gain hands-on experience in our ITM labs with the tools you will need to lead change, whether you are reinventing an established firm or launching a new one. In ITM labs or electives across all the business disciplines, you will learn how technology and information transform business functions and business models." Students concur; one MBA explains, "This school is a global leader in IT." Study at Irvine commences with management of complex organizations, a residential course (held off campus at a nearby hotel) that doubles as a 'get to know your classmates' orientation event. What follows is "a solid core curriculum focused on the fundamental disciplines of management" and electives. The program does not have formal areas of concentration; instead, students are encouraged to "develop depth in a discipline or interdisciplinary area, to gain expertise with a particular set of analytical or technical tools, or to choose electives across disciplines to match [their] individual goals."

While acknowledging the cutting-edge research, world-class facilities, and fine curriculum, students say that "the greatest strength of Irvine is the people at the school—not [only] the students (who are fantastic), but also the administration and faculty." One student says, "There is a culture of teamwork and friendship that has been fostered here, which I don't think a big school can attain. [Professors] are very willing to talk and accommodate any of our needs, for the most part. They are not only researchers, but they also really care about the quality of your learning. I've even had a great time getting to know some of them outside of class." MBAs also appreciate that "Irvine offers excellent opportunities for the students to become a part of the direction for the school. Professors will change curriculum mid-course based on feedback from students."

## Career and Placement

The Irvine MBA program maintains a staff of five who are "dedicated to providing students with career guidance." Available resources include career workshops, interactive Web tools, on-campus recruiting sessions, and career-assessment tools. The office maintains corporate contacts across the country, but they note that "our best company contacts are centered around our geographic location." The school hosts 120 on-campus recruiters each year; 85 employers visit the campus to recruit summer interns.

Employers who most frequently hire UC—Irvine MBAs include Accenture, Beckman Coulter, Bristol Myers Squibb, Conexant, Deloitte Touche Tohmatsu, Experian, Gateway, Hewlett-Packard, Honda Motor Co., IBM, Intel, KPMG, Microsoft, Nissan, PacifiCare, PricewaterhouseCoopers, Roth Capital Partners, Taco Bell, and Wells Fargo. Approximately one in five students finds post-degree work in the Southwestern United States; 1 in 20 finds work outside the country.

## Student Life and Environment

According to students, "UC—Irvine's business school is located in a great area," a spot where "the weather is second to none, and there are many prosperous businesses nearby."

BRYAN MCSWEENEY, ASSOCIATE DIRECTOR, MBA ADMISSIONS
GSM 220, IRVINE, CA 92697-3125 UNITED STATES
PHONE: 949-824-4622 • FAX: 949-824-2235
E-MAIL: MBA@UCI.EDU • WEBSITE: WWW.GSM.UCI.EDU

We have a balanced life. Academics, charity, sports, networking, and family life" can all fit into the mix. Students appreciate that "the campus is very safe, and the location is ideal for studying. Irvine is a quite, beautiful area, with a very well-organized city master plan." The program constitutes "a small community with strong bonds," a place where students "are top-notch, and they are more focused on helping one another than being cutthroat." Remarkably, students feel that this sense of community exists even though "many students are commuters, and a lot of them have lives outside the school, so we barely get together to do things."

The program is also home to a substantial group who participate in campus and social activities within the program. For those seeking extracurricular opportunities, "there is a wide array of opportunities for school involvement and networking. From clubs to community service, executive speakers, or networking events, there are many activities outside of the classroom." One student reports, "I am very involved in club leadership and school life. It's a great experience because I have had opportunities to join into many leadership positions. I also have made a ton of great friends at the school, whom I socialize with during and after school. There is always a happy hour on Thursday nights and get-togethers during the weekends." Socializing isn't limited strictly to students; some students add that "faculty and administration are also a core part of the community. It's not unheard of to meet a professor for coffee or have a beer with the administration staff at the weekly Thursday happy hour."

The student body is relatively diverse, with "a population of about 25 percent internationals, which brings an extra splash of diversity to the school." A student with a family tells us that "[there] are very few students with children my son's age in the program; the area has its own great resources for children, including Boys and Girls Clubs, Boy Scouts, and excellent schools. My family and I have had excellent opportunities to get involved on campus."

## Admissions

The Irvine Graduate School of Management requires incoming students to be proficient in introductory calculus and introductory statistics with probability; students lacking these qualifications can earn a provisional admission but must complete both courses successfully before gaining full admission. The school strongly recommends, but does not require, an introductory accounting course for students with no accounting background. All applicants must submit one copy of official transcripts for all previous academic work, GMAT scores, TOEFL scores (for international students), several "self-evaluation essays," two letters of recommendation, and a resume. The admissions committee looks for evidence of "career progression, well-articulated educational and professional goals, a clear understanding of MBA programs, presentation skills, and leadership potential." The UC Irvine MBA is an Equal Opportunity program.

## FINANCIAL FACTS

| | |
|---|---|
| Annual tuition (in-state/out-of-state) | $21,635/$33,880 |
| Books and supplies | $2,500 |
| Room & board (on/off-campus) | $11,089/$12,443 |
| % of students receiving aid | 85 |
| % of first-year students receiving aid | 70 |
| % of students receiving loans | 80 |
| % of students receiving grants | 48 |
| Average award package | $20,500 |
| Average grant | $9,950 |
| Average student loan debt | $31,500 |

## ADMISSIONS

| | |
|---|---|
| Admissions Selectivity Rating | 93 |
| # of applications received | 530 |
| % applicants accepted | 43 |
| % acceptees attending | 46 |
| Average GMAT | 660 |
| Range of GMAT | 600–710 |
| Average GPA | 3.37 |
| TOEFL required of international students? | yes |
| Minimum TOEFL (paper/computer) | 600/250 |
| Application fee | $110 |
| International application fee | $110 |
| Regular application deadline | 11/15 |
| Regular notification | 1/15 |
| Application deadline/notification | |
| Round 1: | 11/15 / 1/15 |
| Round 2: | 1/15 / 3/1 |
| Round 3: | 2/15 / 4/1 |
| Round 4: | 4/1 / 5/15 |
| Deferment available? | yes |
| Maximum length of deferment | 1 year |
| Non-fall admissions? | yes |
| Need-blind admissions? | yes |

## APPLICANTS ALSO LOOK AT

University of California—Davis, University of California—Los Angeles, University of California—Berkeley, University of Southern California, University of Washington

| EMPLOYMENT PROFILE | | | | |
|---|---|---|---|---|
| Career Rating | 81 | Grads employed by field: | % | avg. salary: |
| Average starting salary | $70,000 | Accounting | 15 | $65,000 |
| | | Finance | 18 | $65,000 |
| | | Marketing | 27 | $64,000 |
| | | MIS | 4 | $72,000 |
| | | Operations | 3 | $67,000 |
| | | Consulting | 20 | $82,000 |
| | | Entrepreneurship | 3 | NR |
| | | General Management | 6 | $68,000 |
| | | Other | 4 | NR |

# UNIVERSITY OF CALIFORNIA—LOS ANGELES
## ANDERSON SCHOOL OF MANAGEMENT

### GENERAL INFORMATION
| | |
|---|---|
| Type of school | public |
| Environment | metropolis |
| Academic calendar | quarters |

### SURVEY SAYS...
Friendly students
Good social scene
Good peer network
*Solid preparation in:*
Marketing

### STUDENTS
| | |
|---|---|
| Enrollment of parent institution | 35,625 |
| Enrollment of business school | 1,250 |
| % male/female | 67/33 |
| % out-of-state | 29 |
| % part-time | 48 |
| % minorities | 25 |
| % international | 27 |
| Average age at entry | 28 |
| Average years work experience at entry | 4.6 |

### ACADEMICS
| | |
|---|---|
| **Academic Experience Rating** | **75** |
| Student/faculty ratio | 8:1 |
| Profs interesting rating | 83 |
| Profs accessible rating | 93 |
| % female faculty | 14 |
| % minority faculty | 8 |

### JOINT DEGREES
MBA/JD; MBA/MD; MBA/DDS; MBA/MPH; MBA/Master of Latin American Studies; MBA/Master of Urban Planning; MBA/Master of Computer Science; MBA/Master of Public Policy; MBA/Master of Library and Information Science; MBA/Master of Nursing; MBA/MPH

## Academics

Students suggest that a good slogan for the UCLA Anderson School of Management might be "excellence without attitude." One student continues the compliment saying, "This school is gold! Students are motivated but not overly competitive. No one's going to rip pages out of books in the library." Anderson's students are crazy about their professors, describing them as "understanding, tremendous, top-notch, [and] distinguished." Most everyone at Anderson, even the occasional administrator, exhibits a "free thinking, entrepreneurial spirit," and students assure that "backstabbers need not apply."

Academics, as one might expect, are "rigorous but fully engaging." And because Anderson is "run by the students, attendees are afforded opportunities to put their skills to work." Many say that, due to its Los Angeles location, MBAs who are "interested in entertainment or entrepreneurship in particular, I can't think of a better place to be."

The academic schedule consists of the five-day "Leadership Foundation" course which initiates the program, the management core (10 classes), and electives, which make up over half of the MBA curriculum. The management core, in which students are divided into cohorts of 65 students, "grounds students in business fundamentals and prepares them for advanced study in areas of their own choosing." Students say the "core teachers are all extremely interesting and cover a lot of material quickly." The broad array of electives, on the other hand, affords students enormous flexibility in designing their own curriculum.

Special aspects of the school include the eight-unit "Management Field Study." In the second year, small field teams of students conduct a six-month investigation on a major strategic consulting project. Field study programs are designed to expand "students' capacity to solve complex business problems in real-world settings." Students say, "The field study program gives students real-life consulting experience working with world-class companies." Another such program is the Advanced International Management program (AIM), in which students tailor their own programs by selecting courses from among many international opportunities at UCLA and UCLA Anderson. Students who opt to participate in AIM work on research with UCLA Anderson's international faculty and interact with business and governmental leaders from around the world.

Students at UCLA Anderson also face an unusually broad selection of joint-degree options (nine in all): MBA/JD, MBA/MD, MBA/master of computer science, MBA/master of Latin American studies, MBA/master of library and information science, MBA/master of nursing, MBA/master of public health, MBA/master of public policy and an MBA/master of urban planning. Because of the broad range of options and the flexibility inherent in the program, students feel confident in the school's "ability to create leaders through teaching and experiential learning."

Students report relatively few complaints, though some wish for "a greater emphasis on life sciences, both in terms of course offerings and career-planning opportunities." And others worry that the entrepreneurial spirit affects the relations with recruiters. "Anderson gets dinged for poor relations because a lot of students start their own businesses."

## Career and Placement

UCLA Anderson students are in the fortunate position of being able to draw upon an alumni network that includes more than 33,000 "corporate executives, entrepreneurs, consultants, film producers, high tech innovators, financiers, and other professionals" in

LINDA BALDWIN, DIRECTOR OF ADMISSIONS
110 WESTWOOD PLAZA, GOLD HALL, SUITE B201, LOS ANGELES, CA 90095-1481 U.S.
PHONE: 310-825-6944 • FAX: 310-825-8582
E-MAIL: MBA.ADMISSIONS@ANDERSON.UCLA.EDU • WEBSITE: WWW.ANDERSON.UCLA.EDU

50 states and 80 countries. Students say, "The school makes good use of its alumni network and the diverse industries in the Los Angeles area." They also really appreciate "the support from everyone, especially the Career Center. They are really making a grand effort to help us find direction and jobs, of course!"

Top recruiters at UCLA Anderson over the past two years include A.T. Kearney, Inc.; Bear, Deutsche Bank; Goldman Sachs; Lehman Brothers; Morgan Stanley; Stearns and Co., Inc.; and Twentieth Century Fox, among many others.

## Student Life and Environment

When imagining life at UCLA Anderson, one student asks you to picture this: "The sun is shining. You stop by In-N-Out for a burger, animal-style, and you're on your way to mingle with the entertainment industry's top executives. Life is good." At UCLA Anderson, you can expect a "healthy mix of Hollywood glamour, fashion, and parties." Students boast of a rigorous social schedule including "Lit Club (a bar event featuring tongue-in-cheek 'readings' by students) on Wednesday nights, beer busts on Thursday afternoons, and surfing, barbecues, golf, and tailgating at football games on the weekends."

Students occasionally complain that their fellow MBAs are "very friendly but way too focused on alcohol. There are very few other social types of events." Still, even for those to whom this lifestyle does not appeal, there's always the "perfect weather, [the] beautiful campus and city, [and of course] top-notch academics" to keep you occupied. The size of the program leaves some people wishing they had more contact with school administrators and "closer relationships between faculty and students." And almost all point out that living in LA is expensive—both in terms of housing and basic amenities. But "that's out of the hands of the school," say the students, who also repeatedly point out that "Los Angeles has something for everyone."

## Admissions

UCLA Anderson receives approximately 2,500 applications every year. Of these, only about 330 students actually enter the school. There is no minimum GMAT or GPA, but they do tend to be high. The mean GMAT was 700, and the mean GPA was 3.6. The average number of years of work experience for the entering class of 2005 was a little over four years. Fellowship support is offered to "exceptional admitted students," and about 20 percent of the incoming class received some sort of fellowship.

### PROMINENT ALUMNI
Jeff Henley, Chair, Oracle Corporation; William Gross, Founder & CIO, PIMCO; Chris Zyda, International CFO, Amazon; Lisa Brummel, VP of Home Products/Microsoft; Mitch Kupchak, General Manager, Los Angeles Lakers.

### FINANCIAL FACTS
| | |
|---|---|
| Annual tuition (in-state/out-of-state) | $12,245 |
| Fees (in-state/out-of-state) | $26,039/$23,330 |
| Books and supplies | $7,237 |
| Room & board | $12,381 |
| % of students receiving aid | 92 |
| % of first-year students receiving aid | 90 |
| % of students receiving loans | 92 |
| % of students receiving grants | 85 |
| Average award package | $48,900 |
| Average grant | $15,000 |
| Average student loan debt | $92,000 |

### ADMISSIONS
| | |
|---|---|
| Admissions Selectivity Rating | 60* |
| # of applications received | 2,523 |
| Average GMAT | 700 |
| Range of GMAT | 640–750 |
| Average GPA | 3.6 |
| TOEFL required of international students? | yes |
| Minimum TOEFL (paper/computer) | 600/260 |
| Application fee | $175 |
| International application fee | $175 |
| Regular application deadline | 4/28 |
| Regular notification | 6/23 |
| Application deadline/notification | |
| Round 1: | 11/3 / 1/26 |
| Round 2: | 1/5 / 3/24 |
| Round 3: | 2/21 / 5/19 |
| Round 4: | 4/28 / 6/23 |
| Early decision program? | yes |
| ED Deadline/notification | 11/3 / 1/26 |
| Deferment available? | yes |
| Maximum length of deferment | Case by case basis |
| Need-blind admissions? | yes |

### APPLICANTS ALSO LOOK AT
Duke University, Harvard University, Northwestern University, Stanford University—DUPE, University of California—Berkeley, University of Pennsylvania

### EMPLOYMENT PROFILE
| Career Rating | 97 | Grads employed by field: | % | avg. salary: |
|---|---|---|---|---|
| Primary source of full-time job acceptances | | Accounting | 1 | NR |
| | | Finance | 32 | $93,736 |
| School-facilitated activities | 146 (60%) | Human Resources | 1 | NR |
| Graduate-facilitated activities | 97 (40%) | Marketing | 26 | $80,811 |
| | | Operations | 1 | $71,667 |
| Average starting salary | $89,545 | Strategic Planning | 6 | $95,000 |
| | | Consulting | 16 | $105,934 |
| | | General Management | 5 | $94,031 |
| | | Venture Capital | 2 | $95,000 |
| | | Other | 10 | $90,000 |

# UNIVERSITY OF CALIFORNIA—RIVERSIDE
## A. GARY ANDERSON GRADUATE SCHOOL OF MANAGEMENT

### GENERAL INFORMATION
| | |
|---|---|
| Type of school | public |
| Environment | city |
| Academic calendar | quarter |

### SURVEY SAYS...
Happy students
*Solid preparation in:*
Accounting
General management
Teamwork Operations
Presentation skills

### STUDENTS
| | |
|---|---|
| Enrollment of parent institution | 17,000 |
| Enrollment of business school | 109 |
| % male/female | 52/48 |
| % out-of-state | 13 |
| % part-time | 12 |
| % minorities | 20 |
| % international | 48 |
| Average age at entry | 26 |
| Average years work experience at entry | 3.7 |

### ACADEMICS
| | |
|---|---|
| **Academic Experience Rating** | **70** |
| Student/faculty ratio | 15:1 |
| Profs interesting rating | 72 |
| Profs accessible rating | 72 |
| % female faculty | 23 |
| % minority faculty | 43 |

## Academics

It may be in part due to the sunny California weather, but students at the A. Gary Anderson Graduate School of Management at UC Riverside are almost nauseatingly enthusiastic about their program. As one student raves, "I am at a fantastic school, and I am having the time of my life. I feel very privileged to be here. As a returning student, having been out in the workforce for some time, this experience is doubly beneficial to me. The rigorous curriculum, the superb professors—what a gift they are!" Students appreciate the fact that "professors are all very accessible, both inside and outside of the classroom." One student says, "[The professors] make an effort to get to know everyone's name, so that you're not just a face in the crowd." And several shy students are enthusiastic about the way the program has "improved [their] professional skills, especially in interpersonal communication, teamwork, and presentational skills."

The six components of an MBA from AGSM are the core courses, an internship, the communication workshop, the electives, "capstone course," and a case project or thesis. Though the core courses take up more time than any other single component, students are most enthusiastic about the wide variety of electives, which are all seminar size and designed to "encourage participative learning." As one student says, the program offers a very "wide diversity of elective courses, and it's very easy to get into any course." There are 10 areas of electives, and students are allowed to take up to nine electives from any area. These areas are accounting, entrepreneurial management, finance, general management, human-resources management/organizational behavior, international management, management information systems, management science, marketing, and production and operations management.

In regard to the teaching style, most students agree that "discussion is greatly encouraged. A lot of courses require presentation with business formal attire; some courses even require group debate." One student notes, "It gives you some pressure, but it's fun." However, others are sorry to point out that "it is a research-oriented university and feel [that they] are not getting attention from some professors. There are one or two professors who [have tenure] and are good at research. Their teaching is very bad, and they don't care about students learning; the university doesn't do anything about them." Other students complain that because "the tuition is very high and is still increasing. Students need to have professors who teach well and care about students, not just good researchers and paper-publishers."

## Career and Placement

Aside from recent budget cuts, the thing that has most students at AGSM up in arms about is the career-resources center. As one student says, "The school desperately needs a stronger career-counseling center designed just for the MBA students." And students consider Career Services, "job placement for MBA graduates, and internships" among the school's greatest failings, although installation of a full-time Career Services coordinator has helped to alleviate these problems. They'd also like to see AGSM work on "improving on-campus recruiting and relationship with alumni," and "community relations and professional networking."

## Student Life and Environment

Lovely Riverside, California, is home to not only UC Riverside, but also three other colleges or universities. Students at AGSM will never have to look far to find like-minded compatriots. And between exams and case studies, there is always something to do. A guide compiled by a group of students from the different schools says, "Riverside has plenty of unique hangouts, interesting shopping, and a wide variety of eats to fit anyone's desires (and budget)." Whatever you're looking for, from "a night out on the town or just a good place to go hiking," Riverside has it. As one student says, "Although I am busy with school, I always have time to mingle with my classmates and outside friends." Another student adds, "Most students go to a local lounge on Thursday nights to listen to a fellow MBA student play bass in a band. We have a great social circle!"

The school itself is housed in a 30,000-square-foot building that features "state-of-the-art research and teaching facilities." MBA students agree that their "computer lab is very nice," but complain that "the undergraduate business majors have the better systems." Other students gripe that they're stuck in "a small building that consists of one lecture room and one classroom. Our school has suffered greatly from the previous budget cuts." Still, the building must have something going for it because "MBA students rarely venture onto the main campus at [UC Riverside], unless it's to go to the library or bookstore."

Students agree that it is worth venturing out to UC Riverside library. It is home to "more than two million bound volumes; 13,000 serials; and 1.6 million microforms, including extensive literature in the management field." This superb research library "provides substantial support for student and faculty research."

## Admissions

At AGSM, students from all undergraduate majors and levels of business experience are eligible for admission. In fact, more than 30 percent of all incoming students come from a background other than business, including social sciences, math, engineering, physical and natural sciences, humanities, and languages. According to the school, "There is no minimum GPA or GMAT requirement for MBA admission consideration. However, please consider that the average GPA for new students admitted for the fall 2005 quarter was 3.37, and the average GMAT score was 574." AGSM does not require prior work experience for its MBA students (though it is, of course, encouraged) and feels that a diverse student body can only add to the learning experience. However, because they don't require prior work experience, they do require that all prospective MBAs complete an internship "to ensure your success upon graduation."

### FINANCIAL FACTS

| | |
|---|---|
| Annual tuition (in-state/out-of-state) | $8,766/$12,246 |
| Fees | $23,289 |
| Books and supplies | $1,650 |
| Room & board | $8,954 |
| % of students receiving aid | 45 |
| % of first-year students receiving aid | 46 |
| % of students receiving grants | 45 |
| Average award package | $21,573 |
| Average grant | $14,276 |

### ADMISSIONS

| | |
|---|---|
| **Admissions Selectivity Rating** | **83** |
| # of applications received | 248 |
| % applicants accepted | 51 |
| % acceptees attending | 47 |
| Average GMAT | 574 |
| Range of GMAT | 540–640 |
| Average GPA | 3.37 |
| TOEFL required of international students? | yes |
| Minimum TOEFL (paper/computer) | 550/213 |
| Application fee | $60 |
| International application fee | $75 |
| Regular application deadline | 5/1 |
| Regular notification | 6/1 |
| Transfer students accepted? | yes |
| Transfer application policy A maximum of 2 graduate courses taken in residence may be transferred. | |
| Non-fall admissions? | yes |
| Need-blind admissions? | yes |

### APPLICANTS ALSO LOOK AT

California State Polytechnic University—Pomona, California State University—Fullerton, Pepperdine University, University of California—Irvine, University of California—San Diego

### EMPLOYMENT PROFILE

| | | | | |
|---|---|---|---|---|
| Career Rating | 61 | **Grads employed by field:** | **% avg. salary:** | |
| **Primary source of full-time job acceptances** | | Accounting | 40 | $44,900 |
| | | Finance | 30 | $44,900 |
| School-facilitated activities | 12 (30%) | Human Resources | 10 | $31,200 |
| Graduate-facilitated activities | 29 (70%) | Marketing | 20 | $30,900 |
| | | | | |
| Average starting salary | $40,600 | | | |
| Percent employed | 47 | | | |

# UNIVERSITY OF CENTRAL ARKANSAS
## COLLEGE OF BUSINESS ADMINISTRATION

## Academics

Affordability, location, the flexibility of the program, and the opportunity to complete a degree in one year are the primary reasons students choose one of the MBA programs at the University of Central Arkansas. UCA offers both a standard MBA and an International MBA. A Pre-MBA Program Certificate Program is also available for students who lack the necessary related undergraduate course work.

UCA's conventional MBA requires 30 credit hours, making it possible for full-time students to complete the program in one year. The program is comprised of 10 three-credit classes offered in the afternoons and evenings. Courses cover information systems, accounting, managerial economics, communication, financial decision making, business law, entrepreneurship, marketing, and strategic management. The program concludes with an integrative class. Elective and specialization options are not available.

The International MBA program requires 36 credit hours, meaning that, too, can be completed in one year by full-time students. The program is comprised of 12 three-credit classes offered in the afternoons and evenings. Courses cover information systems, accounting, managerial economics, financial decision making, business law, global entrepreneurship, marketing, international strategic management, and multicultural communications. In addition, students must take an integrative capstone class and two graduate-level electives in business, international culture, or foreign language. Students may complete an internship with a global company in lieu of the two electives.

Students wishing to receive an MBA but who lack the necessary undergraduate coursework in business may complete that course work through the Pre-MBA Program Certificate Program. Applicants to the program must meet the same requirements as applicants to the MBA program; completion of the Pre-MBA Program does not guarantee admission to the MBA program. The program consists of six courses covering basic concepts in accounting, economics, finance, management, marketing, and quantitative analysis.

Professors get mixed reviews here. More than one respondent points out, "We have some very good professors, but some are unorganized and have a hard time communicating their subjects to students."

## Career and Placement

Because UCA's MBA program is so small and many of the students are part-timers who already have jobs, the school offers few career and placement services directed exclusively to MBAs. Still, several students express a desire for better relations with local companies and overall "better job placement." Students may use the Career Services Office, which serves the entire university; the office provides counseling, training, mock interviews, workshops, access to online job databases, and school-wide career fairs and other recruiting events. Only a handful of employers visit the campus each year for the express purpose of recruiting MBAs. Employers most likely to hire UCA MBAs include Acxiom, ALLTEL, Entergy, First Security Bank, and Kimberly-Clark.

REBECCA GATLIN-WATTS, MBA DIRECTOR
BURDICK BUSINESS BUILDING, ROOM 224, CONWAY, AR 72035 UNITED STATES
PHONE: 501-450-5316 • FAX: 501-450-5302
E-MAIL: MBA@UCA.EDU • WEBSITE: WWW.BUSINESS.UCA.EDU

## FINANCIAL FACTS

| | |
|---|---|
| Annual tuition (in-state/out-of-state) | $4,139/$5,849 |
| Books and supplies | $1,500 |
| Room & board | $6,000 |

## ADMISSIONS

| | |
|---|---|
| **Admissions Selectivity Rating** | **67** |
| # of applications received | 44 |
| % applicants accepted | 86 |
| % acceptees attending | 89 |
| Average GMAT | 494 |
| Range of GMAT | 460–530 |
| Average GPA | 3.25 |
| TOEFL required of international students? | yes |
| Minimum TOEFL (paper/computer) | 550/213 |
| Application fee | $25 |
| International application fee | $40 |
| Regular application deadline | rolling |
| Regular notification | rolling |
| Deferment available? | yes |
| Transfer students accepted? | yes |
| Transfer application policy A maximum of 6 graduate hours is transferrable from an AACSB institution. | |
| Non-fall admissions? | yes |

## APPLICANTS ALSO LOOK AT

University of Arkansas at Little Rock, University of Arkansas—Fayetteville

## Student Life and Environment

The University of Central Arkansas is located in Conway, one of the state's fastest growing cities. The city is home to a number of industries, including Kimberly Clark, AmTran, Virco, and Baldwin Piano. Database magnate Acxiom makes its headquarters in Conway. A number of government headquarters are located in Conway as well. Besides UCA, the city is also home to Hendrix College and Central Baptist College.

The UCA campus is "a unique mix of Georgian-style architecture and up-to-date technology," according to the school's view book. The school has a long and proud tradition in intercollegiate athletics—Scotty Pippin played his college ball here—and the school's 10,000-plus students regularly turn out to cheer on their Bears and Sugar Bears. The MBA program is located in the Burdick Business Administration Building, which was built in 1973.

Because of the International MBA program, the student body here includes "fairly diverse nationalities, which is good." Not so good is the fact that "many American students seem to have come directly from undergraduate programs" and thus lack the practical business experience necessary to contribute meaningfully to classroom discussion.

## Admissions

All applicants to the MBA program at UCA must have earned an undergraduate degree from an accredited U.S. institution or its overseas equivalent, with a minimum GPA of 2.7, or a minimum GPA of 3.0 for the final 60 hours of undergraduate study. Applicants must also submit official GMAT scores; the admissions committee requires a minimum GMAT score of 450 from all applicants. UCA uses formulas to create minimum cut-offs for applicants. Applicants must have a minimum formula index of 1,000 under the formula [(undergraduate GPA 5 200) + GMAT score], or a minimum formula index of 1,050 under the formula [(undergraduate GPA for the final 60 hours of study 5 200) + GMAT score]. International applicants whose first language is not English must also submit TOEFL scores.

# UNIVERSITY OF CENTRAL FLORIDA
## COLLEGE OF BUSINESS ADMINISTRATION

## Academics

Students pursing an MBA at the University of Central Florida have three options: the traditional MBA, a part-time evening program designed for working professionals; the full-time one-year MBA, a daytime program for freshly minted BAs as well as mid-career professionals looking to jumpstart their careers; and an Executive MBA, designed for current executives and managers. The school also offers MS degrees in accounting, economics, taxation, human resources, change management, information systems, and sports business management. Additionally, they have two new certificate programs in entrepreneurship and technology commercialization.

UCF offers concentrations in accounting, economics, finance, entrepreneurship, environmental management and policy, human resources and change management, international business, and management information systems. Both the full-time and part-time MBA programs require between 39 and 51 course hours, depending on one's undergraduate background in business. The school reports that its greatest strengths lie in applied economics, environmental economics, MIS, hi-tech marketing, and entrepreneurship. In addition, students appreciate "the school's focus on technology, which gives it a leg up over more traditional institutions," as well as the program's "strong emphasis on leadership, integrity, academia, and community involvement."

Students interested in the popular Sports Business Management Track must apply for separate admission to the Master in Sports Business Management Program. The program, which awards an MBA as well as the master's degree, requires a 10-week internship.

While students love both the cost and convenience of UCF's graduate business programs, they tell us that the programs are not without their faults. Some complain that "electives aren't clearly laid out, and many of the classes aren't focused enough, making them a repeat of undergraduate business courses." Just as many believe that "the school has more research-oriented teachers than teachers who can actually teach," and that too many professors "lack real-world experience. They are so focused on theory that they do not focus enough on practice." On the other hand, others point out that "professors are generally very experienced in their fields and have a great deal of related knowledge to share."

## Career and Placement

UCF's Career Resource Center operates a satellite office at the College of Business Administration to serve business graduates and undergraduates. The office includes a Career Information Library stocked with job binders, salary surveys, employer databases, and other reading materials. Workshops are offered in resume writing, job search strategies, interviewing techniques, and federal employment opportunities. Students have free access to MonsterTrak during their tenure at the school and for one semester following graduation.

Employers who most frequently hire UCF MBAs include AmSouth Bank, Darden, SunTrust, CitiBank, Coca-Cola Bottling Company, Disney, Aventis, Cendant, Dynetech, IRS, Intersil, and Marriott Vacation Clubs.

JUDY RYDER, DIRECTOR OF GRADUATE ADMISSIONS
PO BOX 161400, BA I, ROOM 240, ORLANDO, FL 32816 UNITED STATES
PHONE: 407-823-4723 • FAX: 407-823-0219
E-MAIL: CBAGRAD@BUS.UCF.EDU • WEBSITE: WWW.BUS.UCF.EDU

## Student Life and Environment

Students in UCF's traditional MBA program attend classes in the evenings, as most are working during the day. These students typically "go to classes and then leave" without participating in the university's extracurricular life. Students in the one-year full-time program, on the other hand, do immerse themselves in the UCF environment. One writes, "You could actually live your whole life on campus—it is almost its own town! We have absolutely everything so you don't even need a car! The gym is spectacular, the food selection is extensive, and there are hundreds of clubs doing great things in the community as well as encouraging students to network." Facilities are equally edifying; one MBA observes, "There are computers everywhere. The dorms are very nice and clean, most even have individual bedrooms and common rooms with kitchens." Everyone here appreciates that "the environment is relatively safe. The campus is well-lit at night and there is a free escort service anywhere on campus if you don't want to walk alone."

Students love Orlando, "a city known throughout the world and one that everyone would like to visit at some point in their lives." The city is an excellent resource for students seeking internships and post-degree jobs. The campus is located "on the outskirts of the city," which some feel is a "great location." Others complain that "it is difficult to access the campus from downtown Orlando. Drive time is between 40 minutes and one hour."

The UCF College of Business Administration attracts "mostly younger professionals or those who are recent graduates and are looking to get a start in a career field," along with "some older students with families and long-time careers. Many students are married." They tend to be "warm and cordial, competitive, yet also good team players who are willing to help others in need." Some feel that "many of the non-business students in the MBA program seem to lag behind, dragging classes to a lower level. More stringent requirements should be implemented for acceptance into the MBA program, possibly including prior business experience."

## Admissions

Applicants to the UCF College of Business MBA program must complete an online application to the UCF School of Graduate Studies. Additionally, applicants must submit official transcripts for each university or college attended, an official GMAT score, a personal essay, a resume, and three letters of recommendation. International students whose first language is not English must also submit TOEFL scores. All international students need to provide translations of non-English documents and an accredited course-by-course evaluation of transcripts from institutions that do not employ the American system. UCF requires a minimum GMAT score of 540 (550 for the one-year full-time program) for its MBA programs; requirements for other master's programs are less restrictive. An undergraduate GPA of at least 3.0 is also required.

### FINANCIAL FACTS

| | |
|---|---|
| Annual tuition (in-state/out-of-state) | $5,788/$21,936 |
| Fees | $158 |
| Books and supplies | $1,500 |
| Room & board (on/off-campus) | $7,000/$10,000 |
| % of students receiving aid | 5 |
| % of first-year students receiving aid | 20 |
| % of students receiving grants | 10 |
| Average award package | $12,000 |
| Average grant | $10,000 |

### ADMISSIONS

| | |
|---|---|
| Admissions Selectivity Rating | 83 |
| # of applications received | 211 |
| % applicants accepted | 59 |
| % acceptees attending | 83 |
| Average GMAT | 561 |
| Range of GMAT | 500–680 |
| Average GPA | 3.3 |
| TOEFL required of international students? | yes |
| Minimum TOEFL (paper/computer) | 575/233 |
| Application fee | $30 |
| International application fee | $30 |
| Regular application deadline | 6/15 |
| Regular notification | rolling |
| Early decision program? | yes |
| ED Deadline/notification | Fall only: 4/15 / 5/15 |
| Transfer students accepted? | yes |
| Transfer application policy Transfer applicants must be from a regionally or nationally accredited university. May transfer in up to 9 hours. | |
| Non-fall admissions? | yes |
| Need-blind admissions? | yes |

### APPLICANTS ALSO LOOK AT

Florida State University, Rollins College, University of Florida, University of South Florida

# UNIVERSITY OF CHICAGO
## GRADUATE SCHOOL OF BUSINESS

## GENERAL INFORMATION

| | |
|---|---|
| Type of school | private |
| Environment | metropolis |
| Academic calendar | quarter |

### SURVEY SAYS...
Happy students
*Solid preparation in:*
Accounting
Quantitative skills

### STUDENTS

| | |
|---|---|
| Enrollment of parent institution | 13,620 |
| Enrollment of business school | 2,574 |
| % male/female | 72/28 |
| % part-time | 58 |
| % minorities | 7 |
| % international | 33 |
| Average age at entry | 28 |
| Average years work experience at entry | 5 |

### ACADEMICS

| | |
|---|---|
| **Academic Experience Rating** | **78** |
| Student/faculty ratio | 15:1 |
| Profs interesting rating | 98 |
| Profs accessible rating | 82 |

### JOINT DEGREES

MBA/AM in Area Studies and Business; MBA/AM in International Relations and Business; JD/MBA; MD/MBA; MBA/MPP Public Policy Studies and Business; MBA/AM Social Service Administration and Business. Students must satisfy the curriculum requirements for each degree. Both degrees must be awarded simultaneously. Students complete the joint program in less time than would be required if each degree were pursued separately.

### PROMINENT ALUMNI

Karen Katen, President, Pfizer Global Pharmaceuticals; Robert Lane, Chair and CEO, Deere & Company; Joe Mansueto, CEO, Morningstar; Jon Corzine, Governor, New Jersey

## Academics

Established in 1898, the University of Chicago's GSB is the second-oldest program in the country. This means, as the students will tell you, that the school has had over a hundred years to perfect its craft. Students tout the impressive qualifications of their teachers: "Professors are Jedi-smart and are passionate about their work. Each [professor] is here because they know that working here exposes them to: the best and the brightest." The word "Nobel" comes up a lot, too—as in, "my faculty advisor is a Nobel laureate." Other students admit that, while "it is daunting to study finance theory at the school where a lot of the theory originated," the "challenge is quite stimulating." However, a few specific departments shine more than others; GSB students say without qualms that their "finance, accounting, entrepreneurship, and marketing are at or near the top across business schools." The one drawback to having the very best in academia at your doorstep is that "most faculty have very limited business experience, so they can teach only the theory and not the practice of business." One student explains, "By far the best courses I have taken are entrepreneurship classes, which are taught by practitioners."

Though the academic program is "intense," students say it's not because of pressures in the program. They explain that it's "because the students are inherently competitive. Grade nondisclosure works very well in increasing the friendliness among students."

Compared to most full-time MBA programs, Chicago's list of requirements is amazingly flexible, and the choice of electives they offer is enormous. Among the few required courses is LEAD (Leadership Effectiveness and Development), which first-year students take as part of a cohort to develop professional personal skills. LEAD is popular and acknowledged as a valuable resource, but some students say that it "could use some revisions. It is a great idea to teach management, negotiation, ethics, and public speaking in the LEAD program, but the modules are not as effective as it could be. The examples used in class are sometimes not relevant, and students don't get as much out of the exercises as they should."

Of the 11 electives, students have the option to take 6 with other departments. This means that, according to the school, GSB students are able to "study with some of the world's most renowned scholars in economics, law, languages, philosophy, or literature." Students appreciate that the curriculum is "flexible enough that students can tailor it to their every need." Students also report that "the flexible curriculum offered at the GSB is one of the [university's] greatest strengths. Recruiters tell us how much more prepared we are for finance internships because we can choose [the] courses we want to take during the first year."

Full-time MBAs can also choose to pursue the international MBA degree. To do this, students must master a foreign language, complete a rigorous course of studies in international business, and study abroad. An internship abroad doesn't hurt either. Joint degrees with other schools within the University of Chicago include an MBA/JD, and MBA/MD, and MBA/master's of public policy studies (MPP), and an MBA/master's of social services administration (AM).

While most students readily applaud the rigor of the academic program, they often wish for diversity, both in the student body and in job opportunities. They would like the GSB to "offer a better mix of different types of marketing, so marketing grads could walk out [of the program] equal to peers at other schools." Other students add that they wish the school "would make more of an effort to develop East Coast career opportunities."

ROSEMARIA MARTINELLI, ASSOCIATE DEAN FOR STUDENT RECRUITMENT & ADMISSION
5807 SOUTH WOODLAWN AVENUE, CHICAGO, IL 60637 UNITED STATES
PHONE: 773-702-7369 • FAX: 773-702-9085
E-MAIL: ADMISSIONS@CHICAGOGSB.EDU • WEBSITE: WWW.CHICAGOGSB.EDU

## Career and Placement

Students have nothing but good things to say about the university's 37,000 alumni. "They're great—perhaps not as proactive as those that cheerlead at other schools, but they are very excited to help and build presence at their firms." Another student points out that Chicago is "one of only a few schools to have been at the top for nearly 100 years, so there is an amazing, deep alumni network of professionals at all levels, especially in finance and general management."

Overall, graduates find jobs and are well-placed in their field. The Career Services Center reports that school-facilitated sources accounted for about 80 percent of all hires for their classes. And three months after graduation, 87 percent of graduates in 2003 had job offers, compared with 82 percent for the class of 2002. The economy was less harsh for the intern class; 99 percent of students who sought an internship in the class of 2004 accepted an offer. Companies that recruit on-campus include Bear Stearns, Goldman Sachs, Merrill Lynch, and McKinsey & Company. Because the career office is so helpful, some students have gone so far as to say that "the Office of Career Services is almost too much of a resource." One student comments, "I think the wealth of materials available to us could be presented in more concise ways in order to free up our schedules a little."

## Student Life and Environment

With a brand new $125 million Hyde Park Center, just a few minutes by train from downtown Chicago, and a handful of blocks from Lake Michigan, "life on campus is relaxed. It is like living in a small village 10 miles from downtown. You can choose when [to] go little and when [to] go big," according to students. Many students live in other Chicago neighborhoods and commute to school; other students complain that "many members of the class have lived in Chicago and [already] have friends in the city, so integrating into the GSB community is not as important to [them]."

Though the neighborhood around Hyde Park is sometimes considered dangerous, students say that "the University of Chicago is striving mightily to improve the surrounding neighborhood. There are areas adjacent to campus that are beautiful and expensive to live in and unfortunately there are areas nearby that are traditionally tough neighborhoods."

## Admissions

Of approximately 3,400 applicants who apply to Chicago GSB every year, only about 800 are admitted and 520 enroll. Approximately 33 percent are international, and about 70 percent are male. All of those admitted have at least some full-time work experience, and their average age is 28. The average GMAT score is 701, and the average undergraduate GPA is 3.5. Many students appreciate that, unlike some other universities, the University of Chicago is "one of the few top schools that gives scholarships. About 25 percent of [those admitted] received some form of scholarship."

### FINANCIAL FACTS

| | |
|---|---|
| Annual tuition | $41,600 |
| Fees | $582 |
| Books and supplies | $1,650 |
| Room & board | $17,100 |
| % of students receiving aid | 80 |
| % of first-year students receiving aid | 80 |
| % of students receiving loans | 70 |
| % of students receiving grants | 16 |
| Average award package | $55,000 |
| Average grant | $21,000 |
| Average student loan debt | $85,000 |

### ADMISSIONS

| | |
|---|---|
| **Admissions Selectivity Rating** | **60*** |
| Average GMAT | 701 |
| Range of GMAT | 640–760 |
| Average GPA | 3.5 |
| TOEFL required of international students? | yes |
| Minimum TOEFL (paper/computer) | 600/250 |
| Application fee | $200 |
| International application fee | $200 |
| Application deadline/notification | |
| Round 1: | 1/26 / 1/11 |
| Round 2: | 1/4 / 3/22 |
| Round 3: | 3/15 / 5/17 |
| Deferment available? | yes |
| Maximum length of deferment | 1 year |
| Need-blind admissions? | yes |

### EMPLOYMENT PROFILE

| | | | |
|---|---|---|---|
| **Career Rating** | **99** | **Grads employed by field:** | **% avg. salary:** |
| **Primary source of full-time** | | Finance | 52 $94,896 |
| **job acceptances** | | Marketing | 11 $89,253 |
| School-facilitated activities | 405 (83%) | Consulting | 27 $105,842 |
| Graduate-facilitated activities | 85 (17%) | General Management | 4 $97,411 |
| | | Other | 5 $98,556 |
| Average starting salary | $95,000 | | |
| Percent employed | 93 | | |

# UNIVERSITY OF CINCINNATI
## COLLEGE OF BUSINESS

## Academics

Future MBAs may choose from multiple options at the University of Cincinnati's College of Business. For full-timers in a hurry, UC offers a full-time 12-month MBA; a 15-month degree that packs the coursework just as tightly but adds a three-month internship; and a 21-month degree that, along with a three-month internship, combines an MBA and MS for those "seeking a high degree of rigorous specialization in addition to an applied general management education." UC's full-time programs take advantage of their ability to sequence classes, allowing advanced classes to build on concepts taught in previous classes.

UC also offers part-time options at a variety of sites, including the Clifton Campus, the Blue Ash Professional Development Center (both evening programs) and Wright Patterson Air Force Base (a mid-afternoon program). The part-time program is by necessity more flexible than its full-time counterpart, but is otherwise similar, employing the same professors and providing the same support services. In both the full-time and part-time programs, concentrations are available in construction management, finance, information systems, international business, management, marketing, operations management, quantitative analysis, and commercial real estate.

The UC MBA program stresses teamwork, which students appreciate. One writes, "The team structure that is fostered from day one is instrumental in making our program unique and successful. The teams are organized in such a way that no one gets left behind. There is almost an imperative that everyone graduates; an instilled sense of community and support, which has been so refreshing. Coming from Procter & Gamble, I recognize the necessity of teaching a team-based structure. It's remarkable." The small size of the program "means students get a lot of attention, something you can never have too much of." However, for many, "the greatest strength of UC is its focus on global business. The College of Business stresses to every student the need to look at business from a global perspective. There are study-abroad opportunities. There are also many foreign students in class with us to give us a different viewpoint of a situation." Offerings in quantitative analysis and commercial real estate also receive high marks.

## Career and Placement

Students tell us that "the MBA Career Office puts extensive effort into assuring us that we have the tools to find a job and brings in various employers for recruiting activities." The office's efforts include one-on-one counseling meetings; career development workshops; career days; online recruiting and contact databases; videotaped mock interviews; and on-campus recruiting events.

Employers most likely to hire UC MBAs include Fifth Third Bank, Deloitte, P & G (Procter & Gamble), The ARS Group, Toyota Motor Manufacturing, L'Oreal, Cincinnati Bell, Sara Lee, Cintas, Eli Lilly and Company, Burke, Inc., Steak 'n Shake, and Charter Consulting.

## Student Life and Environment

The "driven and intelligent" MBAs at UC enjoy a "diverse mix" that includes a one-quarter international population, a range of experience levels ("we have students right out of undergraduate schools, as well as students well into their careers"), and backgrounds ("a lot of the students are engineering undergrads looking to utilize an MBA for the opportunity of advancement in the engineering field; most others are business undergrads looking for career advancement"). The program has an unusually even gender split as

VALERIE O. ROBINSON, ASSOCIATE DIRECTOR, MBA ADMISSIONS
CARL H. LINDNER HALL, SUITE 103, PO BOX 210020, CINCINNATI, OH 45221-0020 U.S.
PHONE: 513-556-7020 • FAX: 513-558-7006
E-MAIL: GRADUATE@UC.EDU • WEBSITE: WWW.BUSINESS.UC.EDU/MBA

well. One student sums up, "UC doesn't recruit a specific mold of what is perceived as 'the MBA Student.' They recruit a diverse mix that makes the experience surprisingly worldly in decidedly Midwestern Cincinnati." The mix "adds a lot of value to the classes."

"The majority of students are commuters" in the UC MBA program, "and it is challenging to have graduate students involved in on-campus activities. We do enjoy the academic strength and fellow classmates, but not all of us feel fully integrated into the campus." The opportunities are there, though, and full-time students generally take advantage of them, reporting that "the administration is focused on activities and connecting students to the university and community. We have weekly networking dinners or happy hours with people from General Electric, Procter & Gamble, and Cincinnati Bell. The MBA Association has been active in organizing social activities for students as well." In addition, "we have a lot of free lunches associated with training sessions and academic and career development sessions. They are wonderful. And we have all kinds of recreational facilities and free movies to broaden our view of the world." UC's men's basketball team is "amazing, and everyone rallies around it. As one student puts it, "For being a mostly commuter campus, there are plenty of opportunities to get involved on campus."

## Admissions

Applicants to the UC MBA program must submit an official GMAT score report, official copies of all post-secondary academic transcripts, two essays, two letters of recommendation, a resume, and a completed application form. Applicants need not have earned undergraduate degrees in business; in fact, only half the students here have. The rest are primarily split among engineering and liberal arts majors, with a few science majors thrown in to the mix. Completion of a college-level calculus course is required of all applicants. International applicants must also submit results for the TOEFL exam and certification of finances. In an effort to increase the population of underrepresented students, "UC offers the Albert C. Yates Scholarships and Fellowships to candidates from underrepresented groups. The scholarships cover full tuition and fees and the fellowship additionally provides a stipend each quarter."

### FINANCIAL FACTS

| | |
|---|---|
| Annual tuition (in-state/out-of-state) | $19,184/$24,188 |
| Fees | $1,932 |
| Books and supplies | $3,300 |
| Room & board (on/off-campus) | $13,000/$14,500 |
| % of students receiving aid | 82 |
| % of first-year students receiving aid | 82 |
| % of students receiving loans | 45 |
| % of students receiving grants | 55 |
| Average award package | $20,795 |
| Average grant | $17,019 |

### ADMISSIONS

| | |
|---|---|
| Admissions Selectivity Rating | 84 |
| # of applications received | 146 |
| % applicants accepted | 58 |
| % acceptees attending | 52 |
| Average GMAT | 587 |
| Range of GMAT | 510–620 |
| Average GPA | 3.35 |
| TOEFL required of international students? | yes |
| Minimum TOEFL (paper/computer) | 600/250 |
| Application fee | $40 |
| International application fee | $40 |
| Regular application deadline | 4/30 |
| Regular notification | rolling |
| Early decision program? | yes |
| ED Deadline/notification | Fall, 2/15 / 3/30 |
| Deferment available? | yes |
| Maximum length of deferment | 1 year |
| Transfer students accepted? | yes |
| Transfer application policy | Transferring from an AACSB-accredited institution, no more than 12 credit hours classes. |
| Non-fall admissions? | yes |
| Need-blind admissions? | yes |

### APPLICANTS ALSO LOOK AT

Indiana University—Bloomington, Miami University, Northern Kentucky University, The Ohio State University, University of Dayton, Wright State University, Xavier University

### EMPLOYMENT PROFILE

| | | Grads employed by field: | % | avg. salary: |
|---|---|---|---|---|
| Career Rating | 69 | Finance | 20 | $50,800 |
| Primary source of full-time job acceptances | | Marketing | 20 | $67,500 |
| Graduate-facilitated activities | 31 (100%) | MIS | 7 | $48,500 |
| | | Operations | 7 | $61,400 |
| Average starting salary | $56,929 | General Management | 26 | NR |
| Percent employed | 30 | Other | 20 | $41,761 |

# UNIVERSITY COLLEGE DUBLIN
## THE MICHAEL SMURFIT GRADUATE SCHOOL OF BUSINESS

## Academics

There are worse ways to spend a year than by getting an MBA in a beautiful, historic city like Dublin, especially when the conferring institution is the well-respected University College Dublin. As Dubliners are well aware, theirs is a city that boasts an appealing blend of commerce, art, and nightlife. Visitors—international business students, for example—may find themselves enthralled by its quaint streets and raucous pubs. On the other hand, they may never find the opportunity to leave the b-school and explore their surroundings. This is one demanding MBA program.

The Smurfit MBA begins with an orientation week, followed by a sequence of nine quant-heavy foundation courses. Corporate and integrative courses, electives, and an applied research project all follow. The program concludes with final examinations. Students warn that "the one-year program is a great test of inner desire to achieve and thrive in a pressure-filled environment." First semester is by far the worst; as one student says, "Semester one in this school is grueling, with very heavy workload and high pressure. It's not as bad, though, for those with a finance background. In semester two, there's more time to actually allow the knowledge to be absorbed." Another MBA agrees, "Second semester is more balanced and sociable than [the] first semester, with the exception that electives run at night and on the weekend, making it less like a full-time course and more like a part-time one!"

MBAs explain that "overall, the greatest strengths of the school [are] the well-developed finance faculty, human-resource faculty, and the team culture that students develop while [at the Smurfit School]. The international business faculty is also great." Smurfit professors are "generally approachable and extremely willing to help out with advice on any quirky idea that emerges," and they "bring together lots of experience and knowledge and, more importantly, a huge amount of enthusiasm that is infectious." Another plus: "Communication facilities, e-mail, Internet, and multimedia facilities are excellent."

## Career and Placement

The Career Management Center at the Smurfit School is, according to the school's website, "a full career-guidance service with a comprehensive array of research and online facilities. These include a large bank of data and publications relating to potential employers around the world, as well as reference materials such as guides to psychometric testing, job hunting, or CV preparation." The service also arranges corporate workshops, one-on-one counseling, and seminars covering interviewing, job search, and resume writing. An MBA-dedicated office is located on the Blackrock campus, home to the Smurfit MBA program.

Employers most likely to hire Smurfit MBAs include A&L Goodbody, Citibank, Elan, Eli Lilly, GE, KPMG, and Riverdeed.

## Student Life and Environment

"Smurfit totally lives up to the phrase 'work hard, play hard,'" according to MBAs. One student writes, "I have never worked so intensely or socialized as much. There are many different committees [that] all students are encouraged to participate in: Smurfit rugby, networking club, or social committee, just to name a few. It has been a life-altering experience [that] I have thoroughly enjoyed." Another student adds, "I never expected an MBA to be so much fun. Sure, if you want to spend every hour studying, you can find the work, but you will miss out on a vital part of the MBA experience."

ELAINE MCAREE, MBA ADMISSIONS OFFICER
UNIVERSITY COLLEGE DUBLIN, CARYSFORT AVENUE, BLACKROCK CO., DUBLIN, IRELAND
PHONE: 011-353-1-716-8862 • FAX: 011-353-1-716-8981
E-MAIL: MBA@UCD.IE • WEBSITE: WWW.UCD.IE/SMURFITSCHOOL

Dublin offers plenty of options for students when they need to blow off steam. Students say that its sometimes necessary for the health of the program; one student explains, "One moment you are in a team meeting, fighting over a strategic posture your team needs to take in case review, and you could be sometimes furious at your inability to get your team members to your point of view. But if you seem really furious at the outcome of this meeting, just hold it; it will be time to meet at the pub soon and all that disagreement will be history. The pub seems to be a place to bury most disagreements." The school also offers "a number of balls and networking events during the course of the year. Other formal events occur from time to time, in which guest speakers, normally CEOs of companies like IBM operating in Ireland, come to give lectures and presentations about their company. Their staff [also comes] in order to get some networks running. These are all a good respite from the tough MBA curricula."

Smurfit students evince "diversity in every dimension you can think of: language, nationality, gender, work experience, age, even hair color." MBAs here enjoy an "open, friendly atmosphere" with a collegial vibe; as one student explains, "The program is set up under one roof, which imparts a strong sense of togetherness and focus."

## Admissions

The Smurfit admissions office requires applicants to provide all of the following: a completed application form and a photocopy of the completed form; two photographs, passport size; one set of official transcripts for all previous undergraduate work, plus a photocopy of all transcripts; two letters of recommendation; three essays; and a resume/curriculum vitae. Non-native English speakers must take the TOEFL to demonstrate English proficiency.

### FINANCIAL FACTS

| | |
|---|---|
| Annual tuition (in-state/out-of-state) | $32,075 |
| Books and supplies | $2,000 |
| Room & board (on-campus) | $6,186 |
| Average grant | $16,000 |

### ADMISSIONS

| | |
|---|---|
| **Admissions Selectivity Rating** | **88** |
| # of applications received | 143 |
| % applicants accepted | 53 |
| % acceptees attending | 51 |
| Average GMAT | 620 |
| Range of GMAT | 560–730 |
| Average GPA | 3.5 |
| TOEFL required of international students? | yes |
| Minimum TOEFL (paper/computer) | 600/250 |
| Application fee | $48 |
| International application fee | $48 |
| Regular application deadline | 5/26 |
| Regular notification | 7/7 |
| Application deadline/notification | |
| Round 1: | 1/20 / 3/3 |
| Round 2: | 3/3 / 4/13 |
| Round 3: | 4/13 / 5/26 |
| Round 4: | 5/26 / 7/7 |
| Deferment available? | yes |
| Maximum length of deferment | 1 year |
| Need-blind admissions? | yes |

### APPLICANTS ALSO LOOK AT

IESE Business School, INSEAD, RSM Erasmus University, University of Dublin, Trinity College, University of London, University of Oxford, University of Warwick

### EMPLOYMENT PROFILE

| Career Rating | 91 | Grads employed by field: | % | avg. salary: |
|---|---|---|---|---|
| Average starting salary | $85,000 | Finance | 25 | NR |
| Percent employed | 96 | Marketing | 21 | NR |
| | | Operations | 10 | NR |
| | | Consulting | 16 | NR |
| | | Entrepreneurship | 7 | NR |
| | | General Management | 6 | NR |
| | | Venture Capital | 2 | NR |
| | | Internet/New Media | 8 | NR |
| | | Other | 5 | NR |

# UNIVERSITY OF COLORADO—BOULDER
## LEEDS SCHOOL OF BUSINESS

## GENERAL INFORMATION
Type of school                public
Environment                   city
Academic calendar           semester

### SURVEY SAYS...
Students love Boulder, CO
Friendly students
Good social scene
*Solid preparation in:*
Entrepreneurial studies

### STUDENTS
Enrollment of parent
  institution                 29,151
Enrollment of business school  175
% male/female                 76/24
% out-of-state                 50
% part-time                   35
% minorities                  5
% international               18
Average age at entry          28
Average years work experience
  at entry                    5.7

### ACADEMICS
**Academic Experience Rating   84**
Student/faculty ratio         4:1
Profs interesting rating      78
Profs accessible rating       82
% female faculty              12
% minority faculty            20

### JOINT DEGREES
JD/MBA, 4 years; MBA/MS in
Telecommunications and/or
Computer Science, 3-3.5 years;
MBA/MA in Fine Arts; MBA/MA in
Theater and Dance; MBA/MA in
Germanic Languages; MBA/MS in
Environmental studies; MBA/MA in
Anthropology, all 3 years

### PROMINENT ALUMNI
Kevin Burns, Managing Principle,
Lazard Technology Partners; John
Puerner, President & CEO, Los
Angeles Times; Patrick Tierney,
CEO, Reed Elsevier; Dick Fuld, CEO,
Lehman Brothers; Michael Leeds,
President & CEO, Flightstar

## Academics

In 2001, the business school at the University of Colorado—Boulder received a $35 million donation—the country's sixth largest such donation in history—from the Leeds family of Long Island, New York (two of the sons attended the school). The school, originally founded in 1923, was renamed the Leeds School of Business as a result, and students feel confident that the huge influx of money "is working to bring top-tier professors to the university, so quality will continue to improve."

The program is small, with only about 50 students per class. As a small school, "Leeds has both the advantages (small class size, easy course access, access to professors, access to entrepreneurship and real-estate center staff) and disadvantages (limited course offerings, reduced access to large corporate recruiters) that are part and parcel of the small school experience." But most agree that the small size lends an intimacy and familiarity that will ensure their future success. "The high caliber of students and faculty is rare for a program of this size," says one student. "Definitely a great group of people that don't take themselves too seriously. If you are looking for a group of people who understand [that] life should be balanced (after first semester), you will love it here."

Leeds has nine required courses and nine electives, and students can choose to take two electives in the spring of the first year, in addition to the required courses. The second year is mainly electives—only two required classes, but the program is very quant-heavy, and students who don't come into the program with a strong background in statistics, college-level algebra, and principles of microeconomics are advised to take college-level courses in these subjects before they enroll. Students say that both the "entrepreneurial course work and real-estate course work are excellent."

Leeds offers more than 25 "career tracks" or sets of electives designed to lead students down specific career paths. Some career paths include "corporate finance, financial consulting, social and ethical venturing, entrepreneurship, real-estate capital markets, marketing management, operations management, and corporate entrepreneurship." When following one of these career paths, students are allowed to enroll in graduate classes in other schools on the university's campus. Dual-degree programs such as an MBA/JD, an MBA/MS in telecommunications or computer science, and an MBA/MA (in anthropology, fine arts, theater and dance, or Germanic languages) are available. And exchange programs are offered at any of the following locations: the ITESM (Monterrey Tec) located in Monterrey, Mexico; and the Instituto de Empresa, located in Madrid, Spain.

Leeds also hosts specialized centers devoted to entrepreneurship, real estate, and financial markets. Students warn, however, that course selection is important: "The professors are a mixed bag. Sometimes you get duds; other times, rock stars." While the new dean has taken steps to address this issue, some say that they'd like to see the teaching style change a bit. "The largest flaw in the academics is not the workload, the professors, or the administration, but the classroom style. Even in case studies, there is limited class debate—this is certainly something that must be directly addressed and changed." The school has taken note of this and has combined the smaller cohorts into one larger one in order to stimulate discussion.

TOBY HEMMERLING, ASSOCIATE DIRECTOR, MBA ADMISSIONS & MARKETING
BUSINESS 204, UCB 419, BOULDER, CO 80309 UNITED STATES
PHONE: 303-492-8397 • FAX: 303-492-1727
E-MAIL: LEEDSMBA@COLORADO.EDU • WEBSITE: LEEDS.COLORADO.EDU/MBA

## Career and Placement

The school only recently appointed someone to the position of Director of Alumni Relations, and so students occasionally complain about the "lack of alumni network." How bad can it be, though, if alumni are donating $35 million to the school? Though students might gripe about the efforts of Career Services, 90 percent of the graduating class of 2005 had found employment within three months of graduation, and the average salary as about $71,000. About 28 percent of students who were hired received a signing bonus, and the average bonus was almost $10,000; 19 percent of the graduates started their own companies, and about 33 percent ended up working for very small companies (between 2 and 50 employees).

## Student Life and Environment

Pretty much all Leeds students agree that living in Boulder can't be topped. Ranked "Best Place to Live" by *Money* magazine, Boulder hosts just over 100,000 residents, and yet is home to multiple high-technology, natural beauty, and multiple cultural institutions. Students say "There is no nicer place to be a student than Boulder, Colorado. The campus is beautiful, architecturally significant, and safe. The school is situated in the foothills of the Rocky Mountains, and world-class ski resorts are but an hour away. The social scene and nightlife are fantastic, and Boulder has an eclectic mix of cafes and restaurants." School or student-organized events include "TNO [Thursday Night Out] at a different bar every week, free tailgates before every football game, a night hike/snowshoe/cross-country ski trip every full moon, and an annual retreat that is a traditional highlight of the year. It's never long before the next event, and with our location, the opportunities are virtually endless."

The only problem with life at Leeds, it seems, is the building in which the school is housed, which students say is "horribly ugly and has a bad feel to it." Construction has begun on a new building, and students have high hopes that it will improve morale when it opens in May of 2007.

## Admissions

When selecting their incoming class of 60 students, admissions officers at Leeds seek out applicants "with a wide variety of backgrounds—both educational and professional. We are not looking for specific work experience in a certain field or for a particular undergraduate degree. Rather, we look for applicants who have compelling reasons to earn an MBA and who will add perspective and experience to their classmates' experiences." The average GPA of this diverse group is a 3.31, and the average GMAT is 643. The student body is 24 percent female, 76 percent male, and 18 percent international. The TOEFL exam is required for international students, and the minimum score is 250 (computer-based) and 600 (paper-based).

## FINANCIAL FACTS

| | |
|---|---|
| Annual tuition (in-state/out-of-state) | $8,982/$24,156 |
| Fees | $869 |
| Books and supplies | $3,000 |
| Room & board | $13,000 |
| % of students receiving aid | 60 |
| % of first-year students receiving aid | 74 |
| % of students receiving loans | 69 |
| % of students receiving grants | 72 |
| Average award package | $23,103 |
| Average grant | $4,132 |
| Average student loan debt | $29,956 |

## ADMISSIONS

| | |
|---|---|
| Admissions Selectivity Rating | 84 |
| # of applications received | 201 |
| % applicants accepted | 64 |
| % acceptees attending | 42 |
| Average GMAT | 643 |
| Range of GMAT | 610–690 |
| Average GPA | 3.31 |
| TOEFL required of international students? | yes |
| Minimum TOEFL (paper/computer) | 600/250 |
| Application fee | $70 |
| International application fee | $70 |
| Regular application deadline | 4/1 |
| Regular notification | 6/15 |
| Application deadline/notification | |
| Round 1: | 12/1 / 2/15 |
| Round 2: | 2/1 / 4/15 |
| Round 3: | 4/1 / 6/15 |
| Early decision program? | yes |
| ED Deadline/notification | 12/1 / 2/15 |
| Transfer students accepted? | yes |
| Transfer application policy | |
| No transfers are allowed in the full-time MBA program. Evening MBA students may transfer up to 6 credits on a case-by-case basis with approval from the MBA Programs Office. | |
| Need-blind admissions? | yes |

## APPLICANTS ALSO LOOK AT

Arizona State University, Colorado State University, The University of Texas at Austin, University of California—Berkeley, University of Colorado at Denver, University of Denver, University of Washington

### EMPLOYMENT PROFILE

| Career Rating | 77 | Grads employed by field: | % avg. salary: |
|---|---|---|---|
| Average starting salary | $70,807 | Finance | 28 | $68,688 |
| Percent employed | 58 | Marketing | 18 | $76,600 |
| | | Operations | 18 | $61,800 |
| | | Consulting | 7 | $60,000 |
| | | General Management | 18 | $79,456 |

# UNIVERSITY OF CONNECTICUT
## SCHOOL OF BUSINESS

### GENERAL INFORMATION
| | |
|---|---|
| Type of school | public |
| Environment | town |
| Academic calendar | semester |

### SURVEY SAYS...
Friendly students
Smart classrooms
*Solid preparation in:*
Teamwork
Computer skills

### STUDENTS
| | |
|---|---|
| Enrollment of parent institution | 26,701 |
| Enrollment of business school | 949 |
| % male/female | 64/36 |
| % out-of-state | 17 |
| % part-time | 89 |
| % minorities | 13 |
| % international | 37 |
| Average age at entry | 29 |
| Average years work experience at entry | 7 |

### ACADEMICS
| | |
|---|---|
| **Academic Experience Rating** | **84** |
| Student/faculty ratio | 13:1 |
| Profs interesting rating | 74 |
| Profs accessible rating | 87 |
| % female faculty | 18 |
| % minority faculty | 27 |

### JOINT DEGREES
MBA/JD; MBA/MD; MBA/MSW;
MBA/MA in International Studies;
MBA/MIM; MBA/MSN, 4 years

### PROMINENT ALUMNI
Mr. Robert W. Crispin, Chair & CEO,
ING Investment Mgmt. Americas;
Mr. Robert E. Diamond, CEO,
Barclays Capital; Ms. Penelope A.
Dobkin, Portfolio Manager, Fidelity
Investments; Mr. John Y. Kim,
President, Prudential Retirement &
Investment Svcs; Mr. Denis Nayden,
Managing Partner, Oakhill Capital

## *Academics*

The University of Connecticut's School of Business stands out as one of the highest-ranked low-cost public schools in the country; students get a bargain and rarely feel that they compromise quality. Students say, "The professors at UConn MBA are first-class. Not only are they your professors, but they are also your friends by the end of the program." Students also point out that "the administration is very much 'for the students.' They listen to concerns and suggestions." In addition, there was a recent multi-million dollar investment in the School of Business. These things combined give students a great deal of confidence in the program. One student says, "The state-of-the-art building is creating a fantastic environment for learning and interaction. The University of Connecticut's School of Business is preparing itself for a bright and prestigious future."

Since there are only about 100 full-time MBA students, classes in the school are small, and "every student has the opportunity to speak their opinions." Academic departments include accounting, finance, health care, information management, management, marketing, operations, and real estate. Students say, "The school really excels in finance, marketing, and application of technology." According to most students, "the technology component of the program, and the diversity of the student body, gives [students] a wide range of experiences in the learning process."

In the first year, students mostly attend core classes and participate in consulting partnerships with real companies. Recent corporate partners in this program include General Electric, United Technologies Corporation, Xerox Engineering Systems, and Aetna. This allows students to apply their knowledge to practical situations almost immediately, under the tutelage of some of the best minds in business. Students will also be better prepared for a summer internship, as they would have already had the experience most students have to wait for. As the school says, "This unique program also mirrors the corporate world by allowing students to integrate all of their course work into one project, thereby realizing the synergistic effect classes in finance, marketing, accounting, management, and operations information management provide." Students say, "The Integration Project was a great way to give students real-world experience, while teaching them important academic skills." Students also have the opportunity to "bridge the gap between theory and practice" with the Student-Managed Fund, edgelab, and the SS&C Technologies Financial Accelerator.

During the second year, there are only two required core courses, and students engage in any two of the five areas of concentration offered by the school. These concentrations are finance, health care management and insurance studies, operations and information management, management consulting, and marketing intelligence. There are also opportunities to design an individualized secondary concentration.

UConn MBA students also have an unusually broad array of dual degree programs from which to choose. These programs include MBA/JD, MBA/master of international management (MIM), MBA/MA international studies, MBA/MS nursing, MBA/MSW, and MBA/MD.

Students gripe that they would like to see more opportunities to pursue studies in entrepreneurship. One student comments, "A part of a business education should prepare [you] to become a business owner."

RICHARD N. DINO, ASSOCIATE DEAN
2100 HILLSIDE ROAD UNIT 1041, STORRS, CT 06269-1041 UNITED STATES
PHONE: 860-486-2872 • FAX: 860-486-5222
E-MAIL: UCONNMBA@BUSINESS.UCONN.EDU • WEBSITE: WWW.BUSINESS.UCONN.EDU

## Career and Placement

Although students typically complain about UConn's Business Placement and Career Center (BPCC), the center has actually done pretty well. For more than 10 years, between 95 and 98 percent of the class have been placed in a position within six months of graduation. The mean salary for the graduating class of 2005 was $70,280, and the median was $70,000; 40 percent of the graduates received some sort of sign-on bonus, and the range for that was between $2,500 and $13,000. UConn's top employers are CIGNA, CitiGroup, Aetna, GE, Bank of America, PricewaterhouseCoopers, ING, and United Technologies Corporation. Other companies include UBS, Textron Financial, British Petroleum, Lehman Brothers, Ernst & Young, Uniprise, CIGNA. Still, students agree that "career placement of international students is a definite sore point, both in terms of internships and permanent jobs after graduation."

## Student Life and Environment

Located in Storrs, Connecticut, UConn's School of Business finds itself placed right in the "*Fortune* 500 Heartland" between Boston and New York, and students take advantage of the abundance of opportunities. A recent influx of money has helped the school a great deal. Students say, "UConn is a big school with a new face-lift. Almost all of the academic buildings have been recently renovated and equipped with top-of-the-line technology. Life on campus is fun and safe, and there's an overall lively spirit that exists."

Still, there's no getting around the fact that the school is in a small town, though most consider that an advantage. One student says, "Because we're in a small town, we have to get creative about doing things together socially. Because of this, I think we have a better time than students do in big cities!" Other students concur, "It's a college town [and] there's not much to do outside of school. But within the school, there is ample opportunity to discover new things all the time, given the huge number of top-rated programs on campus."

## Admissions

When selecting a new class for admission, the UConn MBA program looks for "bright, innovative leaders, who are motivated by change and challenge, and each year [they] strive to create a class with a diversity of professional experience, educational achievement, and cultural background." Approximately 40 percent of students in each class are international students, and 36 percent are female. The average GMAT for last year's class was 610, and the average undergraduate GPA was 3.42. Most students had at least two years of full-time work experience after college, and the average amount of time spent in the work place was 7 years. The average age for those who attended was 29. UConn offers an unusually high amount of financial aid, and graduate assistantship positions are also available.

### FINANCIAL FACTS

| | |
|---|---|
| Annual tuition (in-state/out-of-state) | $7,524/$19,584 |
| Fees | $1,446 |
| Books and supplies | $3,000 |
| Room & board (on/off-campus) | $8,412/$9,000 |
| % of students receiving aid | 58 |
| % of first-year students receiving aid | 61 |
| % of students receiving loans | 12 |
| % of students receiving grants | 40 |
| Average award package | $22,337 |
| Average grant | $27,000 |
| Average student loan debt | $49,724 |

### ADMISSIONS

| | |
|---|---|
| Admissions Selectivity Rating | 88 |
| # of applications received | 221 |
| % applicants accepted | 48 |
| % acceptees attending | 45 |
| Average GMAT | 610 |
| Range of GMAT | 570–660 |
| Average GPA | 3.42 |
| TOEFL required of international students? | yes |
| Minimum TOEFL (paper/computer) | 575/233 |
| Application fee | $65 |
| International application fee | $65 |
| Regular application deadline | 4/15 |
| Regular notification | rolling |
| Deferment available? | yes |
| Maximum length of deferment | 1 year |
| Transfer students accepted? | yes |
| Transfer application policy | |

All students requesting to transfer are required to meet with the Director of the MBA Program. A maximum of 15 credits are accepted.

| | |
|---|---|
| Need-blind admissions? | yes |

### APPLICANTS ALSO LOOK AT

Boston College, Michigan State University, The Ohio State University, The Pennsylvania State University, University of Illinois at Urbana-Champaign, University of Wisconsin

### EMPLOYMENT PROFILE

| Career Rating | 85 | Grads employed by field: | % | avg. salary: |
|---|---|---|---|---|
| **Primary source of full-time job acceptances** | | Accounting | 4 | $60,000 |
| | | Finance | 46 | $71,125 |
| School-facilitated activities | 4 (79%) | Marketing | 17 | $67,000 |
| Graduate-facilitated activities | 11 (21%) | MIS | 11 | $70,750 |
| | | Operations | 5 | $72,500 |
| Average starting salary | $70,190 | Consulting | 11 | $57,250 |
| Percent employed | 94 | Entrepreneurship | 2 | $74,100 |
| | | Other | 4 | $73,666 |

# UNIVERSITY OF DAYTON
## SCHOOL OF BUSINESS ADMINISTRATION

## Academics

An "exceptional integrated core curriculum," "excellent faculty," a "strong alumni base," and "a marvelous Marianist-centered campus life" attract students to the MBA program at the University of Dayton, a midsize Catholic university in southwestern Ohio. Students here assure us that their School of Business Administration offers "one of the best kept secrets in the world of MBA programs."

They are especially enthusiastic about the program's "exceptional process-oriented 'integrated' approach to the core curriculum," which they deem "extremely unique." This integrated approach "allows students to break out of the strict mold of marketing and management," and enroll in "courses involving the integration of two major disciplines (i.e. operations management paired with managerial accounting)." In doing so, students get "the opportunity to have two (or more) senior faculty teaching a class rather than just one (not to mention possibly one executive-in-residence or more)." "Class participation is expected" in all of these classes, forcing "students to think about the interaction between different disciplines, and how decisions or actions in one will affect another."

Dayton MBAs also love the "guaranteed real-world consulting project experience" that, coupled with the school's "integration of its entire curriculum with area industry and its leveraging of professors with industry experience," ensures that students confront "real-life examples in class and elsewhere." Facilities "are terrific," and professors are "a diverse group made up of career teachers, professionals who teach part-time, and retired business leaders. All are accessible and offer a lot to the program." Students busy with careers appreciate that "the program is organized well" and UD "allows for a great amount of flexibility, so you can complete it at your own pace." The Dayton MBA curriculum consists of the integrated core, electives, and a two-semester capstone segment. Students may use their electives to develop a concentration in accounting, entrepreneurship, finance, international business, management information systems, operations management, marketing, and technology-enhanced business/e-commerce. The school is especially noted for its work in finance (driven by the Davis Center for Portfolio Management) and entrepreneurship (Dayton houses the Crotty Center for Entrepreneurial Leadership).

## Career and Placement

MBAs at University of Dayton are served by the Career Services Office, which assists undergraduates, graduates, and alumni in their development and placement needs. The office provides graduate students with the following services: career advisement; job search and résumé critiquing workshops, career fairs, online résumé referral, on-campus recruiting events, and contact with the alumni career network. Employers who typically recruit on the Dayton campus include ACNielsen, Deloitte Touche Tohmatsu, Xerox, Ernst & Young, Ethicon Endo-Surgery, Federal-Mogul, Fifth Third Bank, FM Global, General Electric, Georgia-Pacific, NCR, NVR/Ryan Homes, PricewaterhouseCoopers, Procter & Gamble, Sherwin-Williams, and USG Corporation.

## Student Life and Environment

The degree to which a student is involved in extracurricular life at Dayton "depends on whether you are a full-time or part-time student. Full time students are still connected to undergraduates and the university, while part-time students don't feel as connected." As one part-timer explains, "If someone were interested in getting involved, there are plenty of opportunities, but MBA students typically do not take advantage of these due to a lack of time. Many of us have full-time jobs." Those who can indulge in campus fun report

JANICE GLYNN, DIRECTOR MBA PROGRAM
300 COLLEGE PARK AVENUE, DAYTON, OH 45469-2234 UNITED STATES
PHONE: 937-229-3733 • FAX: 937-229-3882 • E-MAIL: MBA@UDAYTON.EDU
WEBSITE: WWW.SBA.UDAYTON.EDU/MBA

that they enjoy "a very modern gym that contains a pool, track, climbing wall, free weight room, aerobic room, and numerous other things" as well as "a tremendous amount of school spirit at the University of Dayton. Here, I feel like part of a family. I believe UD has struck the perfect balance of being an extremely social campus while upholding academic excellence." Full-timers and part-timers alike note that "the campus is very inviting. There are several places to study before and after class and also places to meet with groups, with plenty of resources for graduate students." Students also report that the school "recently implemented a graduate student social networking event that was very well received. Several more are planned for the upcoming year."

The Dayton MBA program consists of "a diverse mix of individuals from many different walks of life: Some are right out of college, some have been out for 25 years, some have 10-plus years work experience, some have none. In general people are able to share real life examples [that] make the learning environment better."

## Admissions

All applications to the University of Dayton MBA program must include official transcripts for all postsecondary academic work, an official GMAT score report, a completed application form, and a current resume or curriculum vita. Personal statements are encouraged but not required. Letters of recommendation from employers or professors are not required either; however, the admissions committee will consider them if they are submitted. International applicants must meet all of the above requirements and must also provide a translation of any non-English language transcripts and official scores for the TOEFL (minimum score of 550 paper exam, 213 computer exam required for unconditional admission; students with lower scores may be admitted under the condition that they successfully complete English as a Second Language training).

### FINANCIAL FACTS

| | |
|---|---|
| Annual tuition | $11,124 |
| Fees | $75 |
| Books and supplies | $600 |

### ADMISSIONS

| | |
|---|---|
| **Admissions Selectivity Rating** | **76** |
| # of applications received | 161 |
| % applicants accepted | 80 |
| % acceptees attending | 80 |
| Average GMAT | 574 |
| Average GPA | 3.22 |
| TOEFL required of international students? | yes |
| Minimum TOEFL (paper/computer) | 550/213 |
| Regular application deadline | rolling |
| Regular notification | rolling |
| Deferment available? | yes |
| Maximum length of deferment | 1 year |
| Transfer students accepted? | yes |

Transfer application policy
Students may request up to 12 semester hours of approved graduate transfer credits; students must have received a B or better.

| | |
|---|---|
| Non-fall admissions? | yes |
| Need-blind admissions? | yes |

### APPLICANTS ALSO LOOK AT

Miami University, University of Cincinnati, Wright State University, Xavier University

# UNIVERSITY OF DENVER
## DANIELS COLLEGE OF BUSINESS

## Academics

Students at Daniels College of Business at the University of Denver are faced with an almost dizzying array of options. Their classmates are ethnically and nationally diverse and come from a variety of business backgrounds. The city of Denver offers a multitude of cultural, natural, and sporting respites for those looking to take a break from studying. And apart from an 18-month MBA program, the school offers an enormous selection of joint degrees and special concentrations, as well as a part-time evening course of study. For some students, the only problem is narrowing down the field.

Most of the school's curriculum is taken up by the 56 (out of 72) credit hours of core classes, including Daniels' own core, which consists of three classes: values-based leadership, twenty-first-century professional, and global information economy. For the remaining 16 credits, students choose their own electives and are allowed to select any graduate-level courses they like to fulfill these requirements. Travel courses during interim periods are also an option. Of the departments in their school, students say that the "finance department in particular is filled with well-respected, smart teachers." But students add that professors from all departments are good, and "many of the higher-level professors serve as consultants to big players such as First Data, HP/Compaq, and Qwest." The school "has a strong ethics and values program," and students say that these classes "are very thought-provoking. Ethics has been a tradition at Daniels College of Business for many years." Students do gripe, however that there ought to be "better availability and times of core and elective classes."

Another complaint is the relative lack of real-world work experience some students find in their peers. One older student tells us that "some students are getting both an undergraduate degree as well as an MBA, and these students don't seem prepared." Some students feel, "The school should work harder to cater to the needs of the experienced student."

Daniels offers a dual-degree program in which students can earn any two approved graduate level degrees, including the following at once: MBA/international, MBA/master's of accountancy, master's of science in finance, master's of science in information technology, master's of science in management, master's of science in marketing, master's of science in real estate and construction management, master of taxation, and master of data mining.

The school's customized MBA programs include concentrations in applied communication and leadership, art museum administration, environmental policy and management, geographic information systems, human-resource management and development, not-for-profit management, organizational training and development, sport management, strategic management, technology management, and telecommunications. Students are understandably wowed by this smorgasbord of options. One student excitedly notes, "The number of program combinations offered are amazing! If I had the time and money, I would stay on for another year and get another degree."

## Career and Placement

Like so many other schools, Daniels must deal with complaints about its career-resource center. Some students say, "It would help to have a more aggressive job placement service." But others find career resources to be a "helpful advice center for both curriculum

SCOTT CAMPBELL, DIRECTOR OF ADMISSIONS AND FINANCIAL AID
2101 SOUTH UNIVERSITY BOULEVARD #255, RIFKIN CENTER FOR STUDENT SERVICES,
DENVER, CO 80208 U.S. • PHONE: 303-871-3416 • FAX: 303-871-4466
E-MAIL: DANIELS@DU.EDU • WEBSITE: WWW.DANIELS.DU.EDU

and career," and indeed, the school boasts a placement rate of 89 percent. They cite the fact that a student's average salary pre-Daniels was $43,364 while post-Daniels, it was $59,900 as an indicator that they're doing well in spite of the poor economy.

Some of the major companies that recruit on-campus include Accenture, Johnson Controls, Keane Consulting Group, Boston Market, Citibank/Citicorp, Peace Corps, Republic Financial, Enterprise Rent-a-Car, Cap Gemini, Ernst & Young, First Data Corporation, Forest Oil, MicroSystems, and Time Warner Telecom.

## Student Life and Environment

Students at Daniels are surrounded by what they call a "very rich environment." The city of Denver enjoys a relatively mild climate year-round. Outdoor recreation abounds, and students take advantage of hiking, skiing, camping, and myriad sporting events, professional and otherwise. The city hosts numerous music festivals and museums as well as several centers for the performing arts. The school itself boasts the current two-time NCAA Division I national championship hockey team, and, according to the students, among the best aspects of the school's cultural life are that there's "no football team (yay!), a brand-new performing-arts center, and top speakers (like Michael Moore and former presidential cabinet members)." One student enthusiastically adds, "Denver is a great city." As for the student body, MBAs say it is "diverse and has an entrepreneurial edge, though some students just want to get their diploma and a higher salary (how boring!)." People are "warm and friendly, and the atmosphere is light as the building is also used by undergrads." That building, they add, is "world-class [and] provides a good basis for orientation to business technology."

Some students complain that, due to the variety of different programs, and the preponderance of part-time students, the atmosphere can sometimes feel a little "transient. Most students are in and out."

## Admissions

In fall of 2005, the average undergraduate GPA at Daniels was 3.28, and the mean GMAT was 565. Out of 544 students total, 337 were male and 207 were female. The average age was 27, and students hailed from countries as diverse as Serbia, South Africa, Kuwait, Germany, and Canada. A minimum TOEFL score of 600 (paper-based) or 250 (computer-based) is required.

### PROMINENT ALUMNI
Peter Coors, Chaiman, Coors Brewing Company; Andrew Daly, Former President, Vail Resorts; Condoleezza Rice, U.S. Secretary of State; Gale Norton, U.S. Secretary of Interior; Carol Tome, Executive VP and CFO, The Home Depot.

### FINANCIAL FACTS
| | |
|---|---|
| Annual tuition | $27,756 |
| Fees | $474 |
| Books and supplies | $1,300 |
| Room & board | |
| (on/off-campus) | $9,900/$8,620 |
| % of students receiving aid | 59 |
| % of first-year students | |
| receiving aid | 66 |
| % of students receiving loans | 70 |
| % of students receiving grants | 66 |
| Average award package | $9,336 |
| Average grant | $5,034 |

### ADMISSIONS
| | |
|---|---|
| **Admissions Selectivity Rating** | **74** |
| # of applications received | 539 |
| % applicants accepted | 84 |
| % acceptees attending | 48 |
| Average GMAT | 581 |
| Range of GMAT | 540–610 |
| Average GPA | 3.28 |
| TOEFL required of | |
| international students? | yes |
| Minimum TOEFL | |
| (paper/computer) | 600/250 |
| Application fee | $50 |
| International application fee | $50 |
| Regular application deadline | 3/15 |
| Regular notification | 5/1 |
| Application deadline/notification | |
| Round 1: | 1/15 / 3/1 |
| Round 2: | 3/15 / 5/1 |
| Round 3: | 5/15 / 7/1 |
| Deferment available? | yes |
| Maximum length | |
| of deferment | 1 year |
| Transfer students accepted? | yes |
| Transfer application policy | |
| 8 quarter hours (6 semester | |
| hours) toward electives | |
| Non-fall admissions? | yes |
| Need-blind admissions? | yes |

### APPLICANTS ALSO LOOK AT
American University, Arizona State University, Boston University, Brigham Young University, Thunderbird, University of Arizona, University of Colorado

### EMPLOYMENT PROFILE
| Career Rating | 76 | Grads employed by field: | % | avg. salary: |
|---|---|---|---|---|
| **Primary source of full-time** | | Accounting | 16 | $46,917 |
| **job acceptances** | | Finance | 17 | $61,273 |
| School-facilitated activities | 29 (38%) | Human Resources | 1 | $75,000 |
| Graduate-facilitated activities | 43 (57%) | Marketing | 26 | $45,913 |
| Unknown | 4 (5%) | MIS | 5 | $52,750 |
| | | Operations | 8 | $53,667 |
| Average starting salary | $53,613 | Consulting | 12 | $53,944 |
| Percent employed | 59 | General Management | 11 | $68,714 |
| | | Other | 4 | $34,500 |

# UNIVERSITY OF FLORIDA
## WARRINGTON COLLEGE OF BUSINESS

## GENERAL INFORMATION
| | |
|---|---|
| Type of school | public |
| Environment | city |
| Academic calendar | semester |

### SURVEY SAYS...
*Solid preparation in:*
Finance
Teamwork
Communication/interpersonal skills

### STUDENTS
| | |
|---|---|
| Enrollment of parent institution | 49,000 |
| Enrollment of business school | 743 |
| % male/female | 78/22 |
| % part-time | 85 |
| % minorities | 18 |
| % international | 20 |
| Average age at entry | 27 |
| Average years work experience at entry | 4.5 |

### ACADEMICS
| | |
|---|---|
| **Academic Experience Rating** | **98** |
| Student/faculty ratio | 13:1 |
| Profs interesting rating | 93 |
| Profs accessible rating | 90 |
| % female faculty | 13 |
| % minority faculty | 19 |

### JOINT DEGREES
MBA/JD 4 years; MBA/MS in Medical Sciences, Biotechnology; MBA/PhD in Medical Sciences, Biotechnology; MBA/BS in Industrial and Systems Engineering; MBA/Doctor of Pharmacy; MBA/PhD in Medical Sciences; MBA/MD; MBA/Master of Exercise and Sport Science, 3 years

## Academics

Finance "is the greatest strength of the program" at University of Florida's Warrington College of Business, where "entrepreneurship is also a rising star." The school offers students lots of options, everything from course schedules that accommodate UF's many part-timers, to an intensive one-year MBA for those who just want to grind out a degree and get on with their careers.

To maximize opportunities for electives without skimping on core requirements, the school splits each semester into two eight-week modules. Warrington MBAs may choose from 16 areas of concentration including joint ventures with other university branches (for example, arts administration, Latin American business, and sports administration) and six certificate programs (for example, e-commerce and supply-chain management). First, of course, students must master the core curriculum, which includes twelve classes spread over the first four modules. One marketing student writes, "I was challenged by the core classes (especially in unfamiliar topics) as well as my electives. I feel that I was given a great opportunity to learn core business skills while digging deeper and enriching my marketing knowledge."

Despite the enormity of the University of Florida, students report a high degree of personal attention at Warrington. The administration "runs the MBA programs like a business. They do not lose focus of the fact that their primary customer is the student. The MBA programs reflect a milieu that is both student-oriented and student-friendly." According to students, the program does not rest on its considerable laurels; MBAs say, "The school is totally dedicated to improvement. They are always evaluating, changing, modifying, and asking about every part of the program. They are always asking how they can make things better. The best part is that they actually act on what we tell them." MBAs also appreciate their access to "excellent university resources."

Warrington's faculty is yet another feather in the school's cap. As one student notes, "I didn't expect the quality of the professors to be so high. I have been learning from people who [are] educated and worked at the best places in the country. They all say how great it is to teach in Florida. It is awesome to know that your professors could be successful anywhere, and they want to be at your school." Students add that "[faculty accessibility] is amazing. Whether we just stop by the office or send an e-mail at midnight, the administration and professors are always willing to help."

## Career and Placement

The Graduate Business Career Services Office (CSO) earns mixed reviews from Warrington students. The majority of them feel that "the CSO leaves something to be desired. It is moving in the right direction, but most students will need to do their own job search." Some students believe that "the problems may just be a reflection of the economy/environment and not the quality of the department."

Warrington MBAs are most likely to go to work for American Express, Bank America, Citibank, CSX, Darden Restaurants, Disney, Ernst & Young, ExxonMobil, Ford, General Electric, IBM, Johnson & Johnson, Pratt & Whitney, Procter & Gamble, Ryder Systems, and SunTrust. About one-quarter of graduates find their first jobs outside of the United States.

## Student Life and Environment

Florida MBAs can't think of enough good things to say about hometown Gainesville, "a wonderful college town." Students say, "There's plenty of stuff to do, whether it be biking, catching a play, fishing, or hitting downtown for a night out with the gang. Plus, UF has an excellent tradition of strong sports teams!" Another student adds that "the

ROBERT BREWER, ASSOCIATE DIRECTOR OF ADMISSIONS
134 BRYAN HALL, PO BOX 117152, GAINESVILLE, FL 32611-7152 UNITED STATES
PHONE: 877-435-2622 • FAX: 352-392-8791
E-MAIL: FLORIDAMBA@CBA.UFL.EDU • WEBSITE: WWW.FLORIDAMBA.UFL.EDU

beach is close," and "the weather allows for year-round outdoor activities." One student notes, "Gainesville is a great place to live. It was named 'Best Place to Live' by *Money* magazine in the late [1990s]. All of my other b-school opportunities were in the Midwest. My wife and I laugh as we watch the Weather Channel." As an added bonus, "it is also nice being a little over an hour away from Orlando."

The University of Florida campus earns similar plaudits. Students describe it as "awesome" and explain that "[the] university resources like athletics, both personal and varsity (like football and basketball), the libraries, and the caliber of people accentuate a great learning environment." One student says, "It's a huge university, and with so many students (including 10,000 graduate students), I know I can go somewhere any night of the week and see people I know. Meeting people couldn't be any easier [because] people here are friendly, warm, and easy to talk to. I had a group of friends within a week or so. The social life at Florida is wonderful!" MBAs agree that "the combination of student-run activities, competitive athletics, abundant nightlife, and fantastic weather make this a great place to live."

Of course, not everyone has time to enjoy the great town and the great campus. Students in the one-year program have "an incredibly heavy workload, so as a group, we tend to stay close and work together most of the time. We work hard, and we play hard. We may be in the MBA lounge studying at one o'clock on a Saturday night, but we were probably up all night Friday drinking beers and talking. It is easier to deal with so much schoolwork when you like the people you are teamed with," according to students. Everyone else here clears their schedules occasionally to enjoy "school clubs and students who accept everyone, making life here a blast. There is the right balance of studying and fun to make life enjoyable." Warrington's student body includes a large international presence; one student observes, "The ethnic diversity has opened my eyes to a wide range of cultures and opportunities that I have not seen before."

## Admissions

Applicants of the Warrington MBA program are required to have a minimum of two years of full-time, post-undergraduate professional experience; prospective executive MBAs must have at least eight years of experience. Applicants must submit official copies of all undergraduate and graduate transcripts, GMAT scores, TOEFL scores (when applicable), two letters of recommendation (preferably from supervisors at work), personal essays, and a resume. The school "strongly encourages preparation in financial accounting and quantitative skills (like calculus and statistics) prior to enrollment."

### PROMINENT ALUMNI
John Dasburg, MBA 1970, Chair & CEO ASTAR Air Cargo; Cesar Alvarez, MBA 1970, CEO, Managing Partner, Greenberg Traurig LLP; William R. Hough, MBA 1948, President of William R. Hough & Co. & WRH Mortgage; Laurie Burns, MBA 1986, President, Bahama Breeze; Hal Steinbrenner, MBA 1994, General Partner, New York Yankees

### FINANCIAL FACTS
| | |
|---|---|
| Annual tuition (in-state/out-of-state) | $6,234/$21,359 |
| Fees | $500 |
| Books and supplies | $2,645 |
| Room & board (on/off-campus) | $7,090/$7,500 |
| % of students receiving aid | 60 |
| % of first-year students receiving aid | 41 |
| % of students receiving loans | 60 |
| % of students receiving grants | 22 |
| Average award package | $14,772 |
| Average grant | $7,815 |
| Average student loan debt | $10,294 |

### ADMISSIONS
| | |
|---|---|
| Admissions Selectivity Rating | 96 |
| # of applications received | 281 |
| % applicants accepted | 39 |
| % acceptees attending | 58 |
| Average GMAT | 674 |
| Range of GMAT | 680–693 |
| Average GPA | 3.32 |
| TOEFL required of international students? | yes |
| Minimum TOEFL (paper/computer) | 600/250 |
| Application fee | $30 |
| International application fee | $30 |
| Regular application deadline | 4/15 |
| Regular notification | rolling |
| Non-fall admissions? | yes |
| Need-blind admissions? | yes |

### APPLICANTS ALSO LOOK AT
Emory University, Georgetown University, The University of Texas at Austin, University of Georgia, University of North Carolina—Chapel Hill, University of Notre Dame, University of Southern California

### EMPLOYMENT PROFILE
| Career Rating | 87 | Grads employed by field: | % | avg. salary: |
|---|---|---|---|---|
| Primary source of full-time job acceptances | | Finance | 47 | $69,300 |
| | | Marketing | 18 | $62,100 |
| School-facilitated activities | 28 (60%) | MIS | 3 | NR |
| Graduate-facilitated activities | 19 (40%) | Operations | 13 | $63,500 |
| | | Consulting | 11 | $77,100 |
| Average starting salary | $66,800 | General Management | 8 | $59,300 |
| Percent employed | 90 | | | |

# UNIVERSITY OF GEORGIA
## TERRY COLLEGE OF BUSINESS

## Academics

The Terry MBA program at the University of Georgia offers "a good mix of the 'hard' technical skills and 'soft' skills, which are equally required in today's business community." This translates into "a great return on investment," especially for Georgia residents. For a small program—the full-timers number fewer than 200—Terry provides a surprising number of strong concentrations; students praise its programs in entrepreneurship, MIS, real estate, and finance. Students love Terry's "flexibility to create rigorous academic programs suited to the needs of the individual student," and they appreciate how the program draws on the resources of the University of Georgia. One MBA explains, "This a large school with many different opportunities, including taking classes in areas outside of the business school." Students with undergraduate business degrees can earn MBAs in under a year, thanks to the school's eleven-month program, which substitutes a summer of intensive review for the first-year core requirements of the more traditional two-year program. Students in both the eleven-month and two-year programs warn that "the workload is high, especially given that so many of the students have assistantships, which require ten to fifteen hours of work per week." The small size of the program is seen as both an asset and a drawback. In the credit column, the program's size "gives every student complete access to all facilities including lecturers and administrative staff" and "helps build closer relationships between students, create more engaging classes, and make students feel more a part of the school." In the debit column, "the smaller size keeps some recruiters off campus."

Instructors at the University of Georgia include "some very knowledgeable and respected professors," according to one student. "My accounting professor was president of the FASB for 10 years, and my statistics professor was CFO for Kodak." By and large, they are "very good at teaching, not just lecturing about their research," and they deftly communicate "a wealth of real-life experience, which is something that books can't translate." They are also "always very helpful outside of class, whether it's with subject matter or introducing you to people in a particular industry."

## Career and Placement

Because its MBA program is too small to attract some larger recruiters to campus and contrasts with Stanton Chase International, the University of Georgia participates in two consortia (one regional, one national) and contracts with Stanton Chase International. The Career Services Office provides all the standard services—workshops, panel presentations, breakfast speakers, career fairs, and one-on-one counseling. The school also offers students access to Career Leader, an online assessment tool developed by career specialists and psychologists. Students explain that the career office "works very hard" but is hampered by the size of the program. One student says, "Terry needs to grow in order to be considered a top-20 business school. The large schools attract more employers, and employers attract better and better students." Top recruiters of Terry MBAs include Bank of America, BB&T, Capital One, Cintas, Cushman & Wakefield, FedEx, First Union, Hewitt Associates, Home Depot, Liberty Mutual, Prudential, Sun Trust, UPS, and Wachovia. About three-quarters of Terry MBAs take their first jobs in the Southeast.

## Student Life and Environment

The Terry curriculum is demanding, but MBAs here still manage to find some time for "R&R." Students explain that "while we spend a large portion of our time studying, the first-year, 11-month, and second-year students make an effort to continue a normal lifestyle away from campus by organizing social get-togethers, community volunteer opportunities, and athletic activities." Integration into the mainstream is toughest for the

ANNE C. COOPER, DIRECTOR, MBA ADMISSIONS
362 BROOKS HALL, ATHENS, GA 30602-6264 UNITED STATES
PHONE: 706-542-5671 • FAX: 706-542-5351
E-MAIL: TERRYMBA@TERRY.UGA.EDU • WEBSITE: WWW.TERRY.UGA.EDU/MBA

11-month students, "who are rolled in with the returning two-year students for the Fall semester, with no formal get-to-know-each-others." One student says, "While this hasn't been terribly difficult for me to handle, I know other 11-month students who don't know the names of most of the second-year students they are in class with. I think this is unfortunate."

Students tell us that the school "strongly encourages extracurricular activities as much as it drives academic excellence." Terry "offers a wide array of activities [like] guest lectures, seminars, workshops, clubs/organizations, socials, and community service. Strong ties with the external business community means that we get eminent speakers (such as, Vernon Smith, the current Nobel winner for economics) to come to the campus to address us on relevant business topics affecting our world." The university at large offers even more options including Bulldog football and the inevitable tailgating that precedes each home game. The university is also home to the Ramsey Student Center, "the best university sports complex in the United States!"

An up-to-date facility houses the Terry program; students report approvingly that "the main building used for classrooms is fairly new and contains complete multimedia in most classrooms (such as, projection, whiteboards, television, video, PowerPoint, and computer demonstration), is wireless (as is most of north campus), and has many areas where students can work in groups. The main administrative building is an older, grand structure that is easily accessible and beautiful to look at." The program makes its home "on UGA's gorgeous north campus, about 200 yards away from downtown Athens." Students call their hometown "an eclectic Mecca, known mainly because of its contributions to the music scene (like REM, B-52's, and Widespread Panic), [that] is comparable, and often ranked above Austin, Texas, as the best college town. It contains many great eateries and more than [an] adequate nightlife, which is hard to resist." Students also appreciate the "access and proximity to Atlanta."

## Admissions

Applicants to the Terry MBA program must submit two sealed copies of all undergraduate and graduate transcripts, two letters of recommendation, GMAT scores, TOEFL scores (for international students), essays, and a resume. The school regards favorably any evidence of "unique life experiences and growth opportunities." Interviews are encouraged but not required. Candidates are expected to demonstrate computer proficiency and strong math skills; a minimum of two years of work experience is strongly recommended. The admissions office admits students on a rolling basis, beginning in December; the school encourages applicants to apply early.

### FINANCIAL FACTS

| | |
|---|---|
| Annual tuition (in-state/out-of-state) | $6,304/$23,136 |
| Fees | $990 |
| Books and supplies | $1,000 |
| Room & board (on/off-campus) | $12,400/$16,500 |
| % of students receiving aid | 74 |
| % of first-year students receiving aid | 58 |
| % of students receiving grants | 74 |
| Average award package | $23,500 |
| Average grant | $23,500 |

### ADMISSIONS

| | |
|---|---|
| Admissions Selectivity Rating | 93 |
| # of applications received | 321 |
| % applicants accepted | 41 |
| % acceptees attending | 61 |
| Average GMAT | 651 |
| Range of GMAT | 590–700 |
| Average GPA | 3.3 |
| TOEFL required of international students? | yes |
| Minimum TOEFL (paper/computer) | 577/233 |
| Application fee | $62 |
| International application fee | $62 |
| Regular application deadline | 5/12 |
| Regular notification | rolling |
| Application deadline/notification | |
| Round 1: | 11/1 / 12/15 |
| Round 2: | 1/31 / 3/1 |
| Round 3: | 4/15 / 5/15 |
| Round 4: | 5/12 / 6/30 |
| Deferment available? | yes |
| Maximum length of deferment | 1 year |
| Non-fall admissions? | yes |
| Need-blind admissions? | yes |

### APPLICANTS ALSO LOOK AT

Emory University, University of North Carolina—Chapel Hill, Vanderbilt University

### EMPLOYMENT PROFILE

| Career Rating | 77 | Grads employed by field: | % | avg. salary: |
|---|---|---|---|---|
| Average starting salary | $65,438 | Finance | 35 | $62,592 |
| | | Marketing | 18 | $64,444 |
| | | Consulting | 12 | $72,363 |
| | | Other | 25 | $66,969 |

# UNIVERSITY OF HARTFORD
## BARNEY SCHOOL OF BUSINESS

## GENERAL INFORMATION
| | |
|---|---|
| Type of school | private |
| Environment | metropolis |

### SURVEY SAYS...
Friendly students
*Solid preparation in:*
Accounting
Teamwork
Communication/interpersonal skills
Presentation skills

## STUDENTS
| | |
|---|---|
| Enrollment of parent institution | 7,260 |
| Enrollment of business school | 401 |
| % male/female | 57/43 |
| % out-of-state | 7 |
| % part-time | 78 |
| % minorities | 10 |
| % international | 38 |
| Average age at entry | 30 |

## ACADEMICS
| | |
|---|---|
| **Academic Experience Rating** | **72** |
| Student/faculty ratio | 8:1 |
| Profs interesting rating | 75 |
| Profs accessible rating | 80 |
| % female faculty | 28 |
| % minority faculty | 2 |

## Academics

Convenience and a marketable degree are the chief drawing cards for most graduate students at the University of Hartford's Barney School of Business. This predominantly part-time population comes here because the school is local to their homes and employment, flexible to their scheduling needs, and able to deliver a prestigious degree recognized throughout the Northeastern business community.

The Hartford MBA has achieved the gold standard of excellence—AACSB accreditation. The program owes a large measure of its success to an excellent faculty who "are a wealth of knowledge in their areas and are usually very willing to ensure that students get the knowledge they desire." One student says that instructors "come from very diverse backgrounds with a wide array of previous work experience, which I feel helps creates an extremely interesting learning environment." Plus, they know how to teach; according to students, "The professors' methods of class delivery is outstanding. Maintaining interest after [a] full day of work can be difficult. Operations management—amazing. Accounting, which can be so boring—quite the eye-opener. Even the dry statistics were enjoyable."

None of this would do students any good, of course, if it weren't offered in a form adaptable to their busy work schedules. Hartford accommodates its students by scheduling classes once a week on evenings and weekends. Professors here are "very accessible and also understand the demands of the work-school balance," offering "great flexibility to help those who have constraints in both time and money." The administration has pitched in by formulating its "no-hassle" approach which makes books and other curricular materials, identification cards, and parking permits (included in the cost of tuition) available at the same site in which MBA classes are held.

The Hartford MBA consists of 17 three-credit courses. Six core courses cover material mastered by undergraduates with business majors and may be waived on that basis. All other courses—five breadth courses (leadership, managing technology, managing customer interfaces, business law, and performance analysis), five electives, and a capstone course that "integrates functional approaches and environment issues by having students make strategic business decisions" are mandatory. MBAs praise the curriculum's "emphasis on group-based assignments and its emphasis on practical cases and examples in classes."

## Career and Placement

Placement and Career-counseling Services are provided to Barney MBAs by the Career Services Office, which serves the entire undergraduate and graduate student body of the university. Services include resume and cover-letter writing workshops, seminars on networking and interviewing strategies, job banks, on-campus interviewing, and job fairs.

## Student Life and Environment

Nearly all part-timers at the Barney MBA program arrive on campus as classes begin and leave as soon as they end; if they spend any more time there, it's to study, meet with a professor, or participate in a study group. MBA Association, major-related clubs, and pub nights simply aren't part of the equation here. As a typical student explains, "I am a commuter with children at home; therefore, hanging out at the school is not in my schedule. Barbecues and networking get-togethers I do attend, and they are very good." Full-time students benefit from such campus programs as the Lunch and Learn Series, which brings in executives to address students, and non-credit enrichment workshops.

CLAIRE SILVERSTEIN, DIRECTOR OF GRADUATE PROGRAMS
200 BLOOMFIELD AVENUE, CENTER FOR GRADUATE & ADULT SERVICES, CC231
WEST, HARTFORD, CT 06117 UNITED STATES
PHONE: 860-768-4444 • FAX: 860-768-4821
E-MAIL: BARNEY@HARTFORD.EDU • WEBSITE: HTTP://BARNEY.HARTFORD.EDU

The business school makes its home in Beatrice Fox Auerbach Hall, which recently received a partial makeover to renovate its entry hall. The facility houses a "newly refurbished reading room with daily newspapers and periodicals" and two information technology centers on the wireless campus are loaded with computers complete with flat screens. Students appreciate the effort, but many agree that the school needs a more dramatic technological upgrade.

Hartford benefits from its location in one of the nation's insurance centers. The school attracts students from "a wide variety of business and even engineering specialists" whose experiences add to instruction. The school's proximity to "the biggest financial industry in the world—New York City" is also an asset, allowing for guest speakers, internship opportunities, and day trips for interviews and recruiting.

Hartford MBAs "range in age from recent college graduates up to their 50s and higher. It is good, particularly during group projects, to have such diversely experienced co-group members." With about "half the class made up of international students native to foreign countries, the MBA student body is quite diverse, and not just ethnically. Our working backgrounds are so different: engineers, stockbrokers, chemists, a physicist, insurance, business administrators, accountants—oh, boy. You get all of us in a working group [and] it is quite the experience, especially for a class project," notes one MBA.

## Admissions

The Barney admissions office requires all MBA applicants to submit official transcripts from all previously attended postsecondary schools, two letters of recommendation, official GMAT results, a resume, a letter of intent describing the applicant's academic and career goals, and a completed application. Applicants with at least three years of continuous work experience may apply for a GMAT waiver. International students must submit TOEFL scores and a Guarantor's Statement of Financial Support in addition to the above.

## FINANCIAL FACTS

| | |
|---|---|
| Annual tuition | $9,600 |
| Room & board | |
| (on-campus) | $8,786 |
| % of students receiving aid | 18 |
| % of first-year students | |
| receiving aid | 46 |
| % of students receiving loans | 16 |
| % of students receiving grants | 4 |
| Average award package | $14,074 |
| Average grant | $4,351 |

## ADMISSIONS

| | |
|---|---|
| **Admissions Selectivity Rating** | **73** |
| # of applications received | 184 |
| % applicants accepted | 67 |
| % acceptees attending | 72 |
| Average GMAT | 510 |
| Range of GMAT | 460–550 |
| Average GPA | 3 |
| TOEFL required of | |
| international students? | yes |
| Minimum TOEFL | |
| (paper/computer) | 550/213 |
| Application fee | $40 |
| International application fee | $55 |
| Regular application deadline | rolling |
| Regular notification | rolling |
| Deferment available? | yes |
| Maximum length | |
| of deferment | 1 year |
| Transfer students accepted? | yes |
| Transfer application policy | |
| Based on individual cases. | |
| Non-fall admissions? | yes |

# UNIVERSITY OF HAWAII AT MANOA
## COLLEGE OF BUSINESS ADMINISTRATION

## Academics

For most students at the University of Hawaii College of Business, the most exciting thing about their program is "its proximity to Asia and the large number of Chinese and Japanese students." Because so many students plan to go on to work in the rapidly growing markets of Asia, the program is not only helpful to their education, but also to their manners. Through a variety of exchange programs, as well as friendships with students from so many different cultures, students learn how to interact with cultures not their own, and, in many cases, learn how to avoid embarrassing social gaffes that could spoil a deal. As one student says, "[The school's] greatest strengths are the international business ties the school has with countries around the Pacific Rim. The MBA program offers exchange opportunities like the PACIBER program, which requires fluency in a language spoken in the Pacific region other than English, one semester of study abroad, and an internship with a focus on international business." UHM's MBA program is a general one, and its classes are all taught at night to accommodate the needs of its many working students. Students can choose part-time or full-time courses of study and can pick from the following departments: financial economics and institutions, information-technology management, management and industrial relations, marketing, and the school of accountancy. In addition, the school offers a variety of dual degree programs (MBA/MA, or MBA/MS, and JD/MBA), a 21-month China International MBA, and a Japan- or China-focused MBA: a full-time, 15-month specialized program. As far as students are concerned, however, all of the departments have one strength in common: "The professors! They are the ones who point you in the right direction and help with the networking process." Another student concurs, adding that the school is home to "great and knowledgeable faculty. My classmates are also excellent."

Although there are few complaints about the curriculum, some students feel that "the offerings of noncore classes could be increased, especially in the areas of finance and marketing." Others make the case that "academically, the school could make the course work more vigorous, but with more than 50 percent of the students working full-time, those students may not be able to accommodate more rigorous work." Another student agrees and adds that "though the classes require a lot of work, I think that in general they should be more challenging." In keeping with the multinational tone of the school, one of the more popular aspects of the College of Business Administration is their study-abroad program. The school has multiple exchange programs with universities in Asia and Europe and a Summer Asian field-study elective, which "enables students to earn six credits while visiting factories and other businesses in four Asian countries." As one student says, " I went on a three-week long field study, where we visited Korea, Japan, and Thailand. As a group of 15 students with a well-known advisor, we were able to visit with executive managers at companies such as Nissan, POSCO, and K. Cotton." UHM also offers a number of different international activity groups, such as the Academy of International Business; the Asia Pacific Economic Cooperation (APEC) Study Center, the Asia-Pacific Financial Markets Research Center, the Family Business Center of Hawaii, the Pacific-Asian Center for Entrepreneurship and E-Business, and the Native Hawaiian Leadership Project.

## Career and Placement

Many students who graduate from UHM remain in Hawaii to work, though some return to the United States mainland or to Asia, and students are wild about the "networking opportunities for international and local students across Asia and the Pacific Rim." Employers of recent MBAs include AIG Insurance, Bank of Hawaii, Booz Allen Hamilton, PricewaterhouseCoopers, First Hawaiian Bank, Foodland, Frito Lay, Nabisco, Hewlett-Packard, Hilton Hotels, the Internal Revenue Service, and many others. Many MBAs have also been inspired to start their own businesses after their time at UHM.

CINDY HSU, DIRECTOR OF MARKETING
2404 MAILE WAY C-202, HONOLULU, HI 96822 UNITED STATES
PHONE: 808-956-8266 • FAX: 808-956-2657
E-MAIL: MBA@HAWAII.EDU • WEBSITE: WWW.CBA.HAWAII.EDU

Still, some students feel that the alumni network could be improved. One student says, "It would be great if the alumni could get more involved with the program. I am lucky to have a good alumnus who takes participation in my attendance, but I wonder if my other classmates are just as lucky."

## Student Life and Environment

One look at the school's website should tell you all you need to know about campus life at the University of Hawaii, Manoa. Palm trees, mountains, airy beaches, and wide expanses of deep blue sea abound. As one student says on the school's site: "Life in Hawaii... well, what can I say? It's Hawaii!" Another student adds, "Located in beautiful Hawaii, UHM is an ideal location for students who are looking for a change of scenery. The students are extremely diverse, and the program is very flexible to accommodate various needs." And another student points out that the great thing about UHM is that "the location and the diverse student body make it exciting to learn. There are people who are here for different reasons, so it is exciting to meet engineers, psychologists, astronomers, chemists, and economists. The city and community is beautiful and safe." Still, many students feel that "the facilities at this school could stand a lot of improvement, and the negative attitude of most of the faculty toward technology is unacceptable." Many students strongly feel that "the friendships made from the intensive group work make up for all this. In my first semester alone, I have made several friends I am proud to call my friends for life." But others point out that because it's a commuting campus, "extracurriculars are limited, especially with students working full-time. But the Graduate Business Students Association does put on monthly 'relaxers' after classes to get the students to mingle with each other and with professors." Relaxers provide drinks, snacks, and a place to socialize, and students consider them "a good but rare offering." Also, many students feel that "it would be great if the school could involve the spouses and families a bit more. More opportunities to meet socially, instead of just academically (for group work) would be great."

## Admissions

In order to join UHM's diverse community of students, applicants must have a minimum GPA of 3.0 and a minimum GMAT score of 500. The school requires that its applicants have at least two years of postgraduate, full-time work experience. Because international students representing more than 80 countries account for about 20 percent of UHM graduate student population, the TOEFL is required. Students whose native language is not English must score at least a 550 (paper-based) or 213 (computer-based).

## FINANCIAL FACTS

| | |
|---|---|
| Annual tuition (in-state/out-of-state) | $8,928/$14,544 |
| Fees | $172 |
| Books and supplies | $900 |
| Room & board (on/off-campus) | $12,000/$14,000 |
| % of students receiving aid | 25 |
| % of first-year students receiving aid | 5 |
| % of students receiving loans | 22 |
| % of students receiving grants | 10 |
| Average award package | $12,281 |
| Average grant | $25,000 |
| Average student loan debt | $7,644 |

## ADMISSIONS

| | |
|---|---|
| Admissions Selectivity Rating | 89 |
| # of applications received | 313 |
| % applicants accepted | 39 |
| % acceptees attending | 55 |
| Average GMAT | 575 |
| Range of GMAT | 500–710 |
| Average GPA | 3.3 |
| TOEFL required of international students? | yes |
| Minimum TOEFL (paper/computer) | 550/213 |
| Application fee | $50 |
| International application fee | $50 |
| Regular application deadline | 5/1 |
| Regular notification | rolling |
| Transfer students accepted? | yes |
| Transfer application policy | |

Credits may be transferred into the MBA program from other AACSB-accredited business schools, from other University of Hawaii graduate programs, or by petition as follows: Up to half of the program's requirements may be transferred (23 credits). Transfer credit is appropriate for both core classes (upon approval) and electives.

| | |
|---|---|
| Non-fall admissions? | yes |
| Need-blind admissions? | yes |

## EMPLOYMENT PROFILE

| Career Rating | 68 | Grads employed by field: | % | avg. salary: |
|---|---|---|---|---|
| Average starting salary | $50,000 | Accounting | 5 | $45,000 |
| | | Finance | 15 | $45,000 |
| | | Human Resources | 5 | $40,000 |
| | | Marketing | 25 | $50,000 |
| | | MIS | 10 | $55,000 |
| | | Consulting | 5 | $40,000 |
| | | General Management | 10 | $55,000 |
| | | Global Management | 25 | $55,000 |

# UNIVERSITY OF HOUSTON
## C.T. BAUER COLLEGE OF BUSINESS

### GENERAL INFORMATION
| | |
|---|---|
| Type of school | public |
| Environment | metropolis |
| Academic calendar | semester |

### SURVEY SAYS...
Cutting-edge classes
Smart classrooms
*Solid preparation in:*
Accounting

### STUDENTS
| | |
|---|---|
| Enrollment of parent institution | 35,344 |
| Enrollment of business school | 554 |
| % male/female | 57/43 |
| % out-of-state | 40 |
| % part-time | 73 |
| % minorities | 14 |
| % international | 31 |
| Average age at entry | 28 |
| Average years work experience at entry | 4 |

### ACADEMICS
| | |
|---|---|
| **Academic Experience Rating** | **72** |
| Student/faculty ratio | 3:1 |
| Profs interesting rating | 72 |
| Profs accessible rating | 63 |
| % female faculty | 26 |
| % minority faculty | 23 |

### JOINT DEGREES
MBA/JD, 111 credits, 4-6 years;
MBA/MIE, 72 credits, 2-5 years;
MBA/MA in Spanish, 64 credits, 2-5 years; MBA/Master's in Hospitality Management, 78 credits, 2-5 years;
MBA/MSW, 87 credits, 3-5 years;
MBA/MIM, 66 credits, 3-5 years

### PROMINENT ALUMNI
Fran Keeth, President and CEO, Shell Chemical, LP; Karen Katz, President and CEO, Neiman Marcus Stores; David McClanahan, President and CEO, CenterPoint Energy; Harry Lambroussis, President, International Paper-Latin America; John Beard, President, Lyondell Europe Inc.

## Academics

The University of Houston is riding high from a $40 million donation from Charles T. Bauer—so high, in fact, that they renamed the business school in his honor. Bauer's gift, the largest in university history, has spurred the school to greater heights, allowing it to attract top-line faculty, upgrade facilities, and fuel cutting-edge research at its many centers and institutes. Yet, to the delight of students, the school remains "reasonably priced."

Despite the emphasis on big names and research, students at Bauer tell us that "the MBA from UH is definitely a real-life, practical MBA that will be useful in the real world" and that "the best professors are not always the academics, but rather the practitioners of business who bring to the table a lot of relevant real-life experience." Students point out that "some of these teachers are not regular faculty but are rather designated 'Executive Professors' who teach only one or two classes per semester." These teachers "are often drawn from such big-name businesses as ExxonMobil, Royal Dutch Shell, PricewaterhouseCooper, etc."

Bauer's students, two-thirds of whom attend part time, extol the program's "focus on meeting the needs of part-time students who are working full-time." The school offers "cohort scheduling with night classes [and] low tuition costs compared to other schools in the area,"—both high priorities for the school's aspiring MBAs. In addition, the Bauer College has introduced a new full-time day program for Fall 2006 that allows students to complete almost all their required core classes in their first year of study. Bauer's 'mini-lockstep' 30-hour core curriculum helps create cohesion even among the part-time student body. It also allows the school to organize material in thematically related modules, each culminating in an integrative capstone course. This ensures that students learn and apply multiple skills to solve problems and improve their understanding of the business world. MBAs praise the "extensive use of case histories and research papers" in their classes and appreciate the "good selection of advanced electives." The curriculum allows for six electives over the course of the program. In addition to concentrations in accounting, finance, decision and information sciences, management, and marketing, five new specialized concentrations in energy have been added to provide students with industry-specific knowledge in key areas of the energy business. Bauer students' main desire is for the "administration to be more open to change."

The Bauer College also offers an Executive MBA Program as well as graduate certificate programs. Students enrolled in the Executive MBA Program have the option of pursuing the traditional Leadership track, or the new track in Global Energy Management. Graduate certificate program offerings include energy accounting, energy risk management, and financial services management.

## Career and Placement

Bauer students may employ the services of the Elizabeth D. Rockwell Career Services Center. The center offers a number of career-readiness workshops in such areas as resume writing, interviewing strategies, networking, and developing a professional image. The office also assists students in finding jobs and internships, and organizes career fairs. Career counseling services are provided at the Rockwell Center, and students may use the office to access proprietary online job databases. Bauer students may also use a variety of online services free of charge; other career assessment tools are also available through the Rockwell Center.

Employers most likely to take on Bauer MBAs include AIM Management Group, Duke Energy, Hewlett-Packard, ExxonMobil, and Shell Services International.

DAVID SHIELDS, ASSOCIATE DEAN FOR GRADUATE AND PROFESSIONAL PROGRAMS
334 MELCHER HALL, SUITE 275, HOUSTON, TX 77204-6021 UNITED STATES
PHONE: 713-743-5936 • FAX: 713-743-4368
E-MAIL: HOUSTONMBA@UH.EDU • WEBSITE: WWW.BAUER.UH.EDU/MBA

## Student Life and Environment

The Bauer College of Business is housed in Melcher Hall on the east end of the University of Houston campus. The facility includes the AIM Center for Investment Management, a $5-million learning laboratory that students use to manage a mutual fund called The Cougar Fund. The facility is also home to several of Bauer's research institutes, including the Global Energy Management Institute and the Center for Entrepreneurship & Innovation, and programs that serve the Houston business community (e.g. the Center for Executive Development, the Program for Excellence in Selling).

Prior to the introduction of the new full time program in Fall 2006, students describe Bauer as "a commuter school" that "is not really comparable with a conventional MBA program. This one is geared towards working professionals who already live and are working in Houston. We barely have time to handle school and work, much less social activities. Those activities that are scheduled here are geared more towards the international students, many of whom attend full-time." When school is done, "there is no 'Let's hit the bars' attitude. Students generally are tired—they want to go home to their families after class. If we meet on the weekends, it is to do work on group projects, not for fun." MBAs report that "fellow students bring to the table a diversity of experience and background. This makes for really rich discussions."

## Admissions

Applicants to the Bauer MBA program must submit all of the following materials: a completed application; official transcripts for all undergraduate work; an official GMAT score report; a resume; two letters of reference; and a short, personal essay explaining the student's choice of the Bauer MBA Program. International students whose first language is not English must also submit official score reports for the TOEFL or IELTS, unless they have already earned a degree in the U.S. Those with transcripts from overseas must provide translations but need not provide evaluations, as Bauer prefers to make its own assessment of the transcripts. The school admits students for the Fall semester only.

### FINANCIAL FACTS

| | |
|---|---|
| Annual tuition (in-state/out-of-state) | $5,562/$10,530 |
| Fees | $3,243 |
| Books and supplies | $1,400 |
| Room & board (on-campus) | $6,900 |
| % of students receiving aid | 53 |
| % of first-year students receiving aid | 54 |
| % of students receiving loans | 32 |
| % of students receiving grants | 28 |
| Average student loan debt | $22,732 |

### ADMISSIONS

| | |
|---|---|
| Admissions Selectivity Rating | 82 |
| # of applications received | 304 |
| % applicants accepted | 64 |
| % acceptees attending | 70 |
| Average GMAT | 585 |
| Range of GMAT | 540–620 |
| Average GPA | 3.21 |
| TOEFL required of international students? | yes |
| Minimum TOEFL (paper/computer) | 620/260 |
| Application fee | $75 |
| International application fee | $150 |
| Regular application deadline | 5/1 |
| Regular notification | 6/1 |
| Deferment available? | yes |
| Maximum length of deferment | 1 year |
| Need-blind admissions? | yes |

### APPLICANTS ALSO LOOK AT

Rice University, South Texas College of Law, The University of Texas at Austin, University of Houston—Clear Lake

| EMPLOYMENT PROFILE | | | | |
|---|---|---|---|---|
| Career Rating | 75 | Grads employed by field: | % | avg. salary: |
| Average starting salary | $66,000 | Accounting | 14 | $54,500 |
| Percent employed | 77 | Finance | 14 | $71,800 |
| | | Marketing | 14 | $67,200 |
| | | MIS | 19 | $59,700 |
| | | Operations | 10 | $80,000 |
| | | Strategic Planning | 3 | $84,000 |
| | | Consulting | 10 | $76,900 |
| | | Other | 11 | $58,800 |
| | | non-profit | 5 | $38,600 |

# UNIVERSITY OF HOUSTON—VICTORIA
## SCHOOL OF BUSINESS ADMINISTRATION

### GENERAL INFORMATION
| | |
|---|---|
| Type of school | public |
| Academic calendar | 2005-06 |

### SURVEY SAYS...
Happy students
*Solid preparation in:*
General management

### STUDENTS
| | |
|---|---|
| Enrollment of parent institution | 2,491 |
| Enrollment of business school | 522 |
| % male/female | 43/57 |
| % out-of-state | 2 |
| % part-time | 78 |
| % minorities | 75 |
| % international | 16 |
| Average age at entry | 31 |
| Average years work experience at entry | 2 |

### ACADEMICS
| | |
|---|---|
| **Academic Experience Rating** | **70** |
| Student/faculty ratio | 18:1 |
| Profs interesting rating | 96 |
| Profs accessible rating | 82 |
| % female faculty | 15 |
| % minority faculty | 67 |

## Academics

The options are abundant for MBAs at the University of Houston—Victoria. Students here can pursue a traditional MBA, or they can also choose from among several other degree options: a Global MBA, with a focus on international business and management; a master's of economic development and entrepreneurship, with a focus on start-ups and entrepreneurial enterprises; and a fourth-year bridge MBA, designed for ultra-ambitious undergraduates who want to spend their fourth year of school prepping for an MBA program. UHV also allows students several choices of venue: Many programs are available not only at the main campus in Victoria but also at satellite campuses in Sugar Land and Katy (the Cinco Ranch campus). All classes are available to distance learners online.

The highlight of the UHV MBA curriculum, students agree, is the MBA Conference; it's "the culmination of everything that has been learned in the MBA program and applied to an original team case. Each team is competing for top honors and must present its findings at the MBA conference to faculty and students. It is truly a team effort." The competition "really helps us to recapture all the concepts that we have learned through out the program," students say.

Many students—especially those with full-time jobs—opt to take advantage of the well-supported distance-learning options here. Explains one, "Because the course material was online, and because my work in the oil business carried me to very remote locations (e.g., jungles of the Amazon, the Andes mountains, the Caribbean, offshore on a drilling platform), I was always 'present and accounted for.' I could not have finished the MBA if it had not been for the use of technology at UHV." Distance learning allows such students to participate in their courses "while literally working in the global economy, making it easy to learn how the MBA material integrates with the real world." Even those who don't have to trot around the globe appreciate how "we don't waste the time commuting to and from campus, and that results in much more time to devote to researching and studying the material."

## Career and Placement

UHV's MBA program maintains a Career Opportunities Center that houses a collection of job-search resources. Students here also have access to the Career Planning and Placement Office, which serves the entire university community. Students note, however, that the school "is clearly lacking many elements in MBA career placement services. As a relatively new program, they are still working to develop contacts and organize this aspect." As this is a nontraditional program, on-campus recruiting is minimal. However, several employers including 3M, AXA Financial Advisors, Banco Popular, Colgate-Palmolive, Du Pont, GE, Goldman Sachs, Johnson & Johnson, JPMorgan Chase, PricewaterhouseCoopers, the United States Securities and Exchange Commission, and Wachovia.

LINDA PARR, ADMISSIONS COORDINATOR
3007 NORTH BEN WILSON STREET, VICTORIA, TX 77901 UNITED STATES
PHONE: 361-570-4119 • FAX: 361-570-4114 • E-MAIL: ADMISSIONS@UHV.EDU
WEBSITE: WWW.UHV.EDU/BUS/

## Student Life and Environment

UHV holds MBA classes on three campuses. As one student explains, "The UHV main campus is located in Victoria, Texas. There are also large satellite campuses located in South Houston and West Houston. All facilities have state-of-the-art equipment and all campuses offer online courses that run concurrently with the face-to-face classes." Classes "are scheduled at convenient times, and most of the lecturers are understanding in extending our assignment deadlines during personal emergencies. Most of the heavy workload is in a few courses in the second year, but otherwise it is easy to keep up with the classwork." One student sums it up like this: "Life at UHV is unique. You can be as involved or uninvolved as you choose. The technology resources are wonderful, especially the online research tools. The facilities are always clean and attractive inside and out."

Students describe their peers as "mature, experienced, leaders in their communities, smart, current, and well-respected." Many are hard-working professionals with families who still find time and energy to make school a priority. Team projects aren't a problem here, as "it is easy to form teams with enthusiastic students that are willing to share the work together. The diversity of the students allows different views of attacking business problems." One student tells us that the school "is a good fit for students that really want to learn, but not for students who just want to check the box that an MBA was completed."

## Admissions

Applicants to the UVH MBA program are eligible for unconditional admission to the program if they have a four-year undergraduate degree from an accredited institution, earned a GPA of at least 2.5. Students with an admissions index of at least 1,400—calculated under the formula (GPA x 200) + (GMAT x 2)—also qualify for unconditional admission. Students who fail to meet these requirements may qualify for conditional admission. Those students who have previously earned a graduate or professional degree (e.g. MD, PhD, JD) are generally exempted from the GMAT requirement. Under certain circumstances, the school will accept a recent (i.e., less than 5 years old) GRE score in lieu of a GMAT score; a combined verbal-quantitative score of at least 900 is required. A GMAT waiver may also be granted to applicants who meet all the following requirements: an undergraduate GPA of at least 3.0; a grade of B or better in two qualifying courses offered by UVH; and at least two years of relevant professional experience. Such students must submit a personal statement describing their career objectives.

### FINANCIAL FACTS

| | |
|---|---|
| Annual tuition (in-state/out-of-state) | $1,920/$4,632 |
| Fees | $1,164 |
| Books and supplies | $1,200 |
| % of students receiving aid | 57 |
| % of first-year students receiving aid | 48 |
| % of students receiving loans | 43 |
| % of students receiving grants | 43 |
| Average grant | $1,281 |
| Average student loan debt | $31,498 |

### ADMISSIONS

| | |
|---|---|
| Admissions Selectivity Rating | 62 |
| # of applications received | 197 |
| % applicants accepted | 93 |
| % acceptees attending | 78 |
| Average GMAT | 444 |
| Range of GMAT | 390–510 |
| Average GPA | 3.1 |
| TOEFL required of international students? | yes |
| Minimum TOEFL (paper/computer) | 550/213 |
| Deferment available? | yes |
| Maximum length of deferment | 1 year |
| Transfer students accepted? | yes |
| Transfer application policy | |
| Up to 6 hours of graduate business course work may be transferred on department's discretion. | |
| Non-fall admissions? | yes |
| Need-blind admissions? | yes |

### APPLICANTS ALSO LOOK AT

University of Houston, University of Houston—Clear Lake

### EMPLOYMENT PROFILE

| | |
|---|---|
| **Career Rating** | **84** |
| Percent employed | 79 |

# UNIVERSITY OF ILLINOIS—CHICAGO
## LIAUTAUD GRADUATE SCHOOL OF BUSINESS

## Academics

When it comes to resources, the Liautaud Graduate School of Business has two power-houses at its disposal: the University of Illinois—Chicago and the city of Chicago itself. The benefits of location are obvious and bountiful, students tell us; one student writes, "UIC is located in the heart of Chicago. The culturally and economically diverse environment truly makes studying international business not just an in-the-classroom experience. UIC takes advantage of its location by promoting trips to the Federal Reserve and inviting top business leaders in the city to teach professional topics courses. I learn every day about how to function in an international business environment, whether I'm in the classroom or not." Another MBA adds, "We are right in the heart of downtown Chicago, so the city really becomes our campus in a sense. You can access anything you want, and most importantly, you have the resources of Chicago at your disposal."

UIC offers a part-time program you can pursue on a full-time basis, but is flexible enough that students can begin in the Fall or Spring semester. With many classes offered in the evening, "class scheduling makes this a great school for the middle levels to upgrade themselves on the job." The substantial presence of part-timers benefits classroom discussions, which "have more depth due to the high percentage of currently working professionals that attend classes at Liautaud."

UIC MBAs explain that their curriculum "is very intellectually stimulating. The emphasis is not only on the practical/business knowledge, but also on the social-science nature of business (for example, interactions between individuals). Professors challenge students to apply concepts from all aspects of life." Course work places "much emphasis on group effort. If you have difficulty communicating or working with others, this will be a difficult program. If you like group projects, you will do fine." Students are especially keen on the school's programs in entrepreneurship and finance. They also love the low tuition, which gives a UIC MBA a great return on investment. One student sums up, "Arguably, with the exception of Kellogg and Chicago, this is the best MBA program in Chicago, and it is certainly the best public MBA program in the area."

## Career and Placement

UIC students agree that their Business Career Center "is the area of the school in greatest need of improvement." Though there have been complaints in the past regarding the lack of attention given to MBA students over undergraduate students by the Career Services Office, the school opened a separate Career Services office for MBAs in June 2005, so the problem should be fixed. Another student adds, "Other than looking over your resume and doing a mock interview, you're pretty much on your own. The career center doesn't act as though it has a vested interest in showing high placement rates at all."

Employers who have hired UIC MBAs in recent years include Accenture; Aegon Insurance; Alphants Trading; Caterpillar; Citibank; Discover Financial Services; Fujisan.com; KPMG; LG Chemical; MacArthur Foundation; Maytag; Nestle; Netsource; RR Donnelley; SAP America; SC Johnson; Siemens; Takeda Pharmaceuticals; Unilever; and Wirthlin Worldwide.

RITA BIELIAUSKAS, ASSOCIATE DIRECTOR
815 WEST VAN BUREN, SUITE 220, CHICAGO, IL 60607 UNITED STATES
PHONE: 312-996-4573 • FAX: 312-413-0338
E-MAIL: MBA@UIC.EDU • WEBSITE: WWW.MBA.UIC.EDU

## Student Life and Environment

Students say, "Going to school in Chicago is amazing." One student reports that "the city is unbelievable, and, as a business student, it is very important to me that UIC is located in the heart of the Chicago business scene." MBAs explain that "many parts of the city of Chicago have been rejuvenated, and the UIC campus area is one of them. There are plenty of great restaurants and pubs in the area. The United Center where the Bulls and Blackhawks play is within walking distance of campus, and the subway cuts right through the UIC for easy access to everything." However, some students warn that "the safety around the campus isn't the best, but the school has really tried to help with that by putting emergency light posts all over the campus."

The UIC MBA student population includes "a wide variety of students from diverse ethnic and social backgrounds. This helps to make all students more aware of the world and keeps them in touch with the global business environment." Because "it's very much a commuter campus" and "students live all over the city, it's not easy to organize social activities that all may attend." Regular get-togethers include MBA Bar Night, as well as "other great events organized by the MBA Association, so that we can socialize outside of school," according to students.

The MBA program currently shares its facility with business undergraduates, a situation that many here find irksome. "The MBA program wants to build their own building to house classes and offices. This will be the best thing to bring students and the program more cohesion," one student notes.

## Admissions

The admissions committee at UIC considers all the following components of an application: undergraduate and graduate transcripts, GMAT scores, TOEFL scores (international students), employment history (the school "strongly recommends" a minimum of two to three years full-time work experience following undergraduate work), two letters of reference, a personal statement of purpose, and record of organizational involvement. Students are expected to enter with a working knowledge of business statistics. Interviews are encouraged.

### FINANCIAL FACTS

| | |
|---|---|
| Annual tuition (in-state/out-of-state) | $13,202/$25,200 |
| Fees | $2,108 |
| Room & board | $12,000 |

### ADMISSIONS

| | |
|---|---|
| **Admissions Selectivity Rating** | **80** |
| # of applications received | 360 |
| % applicants accepted | 59 |
| % acceptees attending | 51 |
| Average GMAT | 575 |
| Average GPA | 3 |
| TOEFL required of international students? | yes |
| Minimum TOEFL (paper/computer) | 570/230 |
| Application fee | $50 |
| International application fee | $60 |
| Regular application deadline | 5/15 |
| Regular notification | rolling |
| Deferment available? | yes |
| Maximum length of deferment | 1 semester |
| Transfer students accepted? | yes |

Transfer application policy
Need to apply and be accepted to the UIC MBA program. Can submit transcripts from previous course work with a grade of B or better and a course description. Must be from an AACSB-accredited institution. Maximum of 24 semester hours may be transfered.

| | |
|---|---|
| Non-fall admissions? | yes |
| Need-blind admissions? | yes |

### APPLICANTS ALSO LOOK AT

DePaul University, Loyola University Chicago, Northwestern University, The University of Chicago

# UNIVERSITY OF ILLINOIS AT URBANA-CHAMPAIGN
## COLLEGE OF BUSINESS

### GENERAL INFORMATION
| | |
|---|---|
| Type of school | public |
| Environment | city |
| Academic calendar | semester |

### SURVEY SAYS...
Smart classrooms
*Solid preparation in:*
Marketing
Teamwork
Communication/interpersonal skills
Presentation skills

### STUDENTS
| | |
|---|---|
| Enrollment of parent institution | 40,360 |
| Enrollment of business school | 227 |
| % male/female | 73/27 |
| % part-time | 16 |
| % minorities | 14 |
| % international | 55 |
| Average age at entry | 27 |
| Average years work experience at entry | 4 |

### ACADEMICS
| | |
|---|---|
| **Academic Experience Rating** | **72** |
| Student/faculty ratio | 3:1 |
| Profs interesting rating | 96 |
| Profs accessible rating | 85 |
| % female faculty | 23 |
| % minority faculty | 11 |

### JOINT DEGREES
MBA/MA in Architecture, 3 years; MBA/MS in Computer Science, 3 years; MBA/MS in Civil and Environmental Engineering, 3 years; MBA/MS in Electrical Engineering, 3 years; MBA/MS in Industrial Engineering, 3 years; MBA/MS in Mechanical Engineering, 3 years; MBA/MS in Medicine, 5 years; MBA/MS in Journalism, 3 years; MBA/MS in Law, 4 years; MBA/MS in Human Resource Education, 3 years; MBA/ILIR, 3 years.

## Academics

"Our greatest strength lies in research," one satisfied MBA at the University of Illinois—Urbana-Champaign writes. "[The] professors are often on the cutting edge of research, so we are often taught things that won't show up in textbooks for several years." Some of that cutting-edge research goes on outside of the b-school—Urbana-Champaign boasted two Nobel Prize winners in 2003, one in medicine, one in physics—but MBAs can access it all the same through the school's well-regarded joint-degree programs. One student explains pursuing simultaneous degrees in business and engineering: "The MBA program here is excellently paired with the engineering department in the form of a joint degree. It only takes four or five semesters to get both master's degrees."

Throughout the curriculum, "teachers work together to prevent overlapping cases and subjects and to complement one class with another one." This "effective integration of instruction" earns the praise of the students; one MBA writes, "The classes and activities for the first year are well-organized and fully integrated. The program is designed for students to occupy nearly all of their time doing something—homework, study teams, intramurals, clubs, events—related to the school." Things open up in the second year, as the curriculum "offers more flexibility. In fact, there are far too many offerings in the second year for you to do them all."

Illinois MBAs are bullish on their school's future, and they report that "our new administration comprises many folks formerly from Stern Business School of New York University, and it's doing wonders with the MBA program." As one student explains, "Academically, Illinois MBA can take any other business school by its horns and give it a good run for its money. In coming years, I expect the program to catch up with the leading business school in administration domain and then smoothly slip into the tier-one business school rankings." Students comment that finance is the strongest core area.

## Career and Placement

University of Illinois maintains a fully automated resume-posting and job-listing board for its students; the site is called Compass and even e-mails students automatically when positions suiting their qualifications are posted. The school hosts "over 20" career fairs over the course of the school year. Some are exclusively for MBAs, others are open to a wider range of students; in all, there are more than 2,000 employers make recruiting visits to the campus each year. An executive skills program for students sharpens their job-seeking skills; a new internship program gives them a little extra to put on their resumes. While some students complain that "Career Services needs to get their act together and get more alumni support for current students, and more effort needs to be made to support international students in finding careers"; other students feel that "the administration [is working] very hard." Students say, "We can feel the positive effects of its effort in Career Services and organizing business events." Most MBAs understand the handicap under which administrators labor; one MBA writes, "Because the location of our schools is far from the big cities, it's hard to attract as many employers as possible to come here to recruit us."

Companies that most frequently hire Illinois graduates include AC Nielsen, Accenture, Agilent Technologies, Aquila, AT&T, Deloitte Touche Tohmatsu, Dynegy, Ford Motor Company, Gallup Organization, Kraft Foods, Procter & Gamble, and Samsung. The school's alumni network is more than 10,000 strong. Average starting salaries range from $52,000 (production/operations) to over $80,000 (human resources, other). Over one-third of Illinois graduates wind up in finance and accounting (average starting salary in 2003: $71,000).

SARAH ZEHR, ASSOCIATE DIRECTOR OF ADMISSIONS
405 DAVID KINLEY HALL, 1407 WEST GREGORY DRIVE, URBANA, IL 61801 UNITED STATES
PHONE: 217-244-7602 • FAX: 217-333-1156
E-MAIL: MBA@UIUC.EDU • WEBSITE: WWW.MBA.UIUC.EDU

## Student Life and Environment

Urbana-Champaign students report, "[The school] has the best of both worlds: lots of cultural things, but with small-town charm, little traffic, and lots of nature and hiking nearby." While "being located in Champaign does have its drawbacks"—primarily, isolation from the big city and big-city jobs and internships—"there are plenty of opportunities to be involved if you take the initiative." In addition, "it's only a short trip to Chicago or Indianapolis if you crave bigger cities."

Not that there's any need to leave campus because "each day is full, whether it's classes and teamwork, or company presentations and extracurriculars, or simply having fun and relaxing with classmates." The school hosts "many clubs formed by MBA students, MBA softball team, MBA soccer team, [and] MBA volleyball team. Everybody can become friends through various club activities." MBAs say, "Student participation in clubs outside of class is heavy." Students explain that they are particularly proud of Illinois Business Consulting (IBC) (formerly OSBI Consulting), "a student-run consulting organization" that "provides a meaningful interface among MBA students, the faculty, and business leaders." MBAs add that "over two-thirds of students join, even though involvement is not mandatory, and classwork is really demanding." Students also praise the "first-year second-year mentoring program, which is designed to help everyone acclimate to the IMBA program; also, second-year mentors help first-years in the job search. It's totally their own thing on their own time, which is great."

Social life at the University of Illinois piggybacks on university-at-large events, especially Big Ten football and basketball games, which "can't be beat, especially when attending and tailgating with fellow students." Overall, students work hard, but not without a sense of proportion; they also "seem to be very concerned about having fun. Students also report approvingly that "off-campus housing is widely available" and that "public transportation is good; though the campus is large, the transportation provided makes varied destinations accessible."

## Admissions

The University of Illinois admissions department considers GPA, GMAT scores, letters of recommendation, personal essay, interview, and, where appropriate, TOEFL scores; all of these are required. Optional, but also important, are extracurriculars and work experience. The school stresses that "work experience is weighted heavily in admissions decisions. At least two years of full-time, post-undergraduate experience is strongly recommended, although exceptions have been made in the cases of joint-degree applicants and applicants with compelling part-time experience." Prior internships and military experience can also work in the favor of applicants.

### PROMINENT ALUMNI

Mike Tokarz, Chair, The Tokarz Group; Tom Siebel, Founder, Chair & CEO, Siebel Systems, Inc.; Jan Klug Valentic, Executive VP, Young and Rubican; Alan Feldman, President & CEO, Midas, Inc.; Bruce Holecek, CEO, Hobbico

### FINANCIAL FACTS

| | |
|---|---|
| Annual tuition (in-state/out-of-state) | $16,500/$24,400 |
| Fees | $1,718 |
| Books and supplies | $1,190 |
| Room & board | $18,240 |

### ADMISSIONS

| | |
|---|---|
| Admissions Selectivity Rating | 60* |
| # of applications received | 468 |
| Average GMAT | 647 |
| Range of GMAT | 640–690 |
| Average GPA | 3.4 |
| TOEFL required of international students? | yes |
| Application fee | $40 |
| International application fee | $50 |
| Regular application deadline | 3/15 |
| Regular notification | rolling |
| Early decision program? | yes |
| ED Deadline/notification | 12/15 / 2/15 |
| Need-blind admissions? | yes |

### APPLICANTS ALSO LOOK AT

Indiana University—Bloomington, Northwestern University, Purdue University, The University of Chicago, University of Michigan, University of Wisconsin, Washington University

| EMPLOYMENT PROFILE | |
|---|---|
| Career Rating | 88 |
| Average starting salary | $72,212 |
| Percent employed | 96 |

# University of Iowa
## Henry B. Tippie School of Management

### GENERAL INFORMATION
| | |
|---|---|
| Type of school | public |
| Environment | city |
| Academic calendar | semester |

### SURVEY SAYS...
Friendly students
Smart classrooms
*Solid preparation in:*
Finance

### STUDENTS
| | |
|---|---|
| Enrollment of parent institution | 29,642 |
| Enrollment of business school | 805 |
| % male/female | 67/33 |
| % out-of-state | 71 |
| % part-time | 84 |
| % minorities | 4 |
| % international | 48 |
| Average age at entry | 27 |
| Average years work experience at entry | 3.4 |

### ACADEMICS
| | |
|---|---|
| **Academic Experience Rating** | **89** |
| Student/faculty ratio | 6:1 |
| Profs interesting rating | 74 |
| Profs accessible rating | 86 |
| % female faculty | 24 |
| % minority faculty | 13 |

### JOINT DEGREES
MBA combined with: JD, 4 years; Hospital and Health Administration, 2.5 years; Library Science, 3 years; Nursing, 3 years; Medicine, 5 years

### PROMINENT ALUMNI
Steven L. Caves, President, Firstar Bank Iowa (Banking); Kathleen A. Dore, President, TV & Radio CanWest Mediaworks; Kerry Killinger, Chair, President & CEO, Washington Mutual Savings Bank; Michael Maves, MD, Executive VP & CEO, American Medical Association; Ted E. Ziemann, President, Cargill Health & Food.

## Academics

With standout concentrations in finance and marketing, and a dedication to bestowing a "personal touch" on all its students, the Henry B. Tippie School of Management at the University of Iowa provides one of the best publicly funded MBAs in the United States. And thanks to its state-level tuitions, Tippie offers a fabulous return on investment; *Business Week* recently ranked it the MBA with the eighth-fastest payback. Small class sizes and a dedicated administration allow for the personal touches Tippie justly brags about. Students explain that "everyone is very committed to making Tippie as strong a program as possible, and it shows. Just as the primary responsibility of the board is to maximize shareholder value, the faculty [does] a great job of maximizing student value in the MBA program." One student notes, "I've been very impressed. The dean of the school has an open-door policy and is incredibly accessible. He and many professors have made student support a priority. Faculty and staff attend the majority of student social functions and are completely accessible." The University of Iowa's integrated core means "the classes inform each other to a great extent. For example, shortly after we learned regression in statistics, we used regression modeling in marketing to analyze the relationship between the price and market share of several ketchup brands," according to students. The core is flexible enough "to give students the opportunity during the second semester to begin course work in their area of concentration," an option that students appreciate. The core is strongest in Tippie's top disciplines; one student explains, "The finance and marketing faculty are terrific. I'm still in my first semester, and they have already walked us through basic concepts and decision-making tools so well that I scored better on midterms than some students who were already practitioners in those fields."

Overall, Tippie professors "are demanding, but take interest in each student's development. They not only are available for help with a particular subject, but also assist students in exploring career goals." While "the academics are very demanding, especially in relation to quantitative skills," the "small size of the program and the social life allows you to create strong friendships immediately, which in turn helps any academic weakness you might have," according to the students. MBAs love the school's resources, and they explain that "every classroom is perfectly equipped with useful technology. The building itself is modern yet comfortable." However, some students warn that "A lot of the course documents are posted online, and the [support program] goes down a lot. It's a huge time-waster." The university-at-large offers "many fabulous resources," and students say that "there are tons of opportunities to do directed studies with professors or consulting engagements with outside companies. Additionally, we get pushed hard in the classroom which prepares us well for internships and jobs."

## Career and Placement

The MBA Career Services Office at Tippie earns praise for its personalized service. This "dedicated placement center that knows each student individually learns what each of us wants to do, so they can proactively 'sell' us to employers," students say. Career Services are enhanced by "alumni who [help] in networking and opening up internship opportunities. Also, outside speakers are brought in regularly to give another perspective and networking opportunity." Students point out that "perhaps due to its location, Iowa fails to attract a wide range of companies to campus—no high-tech companies or investment banks."

Top employers of Tippie MBAs include AEGON, N.V.; Allstate Corporation; Allsteel, Inc.; Best Buy Co.; CitiGroup; General Electric; HNI Co.; John Deere Credit Co.; Kimberly-Clark Corporation; Lil' Drug Store Products, Inc.; Northwest Airlines Corporation; Pearson; Principal Financial Group, Inc.; Procter & Gamble; and Rockwell Collins, Inc.

MARY SPREEN, DIRECTOR OF MBA ADMISSIONS AND FINANCIAL AID
108 JOHN PAPPAJOHN BUSINESS BUILDING, C140, HEY B. TIPPIE SCHOOL OF MANAGEMENT,
THE UNIVERSITY OF IOWA, IOWA CITY, IA 52242-1000 UNITED STATES
PHONE: 319-335-1039 • FAX: 319-335-3604
E-MAIL: TIPPIEMBA@UIOWA.EDU • WEBSITE: WWW.BIZ.UIOWA.EDU/MBA

## Student Life and Environment

Tippie MBAs have nothing but praise for their classmates and explain that "because Iowa is fairly tough to get into, the students here tend to be highly intelligent and very serious about classes. Some of my classmates include a writer, a musician, a scientist, and, of course, people with business and engineering backgrounds. Iowa accepts people from all disciplines, and I consider this to be a strength." This mutual admiration society loves to hang together; as one student explains, "There is a great deal of camaraderie among the students, which makes for a pleasant class scene. Although it's not as party-intense as college, it's nice to know that grad students can still have fun!"

The high point of the Tippie social calendar arrives on Thursday evening with TGIT (short for "Thank God It's Thursday"). The event "is held each week, and almost all the MBA students of two years attend this fascinating activity." It usually takes place "at one of the many local bars. It's a great atmosphere, and there are always drink specials. It's great because there are no classes on Friday." Besides TGIT, students also convene for "team sports, especially football—the MBA Association sponsors tailgates before each game," and "international lunches where international students prepare food and educate us about their countries and cultures." The many MBA student organizations "provide a wide array of activities to get involved in, either by participating or by assuming a leadership role."

Although not located in a major business center, Tippie's Iowa City location has a lot to recommend it. For one, the cost of living in this "great and very friendly community of students" is "so affordable that a number of students have bought their own houses. Three of my classmates live in my neighborhood, and we do what most late-20s and early-30s couples do, when we have time." Further easing the financial burden of school is the fact that "almost anyone who wants an assistantship (TA or GA) can have one. For out-of-state students, this earns them in-state tuition. For all students, these pay roughly $8,000 for the nine months of school."

## Admissions

Tippie applicants must submit official copies of all undergraduate and graduate transcripts, GMAT scores, TOEFL scores (for the school's considerable pool of international applicants whose first language isn't English), letters of recommendation, a personal statement, and a resume; two years of full-time, post-baccalaureate professional experience is required. Applications are evaluated for evidence of leadership qualities. Tippie is the recipient of a FISPE grant to the Iowa Electronic Markets' initiative, whose goal is to promote knowledge of markets among minority students.

### FINANCIAL FACTS

| | |
|---|---|
| Annual tuition (in-state/out-of-state) | $11,970/$21,960 |
| Fees | $716 |
| Books and supplies | $2,000 |
| Room & board (on/off-campus) | $7,358/$7,875 |
| % of students receiving aid | 53 |
| % of first-year students receiving aid | 62 |
| % of students receiving grants | 43 |
| Average award package | $13,353 |
| Average grant | $5,962 |
| Average student loan debt | $21,250 |

### ADMISSIONS

| | |
|---|---|
| **Admissions Selectivity Rating** | **91** |
| # of applications received | 197 |
| % applicants accepted | 53 |
| % acceptees attending | 60 |
| Average GMAT | 656 |
| Range of GMAT | 600–710 |
| Average GPA | 3.27 |
| TOEFL required of international students? | yes |
| Minimum TOEFL (paper/computer) | 600/250 |
| Application fee | $60 |
| International application fee | $85 |
| Regular application deadline | 7/15 |
| Regular notification | rolling |
| Deferment available? | yes |
| Maximum length of deferment | 1 year |
| Transfer students accepted? | yes |
| Transfer application policy Maximum number of transferable credits is 9 from AACSB-accredited programs only. | |
| Non-fall admissions? | yes |
| Need-blind admissions? | yes |

### APPLICANTS ALSO LOOK AT

Indiana University—Bloomington, Michigan State University, Purdue University, The Ohio State University, University of Illinois at Urbana-Champaign, University of Minnesota, University of Wisconsin

### EMPLOYMENT PROFILE

| Career Rating | 86 | Grads employed by field: | % | avg. salary: |
|---|---|---|---|---|
| **Primary source of full-time job acceptances** | | Finance | 61 | $68,188 |
| | | Human Resources | 4 | NR |
| School-facilitated activities | 30 (61%) | Marketing | 31 | $68,955 |
| Graduate-facilitated activities | 19 (39%) | Operations | 2 | NR |
| | | Consulting | 2 | NR |
| Average starting salary | $68,026 | | | |
| Percent employed | 84 | | | |

# UNIVERSITY OF KANSAS
## SCHOOL OF BUSINESS

### GENERAL INFORMATION
| | |
|---|---|
| Type of school | public |
| Environment | city |
| Academic calendar | semester |

### SURVEY SAYS...
Students love Lawrence, KS
Friendly students
Good peer network
Cutting-edge classes
Helpful alumni
Happy students

### STUDENTS
| | |
|---|---|
| Enrollment of parent institution | 27,890 |
| Enrollment of business school | 165 |
| % male/female | 95/5 |
| % out-of-state | 5 |
| % part-time | 37 |
| % minorities | 10 |
| % international | 10 |
| Average age at entry | 26 |
| Average years work experience at entry | 5 |

### ACADEMICS
| | |
|---|---|
| **Academic Experience Rating** | **81** |
| Student/faculty ratio | 8:1 |
| Profs interesting rating | 75 |
| Profs accessible rating | 75 |
| % female faculty | 30 |
| % minority faculty | 2 |

### JOINT DEGREES
MBA/JD, 3 years; MBA in Petroleum Management, 2 years; MBA/MA Russian and Eastern European Studies, 2 years; MBA/MA Latin American Studies, 2 years; MBA/Masters in Management, 2 years

## Academics

Brand-name recognition is one of the chief drawing cards of the University of Kansas School of Business; students note that the b-school's parent university is "the best school in Kansas and is among the best schools in the Midwest. It has a long tradition as a top university in the nation." Students expect to parlay that reputation into solid job offerings following graduation from this MBA program, whose greatest strengths lie in finance and international business.

KU's core curriculum divides first-year semesters into eight-week half-semester modules "so students can move quickly into electives and areas of concentration." Students approve of the concept but say there are a few kinks in its execution. As one MBA notes, "they need to work on coordinating classes better, as it is difficult to get classes when you need them."

"International business is probably the best part of the KU program," many students feel, citing the school's unique one year MBA in Italy program as well as the presence of the Center for International Business Education and Research on the Lawrence campus. Student say, "There are many excellent opportunities to study abroad." KU MBAs may concentrate in international business; other options include finance, marketing, e-business, information systems, information technology, and human-resource management.

The KU faculty is "very distinguished, very accessible, very open to sharing real-world experiences, and very sensitive to students' needs. They pick up a lot of slack and make the program worthwhile." The administration for the university at large is "a nightmare," but the b-school's administration is much better; students explain that it "has demonstrated knowledge, accuracy, and follow-through." Students also add that "the school needs to develop much more if it wants to go places. But there is a lot of potential, as the administration is very student friendly and will listen to our suggestions and ideas."

## Career and Placement

The Business Career Services Center at KU serves the school's undergraduates and graduates in business disciplines with a variety of workshops, counseling sessions, and career fairs. The school belongs to the 11-school Southwest MBA Alliance, which allows members to "combine efforts each year in order to foster connections between progressive businesses and our outstanding MBA students." The office also maintains a Listserv to notify students when its job listings are updated. Students explain that "career development and placement has been a very low priority in the past.

Top employers of KU MBAs include Accenture, Anderson Consulting, Aquila, Cap Gemini, Cerner Corporation, Deloitte Consulting, Ernst & Young, KPMG, McGladrey & Pullen, Payless ShoeSource, and Sprint. Approximately one in five KU graduates find their first post-MBA job outside the United States.

DEE STEINLE, ASSOCIATE DIRECTOR OF MASTER'S PROGRAMS
206 SUMMERFIELD HALL, 1300 SUNNYSIDE AVENUE, LAWRENCE, KS 66045 UNITED STATES
PHONE: 913-897-8587 • FAX: 913-864-5376
E-MAIL: BSCHOOLGRAD@KU.EDU • WEBSITE: WWW.BUSINESS.KU.EDU

## Student Life and Environment

KU's full-time MBA program is headquartered at the main campus in Lawrence. The campus is "attractive and well-maintained. The classrooms are comfortable and conducive to learning. The library and computer labs are state-of-the-art and very comfortable for studying." Full-time students also take some courses at the Edwards Campus in Overland Park. The drive from Lawrence is approximately 40 minutes; this campus is home to KU's part-time MBA program, and it offers classes in the evening only. Students wish that the bookstore, library services, and similar amenities would keep evening hours. One student complains, "Right now many of these places close at 7:00 P.M., which does us no good at all."

Part-time students also report that there's little more to their program than "getting to class lectures and back. Group and teamwork is carried out, but I think it's looked upon as quite a burden by the students." Extracurricular activity is at a minimum. One student explains, "This is a professional MBA program. Most people work full-time and attend classes at night." Students add that "there is no interaction between full-timers and the part-time business school students other than a 10 to 15 minute break in a 3.5 hour period."

Full-time students tend to be younger than the part-timers, and they enjoy a life that more closely resembles a typical undergraduate social scene. Students explain that "life at KU is very nice, with tons of things to do. Lawrence is a beautiful college town, and basketball is a religion at KU," and "there are plenty of social opportunities. MBA students often go out on the town together." Lawrence, a city of about 100,000, has a vital arts community, great golf courses, and an environment conducive to business; Inc.com named the Lawrence area one of the nation's 20 best in which to start and grow a company. KU's MBA student body is "a pretty good crowd of mid-20-year-olds" with a "substantial international community" figuring into the mix.

## Admissions

Students applying to the University of Kansas School of Business must submit GMAT scores, TOEFL scores (if applicable), two copies of official transcripts from each postsecondary school attended, two letters of recommendation from employers and/or professors, responses to three essay questions, and a resume. Two years of post-baccalaureate full-time professional experience are recommended, and "those without this experience will be at a competitive disadvantage in admissions. However, demonstrating exceptional personal attributes may, to an extent, offset this disadvantage." Limited scholarship funding is available to all students in the full-time program based on academic excellence and/or need.

### FINANCIAL FACTS

| | |
|---|---|
| Annual tuition (in-state/out-of-state) | $19,12/$34,575 |
| Books and supplies | $2,000 |
| Room & board (on-campus) | $10,435 |
| % of students receiving aid | 50 |
| % of first-year students receiving aid | 50 |
| % of students receiving grants | 25 |
| Average grant | $1,500 |

### ADMISSIONS

| | |
|---|---|
| Admissions Selectivity Rating | 82 |
| # of applications received | 268 |
| % applicants accepted | 73 |
| % acceptees attending | 85 |
| Average GMAT | 600 |
| Range of GMAT | 540–690 |
| Average GPA | 3.3 |
| TOEFL required of international students? | yes |
| Minimum TOEFL (paper/computer) | 53/20 |
| Application fee | $60 |
| International application fee | $60 |
| Regular application deadline | 6/1 |
| Regular notification | rolling |
| Deferment available? | yes |
| Maximum length of deferment | 1 year |
| Transfer students accepted? | yes |
| Transfer application policy | Maximum of 6 transferable credit hours. |
| Non-fall admissions? | yes |
| Need-blind admissions? | yes |

### APPLICANTS ALSO LOOK AT

Iowa State University, University of Iowa, University of Missouri—Columbia, University of Nebraska—Lincoln, University of Oklahoma

### EMPLOYMENT PROFILE

| | | | | |
|---|---|---|---|---|
| Career Rating | 74 | Grads employed by field: | % | avg. salary: |
| Primary source of full-time job acceptances | | Finance | 28 | $33,500 |
| | | Marketing | 24 | $43,700 |
| School-facilitated activities | 4 (29%) | Operations | 12 | $40,000 |
| Graduate-facilitated activities | 10 (71%) | Consulting | 12 | $69,000 |
| | | Other | 24 | $80,000 |
| Average starting salary | $50,667 | | | |
| Percent employed | 76 | | | |

# UNIVERSITY OF KENTUCKY

## THE GATTON COLLEGE OF BUSINESS AND ECONOMICS

### GENERAL INFORMATION

| | |
|---|---|
| Type of school | public |
| Environment | city |
| Academic calendar | semester |

### SURVEY SAYS...

Friendly students
Good peer network
*Solid preparation in:*
Accounting
Teamwork
Presentation skills

### STUDENTS

| | |
|---|---|
| Enrollment of parent institution | 26,545 |
| Enrollment of business school | 229 |
| % male/female | 60/40 |
| % out-of-state | 22 |
| % part-time | 42 |
| % minorities | 13 |
| % international | 11 |
| Average age at entry | 25 |
| Average years work experience at entry | 1.8 |

### ACADEMICS

| | |
|---|---|
| **Academic Experience Rating** | **83** |
| Student/faculty ratio | 3:1 |
| Profs interesting rating | 63 |
| Profs accessible rating | 70 |
| % female faculty | 22 |
| % minority faculty | 5 |

### JOINT DEGREES

MBA/JD, 4 years; BS Engineering/MBA, 5 years; MD/MBA, 5 years; PharmD/MBA, 4 years; MBA/MA in International Relations, 3 years

### PROMINENT ALUMNI

Chris Sullivan, Chair of the Board, Outback Steakhouse; Paul Rooke, Executive VP, Lexmark International, Inc.; Gretchen Price, VP, Finance & Accounting, Global Operations, P&G; Greg Burns, Chair and CEO, O'Charley's, Inc.; James E. Rogers, Jr., Chair, President, Cinergy Corp.

## Academics

Everyone from the most experienced businessperson to the liberal-arts undergraduate, who has never before used a calculator, is welcome at the Gatton College of Business and Economics at the University of Kentucky. In fact, the program is set up to accommodate all levels of experience.

In June of 2005, The Gatton College introduced its full-time one year immersive MBA program, which focuses on three fundamental processes: new product development, supply chain management, and mergers and acquisitions. Students participate in "redefined internships" by working with leading companies on projects in each of these modules. Since "many of the students in the program come straight from undergraduate programs directly into the MBA program," students do notice a contingency of MBA candidates with "no or minimal business experience," but students are often required to complete pre-MBA coursework before commencing MBA work (see Admissions). The school's objective is that each student will complete the program with a well-stocked portfolio of accomplishments and certifications.

Students love the friendly vibe of the Gatton program, and they explain that "the non-condescending attitude is the greatest strength at UK. We are a strong academic school, but we are all accepting of others. It makes for a positive working environment. The faculty is available and knowledgeable, making it easy to get one-on-one help." Gatton's administration "is visible, involved, and constantly asking our advice on what improvements should be made to increase the value of our MBA," according to students. Unfortunately, the bureaucracy of the university at large makes it difficult for MBAs to take advantage of UK's many other fine programs. One student complains, "The administration of other programs does not seem to communicate well with the business school to facilitate taking courses in areas outside of the business school."

## Career and Placement

MBAs at Gatton College are served by the James W. Stuckert Career Center. Students explain that one officer handles placement services for both business undergrads and MBAs, but they feel that "[they] need Career Services focused on MBAs alone, not a joint person for undergrad and grad." The office provides opportunities through networking, job fairs, on-campus recruitment (about 180 companies make recruiting trips to the campus each year), job banks, and professional organizations. The career center also provides counseling services.

Top recruiters at Gatton include Bank One, Citigroup, Ernst and Young, PricewaterhouseCoopers, Valvoline, Ernst & Young, Cinergy, and Toyota. About 1 in 20 UK MBAs moves on to a job outside the United States.

## Student Life and Environment

Gatton MBAs enjoy the benefits of a small-program environment within a university community; one student explains, "UK is a large university, but the MBA program has a distinct family feel that is very helpful at times." The advantages conferred by the university include first-class research and fitness facilities, a population large enough to attract prominent guest speakers and famous entertainers, and, of course, competitive and fanatically followed athletic teams. "Be prepared to become a big-time UK fan if you are not already. It's all about football and basketball here," one student observes.

The Gatton program provides students with more cozy environs, including "an MBA center with a big lounge, a big-screen TV, and snacks available. At any given time, there are 5 to 10 students conversing together, laughing [and] hanging out. We eat lunch together at the popular pizza pubs, go to basketball and football games, and we even hang out at Makers' Mark. We are more than classmates: we're friends," students say. The community gels around the MBA Association, which "has been very successful in social activities and bringing the students closer together outside the classroom." All in all, "MBAs spend a lot of time together, in group projects, with homework, and in outside activities. We have all become very close and are all currently trying to help each other find jobs, so we have a unique type of competition." One student says, "I will really miss this program and especially my classmates." Students at UK "have a unique identity. We have a wide range of backgrounds and demographics so that we all learn from each other in one way or another."

Hometown Lexington is yet another one of Gatton's advantages. One student explains, "Location is the greatest asset for the school. It's a relatively small town close to a metropolitan area (Louisville)." There are plenty of businesses headquartered in the area, including Ashland, Bank One, General Electric, Lexmark, Square D, and Toyota. As a result, Lexington provides "many opportunities for outside independent-study projects with companies." The city is home to an active arts scene; fans of the ponies will find plenty to cheer about at the area's two race tracks, Keeneland (thoroughbreds) and Red Mile (harness racing).

## Admissions

A complete application to the Gatton MBA program includes official copies of all undergraduate and graduate transcripts, GMAT scores, TOEFL scores (international students), a personal statement, letters of recommendation, and a resume. The school reports that "the admissions decision is also influenced by communication skills, international experience, and work experience." Proficiency in the basics of financial and managerial accounting, micro- and macro-economics, calculus, and statistics is a prerequisite to entering the evening MBA program. Those lacking proficiency may be admitted provisionally but cannot commence MBA work until they complete pre-MBA foundation course work. The school lists the following programs aimed at recruitment of minority/disadvantaged students: the Academic Excellence Scholarship, Commonwealth Minority Scholarship Program, the Kentucky Scholars program, and Lyman T. Johnson fellowships.

## FINANCIAL FACTS

| | |
|---|---|
| Annual tuition (in-state/out-of-state) | $6,314/$10,646 |
| Fees (in-state/out-of-state) | $6,000/$7,000 |
| Books and supplies | $2,500 |
| Room & board (on/off-campus) | $8,250/$9,100 |
| % of students receiving aid | 35 |
| % of first-year students receiving aid | 20 |
| % of students receiving grants | 35 |
| Average award package | $7,060 |
| Average grant | $3,921 |

## ADMISSIONS

| | |
|---|---|
| Admissions Selectivity Rating | 87 |
| # of applications received | 131 |
| % applicants accepted | 56 |
| % acceptees attending | 71 |
| Average GMAT | 599 |
| Range of GMAT | 550–640 |
| Average GPA | 3.34 |
| TOEFL required of international students? | yes |
| Minimum TOEFL (paper/computer) | 550/213 |
| Application fee | $40 |
| International application fee | $55 |
| Regular application deadline | 6/1 |
| Regular notification | rolling |
| Transfer students accepted? | yes |
| Transfer application policy | |
| File must be compelted and applicant is considered as a regular applicant | |
| Need-blind admissions? | yes |

### APPLICANTS ALSO LOOK AT

Eastern Kentucky University, Indiana University—Bloomington, The Ohio State University, University of Cincinnati, University of Louisville, University of Tennessee—Knoxville, Xavier University

## EMPLOYMENT PROFILE

| | | Grads employed by field: | % | avg. salary: |
|---|---|---|---|---|
| Career Rating | 75 | Accounting | 8 | $41,666 |
| Primary source of full-time | | Finance | 30 | $48,241 |
| job acceptances | | Marketing | 7 | $43,333 |
| School-facilitated activities | 20 (51%) | MIS | 10 | $52,075 |
| Unknown | 5 (12%) | Operations | 10 | $56,450 |
| | | General Management | 12 | $63,333 |
| Average starting salary | $49,726 | Other | 23 | $47,731 |
| Percent employed | 91 | | | |

# UNIVERSITY OF LONDON
## LONDON BUSINESS SCHOOL

### GENERAL INFORMATION
Type of school       private

### SURVEY SAYS...
*Solid preparation in:*
Finance
Doing business in a global economy

### STUDENTS
Average age at entry      28
Average years work experience
  at entry        6

### ACADEMICS
**Academic Experience Rating**  **69**
Student/faculty ratio      8:1
Profs interesting rating    86
Profs accessible rating    81

### JOINT DEGREES
EMBA/Global (part-time) 18 months joint degree with Columbia University, New York. Tuition is split between London and New York.

## *Academics*

"The international slant of the London Business School is its greatest strength," students agree, pointing to both the international focus of the curriculum and the school's location in "the most important financial and business centre of Europe." One MBA explains, "Everything that is done by the school—from creating the study-group teams to the content of the case studies in class—is centered around promoting internationalism. It is very impressive." The school's rare language requirement—students must be proficient in English and a second language (French, Spanish, German, Japanese, or Mandarin) demonstrates the prominence of international business.

LBS's 14-course first-year core is divided into three terms, throughout which "the integration of the different topics is very strong, helping one grasp the big picture quickly and efficiently prepare for the electives." Students caution that "the first-term workload is extremely heavy, but the second term is lighter, which lets time for the milk round." (Note: "Milk round" is a British term for "making the rounds," and usually refers to company-recruiting visits to university campuses.) Students especially appreciate how "the entire stream sits down to give feedback on each of the core classes at the end of the first year, and our comments are immediately fed back to the professors for improvement and/or encouragement. Unpopular electives are either drastically altered or discontinued."

Second year at LBS is a "year of choice," offering seven possible areas of concentration. Students identify strategy, entrepreneurship, and finance as the strongest areas; "London has a great position in the finance centre of Europe. There is no doubt it has deep and strong links with the finance industry with practically every investment bank I have ever heard of presenting at campus," noted one student. Electives in marketing, technology, and decision sciences also earn students' praise. Overall, students describe the LBS curriculum as "balanced, with lots of practical courses and interactions with the outside/real world." They praise the program's shadowing project (in which student's trail a manager for up to five days, then report on the experience) and the capstone second-year consulting project.

LBS faculty "deal daily with today's business issues either through their research or their consulting assignments. It is absolutely fantastic to see them bring that experience to class every week. Moreover, professors recognize they have a class full of bright and intelligent people in front of them and therefore engage them in the discussion and exploration of the latest business thinking. You do not have the feeling that you are back at high school where the teacher reads out what you should know." MBAs point out that professors "have to be good teachers to stay at London Business School. They're rigorously critiqued by students and administration."

## *Career and Placement*

Students give Career Services at London Business School mixed reviews, noting that "in the past, the emphasis of Career Services has been strongly slanted toward finance and consulting, with industry being basically ignored. This focus is starting to shift and hopefully will continue to expand." Several MBAs observed that "the school has recruited new director for the Career Services and things seem to be improving." Until things get entirely up to speed, students can turn to their peers for added job-search assistance, as "the student clubs are especially effective at networking and helping with career strategies and contacts." They can also seek help from the school's 16,000 alumni working in over 100 countries across the globe.

JULIE AHRENS, MBA MARKETING & ADMISSIONS MANAGER
REGENT'S PARK, NW1 4SA, LONDON, ENGLAND
PHONE: 011-44-20-7262-5050 • FAX: 011-44-20-7724-7875
E-MAIL: MBAINFO@LONDON.EDU • WEBSITE: WWW.LONDON.EDU

Top employers of LBS MBAs include A. T. Kearney, Accenture, American Express, Bain, Bank of America, Barclays Capital, Capital One, Booz Allen Hamilton, Citigroup, Deloitte Touche Tohmatsu, Deutsche Bank, Johnson & Johnson, JPMorgan, KPMG, Lehman Brothers, McKinsey, Merrill Lynch, Morgan Stanley, and UBS Warburg.

## Student Life and Environment

LSB attracts a "truly international student and faculty body. More than 80 percent of students comes from outside U.K., giving an indescribable wealth of experience and network." Explains one MBA, "You will never be 'one of the foreign students' at LBS, since there is no dominating nationality. The students are amazingly diverse." Students learn about each others' cultures through the regional clubs, "such as the Indian and Asian clubs, which are very active and host a variety of activities and parties that introduce their country's culture to the student body. In fact, there are so many themed parties that it is sometimes hard to tear yourself away from school and remember that there is an amazing city to explore outside of the school neighborhood." Other clubs "run lectures or other events in the evening, which are good both for learning and networking." Students also have "a plethora of sports options, with men and women's rugby and football being the most popular. Everyone is involved in a club or sport."

Going to school in central London "provides the school access to business leaders from around the globe and direct access to companies," students tell us. One student observed that "London Business School's location limits the school's expanding capabilities—there's really nowhere to expand to in London—but overall the campus is great. It is much smaller than American b-schools, but I'd rather be in a smaller campus in London than in larger one outside the city." "The nightlife and culture are also great" in London; as one student told us, "It is hard to imagine a better social scene at your fingertips at any other school in the world. The only issue is that there may be too many distractions." The chief drawback: "Life in central London can be quite expensive (probably more expensive than Manhattan, even)."

## Admissions

Admission to University of London requires "two to three years of work experience." The school notes that "candidates do not have to have international experience, but they must have international aspirations." Applicants must supply the school with official copies of all undergraduate and graduate transcripts, GMAT scores, two letters of reference, scores on an English proficiency test (where applicable), three essays, and a one-page curriculum vitae. The school reviews applications for evidence of management potential, personal motivation, interpersonal skills, language proficiency, and international orientation.

### FINANCIAL FACTS

| | |
|---|---|
| Annual tuition | $35,675 |
| Books and supplies | $500 |
| Room & board | $25,500 |
| % of students receiving loans | 56 |
| Average grant | $17,980 |

### ADMISSIONS

**Admissions Selectivity Rating 60\***

| | |
|---|---|
| # of applications received | 1,523 |
| Average GMAT | 680 |
| Range of GMAT | 650–710 |
| Average GPA | 3.5 |
| TOEFL required of international students? | yes |
| Application fee | $240 |
| International application fee | $240 |
| Regular application deadline | 4/28 |
| Regular notification | 5/19 |
| Application deadline/notification | |
| Round 1: | 10/21 / 11/23 |
| Round 2: | 1/06 / 2/10 |
| Round 3: | 2/24 / 4/7 |
| Round 4: | 4/28 / 5/19 |
| Deferment available? | yes |
| Maximum length of deferment | 1 year |
| Need-blind admissions? | yes |

### APPLICANTS ALSO LOOK AT

Columbia University, Harvard University, INSEAD, New York University, Northwestern University, Stanford University, University of Pennsylvania

### EMPLOYMENT PROFILE

| Career Rating | 60* | Grads employed by field: | % | avg. salary: |
|---|---|---|---|---|
| | | Finance | 38 | $97,550 |
| | | Consulting | 30 | $110,355 |
| | | General Management | 32 | $99,620 |

# University of Louisiana—Lafayette

## B. I. Moody III College of Business

### GENERAL INFORMATION

| | |
|---|---|
| Type of school | public |
| Environment | city |
| Academic calendar | semester |

### SURVEY SAYS...

Students love Lafayette, LA
Friendly students
Good social scene
Helpful alumni
*Solid preparation in:*
Teamwork

### STUDENTS

| | |
|---|---|
| Enrollment of parent institution | 16,800 |
| Enrollment of business school | 168 |
| % male/female | 55/45 |
| % out-of-state | 9 |
| % part-time | 80 |
| % minorities | 8 |
| % international | 4 |
| Average age at entry | 27 |
| Average years work experience at entry | 7 |

### ACADEMICS

| | |
|---|---|
| **Academic Experience Rating** | **74** |
| Student/faculty ratio | 18:1 |
| Profs interesting rating | 68 |
| Profs accessible rating | 80 |
| % female faculty | 40 |
| % minority faculty | 12 |

### PROMINENT ALUMNI

Mike DeHart, Stuller Management Services, Inc.; Stefni Lotief, UL Women's Softball Coach; Greg Roberts, Director of Aviation, Lafayette Airport; Dr. Ross Judice, Acadian Ambulance and Air Med, EVP and CMO.

## Academics

Students at the University of Louisiana—Lafayette's B.I. Moody College of Business appreciate that theirs is an MBA program constantly in search of improvements. Students explain that "UL has spent a lot of time and effort bringing the university up-to-date with the growing economy, and it has high standards which make getting a degree hard work and valuable." One student notes, "The school continually strives to increase enrollment and improve facilities." The new structure, mostly opened in January 2005, includes wi-fi capabilities, multimedia communications facilities, and new, state-of-the-art classrooms capable of accommodating a larger student body.

According to some students, the new building is the crowning piece of a long, concerted effort to "guide the university from a small, regional university to become the nationally recognized university that it is today." Part of the effort involves "actively [pursuing] the best professors in the field," students report. Best of all, "administrators have grown this university while still providing the small university atmosphere where professors care about their students. Sums up one student, "I am very proud to be part of this institution."

Moody MBAs also speak highly of their instructors. Students say that "many [professors] have or had prestigious careers in the fields they teach. This seems to help in giving students real-world examples of the ideas [they] are teaching." Students only complaint is with the scheduling of classes, which many report is inconvenient for those with full-time jobs. One student warns, "The program was pitched so that you were able to work full time and take night classes. However, if you do not want to take six years to graduate, you are forced to take day classes."

## Career and Placement

Career guidance is provided to Lafayette MBAs by the university's Career Services Center. According to the school's website, "the center serves as a major link between the students and potential employers and confirms its commitment to support and advance university/employer relationship." The office offers students workshops, seminars, one-on-one counseling, and access to various job-listing sources. Students explain that "alumni are supportive" and serve as a major resource in their job searches. Companies recruiting on campus in the spring of 2004 included BJ Services, Cameron Corporation, Drill-Quip, Halliburton, Magnolia Marketing, New York Life, and Union National.

## Student Life and Environment

"UL is located in a part of Louisiana that is known for its hospitality and down-home feel," students say, and they add that "no matter where you are from, you are welcomed to this area with open arms." Lafayette is part of Louisiana's Acadiana region, historical home to French settlers and Creoles, among others. Its location near the Gulf of Mexico feeds the area's many oil- and gas-industry employers; the region has attempted to diversify its economy in recent years and has had some luck attracting manufacturers and companies in the transportation sector.

Students say that campus life "offers the perfect blend of educational opportunities and extracurricular activities." UL "has many different clubs to be involved in, allowing students to feel like a part of the university. The faculty encourages involvement on campus and in the community." Recreational opportunities abound; one student reports, "My undergraduate and graduate life at UL Lafayette has been an even mix of studying and partying. While studies consume most of the week, the city of Lafayette always provides party opportunities such as Mardi Gras, Festival Acadiens, Downtown Alive, and many other cultural gatherings."

DR. C. EDDIE PALMER, DEAN OF THE GRADUATE SCHOOL
MARTIN HALL, ROOM #243, PO BOX 40200, LAFAYETTE, LA 70504-0200 UNITED STATES
PHONE: 337-482-6491 • FAX: 337-482-6195 • E-MAIL: MBA@LOUISIANA.EDU
WEBSITE: WWW.MOODY.LOUISIANA.EDU

While hardly a small school, UL "is not a huge place where you get lost in the crowd, and that is what draws me to it the most," one student says. The MBA program is small enough that "everyone knows each other in the business school, and that creates a family atmosphere for everyone." Minority enrollment in the MBA program is small; nonwhite Americans make up only 8 percent of the student body. International students, who make up 10 percent of the program, arrive from the Caribbean, China, Germany, France, Greece, India, and Southeast Asia. About 50 percent of all MBA students majored in business and commerce as undergrads, another 30 percent majored in math or science, 10 percent studied engineering, and 10 percent were in humanities and social-science programs.

## Admissions

Applicants to the Moody College of Business at UL must provide the school with an undergraduate transcript demonstrating a GPA of at least 2.75; GMAT scores (450 minimum); three letters of recommendation; and a resume "including (at a minimum) the dates and awarding institutions of academic degree(s); employment and salary history; a list of honors, awards, and professional certificates; a summary of basic computer skills; and a list of overseas travels and multilingual abilities. Prospective students are also encouraged to include a resume 'supplement' listing and briefly describing all relevant extracurricular and/or community involvement(s)." Undergraduate grades and GMAT score are "major selection criteria;" recommendations and resume are "significant (of moderate importance)" criteria. Students must also send the school "a written statement of purpose of 750 words or less describing the reasons why the prospective student wishes to pursue an MBA degree."

## FINANCIAL FACTS

| | |
|---|---|
| Annual tuition (in-state/out-of-state) | $3,14/$9,284 |
| Books and supplies | $1,000 |
| Room & board (on/off-campus) | $3,750/$6,750 |
| % of students receiving aid | 60 |
| % of first-year students receiving aid | 50 |
| % of students receiving loans | 40 |
| % of students receiving grants | 25 |
| Average grant | $8,605 |
| Average student loan debt | $5,000 |

## ADMISSIONS

| | |
|---|---|
| Admissions Selectivity Rating | 77 |
| # of applications received | 104 |
| % applicants accepted | 57 |
| % acceptees attending | 76 |
| Average GMAT | 512 |
| Range of GMAT | 470–610 |
| Average GPA | 3.22 |
| TOEFL required of international students? | yes |
| Minimum TOEFL (paper/computer) | 550/213 |
| Application fee | $20 |
| International application fee | $30 |
| Regular application deadline | 6/30 |
| Regular notification | 8/1 |
| Early decision program? | yes |
| ED Deadline/notification | Applications processed as soon as received. / 6/1 |
| Deferment available? | yes |
| Maximum length of deferment | 1 year |
| Transfer students accepted? | yes |
| Transfer application policy | Can transfer in a maximum of 9 credit hours. Must apply through regular process. |
| Non-fall admissions? | yes |
| Need-blind admissions? | yes |

## APPLICANTS ALSO LOOK AT

Louisiana State University, Louisiana Tech University, Loyola University New Orleans, McNeese State University, Nicholls State University, Tulane University, University of New Orleans

| EMPLOYMENT PROFILE | |
|---|---|
| Career Rating | 72 |
| Average starting salary | $55,000 |

# UNIVERSITY OF LOUISVILLE
## COLLEGE OF BUSINESS

## Academics

The College of Business at the University of Louisville offers two primary MBA options. The first is the traditional MBA, presented through an evening program that is designed to fit the needs of working professionals. The second is the IMBA, an integrated, two-year lockstep program that focuses primarily on entrepreneurship. The IMBA is also scheduled for the convenience of working students, meeting twice weekly in the evenings. The university also offers a number of joint-degree MBA programs.

Louisville's traditional MBA for working professionals is a 36-semester hour program that "was just restructured," demonstrating "the commitment of the school to continually improve." Students tell us that "Most of the professors have an innovative approach to teaching, and they look for ways to make their classes better. If I were to restart the program three years after graduating, I am sure it would be a unique experience." Students appreciate that this approach "is essential given the ever-changing business environment," adding that "We may not be a Harvard or Wharton, but we still produce some of the world's leaders in business. In addition, the program offers a great work/life balance." Students praise their professors for "demonstrating meaningful real-world knowledge through prior experiences. The coursework they present is very applicable to situations I face as a manager at a bank each day."

Louisville's IMBA is a lockstep program with an entrepreneurial focus. All courses and meeting times are mandatory. This approach allows for greater integration within the curriculum; classes can be team-taught to highlight the interconnectedness of two or more business disciplines, for example. It also allows the school to vary course lengths. Because all students are taking all courses together, scheduling need not be restrained by traditional semester intervals, and students love the results. One participant writes, "I feel that it's designed to give me everything I wanted in a graduate business program. Everything that I have learned thus far has been applied in my professional life."

## Career and Placement

Louisville MBAs receive career counseling and placement services from the Ulmer Career Management Center, an all-new, state-of-the-art, 3,800 square foot facility that includes a career management resource library, conference rooms, and interview rooms. The office provides resume assistance, training seminars on interviewing skills, and on-campus recruiting events supported by CareerLeader tools and Symplicty software. Students confess that "the career center is just beginning to get off the ground" and that "the school still needs to improve in its career management for graduate students. Although some jobs have been posted, the majority are geared towards undergraduates or students who have graduated from the MBA program and already have several years of experience." On the bright side, students find that attending Louisville creates "many networking opportunities. Most classmates have full-time jobs and experience in the 'real world.' You can make connections with students throughout Louisville that will stay with you a long time."

KEVIN KANE, DIRECTOR, MASTERS PROGRAMS
COLLEGE OF BUSINESS, LOUISVILLE, KY 40292 UNITED STATES
PHONE: 502-852-3969 • FAX: 502-852-4901 • E-MAIL: K0KANE01@GWISE.LOUISVILLE.EDU
WEBSITE: WWW.BUSINESS.LOUISVILLE.EDU/MBA

## Student Life and Environment

Most MBAs at Louisville "have little involvement with the rest of campus (library, gym, etc.) because most work full-time and attend classes in the evenings." Students spend so little time on campus that "they are secluded from other graduate students and, to a certain extent, from the other MBA students." Even the busiest MBAs, however, know that "our basketball team is nationally recognized and dominates both the school and the town during the season." Those who find time to spend on campus boast that it is "very accommodating, with a recently renovated state-of-the-art library and a great athletic program (activities MBAs can attend when not studying!)." One student notes, "Although it's an urban campus, you would never know it given the quaint, friendly atmosphere." MBA 'campus life' will be enhanced in 18-24 months with the planned relocation of the College's graduate business programs to the heart of downtown Louisville.

The metropolitan Louisville area is home to over one million people. Students describe it as "a city full of opportunities for recent or upcoming MBA grads. Openings for MBAs are frequently e-mailed to students by school officials, which is a great service." A recent Wall Street Journal supplement ranked Louisville "the nation's fourth best city for job opportunities for recent graduates." Papa John's, YUM!, Humana Health Insurance, UPS Worldport, and GE all have a large presence in the city; some are headquartered here. Students report that the area surrounding the school "is not the best residential area, it's not good housing. There is good, safe housing about 15 minutes from campus, though, over in the Highlands."

## Admissions

Admission to the University of Louisville MBA program is, without a doubt, competitive. Students in the program rank in the top third of MBA candidates nationwide. Applicants must submit all of the following to the Admissions Office: a completed application; an official copy of all undergraduate transcripts; an official GMAT score report; a one-page personal statement; two letters of recommendation from professors (or employers for applicants who have been out of school for a substantial period); and a current resume. International students must provide, in addition to the above, an official TOEFL score report (minimum score: 170 computer-based test, 550 paper-and-pencil test). All candidates must be proficient in computer and quantitative skills prior to the commencement of their MBA work. Students with undergraduate degrees in areas outside business and management typically must complete 12 hours of preliminary nondegree coursework prior to beginning work on the MBA.

### FINANCIAL FACTS

| | |
|---|---|
| Annual tuition (in-state/out-of-state) | $9,090/$21,166 |
| Books and supplies | $900 |
| Room & board (on/off-campus) | $8,000/$10,600 |
| Average award package | $8,400 |
| Average grant | $10,000 |

### ADMISSIONS

| | |
|---|---|
| Admissions Selectivity Rating | 88 |
| # of applications received | 168 |
| % applicants accepted | 48 |
| % acceptees attending | 89 |
| Average GMAT | 565 |
| Range of GMAT | 505–675 |
| Average GPA | 3.46 |
| TOEFL required of international students? | yes |
| Minimum TOEFL (paper/computer) | 530/170 |
| Application fee | $50 |
| International application fee | $50 |
| Regular application deadline | 5/31 |
| Regular notification | rolling |
| Deferment available? | yes |
| Maximum length of deferment | 2 years |
| Transfer students accepted? | yes |
| Transfer application policy | Up to 6 credits may be accepted from an AACSB-accredited MBA program. |
| Non-fall admissions? | yes |
| Need-blind admissions? | yes |

# UNIVERSITY OF MARYLAND—COLLEGE PARK
## ROBERT H. SMITH SCHOOL OF BUSINESS

## Academics

The Robert H. Smith School of Business at the University of Maryland—College Park places "an extraordinary emphasis on technology in business," refocusing traditional disciplines such as finance, management, and marketing on the emerging world of e-business. Thanks to the largesse of the school's namesake—an area real estate developer who recently donated $30 million to the university—the Smith School has the resources necessary to maintain and develop the state-of-the-art facilities its curriculum requires.

Smith MBAs commence their work with a core curriculum that "is very comprehensive and prepares students well with a solid foundation." Students report that "it is fast-paced and challenging, but the professors make sure the students keep pace." To ensure that students can tailor their MBAs to the areas that interest them most, Smith sets aside "a huge portion of degree requirements for elective courses." Electives can be used to fashion an area of specialization in one of 18 disciplines; students are especially enthusiastic about Smith's offerings in entrepreneurship and information technology. A general management degree without specialization is also an option here. In addition to the traditional curriculum, MBAs may also pursue Experiential Learning Modules (ELMs), such as case competitions, which "provide a great opportunity to continue learning and applying it outside of the classroom."

Smith professors, students agree, "are great. They are genuinely interested in our progress. Very approachable and down-to-earth, too." Observes one student, "Subjects I hated in my undergraduate university—economics and statistics, for example—I enjoy taking at Smith just because of the professors who teach them."

## Career and Placement

Smith's Office of Career Management (OCM) offers MBA students the full complement of career-related services, including a number of high-tech interviewing and job-search facilities. Students report that "the office has made improvements in recent years but has a lot more room for growth." They also tell us that OCM "brings a good number of companies to campus, although more would certainly be better," but they also concede that "the size of the program—each full-time class is about 150 students—makes it more difficult to organize events and attract large companies." International students would love to see "at least one officer devoted exclusively to helping [us] find jobs." These students will be happy to hear that in April 2005 the school retained a leading immigration law firm, Reed Smith LLP, to help recruiters hire international students.

Employers most likely to hire Smith MBAs include: Avaya; Citigroup; Constellation Power Source; Deloitte; Delta; General Electric; Fannie Mae; IBM; Intel; Johnson & Johnson; Navigant; PepsiCo; PricewaterhouseCoopers; UBS; Wachovia; and World Bank.

## Student Life and Environment

Life at Smith is hectic, as "the pressure of the MBA is always looming overhead, with generally two case studies, one to two tests per week, and exams around the corner." Even so, "people still find time to enjoy themselves and hang around with friends." There's "Happy Hour every Thursday, sports clubs for those who like to play intramurals, and cultural clubs (Black, Hispanic, Indian, Asian, Chinese, International, and Jewish) that are very active within the school organizing dinners and fundraising." Students also like to "hit the DC club and bar scene on weekends, and any night of the week you can usually find someone who's willing to join you for a few beers at a local watering hole." One student observes, "There are enough activities inside and outside of the classroom to keep anyone occupied. Formals, tailgates, sporting events, speakers, forums, career development—you name it, we have it." Maryland's part-time students are, of course, much less intimately integrated into extracurricular life. These students, who attend on evenings and weekends, generally spend the minimum amount of time necessary on campus.

Smith MBAs include "a large number of international students" and "a diverse blend of backgrounds, nationalities, ethnicities, and experience. Despite these differences, there is an amazingly strong team-oriented feeling here at Smith School." This "sense of community" is all the more amazing when you realize that "the student body is naturally fragmented by the fact that we live everywhere from Baltimore to Northern Virginia, not just in suburban Maryland and DC."

## Admissions

All applicants to Smith MBA programs at College Park must submit the following to the School: two official copies of transcripts for all postsecondary academic work; an official GMAT score report; personal essays; two letters of recommendation; and a completed application form. Interviews are required for full-time applicants. International students must also provide an official TOEFL score report (minimum required score: 600 paper-based test, 250 computer-based test) and a financial certification form, with supporting documents. The school lists the following outreach programs for minority and disadvantaged students: Kaleidoscope: Advancing Diversity at Smith, a Fall semester recruitment event for underrepresented minority students; Women and the MBA, a symposium oriented to educating women about the advantages of the MBA; Management Leadership for Tomorrow: a partnership that focuses on guiding minority students through the MBA application preparation process; online chats for prospective MBA students from underrepresented groups (Africa, South America, Women, African American, and Hispanics); and participation at conferences of minority professional organizations, including the Society for Hispanic Professional Engineers, the Women's Information Network, Graduate Women in Business, the National Society for Black Engineers, and the Black MBA Association."

## FINANCIAL FACTS

| | |
|---|---|
| Annual tuition (in-state/out-of-state) | $14,454/$23,814 |
| Fees | $6,777 |
| Books and supplies | $1,600 |
| Room & board | $10,500 |
| % of students receiving aid | 50 |
| % of first-year students receiving aid | 52 |
| % of students receiving grants | 11 |
| Average grant | $15,086 |

## ADMISSIONS

| | |
|---|---|
| Admissions Selectivity Rating | 85 |
| # of applications received | 1,153 |
| % applicants accepted | 62 |
| % acceptees attending | 62 |
| Average GMAT | 611 |
| Range of GMAT | 560–660 |
| Average GPA | 3.29 |
| TOEFL required of international students? | yes |
| Minimum TOEFL (paper/computer) | 600/250 |
| Application fee | $60 |
| International application fee | $60 |
| Regular application deadline | rolling |
| Regular notification | rolling |
| Application deadline/notification | |
| Round 1: | 11/1 / 1/15 |
| Round 2: | 12/15 / 2/1 |
| Round 3: | 1/15 / 3/15 |
| Round 4: | 3/15 / 5/1 |
| Early decision program? | yes |
| ED Deadline/notification | 11/1, 12/15 / 2/1 |
| Need-blind admissions? | yes |

## APPLICANTS ALSO LOOK AT

Carnegie Mellon, Georgetown University, Rochester Institute of Technology, The George Washington University, The University of Texas at Austin, University of North Carolina—Chapel Hill, University of Virginia

## EMPLOYMENT PROFILE

| | | Grads employed by field: | % | avg. salary: |
|---|---|---|---|---|
| Career Rating | 88 | Finance | 34 | $78,964 |
| Primary source of full-time job acceptances | | Marketing | 25 | $77,325 |
| | | MIS | 3 | $81,666 |
| School-facilitated activities | 61 (51%) | Operations | 3 | $75,200 |
| Graduate-facilitated activities | 58 (49%) | Consulting | 22 | $85,440 |
| | | General Management | 4 | $79,600 |
| Average starting salary | $78,869 | Other | 9 | $65,800 |
| Percent employed | 92 | | | |

# UNIVERSITY OF MASSACHUSETTS—AMHERST
## ISENBERG SCHOOL OF MANAGEMENT

## GENERAL INFORMATION

| | |
|---|---|
| Type of school | public |
| Environment | town |
| Academic calendar | semester |

## SURVEY SAYS...

Good peer network
Happy students
*Solid preparation in:*
Accounting
Teamwork
Communication/interpersonal skills
Quantitative skills
Computer skills

## STUDENTS

| | |
|---|---|
| Enrollment of parent institution | 25,093 |
| Enrollment of business school | 725 |
| % male/female | 56/44 |
| % out-of-state | 49 |
| % part-time | 89 |
| % minorities | 10 |
| % international | 23 |
| Average age at entry | 28 |
| Average years work experience at entry | 4.6 |

## ACADEMICS

| | |
|---|---|
| **Academic Experience Rating** | **99** |
| Student/faculty ratio | 8:1 |
| Profs interesting rating | 98 |
| Profs accessible rating | 99 |
| % female faculty | 35 |
| % minority faculty | 5 |

## JOINT DEGREES

MBA/MS in Sport Management, 2 years; MBA/MS in Hospitality & Tourism Management, 2 years; MBA/MPP, 2.5 years

## PROMINENT ALUMNI

John P. Flavin, Chair of the Board, Flavin, Blake & Co. Inc.; Eugene M. Isenberg, Chair and CEO, Nabors Industries, Inc.; Jayne A. McMellen, VP Fund Administration, State Street Bank & Trust Co. Inc.; John F. Smith, Jr., Retired Chair, General Motors Corporation

## Academics

Students praise the affordability and the "small size of the program, which makes it extremely possible for students to have one-to-one contact with great faculty" at the Isenberg School of Management at the University of Massachusetts at Amherst. The school's already low public-school tuition is made even more affordable by financial aid and fellowships; in fact, many students receive assistantships that carry a full-tuition waiver plus a stipend. "The university works hard to make sure that students get enough financial aid," MBAs say.

Isenberg offers both full-time and part-time programs; the part-time program is taught at three satellite campuses (Shrewsbury, Pittsfield, and Holyoke) and is also available online in order to maximize convenience for working students. The full-time program dispenses with all core courses during the first year, which "makes it a very fast-paced environment and hard to digest everything. But it is a good program overall." Students build their fields of specialization (accounting, finance and operations management, management, and marketing) through electives offered by the School of Management or by other schools at the University. Full-time students say, "There is a real sense of community. The administration [and the teachers] are always available. I am having an amazing experience!" They also appreciate how "the atmosphere strongly encourages teamwork over cutthroat competition." However these students warn that "the small size of program severely limits the number of electives available. The majority of electives are in finance and operations."

The part-time program, available only to working adults, consists of 12 courses taken at the student's pace. Students typically complete the program in two and a half years, although the program can be completed in as little as 18 months. The online program can be completed entirely in the online format, without visiting the university's campus.

Students brag that Isenberg has "a very impressive faculty. They have the best mix of outstanding intellect and pure teaching skills that I have ever seen. It is one thing to know an incredible amount about a particular subject, [but] it is another thing to actually be able to teach it. UMass has hired individuals capable of accomplishing both." According to the school, faculty specialties include investments, alternative risk management, technology management, organizational change, information technology, corporate creativity, supply-chain management, strategic marketing, and social marketing.

## Career and Placement

Isenberg has a career management service dedicated exclusively to MBAs, which is unusual for a small program. The office schedules networking events and interview sessions, conducts workshops and seminars, and provides students with access to job databases. MBAs say that, unfortunately, it's not enough; although all first-year students are required to take a career management course, they still they say that "students are pretty much on their own finding jobs and internships. If you are not prepared to do your own career research and networking, you will easily be unemployed at graduation. Only a handful of companies recruit on campus." Some students suggest that "off-campus social tours should be organized, and, most importantly, career opportunities and assistance should be improved via more structured courses like the professional seminars."

Employers who most frequently hire Isenberg MBAs include Deloitte Touche Tohmatsu, EMC, Frito-Lay, General Electric, Hamilton Sundstrand, IBM, Liberty Mutual, MassMutual Financial Group, Morgan Stanley, PricewaterhouseCoopers, RSA Security Teradyne, and United Technologies Corporation.

MARYBETH HARRIS, DIRECTOR OF STUDENT SUPPORT SERVICES
305 ISENBERG SCHOOL OF MANAGEMENT, UNIVERSITY OF MASS.—AMHERST, MA 01003 U.S.
PHONE: 413-545-5608 • FAX: 413-577-2234
E-MAIL: GRADPROG@SOM.UMASS.EDU • WEBSITE: WWW.UMASS.EDU/MBA

## Student Life and Environment

Isenberg is housed in "a brand-new building with state-of-the-art computers and multi-media resources, which makes the students more productive and classes easier to comprehend." The completely wireless Alfond Management Center, which opened in 2002, features audio- and videoconferencing facilities as well as a real-time trading center. A number of breakout rooms are available for meetings and recruiting.

Full-timers describe a very socially active program with regular events including a Thursday night pub crawl, "a weekly festivity in which MBA students meet up at a local bar. It provides an opportunity for first- and second-year students to intermingle outside [of] class." Students also have house parties during the weekends. "[The] Graduate Business Association helps with many out-of-school social activities" that are MBA-specific. Students also report that "because we are located in large university campus of 25,000 students, opportunities abound throughout the campus. There are plenty of activities, from watching theater productions at the university's theater to catching a comedy show at the Student Union. UMass has great athletic programs, especially its football program. Students go down and tailgate before Minuteman games at the stadium."

Isenberg students are a group of "handpicked intelligent people. The admission [office] is very selective about who they accept into the program." MBAs explain, "It's delightful to have a high percentage of international students in [a] program located in a relatively rural area." MBAs only wish that there were more students in the program. One student comments, "The school could try to increase the number of students in the full-time program from a current total of 70 (first and second) to 100 or more. This would allow for more critical mass when it comes to recruitment."

Amherst is a quintessential New England college town, home not only to UMass, but also to Amherst College and Hampshire College. The town offers "plenty of things to do. There is no better place to be than New England on a crisp autumn day, and Amherst might be the best place in New England."

## Admissions

According to the Isenberg Admissions office, "no one academic background is favored in the selection of candidates. Academic history, GMAT performance, motivation, aptitude for graduate-level work, and managerial experience are all taken into consideration." The school seeks candidates with two to four years of professional work experience. Applicants must submit two official copies of all undergraduate and graduate transcripts, GMAT scores, TOEFL scores (international students), two letters of recommendation, essays, and a resume. Students applying for fellowships must apply by February 1. Isenberg maintains a Diversity Recruitment Committee that "meets regularly to design and implement effective strategies to continue development of diversity in the program."

### FINANCIAL FACTS

| | |
|---|---|
| Annual tuition (in-state/out-of-state) | $2,640/$9,937 |
| Fees (in-state/out-of-state) | $6,639/$8,319 |
| Books and supplies | $2,000 |
| Room & board (on/off-campus) | $6,189/$8,500 |
| % of students receiving aid | 93 |
| % of first-year students receiving aid | 88 |
| % of students receiving loans | 36 |
| % of students receiving grants | 5 |
| Average award package | $16,427 |
| Average grant | $18,205 |
| Average student loan debt | $16,917 |

### ADMISSIONS

| | |
|---|---|
| Admissions Selectivity Rating | 97 |
| # of applications received | 226 |
| % applicants accepted | 21 |
| % acceptees attending | 77 |
| Average GMAT | 633 |
| Range of GMAT | 590–690 |
| Average GPA | 3.37 |
| TOEFL required of international students? | yes |
| Minimum TOEFL (paper/computer) | 600/250 |
| Application fee | $40 |
| International application fee | $65 |
| Regular application deadline | 2/1 |
| Deferment available? | yes |
| Maximum length of deferment | 1 year |
| Need-blind admissions? | yes |

### APPLICANTS ALSO LOOK AT

Boston College, Boston University, Dartmouth College, Harvard University, University of Connecticut, Yale University

### EMPLOYMENT PROFILE

| Career Rating | 89 | Grads employed by field: | % | avg. salary: |
|---|---|---|---|---|
| Average starting salary | $69,100 | Accounting | 9 | $45,000 |
| Percent employed | 92 | Finance | 37 | $80,000 |
| | | Marketing | 27 | $43,000 |
| | | Consulting | 18 | $80,000 |
| | | Other | 9 | $80,000 |

# UNIVERSITY OF MASSACHUSETTS—DARTMOUTH
## CHARLTON COLLEGE OF BUSINESS

### GENERAL INFORMATION
Type of school      public
Environment      town

### SURVEY SAYS...
Friendly students
Helpful alumni
*Solid preparation in:*
Presentation skills

### ACADEMICS
**Academic Experience Rating**    **61**
Profs interesting rating    70
Profs accessible rating    65

## Academics

The AACSB-accredited MBA program at the University of Massachusetts—Dartmouth is "building its reputation, giving students a great deal of pride in feeling that they are part of something that will be much bigger in the future." For the present, UMass Dartmouth excels at providing its mix of local part-timers and international full-timers a convenient MBA program that can be completed in as little as one year or as many as five years.

All students here must complete a seven-course sequence of core requirements that cover fundamental concepts in accounting, information technology, finance, organization, operations, strategy, and marketing. Three electives are also required; students completing all three electives in a single "concentration stream" may earn an MBA with a concentration. Concentrations are available in accounting, business information, e-commerce, finance, international business, management, marketing, and operations. Students without concentrations graduate with a general MBA.

Entering students who have not satisfactorily completed undergraduate classes in business may be required to complete up to three foundation courses prior to enrolling in any of the 10 courses credited toward the MBA. Completion of an equivalent undergraduate course with a grade of at least a B typically qualifies students to skip a foundation course. Students with undergraduate degrees in business are generally exempt from foundation requirements.

UMass Dartmouth MBA students praise their program's "fine academic facilities and equipment" as well as the school's "favorable student-professor ratio." Administrators and professors are "very helpful and nice" and have a way of "making everything easier to understand." The net result of these positive factors is a "satisfying academic experience."

## Career and Placement

The Career Resource Center at UMass Dartmouth serves all students and alumni of the university. The center provides counseling services, job postings, access to job search engines, and workshops in interviewing, resume writing, and career search. The CRC also maintains the Alumni Career Network and organizes on-campus recruiting events. MBA students receive additional career counseling from the MBA program coordinator. The majority of UMass Dartmouth MBAs attend while working full-time; the primary goal of many is to advance at their current place of employment rather than to find a new career. Thus, many MBAs here do not utilize the university's Career Services.

## Student Life and Environment

Part-time students constitute the majority in UMass Dartmouth's MBA program, and they are drawn almost exclusively from the surrounding area. These "motivated, interesting and intelligent individuals" include a number of students who are "relatively older, with years of experience in the professional world. Many of them bring their experiences to bear in our classroom discussions." The school also hosts a number of full-timers, many of them "international students with different backgrounds, most of whom are younger than 30." Their ranks include "lots of scholarship students from Germany." MBAs from both populations bond well. As one explains, "I have found my fellow students to be team-oriented and I have made lasting friendships. We have formed informal study groups and we have helped each other through difficult class times."

All classes at UMass Dartmouth are offered in the evenings in order to accommodate students with jobs. Many part-timers juggle family and career responsibilities with work and accordingly spend as little time on campus as possible. "Generally, because the school is

NANCY FLINN LUDWIN, MBA PROGRAM COORDINATOR
285 OLD WESTPORT ROAD, NORTH DARTMOUTH, MA 02747-2300 UNITED STATES
PHONE: 508-999-8543 • FAX: 508-910-6935 • E-MAIL: NFLINN@UMASSD.EDU
WEBSITE: WWW.UMASSD.EDU/CHARLTON/PROGRAMS/MBA.CFM

**FINANCIAL FACTS**
Annual tuition (in-state/out-of-state)
$1,553/$6,074

**ADMISSIONS**
**Admissions Selectivity Rating  60***
% applicants accepted                    87
Application fee                        $35
Regular application deadline  rolling
Regular notification            rolling

oriented towards commuter students and people who take night classes, there really is no campus life for MBA students per se," explains one part-time student. Full-timers socialize more often; they "come together before and after class and perform some teamwork and long discussions. Outside the classroom, there are many social activities, from karate courses to chess, from sport activities to art. It is easy to find many things (to do)."

The main UMass Dartmouth campus is located in the southeast corner of the state, about one hour's drive from Boston and about a half hour away from Providence, Rhode Island. Wholesale trade helps fuel the local economy, as do fishing, cranberry farming, retail, and the remnants of the region's once-robust manufacturing industry.

## Admissions

UMass Dartmouth considers all of the following in evaluating candidates for its MBA program: previous undergraduate and graduate academic record; GMAT scores or scores on an equivalent test; two letters of recommendation (one from a faculty member and one from an employer preferred); a personal statement of 200 to 300 words describing one's academic and career goals; and employment experience. TOEFL scores are required of all international applicants whose first language is not English. UMass Dartmouth offers certificate programs that, for some, provide a back-door entryway to the MBA program. One such student writes, "I came here because they offer certificate programs. I entered a certificate program first, then applied again to be a formal MBA student."

# UNIVERSITY OF MEMPHIS
## FOGELMAN COLLEGE OF BUSINESS AND ECONOMICS

### GENERAL INFORMATION
| | |
|---|---|
| Type of school | public |
| Environment | city |
| Academic calendar | semester |

### SURVEY SAYS...
Friendly students
*Solid preparation in:*
Teamwork
Presentation skills

### STUDENTS
| | |
|---|---|
| Enrollment of parent institution | 20,668 |
| Enrollment of business school | 186 |
| % male/female | 67/33 |
| % part-time | 62 |
| % minorities | 10 |
| % international | 20 |
| Average age at entry | 30 |
| Average years work experience at entry | 5 |

### ACADEMICS
| | |
|---|---|
| **Academic Experience Rating** | **72** |
| Student/faculty ratio | 29:1 |
| Profs interesting rating | 69 |
| Profs accessible rating | 62 |
| % female faculty | 19 |
| % minority faculty | 4 |

### JOINT DEGREES
MBA/JD, 4 years

## Academics

The Fogelman College of Business and Economics at the University of Memphis is a program on the rebound. Students report that "the school had lost its focus during the mid-to-late '90s but has really pulled things together lately." One MBA student writes, "I have been here off and on since 1987, and it is now regaining its previous level." Central to the school's rehabilitation is a recent curriculum overhaul, from which the school identifies four resulting improvements: the creation of a more structured, more focused program stressing integration and thematic links among different courses and areas of study; an upgrade to program prerequisites that relegates remedial work to pre-MBA study; a "beefing up" of the MIS program; and the elimination of concentrations (in order to allow students to complete the program in a reasonable amount of time).

To better serve the majority of students, who attend part-time while working full-time, Fogelman offers most classes in the evenings. Students appreciate the convenience but warn that scheduling can be difficult. One MBA complains, "Every decent class is offered from 5:30 to 7:00 [P.M.] only on Tuesdays and Thursdays." Another student notes, "The scheduling of various courses is determined by each department with no input from the students. Class conflicts between departments offering core courses are unfortunately not taken into consideration." Most classes at Fogelman are required, which complicates matters further; only 3 of the 11 classes required for graduation are electives, and one elective must cover international business.

Fogelman faculty members earn good marks from students, who explain that "the majority of the professors are well-known in their academic fields and are very nice individuals. [They] have gone out of their way to be helpful with questions asked." "[Many professors] have life experiences that relate [to] the material," which "enhances their ability to teach. Once you've studied with these professors, you can understand why they have such well-deserved reputations." Students also appreciate the school's "partnerships with local corporations," which facilitate internships, and also that "tuition is very reasonable."

## Career and Placement

There is no dedicated career office for the Fogelman MBA program; all students at the university utilize the school's Career and Employment Services (C&ES) Office, which "provides leadership and administers university-wide part-time and full-time placement programs; works with local and regional employers to identify part-time jobs and full-time career opportunities for University of Memphis students and alumni, prepares students with proficient job-search skills that will enable them to effectively present themselves to prospective employers, provides an opportunity for prospective employers and University of Memphis students/alumni to meet, and enhances faculty support of and interest in the professional employment process."

## Student Life and Environment

Fogelman welcomes full-time MBA students, but "the college is designed for part-time students with all classes offered in the evening" because part-timers make up the bulk of the population. Accordingly, "it's a commuter school" where "[the] only real campus experience [for most students] is taking classes" and studying. Students grouse that facilities are "in poor shape" and that "more computers are needed in the classrooms." One student writes, "I'm taking a programming class in a room with no computers [and] where the instructor has to bring in his own laptop to teach us." In the asset column, the campus is surprisingly cozy for such a large-scale university. One student explains, "I came from a small, private university in my undergrad and was afraid of the large uni-

CAROL DANEHOWER, DIRECTOR OF MASTER'S PROGRAMS
GRADUATE SCHOOL, ADMINISTRATION BUILDING, ROOM 216, MEMPHIS, TN 38152-3370 U.S.
PHONE: 901-678-2911 • FAX: 901-678-5023
E-MAIL: GRADSCH@MEMPHIS.EDU • WEBSITE: WWW.FCBE.MEMPHIS.EDU

versity feel, but the proximity of all the buildings and all my classes makes the feel less overbearing."

Hometown Memphis is the headquarters of FedEx shipping; it is also a major manufacturing center. The city is home to an NBA franchise, a AAA baseball team, and more great barbecue joints and live music venues than you can count. Tourist attractions include Graceland, Elvis Presley's home and burial place; Beale Street, where blues legend B.B. King (among others) built his reputation as a blues master; and the National Civil Rights Museum, located on the site where Martin Luther King, Jr. was assassinated. Memphis is home to seven colleges and universities.

## Admissions

Applicants to the Fogelman College of Business and Economics must submit official copies of all undergraduate transcripts, official GMAT scores, TOEFL scores (international students), a current resume reflecting at least one year of professional work experience, a personal statement of purpose for pursuing a Fogelman MBA, and a written response to an essay question provided by the school. The school does not require letters of recommendation or an interview; however, letters of recommendation are "suggested." Fogelman recently raised admissions standards; a work requirement was added, the minimum GPA score was increased, and standardized test scores are now required for consideration of admission.

## FINANCIAL FACTS

| | |
|---|---|
| Annual tuition (in-state/out-of-state) | $6,524/$16,370 |
| Fees (in-state/out-of-state) | $44/$3,022 |
| Books and supplies | $10,000 |
| Room & board | $6,000 |

## ADMISSIONS

| | |
|---|---|
| Admissions Selectivity Rating | 86 |
| # of applications received | 100 |
| % applicants accepted | 39 |
| % acceptees attending | 100 |
| Average GMAT | 530 |
| Range of GMAT | 530–700 |
| Average GPA | 3.2 |
| TOEFL required of international students? | yes |
| Minimum TOEFL (paper/computer) | 550/213 |
| Application fee | $35 |
| International application fee | $60 |
| Regular application deadline | 7/1 |
| Regular notification | rolling |
| Deferment available? | yes |
| Maximum length of deferment | 1 year |
| Non-fall admissions? | yes |

## EMPLOYMENT PROFILE

| | |
|---|---|
| Career Rating | 63 |
| Average starting salary | $63,800 |

# University of Miami
## School of Business

## Academics

A rigorous MBA program with a strong international focus, the University of Miami School of Business prides itself on attracting a diverse and multinational faculty and student body, and on offering challenging and relevant coursework for today's global professional. For students who did not study business as an undergraduate, the school offers a full-time, 48-unit program, which must be completed over the course of two years. Those with an undergraduate business degree may apply for the accelerated one-year program, which requires the completion of 32 credits over the course of two semesters. Each of these programs is targeted at young professionals, who have graduated from college within the past five years.

Both the one-year and two-year programs boast a lockstep curriculum, in which the entire entering class moves through required coursework in unison. As a result, students form strong professional, scholarly, and social relationships with their classmates. On this campus, a third of students hail from outside the United States and comprise "a wide range of ages," so these relationships form an integral part of the learning experience at the University of Miami. A current student enthuses, "fellow classmates interest me, challenge me, and contribute to a productive class/team environment." With a "small student to teacher ratio," the environment is truly collaborative and "people work together on every aspect of education and life."

Elective classes are available to students in both programs. While students say the program is excellent, some feel it could be improved by becoming "much more challenging" and incorporating a heavier workload. Students may choose to focus their electives to receive a concentration in accounting, computer information systems, finance, international business, management, management science, or marketing. In general, students have high praises for University of Miami professors, especially for those in their area of concentration. One student reports, "The professors in my chosen concentration of management science are outstanding and have prepared me very well for my career post-graduation. The school has afforded me opportunities within management science that are not available elsewhere and has helped me to pursue different career paths."

## Career & Placement

The Ziff Career Center at the University of Miami is available to graduate business students and offers career advising, online and on-campus recruiting, a career library, and periodic workshops on resume writing and job search strategy. Boasting the sixth largest alumni network in the world, University of Miami students have access to a large, international employment base. As the program is targeted toward younger students who graduated from college within the past five years, "work experience is, for all practical purposes, nonexistent" within the business school student body. Therefore, the career office tends to focus their efforts on placing recent grads in entry-level management positions. Students report that, "on-campus recruiting is sufficient for students with no real work experience," while more advanced professional positions are harder to come by.

DANIELA MUNIZ, ASSOCIATE DIRECTOR
PO BOX 248505, CORAL GABLES, FL 33124-6524 UNITED STATES
PHONE: 305-284-4607 • FAX: 305-284-1878 • E-MAIL: MBA@MIAMI.EDU
WEBSITE: WWW.BUS.MIAMI.EDU/GRAD

## Student Life and Environment

For a business student, you couldn't ask for a more comfortable lifestyle and environment than at the University of Miami. With a "perfect location" on the university's Coral Gables campus, the business school is housed in an "absolutely beautiful" $24-million facility, in which, "each classroom has big, comfy leather executive chairs for the students and great computers for the professor." There is even "a lounge for graduate business students that has free coffee and bagels every morning."

The campus vibe is highly social, as "most everyone moved to Miami from different states/cities, and it was very easy to make new friends who will last a lifetime." On top of that, "There is a great student run organization, Graduate Business Student Association, that arranges and sponsors many events. It is easy to meet new people and make many friends." For those who like to get involved, "There are clubs for every concentration plus a few others. A lot of the students form intramural teams for flag football, soccer, and softball." Students are quick to mention that "The football team is a big deal here and everyone goes to the games together, and the business school always has a tailgate before the games." Situated in Miami, the party capital of the Southeast, "there is a very active social life both on and off campus," as students further enjoy world-class cultural and recreational opportunities—not to mention, perfect weather—in their immediate vicinity.

## Admissions

To apply to the MBA program, students must submit a completed application, official transcripts from any undergraduate and postgraduate coursework, a current resume, one letter of recommendation, official GMAT score reports, and TOEFL test scores for non-native speakers of English. Students are evaluated on the strength of all application materials. Students wishing to enter the two-year program do not need to have undergraduate business degrees. However, those wishing to enter the accelerated one-year program must have an undergraduate business degree. Admissions decisions are made on a rolling basis until the class is full, though students are encouraged to apply at least two months before the beginning of the term. Students who wish to be considered for scholarships, fellowships, or graduate assistantship are advised to apply early.

### FINANCIAL FACTS

| | |
|---|---|
| Annual tuition | $28,992 |
| Room & board | $8,906 |
| Fees | $498 |
| Books and supplies | $1,080 |
| % of students receiving aid | 65 |
| % of first-year students receiving aid | 66 |
| % of students receiving loans | 40 |
| % of students receiving grants | 47 |
| Average award package | $27,910 |
| Average grant | $16,432 |
| Average student loan debt | $49,225 |

### ADMISSIONS

| | |
|---|---|
| **Admissions Selectivity Rating** | **79** |
| # of applications received | 357 |
| % applicants accepted | 72 |
| % acceptees attending | 43 |
| Average GMAT | 605 |
| Range of GMAT | 560–650 |
| Average GPA | 3.29 |
| TOEFL required of international students? | yes |
| Minimum TOEFL (paper/computer) | 550/213 |
| Application fee | $50 |
| International application fee | $50 |
| Regular application deadline | rolling |
| Regular notification | rolling |
| Deferment available? | yes |
| Maximum length of deferment | 1 year |
| Non-fall admissions? | yes |
| Need-blind admissions? | yes |

### EMPLOYMENT PROFILE

| Career Rating | 67 | Grads employed by field: | % | avg. salary: |
|---|---|---|---|---|
| **Primary source of full-time job acceptances** | | Finance | 46 | $60,799 |
| | | Human Resources | 2 | $45,000 |
| School-facilitated activities | 31 (53%) | Marketing | 15 | $69,286 |
| Graduate-facilitated activities | 17 (29%) | MIS | 2 | $67,200 |
| Unknown | 11 (18%) | Operations | 2 | $80,000 |
| | | Consulting | 9 | $61,000 |
| Average starting salary | $63,156 | General Management | 17 | $68,000 |
| Percent employed | 35 | Other | 7 | $52,000 |

# UNIVERSITY OF MICHIGAN—ANN ARBOR
## STEPHEN M. ROSS SCHOOL OF BUSINESS

## Academics

The University of Michigan Business School made history in 2004 when it accepted the largest gift to any U.S. business school—$100 million—from New York real estate developer and alumnus Stephen M. Ross. In honor of the unprecedented gift, the school was renamed the Stephen M. Ross School of Business. Early in 2005, the Ross School announced plans to build a new $145 million facility to support its action-based curriculum. This announcement came on the heels of the school rolling out for the Class of 2006 a revised MBA curriculum. Benefits include carefully sequenced core courses, more electives, and the opportunity to focus on specific areas of interest prior to internship interviews.

Most students agree that the program was and remains "extremely strong in corporate strategy, entrepreneurial studies, management accounting, marketing, organizational behavior, nonprofit organizations, social venturing, and venture-capital/private-equity/entrepreneurial finance." Because of the size of the program, Michigan is able to offer a wide variety of choices—more than 100 electives in nine disciplines by the school's reckoning, plus entrepreneurial studies and plenty of dual-degree options. In addition, because the Business School does not require students to specialize, MBAs "have a lot of flexibility in the second-year schedule to focus on the classes [they] want." Students must first complete a rigorous core [curriculum], however, before moving on to electives. For full-time students, the core takes up their entire first year with 10 courses "in elemental business functions" as well as a seven-week Multidisciplinary Action Project (MAP). Students say, "[The program] essentially allows us to get real-world experience and learn a heck [of a] lot while we're doing it." MBAs add that the workload is fairly heavy. One student reports, "We take five classes per semester, and each class usually meets twice a week for one and [one] half hours at a time. For every one and [one] half hour class, there's probably about that much preparation time that is put in outside of class." The evening MBA core is no less demanding, although it does not include a MAP Team-Project experience. As a major research institution, U of M gives its MBAs access to world-class research facilities including institutes in emerging and transitional economies worldwide, entrepreneurial studies, environmental management, and manufacturing. Students especially praise the environmental management and transitional economies worldwide institutes. MBAs say, "[The] U of M's self-positioning [is] on the cutting edge of corporate-responsibility issues."

## Career and Placement

"[The university] literally [has] the largest alumni network of any business school in the world." U of M's Student Career Services Office at the Ross School of Business, serves both undergraduates and graduate students. Among 2003 graduates, approximately three-fifths reported that they found positions through school-affiliated channels (on-campus recruiting, 35 percent; on-campus job posting, 17 percent; return to place of first-year summer internship, 10 percent).

Top employers of Michigan MBAs include Citigroup, Booz Allen Hamilton Inc., Dell, Inc., McKinsey & Company, Deloitte Consulting, Johnson & Johnson, A Family of Companies, American Express Company, JPMorgan Chase & Co., A.T. Kearney, Inc., Eli Lilly & Company, Bain & Company, Inc., Ford Motor Company, Medtronic, Inc., 3M Company, Cummins Inc., DiamondCluster International, Inc., General Mills, Inc.,

JAMES P. HAYES, DIRECTOR OF ADMISSIONS
701 TAPPAN STREET, D2260, ANN ARBOR, MI 48109-1234 UNITED STATES
PHONE: 734-763-5796 • FAX: 734-763-7804
E-MAIL: ROSSMBA@UMICH.EDU • WEBSITE: WWW.BUS.UMICH.EDU

Guidant Corporation, Intel Corporation, Kraft Foods Inc., Lehman Brothers, Microsoft Corporation, National City Corporation and S.C. Johnson & Son, Inc. The desirability of U of M MBAs can be seen in the geographic diversity of their first-job locations. While one in three remains in the Midwest, others head everywhere from the mid-Atlantic (9 percent) to the Pacific Coast (13 percent) to companies outside the United States (12 percent).

## Student Life and Environment

"If you like college towns, you will love Ann Arbor," students at U of M agree. MBAs add that "there's happy hour every Thursday, tailgates every Football Saturday, and numerous club parties in between." The hub of campus life is the school's athletic program; one student explains, "You can't beat Michigan football, hockey, and basketball. Tailgates make a great way to bond in the spirit of the university." The city also "offers a lot of entertainment options like jazz, dance clubs, and restaurants." About the only drawback to Ann Arbor life is that "the weather is cold in the winter, and students do spend too much time studying because there's not much else to do when it's 15 degrees out." The MBA program offers "abundant opportunities to get involved, from professional to social clubs, newspaper, admissions, and career counseling. There's even a wine-tasting club." The program also "provides lots of opportunities for spouses to get together. It also has joint programs with other schools in the university, which provide meaningful activities." All in all, students agree that the program provides a "good work-life balance. We work quite hard, but on Thursday evenings, practically all MBAs flock to the b-school happy-hour bar, Mitch's. No weekend goes by without lots of prep for class, several group meetings, and at least one party or social/fun activity. We live the two years at b-school [like they] are the last of our lives. We've gotta do everything while having fun!"

## Admissions

Applications to the University of Michigan MBA program must include undergraduate transcripts, GMAT test scores, TOEFL test scores (international students—see website for exceptions), letters of recommendation, a personal statement, and a resume. The school also looks at an applicant's track record of success, clarity of goals, and management and leadership potential. The program does require previous work experience. Interviews are "highly recommended" but not required. Minority recruitment efforts include membership in the Consortium for Graduate Study in Management; the UpClose Program a weekend for prospective minority students; Robert F. Toigo Fellowships in Finance, Management Leadership for Tomorrow (MLT)-mentorship opportunities, National Society of Hispanic MBA Conference, National Black MBA Conference, faculty and alumni outreach and a student phonathon.

### PROMINENT ALUMNI
John M. Devine, Vice Chair and CFO, General Motors Corp; Mary Kay Haben, Group VP, Kraft North America; President, Kraft Cheese; John W. Madigan, Chair and CEO, Tribune Company; Stephen W. Sanger, Chair and CEO, General Mills; Robert K. Shaye, Co-Chair and Co-CEO, New Line Cinema

### FINANCIAL FACTS
| | |
|---|---|
| Annual tuition | $33,800 |
| Fees | $189 |
| Books and supplies | $7,730 |
| Room & board | $9,752 |
| % of students receiving aid | 75 |
| % of first-year students receiving aid | 75 |
| % of students receiving loans | 47 |
| % of students receiving grants | 48 |
| Average award package | $56,655 |
| Average grant | $11,044 |
| Average student loan debt | $61,600 |

### ADMISSIONS
| | |
|---|---|
| Admissions Selectivity Rating | 96 |
| # of applications received | 2,067 |
| % applicants accepted | 32 |
| % acceptees attending | 63 |
| Average GMAT | 690 |
| Range of GMAT | 640–740 |
| Average GPA | 3.3 |
| TOEFL required of international students? | yes |
| Minimum TOEFL (paper/computer) | 600/250 |
| Application fee | $180 |
| International application fee | $180 |
| Regular application deadline | 11/4 |
| Regular notification | 1/5 |
| Application deadline/notification | |
| Round 1: | 11/1 / 1/15 |
| Round 2: | 1/7 / 3/15 |
| Round 3: | 3/1 / 5/15 |
| Deferment available? | yes |
| Maximum length of deferment | 1 year |
| Transfer students accepted? | yes |
| Transfer application policy | |
| Transfer applicants are welcome to apply, but no credits will transfer into our program. | |
| Need-blind admissions? | yes |

### APPLICANTS ALSO LOOK AT
Duke U., Northwestern U., The U. of Chicago, U. of Pennsylvania

### EMPLOYMENT PROFILE
| Career Rating | 99 | Grads employed by field: | % | avg. salary: |
|---|---|---|---|---|
| Primary source of full-time job acceptances | | Finance | 34 | $90,850 |
| | | Marketing | 24 | $85,378 |
| School-facilitated activities | 244 (68%) | Operations | 3 | $90,000 |
| Graduate-facilitated activities | 110 (31%) | Strategic Planning | 3 | $84,679 |
| Unknown | 4 (1%) | Consulting | 22 | $104,267 |
| | | General Management | 6 | $90,059 |
| Average starting salary | $91,835 | Other | 8 | $84,810 |

# UNIVERSITY OF MICHIGAN—FLINT
## SCHOOL OF MANAGEMENT

### GENERAL INFORMATION
| | |
|---|---|
| Type of school | public |
| Environment | city |
| Academic calendar | semesters |

### SURVEY SAYS...
Smart classrooms
*Solid preparation in:*
Communication/interpersonal skills
Presentation skills

### STUDENTS
| | |
|---|---|
| Enrollment of business school | 167 |
| % part-time | 100 |
| Average age at entry | 31 |
| Average years work experience at entry | 3 |

### ACADEMICS
| | |
|---|---|
| **Academic Experience Rating** | **68** |
| Student/faculty ratio | 11:1 |
| Profs interesting rating | 74 |
| Profs accessible rating | 71 |
| % female faculty | 27 |
| % minority faculty | 13 |

### JOINT DEGREES
BA/MBA, 5 years

## Academics

The School of Management at University of Michigan—Flint offers its entirely part-time student body two MBA options: a traditional MBA conducted on the Flint campus, and the NetPlus! MBA, a "mixed-mode" program that combines online instruction with classroom interaction. The NetPlus! calendar includes a mandatory campus session one weekend every six weeks.

U of M Flint's traditional MBA program is unusual among part-time programs, in that, it is cohort-based, which "enables students to develop a strong support network for personal and professional development beyond the time they are in the MBA program." This 18-course program does not allow students to develop an area of specialization—in fact, it allows for only two electives, chosen from a limited list of options—preferring instead to emphasize generalization. This program "provides [students] with a solid foundation for making decisions, which has an impact beyond one functional area." Students in the program explain that it is "outstanding in every way; however, the work involved to get through the program is incredible!" One student says, "I still question whether I'll make it through, with all the other work, home, and parenting responsibilities of life competing for [my] time."

Students seeking more flexibility and convenience should consider the NetPlus! MBA because it allows students to view online lectures "anytime [and] anywhere." In this program, each 12-week term commences with a one-day on-campus orientation; subsequent campus visits are required three and nine weeks into each term. On-campus sessions mean that students reap the benefits of cohort-based instruction. One participant explains, "The mixed-mode concept provides networking opportunities, classroom interaction, and flexible scheduling for studies, assignments, and exams." However, "all students and professors new to the program experience behavioral challenges switching from a traditional classroom environment to an online classroom dependent on evolving technology;" some professors are reportedly better at handling the technical demands of the program than are others. Students point out that "this is a new program. There have been some kinks, but overall, I am impressed with the attention to detail in administering this program."

In both programs, U of M—Flint features "committed, interested professors who are willing to assist and provide up-to-date information and discussion on today's business trends and events; extremely up-to-date textbooks with recent business case studies and trends incorporated into the syllabus;" and perhaps best of all, "an affordable tuition." The cherry on the sundae: "The name 'University of Michigan' on a resume is valuable to employers."

## Career and Placement

The U of M—Flint Career Development Center serves all undergraduate and graduate students at the university. Because MBA students are already employed full-time, relatively few use the office's services.

D. Nicol Taylor, MBA, MBA Program Coordinator
School of Management, UM-Flint, 3139 William South White Building, 303 East
Kearsley Street, Flint, MI 48502-1950 United States
Phone: 810-762-3163 • Fax: 810-237-6685
E-mail: UMFlintMBA1@umich.edu • Website: www.mba.umflint.edu

## Student Life and Environment

U of M—Flint is "a commuter college with very little life at the school," students say. That's especially true for students in the NetPlus! program, who only see each other a few times a year. One participant in the program explains, "The online concept minimizes school-activity involvement unless you are local to the area. Most students commute to the town for weekend residencies and spend the majority of the time in the classroom or dining in the evening with classmates." Those who travel note with approval that "there are excellent discounts provided with area hotels through the school program. Breakfast and lunch are catered-in to increase class networking time, and many professors in the school of business join us for the meals providing additional networking opportunities."

Those amenities minimize the time that students spend venturing about Flint, which most see as a very good thing. "The city is not the best," say students of this "mostly unsafe" town, "but the campus and especially the business building is well-equipped and very nice." The program's facility "has state-of-the-art technology for presentations and Internet access. It makes it easy to prepare professional projects for class." One student observes, "The facilities are excellent. They are clean and consistent with what you see in top corporations. You feel like you are in a business meeting and not just a classroom."

## Admissions

All applicants to the School of Management at U of M—Flint must provide the school with official copies of all undergraduate and graduate transcripts, GMAT scores, TOEFL scores (international students), three letters of recommendation (preferably from employers and/or professors), a statement of purpose, and a resume. One year of finite mathematics or college algebra is a prerequisite. A background in statistics, economics, or accounting is not required, but it is helpful in getting the entire class quickly up to speed. Work experience is preferred; the average student arrives with three years of professional experience.

### FINANCIAL FACTS

| | |
|---|---|
| Annual tuition | $8,694 |
| Fees | $316 |
| Books and supplies | $258 |
| Average award package | $15,472 |
| Average grant | $2,273 |

### ADMISSIONS

| | |
|---|---|
| **Admissions Selectivity Rating** | **71** |
| # of applications received | 72 |
| % applicants accepted | 85 |
| % acceptees attending | 87 |
| Average GMAT | 528 |
| Range of GMAT | 460–590 |
| Average GPA | 3.18 |
| TOEFL required of international students? | yes |
| Minimum TOEFL (paper/computer) | 550/213 |
| Application fee | $55 |
| International application fee | $55 |
| Regular application deadline | rolling |
| Regular notification | rolling |
| Deferment available? | yes |
| Maximum length of deferment | 1 year |
| Transfer students accepted? | yes |
| Transfer application policy AACSB-accredited, "B" or better, grad level, 9 credit hours only, not part of any other degree program. | |
| Non-fall admissions? | yes |
| Need-blind admissions? | yes |

# UNIVERSITY OF MINNESOTA
## CARLSON SCHOOL OF MANAGEMENT

### GENERAL INFORMATION
| | |
|---|---|
| Type of school | public |
| Environment | metropolis |
| Academic calendar | semester |

### SURVEY SAYS...
Students love Minneapolis, MN
Smart classrooms
*Solid preparation in:*
Marketing
Teamwork
Communication/interpersonal skills

### STUDENTS
| | |
|---|---|
| Enrollment of parent institution | 50,954 |
| Enrollment of business school | 1,933 |
| % male/female | 77/23 |
| % out-of-state | 73 |
| % part-time | 90 |
| % minorities | 6 |
| % international | 36 |
| Average age at entry | 29 |
| Average years work experience at entry | 5 |

### ACADEMICS
| | |
|---|---|
| **Academic Experience Rating** | **91** |
| Student/faculty ratio | 15:1 |
| Profs interesting rating | 84 |
| Profs accessible rating | 85 |
| % female faculty | 22 |
| % minority faculty | 20 |

### JOINT DEGREES
JD/MBA, 4 years; MHA/MBA, 3 years; MD/MBA, 5 years

### PROMINENT ALUMNI
Charles W. Mooty, CEO, International Dairy Queen; William G. Van Dyke, Chair, President & CEO, Donaldson Company, Inc.; Curtis C. Nelson, President & COO, Carlson Companies; Robert A. Kierlin, Chair, Fastenal Company; Barbara J. Mowry, President & CEO, TMC Consulting

## Academics

The Carlson School of Management MBA program "combines research and reality" in a curriculum that capitalizes on university resources and the school's urban location. The business school's 11 research centers have elevated it to the nation's 13th-ranked institution in business-research productivity, according to the school. MBAs benefit from Carlson cutting-edge work, but their greatest enthusiasm is for the "reality" portion of the equation. They love the program's emphasis on experiential learning, especially through its four enterprise programs: Carlson Funds Enterprise, Carlson Consulting Enterprise, Carlson Ventures Enterprise, and Carlson Brand Enterprise. These programs "allow students to get real-world experience before entering the job market, while working with local and national companies" through their "student-led businesses within the school."

The Carlson School's "unbelievably integrated curriculum is one of the school's major strengths. Carlson breeds outstanding generalists who are capable of working well in teams." Course work commences with an intensive—some say too intensive—core. One student warns, "The workload during the first semester is too much. It's seven classes (19 credits), two required workshops, Leadership Edge (a co curricular program designed to help students cultivate their leadership skills), Career Exploration (a career conference), and the hunt for a summer internship." Students generally survive the grind, and the pressure lessens somewhat thereafter. Throughout the first year, "there is a huge focus on group projects. Teams are hand-picked before classes begin to ensure a good mix of first-year students. These teams work on over a dozen projects together during the first semester; plus, they often form strong friendships while socializing after helping each other with homework. The school places significant emphasis on networking with fellow students, faculty, and alumni," according to students.

Students also love that the focus of the university "is on creating leaders. There's a real emphasis on so-called 'soft skills' such as, negotiations, group dynamics, and new technology sales." One student says, "Coming into the program I expected that most, if not all of my classes would be focused on finance, statistics, or operations. But having been encouraged and having taken the opportunity to take these soft-skill classes, I believe I am much better qualified to work as a manager." The program has "a very strong brand-management faculty" and "is a prominent leader in strategic and marketing research." The Carlson School "also has a very strong finance and accounting department."

## Career and Placement

Carlson MBAs appreciate their program—dedicated Career Services Office—the Graduate Business Career Center (GBCC)—and explain that "the initiatives introduced by the GBCC to build skills such as networking, interviewing, and leadership are one of the great strengths of the program." The office "counsels each and every student one-on-one on a constant basis, giving feedback on strengths and weaknesses." Students report that "alumni connections and career opportunities within the Twin Cities area [of Minneapolis/St. Paul] specifically are strong." However, some students feel that "the GBCC needs to work with more companies outside the Twin Cities as well as working with companies that are smaller, providing more diverse on-campus opportunities." Employers of Carlson School MBAs include 3M, Boston Scientific Scimed, Ernst & Young, Cargill, Carlson Companies, Deloitte Consulting, Ecolab, General Electric, General Mills, Guidant, Honeywell, Johnson & Johnson, Kimberly-Clark, Kurt Salmon Associates, McKinsey, Medtronic, Multifoods, Northwest Airlines, Philip Morris, RBC Capital Markets, RBC Dain Rauscher, Samsung Electronics, Taylor Corporation, Target, U.S. Bancorp, and U.S. Bancorp Piper Jaffray.

Dustin Cornwell, Director of Admissions & Recruiting
321 Nineteenth Avenue South, Suite 2-210, Minneapolis, MN 55455 United States
Phone: 612-625-5555 • Fax: 612-626-7785
E-mail: full-timembainfo@carlsonschool.umn.edu • Website: www.carlsonschool.umn.edu

## Student Life and Environment

The Carlson School has substantial populations of both full-time and part-time MBAs. The full-timers take a mix of daytime and evening courses; part-time students attend courses in the evenings and Saturdays. The part-timers have less available time to participate in non academic activities, but all students enjoy the "excellent camaraderie between students and between students and faculty." Students say, "We have lounge parties every Thursday, monthly interaction with the alumni base, the MBA Follies (a talent show), and almost-daily speakers or company information sessions." One student reports, "I have made many friends at the school, and we spend quite a bit of time together, whether it is by going out on the town, dinners at [our] homes with our significant others, competing in intramural sports, or by getting a block of tickets to cheer on the university's football, basketball, or hockey teams."

The full-timers, though, are hard-pressed to enjoy extracurriculars during their first semester because the core is extremely demanding. One student writes, "During the first semester (for example, the 'core'), life is totally focused on studies. It was all day on the weekdays, and then I usually studied every evening from 6:00 P.M. until 12:00 or 1:00 A.M. I also studied both weekend days, trying to take one weekend night off to do something with my fiancée or friends outside of the program. Total time spent studying or preparing [for courses] (outside of class) was about 65 to 75 hours a week." The second year is a little better because "during the second year, less time is spent on studying, but students are still very busy focusing on internships, job searching, [and] working in Carlson Enterprise programs."

The Carlson School's recently constructed facilities "offer a great environment for learning with wireless and other new technology enhancing the educational experience." Students comment that "the campus is large but nice. It sits on both sides of the Mississippi River and is very attractive." Students with families complain that "the school is not really set-up to be kid- or spouse-friendly. Few people bring their spouse or kids to extracurricular activities."

## Admissions

The University of Minnesota Admissions Office considers applicants' undergraduate records, GMAT scores, TOEFL or IELTS scores (international students), letters of recommendation from employers and/or professors, a personal statement, and a resume. An interview is "required," and "a minimum of two years' work experience is strongly recommended." The school reports that "Minnesota Boulevard is a group of locally based companies working jointly with the Carlson School to bring minority MBA candidates to Twin Cities for jobs, mentoring, and the MBA. The school maintains close ties with the National Black MBA Association (NBMBAA) and NSHMBA, who help and call students for recruiting, scholarships, and retention."

### FINANCIAL FACTS

| | |
|---|---|
| Annual tuition (in-state/out-of-state) | $21,300/$30,320 |
| Fees | $2,500 |
| Books and supplies | $4,000 |
| Room & board (on/off-campus) | $13,000/$15,000 |
| % of students receiving aid | 77 |
| % of students receiving loans | 41 |
| % of students receiving grants | 63 |
| Average award package | $29,260 |
| Average grant | $19,200 |
| Average student loan debt | $41,877 |

### ADMISSIONS

| | |
|---|---|
| Admissions Selectivity Rating | 90 |
| # of applications received | 453 |
| % applicants accepted | 48 |
| % acceptees attending | 44 |
| Average GMAT | 650 |
| Range of GMAT | 610–700 |
| Average GPA | 3.33 |
| TOEFL required of international students? | yes |
| Minimum TOEFL (paper/computer) | 580/240 |
| Application fee | $60 |
| International application fee | $90 |
| Regular application deadline | 4/15 |
| Regular notification | 5/15 |
| Application deadline/notification | |
| Round 1: | 12/15 / 2/15 |
| Round 2: | 2/15 / 4/15 |
| Round 3: | 4/15 / 5/15 |
| Early decision program? | yes |
| ED Deadline/notification | 12/15 / 2/15 |
| Deferment available? | yes |
| Maximum length of deferment | 1 year |
| Need-blind admissions? | yes |

### EMPLOYMENT PROFILE

| Career Rating | 92 | Grads employed by field: | % | avg. salary: |
|---|---|---|---|---|
| Primary source of full-time job acceptances | | Finance | 24 | $78,100 |
| | | Marketing | 33 | $80,574 |
| School-facilitated activities | 68 (77%) | MIS | 1 | NR |
| Graduate-facilitated activities | 20 (23%) | Operations | 7 | $75,417 |
| | | Consulting | 12 | $93,732 |
| Average starting salary | $82,436 | General Management | 3 | NR |
| Percent employed | 97 | Other | 8 | NR |

# UNIVERSITY OF MISSISSIPPI
## SCHOOL OF BUSINESS ADMINISTRATION

### GENERAL INFORMATION
| | |
|---|---|
| Type of school | public |
| Environment | village |
| Academic calendar | semester |

### SURVEY SAYS...
Students love University, MS
Friendly students

### STUDENTS
| | |
|---|---|
| Enrollment of parent institution | 13,500 |
| Enrollment of business school | 96 |
| % male/female | 59/41 |
| % out-of-state | 41 |
| % minorities | 4 |
| % international | 8 |
| Average age at entry | 26 |
| Average years work experience at entry | 2 |

### ACADEMICS
| | |
|---|---|
| **Academic Experience Rating** | **63** |
| Student/faculty ratio | 30:1 |
| Profs interesting rating | 63 |
| Profs accessible rating | 80 |
| % female faculty | 18 |

## Academics

The University of Mississippi—known affectionately as "Ole Miss" to its many students and supporters—offers students two MBA options. The first is an intensive, one-year full-time MBA, which does not require post-undergraduate professional experience for admission; the other is the two-year professional MBA for working adults, which gives strong preference to students with at least two years of post-undergraduate business-related employment.

Ole Miss' one-year program runs 11 months, commencing in July and ending in May. The curriculum consists of 13 prescribed courses, taught cohort-style with an emphasis on "the integration of subjects into real business applications." Students warn that the program is intense. As one explains, "Overall, you have to be very serious if you want to be in a one-year program. Don't let the kind recruiters fool you: You are in for hell if you are not 100 percent committed...There is hardly any time to breathe. This is only for the extremely serious." Instructors "expect a lot out of us," and even "the administration is concerned with our performance and takes measures to continually monitor our progression through the classes. Overall, the academic experience is rigorous." One student concurs, "The program could use more breaks. Or, they could lengthen it to ease the stress."

The part-time MBA at Ole Miss is more flexible, using "alternate methods of delivering course content" that include interactive CD-ROMs, DVDs, videoconferencing, conference calls, and Internet learning. Some on-campus sessions are required, but most of the program can be completed remotely. In both the part-time and full-time program, "Professors all have business backgrounds and have been tenured for a long time, or they have short academic careers and long, successful business careers in the fields they teach." Instructors typically employ "real-world examples and tie your education from them into your own work experiences. Dictation seldom happens. Discussion of the assigned readings is the primary classroom focus."

## Career and Placement

Ole Miss MBAs receive career support from the university's Career Center. Students report that many of the best career opportunities come via the alumni network, which is "very supportive. The Ole Miss 'brand' is well-respected in the Southeast." Employers that recruit on the Ole Miss campus include Acxiom, Allstate, Bancorp South, FedEx, Harrah's, IBM Consulting, International Paper, Regions Bank, and the Tennessee Valley Authority.

## Student Life and Environment

The swift pace of the full-time MBA program means that many students "study so much that it is hard to have a life. But when there are small breaks, the potential to have a great time is definitely there." First and foremost, is Ole Miss football and the requisite tailgate parties beforehand, but there's much more to the social scene than sports. The school "offers a wide variety of activities socially and academically that you can become involved in. This place has a lot of great traditions." Students appreciate the Ole Miss grounds, which one describes as "a walking campus that promotes and produces beautiful people!"

Dr. John Holleman, Director of MBA Administration
319 Conner Hall, University, MS 38677 United States
Phone: 662-915-5483 • Fax: 662-915-7968 • E-mail: jholleman@bus.olemiss.edu
Website: www.mba.olemiss.edu

Hometown Oxford is a small, Southern college town distinguished by the university and the residences of several famous writers, including John Grisham. The town has become a travel destination for many, not only for Ole Miss sporting events but also for festivals such as the Double Decker Arts Festival and conferences as the Faulkner & Yoknapatawpha Conference (named after the author William Faulkner, who made his home in Oxford, and the fictional county in which much of his work is set). The city of Memphis is just 70 miles to the north.

Full-timers at Ole Miss tend to be "very young. The majority are 22 years old. Some have had internships, but none have actually worked. It's very difficult to have a discussion about business if you've never been involved in one. The few students with work experience talk 95 percent of the time." The student community is close. As one student explains, "One thing about going through an MBA 'boot camp' like this is that you come together very quickly. Because you're all suffering together, people are very friendly and quick to help you out."

## Admissions

All applicants to the full-time MBA program at Ole Miss must provide an official transcript of undergraduate work showing a minimum 3.0 GPA for the final 60 semesters hours of academic work; an official GMAT score report (the school lists 550 as the cut-off for "acceptable" scores); two letters of recommendation; and a 400-word personal statement of purpose. Students who have not completed prerequisite course work in undergraduate business disciplines will be required to complete such courses successfully before commencing work on their graduate degrees. International students must meet all of the above requirements and submit TOEFL scores (minimum acceptable score is 600). Applicants to the professional MBA program "with two or more years of post-baccalaureate degree professional work experience" receive "particular consideration" from the Admissions Committee. The professional MBA program is "very competitive."

## FINANCIAL FACTS

| | |
|---|---|
| Annual tuition (in-state/out-of-state) | $7,000/$13,000 |
| Books and supplies | $5,000 |
| Room & board (on/off-campus) | $8,800/$10,000 |
| Average grant | $1,469 |

## ADMISSIONS

| | |
|---|---|
| Admissions Selectivity Rating | 81 |
| # of applications received | 225 |
| % applicants accepted | 45 |
| % acceptees attending | 55 |
| Average GMAT | 550 |
| Range of GMAT | 500–610 |
| Average GPA | 3.0 |
| TOEFL required of international students? | yes |
| Minimum TOEFL (paper) | 600 |
| Regular application deadline | 4/1 |
| Regular notification | 5/1 |
| Non-fall admissions? | yes |
| Need-blind admissions? | yes |

## EMPLOYMENT PROFILE

| Career Rating | 65 | Grads employed by field: | % | avg. salary: |
|---|---|---|---|---|
| Average starting salary | $52,500 | Accounting | 5 | NR |
| | | Finance | 15 | NR |
| | | Marketing | 15 | NR |
| | | MIS | 20 | NR |
| | | Consulting | 10 | NR |
| | | Entrepreneurship | 5 | NR |
| | | General Management | 5 | NR |
| | | Internet/New Media | 25 | NR |

# UNIVERSITY OF MISSOURI—COLUMBIA
## COLLEGE OF BUSINESS

### GENERAL INFORMATION
Type of school                public
Environment                   city
Academic calendar           semester

### SURVEY SAYS...
Happy students
Smart classrooms
*Solid preparation in:*
Marketing
Presentation skills

### STUDENTS
Enrollment of parent
  institution                27,000
Enrollment of business school  204
% male/female                 65/35
% out-of-state                   15
% part-time                       5
% minorities                      4
% international                  34
Average age at entry             25
Average years work experience
  at entry                        2

### ACADEMICS
**Academic Experience Rating    86**
Student/faculty ratio          20:1
Profs interesting rating         83
Profs accessible rating          76

### JOINT DEGREES
MBA/MSIE, 3 years; MBA/JD, 4
years; MBA/MHA, 3 years

## Academics

Boasting modern facilities, a cool campus culture, talented students, and superbly friendly faculty and staff, the University of Missouri—Columbia is a great place to earn a degree while enjoying the best aspects of academic life. With just 200 graduate students in the business program each year, "class sizes are kept low so there is a lot of student-teacher interaction." As a result, the academic environment is highly supportive, and "the professors are wonderful at providing help outside of the classroom for both class-related items and professional development." In addition, students dole out praise for the school's super-friendly administrators, whom they describe as "very congenial and efficient" as well as highly responsive to student needs. A current student attests, "The administration has a great flow of communication. I can go to them when I need assistance with class work or if I simply want advice."

While the majority of students focus on management, marketing, finance, or management information systems, "Mizzou" likes to stay on top of the trends—"whenever a new market trend emerges, it is incorporated into the classroom environment, either in a class or in a seminar." Coursework is just one component of this highly integrated program, which also draws heavily on teamwork, networking, and hands-on projects. For example, the school boasts "something called the Integrated Functional Perspective project, [where] students work together without a classroom setting and do a case analysis that involves several functions, instead of simply the one that you are studying." In general, Mizzou's "programs are designed to encourage networking between students, alumni, and faculty"; work outside the classroom is as important as work within it. Students dole out endless praise for the caliber of their talented classmates, whom they characterize as "very active in the program, extremely bright, hardworking, and [possess] diverse talents and career aspirations that make for a great learning environment."

Given the focus on extracurricular learning, Mizzou "strikes a great balance between exceptional in-class learning while not making the workload too rigorous." Students feel they are definitely learning techniques that will be essential outside the classroom. "However, the reasonably manageable workload provides the opportunity to do outside research and independent study that pertain to my niche interests." Even so, don't expect to coast through the program. Mizzou MBAs definitely keep busy with "a great amount of networking, socializing, teamwork, and career development activities outside of the classroom. So, when you factor in all the MBA-related events, classes, studying, and outside events, you will spend 40 hours a week involved with the program."

## Career and Placement

The MBA program at Mizzou "does a great job of polishing young businesspeople into professionals," and students at the University of Missouri feel confident entering the workforce after graduation. In addition to coursework, "professional development opportunities add the finesse that is needed to succeed in a competitive business environment."

Through the Career Services Office, students have access to career and internship fairs, career-building workshops, and online job databases. The office also maintains contact with a number of recruiting firms across the United States. The school has an especially excellent reputation in the Columbia area and the state of Missouri, and "several recruiters are discovering the value of students who come out of this university, so the on-campus recruiting opportunities are phenomenal!" Some students, however, feel that the school is still too regionally focused, and that "Career Services could offer more [recruiting opportunities with] companies outside of Missouri."

BARBARA SCHNEIDER, COORDINATOR RECRUITING AND ADMISSIONS
213 CORNELL HALL, COLUMBIA, MO 65211 UNITED STATES
PHONE: 573-882-2750 • FAX: 573-882-6838 • E-MAIL: MBA@MISSOURI.EDU
WEBSITE: WWW.MBA.MISSOURI.EDU

## Student Life and Environment

A MBA at Mizzou is "not only about academics; it's also about socializing, networking, and finding out who you really are." The students form a "very tight-knit" group. Most hail from Missouri yet come from "very diverse backgrounds ethnically and education- ally." After class, students are enthusiastic to "kick back and relax together"; they also "love to celebrate the diversity of the program with special international days, language partner programs, and impromptu dinners and cultural activities."

Extracurricular opportunities are ample, and "about half of the students are involved in the MBA Association. Through this organization, students participate in philanthropy activities (such as Big Brothers, Big Sisters, and Relay for Life), professional development activities (networking receptions, workshops, and alumni events), and social events (weekly happy hours, parties, and wine tastings)." Students with families should take note, however: The programs primarily cater to a younger set, and while "some spouses come to MBA events, most are left out."

On campus, MBA students enjoy "an outstanding library, tons of cultural events, beautiful architecture, and lots of brand new student housing," as well as a state-of-the-art rec center. On top of that, "The business school is housed in a brand-new, technologically-advanced building that is full of resources for the students." According to students here, there's no better location than Columbia, Missouri, which many characterize as "a very forward- thinking city, perfect for both families and younger singletons." The consummate college town, Columbia is home to a host of "schools, parks, libraries, hike-and-bike trails, and arts programs, as well as standard college-town nightlife and activities."

## Admissions

The University of Missouri evaluates prospective students based on the strength of their undergraduate work, leadership skills, and GMAT scores. Work experience is not a requirement of the program, but is a factor that is considered in the admissions decision. In the previous year, successful applicants to University of Missouri—Columbia's graduate business program submitted an average GPA of 3.38 and an average GMAT score of 625. Applicants must submit an MU Graduate School Application and MBA Department Application. Admissions decisions are made on a rolling basis, and students are usually notified of a decision within three weeks of submitting all of the necessary application materials. Students can enter in the Fall, Winter or Summer terms and graduate in three or four semesters depending upon their academic background.

## FINANCIAL FACTS

| | |
|---|---|
| Annual tuition (in-state/out-of-state) | $7,032/$17,016 |
| Fees | $700 |
| Room & board | $7,848 |
| Books and supplies | $908 |
| % of students receiving aid | 44 |
| % of first-year students receiving aid | 44 |
| % of students receiving grants | 44 |
| Average award package | $13,000 |
| Average grant | $13,000 |

## ADMISSIONS

| | |
|---|---|
| Admissions Selectivity Rating | 91 |
| # of applications received | 348 |
| % applicants accepted | 46 |
| % acceptees attending | 58 |
| Average GMAT | 625 |
| Range of GMAT | 590–670 |
| Average GPA | 3.38 |
| TOEFL required of international students? | yes |
| Minimum TOEFL (paper/computer) | 550/213 |
| Application fee | $45 |
| International application fee | $60 |
| Regular application deadline | rolling |
| Regular notification | rolling |
| Deferment available? | yes |
| Maximum length of deferment | 1 year |
| Transfer students accepted? | yes |
| Transfer application policy | |
| Students may waive up to 27 credit hours and may transfer 6 credit hours from an AACSB MBA program. | |
| Non-fall admissions? | yes |
| Need-blind admissions? | yes |

## EMPLOYMENT PROFILE

| Career Rating | 78 | Grads employed by field: | % | avg. salary: |
|---|---|---|---|---|
| Primary source of full-time job acceptances | | Finance | 15 | $54,460 |
| | | Marketing | 13 | $64,375 |
| School-facilitated activities | 17 (33%) | MIS | 3 | $51,500 |
| Graduate-facilitated activities | 15 (29%) | Operations | 6 | $54,500 |
| Unknown | 19 (37%) | Consulting | 34 | $48,364 |
| | | General Management | 15 | $59,000 |
| Average starting salary | $54,083 | Other | 14 | $62,077 |
| Percent employed | 80 | | | |

# University of Missouri—Kansas City
## Henry W. Bloch School of Business and Public Administration

## GENERAL INFORMATION
| | |
|---|---|
| Type of school | public |
| Environment | metropolis |
| Academic calendar | semester |

## SURVEY SAYS...
Students love Kansas City, MO
Happy students
Smart classrooms
*Solid preparation in:*
Teamwork
Communication/interpersonal skills

## STUDENTS
| | |
|---|---|
| Enrollment of parent institution | 14,310 |
| Enrollment of business school | 359 |
| % part-time | 100 |
| Average age at entry | 30 |
| Average years work experience at entry | 4 |

## ACADEMICS
| | |
|---|---|
| **Academic Experience Rating** | **75** |
| Student/faculty ratio | 14:1 |
| Profs interesting rating | 73 |
| Profs accessible rating | 62 |
| % female faculty | 16 |
| % minority faculty | 8 |

## JOINT DEGREES
JD/MBA, 81 law school credit hours + 30-48 MBA credit hours;
JD/MPA, 81 law school credit hours + 36-39 MPA credit hours

## PROMINENT ALUMNI
Kay Waldo Barnes, Mayor, Kansas City, Missouri; Terry Dunn, President and CEO, Dunn Industries, Inc.; Bob Regnier, President, Bank of Blue Valley; Tom Holcom, President, Pioneer Financial Services, Inc.

## Academics

"A convenient location" and "a strong reputation" in the region attract students to the Henry W. Bloch School of Business and Public Administration at the University of Missouri—Kansas City, a large public institution serving nearly 15,000 undergraduates and graduate students. As you would expect of a school named after a founder of tax-preparation giant H & R Block, accounting is among the strongest programs here. Many also praise the finance emphasis, pointing out that "many of the professors [in this discipline] are distinguished and have impressive backgrounds in publications."

The Bloch MBA requires a minimum of 30 semester hours of coursework, and students who enter the program with deficiencies in core skills (e.g. students who did not satisfactorily complete a business major at the undergraduate level) may be required to complete up to 18 additional semester hours as well as introductory classes in mathematics and computer applications. All students must complete a minimum of 18 semester hours outside their area of emphasis. Twelve semester hours are required to complete an emphasis; emphases are available in entrepreneurship, finance, general management, international business, leadership and change in human systems, management information systems, marketing, and operations management.

Students appreciate the "availability of experiential learning" throughout the program and observe that "the quality of the faculty is very high and the overall program is quite thorough." Small class sizes encourage strong relationships between students and teachers—a boon for those MBAs hoping to develop a mentor while here. UMKC's administration "is not very noticeable, which is a good thing. They don't get in the way. They are accessible, though."

## Career and Placement

UMKC's Career Services Center, which serves the entire university population, recently opened a satellite office at the Bloch School to serve business graduates and undergraduates. Unfortunately, the office only stays open until 5:00 P.M., making it difficult for Bloch's many part-time students who hold full-time jobs to benefit from its services. It's only an issue for some—many students here have little interest in leaving their current employers—but it is a nuisance for those it affects. Employers who recruit on the UMKC campus include Ameriprise Financial Services, Inc., Cerner, Commerce Bank, Eli Lilly & Company, Etelligent Consulting Inc., the Farmers Insurance Group, the Federal Bureau of Investigation, First Investors Corp., the Internal Revenue Service, John Hancock Financial Services, State Street, US Bank, Wells Fargo, and Zen Infotech.

## Student Life and Environment

"Most MBA students are working professionals during the day and students at night" at UMKC. "Many are married and have kids, most are hard working and competitive," and nearly all are "looking for more out of their careers." This population is supplemented by "a significant international presence" and "some executive students. UMKC is an urban school that fits the mold." For the most part, students' careers and familial obligations leave them "minimal time for extracurricular interaction." They attend classes, participate in team projects, and try to make time for study groups. Aside from that, they do not spend much time on campus.

DIRECTOR OF ADMISSIONS
5100 ROCKHILL ROAD, KANSAS CITY, MO 64110 UNITED STATES
PHONE: 816-235-1111 • FAX: 816-235-5544 • E-MAIL: ADMIT@UMKC.EDU
WEBSITE: WWW.UMKC.EDU/BLOCH

The Bloch School is located in a renovated and expanded facility that is also one of the city's historic mansions. The building has been updated to meet the requirements of twenty-first century business education. Students have access to modern classrooms and to computer and research laboratories. The school "operates a Digital Open VMS Cluster providing many programming languages, statistical packages, e-mail, and other Internet applications to students. PPP dial-up access to the VMS computer and to the Internet is also available to students."

The Kansas City metropolitan area sprawls over six counties in two states, Missouri and Kansas. The region is home to nearly two million residents, placing it among the 30 largest metropolitan regions in the country. Naturally, numerous companies and national organizations are headquartered in the city. They include American Century, Applebee's, Aquila, Black and Veatch, Ferrallgas, Hallmark, H & R Block, Interstate Bakeries, Russell Stover, and Sprint.

## Admissions

Applicants to the MBA program at the University of Missouri—Kansas City must submit official copies of transcripts for all academic work completed after high school and an official score report for the GMAT. The school will consider graduate-level admissions tests other than the GMAT (e.g. LSAT, GRE) so long as scores exceed the fiftieth percentile in all parts of the exam. Candidates must also provide the admissions committee with all of the following: a completed application form (available online); a current resume showing both work history and professional certifications; a personal statement of purpose in pursuing the MBA; and a summary of the candidate's current commitments to work (i.e., hours of work per week, amount of business travel). International students must provide all of the above and must also provide an official score report for the TOEFL; a minimum score of 550 on the paper-based exam or 213 on the computer-based exam is required.

### FINANCIAL FACTS
Annual tuition (in-state/out-of-state) $5,196/$13,018
Fees $1,392
% of first-year students receiving aid 41
Average award package $15,932
Average grant $4,660
Average student loan debt $28,891

### ADMISSIONS
**Admissions Selectivity Rating 80**
# of applications received 288
% applicants accepted 60
% acceptees attending 85
Average GMAT 536
Range of GMAT 510–620
Average GPA 3.25
TOEFL required of international students? yes
Minimum TOEFL (paper/computer) 550/213
Application fee $35
International application fee $50
Regular application deadline 5/1
Regular notification rolling
Deferment available? yes
Maximum length of deferment 1 year
Transfer students accepted? yes
Transfer application policy Students may transfer up to 6 credits from an AACSB-accredited institution.
Non-fall admissions? yes
Need-blind admissions? yes

# University of Missouri—St. Louis
## College of Business Administration

## Academics

The College of Business Administration at the University of Missouri—St. Louis offers two options to the busy professional who is in search of the MBA. Its traditional MBA is a 39 to 54-hour program (depending on the number of general requirements courses a student can place out of) that convenes on weeknights. The school's professional MBA online is a 48-hour program that requires students to visit campus only one weekend per month; most other work is completed via the Internet. Students in this program "love its flexibility" and note that "although we are only at school for two full days per month, the class schedules and assignments require us to meet in groups almost weekly and sometimes more. Each class requiring at least one presentation allows us to polish our communication skills for the real world quite often."

The degree of convenience is not the only difference between UM—St. Louis's two MBA options. The professional MBA online curriculum is entirely prescribed, while the traditional MBA afford the opportunity to take electives and develop an area of specialization (accounting, finance, logistics and supply-chain management, management, marketing, operations management) or earn a graduate certificate (e-commerce, human-resources management, information-resource management, information-systems development, logistics and supply-chain management, marketing management, telecommunications management). Students in our survey were especially enthusiastic about accounting, logistics, marketing, and operations management.

UM—St. Louis professors "are top rate. They have almost all authored books or teach at other well-known and more expensive schools." Students also report that instructors "are all very willing to help with any problems you may have and especially seem to enjoy working with professionals who are working within industry. I have approached several professors who have helped me develop processes that assist me at work. Additionally, the professors are easy to access and seem to be available whenever you need help or will make time to meet your schedule." That's important since this program is no walk in the park; warns one student, "The course load is very intensive, considering that the entire class is full of professionals who work forty hours a week, have families, and are trying to get their MBAs." Students predict a bright future for the program; as one told us, "It is overall a progressive school that changes to current needs of students. Because of this and their continuous surveys, UM—St. Louis is always improving their education experience."

## Career and Placement

The Career Services Office at UM—St. Louis serves the entire university's undergraduate and graduate student bodies. Available services include a research library, counseling, workshops, seminars, e-recruiting resources, Web-based support, job fairs, and alumni events. Each degree program maintains its own Listserv through which subscribers can learn immediately about new job openings in their area. Top employers of UM—St. Louis MBAs include Boeing Company, CitiMortgage, Edward Jones, and May Company.

Thomas H. Eyssell, Director, Graduate Programs in Business
One University Boulevard, 250 University Center, St. Louis, MO 63121-4499 United States
Phone: 314-516-5885 • Fax: 314-516-7202
E-mail: mba@umsl.edu • Website: www.mba.umsl.edu

## Student Life and Environment

The MBA program at UM—St. Louis "is split between students who work full-time and try to spend the least amount of time on campus and those that are involved on campus with every aspect of their lives." Those most involved tell us that "we have an active Student Union and a good student newspaper. Student life is enriched by the diversity of student backgrounds and culture. For example, African students put up an annual dinner at which they share their different cultures with U.S. students and others. My school is a rich mix of social life." Nearly all international students attend the full-time program; the majority of local students are enrolled part-time. The full-time/part-time mix prevents cohort-based instruction, which in turn reduces communal spirit. One part-timer writes, "It would be nice to have more of a sense of community with others in my year. I am in class with people in their first and last semesters, and I don't know who is who."

The program's facility receives mixed reviews. Students report approvingly that "most classrooms have a computer and overhead screen that instructors and students have access to" but complain that "there is really nowhere in the business building to study except one small room." They also complain that "the campus grounds at UM—St. Louis are not what I'd hoped they'd be; they're not kept very well." On a positive note, the campus is easy to reach by public transportation.

St. Louis is a sizeable city, home to major league sports teams, one of the nation's best zoos, and numerous cultural sites and ethnic neighborhoods. Its most famous attraction, of course, is the Gateway Arch, and its most famous business is probably Anheuser-Busch. Other major employers in the city include Monsanto, Ralston Purina, Boeing, and many of the major automobile manufacturers. St. Louis was once a major center of shoe manufacturing; while that is no longer the case, many shoe companies continue to run their corporate operations from the city. The city is well-known for great music and great barbecue, two commodities that are still available in abundance.

## Admissions

Applicants to the UM—St. Louis MBA program must submit official copies of all undergraduate and graduate transcripts, official GMAT score reports, TOEFL scores (international students), a brief personal statement, two letters of recommendation, and a resume. The admissions committee looks for "professional experience since graduation, motivation, and other indicators of ability" in assessing applicants' fitness for the program. A minimum GMAT score of 500 (with both Math and Verbal scores above the 30th percentile) and a minimum undergraduate GPA of 3.0 are both required for unrestricted admission. Interviews are not required, but they are available to those who are interested.

### FINANCIAL FACTS

| | |
|---|---|
| Annual tuition (in-state/out-of-state) | $6,316/$16,313 |
| Fees | $1,287 |
| Books and supplies | $3,000 |
| Room & board (on/off-campus) | $5,600/$6,180 |
| % of students receiving aid | 53 |
| % of first-year students receiving aid | 48 |
| % of students receiving loans | 32 |
| % of students receiving grants | 24 |
| Average award package | $10,139 |
| Average grant | $6,159 |
| Average student loan debt | $5,933 |

### ADMISSIONS

| | |
|---|---|
| Admissions Selectivity Rating | 73 |
| # of applications received | 106 |
| % applicants accepted | 80 |
| % acceptees attending | 71 |
| Average GMAT | 550 |
| Range of GMAT | 470–590 |
| Average GPA | 3.2 |
| TOEFL required of international students? | yes |
| Minimum TOEFL (paper/computer) | 550/213 |
| Application fee | $35 |
| International application fee | $40 |
| Regular application deadline | 7/1 |
| Regular notification | rolling |
| Deferment available? | yes |
| Maximum length of deferment | 1 year |
| Transfer students accepted? | yes |
| Transfer application policy Transcripts are evaluated for relevant course work. Maximum of 9 hours of acceptable graduate credit allowed to be transfered in. | |
| Non-fall admissions? | yes |
| Need-blind admissions? | yes |

### EMPLOYMENT PROFILE

| Career Rating | 65 | Grads employed by field: | % | avg. salary: |
|---|---|---|---|---|
| Average starting salary | $48,067 | Finance | 50 | $51,600 |
| | | Consulting | 17 | $42,500 |
| | | Communications | 16 | $43,000 |
| | | Other | 17 | $48,000 |

# UNIVERSITY OF NEBRASKA AT OMAHA
## COLLEGE OF BUSINESS ADMINISTRATION

## Academics

"The MBA program at UNO's College of Business Administration concentrates on the working professional, and most, if not all, classes are offered at night. This is a big plus for me," one typical student in this solid local program writes. Students are pragmatic about what the CBA can and cannot offer, and they are confident that it is by far the best option for Omaha-area students. One student writes, "It's a great school if you're working full-time. There's good, cheap parking; a safe campus, business-focused classes; and professors with real-world experience." Another student agrees, "I'm glad that I chose UNO because, I think proportionally, there are just as many students and teachers that aren't the highest caliber at other graduate schools. I would be highly upset if I had to drive twice the distance and pay three times as much for teachers and students who weren't all smarter than the best at UNO. It's not realistic to expect that much from any local school."

Students entering the CBA must demonstrate proficiency in accounting and finance fundamentals, basic business statistics, and foundations of economics; those lacking these skills must take the corresponding foundation courses at the outset of the program. The MBA curriculum includes nine core courses (27 hours) and nine hours of electives; students may elect to devote six curriculum hours to writing and subsequently defending orally a thesis paper. Students must also participate in at least three business leadership seminars during their tenure; complete a business case study as part of the capstone course policy, planning, and strategy; and pass a comprehensive exam that requires them to synthesize core skills and concepts.

While some students wish that the program were even broader and more demanding one student, for example, complains that "the conventional MBA program does not even offer a specialization in finance," most are satisfied with what UNO offers. Professors are generally good; they "make the material very interesting, and most [professors] teach the material as it applies to both academic and real-world settings." In addition, they are "very supportive, very prepared, and always available for questions." On the downside, "some are a bit long in the tooth and do not relate well to current technology for the students. That's frustrating and a waste of time in class." MBAs also complain that "state budget cuts have led to fewer times available for some classes."

## Career and Placement

UNO's Career Center "assists undergraduates, graduate candidates, and alumni from all colleges of the university in their search for career employment." According to the school's catalog, the center provides counseling services, a library of information on local and national employers, and recruiting and referral programs. The school also offers university-wide career fairs. Students explain that "the local reputation is key" in parlaying their degrees into successful careers; in addition, "good corporations in town and working adult students bring in current information" that assists in their job searches. Companies recruiting on campus during the spring of 2004 included Deloitte Touche Tohmatsu, EFG Companies, First National Bank of Omaha, Mutual of Omaha, the state of Nebraska, Northwestern Mutual, State Farm, and Union Pacific.

## Student Life and Environment

According to students, UNO MBAs form a "close-knit group, even though [they] have few out-of-class activities because most of the students have responsibilities outside of school." As one student says, "Other than networking through the various clubs and associations, the extracurriculars are limited to the undergraduate population." MBAs are friendly enough to watch out for each other, students say. One student adds, "We become friends, and we all use the friendships developed at school to network and that eventually leads to new jobs. Also, because all the students know each other, they get guidance from each other on what classes are better and the teaching styles of the professors."

UNO is the state's only metropolitan-area university, and this allows it to offer some of the best student-business connections available in Nebraska. Major employers in the city include Alegent Health, ConAgra, First Data Corporation, Methodist Health, Mutual of Omaha, Odyssey Staffing, Staff Mid-America, Union Pacific, and West Corporation. Omaha's metropolitan population of over 600,000 supports a variety of museums, the world's best-endowed community theater, and a zoo.

## Admissions

Students applying to the University of Nebraska—Omaha must provide the admissions department an official transcript for each undergraduate and graduate program attended, official GMAT test results, and a current resume detailing work experience. Letters of recommendation, an essay or personal statement, and an interview are all optional for domestic applicants. International applicants "must provide letters of recommendation, statements of financial independence, and evidence of ability to speak and write the English language." The CBA accepts applications for admission three times a year; students may enter in the Fall, Spring, or Summer.

### FINANCIAL FACTS

| | |
|---|---|
| Room & board | |
| (on/off-campus) | $6,500/$9,500 |
| Average award package | $8,414 |
| Average grant | $2,981 |
| Average student loan debt | $7,625 |

### ADMISSIONS

| | |
|---|---|
| **Admissions Selectivity Rating** | **77** |
| # of applications received | 86 |
| % applicants accepted | 79 |
| % acceptees attending | 78 |
| Average GMAT | 568 |
| Range of GMAT | 500–610 |
| Average GPA | 3.45 |
| TOEFL required of international students? | yes |
| Minimum TOEFL (paper/computer) | 550/213 |
| Application fee | $45 |
| International application fee | $45 |
| Regular application deadline | 7/1 |
| Regular notification | rolling |
| Deferment available? | yes |
| Maximum length of deferment | 1 year |
| Transfer students accepted? | yes |
| Transfer application policy | |
| A maximum of nine hours of transfer credit may be accepted from another accredited (AACSB) institution. Requires submission of course syllabi and relevant catalog information. | |
| Non-fall admissions? | yes |
| Need-blind admissions? | yes |

### APPLICANTS ALSO LOOK AT

Creighton University, University of Nebraska—Lincoln

# UNIVERSITY OF NEVADA—LAS VEGAS
## COLLEGE OF BUSINESS

**GENERAL INFORMATION**

| | |
|---|---|
| Type of school | public |
| Environment | metropolis |
| Academic calendar | semesters |

**SURVEY SAYS...**

Students love Las Vegas, NV
Friendly students
Good peer network
Happy students

**STUDENTS**

| | |
|---|---|
| Enrollment of parent institution | 27,344 |
| Enrollment of business school | 265 |
| Average age at entry | 28 |
| Average years work experience at entry | 5.4 |

**ACADEMICS**

| | |
|---|---|
| **Academic Experience Rating** | **70** |
| Student/faculty ratio | 30:1 |
| Profs interesting rating | 61 |
| Profs accessible rating | 65 |
| % female faculty | 23 |
| % minority faculty | 21 |

**JOINT DEGREES**

MBA/MS in Hotel Administration, 2.5 years; JD/MBA, 4 years full time, 5 years part-time; MBA/DDM (Dental Medicine)

## Academics

The College of Business at the University of Nevada—Las Vegas offers both a full-time and part-time evening MBA as well as a cohort-based weekend Executive MBA program for more experienced professionals. Roughly half the students in these programs attend the college full time.

UNLV's evening MBA consists of 48 credit hours, 33 of which are devoted to core courses. Students must devote five electives to a single area in order to achieve a concentration; the college offers concentrations in finance, management information systems, service marketing, and venture management. An accelerated program is open to students who score at least a 600 on the GMAT (with a score exceeding the 50th percentile in both verbal and quantitative skills) and an undergraduate business degree from an AACSB-accredited university. Students who meet these conditions may be allowed to waive up to six of the ten required core courses.

The 18-month Executive MBA program offers a general management degree; in order to preserve the program's cohort-based approach to learning, all students follow the same curriculum. The program begins with a week of intensive work; afterwards, students meet every Friday and Saturday from 8:30 A.M. to 5:30 P.M. Applicants to the program must have at least seven years of professional experience, at least three of which have been spent in "a key decision-making role."

UNLV also offers combined-degree programs in hotel administration, dental medicine, and a JD/MBA. Students point out that the "hotel concentration feeds off the Las Vegas resort market."

## Career and Placement

The UNLV College of Business Career Services Center serves only graduate students in business. According to the College's website, the office seeks to help students define career goals, develop a career plan, market themselves, develop job-search skills, sharpen interviewing skills, and contact alumni. The office serves as a liaison to the local business community, maintains a number of hard-copy and online job databases, and organizes lectures and on-campus recruiting events.

Employers most likely to hire UNLV MBAs include Bechtel Nevada, Bechtel SAIC, Citibank, Harrah's Entertainment, Pulte Homes, US Bank, and Wells Fargo. A plurality of the class of 2004 wound up in the finance sector, and almost everyone had found employment by graduation.

ROBERT CHATFIELD, MBA PROGRAMS DIRECTOR
4505 MARYLAND PARKWAY, BOX 456031, LAS VEGAS, NV 89154-6031 UNITED STATES
PHONE: 702-895-3655 • FAX: 702-895-4090
E-MAIL: COBMBA@CCMAIL.NEVADA.EDU • WEBSITE: WWW.BUSINESS.UNLV.EDU

## Student Life and Environment

Las Vegas is one of America's top tourist destinations, primarily because "it's fun every single night." Those who live here know that Vegas has a lot more to offer than just gambling, over-the-top floor shows, and cheap buffets. The Las Vegas metropolitan region is home to 1.5 million residents, many of whom never set foot inside a casino. The city boasts all the amenities of a midsize metropolis and adds to the mix a perennially sunny climate and proximity to plenty of outdoor fun; Lake Mead, the Colorado River, and the Hoover Dam are all within a half-hour's drive of the city. Some fabulous skiing and hiking awaits residents on Mount Charleston, less than an hour northwest of Sin City.

UNLV does its part to keep things interesting, providing "new cultural and entertainment attractions to the community every day," according to the college's website. Prominent lecturers and touring performing artists regularly stop by this desert campus.

## Admissions

Applicants to the MBA program at UNLV must submit the following to the Admissions Committee: official transcripts for all postsecondary academic work undertaken; an official score report for the GMAT; two letters of recommendation; a personal essay; and a resume. An interview is required for admission to the Executive MBA program, but not for other graduate programs. The TOEFL is not required of students who completed degree programs conducted in English or the U.S., U.K., Australia, Canada, or New Zealand. All international applicants must provide financial certification documents.

### FINANCIAL FACTS

| | |
|---|---|
| Annual tuition (in-state/out-of-state) | $8,674 |
| Fees | $456 |
| Books and supplies | $800 |
| Room & board (on/off-campus) | $5,000/$7,000 |
| % of students receiving aid | 24 |
| % of first-year students receiving aid | 34 |
| % of students receiving loans | 23 |
| % of students receiving grants | 3 |
| Average award package | $16,000 |
| Average grant | $2,500 |
| Average student loan debt | $30,957 |

### ADMISSIONS

| | |
|---|---|
| Admissions Selectivity Rating | 87 |
| # of applications received | 193 |
| % applicants accepted | 48 |
| % acceptees attending | 68 |
| Average GMAT | 586 |
| Range of GMAT | 520–760 |
| Average GPA | 3.26 |
| TOEFL required of international students? | yes |
| Minimum TOEFL (paper/computer) | 550/213 |
| Application fee | $60 |
| International application fee | $75 |
| Regular application deadline | 6/1 |
| Regular notification | 7/1 |
| Deferment available? | yes |
| Maximum length of deferment | 1 semester |
| Transfer students accepted? | yes |
| Transfer application policy | Total of 6 credits from an AACSB-accredited school |
| Non-fall admissions? | yes |
| Need-blind admissions? | yes |

### EMPLOYMENT PROFILE

| Career Rating | 64 | Grads employed by field: | % | avg. salary: |
|---|---|---|---|---|
| Average starting salary | $57,000 | Accounting | 10 | $50,000 |
| | | Finance | 40 | $52,000 |
| | | Human Resources | 2 | $50,000 |
| | | Marketing | 20 | $45,000 |
| | | MIS | 3 | $50,000 |
| | | Operations | 2 | $65,000 |
| | | Consulting | 3 | $60,000 |
| | | General Management | 10 | $70,000 |
| | | Other | 10 | $35,000 |

# UNIVERSITY OF NEW HAMPSHIRE
## WHITTEMORE SCHOOL OF BUSINESS AND ECONOMICS

## Academics

Things are changing at the University of New Hampshire's Whittemore School of Business and Economics: In 2005–2006, the school introduced a brand-new MBA program designed to streamline the degree-earning process. The new program hustles full-time students through in less than one year (through an "intense program" that leaves "little time for anything else," according to the school's website), while part-timers graduate in fewer than two years. Students here frequently cite the speed with which the program can be completed as one of its biggest draws.

Whittemore's full-time program begins in late August with a five-week term, during which students study management, accounting, and organizational behavior. The second term, which runs for three months, consists entirely of required courses in economics, marketing, information systems and enterprise integration, and financial management. Term three is split between two required courses (one in organizations and leadership, the other in managerial decision making) and two electives. Term four consists of two required courses covering operations management and business strategy, an elective, and the first segment of the Corporate Roundtable Project (CRT). This provides student teams the opportunity to work on a real-world project with a major company, such as Fidelity Investments or Liberty Mutual Life. The program concludes with term five, during which students take one elective and conclude the CRT. Students may use electives to develop a concentration in marketing and supply chain management, entrepreneurial venture creation, or financial management. Many students single out the entrepreneurship classes as a highlight of the program.

Whittemore's part-time program follows a similar curriculum to the full-time program, although it replaces the CRT with two extra electives. The part-time program offers the same selection of concentrations as the full-time program.

MBAs at Whittemore detect an "an emphasis on academic greatness that fosters a great study environment." They report approvingly that "the faculty is always willing to help out" and that "the school offers lots of resources for going into the workplace." They also note that "because this is the first year of the redesigned program, there are definitely some kinks that have to be worked out at our expense," but students expect things to improve soon—especially because "professors are, for the most part, very good and have extensive experience and research in their fields. The experience from the Whittemore School of Business and Economics is one of academic intensity as well as a lot of fun."

## Career and Placement

Business students at UNH have their own placement facility, the Whittemore School Placement Office, which works in partnership with the university-at-large placement office, the University Advising and Career Center. The b-school placement office works with business undergraduates, graduates, and alumni to forge career strategies, identify potential employers, and navigate the recruitment process. Recent employers of Whittemore School graduates include Anthem Blue Cross Blue Shield, AT&T, Boise Cascade, Chubb Life-America, Cigna, Credit Suisse, Fidelity Investments, General Electric, IBM, LL Bean, Inc., McGraw-Hill, Osram Sylvania, Pfizer Pharmaceuticals, Raytheon Company, Sprague Energy, Timken Aerospace, Verizon, and Westinghouse.

GEORGE ABRAHAM, DIRECTOR, GRADUATE AND EXECUTIVE PROGRAMS
116 MCCONNELL HALL, 15 COLLEGE ROAD, DURHAM, NH 3824 UNITED STATES
PHONE: 603-862-1367 • FAX: 603-862-4468 • E-MAIL: WSBE.GRAD@UNH.EDU
WEBSITE: WWW.MBA.UNH.EDU

## Student Life and Environment

"Most of us are in the same boat here: all fresh out of undergrad with no business knowledge whatsoever," explains one full-time student. "This alone gives us a strong bond. But add myriad team-building exercises and an intense workload, and we've become very close in our time together thus far." MBAs here describe themselves as "overachievers—we were hand-picked by the program's creator—but we manage to maintain a balance between our academic lives and our social lives." Outside the classroom, students participate in international competitions, such as I2P Idea to Product and the NASA Means Business Competition. Discipline-related clubs are also available. Like full-timers, part-timers tend to be young; however, they typically have full-time jobs, and their extracurricular experiences are more limited.

The UNH campus and surrounding area provide "a fun, beautiful environment to be in. The seasons are amazing, and the skiing is great." Durham is "a small college town" with "a few bars, three or four pizza places, and a cell phone service provider," but fortunately "Portsmouth and the beaches are close by." Students tell us that "it is desirable to take trips down to Boston for some excitement."

## Admissions

Applicants to the MBA program at UNH's Whittemore School must provide the admissions department with all of the following: official copies of transcripts for all postsecondary academic work; an official score report for the GMAT; three letters of reference focusing on the candidate's "strengths, weaknesses, and potential for academic and managerial success"; responses to essay questions, which the school deems a "crucial" aspect of the application; a current resume; and any evidence of leadership skills that the applicant wishes to provide. Applicants to the Executive MBA program must undergo an admissions interview. Applicants to other MBA programs may request an interview but are not required to do so. (It is, however, "strongly recommended" that such applicants who have "one or more weak components in their profile" schedule an appointment.) Two years of work experience is "recommended but not required" for the full-time and part-time MBA programs; a minimum of seven years of professional experience is required for the Executive MBA program. International applicants must meet all of the above requirements and must submit an official score report for the TOEFL (minimum required score: 550 paper-based test, 213 computer-based test).

### FINANCIAL FACTS

| | |
|---|---|
| Annual tuition (in-state/out-of-state) | $12,500/$23,000 |
| Fees | $1,386 |
| Books and supplies | $2,000 |
| Room & board (on/off-campus) | $7,540/$8,400 |
| % of students receiving aid | 89 |
| % of first-year students receiving aid | 84 |
| % of students receiving loans | 60 |
| % of students receiving grants | 53 |
| Average award package | $16,002 |
| Average grant | $6,807 |
| Average student loan debt | $24,487 |

### ADMISSIONS

| | |
|---|---|
| Admissions Selectivity Rating | 74 |
| # of applications received | 124 |
| % applicants accepted | 87 |
| % acceptees attending | 77 |
| Average GMAT | 569 |
| Range of GMAT | 510–620 |
| Average GPA | 3.35 |
| TOEFL required of international students? | yes |
| Minimum TOEFL (paper/computer) | 550/213 |
| Application fee | $60 |
| International application fee | $60 |
| Regular application deadline | 7/6 |
| Regular notification | rolling |
| Early decision program? | yes |
| ED Deadline/notification | 4/1 / 5/15 |
| Deferment available? | yes |
| Maximum length of deferment | 1 year |
| Transfer students accepted? | yes |
| Transfer application policy | |
| Students may transfer a maximum of 9 credits upon departmental approval. | |
| Non-fall admissions? | yes |
| Need-blind admissions? | yes |

### APPLICANTS ALSO LOOK AT

Babson College, Bentley College, Boston University, Suffolk University

### EMPLOYMENT PROFILE

| Career Rating | 77 | Grads employed by field: | % avg. salary: |
|---|---|---|---|
| Primary source of full-time job acceptances | | Accounting | 12 $88,725 |
| | | Finance | 12 $88,725 |
| School-facilitated activities | 6 (35%) | Human Resources | 6 NR |
| Graduate-facilitated activities | 4 (24%) | Marketing | 18 $51,500 |
| Unknown | 7 (41%) | MIS | 5 $50,000 |
| | | Operations | 17 $76,800 |
| Average starting salary | $61,862 | Consulting | 18 $54,000 |
| Percent employed | 84 | General Management | 12 $57,500 |

# University of New Mexico
## Robert O. Anderson Graduate School of Management

## Academics

Students turn to the Robert O. Anderson Graduate School of Management at the University of New Mexico for "an excellent education at a reasonable cost," and most students are extremely satisfied with the results. MBAs can choose from nine areas of concentration including organizational behavior/human resources, management of technology ("the most reputable program at the business school," one MBA notes), and policy and planning (the last abroad, cross-functional approach to problem-solving analysis). One student says, "[The policy and planning concentration] really sets the school apart from any of the others I considered." The Anderson School also offers a master's of accounting, and dual degrees that incorporate law, engineering, or Latin American studies.

Although many of its students register for full-time instruction, Anderson provides "plenty of flexibility for working professionals," with "classes usually held in the evenings." The core curriculum consists of ten classes; students with undergraduate business degrees may be able to receive a waiver for some of these; six management electives round out the requirements. Students pursuing a specialization may arrange the six electives to satisfy concentration requirements. The curriculum concludes with a capstone course in strategic management.

Students praise the Anderson faculty "in both core and concentration areas." One MBA writes, "The professors are wonderful, supportive, and challenging. I have had the opportunity to make friends with them and will be in touch with them after graduation." Another student adds, "The professors are incredibly helpful and have open minds about teaching. More than book work, the professors often engage the class in case studies, group work, interactive discussions, and role-play negotiations. Nearly every course is unique in the way the teacher presents the material." One student neatly sums up, "Who could make accounting interesting? Our faculty does!"

While some students feel that standards should be raised in order to increase the program's ranking and national profile, most of them believe that Anderson serves a valuable function for its mostly local student body. As one student concludes, "The academic experience has been rewarding for me, and I have grown as an individual and a professional. My analytical and problem-solving skills have been sharpened, and I have had the opportunity to explore where I would like for my career path to head."

## Career and Placement

The school's Career Planning and Placement Office manages Career Services for all Anderson undergraduate and graduate students. The office provides information sessions, schedules on-campus interviews, organizes job fairs, manages access to online job databases, and provides job search skills coaching. The school reports that 60 employers recruit full-time employees on campus each year; 25 recruit first-year students for summer internships.

Employers who most frequently hire Anderson MBAs include Cardinal Health, Eli Lilly & Company, the EPA—Office of Inspector General, Goldman Sacks & Co., IBM, Intel, Lawrence Livermore National Laboratory, Los Alamos National Laboratory, Pulte Homes, Sandia National Laboratories, the state of New Mexico, University of New Mexico, and the U.S. General Accounting Office.

LOYOLA CHASTAIN, GRADUATE PROGRAMS MANAGER
UNIVERSITY OF NEW MEXICO, 1924 LAS LOMAS BOULEVARD, ALBUQUERQUE, NM 87131 U.S.
PHONE: 505-277-3147 • FAX: 505-277-9356
E-MAIL: CHASTAIN@MGT.UNM.EDU • WEBSITE: WWW.MGT.UNM.EDU

## Student Life and Environment

The Anderson Graduate School of Management is "a total commuter school" that "tends to be for working professionals." Those who don't work will find that "there are several internships that are available to graduate students as well as TA and GA positions," which will give them something to do during the daytime hours (classes are largely conducted in the evening). One student observes, "It is not a lively campus. There is little connection between MBA students because [the University of New Mexico] is a commuter campus. Everyone comes to class [and] then leaves."

Hometown Albuquerque "is okay, but nightlife is substandard in comparison to other towns. There isn't any specific hang out that students frequent, so between classes, students hang out and talk or usually go to the computer lab." They also head outside because "the warm weather allows lots of interaction outdoors between classes." Students also appreciate the opportunities afforded by Albuquerque's setting, which is "in the midst of a growing Southwestern community with tons of local opportunities for entrepreneurship."

Although UNM is a sizeable university, "the business school has a small-school feel with students, instructors, [and] professors getting to know each other well." Students explain that "the diversity of the student population is one of the greatest strengths of the school. It is cultural, geographic, and gender-based." Hispanic Americans constitute the largest minority population here (approximately 20 percent of the student body).

## Admissions

A completed application to the Anderson MBA program includes all of the following: two official transcripts from each undergraduate and graduate school attended, GMAT scores, TOEFL scores (international students), a brief statement of purpose, three letters of recommendation ("the most meaningful evaluations come from people who been responsible for evaluating your academic or managerial performance"), two application forms, and a resume. Students may apply for admission for the Fall, Spring, or Summer term.

### FINANCIAL FACTS

| | |
|---|---|
| Annual tuition (in-state/out-of-state) | $4,110/$12,811 |
| Fees | $280 |
| Books and supplies | $2,000 |
| Room & board (on/off-campus) | $10,270/$8,520 |
| % of students receiving aid | 55 |
| % of first-year students receiving aid | 52 |
| % of students receiving loans | 36 |
| % of students receiving grants | 30 |
| Average award package | $5,424 |
| Average grant | $2,849 |
| Average student loan debt | $25,134 |

### ADMISSIONS

| | |
|---|---|
| Admissions Selectivity Rating | 88 |
| # of applications received | 168 |
| % applicants accepted | 51 |
| % acceptees attending | 100 |
| Average GMAT | 561 |
| Range of GMAT | 420–760 |
| Average GPA | 3.54 |
| TOEFL required of international students? | yes |
| Minimum TOEFL (paper/computer) | 550/213 |
| Application fee | $40 |
| International application fee | $40 |
| Regular application deadline | 6/1 |
| Regular notification | rolling |
| Deferment available? | yes |
| Maximum length of deferment | 1 year |
| Transfer students accepted? | yes |
| Transfer application policy | Up to 6 credit hours may be transfered. |
| Non-fall admissions? | yes |

### EMPLOYMENT PROFILE

| Career Rating | 71 | Grads employed by field: | % | avg. salary: |
|---|---|---|---|---|
| Average starting salary | $53,025 | Accounting | 18 | $47,800 |
| | | Finance | 18 | $54,500 |
| | | Marketing | 9 | $34,000 |
| | | MIS | 9 | $61,100 |
| | | Operations | 9 | $54,600 |
| | | General Management | 22 | $44,200 |
| | | Other | 15 | $50,045 |

# UNIVERSITY OF NORTH CAROLINA AT CHAPEL HILL
## KENAN-FLAGLER BUSINESS SCHOOL

## GENERAL INFORMATION

| | |
|---|---|
| Type of school | public |
| Environment | town |
| Academic calendar | semester |

## SURVEY SAYS...

Friendly students
Good peer network
Happy students
Smart classrooms
*Solid preparation in:*
Teamwork

## STUDENTS

| | |
|---|---|
| Enrollment of parent institution | 23,000 |
| Enrollment of business school | 558 |
| % male/female | 74/26 |
| % out-of-state | 75 |
| % minorities | 11 |
| % international | 28 |
| Average age at entry | 28 |
| Average years work experience at entry | 5 |

## ACADEMICS

| | |
|---|---|
| **Academic Experience Rating** | **96** |
| Student/faculty ratio | 5:1 |
| Profs interesting rating | 94 |
| Profs accessible rating | 98 |
| % female faculty | 17 |
| % minority faculty | 1 |

## JOINT DEGREES

MBA/JD, 4 years; MBA/Master of Regional Planning, 3 years; MBA/Master of Health Care Administration, 3 years; MBA/MS in Information Sciences, 3 years

## PROMINENT ALUMNI

Claire Babrowski, Executive VP and COO, Radioshack Corp.; Brent Callinicos, Corp VP, Worldwide Licensing, Microsoft; Peter Mallinson, Managing Director, Goldman Sachs Intl; Lee Ainslie, Managing Partner, Maverick Capital Management; Daryl Brewster, President & CEO, Krispy Kreme Doughnuts Inc.

## Academics

Students have a lot of reasons to be happy at Kenan-Flagler Business School at UNC at Chapel Hill. Students explain that "there is an intense focus on student satisfaction, and the administration is really focused on the MBA program as key to UNC's success." UNC Kenan-Flagler MBAs get to voice their opinions at "monthly town-hall meetings; [students] are also highly encouraged to give feedback to the dean of the MBA program and the business school dean." Students report that their feedback is quickly acted upon. Some students note, "There was weakness in the core finance curriculum for the class of 2004. We told the dean about it, and it was dramatically improved for the 2005 class."

This student-friendly attitude is emblematic of UNC Kenan-Flagler, where collegiality and learning constantly trump competitiveness and grade-grubbing. "Any student will drop what they are doing and help you with your work," according to students. This is because the grading system (high pass, pass, low pass, and fail, rather than the traditional A-through-F grades) "is such that one needs to be almost flawless on exams to earn a high pass. This leaves the vast majority of students with no incentive to restrict the aid they give to other students." Another student adds, "Not having grades creates an atmosphere that encourages learning, but more importantly, challenges students to take courses outside of their comfort zone. This is critical for those that want to be well-rounded leaders."

Even without its approach to customer service, UNC Kenan-Flagler would still be among the nation's top MBA programs, one with "excellent entrepreneurship and real estate efforts, great strength in marketing and finance, [a] sustainable enterprise program that's the best in the country," and a "strong general-management focus." Students love how "international opportunities abound: you can take a language class [or] a business-outside-the-United States course that culminates in a trip overseas (there are about eight of these per year [in] various countries), get an internship overseas (we have strong connections in Southeast Asia), or spend half a semester to [one] year abroad studying at another school."

The quality of the program justifies the effort needed to complete it, which is considerable. The grueling core curriculum "is like a pain you know you must live with for a little while, but in the end you will be stronger for it." Students also point out that "while the first-year course load is heavy, most concepts are covered again in the second year, which allows you to thoroughly understand the topics in a way that is relevant to your career interest." Comprehension is also enhanced by "outstanding coordination among the faculty, which allows for the 'a-ha' effect to be much more profound." The faculty, "a split of all-stars and good younger professors, who are trying to make it," are "amazingly capable, challenging, and engaging."

## Career and Placement

UNC b-students praise the MBA Career Management Center; they explain that the office makes MBAs feel as though it "has a personal stake in [their] careers and wants [them] to succeed." Students also note that the office "does an outstanding job of preparing students for the interview process and helping them find full-time and intern positions. In addition, they put a great deal of energy into maintaining current corporate relationships as well as building and improving new corporate relationships. The companies that recruit at Carolina come here because of the quality of the people. Once they recruit from UNC, they rarely leave!" As at most career offices, the services are strongest within the immediate region of the school; "MBA Career Mangement Center is not incredibly helpful if you're looking for positions outside of the East Coast," students observe.

SHERRY WALLACE, DIRECTOR, MBA ADMISSIONS
CB #3490, McCOLL BUILDING, CHAPEL HILL, NC 27599-3490 UNITED STATES
PHONE: 919-962-3236 • FAX: 919-962-0898
E-MAIL: MBA_INFO@UNC.EDU • WEBSITE: WWW.KENAN-FLAGLER.UNC.EDU

Companies that most frequently hire Kenan-Flagler MBAs include Bank of America, Bayer Corporation, BellSouth Corporation, Blue Cross Blue Shield of North Carolina, Deloitte Consulting, Hewlett-Packard, IBM, Johnson & Johnson, Kraft Foods, Lehman Brothers, Microsoft, Pulte Homes, Scott Madden & Associates, Wachovia, and Wood Partners.

## Student Life and Environment

"Life at Kenan-Flagler is always challenging and usually a lot of fun," students note. One student adds, "The school operates on a modular system, so your class schedule changes regularly. I like the mod system because it makes the most of your time here. If the school feels like they only need eight weeks to teach intro statistics, then the class is only eight weeks long. They don't make it 12 weeks just because finance needs to be 12 weeks." Outside of class, "social and cultural activities can't be beat. [Some activities include] semi-annual bar golf, golf tournaments every week, free golf lessons for women, small group potluck dinners every quarter (with a new mix of people each time), Asia night, Latin parties, speaker series, bonfires, 'Prom,' and a slew of athletic activities." In addition, students say, "Club activities abound. We have a very active student-run career network for every conceivable track," as well as "a very active partners' club for spouses."

Hometown Chapel Hill—part of Raleigh's Triangle region (Raleigh and Durham round out the triumvirate)—is highly regarded by all. One student observes, "The community is diverse in cultural background, is beautifully kept, and is safe; the bus system is free; the public library is top-notch; the elementary school system is in the top 10 in the country, which is great for my family. You really couldn't ask for more." The town serves up "a great nightlife, especially if you like music." The university at large contributes "great sporting events, super social interactions, stimulating reading clubs, and lecture series," as well as "a beautiful campus."

## Admissions

Applicants to UNC Kenan-Flagler must submit the following to the school: official copies of all undergraduate and graduate transcripts, GMAT scores, TOEFL scores (international students), two letters of recommendation, three essays, and a resume. An interview is also required. Applicants must have at least two years of post-baccalaureate professional experience; the school notes that "most successful candidates have closer to five years of work experience." The school also reports that "at UNC Kenan-Flagler, current minority students play an active role in recruiting other high-achieving students of color." The school hosts on-campus recruiting events for minority and underprivileged students, participates in the National Black MBA Association annual conference and the National Society of Hispanic MBAs annual conference, and recruits talented minorities to compete for merit-based fellowships.

### FINANCIAL FACTS

| | |
|---|---|
| Annual tuition (in-state/out-of-state) | $16,375/$32,749 |
| Fees | $2,551 |
| Books and supplies | $4,538 |
| Room & board | $15,032 |
| % of students receiving aid | 78 |
| % of first-year students receiving aid | 81 |
| % of students receiving loans | 71 |
| % of students receiving grants | 65 |
| Average award package | $28,953 |
| Average grant | $5,033 |
| Average student loan debt | $62,361 |

### ADMISSIONS

| | |
|---|---|
| Admissions Selectivity Rating | 91 |
| # of applications received | 1,318 |
| % applicants accepted | 49 |
| % acceptees attending | 43 |
| Average GMAT | 672 |
| Range of GMAT | 640–710 |
| Average GPA | 3.22 |
| TOEFL required of international students? | yes |
| Minimum TOEFL (paper/computer) | 600/250 |
| Application fee | $125 |
| International application fee | $125 |
| Regular application deadline | 3/3 |
| Regular notification | 4/28 |
| Application deadline/notification | |
| Round 1: | 10/28 / 12/12 |
| Round 2: | 12/3 / 2/6 |
| Round 3: | 1/6 / 3/13 |
| Round 4: | 3/3 / 4/28 |
| Early decision program? | yes |
| ED Deadline/notification | |
| | Early Action deadline is 10/28 / 12/12 |
| Deferment available? | yes |
| Maximum length of deferment | 1 year emergency only |
| Need-blind admissions? | yes |

### APPLICANTS ALSO LOOK AT

Duke University, Northwestern University, University of Michigan, University of Virginia

## EMPLOYMENT PROFILE

| Career Rating | 96 | Grads employed by field: | % | avg. salary: |
|---|---|---|---|---|
| Primary source of full-time job acceptances | | Finance | 36 | $87,907 |
| | | Marketing | 21 | $84,374 |
| School-facilitated activities | 111 (57%) | Operations | 5 | $68,900 |
| Graduate-facilitated activities | 84 (43%) | Consulting | 12 | $97,918 |
| | | General Management | 4 | $79,721 |
| Average starting salary | $85,589 | Other | 19 | $81,672 |
| Percent employed | 86 | | | |

# UNIVERSITY OF NORTH CAROLINA AT CHARLOTTE
## BELK COLLEGE OF BUSINESS ADMINISTRATION

### GENERAL INFORMATION
Type of school                public
Environment                 metropolis
Academic calendar           semesters

### SURVEY SAYS...
Students love Charlotte, NC
Cutting-edge classes
Happy students
*Solid preparation in:*
Teamwork
Quantitative skills

### STUDENTS
Enrollment of parent
  institution                 19,846
Enrollment of business school   310
% male/female                    69/31
% out-of-state                      6
% part-time                        80
% minorities                        8
% international                    28
Average age at entry               30
Average years work experience
  at entry                         8.7

### ACADEMICS
**Academic Experience Rating**    85
Student/faculty ratio              5:1
Profs interesting rating           82
Profs accessible rating            76
% female faculty                   15
% minority faculty                 13

### PROMINENT ALUMNI
Verl Purdy, Executive VP and
President, AGDATA; Manuel Zapata,
President, Zapata Engineering;
David Hauser, CFO, Duke Energy;
Dr. Robert Rucho, DDS, Senator,
North Carolina General Assembly;
Kathy B. Harris, VP, Software Sector
Chief of Research, Gartner, Inc.

## Academics

A large part-time program "allows working professionals to earn their degree in the evening without interrupting their careers" at the University of North Carolina at Charlotte, a state school located in one of the nation's major banking centers. MBAs in this "incredibly flexible program" can take one to four courses per term at two convenient locations, and as long as they're North Carolina residents, they can do it for a remarkably low price. "I think it's probably one of the top five business schools in terms of return on investment," one Tar Heel tells us.

Belk offers a whopping 9 areas of concentration (business finance, information & technology management, international business, management, marketing, economics, real estate finance and development, supply chain management, and financial institutions/commercial banking), as well as the option to design one of your own. Banking and finance-related disciplines are strong, benefiting from the school's location. Other disciplines also benefit from Charlotte's status as a business center. One MBA explains, "Many of the professors are very active within their fields as well as in the community, and often run their own businesses. They bring valuable knowledge and experience into the classroom, and keep current events in the forefront of class discussion." The program has recently intensified its focus on international business, employing technology to run joint learning ventures with students in Mexico, Europe, Asia, and Latin America.

Students here warn that "Most of the time, the course load is very heavy, but that's the only way you learn a lot from a master's program." Fortunately, when work becomes overwhelming, the professors "are very helpful and knowledgeable" and administrators "are willing to meet one-on-one and they respond to your e-mails almost immediately, even during registration week." Best of all, the school's leaders are "very committed to implement students' input and develop a stronger program." No wonder MBAs express a high degree of satisfaction with Belk, telling us that "it offers a well-diversified and challenging program that's most likely as good as any."

## Career and Placement

Belk students receive career and placement assistance from both the administration of their program and the university's Career Center. The Career Center maintains a list of job postings and recruiting schedules; conducts workshops and counseling sessions in resume writing, interviewing, and networking; and provides assistance in employment searches. A total of 37 companies visit the UNC at Charlotte campus each year to recruit MBAs for full-time employment; another seven recruit summer interns here. Many students attend part-time on their employer's dime and do not use the school's career services—some because they deem the services "weak."

Top employers of Belk MBAs include AG Edwards, Bank of America, BB&T, Belk Stores Services, Carolina Health Care System, Cisco Systems, Compass Group, Duke Energy, IBM, Ingersoll-Rand, Northwestern Mutual, TIAA-CREF, and Wachovia.

## Student Life and Environment

Belk MBAs "are very career-focused . . . working adults" who "spend very little time on campus," and accordingly "many do not have time for much outside of class." When attending classes, students appreciate the "clean, safe, new buildings, and well-kept grounds," but they rarely stick around long once classes end. Full-timers note that "there

RON VEITH, DIRECTOR OF THE MBA PROGRAM
9201 UNIVERSITY CITY BOULEVARD, CHARLOTTE, NC 28223-0001 UNITED STATES
PHONE: 704-687-2569 • FAX: 704-687-2809
E-MAIL: MBA@EMAIL.UNCC.EDU • WEBSITE: WWW.MBA.UNCC.EDU

are a lot of activities which are cocurricular [and] a lot of extracurricular activities, like plays, dramas, and movies to watch together on weekends here on campus. There are also a few international festivals organized by UNC at Charlotte each year." Even so, most feel that "the MBA program needs to be more involved in the community and more active in sponsoring seminars, etc. The school in general should do more to make it a 'non-commuter' school." They report optimistically, "The association representing business school students is trying to bring about these changes."

Students see great benefit in attending school in Charlotte, a "growing city" with "diverse companies that allow UNC at Charlotte to attract students who could go to better schools." Charlotte is a major global banking center and is the U.S. headquarters to over 400 global corporations (among which are nine *Fortune* 500 companies). Health care and technology are also major players in the employment market here. The program's thousand-acre main campus is both beautiful and easily accessible. Students may also attend classes at the uptown campus in the Mint Museum of Craft & Design.

The Belk student body consists primarily of "two general types of students. One type is the recent undergraduate who has either not found employment or is not ready to commit to a full-time job yet. The other type is the achieving professional, typically with four or more years of experience and family commitments that prevent him or her from attending a 'name school' full-time. Thankfully, UNC at Charlotte is devoting its resources to attracting the second type of student." Of the latter, MBAs agree that "Full-time employment gives students excellent working experience to bring to class, probably more so than in a full-time program." Wachovia, Bank of America, Duke Energy, IBM, and Bell South are all major feeders into the program, but over 210 companies are represented here, including nonprofits, real estate developers, and sole proprietorships.

## Admissions

Belk prefers students with at least three years of professional experience. Eighty percent of its students are part-timers who also work full-time. Applicants must provide the school with two official copies of all transcripts for postsecondary-school work, GMAT scores, a personal essay "describing the applicant's experience and objectives in undertaking graduate study," a resume, and three evaluations from "persons familiar with the applicant's personal and professional qualifications." International applicants must provide TOEFL scores (minimum 557 paper-and-pencil, 220 computer-based), IELTS scores (minimum overall band score 6.5), or MELAB scores (minimum 78), as well as a statement of sufficient financial resources to cover the cost of education and living in Charlotte.

## FINANCIAL FACTS

| | |
|---|---|
| Annual tuition (in-state/out-of-state) | $6,052/$16,259 |
| % of students receiving aid | 53 |
| % of students receiving loans | 16 |

## ADMISSIONS

| | |
|---|---|
| **Admissions Selectivity Rating** | **82** |
| # of applications received | 170 |
| % applicants accepted | 62 |
| % acceptees attending | 68 |
| Average GMAT | 575 |
| Range of GMAT | 530–630 |
| Average GPA | 3.25 |
| TOEFL required of international students? | yes |
| Minimum TOEFL (paper/computer) | 557/220 |
| Application fee | $55 |
| International application fee | $55 |
| Regular application deadline | 5/1 |
| Regular notification | rolling |
| Deferment available? | yes |
| Maximum length of deferment | 1 year |
| Transfer students accepted? | yes |
| Transfer application policy | |

All students have to complete the graduate application materials and submit official test scores. With permission, it may be possible to transfer graduate level work from an AACSB-accredited university. This will be considered when the application materials are officially reviewed. At least 30 hours of graduate level course work must be completed in residence at UNC at Charlotte.

| | |
|---|---|
| Non-fall admissions? | yes |
| Need-blind admissions? | yes |

## EMPLOYMENT PROFILE

| Career Rating | 79 | Grads employed by field: | % | avg. salary: |
|---|---|---|---|---|
| Average starting salary | $68,251 | Accounting | 2 | NR |
| | | Finance | 35 | NR |
| | | Human Resources | 2 | NR |
| | | Marketing | 7 | NR |
| | | MIS | 5 | NR |
| | | Operations | 14 | NR |
| | | Consulting | 12 | NR |
| | | General Management | 5 | NR |
| | | Other | 18 | NR |

# THE UNIVERSITY OF NORTH CAROLINA AT GREENSBORO
## JOSEPH M. BRYAN SCHOOL OF BUSINESS & ECONOMICS

## Academics

Most of the students in the Bryan MBA program at The University of North Carolina Greensboro are part-timers, and the school accordingly tailors its evening program to their needs. MBAs tell us that their school gets the job done, praising the flexible scheduling system that allows them to shoehorn schoolwork into their busy lives. They also appreciate a "very affordable price" that doesn't impinge on the "outstanding quality of the program" and technological assets that are "a huge plus for UNCG," including a wireless network that supports "a variety of computing environments and provides access to a wide range of software to support instructional and research activities," numerous computer labs, and modern computing and projection equipment in classrooms.

Classes for experienced students at Bryan are offered in the evening, a system that "allows maximum flexibility for working students, and allows daytime internship opportunities for full-time students." In addition to prerequisite courses (which can be waived for students with appropriate academic or professional backgrounds) and foundation courses, Bryan offers electives in advanced accounting, finance, management information systems, marketing, international business, and economics. Students may also take electives through the masters of textile design and marketing program, a program that capitalizes on Greensboro's historic role as a textile manufacturer. All classes "are taught in seven-week increments, so the pace of the courses is fast. Having this type of class enables you to learn quickly and then apply that knowledge to the next layer of classes you take."

Bryan "does well in pulling experts from the field to teach one or two courses, including CEOs from top firms. Some still practice in their field but most are on a 'second' career as a teacher." The professors "demand that students set high standards ethically, professionally, and academically," but are also "understanding of the multitude of priorities in life in addition to coursework. It takes self-motivation to excel in this program," in which "class interaction is encouraged and stressed." The MBA program recently introduced a full-time day MBA option in August 2004 to attract recent graduates with little or no work experience. The course structure is similar to the evening option but more emphasis is placed on practical learning experiences through summer internships, study abroad, and a capstone consulting course. The students in the daytime option go through "Boot camp"—a four day skill and team building program before they begin graduate level course work.

## Career and Placement

The office providing Career Services to Bryan MBAs is new and dedicated to providing service to MBA and MS in information technology and management students. It will assist current students and alumni, at no charge, in career and internship placement services.

Top employers of Bryan MBAs include Wachovia, VF Corporation, Sara Lee, Volvo Finance, American Express, Gilbarco Veeder-Root, Syngenta, the Moses Cone Health Care System, the Center for Creative Leadership, Eveready, Kayser-Roth, Stockhausen Inc., Dow Corning, Labcorps, Banner Pharmacaps, North Carolina Baptist Hospital, Cone Mills Corporation, Deloitte Touche Tohmatsu, Procter & Gamble, Reynolds American, Dixon Hughes PLLC, Merck, and a variety of regional organizations.

## Student Life and Environment

Because the Bryan MBA is largely a part-time evening program, "Most of the students work a full week and attend classes at night. Add to that the pressures of family and basic household responsibilities, and there's not much time for social clubs and organizations." Even so, the program makes "some attempts at activities, but it's hard because

DR. CATHERINE HOLDERNESS, ADMINISTRATIVE DIRECTOR, MBA PROGRAM
PO BOX 26165, GREENSBORO, NC 27402-6165 UNITED STATES
PHONE: 336-334-5390 • FAX: 336-334-4209
E-MAIL: MYBRYANMBA@UNCG.EDU • WEBSITE: WWW.MYBRYANMBA.COM

most of us work and go to school." On a positive note, "a lot of the MBA social events try to include alumni, which is important and helps with networking for jobs when you get out." The university at large is busy, with plenty of athletic events, theatrical productions, and lectures. As one MBA puts it, "Many of us in the MBA program are too tired to take advantage of all that's offered by the university."

Bryan students enjoy a genial classroom atmosphere in which "the environment is competitive, but students look out for one another and try to help one another out." Full-timers "tend to stick together. Almost any time of day you can find a group of them in the business school studying, conversing, eating, etc." Full-timers also note that "the recreational facilities are outstanding [and] the campus is well-lit and safe." All students complain that "parking is an issue, due to the increased enrollment in the MBA program."

Students tell us that hometown Greensboro, a midsize city with a small-town feel, "is full of entertainment options." The city is part of North Carolina's Triad metropolitan region (which also includes High Point and Winston-Salem), home to 11 colleges and universities as well as a 24,000-seat arena (home of the ACC basketball tournaments), minor-league baseball, and numerous theaters, galleries, and restaurants. The location provides easy access to mountain getaways, Sandhills golf, and North Carolina's two largest cities, Charlotte (a major banking center) and Raleigh (the state capital).

"There is a large group of international students" in the Bryan MBA program, "which enables U.S. students to understand the global business world more clearly." Students come from Germany, France, Italy, China, India, Japan, Thailand, and Holland, we're told. Local students "are a good mix of younger students who recently graduated from undergrad school and students in their 30s or 40s (or higher) who have been in the work force for some time." Many "are technically oriented by degree and experience."

## Admissions

Applicants to the Bryan MBA program must provide the admissions office with a completed application, two sets of official undergraduate transcripts, GMAT scores, a personal essay, and three letters of recommendation from coworkers and/or current/former instructors. International students must also submit TOEFL scores and an affidavit of financial support. The school reports that the average successful applicant has a GMAT score of 552 and an undergraduate GPA of 3.4. Note, however, that half of all successful applicants fail to meet at least one of those benchmarks. Previous work experience is preferred but not required. Bryan fellowships, scholarships, and graduate assistantships are available to outstanding and well deserving students.

### FINANCIAL FACTS

| | |
|---|---|
| Annual tuition (in-state/out-of-state) | $4,092/$15,142 |
| Fees | $720 |
| Books and supplies | $1,200 |
| Room & board | $7,000 |
| % of students receiving aid | 7 |
| % of first-year students receiving aid | 17 |
| % of students receiving grants | 1 |
| Average award package | $6,367 |
| Average grant | $16,581 |

### ADMISSIONS

| | |
|---|---|
| Admissions Selectivity Rating | 75 |
| # of applications received | 131 |
| % applicants accepted | 72 |
| % acceptees attending | 44 |
| Average GMAT | 552 |
| Range of GMAT | 510–590 |
| Average GPA | 3.4 |
| TOEFL required of international students? | yes |
| Minimum TOEFL (paper/computer) | 550/213 |
| Application fee | $45 |
| International application fee | $45 |
| Regular application deadline | 7/1 |
| Regular notification | rolling |
| Deferment available? | yes |
| Maximum length of deferment | 1 year |
| Transfer students accepted? | yes |
| Transfer application policy They must be in good standing at a fellow AACSB-accredited MBA program and may transfer no more than 12 semester credit hours of approved course work. | |
| Non-fall admissions? | yes |
| Need-blind admissions? | yes |

### APPLICANTS ALSO LOOK AT

North Carolina State University, University of North Carolina—Chapel Hill, Wake Forest University, Evening MBA—Winston-Salem

| EMPLOYMENT PROFILE | |
|---|---|
| **Career Rating** | **83** |
| Average starting salary | $70,605 |
| Percent employed | 85 |

# University of North Dakota
## College of Business and Public Administration

### GENERAL INFORMATION
| | |
|---|---|
| Type of school | public |
| Environment | town |

### SURVEY SAYS...
Friendly students
Happy students
Smart classrooms
*Solid preparation in:*
Computer skills

### STUDENTS
| | |
|---|---|
| Enrollment of parent institution | 11,300 |
| Enrollment of business school | 106 |
| % male/female | 60/40 |
| % out-of-state | 30 |
| % part-time | 60 |
| % minorities | 15 |
| % international | 10 |
| Average age at entry | 27 |
| Average years work experience at entry | 5 |

### ACADEMICS
| | |
|---|---|
| **Academic Experience Rating** | **75** |
| Student/faculty ratio | 3:1 |
| Profs interesting rating | 76 |
| Profs accessible rating | 70 |
| % female faculty | 23 |
| % minority faculty | 20 |

### PROMINENT ALUMNI
Jason Coffel, Finance Manager; Dave Goodin, Vice President of Operations; Odella M. Fuqua, Assistant Dean of Finance & Information Technology; Rick Pauls, Managing Director

## Academics

Affordability, convenience, a "solid reputation in the area," and a popular 3/2 combined bachelor's-MBA program draw students to the College of Business and Public Administration at the University of North Dakota, one of only two AACSB-accredited programs in the state. More than half the students here attend full-time, many under the Combined Model that yields a baccalaureate in business and a MBA in five years' time. The part-time population include a number of distance learners; UND has offered long-distance learning for more than 10 years through IVN, the state-run interactive video network.

The UND MBA consists of 32 hours of coursework (35 hours for students pursuing a concentration). Twenty-four hours are committed to core classes, two hours are set aside for independent study, and the remaining hours are allotted to electives. Because this is a small program, concentrations are available in two areas only: accounting, and international business. The former program can be used to help fulfill the 150-hour requirement for taking the CPA exam; the latter program requires students to complete nine hours of coursework at the Business Institute University of Norway. Students here praise the "outstanding accounting concentration" and also love the college's courses in entrepreneurship. In all areas, classes at UND are "small and discussion based," leading to "a more intimate student-teacher relationship." Sums up one student, "This is the best school in the state of North Dakota. It's also great having a Division I hockey team. It helps with recruiting, believe it or not."

## Career and Placement

The UND Career Services Office provides counseling and placement services for all enrolled students of the university. The office organizes career fairs and on-campus recruiting events. On average, about 25 companies visit the campus to recruit MBAs each year; another three visit to recruit summer interns. Employers most likely to hire UND MBAs include Cargill, Deloitte Touche Tohmatsu, PricewaterhouseCoopers, Honeywell, Microsoft Great Plains, Eide Bailley, and McGladdrey Pullen.

## Student Life and Environment

The College of Business and Public Administration building at UND boasts a number of high-tech facilities, including the A. Kirk Lanterman Investment Center, which "provides students access to real-time financial market data and research information, which augments student education at the graduate and undergraduate levels," according to the college's website. The Page Family Marketing Center provides marketing students with a research lab, breakout rooms, a conference room, and a focus group area equipped with video cameras for taping focus-group sessions. Students appreciate these assets, but are most pleased that "all the classes are in the same building, which means we don't have to go outside in the winter!"

Students can make their extracurricular lives at UND as busy as they want. The program hosts a solid complement of professional groups and student organizations. There are plenty of opportunities for physical activity, both indoor and out: students have access to an Arnold Palmer-designed golf course, parks, swimming pools, and a gym. The university's hockey team draws large crowds of winter sports enthusiasts. The area is also ideal for skaters, sledders, snowmobilers, and cross-country skiers. Students report that "the various seasons provide a diverse climate" in Grand Forks, but warn that "the Winter session is very harsh because of the weather."

SUSAN NELSON, MBA DIRECTOR
GAMBLE HALL, PO BOX 8098, GRAND FORKS, ND 58202 UNITED STATES
PHONE: 701-777-2975 • FAX: 701-777-2019
E-MAIL: MBA@UND.NODAK.EDU • WEBSITE: WWW.BPA.UND.NODAK.EDU/MBA/

"Many students come straight out of undergraduate school and into the program" at UND, but the student body as a whole is drawn "from all different backgrounds and all different locations." Nearly one-third of the student body originates from outside North Dakota. Students form a "friendly community" of "smart and self-sufficient" future MBAs.

## Admissions

Admissions requirements to the MBA program at UND include: an undergraduate degree from an accredited institution, with a GPA of at least 2.75 for the full four years or 3.00 for the final two years of undergraduate work (a 3.00 GPA is required for admission under the Combined Model, which allows students to begin their MBA work after three years of undergraduate work); and demonstrated proficiency in basic accounting, administrative process, economics, functional areas of business, mathematics, and quantitative methods. Applicants who do not meet this final requirement may be admitted conditionally, pending completion of coursework in the prescribed areas. International students whose first language is not English must additionally demonstrate language mastery through the TOEFL.

## FINANCIAL FACTS

| | |
|---|---|
| Books and supplies | $3,300 |
| Room & board | $3,932 |
| % of students receiving aid | 40 |
| % of first-year students receiving aid | 25 |
| % of students receiving grants | 2 |
| Average grant | $7,000 |

## ADMISSIONS

| | |
|---|---|
| Admissions Selectivity Rating | 78 |
| # of applications received | 36 |
| % applicants accepted | 64 |
| % acceptees attending | 70 |
| Average GMAT | 545 |
| Range of GMAT | 390–680 |
| Average GPA | 3.2 |
| TOEFL required of international students? | yes |
| Minimum TOEFL (paper/computer) | 550/213 |
| Application fee | $35 |
| International application fee | $35 |
| Regular application deadline | rolling |
| Regular notification | rolling |
| Deferment available? | yes |
| Maximum length of deferment | Up to 1 year |
| Transfer students accepted? | yes |
| Transfer application policy | Up to 9 credits of approved course work can be transferred. |
| Non-fall admissions? | yes |
| Need-blind admissions? | yes |

### APPLICANTS ALSO LOOK AT
North Dakota State University, University of Minnesota

## EMPLOYMENT PROFILE

| Career Rating | 63 | Grads employed by field: | % | avg. salary: |
|---|---|---|---|---|
| Average starting salary | $39,000 | Accounting | 25 | $50,000 |
| | | Finance | 20 | $45,000 |
| | | Human Resources | 15 | $38,000 |
| | | Marketing | 20 | $45,000 |
| | | MIS | 5 | $40,000 |
| | | Consulting | 5 | $42,000 |
| | | Communications | 5 | $37,000 |
| | | General Management | 5 | $40,000 |

# UNIVERSITY OF NORTH FLORIDA
## COGGIN COLLEGE OF BUSINESS

### GENERAL INFORMATION

| | |
|---|---|
| Type of school | public |
| Environment | metropolis |
| Academic calendar | 2005-2006 |

### SURVEY SAYS...
*Solid preparation in:*
Teamwork
Doing business in a global economy

### STUDENTS

| | |
|---|---|
| Enrollment of parent institution | 15,353 |
| Enrollment of business school | 452 |
| % male/female | 55/45 |
| % out-of-state | 3 |
| % part-time | 68 |
| % minorities | 17 |
| % international | 8 |
| Average age at entry | 27 |

### ACADEMICS

| | |
|---|---|
| **Academic Experience Rating** | **80** |
| Student/faculty ratio | 17:1 |
| Profs interesting rating | 85 |
| Profs accessible rating | 82 |
| % female faculty | 15 |
| % minority faculty | 17 |

## Academics

When you consider the cost-benefit ratio, The University of North Florida Coggin College of Business is an excellent choice for the sensible business student, as it offers "quality instructors and overall programs at an affordable price." Intended for students with a bachelor's degree in any field, Coggin offers general graduate level coursework in a wide range of business topics, including accounting, finance, international business and e-commerce. As a vast majority of the school's 450 graduate students are working professionals, the school offers a flexible evening schedule, and classes are also offered on the weekends.

Coggin has a strong "focus on application-based learning." All UNF professors join the faculty with real world experience, and students are expected to take a hands-on, practical approach to their education. A student reports, "I have been very pleased with my professors at UNF. A majority of them have published several books, journal articles, and have also been part of corporate America, such as Dun & Bradstreet and *Fortune* 500 companies. They have brought valuable corporate experience into the classroom." Another student adds, "I have seen a direct correlation between my performance at work and the additional knowledge gained through my MBA courses. Most professors have done an excellent job relating the course material to real-world business examples."

A distinguishing characteristic of the Coggin MBA program is its strong focus on international business. In particular, Coggin offers the unique GlobalMBA program, a business school exchange operated in conjunction with three partner universities in France, Germany, and Poland. The GlobalMBA brings "a ton of international students" to the UNF campus each year, a benefit to the entire student community. "The GlobalMBA attracts students from across the world," writes one student. "My current cohort has nationalities of Greece, Iran, Bulgaria, Germany, France, Poland, and the U.S.A. This makes for a great intercultural experience, as well as a wonderful interactive learning environment." For students in the regular MBA program, "There are several opportunities for UNF students to study abroad all over the world."

Coggin offers a number of concentrations for those who wish to focus their education on a specific business field. Currently, the faculty has approved concentrations in the following fields of study: accounting, construction management, e-commerce, economics, finance, human resource management, international business, logistics, or management application. Students also point out that UNF offers the unique "opportunity to be selected in the Osprey Financial Group, the student run investment portfolio" that manages a $600,000 portfolio of equity and fixed income securities. Still, many students believe Coggin could offer "more options for electives." Many tell us that the research facilities need to be updated; "Really, the biggest improvement [is] the library. It is dated and the material is lacking. You have to go to your local library or order the book you need from another university," writes a second-year student. Luckily, a library extension is underway.

## Career & Placement

Coggin students "mostly consist of local Jacksonville residents who intend to continue their careers in the area." As such, the school is an excellent choice for those interested in finding quality employment in the burgeoning Jacksonville region, as it is "well regarded in the community." This is mainly due to that fact that faculty and administrators work "diligently at keeping their business school on the cutting edge and involving the local business community."

PEGGY TATTERSALL, GRADUATE STUDIES COORDINATOR
4567 ST. JOHN'S BLUFF ROAD SOUTH, BUILDING 2, JACKSONVILLE, FL 32224 UNITED STATES
PHONE: 904-620-1361 • FAX: 904-620-1362
E-MAIL: PTATTERS@UNF.EDU • WEBSITE: WWW.UNF.EDU/CCB/

## Student Life & Environment

With its international focus and active part-time program, Coggin attracts "a very diverse group of students. Some with families, some...straight out of undergrad." Satisfied part-time students praise the fact that "for the working student, UNF is a great university that allows you to balance your educational objectives." While the campus vibe is low-key and friendly, most business students "have busy lives and would really like to minimize the time spent on campus." Therefore, most are uninterested in participating in campus clubs or social activities. In fact, "many of us only attend functions that are mandatory on campus or for our group work."

Nonetheless, UNF still also manages to appeal to full time students. For those who want a more traditional college experience, "the campus housing is pretty good," and "UNF has tons of clubs, sororities, and sports" in which MBA students are free to participate. Students also note that "the weather, the people, the campus are all wonderful." In fact, "the city itself is full of activities from the beach to NFL football games, to clubs to hockey games. You can't get bored!"

## Admissions

To apply to the Coggin School of Business, you must submit a completed application, an application fee, undergraduate transcripts, and GMAT scores. Admission to the regular MBA program is based on undergraduate GPA and GMAT scores. To be admitted, a minimum 1,000 index must be obtained on the formula (GPA x 200) + GMAT total score. GMAT: In addition to the minimum 1,000 index, a minimum 20 Verbal and 22 Quantitative GMAT sub-score and a 450 score total are required for graduate admission. Currently, the Analytical Writing Analysis sub-score is not used as an admission criterion.

Students must apply separately for the GlobalMBA program. To apply to the GlobalMBA, students must submit a completed application and fee, undergraduate transcripts, and GMAT scores. The minimum GMAT score for the GlobalMBA is 500. These documents are carefully reviewed and qualified candidates are then invited for personal interviews with the admissions committee. All applications for the GlobalMBA must be submitted by 4/1.

### FINANCIAL FACTS

| | |
|---|---|
| Annual tuition (in-state/out-of-state) | $5,855/$20,047 |
| Books and supplies | $900 |
| Room & board (on/off-campus) | $3,500/$4,500 |
| % of students receiving aid | 21 |
| % of first-year students receiving aid | 28 |
| % of students receiving loans | 18 |
| % of students receiving grants | 10 |
| Average award package | $3,247 |
| Average grant | $997 |

### ADMISSIONS

| | |
|---|---|
| **Admissions Selectivity Rating** | **77** |
| # of applications received | 266 |
| % applicants accepted | 57 |
| % acceptees attending | 73 |
| Average GMAT | 521 |
| Range of GMAT | 460–560 |
| Average GPA | 3.2 |
| TOEFL required of international students? | yes |
| Minimum TOEFL (paper) | 550 |
| Application fee | $30 |
| International application fee | $30 |
| Regular application deadline | 7/1 |
| Regular notification | rolling |
| Deferment available? | yes |
| Maximum length of deferment | 1 semester |
| Transfer students accepted? | yes |
| Transfer application policy | On a case by case basis |
| Non-fall admissions? | yes |
| Need-blind admissions? | yes |

# UNIVERSITY OF NORTHERN IOWA
## COLLEGE OF BUSINESS ADMINISTRATION

### GENERAL INFORMATION

| | |
|---|---|
| Type of school | public |
| Environment | town |
| Academic calendar | trimester |

### SURVEY SAYS...

Friendly students
Good peer network
Happy students
*Solid preparation in:*
General management
Teamwork

### STUDENTS

| | |
|---|---|
| Enrollment of parent institution | 12,513 |
| Enrollment of business school | 59 |
| % male/female | 50/50 |
| % part-time | 97 |
| Average age at entry | 29 |
| Average years work experience at entry | 7 |

### ACADEMICS

| | |
|---|---|
| **Academic Experience Rating** | **89** |
| Student/faculty ratio | 25:1 |
| Profs interesting rating | 87 |
| Profs accessible rating | 84 |
| % female faculty | 17 |
| % minority faculty | 19 |

### PROMINENT ALUMNI

Nancy Aossey, CEO, International Medical Corporation; Mark Baldwin, CEO, Iowa Laser Technology; Kevin Lentz, Sr. VP, Cuna Mutual Insurance; Gary Rolling, President and CEO, J-Tec Associates, Inc.; Kyle Selberg, VP Marketing, Principal Financial Group

## *Academics*

Combining state-of-the-art facilities, "impossibly friendly" faculty, and a low, public school price tag, it's no wonder that University of Northern Iowa students feel theirs is "the best business program in the Midwest." A friendly environment is balanced with a high caliber of academics creating "a small-college feel and university opportunities," at UNI. Professors are, "knowledgeable, efficient, friendly, concerned, creative, and provide a learning- and result-oriented atmosphere with as little psychological pressure as possible." One current student tells us, "Most of the professors are above standard academically speaking, and are willing to help the students as much as possible." Another adds, "It's a great value and the faculty are very accessible. They are passionate about their work and strive to continually improve programs." On that note, the university is dedicated to offering coursework that addresses current issues in business, and one of the school's greatest strengths is "the diversity of the classes and the desire to incorporate current issues and trends into the various classes."

Committed to providing a thorough but expeditious education, the University of Northern Iowa's curriculum can be tailored to fit the objectives and needs of each individual student. In fact, before beginning the program, every student's educational and professional background is evaluated to determine which foundational courses they will be required to take in order to complete the degree. As a result, students entering the program with business experience may be able to complete the program more quickly, and therefore save on tuition costs. In this and other ways, the school's "great and efficient administration," displays their commitment to students needs. By all accounts, "the school is running smoothly" and "the administration is very active in making sure all students have the resources they need to succeed in the program and beyond."

All courses in the graduate program at University of Northern Iowa are offered in the evening to accommodate students who work full-time or who wish to pursue an internship during business hours. Of UNI master's students, "the majority are working or have work experience" and are able to directly integrate their course work into their current position. In terms of practical, hands-on components, the MBA at UNI culminates in the business capstone experience, a one-credit course in which the student serves as a consultant to a local company under the advisement of a UNI faculty member. In addition, students may gain real-world experience through one of the school's two-week international programs in Hong Kong and Paris, France.

## *Career and Placement*

In the Cedar Falls area, UNI is "well known for its finance and business degrees," giving graduates a step-up in the local market. For extra support, the Academic Advising and Career Services Center at UNI offers workshops, resume reviews, cover letter advice, mock interviews, and Internet resources for job seekers. Recruiters visit the campus throughout the year, and the school also hosts the Fall Career Fair Day, and the Spring Job and Internship Fair for job seekers.

NANCY L. HOFFMAN, MBA PROGRAM ASSISTANT
COLLEGE OF BUSINESS ADMINISTRATION, CURRIS BUSINESS BUILDING 325, CEDAR FALLS, IA 50613-0123 UNITED STATES • PHONE: 319-273-6243 • FAX: 319-273-6230
E-MAIL: MBA@UNI.EDU • WEBSITE: WWW.CBA.UNI.EDU/MBA/

## Student Life and Environment

Housed in the thoroughly modern Curris Business Building, UNI offers "excellent facilities and technology," to undergraduate and graduate business students. A surprisingly diverse community, "MBA students at the University of Northern Iowa represent a wide variety of ethnic, cultural and educational backgrounds, as well as a breadth of future endeavors. The diversity helps to create a dynamic and intellectually challenging learning environment." As one current student enthuses: "I was amazed at the diversity of students in the MBA program (in regards to) marital status, age, ethnicity, and work experience. This was great for classroom discussion." Despite the diversity within the student body, everyone finds a place, as "life at the University of Northern Iowa is well suited to a variety of needs."

Outside the classroom, "There are a wide variety of activities offered through the university at large. In addition, there are a large number of extracurricular and social activities offered through the School of Business." Students note that "the athletic teams are spectacular at UNI," and a source of pride for the whole school community. A number of academic organizations are represented on campus, including the Economics Club, Accounting Club, American Marketing Association, as well as honor organizations such as Beta Gamma Sigma and Mu Kappa Tau, among others. However, the level of extracurricular involvement is laid back and entirely up to each student. "If a student is interested in community or campus involvement, there are numerous groups to join. If the student would rather not be involved, there is no pressure to join extracurricular activities."

## Admissions

Applicants to the University of Northern Iowa must submit official GMAT scores, transcripts from all colleges and universities attended, and three essays, which address the applicant's professional and personal background. The Admissions Committee selects applicants based on their communication skills, demonstrated leadership potential, intellectual capability, and academic success during undergraduate and graduate work. The Admissions Committee considers each applicant's particular accomplishments individually, and admissions essays are strongly weighted in a decision. Applicants must have a bachelor's degree from an accredited university or college. In the past three years, successful applicants have submitted GMAT scores averaging 560–580.

### FINANCIAL FACTS

| | |
|---|---|
| Annual tuition (in-state/out-of-state) | $5,708/$13,532 |
| Fees | $712 |
| Books and supplies | $1,000 |
| Room & board | $5,537 |
| % of students receiving loans | 27 |
| % of students receiving grants | 5 |
| Average award package | $10,664 |
| Average grant | $12,500 |
| Average student loan debt | $5,151 |

### ADMISSIONS

| | |
|---|---|
| Admissions Selectivity Rating | 85 |
| # of applications received | 53 |
| % applicants accepted | 55 |
| % acceptees attending | 79 |
| Average GMAT | 575 |
| Range of GMAT | 500–690 |
| Average GPA | 3.24 |
| TOEFL required of international students? | yes |
| Minimum TOEFL (paper/computer) | 600/250 |
| Application fee | $30 |
| International application fee | $50 |
| Regular application deadline | 7/20 |
| Regular notification | rolling |
| Deferment available? | yes |
| Maximum length of deferment | 1 year |
| Transfer students accepted? | yes |
| Transfer application policy Students may transfer up to 11 hours of AACSB-accredited graduate credits. | |
| Non-fall admissions? | yes |
| Need-blind admissions? | yes |

### APPLICANTS ALSO LOOK AT

Iowa State University, The University of Iowa, University of Minnesota, University of Nebraska—Lincoln

### EMPLOYMENT PROFILE

| | |
|---|---|
| Career Rating | 91 |
| Primary source of full-time job acceptances | |
| School-facilitated activities | 1 (20%) |
| Graduate-facilitated activities | 4 (80%) |
| Percent employed | 100 |

# University of Notre Dame
## Mendoza College of Business

## Academics

Students who enroll in the University of Notre Dame's Mendoza College of Business know what they're getting into. With its storied past, Notre Dame gives MBAs more than just a business education. They get the Golden Dome, Knute Rockne, the Grotto, the Basilica, an education grounded in Catholic values and, of course, some of the biggest football fans in the world. Students say, "Your acceptance letter welcomes you to the Notre Dame Family and means it. I can't imagine a lot of institutions that take such a warm, committed approach to their students. This is one of the reasons why the alumni are tight and supportive." Professors are dedicated to students; one student reports, "I even have a professor who came in to school on a weekend to answer a question that I had about a subject that he did not teach." With all this good will, it's no wonder "the school has a lot of energy."

Because of the school's grounding in Catholicism, ethical studies are a component of most of the classes. Students say that "the focus on ethics make sure [they] keep in mind the most important things when they make business decisions." Still, students need not be Catholic to apply or succeed. As one student says, "I have never met a more religiously diverse group of students. I have learned more about world religions over beers at the bars than in any history or theology course that I have ever studied. People are very open to discussing these 'deep' topics."

Students who entered the program in May and August of 2005 experienced a new curriculum and modular format. Centered on the themes of thought, action, and values leadership, the curriculum combines rigorous training in the basic business disciplines with an in-depth treatment of business ethics and applied courses and projects that require students to put their knowledge into action. Unique to the curriculum are required courses in ethics, values in decision making, business communications, and integrated problem solving.

Mendoza offers elective concentration tracks in operations management, general management, corporate finance, investments, entrepreneurship, business-to-business marketing, consumer marketing, and consulting. Students largely agree that the "finance faculty is outstanding" but believe that the school should offer "more course offerings in nonprofits, law, and accounting." Others add that the school "could use better courses in technology." Students note that it could "do a better job of getting us up to speed on the technology and software that would be beneficial to us as businesspeople and make us stand out in the workplace."

Though Notre Dame has campuses all over the world and Mendoza offers opportunities to study in China, Belgium, and Chile, students wish the school had "more of an international outlook." In addition, in cooperation with Notre Dame's law school, Mendoza also offers a four-year MBA/JD.

## Career and Placement

Notre Dame, like many other schools, has suffered from the poor economy, but its Career Services Department has done their best to combat it. According to one student, "There has been a great deal of restructuring in the Career Services Office. It appears to be working to provide more opportunities for the students, but only time will tell." One student says, "Recruiting is impressive, but it is very regional and there aren't many opportunities for people looking to go back to the East Coast as I am. With that said, I have had great success getting a job on the East Coast, thanks to the active alumni (both grad and undergrad networks)."

MARY GOSS, DIRECTOR OF ADMISSIONS
276 MENDOZA COLLEGE OF BUSINESS, NOTRE DAME, IN 46556-4656 UNITED STATES
PHONE: 219-631-8488 • FAX: 219-631-8800
E-MAIL: MBA.1@ND.EDU • WEBSITE: WWW.ND.EDU/~MBA

With more than 240 alumni clubs worldwide, Notre Dame's network is among the strongest in the country, and the almost-fanatic pride that graduates take in their school means that most alumni are more than willing to lend a hand. As one student says, alumni are "absolutely outstanding in terms of helping students find what jobs they want and helping them get those jobs." Another student adds, "I have yet to call or e-mail an alum that didn't give a positive response."

Companies that recruit regularly on campus include General Electric, Johnson & Johnson, and IBM. The median base salary for students graduating in 2004 was $80,000. About 41 percent of those graduates ended up working in the Midwest and 59 percent ended up working in finance/consulting.

## Student Life and Environment

It turns out that Notre Dame really does inspire a *Rudy*-like devotion in its students, who wax poetic about the trees that "line enormous quads filled with bustling students. Wondrous brick buildings mark the university's growth during the past 150 years. To the south, a modern-day coliseum sits waiting to erupt six Saturdays each fall. And at the center of it all, a magnificent golden dome and a basilica spire rise above the trees, toward the heavens, communicating Notre Dame's grace and power to the world." Because of the school's reputation and fanatic loyalists, students who end up there have often waited their entire lives to be a part of Notre Dame.

One student also points out that another advantage to a small town is that "on any particular evening out, I am likely to run into half my class. The MBA program is a tight-knit group, and I think we respect one another's abilities and appreciate our unique personalities." No wonder the alumni keep coming back. As one student says, most students at Notre Dame are "honored to be a part of the school and determined to be successful partners in its future."

## Admissions

The Notre Dame admissions staff looks for three characteristics in the students they accept: "a demonstrated track record and aptitude for academic success, a track record of professional success, and leadership qualities that show you will be an active participant in the MBA community." Diversity is important to the school, so admissions encourage "you to apply even if your profile is atypical." Despite this, in a class of about 130 students, only about 22 percent are female and 13 percent are minority students (from the United States). The average work experience was 4.4 years, and the middle GPA range was 2.7–3.9. The middle GMAT range was 570 to 740. About 26 percent of students were international in 2005, and 30 different countries were represented.

### FINANCIAL FACTS

| | |
|---|---|
| Annual tuition | $33,400 |
| Fees | $375 |
| Books and supplies | $1,510 |
| Room & board (on/off-campus) | $7,250/$12,260 |
| % of students receiving aid | 88 |
| % of first-year students receiving aid | 56 |
| % of students receiving loans | 48 |
| % of students receiving grants | 67 |
| Average award package | $36,549 |
| Average grant | $15,295 |
| Average student loan debt | $51,573 |

### ADMISSIONS

| | |
|---|---|
| Admissions Selectivity Rating | 89 |
| # of applications received | 598 |
| % applicants accepted | 51 |
| % acceptees attending | 40 |
| Average GMAT | 662 |
| Range of GMAT | 570–740 |
| Average GPA | 3.3 |
| TOEFL required of international students? | yes |
| Minimum TOEFL (paper/computer) | 600/250 |
| Application fee | $100 |
| International application fee | $100 |
| Regular application deadline | 1/15 |
| Regular notification | 2/15 |
| Early decision program? | yes |
| ED Deadline/notification | 11/15 / 12/15 |
| Deferment available? | yes |
| Maximum length of deferment | 1 year |
| Non-fall admissions? | yes |
| Need-blind admissions? | yes |

### APPLICANTS ALSO LOOK AT
Northwestern University, The University of Texas at Austin, University of Michigan, Vanderbilt University

### EMPLOYMENT PROFILE

| Career Rating | 88 | Grads employed by field: | % | avg. salary: |
|---|---|---|---|---|
| **Primary source of full-time job acceptances** | | Finance | 35 | $76,000 |
| | | Human Resources | 1 | NR |
| School-facilitated activities | 80 (54%) | Marketing | 24 | $76,000 |
| Graduate-facilitated activities | 45 (30%) | MIS | 2 | NR |
| Unknown | 24 (16%) | Operations | 5 | $77,500 |
| | | Consulting | 25 | $82,500 |
| Average starting salary | $78,500 | General Management | 6 | $77,000 |
| Percent employed | 93 | Other | 2 | NR |

# University of Oklahoma

## Michael F. Price College of Business

### GENERAL INFORMATION

| | |
|---|---|
| Type of school | public |
| Environment | city |
| Academic calendar | semester |

### SURVEY SAYS...

Students love Norman, OK
Happy students
*Solid preparation in:*
Finance
Teamwork
Quantitative skills

### STUDENTS

| | |
|---|---|
| Enrollment of parent institution | 27,910 |
| Enrollment of business school | 243 |
| % male/female | 62/38 |
| % out-of-state | 19 |
| % part-time | 63 |
| % minorities | 4 |
| % international | 21 |
| Average age at entry | 25 |
| Average years work experience at entry | 1.2 |

### ACADEMICS

| | |
|---|---|
| **Academic Experience Rating** | **87** |
| Student/faculty ratio | 4:1 |
| Profs interesting rating | 69 |
| Profs accessible rating | 82 |
| % female faculty | 17 |
| % minority faculty | 2 |

### JOINT DEGREES

MBA/JD, 4-5 years; MBA/MSMIS, 2-3 years; MBA/MAcc, 3 years; BS in IE/MBA, 5 years; BBA/MAcc, 5 years; Generic dual (MBA and any other masters program) length varies

### PROMINENT ALUMNI

Michael F. Price, Mutual Fund Investor; Richard Moore, President, Lazard Freres and Co.; Steve Moore, CEO, OG&E; Archie Dunham, CEO, ConocoPhillips

## Academics

Students at the Price College of Business at the University of Oklahoma are drawn to "the biggest and best university in the region" because of the reasonable tuition and the perception that "Price is a good school, with a ton of potential, and the support of some heavy-hitters to make it happen." Finance and entrepreneurship are the star attractions at this "small program with lots of one-on-one contact with professors." As one student explains, "The small class size of the program is an asset in that every professor knows who you are and are willing to help you where they can." Another student adds, "The greatest strengths of the Price College lie in the character of the staff at OU. The facilities are nice and [are] getting better, but the desire of the faculty to see us succeed is what's most impressive."

Price works first-year students hard, requiring six core courses from them each semester. Students report that "there's a lot of team and individual work the first year. It's a hard-core lockstep program." While students like the teamwork concept, some complain that the execution is lacking, in large part due to teammates who refuse to pull their own weight. We heard several complaints from students who felt that "the overall academic experience would have been fine except for the group situation. [Students] are forced into groups at the beginning of the year, and typically two of you do all the work, and the three others freeload. I suppose if you are a freeloader, this is a good deal, as you will suffer no ill effects from your freeloading. In fact, you will likely do better than those who do the work; you can study for exams while others are working on projects and papers."

Second-year studies, in contrast to first-year, are "easy and relaxed." However, students feel that too many of the second-year electives "are taught at night as part of the part-time program" at a satellite campus in Oklahoma City. The source of this problem, students feel, is the size of the program; one student explains, "Course offerings are too slim because of the small number of students, so holes exist in student training. If someone does get hired at a top-notch firm, they start behind the curve and most of their learning is on the job." On the upside, Price offers "great summer special programs (both nationally and abroad)." Students feel that the school has a promising future. One student writes, "This isn't a bad place, although sometimes it feels like it's building from scratch. Any opportunities you find in this program will be seeds that you'll need to grow on your own. But the dean has a real vision for this program, so it could go places."

## Career and Placement

The Michael F. Price College of Business Student Support Center offers Oklahoma business students all the following services: workshops in resume and cover-letter creating; mock interviews, videotaped for review; self-assessment tests and other tools; personal counseling; alumni networking opportunities; an executive speaker series; and the opportunity to participate in mentoring programs. In addition, the school participates in the Southwest MBA Alliance to sponsor job fairs and other recruiting events. The office also helps students find domestic and international internships between the first and second years of the program. Students feel the office "is pretty good" and recognize that it labors under a handicap. One MBA explains, "Recruiters won't make a stop here because the pool of candidates is too small to justify it, and more students won't come here because jobs are too scarce in Oklahoma."

Top employers of Price MBAs include American Airlines, Bank of Oklahoma, ConocoPhillips, Devon Energy, Exxon, Kerr-McGee Corporation, OGE, RiskMetrics, SBC Communication, and TXU.

GINA AMUNDSON, DIRECTOR OF GRADUATE PROGRAMS
1003 ASP AVENUE, PRICE HALL, SUITE 1040, NORMAN, OK 73019-4302 UNITED STATES
PHONE: 405-325-4107 • FAX: 405-325-7753
E-MAIL: GAMUNDSON@OU.EDU • WEBSITE: PRICE.OU.EDU/MBA/

## Student Life and Environment

Students report that the University of Oklahoma "has a great atmosphere to work in and a lot of options, when you want to get away from the school life." Most students agree that "Norman is cool, and you are close to Oklahoma City. We have great athletics, and they are a good distraction from studies. Norman is affordable and has a few good bars, although the town dies in the summer."

The MBA program itself, however, has little life of its own. "It's nonexistent," one student writes and adds that "if you don't put it together on your own, there's nothing going on. It's getting better with this year's incoming class, but [there] is no support from the administration for quality-of-life issues (other than the occasional faculty member visiting a get-together)." A good start, one student suggests, would be for the school to "plan extensive social activities for students' spouses and children. Right now the school does not have such activities."

Price students "are driven, friendly, and will amount to something. They are the greatest strength of the program." Each class includes between 30 and 40 full-timers with part-time students filling out the ranks. Price also has a large international population.

## Admissions

The University of Oklahoma considers all the following elements of an MBA application: GMAT score (typically at least 600, minimum 50th percentile in math and verbal, and at least 3.5 on the analytical writing section); final 60 hours of undergraduate course work (students typically have at least a 3.2 GPA for this period); a resume (two or more years full-time experience is desired but not required); three letters of recommendation; and the applicant's personal statement of career and educational goals. The admissions committee also considers undergraduate extracurricular involvement and commitment to community service.

### FINANCIAL FACTS

| | |
|---|---|
| Annual tuition (in-state/out-of-state) | $4,598/$13,349 |
| Fees | $2,838 |
| Books and supplies | $1,067 |
| Room & board | $7,677 |
| Average grant | $6,808 |

### ADMISSIONS

| | |
|---|---|
| **Admissions Selectivity Rating** | **87** |
| # of applications received | 107 |
| % applicants accepted | 62 |
| % acceptees attending | 64 |
| Average GMAT | 621 |
| Range of GMAT | 580–672 |
| Average GPA | 3.52 |
| TOEFL required of international students? | yes |
| Minimum TOEFL (paper/computer) | 550/213 |
| Application fee | $40 |
| International application fee | $90 |
| Regular application deadline | 7/1 |
| Regular notification | rolling |
| Deferment available? | yes |
| Maximum length of deferment | 1 year |
| Transfer students accepted? | yes |
| Transfer application policy | |
| Students may transfer into our PT MBA program from other AACSB-accredited institutions. | |
| Need-blind admissions? | yes |

### APPLICANTS ALSO LOOK AT

Oklahoma State University, South Texas College of Law, The University of Texas at Austin

### EMPLOYMENT PROFILE

| Career Rating | 80 | Grads employed by field: | % | avg. salary: |
|---|---|---|---|---|
| **Primary source of full-time job acceptances** | | Finance | 39 | $55,222 |
| | | Marketing | 9 | $48,000 |
| School-facilitated activities | 18 (78%) | MIS | 9 | $42,500 |
| Graduate-facilitated activities | 5 (22%) | Operations | 4 | $55,000 |
| | | Consulting | 13 | $65,833 |
| Average starting salary | $56,674 | Other | 26 | $62,166 |
| Percent employed | 87 | | | |

# UNIVERSITY OF OREGON
## THE CHARLES H. LUNDQUIST COLLEGE OF BUSINESS

## Academics

Despite its small size and off-the-beaten-path location, the Charles H. Lundquist College of Business MBA program at the University of Oregon is quickly developing a national reputation. Credit lies primarily with two nationally recognized programs. The first, in sports business, provides MBAs with "invaluable connections in the sports industry" through "coursework and opportunities to meet and work with top execs." The other program, in entrepreneurship, thrives thanks to its excellent faculty, who "have propelled this small program into many national top 25 lists over the past three years. This program gives Oregon MBAs unique access to, and preparation for, the top domestic and international business plan competitions." Oregon also offers programs in corporate finance, financial analysis, marketing, MIS, and supply chain management.

No matter what area students choose, they agree that "the greatest strengths of this school are the faculty and small class size. The staff and faculty go out of their way to help students, and the small class size makes them very accessible to each and every student." All 110 MBAs here are full-time students, a situation that fosters a close academic community. This makes it easier for students to face down "a rigorous presentation-skills module that runs for the entire first year" as well as "challenging, team-based projects such as SPP (the Strategic Planning Project), in which students gain experience in planning marketing strategy." Professors earn high marks for "trying very hard to ride the forefront of thought in marketing, strategy, and sustainable business. It is the strength of the institution that the desire is so strong and resources are available to us," vouches one student.

MBAs also benefit from the university at large ("We are encouraged to draw from other schools in the university in order to meet our own needs, which allows great flexibility," writes one student) and "facilities and classroom technology that are highly superior."

## Career and Placement

Success in recruitment faces two hurdles at the University of Oregon. First is the small class size, which many companies see as a disincentive to visit the campus. Second is the school's relatively out-of-the-way location, which is not ideal for a quick visit. One student explains, "Eugene, Oregon is not easily accessible for business recruiters, but there is nothing that can fix that. It is especially difficult to get companies from outside the Northwest to visit the school."

There are other factors, too. One student writes, "In comparative average salary rankings, the Oregon MBA often ranks below other schools for two reasons: 1) Many students interested in nonprofit and competitive sports marketing careers attend the program. 2) Regional unemployment rates have affected salaries in many areas for graduating students." Fortunately, "the Oregon MBA also has a great network of alumni who are willing to work with current students."

All told, 18 employers typically visit campus each year to seek full-time employees; another 7 come looking for summer interns. Top employers include Hewlett-Packard, Intel, Tektronik, ESPN, and Bear Creek. An interesting stat: nearly one in four Oregon MBAs finds his/her first job outside the U.S.

## Student Life and Environment

Even if the location isn't always recruiter-friendly, it is absolutely friendly to the MBAs who attend school here. "Located in one of the most beautiful parts of the country," the University of Oregon bestows an extremely high quality of life on its students. "The town and campus are amazing," and beyond both are abundant natural resources in which

Ms. Laura Balaty, Admissions Assistant
300 Peterson Hall, 1208 University of Oregon, Eugene, OR 97403-1208 United States
Phone: 541-346-1462 • Fax: 541-346-0073
E-mail: info@oregonmba.com • Website: www.oregonmba.com

"outdoor activities abound." While "the workload is heavy" in the program, students here usually find time to unwind. One MBA explains, "Life at the U of O is all about having a healthy environment to support your hard work. I put in a good 60-plus hours a week on school, but when we have free time, students get together and take advantage of what the area has to offer. For example, I had class all morning, then went for a quick hike to reenergize to study until 8 or 9, and then I'll be off to meet classmates for a beer at a local microbrewery. That's a 10-hour day of studying, but I can avoid burning out." MBAs don't have to worry about driving home from the bars, either, since "students enjoy free public bus transportation, which is more than ample."

MBAs don't even need to leave campus to enjoy themselves. "In the university at large, there are plenty of events to go to," such as lectures, performances, movies, and sporting events. MBAs within the program say they enjoy "great team-building activities, rafting trips, golf outings, and bagel lunches. There are also football games and low-key and informal social events where we interact with fellow students and faculty." The Lundquist facility is homey and comfortable, a "beautiful new building that serves as a hub for the MBA students and others taking business classes. And it has all the latest technology." One MBA sums up, "The outdoor and on-campus activities are endless, which makes it very easy to get a good balance of schoolwork and social interaction."

Because of the small class size, Oregon MBAs "all know each other after only three weeks. It makes the experience much more enjoyable." Broadening the social circle is the fact that "the MBA and JD programs have good and frequent interaction, attending each other's events." The program has a "very strong Asian population," but otherwise "there is little racial diversity." Students are "very friendly [and] are very willing to use and share their experiences for the benefit of the class." Although "everyone is competitive, there are no egos."

## Admissions

With a program that is small by design, Oregon allows itself the luxury to hand-pick each student admitted. Students are chosen for their potential in the business world and for their fit with the program. Admissions officers look for those who are eager for experiential learning, who have good team skills, and who are comfortable with complexity and uncertainty. In addition, successful applicants typically have a minimum GMAT score of 600 (and at least a 60th percentile rank on the quantitative section), an undergraduate GPA of at least 3.0, and two years of full-time, post-undergraduate work experience. Prior to enrollment, students must complete one term each of microeconomics and macroeconomics.

### FINANCIAL FACTS

| | |
|---|---|
| Annual tuition (in-state/out-of-state) | $10,560/$15,150 |
| Fees | $1,650 |
| Books and supplies | $900 |
| Room & board | |
| (on/off-campus) | $7,173/$9,800 |
| % of students receiving loans | 57 |
| Average award package | $23,349 |
| Average grant | $4,250 |
| Average student loan debt | $36,000 |

### ADMISSIONS

| | |
|---|---|
| Admissions Selectivity Rating | 89 |
| # of applications received | 140 |
| % applicants accepted | 54 |
| % acceptees attending | 53 |
| Average GMAT | 631 |
| Range of GMAT | 590–670 |
| Average GPA | 3.29 |
| TOEFL required of | |
| international students? | yes |
| Minimum TOEFL | |
| (paper/computer) | 600/250 |
| Application fee | $50 |
| International application fee | $50 |
| Regular application deadline | 4/15 |
| Regular notification | 5/15 |
| Application deadline/notification | |
| Round 1: | 12/15 / 1/31 |
| Round 2: | 2/15 / 3/31 |
| Round 3: | 3/15 / 5/15 |
| Early decision program? | yes |
| ED Deadline/notification | |
| | 12/15 / 1/31 |
| Deferment available? | yes |
| Maximum length | |
| of deferment | 1 year |
| Need-blind admissions? | yes |

### APPLICANTS ALSO LOOK AT

Arizona State University, University of Colorado, University of Washington

### EMPLOYMENT PROFILE

| | | | | |
|---|---|---|---|---|
| Career Rating | 81 | Grads employed by field: | % | avg. salary: |
| Primary source of full-time | | Finance | 38 | $56,929 |
| job acceptances | | Human Resources | 2 | $45,000 |
| Unknown | 64 (100%) | Marketing | 34 | $59,309 |
| | | Consulting | 4 | $62,250 |
| Average starting salary | $57,024 | General Management | 13 | $53,480 |
| Percent employed | 92 | Other | 7 | $45,000 |

# UNIVERSITY OF OTTAWA
## SCHOOL OF MANAGEMENT

## GENERAL INFORMATION

| | |
|---|---|
| Type of school | public |
| Academic calendar | Aug.-Aug. |

### SURVEY SAYS...
Friendly students
Helpful alumni
*Solid preparation in:*
Teamwork
Presentation skills

### STUDENTS

| | |
|---|---|
| Enrollment of parent institution | 33,576 |
| Enrollment of business school | 229 |
| % male/female | 55/45 |
| % part-time | 55 |
| % international | 24 |
| Average age at entry | 31 |
| Average years work experience at entry | 7.2 |

### ACADEMICS

| | |
|---|---|
| **Academic Experience Rating** | **79** |
| Student/faculty ratio | 3:1 |
| Profs interesting rating | 61 |
| Profs accessible rating | 70 |
| % female faculty | 25 |

### JOINT DEGREES
MBA/LLB, 40 months

### PROMINENT ALUMNI
Paul Desmarais, Chair of the Executive Committee, Power Corp.; Robert Ashe, President & CEO, Cognos Inc.; Guy Laflamme, VP Mkg & Comm., National Capital Commission; Mark R. Bruneau, Executive Vice-President, and Chief Strategy Office, Bell Canada Enterprises; André Marcheterre, President, Merck Frosst Canada

## Academics

The School of Management at the University of Ottawa "keeps on top of trends and adapts the program to new trends and the changes in global business practices," students report. The school is ideally located to ride the breaking waves of modern business; Ottawa is the self-proclaimed Silicon Valley North, and it is home to many of the nation's telecom and IT companies including Cognos, Inc.; Corel Corporation; Mitel Corporation; Nortel; and Zarlink. Ottawa's MBA program is geared toward these industries and maintains "a high tech focus. Plus, our proximity to the thriving high-tech sector brings in guest speakers who have relevant experiences." Ottawa's focus on international business is also particularly intense, especially when compared with many American programs.

Ottawa's MBA program is organized thematically with clusters of courses emphasizing issues in integrating business functions, international business, strategy, the developing tech-intensive global economy, and providing value to the business community. Highlights of the curriculum include "a one-term team consulting project, in which students help real businesses with business problems and prepare business plans," among other things. One student notes, "In our project, we are working with the ambassador of Thailand to improve economic relations (export and import) between Canada and Thailand. The focus is about closing a deal. It's very real, and that's great." The MBA can be completed in an intensive full-time program (one year) or a part-time program (28–36 months). Either way, course work consists of a mix of 12-week classes and 6-week modules. The entire program is cohort-based, with no electives and thus no specialization options. In many courses, students have the choice of instruction in English or French.

Students comment, "[Ottawa professors] are extremely interesting," and they observe that "the experience and insight they bring to the classes are invaluable!" Some students warn, "[the professors] have great qualifications on paper but have a hard time engaging [the students]." Generally, MBAs agree that the faculty is "very professional and knowledgeable."

## Career and Placement

The student-funded Career Center at the School of Management offers career-planning services to all business undergraduates, graduate students, and alumni of the university. The office's relationship managers conduct workshops and mock interviews, coordinate recruiting events, assist in the search for internships, and maintain extensive online and hard-copy job databases. The office offers all MBAs a 12-month, 3-stage program; students first learn job-search skills and undergo self-assessment, then commence networking and searching for jobs, and finally learn the finer points of business conduct ranging from etiquette to salary negotiation. Students praise the "many career-oriented workshops/events available."

DIANE SARRAZIN, MBA PROGRAM ADMINISTRATOR
136 JEAN-JACQUES LUSSIER, ROOM 252, OTTAWA, ON K1N 6N5 CANADA
PHONE: 613-562-5884 • FAX: 613-562-5912
E-MAIL: MBA@MANAGEMENT.UOTTAWA.CA • WEBSITE: WWW.MANAGEMENT.UOTTAWA.CA/

## Student Life and Environment

In a typical year, slightly less than half the graduating MBAs at the University of Ottawa are full-time students; the rest attend part-time. Because full-timers move much more quickly through the program than part-timers, this means that the vast majority of enrollees are part-time students. Many students have schedules similar to this student, who writes, "I work full-time and attend school part-time. I go to class twice a week for three hours (Tuesday and Thursday from 7:00 P.M. to 10:00 P.M.). I show up on time and leave afterwards. When projects [are required], our group gets together at the school to plan the project. Otherwise, we communicate mostly by e-mail. Once in a while, we do a conference bridge that one of the team members has access to at work. We sometimes go out for a beer (usually the same group), but then you don't get home until 11:00 P.M. or midnight, which makes the next day [a very long day]." Such students appreciate that "the part-time MBA program caters to students who work full-time. Classes are scheduled in the evenings, and the course work can be completed in three years, or less, while working full-time."

Full-time students must deal with the academic burden of an accelerated program, yet most still find time to enjoy "the well-organized social activities." Some activities include "an annual Halloween party, a Christmas celebration, a food drive, theater night, movie night, and a skating party." Students explain that "the School of Management also organizes many conferences with CEOs of well-established companies, such as Cognos and Mitel." Ottawa students "come from 18 different countries. The diversity is fantastic and crucial in our global business environment." Students say that they appreciate their "competitive and friendly peers."

## Admissions

Applicants to the School of Management MBA program must provide the school with official transcripts covering all previous academic work (demonstrating a 70 percent overall standing of 3.0), GMAT scores (minimum 50th percentile, with a minimum 4.5 score on the analytical writing section), two letters of recommendation, a resume demonstrating at least two years of managerial or professional work experience postdating undergraduate schooling, evidence of proficiency in either English or French, and evidence of mastery of calculus and linear algebra. Students lacking the necessary math competencies may be admitted provisionally and are required to complete the school's "Fundamentals of Quantitative Analysis" course successfully before commencing MBA work.

### FINANCIAL FACTS

| | |
|---|---|
| Annual tuition (in-state/out-of-state) | $12,100/$20,743 |
| Fees | $891 |
| Books and supplies | $1,300 |
| Room & board (on/off-campus) | $4,625/$5,760 |
| Average grant | $5,185 |

### ADMISSIONS

| | |
|---|---|
| Admissions Selectivity Rating | 86 |
| # of applications received | 273 |
| % applicants accepted | 58 |
| % acceptees attending | 65 |
| Average GMAT | 617 |
| Range of GMAT | 580–710 |
| Average GPA | 3.15 |
| TOEFL required of international students? | yes |
| Minimum TOEFL (paper/computer) | 600/250 |
| Application fee | $75 |
| International application fee | $65 |
| Regular application deadline | 4/1 |
| Regular notification | rolling |
| Transfer students accepted? | yes |
| Transfer application policy A maximum of 24 credits could be retained for graduate courses in management completed in a Canadian MBA program or an AACSB-accredited program. | |
| Need-blind admissions? | yes |

### EMPLOYMENT PROFILE

| Career Rating | 86 | Grads employed by field: | % | avg. salary: |
|---|---|---|---|---|
| Average starting salary | $74,884 | Accounting | 5 | NR |
| Percent employed | 96 | Finance | 16 | NR |
| | | Marketing | 25 | NR |
| | | MIS | 7 | NR |
| | | Operations | 7 | NR |
| | | Other | 40 | NR |

# UNIVERSITY OF THE PACIFIC
## EBERHARDT SCHOOL OF BUSINESS

## Academics

At the Eberhardt School of Business at the University of the Pacific, a small cohort of MBAs enjoys a surprising range of degree options, including one- and two-year programs, a part-time option for working professionals, and joint-degree programs in law and pharmacology. The school also offers a unique master's international peace corps/MBA, which includes two years of on-campus study and a two-year Peace Corps assignment.

In all programs, "small class sizes that allow professors to engage students in their education" and a "strong emphasis on field experience" distinguish an Eberhardt degree. Field experience opportunities include participation in an annual global business couse that has taken students to South Korea, Singapore, Chile, Malaysia, Spain, Ireland, France, England, Finland, and Estonia.

Eberhardt offers specialization in five areas: MIS, finance, marketing, management, and entrepreneurship. To accommodate working professionals, many classes are held in the evening. Students with a solid foundation in business principles generally opt for the one-year accelerated program; others choose the two-year track, which begins with a year of classes in MIS, accounting, business law, management, quantitative analysis, managerial economics, finance, marketing, and organizational behavior. Classes are taught by professors who "have great experience in different industries, and apply their experiences to the applications of the course." Students appreciate how "the team aspect of business is stressed within the classroom. The students here apply it to all aspects of Pacific. They have made this a great learning experience." They also give the administration a thumbs up, telling us that administrators "have always been helpful in achieving goals, as well as providing solutions to any problems faced in the past. They've always been reliable."

## Career and Placement

Eberhardt MBAs receive career assistance through the ESB's Career Services Office, which serves both undergraduates and graduates in business. Services include monthly career development seminars, one-on-one career counseling, e-recruiting tools, and access to alumni and employers. Many here commend the office's "major push on networking and finding a job before you graduate. The ESB Career Services Office is very helpful." A few, however, feel "the school could increase the number of alumni involved with job recruitment, possibly aiding with internships too."

Twenty-five employers visit the Pacific campus to recruit MBAs each year. Another 25 recruit here for summer interns. Employers who most frequently hire Eberhardt MBAs include Boboli International, Deloitte Touche Tohmatsu, Ernest & Julio Gallo Winery, Ernst & Young, Accenture, Johnson & Johnson, Kraft Foods, Monier Life Tile, Pacific Southwest Containers, Pac West Telecomm, and the U.S. Government.

## Student Life and Environment

Both the size and the nature of the Eberhardt MBA contribute to a low-key extracurricular scene. The small student body is subdivided into one-year and two-year students, full-timers and part-timers, and joint-degree/non-joint-degree MBAs. With many classes held at night and many students commuting to campus, there can be a lack of social activity. One MBA comments, "It's easy for students to feel isolated, as it seems we aren't as unified outside school as [we] are in class." The MBA Association does its best, "trying to gather students every Thursday for socializing, wine tasting, movie nights, bar nights, trips, and other community services as a means of helping others and getting together." An MBA reports, "About half the MBA population goes to these events. They're usually fun."

## FINANCIAL FACTS

| | |
|---|---|
| Annual tuition | $24,060 |
| Fees | $450 |
| Books and supplies | $2,500 |
| Room & board | $11,112 |
| % of students receiving aid | 58 |
| % of first-year students receiving aid | 70 |
| % of students receiving loans | 29 |
| % of students receiving grants | 50 |
| Average award package | $8,682 |
| Average grant | $7,516 |
| Average student loan debt | $16,033 |

## ADMISSIONS

| | |
|---|---|
| Admissions Selectivity Rating | 86 |
| # of applications received | 80 |
| % applicants accepted | 52 |
| % acceptees attending | 62 |
| Average GMAT | 581 |
| Range of GMAT | 530–640 |
| Average GPA | 3.54 |
| TOEFL required of international students? | yes |
| Minimum TOEFL (paper/computer) | 550/213 |
| Application fee | $75 |
| International application fee | $75 |
| Regular application deadline | 3/1 |
| Regular notification | rolling |
| Deferment available? | yes |
| Maximum length of deferment | 1 year |
| Transfer students accepted? | yes |
| Transfer application policy | They may waive all first-year courses, if they have completed them with a B or better from another AACSB-accredited college at the undergraduate level. Students may also transfer up to 2 advanced courses from another AACSB-accredited MBA program. |
| Non-fall admissions? | yes |
| Need-blind admissions? | yes |

The Pacific community at large offers a great deal more, and MBAs are welcome to partake. One student writes, "Within the university, there are many different schools which include pharmacy, education, engineering, and music (to name a few). By being in a diverse environment, business students can meet other students who come from a wide variety of backgrounds." The campus "has a strong Greek influence, as well as lots of clubs and organizations. If anyone wants to get involved, one does not need to look hard." Another agrees, "Overall, I'm having a great experience at Pacific. Clubs provide a great opportunity to get involved in the community and meet other students. The school also has a lacrosse team that I joined and really enjoy." MBAs approve of the beautiful campus, which "is built much like many of the campuses on the East Coast: brick buildings and ivy-covered walls." The campus so closely follows the Ivy League model, in fact, that moviemakers often use it as a stand-in for Harvard or Yale. On campus, "Students have access to many facilities including the Conservatory, Pacific Theatre, an Olympic swimming pool, track, and many others." The only downside: "While the campus is generally a safe place to be, the surrounding area can be dangerous at night. Campus police do a good job of keeping the university safe, but an escort service would be nice."

Eberhardt MBA's tend to be "young and excited, eager sharks waiting to venture into the depths of the unknown [but] with little to no experience in the work field." Their shark-like qualities notwithstanding, students tend to be "very supportive and enthusiastic about the program." A considerable number "come from other countries such as France, Brazil, and the Philippines, and they bring a wide array of experiences to the education."

## Admissions

Applicants to Eberhardt must submit official transcripts for all undergraduate, graduate, and professional schools attended; two letters of recommendation (one from an instructor, one from a work supervisor); GMAT scores; a completed application; and an interview. The Admissions Committee studies grade trends and ranks students by formula score, applying the formula [(undergraduate GPA 5 200) + GMAT score] and looking for scores of at least 1,200. International students must also submit TOEFL scores (minimum 550 paper-and-pencil, 213 computer-based) and a Certification of Finances. Prior to beginning the MBA program, students must have completed the following prerequisite courses: intro microeconomics, intro macroeconomics, probability and statistics, calculus, and computers and information processing.

## APPLICANTS ALSO LOOK AT

California State University—Sacramento, California State University—East Bay, Pepperdine University, San Francisco State University, Santa Clara University, University of California—Davis, University of San Francisco

## EMPLOYMENT PROFILE

| Career Rating | 82 | Grads employed by field: | % | avg. salary: |
|---|---|---|---|---|
| Primary source of full-time job acceptances | | Accounting | 23 | $49,250 |
| | | Finance | 23 | $46,250 |
| School-facilitated activities | 7 (41%) | Marketing | 18 | $55,000 |
| Graduate-facilitated activities | 10 (59%) | MIS | 6 | NR |
| | | Operations | 6 | NR |
| Average starting salary | $50,857 | Consulting | 12 | $55,000 |
| Percent employed | 94 | General Management | 6 | $58,000 |
| | | Quantitative | 6 | $52,000 |

# UNIVERSITY OF PENNSYLVANIA
## WHARTON SCHOOL GRADUATE DIVISION

## *Academics*

The University of Pennsylvania's Wharton School, one of the premier MBA programs in the world, is best known for its "strong finance reputation," but the curriculum's "strong emphasis on quantitative analysis" extends "across many disciplines, not just finance but marketing, entrepreneurship, operations, international business, real estate, etc." as well. All areas present a "holistic program with a mix of case studies, traditional lecture formats, experiential learning opportunities, and strong co-curricular programs."

Students brag that Wharton "provides all the resources necessary for us to succeed, and then some," reporting that "the difficult part here is deciding between which resources— lectures, seminars, simulations, clubs, special events—one can fit into one's schedule." Writes one student, "The breadth and depth of the academic curriculum and the extracurricular activities is so huge that I would need at least six MBA years to experience 20 percent of it all." A heavy workload, described as "difficult for everyone but the most brilliant to manage," makes those choices even tougher. But what impresses students most here is the degree to which students themselves contribute to the learning experience. Wharton uses a "co-production model of learning" that "requires engagement from all participants in the Wharton community." One MBA observes, "Students sometimes add more value than assigned readings. Students make Wharton. 'Student-run' is an understatement." Another agrees, "The 'co-production model' is not just a buzz word; it really exists here."

Under the Wharton pedagogic system, "Classes build on each other. Professors are known to coordinate timing of discussing certain topics to ensure that the student has mastered the concept in another class." Much work here is done in teams. To promote cooperation and reduce competitiveness, Wharton policy currently forbids grade disclosure to recruiters. Students report that the policy "fosters an environment of helping at the school." Nondisclosure apparently has little impact on students' motivation to work. One notes, "The school has high expectations for each admit, and the overall performance of the students rises to that expectation."

## *Career and Placement*

Wharton is a brand that pretty much sells itself, so it's no surprise that the school's career services are highly regarded and widely appreciated by students. Each year brings the following career placement services to the campus: over 200 employer information sessions; almost 300 recruiting companies; and, more than 5,000 job-board postings. Wharton's Career Management Services Office also offers resume review and distribution, mock interviews, internship placement, one-on-one counseling, and over 25 career treks both in and outside the U.S. No wonder students praise the "fantastic career opportunities and resources." About 40 percent of Wharton MBAs take jobs in the finance sector; 23 percent wind up in consulting; and 10 percent find jobs in the health care/pharma/biotech arena.

ROSEMARIA MARTINELLI, DIRECTOR OF ADMISSIONS AND FINANCIAL AID
420 JON M. HUNTSMAN HALL, 3730 WALNUT STREET, PHILADELPHIA, PA 19104-6340 UNITED STATES
PHONE: 215-898-6183 • FAX: 215-898-0120 • E-MAIL: MBA.ADMISSIONS@WHARTON.UPENN.EDU
WEBSITE: WWW.WHARTON.UPENN.EDU/MBA

## Student Life and Environment

Life at Wharton offers "an amazing number of choices in terms of classes, activities, clubs, etc." It's an atmosphere students tell us is filled with a constant stream of unique opportunities they wouldn't otherwise have. One student cites these personal examples: "At Wharton I have done a four-week study trip to greater China; a consulting project to an Israeli company that wanted to enter the U.S. market; a marketing consulting project for AOL for the mobile location-based services product; a leadership venture to Ecuador next spring to learn about teamwork through a mountain climbing expedition; dozens of fantastic speakers; and finally, some great parties." MBAs appreciate that their "partners are involved in almost all campus-related activities here." One reports, "My wife and one-year-old daughter enjoy going to activities every Wednesday and Friday with the Wharton Kids Club. This has proved to be very helpful in providing an environment where my wife can make lots of friends in a new city, and my daughter can play with other kids her own age."

Hometown Philadelphia "is underrated but still needs work." One Bay Area native notes, "I was worried about Philadelphia after living in San Francisco, but I have been pleasantly surprised by the depth of culture, fun, and good food." Wharton's new facility, Huntsman Hall, is "top-of-the-line" but MBAs gripe that "sharing the building with undergraduates leads to scarce group study rooms. Most students do not use the library because it is overrun with undergrads." Still, Wharton does most things right. You realize this when you ask students what most needs improving here and all they can think to mention is "full-size lockers for each student."

## Admissions

Wharton is among the most selective MBA programs in the country. On average, the school receives between 7 and 10 applications for each available slot. The school's website notes that "approximately 75 to 80 percent of all applicants are qualified for admission." Applicants are evaluated holistically by at least three members of the Admissions Committee. All prior academic experience, including graduate work and certifications, is considered. GMAT scores also figure into the decision. Quality of professional experiences, career choices, and stated goals for entering the program are all carefully reviewed. Committee members also look for evidence of leadership, interpersonal skills, entrepreneurial spirit, and good citizenship. International students must demonstrate competency in English through essays and interviews. Applying as early as possible is strongly advised.

## FINANCIAL FACTS

| | |
|---|---|
| Annual tuition | $39,835 |
| Fees | $5,900 |
| Books and supplies | $2,478 |
| Room & board (on-campus) | $14,200 |
| % of students receiving aid | 87 |
| % of first-year students receiving aid | 60 |
| % of students receiving loans | 60 |
| % of students receiving grants | 40 |
| Average award package | $35,000 |
| Average grant | $5,000 |
| Average student loan debt | $85,000 |

## ADMISSIONS

| | |
|---|---|
| Admissions Selectivity Rating | 99 |
| # of applications received | 7,215 |
| % applicants accepted | 16 |
| % acceptees attending | 71 |
| Average GMAT | 714 |
| Range of GMAT | 660–760 |
| Average GPA | 3.5 |
| TOEFL required of international students? | yes |
| Application fee | $200 |
| International application fee | $200 |
| Application deadline/notification | |
| Round 1: | 10/14 / 12/23 |
| Round 2: | 1/6 / 3/24 |
| Round 3: | 3/3 / 5/19 |
| Deferment available? | yes |
| Maximum length of deferment | case-by-case |
| Need-blind admissions? | yes |

## EMPLOYMENT PROFILE

| Career Rating | 98 | Grads employed by field: | % | avg. salary: |
|---|---|---|---|---|
| Average starting salary | $115,000 | Consulting | 21 | $120,000 |

# UNIVERSITY OF PITTSBURGH
## JOSEPH M. KATZ GRADUATE SCHOOL OF BUSINESS

## Academics

In 1960, the University of Pittsburgh's Joseph M. Katz Graduate School of Business added the country's first one-year, full-time MBA program, which is still the school's signature program. In it, students' brains are crammed with all the knowledge they would normally get from a two-year program in the span of 11 months. Students, especially those with other commitments, love the program. The school experience is "strenuous; you come up to breathe on Fridays, but the week is so busy." Students say that the "program is top-notch in terms of curriculum and pace."

Because the program is relatively small, with only about 200 full-timers in the one- and two-year tracks, students benefit from individual attention of both the faculty and staff of the school. As one student says, "The faculty care about the students much more so than [the] other schools I looked into." Another student adds that "the teachers are exceptional, the dean is energetic, and everyone has a passion to succeed." The attitude of the administration and faculty also rubs off on its students. "Katz has great students that cooperate with each other and help each other whenever they can. It is not cutthroat around here; it is much more collaborative and caring."

The academic schedule for Katz's one-year program is designed for flexibility. The school offers electives during the day and the evening, in addition to some Saturday courses. In this way, students are able to design a schedule that fits their own needs. The first year of the two-year program is mostly core courses (with one flexible option), and an internship is required during the summer.

In addition to the regular concentrations offered at most schools, Katz offers a few "signature programs" that have a multidisciplinary focus. The three areas are the marketing of technology-based products and services, process management and integration, and valuation and corporate finance. The school offers the following dual degrees: MBA/MS-MIS, MBA/MSIE, MBA/MS BioE, MBA/MIB, and the MBA/JD.

## Career and Placement

Though students would like to see more companies coming to campus to solicit their employment, a number of big names have hired from the Katz program in the past five years, including Dell, Deloitte Touche Tohmatsu, Eli Lilly, FedEx, IBM, Playtex Products, PricewaterhouseCoopers, Villeroy & Boch, and WhiteStone Technology. In addition, students proudly proclaim that alumni are "a great resource for the current students."

Even in a difficult economy, employment prospects at Katz don't seem to be dire. Four months after graduation, 84 percent of Katz's 2003 graduates had accepted offers. The average salary for U.S. citizens was $66,000, and the average salary for a non-U.S. citizen was $60,000.

KELLY R. WILSON, ASSISTANT DEAN AND DIRECTOR
276 MERVIS HALL, ROBERTO CLEMENTE DRIVE, PITTSBURGH, PA 15260 UNITED STATES
PHONE: 412-648-1700 • FAX: 412-648-1659
E-MAIL: MBA@KATZ.PITT.EDU • WEBSITE: WWW.KATZ.PITT.EDU

## Student Life and Environment

Katz is located in the area known as Oakland, one of Pittsburgh's "most diverse and intense neighborhoods." Students say, "Pittsburgh is a great, student-oriented city with lots of cheap housing and opportunities for students to participate in cultural activities at reduced rates." If the city isn't giving them everything they want, "the university is large and affords many opportunities for socializing." One student says, "We usually go out and bar hop every couple of weeks as a group. I have made many good friends because of the team activities we do." Katz's one-year program does provide some unusual stresses because so much information is packed into such a short period of time. To combat these stresses, Katz students (like many b-school students) have a weekly drinking appointment that they like to keep. As one student says, "There is a group that goes out every weekend and just relaxes—something that is needed in this type of program." Another student adds that, "socially speaking, the KGSB is excellent at bringing people together. It's good that they finally have a two-year program in which to solidify those relationships."

## Admissions

About 50 percent of Katz's approximately 130 students had one or more years of full-time work experience before they sought to further their education; 36 percent were international students and 27 percent were female. The average GMAT score was 624, and the average undergraduate GPA was 3.32. The average age of a Katz student was 25, and about 19 different countries were represented in the MBA student body including Armenia, Jamaica, Latvia, Morocco, and South Korea.

### FINANCIAL FACTS

| | |
|---|---|
| Annual tuition (in-state/out-of-state) | $13,180/$20,636 |
| Fees | $5,160 |
| Books and supplies | $1,050 |
| Room & board | $11,500 |
| % of students receiving aid | 53 |
| % of first-year students receiving aid | 33 |
| % of students receiving grants | 53 |
| Average award package | $13,000 |
| Average grant | $13,000 |

### ADMISSIONS

| | |
|---|---|
| Admissions Selectivity Rating | 86 |
| # of applications received | 472 |
| % applicants accepted | 55 |
| % acceptees attending | 37 |
| Average GMAT | 624 |
| Range of GMAT | 570–680 |
| Average GPA | 3.32 |
| TOEFL required of international students? | yes |
| Minimum TOEFL (paper/computer) | 600/250 |
| Application fee | $50 |
| International application fee | $50 |
| Regular application deadline | 12/1 |
| Regular notification | 2/1 |
| Application deadline/notification | |
| Round 1: | 12/1 / 2/1 |
| Round 2: | 1/15 / 3/15 |
| Round 3: | 3/1 / 4/15 |
| Round 4: | 4/15 / 5/15 |
| Transfer students accepted? | yes |
| Transfer application policy | |

Matching course work, accepting up to 17 credits from an AACSB-accredited MBA program, provided that credits were not used to complete a previous MBA degree.

| | |
|---|---|
| Need-blind admissions? | yes |

### APPLICANTS ALSO LOOK AT

Carnegie Mellon, Duquesne University, The Ohio State University, The Pennsylvania State University, University of Illinois at Urbana-Champaign, University of Maryland—College Park, University of Pennsylvania

### EMPLOYMENT PROFILE

| | | Grads employed by field: | % | avg. salary: |
|---|---|---|---|---|
| Career Rating | 86 | Accounting | 4 | $52,200 |
| Primary source of full-time job acceptances | | Finance | 39 | $70,100 |
| | | Human Resources | 2 | NR |
| School-facilitated activities | 36 (52%) | Marketing | 20 | $63,400 |
| Graduate-facilitated activities | 33 (48%) | MIS | 6 | $72,000 |
| | | Operations | 10 | $59,300 |
| Average starting salary | $67,000 | Consulting | 9 | $58,000 |
| Percent employed | 93 | Other | 10 | $71,000 |

# UNIVERSITY OF PORTLAND
## PAMPLIN SCHOOL OF BUSINESS ADMINISTRATION

## *Academics*

The Pamplin MBA at the University of Portland is structured to suit the needs of its largely part-time student body. A flexible schedule built around evening classes accommodates a student body that typically is also part of the full-time work force of Portland. About 30 percent of the students here have full-time status; their numbers primarily include international students and students in the five-year BBA/MBA program.

For students with undergraduate degrees in non-business areas, the Pamplin MBA begins with a Foundation Core, a series of college-level courses covering basic principles of economics, marketing, finance, and accounting. Students who majored in business during college skip the Foundation Core and proceed directly to the Integration Core, a cross-disciplinary sequence focusing on "solving common business problems." The Advanced Core, covering advanced analysis of statistics, information systems, finance, marketing, and international business follows. Students may use electives to establish a concentration in entrepreneurship, finance, global business, health care, management, or marketing. Alternatively, students can design their own concentrations in consultation with a faculty advisor. Students may also choose electives from a variety of disciplines and graduate with a degree in general management.

Students praise the Pamplin School for its willingness to experiment and innovate. The school "has the flexibility to allow students to take classes in any area of business," writes one student, adding that she is "working on earning a CPA and CMA licenses in addition to my MBA. There were no other programs in this area that offered all of this!" Another student approvingly notes that "UP seems to always hire guest professors to offer new classes, such as special 'Summer only' classes in areas like real estate or nonprofit accounting and management." Participation in JEBNET, "a network of 30 universities nationwide," allows students who must relocate to complete their MBAs at another school without losing credits.

Portland business professors "are very good. They all have their doctorates, have decades of professional experience in their fields, know other professionals in their respective fields, and invite these professionals into class to give real-world examples of what we are learning." Students also value the school's "great local reputation." The program is "administered extremely well, with regular communications from the school, including schedules, a newsletter, etc. The same cannot be said for the university at large, unfortunately."

## *Career and Placement*

The University of Portland's Office of Career Services provides career and placement services for the school's undergraduate students, graduate students, and alumni. Office staff maintain job and internship listings, company research, and lists of alumni contacts. The office also organizes resume-writing and interviewing workshops, job fairs, and networking events. Students feel that the office, like much of the university, "sees UP primarily as an undergraduate institution and provides services accordingly" and believe that the school "should network better with local companies to get them to recruit on campus." Employers that recruit on campus include Black and Veatch, Deloitte Touche Tohmatsu, Ernst & Young, KPMG, and PricewaterhouseCoopers.

MELISSA MCCARTHY, MBA PROGRAM COORDINATOR
5000 NORTH WILLAMETTE BOULEVARD, PORTLAND, OR 97203 UNITED STATES
PHONE: 503-943-7225 • FAX: 503-943-8041 • E-MAIL: MBA-UP@UP.EDU
WEBSITE: WWW.BUSINESS.UP.EDU/

## Student Life and Environment

"There are no real clubs on campus" for Pamplin MBAs, "and no one seems to care. Because of the scheduling—classes are from 4:00 P.M. to 7:00 P.M. or 7:00 P.M. to 10:00 P.M. Monday through Thursday—it is almost impossible to get out into the community and attend business-related events, or even most school events, since they are scheduled right during the middle of most of our classes." One student observes, "The University of Portland's MBA program is mostly attended by working professionals who are only on campus long enough to go to class and then go home to their families. While there is not really a sense of community with this group, there is a strong sense of pride that we are attending the best MBA program in the city, and one of the best in the Northwest."

The average Pamplin student "is about 29 years old. There are a few of us with a couple of years of work experience but the majority of the students have been out for four or five years and there are also others who have been out for eight to fifteen years." The program is "diverse both ethnically and financially, populated by people who are always willing to help while at the same time are very competitive."

The city of Portland is among the most appealing in the Pacific Northwest. An arts Mecca, the city also hosts numerous fine restaurants, great shopping, and major-league professional basketball. The city's location provides easy access to numerous locations ideal for outdoor activity.

## Admissions

Applicants to the MBA program at the University of Portland must meet the following minimum requirements: an undergraduate GPA of at least 3.0; a GMAT score of at least 500; and an "admission index" of at least 1,100 under the formula [(undergraduate GPA x 200) + GMAT score]. Work experience, though strongly recommended, is not required; applicants with at least three years of post-baccalaureate professional experience are considered optimal candidates for the program. International students must score at least 570 on the TOEFL paper test or 230 on the computer-adaptive version of the TOEFL. All applications to the University of Portland must include a completed application form, a personal statement of goals, official transcripts for all postsecondary academic work, an official GMAT score report, and two letters of recommendation. International students must submit all of the above as well as an official TOEFL score report and a financial statement that indicates they will have adequate support throughout the duration of study. This is required before the I-20 form will be issued to them.

### FINANCIAL FACTS

| | |
|---|---|
| Annual tuition | $24,768 |
| Fees | $420 |
| Books and supplies | $600 |
| % of students receiving aid | 90 |
| % of first-year students receiving aid | 60 |
| % of students receiving grants | 20 |
| Average award package | $18,500 |
| Average grant | $4,500 |

### ADMISSIONS

| | |
|---|---|
| **Admissions Selectivity Rating** | **68** |
| # of applications received | 78 |
| % applicants accepted | 88 |
| % acceptees attending | 51 |
| Average GMAT | 535 |
| Average GPA | 3.2 |
| TOEFL required of international students? | yes |
| Minimum TOEFL (paper/computer) | 570/230 |
| Application fee | $50 |
| International application fee | $50 |
| Regular application deadline | rolling |
| Regular notification | rolling |
| Deferment available? | yes |
| Maximum length of deferment | 1 year |
| Transfer students accepted? | yes |
| Transfer application policy Students may transfer 6 semester hours from an AACSB-accredited program, or all credits in the Jesuit Transfer Agreement. | |
| Non-fall admissions? | yes |
| Need-blind admissions? | yes |

### APPLICANTS ALSO LOOK AT

Portland State University

# UNIVERSITY OF RHODE ISLAND
## COLLEGE OF BUSINESS

### GENERAL INFORMATION
| | |
|---|---|
| Type of school | public |
| Environment | village |
| Academic calendar | semesters |

### SURVEY SAYS...
Friendly students
Happy students
Smart classrooms
*Solid preparation in:*
Accounting

### STUDENTS
| | |
|---|---|
| Enrollment of parent institution | 15,095 |
| Enrollment of business school | 186 |
| % male/female | 57/43 |
| % out-of-state | 42 |
| % part-time | 88 |
| % minorities | 4 |
| % international | 26 |
| Average age at entry | 29 |

### ACADEMICS
| | |
|---|---|
| **Academic Experience Rating** | **73** |
| Student/faculty ratio | 4:1 |
| Profs interesting rating | 72 |
| Profs accessible rating | 78 |
| % female faculty | 24 |

### JOINT DEGREES
MBA/PharmD, 7 years;
MBA/Engineering, 5 years

## Academics

The College of Business at the University of Rhode Island offers a one-year, full-time MBA program with "a very compact curriculum that focuses on the most important fields." Students "like the one-year aspect," noting that "it costs less and is more efficient" than traditional two-year programs. The school also offers a part-time program, which is favored by area students who wish to continue their careers while attending school. The full-time program convenes on URI's main campus in Kingston, while the evening classes for part-time students meet at the Allen Shawn Feinstein College of Continuing Education in Providence. URI's relatively small graduate business program—fewer than 200 students pursue MBAs here—allows students to forge close relationships with their professors.

URI's one-year full-time MBA is a non-thesis program consisting of 48 class-hour credits. The entire curriculum is integrated, with only six credits of electives allowed. Students love how the program is "designed to have us working with real-life small businesses" by "setting up consulting relationships with local companies." They also tell us that "the program incorporates teamwork into every aspect of the program, which is a great strength," and that "all the professors are very competent and demand student participation in class." Some wish that "the core curriculum would offer a little more flexibility" so that "we could develop concentrations for our MBAs," or that faculty would "do a better job of creating a competitive atmosphere and challenging the students to improve the overall quality of the program." Some also feel that "the focus of the program is too regional, preparing you for working in Rhode Island (vs. NYC or Boston)" and that "a greater focus on global business would improve the program."

Part-time MBA students must complete at least 36 class-hour credits. Students lacking in foundation skills may be required to take up to 17 additional credits of prerequisite classes covering undergraduate business material. The part-time curriculum is similar to the full-time curriculum, although it allows students a few more elective options.

## Career and Placement

Career and placement services are provided to URI MBAs by the university's Career Services Office, which serves the entire university population. All MBA students receive a BEACON ("Become Employed at Career Online Network") account in order to access the university's online recruitment system, which is powered by MonsterTRAK. BEACON notifies students by e-mail when opportunities that fit their skill set are posted; it also enables students to monitor the on-campus interviewing schedule and to search a database of job postings. Other services available to grad students include one-on-one counseling; personal assessments; workshops on resume writing, interviewing, and job search skills; mock interviews; resume review; job and internship fairs; and networking events.

LISA LANCELLOTTA, COORDINATOR, MBA PROGRAMS
7 LIPPITT ROAD, BALLENTINE HALL, KINGSTON, RI 2881 UNITED STATES
PHONE: 401-874-5000 • FAX: 401-874-4312 • E-MAIL: MBA@URI.EDU
WEBSITE: WWW.CBA.URI.EDU/MBA

## Student Life and Environment

URI's College of Business has "great technology in the classrooms." Larger classes are held in a tiered-seating facility equipped with touch-screen controls, a computer, a projector, audiovisual equipment, and both wired and wireless Internet access. Smaller classrooms boast many of the same amenities. The business facility also has two computer labs with 40 computers each, a seminar room, and two conference rooms. Wireless service is supported throughout Ballentine Hall, home to the College of Business.

URI is located in Kingston, where "the beach is close" and "apartments are clean and spacious as well as low cost." It's not hard to find housing close to campus. Many students "live in houses on the beach, the type of places that are rented to vacationers in the summer." The school itself makes up a large portion of the town of Kingston, but larger cities and big-city fun are within easy reach. Providence sits a short drive from campus, and Boston, MA and New Haven, CT are both easily reachable by car or train.

URI's campus "is mostly populated by undergrads," and students in the MBA program also "are mostly young—either recent grads or only a few years out of school. Everyone is very nice and social, easy to talk to, and willing to work as a team." "Some are married" and "many have an international background or are exchange students," although "there are also plenty of local kids here, too."

## Admissions

URI offers many components of its application online and encourages applicants to submit materials online whenever possible. Students may provide all of the following materials via the Internet: a current resume, a personal statement of purpose, and letters of recommendation (applicants e-mail referees, who then send their recommendations directly to the school). Students must also provide the admissions office with official transcripts for all postsecondary academic work and an official score report for the GMAT (scores must be no more than five years old). International applicants must provide all of the above plus an official TOEFL score report (scores must be no more than five years old); the minimum required score for admission is 575 on the paper-based test, 233 on the computer-based test. The school notes that applicants with a GPA below 3.0 and GMAT scores below the 50th percentile "have a low probability of admission," but allows that grades and test scores are not the sole criteria for admission. The school seeks candidates with demonstrated strength in quantitative skills, work experience ("valued," but not required, according to university materials), leadership potential, motivation, and communication skills.

### FINANCIAL FACTS

| | |
|---|---|
| Annual tuition (in-state/out-of-state) | $11,048/$31,976 |
| Fees | $2,892 |
| Books and supplies | $3,500 |

### ADMISSIONS

| | |
|---|---|
| Admissions Selectivity Rating | 76 |
| # of applications received | 92 |
| % applicants accepted | 80 |
| % acceptees attending | 85 |
| Average GMAT | 570 |
| Average GPA | 3.2 |
| TOEFL required of international students? | yes |
| Minimum TOEFL (paper/computer) | 575/233 |
| Application fee | $50 |
| International application fee | $50 |
| Regular application deadline | 4/15 |
| Regular notification | rolling |
| Deferment available? | yes |
| Maximum length of deferment | 1 year |
| Transfer students accepted? | yes |
| Transfer application policy Students may transfer up to 20 percent of total credits from another AACSB-accredited college/university. | |
| Non-fall admissions? | yes |
| Need-blind admissions? | yes |

### APPLICANTS ALSO LOOK AT

Babson College, Boston College, Boston University, Bryant University, Northeastern University, Suffolk University, University of Connecticut

### EMPLOYMENT PROFILE

| | |
|---|---|
| Career Rating | 67 |
| Average starting salary | $62,576 |

# UNIVERSITY OF RICHMOND
## ROBINS SCHOOL OF BUSINESS

## GENERAL INFORMATION
| | |
|---|---|
| Type of school | private |
| Environment | metropolis |
| Academic calendar | semester |

## SURVEY SAYS...
Friendly students
Good peer network
Happy students
Smart classrooms
*Solid preparation in:*
Accounting

## STUDENTS
| | |
|---|---|
| Enrollment of parent institution | 4,487 |
| Enrollment of business school | 153 |
| % part-time | 100 |
| Average age at entry | 27 |
| Average years work experience at entry | 4 |

## ACADEMICS
| | |
|---|---|
| **Academic Experience Rating** | **84** |
| Student/faculty ratio | 3:1 |
| Profs interesting rating | 87 |
| Profs accessible rating | 86 |
| % female faculty | 22 |
| % minority faculty | 7 |

## JOINT DEGREES
JD/MBA, 3–4 years

## PROMINENT ALUMNI
David Beran, Senior VP, Philip Morris USA; Lyn McDermid, CIO, Dominion Resources; Lew Boggs, President, Property Investment Advisors; Rex Smith, President & CEO, Bank of Richmond; Mark Hourigan, President, Hourigan Construction

## Academics

Offering "an excellent MBA program for part-time working students," the University of Richmond is ideal for business professionals looking to expand their skill set and advance their career opportunities. The curriculum is "geared toward business in the real world and not just conceptual skills" and, from the first day of classes, practical applications of business issues are stressed. In fact, the program begins with the opening residency, a case-based course that introduces students to business topics through a "live" case.

In the classroom, professors "are not strict academics, but bring an extensive amount of background from the professional world;" "classes focus on cases and discussions more so than on lectures and books." Group work and student participation is encouraged, and the classroom environment is characterized by "rich discussions and a laid back atmosphere that fosters contributions from all points of view." Students tell us that "the atmosphere is collaborative and genuinely friendly" and "the professors are terrific and interested in learning from us as we learn from them."

"The past two associate deans of the school have been very progressive," one student asserts, "and as a result they have been able to create a strong, relevant, and current MBA program." This program includes course work in current topics such as leadership, ethics, and international business. A unique requirement of the Richmond MBA is that all students must participate in the international residency, a weeklong consulting project in a foreign country in Asia, Latin America, or Central or Eastern Europe.

Given the program's focus on working students, professors are sensitive to the needs of part-time students. All classes are taught at night and students "can even meet with some faculty on Sunday afternoons." Even so, students warn us that the "workload is slightly overboard given that 95 percent of us are trying to juggle school with very demanding day jobs." However, one student contests: "The school is academically challenging but not busy work; it is work that actually helps me to be more successful at work. I feel more knowledgeable regarding the global economy and trends than ever before."

## Career and Placement

Many students choose University of Richmond based on the advice of their colleagues and employers, as it has a "fine reputation for being a challenging program that allows its graduates to advance in their careers." While the school is very efficient at accomplishing this goal, students complain that "because the program is part-time and most students go through the program while continuing to work full-time during the day, there is no career office to help in a job search besides the general one that's focused on undergraduate students." In fact, "the careers services branch is strong for undergrads and the law school," but "the school has made little effort to attract area employers to campus to target MBA students or program graduates." Many suggest that while "a formal office may not be needed, it would be nice to have a few faculty members who function as career counselors and are able to attract employers to campus specifically for MBAs when appropriate." Even so, students say they benefit immensely from the school's strong standing in the local community, as well as its "great reputation throughout the Southeast with a growing national reputation."

Dr. Richard S. Coughlan, Associate Dean for Graduate and Executive Programs
MBA Office, Robins School of Business University of Richmond, Richmond, VA 23173 U.S.
Phone: 804-289-8553 • Fax: 804-287-1228 • E-mail: mba@richmond.edu
Website: www.business.richmond.edu/mba

## Student Life and Environment

With a lovely academic environment—even for graduate students screeching in after a long day of work—the University of Richmond's "campus is beautiful and the classrooms have the latest in technology tools." Generally speaking, the Richmond MBA caters to "very hard working professionals from the Richmond area." However, professionally speaking, students hail from a wide variety of backgrounds, "from the military to corporate America to government and nonprofit."

As the program is primarily part-time, there "is not much campus activity associated with the program. Its classes and that's it." Even so, you might be surprised to learn that U of R students "are relatively social, so they gather on their own a great deal." A student explains: "We don't have all the bells and whistles of a normal, full-time MBA program, such as student clubs and organizations. That's not to say we're not social and never get together after classes, though." Another adds, "We have a good time with each other, get to know each other really well, and enjoy our experience." Even those who have little time outside the program find that "the international residency program, where you spend a week abroad with your classmates working on a business case [in] a foreign company, is a great bonding experience." However, some would like to see "more activities catered to families with children. I have not seen any such activities advertised by the business school; if they are, they aren't very noticeable."

## Admissions

Applicants to the Robins School of Business must submit a completed application form, official GMAT scores, official transcripts from each college and university attended, and a current resume. As the program is designed for working professionals, students are required to have at least two years of relevant work experience after completion of their bachelor's degree, though the average student applies with more than 4 years of experience. There are no minimum GPA or GMAT requirements. As a point of reference, in the past year accepted students had an average GMAT score of 586 and an average undergraduate GPA of 3.27. While the majority of students attend part-time, students may apply to complete the program full-time, or apply to the JD/MBA joint-degree program. Applicants to either the full-time or joint-degree program may be considered without prior work experience.

### FINANCIAL FACTS

| | |
|---|---|
| Annual tuition | $26,300 |
| Books and supplies | $2,300 |
| Average award package | $10,020 |
| Average student loan debt | $31,800 |

### ADMISSIONS

| | |
|---|---|
| **Admissions Selectivity Rating** | **76** |
| # of applications received | 76 |
| % applicants accepted | 88 |
| % acceptees attending | 88 |
| Average GMAT | 586 |
| Range of GMAT | 540–640 |
| Average GPA | 3.27 |
| TOEFL required of international students? | yes |
| Minimum TOEFL (paper/computer) | 600/250 |
| Application fee | $50 |
| International application fee | $50 |
| Regular application deadline | 5/1 |
| Regular notification | 6/1 |
| Deferment available? | yes |
| Maximum length of deferment | 1 year |
| Transfer students accepted? | yes |
| Transfer application policy Students may transfer a maximum of 12 hours from other AACSB-accredited schools. | |
| Need-blind admissions? | yes |

### APPLICANTS ALSO LOOK AT

The College of William and Mary, University of Virginia, Wake Forest University—Babcock

# UNIVERSITY OF ROCHESTER
## WILLIAM E. SIMON GRADUATE SCHOOL OF BUSINESS ADMINISTRATION

## Academics

"The hallmarks of a Simon Graduate School education are its integration around economic principles and its long-term applicability," school representatives tell us, and students concur. One MBA notes, "Particularly consistent is the economics-based approach that returns in every (yes, every single) class. Sending consistent messages to the students is so very important and creates a solid understanding of business processes that is timeless. If you are looking for the most solid, no-nonsense MBA with a great return on investment, this is the school for you." The Simon approach includes a "heavy quantitative emphasis" that fits well with the school's strongest discipline: finance. Brand management and strategy are among Simon Graduate School's other strong areas.

The Simon Graduate School curriculum lays the work on heavy in the first-year core. One student explains, "The academic workload is different in the first year from what it is in the second year. The first year is brutal—constant team assignments, exams, studying, and labs. I spent most of the first year on campus, scared that I wasn't going to learn enough to keep up with my classmates." Accordingly, first year requires "great time management skills. You are assigned so much homework, reading assignments, and team projects, it's impossible to finish everything. In addition, you have to prepare your resume and cover letters and research for summer internship. Not to mention that networking experience is a big part of b-school, and that requires time to contribute to club activities." The second year "is much more relaxed, in that all the time and effort put into learning the concepts in the first year now allows you to understand concepts in class and apply things better. Teamwork is still extensive in the second year but the pressure to perform doesn't feel as great."

Throughout, students get to know their classmates and professors well because of the "warm and friendly climate" fostered by the small size of the program. One MBA reports, "The professors really get to know you with the smaller size of the classes. It isn't uncommon for professors to cold-call, but not in an intimidating manner. With classes small and classmates and professors comfortable with each other, lectures are interesting and entertaining, personal, and friendly. The school encourages an environment where students ask questions throughout the class, and what started as a lecture becomes a discussion. The small size also means that you know your classmates well and you can approach them with pretty much any question, be it about an assignment, career-related, or just a ride to the happy hour."

The Simon Graduate School "offers 14 concentrations ranging from the more broad-based (finance) to the more specialized (e-commerce and health-sciences management).

## Career and Placement

The Career Management Center at the Simon Graduate School recognizes that its remote location is a handicap to students' job searches. To address this situation, the school holds annual interview sessions in New York City and participates in several national consortia to sponsor twice-yearly job fairs in New York City and Atlanta. On-campus interviews, as well as speakers, career panels, video interviewing, and alumni programs supplement these efforts. A recent restructuring of the CMC has made it more amenable to the needs of students planning careers in fields other than finance, and it is working to increase on-campus recruiting.

GREGORY V. MacDONALD, EXECUTIVE DIRECTOR FOR MBA ADMISSIONS AND ADMINISTRATION
305 SCHLEGEL HALL, ROCHESTER, NY 14627 UNITED STATES
PHONE: 585-275-3533 • FAX: 585-271-3907
E-MAIL: ADMISSIONS@SIMON.ROCHESTER.EDU • WEBSITE: WWW.SIMON.ROCHESTER.EDU

## FINANCIAL FACTS

| | |
|---|---|
| Annual tuition | $34,710 |
| Fees | $897 |
| Books and supplies | $1,510 |
| Room & board | $8,504 |
| % of students receiving grants | 65 |

## ADMISSIONS

| | |
|---|---|
| **Admissions Selectivity Rating** | **93** |
| # of applications received | 644 |
| % applicants accepted | 42 |
| % acceptees attending | 40 |
| Average GMAT | 664 |
| Average GPA | 3.45 |
| TOEFL required of international students? | yes |
| Application fee | $125 |
| International application fee | $125 |
| Regular application deadline | 12/1 |
| Regular notification | 2/15 |
| Application deadline/notification | |
| Round 1: | 12/1 / 2/15 |
| Round 2: | 2/1 / 3/31 |
| Round 3: | 4/1 / 5/15 |
| Round 4: | 6/1 / 7/1 |
| Early decision program? | yes |
| ED deadline/notification | 11/1 / 1/15 |
| Transfer students accepted? | yes |
| Transfer application policy | |
| No more than 9 credit hours, may not be core courses. | |
| Non-fall admissions? | yes |
| Need-blind admissions? | yes |

Employers who most often hire Simon MBAs include American Express, Barclays, Bausch and Lomb, Citigroup, Deloitte Touche Tohmatsu, Diageo, Ford, General Electric, Harris RF Communications, JPMorgan Chase, Johnson & Johnson, Kraft Foods, M & T Bank, Manning & Napier Advisors, OppenheimerFunds, PAETEC Communications, PricewaterhouseCoopers, Playtex, Reckitt & Benckiser, UBS Financial Services, and Xerox.

## Student Life and Environment

"Due to the quarter system, with midterms and finals arriving quickly, there's a very intense workload" at the Simon school, "so most of school life is spent studying and working on team projects." That's especially true during the demanding first year of the program. Even so, "we also have a great social life here, with all sorts of events to go to and interact with peers. They are usually very well attended, too: Simon Games, Flip Cup, happy hours, bowling, and karaoke. Many events are family-oriented. There are also a lot of professional opportunities for students through clubs, special organizations, and speakers." Happy hours are frequent; the MBA Association holds one every other week, and most clubs hold them almost as frequently. Occasional road trips take students to "professional sporting events in Buffalo, theater, and shopping trips to Toronto—that sort of thing."

Hometown Rochester is "a good, midsize city" and "a charming town," but its "winter is ridiculously long, cold, and snowy." The U of R campus "has excellent amenities, and Simon Graduate School has three of its own buildings, constructed in 1991 and 2001," which "are very nice, as is not having to mix with undergraduates (no undergrad business school)." The program has a large international population, whom students welcome with a single caveat: "Many international students have poor language skills, which is a big problem with team projects," some students warn.

## Admissions

According to the school's website, the Simon admissions committee "does not apply specific weights to the main criteria, but rather makes evaluations on the cumulative strength of each application as it compares to others received that year. Work experience, undergraduate record, GMAT results, personal recommendations, and required essays provide the basis for evaluation." Verbal skills count; applicants must score a minimum 40th percentile on the GMAT Verbal section, with at least a 3.5 on the Writing Sample. The Simon School is a member of the Consortium for Graduate Study in Management (headquartered in St. Louis) and participates in its programs to recruit minority and disadvantaged students.

## APPLICANTS ALSO LOOK AT

Carnegie Mellon University, Columbia University, Cornell University, Indiana University—Purdue, University at Fort Wayne, New York University

## EMPLOYMENT PROFILE

| | | | | |
|---|---|---|---|---|
| Career Rating | 83 | **Grads employed by field:** | **%** | **avg. salary:** |
| **Primary source of full-time** | | Finance | 56 | $83,461 |
| **job acceptances** | | Marketing | 20 | $76,658 |
| School-facilitated activities | 68 (67%) | Consulting | 15 | $87,889 |
| Graduate-facilitated activities | 34 (33%) | General Management | 6 | $78,667 |
| | | Other | 3 | $74,667 |
| Average starting salary | $81,735 | | | |
| Percent employed | 88 | | | |

# UNIVERSITY OF SAN FRANCISCO
## MASAGUNG GRADUATE SCHOOL OF MANAGEMENT

## GENERAL INFORMATION
| | |
|---|---|
| Type of school | private |
| Affiliation | Jesuit |
| Environment | metropolis |

### SURVEY SAYS...
Students love San Francisco, CA
Friendly students
*Solid preparation in:*
Teamwork
Doing business in a global economy

### STUDENTS
| | |
|---|---|
| Enrollment of parent institution | 8,110 |
| Enrollment of business school | 309 |
| % male/female | 56/44 |
| % minorities | 30 |
| % international | 35 |
| Average age at entry | 28 |
| Average years work experience at entry | 5 |

### ACADEMICS
| | |
|---|---|
| **Academic Experience Rating** | **82** |
| Student/faculty ratio | 10:1 |
| Profs interesting rating | 82 |
| Profs accessible rating | 72 |
| % female faculty | 20 |
| % minority faculty | 25 |

### JOINT DEGREES
JD/MBA; MAPS/MBA (Asian Pacific Studies); MSEM/MBA (Master of Science in Environmental Management); MSFA/MBA

### PROMINENT ALUMNI
Gordon Smith, CEO, PG&E; Lip Bu-Tan, Founder, Walden International Investment Group; Mary Callanan, Retired Treasurer for the County/City of San Francisco; Angela Alioto, Attorney, Political Leader; Pierre Salinger, Former Press Secretary to the U.S. President

## Academics

"You will receive a grounded, broad-based business degree with lots of teamwork experience" at University of San Francisco's Masagung Graduate School of Management, according to students. If you choose to, you can also pursue an emphasis in telecommunications; USF's unique telecom program takes advantage of the school's "strategic location" among the headquarters of many IT and telecom giants. Hometown San Francisco is also a major financial center of the Pacific Coast; it should come as no surprise, then, that the school also boasts solid programs in finance and entrepreneurship. One student writes, "Our greatest strength is the extensive entrepreneur program. We host the business-plan competition, have venture-capital classes, and have instructors who are real entrepreneurs."

Location plays a key role in many of Masagung's successes. Students explain that "the school has close ties to the surrounding business community, which will be helpful after graduation." Because San Francisco is a world-class city, it is a magnet for great minds and great business people, and some of these folks wind up teaching courses at USF.

Masagung instructors "do a good job bringing relevant experience to the classroom. Some are "spectacular" and "very motivating," and "all seem genuinely interested in each student's education. They encourage open discussions, and the use of teams for research projects/presentations is integrated into most classes," according to students. One MBA observes, "Having attended a large public undergraduate institution, I was completely unprepared for the amount of face-time I get with my professors at the USF MBA program. Overall, they make an effort to be accessible and are fantastic instructors. [That's the] best thing about this program." And if a professor fails to meet expectations, students can take comfort in the fact that "USF has a good feedback process among the students independent of the administrative review."

Masagung allows students to develop an emphasis in entrepreneurship, finance, international business, marketing, or telecommunications. They may also choose a broad range of electives to earn a degree in general management. International study tours are available, as is a semester in Beijing. Students may take advantage of the Jesuit Network to earn exchange-student privileges at numerous institutions around the world.

## Career and Placement

The USF Career Services Center offers networking opportunities, a resource center, workshops, counseling, and MBA Alumni Society events. Career Forums and the Job and Internship Fair bring approximately 30 recruiting companies to campus each year, including Accenture; Sprint; Wells Fargo; Fair Isaac; Eastman Kodak; and Infoex International, Inc.

Employers most likely to hire Masagung MBAs include Advanced Fibre Communications; Bank of the West; BioMarin Pharmaceutical, Inc.; California Bank and Trust; Charles Schwab; Cisco Systems; EMQ Children & Family Services; Ernst & Young, LLP; Franchise Tax Board; IBM Global Services; Inverito, Inc.; KPMG; The LaRose Group; Lautze & Lautze; Live Capital; Marcus & Millichap; Marsh, Inc.; Mervyns; OPT Derivatives; Pacific Gas and Electric Company; Peat Marwick; Persona, International; Prudential; Salomon Smith Barney; Systron-Donner; Walden International Investment Group; and Wells Capital Management.

MELISSA DELANEY, ACTING DIRECTOR
2130 FULTON STREET, LONE MOUNTAIN, SAN FRANCISCO, CA 94117-1045 UNITED STATES
PHONE: 415-422-2089 • FAX: 415-422-2066
E-MAIL: GRADUATE@USFCA.EDU • WEBSITE: WWW.USFCA.EDU/SOBAM

## Student Life and Environment

Like the population of the city that it calls home, "USF students are diverse in cultures and professions. We enjoy an open atmosphere for dialogue among different views and backgrounds, which aids in learning." Students agree that the school has a large international population, "so if you want to learn about the global business, this is the school."

Students also explain that "because the University of San Francisco is a Jesuit private school, students are mostly calm, well-educated, and compassionate. We have many community activities that our school minister organizes." The small student body makes it "easy to make friends who stick with you through the program. We have enjoyable working relationships, and the school atmosphere promotes social interaction in group studies/work and facilitates proper teamwork." Another benefit of the size of the program is that "we don't need to fight for things like parking spaces, computers, or classes as often as students in public schools."

Students enjoy USF's new School of Business and Management facility. One student writes, "We have all our classes at smart classrooms, and there [is] a lounge area [where] we can study or socialize."

## Admissions

Students admitted to the Masagung MBA program are expected to arrive with proficiency in mathematics through college algebra, statistics through hypothesis testing and standard deviation, fundamental accounting, basic computer skills (word processing, spreadsheet functions), and business writing. The school offers foundation courses in all these areas; these courses are waived for students who demonstrate the required skills. Applicants must submit official copies of all undergraduate and graduate transcripts, GMAT scores, TOEFL scores (international students), two letters of recommendation, two personal essays, and a resume. Interviews are encouraged but not required. Students may enter in either the Fall or Spring semester.

### FINANCIAL FACTS

| | |
|---|---|
| Annual tuition | $23,125 |
| Fees | $444 |
| Books and supplies | $1,250 |
| Room & board (on-campus) | $8,324 |

### ADMISSIONS

| | |
|---|---|
| Admissions Selectivity Rating | 86 |
| # of applications received | 372 |
| % applicants accepted | 40 |
| % acceptees attending | 54 |
| Average GMAT | 573 |
| Range of GMAT | 500–650 |
| Average GPA | 3.13 |
| TOEFL required of international students? | yes |
| Minimum TOEFL (paper/computer) | 600/250 |
| Application fee | $55 |
| International application fee | $65 |
| Regular application deadline | 6/1 |
| Regular notification | rolling |
| Deferment available? | yes |
| Maximum length of deferment | 1 year |
| Transfer students accepted? | yes |
| Transfer application policy Transfer up to 6 credits for students coming from another AACSB-accredited program. | |
| Non-fall admissions? | yes |

### APPLICANTS ALSO LOOK AT

Pepperdine University, Santa Clara University, University of California—Irvine, University of San Diego

### EMPLOYMENT PROFILE

| Career Rating | 78 | Grads employed by field: | % | avg. salary: |
|---|---|---|---|---|
| Average starting salary | $68,000 | Finance | 14 | $72,000 |
| | | Marketing | 39 | $70,000 |
| | | MIS | 7 | $63,000 |
| | | Consulting | 4 | $65,000 |
| | | General Management | 4 | $59,000 |
| | | Nonprofit | 1 | $52,000 |
| | | Other | 31 | $55,000 |

# UNIVERSITY OF SCRANTON
## KANIA SCHOOL OF MANAGEMENT

## *Academics*

Offering Northeast Pennsylvania's only AACSB-accredited MBA program, the University of Scranton delivers graduate business study that not only "emphasizes a set of skills and perspectives needed to succeed in the increasingly fast-paced, global and technology-oriented business environment" but does so within the ethical framework of a Catholic education. Typical of Jesuit institutions, the University of Scranton expects its professors to dedicate themselves to teaching. Apparently they meet that expectation; students report, "The faculty here is outstanding. Our professors are very accessible outside the classroom to review course material and offer career guidance."

For students with little academic or professional background in business, the Scranton MBA begins with qualifying modules covering basic concepts in statistics, management, information management, finance, accounting, and marketing. Qualified students may skip these modules and proceed directly to 10 extending courses of their choosing, including at least one international course. The extending courses advance the basic functional areas of business: accounting, enterprise management technology, marketing, management, managerial economics, organizational behavior, financial management, management information systems, and operations management.

The Scranton MBA curriculum also allows for four advanced electives, at least one of which must cover material pertaining to international business. Students may fashion a field of specialization by taking no more than four extending courses in one of the following areas: accounting, finance, international business, marketing, operations management, management information systems, and enterprise management technology. Students may also complete a dual specialization by taking four unique courses in each of the two specialization areas. Specialization is not required; students may choose instead to earn a general MBA degree.

To complete the MBA degree, Scranton students must take two mission specific courses. business policy, which is designed to "synthesize the knowledge students have gained in every other extending course in the program." In this course, MBAs "develop, present, and defend their own policy recommendations in case studies which require an understanding of all areas of business to make sound judgments." The other required course is responsibility, sustainability, and justice, which reflects upon the relationship between sustainable development, business, and all affected stakeholders.

In recent years, The University of Scranton has entered into a unique relationship with the Beijing International MBA Program held on the campus of Peking University in Beijing. Through their arrangement, Scranton sends professors to teach in China. Professors return to Scranton with new insights about the world's fastest-growing economy, to the benefit of all Scranton MBAs.

## *Career and Placement*

Scranton MBAs receive career and placement services from the school's Office of Career Services, which serves the university at large. The office, "guided by the principles of Jesuit education and aware of the need to impart knowledge that has immediate and long-term value," seeks to "assume the roles of advisor, teacher, and mentor" for MBAs seeking postgraduation employment. Many do not; full-timers are the minority here, and the majority of part-time students are already employed and looking to advance within their companies.

JAMES L. GOONAN, DIRECTOR, GRADUATE ADMISSIONS
THE GRADUATE SCHOOL, UNIVERSITY OF SCRANTON, SCRANTON, PA 18510-4631 UNITED STATES
PHONE: 570-941-7600 • FAX: 570-941-5995
E-MAIL: GRADUATESCHOOL@SCRANTON.EDU • WEBSITE: WWW.SCRANTON.EDU

## Student Life and Environment

Scranton's MBA program is a small one, "scheduled specifically for students who work full-time." Approximately seven in ten Scranton MBAs attend part-time. Because many Scranton MBAs are full-time workers/part-time students, the school offers all classes in the early evening and at night; all classes meet once per week.

Due to the demands of their schedules and the infrequency of their visits to campus, part-time students report, "Many of the school-life activities are not available to MBA students, especially those of us who are working professionals." Those who do have the time to enjoy campus life usually take in university sporting events, enroll in interest-based and background-based clubs and organizations, and participate in the frequent spiritual retreats offered by the campus ministry. Hometown Scranton is located in the Pocono Mountains, approximately 125 miles from New York City, Philadelphia, Syracuse, and Trenton. This city of 70,000 is large enough to provide students with valuable internship and practicum opportunities.

Brennan Hall serves as the home to Scranton's business graduates and undergraduates. The facility, completed in 2000, boasts up-to-date computer labs and high-tech classrooms, as well as ample executive meeting rooms. A campus-wide voice, video, and data network allows students Internet access from just about anywhere on campus.

The University of Scranton's MBA program attracts a large international population; approximately one in three students here originates from outside the United States.

## Admissions

According to The University of Scranton website, admissions decisions here are based on a combination of four factors: previous academic performance, as indicated by transcripts; GMAT score, used to "measure certain mental abilities which have been found to be indicators of success" in graduate business programs of business; three letters of recommendation; and, when applicable, prior work experience (work experience is not a prerequisite to admission to the program). Of the four factors, previous academic performance and GMAT scores are considered most important. International students whose first language is not English must provide TOEFL scores in addition to academic records, test scores, and letters of recommendation. A minimum score of 550 paper-and-pencil or 213 computer-based is required for unconditional admission to the program. A score of at least 500 paper-and-pencil/173 computer-based allows conditional admission contingent on the completion of an English language proficiency course.

### FINANCIAL FACTS

| | |
|---|---|
| Annual tuition | $16,716 |
| Fees | $2,500 |
| Books and supplies | $1,584 |
| Room & board | $10,950 |
| % of students receiving aid | 10 |
| Average award package | $25,116 |

### ADMISSIONS

| | |
|---|---|
| Admissions Selectivity Rating | 62 |
| # of applications received | 115 |
| % applicants accepted | 93 |
| % acceptees attending | 22 |
| Average GMAT | 500 |
| Average GPA | 3.3 |
| TOEFL required of international students? | yes |
| Minimum TOEFL (paper/computer) | 550/213 |
| Application fee | $50 |
| International application fee | $50 |
| Regular application deadline | rolling |
| Regular notification | rolling |
| Deferment available? | yes |
| Maximum length of deferment | 2 years |
| Transfer students accepted? | yes |
| Transfer application policy | A transfer from an AACSB-accredited Jesuit school; otherwise, 6 credits max. |
| Non-fall admissions? | yes |

| EMPLOYMENT PROFILE | |
|---|---|
| Career Rating | 72 |
| Average starting salary | $50,494 |

# UNIVERSITY OF SOUTH CAROLINA
## MOORE SCHOOL OF BUSINESS

## *Academics*

In 2001, the Moore School of Business upgraded its MIBS program to the international master of business administration (IMBA), within which students can choose from three different tracks. Furthering the school's dedication to exploring the global market, all three include some sort of international component. Students say the "international focus of the school is reflected in every course, the international students, and the international internship experience." Students feel that, with a Moore IMBA under their belts, they'll be "well-positioned for the trend of increasing global commerce." Though the transition to the IMBA wasn't always smooth, students happily acknowledge that the program "is a fresh and newly conceived program, and there are still several tasks to be improved in terms of administration. But its freshness helps to add things in the long run. The best part is diversity. IMBA is a program that speaks many languages, and it should be kept that way."

The three different tracks of study offered by the school are Language Track, which focuses on "intense study and immersion in the language and culture of a region;" Global Track, "for those who may not need another language, [this is] a global approach to the culture and economies of the world"; and the acclaimed Vienna Program, a partnership with the Wirtschaftsuniversität Wien, the acclaimed business and economic university in Austria. Though the programs differ substantially from one another in content and concentration, they are all united by one thing: an intensive core curriculum. All students take the same core classes, which are rarely made up of more than 50 students. Because the core curriculum is compressed and students rush off to overseas studies, "first-year life equals study squared (now you know they're doing a good job teaching quantitative methods)."

Languages offered in Language Track include French, German, Italian, Portuguese, and Spanish. Students who choose one of these options pass through a two-year course. For students who opt to learn Arabic, Japanese, or Chinese language and culture, a three-year program is available. In this, "students follow the same format as the two-year language tracks, but they live and study for 12 months in Japan or China before they participate in the internship."

In the second year, after completing their internships, students return to the South Carolina campus and take seven electives in order to specialize in a particular field. Concentrations include marketing and brand management, customer relationship management, economic development, corporate accounting and finance, human resources, operations, and information systems. That same year, students are required to take a two-part management class. The first half "focuses on how to manage in multicultural organizations." The second "examines entrepreneurial practices and organizational transformation." According to one student, who returned from studying in Vienna, students are "happy upon returning to find that the professors that came to Vienna were teaching identical classes in South Carolina. I feel that we all share a common experience with many shared professors, which makes our whole class a strong network, and our professors and course work are an essential part of that."

REENA LICHTENFELD, MANAGING DIRECTOR-GRADUATE ADMISSIONS
1705 COLLEGE STREET, COLUMBIA, SC 29208 UNITED STATES
PHONE: 803-777-4346 • FAX: 803-777-0414
E-MAIL: GRADADMIT@MOORE.SC.EDU • WEBSITE: WWW.MOORESCHOOL.SC.EDU

## Career and Placement

The main complaint Moore students seem to have with their Career Resources Center is that, despite the program's focus on international studies, there are not enough international employment opportunities. Students complain that the center thinks too regionally and "could do more to pull in companies who are looking for the kind of globally minded students they are graduating and propel them all over the world, and not just the Southeast." Another student complains that though the school "runs a partnership program with Vienna, [it won't lift] a finger about a job in Europe."

Many students counter this by saying, "The Career Center goes out of its way to try to help us out. They are very accessible." Companies as diverse as Accenture; Alcoa Fujikura Ltd.; Anheuser-Busch, Inc.; Bali; Bayerische Vereinsbank; Bertelsmann; BMW; Credit Suisse; and Industrial Bank of Japan have all recruited from Moore (among many others).

## Student Life and Environment

Located in downtown Colombia, South Carolina, Moore School of Business has a lot going for it. The city is in the middle of an urban revitalization effort, and the downtown, in particular, is proof. "Nightlife is good," one student says. The city's efforts to redevelop are "bringing the younger crowd back into the inner city. The Vista (downtown nightlife area) on the river is very fun."

If, as one student says, "South Carolina is a different country inside the U.S. and a very peculiar window to American culture," what better place for a school with an international focus? The diversity of the environment is a deciding factor for many students, and "the social scene is wonderful. We have international potlucks, gatherings at Chinese New Year, and Diwali (an Indian Hindu holiday). When I organized a Diwali dinner, 100 out of the 140 students showed up." Students say their fellow IMBAs are "competitive—but in a fun way, not a detrimental way. Classmates are so giving and willing to help each other with class work and in personal situations. I could not imagine fitting in as well and feeling as welcomed anywhere else."

### FINANCIAL FACTS

| | |
|---|---|
| Annual tuition (in-state/out-of-state) | $32,000/$47,000 |
| Fees | $525 |
| Books and supplies | $2,000 |
| Room & board | $10,000 |
| % of students receiving aid | 75 |
| % of first-year students receiving aid | 76 |
| % of students receiving loans | 85 |
| % of students receiving grants | 75 |
| Average award package | $24,000 |
| Average grant | $14,000 |
| Average student loan debt | $36,000 |

### ADMISSIONS

| | |
|---|---|
| Admissions Selectivity Rating | 86 |
| # of applications received | 262 |
| % applicants accepted | 64 |
| % acceptees attending | 63 |
| Average GMAT | 628 |
| Range of GMAT | 590–660 |
| Average GPA | 3.29 |
| TOEFL required of international students? | yes |
| Minimum TOEFL (paper/computer) | 600/250 |
| Application fee | $40 |
| International application fee | $40 |
| Regular application deadline | 11/6 |
| Regular notification | 12/6 |
| Application deadline/notification | |
| Round 1: | 10/6 / 11/6 |
| Round 2: | 11/6 / 12/6 |
| Round 3: | 2/7 / 3/7 |
| Round 4: | 5/7 / 6/7 |
| Early decision program? | yes |
| ED deadline/notification | IMBA, 10/1, IMBA Vienna, 10/1 / 11/06 |
| Transfer students accepted? | yes |
| Transfer application policy | Can transfer up to a maximum of 12 credit hours, 4 courses. |
| Non-fall admissions? | yes |
| Need-blind admissions? | yes |

### APPLICANTS ALSO LOOK AT

Georgetown University, Thunderbird, University of Virginia, Vanderbilt University, Wake Forest University

| EMPLOYMENT PROFILE | | | | |
|---|---|---|---|---|
| Career Rating | 81 | Grads employed by field: | % | avg. salary: |
| Primary source of full-time | | Finance | 35 | $76,861 |
| job acceptances | | Marketing | 24 | $69,000 |
| School-facilitated activities | 54% | MIS | 6 | $70,000 |
| Graduate-facilitated activities | 46% | Operations | 11 | $65,166 |
| | | Consulting | 7 | $67,500 |
| Average starting salary | $72,500 | General Management | 11 | $70,686 |
| Percent employed | 80 | Other | 6 | $83,166 |

# UNIVERSITY OF SOUTH DAKOTA
## SCHOOL OF BUSINESS

## GENERAL INFORMATION
| | |
|---|---|
| Type of school | public |
| Environment | village |
| Academic calendar | semester |

## SURVEY SAYS...
Happy students
*Solid preparation in:*
Finance
Accounting
Teamwork
Quantitative skills

## STUDENTS
| | |
|---|---|
| Enrollment of parent institution | 7,500 |
| Enrollment of business school | 200 |
| % male/female | 50/50 |
| % out-of-state | 7 |
| % part-time | 75 |
| % minorities | 3 |
| % international | 5 |

## ACADEMICS
| | |
|---|---|
| **Academic Experience Rating** | **70** |
| Student/faculty ratio | 15:1 |
| Profs interesting rating | 73 |
| Profs accessible rating | 79 |
| % female faculty | 3 |
| % minority faculty | 2 |

## JOINT DEGREES
JD/MBA, 3 years of full time study

## PROMINENT ALUMNI
John Thune, U.S. Senator from
South Dakota

## *Academics*

If you're looking for an accredited MBA program in South Dakota, there's only one game in town. It's the MBA program at USD, the only one in the state to receive AACSB international accreditation. That distinction places the USD MBA among the top 10 percent of all business programs in the United States. Students frequently cite the school's "strong reputation," both locally and nationally, when asked why they choose this program over others.

USD's curriculum stresses "decision-making, problem-solving, understanding the role of business in society, and developing the leadership ability and social responsibility" to help its students "progress to positions of executive responsibility," according to university materials. The goal is not only to "develop future executive leadership for business, industry, and government," but also to "encourage those who have an interest in college teaching and an aptitude for an academic career to continue their work at the doctoral level." For the convenience of its students—many of whom work full-time in addition to attending school—USD offers both a part-time and full-time program, with full-time participation in Vermillion and part-time participation in Vermillion, Sioux Falls, Pierre, Rapid City, Sioux City, IA and statewide through the Digital Dakota Network. This is a closed circuit telecommunicated network of South Dakota schools which allows the interactive delivery of university courses across South Dakota.

In Spring 2005, USD introduced yet another option for part-timers: Cohort Express, available in Sioux Falls, Pierre, and Sioux City, IA, is a program designed to combine the convenience of part-time instruction with the benefits of cohort learning. Participants will complete the entire 22-month program with the same peer group, allowing them to develop the same strong long-term relationships and networking contacts that full-time students enjoy. They'll accomplish this without having to increase the amount of time they spend on campus. Cohort Express requires students to attend classes only one evening a week, or, alternatively, for every other weekend. Plus, they'll be able to do so for the same low tuition and fees that other MBAs here pay.

USD MBAs brag that "the professors are terrific [and] the administration has been flawless. They are very friendly and helpful and have made registration easy." They especially appreciate the school's "no-nonsense approach to learning. It is understood that we are all working adults and there is very little fluff." They report that a new b-school facility is in the planning stages.

## *Career and Placement*

USD MBAs receive career and placement services from the Business School Employment Services Office, which coordinates its efforts with the university's Career Development Center. The office provides assistance with job-search strategy, job listings, a weekly e-mail of useful info, on-campus interviews, resume reviews, mock interviews, resume referrals, career counseling, and an electronic resume book. In 2003, the last year for which such figures were available, a job fair cosponsored by the Employment Services Office and the South Dakota Career Planning and Placement Association brought 130 employers to recruit business undergraduates and graduate students. In that same year, the median starting salary for MBAs was approximately $40,500. Employers of USD business students include AFLAC, Aramark, Citibank, New York Life, Northwestern Mutual, and Wells Fargo.

Dr. Angeline Lavin, MBA Director
414 East Clark, School of Business, Vermillion, SD 57069 United States
Phone: 605-677-5232 • Fax: 605-677-5058 • Toll Free: 866-890-IMBA (1622)
E-mail: MBA@USD.EDU • Website: WWW.USD.EDU/MBA

## Student Life and Environment

Students at USD evince "strong Midwest values and are very caring individuals" who are "personable and understanding of work and home commitments." The student body is split among adults with considerable professional experience and younger students "fresh out of undergraduate school with few years of experience and the idea of having fun prominently on their minds."

USD is small by state-school standards, with a typical full-time enrollment of just under 8,000. The school competes in NCAA Division II athletics and supports a strong arts community active in music and theater, as well as "a wide range of other recreational, cultural, social, and professional activities and organizations." Hometown Vermillion is small and quiet, a typical city of 10,000. The surrounding area is gorgeous and offers plenty of outdoor fun, but more urbane entertainments are in relatively short supply. For those, students head southeast to Sioux City, Iowa, or north to Sioux Falls.

## Admissions

Applicants to the MBA program at the University of South Dakota must submit two official transcripts for all prior academic work, GMAT scores, two letters of recommendation, a resume, a statement of purpose, and a completed application. A minimum undergraduate GPA of 2.7 is required. All international applicants must also submit a Statement of Finance form, a certified bank statement or sponsor's letter, and TOEFL scores if their native language is other than English (minimum acceptable score is 550 on the written exam). Applicants must have completed all of the following before beginning the MBA program: principles of micro and macro economics, six hours; principles of accounting I & II, six hours; business finance, three hours; management (principles or organizational theory), three hours; business statistics, three hours; calculus, three to four hours; introduction to management information systems, three hours; production and operations management, three hours; and marketing, three hours. Equivalent foundation courses are available at USD, but cannot be counted toward the MBA degree. According to printed material from the school, the School of Business reviews applications, then "recommends the admission status of the applicant to the dean of the Graduate School based on the applicant's undergraduate record, GMAT score, and recommendations. Students may be accepted to a University of South Dakota Graduate School degree program with full admission or provisional admission."

### FINANCIAL FACTS
Annual tuition (in-state/out-of-state) $3,821/$11,268
Fees $1,069

### ADMISSIONS
Admissions Selectivity Rating 70
# of applications received 134
% applicants accepted 84
% acceptees attending 90
Average GMAT 500
Average GPA 3.3
TOEFL required of international students? yes
Minimum TOEFL (paper/computer) 550/213
Application fee $35
International application fee $35
Regular application deadline 6/1
Regular notification rolling
Deferment available? yes
Maximum length of deferment 3 years
Transfer students accepted? yes
Transfer application policy Maximum of 9 credit hours from an AACSB-accredited institution may be transferred.
Non-fall admissions? yes
Need-blind admissions? yes

### EMPLOYMENT PROFILE
Career Rating 73
Average starting salary $40,500
Percent employed 95

# UNIVERSITY OF SOUTHERN CALIFORNIA
## MARSHALL SCHOOL OF BUSINESS

## Academics

The Marshall School of Business at University of Southern California first made its mark with its groundbreaking entrepreneurship program—the school was the nation's first to institute such a program—but today, Marshall is much more than an entrepreneurial maverick. With solid departments in finance, strategy, marketing, operations, human resources, and accounting, and emphasis in the business of entertainment, as well as innovative programs that introduce global business issues throughout the curriculum, Marshall has catapulted itself to the top ranks of U.S. MBA programs.

Marshall divides each semester into two terms, concentrating course material to the point that "the workload is killer in both quality and quantity," especially during the first-year core curriculum. Even the most experienced students find the material novel and challenging; one writes, "I had 10 years of very strong work experience (strategy consulting) and wasn't really expecting to learn much during my first-year core classes. Was I ever in for a surprise! I feel so much more prepared for a successful business career after only one semester. It's a great feeling of time and money well spent." Core courses are "extremely well-linked. Professors constantly refer to the other courses we are currently in or have taken to show how well all aspects of business are interrelated." Students appreciate that core professors "are nearly all senior faculty members who have won teaching awards and written books. Each of them chose to teach first-year MBAs because of their passion to engage students in the classroom."

Students report that "Marshall has a very international perspective," evidenced by the seven-week PRIME (Pacific Rim Education Program) course that caps off first year. PRIME incorporates case studies, teamwork, lectures, and a 10-day research trip to a Pacific Rim country (Chile, Brazil, China, Japan, Singapore, Thailand, Cuba, or Mexico) to combine expert instruction and on-site, real-time experiential learning. Students agree that "the PRIME class and field trip is a definite highlight at the end of the first year." Students may also opt to participate in the MBA international exchange program, which sends second-year students abroad for a semester.

Throughout all departments, students brag that "professors are friendly and accessible. They are master teachers. They seem to have more of an interest in teaching versus other professors who seemed more interested in making themselves more known in their fields (experienced as a Wharton undergraduate taking MBA level courses)."

## Career and Placement

Students applaud USC for improving Marshall's national rankings. They also recognize that the Career Resource Center is on its way to catching up to the other initiatives underway throughout the Business School. An aggressive employer outreach program, a new operational model focused on industry and functional alignment of students and advisors, along with a more robust career-oriented training/educational curriculum are steps in the rights direction. With over 375 employers interacting with graduate students this year, Marshall no longer competes for the attention of employers with their cross-town rival. One MBA notes, "The administration and Career Resource Center have spent great effort and financial resources to continue to improve the recruiting opportunities at Marshall. I am confident on-campus recruiting opportunities will continue to improve as more companies come to Marshall for recruiting and the economy rebounds in the coming years."

Likely employers of Marshall MBAs (besides private firms and corporations) include federal judges and government and public-interest nonprofits. Private firms and corporations include AIG Global Investment, Amgen, AT Kearney, Bank of America, Black & Decker, Bristol-Myers Squibb, Broadcom, CIBC, Citigroup, Clorox, ConAgra,

A. Keith Vaughn, Director of MBA Admissions
Popovich Hall Room 308, Los Angeles, CA 90089-2633 United States
Phone: 213-740-7846 • Fax: 213-749-8520
E-mail: marshallmba@marshall.usc.edu • Website: www.marshall.usc.edu

Countrywide, Deloitte, Deutsche Banc, Farmers Insurance, Federal Reserve Bank, Fidelity, Gap, GE, Goldman Sachs, Honeywell, Intel, Lehman Brothers, Mattel, Merrill Lynch, Microsoft, Nestlé USA, Northrup Grumman, PricewaterhouseCoopers, Procter & Gamble, Shea Homes, Toyota, Twentieth Century Fox, UBS, and Wells Fargo.

## Student Life and Environment

The school spirit of USC students and alumni is legendary. It's also a lifelong passion, as evidenced by the school's vaunted Trojan Network, a 68,000-strong alumni base that "rabidly works to help students, pulling them into the Trojan family to help them meet the industry players who will eventually connect them with jobs, business partners, clients, and investors." Where better to meet those contacts than at Trojan football games? Students report that "for all home football games, the students sponsor an alumni tailgate, and over 1,000 alumni show up to enjoy each others' company and to network."

Despite the demands of their program, Marshall students find time not only to attend football games but also to get involved with the community. They participate in "Challenge-4-Charity Weekend up at Stanford, which supports Special Olympics. There is something that involves all of us each month [like] parties or gym days with underprivileged kids. Volunteering is very strong here." Professional clubs are also popular, as "there is a club for virtually any interest a student could have, and if for some reason a club doesn't exist, it is very easy for students to create one. Many clubs bring in excellent speakers from both big and small companies to share their experiences, and a few clubs have 'Industry Nights' during which many professionals come to USC to share their experience in a more intimate, roundtable setting." The school is located "in the heart of downtown Los Angeles. However, the majority of graduate business students live off campus, typically about a 20-minute commute. Students have the opportunity to experience a variety of cultures and neighborhoods no matter where they decide to live, ranging from the low-key beach cities (Manhattan Beach, Hermosa Beach) to the entertainment-rich areas (Hollywood)." Like Randy Newman, they love LA.

## Admissions

The Marshall MBA program is "highly selective," and the admissions committee carefully considers all aspects of an application to determine which candidates have "outstanding leadership potential as well as intellectual and interpersonal abilities to contribute to our academic and extracurricular programs." All applicants must submit official academic transcripts, letters of recommendation, a personal statement, GMAT scores, and a resume. Non-English speaking international students must submit TOEFL scores. USC reports that "Marshall is a member of the Consortium for Graduate Study in Management, an alliance of 14 graduate schools of business committed to creating career opportunities for African Americans, Hispanic Americans, and Native Americans. Marshall also hosts an annual Diversity Weekend geared toward prospective minority applicants."

### PROMINENT ALUMNI

Cho Yang Ho, Chair and CEO, Korean Air Lines Co., Ltd.; Stephen C. Goodall, CEO, J.D. Power and Associates; J. Terrence Lanni, Chair and CEO, MGM MIRAGE; Paul Orfalea, Founder and Chair Emeritus, Kinko's; Robert B. McKnight, Chair and CEO, Quicksilver Inc.

### FINANCIAL FACTS

| | |
|---|---|
| Annual tuition | $35,904 |
| Fees | $1,634 |
| Books and supplies | $2,400 |
| Room & board | $14,000 |
| % of students receiving aid | 74 |
| % of first-year students receiving aid | 73 |
| % of students receiving loans | 62 |
| % of students receiving grants | 30 |
| Average award package | $33,930 |
| Average grant | $26,393 |

### ADMISSIONS

| | |
|---|---|
| Admissions Selectivity Rating | 94 |
| # of applications received | 1,501 |
| % applicants accepted | 38 |
| % acceptees attending | 39 |
| Average GMAT | 680 |
| Range of GMAT | 650–710 |
| Average GPA | 3.3 |
| TOEFL required of international students? | yes |
| Minimum TOEFL (paper/computer) | 600/250 |
| Application fee | $150 |
| International application fee | $150 |
| Regular application deadline | 4/1 |
| Regular notification | 5/22 |
| Application deadline/notification | |
| Round 1: | 12/1 / 2/1 |
| Round 2: | 1/15 / 3/27 |
| Round 3: | 2/15 / 4/24 |
| Round 4: | 4/1 / 5/22 |
| Need-blind admissions? | yes |

### APPLICANTS ALSO LOOK AT

New York University, Stanford University, University of California—Los Angeles, University of California—Berkeley

| EMPLOYMENT PROFILE | | | | |
|---|---|---|---|---|
| Career Rating | 87 | Grads employed by field: | % | avg. salary: |
| Primary source of full-time job acceptances | | Accounting | 3 | $84,666 |
| | | Finance | 39 | $86,147 |
| School-facilitated activities | 59 (45%) | Human Resources | 2 | NR |
| Graduate-facilitated activities | 43 (33%) | Marketing | 21 | $78,142 |
| Unknown | 29 (22%) | MIS | 2 | $120,000 |
| | | Operations | 2 | $85,000 |
| Average starting salary | $82,405 | Consulting | 8 | $83,773 |
| Percent employed | 82 | General Management | 2 | $74,334 |
| | | Nonprofit | 2 | NR |
| | | Other | 19 | $78,500 |

# UNIVERSITY OF SOUTHERN INDIANA
## COLLEGE OF BUSINESS

## Academics

The MBA program at the University of Southern Indiana benefits from the huge undergraduate population of business and marketing majors at USI's College of Business. With nearly 2,000 such undergraduates, USI can maintain a much broader range of graduate business offerings than could most schools of its size. The school offers an MBA in general management.

USI's MBA program offers up to 18 hours of foundation courses for students with little or no undergraduate background in business. Students must complete or place out of these courses before turning to the 30-hour core sequence. This system allows part-time students to complete their MBAs within three years and full-timers to complete the degree within two years.

Students report that USI's approach "is very good at giving the student a core basis in everything business-related," but that the program would benefit from "more focus on specialized business areas such as entrepreneurship, global marketing, international business, Internet technology, and other specialized fields of study as opposed to [a] broad scope of [the] MBA program." Some students also believe that the school goes too far to accommodate students whose jobs leave them too busy for intensive study. One MBA observes, "Some classes are 'watered down' for the nontechnical students. For instance, most classes take all calculus-based problems out of the curriculum so that most of the students would not be intimidated. I believe that real-life economic and operations problems require one to develop models and perform standard calculus computations to arrive at an answer."

Students who want to dig deeper will find willing accomplices in the faculty. USI professors "are very knowledgeable in their chosen field. Marketing, finance, and economics professors all do very well with their material." Their "diverse backgrounds and experiences help students to gain a better understanding of all the fields represented in the program." USI's busy MBAs also love "being able to resolve most of administrative issues over the Internet. That's extremely convenient," one student comments. Overall, the students feel they receive "good academic 'bang for the buck,'" and that "you can definitely take pride in this school," according to a survey.

## Career and Placement

The Career Counseling Center at USI assists students through assessment testing, personalized counseling, workshops, online job databases, and resume books. The office maintains a library of electronic and print resources pertaining to all aspects of the job search. Students may also access the electronic resources of the entire University of Indiana system. MBAs explain that "career placement seems greatly tailored toward accounting majors. It could be more broad." Because most USI MBAs have jobs, which frequently contribute toward the students' tuition, the school places a relatively low priority on career services for its MBA students.

PEGGY HARREL, DIRECTOR OF GRADUATE STUDIES
8600 UNIVERSITY BOULEVARD, EVANSVILLE, IN 47712 UNITED STATES
PHONE: 812-465-7015 • FAX: 812-464-1956
E-MAIL: GSSR@USI.EDU • WEBSITE: WWW.BUSINESS.USI.EDU

## Student Life and Environment

Evansville, with a population of 120,000, is a small industrial city in southern Indiana; about one-third of its jobs are in manufacturing (Toyota is the metro area's biggest employer). The closest large city is Louisville, Kentucky, about 120 miles away; Nashville, Indianapolis, and St. Louis are all within a 200-mile radius. Students appreciate the small-town setting, which they find conducive to study. "Coming from a much larger city, I think Evansville is wonderful. The community is great," one MBA writes.

Students also love the "nice atmosphere on campus and up-to-date facilities." One MBA writes, "There are many things a person can do. The gym facilities are brand new. New buildings are popping up every year. It's a great place [that] has many community builders and activities for students. It is a great campus to just hang out at and get to know people." One student notes, "USI provides a close community for the students who wish to be involved. There is always help and always activities to participate in."

Most students, however, are simply too busy to get involved with campus life. One student explains, "The MBA degree program at USI is designed for working adults. Most of us don't spend much extra time after class unless [it is] necessary." One typical student writes, "I commute one hour to school, work a full-time job as a health-system quality leader, travel two hours one way to sing in a chorus each week, am a cantor, and am very active in my church with my husband. [I also] have a grown daughter who is married with an eight-month-old son and take two to three courses at a time. The amount of time necessary to be an active participant in all of this keeps me from being more active in school activities—other than the MBA program and requirements." Professors recognize "that the MBA student has a tough schedule to juggle" and usually create assignments accordingly.

## Admissions

Admission to the College of Business at USI is based primarily on GMAT score and undergraduate transcript. The admissions office also considers leadership potential and work experience. Students may supplement their applications with letters of recommendation, personal statements, and an interview, but none of these are required. According to the school's website, "all candidates for admission to the MBA program must demonstrate proficiency in computer skills. Proficiency may be established by successfully completing college-level course work within five years of admission to the MBA program or by passing a proficiency exam provided through the MBA office."

### FINANCIAL FACTS

| | |
|---|---|
| Annual tuition (in-state/out-of-state) | $3,697/$7,302 |
| Fees | $220 |
| Books and supplies | $850 |
| Room & board (on/off-campus) | $6,368/$7,872 |
| % of students receiving aid | 38 |
| % of first-year students receiving aid | 33 |
| % of students receiving loans | 28 |
| % of students receiving grants | 1 |
| Average award package | $8,025 |
| Average grant | $2,545 |

### ADMISSIONS

| | |
|---|---|
| Admissions Selectivity Rating | 89 |
| # of applications received | 55 |
| % applicants accepted | 49 |
| % acceptees attending | 100 |
| Average GMAT | 576 |
| Range of GMAT | 530–580 |
| Average GPA | 3.11 |
| TOEFL required of international students? | yes |
| Minimum TOEFL (paper/computer) | 550/213 |
| Application fee | $25 |
| International application fee | $25 |
| Regular application deadline | rolling |
| Regular notification | rolling |
| Transfer students accepted? | yes |
| Transfer application policy 12 accepted hours can be transferred into the program. | |
| Non-fall admissions? | yes |
| Need-blind admissions? | yes |

### EMPLOYMENT PROFILE

| | |
|---|---|
| Career Rating | 76 |
| Average starting salary | $57,451 |
| Percent employed | 94 |

# UNIVERSITY OF SOUTHERN MAINE
## SCHOOL OF BUSINESS

### GENERAL INFORMATION
Type of school                public
Environment                   town
Academic calendar          semester

### SURVEY SAYS...
Students love Portland, ME
Friendly students
*Solid preparation in:*
Teamwork
Computer skills

### STUDENTS
Enrollment of parent
  institution                 10,974
Enrollment of business school  130
% male/female                  70/30
% out-of-state                    14
% part-time                       88
% international                   14
Average age at entry              32
Average years work experience
  at entry                         6

### ACADEMICS
**Academic Experience Rating    74**
Student/faculty ratio           20:1
Profs interesting rating          73
Profs accessible rating           68
% female faculty                  24

### JOINT DEGREES
3-2 MBA, 5 years; BS/MBA; 3-2
MSA, 5 years; BS/MSA;
MBA/MSN, 3–4 years; JD/MBA, 4–5
years

## Academics

The MBA program at the University of Southern Maine focuses its attention primarily on students "who wish to advance their careers and contribute to their companies." It serves a largely part-time student body whose members hold full-time jobs in the area and seek a degree that will help them "develop cross-functional business solutions to real-world problems [and] cultivate a broad critical perspective, interpersonal skills, and the analytical tools of management." USM's full-time student body is primarily enrolled in the 3-2 MBA program, which allows undergraduates to earn a bachelor's degree and an MBA in five years.

Part-time students can complete USM's 33-credit sequence in two years, although some take longer. The curriculum consists of nine three-hour core courses and two three-hour electives. "All classes are held in the evening" so that working students can attend the MBA program, which students appreciate. One such student writes, "This school is well-located for part-time students and it caters well to them. The administration strongly supports the students." Because of the limited number of electives available, students cannot fashion an area of concentration here, a situation some would like to see addressed. One says, "I work in the financial services industry and would love to be able to come out of USM with a finance concentration MBA."

USM professors "are well integrated into the local business community, opening up several great opportunities for enriching projects." Their quality as classroom instructors varies; "Some seem to teach to the lowest common denominator, but generally they are good to very strong," students tell us. They single out instructors in operations, accounting, and finance for their expertise and "ability to inspire learning in their students." Many agree the b-school facility "needs to be vastly improved," adding that "the school desperately needs a new building of their own with more modern, comfortable facilities."

## Career and Placement

USM's website states: "Because many of our students are already employed in management positions, we do not have a formal placement service for MBA or MSA students." The site adds that "opportunities for employment often come to our attention," and these opportunities "are passed on to students for consideration." Students may use the services of the USM Career Services Office, which serves the entire university population. Students may also work with the Office of Graduate Studies, which employs a career advisor to administer career assessments, counsel students in resume building and interviewing skills, and arrange networking opportunities.

## Student Life and Environment

Because "the University of Southern Maine is mainly a commuter college," "there is really very little in the way of organized outside activities. We all have a local life outside of school which demands our time." One student observes, "There isn't a whole lot of school spirit and clubs like at other universities. The only club I've heard of for the MBA program is the MBA Association. Unfortunately, any clubs that students are asked to participate in have meetings when many students are in class. That also goes for most networking opportunities that are available." Extracurricular life isn't totally dead, though; according to one MBA, "The school does try to bring students together for occasional special events, and many professors hold off-campus gatherings on the last night of class that provide a good networking opportunity with other students."

ALICE B. CASH, GRADUATE PROGRAMS DIRECTOR
PO BOX 9300, PORTLAND, ME 04104 UNITED STATES
PHONE: 207-780-4184 • FAX: 207-780-4662
E-MAIL: MBA@USM.MAINE.EDU • WEBSITE: WWW.USM.MAINE.EDU/SB

USM's MBA program is a small one, the majority of whose students attend part time. They are "good-natured, intelligent individuals" who are "motivated but not extremely driven in a business sense. They are hard-working and striving for knowledge," creating "a positive learning environment." The mix of "older students with families and substantial professional backgrounds and younger students with less work experience but more recent educational experience" is a "positive mix," students say. They also love that "the academic community is quiet and the scenery is wonderful, very relaxing."

Portland is home to the School of Business' main campus. With a population just under a quarter of a million, Portland is the largest city in Maine. It serves as the state's financial, business, and retail center; its major industries include tourism, telecommunications, technology, light manufacturing, and insurance.

## Admissions

All applicants to the MBA program at USM must submit a completed application, two copies of official transcripts for all postsecondary work (including work at USM), GMAT scores, three letters of recommendation, a resume, and a personal essay. In addition, international students must also submit a certificate of finances and, if English is not their first language, TOEFL scores. Fully admitted students must have a formula score of 1,100 under the formula [(undergraduate GPA 5 200) + GMAT score] and a minimum GMAT score of 500. The GMAT requirement is waived for students who have completed a terminal degree (e.g. PhD, JD, MD). The admissions office considers rigor of undergraduate field of study, reputation of undergraduate institution, potential, likelihood of enhancing the educational environment at USM, demonstrated leadership, evidence of creativity, and record of accomplishment in business in making its admissions decisions. Prior to commencing the MBA program, all students must complete, or demonstrate competency in, the following 'foundation' areas: managing organizational behavior, IT/MIS, economics, accounting, probability and statistics, finance, marketing, and management science. Students with deficiencies in these areas will be notified at the time of their admission.

## FINANCIAL FACTS

| | |
|---|---|
| Annual tuition (in-state/out-of-state) | $4,464/$12,456 |
| Fees | $534 |
| Books and supplies | $1,000 |
| Room & board (on-campus) | $6,800 |

## ADMISSIONS

| | |
|---|---|
| Admissions Selectivity Rating | 83 |
| # of applications received | 60 |
| % applicants accepted | 68 |
| % acceptees attending | 88 |
| Average GMAT | 577 |
| Range of GMAT | 540–610 |
| Average GPA | 3.36 |
| TOEFL required of international students? | yes |
| Minimum TOEFL (paper/computer) | 550/213 |
| Application fee | $50 |
| International application fee | $50 |
| Regular application deadline | 8/1 |
| Regular notification | rolling |
| Deferment available? | yes |
| Maximum length of deferment | 1 year |
| Transfer students accepted? | yes |
| Transfer application policy | |
| A maximum of 6 semester hours of transfer credit may be accepted. Please see catalog. www.usm.maine.edu/catalogs/graduate/ | |
| Non-fall admissions? | yes |
| Need-blind admissions? | yes |

# UNIVERSITY OF SYDNEY/UNIVERSITY OF NEW SOUTH WALES
## AUSTRALIAN GRADUATE SCHOOL OF MANAGEMENT

## Academics

Students praise the "well-developed generalist course taught by renowned faculty" at the Australian Graduate School of Management, the b-school affiliate of both the University of Sydney and the University of New South Wales. The school, which is "well-known in the Asian Pacific" (especially at home and in Southeast Asia), has made its mark through its "world-class research." In 2005, the *Financial Times* ranked the school 40th in the world for research output.

AGSM's research institutes include the Center for Corporate Change (CCC), described by the school as "Australia's leading center for the study of organizational transformation." Other institutes include the Center for Research in Finance (which "was set up to collect, store, and analyze data for both pure and applied research in finance and related disciplines"), and the Center for Applied Marketing (which "aims to further marketing knowledge and encourage state-of-the-art marketing practice [and which] sponsors an overseas visitor program to ensure that the latest in international thinking is available to Australian researchers and practitioners").

Research is not AGSM's only asset, however. Professors are not just brilliant, innovative thinkers, they are also "very motivating, approachable, and inspiring, with good teaching style and diverse teaching methods." Students caution that "a couple of them are much better on a one-to-one basis than lecturing to a class, so sometimes you have to make use of their openness," but since most professors are "extremely approachable," this rarely causes problems. Students single out the school's "recognized experts in organizational behavior, organizational design, statistics, and negotiations" for praise.

The AGSM curriculum draws on an "innovative, research-driven knowledge base that provides the framework for management decision-making and development of leadership competencies," according to the school. Students approve, but warn that "grading is on a bell curve," making it tougher than usual for students to earn their accustomed As and Bs. They also warn that "for some reason, qualitative subjects are always graded harder than quantitative ones." In other words, don't expect to cruise through. The workload, we're told, is "heavy, but not all that extreme."

## Career and Placement

The Career Center of AGSM offers students the usual potpourri of services: workshops, one-on-one counseling, maintenance of a resume book, self-assessment tools, and networking events. The office also runs the Management Projects Program, which "creates, develops, and facilitates opportunities for AGSM students to work in teams with [senior executives] on issues of strategic importance [to] define and analyze a business issue and make recommendations for action through written and oral presentations." Students tell us that AGSM is most effective in placing students in consultancy positions. In 2004, 60 percent of all graduates reported that their job offers were the result of networking; 20 percent attributed their job offer to contacts made through the Career Center.

Those most likely to employ AGSM MBAs include: Accenture, AT Kearney, Colgate Palmolive, KPMG, Macquarie Bank, McKinsey, and Westpac.

## FINANCIAL FACTS

| | |
|---|---|
| Annual tuition | $39,441 |
| Books and supplies | $1,160 |
| % of first-year students receiving aid | 53 |
| Average award package | $165,059 |
| Average grant | $8,253 |

## Student Life and Environment

The students at AGSM form "a very close-knit and supportive environment, and everyone is made to feel very welcome. The students are high-achieving but not too competitive." One student explains, "The full-time MBA program is intimate. The class size will vary from 90 to 140 for an incoming class. This means that relationships grow quickly and grow strong. Additionally, there is no undergraduate program, so the facilities are dedicated to the graduate students." Students bring "good breadth and depth of experience, and there are many multicultural students from different backgrounds," all of which enhance the AGSM experience. Some students feel the only component missing is an outreach to students' spouses and children. "Inclusion of families through establishment of a formal network/association to help families survive our 'MBA experience' would be great," students tell us.

Because the school sits on the University of New South Wales campus, it has "several thousand post and undergraduate students and a wide range of clubs and societies to join." MBAs enjoy "various networking opportunities for present students, such as barbecues, cruises, courtyard lunches in the sun, presentations, and contests run by clubs. The school has a commitment to ensuring extra-curricular programs accompany demanding course work." All told, AGSM provides "a relaxed atmosphere that accommodates focused students well." Students also love the "clean and tidy" campus, which has "good technology and plenty of appropriate areas to study."

As for hometown Sydney, well, "How can anyone not like Sydney?" The school is located "close to Sydney CBD and Bondi Beach," and the area offers "wonderful weather [and] lots of sunshine." With a population of four million, Sydney is a major business and cultural center.

## Admissions

Applicants to the MBA program must have an undergraduate bachelor's degree and at least two years' full-time professional or managerial work experience postdating their undergraduate degree. Students must score a minimum of 550 on the GMAT (a score of 600+ is preferred; those with lower scores must "excel in all other areas"). Students whose native language is not English must score at least a 600 on the TOEFL. Completed applications must include transcripts, test scores, two letters of recommendation (one from a current or recent employer), a detailed resume, and personal-statement essays. Applications "are processed as they are received, [therefore,] the earlier the application, the longer the period of time available for international students to have their student visas approved—this can take up to six months in extreme cases. An early application helps to ensure a place is still available for you."

## ADMISSIONS

| | |
|---|---|
| **Admissions Selectivity Rating** | **85** |
| # of applications received | 148 |
| % applicants accepted | 56 |
| % acceptees attending | 46 |
| Average GMAT | 624 |
| Range of GMAT | 590–680 |
| Average GPA | 3 |
| Minimum TOEFL (paper/computer) | 600/250 |
| Application fee | $78 |
| International application fee | $78 |
| Regular application deadline | 9/30 |
| Regular notification | rolling |
| Deferment available? | yes |
| Maximum length of deferment | 1 year |

| EMPLOYMENT PROFILE | |
|---|---|
| **Career Rating** | **85** |
| **Primary source of full-time job acceptances** | |
| School-facilitated activities | 15 (23%) |
| Graduate-facilitated activities | 51 (77%) |
| | |
| Average starting salary | $85,930 |

# University of Tampa
## John H. Sykes College of Business

## Academics

MBAs considering the John H. Sykes College of Business at the University of Tampa have three options: a full-time program that can be completed in 16 months, a part-time program that is typically completed in about three years, and a six-term Saturday professional MBA program. Roughly one-third of the student body attends full time.

All MBA programs at Sykes consist of foundation courses, which can be waived for students completing equivalent undergraduate courses in the prior seven years with a minimum grade of B, or by passing a departmental examination. The integrated core curriculum here "stresses case studies and group work, allowing students to obtain knowledge and corporate values." All students also complete course work leading to a concentration, a leadership development program centered on mentoring and one-on-one coaching, and a capstone team project in which students create a strategic business assessment and present it to the top leadership of an area company. Concentrations are available in accounting, entrepreneurship, finance, information systems management, international business, management, and marketing.

"Teamwork and leadership skills" are "the focus of this MBA program," students tell us. Professors here "have a genuine interest in students' success and academic endeavors" and "find ways to stimulate our thinking. They're not just giving us required material. If one doesn't understand the class material, he or she can always talk to professor during consultation hours. If even that is not enough, there is free tutoring available." Students praise Sykes' "strong relationship with the business community" and its "ability to include local area businesses in projects." Many, however, complain that "the school doesn't offer enough electives each semester," making it difficult to complete some concentrations.

## Career and Placement

UT's Office of Career Services provides Sykes MBAs with a battery of services, including assessment tests, workshops in business etiquette and business dress, one-on-one counseling, and job fairs. Attendees of a recent on-campus career fair included the Allegis Group, Colonial Bank, Enterprise Rent-A-Car, Federated Mutual Insurance Company, Franklin Templeton Investments, GEICO, MacDill Federal Credit Union, Northwestern Mutual Financial Network/Teague, Smith Barney—The Jaffe Group, Sprint Nextel, and T. Rowe Price.

FERNANDO NOLASCO, ASSOCIATE DIRECTOR, GRADUATE STUDIES
401 WEST KENNEDY BOULEVARD, TAMPA, FL 33606-1490 UNITED STATES
PHONE: 813-258-7409 • FAX: 813-259-5403 • E-MAIL: UTGRAD@UT.EDU
WEBSITE: WWW.GRAD.UT.EDU

## Student Life and Environment

A "beautiful campus" with "state-of-the-art facilities" makes the University of Tampa a pleasant and supportive place for students pursuing their MBAs. Many here do not get to enjoy the extra amenities very often, however. Part-time students have too many other responsibilities (e.g. work, family) to linger on campus a second longer than necessary, although they do appreciate that "there are plenty of places to relax or grab a bite to eat for a student coming from a full-time job to school."

Full-time students "are typically on campus all day. Many live on campus." And since there are "a lot of activities to do," why shouldn't they? For example, "There is the Student Organization of MBAs (SOMBA), which meets about once every two weeks. Any MBA student can come, and pizza and sodas are served. The Dean of Graduate Studies always comes. Meetings have a very relaxed yet very productive atmosphere: We talk about how to promote our school, what events we would like to happen and how to organize them, and what we would like to see different in our school." An MBA lounge is another "great feature because it is a place where MBA students can study and meet for group projects. You can usually always find a seat there because it isn't flooded with undergrads."

Sykes MBAs are predominantly from the Southeast U.S., although "a lot of international students" are in the mix as well. This "enthusiastic, diverse group of professionals from all around the globe, brought together to share in growth and learning" is "competitive, but in a cooperative atmosphere: lots of e-mails, phone calls, and meetings." Full-time students tend to have "little to no work experience," while "evening classes have many working professionals in them." Nearly everyone feels that Tampa Bay is the place to be, a metropolis that "is showing very strong signs of healthy growth to use MBAs in the coming years."

## Admissions

Admission to the full-time and part-time MBA programs at Sykes is based on under-graduate work (a minimum GPA of 3.0 is required of degree-seeking students; non-degree seeking students need a minimum GPA of 3.0 for their final 60 hours of undergraduate credit); GMAT score (a minimum score of 450 is required) or GRE score (a minimum combined verbal-quantitative score of 1,000 is required); demonstration of proficiency in mathematics, computers, and written and oral communications skills; and professional experience. International students must demonstrate proficiency in English by scoring at least 577 on the written TOEFL or 230 on the computer-based TOEFL. Admission to the Saturday MBA program requires relevant work experience. Applicants to the Saturday program who have a minimum undergraduate GPA of 3.0 may receive a waiver on the GMAT requirement. Applicants to all programs must submit two letters of recommen-dation, a resume, and a personal statement.

### FINANCIAL FACTS

| | |
|---|---|
| Annual tuition | $6,528 |
| Fees | $70 |
| Books and supplies | $576 |
| Room & board (on/off-campus) | $6,936/$4,200 |
| % of students receiving aid | 52 |
| % of first-year students receiving aid | 15 |
| % of students receiving loans | 39 |
| % of students receiving grants | 28 |
| Average award package | $10,968 |
| Average grant | $9,528 |
| Average student loan debt | $21,505 |

### ADMISSIONS

| | |
|---|---|
| Admissions Selectivity Rating | 82 |
| # of applications received | 401 |
| % applicants accepted | 52 |
| % acceptees attending | 77 |
| Average GMAT | 536 |
| Range of GMAT | 470–583 |
| Average GPA | 3.35 |
| TOEFL required of international students? | yes |
| Minimum TOEFL (paper/computer) | 577/230 |
| Application fee | $40 |
| International application fee | $40 |
| Regular application deadline | rolling |
| Regular notification | rolling |
| Deferment available? | yes |
| Maximum length of deferment | 1 year |
| Transfer students accepted? | yes |
| Transfer application policy Up to 9 hours from an AACSB-accredited school. | |
| Non-fall admissions? | yes |
| Need-blind admissions? | yes |

### APPLICANTS ALSO LOOK AT

University of Florida, University of South Florida

### EMPLOYMENT PROFILE

| Career Rating | 80 | Grads employed by field: | % | avg. salary: |
|---|---|---|---|---|
| Average starting salary | $50,571 | Accounting | 20 | NR |
| Percent employed | 100 | Finance | 30 | $62,500 |
| | | Human Resources | 10 | $26,000 |
| | | Marketing | 10 | $75,000 |
| | | MIS | 20 | $40,000 |
| | | Other | 10 | NR |

# UNIVERSITY OF TENNESSEE—CHATTANOOGA
## COLLEGE OF BUSINESS ADMINISTRATION

### GENERAL INFORMATION
| | |
|---|---|
| Type of school | public |
| Environment | city |
| Academic calendar | semester |

### SURVEY SAYS...
Students love Chattanooga, TN
Friendly students
*Solid preparation in:*
General management

### STUDENTS
| | |
|---|---|
| Enrollment of parent institution | 8,689 |
| Enrollment of business school | 272 |
| % male/female | 50/50 |
| % out-of-state | 21 |
| % part-time | 91 |
| % minorities | 10 |
| % international | 10 |
| Average age at entry | 29 |
| Average years work experience at entry | 3 |

### ACADEMICS
| | |
|---|---|
| **Academic Experience Rating** | **70** |
| Student/faculty ratio | 23:1 |
| Profs interesting rating | 86 |
| Profs accessible rating | 93 |
| % female faculty | 46 |
| % minority faculty | 15 |

### PROMINENT ALUMNI
General B. B. Bell, Four-Star General in U. S. Army

## Academics

Change is coming to the MBA program at the University of Tennessee—Chattanooga. The school recently revamped its MBA curriculum, with changes to be implemented in the fall of 2006. The new curriculum increases the length of the program from a minimum of 30 class hours to a minimum of 36 class hours. The school has reduced the number of foundation/background courses (classes that cover pre-MBA material and which can be waived by students with undergraduate business degrees), increased the number of core and elective options, and added a second capstone class (in entrepreneurship). Students admitted after August 2006 must complete the new curriculum to graduate.

UTC's predominantly part-time student body will most likely be satisfied with the changes so long as the school maintains "a reputation for academic rigor" and, perhaps more importantly, the "great convenience of evening class scheduling, which makes it possible to work full-time while attending." As one student observes, "The program is tailored to individuals who work full-time. The faculty and staff go above and beyond to help make the program feasible without compromising the quality of the academics." Even without the coming upgrades, students here are "very impressed" by the perception that "for a small school, this program has some professors who are high profile and important in their field, yet also accessible to the students. The professors really seem to love teaching."

Other assets here include "modern classroom facilities and computer labs" and "an administration that is professional and meticulous." While some here feel that the school should get a little pickier about "whom they select for the program, because some students are not quite ready" and others wish that "there were more options for students who aren't engineers, computer scientists, or in the manufacturing and production industries," most here recognize UTC as "an excellent value for the money. The professors have real-world experience and want to help you be as prepared as possible. The work for each course is designed to give real-world experience and help you understand better the macro business perspective. Overall this is an excellent school that will only get better as more money is funded toward it."

## Career and Placement

UTC maintains a Career Resource Center for all students. The center houses a library of job-search related materials, including literature, annual reports, and job postings. The school's Placement and Student Employment Center also hosts on-campus recruitment interview sessions, one major annual career fair, and a number of special career fairs each year. Students and alumni may post their resumes online with the Placement Center.

## Student Life and Environment

Students at UTC tell us that they experience an "excellent atmosphere for learning." Facilities "have integrated multimedia capability and are thoroughly up-to-date" and "small class sizes are conducive to student participation and enhance learning." Students here "for the most part take classes at night and are not a part of the life of the university." And while "the Grad School is attempting to create more of a community for all of the graduate students on campus by distributing interest surveys and planning activities," "not that many people participate."

MELISSA BLAZEK, GRADUATE PROGRAM LIAISON
GRADUATE SCHOOL, DEPARTMENT 5305, 615 MCCALLIE AVENUE, CHATTANOOGA, TN 37403 U.S.
PHONE: 423-425-4667 • FAX: 423-425-5223 • E-MAIL: MELISSA-BLAZEK@UTC.EDU
WEBSITE: WWW.UTC.EDU

Many simply don't have the time for extracurricular commitments. Most students here "are working professionals who are committed to achieving the highest grade possible." These "hard workers are here to learn everything they can," and they "take the MBA program very seriously." Work and family obligations leave them with just enough time to study, but not to do much else. Students report that "there seem to be a lot of engineers in the program, but there are also many people from local insurance companies and other businesses in the area. It is not unusual to have classes with engineers, nurses, teachers, computer science professionals, etc."

Chattanooga is located on Tennessee's southern border, about halfway between Nashville and Atlanta. The city is home to a number of colleges and universities. UTC, the second-largest school in the University of Tennessee system, is the biggest. Others include Tennessee Temple University and Covenant College (located just outside the city, on Lookout Mountain).

## Admissions

Applicants to the MBA program at UTC must provide the Admissions Committee with two official copies of transcripts for all academic work completed after high school and an official GMAT score report. The academic record must show either a minimum GPA of 2.5 for the applicant's entire undergraduate career or a GPA of at least 3.0 during the senior year in order for the applicant to gain unconditional admission. Successful applicants must have a minimum "admissions index" score of 950, calculated under the formula [(undergraduate GPA x 200) + GMAT Score]. Students who do not meet the above-mentioned qualifications may still earn conditional admission. International students whose first language is not English must submit an official score report for the TOEFL (minimum grade required: 550, paper-based; 213, computer-based).

### FINANCIAL FACTS

| | |
|---|---|
| Annual tuition (in-state/out-of-state) | $5,210/$14,234 |
| Books and supplies | $1,000 |
| Room & board (on/off-campus) | $6,450/$7,800 |
| % of students receiving aid | 72 |
| % of first-year students receiving aid | 70 |
| % of students receiving loans | 61 |
| % of students receiving grants | 4 |
| Average grant | $9,500 |

### ADMISSIONS

| | |
|---|---|
| **Admissions Selectivity Rating** | **64** |
| # of applications received | 123 |
| % applicants accepted | 89 |
| % acceptees attending | 70 |
| Average GMAT | 489 |
| Range of GMAT | 350–700 |
| Average GPA | 3.18 |
| TOEFL required of international students? | yes |
| Minimum TOEFL (paper/computer) | 550/213 |
| Application fee | $25 |
| International application fee | $25 |
| Regular application deadline | rolling |
| Regular notification | rolling |
| Deferment available? | yes |
| Maximum length of deferment | 1 year |
| Transfer students accepted? | yes |
| Transfer application policy | Students may transfer a maximum of 6 hours from an AACSB-accredited school. All transfer courses are subject to department approval. |
| Non-fall admissions? | yes |
| Need-blind admissions? | yes |

### APPLICANTS ALSO LOOK AT

East Tennessee State University, Georgia State University, Middle Tennessee State University, Tennessee Tech University, University of Georgia, University of Tennessee—Knoxville, Vanderbilt University

# UNIVERSITY OF TENNESSEE—KNOXVILLE
## COLLEGE OF BUSINESS ADMINISTRATION

## Academics

The University of Tennessee's College of Business Administration has recently compressed their full-time program so that it now spans a mere 17 months. The school explains their decision thus: "Although compressed in time, this program maintains all of the quality instruction that has made our graduates attractive to corporate recruiters. At the same time, we understand that students make great sacrifices to attend full-time MBA programs, and we are working to reduce that sacrifice. Unconventional? Sure. Challenging? Absolutely." And students concur, calling the 17-month program one of the school's "greatest strengths."

The other great strength of the program is their integrated core curriculum. UTK was the first MBA program in the country to implement a fully integrated core curriculum, which is taught by a "cross-functional faculty team." The school points out that this resulted in the UT MBA program being ranked number two in the country for return on investment. Students also appreciate this, pointing out that since "classes for first-year students are lockstep," they have the opportunity to "become very familiar with peers."

The list of possible concentrations for students isn't long—finance, logistics and transportation, marketing, operations management, JD/MBA—and an MBA/MS in engineering—but students point out with pride that the logistics and transportation program is top-notch. Students say, "It has professors with real-life experiences." And the school points out that their marketing program is sixth in the country for the teaching of marketing skills, while logistics and transportation is ranked number one for educating future logistics/procurement executives. "So far," one student says, "I have learned volumes and have been exposed to a plethora of different real-world case scenarios. I feel that this has been a fabulous investment."

The extras are what makes the program stand out. The school offers a cultural exchange program in Prague. After-class activities "provide the opportunity to hear speakers or participate in activities that enhance the learning experience," and "professors always make themselves available to the students, sometimes even missing a lunch if time is pressing."

Students wish there was "more of an entrepreneurial focus" and complain that the program "just doesn't spend enough time on finance," but apart from that, they agree that it's a "great school" and that "life overall is good."

## Career and Placement

Although it has had something of a rocky past, students say that "Career Services is really picking up under new direction." The average salary for the class of 2001 was about $72,000. More people ended up in logistics and transportation than in any other area, and students who concentrated in supply-chain management and logistics and transportation typically earned several thousand more than those who studied other areas.

Companies who have recruited on campus include Accenture; Amazon.com; AmSouth Bank; Andersen Consulting; Burke, Inc.; Eli Lilly; FedEx; and Hewlett-Packard (among many others).

DONNA POTTS, DIRECTOR OF ADMISSIONS, MBA PROGRAM
527 STOKELY MANAGEMENT CENTER, KNOXVILLE, TN 37996-0552 UNITED STATES
PHONE: 865-974-5033 • FAX: 865-974-3826
E-MAIL: MBA@UTK.EDU • WEBSITE: WWW.MBA.UTK.EDU

## Student Life and Environment

Knoxville, Tennessee, was recently ranked the "best place to live in the United States and Canada" among cities with a population of fewer than 1 million. This may have something to do with the fact that it's nestled between the Great Smokey Mountains and the Cumberland Mountains, or that it's about a two-hour drive from five national parks, seven state parks, and seven lakes. It is the largest city in East Tennessee; it's also the third largest in the state. The shelter of the mountain ranges ensures that the climate is relatively temperate, with an annual average temperature of about 60°F. Even students coming from big cities have come to enjoy life in a smaller city. "I am enjoying the pace of life and getting to relive college to a certain degree, but this time I have a plan and more responsibility," one former New Yorker says. And other students report that "students do go out together and enjoy the Knoxville nightlife."

Students say that while the 17-month program keeps them very busy, "there is a good balance between school and social life. I have made great contacts." Much of an MBA's free time, apparently, is consumed by football. "Football season is a very exciting time around here!" one student says. "I only wish that the football team was better the past two years." Though most MBAs enjoy the opportunity to socialize over beers at a tailgate party, some complain that "besides the football games, there really isn't much to do."

## Admissions

Of the 80-odd students who will enter each fall, 66 percent are male, 34 percent are female, and 18 percent are international. The average age of an incoming student is 26, and the average undergraduate GPA is 3.34. The average GMAT score is 600, and the average amount of work experience is 3.5 years. About 20 percent of the students had worked for less than one year, but 50 percent had worked for three or more. Students came from China, Ecuador, Germany, India, Italy, Japan, Panama, Russia, and South Korea. About 24 percent had an arts-and-sciences background, and 45 percent were business undergrads.

### FINANCIAL FACTS

| | |
|---|---|
| Annual tuition (in-state/out-of-state) | $5,376/$15,156 |
| Fees | $1,000 |
| Books and supplies | $3,000 |
| Room & board (on/off-campus) | $7,400/$12,500 |
| % of students receiving aid | 43 |
| % of first-year students receiving aid | 27 |
| % of students receiving grants | 14 |
| Average award package | $17,784 |
| Average grant | $8,514 |

### ADMISSIONS

| | |
|---|---|
| Admissions Selectivity Rating | 89 |
| # of applications received | 230 |
| % applicants accepted | 45 |
| % acceptees attending | 62 |
| Average GMAT | 600 |
| Range of GMAT | 560–640 |
| Average GPA | 3.3 |
| TOEFL required of international students? | yes |
| Minimum TOEFL (paper/computer) | 600/250 |
| Application fee | $35 |
| International application fee | $35 |
| Regular application deadline | 2/1 |
| Regular notification | rolling |
| Need-blind admissions? | yes |

### APPLICANTS ALSO LOOK AT

Arizona State University, The Pennsylvania State University, University of Georgia, Vanderbilt University, Wake Forest University

### EMPLOYMENT PROFILE

| Career Rating | 76 | Grads employed by field: | % | avg. salary: |
|---|---|---|---|---|
| Average starting salary | $55,400 | Finance | 17 | $54,300 |
| | | Marketing | 22 | $52,000 |
| | | Operations | 31 | $59,800 |
| | | Consulting | 6 | $60,300 |
| | | General Management | 20 | $53,600 |
| | | Other | 4 | $45,200 |

# THE UNIVERSITY OF TEXAS—ARLINGTON
## COLLEGE OF BUSINESS ADMINISTRATION

## GENERAL INFORMATION
| | |
|---|---|
| Type of school | public |
| Environment | metropolis |
| Academic calendar | semester |

### SURVEY SAYS...
Friendly students
Helpful alumni
Smart classrooms
*Solid preparation in:*
Accounting

## STUDENTS
| | |
|---|---|
| Enrollment of parent institution | 25,297 |
| Enrollment of business school | 457 |
| % male/female | 54/46 |
| % part-time | 66 |
| % minorities | 28 |
| % international | 35 |
| Average age at entry | 31 |
| Average years work experience at entry | 5 |

## ACADEMICS
| | |
|---|---|
| **Academic Experience Rating** | **77** |
| Student/faculty ratio | 20:1 |
| Profs interesting rating | 74 |
| Profs accessible rating | 73 |
| % female faculty | 16 |
| % minority faculty | 5 |

## JOINT DEGREES
May combine any 2 degrees (usually MBA and specialized program) or a business degree with others, such as Engineering, Architecture, Science, Nursing. Can obtain second degree with as few as 18 additional hours. May pursue MBA at UTA with MIM at Thunderbird, the American Graduate School, or international management, with reduced requirements.

## PROMINENT ALUMNI
John McMichael, Executive VP & CFO, Finley Resources, Inc.; Lee Thurburn, President, NetOffer.com

## Academics

In its efforts to meet the needs of its diverse student population, the College of Business Administration at University of Texas at Arlington offers several MBA options. There's the Flexible MBA–often referred to simply as "the MBA" because it is regarded as the default option. The Flexible MBA can be completed part-time or full-time, and it jettisons the conventional lockstep MBA curriculum and cohort learning to maximize convenience. This option is offered only on the Arlington campus. Then there's the Accelerated MBA (also known as the Cohort MBA, because students travel through the program with the same group of peers), with its mini-terms scheduled for the convenience of its part-time-student/full-time-worker student body. The Accelerated MBA is offered only at UTA/Fort Worth. UTA also offers an online MBA, which can be completed "without ever setting foot on campus," and the school participates in an Executive MBA (EMBA) program in Taipei, Beijing, and Shanghai.

Students in the Flexible MBA program may choose a specialization from among the following: finance, accounting, information systems, international business, marketing research, real estate, human resource management, electronic commerce, and enterprise resource planning. Current students praise the economics department ("the professors are producing advanced research and presenting it in class along with other new research done in the field"), the accounting and operations management department, and the marketing research program, which "is offered only in limited schools across the country."

The Accelerated MBA program receives even more enthusiastic endorsements from students, one tells us, "There is tremendous value in being in with the same classmates for 2.5 years and who all have industry experience. Through presentations from classmates with experience in the field, I have learned more about the defense industry, the pharmaceutical industry, the health care industry, the banking industry, and manufacturing in general." This "extremely focused" program "is excellent for working adults." Students in the online MBA programs can earn only general MBAs without concentrations.

In all programs, students love "the overall value, [the] up-to-date technology, [and the] user-friendly registration, enrollment, and work processes." Professors here "are really good and very engaging with the class. They come from all walks of life: Some write their own textbooks, some have owned their own businesses, some are teaching for fun, some have taught forever! Given the strong professional presence of the students, they are always kept on their toes and questioned regarding anything that might not make sense."

## Career and Placement

Career Services at UTA include "comprehensive assessment, industry analysis, career exploration and informational interviews, managing in a diverse environment, career-focused academic advising, and internships," the school tells us. In addition, students take a careers class that "presents both practical and theoretical perspectives on careers and managing in a changing work environment." Students gripe that "the school still needs to work hard on getting more known companies to visit the campus for recruitment." They also identify alumni connections as an area needing improvement. Employers most likely to hire UTA MBAs include Alcon Laboratories, Sabre Group Holdings, Inc, Nokia, American Airlines, and Bank of America.

## Student Life and Environment

UTA's MBA programs are "made for working professionals looking to earn a degree, but not necessarily a second "college experience." Students yearning to meet new friends and embellish another undergraduate experience should look for more personalized service at other institutions. To be sure, UTA is a very large, growing institution that offers all the facilities and resources of most major academic institutions at a much lower cost. However, "most students are part-times with full-time jobs, so mingling is not a top priority." The full-timers in the Flexible MBA program are the exception—they do spend considerable time together. They tell us that "life at school is moderately paced, which allows most students to get into other activities apart from academics." One full-time student explains, "There are many opportunities for students to get involved, if they want them. UTA is a school where you have to seek out the opportunities—you will find them if you look. I am very involved on campus on the part of the graduate school. Yet such opportunities are not always advertised and made known to all the students eligible."

All programs at UTA boast impressive diversity stats. One student reports, "The school is extremely diverse; almost any class has a spread of Asians, Africans, Europeans, Middle Easterners, and Hispanics." Students in the Flexible MBA program are "a mixed bag. Like any academic program, you have foreign students, students with a lot of work experience, and students who are fresh out of undergrad. It's a very stimulating and rewarding combination." Cohort MBAs are all "industry professionals from the Dallas/Fort Worth area," notes a part-timer. They are all very vocal, intelligent, and engaging in the classroom. I've never had this much fun in a real classroom before. Vacations, gatherings, and celebrations among students is common." Everyone here is "very career-oriented and outgoing. Many students have families and are married."

Students observe that "one of the greatest strengths of UTA is that we are located in a very active business market. This large metroplex allows for many opportunities to go outside the classroom as well as bring in local experts."

## Admissions

Admissions officers at UTA consider all of the following: GMAT score, undergraduate GPA and curriculum, work experience, essays (including a 200-word statement of academic intent), and letters of recommendation. Applicants are ranked using the formula [(undergraduate GPA × 200) + GMAT score], and the average admitted student scores approximately 1,100 (which, of course, means that many admitted students score lower than 1,100). Students whose first language is not English must also submit TOEFL scores (this requirement is waived for students who have earned a postsecondary degree from a U.S. college or university). International students must also provide a bank affidavit and financial statement. To promote diversity within the student body, UTA College of Business Education supports activities sponsored by the McNair Scholar Program and the National Black MBA Association.

## FINANCIAL FACTS

| | |
|---|---|
| Annual tuition (in-state/out-of-state) | $4,944/$13,998 |
| Fees (in-state/out-of-state) | $2,058/$2,253 |
| Books and supplies | $1,000 |
| Room & board (on/off-campus) | $4,800/$6,000 |
| % of students receiving aid | 20 |
| Average award package | $8,500 |
| Average grant | $1,000 |
| Average student loan debt | $23,475 |

## ADMISSIONS

| | |
|---|---|
| **Admissions Selectivity Rating** | **80** |
| # of applications received | 413 |
| % applicants accepted | 49 |
| % acceptees attending | 65 |
| Average GMAT | 530 |
| Range of GMAT | 470–620 |
| Average GPA | 3.28 |
| TOEFL required of international students? | yes |
| Minimum TOEFL (paper/computer) | 550/213 |
| Application fee | $30 |
| International application fee | $60 |
| Regular application deadline | 6/10 |
| Regular notification | rolling |
| Early decision program? | yes |
| ED deadline/notification | rolling / 6/15 |
| Deferment available? | yes |
| Maximum length of deferment | 1 year |
| Transfer students accepted? | yes |
| Transfer application policy | Maximum number of transferable credits is 9. Grades of B or better from an AACSB-accredited university. |
| Non-fall admissions? | yes |
| Need-blind admissions? | yes |

# THE UNIVERSITY OF TEXAS—AUSTIN
## MCCOMBS SCHOOL OF BUSINESS

## Academics

For a combination of an excellent graduate business program and an equally fine quality of life, it's hard to beat the McCombs School of Business at The University of Texas at Austin. Students here agree that "Austin is a very cool town, Texas is a great state, and UT has a top 20 MBA program." They also praise "an atmosphere that is very collaborative and laid-back, but still professional." Students also love the fact that the larger university is big enough to be strong in many disciplines. Our survey respondents see strengths in such b-school staples as accounting, IT, entrepreneurship, real estate and marketing; they're also enthusiastic about the school's unique offerings in investment management, private equity, and energy finance.

The McCombs curriculum consists of 27 credits of core requirements and a minimum of 33 elective credits. If 15 of those credits are devoted to one of five specific functional areas (accounting, finance, management, information technology, or marketing), then one graduates with a concentration. In addition to concentrations, McCombs offers students the option of a specialization, which is basically a "specifically designed set of courses" within a particular discipline. Teamwork and group projects figure heavily in the McCombs curriculum; observes one student, "The cooperative and team environment is the greatest attribute of McCombs. Most classes require some form of group interaction, which is important to life in the professional world." Students report that "most professors use the methods most appropriate for their specific fields of study; from the case method to class discussion, lectures to problem sets, they use them all as required by the material."

Among McCombs' standout features is the Plus Program, a relatively recent addition to the curriculum spurred on by "the school's commitment to hands-on learning and market-driven education." The Plus Program consists of short programs "ranging from international business tours to professional development seminars." Future MBAs report that the Plus Program "helps us gain real-world experience very quickly." Writes one student, the "program gives students excellent opportunities to improve communications skills and work on real-life projects with local companies outside of the academic schedule."

## Career and Placement

According to the school, each year "recruiters from hundreds of the world's leading companies" visit the Ford Career Center to recruit McCombs MBAs. Corporate relationships, including "affiliations with high-tech companies," mean employers are a major presence on campus all year round, not just at recruiting time. This allows students to forge strong relationships with potential employers, which, unsurprisingly, pleases McCombs students quite a bit. Almost all the students in our survey reported satisfaction with McCombs' ability to attract recruiters and to place students in internships and jobs.

Top employers of McCombs MBAs include American Airlines; Capital One; Citibank; Dell; Deloitte Consulting; Exelon; Frito Lay; General Mills; HEB; IBM; Johnson & Johnson; Procter & Gamble; SBC Communications; Samsung; Standard & Poor's; and Union Bank of Switzerland. About half of all graduates remain in the Southwest; the remaining students scatter pretty evenly around the country and the world for their first post-degree jobs.

TINA MABLEY, DIRECTOR OF ADMISSION, MBA PROGRAMS
ADMISSIONS, MBA PROGRAM OFFICE, 1 UNIVERSITY STATION, B6004, AUSTIN, TX 78712 U.S.
PHONE: 512-471-7612 • FAX: 512-471-4243
E-MAIL: MCCOMBSMBA@MCCOMBS.UTEXAS.EDU • WEBSITE: WWW.MBA.MCCOMBS.UTEXAS.EDU

## Student Life and Environment

Like seemingly everyone else who lives in Austin, students love their school's hometown. Explains one student, "It's unlike any other environment. It is not New York City, so it doesn't stress you out, and it's not rural America, so it doesn't bore you to death. If you are outgoing, then this is the place to be. Forbes rated Austin as the best city for singles, and that kind of explains it." Students here laud the "many outdoor activities, like biking, running, hiking, and camping that are available in the city. There's also a big lake that provides a great place to relax during the spring and summer." They also praise the "incredible Tex-Mex food" (the barbecue's not half bad, either) and "the night life on Sixth Street, which is better than just about anywhere." If you like live music, you'll love Austin.

On campus, "social life is excellent" at McCombs, with "a great deal of camaraderie among the students." Student organizations "are very involved and very well run," and extracurricular fun is always close at hand, as "Every Thursday night we have Think and Drinks which allow students to mingle at a bar over a beer or two. It's a work hard, play hard culture." Tailgate parties before football games "are always fantastic, with free food, free drinks, and free fun." Married students happily note that "The Student and Significant Others Group is great for those students who bring a partner. The school has great programs for my spouse as well as for my kids."

"Teamwork and cooperation overshadows intense competition" at McCombs; students' awareness that they are in a top-flight program that can yield good jobs for all of them, and also helps keep competitiveness low. A large portion of the student body originates from outside the United States; writes one American student, "I was amazed at the broad spectrum of countries and nationalities represented. This alone has been a tremendous learning experience."

## Admissions

Application to McCombs must be submitted online. Admission is extremely competitive. A completed application must include: a resume detailing work history; personal essays; official copies of transcripts for all postsecondary academic work; letters of recommendation; an official score report for the GMAT; and, for international students whose first language is not English, an official score report for the TOEFL. Programs designed to increase minority and disadvantaged populations at McCombs include Jump Start, "which targets undergraduate seniors who are academically qualified for a top-ranked MBA but lack the required work experience;" Explore McCombs, "a three-day preview of the School for qualified African American, Hispanic American, and Native American applicants;" and participation in a number of alliances, associations, and consortia dedicated to the goal.

### PROMINENT ALUMNI

Jim Mulva, President & CEO, Conoco Phillips; William Johnson, Chair, President & CEO, Heinz; Don Evans, former Secretary of Commerce, U.S. Government; Sara Martinez Tucker, President & CEO, Hispanic Scholarship Fund; Gerard Arpey, Chair, President & CEO, American Airlines.

### FINANCIAL FACTS

| | |
|---|---|
| Annual tuition (in-state/out-of-state) | $9,360/$24,450 |
| Fees (in-state/out-of-state) | $7,912/$9,680 |
| Books and supplies | $1,477 |
| Room & board | $12,980 |
| % of students receiving aid | 64 |
| % of first-year students receiving aid | 64 |
| % of students receiving loans | 64 |
| % of students receiving grants | 20 |
| Average award package | $24,048 |
| Average grant | $10,564 |
| Average student loan debt | $40,631 |

### ADMISSIONS

| | |
|---|---|
| Admissions Selectivity Rating | 95 |
| # of applications received | 1,335 |
| % applicants accepted | 39 |
| % acceptees attending | 49 |
| Average GMAT | 672 |
| Range of GMAT | 610–720 |
| Average GPA | 3.38 |
| TOEFL required of international students? | yes |
| Minimum TOEFL (paper/computer) | 620/260 |
| Application fee | $125 |
| International application fee | $125 |
| Regular application deadline | 4/15 |
| Regular notification | 5/1 |
| Deferment available? | yes |
| Maximum length of deferment | 1 year |
| Need-blind admissions? | yes |

### APPLICANTS ALSO LOOK AT

Duke University, Harvard University, Northwestern University, University of California—Berkeley, University of Michigan, University of North Carolina—Chapel Hill, University of Pennsylvania

### EMPLOYMENT PROFILE

| Career Rating | 95 | Grads employed by field: | % | avg. salary: |
|---|---|---|---|---|
| Primary source of full-time job acceptances | | Finance | 39 | $82,328 |
| | | Marketing | 21 | $81,176 |
| School-facilitated activities | 173 (56%) | MIS | 3 | $86,188 |
| Graduate-facilitated activities | 133 (44%) | Operations | 4 | $83,364 |
| | | Consulting | 16 | $94,940 |
| Average starting salary | $84,025 | General Management | 12 | $81,816 |
| Percent employed | 90 | Other | 5 | $77,970 |

# THE UNIVERSITY OF TEXAS—DALLAS
## SCHOOL OF MANAGEMENT

## GENERAL INFORMATION
| | |
|---|---|
| Type of school | public |
| Academic calendar | semester |

## SURVEY SAYS...
Smart classrooms
*Solid preparation in:*
Teamwork
Computer skills

## STUDENTS
| | |
|---|---|
| Enrollment of parent institution | 14,774 |
| Enrollment of business school | 1,185 |
| % male/female | 72/28 |
| % out-of-state | 1 |
| % part-time | 94 |
| % minorities | 11 |
| % international | 49 |
| Average age at entry | 29 |
| Average years work experience at entry | 5 |

## ACADEMICS
| | |
|---|---|
| **Academic Experience Rating** | **86** |
| Student/faculty ratio | 24:1 |
| Profs interesting rating | 76 |
| Profs accessible rating | 66 |
| % female faculty | 15 |
| % minority faculty | 5 |

## JOINT DEGREES
MBA/MS in Electrical Engineering, 3 years; MBA/MD, 4 years

## Academics

Most students attend The University of Texas at Dallas' MBA program on a part-time basis, enrolling in either the professional part-time MBA program (available either on-site or online) or one of a number of executive MBA options. Sixty students each year enter the more competitive cohort full-time MBA program, a relatively new offering at the school (the program was established in 1996).

Full-time students call the cohort MBA "one of the best bang-for-the-buck programs out there," one that benefits from "truly outstanding professors, many of whom have real-world work experience as business leaders. Also, all of them are excited about what they teach, and that enthusiasm rubs off on the students." Part-time students agree that professors are "very good and very knowledgeable," and also appreciate that "the school runs a tight ship." Reports one global leadership executive MBA (GLEMBA) student, "The supportive administrators really help out making the 'chore' of all the paperwork much easier so students can concentrate on learning."

All students follow the same basic curriculum, commencing with a "heavy" 29-credit core: "Some of us would rather be able to pick and choose some courses to have a more customized educational experience." Electives allow students to develop specializations in accounting, innovation and entrepreneurship, finance, international management, managerial economics, marketing management, MIS, operations management, or organization and strategy. Students single out the school's "analytic and quantitative approach to business management, with a full scope of leadership/soft skills" as its greatest curricular strength. Writes one student, "Materials are highly relevant and contemporary, the delivery is high quality and interactive, the assignments build upon the material, and the core courses build on one another." Graduate study is further enhanced by the fact that "UTD is a highly research-oriented school, and we have many professors who are well noted for their excellence in research."

## Career and Placement

Students at UTD's School of Management have access to two Career Services Offices: the SOM Career Management Center (CMC), and the UTD Career Center. The offices coordinate efforts to serve both undergraduates and graduate students in business; the CMC focuses primarily on the needs of graduate students. The CMC coordinates career fairs, company information sessions, and on-campus interviews. The office also maintains online bulletin boards and job databases. Students looking for more are encouraged to use school resources to achieve their goals; writes one MBA, "The administration is wonderful. They helped a group I was in develop, implement, and finance a career fair for MBAs specifically."

Employers most likely to hire UTD MBAs include Alliance Data Systems, Bank of New York, Dell, Deloitte Touche Tohmatsu, Ernst & Young, KPMG, Lennox, Nortel, and Sabre Holdings.

## Student Life and Environment

UTD's School of Management "recently transitioned into a single on-campus facility" that "has everything we need for the business school." Amenities include "wireless internet, technologically advanced classrooms, plenty of computer labs," "a nice lounge area," breakout rooms, and a 350-seat auditorium. Despite the upgrade, some here are not entirely satisfied; they complain that "the campus is boring. The atmosphere within the buildings is not welcoming, there are few trees around, and there are few places to sit outside and enjoy the day while studying."

JYOTU MALLICK, DIRECTOR OF THE COHORT MBA PROGRAM
SCHOOL OF MANAGEMENT BUILDING, 2601 NORTH FLOYD ROAD, RICHARDSON, TX 75080 U.S.
PHONE: 972-883-6191 • FAX: 972-883-6823
E-MAIL: MBA@UTDALLAS.EDU • WEBSITE: HTTP://SOM.UTDALLAS.EDU/GRADUATE/COHORTMBA

Because "the majority of graduate students commute" at UTD, "there is not a strong community" among most MBA students. Reports one part-time student, "The professional MBA program is more geared toward working professionals. Classes are in the evening or on weekends, and the professors are well aware that most of the students are working 40 to 60 hours per week (as well as traveling)." Full-time students are more likely to spend free time on campus. They tell us that "there are a lot of activities going on all the time. There are several student academic and nonacademic clubs. Every Friday, the International Student Services Office arranges for the celebration of the culture of a country, with food, song, [and] dance. The school frequently organizes CEO lecture series. The Institute for Excellence in Corporate Governance in the school organizes seminars from time to time where top management people from big corporations come for brainstorming on contemporary business issues. Field trips to companies are organized."

UTD's part-time student body "mostly consists of working, married people, many with children. They are interested in performing well in school, but are not highly competitive for grades. In fact, some just want the degree and don't care about the grades. Most students already have a career path and are attending school to further careers that have been started, so you don't feel that you are competing for jobs with them." In the full-time program, "the atmosphere is very family-like. The batches work together in community outreach programs, form study groups, and have parties at each other's homes." Both programs have substantial international populations who "lend interesting insights and viewpoints."

## Admissions

All applicants to UTD business graduate programs must submit the following: an online application; official copies of all postsecondary transcripts; an official score report for the GMAT; three letters of recommendation; and a personal statement/essay. International students whose native language is not English must provide an official score report for the TOEFL in addition to the materials listed above. The UTD admissions office looks most closely at the undergraduate transcript and GMAT scores; letters of recommendation and the essay are also considered important factors. Other aspects of the application are considered but are given less weight in the final decision. Admission to the full-time cohort program is more competitive than is admission to part-time programs. All programs require calculus as a prerequisite.

### FINANCIAL FACTS

| | |
|---|---|
| Annual tuition (in-state/out-of-state) | $5,700/$10,668 |
| Books and supplies | $1,000 |
| Room & board (on/off-campus) | $9,424 |
| % of students receiving aid | 80 |
| % of first-year students receiving aid | 85 |
| % of students receiving grants | 48 |
| Average award package | $11,915 |
| Average grant | $14,143 |

### ADMISSIONS

| | |
|---|---|
| Admissions Selectivity Rating | 95 |
| # of applications received | 164 |
| % applicants accepted | 36 |
| % acceptees attending | 56 |
| Average GMAT | 654 |
| Range of GMAT | 600–720 |
| Average GPA | 3.4 |
| TOEFL required of international students? | yes |
| Minimum TOEFL (paper/computer) | 550/215 |
| Application fee | $50 |
| International application fee | $100 |
| Regular application deadline | 5/1 |
| Regular notification | 6/15 |
| Application deadline/notification | |
| Round 1: | 1/15 / 3/1 |
| Round 2: | 3/1 / 4/15 |
| Round 3: | 6/1 / 6/15 |
| Deferment available? | yes |
| Maximum length of deferment | 1 year |
| Need-blind admissions? | yes |

### APPLICANTS ALSO LOOK AT
Southern Methodist University

### EMPLOYMENT PROFILE

| | | Grads employed by field: | % | avg. salary: |
|---|---|---|---|---|
| Career Rating | 85 | Accounting | 20 | NR |
| Primary source of full-time job acceptances | | Finance | 20 | NR |
| | | Marketing | 5 | NR |
| School-facilitated activities | 40% | MIS | 10 | NR |
| Graduate-facilitated activities | 60% | Operations | 5 | NR |
| | | Consulting | 20 | NR |
| Average starting salary | $66,667 | General Management | 20 | NR |
| Percent employed | 85 | | | |

# THE UNIVERSITY OF TEXAS—PAN AMERICAN
## COLLEGE OF BUSINESS ADMINISTRATION

### GENERAL INFORMATION

| | |
|---|---|
| Type of school | public |
| Environment | town |
| Academic calendar | semester |

### SURVEY SAYS...

Friendly students
Cutting-edge classes
Happy students
*Solid preparation in:*
Communication/interpersonal skills
Presentation skills

### STUDENTS

| | |
|---|---|
| Enrollment of parent institution | 17,500 |
| Enrollment of business school | 186 |
| % male/female | 68/32 |
| % part-time | 69 |
| % minorities | 75 |
| % international | 15 |
| Average age at entry | 31 |
| Average years work experience at entry | 2 |

### ACADEMICS

| | |
|---|---|
| **Academic Experience Rating** | **61** |
| Student/faculty ratio | 27:1 |
| Profs interesting rating | 70 |
| Profs accessible rating | 67 |
| % female faculty | 30 |

## Academics

The College of Business Administration at the University of Texas—Pan American offers both an evening MBA program and an online MBA program. The college and the MBA program are accredited by the American Assembly of Collegiate Schools of Business (AACSB).

UTPA's evening MBA program may be completed on either a full-time or a part-time basis. Full-time students with undergraduate degrees in business may complete the program in as little as 18 months. Part-time students may take up to seven years to earn their degrees. Those lacking an academic background in business are required to commence the program with a sequence of foundation courses that cover principles of accounting, economics, management, marketing, statistics, and finance. All students must complete nine core courses and three electives for a total of 36 course hours of work. Students may choose to write a thesis instead of taking six of the nine hours of required electives; thesis topics are subject to approval from the MBA director. Students in the program praise its emphasis on teamwork and the "good availability of classes at night." Yet they also tell us that the facility housing the program "needs to be renovated."

The online MBA is administered jointly with seven other UT campuses (Arlington, Brownsville, Dallas, El Paso, Permian Basin, San Antonio, and Tyler). The online curriculum consists of 48 course hours. Students with sufficient backgrounds in business may have up to four core courses waived, reducing the number of required hours to 36. Online students must take at least two courses in person at their home campuses; all other courses can be completed at home via computer.

## Career and Placement

Because UTPA's MBA program is relatively small, graduate students here share a Career Services Office with business undergraduates. That office, called the Center for Advisement, Recruitment, Internships and Retention (CARIR), provides career counseling services, job-related reference materials, and assistance in internship placements. The office participates in numerous regional and national online job databases, which students may access through their UTPA accounts. CARIR also organizes on-campus recruitment events each semester, although most of the recruitment is geared toward undergraduate students.

## Student Life and Environment

UTPA is "a commuter campus" that "is not very eventful for graduate students." Aside from "occasional group meetings," MBAs here spend little time on campus. They attend classes, take care of other school-related obligations, and then head home. For all of the students who commute, the school's "parking facilities could be better."

UTPA is located in Edinburg, Texas, a city of nearly 50,000 in the southernmost section of the state. Edinburg is the county seat of Hidalgo County. The majority population is Hispanic, with most residents of Mexican descent. Education and health care are the area's major employment sectors; retail trade capitalizes on the city's location near the Mexico border.

The "career-minded" students in the program are "varied in nationalities and goals," according to their peers. These "resourceful, energetic, focused, and interesting" future MBAs "are typically employed full time, many with families and major commitments. We are nearly all night students. Students are disciplined and group-oriented."

Jerry Prock, Director of MBA Programs
1201 West University Drive, Edinburg, TX 78541-2999 United States
Phone: 956-381-3313 • Fax: 956-381-2970
E-mail: mbaprog@utpa.edu • Website: www.coba.panam.edu/mba/index.htm

## Admissions

Applicants to University of Texas—Pan American must submit all the following materials to the Admissions Committee: an application to the UTPA Graduate School; sealed copies of official transcripts for all previously attended postsecondary institutions; a sealed copy of an official GMAT score report. In addition, international students whose first language is not English must submit a sealed copy of an official TOEFL score report. Applicants who receive a score of at least 950 under the formula [(undergraduate GPA for final 60 semester hours of academic work 5 200) + GMAT score] have the best chance of gaining admission to the program. Those who fail to meet this benchmark may still be admitted on the basis of "strong supporting documentation," such as letters of recommendation, resume, and "other evidence of potential success based on relevant work and leadership experience."

### FINANCIAL FACTS

| | |
|---|---|
| Annual tuition (in-state/out-of-state) | $2,797/$8,900 |
| Fees (in-state/out-of-state) | $314/$402 |
| Books and supplies | $1,500 |
| Average grant | $9,999 |

### ADMISSIONS

| | |
|---|---|
| **Admissions Selectivity Rating** | **71** |
| # of applications received | 78 |
| % applicants accepted | 47 |
| % acceptees attending | 73 |
| Average GMAT | 420 |
| Average GPA | 3 |
| TOEFL required of international students? | yes |
| Minimum TOEFL (paper/computer) | 500/173 |
| Application fee | $35 |
| International application fee | $35 |
| Regular application deadline | 8/1 |
| Regular notification | rolling |
| Transfer students accepted? | yes |
| Transfer application policy Accept maximum 4 courses | |
| Non-fall admissions? | yes |
| Need-blind admissions? | yes |

# THE UNIVERSITY OF TEXAS—SAN ANTONIO
## COLLEGE OF BUSINESS

## Academics

You can earn your MBA at exactly the speed you choose at the University of Texas at San Antonio, a "self-paced" program geared toward the needs of busy area professionals. "Most students work full-time and take one or two classes a semester (three or six semester credit hours) and finish in approximately two years," according to the school's website. Students may take up to six years to complete the degree. Classes are usually offered on weekday evenings and on weekends.

The UTSA MBA program enjoys a boost from the school's PhD programs in accounting, finance, management and organizational studies, and information technology. Faculty in these areas are active in current research in their fields. In addition, faculty members in economics and real estate also publish frequently. The school also positions itself at the vanguard of business education by seeking new and promising disciplines; it has developed an expertise and an academic program in infrastructure assurance and security. Students here praise their professors, noting that "the majority of professors are PhDs with published work and prior experience in their field. Their real-world experience allows them to relate teachings to real-world situations, which help students assimilate new material." They appreciate how "most of the professors are very interested in making sure that their students learn the material and are very accessible and very willing to help." One MBA reports, "Several professors took time on weekends for additional exam preparation for students." Students also love the relatively low cost of the program. One writes, "The greatest strength of this program is the value when comparing tuition costs to the quality of the education and the resources available."

UTSA offers three basic MBA options: a general MBA, nonthesis; a general MBA with a thesis; and a nonthesis MBA with a concentration. All options require 33 hours of coursework (beyond preparatory core courses), 21 hours of which are devoted to Foundations of Knowledge requirements (advanced courses in accounting, managerial economics, financial management, management and behavior, strategy, marketing, and decision analysis). The thesis option requires an additional six hours of electives and six hours of master's thesis credit. The nonthesis option requires 12 hours of electives. Students may use their electives to concentrate in business economics, finance, health care management, information systems, management accounting, management of technology, management science, marketing management, project management, and taxation.

## Career and Placement

UTSA employs a career officer dedicated to providing counseling and placement services to graduate business students. Services include career assessment; one-on-one counseling; library services; online resume books and job postings; resume reviews; mock interviews; internships; career fairs and on-campus recruiting; career skills workshops; and networking events. UTSA MBAs appreciate the efforts but wish for something more; "We need more activities for graduate business students, more networking with alumni, and better companies to come recruit on campus," writes one student. Employers most likely to hire UTSA business graduates include HEB Grocery Company, USAA, and Dell Computers.

## Student Life and Environment

UTSA is a school in transition; it "was established as a commuter school," but students note that "the last few years have seen a trend towards more traditional students and programs. It is exciting to be on a campus that is becoming a real college campus for the first time. The

VERONICA RAMIREZ, SUPERVISOR, GRADUATE ADMISSIONS
6900 NORTH LOOP, 1604 WEST, SAN ANTONIO, TX 78249-0603 UNITED STATES
PHONE: 210-458-4330 • FAX: 210-458-4332
E-MAIL: GRADUATESTUDIES@UTSA.EDU • WEBSITE: BUSINESS.UTSA.EDU/GRADUATE/

gym is busy even at 10:00 or 11:00 at night, and it's amazing to see the amount of activity that persists on campus even in the afternoon and evening." Students also report that "the addition of the downtown campus in the urban center has allowed for full-time professionals to more efficiently intermix the professional with the academic lives." Even so, this is hardly a lively extracurricular scene for MBA. One student explains, "Most of the courses are offered after 5:00 P.M., which lends itself to many working, commuting students. In this type of environment, it is sometimes difficult to establish a sense of community." However, approximately one-third of the students in the graduate program attend school on a full-time basis. These students tend to work on campus as research and teaching assistants and are on campus most of the day. The MBA Association does its best; it is "active and aggressive in providing MBA students with access to lectures, etiquette dinners, networking opportunities, resume seminars, [and] job fairs."

UTSA's facilities earn students' praise; MBAs tell us the campus "is beautiful and safe," and that "the business building has excellent learning technology in the classrooms. Also, access to computers and research materials is widely available throughout the campus." Things are so good here that many students identify the lack of a football team as the university's most glaring weakness.

The population of the MBA program at UTSA "is very diverse," although "the predominant type is the full-time employed individual, [typically] married, in [their] late 20s or early 30s, and whose time is at a premium." Students represent "an incredibly diverse mix of professions as well as backgrounds. For example, I had a physicist from MIT and an Air Force Colonel in the same class." says one MBA. The school attracts many internationals; one student writes, "There are people from Asia, the U.S., India, and Mexico."

## Admissions

Applicants to the UTSA MBA program are required to provide the school with a completed application form, official copies of transcripts from all colleges and universities attended, official GMAT scores, and a personal statement stating the applicant's career and academic goals. A current resume and two letters of reference are officially optional but are "strongly recommended" by the Admissions Office. Applicants need not have majored in business as undergraduates to gain admission. Students with non-business undergraduate degrees are typically required to complete core courses in accounting, business law, economic theory, business finance, information systems, marketing, and quantitative methods prior to beginning work on the MBA. Students who completed undergraduate work in a business field more than seven years prior to admission may also be required to complete some or all core courses.

### FINANCIAL FACTS
Annual tuition (in-state/out-of-state)
$5,590/$15,626

### ADMISSIONS
| | |
|---|---|
| **Admissions Selectivity Rating** | **79** |
| # of applications received | 198 |
| % applicants accepted | 65 |
| % acceptees attending | 63 |
| Average GMAT | 569 |
| Range of GMAT | 513–610 |
| Average GPA | 3.28 |
| TOEFL required of international students? | yes |
| Minimum TOEFL (paper/computer) | 500/173 |
| Application fee | $45 |
| International application fee | $80 |
| Regular application deadline | 7/1 |
| Regular notification | rolling |
| Deferment available? | yes |
| Maximum length of deferment | 2 terms |
| Transfer students accepted? | yes |
| Transfer application policy Please refer to Current Graduate Catalog. | |
| Non-fall admissions? | yes |
| Need-blind admissions? | yes |

| EMPLOYMENT PROFILE | |
|---|---|
| **Career Rating** | **61** |
| **Primary source of full-time job acceptances** | |
| School-facilitated activities | 5 (63%) |
| Graduate-facilitated activities | 3 (38%) |
| Unknown | 59 |
| | |
| Average starting salary | $42,934 |
| Percent employed | 4 |

# THE UNIVERSITY OF TULSA
## COLLEGE OF BUSINESS ADMINISTRATION

## Academics

The College of Business Administration at The University of Tulsa (TU) offers a number of options to meet the needs of a wide variety of students. For those in a hurry to get their degrees, TU offers a full-time MBA that can be completed (by those with undergraduate degrees in business) in 18 months. For those who work full-time, the school has a part-time program with classes that meet once a week on evenings. And for those who can't make it to campus, TU has an iMBA (Internet-mediated MBA) that requires only two visits to campus: one for orientation, the other for graduation. Many students love this final option; one iMBA student writes, "In the online MBA program, they continue to develop an understanding of 'best practices' in online education and incorporate new knowledge into the delivery of the program." Plus, "the online program also is taught by the same full-time professors who teach the campus-based courses, so the quality of instruction and level of expertise are high."

For students lacking expertise in some or all fundamental business areas, the TU MBA program commences with 8 basic foundation courses; students may apply for a waiver from any or all of these courses. The remainder of the curriculum consists of a one-hour ethics course plus eight core courses and two electives. Students may use the electives to create a specialization in accounting, taxation, finance, or MIS. MBAs report that "the finance program in risk management is great. It's very challenging and very interesting." They also appreciate how the curriculum "helps students become very comfortable and confident in their presentation and speaking skills." Students also add that "several classes provide the opportunity to express [their] own experiences and ideas, which gives a more practical feel to the material." However, some students complain that "there is too much emphasis on quantitative problems, as opposed to learning to read what the output really means." All MBAs agree, "This is a tough school that cannot be breezed through with ease."

TU is a small program, which translates into "very low student-teacher ratios" and "small class sizes," but it also means that there's a limited availability of class times. "We don't have the choice of taking some classes during the day," students say. "The program is set up for the working adults, not for the few full-timers." Luckily, "the professors at The University of Tulsa are fantastic." One student reasons, "A good professor may teach you concepts, but a great professor will teach you to think. Here at TU, the emphasis is more on understanding than remembering." Plus, "professors are very accessible," fulfilling their roles "not only as teachers, but also as professional coaches."

## Career and Placement

The Career Services Office at The University of Tulsa works with all students (undergraduate and graduate) and alumni, while the College of Business provides some supplemental services, including assistance in finding summer internships for MBAs. Students report that the school provides "good networking opportunities." One student attests, "I met the CEO of my company (ConocoPhillips) in one of the business forums." But, still, other students say, "Career Services needs to make more contacts and deliver a bigger variety of companies for job fairs and job opportunities." As one student explains, "Currently most of the employers recruiting from TU are local companies or government organizations. The school would increase its stature if it could get more national placements than regional ones." Currently more than 80 percent of TU graduates find jobs in the immediate region; [the majority] of the rest are international students who return home after graduation.

Top employers of TU MBAs include AFN Communications, ALLTEL, Bank of Oklahoma, Citgo, Crosby Group, Datatel, First Omni, IBM, KPMG, MCI Worldcom, Nordam, Williams, and Wiltel (formerly Williams Communications).

## Student Life and Environment

The University of Tulsa "is not a party school," because "students have to study 24/7 to survive," students say. For those who can afford to take a breather, "there are a number of clubs at the university" with themes ranging "from the outdoors to sports cars." And if you want to let off some steam, "the new gym facility is wonderful. It includes three basketball courts, an indoor and outdoor track, and the latest in cardio and weight-lifting equipment."

MBAs like that "TU attracts focused, career-minded students who tend to be achievement-oriented without being competitive." MBAs say, "Students are mature enough to invest in relationships and group activities that add educational value," which creates "a warm family atmosphere where students and professors can develop a rapport with one another." The only fly in the ointment is the occasional slacker. It seems the administration "needs to be more selective about who they allow into the MBA program. There are too many students on probation for poor grades," according to some MBAs.

Hometown Tulsa—Oklahoma's second-largest city—is large enough to support an AA baseball team, an arena football franchise, and a motor racing circuit. The city is home to Oral Roberts University, an opera company, a theater, and a performing-arts center.

## Admissions

Applicants to the MBA program at TU must provide the school with a completed application, official transcripts for all undergraduate and graduate work, GMAT scores, TOEFL scores (international students only), three letters of recommendation, and a resume. TU offers a GM minority scholarship in an effort to increase the program's diversity.

### FINANCIAL FACTS

| | |
|---|---|
| Annual tuition | $13,230 |
| Books and supplies | $1,000 |
| Room & board | |
| (on/off-campus) | $5,886/$6,300 |
| % of students receiving aid | 20 |
| Average award package | $15,330 |
| Average grant | $10,080 |
| Average student loan debt | $23,375 |

### ADMISSIONS

| | |
|---|---|
| Admissions Selectivity Rating | 76 |
| # of applications received | 85 |
| % applicants accepted | 67 |
| % acceptees attending | 51 |
| Average GMAT | 546 |
| Range of GMAT | 450–750 |
| Average GPA | 3.44 |
| TOEFL required of international students? | yes |
| Minimum TOEFL (paper/computer) | 575/232 |
| Application fee | $30 |
| International application fee | $30 |
| Regular application deadline | rolling |
| Regular notification | rolling |
| Deferment available? | yes |
| Maximum length of deferment | 1 year |
| Transfer students accepted? | yes |
| Transfer application policy Up to 6 credit hours may be transferred. | |
| Non-fall admissions? | yes |
| Need-blind admissions? | yes |

### APPLICANTS ALSO LOOK AT
Oklahoma State University,
University of Oklahoma

| EMPLOYMENT PROFILE | |
|---|---|
| Career Rating | 72 |
| Average starting salary | $56,100 |

# UNIVERSITY OF UTAH
## DAVID ECCLES SCHOOL OF BUSINESS

### GENERAL INFORMATION
| | |
|---|---|
| Type of school | public |
| Environment | city |
| Academic calendar | semester |

### SURVEY SAYS...
Students love Salt Lake City, UT
Friendly students
Smart classrooms

### STUDENTS
| | |
|---|---|
| Enrollment of parent institution | 30,000 |
| Enrollment of business school | 416 |
| % male/female | 70/30 |
| % out-of-state | 49 |
| % part-time | 75 |
| % minorities | 5 |
| % international | 21 |
| Average age at entry | 28 |
| Average years work experience at entry | 5.5 |

### ACADEMICS
| | |
|---|---|
| **Academic Experience Rating** | **88** |
| Student/faculty ratio | 5:1 |
| Profs interesting rating | 85 |
| Profs accessible rating | 81 |
| % female faculty | 28 |
| % minority faculty | 16 |

### JOINT DEGREES
MBA/JD, 3-4 years; MBA/MArch, 3-4 years

### PROMINENT ALUMNI
Pierre Lassonde, President, Franco-Nevada Mining; Spencer Kirk, Retired CEO, Megahertz Corp.; Robert McDonald, Vice-Chair Global Operations, Procter & Gamble; Jerry Atkin, President, CEO, Skywest Airlines; Geoffrey Wooley, Founding Partner, Dominion Ventures

## Academics

The David Eccles School of Business (DESB) at the University of Utah is an up-and-coming business program that students say is "still figuring out its culture and personality." Currently its strengths lie in accounting, finance, and marketing, but lots of interesting and unusual areas are also developing on the school's Salt Lake City campus. Students report that "DESB has unique offerings, like a nonprofit consulting class (set up by the Net Impact chapter)" and the New Venture Development Center, which capitalizes on developments throughout the university. One student explains, "There are some very exciting opportunities in genetic-based medicine, biotechnologies, medical testing, and medical digital-imaging technologies coming out of this university, and I am working to bring these to market through the New Venture Development Center. It is a fabulous opportunity."

Because Eccles "is still a small program, it is very personalized," which students appreciate. They also like the "class curriculum that provides a strong foundation for business students, yet allows them to tailor a unique program to fit their own wants and needs." The school is also flexible enough to adapt to the schedules of its part-timers; one student writes, "The business school has done a great job implementing a professional-based MBA program for working students."

Students cite many areas of strength at the university. The entrepreneurial program, students say, is "extremely pragmatic with professors that have more than succeeded out in the dog-eat-dog world." Finance professors "approach their responsibility with incredible seriousness, with a challenging program that teaches students the critical eye of analysis [and] shows them how to dig deep to find the critical details that make or break investments. This is so much more than the plug-and-chug model." The marketing program "includes a Nobel Prize nominee." Students say, "These people know their stuff. And if you want to learn, they're willing to take the time and make the effort to teach you, inside and outside of class." Throughout the program, "the faculty and administration at the University of Utah provides a broad mix of people and styles. There are definite thought leaders in each respect and field that are able to teach and do things that make being here a very worthwhile experience," some students note.

## Career and Placement

The MBA Career Services Office at Eccles is "very active. They are always having student networking nights and sending out info for new job postings." Students agree that their strengths lie in specialized areas. One student explains, "There are good opportunities to network in accounting and finance, but there is limited on-campus recruiting in investment banking and venture capital. For most careers in accounting and finance, there are many great opportunities for on-campus interviews. I already have a full-time job set up for after graduation. I got [a job] offer early in November, and I would say that more than half of my fellow students are in the same boat. Believe me, that takes off a lot of stress." Some MBAs—especially those in areas that are not optimally served—feel that "Career Services is understaffed, making job searching an additional responsibility for the student above and beyond their classes and course work."

Top employers of Eccles MBAs include 3M, Accenture, Deloitte Touche Tohmatsu, eBay, FedEx, GE-OEC Medical Systems, Goldman Sachs, IBM, Ford, Intel, Intermountain Health Care, KPMG, PacifiCorp, PricewaterhouseCoopers, UPS, Wells Fargo, and Zions Bank.

## Student Life and Environment

The DESB is housed in a new, up-to-date building in which "almost all classrooms have amphitheater seating with wireless connections and power plugs at each workstation. The professor can show you something in Excel, and you can follow along right there instead of trying to write notes and practice it on your laptop later." One student adds, "The tie-in to technology has been a great asset. All professors use WebCT to post syllabi and course work. I love this easy access to everything." Eccles MBAs agree that "the program technology is cutting-edge. Everyone in my program got a free laptop. They just work it into the tuition, but you keep the laptop at the end of the program, and you have three years of free tech support."

While "the Eccles program allows for a social life, not many students take advantage of it." One professional MBA student explains, "Most everyone in my classes works full-time. Also, many people have families. Therefore, life at school is limited to class time and job searches. There is not a strong sense of community or social connection." Full-timers do enjoy a more well-rounded MBA experience that includes "excellent clubs: the U Venture Fund, the Lassonde New Venture Development Center, the Utah Entrepreneur Center, UTEC, and the Smart Start Mentor program." Eccles also hosts "great guest lecturers. I just got back from a lecture given by Lynn Turner, the former chief accountant of the SEC. There were about 40 of us in a classroom and the discussion was very informal with plenty of time for everyone to get their questions answered," one student says. They also "schedule occasional 'Attitude Adjustment Seminars' where MBA students network with the wider community. Actually, the 'seminars' are just people getting together at a club for a few drinks. Alumni, mentors, faculty, and staff are all invited. The Graduate Business Student Association also sponsors exciting campouts, tailgate parties, and pizza parties."

Students agree that "the Utah community is very friendly, safe, and active. Housing near the school is plentiful and public transportation is new this year but very accessible and helpful."

## Admissions

The Eccles Admissions Department requires applicants to provide the following: an undergraduate transcript demonstrating a GPA of at least 3.0, proof of completion of a college-level statistics course, GMAT scores (minimum score of 50th percentile in math required or college algebra must be retaken), letters of recommendation, personal statements, and a resume. International students whose first language is not English must take the TOEFL and TSE. To increase campus diversity, the school has "several privately donated scholarships reserved for underrepresented groups and to help [them] build the gender, ethnic, and geographic diversity of [their] student body."

### FINANCIAL FACTS

| | |
|---|---|
| Annual tuition (in-state/out-of-state) | $9,291/$20,936 |
| Fees | $341 |
| Books and supplies | $1,500 |
| Room & board (on/off-campus) | $8,000/$11,000 |
| % of students receiving aid | 44 |
| % of first-year students receiving aid | 44 |
| % of students receiving grants | 44 |
| Average award package | $14,350 |
| Average grant | $14,350 |

### ADMISSIONS

| | |
|---|---|
| Admissions Selectivity Rating | 87 |
| # of applications received | 159 |
| % applicants accepted | 53 |
| % acceptees attending | 61 |
| Average GMAT | 601 |
| Range of GMAT | 540–640 |
| Average GPA | 3.36 |
| TOEFL required of international students? | yes |
| Minimum TOEFL (paper/computer) | 600/250 |
| Application fee | $45 |
| International application fee | $65 |
| Regular application deadline | 2/15 |
| Regular notification | 4/10 |
| Transfer students accepted? | yes |
| Transfer application policy | In special circumstances, up to 6 credit hours may be transferred into the program from another program. |
| Need-blind admissions? | yes |

### APPLICANTS ALSO LOOK AT

Brigham Young University

### EMPLOYMENT PROFILE

| Career Rating | 82 | Grads employed by field: | % | avg. salary: |
|---|---|---|---|---|
| **Primary source of full-time job acceptances** | | Accounting | 19 | $44,500 |
| | | Finance | 30 | $52,833 |
| School-facilitated activities | 28 (88%) | Human Resources | 10 | $53,667 |
| Graduate-facilitated activities | 2 (6%) | Marketing | 16 | $56,400 |
| Unknown | 2 (6%) | Consulting | 3 | $80,000 |
| | | Nonprofit | 3 | $35,000 |
| Average starting salary | $58,823 | Other | 9 | $56,167 |
| Percent employed | 94 | | | |

# UNIVERSITY OF VERMONT
## SCHOOL OF BUSINESS ADMINISTRATION

### GENERAL INFORMATION
| | |
|---|---|
| Type of school | public |
| Environment | city |
| Academic calendar | fall/spring |

### SURVEY SAYS...
Students love Burlington, VT
Friendly students
Happy students

### STUDENTS
| | |
|---|---|
| Enrollment of parent institution | 11,597 |
| Enrollment of business school | 51 |
| % male/female | 23/77 |
| % out-of-state | 23 |
| % part-time | 75 |
| % minorities | 6 |
| % international | 8 |
| Average age at entry | 30 |
| Average years work experience at entry | 9 |

### ACADEMICS
| | |
|---|---|
| **Academic Experience Rating** | **83** |
| Student/faculty ratio | 3:1 |
| Profs interesting rating | 83 |
| Profs accessible rating | 86 |
| % female faculty | 27 |

### PROMINENT ALUMNI
Doug Goldsmith, CFO & VP, Finance & Admin; Corp. Finance, Rock of Ages; Elisabeth Robert, President, CFO & Treasurer, VT Teddy Bear, Inc.; direct consumer retail; Katherine B. Crosett, Principal; Kalex Enterprises, Inc.; Alexander D. Crosett, III, Principal; Kalex Enterprises, Inc.

## Academics

"The best—make that 'only'—MBA program in Burlington" is how one student at the UVM School of Business Administration wryly encapsulates his school, but this program has a lot more going for it than just its geographic monopoly. With approximately 70 students in the program, UVM can offer its MBA students all the personal attention they desire. Plus, with a large university (and large university resources) looming in the background, UVM MBAs can benefit from "interaction with other programs." An environmental engineer earning his MBA here, for example, praises his easy access to the Rubenstein School of Environment and Natural Resources and the Gund Institute of Ecological Economics.

UVM offers both full-time and part-time options in the MBA but schedules classes for the convenience of part-timers, most of whom have full-time jobs. Nearly all classes meet twice weekly in 75-minute evening sessions. "The night classes offer more flexibility to those who work," one student explains. The program is divided into two parts: the core level, comprised of six required courses covering business fundamentals (marketing, accounting, organization, finance, business law, and production and operations management); and the advanced level, comprised of six distribution requirements covering six functions, three electives, and an integrative capstone course.

Students praise the UVM faculty for "bringing in current events into the classroom." They also appreciate that "professors are very accessible, willing to help with coursework or networking, and are generally good at encouraging stimulating discussion in the classroom." Administrators are also "readily accessible. In fact, the director of the program offers to talk with every student at course-registration time." There are, of course, drawbacks to all small programs, and UVM is no exception. One student warns, "The frustrating part is the limited number of courses offered each semester. Moreover, many of the courses are offered at the same time, making it impossible to take all the courses you want."

## Career and Placement

The Career Services Office at UVM, students tell us, "puts very little effort into graduate placement for careers. The people currently in career services are trying hard, but they are starting from scratch in the graduate area as there is no history of on-campus recruiting. There needs to be!" The office could start, one student suggests, by "offering more networking events. I think that they are trying to improve on this area by putting career counselors in place in the business building. We'll see."

## Student Life and Environment

Students tell us that "there is a big difference between part-time students," who make up about two-thirds of the UVM MBA student body, "and full-time students. Part-timers and older, have full-time jobs and have done little or no prior business coursework. Full-timers are younger, typically have a business-related undergraduate degree, and are unemployed. Full-timers and part-timers mingle well despite being in different life stages. They frequently hang out together outside of school." Part-timers "often work, attend classes at night, and have families to attend to. They burn the candle at both ends—and look like it!" The student body boasts a solid contingent of engineers as well as a sizeable international population.

RALPH SWENSON, DIRECTOR OF GRADUATE ADMISSIONS
333 WATERMAN BUILDING, BURLINGTON, VT 05405 UNITED STATES
PHONE: 802-656-0655 • FAX: 802-656-4078 • E-MAIL: MBA@BSAD.UVM.EDU
WEBSITE: WWW.BSAD.UVM.EDU/ACADEMICS/DEGREE+PROGRAMS/MBA/

Full-timers here report "a healthy balance of work and leisure. We work hard but have plenty of valuable diversions, such as snowboarding at nearby mountains." While some feel that "it would be better to have more events for the MBA students so that [they] could network amongst [them]selves as well as potentially other members in the community," most here accept the current situation as the unavoidable result of a tiny MBA program. Students tell us, "Burlington is a great small city with lots to offer, especially the quality and variety of live music and restaurants." Montreal is only a two-hour drive from Burlington; Ottawa, Ontario, and Albany, NY, can be reached in three hours.

## Admissions

The Admissions Committee for the UVM MBA program considers academic record, previous work experience, GMAT scores, writing ability, and letters of recommendation in making its decisions. Applicants must submit official transcripts for all college and graduate work, an official GMAT score report, a resume, a personal essay, and a completed application. The average GMAT score of admitted students is 600; their average undergraduate GPA is 3.2. No student may begin the MBA program without first completing prerequisite courses in macroeconomics, microeconomics, calculus, statistics, and computer usage. Students who have completed undergraduate degrees in business within the last five years may waive the prerequisite courses; others may place out of the classes by passing qualifying examinations.

### FINANCIAL FACTS

| | |
|---|---|
| Annual tuition (in-state/out-of-state) | $9,088/$22,728 |
| Fees | $1,138 |
| Books and supplies | $400 |
| Room & board (on-campus) | $7,600 |
| Average grant | $2,000 |

### ADMISSIONS

| | |
|---|---|
| **Admissions Selectivity Rating** | **80** |
| # of applications received | 46 |
| % applicants accepted | 61 |
| % acceptees attending | 79 |
| Average GMAT | 610 |
| Range of GMAT | 480–730 |
| Average GPA | 3.18 |
| TOEFL required of international students? | yes |
| Minimum TOEFL (paper/computer) | 550/213 |
| Application fee | $25 |
| International application fee | $25 |
| Regular application deadline | rolling |
| Regular notification | rolling |
| Deferment available? | yes |
| Maximum length of deferment | 1 year |
| Non-fall admissions? | yes |
| Need-blind admissions? | yes |

### APPLICANTS ALSO LOOK AT

Boston College, Boston University, University of Connecticut, University of Massachusetts—Amherst, University of New Hampshire

| EMPLOYMENT PROFILE | |
|---|---|
| Career Rating | 75 |

# UNIVERSITY OF VIRGINIA
## DARDEN GRADUATE SCHOOL OF BUSINESS ADMINISTRATION

### GENERAL INFORMATION
| | |
|---|---|
| Type of school | public |
| Environment | city |
| Academic calendar | semester |

### SURVEY SAYS...
Smart classrooms
*Solid preparation in:*
General management
Teamwork

### STUDENTS
| | |
|---|---|
| Enrollment of parent institution | 20,399 |
| Enrollment of business school | 617 |
| % male/female | 76/24 |
| % out-of-state | 73 |
| % minorities | 13 |
| % international | 25 |
| Average age at entry | 28 |
| Average years work experience at entry | 4.5 |

### ACADEMICS
| | |
|---|---|
| **Academic Experience Rating** | **95** |
| Student/faculty ratio | 7:1 |
| Profs interesting rating | 99 |
| Profs accessible rating | 98 |
| % female faculty | 20 |
| % minority faculty | 4 |

### JOINT DEGREES
MBA/JD, 4 years; MBA/MA in Asian Studies, 3 years; MBA/MA in Government or Foreign Affairs, 3 years; MBA/ME, 3 years; MBA/MSN, 3 years; MBA/PhD, 4 years

### PROMINENT ALUMNI
Mr. Douglas R. Lebda, Founder and former CEO, Lending Tree, Inc.; Mr. Steven S Reinemund, Chair of the Board and CEO, PepsiCo, Inc.; Ms. Lawton Fitt, Director Reuters Group, PLC; Mr. George David, Chair and CEO of United Technologies Corp.; Ms. E. Follin Smith, Exe. VP, CFO, CAO Constellation Energy Group

## Academics

Most business schools employ case studies in their curricula, but few incorporate them so integrally or so thoroughly as the Darden Graduate School of Business Administration at the University of Virginia. The case method, which permeates the entire first-year curriculum, requires both a faculty capable of teaching multidisciplinary approaches to problem-solving, and a student body dedicated enough to spend hours a day preparing, reviewing, and discussing cases outside the classroom. The case method process simulates the function of modern managers in a wide variety of different industries, products, processes and styles of management. Fortunately, Darden has both.

Students agree that the case method is demanding. One student notes, "The learning curve is incredibly steep, and the workload is high, but this gives the best base for learning." Another student observes, "There is no doubt that the workload at Darden, especially during the first semester, is probably the toughest of any business school, but you learn to prioritize, rely on your learning team, and think on your feet in a dynamic classroom environment led by exceptional faculty." Because the case method stresses in-class discussion, "you really learn the importance of being able to articulate your arguments."

First-year studies at Darden are especially grueling. Students have revealed that "all the courses are required, you have no scheduling freedom, and the workload is [a] killer. This boot camp ensures that everyone is equally prepared in all core courses." Fortunately, students now report that "curriculum is changing for the first-year, where students will be able to choose electives in the fourth quarter." Indeed, first-year students will now be able to choose three first-year program electives from eleven options during the fourth quarter. The first-year program electives are extensions of the core courses and all relate to preparing students for summer internships. Some students complain that "the course work can be too demanding. At certain times of the year, the volume of work necessary exceeds the hours in the day. You have to learn to prioritize, or you won't succeed." Most, however, say that they "wouldn't change a thing." The second-year curriculum "is more like other schools. You pick all your courses, times, and professors, and the workload is much lighter," one student comments.

Through it all, Darden MBAs benefit from what they perceive to be "the best teaching faculty of any business school. The professors are outstanding, and they are very accessible to students. You simply fire an e-mail, and within a day or two, you have an appointment set up with them." One student notes, "It is amazing how well the faculty runs case discussions, which is the most difficult type of teaching. Not many professors could survive in an atmosphere of constant questions and the need to link together so many diverse approaches to create a better understanding for the class."

## Career and Placement

Many Darden MBAs would like to see a wider range of companies recruiting on campus. One student explains, "A lot of banks and financial institutions recruit here; we could use more marketing and general-management type opportunities." The school reports that this issue is being addressed as many new companies from marketing and general Management industries have joined on-grounds recruiting. Students do however, applaud the "extremely helpful and tight-knit alumni network." MBAs say, "[The alumni network] is among the greatest strengths of Darden. The alumni are extremely helpful when looking for employment."

The 2004 to 2005 MBA recruiters at Darden included Citigroup Global Corporate & Investment Bank, McKinsey & Company, Lehman Brothers, The Boston Consulting Group, General Electric Company, Pfizer, Booz Allen Hamilton, Capital One Financial, Bank of America Securities, Bank of America, Cargill, Bain and Company, and Bear Sterns and Co.

DAWNA CLARKE, DIRECTOR OF ADMISSIONS
PO BOX 6550, CHARLOTTESVILLE, VA 22906 UNITED STATES
PHONE: 434-924-7281 • FAX: 434-243-5033
E-MAIL: DARDEN@VIRGINIA.EDU • WEBSITE: WWW.DARDEN.VIRGINIA.EDU

## Student Life and Environment

Life at Darden is dictated in large part by the curriculum. Students warn that "the first year is really tough, and the stress is enormous. There is very little time in the first semester for anything but school and resume [preparation]. Many of us are here from 8:00 A.M. to 10:00 or 11:00 P.M. It eases up in the spring, although at that point, recruiting takes up a lot of time." Most MBAs try to find time for at least a little work break, as the popular "Thursday Night Drinking Club (TNDC). The students are a blast when you get them out. There isn't a ton of weekday socialization for first-years who have learning team at night, but once the weekend comes, watch out."

The emphasis on teamwork builds a strong student community, making the program "like a family. There are always school-related activities going on ranging from the Chili Cookoff to the Latin American Student Association Carnival." Extracurricular clubs abound; students say that "the [Darden Leadership Forum] is superb, inviting phenomenal business executives to speak and raise our awareness of the power of business today," while the student-run Darden Capital Management "manages over $2 million of the school's endowment. It provides a fantastic hands-on learning experience for future asset managers that few other top MBA schools offer. It's been a blast!"

Students love "cosmopolitan" hometown Charlottesville and call it "a great college town." One student says, "I can't think of a better place to spend two years than at Mr. Jefferson's university. [There are] lots of things to do outside of class; great football and ACC basketball." One student adds, "The city is both quaint and refined. If you are into the outdoors, hiking, camping, and seasonal skiing are just 30 minutes away. If you are into food, C'ville has a ton of good restaurants and bars. If you are single, there are tons of other grad students in the law, medicine, and other grad schools, as well as a huge undergrad population. As for family folks, the city is safe and very family-friendly. I am enjoying myself."

## Admissions

According to Darden's viewbook, the admissions committee looks for "breadth of perspective, international exposure, and diversity," as well as evidence of motivation, interpersonal skills, and leadership in prospective students. The school points out that over 99 percent of successful applicants have full-time work experience. Applicants must submit academic transcripts, GMAT scores, TOEFL scores (non-native English speakers only), four essays, two letters of recommendation, and a resume. All prospects should have a personal interview.

### FINANCIAL FACTS

| | |
|---|---|
| Annual tuition (in-state/out-of-state) | $32,198/$37,198 |
| Fees | $102 |
| Books and supplies | $2,577 |
| Room & board | $13,923 |
| % of students receiving aid | 79 |
| % of first-year students receiving aid | 79 |
| % of students receiving loans | 76 |
| % of students receiving grants | 49 |
| Average award package | $33,170 |
| Average grant | $15,826 |
| Average student loan debt | $63,811 |

### ADMISSIONS

| | |
|---|---|
| Admissions Selectivity Rating | 91 |
| # of applications received | 1,598 |
| % applicants accepted | 49 |
| % acceptees attending | 39 |
| Average GMAT | 670 |
| Range of GMAT | 640–700 |
| Average GPA | 3.29 |
| TOEFL required of international students? | yes |
| Minimum TOEFL (paper/computer) | 650/270 |
| Application fee | $140 |
| International application fee | $140 |
| Regular application deadline | 12/5 |
| Regular notification | 2/6 |
| Application deadline/notification | |
| Round 1: | 10/5 / 12/5 |
| Round 2: | 12/5 / 2/6 |
| Round 3: | 1/6 / 3/6 |
| Round 4: | 3/6 / 4/6 |
| Deferment available? | yes |
| Maximum length of deferment | Managed case by case |
| Transfer students accepted? | yes |
| Transfer application policy | Transfer students are accepted but credits cannot be transferred. |
| Need-blind admissions? | yes |

### EMPLOYMENT PROFILE

| Career Rating | 96 | Grads employed by field: | % | avg. salary: |
|---|---|---|---|---|
| Primary source of full-time job acceptances | | Finance | 43 | $89,968 |
| | | Marketing | 11 | $82,401 |
| School-facilitated activities | 194 (77%) | Strategic Planning | 5 | $101,056 |
| Graduate-facilitated activities | 59 (23%) | Consulting | 21 | $100,883 |
| | | General Management | 16 | $89,829 |
| Average starting salary | $91,740 | Other | 4 | $36,000 |
| Percent employed | 93 | | | |

# UNIVERSITY OF WASHINGTON
## BUSINESS SCHOOL

## Academics

"If you want to get a job in the Pacific Northwest, the University of Washington is the best place you can go," students at this small, prestigious b-school say. That's especially true for folks looking to remain in Seattle after graduation; UW has a big leg up on the competition there because "there is no other major school in Seattle, where there [are] a number of first-class companies." But it's not just location that gives UW its competitive edge; MBAs explain that "the overall academic experience is great here. We are learning all the classic elements of a b-school education in marketing, finance, and operations. There are also innovative programs, such as the e-business program."

UW's areas of strength are extensive; students praise the programs in accounting, e-business, entrepreneurship, finance, and IT. They also love the "outstanding core faculty," who deliver "a first-year core that is extremely challenging, with a broad exposure to the kind of wide variety of disciplines that any businessperson should know about." MBAs report favorably that "all of the first-year core professors make themselves available for a professor-night dinner once each quarter, where we get to sit down with them, drink wine, and get to know them better. It's a great example of how accessible our faculty are."

Second-year students say that their biggest problem is that the school offers too much value. One student explains, "I wish I could make more time in my second year to take more of the electives. There are more must-have courses from must-have professors than I have room in my schedule. It's almost too bad I have to go back out into the workplace, but then I'm excited to practice what I've learned." The administration earns students' thumbs up because "they run things smoothly. They facilitate integration of speakers, networking events, and other activities with classes very well," and they "are behind students and like to make sure [that] students are having a great experience in b-school. They are [also] open to new ideas and willing to try new things." Administrators are currently at work on remedying the school's chief drawback, which is the facility in which it's housed. One MBA notes, "We need a new building. The building we're in is dated and unattractive. Fortunately, there is a plan to build a new building in the next four or five years."

## Career and Placement

The Business Connections Center at the University of Washington Business School connects students to area businesses through its MBA mentor program, which "offers students the opportunity to learn about the way business is practiced today, under the guidance of top executives." The school also sets up "Road Shows," in which, UW MBAs travel to major cities (like New York, Los Angeles, San Francisco, and San Diego) to network with alumni and area businesses. Students are generally satisfied with the services provided by the BCC, although a number complained that the office is "a bit understaffed."

Top employers of UW MBAs include Alaska Airlines, Amazon.com, AT&T Wireless, Bank of America, Boeing Company, Booz Allen Hamilton, Cap Gemini Ernst & Young, Deloitte Touche Tohmatsu, GE Capital, Hewlett-Packard, Hitachi Consulting, Intel, Microsoft, Paccar, Phillips Medical Systems, Samsung Electronics, Starbucks, Tektronix, Washington Mutual, and Wells Fargo. Approximately 1 in 10 MBAs begins their post-degree career outside the U.S.

## Student Life and Environment

UW MBAs agree that there's "great camaraderie among students" in their program. One student says, "The culture is one where students are friendly and helpful in making sure that no one is left behind. Second-year MBA students here lead review sessions to help

SUNNI BANNON, DIRECTOR OF ADMISSIONS
110 MACKENZIE HALL, BOX 353200, SEATTLE, WA 98195-3200 UNITED STATES
PHONE: 206-543-4661 • FAX: 206-616-7351
E-MAIL: MBA@U.WASHINGTON.EDU • WEBSITE: WWW.MBA.WASHINGTON.EDU

the first-year students get through the first quarter of the core. In addition, every student is easily approachable and more than willing to share his or her insights into a particular class, the job search, or even how to handle one's personal life. The culture here has allowed me to make friends for life!" Students also appreciate that their classmates are "smart and ambitious but very down-to-earth," with "strong individual and entrepreneurial mind-sets."

Students are also "very active in clubs and efforts to continue developing the program." The program also enjoys a "strong sense of community involvement through volunteerism and fund-raising for charity organizations." For example, "everyone participates in Challenge for Charity! We are the West Coast winner year after year, despite the fact that we are the smallest school." As one student explains, "Life here is balanced. We have a finance club, but we also have a hiking club. The same person who interned at a Venture Capital firm over the summer volunteers with the Special Olympics on weekends." Quite a few students at the university "are also involved in initiatives to study how to better market the school."

Leisure fun is abetted by the many options available in Seattle with "its proximity to great hiking, biking, and skiing" and "great microbrews." There's plenty of socializing within the school, too; for example, students "have a program where [they] invite professors to students' homes for potlucks with other students. Typically 10 to 12 students attend each potluck, which creates a relaxed atmosphere [for students] to get to know the professor." Students add that "every other week, there is a 'TG' in the MBA lounge with food and a keg. We get a chance to relax at the end of a hard week and party a little bit with our classmates. Some of my classmates have become my best friends, and we often go out together." All in all, "social interaction [is] very strong through formal and informal student gatherings and bar nights."

## Admissions

The admissions office at University of Washington says, "We consider a broad spectrum of factors. No one factor is weighed more heavily than others. We also seek a highly diverse class in terms of academic background, work experience, and personal experience. Applicants from nonbusiness backgrounds and unique backgrounds are encouraged to apply." Applicants must submit all undergraduate and graduate transcripts, letters of recommendation, a personal statement, a resume, and GMAT scores; an interview is by invitation. To increase minority representation in the MBA program, "the University of Washington sponsors campus-visit programs and receptions for students from underrepresented minority groups. We have scholarships specifically targeting underrepresented minority candidates."

### FINANCIAL FACTS

| | |
|---|---|
| Annual tuition (in-state/out-of-state) | $16,500/$26,000 |
| Fees | $510 |
| Books and supplies | $1,800 |
| Room & board | $10,600 |
| % of students receiving aid | 66 |
| % of first-year students receiving aid | 78 |
| % of students receiving loans | 68 |
| % of students receiving grants | 46 |
| Average award package | $12,898 |
| Average grant | $8,683 |
| Average student loan debt | $20,480 |

### ADMISSIONS

| | |
|---|---|
| Admissions Selectivity Rating | 94 |
| # of applications received | 564 |
| % applicants accepted | 43 |
| % acceptees attending | 49 |
| Average GMAT | 672 |
| Range of GMAT | 630–730 |
| Average GPA | 3.38 |
| TOEFL required of international students? | yes |
| Minimum TOEFL (paper/computer) | 600/250 |
| Application fee | $75 |
| International application fee | $75 |
| Regular application deadline | 1/15 |
| Regular notification | 4/5 |
| Application deadline/notification | |
| Round 1: | 11/15 / 1/15 |
| Round 2: | 1/15 / /4/5 |
| Round 3: | 3/15 / 5/15 |
| Transfer students accepted? | yes |
| Transfer application policy | |
| Transfer applicants should apply as any other new student. The status of a transfer student is determined on a case by case basis, depending on the work completed at another school. | |
| Need-blind admissions? | yes |

### APPLICANTS ALSO LOOK AT

Arizona State University, Stanford University, The University of Texas at Austin, University of California—Berkeley, University of Illinois at Urbana-Champaign, University of North Carolina—Chapel Hill, University of Southern California

## EMPLOYMENT PROFILE

| Career Rating | 93 | Grads employed by field: | % avg. salary: |
|---|---|---|---|
| Primary source of full-time job acceptances | | Finance | 30 $76,670 |
| | | Marketing | 25 $86,941 |
| School-facilitated activities | 48 (56%) | Consulting | 21 $74,000 |
| Graduate-facilitated activities | 22 (26%) | General Management | 24 $66,681 |
| Unknown | 15 (18%) | | |
| | | | |
| Average starting salary | $76,333 | | |
| Percent employed | 95 | | |

# UNIVERSITY OF WEST GEORGIA
## RICHARDS COLLEGE OF BUSINESS

## GENERAL INFORMATION
Type of school   public
Environment   city
Academic calendar   semester

### SURVEY SAYS...
Friendly students
Smart classrooms

### STUDENTS
Enrollment of parent
  institution   10,154
Enrollment of business school   48
% male/female   57/43
% out-of-state   57
% part-time   56
% minorities   38
% international   57
Average age at entry   25

### ACADEMICS
**Academic Experience Rating**   **67**
Student/faculty ratio   19:1
Profs interesting rating   67
Profs accessible rating   79
% female faculty   26
% minority faculty   16

## Academics

The MBA program at University of West Georgia is designed primarily to address the needs of part-time students who work full-time in the area (the school's Carrollton campus is located about 40 miles west of Atlanta). A number of full-time students also attend. Their ranks include American students making the jump directly from undergraduate programs and international students who "usually return to their own country after graduation," according to the school catalogue.

West Georgia offers both an MBA and a masters of professional accounting. Either program can be completed in 12 months by a full-time student who is entering with an undergraduate degree in business. Students whose undergraduate work is in a nonbusiness related discipline typically must complete 24 semester hours of preparation-level coursework (covering the basics of marketing, statistics, information systems, corporate finance, business law, accounting theory, microeconomics, and macroeconomics). Excluding prep-level courses, the MBA requires 30 semester hours of course work, 24 of which are dedicated to required classes. Students may choose elective courses from the fields of economics, information technology, finance, international business, cost accounting, theory and philosophy of management, and business and society.

Students attending classes at the Carrollton campus tell us that "the school has a lot of good professors who are from all over the country and the world. The teachers are very knowledgeable in what they do." Professors are also "surprisingly easy to reach, and most are willing to provide time and energy to help students succeed." Small classes create a "great learning environment," as do "the many guest speakers who lecture about their field or a topic in [their] field."

University of West Georgia also offers a web MBA, in which "all classes are taught online via the Web." Admission to the web MBA program requires a minimum of two years of post-baccalaureate professional work experience (though admission to the traditional MBA program carries no such requirement). The web MBA curriculum roughly mirrors the conventional MBA curriculum; however, no electives are available to web MBA students. One student in the program tells us that "I chose the web MBA program because it was affordable and allowed me flexibility in my study schedule. I travel during the week and would not be able to attend classes in a traditional setting."

## Career and Placement

MBA students at West Georgia use the Department of Career Services, which provides "a comprehensive career development and employment plan for all students and alumni" of the school. The office provides assistance with job searches and career strategy, resume referrals, and help with finding internships. It also coordinates on-campus recruitment events, maintains job listings and a career resource library, offers seminars and workshops in resume writing and interviewing, and organizes career and job fairs.

JONATHAN R. ANDERSON, DIRECTOR, MBA PROGRAM, ASSOCIATE DEAN
1601 MAPLE STREET, CARROLLTON, GA 30118-3000 UNITED STATES
PHONE: 678-839-6467 • FAX: 678-839-5040 • E-MAIL: JANDERSON@WESTGA.EDU
WEBSITE: WWW.WESTGA.EDU

## FINANCIAL FACTS

| | |
|---|---|
| Annual tuition (in-state/out-of-state) | $2,196/$8,784 |
| Fees | $681 |
| Books and supplies | $1,200 |
| Room & board | |
| (on/off-campus) | $5,568/$7,000 |
| % of students receiving aid | 20 |
| % of first-year students | |
| receiving aid | 6 |
| % of students receiving loans | 20 |
| % of students receiving grants | 20 |
| Average award package | $7,780 |
| Average student loan debt | $17,857 |

## ADMISSIONS

| | |
|---|---|
| **Admissions Selectivity Rating** | **77** |
| # of applications received | 34 |
| % applicants accepted | 59 |
| % acceptees attending | 75 |
| Average GMAT | 523 |
| Range of GMAT | 460–560 |
| Average GPA | 3.18 |
| TOEFL required of | |
| international students? | yes |
| Minimum TOEFL | |
| (paper/computer) | 550/213 |
| Application fee | $20 |
| International application fee | $20 |
| Regular application deadline | 8/2 |
| Transfer students accepted? | yes |
| Transfer application policy | |
| Students may transfer a maximum of 6 hours from other AACSB-accredited schools. | |
| Non-fall admissions? | yes |

## Student Life and Environment

The University of West Georgia campus in Carrollton "is attractive and well located. It's outside of Atlanta but within an easy commute [from] work." Students enjoy "a relaxed, easygoing mood on the campus and in the MBA program," although they complain that "parking on campus is horrible." Because the program here is small and predominantly part-time, there is little extracurricular life for MBAs.

The conventional MBA program includes "a great diversity of international students." One MBA writes, "I have classes with students from Bulgaria, Turkey, India, and Colombia. I didn't have this much diversity as an undergraduate in a school of 25,000 students." Most of the American students in the program "have little work experience, and many have lived in Georgia all their lives." Students in the web MBA bring more experience to their studies, partly due to the nature of the requirements. Writes one student in the program, "We have a diverse group in our virtual team. The fact that our ages, life experiences, and backgrounds are so different seems to add to our focus and enables us to leverage individual strengths when tackling group projects. I'd say we are a friendly bunch, [and] willing to lean on each other when necessary, but also [to] hold each individual accountable for [his or her] share of work."

## Admissions

All applicants to the MBA program at the University of West Georgia must submit official copies of transcripts for all postsecondary academic work, an official GMAT score report, and letters of recommendation. Applicants must meet the following minimum requirements to be considered for admission with "regular status": an analytical writing score of at least 3.0 on the GMAT, a total GMAT score of at least 450, and an admissions score of at least 950 under the formula [(undergraduate GPA × 200) + GMAT score] or a score of at least 1,000 under the formula [(undergraduate GPA for final 60 semester hours of undergraduate work × 200) + GMAT score]. International students whose first language is not English must earn at least a 550 on the paper-based TOEFL or at least a 213 on the computer-based TOEFL. Students not meeting these minimum requirements may be granted admission with "provisional status." Such students are "reviewed for retention on regular status after completing nine hours toward the MBA," according to the school.

# UNIVERSITY OF WISCONSIN—MADISON
## SCHOOL OF BUSINESS

### GENERAL INFORMATION
Type of school                  public
Environment                       city
Academic calendar            semester

### SURVEY SAYS...
Happy students
Smart classrooms
*Solid preparation in:*
Marketing
Communication/interpersonal skills
Presentation skills

### STUDENTS
Enrollment of parent
  institution                 41,480
Enrollment of business school  345
% male/female                  67/33
% out-of-state                    59
% part-time                       34
% minorities                      11
% international                   22
Average age at entry              27
Average years work experience
  at entry                         4

### ACADEMICS
**Academic Experience Rating**   95
Student/faculty ratio            4:1
Profs interesting rating          87
Profs accessible rating           88
% female faculty                  19
% minority faculty                16

### JOINT DEGREES
JD/MBA, 4 years

### PROMINENT ALUMNI
Steve Bennett, President & CEO,
Intuit; Curt Culver, President & CEO,
MGIC; Tadashi Okamura,
Chair/President/CEO, Toshiba
Corporation; Thomas J. Falk, Chair
of the Board & CEO, Kimberly Clark
Corp.; John P. Morgridge, Chair of
the Board, Cisco Systems

## Academics

The MBA program at University of Wisconsin—Madison has always been a solid, afford-able choice, but it has set its aim higher in recent years. Students report that "the MBA program is undergoing a significant change in its structure." All students are required to align with an academic center "associated with a field of specialization. These centers maintain alumni contacts and a close connection to the business community, and they allow for outstanding faculty and student preparation for cutting-edge aspects of busi-ness management." Students recognize many advantages to the new approach. One stu-dent writes, "My specialization, the AC Nielsen Center for Marketing Research, is the best in the field. We had over 10 companies come to campus recruiting interns in the first semester extending multiple offers. I stopped interviewing at three offers. I couldn't be happier with my career prospects and the power of the network I will develop through my center!"

Other recent changes to the program include a transition to a lockstep curriculum in the past couple of years; students believe "this new system will allow for more overlap between courses." The future will also bring a facilities upgrade—a $40 million MBA addition to the School of Business is scheduled to open in fall 2008. Even without these changes, students would probably find little to fault at UW—Madison. They praise the school's offerings in arts administration, brand management, entrepreneurship, market-ing, real-estate, and supply-chain management. Students also boast that "there are a number of resources for graduate students including the graduate computing lab, grad-uate advisors, and the Academic Center. The amount of academic support available to graduate students is impressive."

All MBAs at UW—Madison are a happy lot. Why shouldn't they be, given that "Madison consistently ranks high across all business majors, not to mention many other programs on campus. It is the ability to do many things and do them better than anyone else that sets Madison apart. Many schools excel in academics, while others are in support for students, and some in diversity. In comparison, Madison is at the top of its game across the board."

## Career and Placement

Students report that, through MBA Career Services, their peers "have had great success get-ting interviews, internships, and job offers." Students' job searches are aided by alumni, "who have very strong ties to the school and are very helpful when students approach them," and especially by the directors of the Academic Centers.

Major employers of UW—Madison MBAs include Abbott Laboratories, Allstate Investments, Best Buy, Deloitte Touche Tohmatsu, Freddie Mac, General Electric, General Motors Corporation, W.W. Grainger Corporation, Guidant Corporation, Hewlett-Packard, IBM, Intel Corporation, and Kraft Foods. UW—Madison grads find employment across the country and around the world. About 8 percent head west and 17 percent head east for their first postgraduation jobs; approximately five percent take jobs outside the United States.

## Student Life and Environment

Life in the UW—Madison MBA program offers "a great balance between studying, social life, involvement on campus and in the community, and forward-looking career-networking opportunities," according to students. "Because the school is small, everyone knows everyone else," and "as a result, it's a very close-knit group of people. We hang out together outside of class a lot, which is great," MBAs say. Though the majority of stu-dents are from out of state, few have trouble adjusting to the UW milieu. One sanguine student reports, "We like cheese, bratwurst, beer, and sunny days. We boast a hard-work-

BETSY KACIZAK, DIRECTOR OF ADMISSIONS AND FINANCIAL AID
3150 GRAINGER HALL, 975 UNIVERSITY AVENUE, MADISON, WI 53706 UNITED STATES
PHONE: 608-262-4000 • FAX: 608-265-4192
E-MAIL: MBA@BUS.WISC.EDU • WEBSITE: WWW.BUS.WISC.EDU/MBA

ing Midwestern work ethic and yet everyone is happy. I mean, everyone waves, smiles, and says hello."

MBAs observe that "the graduate student organizations have a huge impact on student life at UW. The Graduate Business Association sponsors a weekly happy hour, 'TAPS,' that is well attended," as well as town-hall meetings, community-service projects, lunches with the dean, and social gatherings. UW—Madison has clubs and associations dedicated to nearly every major and interest. MBAs also tell us that UW—Madison is especially accommodating to students with families. One student writes, "My family is hugely important to me. We are absolutely ecstatic to be here at UW—Madison. The Joint Ventures Club has been a key source of family and couples activities for us, and we have made many great friends through the club."

The city of Madison is widely regarded as a great place to live, and UW—Madison MBAs don't diverge from the consensus. They explain that "Madison is a great city for students" because it "gives students a positive, exciting environment in which to learn. There are great public libraries to augment the university's extensive resources. Also, there's a plethora of social and recreational options when students need a break (everything from a beer at the union to sailing on the lakes)." One student observes, "There are a ton of things to do here: sporting/outdoor activities, dance, music, films, theater, bars, and everything in between. Graduate students enjoy the myriad of sporting events at UW, and it is easy to get caught up in the Badger hysteria!" Another student notes, "The advantage of a large university is how much free or cheap stuff is available including the fact that most of the arts organizations in town offer discounted student tickets." The only drawback: "Winters are tough. But spring and fall are spectacular."

## Admissions

"The admissions committee looks at all aspects of an applicant's profile including work experience, academic performance, standardized test scores, essays, and letters of recommendation," according to UW—Madison. All applicants must submit transcripts, recent GMAT scores (within the past five years), TOEFL scores (international students), letters of recommendation, essays, and a resume showing a minimum of two years of work experience (exceptional candidates may be admitted with less work experience). The school uses all of the following to increase its population of minority/disadvantaged students: the Consortium for Graduate Study in Management, Minority Fellowship Program, and advanced opportunity fellowships.

## FINANCIAL FACTS

| | |
|---|---|
| Annual tuition (in-state/out-of-state) | $10,194/$25,632 |
| Fees | $666 |
| Books and supplies | $860 |
| Room & board (on-campus) | $7,650 |
| % of students receiving aid | 65 |
| % of first-year students receiving aid | 50 |
| % of students receiving grants | 65 |
| Average award package | $14,399 |
| Average grant | $19,804 |

## ADMISSIONS

| | |
|---|---|
| Admissions Selectivity Rating | 95 |
| # of applications received | 432 |
| % applicants accepted | 40 |
| % acceptees attending | 65 |
| Average GMAT | 659 |
| Range of GMAT | 620–700 |
| Average GPA | 3.36 |
| TOEFL required of international students? | yes |
| Minimum TOEFL (paper/computer) | 600/250 |
| Application fee | $45 |
| International application fee | $45 |
| Regular application deadline | 6/1 |
| Regular notification | rolling |
| Application deadline/notification | |
| Round 1: | 1/12 / 2/20 |
| Round 2: | 3/2 / 4/10 |
| Round 3: | 4/20 / 5/30 |
| Round 4: | 6/1 / 6/26 |
| Early decision program? | yes |
| ED Deadline/notification | 11/17 / 12/19 |
| Need-blind admissions? | yes |

| EMPLOYMENT PROFILE | | | |
|---|---|---|---|
| Career Rating | 88 | Grads employed by field: | % avg. salary: |
| Average starting salary | $74,332 | Finance | 32 $70,306 |
| Percent employed | 92 | Human Resources | 3 $74,333 |
| | | Marketing | 21 $79,190 |
| | | Operations | 12 $78,229 |
| | | Consulting | 2 $77,500 |
| | | General Management | 3 $74,333 |
| | | Other | 1 NR |

# UNIVERSITY OF WISCONSIN—MILWAUKEE
## SHELDON B. LUBAR SCHOOL OF BUSINESS

## GENERAL INFORMATION
Type of school               public
Environment                    city
Academic calendar          semester

## SURVEY SAYS...
Friendly students
Helpful alumni
Happy students
Smart classrooms
*Solid preparation in:*
Teamwork

## STUDENTS
Enrollment of parent
  institution              26,792
Enrollment of business school  318
% male/female              61/39
% out-of-state                14
% part-time                   65
% minorities                   8
% international               14
Average age at entry          27
Average years work experience
  at entry                   4.4

## ACADEMICS
**Academic Experience Rating**   **77**
Student/faculty ratio        10:1
Profs interesting rating       68
Profs accessible rating        68
% female faculty               33
% minority faculty              5

## JOINT DEGREES
Master of Human Resources and
Labor Relations, 2-7 years; MPA,
Nonprofit Management, 2-7 years;
MBA/MSN, 3-7 years

## PROMINENT ALUMNI
Robert Probst, Executive VP,
Tamarack Petroleum Co.; Mary Ellen
Stanek, Managing Director, Robert
Baird & Co; Roger Fitzsimonds,
Retired Chairman & CEO, Firstar
Corporation; Keith Nosbusch, CEO,
Rockwell Automation; Dennis Glaso,
President & CEO, Jefferson Pilot
Corporation

## *Academics*

Students choose the MBA program at the University of Wisconsin—Milwaukee's Sheldon B. Lubar School of Business because it is convenient and affordable, and because it can be completed on a flexible schedule. Students here agree that "the greatest strength of the program is the school's ability to accommodate the full-time working student via flexible class times, and the next greatest strength is the low cost." MBAs here also appreciate that the university "has a strong connection to the surrounding community, and the school and community often work together on initiatives to make both better places."

Offering classes in the evening, UW—Milwaukee's MBA program is designed for the part-time student who can complete the program in two years by taking three courses per semester (provided the student has an undergraduate degree in business—students with nonbusiness degrees must complete introductory courses before beginning work on the MBA). The program offers the option of graduating with a career-focused concentration in health care management, international business, supply chain management, or managing change. Students may also opt for a general MBA. Either way, students are required to complete 39 to 42 semester credits.

UW—Milwaukee offers "a great atmosphere" with "classes that are filled with discussion and group work." Instruction is "very case study-focused so you get a lot of real world applications for the concepts you are learning." Students also appreciate "the many different academic resources available here, including the computer labs, library, and faculty." Some complain, however, that "many of the courses seem limited in scope" and that "some core courses could be combined to form one comprehensive course. "Students tell us that the program could benefit from "improv[ing] the quality of the courses," "more mandatory academic counseling," and "better instructors" for "a handful of classes."

UW—Milwaukee students may also opt to pursue the MBA at Waukesha. This program, taught by the same faculty who teach at the Milwaukee campus, is a cohort-based program that takes 16 months to complete. The program consists of 24 to 27 semester credits worth of core courses and 12 credits of electives, which are chosen as a group by each cohort.

## *Career and Placement*

The Sheldon B. Lubar School of Business Career Services Center serves undergraduates, graduate students, and alumni of the UW Milwaukee business school. The staff includes two career advisors and a director of career services. The office schedules on-campus interviews online via the eRecruiting system; coordinates internships; organizes career fairs; maintains a list of job postings; conducts workshops on resume writing, interviewing, and job-search skills; and hosts company information sessions.

SARAH SANDIN, MBA/MS PROGRAM MANAGER
PO BOX 742, MILWAUKEE, WI 53201-0742 UNITED STATES
PHONE: 414-229-5403 • FAX: 414-229-2372
E-MAIL: MBA-MS@UWM.EDU • WEBSITE: WWW.UWM.EDU/BUSINESS

## Student Life and Environment

UW—Milwaukee is "mainly a commuter school," with "the majority of all students (graduate and undergraduate) living off campus. Some drive one hour each way to class." As one MBA candidate puts it, "Students tend to identify as members of society first, and students at this school second. Even though people come to class and leave, there are no slackers here. They are dedicated, sincere academics." Students "range in age from 22 to 40. Many are married or engaged, and all are friendly. Most are employed by major firms around Milwaukee (Briggs, GE Medical, Harley, Kohler, SC Johnson, US Bank, etc.) and want to differentiate themselves."

The UW—Milwaukee campus is not without its amenities. Students report that "the library is great for research, the student union is great for relaxing and eating, and parking isn't all that difficult. The school offers a comfortable atmosphere." There are "lots of student activities going on in the union for the campus at large," though "business school activities seem more career-focused, more concerned with additional learning and career opportunities than with socialization. There are not as many social opportunities for graduate students as there are for undergrads." Students also point out that some "campus services do not revolve around the evening class time period, nor are there standard accommodations for those who attend classes from 5:30 P.M. to 8:10 P.M. or 6:00 P.M. to 8:40 P.M."

UW—Milwaukee is located "on the east side of the city" and "it would be difficult to find a better location. There is always plenty to do, with bars and clubs everywhere. There is plenty of live music as well."

## Admissions

Applicants to UW—Milwaukee's MBA program must apply to the university's Graduate School, which refers b-school applications to the School of Business Administration for review and recommendation. The Graduate School Admissions Office makes all final admissions decisions. All applicants must submit a completed application form, an official GMAT score, two official copies of transcripts for all undergraduate work, and two copies of a personal statement. Students must achieve a minimum undergraduate GPA of 2.75 and have a "satisfactory" score on the GMAT to be considered for "admission in good standing." Applicants who fail to meet these minimum requirements may be granted "admission on probation" status. International students must meet all of the above requirements and must also submit an official TOEFL score report (the minimum required score is 550 on the paper test, 213 on the computer test).

## FINANCIAL FACTS

| | |
|---|---|
| Annual tuition (in-state/out-of-state) | $9,914/$24,350 |
| Books and supplies | $800 |
| Room & board (on/off-campus) | $8,000/$10,000 |
| % of students receiving aid | 30 |
| % of first-year students receiving aid | 40 |
| % of students receiving loans | 29 |
| Average award package | $14,688 |
| Average grant | $5,869 |

## ADMISSIONS

| | |
|---|---|
| Admissions Selectivity Rating | 84 |
| # of applications received | 199 |
| % applicants accepted | 48 |
| % acceptees attending | 71 |
| Average GMAT | 547 |
| Range of GMAT | 500–590 |
| Average GPA | 3.25 |
| TOEFL required of international students? | yes |
| Minimum TOEFL (paper/computer) | 550/213 |
| Application fee | $45 |
| International application fee | $75 |
| Regular application deadline | rolling |
| Regular notification | rolling |
| Deferment available? | yes |
| Maximum length of deferment | 1 year |
| Transfer students accepted? | yes |
| Transfer application policy The application process is the same for all applicants. | |
| Non-fall admissions? | yes |
| Need-blind admissions? | yes |

## APPLICANTS ALSO LOOK AT

Marquette University, University of Wisconsin, University of Wisconsin—Whitewater

## EMPLOYMENT PROFILE

| Career Rating | 71 | Grads employed by field: | % | avg. salary: |
|---|---|---|---|---|
| Primary source of full-time job acceptances | | Accounting | 30 | $59,833 |
| | | Finance | 10 | $92,000 |
| School-facilitated activities | 15 (40%) | Marketing | 10 | $55,000 |
| Graduate-facilitated activities | 16 (43%) | Operations | 10 | $69,000 |
| Unknown | 6 (17%) | General Management | 30 | $69,500 |
| | | Other | 10 | $61,000 |
| Average starting salary | $68,000 | | | |
| Percent employed | 100 | | | |

# UNIVERSITY OF WISCONSIN—WHITEWATER
## COLLEGE OF BUSINESS AND ECONOMICS

## GENERAL INFORMATION

| | |
|---|---|
| Type of school | public |
| Environment | village |
| Academic calendar | semester |

### SURVEY SAYS...
Happy students
*Solid preparation in:*
General management
Teamwork
Communication/interpersonal skills
Computer skills
Doing business in a global economy

### STUDENTS

| | |
|---|---|
| Enrollment of parent institution | 10,520 |
| Enrollment of business school | 460 |
| % male/female | 45/55 |
| % out-of-state | 10 |
| % part-time | 85 |
| % minorities | 1 |
| % international | 30 |
| Average age at entry | 34 |
| Average years work experience at entry | 7 |

### ACADEMICS

| | |
|---|---|
| **Academic Experience Rating** | **64** |
| Student/faculty ratio | 28:1 |
| Profs interesting rating | 76 |
| Profs accessible rating | 71 |
| % female faculty | 29 |
| % minority faculty | 22 |

## Academics

Since the early 1900s, University of Wisconsin—Whitewater has been known as "the state business school of Wisconsin," a place where students can receive solid, affordable undergraduate and graduate business degrees at a reasonable cost. Whitewater serves its admirable role with distinction; its accounting department, for example, is widely regarded as one of the most effective in the nation due to its graduates' excellent success rate on the CPA exam. Whitewater also excels in several technology-driven areas. Its Management Computer Systems Program is consistently ranked among the best of its kind by the Association of Information Technology Professionals, while the joint-degree offered by the Department of Business Education and the Computer and Network Administration has been repeatedly recognized as a Program of Excellence by the National Association for Career and Technical Education (ACTE).

The Whitewater MBA program offers concentrations in finance, human resource management, international business, IT management, management, marketing, technology and training, and operations and supply chain management, as well as a master of science in computer information systems and a master of professional accountancy. Students appreciate the breadth of choices as well as the variety of full-time and part-time options the school provides for their convenience. Most students opt for either part-time evening courses (offered at both the Whitewater and Waukesha Center campuses) or distance learning, which is growing increasingly popular despite the fact that distance courses are considerably more expensive. One MBA writes, "I chose UW—Whitewater for the flexible class times and the multiple locations. The school truly understands the demanding schedules of students who work full-time and/or have children." Another adds, "The online program is great because it allows you to complete the entire degree off campus."

Satisfaction rates are high among MBAs, who regard Whitewater as "an excellent school with an excellent administration [that] helps you achieve your academic goals by suggesting classes and providing other valuable assistance." They praise professors who "are extremely knowledgeable, yet easy to interact with on a daily basis, [are] very accessible at all times, [and who] strive to have students participate and work together in groups." Most important, they appreciate how "IT is used very well, the subject matter is always current and relevant, and the skills/techniques are easily transferred into the business environment."

## Career and Placement

The Career Services Office at Whitewater provides career counseling and placement services to all undergraduate and graduate students at the university. The office coordinates on-campus interviews, career fairs, online job-search tools, the administration of self-assessment instruments, and advisement in resume creation, interviewing, and job-search strategies. Many students tell us that the quality of the office is not a major concern to them, as their primary goal in attending Whitewater is to improve their status at their current jobs.

DONALD K. ZAHN, ASSOCIATE DEAN
800 WEST MAIN STREET, WHITEWATER, WI 53190-1790
PHONE: 262-472-5588 • FAX: 262-472-4863
E-MAIL: CLEMENTC@UWW.EDU • WEBSITE: HTTP://.UWW.EDU/BUSINESS

## Student Life and Environment

The Whitewater MBA program is home to "a diverse student body that includes single, married, and international students" who "really bring the global work environment into perspective." There is also "a good mix of full-time and part-time students" as well as "a wide variety of ages and experience from students in their 50s to new undergrads." Teamwork is important here, so it's fortunate that "most students are friendly and work well in teams [and] "most everyone has a great sense of humor and is willing to compromise for the better of group projects."

Because so many students attend part-time, "there really is no 'presence' of graduate student organizations on campus. Most students seem to be interested only in school; there really aren't any graduate student activities offered to students." Full-timers—there are about 80 of them here—note that "you can be involved in a variety of business organizations or the Graduate Student Organization" if you choose to be. One student writes, "I particularly love the assistantship I have on campus because I get to continue to interact with undergraduates and watch them grow as well." The school is in the early stages of planning a new dedicated business facility. The completion of the facility should lead to an uptick in MBA-related extracurricular activity.

Whitewater is a popular vacation destination, especially for boating and fishing enthusiasts. The town is also known as "the hang gliding capital of the Midwest" due to the popularity of the sport here. One student notes, "There is not a great deal of crime in Whitewater. It is isolated and peaceful." Although Whitewater is a small town, its proximity to large cities provides access to valuable internships. Both Milwaukee and Madison are 45 minutes off by car; Chicago is 100 miles to the southeast.

## Admissions

To gain admission to the MBA program at Whitewater, students must have either 1) at least a 2.75 GPA for all undergraduate work; 2) at least a 2.90 GPA for the final half of their undergraduate work; 3) 12 credits of graduate work completed successfully at Whitewater; 4) at least a 2.50 GPA for all undergraduate work, a minimum GMAT score of 570, and a minimum of five years of professional experience; 5) a formula score of at least 1,000 under the formula [(undergraduate GPA × 200) + GMAT score]; or 6) a formula score of at least 1,050 under the formula [(GPA for last half of undergraduate work × 200) + GMAT score]. Students who have previously completed graduate work at Whitewater must have a minimum GPA of 3.00 in those classes with no grades of 'I' (Incomplete) or 'P' (Pending). Non-native English speakers must demonstrate proficiency by achieving a minimum TOEFL score of 550.

### FINANCIAL FACTS

| | |
|---|---|
| Annual tuition (in-state/out-of-state) | $6,876/$17,512 |
| Books and supplies | $2,600 |
| Room & board (on-campus) | $4,800 |
| Average grant | $500 |

### ADMISSIONS

| | |
|---|---|
| **Admissions Selectivity Rating** | **65** |
| # of applications received | 134 |
| % applicants accepted | 88 |
| % acceptees attending | 92 |
| Average GMAT | 482 |
| Range of GMAT | 210–730 |
| Average GPA | 3.13 |
| TOEFL required of international students? | yes |
| Minimum TOEFL (paper/computer) | 550/213 |
| Application fee | $45 |
| Regular application deadline | rolling |
| Regular notification | rolling |
| Deferment available? | yes |
| Maximum length of deferment | 1 year |
| Transfer students accepted? | yes |
| Transfer application policy | |
| They must meet the same requirements as a non-transfer student. Nine credits may be transferred into the program. | |
| Non-fall admissions? | yes |

### APPLICANTS ALSO LOOK AT

Marquette University, University of Wisconsin, University of Wisconsin—Milwaukee, University of Wisconsin—Oshkosh, University of Wisconsin—Parkside

| EMPLOYMENT PROFILE | |
|---|---|
| **Career Rating** | **62** |
| Average starting salary | $49,000 |

# VALPARAISO UNIVERSITY
## COLLEGE OF BUSINESS ADMINISTRATION

## Academics

Although long established as a quality Midwestern university, Valparaiso is a fledgling in the world of MBA programs. The school only began offering the MBA in the 2002–2003 academic year, and as of this writing, you could still count its graduates on your fingers. Yet, despite its nascency, the Valpo MBA has already found ways to distinguish itself from the pack, primarily by incorporating ethical issues throughout the curriculum. The program places a special focus on environmental stewardship; the school points out that "often the most effective and efficient decisions are those that include environmental issues from the beginning. Making decisions that include the wise use and conservation of environmental resources is not only the ethical choice, but also is often the most profitable." Students tell us that "the way they incorporate the business world, technology, ethics, and environmental issues into each and every class adds tremendous value" to the program.

Valpo's MBA program is designed with the needs of part-timers in mind. All courses are offered once a week in the evenings. Terms run only seven weeks (six in the summer); this creates six different junctures during the year when students can begin the program. All this flexibility means students can pace themselves and complete the program in as little or as much time as they want; a full-time student can complete the degree in one year. Students endorse the approach; one MBA writes, "I think [it is a strength] that classes are only seven weeks long because they focus on what you need to know rather than provide too much 'useless' material that [you] will never use. This way you [don't] get too bogged down in any course." Students also appreciate the "small-school atmosphere and the leading-edge business topics. We use current topics from magazines and journals often, and I can apply what I'm learning to my work life."

Students give their professors high marks, and they report that "almost all are doctorate-level professionals. They have good, applicable real-world experience. They are also good 'people' persons who can present material clearly and relate well to students (mainly the students in the workforce). They are passionate about what they do and are always available for questions and/or discussion on different topics." Administrators are similarly highly regarded; students explain that they "are always willing to help" and listen attentively to student feedback, "recognizing that it is important for developing future programs" at Valpo.

## Career and Placement

"We need to initiate a placement program" for Valpo MBAs, students say; currently students receive career services through the university's Career Center, which serves all undergraduates and graduate students. The MBA program offers an elective called "Career Development, Survival, and Success," which focuses on many of the skills usually taught at MBA career services offices: self-assessment and understanding, time management, career development, stress management, balancing work and nonwork issues, perspective and bias, surviving office politics, and personal ethical philosophy and behavior. Many Valpo MBAs explain that they have no need for career services since they are employed and intend to remain with their employer after graduation.

Erin L. Brown, Program Coordinator
104 Urschel Hall, 1909 Chapel Drive, Valparaiso, IN 46383 United States
Phone: 800-599-0840 • Fax: 219-464-5789
E-mail: mba@valpo.edu • Website: www.valpo.edu/mba

## Student Life and Environment

Valpo MBAs envision a day when their program will draw applicants from around the world, but they admit that that day is still a way off. One student explains, "Since the MBA program is so new, there is no critical mass of people from which to draw a truly diverse group. This will change over time, but for now it impedes a true exchange of ideas." Some MBAs also point out that "there are so many fresh undergrad graduates in the program that the older students are obliged to become perhaps overly facilitating in discussions. The younger students do not yet know how to interact in a truly adult/mature way in class." On the plus side, "because Valparaiso University is semi-religiously affiliated, many of the students come equipped with a strong moral compass. This helps students to comfortably engage in moral/ethical conversations."

For now, "most students are part-time, and the program seems to be oriented toward part-timers, both academically and socially. All classes are in the evening, which means MBA students aren't exposed to other students or professors" within the university. One student says that there "is not much of a social aspect [for] the students in the program (at least not one I have seen)." Another student observes, "More socializing will improve networking and lasting friendships, which is what you need to get jobs." Still, "MBA students get along well, and they do occasionally get together outside class in clusters." Big get-togethers are confined to a couple of events each year; students say, "We do have semi-annual parties with spouses invited to help get to know each other outside of the classroom."

Despite any drawbacks, most MBAs agree that "Valparaiso treats its graduate students so well. Resources are abundant, and there are no problems completing any tasks due to the way the school is set up." Hometown Valparaiso is small, but students brag that it "is extremely vibrant and a great place to live and work." One student says, "I would recommend a visit to anyone looking for a great place to complete their business education." Chicago is about 60 miles to the northwest.

## Admissions

Applicants to Valpo's MBA program must submit a completed application with a cover letter (explaining their reasons for pursuing the degree), official copies of all undergraduate and graduate transcripts, GMAT scores, and two letters of recommendation. Professional experience, as demonstrated by a resume, is not required but is taken into consideration. Entering students must be proficient in calculus/finite math and have basic computer skills. Applications are processed on a rolling basis; applicants are typically notified of the school's decision within 10 days of receipt of a completed application.

**FINANCIAL FACTS**

| | |
|---|---|
| Annual tuition | $19,760 |
| Fees | $60 |
| Books and supplies | $1,000 |
| % of students receiving aid | 51 |
| % of first-year students receiving aid | 51 |
| % of students receiving loans | 51 |
| Average student loan debt | $11,887 |

**ADMISSIONS**

| | |
|---|---|
| Admissions Selectivity Rating | 95 |
| # of applications received | 183 |
| % applicants accepted | 23 |
| % acceptees attending | 88 |
| Average GMAT | 584 |
| Average GPA | 3.26 |
| TOEFL required of international students? | yes |
| Minimum TOEFL (paper/computer) | 575/236 |
| Application fee | $30 |
| International application fee | $50 |
| Deferment available? | yes |
| Maximum length of deferment | 1 year |
| Transfer students accepted? | yes |
| Transfer application policy | Students must meet admissions requirements and be in good standing at their current institution. Up to 6 credit hours may be transferred. |
| Non-fall admissions? | yes |
| Need-blind admissions? | yes |

# VANDERBILT UNIVERSITY
## OWEN GRADUATE SCHOOL OF MANAGEMENT

## GENERAL INFORMATION
| | |
|---|---|
| Type of school | private |
| Environment | metropolis |
| Academic calendar | module |

### SURVEY SAYS...
Happy students
*Solid preparation in:*
Teamwork
Communication/interpersonal skills

### STUDENTS
| | |
|---|---|
| Enrollment of parent institution | 11,481 |
| Enrollment of business school | 373 |
| % male/female | 78/22 |
| % out-of-state | 72 |
| % minorities | 9 |
| % international | 35 |
| Average age at entry | 29 |
| Average years work experience at entry | 5 |

### ACADEMICS
| | |
|---|---|
| **Academic Experience Rating** | **90** |
| Student/faculty ratio | 10:1 |
| Profs interesting rating | 85 |
| Profs accessible rating | 92 |
| % female faculty | 14 |
| % minority faculty | 20 |

### JOINT DEGREES
MBA/JD, 4 years; MBA/MD, 5 years; MBA/MSN, 5 semesters; MBA/ME, 5 semesters; MBA/MLAS, 3 years; MBA/BA or MBA/BS, 5 years; MBA/DIV, 7 semesters

### PROMINENT ALUMNI
David Farr, CEO, Emerson Electric; David Ingram, Chair & President, Ingram Entertainment; Brad Martin, Chair & CEO, Saks, Inc.; Doug Parker, Chair, President & CEO, America West Airlines

## Academics

Over and over in our survey, MBA students at Vanderbilt praise the "great sense of community" at the first-rate Owen Graduate School of Management. Observes one student, "There is competition here and fellow students and faculty do not let you off easily, but they also help you through the challenges. Whether it is helping you prepare for an interview that they are preparing for themselves or tutoring you in finance because you tutored them in marketing, students are there for each other." It's not just the student body immersed in community spirit; the administration and faculty also join in. One MBA writes, "The most striking thing at Vanderbilt is the ability to really get to know your professors and the administration. Every Thursday night, we have a social where students can kick back and relax from the hard work week. Many professors will join us for the event and make the effort to get to know the student body outside of the classroom. Another example: [In 2003-2004], we had a student-led initiative to assist all first-year students who didn't have internships secure one. The professors volunteered to help students by reaching out to their industry contacts and finding positions for qualified first-year students. Their assistance helped us achieve a 99.1 percent internship-placement statistic."

Such personal touches are rarely accompanied by crack research, but Owen is also a leader in a variety of fields, and students benefit from their professors' cutting-edge work. The faculty excels in finance and marketing; e-commerce, operations management, and organizational management are also considered extremely strong. One MBA writes, "The greatest strengths of Owen are the various strong concentrations, along with a well-organized academic calendar. Moreover, if we want, we can take more electives depending on personal special interest." The strength of other Vanderbilt divisions adds further value to Owen; "The fact that Owen offers jointly taught courses with other highly ranked programs in the Vanderbilt system like the law, medical, and engineering schools is a huge advantage to Owen students."

Vandy's curriculum is "very rigorous, with challenging assignments that stimulate intellect and creativity." Lectures "incorporate real-world practices and situations into the courses and try and make the courses fun, which encourages active participation among the students." And the administration, which "works very hard to deliver an outstanding product to the students," is "doing an excellent job redefining the strategy, positioning, and mission of the school and is very flexible to include student requests." Looks like a good thing may soon be getting even better in Music City.

## Career and Placement

Owen MBAs praise "the creativity of the Career Management Center to react to the changing needs of the students" and tell [them] that "the Career Management Center has been great in this depressed job market, keeping [them] focused on the job search and pointing the way to great job opportunities." Things weren't always so rosy—students report that "the office has gone through a noticeable change in the last couple of years" and that "the administration increased funding to the Career Management Center to respond to the poor recruiting environment"—but the problems, apparently, are all in the past.

Employers most likely to hire Owen MBAs include American Express, Banc America Securities, Citigroup, Dell Computer, Deloitte Touche Tohmatsu, Deutsche Bank, Eli Lilly, Emerson Electric, Ford Motor Company, Gaylord Entertainment, GE Capital, Harrah's Entertainment, Hewlett-Packard, Home Depot, Honeywell, IBM, Johnson & Johnson, Mattel[v] Toys, Merrill Lynch, Procter & Gamble, Salomon Smith Barney, Sara Lee Corporation, Southern Company, SunTrust Bank, Unilever, and Wachovia Securities.

MELINDA ALLEN, ASSISTANT DEAN, ADMISSIONS & CAREER MANAGEMENT CENTER
401 21ST AVENUE SOUTH, NASHVILLE, TN 37203 UNITED STATES
PHONE: 615-322-6469 • FAX: 615-343-1175
E-MAIL: ADMISSIONS@OWEN.VANDERBILT.EDU • WEBSITE: OWEN.VANDERBILT.EDU

## Student Life and Environment

Although the MBA curriculum is time-consuming, "at Vanderbilt, you don't only live with books. The community helps you to keep a balanced life, so you also have time to play sports or meet outside the school." As one student put it, "One minute you're doing bond arbitrage, another minute you're playing flag football with the same great people." The school sponsors social events "that allow students to network and take a break from class work" (e.g., Thursday night kegs), program-based clubs and organizations serve students of every interest and background, and intramural sports are extremely popular. Plus, there are plenty of restaurants and bars (and student housing, dispensing with the need for designated drivers) within walking distance of the campus. "The real dilemma," one student explained, "is choosing where to spend your time."

Students also make time to enjoy hometown Nashville, "an excellent city in that it offers all the entertainment of a big city but all in close proximity to campus." The city "has the best music scene in the country," one MBA who's "not even a huge country music fan," writes, noting that "there's all types of music here because Nashville attracts incredible musicians. The fact that everything is so close together, easy to get to, and cheap makes this a better music city than Los Angeles or New York City." Nashville also offers "good food, great parks, and a surprising number of very good employment opportunities." The city is home to big-league hockey and football teams, as well as a AAA minor-league baseball team.

Owen's facility offers "everything and everyone is in one building," with "full integration of technology in the classrooms and Intranet. Class assignments, syllabi, and grades are all at the school's Blackboard website. All students have a laptop, with full support provided by Vandy's IT department."

## Admissions

Vanderbilt bases admissions decisions on all the following factors: "Caliber of undergraduate institution, difficulty of major, quality and duration of prior work experience, professional responsibilities and accomplishments, career advancement, career goals, extracurricular/professional/community involvement, leadership potential, interpersonal skills, communication skills, team orientation, diversity, and cross-cultural awareness/understanding/experience/appreciation." Recruitment efforts aimed at minority/disadvantaged students include a Diversity Weekend, "which is open to all prospective students, but specially targeted to prospective U.S. minority students."

### FINANCIAL FACTS

| | |
|---|---|
| Annual tuition | $33,830 |
| Fees | $686 |
| Books and supplies | $1,484 |
| Room & board | $11,268 |
| % of students receiving aid | 71 |
| % of first-year students receiving aid | 71 |
| % of students receiving loans | 51 |
| % of students receiving grants | 50 |
| Average award package | $38,688 |
| Average grant | $14,017 |
| Average student loan debt | $65,652 |

### ADMISSIONS

| | |
|---|---|
| Admissions Selectivity Rating | 88 |
| # of applications received | 722 |
| % applicants accepted | 51 |
| % acceptees attending | 53 |
| Average GMAT | 624 |
| Range of GMAT | 590–660 |
| Average GPA | 3.25 |
| TOEFL required of international students? | yes |
| Minimum TOEFL (paper/computer) | 600/250 |
| Application fee | $100 |
| International application fee | $100 |
| Regular application deadline | 3/1 |
| Regular notification | 4/1 |
| Application deadline/notification | |
| Round 1: | 11/15 / 1/15 |
| Round 2: | 1/15 / 3/15 |
| Round 3: | 3/1 / 4/1 |
| Need-blind admissions? | yes |

### APPLICANTS ALSO LOOK AT

Duke University, Emory University, Georgetown University, Indiana University—Bloomington, The University of Texas at Austin, University of North Carolina—Chapel Hill, University of Virginia

### EMPLOYMENT PROFILE

| Career Rating | 89 | Grads employed by field: | % | avg. salary: |
|---|---|---|---|---|
| **Primary source of full-time job acceptances** | | Finance | 44 | $81,246 |
| | | Human Resources | 5 | $73,857 |
| School-facilitated activities | 85 (62%) | Marketing | 28 | $80,188 |
| Graduate-facilitated activities | 53 (38%) | Operations | 7 | $77,500 |
| | | Consulting | 12 | $86,031 |
| Average starting salary | $81,017 | General Management | 4 | $82,000 |
| Percent employed | 81 | | | |

# VILLANOVA UNIVERSITY
## VILLANOVA SCHOOL OF BUSINESS

### GENERAL INFORMATION
| | |
|---|---|
| Type of school | private |
| Affiliation | Augustinian Catholic |
| Environment | village |
| Academic calendar | semester |

### SURVEY SAYS...
Cutting-edge classes
Helpful alumni
Smart classrooms

### STUDENTS
| | |
|---|---|
| Enrollment of parent institution | 10,267 |
| Enrollment of business school | 598 |
| % male/female | 69/31 |
| % part-time | 90 |
| Average age at entry | 28 |
| Average years work experience at entry | 5 |

### ACADEMICS
| | |
|---|---|
| **Academic Experience Rating** | **71** |
| Student/faculty ratio | 12:1 |
| Profs interesting rating | 88 |
| Profs accessible rating | 75 |
| % female faculty | 22 |

### JOINT DEGREES
JD/MBA, 3-4 years

## Academics

With three MBA programs offered, including a professional MBA and executive MBA, as well as a JD/MBA, Villanova's crowning glory may have been in finding the perfect solution for Philly area students who can't decide between a full-time and part-time MBA program. The school's new full-time equivalent (FTE) MBA offers many of the conveniences of a part-time program—including evening classes—with the best aspects of a full-time program; namely, cohort-based instruction and a quick return on time invested. Of the former, MBAs say, "The cohort factor is the greatest strength of the FTE program. Because we will be studying together for two years, we are able to develop deeper relationships and make more connections that will aid us both during and after the program."

According to a survey, students had a lot to say about the FTE MBA program. One MBA comments, "The FTE MBA program at Villanova has the best of the best, which is why it is separate from the traditional MBA program. This program has an all-star class of professors and an administration second to none. This is the reason I chose this school." The administration "is trying very hard to make this flagship program world-class," and students are confident that it will succeed soon. The first year (2003 to 2004), they admit, was a somewhat bumpy ride; one student reports, "Classes are often disjointed, as professors work to fit too much into a 15-week semester. Also, we were told that prerequisites in [classes like] accounting and statistics were unnecessary, yet I sit in my accounting class (the first in my career) next to CPAs and financial analysts. The program doesn't allow them to skip such classes, but it also doesn't provide the foundation on which I can build a deeper understanding." Our survey respondents say that "the administration and the faculty try their best to remedy any issues that come up as a result of disorganization," and they are confident that administrators "are taking these issues into account as they plan for next year's cohort."

Villanova also enrolls students full-time in the professional MBA program which offers a highly flexible schedule that can incorporate a number of distance-learning options. All classes meet in the evening and all "are heavily focused on technology, ethics, and the latest business trends and practices." Part-timers explain that "both the faculty and the administration recognize the challenges of working full-time, going to school, and managing a family life, and they are willing to work with us to ensure that we have the best educational experience possible. However, they do not use the aforementioned challenges as excuses to give us a less rigorous program—they still provide us with challenging courses and demand rigorous academic study." Villanova offers specializations in finance, health care administration, international business, MIS, and marketing; students are not required to select a specialization in order to graduate.

## Career and Placement

Villanova's Career Services Office provides workshops, recruiting events, online job databases, alumni networking opportunities, and online support for all undergraduate and graduate students at the university. The school combines forces with 10 other area schools to sponsor Talent Finder, a job fair dedicated exclusively to MBAs; most other recruiting events are open to the university at large. Most students agree that Villanova needs to make a greater effort to attract recruiters specifically for MBAs. Employers of Villanova MBAs have included AIG, American Express, Ernst & Young, Goldman Sachs, Lincoln Financial, Merrill Lynch, Morgan Stanley, Pfizer, PricewaterhouseCoopers, Prudential, and the Vanguard Group.

Ms. Elizabeth Eshleman, Associate Director & Corporate Liaison
800 Lancaster Avenue, Bartley Hall, Suite 1054, Villanova, PA 19085 United States
Phone: 610-519-4336 • Fax: 610-519-6273
E-mail: MBA@VILLANOVA.EDU • Website: WWW.MBA.VILLANOVA.EDU

## Student Life and Environment

All MBA classes at Villanova are held in the evenings for the convenience of students, the vast majority of whom hold full-time jobs. Because of these circumstances, "time spent at school is usually limited to class time and time spent in study groups." MBAs also note that "before class and during breaks; however, it is easy to find classmates socializing either in the cafe on the ground floor or outside the room." Students enjoy a collegial atmosphere, especially in the cohort-based FTE program. One student writes, "The work can be hard, but it's made a little easier by knowing that you have 44 other people going through the exact same thing."

The program's main organization is the MBA Society of Alumni and Students, whose mission "is to leverage the diverse professional and personal experiences and relationship of its members by creating opportunities to network, share information, and continue education. Keynote speakers have included the CEOs of Rohm-Haas, SAP America, and the Philadelphia Stock Exchange.

Villanova's location, students say, is "absolutely fantastic. The campus is beautiful as is the location of the school relative to Philadelphia." The SEPTA train stops right on campus and provides quick, convenient transport to Philly's downtown area.

## Admissions

The primary criteria for admission to Villanova's Professional and FTE MBA programs include undergraduate record (GPA and quality of course work), GMAT scores, TOEFL scores (international students), quality of essays (two), quality of recommendations (two), and work experience. Work experience is not required of most applicants; however, in all Villanova MBA programs, the average student has five years of post-undergraduate professional experience.

### FINANCIAL FACTS

| | |
|---|---|
| Annual tuition | $19,500 |
| Fees | $60 |
| Books and supplies | $800 |

### ADMISSIONS

| | |
|---|---|
| Admissions Selectivity Rating | 60* |
| Average GMAT | 580 |
| Average GPA | 3.2 |
| TOEFL required of international students? | yes |
| Minimum TOEFL (paper/computer) | 600/250 |
| Application fee | $50 |
| International application fee | $50 |
| Regular application deadline | 6/30 |
| Regular notification | rolling |
| Deferment available? | yes |
| Maximum length of deferment | up to 1 year |
| Transfer students accepted? | yes |
| Transfer application policy Up to 9 credits from an AACSB-accredited MBA programs | |
| Non-fall admissions? | yes |
| Need-blind admissions? | yes |

### APPLICANTS ALSO LOOK AT

Drexel University, Temple University

# Virginia Polytechnic Institute and State University

## Pamplin College of Business

### GENERAL INFORMATION

| | |
|---|---|
| Type of school | public |
| Environment | town |
| Academic calendar | fall 2003 |

### SURVEY SAYS...

Friendly students
Happy students
Smart classrooms
*Solid preparation in:*
Teamwork

### STUDENTS

| | |
|---|---|
| Enrollment of parent institution | 27,979 |
| Enrollment of business school | 346 |
| % male/female | 75/25 |
| % out-of-state | 36 |
| % part-time | 49 |
| % minorities | 5 |
| % international | 50 |
| Average age at entry | 25 |
| Average years work experience at entry | 3 |

### ACADEMICS

| | |
|---|---|
| **Academic Experience Rating** | **86** |
| Student/faculty ratio | 2:1 |
| Profs interesting rating | 82 |
| Profs accessible rating | 85 |
| % female faculty | 25 |
| % minority faculty | 2 |

### JOINT DEGREES

MBA/MIM, 33 semester hours in the Pamplin MBA Program and 30 trimester hours at Thunderbird; l'Institute National des Telecommunications (INT) in France

## Academics

"It's a combination of everything"—including "an outstanding MBA program with very nice faculty, staff, and students; a beautiful campus where you can do a lot of activities (sports, cultural); and a program small enough to give you personal attention in a school that's big enough to put everything at your fingertips"—that makes the Pamplin MBA at Virginia Tech so appealing to students. MBAs here also love that their program is a "great value" and that the curriculum places an emphasis "particularly on liking what you do and doing what's important to you, and on building not only a career but a life."

Pamplin offers both a full-time and part-time MBA. The curricula for the two are identical; each requires 48 credit hours divided almost evenly among required core courses and electives. The full-time program is cohort-based; the part-time program is not. Full-time students praise the cohort system, which gets them "focused on learning from the other students in the program, in addition to the normal course material." Part-timers enjoy the convenience of their program, which offers classes on six campuses throughout Virginia as well as on the Blacksburg campus. Students in both programs tell us that "the curriculum is much more technical and hands-on as opposed to theoretical" and that "the integration of technology to courses is remarkable." Finance and IT departments both receive high marks. Across departments, professors are described as "very knowledgeable and willing to answer any questions we have, willing to give extra help when required, and available for questions and conversations outside of class." The administration "is active as well, keeping in frequent contact by sending out announcements and asking for feedback from students."

Asked how they would improve their program, most students here suggest tweaks rather than an overhaul. A typical student proposes that "the MBA program would benefit from a larger number of students. There are currently less than 50 first-year MBAs in the full-time program. This can cause problems with some concentrations not being offered due to lack of interest. The program would benefit from having closer to 100 students in each class." The school lists the following available concentrations: corporate financial management, e-business technology, global business, hospitality and tourism management, information systems and technology, investment and financial services management, marketing, organizational leadership, and systems engineering management.

## Career and Placement

Pamplin MBAs receive placement help both from the university's Career Services Office and from the MBA-dedicated Career Advising Office, which students call "perhaps the program's greatest strength. Barry O'Donnell is in charge of the program and teaches one-credit courses on career search. It's an incredible program." His office also plans MBA recruitment campaigns, "including MBA Corporate Briefings, posting MBA internships and career opportunities, or gaining access to the MBA Association (MBAA), the professional student organization."

Employers most likely to hire Pamplin MBAs include Black & Decker, Giant Food Stores LLC, Air Products and Chemicals, U.S. General Services Administration (GSA), Eastman Chemical Company, Branch Banking and Trust Company, Freddie Mac, Gildner and Associates, Inc., Cox Communications, J.E. Jamerson and Sons, Bank One, and Toyo Tires.

Susan Vest, Enrollment Coordinator
1044 Pamplin Hall, Virginia Tech, Blacksburg, VA 24061 United States
Phone: 540-231-6152 • Fax: 540-231-4487
E-mail: mba_info@vt.edu • Website: www.mba.vt.edu

## Student Life and Environment

"Because of the large size of VT, there is an abundance of things to get involved with" around the Blacksburg campus, including "lots of outdoor activities" such as hiking, camping, skiing, and whitewater rafting in the nearby mountains. One parent/student notes that the campus itself offers "lots of green spaces where our kids can run and play" and plenty of opportunities to participate in intramural sports and pickup games. Social life among full-time MBAs is "active, partly because there are a lot of bars around here." One writes, "We have a dependable social circle and do many things together like going out on Thursday nights, eating dinner together at our favorite Mexican restaurant, and tailgating before football games." Many students here note that "Virginia Tech is a big football school. Especially in the fall, life around here seems to revolve around the Hokies." The MBA Association is "very active," and many MBAs devote some of their spare time to community service. Overall, as one student sums up, "life at school is really enjoyable; not too stressful, but learning a lot."

VT MBAs include "many students with engineering backgrounds," including a number of international students. One MBA observes, "Our class is very ethnically diverse, with many [students] from India and Asia, but all the different cultures seem to mesh extremely well" and the mix creates "a great learning atmosphere." Students also represent a variety of experience levels; "Many students came straight from undergrad while several others have worked for years and have children," students report. Most importantly, "students generally cooperate with one another and help each other. They don't try to run each other down in competition. There is a good camaraderie among first-year students and second-year students are very helpful to first-years."

## Admissions

All applications to the Pamplin MBA program must include a completed application form, official GMAT scores, a resume, and two copies of official transcripts from all post-secondary institutions attended. Students may choose to submit two letters of recommendation, but they are not required. International students whose first language is not English must also submit TOEFL scores. The Admissions Office considers all pieces of the application, with emphasis placed on academic record and preparedness for graduate business work, GMAT scores, professional experience, communication skills, goals, and compatibility with the program. One semester of calculus and two semesters of undergraduate accounting are prerequisite to commencing the MBA program.

### FINANCIAL FACTS

| | |
|---|---|
| Annual tuition (in-state/out-of-state) | $6,558/$11,296 |
| Fees (in-state/out-of-state) | $1,350/$1,419 |
| Books and supplies | $20,000 |
| % of students receiving grants | 68 |
| Average award package | $6,000 |
| Average grant | $3,000 |

### ADMISSIONS

| | |
|---|---|
| **Admissions Selectivity Rating** | **88** |
| # of applications received | 144 |
| % applicants accepted | 52 |
| % acceptees attending | 65 |
| Average GMAT | 623 |
| Range of GMAT | 620–690 |
| Average GPA | 3 |
| TOEFL required of international students? | yes |
| Minimum TOEFL (paper/computer) | 550/213 |
| Application fee | $45 |
| International application fee | $45 |
| Regular application deadline | 2/1 |
| Regular notification | rolling |
| Deferment available? | yes |
| Maximum length of deferment | 1 year |
| Need-blind admissions? | yes |

### EMPLOYMENT PROFILE

| Career Rating | 77 | Grads employed by field: | % | avg. salary: |
|---|---|---|---|---|
| **Primary source of full-time job acceptances** | | Finance | 36 | $50,942 |
| | | Marketing | 9 | $58,350 |
| School-facilitated activities | 9 (41%) | MIS | 23 | $58,000 |
| Graduate-facilitated activities | 13 (59%) | Operations | 5 | $57,000 |
| | | Consulting | 27 | $60,800 |
| Average starting salary | $56,016 | | | |
| Percent employed | 70 | | | |

# WAKE FOREST UNIVERSITY
## BABCOCK GRADUATE SCHOOL OF MANAGEMENT

## Academics

The Babcock Graduate School of Management at Wake Forest University excels in the financial concentrations and quantitative analytical skills prized by the banking industry. That should come as no surprise because many of the region's major banks are headquartered in nearby Charlotte. The Babcock MBA program commences with a "lockstep core program that is fully integrated; functional tracks are not offered until the second year," though students are allowed to take two electives in their chosen tracks at the end of their first year. Students have high praise for the core, and they describe it as "an integrated program, not a list of courses. Each class builds directly on the last, across all disciplines. You may have accounting four times in one week and not at all the next because you need to learn certain quantitative skills before you can proceed to the next accounting topic." Throughout the core year, "students work with four-to-five member teams, assigned during orientation. The teams are designed to include students from a range of backgrounds. All of the classes are with these teams, and much of the work is done with these people. This gives students an opportunity to work with others, as [they] will in the workforce. It also gives the school an atmosphere of cooperation."

Both years of the program "can be very challenging" because "the workload is heavy and the expectations are high." Fortunately, "students are always willing to help each other out. Working in teams is an essential part of almost every class. You learn from each others' experiences as much as you do from the professors." Small class sizes "allow for good in class discussions and opportunities to participate, but if you want to blend in and coast through b-school unnoticed, this is not the place. Because it is so small, you really can't get away with being unprepared or not participating. [There is a] big emphasis on class participation; it is a large part of [the] grading system." Babcock professors are "extremely helpful and easy to access. Setting up meetings regarding class material, job hunting, or other career information, has been an excellent way for me to learn about opportunities." Students also love how professors "encourage real-world cases." For example, one student explains, "A professor brought the director of a seminary in from Haiti to use as a case study for cost analysis. Another faculty member included branding a local winery in the class deliverables. These projects allow us to practice working with clients, integrate course materials into existing situations, and actually provide beneficial information to nonprofits or start-ups." Teaching here is highly tech-reliant, so "all students are provided with a laptop computer as part of tuition, and all classrooms are outfitted with integrated computer and audio-visual equipment."

## Career and Placement

"The help of the Career Management Center is wonderful," students report. Of course, the down economy of the early 2000s has challenged the office; students explain that "the Career Management Center has had a tough time placing people in full-time and internship positions over the last couple of years." Because "we are in an area with lots of bank headquarters, finance is heavily emphasized, and banks recruit heavily here." Students in these areas are most likely to be happy with career services at Wake Forest. MBAs in operations and IT, on the other hand, feel that "the Career Management Center needs to attract more positions/recruiters." Top employers of Wake Forest MBAs include Alex Lee, Philip Morris, Accenture, Key Bank, Bank of America, BearingPoint, Booz Allen Hamilton, General Electric, Lowe's, Sara Lee, and Wachovia. Nearly two-thirds of Wake MBAs find their first jobs in the South Atlantic region; about 3 in 10 find jobs outside the United States.

STACY POINDEXTER OWEN, DIRECTOR OF ADMISSIONS
PO BOX 7659, WINSTON-SALEM, NC 27109-7659 UNITED STATES
PHONE: 336-758-5422 • FAX: 336-758-5830
E-MAIL: ADMISSIONS@MBA.WFU.EDU • WEBSITE: WWW.MBA.WFU.EDU

## Student Life and Environment

Wake's MBA program has students burning the candle at both ends; one MBA explains, "Classes and homework require approximately 12 hours per day in both years. There are lots of activities, clubs, and opportunities to meet staff, faculty, other students, and local business leaders. We work hard and there is an opportunity to play hard." Another student agrees, "It is extremely challenging to manage all aspects of life here. Academics, clubs, and social opportunities are very time-consuming. It is worth every bit of pressure and time, though. The environment here is one of teamwork and stimulation. Everyone is looking out for each other and is excited to be here, learning new things, and meeting new people."

Babcock "does a great job of presenting opportunities to balance your life. There are many social events outside of academics so that students and spouses/girlfriends/boyfriends can mingle and be social. This is key as the real business world requires a social side to your personality," according to MBAs. Students enjoy such extracurricular options as "happy hours at school on Fridays and tailgates at home football games. Social events often coincide with career-related opportunities, such as cocktails and hors d'oeuvres after a club event involving outside speakers (like alumni and corporate recruiters)." MBAs agree that "this is a very social program," in which, "everyone knows each other since the class size is so small. Thus, whenever we all go out, we all go out. It's great to build strong relationships and networking." The student body includes a large international population; one MBA observes, "Thirty percent of the class is reserved for international students and this has really widened my perceptions. Getting input from a Chinese student about a case set in China is really helpful." Hometown Winston-Salem "is not the most hip, but there are opportunities to go out." Those who love the Southern style of living will be most comfortable here. As one MBA notes, "Even though Winston-Salem is struggling economically, it is a great city to live in, due to its relaxing environment. The Southern culture is pervasive, even to those from outside the South." Two larger cities, Charlotte and Raleigh, are within a one-and-a-half hour drive of campus.

## Admissions

Wake Forest's admissions decisions "are influenced by demonstrated potential for management careers through academic achievement, professional experience, and community involvement." The school considers all of the following components of the application: GMAT scores, TOEFL scores (international applicants), undergraduate and graduate transcripts, personal statements, letters of recommendation, resume, and an interview. To recruit minority students, "Babcock offers Diversity Weekend, an event for prospective minority, female, and international candidates, and [the university] participates in the National Black MBA Association and the National Hispanic Society of MBAs Career Forums. Through the Wachovia Scholars Program, Babcock is able to offer scholarships to underrepresented full-time students. These scholarships include a full-tuition waiver, stipend, and an international summer study trip."

## FINANCIAL FACTS

| | |
|---|---|
| Annual tuition | $31,500 |
| Fees | $150 |
| Books and supplies | $1,500 |
| Room & board | $7,000 |
| % of students receiving aid | 87 |
| % of first-year students receiving aid | 82 |
| % of students receiving loans | 56 |
| % of students receiving grants | 61 |
| Average award package | $22,476 |
| Average grant | $14,127 |
| Average student loan debt | $49,890 |

## ADMISSIONS

| | |
|---|---|
| Admissions Selectivity Rating | 81 |
| # of applications received | 302 |
| % applicants accepted | 72 |
| % acceptees attending | 40 |
| Average GMAT | 630 |
| Range of GMAT | 580–660 |
| Average GPA | 3.2 |
| TOEFL required of international students? | yes |
| Minimum TOEFL (paper/computer) | 600/250 |
| Application fee | $75 |
| International application fee | $75 |
| Regular application deadline | 4/1 |
| Regular notification | rolling |
| Early decision program? | yes |
| ED Deadline/notification | 11/1 / 12/1 |
| Need-blind admissions? | yes |

## APPLICANTS ALSO LOOK AT

Duke University, Indiana University—Bloomington, University of North Carolina—Chapel Hill, University of Notre Dame, University of Virginia, Vanderbilt University, Washington University

### EMPLOYMENT PROFILE

| | | Grads employed by field: | % | avg. salary: |
|---|---|---|---|---|
| Career Rating | 86 | Finance | 44 | $75,351 |
| Primary source of full-time job acceptances | | Marketing | 36 | $72,850 |
| | | MIS | 1 | NR |
| School-facilitated activities | 47 (64%) | Operations | 7 | $69,760 |
| Graduate-facilitated activities | 26 (36%) | Consulting | 7 | $83,000 |
| | | General Management | 5 | $74,233 |
| Average starting salary | $74,546 | | | |
| Percent employed | 86 | | | |

# WASHINGTON UNIVERSITY IN ST. LOUIS
## JOHN M. OLIN SCHOOL OF BUSINESS

## Academics

The emphasis is on "learning by doing" at the Olin School of Business at Washington University, and it is this focus that draws future business leaders to the venerable St. Louis institution. Key to Olin's approach is its Center for Experiential Learning, which puts aspiring MBAs to work solving the actual problems of actual businesses in the area. Students love the experience, and they report that "the Center for Experiential Learning (CEL) provides students the opportunity to benefit from working with St. Louis companies on consulting projects, entrepreneurial projects, and nonprofit consulting projects. It does a great job recruiting companies to participate in its activities on behalf of Olin students."

Olin MBAs also appreciate the flexibility of their curriculum, which "allows students to tailor the program to their liking, taking electives as early as the first semester." The school facilitates both electives and core courses through a unique hybrid academic calendar that is equal parts semester- and quarter-system; each semester is divided into two "mini-semesters," resulting in a pace more commonly associated with a quarter system. Students appreciate that "mini-semesters enable lots of electives and a broad base of knowledge," but they warn that the timing "is a bit aggressive. It's hard for everything to sink in over such a short term." One student puts a positive spin on the accelerated pace; he explains that "the program itself is streamlined to maximize learning in a minimal amount of time. The professors even coordinate material among the core courses to enhance the process." Most students agree that "it's a killer workload, but it means that [students are] better prepared for electives and summer internships."

Olin excels in strategy "(some strategy professors are at the cutting edge)," finance, operations, and accounting. A global-management studies course, offered through CEL, includes a two-week in-country immersion experience. Students explain that professors are "experienced, on the cutting edge of research, and know what's happening in industry, due to regular consulting assignments." Students add, "[The professors] are great researchers and great teachers, are eager to help students, and are also very involved in our successes. They are great resources both while in school and after graduation." The small size of the Olin program means that student interaction with professors and administrators is frequent. Students report that "the school's administration is extremely receptive to students' feedback. The administration really bends over backwards to serve its customers, the students. The dean has an open-door policy, which makes him quite accessible. He's always interested in listening to students' suggestions and feedback."

## Career and Placement

Washington University's Weston Career Resources Center (WCRC) enrolls all Olin MBAs in a first-year, first-semester course called "Managing Your Career Strategies." During this course, students "plan a series of key actions that [they] will engage in throughout [their] MBA education and into [their] first year of post-MBA employment." Students explain that their greatest career contacts come not through the WCRC, but rather through their participation in Olin's Experiential Learning program. Students also praise the alumni network and say that "the alumni are very active, and this is reflected in their support of current students, the endowment of the college, and the average gift given by an alumnus." Alumni provide numerous job leads for current Olin MBAs.

Top employers of Olin MBAs include 3M; Anheuser-Busch; Bank of America; Cisco Systems, Inc.; Citibank; Emerson; ExxonMobil; FedEx; GE Capital; Guidant; Honeywell; IBM Corp.; LG Electronic; Mead Johnson; The Hartford; and Wells Fargo. Nearly one in five graduates find a first job outside the United States; about half remain in the St. Louis region.

BRAD PEARSON, DIRECTOR OF MBA ADMISSIONS AND FINANCIAL AID
CAMPUS BOX 1133, ONE BROOKINGS DRIVE, ST. LOUIS, MO 63130 UNITED STATES
PHONE: 314-935-7301 • FAX: 314-935-6309
E-MAIL: MBA@OLIN.WUSTL.EDU • WEBSITE: WWW.OLIN.WUSTL.EDU

## Student Life and Environment

Olin has "a great social feel," students say. MBAs also note that "students are at school whether it is the weekend or not. It is a central social hub, and there are days spent in study rooms [or] hanging out in the MBA lounge and courtyard." The Friday Afternoon Club (FAC) is a much-anticipated weekly event, in which, "everyone is invited: students, spouses, significant others, children, faculty, and staff. It's a great time to catch up with people you don't see every day and find out what people are doing over the weekend." The event is sponsored by a different club each week and almost always involves a keg, which pleases students; many students agree, "We work hard and play hard."

Olin's facility is a homey building with "comfortable study spaces, adequate meeting rooms, a kitchen, and access to prepared foods, which make the extensive time in the school tolerable." The computer facilities "got a total makeover in 2003," so now "students have the option of using wireless connections in addition to the traditional PCs that have been available in the past. The wireless LAN provides coverage to all student-accessible public areas such as student lounges, the library, study rooms, May Auditorium, and the Lopata Courtyard." The school also has a Polycom video conferencing system that "is often used by students for interviewing with companies."

Olin students tend to be on the youngish side; they are a "great bunch of fun, intelligent personalities, with a diversity of work and cultural backgrounds. We have a great mix of international and domestic students." They "take their academics seriously, but they are not weighed down by enormous, cutthroat pressure." Many MBAs tell us that school keeps them too busy to enjoy the metropolitan life afforded by their St. Louis location.

## Admissions

The Olin admissions office scours applicants' records for evidence of "a history of setting and achieving goals." The school also takes into strong consideration the "quality of previous education, the quality of previous work experience, and the quality of the match between the applicant's stated educational and professional objectives and the MBA program's content." Leadership and community service are seen as leading indicators of fitness for the Olin program. Applicants must submit official copies of all undergraduate and graduate transcripts, GMAT scores, TOEFL scores (where appropriate), two letters of recommendation, a personal statement, and a resume. Olin participates in the Consortium for Graduate Study in Management, which funds fellowships for talented minorities.

### FINANCIAL FACTS

| | |
|---|---|
| Annual tuition | $34,500 |
| Fees | $705 |
| Books and supplies | $2,500 |
| Room & board (off-campus) | $26,000 |
| % of first-year students receiving aid | 90 |
| Average award package | $35,451 |

### ADMISSIONS

| | |
|---|---|
| Admissions Selectivity Rating | 87 |
| # of applications received | 576 |
| % applicants accepted | 56 |
| % acceptees attending | 37 |
| Average GMAT | 635 |
| Range of GMAT | 590–680 |
| Average GPA | 3.3 |
| TOEFL required of international students? | yes |
| Minimum TOEFL (paper/computer) | 590/243 |
| Application fee | $100 |
| International application fee | $100 |
| Regular application deadline | 1/2 |
| Regular notification | 3/17 |

Application deadline/notification
| | |
|---|---|
| Round 1: | 11/14 / 1/27 |
| Round 2: | 1/2 / 3/17 |
| Round 3: | 2/27 / 4/21 |
| Round 4: | 5/1 / 6/19 |
| Deferment available? | yes |
| Maximum length of deferment | 1 year |
| Transfer students accepted? | yes |

Transfer application policy
Up to 9 credits from an AACSB-accredited graduate program.
| | |
|---|---|
| Need-blind admissions? | yes |

### APPLICANTS ALSO LOOK AT

Duke University, Emory University, Georgetown University, Indiana University—Bloomington, The University of Texas at Austin, University of Michigan, University of North Carolina—Chapel Hill

### EMPLOYMENT PROFILE

| | | Grads employed by field: | % | avg. salary: |
|---|---|---|---|---|
| Career Rating | 92 | Finance | 38 | $79,106 |
| Primary source of full-time job acceptances | | Human Resources | 1 | NR |
| School-facilitated activities | 57 (65%) | Marketing | 22 | $77,961 |
| Graduate-facilitated activities | 30 (34%) | Operations | 1 | NR |
| Unknown | 1 (1%) | Consulting | 28 | $84,165 |
| | | General Management | 9 | $84,063 |
| Average starting salary | $80,204 | Other | 1 | NR |
| Percent employed | 91 | | | |

# WEST VIRGINIA UNIVERSITY
## COLLEGE OF BUSINESS AND ECONOMICS

## Academics

West Virginia University offers two distinct MBA options, each designed for a specific demographic. For young students with little professional experience and a desire to move forward quickly, WVU has designed a full-time MBA program that can be completed in just over a year. For more experienced students with a stronger business background and ongoing professional obligations, WVU offers a part-time executive MBA in eight West Virginia cities.

Both MBA options stress the integral nature of technology in modern business. One student observes, "The greatest strength of this program is the broad use of technology in the classes. I would have rated myself as an advanced user of information technology in my role of managing a number of databases before this class, and yet I have learned so much more and become even more comfortable with technology and common software packages." Although the curricula for the two programs vary, both stress the importance of teamwork and cover all major functions of business study.

The full-time program, located in Morgantown, begins with a pre-professional session designed to polish necessary business skills. It then moves through the curriculum thematically, covering such subjects as business planning, organizational skills, implementation, control, and change. Students "take one class for a period of weeks, and then a different class begins. It's a really great structure that allows you to fully concentrate on the material." The program's emphasis on "practical thinking and experience," MBAs tell us, is helpful. One explains, "I am young and do not have much business and working experience, and the MBA program has done an excellent job of easing me into the business atmosphere while challenging me to go further." Professors "make themselves available to help each student, even into the late hours of the evening, and go above and beyond the call of duty for the WVU MBA students"—another plus.

The part-time EMBA brings students to a satellite classroom, where interactive technology allows them to participate in classes with each other and the professor. Classes are videotaped to accommodate working professionals who miss class due to travel. An MBA tells us that "given the complexity of coordinating things, it is amazing how well everything has worked. Any time you are heavily dependent on technology, you expect a certain amount of inconvenience, but I have been pleasantly surprised at how well-maintained the systems are and how committed the school has been to making sure that we are all comfortable with the learning experience." Students also appreciate that "professors visit the various sites during the classes so that we actually meet them and each site gets to experience being remote and being on-site." They also tell us, "The online support given is outstanding. Anything and everything you need to know can be found by a simple Internet connection." A student complains that "too many group projects are required, meaning that additional travel to a central meeting place (one hour for me) was a common occurrence. Usually 20 to 40 percent of your grade is based upon group efforts. This undercuts a lot of the convenience of the program."

## Career and Placement

The College of Business and Economics at WVU has its own dedicated Career Development Center to serve business undergraduates and graduate students. The office provides counseling services, workshops, seminars, and on-campus recruiting events.

BONNIE ANDERSON, ASSOCIATE DIRECTOR
PO BOX 6027, MORGANTOWN, WV 26506-6027 UNITED STATES
PHONE: 304-293-5408 • FAX: 304-293-2385
E-MAIL: MBA@WVU.EDU • WEBSITE: WWW.BE.WVU.EDU

Students tell us that the office seems geared mostly toward the needs of undergraduates. One writes, "The largest improvement to the program could be made with career services tailored specifically to the MBA students. The MBA program would benefit greatly by bringing reputable companies to directly meet with business students. The accounting program at WVU has an excellent relationship with the big four accounting firms. The MBA program should seek to achieve a similar relationship with a selected group of organizations."

## Student Life and Environment

WVU is a pretty typical large state university, with plenty of extracurricular options for those who seek them. One student notes, "There are many things that WVU offers as special activities. They offer movies, up-all-night activities, that sort of thing. They also have a lot of shows and performers that come to campus." Football games "are always great," and "keg parties, bar crawls, and burning couches are fairly regular affairs. This is a renowned party school." Most MBAs, though, "do not have as much time to enjoy these activities as [they] did as undergrads." Hometown Morgantown "is the kind of wonderful town that you never tire of. It offers absolutely anything and everything you could want, while still holding true to a small-town atmosphere. You would have to search long and hard to match all that it offers."

It's a different story for EMBAs, whose students are "not very focused on campus life. Most people have non-university centered lives."

WVU MBAs are "a diverse group," with "work experience from a number of industries, government, and health care. Some are managers, directors, or vice presidents, while others are in staff positions. They are all willing to share their experiences and opinions." One student writes, "Even though we are so different in the class, we all pull together and work as a team and learn from each other just as much as we learn in the classes. It has been amazing."

## Admissions

Applicants to the MBA program must submit official transcripts for all postsecondary academic work, an official GMAT score report, and a resume. Letters of recommendation and a statement of purpose are optional. All students must have full use of a laptop PC that meets prescribed minimum software, memory, and processor-speed requirements; contact the school or visit the website for details. Applicants to the EMBA program must have at least two years of "significant work experience." For applicants with less than five years experience, GPA and GMAT figure most heavily in the admissions decision. Professional experience, especially managerial experience, is the greater factor for applicants with at least five years of experience.

### FINANCIAL FACTS
| | |
|---|---|
| Annual tuition (in-state/out-of-state) | $8,560/$23,300 |
| Books and supplies | $1,600 |
| Room & board | $6,900 |

### ADMISSIONS
| | |
|---|---|
| Admissions Selectivity Rating | 90 |
| # of applications received | 284 |
| % applicants accepted | 33 |
| % acceptees attending | 87 |
| Average GMAT | 560 |
| Range of GMAT | 520–640 |
| Average GPA | 3.34 |
| TOEFL required of international students? | yes |
| Minimum TOEFL (paper/computer) | 580/237 |
| Application fee | $50 |
| International application fee | $50 |
| Regular application deadline | 2/28 |
| Regular notification | 3/15 |
| Deferment available? | yes |
| Maximum length of deferment | 1 years |
| Transfer students accepted? | yes |
| Transfer application policy | Applicants request transfer credits and the Admission Committee reviews the request. |
| Non-fall admissions? | yes |
| Need-blind admissions? | yes |

### APPLICANTS ALSO LOOK AT
Marshall University, The Pennsylvania State University, Syracuse University, Temple University, University of Kentucky, University of Pittsburgh, Virginia Tech

### EMPLOYMENT PROFILE
| | |
|---|---|
| Career Rating | 66 |
| Average starting salary | $49,200 |

# WESTERN CAROLINA UNIVERSITY
## COLLEGE OF BUSINESS

### GENERAL INFORMATION
| | |
|---|---|
| Type of school | public |
| Environment | rural |
| Academic calendar | semester |

### SURVEY SAYS...
Smart classrooms
*Solid preparation in:*
Accounting
General management
Presentation skills

### STUDENTS
| | |
|---|---|
| Enrollment of parent institution | 8,665 |
| Enrollment of business school | 131 |
| % male/female | 68/32 |
| % part-time | 60 |
| % international | 42 |
| Average age at entry | 28 |
| Average years work experience at entry | 7 |

### ACADEMICS
| | |
|---|---|
| **Academic Experience Rating** | **63** |
| Student/faculty ratio | 15:1 |
| Profs interesting rating | 75 |
| Profs accessible rating | 67 |
| % female faculty | 26 |
| % minority faculty | 2 |

## Academics

Students may pursue the Western Carolina University MBA at the school's main campus in Cullowhee or at its resident credit center in Asheville. WCU also offers a master of accountancy at the Asheville campus and a master of entrepreneurship and a master of project management as web-based programs.

WCU keeps MBA class sizes below 35 students, with many classes having as few as 15 students. Small classes free professors to employ a range of teaching techniques including team projects, case studies, in-class discussion, and lecture. Students tell us that the small size of their program means that "administration and professors are always available and easy to talk to. Most students have very good relationships with their professors. Since the MBA program here at Western is not too large, students can get to know their professors other than just in the classroom."

The WCU MBA curriculum consists of 24 credits in core courses covering managerial accounting, decision support systems, managerial economics, financial management, organizational behavior and analysis, quantitative analysis for business, strategic management, and marketing management. Students must also successfully complete 12 hours of coursework in electives. Elective classes are available in the following areas: accounting; business law; information systems; economics; entrepreneurship; finance; international business; management; and marketing. Instruction is provided by "professors who are at the PhD level and are experienced teachers," though some here "wish the instructors had more experience with big business." The administration earns student praise for being "helpful in every way it can be, from signing students up for classes to sending out job vacancies from businesses."

## Career and Placement

The Office of Career Services and Cooperative Education handles counseling and placement services for all undergraduate and graduate students at WCU. Services include a career library, co-op placement, one-on-one counseling, interviewing workshops, resume critiquing, online job listings, career-related personality assessment, career days, and on-campus recruitment events. Companies recruiting on campus in 2004 included Allegis Group, BB&T, Builders First Source, Cintas Corporation, Consolidated Electrical Distributors, Edward Jones, Ferguson Enterprises, Home Trust Bank, and Liberty Mutual.

## Student Life and Environment

Western Carolina's main campus is located in Cullowhee, which has a "small-town atmosphere that makes it easy to focus on your studies." Cullowhee is surrounded by a rural valley between the Great Smoky Mountains and the Blue Ridge Mountains. Nearby amenities include the Blue Ridge Parkway, the Cherokee Indian Reservation, Great Smoky Mountain National Park, and a number of resorts offering golf, fishing, skiing, and other outdoor activities. Not everyone sees the town's merits, however. Complains one MBA, "To me, the town WCU is a little small. Some people enjoy that there aren't a lot of buildings and cars and people, but I enjoy larger cities with a little more going on. However, Asheville, NC is only 45 minutes away, and [it has] a lot to offer." For a real taste of city life, Atlanta, Georgia, lies two and a half hours to the southwest.

MICHAEL SMITH, DIRECTOR OF MBA PROGRAM
112 FORSYTH BUILDING, CULLOWHEE, NC 28723 UNITED STATES
PHONE: 828-227-3588 • FAX: 828-227-7414 • E-MAIL: FDEITZ@EMAIL.WCU.EDU
WEBSITE: WWW.WCU.EDU/COB/MBA/

WCU's MBA program includes "many students from all over the world, including Germany, Ireland, Egypt, and India" who "are very friendly and are as curious about our culture as we are of theirs." Writes one American MBA, "Here at WCU, I have learned a lot about different cultures by just simply getting to know my fellow students. It has been a fun and educational experience for me." The program also attracts many "younger part-time students with families." Most have been "pleasantly surprised by the qualities of [their] fellow students" who are, as one student puts it, "bright, friendly, motivated, and interesting people. They come from a variety of backgrounds and work experiences and are well-rounded." But a few students still feel that "the school needs to increase its selectivity. As a relatively new program attempting to increase enrollment, standards for admission are a little too low." An admission rate of over 90 percent lends support to that assessment.

WCU hosts "many clubs and organizations" and has "a movie theater on campus," all of which help to foster a "close-knit community" among full-time students. The many part-timers here, however, have little time for such diversions; explains one, "My life at school is insignificant compared to my life at work and [as] a mother of three children. However, if I had the time, there would be many opportunities to do really cool stuff at school. I read the announcements of events longingly."

## Admissions

Applicants to the MBA program at Western Carolina University must submit official copies of transcripts for all academic work completed after high school and an official score report for the GMAT. The school may additionally request letters of recommendation and an interview of some applicants, but otherwise they are not required. Applicants most likely to gain admission to the program have a score of at least 1,000 under the formula [(undergraduate GPA for final 60 semester hours of undergraduate work × 200) + GMAT score]. International applicants must also submit official score reports for the TOEFL and achieve a minimum score of 550 on the paper test or 213 on the computer test. International applications are due by April 1 for the Fall semester and by September 1 for the Spring semester.

## FINANCIAL FACTS

| | |
|---|---|
| Annual tuition (in-state/out-of-state) | $2,023/$11,608 |
| Fees | $1,759 |
| Books and supplies | $2,000 |
| Room & board | $6,800 |
| % of students receiving aid | 79 |
| % of first-year students receiving aid | 75 |
| % of students receiving loans | 39 |
| % of students receiving grants | 31 |
| Average award package | $11,187 |
| Average grant | $3,350 |
| Average student loan debt | $19,923 |

## ADMISSIONS

| | |
|---|---|
| **Admissions Selectivity Rating** | **64** |
| # of applications received | 57 |
| % applicants accepted | 98 |
| % acceptees attending | 73 |
| Average GMAT | 486 |
| Range of GMAT | 440–530 |
| Average GPA | 3.35 |
| TOEFL required of international students? | yes |
| Minimum TOEFL (paper/computer) | 550/213 |
| Application fee | $40 |
| International application fee | $40 |
| Regular application deadline | rolling |
| Regular notification | rolling |
| Deferment available? | yes |
| Maximum length of deferment | 1 year |
| Transfer students accepted? | yes |
| Transfer application policy Students may transfer a maximum of 6 hours from other AACSB-accredited schools. | |
| Non-fall admissions? | yes |
| Need-blind admissions? | yes |

## APPLICANTS ALSO LOOK AT

Appalachian State University, University of North Carolina at Charlotte

# WICHITA STATE UNIVERSITY
## BARTON SCHOOL OF BUSINESS

## GENERAL INFORMATION

| | |
|---|---|
| Type of school | public |
| Environment | metropolis |
| Academic calendar | semesters |

### SURVEY SAYS...
*Solid preparation in:*
General management
Teamwork
Presentation skills

### STUDENTS

| | |
|---|---|
| Enrollment of parent institution | 15,000 |
| Enrollment of business school | 183 |
| % male/female | 64/36 |
| % part-time | 76 |
| % minorities | 30 |
| Average age at entry | 25 |
| Average years work experience at entry | 2 |

### ACADEMICS

| | |
|---|---|
| **Academic Experience Rating** | **77** |
| Student/faculty ratio | 4:1 |
| Profs interesting rating | 70 |
| Profs accessible rating | 73 |
| % female faculty | 3 |
| % minority faculty | 21 |

### JOINT DEGREES
MBA/MSN

## Academics

There's one obvious and indisputable reason that students choose the Barton School of Business at Wichita State University: "It's the only accredited program in the city of Wichita, Kansas," as one student says. Thus, it is the most convenient choice for the many full-time worker/part-time student MBAs who attend the school. Yet, convenience is hardly Barton's only virtue. The program "concentrates on general management, with particular attention given to developing an understanding of the organization as an integrated system." It also provides students access to "professors who all have PhDs, and most of whom participate in industry consulting. [This] provides a real edge for dealing with real-world business challenges."

With a large part-time enrollment, Barton "has to be flexible, and it is. [Because] there are so many nontraditional students, they take the time to work with each student individually." This is especially important because classes tend to be large. One MBA observes, "We need smaller class sizes. Forty is too many, and I even had class in a room that was too small for the number enrolled. Because of this, class discussion does not take place, and neither does the learning that's associated with discussion. We need more emphasis on thinking through concepts by doing things like writing papers." Students also feel the school needs a tech upgrade, and they explain that "we don't have enough computers and wi-fi services in classrooms."

While Barton has "many great professors," students must also endure "a couple of bad apples." Experience is a factor; students comment that "there's a large percentage of 'this is the first time I have taught this class' professors. Sometimes they assign too much work, maybe to prove a point, and at other times they haven't had a clue what they were doing." One part-time student adds, "Professors tend to think just because we meet once per week that we have time to do lots of reading. Most students are in two-night classes, work, and have personal responsibilities like families, homes, and pets." Barton MBAs are most positive about the instructors in management; they are least enthused about the accounting faculty and warn that "the professors do not teach in an understandable way." The school offers MBA concentrations in five areas: entrepreneurship, finance, healthcare administration, marketing, and operations management. It also offers a master's in accountancy, an MA in economics, and a unique combined MBA/MS in nursing degree.

Barton has research centers devoted to economic development, entrepreneurship, international business advancement, management development, and real estate. All provide services to the Wichita business community and allow participating students to learn while developing valuable contacts.

## Career and Placement

Wichita State's Career Development Office maintains a satellite office at Barton's Clinton Hall, although the main office that serves all WSU students remains in Grace Wilkie Hall. The office offers resume and cover letter review, mock interviews, job-search counseling, career counseling, and Crossroads, an online service that allows students to coordinate applications and interviews from their own computers. The CDO also sponsors job fairs for the university at large but none specifically for MBAs.

DOROTHY HARPOOL, DIRECTOR OF MBA PROGRAMS
1845 NORTH FAIRMOUNT, WICHITA, KS 67260-0048 UNITED STATES
PHONE: 316-978-3230 • FAX: 316-978-3767
E-MAIL: MBA@WICHITA.EDU • WEBSITE: WWW.WICHITA.EDU/MBA

## Student Life and Environment

WSU's large nontraditional student body is generally too busy to linger long on campus. They flood in during the evenings for class, and if they remain afterward, it is to study in the library or to participate in required team projects. One typical student explains, "I have a full-time career, [and] I attend school in the evenings. Life at school is strictly learning by attending class. I do everything else like homework and group work at home or at the library." Another part-timer adds, "There is no life at school. It is a commuter school."

Barton is home to a number of clubs, enjoyed primarily by full-time students, but also by some particularly ambitious part-timers. These include several national honor societies as well as groups devoted to entrepreneurship, international business, human-resource management, and promotion of free enterprise. One part-time MBA explains, "Our business school organizations are well-organized and the school caters to evening students."

Besides the conventional part-timers and full-timers, Barton also hosts participants in the executive MBA program, open only to those with a minimum of five years full-time work experience. One participant reports that "the EMBA program is very demanding and requires significant dedication. The school helps by handling all registration themselves and providing resources so that students do not have to waste precious time. Annual EMBA gatherings are great places for networking."

Hometown Wichita is a city of approximately 350,000. The birthplace of Pizza Hut, Wichita prides itself as a fertile ground for entrepreneurial innovation. From opera to greyhound racing, Wichita has more to offer than most outsiders would suspect. Students tell us that their campus' West Side location "is very convenient, safe, and offers reasonable parking," and that it also boasts "a great gym facility, good student health care, and an overall friendly atmosphere."

## Admissions

A completed application to the Barton School of Business must include GMAT scores (the school considers both overall score and component scores), official transcripts for all postsecondary schools attended, a "personal goals" essay, two letters of reference, and a current resume. The school notes that "the specific content of a student's previous education is less important than evidence that the student has sound scholarship, strong personal motivation, and the ability to develop skills necessary to assume a position of leadership." Barton prefers, but does not require, its applicants to have professional work experience.

### FINANCIAL FACTS

| | |
|---|---|
| Annual tuition (in-state/out-of-state) | $4,128/$11,280 |
| Books and supplies | $1,200 |
| Average grant | $6,000 |

### ADMISSIONS

| | |
|---|---|
| **Admissions Selectivity Rating** | **85** |
| # of applications received | 93 |
| % applicants accepted | 52 |
| % acceptees attending | 100 |
| Average GMAT | 544 |
| Average GPA | 3.38 |
| TOEFL required of international students? | yes |
| Minimum TOEFL (paper/computer) | 570/230 |
| Application fee | $35 |
| International application fee | $50 |
| Regular application deadline | 6/1 |
| Regular notification | 6/15 |
| Deferment available? | yes |
| Maximum length of deferment | 1 year |
| Transfer students accepted? | yes |
| Transfer application policy Only AACSB-accredited classes may be transferred. | |
| Non-fall admissions? | yes |
| Need-blind admissions? | yes |

### EMPLOYMENT PROFILE

| | |
|---|---|
| **Career Rating** | **62** |
| Average starting salary | $55,000 |

# WILLAMETTE UNIVERSITY
## ATKINSON GRADUATE SCHOOL OF MANAGEMENT

## GENERAL INFORMATION

| | |
|---|---|
| Type of school | private |
| Affiliation | Methodist |
| Environment | city |
| Academic calendar | semester |

### SURVEY SAYS...
Friendly students
Smart classrooms
*Solid preparation in:*
Marketing
Teamwork

### STUDENTS

| | |
|---|---|
| Enrollment of parent institution | 2,500 |
| Enrollment of business school | 136 |
| % male/female | 65/35 |
| % out-of-state | 50 |
| % part-time | 8 |
| % minorities | 16 |
| % international | 21 |
| Average age at entry | 25 |
| Average years work experience at entry | 2 |

### ACADEMICS

| | |
|---|---|
| **Academic Experience Rating** | **72** |
| Student/faculty ratio | 9:1 |
| Profs interesting rating | 67 |
| Profs accessible rating | 74 |
| % female faculty | 24 |

### JOINT DEGREES
MBA/JD, 4 years

### PROMINENT ALUMNI
Grace Crunican, Director, Seattle Dept. of Transportation; James Fitzhenry, Senior VP, FLIR Systems, Inc.; Thomas Neilsen, Chair, Neilsen Manufacturing, Inc.; Ann Jackson, Executive Director/CEO, Oregon Hospice Association; James McCluskey, Senior Managing Director, Bear Stearns Asset Management

## Academics

The Atkinson Graduate School of Management at Willamette University offers a distinctive MBA that places an unusual "emphasis on harmonizing private enterprise, not-for-profit, and government with community" to "educate and produce highly intelligent and socially responsible individuals." Although 75 percent of Atkinson graduates pursue careers in business, one in four Atkinson graduates moves on to work in the public or not-for-profit sector. Students tell us that "the school excels in nonprofit management and management in general," and they like the fact that Willamette's MBA is accredited for business (AACSB International) and public administration (NASPAA).

The highlight of the Atkinson program is the PACE project, a two year long endeavor that first has student teams delivering management services to a real not-for-profit organization and later writing and presenting a complete business plan. One student explains, The PACe experience is amazing because the students must create a business plan, receive funding, and market their product or service, and exit the business within 10 months. There is more learning to be had in this project than anything else I have ever had to do."

PACE I and the core curriculum encompass the first year; the second year is given over to "tremendous electives," with especially distinguished offerings in marketing, finance, economics, and organizational development/HR. Professors "genuinely seem to care about the students, whether we are learning in their classes, are finding internships and employment, or need a place to go for a holiday dinner." Faculty members "know their subject matter extremely well, as most are working as consultants in business, government, or not-for-profit organizations." However, "like most schools, there are strong professors and weak professors. All of our professors are incredibly intelligent, but some of them are better at teaching what they know." Administrators earn high marks; students tell us that they are "very involved in the education process, facilitating and celebrating success while seeking to mitigate or resolve conflicts and problems." MBAs love Atkinson's high tech compatibility, reporting that "all students use laptops in class, and with [their] wireless Web, professors give handouts online during class rather than using paper, assignments are submitted through [their] class tools website, and exams can be taken online with a secure program."

## Career and Placement

The Career Services Office at the Atkinson School offers a wide range of services, including career fairs, counseling, online job databases, online resume books, self-assessment tools (e.g., CareerLeader), and workshops in interviewing, networking, and resume-building skills. Students feel the office does a good job with local placement, but that "further expanding the emphasis of the career center beyond our metro area and traditional areas of MBA emphasis is necessary. While there are postings for opportunities around the world, the on-campus efforts do tend to focus on traditional roles (mid-level manager to director positions in finance, marketing, and HR departments throughout the mid to upper Willamette Valley and Pacific Northwest coast)." Top employers of Atkinson MBAs include Bonneville Power Administration, Hewlett-Packard, Hollywood Entertainment, Intel Corporation, and Nike.

## Student Life and Environment

Willamette's emphasis on "learning by doing" makes it a popular choice for early-career students. This, and the lack of a work-experience prerequisite for admission, means that

Judy O'Neill, Director of Admission
900 State Street, Salem, OR 97301 United States
Phone: 503-370-6167 • Fax: 503-370-3011
E-mail: mba-admission@willamette.edu • Website: www.willamette.edu/mba

the student body is on the young side. One student explains, "Although students are of all ages and have different family types, most students are in their mid 20s and unmarried. However, the school does not come across as unfriendly to children or spouses." Another student adds, "I feel that if you are not young (right out of undergrad), you are going to have a hard time feeling that you fit in with the majority of the student body." Others disagree, telling us that "we have many different people here, so it's easy to find a niche that fits your way of life. Don't like to party? Plenty just like you. Like to party? Great; you'll have many to go out with. For those who like to keep their personal and academic lives separate, that's fine—they aren't treated any differently at school."

MBAs tell us that "all students are involved somehow in an extracurricular activity. The school has all professional associations, including the American Marketing Association, Atkinson Student Association, Public Management Association, and SHRM. There are many activities and opportunities to learn and network." Students also enjoy getting together socially, especially for Thursday Night Out (TNO), "a great opportunity to get together with other students and socialize; and with no classes on Fridays, you can begin to wind down from the week. (Also, no classes on Fridays allows students to take on internships, schedule job interviews, and arrange study groups, all without cutting into your weekend time that you want to spend with family.)" Athletic types will be happy to learn that "there is an intramural team for everybody, and you can easily find companions if you are interested in nonteam activities like cycling or hiking."

Willamette is located in Salem, Oregon, "a location that highly encourages studying. The city is safe, not too small, not too big, and not expensive to live. It also offers easy access to a metropolitan city (Portland is only 45 minutes away), outdoor recreation, natural attractions, and other universities." Students brag that "Willamette is one of the most beautiful campuses in the Northwest. The climate is excellent, the people are friendly, and the staff is excellent."

## Admissions

The Atkinson admissions office requires applicants to submit GMAT or GRE scores, official transcripts for all undergraduate and graduate work, a personal statement, an interview, and two letters of recommendation. International students whose native language is not English must score at least a 570 on the paper-based TOEFL or at least a 230 on the computer-based TOEFL. No work experience is required, except for the accelerated program (which requires two years' post-baccalaureate work experience and an undergraduate degree in business). Interviews are not required. Willamette offers a strong merit-based scholarship program.

### FINANCIAL FACTS

| | |
|---|---|
| Annual tuition | $21,600 |
| Fees | $50 |
| Books and supplies | $1,200 |
| Room & board (on/off-campus) | $12,000/$11,000 |
| % of students receiving aid | 79 |
| % of first-year students receiving aid | 79 |
| % of students receiving loans | 70 |
| % of students receiving grants | 70 |
| Average award package | $24,368 |
| Average grant | $9,394 |
| Average student loan debt | $31,642 |

### ADMISSIONS

| | |
|---|---|
| Admissions Selectivity Rating | 72 |
| # of applications received | 131 |
| % applicants accepted | 93 |
| % acceptees attending | 52 |
| Average GMAT | 591 |
| Range of GMAT | 530–670 |
| Average GPA | 3.24 |
| TOEFL required of international students? | yes |
| Minimum TOEFL (paper/computer) | 570/230 |
| Application fee | $50 |
| International application fee | $50 |
| Regular application deadline | 5/1 |
| Regular notification | rolling |
| Application deadline/notification | |
| Round 1: | 1/9 / rolling |
| Round 2: | 3/1 / rolling |
| Round 3: | 5/1 / rolling |
| Deferment available? | yes |
| Maximum length of deferment | 1 year |
| Transfer students accepted? | yes |
| Transfer application policy May transfer up to 6 credits of MBA course work with the approval of the dean. | |
| Need-blind admissions? | yes |

### APPLICANTS ALSO LOOK AT

Oregon State University, Pepperdine University, Portland State University, Stanford University, University of Oregon, University of Portland, University of Washington

### EMPLOYMENT PROFILE

| Career Rating | 78 | Grads employed by field: | % avg. salary: |
|---|---|---|---|
| Primary source of full-time job acceptances | | Accounting | 7 | NR |
| | | Finance | 16 | NR |
| School-facilitated activities | 25 (63%) | Human Resources | 7 | NR |
| Graduate-facilitated activities | 15 (37%) | Marketing | 18 | NR |
| | | Operations | 2 | NR |
| Average starting salary | $54,000 | Strategic Planning | 2 | NR |
| Percent employed | 87 | Consulting | 7 | NR |
| | | Entrepreneurship | 5 | NR |
| | | General Management | 16 | NR |
| | | non-profit | 20 | NR |

# WORCESTER POLYTECHNIC INSTITUTE
## DEPARTMENT OF MANAGEMENT

## Academics

"WPI's greatest strength is its ability to stay ahead of the curve with respect to technology," students at this small, predominantly part-time MBA program in central Massachusetts tell us. Through "a synergy of technical and business factors and real-life scenarios/case studies," WPI delivers an MBA program whose "focus is in the management of technology, with specialty areas that include IT, tech-based entrepreneurship, tech marketing, operations management, and e-business." As one student puts it, "Technology is here to stay, and WPI has done an excellent job establishing a program that addresses the need for better technical managers."

Computing resources are uniformly first-rate. The school reports that "computing services at WPI include powerful UNIX workstations, high-performance computing, electronic classrooms, a campus-wide high-speed data network, high-speed Internet connections, extensive roaming wireless coverage that lets students with wireless-enabled laptops or PDAs to work unplugged, and a web-based information system."

Not surprisingly—given the technological emphasis—WPI is well set up to accommodate distance learners, and in fact its advanced distance learning network (ADLN) program is extremely popular. Students love "the flexibility of the MBA program catering to online students. I am able to work no matter where my job takes me. I'm currently in London and still working on my MBA." Another ADLN student adds, "The facilities are excellent online and in person. I log in to get class materials, download presentations and documents, and participate in online discussions. I am paired up with a person who is taking the class on-site. I can order books online or in person. I can sign up for classes and get help online. It has been a positive experience. The online program is very well done."

WPI's "challenging but rewarding" curriculum means "it's hard work in each and every class" for MBAs. Academics "frequently mimic work scenarios by incorporating real cases for studies, teamwork, and hands-on experience. The school gives us the skills to work in business by increasing our quantitative and qualitative knowledge. The emphasis on teamwork and the integration of diversity of other student's cultures and professional experiences are also strengths of the program." MBAs feel that "the concepts learned in the classroom allow us to better manage our employees, relate to customers, and do our jobs more effectively. We can bring new knowledge to work right away."

WPI's professors are "excellent, knowledgeable, always accessible, willing to help, and go above and beyond." Students also appreciate how "all the faculty at WPI have strong connections with industry, which allows them to integrate their experiences with lecture."

## Career and Placement

The Career Development Center (CDC) serves all WPI students, undergraduate, and graduate; the school has no office dedicated exclusively to its business students. The CDC provides students with self-assessment tools, individual counseling, research materials, workshops, job fairs, online job databases, company visits, and assistance in landing summer internships. According to the CDC website, the school "utilizes state-of-the-art technology that makes [them] accessible from any location worldwide. [They] take exceptional pride in [their] services and staff members and will continue to design products that support career-related goals." Companies most likely to hire WPI MBAs include BAE Systems, EMC, Fidelity, GE, Raytheon, Teradyne, and Textron. Following graduation, 85 percent of WPI MBAs remain in New England; 1 in 20 finds work outside the U.S.

NORM WILKINSON, DIRECTOR, GRADUATE MANAGEMENT PROGRAMS
100 INSTITUTE ROAD, WORCESTER, MA 01609 UNITED STATES
PHONE: 508-831-5218 • FAX: 508-831-5720
E-MAIL: GMP@WPI.EDU • WEBSITE: WWW.MGT.WPI.EDU

## Student Life and Environment

"WPI has tons of programs going on during the week and weekend and is a great place for students to kick back and relax or go out with friends," MBAs tell us, although they also report that the majority—made up of part-time and distance-learning students—spend little time on campus. Those who do stick around after class tell us that "WPI recognizes that students need options and must escape from academics occasionally. As a result, the school offers programs to intrigue the mind or engage the student in something different. Students enjoy meeting new students and doing new and exciting things while at WPI (one student learned to juggle and play the flute in addition to learning about chemistry instruments). There are millions of clubs and intramural sports that students can enjoy as well as opportunities to do independent or team research. The opportunities are plentiful."

Hometown Worcester "is a great city that has much historical charm and is up-and-coming in terms of modern development." The city (population approximately 175,000) is home to nine colleges and universities, and it supports an active arts community and a number of fine restaurants. Boston, New England's largest city, "is only a 45 to 60-minute commute away, and WPI offers transportation to those without cars."

## Admissions

WPI's website states: "In keeping with our focus on the management of technology, we look for candidates who have a high likelihood of success in a challenging, technology-focused management program, based on their academic and professional records. Applicants should have the analytic aptitude and academic preparation necessary to complete a technology-oriented management program. This includes a minimum of three semesters of college-level math or two semesters of college-level calculus. Applicants are also required to have an understanding of computer systems." The admissions office requires applicants to provide official transcripts from all previously attended undergraduate and graduate institutions, GMAT scores (GRE acceptable for master of science and certificate programs), TOEFL scores (where appropriate), a personal statement, and three letters of recommendation. The Department of Management "works closely with WPI's Office of Diversity & Women's Programs to recruit qualified minority students" and recruits through NSBE and SWE.

### FINANCIAL FACTS

| | |
|---|---|
| Annual tuition | $23,055 |
| Fees | $85 |
| Books and supplies | $1,100 |
| Room & board | $8,100 |
| % of students receiving aid | 50 |
| % of first-year students receiving aid | 50 |
| % of students receiving loans | 33 |
| % of students receiving grants | 50 |
| Average award package | $4,800 |
| Average grant | $34,140 |

### ADMISSIONS

| | |
|---|---|
| Admissions Selectivity Rating | 78 |
| # of applications received | 52 |
| % applicants accepted | 87 |
| % acceptees attending | 76 |
| Average GMAT | 608 |
| Range of GMAT | 560–660 |
| Average GPA | 3.23 |
| TOEFL required of international students? | yes |
| Minimum TOEFL (paper/computer) | 550/213 |
| Application fee | $70 |
| International application fee | $70 |
| Regular application deadline | 8/1 |
| Regular notification | rolling |
| Deferment available? | yes |
| Maximum length of deferment | 1 year |
| Transfer students accepted? | yes |
| Transfer application policy Accepted transfer applicants may transfer in up to 9 prior graduate-level credits toward the WPI MBA. | |
| Non-fall admissions? | yes |
| Need-blind admissions? | yes |

### APPLICANTS ALSO LOOK AT
Babson College, Bentley College, Boston College, Boston University, Massachusetts Institute of Technology, Northeastern University, University of Massachusetts—Amherst

### EMPLOYMENT PROFILE

| Career Rating | 93 | Grads employed by field: | % | avg. salary: |
|---|---|---|---|---|
| Primary source of full-time job acceptances | | Marketing | 20 | $90,000 |
| | | Operations | 20 | $102,000 |
| School-facilitated activities | 1 (17%) | Consulting | 40 | $83,000 |
| Graduate-facilitated activities | 4 (66%) | General Management | 20 | $65,000 |
| Unknown | 1 (17%) | | | |
| Average starting salary | $84,600 | | | |
| Percent employed | 83 | | | |

# XAVIER UNIVERSITY
## WILLIAMS COLLEGE OF BUSINESS

## GENERAL INFORMATION
| | |
|---|---|
| Type of school | private |
| Affiliation | Roman Catholic/Jesuit |
| Environment | metropolis |
| Academic calendar | semester |

## SURVEY SAYS...
Friendly students
Happy students
Smart classrooms
*Solid preparation in:*
Communication/interpersonal skills

## STUDENTS
| | |
|---|---|
| Enrollment of parent institution | 6,665 |
| Enrollment of business school | 823 |
| % male/female | 70/30 |
| % out-of-state | 11 |
| % part-time | 81 |
| % minorities | 22 |
| % international | 11 |
| Average age at entry | 29 |
| Average years work experience at entry | 8 |

## ACADEMICS
| | |
|---|---|
| **Academic Experience Rating** | **76** |
| Student/faculty ratio | 16:1 |
| Profs interesting rating | 79 |
| Profs accessible rating | 76 |
| % female faculty | 34 |
| % minority faculty | 17 |

## JOINT DEGREES
MBA/MHSA, 3 years; MBA/MSN, 3 years

## PROMINENT ALUMNI
George Schaefer, President/CEO, Fifth Third Bancorp; Robert J. Kohlhepp, CEO, Cintas Corp.; Ken Lucas, US Congressman; Carlos Alcantara, President of International Penzoil-Quaker State; Lloyd Ward, President, US Olympic Committee

## Academics

The MBA programs at Xavier University's Williams College of Business "are geared toward the working professional," so much so, in fact, that one of its MBA programs is called "the working professional's evening MBA." Other programs—the weekend MBA and the executive MBA, for example—all are designed with the busy professional in mind.

Consider the executive MBA program, for example, which students tell us "is very well run; Xavier even relieves all administrative tasks for their XMBA students. They prepare packages and provide the textbooks for each class in the classroom prior to our arrival. Lunch is provided in the lobby of the business school building. Generally speaking, our only task at Xavier is to learn, as opposed to worrying about things such as getting parking permits." Writes one enrollee, "When someone like me is working full-time, raising a family, and trying to further my education at the same time, the assistance and support that Xavier gives is wonderful."

Xavier professors "are aware that students work full-time and are both accommodating and understanding about missing class for a business trip. All they ask is that you keep up with the work and learn what you missed, and to be told of conflicts in advance. They are terrific about sticking to their syllabi so students can schedule business trips around exams and presentations." The faculty is praised as "no nonsense. We learn what's important in today's markets and today's businesses rather than wasting collaborative time hashing out the past. The foundations (or the past) are important to know, but the expectation is that you will read and learn about that to prepare for classroom discussions about the present. I like the format because it makes you think more and challenges the professors to keep learning right alongside the students." Students also brag that "the adjunct professors that the university utilizes are a tremendous asset to the overall knowledge gained at the university. It is essential to the education of any MBA student to be taught by someone who works 40 to 50 hours a week in the subject material that they are teaching."

Xavier offers concentrations in six areas: e-business, finance, general business, international business, management-information systems, and marketing. MBAs warn that "the workload is demanding, but you really get a lot out of the program, and it's a very enjoyable experience."

## Career and Placement

In January 2004, the Xavier MBA program introduced Corporate Connections, an office dedicated to assist Williams College of Business MBA students and alumni by providing students with the opportunities to network with employers and with one another, as well as serving as a link between the Williams MBA student population and the corporate community. Many students are here to enhance their positions at their current place of employment, and therefore have no need for the CLDO. Those who are seeking employment tell us that Xavier's greatest asset is its local reputation with employers. One student writes, "It gets great respect within the Cincinnati area. People are very impressed when I say 'I am an MBA student at Xavier.'"

Employers who have visited the campus this year include: Cinergy Corporation, Deloitte Touche Tohmatsu, Kforce, Merrill Lynch, Northwestern Mutual, Novartis, Resources Global Professionals, RLG Associates, State Farm, and U.S. Bank.

JENNIFER BUSH, DIRECTOR, MBA ENROLLMENT SERVICES
3800 VICTORY PARKWAY, CINCINNATI, OH 45207 UNITED STATES
PHONE: 513-754-3525 • FAX: 513-745-2929
E-MAIL: XUMBA@XAVIER.EDU • WEBSITE: WWW.XAVIER.EDU/MBA

## Student Life and Environment

Xavier's MBA program serves "mostly working people who come to class then leave. Most have little time to enjoy the campus and its offerings." The few extracurricular activities they participate in include "local activities with local companies, clubs, and lots of networking opportunities." Some students stick around after class to participate in study groups, "then go out together to a restaurant or bar."

Cincinnati "is home to some of the greatest employers around: Procter & Gamble, Cintas Corporation, Fifth Third Bancorp, General Electric, Kroger, GE, and Toyota. These companies play a key role in speaking on job placement, and direction within the MBA program." The Cincinnati metropolitan region is home to about two million people, large enough to support thriving arts, sports, and commercial scenes.

Xavier University, students report, "has changed for the better over the last 10 years. The university has undergone a number of construction projects that have beautified the campus. I feel as though this has contributed positively to the overall enrollment at the school. More people are selecting Xavier as their school of choice than ever before." Students love the fact that "the school is small, the campus is pretty and well-maintained, and classrooms, student lounges, and restrooms are always very clean." They also appreciate how "everyone is nice to everyone here, no matter their age, color, race, religion, or sex. Everyone is an equal."

## Admissions

Applicants to Xavier's MBA programs must submit official copies of all academic transcripts, GMAT scores, and a resume. Students with GMAT scores below 400, or quantitative scores below the 25th percentile, are not considered for admission. Work experience is highly recommended but not required for the full-time and working professional MBA programs; the average applicant has eight years work experience. For the executive MBA (XMBA), however, candidates must be employed full-time at the time they enter the program and have a significant managerial and leadership experience in middle and upper levels of corporation.

### FINANCIAL FACTS

| | |
|---|---|
| Annual tuition | $10,800 |
| Books and supplies | $900 |
| % of students receiving loans | 26 |
| % of students receiving grants | 47 |
| Average grant | $676 |

### ADMISSIONS

| | |
|---|---|
| **Admissions Selectivity Rating** | **74** |
| # of applications received | 544 |
| % applicants accepted | 74 |
| % acceptees attending | 71 |
| Average GMAT | 540 |
| Range of GMAT | 490–580 |
| Average GPA | 3.2 |
| TOEFL required of international students? | yes |
| Minimum TOEFL (paper/computer) | 550/213 |
| Application fee | $35 |
| International application fee | $35 |
| Deferment available? | yes |
| Maximum length of deferment | 1 year |
| Transfer students accepted? | yes |
| Transfer application policy 6 hours of core curriculum from an AACSB-accredited programs only. Up to 18 hours of core curriculum from AACSB-accredited Jesuit MBA network schools. | |
| Non-fall admissions? | yes |
| Need-blind admissions? | yes |

### APPLICANTS ALSO LOOK AT

Miami University, Northern Kentucky University, University of Cincinnati

## EMPLOYMENT PROFILE

| Career Rating | 82 | Grads employed by field: | % | avg. salary: |
|---|---|---|---|---|
| Average starting salary | $70,961 | Accounting | 4 | $55,000 |
| | | Finance | 19 | $51,000 |
| | | Human Resources | 8 | $35,000 |
| | | Marketing | 4 | $55,000 |
| | | MIS | 12 | $70,000 |
| | | Operations | 19 | $83,000 |
| | | Strategic Planning | 8 | $45,000 |
| | | Communications | 4 | $35,000 |
| | | Entrepreneurship | 4 | $75,000 |
| | | Quantitative | 4 | $55,000 |
| | | Other | 14 | $72,500 |

# YALE UNIVERSITY
## SCHOOL OF MANAGEMENT

## Academics

Although Yale the institution has been around centuries longer than its business school, the school owes its reputation (and its name) to a businessman named Elihu Yale, who made the school's first large donation in 1717. And ever since Yale's School of Management was founded in 1974, the school has been eager to acknowledge its debt to a captain of industry. The School of Management is well-integrated into the university as a whole, and students say, "being part of one of the world's most renowned universities has given me access to unparalleled intellectual experiences." One student says, "I met Joe Stiglitz (Nobel Prize in Economics) at a globalization conference. On Friday, I am attending a talk by Bill Clinton." And more recently, students have encountered George Soros and New York mayor Michael Bloomberg. Students report that this kind of jam-packed and challenging schedule is exactly what you should expect. Another student says, "So far this week I've prepared and presented the marketing strategy for a new medication to senior execs from two major pharmaceutical companies in a case competition, organized an alumni event in New York to improve networking opportunities, had beers with friends after hockey practice, and attended class with the former CEO of Medtronic where we discussed authentic leadership in modern business. It's been a busy week, and it's only Wednesday night!"

According to most, Yale's "program is very quantitative. It attracts many finance and nonprofit gurus." Some students complain that the first year, which consists entirely of core courses, is "much too theoretical," but others see that as a strength. They say, "we spend our time learning fundamental theory instead of business fads, and while this may not give us an advantage during recruiting, our knowledge will stand the test of time and give us an advantage over the course of our career." The "professors are incredible, especially in finance, strategy, game theory, and statistics." They "make themselves totally available. There are more than enough study sessions and TA office hours to ask questions, and my classmates with more experience in these areas are enthusiastic about helping me get to the same level as themselves."

Yale students can also opt for joint degrees in any of the following areas: an MBA/JD with Yale Law School, an MBA/MEM or MF with Yale School of Forestry and Environmental Studies, an MBA/MPH with Yale School of Public Health, an MBA/MD with Yale School of Medicine, an MBA/MArch with Yale School of Architecture, an MBA/MFA with Yale School of Drama, an MBA/MDIV or MAR with Yale Divinity School. The school also offers an MBA/MA in any of the following areas of international studies: International Relations, and Russian and East European studies. Additionally, an MBA/PhD with the Yale Graduate School of Arts and Sciences is now offered.

## Career and Placement

Unlike most schools, Yale has a career-service program that more or less gets the approval of its students. Students call it "extremely supportive," and say it "provides one-on-one attention." Some students qualify this by saying it could work on "attracting firms other than banks and management-consulting firms for recruiting." Students also point out that "being close to NYC and Boston is ideal for short trip to interview and visit for jobs and internships." They also appreciate the internship fund, which "provides summer stipends for students taking unpaid or low-paid internships with 501-C3 nonprofits. It is totally student run!"

ANNE COYLE, DIRECTOR OF ADMISSIONS
135 PROSPECT STREET, PO BOX 208200, NEW HAVEN, CT 06520-8200 UNITED STATES
PHONE: 203-432-5932 • FAX: 203-432-7004
E-MAIL: MBA.ADMISSIONS@YALE.EDU • WEBSITE: WWW.MBA.YALE.EDU

Another strength is the alumni network. One student says, "The alumni network I graduate into will be one where strong connections are felt amongst its members due to the unique close-knit atmosphere the school provides. On top of that, I will have the power of the Yale name to help me in my career pursuits."

Companies that regularly recruit on campus include Bear Stearns, Citigroup, Credit Suisse First Boston, Deutsche Bank AG, Goldman Sachs, American Express, Lehman Brothers, Dupont, JPMorgan Chase, Morgan Stanley, Procter & Gamble, IBM, and Intel Corporation

## Student Life and Environment

"Yale goes out of its way to make quality of life important for its students. They definitely encourage a sense of community through weekly happy hours and social events to get peoples' minds off the academic demands. There are fun student groups like the wine club, and many recreational sports groups, like rowing or hockey. Everyone is encouraged to participate, regardless of experience." MBAs don't have Friday classes, "so every Thursday at 4:00, the Social Committee brings in a keg (or two) and everyone hangs out in the courtyard and socializes. On Tuesday nights, a number of SOMers can be found at Anna Liffey's playing in the trivia competition and downing some Guinness. Recently, more than 40 students spent a day touring local wineries together on the 'Wine SIG Party Bus.' There are also plenty of parties, Thursday nights at GPSCY, martinis downtown, symphony, and theater—plenty of social opportunities for those who are interested in getting out of the house."

Apart from their superb skills with a keg, however, Yale's MBAs are also praised for their "incredibly high ethical standards. Students are socially responsible but not in-your-face about it." Students are said to be very "active in the community, offering pro bono consulting services to local nonprofits."

Most students agree, however, that the facilities could stand improvement—they're too old and too cold. Another common gripe involves the long distance to the gym.

## Admissions

When selecting the 250-odd students who will eventually make up their class, the admissions board at Yale's SOM "seeks a rich, highly interactive community in which students stimulate each other to grow, both intellectually and professionally. The school looks for students from a broad range of backgrounds and with widely differing experiences." In the class of 2005, the average GMAT score was 683, and the average college GPA was 3.42. The entering minimum TOEFL score required for admission is a 600 (paper-based).

### PROMINENT ALUMNI

John Thornton, Former Co-COO & President, Goldman Sachs; Nancy Peretsman, Managing Director, Allen & Company; Indra Nooyi, President & CFO, PepsiCo Inc.; Fred Terrell, Managing Partner & CEO, Provender Capital Group; Timothy Collins, CEO & Senior Managing Director, Ripplewood Holding

### FINANCIAL FACTS

| | |
|---|---|
| Annual tuition | $36,800 |
| Fees | $1,515 |
| Books and supplies | $7,200 |
| Room & board | $12,000 |
| % of students receiving aid | 76 |
| % of first-year students receiving aid | 79 |
| % of students receiving loans | 74 |
| % of students receiving grants | 37 |
| Average award package | $29,075 |
| Average grant | $10,575 |
| Average student loan debt | $68,429 |

### ADMISSIONS

| | |
|---|---|
| Admissions Selectivity Rating | 96 |
| # of applications received | 2,033 |
| % applicants accepted | 28 |
| % acceptees attending | 37 |
| Average GMAT | 683 |
| Range of GMAT | 650–710 |
| Average GPA | 3.42 |
| TOEFL required of international students? | yes |
| Minimum TOEFL (paper/computer) | 600/250 |
| Application fee | $180 |
| Regular application deadline | 3/15 |
| Regular notification | 5/19 |
| Application deadline/notification | |
| Round 1: | 10/26 / 1/20 |
| Round 2: | 1/11 / 3/31 |
| Round 3: | 3/15 / 5/19 |
| Deferment available? | yes |
| Maximum length of deferment | 1 year |
| Need-blind admissions? | yes |

### APPLICANTS ALSO LOOK AT

Harvard University, University of Pennsylvania

### EMPLOYMENT PROFILE

| Career Rating | 95 | Grads employed by field: | % | avg. salary: |
|---|---|---|---|---|
| Average starting salary | $89,527 | Finance | 40 | $90,274 |
| Percent employed | 89 | Marketing | 10 | $83,647 |
| | | Consulting | 9 | $96,211 |
| | | General Management | 9 | $90,058 |
| | | Other | 32 | $87,778 |

# Part III-B
# Business School Data
# Listings

# Arizona State University— Global Management

## School of Global Management & Leadership

*Admissions Contact:* MBA Admissions
*Address:* PO Box 37100, Phoenix, AZ 85069-7100
*Phone:* 602-543-6201 • *Fax:* 602-543-6249
*E-mail:* MBAINFO@ASU.EDU
*Website:* WWW.WEST.ASU.EDU/SGML/MBA

### GENERAL INFORMATION

**Type of School:** public **Environment:** metropolis **Academic Calendar:** semester

### STUDENTS

**Enrollment of business school:** 315 **% part-time:** 100 **Average age at entry:** 33 **Average years work experience at entry:** 9

### ACADEMICS

**Student/faculty ratio:** 20:1 **% female faculty** 29 **% minority faculty** 12 **Joint Degrees:** MBA/MIM jointly offered with Thunderbird, 3 years

### FINANCIAL FACTS

**% of students receiving aid:** 20 **% of first-year students receiving aid:** 5

### ADMISSIONS

**Admissions Selectivity Rating:** 78

**# of applications received:** 139 **% applicants accepted:** 81 **% acceptees attending:** 71 **GMAT Range (25th to 75th percentile):** 500-700 **Average GMAT:** 590 **Average GPA:** 3.5 **TOEFL required of int'l applicants?** yes **Minimum TOEFL (paper/computer):** 600/250 **Application Fee:** $50 **Deferment Available?** yes **Maximum length of deferment:** 1 semester **Transfer Students Accepted?** yes **Non-fall Admissions?** yes **Need-Blind Admissions?** yes **Applicants also look at:** Arizona State University, Northern Arizona University, University of Arizona

### EMPLOYMENT PROFILE

| Grads employed by field: | ..........% |
| --- | --- |
| Accounting | 6 |
| Finance | 15 |
| Human Resources | 1 |
| Marketing | 20 |
| MIS | 6 |
| Operations | 24 |
| Strategic Planning | 1 |
| Consulting | 6 |
| Communications | 1 |
| General Management | 7 |
| Other | 10 |

# Arkansas State University

## College of Business

*Admissions Contact:* Dr. Thomas Wheeler, Dean, Graduate School
*Address:* PO Box 60, State University, AR 72467
*Phone:* 870-972-3029 • *Fax:* 870-972-3857
*E-mail:* GRADSCH@CHOCTAW.ASTATE.EDU
*Website:* HTTP://BUSINESS.ASTATE.EDU

### GENERAL INFORMATION

**Type of School:** public **Environment:** town **Academic Calendar:** semester

### STUDENTS

**Enrollment of business school:** 104

### ACADEMICS

**Student/faculty ratio:** 25:1 **% female faculty** 24 **% minority faculty** 1

### FINANCIAL FACTS

**Tuition (in-state/out-of-state):** $1,488/$3,744 **Books and supplies:** $2,100 **Room & board:** $3,500 **Average grant:** $6,427

### ADMISSIONS

**Admissions Selectivity Rating:** 60*

**# of applications received:** 53 **% applicants accepted:** 85 **% acceptees attending:** 80 **TOEFL required of int'l applicants?** yes **Minimum TOEFL (paper):** 550 **Regular Application Deadline:** rolling **Regular Notification:** rolling

# Ashridge (United Kingdom)

*Admissions Contact:* MBA Admissions
*Address:* Berkhamsted, Hertfordshire, HP4 1NS England
*Phone:* 001-44-1442-841142 • *Fax:* 001-44-1442-841144
*E-mail:* MBA@ASHRIDGE.ORG.UK
*Website:* WWW.ASHRIDGE.COM

### GENERAL INFORMATION

**Type of School:** private

### STUDENTS

### ACADEMICS

**Student/faculty ratio:** 1:1 **% female faculty** 26

### FINANCIAL FACTS

**Tuition:** $51,911 **Books and supplies:** $880 **Room & board (on/off campus):** $13,198/$17,597 **Average award package:** $50,000

### ADMISSIONS

**Admissions Selectivity Rating:** 60*

**GMAT Range (25th to 75th percentile):** 520-640 **Average GMAT:** 560 **Average GPA:** 1 **TOEFL required of int'l applicants?** yes

Minimum TOEFL (paper/computer): 600/250 **Regular Application Deadline:** 1/5 **Regular Notification:** 1/5 **Deferment Available?** yes **Maximum length of deferment:** 1 year **Non-fall Admissions?** yes

## EMPLOYMENT PROFILE

Grads employed by field: ..........%

Finance ............................................15
Marketing .........................................15
Operations.........................................20
Consulting.........................................10
General Management ....................10
Internet/New Media........................15
Other.................................................15

# AUGUSTA STATE UNIVERSITY
## COLLEGE OF BUSINESS ADMINISTRATION

**ADMISSIONS CONTACT:** MIYOKO JACKSON, DEGREE PROGRAM SPECIALIST **ADDRESS:** COLLEGE OF BUSINESS ADMINISTRATION MBA OFFICE, 2500 WALTON WAY, AUGUSTA, GA 30904-2200 **PHONE:** 706-737-1565 • **FAX:** 706-667-4064 **E-MAIL:** MBAINFO@AUG.EDU **WEBSITE:** WWW.AUG.EDU/COBA/

### GENERAL INFORMATION

**Type of School:** public **Environment:** village **Academic Calendar:** trimester

### STUDENTS

**Enrollment of parent institution:** 6,333 **Enrollment of business school:** 89 **% male/female:** 53/47 **% out-of-state:** 18 **% part-time:** 62 **% minorities:** 3 **% international:** 29 **Average age at entry:** 26 **Average years work experience at entry:** 4

### ACADEMICS

**Student/faculty ratio:** 11:1 **% female faculty** 42

### FINANCIAL FACTS

**Tuition (in-state/out-of-state):** $2,196/$8,784 **Fees:** $482 **Books and supplies:** $500 **Room & board (on/off campus):** $9,000/$9,500

### ADMISSIONS

**ADMISSIONS SELECTIVITY RATING: 77**

**# of applications received:** 33 **% applicants accepted:** 58 **% acceptees attending:** 79 **GMAT Range (25th to 75th percentile):** 450-590 **Average GMAT:** 520 **Average GPA:** 3.12 **TOEFL required of int'l applicants?** yes **Minimum TOEFL (paper/computer):** 550/213 **Application Fee:** $20 **International Application Fee:** $20 **Regular Application Deadline:** rolling **Regular Notification:** rolling **Deferment Available?** yes **Maximum length of deferment:** 1 year **Transfer Students Accepted?** yes **Non-fall Admissions?** yes

# BALL STATE UNIVERSITY
## MILLER COLLEGE OF BUSINESS

**ADMISSIONS CONTACT:** DR. INGA HILL, ASSISTANT TO THE DEAN FOR GRADUATE BUSINESS PROGRAMS **ADDRESS:** WB 147, MUNCIE, IN 47306 **PHONE:** 765-285-1931 • **FAX:** 765-285-8818 **E-MAIL:** MBA@BSU.EDU **WEBSITE:** WWW.BSU.EDU/MBA

### GENERAL INFORMATION

**Type of School:** public **Environment:** city **Academic Calendar:** semester

### STUDENTS

**Enrollment of parent institution:** 18,161 **Enrollment of business school:** 191 **% male/female:** 64/36 **% out-of-state:** 40 **% part-time:** 72 **% minorities:** 4 **% international:** 30 **Average age at entry:** 28 **Average years work experience at entry:** 5

### ACADEMICS

**Student/faculty ratio:** 30:1

### FINANCIAL FACTS

**Tuition (in-state/out-of-state):** $7,843/$19,851 **Fees:** $642 **Books and supplies:** $1,600 **Room & board (on/off campus):** $8,314/$8,000

### ADMISSIONS

**ADMISSIONS SELECTIVITY RATING: 69**

**# of applications received:** 50 **% applicants accepted:** 92 **% GMAT Range (25th to 75th percentile):** 460-630 **Average GMAT:** 556 **Average GPA:** 3.28 **TOEFL required of int'l applicants?** yes **Minimum TOEFL (paper/computer):** 550/213 **Application Fee:** $35 **International Application Fee:** $40 **Regular Application Deadline:** rolling **Regular Notification:** rolling **Deferment Available?** yes **Maximum length of deferment:** 2 years **Transfer Students Accepted?** yes **Non-fall Admissions?** yes **Need-Blind Admissions?** yes **Applicants also look at:** Butler University, Indiana University Kokomo, Indiana University-Purdue University at Fort Wayne, Indiana University-Purdue University Indianapolis

# BOCCONI UNIVERSITY
## SDA BOCCONI SCHOOL OF MANAGEMENT

**ADMISSIONS CONTACT:** ROSSANA CAMERA, ADMISSIONS OFFICER **ADDRESS:** VIA BALILLA 18, MILANO, 20136 ITALY **PHONE:** 0039-0258363297 • **FAX:** 0039-0258363272 **E-MAIL:** ADMISSIONS@SDABOCCONI.IT **WEBSITE:** WWW.SDABOCCONI.IT

### GENERAL INFORMATION

**Type of School:** private

## STUDENTS

Enrollment of business school: 269 **% male/female:** 73/27 **% part-time:** 45 **% international:** 50 **Average age at entry:** 29 **Average years work experience at entry:** 5

## FINANCIAL FACTS

**Tuition (in-state/out-of-state):** $38,452/$38,452 **Fees (in-state/out-of-state):** $38,452/$38,452 **Room & board:** $1,564

## ADMISSIONS

**ADMISSIONS SELECTIVITY RATING: 60\***

**# of applications received:** 410 **% applicants accepted:** 35 **% acceptees attending:** 80 **TOEFL required of int'l applicants?** yes **Minimum TOEFL (paper/computer):** 600/250 **Application Fee:** $120 **International Application Fee:** $120 **Regular Application Deadline:** 4/28 **Regular Notification:** rolling **Deferment Available?** yes **Maximum length of deferment:** 2 years **Applicants also look at:** IESE Business School, Institute of Undergraduate Business Studies, Instituto de Empresa, London Business School

# BOISE STATE UNIVERSITY
## COLLEGE OF BUSINESS AND ECONOMICS

**ADMISSIONS CONTACT:** J. RENEE ANCHUSTEGUI, PROGRAMS ADMINISTRATOR
**ADDRESS:** BUSINESS GRADUATE STUDIES, 1910 UNIVERSITY DRIVE B318, BOISE, ID 83725-1600
**PHONE:** 208-426-1126 • **FAX:** 208-426-1135
**E-MAIL:** RANCHUST@BOISESTATE.EDU
**WEBSITE:** HTTP://COBE.BOISESTATE.EDU/GRADUATE

## GENERAL INFORMATION

**Type of School:** public **Environment:** city

## STUDENTS

**Enrollment of parent institution:** 17,883 **Enrollment of business school:** 122 **% male/female:** 57/43 **% out-of-state:** 40 **% part-time:** 82 **% minorities:** 1 **% international:** 17 **Average age at entry:** 32 **Average years work experience at entry:** 6.4

## ACADEMICS

**Student/faculty ratio:** 30:1 **% female faculty** 11 **% minority faculty** 5 **Prominent Alumni:** Jan Packwood, President & COO, Idaho Power Co.; William Glynn, President, Intermountain Gas; Steve Heyl, VP Strategic Planning, Arby's; Norm Schlachter, VP Finance, Micron Technology; Mary Schofield, Controller, Boise Division, Hewlett-Packard

## FINANCIAL FACTS

**Tuition (out-of-state):** $7,408 **Fees:** $5,530 **Books and supplies:** $2,000 **Room & board (on/off campus):** $6,800/$7,200 **% of students receiving aid:** 20 **% of first-year students receiving aid:** 12 **% of students receiving loans:** 10 **% of students receiving grants:** 11 **Average grant:** $17,420 **Average student loan debt:** $12,000

## ADMISSIONS

**ADMISSIONS SELECTIVITY RATING: 89**

**# of applications received:** 120 **% applicants accepted:** 42 **% acceptees attending:** 70 **GMAT Range (25th to 75th percentile):** 530-640 **Average GMAT:** 585 **Average GPA:** 3.3 **TOEFL required of int'l applicants?** yes **Minimum TOEFL (paper/computer):** 587/240 **Application Fee:** $55 **International Application Fee:** $55 **Regular Application Deadline:** 6/1 **Regular Notification:** rolling **Early decision program?** yes **ED deadline /notification:** Fall 2/15; Spring 8/1 / 3/15 **Deferment Available?** yes **Maximum length of deferment:** 1 year **Transfer Students Accepted?** yes **Non-fall Admissions?** yes **Need-Blind Admissions?** yes **Applicants also look at:** University of Minnesota

## EMPLOYMENT PROFILE

**Primary source of full-time job acceptances**

Unknown.......................................16 (100%)

**Average starting salary:** $53,330

**Percent employed:** 90

| Grads employed by field: | .........% | avg. salary: |
|---|---|---|
| Accounting | 19 | $67,667 |
| Finance | 25 | $37,500 |
| Marketing | 6 | $41,000 |
| Operations | 6 | $60,000 |
| Consulting | 6 | $58,000 |
| General Management | 19 | $49,250 |
| Nonprofit | 6 | $42,000 |
| Other | 13 | $85,000 |

# BRADLEY UNIVERSITY
## FOSTER COLLEGE OF BUSINESS ADMINISTRATION

**ADMISSIONS CONTACT:** DR. EDWARD SATTLER, DIRECTOR OF GRADUATE PROGRAMS
**ADDRESS:** BAKER HALL, PEORIA, IL 61625
**PHONE:** 309-677-2253 • **FAX:** 309-677-3374
**E-MAIL:** ADE@BRADLEY.EDU
**WEBSITE:** WWW.BRADLEY.EDU/FCBA/INDEX.HTML

## GENERAL INFORMATION

**Type of School:** private **Environment:** city **Academic Calendar:** semester

## FINANCIAL FACTS

**Tuition:** $8,832 **Fees:** $15 **Books and supplies:** $700

## ADMISSIONS

**ADMISSIONS SELECTIVITY RATING: 60\***

**# of applications received:** 47 **% applicants accepted:** 100 **% acceptees attending:** 57 **TOEFL required of int'l applicants?** yes **Minimum TOEFL (paper):** 500 **Application Fee:** $50 **Regular**

Application Deadline: rolling **Regular Notification:** rolling
**Deferment Available?** yes **Maximum length of deferment:** 1 year
**Non-fall Admissions?** yes **Need-Blind Admissions?** yes **Applicants
also look at:** Illinois State University, University of Phoenix Online

# BRYANT UNIVERSITY
## SCHOOL OF GRADUATE STUDIES

**ADMISSIONS CONTACT:** KRISTOPHER SULLIVAN, DIRECTOR OF GRADUATE STUDIES
**ADDRESS:** 1150 DOUGLAS PIKE, SMITHFIELD, RI 02917-1284
**PHONE:** 401-232-6230 • **FAX:** 401-232-6494
**E-MAIL:** GRADPROG@BRYANT.EDU
**WEBSITE:** WWW.BRYANT.EDU

### GENERAL INFORMATION
**Type of School:** private **Environment:** town **Academic Calendar:**
semester

### STUDENTS
**Enrollment of parent institution:** 3,642 **Enrollment of business
school:** 339 **% male/female:** 44/56 **% part-time:** 90 **% minorities:**
12 **% international:** 24 **Average age at entry:** 27 **Average years
work experience at entry:** 6

### ACADEMICS
**Student/faculty ratio:** 20:1 **% female faculty** 19 **% minority faculty**
17 **Joint Degrees:** MBA with a concentration in computer informa-
tion systems and MSIS, 54 to 66 credits, 7 years to complete both
programs **Prominent Alumni:** David M. Beirne, General Partner,
Benchmark Capital Partners; William J. Conaty, Senior VP, General
Electric; Robert P. Mead, President, Tyco Engineered Products &
Services; Thomas Taylor, President & CEO, Amica Insurance;
Kristian P. Moor, Executive VP, Domestic General Insurance.

### FINANCIAL FACTS
**Books and supplies:** $1,200 **Room & board:** $9,000

### ADMISSIONS
**ADMISSIONS SELECTIVITY RATING: 73**
**# of applications received:** 119 **% applicants accepted:** 69 **%
acceptees attending:** 71 **GMAT Range (25th to 75th percentile):**
410-630 **Average GMAT:** 515 **Average GPA:** 3.0 **TOEFL required of
int'l applicants?** yes **Minimum TOEFL (paper/computer):** 580/237
**Application Fee:** $60 **International Application Fee:** $80 **Regular
Application Deadline:** 7/15 **Regular Notification:** rolling **Deferment
Available?** yes **Maximum length of deferment:** 1 year **Transfer
Students Accepted?** yes **Non-fall Admissions?** yes **Need-Blind
Admissions?** yes **Applicants also look at:** Babson College, Bentley
College, Suffolk University, University of Rhode Island

# CALIFORNIA STATE UNIVERSITY— BAKERSFIELD
## SCHOOL OF BUSINESS AND PUBLIC ADMINISTRATION

**ADMISSIONS CONTACT:** DEBBIE BLOWERS, EVALUATIONS
**ADDRESS:** 9001 STOCKDALE HIGHWAY, BAKERSFIELD, CA 93311-1099
**PHONE:** 661-664-3036 • **FAX:** 661-664-3389
**E-MAIL:** ADMISSIONS@CSUB.EDU
**WEBSITE:** WWW.CSUBAK.EDU/BPA/

### GENERAL INFORMATION
**Type of School:** public **Environment:** village **Academic Calendar:**
quarter

### STUDENTS
**Enrollment of parent institution:** 6,700 **Enrollment of business
school:** 84 **% male/female:** 33/67 **% part-time:** 86 **% minorities:**
25 **% international:** 25 **Average age at entry:** 32

### ACADEMICS
**Student/faculty ratio:** 17:1 **% female faculty** 10 **% minority faculty**
10

### FINANCIAL FACTS
**Tuition (in-state/out-of-state):** $2,126/$6,646 **Books and supplies:**
$2,200 **Room & board (on/off campus):** $4,950/$7,679

### ADMISSIONS
**ADMISSIONS SELECTIVITY RATING: 88**
**# of applications received:** 80 **% applicants accepted:** 28 **%
acceptees attending:** 73 **GMAT Range (25th to 75th percentile):**
490-570 **Average GMAT:** 530 **Average GPA:** 3.3 **TOEFL required of
int'l applicants?** yes **Minimum TOEFL (paper):** 550 **Application
Fee:** $55 **Regular Application Deadline:** rolling **Regular
Notification:** rolling **Non-fall Admissions?** yes

# CALIFORNIA STATE UNIVERSITY— LOS ANGELES
## COLLEGE OF BUSINESS AND ECONOMICS

**ADMISSIONS CONTACT:** JOAN WOOSLEY, ADMISSIONS OFFICER
**ADDRESS:** 5151 STATE UNIVERSITY DRIVE, LOS ANGELES, CA 90032
**PHONE:** 323-343-3904 • **FAX:** 323-343-6306
**E-MAIL:** ADMISSIONS@CALSTATELA.EDU
**WEBSITE:** HTTP://CBE.CALSTATELA.EDU/

### GENERAL INFORMATION
**Type of School:** public **Environment:** city **Academic Calendar:** quarter

## STUDENTS

**Enrollment of parent institution:** 18,849 **Enrollment of business school:** 330 **% male/female:** 47/53 **% part-time:** 100 **% minorities:** 50 **Average age at entry:** 31

## FINANCIAL FACTS

**Tuition (in-state/out-of-state):** $1,796/$5,732

## ADMISSIONS

**ADMISSIONS SELECTIVITY RATING:** 84

**# of applications received:** 388 **% applicants accepted:** 43 **% acceptees attending:** 52 **Average GMAT:** 560 **Average GPA:** 3.0 **TOEFL required of int'l applicants?** yes **Minimum TOEFL (paper/computer):** 550/213 **Application Fee:** $55 **Regular Application Deadline:** 6/15 **Regular Notification:** 1/1 **Non-fall Admissions?** yes

# CALIFORNIA STATE UNIVERSITY— NORTHRIDGE
## COLLEGE OF BUSINESS AND ECONOMICS

**ADMISSIONS CONTACT:** RON ANDRADE, ASSISTANT DIRECTOR OF GRADUATE PROGRAMS
**ADDRESS:** 18111 NORDHOFF STREET, NORTHRIDGE, CA 91330-8380
**PHONE:** 818-677-2467 • **FAX:** 818-677-3188
**E-MAIL:** MBA@CSUN.EDU
**WEBSITE:** HTTP://CSUN.EDU/MBA

## GENERAL INFORMATION

**Type of School:** public **Environment:** city **Academic Calendar:** semester

## STUDENTS

**Enrollment of parent institution:** 30,000 **Enrollment of business school:** 275 **% male/female:** 50/50 **% minorities:** 50 **Average age at entry:** 29 **Average years work experience at entry:** 7

## ACADEMICS

**Student/faculty ratio:** 22:1 **% female faculty** 18 **% minority faculty** 6

## FINANCIAL FACTS

**Fees:** $3,618 **Books and supplies:** $1,300 **Room & board:** $9,328

## ADMISSIONS

**ADMISSIONS SELECTIVITY RATING:** 91

**# of applications received:** 249 **% applicants accepted:** 30 **% acceptees attending:** 73 **Average GMAT:** 552 **Average GPA:** 3.2 **TOEFL required of int'l applicants?** yes **Minimum TOEFL (paper/computer):** 550/213 **Application Fee:** $55 **International Application Fee:** $55 **Regular Application Deadline:** 5/1 **Regular Notification:** rolling **Deferment Available?** yes **Maximum length of deferment:** 1 semester **Transfer Students Accepted?** yes **Non-fall Admissions?** yes **Need-Blind Admissions?** yes

# CALIFORNIA STATE UNIVERSITY— SACRAMENTO
## COLLEGE OF BUSINESS ADMINISTRATION

**ADMISSIONS CONTACT:** JEANIE ALLAM, GRADUATE PROGRAM ACADEMIC COUNSELOR
**ADDRESS:** 6000 J STREET, SACRAMENTO, CA 95819-6088
**PHONE:** 916-278-6772 • **FAX:** 916-278-4233
**E-MAIL:** CBAGRAD@CSUS.EDU
**WEBSITE:** WWW.CSUS.EDU/CBAGRAD/INDEX.HTML

## GENERAL INFORMATION

**Type of School:** public **Environment:** metropolis **Academic Calendar:** semester

## STUDENTS

**Enrollment of parent institution:** 28,375 **Enrollment of business school:** 311 **% male/female:** 56/44 **% part-time:** 63 **% minorities:** 49 **% international:** 10 **Average age at entry:** 30 **Average years work experience at entry:** 3

## ACADEMICS

**Student/faculty ratio:** 13:1 **% female faculty** 28 **Joint Degrees:** MBA/JD with McGeorge School of Law, 4.5 years needed to complete combined program **Prominent Alumni:** Dennis Gardemeyer, Executive VP, Zuckerman-Hertog; Tom Weborg, CEO, Cucina Holdings; William Keever, President/Vodafone Airtouch; Margo Murray, President, CEO, MMHA The Mangers' Mentors Inc.; Scott Syphax, President, CEO, Nehemiah Corporation.

## FINANCIAL FACTS

**Tuition (in-state/out-of-state):** $3,310/$9,160 **Books and supplies:** $1,700 **Room & board (on/off campus):** $9,400/$8,400

## ADMISSIONS

**ADMISSIONS SELECTIVITY RATING:** 81

**# of applications received:** 247 **% applicants accepted:** 61 **% acceptees attending:** 66 **GMAT Range (25th to 75th percentile):** 420-750 **Average GMAT:** 575 **Average GPA:** 3.1 **TOEFL required of int'l applicants?** yes **Minimum TOEFL (paper/computer):** 550/213 **Application Fee:** $55 **International Application Fee:** $55 **Regular Application Deadline:** 4/1 **Regular Notification:** 5/30 **Transfer Students Accepted?** yes **Non-fall Admissions?** yes **Need-Blind Admissions?** yes

# CANISIUS COLLEGE
## RICHARD J. WEHLE SCHOOL OF BUSINESS

**ADMISSIONS CONTACT:** LAURA MCEWEN, DIRECTOR, GRADUATE BUSINESS PROGRAMS
**ADDRESS:** CANISIUS COLLEGE, 2001 MAIN STREET, BAGEN HALL 201, BUFFALO, NY 14208-1098
**PHONE:** 716-888-2140 • **FAX:** 716-888-2145
**E-MAIL:** GRADUBUS@CANISIUS.EDU
**WEBSITE:** WWW.CANISIUS.EDU/MBA

### GENERAL INFORMATION
**Type of School:** private **Affiliation:** Roman Catholic-Jesuit **Environment:** metropolis **Academic Calendar:** semester

### STUDENTS
**Enrollment of parent institution:** 4,979 **Enrollment of business school:** 261 **% male/female:** 51/49 **% part-time:** 74 **% minorities:** 9 **% international:** 9 **Average age at entry:** 28

### ACADEMICS
**% female faculty** 13 **% minority faculty** 8 **Joint Degrees:** Bachelor and MBA, 5 years.

### FINANCIAL FACTS
**Tuition:** $31,942 **Books and supplies:** $1,000 **Room & board:** $8,100

### ADMISSIONS
**ADMISSIONS SELECTIVITY RATING: 60\***
**# GMAT Range (25th to 75th percentile):** 410-550 **Average GMAT:** 474 **TOEFL required of int'l applicants?** yes **Minimum TOEFL (paper/computer):** 500/200 **Application Fee:** $25 **Regular Application Deadline:** rolling **Regular Notification:** rolling **Deferment Available?** yes **Maximum length of deferment:** 1 year **Transfer Students Accepted?** yes **Non-fall Admissions?** yes **Applicants also look at:** The State University of New York

### EMPLOYMENT PROFILE
**Average starting salary:** $48,900


# CENTRAL MICHIGAN UNIVERSITY
## COLLEGE OF BUSINESS ADMINISTRATION

**ADMISSIONS CONTACT:** PAMELA STAMBERSKY, DIRECTOR OF GRADUATE PROGRAMS
**ADDRESS:** 105 WARRINER HALL, MOUNT PLEASANT, MI 48859
**PHONE:** 517-774-3150 • **FAX:** 517-774-2372
**E-MAIL:** CBAWORK@CMICH.EDU
**WEBSITE:** WWW.CBA.CMICH.EDU

### GENERAL INFORMATION
**Type of School:** public **Environment:** town **Academic Calendar:** semester

### STUDENTS
**Enrollment of parent institution:** 16,613 **Enrollment of business school:** 471 **% male/female:** 59/41 **% part-time:** 50 **% minorities:** 1 **% international:** 34 **Average age at entry:** 28

### ADMISSIONS
**ADMISSIONS SELECTIVITY RATING: 60\***
**# of applications received:** 151 **% applicants accepted:** 80 **TOEFL required of int'l applicants?** yes **Minimum TOEFL (paper):** 550 **Application Fee:** $30 **Regular Application Deadline:** rolling **Regular Notification:** rolling **Deferment Available?** yes


# CENTRAL MISSOURI STATE UNIVERSITY
## HARMON COLLEGE OF BUSINESS ADMINISTRATION

**ADMISSIONS CONTACT:** LAURIE DELAP, ADMISSIONS EVALUATOR, GRADUATE SCHOOL
**ADDRESS:** WARD EDWARDS 1800, WARRENSBURG, MO 64093
**PHONE:** 660-543-4328 • **FAX:** 660-543-4778
**E-MAIL:** DELAP@CMSU.EDU
**WEBSITE:** WWW.CMSU.EDU/GRADUATE

### GENERAL INFORMATION
**Type of School:** public **Environment:** rural **Academic Calendar:** semester

### STUDENTS
**Enrollment of parent institution:** 10,313 **Enrollment of business school:** 64 **% male/female:** 62/38 **% out-of-state:** 40 **% part-time:** 38 **% minorities:** 22 **% international:** 46 **Average age at entry:** 27 **Average years work experience at entry:** 2

### ACADEMICS
**Student/faculty ratio:** 2:1 **% female faculty** 29 **% minority faculty** 1

### FINANCIAL FACTS
**Tuition (in-state/out-of-state):** $5,496/$10,656 **Books and supplies:** $800 **Room & board:** $5,180 **% of students receiving grants:** 50

### ADMISSIONS
**ADMISSIONS SELECTIVITY RATING: 83**
**# of applications received:** 75 **% applicants accepted:** 40 **% acceptees attending:** 100 **GMAT Range (25th to 75th percentile):** 440-520 **Average GMAT:** 485 **Average GPA:** 3.28 **TOEFL required of int'l applicants?** yes **Minimum TOEFL (paper/computer):** 550/213 **Application Fee:** $30 **International Application Fee:** $50 **Regular Application Deadline:** rolling **Regular Notification:** rolling **Deferment Available?** yes **Maximum length of deferment:** 2 semesters **Transfer Students Accepted?** yes **Non-fall Admissions?** yes **Need-Blind Admissions?** yes **Applicants also look at:** Missouri State University (Formerly SW MSU), Southeast Missouri State University, University of Missouri—Kansas City

# CLARION UNIVERSITY
## COLLEGE OF BUSINESS ADMINISTRATION

*ADMISSIONS CONTACT:* DR. ROBERT S. BALOUGH, DIRECTOR OF MBA PROGRAM
*ADDRESS:* 302 STILL HALL, CLARION UNIVERSITY, CLARION, PA 16214
*PHONE:* 814-393-2605 • *FAX:* 814-393-1910
*E-MAIL:* MBA@CLARION.EDU
*WEBSITE:* WWW.CLARION.EDU/MBA

### GENERAL INFORMATION
**Type of School:** public **Environment:** rural **Academic Calendar:** semester

### STUDENTS
**Enrollment of parent institution:** 6,338 **Enrollment of business school:** 36 **% male/female:** 64/36 **% out-of-state:** 8 **% part-time:** 14 **% minorities:** 6 **% international:** 31 **Average age at entry:** 23 **Average years work experience at entry:** 6.3

### ACADEMICS
**female faculty** 18 **% minority faculty** 23

### FINANCIAL FACTS
**Tuition (in-state/out-of-state):** $5,888/$9,422 **Fees (in-state/out-of-state):** $1,778/$1,843 **Books and supplies:** $3,650 **Room & board (on/off campus):** $5,246/$4,000

### ADMISSIONS
**ADMISSIONS SELECTIVITY RATING:** 66

**# of applications received:** 36 **% applicants accepted:** 86 **% acceptees attending:** 65 **Average GMAT:** 489 **Average GPA:** 3.43 **TOEFL required of int'l applicants?** yes **Minimum TOEFL (paper/computer):** 550/213 **Application Fee:** $30 **International Application Fee:** $30 **Regular Application Deadline:** rolling **Regular Notification:** rolling **Deferment Available?** yes **Maximum length of deferment:** 1 year **Transfer Students Accepted?** yes **Non-fall Admissions?** yes **Need-Blind Admissions?** yes

# CLARK ATLANTA UNIVERSITY
## SCHOOL OF BUSINESS ADMINISTRATION

*ADMISSIONS CONTACT:* CRYSTA L. BOLTON, DIRECTOR OF ADMISSIONS AND STUDENT AFFAIRS
*ADDRESS:* 223 JAMES P. BRAWLEY DRIVE, ATLANTA, GA 30314
*PHONE:* 404-880-8447 • *FAX:* 404-880-6159
*E-MAIL:* CBOLTON@CAU.EDU
*WEBSITE:* WWW.CAU.EDU

### GENERAL INFORMATION
**Type of School:** private **Affiliation:** Methodist **Environment:** city

### STUDENTS
**Enrollment of business school:** 120 **% male/female:** 38/62 **% minorities:** 38 **% international:** 7 **Average age at entry:** 29 **Average years work experience at entry:** 5

### ACADEMICS
**Student/faculty ratio:** 11:1 **% female faculty** 19

### FINANCIAL FACTS
**Tuition:** $16,709 **Fees:** $200 **Books and supplies:** $1,000 **Room & board:** $5,000 **% of students receiving aid:** 95 **% of first-year students receiving aid:** 95 **% of students receiving loans:** 95 **% of students receiving grants:** 95 **Average award package:** $32,000 **Average grant:** $32,000 **Average student loan debt:** $65,000

### ADMISSIONS
**ADMISSIONS SELECTIVITY RATING:80**

**# of applications received:** 346 **% applicants accepted:** 26 **% acceptees attending:** 82 **Average GMAT:** 446 **Average GPA:** 2.83 **TOEFL required of int'l applicants?** yes **Application Fee:** $40 **International Application Fee:** $55 **Regular Application Deadline:** 3/1 **Regular Notification:** rolling **Deferment Available?** yes **Maximum length of deferment:** 2 years **Applicants also look at:** Emory University, Georgia State University

### EMPLOYMENT PROFILE
**Average starting salary:** $84,000

# CLEVELAND STATE UNIVERSITY
## JAMES J. NANCE COLLEGE OF BUSINESS ADMINISTRATION

*ADMISSIONS CONTACT:* BRUCE M. GOTTSCHALK, MBA PROGRAMS ADMINISTRATOR
*ADDRESS:* 2121 EUCLID AVENUE, BU 219, CLEVELAND, OH 44115
*PHONE:* 216-687-3730 • *FAX:* 216-687-5311
*E-MAIL:* CBACSU@CSUOHIO.EDU
*WEBSITE:* WWW.CSUOHIO.EDU/CBA/ACADEMIC//GRADUATE/GRADUATE.HTML

### GENERAL INFORMATION
**Type of School:** public **Environment:** city **Academic Calendar:** semester

### STUDENTS
**Enrollment of parent institution:** 15,650 **Enrollment of business school:** 655 **% male/female:** 63/37 **% out-of-state:** 40 **% part-time:** 78 **% minorities:** 19 **% international:** 38 **Average age at entry:** 27 **Average years work experience at entry:** 5

### ACADEMICS
**Student/faculty ratio:** 27:1 **% female faculty** 22 **% minority faculty** 15 **Joint Degrees:** JD/MBA 4 years, MBA/MSN 3 years **Prominent Alumni:** Monte Ahuja, Chair, President & CEO, Transtar Industries; Michael Berthelot, Chair & CEO, Transtechnolgy Corporation; Ted Hlavaty, Chair & CEO, Neway Stamping & Manufacturing; Thomas Moore, President, Wolf Group; Kenneth Semelsberger, President, COO & Director, Scott Fetzer, Inc.

## FINANCIAL FACTS

**Tuition (in-state/out-of-state):** $9,240/$17,640 **Books and supplies:** $1,300 **Room & board (on/off campus):** $10,000/$12,000 **% of students receiving aid:** 4 **% of first-year students receiving aid:** 8 **% of students receiving loans:** 34 **% of students receiving grants:** 1 **Average award package:** $15,000

## ADMISSIONS

**ADMISSIONS SELECTIVITY RATING: 70**

**# of applications received:** 379 **% applicants accepted:** 73 **% acceptees attending:** 60 **GMAT Range (25th to 75th percentile):** 460-590 **Average GMAT:** 500 **Average GPA:** 3.14 **TOEFL required of int'l applicants?** yes **Minimum TOEFL (paper/computer):** 525/197 **Application Fee:** $30 **International Application Fee:** $30 **Regular Application Deadline:** 7/1 **Regular Notification:** rolling **Deferment Available?** yes **Maximum length of deferment:** 1 year **Transfer Students Accepted?** yes **Non-fall Admissions?** yes **Need-Blind Admissions?** yes **Applicants also look at:** Case Western Reserve University, John Carroll University, Kent State University, The University of Akron

## EMPLOYMENT PROFILE

**Average starting salary:** $54,100
**Percent employed:** 10

| Grads employed by field: | % | avg. salary: |
|---|---|---|
| Accounting | 11 | $54,800 |
| Finance | 22 | $57,500 |
| Human Resources | 3 | $53,000 |
| Marketing | 18 | $54,900 |
| MIS | 3 | $53,600 |
| Operations | 15 | $57,600 |
| General Management | 6 | $56,000 |
| Nonprofit | 10 | $47,800 |
| Other | 12 | $51,000 |

# COLORADO STATE UNIVERSITY— DENVER EXECUTIVE MBA
## COLLEGE OF BUSINESS EXECUTIVE MBA PROGRAM

**ADMISSIONS CONTACT:** JOHN HOXMEIER, ASSOCIATE DEAN OF GRADUATE PROGRAMS
**ADDRESS:** DENVER EXECUTIVE MBA OFFICES, 1445 MARKET STREET, SUITE 208, DENVER, CO 80202
**PHONE:** 303-534-3191 • **FAX:** 303-534-3194
**E-MAIL:** DENVERMBA@BUSINESS.COLOSTATE.EDU
**WEBSITE:** WWW.CSUDENVERMBA.COM

## GENERAL INFORMATION

**Type of School:** public **Academic Calendar:** Aug-May

## STUDENTS

**Enrollment of parent institution:** 25,090 **Enrollment of business school:** 40 **% part-time:** 100 **Average age at entry:** 38 **Average years work experience at entry:** 14

## ACADEMICS

**Student/faculty ratio:** 20:1 **% female faculty** 10 **Joint Degrees:** The executive MBA program is not a combined program; however, there is DVM/MBA combination degree offered on campus in Fort Collins, Colorado through the College of Veterinary Medicine and the College of Business.

## FINANCIAL FACTS

**Fees:** $30

## ADMISSIONS

**ADMISSIONS SELECTIVITY RATING: 83**

**# of applications received:** 32 **% applicants accepted:** 75 **% acceptees attending:** 92 **Average GMAT:** 610 **Average GPA:** 3.2 **TOEFL required of int'l applicants?** yes **Minimum TOEFL (paper/computer):** 565/227 **Application Fee:** $50 **International Application Fee:** $50 **Regular Application Deadline:** 7/15 **Regular Notification:** 8/1 **Deferment Available?** yes **Maximum length of deferment:** 1 year **Need-Blind Admissions?** yes

# COLORADO STATE UNIVERSITY— DISTANCE MBA PROGRAM
## COLLEGE OF BUSINESS DISTANCE MBA PROGRAM

**ADMISSIONS CONTACT:** RACHEL STOLL, GRADUATE ADMISSIONS
**ADDRESS:** COLLEGE OF BUSINESS, 1270 CAMPUS DELIVERY, FORT COLLINS, CO 80523-1270
**PHONE:** 800-491-4622 • **FAX:** 970-491-2348
**E-MAIL:** BIZINFO@LAMAR.COLOSTATE.EDU
**WEBSITE:** WWW.CSUMBA.COM

## GENERAL INFORMATION

**Type of School:** public **Academic Calendar:** Aug-May

## STUDENTS

**Enrollment of parent institution:** 25,090 **Enrollment of business school:** 413 **% part-time:** 100 **Average age at entry:** 34 **Average years work experience at entry:** 13

## ACADEMICS

**Student/faculty ratio:** 40:1 **% female faculty** 10 **Joint Degrees:** DVM/MBA program is a 5-year program and is a joint program with the College of Business and the College of Veterinary Medicine.

## FINANCIAL FACTS

**Fees:** $30 **Books and supplies:** $2,100

## ADMISSIONS

**ADMISSIONS SELECTIVITY RATING: 78**

**# of applications received:** 143 **% applicants accepted:** 85 **% acceptees attending:** 85 **Average GMAT:** 612 **Average GPA:** 3.1 **TOEFL required of int'l applicants?** yes **Minimum TOEFL (paper/computer):** 565/227 **Application Fee:** $50 **International Application Fee:** $50 **Regular Application Deadline:** 7/15 **Regular Notification:** 8/1 **Deferment Available?** yes **Maximum length of deferment:** 1 year **Non-fall Admissions?** yes **Need-Blind Admissions?** yes

# COLUMBUS STATE UNIVERSITY

## D. ABBOTT TURNER COLLEGE OF BUSINESS

**ADMISSIONS CONTACT:** MS. KATIE THORNTON, GRADUATE ADMISSIONS
**ADDRESS:** 4225 UNIVERSITY AVENUE, COLUMBUS, GA 31907
**PHONE:** 706-568-2035 • **FAX:** 706-568-5091
**E-MAIL:** ADMISSIONS@COLSTATE.EDU
**WEBSITE:** HTTP://DATCOB.COLSTATE.EDU/

### GENERAL INFORMATION

**Type of School:** public **Academic Calendar:** semester

### STUDENTS

**Enrollment of business school:** 48 **% male/female:** 33/67 **% minorities:** 56

### ACADEMICS

**Student/faculty ratio:** 12:1

### FINANCIAL FACTS

**Tuition (in-state/out-of-state):** $3,500/$14,000 **Fees:** $876 **Books and supplies:** $1,000 **Average grant:** $3,000

### ADMISSIONS

**ADMISSIONS SELECTIVITY RATING: 86**

**# of applications received:** 33 **% applicants accepted:** 36 **% acceptees attending:** 100 **Average GMAT:** 500 **Average GPA:** 3.42 **TOEFL required of int'l applicants?** yes **Minimum TOEFL (paper/computer):** 550/213 **Application Fee:** $25 **International Application Fee:** $25 **Regular Application Deadline:** 7/20 **Regular Notification:** rolling **Transfer Students Accepted?** yes **Non-fall Admissions?** yes **Need-Blind Admissions?** yes

# CREIGHTON UNIVERSITY

## COLLEGE OF BUSINESS ADMINISTRATION

**ADMISSIONS CONTACT:** GAIL HAFER, COORDINATOR OF GRADUATE BUSINESS PROGRAMS
**ADDRESS:** COLLEGE OF BUSINESS ADMINISTRATION, ROOM 212C, 2500 CALIFORNIA PLAZA, OMAHA, NE 68178
**PHONE:** 402-280-2853 • **FAX:** 402-280-2172
**E-MAIL:** COBAGRAD@CREIGHTON.EDU
**WEBSITE:** HTTP://COBWEB.CREIGHTON.EDU

### GENERAL INFORMATION

**Type of School:** private **Affiliation:** Roman Catholic **Environment:** metropolis **Academic Calendar:** 8/7

### STUDENTS

**Enrollment of parent institution:** 6,723 **Enrollment of business school:** 118 **% male/female:** 58/42 **% part-time:** 84 **% minorities:** 1 **% international:** 31 **Average age at entry:** 25 **Average years work experience at entry:** 3

### ACADEMICS

**Student/faculty ratio:** 2:1 **% female faculty** 10 **Joint Degrees:** MBA/JD, 3 years; MBA/PharmD, 4 years; MBA/MIR, 3 years; MBA/MS

### FINANCIAL FACTS

**Tuition:** $10,206 **Fees:** $764 **Books and supplies:** $1,600 **Room & board (on/off campus):** $7,000/$6,000 **% of students receiving aid:** 15 **% of first-year students receiving aid:** 8 **Average award package:** $19,653

### ADMISSIONS

**ADMISSIONS SELECTIVITY RATING: 72**

**# of applications received:** 24 **% applicants accepted:** 96 **% acceptees attending:** 78 **Average GMAT:** 570 **Average GPA:** 3.39 **TOEFL required of int'l applicants?** yes **Minimum TOEFL (paper/computer):** 550/213 **Application Fee:** $40 **International Application Fee:** $40 **Regular Application Deadline:** rolling **Regular Notification:** rolling **Deferment Available?** yes **Maximum length of deferment:** 1 year **Transfer Students Accepted?** yes **Non-fall Admissions?** yes **Applicants also look at:** University of Nebraska at Omaha

# DePaul University
## Kellstadt Graduate School of Business

**Admissions Contact:** Robert Ryan, Assistant Dean
**Address:** 1 East Jackson Boulevard Suite 7900, Chicago, IL 60604
**Phone:** 312-362-8810 • **Fax:** 312-362-6677
**E-mail:** KGSB@DEPAUL.EDU
**Website:** WWW.KELLSTADT.DEPAUL.EDU

### GENERAL INFORMATION
**Type of School:** private **Affiliation:** Roman Catholic **Environment:** metropolis **Academic Calendar:** quarter

### STUDENTS
**Enrollment of parent institution:** 23,148 **Enrollment of business school:** 1,813 **% male/female:** 72/28 **% part-time:** 97 **% minorities:** 18 **% international:** 18 **Average age at entry:** 28 **Average years work experience at entry:** 5

### ACADEMICS
**Student/faculty ratio:** 11:1 **% female faculty** 20 **% minority faculty** 23 **Joint Degrees:** MBA/JD, 140 total credits required, full-time or part-time, 2.8 to 3.8 years to complete. Any of the concentrations listed for evening MBA can be selected for this combined degree. **Prominent Alumni:** Jim Jenness, CEO, Kellogg's; Richard Driehaus, President, Driehaus Capital Management; Edward Bosowski, President, USG Corporation; Daniel Ustian, Chair, President and CEO, Navistar International

### FINANCIAL FACTS
**Tuition:** $34,840 **Fees:** $200 **Books and supplies:** $1,300 **Room & board (on/off campus):** $12,316/$10,800 **% of students receiving aid:** 37 **% of first-year students receiving aid:** 26 **% of students receiving loans:** 22 **% of students receiving grants:** 21 **Average award package:** $21,120 **Average grant:** $16,080 **Average student loan debt:** $46,005

### ADMISSIONS
**Admissions Selectivity Rating: 75**

**# of applications received:** 389 **% applicants accepted:** 78 **% acceptees attending:** 74 **GMAT Range (25th to 75th percentile):** 520-600 **Average GMAT:** 556 **Average GPA:** 3.12 **TOEFL required of int'l applicants?** yes **Minimum TOEFL (paper/computer):** 550/213 **Application Fee:** $60 **International Application Fee:** $60 **Regular Application Deadline:** 7/1 **Regular Notification:** rolling **Deferment Available?** yes **Maximum length of deferment:** 1 year **Transfer Students Accepted?** yes **Non-fall Admissions?** yes **Need-Blind Admissions?** yes **Applicants also look at:** Loyola University Chicago, Northwestern University, The University of Chicago

### EMPLOYMENT PROFILE
School-facilitated activities 12 (50%)
Graduate-facilitated activities 12(50%)
**Average starting salary:** $63,000
**Percent employed:** 83

| Grads employed by field: | .........% | avg. salary: |
|---|---|---|
| Finance | 50 | $60,889 |
| Marketing | 30 | $70,500 |
| Operations | 8 | $56,000 |
| General Management | 8 | NR |
| Other | 4 | $40,000 |

# Drake University
## College of Business and Public Administration

**Admissions Contact:** Danette Kenne, Director of Graduate Programs
**Address:** 2507 University Avenue, Aliber Hall, Des Moines, IA 50311
**Phone:** 515-271-2188 • **Fax:** 515-271-2187
**E-mail:** CBPA.GRADPROGRAMS@DRAKE.EDU
**Website:** WWW.CBPA.DRAKE.EDU/ASPX/PROGRAMS

### GENERAL INFORMATION
**Type of School:** private **Environment:** metropolis **Academic Calendar:** semester

### STUDENTS
**Enrollment of parent institution:** 5,277 **Enrollment of business school:** 194 **% male/female:** 98/2 **% part-time:** 94 **% minorities:** 6 **% international:** 10 **Average age at entry:** 26

### ACADEMICS
**Student/faculty ratio:** 19:1 **% female faculty** 1 **Joint Degrees:** MBA/PharmD, 6 years; MBA/JD, 3 years; MPA/JD, 3 years; MPA/PharmD, 6 year **Prominent Alumni:** Robert D, Ray, Former Governor State of Iowa; Sherrill Milnes, Opera; Daniel Jorndt, Former Chair/CEO, Walgreen's; Dwight Opperman, Former CEO of West Publishing; Marie Wilson, President of MS Foundation for Women

### FINANCIAL FACTS
**Tuition (in-state/out-of-state):** $8,600/$8,600 **Fees (in-state/out-of-state):** $306/$306 **Books and supplies:** $800 **Room & board (on/off campus):** $5,870/$6,170 **% of students receiving loans:** 10 **% of students receiving grants:** 1

### ADMISSIONS
**Admissions Selectivity Rating: 71**

**# of applications received:** 86 **% applicants accepted:** 64 **% acceptees attending:** 78 **GMAT Range (25th to 75th percentile):** 410-560 **Average GMAT:** 470 **Average GPA:** 3.1 **TOEFL required of int'l applicants?** yes **Minimum TOEFL (paper/computer):** 550/213 **Application Fee:** $25 **International Application Fee:** $25 **Regular Application Deadline:** 6/6 **Regular Notification:** rolling **Deferment Available?** yes **Maximum length of deferment:** one term **Transfer Students Accepted?** yes **Non-fall Admissions?** yes **Need-Blind Admissions?** yes **Applicants also look at:** Iowa State University, University of Iowa

## EMPLOYMENT PROFILE

**Average starting salary:** $54,167

**Grads employed by field: ..........% avg. salary:**

| | | |
|---|---|---|
| Accounting | 12 | $52,500 |
| Marketing | 12 | $52,500 |
| Operations | 12 | NR |
| Strategic Planning | 6 | $47,500 |
| Entrepreneurship | 1 | NR |
| General Management | 25 | NR |
| Quantitative | 6 | NR |
| Other | 26 | $57,500 |

# DREXEL UNIVERSITY— PROFESSIONAL MBA

## DUPE—LEBOW COLLEGE OF BUSINESS

**ADMISSIONS CONTACT:** ROB PALACHICK, DIRECTOR OF GRADUATE ENROLLMENT SERVIC
**ADDRESS:** 3141 CHESTNUT STREET, 207 MATHESON HALL, PHILADELPHIA, PA 19104-2875
**PHONE:** 215-895-6804 • **FAX:** 215-895-1725
**E-MAIL:** RAP36@DREXEL.EDU
**WEBSITE:** WWW.LEBOW.DREXEL.EDU

### GENERAL INFORMATION

**Type of School:** private **Environment:** metropolis **Academic Calendar:** quarter

### STUDENTS

**Enrollment of business school:** 858 **% male/female:** 49/51 **% part-time:** 74 **% minorities:** 14 **% international:** 12 **Average age at entry:** 27

### ACADEMICS

**Student/faculty ratio:** 16:1 **% female faculty** 26 **% minority faculty** 15 **Joint Degrees:** MBA/MS

### FINANCIAL FACTS

**Tuition:** $42,000 **Books and supplies:** $12,000

### ADMISSIONS

**ADMISSIONS SELECTIVITY RATING: 88**

**# of applications received:** 770 **% applicants accepted:** 43 **% acceptees attending:** 51 **Average GMAT:** 590 **Average GPA:** 3.25 **TOEFL required of int'l applicants?** yes **Minimum TOEFL (paper/computer):** 600/250 **Application Fee:** $50 **International Application Fee:** $50 **Regular Notification:** rolling **Early decision program?** yes **ED deadline /notification:** 10/1;12/1 / 1/1 **Deferment Available?** yes **Maximum length of deferment:** 12 months **Transfer Students Accepted?** yes **Non-fall Admissions?** yes **Need-Blind Admissions?** yes

## EMPLOYMENT PROFILE

**Average starting salary:** $57,710

**Grads employed by field: ..........% avg. salary:**

| | | |
|---|---|---|
| Finance | 43 | $55,000 |
| Human Resources | 4 | $68,000 |
| Marketing | 14 | $61,000 |
| Operations | 18 | $58,600 |
| Consulting | 7 | $50,500 |
| General Management | 7 | $65,000 |
| Other | 7 | NR |

# EASTERN ILLINOIS UNIVERSITY
## LUMPKIN COLLEGE OF BUSINESS AND APPLIED SCIENCES

**ADMISSIONS CONTACT:** DR. CHERYL NOLL, COORDINATOR, GRADUATE BUSINESS STUDIES
**ADDRESS:** 600 LINCOLN AVENUE, 4025 LUMPKIN HALL, CHARLESTON, IL 61920-3099
**PHONE:** 217-581-3028 • **FAX:** 217-581-6642
**E-MAIL:** MBA@EIU.EDU
**WEBSITE:** WWW.EIU.EDU/~MBA

### GENERAL INFORMATION

**Type of School:** public **Environment:** village **Academic Calendar:** semester

### STUDENTS

**Enrollment of parent institution:** 12,000 **Enrollment of business school:** 146 **% male/female:** 61/39 **% part-time:** 49 **% minorities:** 8 **% international:** 19 **Average age at entry:** 29 **Average years work experience at entry:** 7

### ACADEMICS

**Student/faculty ratio:** 22:1 **% female faculty** 32 **% minority faculty** 8

### FINANCIAL FACTS

**Tuition (in-state/out-of-state):** $4,983/$14,916 **Fees (in-state/out-of-state):** $2,213/$2,213 **Books and supplies:** $325 **Room & board (on/off campus):** $7,000/$8,000 **% of students receiving aid:** 20 **% of first-year students receiving aid:** 30 **% of students receiving grants:** 20 **Average grant:** $7,000

### ADMISSIONS

**ADMISSIONS SELECTIVITY RATING: 72**

**# of applications received:** 85 **% applicants accepted:** 81 **% acceptees attending:** 88 **GMAT Range (25th to 75th percentile):** 480-570 **Average GMAT:** 520 **Average GPA:** 3.3 **TOEFL required of int'l applicants?** yes **Minimum TOEFL (paper/computer):** 550/213 **Application Fee:** $30 **International Application Fee:** $30 **Regular Application Deadline:** rolling **Regular Notification:** rolling **Deferment Available?** yes **Maximum length of deferment:** 1 year

Transfer Students Accepted? yes Non-fall Admissions? yes Need-Blind Admissions? yes

# EDHEC BUSINESS SCHOOL
## THESEUS-EDHEC MBA

**ADMISSIONS CONTACT:** MAUREEN BYRNE, ADMISSIONS MANAGER
**ADDRESS:** CAMPUS LILLE, 58 RUE DU PORT, LILLE, 59046 FRANCE
**PHONE:** 011-33-3-2015-4465 • **FAX:** 011-33-3-2015-4841
**E-MAIL:** MAUREEN.BYRNE@EDHEC.EDU
**WEBSITE:** WWW.THESEUS-MBA.COM

### GENERAL INFORMATION
**Type of School:** private **Academic Calendar:** 9/7

### STUDENTS
**Enrollment of business school:** 17 **% male/female:** 83/17 **% international:** 72 **Average age at entry:** 34 **Average years work experience at entry:** 7

### FINANCIAL FACTS
**Tuition :** $27,000 **Room & board:** $700

### ADMISSIONS
**ADMISSIONS SELECTIVITY RATING:** 68
**# of applications received:** 17 **% applicants accepted:** 100 **% acceptees attending:** 100 **Average GMAT:** 600 **Regular Application Deadline:** 5/31 **Application Deadline/Notification Round 1:** Dec / Jan **Round 2:** Feb / Mar **Round 3:** Apr / May **Round 4:** May / Jun

# EMPORIA STATE UNIVERSITY
## SCHOOL OF BUSINESS

**ADMISSIONS CONTACT:** MARY SEWELL, GRADUATE ADMISSIONS COORDINATOR
**ADDRESS:** EMPORIA STATE UNIVERSITY, CAMPUS BOX 4003, 1200 COMMERCIAL STREET, EMPORIA, KS 66801
**PHONE:** 620-341-5403 • **FAX:** 620-341-5909
**E-MAIL:** GRADINFO@EMPORIA.EDU
**WEBSITE:** WWW.EMPORIA.EDU

### GENERAL INFORMATION
**Type of School:** public

### STUDENTS
**Enrollment of parent institution:** 6,000 **Enrollment of business school:** 76 **% male/female:** 50/50 **% out-of-state:** 2 **% part-time:** 32 **% minorities:** 2 **% international:** 32 **Average age at entry:** 25

### ACADEMICS
**Student/faculty ratio:** 5:1 **% female faculty** 10 **% minority faculty** 26 **Prominent Alumni:** Donna Jacobs, VP, Nuclear Services, Diablo Corporation; Shawn Keough, PhD, Professor, University of Texas/Tyler

## FINANCIAL FACTS
**Tuition (in-state/out-of-state):** $3,836/$10,796 **Books and supplies:** $600 **Room & board (on/off campus):** $4,850/$4,850 **Average grant:** $6,492

## ADMISSIONS
**ADMISSIONS SELECTIVITY RATING:** 66
**# of applications received:** 58 **% applicants accepted:** 83 **% acceptees attending:** 35 **Average GMAT:** 524 **Average GPA:** 3.27 **TOEFL required of int'l applicants?** yes **Minimum TOEFL (paper/computer):** 550/213 **Application Fee:** $30 **International Application Fee:** $75 **Regular Application Deadline:** rolling **Regular Notification:** rolling **Deferment Available?** yes, contingent **Transfer Students Accepted?** yes **Non-fall Admissions?** yes **Need-Blind Admissions?** yes **Applicants also look at:** Institute of Undergraduate Business Studies

## EMPLOYMENT PROFILE
**Grads employed by field: ..........%:**
| | |
|---|---|
| Finance | 33 |
| Marketing | 33 |
| General Management | 33 |

# ESCP-EAP EUROPEAN SCHOOL OF MANAGEMENT
## ESCP-EAP PARIS LONDON MADRID BERLIN TORINO

**ADMISSIONS CONTACT:** FRANCYNE MARCAR, UK MARKETING COMMUNICATIONS MANAGER
**ADDRESS:** 527, FINCHLEY ROAD, HAMPSTEAD, LONDON, NW3 7BG ENGLAND
**PHONE:** 011-44-207-443-88-73 • **FAX:** 011-44-207-443-88-74
**E-MAIL:** UKADMISSION@ESCP-EAP.NET
**WEBSITE:** WWW.ESCP-EAP.NET

### GENERAL INFORMATION
**Type of School:** private **Academic Calendar:** Sept

### STUDENTS
**Enrollment of parent institution:** 3,300 **Enrollment of business school:** 229 **% male/female:** 45/55 **% international:** 86 **Average age at entry:** 25 **Average years work experience at entry:** 1

### ACADEMICS
**Student/faculty ratio:** 20:1 **% female faculty** 25 **Prominent Alumni:** Jean Pierre Raffarin, Former Prime Minister of France; Henri Sturz, President, Cap Gemini, Ernst & Young; Ignacio Garcia Alves, President, Arhur D. Little; Werner Josef Lubberink, Director, Deutsche Bahn; Antoine Riboud, Danone

### FINANCIAL FACTS
**Tuition:** $15,000 **Books and supplies:** $1,000 **Room & board:** $10,000

**ADMISSIONS SELECTIVITY RATING: 60***

**# of applications received:** 523 **% applicants accepted:** 62 **% acceptees attending:** 70 **Application Fee:** $200 **International Application Fee:** $200 **Application Deadline/Notification Round 1:** 3/1 / 5/1 **Round 2:** 5/1 / 6/1 **Round 3:** 6/5 / 7/1 **Deferment Available?** yes **Maximum length of deferment:** 1 year **Need-Blind Admissions?** yes

## EMPLOYMENT PROFILE

School-facilitated activities 45 (20%)

Graduate-facilitated activities 75 (34%)

Unknown......................................103 (46%)

**Average starting salary:** $53,000

**Percent employed:** 13

**Grads employed by field:** ..........% avg. salary:

Finance ........................................17 $66,000

Marketing .....................................45 $55,000

Consulting ....................................19 $60,000

Other............................................19 $52,000

# FAIRLEIGH DICKINSON UNIVERSITY—COLLEGE AT FLORHAM

## SILBERMAN COLLEGE OF BUSINESS

**ADMISSIONS CONTACT:** THOMAS M. SHEA, UNIVERSITY DIRECTOR OF INTERNATIONAL & GRADUATE ADMISSIONS
**ADDRESS:** 1000 RIVER ROAD, T-KB1-01, TEANECK, NJ 07666
**PHONE:** 201-692-2563 • **FAX:** 201-692-2560
**E-MAIL:** GRAD@FDU.EDU
**WEBSITE:** WWW.FDU.EDU

### GENERAL INFORMATION

**Type of School:** private

### STUDENTS

**Enrollment of parent institution:** 3,743 **Enrollment of business school:** 364 **% male/female:** 47/53 **% out-of-state:** 29 **% part-time:** 68 **% international:** 14 **Average age at entry:** 28

### ACADEMICS

**Prominent Alumni:** Michael King, King World; Patrick Zenner, Former President & CEO, Hoffman LaRoche, Inc.; Anthony Cuti, Chair, President, CEO, Duane Reade Corp.; George Martin, NFL Giants Captain; Gary Balkema, President, Worldwide Bayer Cust Care Division, Bayer Corp.

## FINANCIAL FACTS

**Fees:** $480

## ADMISSIONS

**ADMISSIONS SELECTIVITY RATING: 60***

**# of applications received:** 203 **% applicants accepted:** 67 **% acceptees attending:** 60 **TOEFL required of int'l applicants?** yes **Minimum TOEFL (paper/computer):** 550/213 **Application Fee:** $40 **International Application Fee:** $40 **Deferment Available?** yes **Transfer Students Accepted?** yes **Non-fall Admissions?** yes **Need-Blind Admissions?** yes

# FLORIDA INTERNATIONAL UNIVERSITY

## ALVAH H. CHAPMAN, JR., GRADUATE SCHOOL OF BUSINESS

**ADMISSIONS CONTACT:** ELLIE BROWNER, DIRECTOR, ADMISSIONS AND STUDENT SERVICES
**ADDRESS:** 11200 SOUTHWEST 8TH STREET - MARC 210, MIAMI, FL 33199
**PHONE:** 305-348-7398 • **FAX:** 305-348-2368
**E-MAIL:** CHAPINFO@FIU.EDU
**WEBSITE:** HTTP://CHAPMAN.FIU.EDU

### GENERAL INFORMATION

**Type of School:** public **Environment:** metropolis **Academic Calendar:** varies

### STUDENTS

**Enrollment of parent institution:** 36,975 **Enrollment of business school:** 290 **% male/female:** 58/42 **% part-time:** 86 **% minorities:** 25 **% international:** 45 **Average age at entry:** 27 **Average years work experience at entry:** 6

### ACADEMICS

**Student/faculty ratio:** 30:1 **% female faculty** 22 **% minority faculty** 31 **Joint Degrees:** MBA/MSF, 2-3 years; MBA/MSMIS, 2-3 years; MBA/JD, 5-7 years **Prominent Alumni:** Augusto Vidaurreta, Founder, Systems Consulting Group & Adjoined Techn; Carlos Migoya, President, Wachovia/First Union Bank, Miami; Anthony Argiz, Managing Partner, KPMG, LLP; Bob Bell, Founder, Banana Boat and Sea & Ski; Anthony Ronconi, Founder/President, Stratasys, Inc.

### FINANCIAL FACTS

**Tuition (in-state/out-of-state):** $27,500/$31,500 **Books and supplies:** $1,800 **Room & board (on/off campus):** $12,000/$18,000 **% of students receiving aid:** 39 **% of first-year students receiving aid:** 77 **% of students receiving loans:** 92 **% of students receiving grants:** 21 **Average award package:** $7,936 **Average grant:** $2,438 **Average student loan debt:** $31,850

## ADMISSIONS

**ADMISSIONS SELECTIVITY RATING: 78**

**# of applications received:** 249 **% applicants accepted:** 49 **%
acceptees attending:** 50 **GMAT Range (25th to 75th percentile):**
490-570 **Average GMAT:** 528 **Average GPA:** 3.14 **TOEFL required of
int'l applicants?** yes **Minimum TOEFL (paper/computer):** 550/213
**Application Fee:** $30 **International Application Fee:** $30 **Regular
Application Deadline:** rolling **Regular Notification:** rolling
**Deferment Available?** yes **Maximum length of deferment:** 1 year
**Transfer Students Accepted?** yes **Non-fall Admissions?** yes
**Applicants also look at:** Florida State University, University of
Florida, University of Miami, University of South Carolina

## EMPLOYMENT PROFILE

School-facilitated activities 8 (50%)

Graduate-facilitated activities 7 (44%)

Unknown......................................1 (6%)

**Average starting salary:** $60,333

**Percent employed:** 18

**Grads employed by field: ..........% avg. salary:**

Finance ..........................................20 $71,667

Human Resources..........................7 $50,000

Marketing ....................................33 $51,600

Consulting....................................20 $61,000

General Management ...................13 $52,500

# FU JEN CATHOLIC UNIVERSITY
## COLLEGE OF MANAGEMENT

**ADMISSIONS CONTACT:** *PEI-GI SHU, ASSOCIATE DEAN*
**ADDRESS:** *510 CHUNG CHENG ROAD, HSINCHUANG, TAIPEI HSIEN, 24205
TAIWAN*
**PHONE:** *011-886-2-2905-2613* • **FAX:** *011-886-2-2905-2186*
**E-MAIL:** *CLARE@MAILS.FJU.EDU.TW*
**WEBSITE:** *WWW.MANAGEMENT.FJU.EDU.TW*

## GENERAL INFORMATION

**Type of School:** private **Affiliation:** Roman Catholic-Jesuit

## STUDENTS

**Enrollment of business school:** 86 **% male/female:** 81/19 **% out-of-
state:** 3 **% part-time:** 39 **% international:** 3 **Average age at entry:**
25

## ACADEMICS

**Prominent Alumni:** Yi-Jeng Peng, VP, Bank of Overseas Chinese;
Wan-Li Wang, VP, CFSB; Wen-Zong Shu, General Manager, Home
Box; Ying-Chung Lyu, Senior VP; Yen-Mu Chen, President, Furniture
Company

## ADMISSIONS

**ADMISSIONS SELECTIVITY RATING: 60\***

**# of applications received:** 2397 **% applicants accepted:** 4 %

**acceptees attending:** 98 **International Application Fee:** $6 **Regular
Application Deadline:** 7/25 **Regular Notification:** 8/7

## EMPLOYMENT PROFILE

**Primary source of full-time job acceptances**

Graduate-facilitated activities 2 (9%)

Unknown.......................................21 (91%)

**Average starting salary:** ..........$1,180

**Percent employed:** 85

**Grads employed by field: ..........% avg. salary:**

Finance ........................................13 $1,250

Human Resources..........................9 $950

Marketing ....................................48 $1,250

MIS ...............................................9 $1,100

General Management ...................17 $1,100

Other.............................................4 $1,200

# GEORGE MASON UNIVERSITY
## SCHOOL OF MANAGEMENT

**ADMISSIONS CONTACT:** *CAROL HOSKINS, MBA PROGRAM COORDINATOR*
**ADDRESS:** *4400 UNIVERSITY DRIVE, MSN 5A2, ENTERPRISE HALL, ROOM 37,
FAIRFAX, VA 22030*
**PHONE:** *703-993-2136* • **FAX:** *703-993-1778*
**E-MAIL:** *SOMGRAD@GMU.EDU*
**WEBSITE:** *WWW.SOM.GMU.EDU*

## GENERAL INFORMATION

**Type of School:** public **Environment:** city **Academic Calendar:**
semester

## STUDENTS

**Enrollment of parent institution:** 6,734 **Enrollment of business
school:** 87 **% male/female:** 55/45 **% out-of-state:** 75 **% part-time:**
75 **% minorities:** 15 **% international:** 75 **Average age at entry:** 29
**Average years work experience at entry:** 7

## ACADEMICS

**Student/faculty ratio:** 5:1 **Prominent Alumni:** Michael G. Anzilotti,
MBA, President/CEO, First Virginia Bank; William Page Johnson II,
BS Finance, The Commissioner for Revenue, City of Fairfax, VA; Terri
Malone, MBA, Washington National Opera Singer, Northrop
Grumman Executive; Bill Henry, MBA, National President of The
American Society of Civil Engineers; Walter Howell, MBA, Senior VP
of Computer Associates International, Inc.

## FINANCIAL FACTS

**Tuition (in-state/out-of-state):** $10,848/$19,152 **Fees:** $260 **Books
and supplies:** $3,600

## ADMISSIONS

**ADMISSIONS SELECTIVITY RATING: 88**

**# of applications received:** 277 **% applicants accepted:** 45 %

acceptees attending: 69 **GMAT Range (25th to 75th percentile):** 580-590 **Average GMAT:** 590 **Average GPA:** 3.2 **TOEFL required of int'l applicants?** yes **Minimum TOEFL (paper/computer):** 600/230 **Application Fee:** $60 **International Application Fee:** $60 **Regular Application Deadline:** 4/1 **Regular Notification:** 4/30 **Application Deadline/Notification Round 1:** 4/1 / 4/30 **Round 2:** 6/1 / 6/30 **Deferment Available?** yes **Maximum length of deferment:** 1 semester **Transfer Students Accepted?** yes **Non-fall Admissions?** yes **Need-Blind Admissions?** yes

### EMPLOYMENT PROFILE
**Average starting salary:** $70,328

# GEORGIA COLLEGE & STATE UNIVERSITY
## THE J. WHITNEY BUNTING SCHOOL OF BUSINESS

**ADMISSIONS CONTACT:** MIKE AUGUSTINE, DIRECTOR OF ADMISSIONS
**ADDRESS:** GC&SU CAMPUS BOX 23, MILLEDGEVILLE, GA 31061
**PHONE:** 478-445-6289 • **FAX:** 478-445-1914
**E-MAIL:** CHRISTY.SMITH@GCSU.EDU
**WEBSITE:** WWW.GCSU.EDU

### GENERAL INFORMATION
**Type of School:** public **Environment:** town **Academic Calendar:** semester

### STUDENTS
**% part-time:** 100 **Average age at entry:** 26

### ACADEMICS
**Student/faculty ratio:** 17:1 **% female faculty** 35 **Prominent Alumni:** Tony Nicely, President and CEO, GEICO; Alex Gregory, President and CEO, YKK Corporation of America; Mike Garrett, President and CEO, Georgia Power Company.

### FINANCIAL FACTS
**Tuition (in-state/out-of-state):** $4,185/$13,365 **Fees:** $710 **Books and supplies:** $700 **Room & board (on/off campus):** $6,282/$6,850 **Average award package:** $7,005 **Average grant:** $2,336

### ADMISSIONS
**ADMISSIONS SELECTIVITY RATING: 60\***
**# of applications received:** 71 **% applicants accepted:** 83 **% acceptees attending:** 75 **GMAT Range (25th to 75th percentile):** 430-510 **Average GMAT:** 485 **Average GPA:** 3.2 **TOEFL required of int'l applicants?** yes **Minimum TOEFL (paper/computer):** 500/173 **Application Fee:** $25 **Regular Application Deadline:** rolling **Regular Notification:** rolling **Deferment Available?** yes **Maximum length of deferment:** 1 year **Transfer Students Accepted?** yes **Non-fall Admissions?** yes

# GRENOBLE ECOLE DE MANAGEMENT (FRANCE)
## GRENOBLE GRADUATE SCHOOL OF BUSINESS

**ADMISSIONS CONTACT:** MRS. KRIS LEROY, MARKETING AND ADMISSIONS MANAGER
**ADDRESS:** 12 RUE PIERRE SÉMARD, BP 127, GRENOBLE, 38530 FRANCE
**PHONE:** 011-33-04-76-70-62-31 • **FAX:** 011-33-04-76-70-61-77
**E-MAIL:** KRIS.LEROY@GGSB.COM
**WEBSITE:** WWW.GRENOBLE-EM.COM

### GENERAL INFORMATION
**Type of School:** private

### STUDENTS
**Enrollment of business school:** 200 **% male/female:** 67/33 **% international:** 74 **Average age at entry:** 32 **Average years work experience at entry:** 7.5

### FINANCIAL FACTS
**Fees:** $21,285 **Room & board:** $800 **% of students receiving grants:** 100

### ADMISSIONS
**ADMISSIONS SELECTIVITY RATING: 99**
**# of applications received:** 700 **% applicants accepted:** 4 **% acceptees attending:** 100 **GMAT Range (25th to 75th percentile):** 550-700 **Average GMAT:** 600 **Average GPA:** 3.3 **TOEFL required of int'l applicants?** yes **Minimum TOEFL (paper/computer):** 677/240 **Application Fee:** $77 **International Application Fee:** $77 **Regular Application Deadline:** 6/26 **Regular Notification:** 7/17 **Application Deadline/Notification Round 1:** 2/6 / 2/28 **Round 2:** 3/20 / 5/1 **Round 3:** 4/10 / 5/22 **Round 4:** 5/22 / 6/12 **Deferment Available?** yes **Maximum length of deferment:** 1 year **Transfer Students Accepted?** yes **Non-fall Admissions?** yes

### EMPLOYMENT PROFILE
School-facilitated activities 21%
Graduate-facilitated activities 10%
Unknown.......................................69%
**Average starting salary:** $65,000
**Grads employed by field: ..........%**
Accounting ....................................10
Human Resources.........................18
Marketing ......................................4
MIS .................................................45
Operations.....................................5
General Management ...................10
Other .............................................4

# GROUPE ESC TOULOUSE
## ESC TOULOUSE GRADUATE SCHOOL OF MANAGEMENT

**ADMISSIONS CONTACT:** DIRECTOR ESC TOULOUSE
**WEBSITE:** WWW.ESC-TOULOUSE.FR

### GENERAL INFORMATION

**Type of School:** private **Academic Calendar:** trimester

### STUDENTS

**Enrollment of parent institution:** 1,424 **Enrollment of business school:** 850 **% male/female:** 52/48 **% international:** 16 **Average age at entry:** 23

### ADMISSIONS

**ADMISSIONS SELECTIVITY RATING: 60\***
**# of applications received:** 2,500 **% applicants accepted:** 20 **% acceptees attending:** 90 **Regular Application Deadline:** 7/30 **Regular Notification:** rolling **Deferment Available?** yes

### EMPLOYMENT PROFILE

**Average starting salary:** $175,000

# HENDERSON STATE UNIVERSITY
## SCHOOL OF BUSINESS ADMINISTRATION

**ADMISSIONS CONTACT:** MISSIE BELL, GRADUATE SCHOOL ADMINISTRATIVE ASSISTANT
**ADDRESS:** 1100 HENDERSON STREET, BOX 7802, ARKADELPHIA, AR 71999-0001
**PHONE:** 870-230-5126 • **FAX:** 870-230-5479
**E-MAIL:** GRAD@HSU.EDU
**WEBSITE:** WWW.HSU.EDU/SCHOOLOFBUSINESS/

### GENERAL INFORMATION

**Type of School:** public **Environment:** rural

### STUDENTS

**Enrollment of parent institution:** 3,754 **Enrollment of business school:** 45 **% male/female:** 50/50 **% out-of-state:** 5 **% part-time:** 25 **% minorities:** 10 **% international:** 20

### ACADEMICS

**Student/faculty ratio:** 6:1 **% female faculty** 38 **Prominent Alumni:** Theresa Brown, Senior Systems Software Analyst; Junious Babbs, Assist. Superintendent of Little Rock School District; Richard Hoover, NASA; Billy Hudson, Professor at Vanderbilt University; Bob Fisher, President of Belmont University

### FINANCIAL FACTS

**Tuition (in-state/out-of-state):** $2,916/$5,832 **Fees:** $411 **Room & board:** $3,874

### ADMISSIONS

**ADMISSIONS SELECTIVITY RATING: 61**
**# of applications received:** 19 **% applicants accepted:** 100 **% acceptees attending:** 32 **GMAT Range (25th to 75th percentile):** 390-670 **Average GMAT:** 450 **Average GPA:** 3.0 **TOEFL required of int'l applicants?** yes **Minimum TOEFL (paper/computer):** 550/213 **International Application Fee:** $40 **Regular Application Deadline:** rolling **Regular Notification:** rolling

**Transfer Students Accepted?** yes **Non-fall Admissions?** yes **Need-Blind Admissions?** yes

# IDAHO STATE UNIVERSITY
## COLLEGE OF BUSINESS

**ADMISSIONS CONTACT:** GORDON B. BROOKS, SR., ASSISTANT DEAN FOR GRADUATE PROGRAMS
**ADDRESS:** BOX 8020, POCATELLO, ID 83209
**PHONE:** 208-282-2504 • **FAX:** 208-236-4367
**E-MAIL:** BROOGORD@ISU.EDU
**WEBSITE:** HTTP://COB.ISU.EDU

### GENERAL INFORMATION

**Type of School:** public **Environment:** town **Academic Calendar:** semester

### STUDENTS

**Enrollment of parent institution:** 13,977 **Enrollment of business school:** 109 **% male/female:** 75/25 **% part-time:** 56 **% minorities:** 4 **% international:** 10 **Average age at entry:** 32

### ACADEMICS

**Student/faculty ratio:** 23:1 **% female faculty** 20 **% minority faculty** 2

### FINANCIAL FACTS

**Tuition (in-state/out-of-state):** $5,520/$13,220 **Books and supplies:** $1,000 **Room & board:** $7,500

### ADMISSIONS

**ADMISSIONS SELECTIVITY RATING: 82**
**# of applications received:** 73 **% applicants accepted:** 59 **% acceptees attending:** 74 **GMAT Range (25th to 75th percentile):** 440-710 **Average GMAT:** 562 **Average GPA:** 3.39 **TOEFL required of int'l applicants?** yes **Minimum TOEFL (paper/computer):** 550/213 **Application Fee:** $55 **Regular Application Deadline:** 6/1 **Regular Notification:** 6/7 **Deferment Available?** yes **Maximum length of deferment:** 2 years **Transfer Students Accepted?** yes **Non-fall Admissions?** yes

# INCAE

## GRADUATE PROGRAM

**ADDRESS:** COSTA RICA
**WEBSITE:** WWW.INCAE.AC.CR

### GENERAL INFORMATION

**Type of School:** private **Academic Calendar:** trimester

### STUDENTS

**Enrollment of parent institution:** 441 **Enrollment of business school:** 441 **% male/female:** 70/30 **% part-time:** 20 **Average age at entry:** 28

### ACADEMICS

**Student/faculty ratio:** 15:1

### FINANCIAL FACTS

**Tuition (in-state/out-of-state):** $11,500 **% of students receiving aid:** 3

### ADMISSIONS

**ADMISSIONS SELECTIVITY RATING: 60\***

**# of applications received:** 530 **% applicants accepted:** 60 % **acceptees attending:** 37 **Application Fee:** $50 **Regular Application Deadline:** 7/15 **Regular Notification:** rolling **Deferment Available?** yes

### EMPLOYMENT PROFILE

**Average starting salary:** $53,000


# INDIANA UNIVERSITY NORTHWEST

## SCHOOL OF BUSINESS AND ECONOMICS

**ADMISSIONS CONTACT:** JOHN GIBSON, DIRECTOR, UNDERGRADUATE AND GRADUATE PROGRAMS IN BUSINESS
**ADDRESS:** 3400 BROADWAY, GARY, IN 46408-1197
**PHONE:** 219-980-6635 • **FAX:** 219-980-6916
**E-MAIL:** JAGIBSON@IUN.EDU
**WEBSITE:** WWW.IUN.EDU/~BUSNW

### GENERAL INFORMATION

**Type of School:** public **Environment:** city **Academic Calendar:** semester

### STUDENTS

**Enrollment of parent institution:** 4,000 **Enrollment of business school:** 110 **% part-time:** 98 **Average age at entry:** 36

### ACADEMICS

**Student/faculty ratio:** 10:1 **% female faculty** 26 **% minority faculty** 37

### FINANCIAL FACTS

**Tuition (in-state/out-of-state):** $4,500/$10,400 **Fees:** $500

## ADMISSIONS

**ADMISSIONS SELECTIVITY RATING: 61**

**# of applications received:** 215 **% applicants accepted:** 91 % **acceptees attending:** 100 **Average GMAT:** 430 **TOEFL required of int'l applicants?** yes **Minimum TOEFL:** 550 **Application Fee:** $25 **International Application Fee:** $55 **Deferment Available?** yes **Maximum length of deferment:** 1 year **Transfer Students Accepted?** yes **Non-fall Admissions?** yes **Need-Blind Admissions?** yes **Applicants also look at:** Purdue University—Calumet, Valparaiso University


# INDIANA UNIVERSITY-PURDUE UNIVERSITY AT FORT WAYNE

## SCHOOL OF BUSINESS AND MANAGEMENT

**ADMISSIONS CONTACT:** SANDY FRANKE, SECRETARY, MBA PROGRAM
**ADDRESS:** NEFF 366, 2101 COLISEUM BOULEVARD EAST, FORT WAYNE, IN 46805-1499
**PHONE:** 260-481-6498
**E-MAIL:** EMAIL@SCHOOL.EDU
**WEBSITE:** WWW.IPFW.EDU/BMS/MBA1.HTM

### GENERAL INFORMATION

**Type of School:** public **Environment:** village **Academic Calendar:** semester

### STUDENTS

**Enrollment of parent institution:** 10,749 **Enrollment of business school:** 191 **% male/female:** 65/35 **% part-time:** 91 **Average age at entry:** 32

### ACADEMICS

**Student/faculty ratio:** 1:1

### ADMISSIONS

**ADMISSIONS SELECTIVITY RATING: 60\***

**# of applications received:** 45 **% applicants accepted:** 91 % **acceptees attending:** 95 **Application Fee:** $30 **Regular Application Deadline:** 7/15 **Regular Notification:** 1/1 **Deferment Available?** yes **Maximum length of deferment:** 1 **Non-fall Admissions?** yes

# INSTITUTO DE EMPRESA

INSTITUTO DE EMPRESA

*ADMISSIONS CONTACT:* DAVID STANDEN, ADMISSIONS OFFICER
*ADDRESS:* MARÍA DE MOLINA 11-13-15, MADRID, 28006 SPAIN
*PHONE:* 011-34-91-568-9610 • *FAX:* 011-34-91-568-9710
*E-MAIL:* ADMISSIONS@IE.EDU
*WEBSITE:* WWW.IE.EDU

## GENERAL INFORMATION
**Type of School:** private

## STUDENTS
**Enrollment of business school:** 292 **% male/female:** 60/40 **% part-time:** 34 **% minorities:** 26 **% international:** 84 **Average age at entry:** 29 **Average years work experience at entry:** 6.3

## ACADEMICS
**Student/faculty ratio:** 11:1 **Prominent Alumni:** Fernando Barnuevo, JPMorgan Chase, Head of Global Investment Mgmt; Pilar de Zulueta; Warner Bros. Southern Europe Director; José María Cámara, President of Sony Music, Spain; Juan PableSan Agustín, Vice President, CEMEX; Isabel Aguilera, COO, NH Hotels

## FINANCIAL FACTS
**Tuition:** $33,850 **Books and supplies:** $400 **Average grant:** $17,000

## ADMISSIONS
**ADMISSIONS SELECTIVITY RATING: 99**
**# of applications received:** 2356 **% applicants accepted:** 14 **% acceptees attending:** 88 **Average GMAT:** 670 **Average GPA:** 3.7 **Application Fee:** $120 **Regular Application Deadline:** rolling **Regular Notification:** rolling **Deferment Available?** yes **Maximum length of deferment:** 2 years **Non-fall Admissions?** yes **Need-Blind Admissions?** yes **Applicants also look at:** ESADE, IESE Business School, IMD (International Institute for Management Development), INSEAD

## EMPLOYMENT PROFILE
**Average starting salary:** $72,730
**Grads employed by field: ..........%**
Finance .............................................17
Human Resources.........................3
Marketing .....................................10
Operations......................................3
Strategic Planning........................9
Consulting....................................14
Communications..........................13
Entrepreneurship..........................8
General Management ...................7
Global Management ....................7
Venture Capital ............................4
Other.............................................5

# INSTITUTO TECNOLOGICO Y DE ESTUDIOS SUPERIORES DE MONTERREY (ITESM)

## EGADE, MONTERREY CAMPUS

*ADMISSIONS CONTACT:* LIC. OLGA RENÉE DE LA TORRE, ACADEMIC SERVICES DIRECTOR
*ADDRESS:* AV. FUNDADORES Y RUFINO TAMAYO, COL. VALLE ORIENTE, SAN PEDRO GARZA GARCÍA, NL 66269 MEXICO
*PHONE:* 011-52-818-625-6204 • *FAX:* 011-52-818-625-6208
*E-MAIL:* ADMISIONES.EGADE@ITESM.MX
*WEBSITE:* WWW.EGADE.ITESM.MX

## GENERAL INFORMATION
**Type of School:** private **Academic Calendar:** quarter

## STUDENTS
**Enrollment of parent institution:** 19,358 **Enrollment of business school:** 597 **% male/female:** 79/21 **% part-time:** 90 **% international:** 66 **Average age at entry:** 28 **Average years work experience at entry:** 5

## ACADEMICS
**Student/faculty ratio:** 14:1 **% female faculty** 25 **Joint Degrees:** Double Degree MBA. **Prominent Alumni:** Eugenio Clariond Reyes-Retana, General Director of IMSA Group; Fernando Canales Clariond, Ministery of Economic Affairs, Mexico Government; Jose Antonio Rivero Larrea, President of Administration Board, Autlan Group; Jose Antonio Fernandez Carbajal, General Director of FEMSA Group; Luis Sada Gonzalez, General Director of John Deere, Mexico

## FINANCIAL FACTS
**Tuition:** $17,500 **Books and supplies:** $780 **Room & board (on/off campus):** $7,800/$6,400 **% of students receiving aid:** 26 **% of first-year students receiving aid:** 24 **% of students receiving loans:** 3 **% of students receiving grants:** 23 **Average grant:** $11,375

## ADMISSIONS
**ADMISSIONS SELECTIVITY RATING: 84**
**# of applications received:** 199 **% applicants accepted:** 73 **% acceptees attending:** 74 **Average GMAT:** 615 **Average GPA:** 3.5 **Application Fee:** $115 **International Application Fee:** $115 **Regular Application Deadline:** 5/1 **Regular Notification:** 6/1 **Deferment Available?** yes **Maximum length of deferment:** 1 year **Transfer Students Accepted?** yes **Non-fall Admissions?** yes

## EMPLOYMENT PROFILE
Grads employed by field: .............%:
Finance ...........................................38
Marketing .......................................12
Operations......................................25
Strategic Planning........................6
Other...............................................19

# Iowa State University
## College of Business

***Admissions Contact:*** *Amy Hutter, Director, MBA Recruitment & Marketing*
***Address:*** *1360 Gerdin Business Building, Ames, IA 50011*
***Phone:*** *515-294-8118 • Fax: 515-294-2446*
***E-mail:*** *busgrad@iastate.edu*
***Website:*** *www.bus.iastate.edu/grad/*

### GENERAL INFORMATION
**Type of School:** public **Environment:** town **Academic Calendar:** semester

### STUDENTS
**Enrollment of parent institution:** 26,380 **Enrollment of business school:** 210 **% male/female:** 54/46 **% out-of-state:** 18 **% part-time:** 65 **% minorities:** 3 **% international:** 35 **Average age at entry:** 27 **Average years work experience at entry:** 4

### ACADEMICS
**Student/faculty ratio:** 4:1 **% female faculty** 9 **% minority faculty** 12 **Joint Degrees:** MBA/MS in Statistics, 72 credit hours, 3 years; MBA/MS in Community and Regional Planning, 73 credit hours, 3 years; MBA/BS in Engineering, 5 years.

### FINANCIAL FACTS
**Tuition (in-state/out-of-state):** $7,417/$17,430 **Fees:** $702 **Books and supplies:** $1,000 **Room & board:** $10,200 **% of students receiving aid:** 50 **% of first-year students receiving aid:** 50 **Average award package:** $8,120

### ADMISSIONS
**Admissions Selectivity Rating:** 76

**# of applications received:** 188 **% applicants accepted:** 71 **% acceptees attending:** 26 **Average GMAT:** 577 **Average GPA:** 3.33 **TOEFL required of int'l applicants?** yes **Minimum TOEFL (paper/computer):** 590/250 **Application Fee:** $30 **International Application Fee:** $70 **Regular Application Deadline:** rolling **Regular Notification:** rolling **Deferment Available?** yes **Maximum length of deferment:** 1 year **Non-fall Admissions?** yes **Need-Blind Admissions?** yes **Applicants also look at:** Drake University, University of Iowa

### EMPLOYMENT PROFILE
**Primary source of full-time job acceptances**
School-facilitated activities 20 (67%)
Graduate-facilitated activities 10 (33%)
Unknown......................................5
**Average starting salary:** $50,319
**Percent employed:** 89

**Grads employed by field: ..........% avg. salary:**
Accounting ....................................4 NR
Finance ...........................................12 $47,750
Human Resources.........................10 NR
Marketing .....................................25 $60,000
MIS .................................................5 NR
Operations.....................................15 $50,000
Entrepreneurship..........................4 NR
General Management ...................25 $43,500

# Jackson State University
## School of Business

***Admissions Contact:*** *Jesse Pennington, Director of Graduate programs*
***Address:*** *PO Box 18660, Jackson, MI 39217*
***Phone:*** *601-432-6315 • Fax: 601-987-4380*
***E-mail:*** *gadmappl@ccaix.jsums.edu*
***Website:*** *http://ccaix.jsums.edu/business/*

### GENERAL INFORMATION
**Type of School:** public **Environment:** city **Academic Calendar:** semester

### STUDENTS
**Enrollment of parent institution:** 6,292 **Enrollment of business school:** 1,104

### ACADEMICS
**Student/faculty ratio:** 99:1

### FINANCIAL FACTS
**Tuition (in-state/out-of-state):** $1,920/$2,378 **% of students receiving aid:** 8

### ADMISSIONS
**Admissions Selectivity Rating:** 60*

**# of applications received:** 160 **% applicants accepted:** 77 **% acceptees attending:** 89 **TOEFL required of int'l applicants?** yes **Minimum TOEFL:** 525 **Regular Application Deadline:** rolling **Regular Notification:** rolling **Deferment Available?** yes

### EMPLOYMENT PROFILE
**Average starting salary:** $30,000

# JAMES MADISON UNIVERSITY
## COLLEGE OF BUSINESS

**ADMISSIONS CONTACT:** *KRISTA D. DOFFLEMYER, ADMINISTRATIVE ASSISTANT*
**ADDRESS:** *ZANE SHOWKER HALL, MSC 0206, ROOM 620, HARRISONBURG, VA 22807*
**PHONE:** *540-568-3253 • FAX: 540-568-3587*
**E-MAIL:** *MBA@JMU.EDU*
**WEBSITE:** *WWW.JMU.EDU/MBA*

### GENERAL INFORMATION
**Type of School:** public **Environment:** town **Academic Calendar:** Aug-July

### STUDENTS
**Enrollment of parent institution:** 16,938 **Enrollment of business school:** 83 **% male/female:** 72/28 **% out-of-state:** 28 **% part-time:** 78 **% minorities:** 6 **% international:** 33 **Average age at entry:** 31 **Average years work experience at entry:** 4

### ACADEMICS
**% female faculty** 33 **% minority faculty** 17

### FINANCIAL FACTS
**Tuition (in-state/out-of-state):** $5,904/$16,824 **Books and supplies:** $2,000 **% of students receiving aid:** 42 **% of first-year students receiving aid:** 24 **% of students receiving loans:** 20 **% of students receiving grants:** 30 **Average award package:** $10,642 **Average grant:** $5,861 **Average student loan debt:** $11,622

### ADMISSIONS
**ADMISSIONS SELECTIVITY RATING: 76**
**# of applications received:** 35 **% applicants accepted:** 86 **% acceptees attending:** 93 **GMAT Range (25th to 75th percentile):** 520-670 **Average GMAT:** 575 **Average GPA:** 3.2 **TOEFL required of int'l applicants?** yes **Minimum TOEFL (paper/computer):** 550/230 **Application Fee:** $55 **International Application Fee:** $55 **Regular Application Deadline:** 7/1 **Regular Notification:** rolling **Deferment Available?** yes **Maximum length of deferment:** 1 year **Transfer Students Accepted?** yes

### EMPLOYMENT PROFILE
**Average starting salary:** $75,000

# KANSAS STATE UNIVERSITY
## COLLEGE OF BUSINESS ADMINISTRATION

**ADMISSIONS CONTACT:** *LYNN WAUGH, GRADUATE STUDIES ASSISTANT*
**ADDRESS:** *110 CALVIN HALL, MANHATTAN, KS 66506-0501*
**PHONE:** *785-532-7190 • FAX: 785-532-7216*
**E-MAIL:** *FLYNN@KSU.EDU*
**WEBSITE:** *WWW.CBA.KSU.EDU*

### GENERAL INFORMATION
**Type of School:** public **Environment:** village **Academic Calendar:** semeters

### STUDENTS
**Enrollment of business school:** 91 **% male/female:** 70/30 **% out-of-state:** 4 **% part-time:** 18 **% minorities:** 9 **% international:** 22 **Average age at entry:** 24 **Average years work experience at entry:** 2

### ACADEMICS
**Student/faculty ratio:** 5:1 **% female faculty** 22 **% minority faculty** 4

### FINANCIAL FACTS
**Tuition (in-state/out-of-state):** $6,855/$19,340 **Fees:** $666 **Books and supplies:** $1,000 **Room & board (on/off campus):** $5,000/$6,000 **% of students receiving aid:** 18 **% of first-year students receiving aid:** 12 **Average grant:** $2,500

### ADMISSIONS
**ADMISSIONS SELECTIVITY RATING: 89**
**# of applications received:** 86 **% applicants accepted:** 40 **% acceptees attending:** 100 **Average GMAT:** 548 **Average GPA:** 3.39 **TOEFL required of int'l applicants?** yes **Minimum TOEFL (paper/computer):** 550/213 **Application Fee:** $50 **Regular Application Deadline:** 7/1 **Deferment Available?** yes **Maximum length of deferment:** 1 year **Transfer Students Accepted?** yes **Need-Blind Admissions?** yes **Applicants also look at:** Oklahoma State University, University of Kansas, University of Nebraska—Lincoln, University of Oklahoma, Wichita State University.

### EMPLOYMENT PROFILE
**Average starting salary:** $42,000

| Grads employed by field: | % | avg. salary: |
| --- | --- | --- |
| Accounting | 8 | $42,000 |
| Finance | 30 | $46,000 |
| Human Resources | 8 | $52,000 |
| Marketing | 8 | $38,000 |
| MIS | 8 | $55,000 |
| Consulting | 22 | $42,000 |
| Communications | 8 | $57,000 |
| Entrepreneurship | 8 | $38,000 |

# KING FAHD UNIVERSITY OF PETROLEUM AND MINERALS (SAUDI ARABIA)
## COLLEGE OF INDUSTRIAL MANAGEMENT

**ADMISSIONS CONTACT:** *ASSISTANT DEAN FOR GRADUATE PROGRAMS, CIM, OFFICE OF THE ASSISTANT DEAN FOR GRADUATE PROGRA*
**ADDRESS:** *PO BOX 1570, DHAHRAN, 31261 SAUDI ARABIA*
**PHONE:** *00966-3-860-1143 • FAX: 00966-3-860-3850*
**E-MAIL:** *SGHAMDI@KFUPM.EDU.SA*
**WEBSITE:** *WWW.KFUPM.EDU.SA/*

### GENERAL INFORMATION
**Type of School:** public **Academic Calendar:** Sept-June

### STUDENTS
**Enrollment of business school:** 193 **% part-time:** 87 **% international:** 3 **Average age at entry:** 29 **Average years work experience at entry:** 3.5

### ACADEMICS
**Student/faculty ratio:** 20:1

### ADMISSIONS
**ADMISSIONS SELECTIVITY RATING: 70**
**# of applications received:** 108 **% applicants accepted:** 62 **% acceptees attending:** 100 **Average GMAT:** 445 **Average GPA:** 2.8 **TOEFL required of int'l applicants?** yes **Regular Application Deadline:** 10/31 **Regular Notification:** 11/21 **Deferment Available?** yes **Maximum length of deferment:** none **Transfer Students Accepted?** yes **Non-fall Admissions?** yes

# KUWAIT UNIVERSITY
## COLLEGE OF BUSINESS ADMINISTRATION

**ADMISSIONS CONTACT:** *ADMISSION OFFICER*
**ADDRESS:** *KUWAIT UNIVERSITY, COLLEGE OF GRADUATE STUDY, KHALDIA, BULDING 2, KUWAIT PO BOX 5969, SAFAT 13060 KUWAIT*
**PHONE:** *965-498-7102 • FAX: 965-481-0499*
**E-MAIL:** *GRADADM@KUC01.KUNIV.EDU.KW*
**WEBSITE:** *WWW.GRADUATE.EDU.KW*

### GENERAL INFORMATION
**Type of School:** public

### STUDENTS
**Enrollment of parent institution:** 45 **Enrollment of business school:** 130 **% male/female:** 30/70 **% part-time:** 95 **% international:** 30 **Average age at entry:** 25 **Average years work experience at entry:** 3

### ACADEMICS
**Student/faculty ratio:** 7:1

### FINANCIAL FACTS
**Tuition (in-state):** $1,060 **Fees (in-state):** $320

### ADMISSIONS
**ADMISSIONS SELECTIVITY RATING: 70**
**# of applications received:** 16 **% applicants accepted:** 88 **% acceptees attending:** 93 **GMAT Range (25th to 75th percentile):** 470-520 **Average GMAT:** 506 **Average GPA:** 3.27 **TOEFL required of int'l applicants?** yes **Minimum TOEFL (paper/computer):** 550/213 **Regular Application Deadline:** 1/31 **Regular Notification:** 5/15 **Application Deadline/Notification Round 1:** 1/31 / 5/15 **Deferment Available?** yes **Maximum length of deferment:** 1 year **Transfer Students Accepted?** yes

# LA SALLE UNIVERSITY
## SCHOOL OF BUSINESS ADMINISTRATION

**ADMISSIONS CONTACT:** *KATHY BAGNELL, DIRECTOR, MARKETING AND GRADUATE ENROLLMENT*
**ADDRESS:** *1900 WEST OLNEY AVENUE, PHILADELPHIA, PA 19141*
**PHONE:** *215-951-1057 • FAX: 215-951-1886*
**E-MAIL:** *EMAIL@SCHOOL.EDU*
**WEBSITE:** *WWW.LASALLE.EDU/ACADEM/SBA/GRAD/INDEX.SHTML*

### GENERAL INFORMATION
**Type of School:** private **Environment:** metropolis **Academic Calendar:** trimester

### STUDENTS
**Enrollment of parent institution:** 5,408 **Enrollment of business school:** 687 **% male/female:** 59/41 **% part-time:** 90 **% minorities:** 12 **% international:** 11 **Average age at entry:** 32

### FINANCIAL FACTS
**Tuition:** $12,800 **Fees:** $85

### ADMISSIONS
**ADMISSIONS SELECTIVITY RATING: 60\***
**# of applications received:** 142 **% applicants accepted:** 85 **% acceptees attending:** 89 **TOEFL required of int'l applicants?** yes **Minimum TOEFL:** 550 **Application Fee:** $35 **Regular Application Deadline:** 8/14 **Regular Notification:** rolling **Deferment Available?** yes **Non-fall Admissions?** yes

# LEHIGH UNIVERSITY
## COLLEGE OF BUSINESS AND ECONOMICS

*ADMISSIONS CONTACT:* MARY THERESA TAGLANG, DIRECTOR OF RECRUITMENT
AND ADMISSIONS
*ADDRESS:* 621 TAYLOR STREET, BETHLEHEM, PA 18015
*PHONE:* 610-758-5280 • *FAX:* 610-758-5283
*E-MAIL:* MBA.ADMISSIONS@LEHIGH.EDU
*WEBSITE:* WWW.LEHIGH.EDU/MBA

### GENERAL INFORMATION
**Type of School:** private **Environment:** city **Academic Calendar:**
semester

### STUDENTS
**Enrollment of parent institution:** 6,748 **Enrollment of business
school:** 228 **% male/female:** 69/31 **% part-time:** 83 **% minorities:**
8 **% international:** 59 **Average age at entry:** 30 **Average years work
experience at entry:** 7

### ACADEMICS
**Student/faculty ratio:** 6:1 **% female faculty** 20 **% minority faculty**
27 **Joint Degrees:** MBA & Engineering, 45 credit hours; MBA/MEd,
45 credit hours.

### FINANCIAL FACTS
**Tuition:** $11,340 **Fees:** $240 **Books and supplies:** $1,300 **Room &
board:** $10,800 **% of students receiving aid:** 8 **% of first-year stu-
dents receiving aid:** 15 **Average award package:** $24,260 **Average
grant:** $11,000

### ADMISSIONS
**ADMISSIONS SELECTIVITY RATING: 87**

**# of applications received:** 185 **% applicants accepted:** 62 **%
acceptees attending:** 80 **GMAT Range (25th to 75th percentile):**
590-640 **Average GMAT:** 617 **Average GPA:** 3.24 **TOEFL required of
int'l applicants?** yes **Minimum TOEFL (paper/computer):** 600/250
**Application Fee:** $60 **International Application Fee:** $60 **Regular
Application Deadline:** 5/1 **Regular Notification:** rolling **Deferment
Available?** yes **Maximum length of deferment:** 1 year **Transfer
Students Accepted?** yes **Non-fall Admissions?** yes **Need-Blind
Admissions?** yes

### EMPLOYMENT PROFILE
**Primary source of full-time job acceptances**
School-facilitated activities 3 (27%)
Graduate-facilitated activities 2 (18%)
Unknown......................................6 (55%)
**Average starting salary:** $81,500

| Grads employed by field: | .........% | avg. salary: |
|---|---|---|
| Accounting | 9 | $53,000 |
| Finance | 37 | $109,000 |
| Marketing | 9 | NR |
| MIS | 9 | NR |
| Operations | 9 | $76,000 |
| Consulting | 9 | $145,000 |
| Entrepreneurship | 9 | $60,000 |
| Other | 9 | $80,000 |

# LOUISIANA STATE UNIVERSITY— SHREVEPORT
## COLLEGE OF BUSINESS ADMINISTRATION

*ADMISSIONS CONTACT:* SUSAN WOOD, MBA DIRECTOR
*ADDRESS:* ONE UNIVERSITY PLACE, SHREVEPORT, LA 71115
*PHONE:* 318-797-5213 • *FAX:* 318-797-5017
*E-MAIL:* SWOOD@PILOT.LSUS.EDU
*WEBSITE:* WWW.LSUS.EDU/BA/MBA/

### GENERAL INFORMATION
**Type of School:** public **Environment:** city **Academic Calendar:**
semester

### STUDENTS
**Enrollment of parent institution:** 4,237 **Enrollment of business
school:** 150 **% male/female:** 47/53 **% part-time:** 93 **% minorities:**
10 **% international:** 5

### ACADEMICS
**Student/faculty ratio:** 20:1

### FINANCIAL FACTS
**Tuition (in-state/out-of-state):** $3,245/$9,420 **% of students receiving aid:** 60

### ADMISSIONS
**ADMISSIONS SELECTIVITY RATING: 60\***

**# of applications received:** 70 **% applicants accepted:** 71 **%
acceptees attending:** 80 **TOEFL required of int'l applicants?** yes
**Minimum TOEFL:** 550 **Application Fee:** $10 **Regular Application
Deadline:** 6/30 **Regular Notification:** rolling **Non-fall Admissions?**
yes

### EMPLOYMENT PROFILE
**Average starting salary:** $40,000

# LOUISIANA TECH UNIVERSITY
## COLLEGE OF ADMINISTRATION AND BUSINESS

**ADMISSIONS CONTACT:** DR. MARC C. CHOPIN, ASSOCIATE DEAN OF GRADUATE STUDIES & RESEARCH
**ADDRESS:** PO BOX 10318, RUSTON, LA 71272
**PHONE:** 318-257-4528 • **FAX:** 318-257-4253
**E-MAIL:** GSCHOOL@CAB.LATECH.EDU
**WEBSITE:** WWW.CAB.LATECH.EDU

### GENERAL INFORMATION
**Type of School:** public **Environment:** rural **Academic Calendar:** quarter

### STUDENTS
**Enrollment of parent institution:** 11,611 **Enrollment of business school:** 72 **% male/female:** 64/36 **% part-time:** 10 **% international:** 21

### ACADEMICS
**Student/faculty ratio:** 25:1 **% female faculty** 17 **% minority faculty** 12

### FINANCIAL FACTS
**Tuition (in-state/out-of-state):** $3,376/$6,956 **Fees:** $40 **Books and supplies:** $900 **Room & board:** $6,580

### ADMISSIONS
**ADMISSIONS SELECTIVITY RATING:** 75
**# of applications received:** 50 **% applicants accepted:** 70 **% acceptees attending:** 77 **GMAT Range (25th to 75th percentile):** 450-700 **Average GMAT:** 530 **Average GPA:** 3.2 **TOEFL required of int'l applicants?** yes **Minimum TOEFL (paper/computer):** 550/213 **Application Fee:** $20 **International Application Fee:** $30 **Regular Application Deadline:** 8/1 **Deferment Available?** yes **Maximum length of deferment:** 1 year **Transfer Students Accepted?** yes **Non-fall Admissions?** yes

# MARSHALL UNIVERSITY
## LEWIS COLLEGE OF BUSINESS

**ADMISSIONS CONTACT:** DR. MICHAEL A. NEWSOME, MBA DIRECTOR
**ADDRESS:** CORBY HALL 217, 400 HAL GREER BOULEVARD, HUNTINGTON, WV 25755-2305
**PHONE:** 304-696-2613 • **FAX:** 304-696-3661
**E-MAIL:** EMAIL@SCHOOL.EDU
**WEBSITE:** HTTP://LCOB.MARSHALL.EDU/

### GENERAL INFORMATION
**Type of School:** public **Environment:** town **Academic Calendar:** semesters

### STUDENTS
**Enrollment of business school:** 80 **% male/female:** 40/60 **% minorities:** 15 **% international:** 30 **Average years work experience at entry:** 2

### ACADEMICS
**Student/faculty ratio:** 5:1 **% female faculty** 10 **% minority faculty** 10

### FINANCIAL FACTS
**Tuition (in-state/out-of-state):** $2,020/$5,653 **Fees (in-state/out-of-state):** $1,100/$1,250 **Books and supplies:** $1,000 **Room & board:** $4,000 **% of students receiving aid:** 50 **% of first-year students receiving aid:** 50

### ADMISSIONS
**ADMISSIONS SELECTIVITY RATING:** 73
**# of applications received:** 100 **% applicants accepted:** 84 **% acceptees attending:** 95 **Average GMAT:** 530 **Average GPA:** 3.5 **TOEFL required of int'l applicants?** yes **Minimum TOEFL (paper/computer):** 525/195 **Application Fee:** $30 **International Application Fee:** $25 **Regular Application Deadline:** rolling **Regular Notification:** rolling
**Transfer Students Accepted?** yes **Non-fall Admissions?** yes

### EMPLOYMENT PROFILE
**Average starting salary:** $50,000
Grads employed by field: ..............%:
Accounting ...................................75

# MCMASTER UNIVERSITY
## DEGROOTE SCHOOL OF BUSINESS

**ADMISSIONS CONTACT:** LOU CAFAZZO, RECRUITING ADMINISTRATOR
**ADDRESS:** MGD A114, 1280 MAIN STREET WEST, HAMILTON, ONTARIO, ON L8S 4M4 CANADA
**PHONE:** 905-525-9140 • **FAX:** 905-521-8995
**E-MAIL:** MBAINFO@MCMASTER.CA
**WEBSITE:** WWW.DEGROOTE.MCMASTER.CA

### GENERAL INFORMATION
**Type of School:** public

### STUDENTS
**Enrollment of parent institution:** 18,000 **Enrollment of business school:** 371 **% male/female:** 61/39 **% part-time:** 25 **% international:** 15 **Average age at entry:** 27 **Average years work experience at entry:** 3

### ACADEMICS
**Student/faculty ratio:** 10:1 **% female faculty** 13
**Prominent Alumni:** Wayne C. Fox, CIBC, Vice Chairman & Chief Risk Officer; Edward Minich, President, Otis Canada; Paul Cummings, President & CEO, Volvo Canada; Jim Alfana, President, Stelco; Mossadiq Umedaly, Chairman & CEO Xantrex Technology

### FINANCIAL FACTS
**Tuition:** $17,245 **Books and supplies:** $3,850 **Room & board:** $5,000 **% of students receiving grants:** 8 **Average grant:** $2,000

## ADMISSIONS

**ADMISSIONS SELECTIVITY RATING: 60\***

**# of applications received:** 301 **% applicants accepted:** 58 **% acceptees attending:** 59 **Average GMAT:** 641 **Average GPA:** 3.5 **TOEFL required of int'l applicants?** yes **Minimum TOEFL (paper/computer):** 600/250 **Application Fee:** $125 **International application fee:** $125 **Regular Application Deadline:** 5/1 **Regular Notification:** rolling

**Applicants also look at:** University of Toronto, York University

### EMPLOYMENT PROFILE

**Primary source of full-time job acceptances**

School-facilitated activities 45%

Graduate-facilitated activities 45%

Unknown.........................................1%

Average starting salary .................$54,782

**Grads employed by field: ..........% avg. salary:**

Accounting .....................................5 $34,240

Finance ..........................................29 $59,223

Human Resources.........................2 $58,000

Marketing ......................................33 $55,536

MIS .................................................6 $61,300

Operations.....................................5 $41,000

Consulting......................................8 $53,920

General Management ....................12 $51,914

# MCNEESE STATE UNIVERSITY
## MBA PROGRAM

*ADMISSIONS CONTACT: TAMMY PETTIS, UNIVERSITY ADMISSIONS*
*ADDRESS: PO BOX 92495, LAKE CHARLES, LA 70609-2495*
*PHONE: 337-475-5147 • FAX: 337-475-5151*
*E-MAIL: INFO@MCNEESE.EDU*
*WEBSITE: WWW.MCNEESE.EDU/COLLEGES/BUSINESS/MBA*

### GENERAL INFORMATION

**Type of School:** public **Environment:** city **Academic Calendar:** semester

### STUDENTS

**Enrollment of parent institution:** 8,423 **Enrollment of business school:** 81 **% male/female:** 68/32 **% out-of-state:** 3 **% part-time:** 64 **% international:** 33 **Average age at entry:** 30

### ACADEMICS

**Student/faculty ratio:** 16:1 **% female faculty** 1 **% minority faculty** 45

### FINANCIAL FACTS

**Tuition (in-state/out-of-state):** $1,527/$4,560 **Books and supplies:** $1,000 **Room & board (on/off campus):** $3,200/$3,600

## ADMISSIONS

**ADMISSIONS SELECTIVITY RATING: 63**

**# of applications received:** 36 **% applicants accepted:** 97 **% acceptees attending:** 51 **GMAT Range (25th to 75th percentile):** 250-690 **Average GMAT:** 480 **Average GPA:** 3.6 **TOEFL required of int'l applicants?** yes **Minimum TOEFL:** 550 **Application Fee:** $20 **International Application Fee:** $30 **Regular Application Deadline:** rolling **Regular Notification:** rolling **Deferment Available?** yes **Maximum length of deferment:** 1 year **Transfer Students Accepted?** yes **Non-fall Admissions?** yes **Need-Blind Admissions?** yes

# MICHIGAN TECHNOLOGICAL UNIVERSITY
## SCHOOL OF BUSINESS AND ECONOMICS

*ADMISSIONS CONTACT: NANCY REHLING, DIRECTOR OF ADMISSIONS*
*ADDRESS: ADMISSIONS OFFICE, 1400 TOWNSEND DRIVE, HOUGHTON, MI 49931*
*PHONE: 906-487-2335 • FAX: 906-487-2125*
*E-MAIL: MTU4U@MTU.EDU*
*WEBSITE: WWW.SBE.MTU.EDU*

### GENERAL INFORMATION

**Type of School:** public

### ACADEMICS

**Student/faculty ratio:** 14:1 **Joint Degrees:** A second degree program is available. This is a 47 credit hour program and is available to students who have earned or are earning another bachelors degree. The second degree in business is in business administration.

### FINANCIAL FACTS

**Tuition (in-state):** $7,776 **Room & board (on campus):** $8,830

### ADMISSIONS

**ADMISSIONS SELECTIVITY RATING: 80**

**# of applications received:** 150 **% applicants accepted:** 63 **% acceptees attending:** 68 **Average GMAT:** 570 **Average GPA:** 3.3 **Application Fee:** $40 **Regular Application Deadline:** rolling **Regular Notification:** rolling

# MIDDLE TENNESSEE STATE UNIVERSITY
## JENNINGS A. JONES COLLEGE OF BUSINESS

**ADMISSIONS CONTACT:** TROY A. FESTERVAND, DIRECTOR, GRADUATE BUSINESS STUDIES
**ADDRESS:** PO Box 290, BAS N222, MURFREESBORO, TN 37132
**PHONE:** 615-898-2368 • **FAX:** 615-904-8491
**E-MAIL:** GBS@MTSU.EDU
**WEBSITE:** WWW.MTSU.EDU/~GRADUATE/PROGRAMS/BUAD.HTM

### GENERAL INFORMATION
**Type of School:** public **Environment:** village

### STUDENTS
**Enrollment of business school:** 396 **% male/female:** 77/23 **% minorities:** 12 **Average age at entry:** 24

### ACADEMICS
**Student/faculty ratio:** 20:1

### FINANCIAL FACTS
**Tuition (in-state/out-of-state):** $2,250/$6,100 **Fees:** $300 **Books and supplies:** $1,000 **Room & board:** $2,500

### ADMISSIONS
**ADMISSIONS SELECTIVITY RATING: 64**
**# of applications received:** 231 **% applicants accepted:** 83 **Average GMAT:** 490 **Average GPA:** 3.20 **TOEFL required of int'l applicants?** yes **Minimum TOEFL (paper/computer):** 525/197 **Application Fee:** $25 **International Application Fee:** $30 **Regular Application Deadline:** 7/1 **Regular Notification:** 8/1 **Deferment Available?** yes **Maximum length of deferment:** varies **Transfer Students Accepted?** yes **Non-fall Admissions?** yes

# MONTANA STATE UNIVERSITY
## COLLEGE OF BUSINESS

**ADMISSIONS CONTACT:** MARC A. GIULLIAN, MPAC DIRECTOR
**ADDRESS:** 338 REID HALL, PO BOX 173040, BOZEMAN, MT 59717-3040
**PHONE:** 406-994-4681 • **FAX:** 406-994-6206
**E-MAIL:** MGIULLIAN@MONTANA.EDU
**WEBSITE:** WWW.MONTANA.EDU/COB/

### GENERAL INFORMATION
**Type of School:** public **Environment:** town **Academic Calendar:** semester

### STUDENTS
**Enrollment of business school:** 40 **% male/female:** 25/75 **% part-time:** 8 **Average age at entry:** 25

### ACADEMICS
**Student/faculty ratio:** 20:1 **% female faculty** 33

### FINANCIAL FACTS
**Tuition (in-state/out-of-state):** $6,562/$16,162 **Fees:** $311 **% of students receiving aid:** 50 **Average grant:** $5,000

### ADMISSIONS
**ADMISSIONS SELECTIVITY RATING: 79**
**# of applications received:** 50 **% applicants accepted:** 62 **% acceptees attending:** 94 **Average GMAT:** 520 **Average GPA:** 3.5 **TOEFL required of int'l applicants?** yes **Minimum TOEFL:** 550 **Application Fee:** $50 **Regular Application Deadline:** 6/30 **Regular Notification:** rolling **Deferment Available?** yes **Maximum length of deferment:** 1 year **Transfer Students Accepted?** yes **Non-fall Admissions?** yes

### EMPLOYMENT PROFILE
**Average starting salary:** $38,000
**Grads employed by field:** ..........% avg. salary:
Accounting ...................................85 $38,000

# MOREHEAD STATE UNIVERSITY
## COLLEGE OF BUSINESS

**ADMISSIONS CONTACT:** JESSICA COX, ADMISSIONS SPECIALIST
**ADDRESS:** 701 GINGER HALL, MOREHEAD, KY 40351
**PHONE:** 606-783-2039 • **FAX:** 606-783-5061
**E-MAIL:** GRADUATE@MOREHEADSTATE.EDU
**WEBSITE:** WWW.MOREHEADSTATE.EDU

### GENERAL INFORMATION
**Type of School:** public

### FINANCIAL FACTS
**Tuition (in-state/out-of-state):** $5,670/$8,370

### ADMISSIONS
**ADMISSIONS SELECTIVITY RATING: 60\***
**TOEFL required of int'l applicants?** yes **Minimum TOEFL (paper):** 525 **Regular Application Deadline:** 8/1 **Regular Notification:** 8/1 **Transfer Students Accepted?** yes **Non-fall Admissions?** yes

# MORGAN STATE UNIVERSITY
## EARL GRAVES SCHOOL OF BUSINESS AND MANAGEMENT

**ADMISSIONS CONTACT:** DIRECTOR OF GRADUATE ADMISSIONS
**WEBSITE:** WWW.MORGAN.EDU/ACADEMICS/SBM

### GENERAL INFORMATION
**Type of School:** public **Environment:** city **Academic Calendar:** semester

## STUDENTS

**Enrollment of parent institution:** 5,900 **Enrollment of business school:** 103 **% part-time:** 100

## ACADEMICS

**Student/faculty ratio:** 12:1

## FINANCIAL FACTS

**Room & board (on campus):** $2,990

## ADMISSIONS

**ADMISSIONS SELECTIVITY RATING: 60\***

**TOEFL required of int'l applicants?** yes **Minimum TOEFL:** 600 **Application Fee:** $20 **Regular Application Deadline:** rolling **Regular Notification:** rolling **Deferment Available?** yes

# MURRAY STATE UNIVERSITY
## COLLEGE OF BUSINESS AND PUBLIC AFFAIRS

**ADMISSIONS CONTACT:** DR. GERRY NKOMBO MUUKA, ASSISTANT DEAN AND MBA DIRECTOR
**ADDRESS:** 109 BUSINESS BUILDING, GRADUATE ADMISSIONS OFFICE, SPARKS HALL, MURRAY, KY 42071
**PHONE:** 270-762-6970 • **FAX:** 270-762-3482
**E-MAIL:** CBPA@MURRAYSTATE.EDU
**WEBSITE:** WWW.MURSUKY.EDU/QACD/CBPA/MBA/INDEX.HTM

## GENERAL INFORMATION

**Type of School:** public **Environment:** village **Academic Calendar:** semester

## STUDENTS

**Enrollment of parent institution:** 9,000 **Enrollment of business school:** 160 **% part-time:** 53 **Average age at entry:** 31

## ACADEMICS

**Student/faculty ratio:** 20:1

## FINANCIAL FACTS

**Tuition (in-state/out-of-state):** $4,185/$11,700 **Room & board:** $3,800

## ADMISSIONS

**ADMISSIONS SELECTIVITY RATING: 60\***

**# of applications received:** 121 **% applicants accepted:** 75 **% acceptees attending:** 52 **TOEFL required of int'l applicants?** yes **Minimum TOEFL (paper):** 525 **Application Fee:** $25 **Regular Application Deadline:** rolling **Regular Notification:** rolling **Deferment Available?** yes **Transfer Students Accepted?** yes **Non-fall Admissions?** yes

# NANYANG TECHNOLOGICAL UNIVERSITY
## NANYANG BUSINESS SCHOOL

**ADMISSIONS CONTACT:** ASSOCIATE PROFESSOR OOI LEE LEE, DIRECTOR MBA
**ADDRESS:** THE NANYANG MBA, NANYANG BUSINESS SCHOOL, NANYANG AVENUE, SINGAPORE, 639789 SINGAPORE
**PHONE:** 011-65-67906183 • **FAX:** 011-65-67913561
**E-MAIL:** NBSMBA@NTU.EDU.SG
**WEBSITE:** WWW.NANYANGMBA.NTU.EDU.SG

## GENERAL INFORMATION

**Type of School:** public **Academic Calendar:** 2006-07

## STUDENTS

**Enrollment of business school:** 121 **% male/female:** 72/28 **% part-time:** 36 **% international:** 81 **Average age at entry:** 32 **Average years work experience at entry:** 7

## ACADEMICS

**Student/faculty ratio:** 30:1 **% female faculty** 21 **Joint Degrees:** NTU-Waseda Double MBA, 1 year; NTU-St. Gallen Double MBA, 24 months; NTU-ESSEC Double MBA, 2 years. **Prominent Alumni:** Terence Chan, CEO, CAD-IT Consultants (Asia) Pte Ltd; Mr. Christopher Tay, CEO, NTUC Healthcare Co-op Limited; Chew Hong Gian, Senior VP, Singapore Exchange

## FINANCIAL FACTS

**Tuition (out-of-state):** $14,500 **Books and supplies:** $8,500 **Room & board (on/off campus):** $3,000/$5,000 **% of students receiving grants:** 13

## ADMISSIONS

**ADMISSIONS SELECTIVITY RATING: 92**

**# of applications received:** 633 **% applicants accepted:** 36 **% acceptees attending:** 52 **GMAT Range (25th to 75th percentile):** 600-710 **Average GMAT:** 650 **TOEFL required of int'l applicants?** yes **Minimum TOEFL (paper/computer):** 600/250 **Application Fee:** $30 **International Application Fee:** $30 **Application Deadline/Notification Round 1:** 12/31 / 1/31 **Round 2:** 1/31 / 2/28 **Round 3:** 2/28 / 3/31 **Round 4:** 3/31 / 4/30 **Deferment Available?** yes **Maximum length of deferment:** 1 year **Transfer Students Accepted?** yes **Non-fall Admissions?** yes

## EMPLOYMENT PROFILE

**Primary source of full-time job acceptances**

School-facilitated activities 22%

Graduate-facilitated activities 78%

**Average starting salary:** $39,890

**Percent employed:** 24

**Grads employed by field:** ..........%

Finance ...........................................38

Marketing .....................................31

Operations.....................................10

Consulting......................................16
General Management ...................3
Other...........................................2

# NEW YORK UNIVERSITY
## STERN EXECUTIVE MBA PROGRAM

**ADMISSIONS CONTACT:** PETER TODD, ADMISSIONS COORDINATOR
**ADDRESS:** 44 WEST 4TH STREET, SUITE 10-66, NEW YORK, NY 10012
**PHONE:** 212-998-0789 • **FAX:** 212-995-4222
**E-MAIL:** EXECUTIVE@STERN.NYU.EDU
**WEBSITE:** WWW.STERN.NYU.EDU/EXECUTIVE/EMBA

### GENERAL INFORMATION
**Type of School:** private

### STUDENTS
**Enrollment of business school:** 100 **% male/female:** 71/29 **%
minorities:** 12 **% international:** 20 **Average age at entry:** 33
**Average years work experience at entry:** 10

### ADMISSIONS
**ADMISSIONS SELECTIVITY RATING: 97**

**# of applications received:** 600 **% applicants accepted:** 25 **%
acceptees attending:** 67 **Average GMAT:** 660 **Average GPA:** 3.4
**Application Fee:** $150 **International Application Fee:** $150 **Regular
Application Deadline:** 2/27 **Regular Notification:** rolling **Deferment
Available?** yes **Maximum length of deferment:** 1 year **Non-fall
Admissions?** yes

# NIAGARA UNIVERSITY
## COLLEGE OF BUSINESS ADMINISTRATION

**ADDRESS:** COLLEGE OF BUSINESS ADMINISTRATION, MBA, NIAGARA UNIVERSITY,
NY 14109
**PHONE:** 716-286-8300
**E-MAIL:** SQC@NIAGARA.EDU
**WEBSITE:** WWW.NIAGARA.EDU/MBA/

### GENERAL INFORMATION
**Type of School:** private

### FINANCIAL FACTS
**Tuition:** $7,440

### ADMISSIONS
**ADMISSIONS SELECTIVITY RATING: 60\***
**Application Fee:** $35 **Regular Application Deadline:** rolling **Regular
Notification:** rolling

# NICHOLLS STATE UNIVERSITY
## COLLEGE OF BUSINESS ADMINISTRATION

**ADMISSIONS CONTACT:** BECKY LEBLANC-DUROCHER, DIRECTOR OF ADMIS-
SIONS
**ADDRESS:** PO BOX 2004, THIBODAUX, LA 70310
**PHONE:** 877-642-4655 • **FAX:** 985-448-4929
**E-MAIL:** ESAI-BL@NICHOLLS.EDU
**WEBSITE:** WWW.NICHOLLS.EDU

### GENERAL INFORMATION
**Type of School:** public **Environment:** village **Academic Calendar:**
semester

### STUDENTS
**Enrollment of parent institution:** 7,482 **Enrollment of business
school:** 116 **% male/female:** 49/51 **% out-of-state:** 1 **% part-time:**
59 **% minorities:** 6 **% international:** 12

### ACADEMICS
**Student/faculty ratio:** 15:1 **% female faculty** 19 **Prominent Alumni:**
Barry Melancon, President, AICPA; John Weimer, Justice, Louisiana
Supreme Court; Billy Tauzin, U.S. Representative

### FINANCIAL FACTS
**Tuition (in-state/out-of-state):** $3,075/$8,523 **Books and supplies:**
$2,000 **Room & board:** $4,584 **% of students receiving aid:** 20
**Average grant:** $4,000

### ADMISSIONS
**ADMISSIONS SELECTIVITY RATING: 62**

**# of applications received:** 70 **% applicants accepted:** 99 **%
acceptees attending:** 57 **Average GMAT:** 486 **Average GPA:** 3.1
**TOEFL required of int'l applicants?** yes **Minimum TOEFL
(paper/computer):** 550/213 **Application Fee:** $20 **International
Application Fee:** $30 **Regular Application Deadline:** 7/1 **Regular
Notification:** rolling **Deferment Available?** yes **Maximum length of
deferment:** 1 semester **Transfer Students Accepted?** yes **Non-fall
Admissions?** yes **Need-Blind Admissions?** yes

# NORTH DAKOTA STATE UNIVERSITY
## COLLEGE OF BUSINESS ADMINISTRATION

**ADMISSIONS CONTACT:** PAUL BROWN, MBA DIRECTOR
**ADDRESS:** PO BOX 5137, FARGO, ND 58018
**E-MAIL:** PAUL.BROWN@NDSU.EDUX
**WEBSITE:** WWW.NDSU.EDU/CBA/

### GENERAL INFORMATION
**Type of School:** public **Environment:** city

## STUDENTS

Enrollment of business school: 537 **% male/female:** 60/40 **% part-time:** 89 **% international:** 8 **Average age at entry:** 29

## ACADEMICS

**Student/faculty ratio:** 19:1 **Joint Degrees:** MBA/JD, 3.5-5 years

## FINANCIAL FACTS

**Tuition (in-state/out-of-state):** $4,600/$10,800 **Fees:** $340

## ADMISSIONS

**ADMISSIONS SELECTIVITY RATING: 60\***

**# of applications received:** 162 **% applicants accepted:** 90 **% acceptees attending:** 80 **TOEFL required of int'l applicants?** yes **Minimum TOEFL:** 550 **Application Fee:** $35 **Regular Application Deadline:** 7/15 **Regular Notification:** rolling **Deferment Available?** yes **Non-fall Admissions?** yes

# NORTHERN ILLINOIS UNIVERSITY, COLLEGE OF BUSINESS
## MBA PROGRAMS

**ADMISSIONS CONTACT:** MONA SALMON, ASSISTANT DIRECTOR
**ADDRESS:** BARSEMA 203, DEKALB, IL 60115
**PHONE:** 866-648-6221 • **FAX:** 815-753-1668
**E-MAIL:** MBA@NIU.EDU
**WEBSITE:** WWW.COB.NIU.EDU/MBAPROGRAMS

## GENERAL INFORMATION

**Type of School:** public **Environment:** rural

## STUDENTS

**Enrollment of parent institution:** 25,000 **Enrollment of business school:** 528 **% part-time:** 99 **Average age at entry:** 32 **Average years work experience at entry:** 9

## ACADEMICS

**Student/faculty ratio:** 24:1 **% female faculty** 19 **% minority faculty** 4

## FINANCIAL FACTS

**Tuition (in-state/out-of-state):** $8,154/$11,538 **Books and supplies:** $750

## ADMISSIONS

**ADMISSIONS SELECTIVITY RATING: 68**

**# of applications received:** 262 **% applicants accepted:** 97 **% acceptees attending:** 70 **Average GMAT:** 550 **Average GPA:** 3.20 **TOEFL required of int'l applicants?** yes **Minimum TOEFL (paper/computer):** 550/213 **Application Fee:** $30 **Regular Application Deadline:** 6/1 **Regular Notification:** rolling **Deferment Available?** yes **Maximum length of deferment:** 2 years **Transfer Students Accepted?** yes **Non-fall Admissions?** yes **Need-Blind Admissions?** yes

# NORTHERN KENTUCKY UNIVERSITY
## COLLEGE OF BUSINESS

**ADMISSIONS CONTACT:** AMANDA STARZEC, GRADUATE ASSISTANT
**ADDRESS:** COLLEGE OF BUSINESS, NUNN DRIVE, HIGHLAND HEIGHTS, KY 41099
**PHONE:** 859-572-6336 • **FAX:** 859-572-6177
**E-MAIL:** MBUSINESS@NKU.EDU
**WEBSITE:** WWW.NKU.EDU/~MBUSINESS

## GENERAL INFORMATION

**Type of School:** public **Environment:** metropolis

## STUDENTS

**Enrollment of parent institution:** 14,000 **Enrollment of business school:** 250 **% male/female:** 59/41 **% out-of-state:** 16 **% part-time:** 85 **Average age at entry:** 27

## ACADEMICS

**Student/faculty ratio:** 20:1 **Joint Degrees:** JD/MBA, minimum 2.8 years

## FINANCIAL FACTS

**Tuition (in-state/out-of-state):** $4,200/$9,800 **Fees:** $575 **% of students receiving aid:** 33 **% of students receiving loans:** 23 **% of students receiving grants:** 10 **Average award package:** $8,356 **Average grant:** $3,359 **Average student loan debt:** $27,880

## ADMISSIONS

**ADMISSIONS SELECTIVITY RATING: 72**

**# of applications received:** 71 **% applicants accepted:** 73 **% acceptees attending:** 58 **GMAT Range (25th to 75th percentile):** 440-630 **Average GMAT:** 529 **Average GPA:** 3.28 **TOEFL required of int'l applicants?** yes **Minimum TOEFL:** 550 **Application Fee:** $30 **Regular Application Deadline:** 8/1 **Regular Notification:** rolling **Deferment Available?** yes **Transfer Students Accepted?** yes **Non-fall Admissions?** yes **Need-Blind Admissions?** yes **Applicants also look at:** University of Cincinnati, Xavier University

# OAKLAND UNIVERSITY
## SCHOOL OF BUSINESS ADMINSTRATION

**ADMISSIONS CONTACT:** DONNA D. FREE, COORDINATOR OF GRADUATE BUSINESS PROGRAMS
**ADDRESS:** 432 ELLIOTT HALL, ROCHESTER, MI 48309-4493
**PHONE:** 248-370-3287 • **FAX:** 248-370-4964
**E-MAIL:** GBP@LISTS.OAKLAND.EDU
**WEBSITE:** WWW.SBA.OAKLAND.EDU

## GENERAL INFORMATION

**Type of School:** public **Environment:** town **Academic Calendar:** semester

## STUDENTS

**Enrollment of parent institution:** 17,339 **Enrollment of business school:** 460 **% male/female:** 66/34 **% out-of-state:** 5 **% part-time:**

95 **% international:** 5 **Average age at entry:** 28 **Average years work experience at entry:** 5

### ACADEMICS

**Student/faculty ratio:** 19:1 **% female faculty** 19 **% minority faculty** 5

### FINANCIAL FACTS

**Tuition (in-state/out-of-state):** $6,894/$11,993 **Books and supplies:** $800 **Room & board:** $7,170 **Average grant:** $4,500

### ADMISSIONS

**ADMISSIONS SELECTIVITY RATING:** 73

**# of applications received:** 116 **% applicants accepted:** 84 **% acceptees attending:** 90 **Average GMAT:** 535 **Average GPA:** 3.23 **TOEFL required of int'l applicants?** yes **Minimum TOEFL (paper/computer):** 550/213 **Application Fee:** $50 **International Application Fee:** $50 **Regular Application Deadline:** 8/1 **Regular Notification:** rolling **Deferment Available?** yes **Maximum length of deferment:** 1 year **Transfer Students Accepted?** yes **Non-fall Admissions?** yes **Need-Blind Admissions?** yes **Applicants also look at:** Wayne State University

### EMPLOYMENT PROFILE

**Average starting salary:** $70,000

# OHIO UNIVERSITY
## COLLEGE OF BUSINESS

**ADMISSIONS CONTACT:** JAN ROSS, ASSISTANT DIRECTOR, GRADUATE PROGRAM
**ADDRESS:** 514 COPELAND HALL, ATHENS, OH 45701
**PHONE:** 740-593-4320 • **FAX:** 740-593-1388
**E-MAIL:** ROSSJ@OHIO.EDU
**WEBSITE:** WWW.COB.OHIOU.EDU/GRAD/

### GENERAL INFORMATION

**Type of School:** public **Environment:** rural **Academic Calendar:** quarters

### STUDENTS

**Enrollment of parent institution:** 19,000 **Enrollment of business school:** 105 **% male/female:** 55/45 **% out-of-state:** 50 **% minorities:** 7 **% international:** 20 **Average age at entry:** 25 **Average years work experience at entry:** 2

### ACADEMICS

**Student/faculty ratio:** 10:1 **% female faculty** 10 **% minority faculty** 10 **Joint Degrees:** MBA/MSpAd, 2 years; MBA/MA International Affairs, 2 years

### FINANCIAL FACTS

**Tuition (in-state/out-of-state):** $8,800/$18,400 **Fees:** $4,000 **Books and supplies:** $4,700 **Room & board:** $10,000 **% of students receiving aid:** 70 **% of first-year students receiving aid:** 70

**Average award package:** $15,000 **Average grant:** $8,000

### ADMISSIONS

**ADMISSIONS SELECTIVITY RATING:** 77

**# of applications received:** 264 **% applicants accepted:** 64 **% acceptees attending:** 62 **GMAT Range (25th to 75th percentile):** 470-670 **Average GMAT:** 555 **Average GPA:** 3.0 **TOEFL required of int'l applicants?** yes **Minimum TOEFL (paper/computer):** 600/250 **Application Fee:** $30 **Regular Application Deadline:** 1/15 **Regular Notification:** 4/1 **Deferment Available?** yes **Maximum length of deferment:** 1 year **Need-Blind Admissions?** yes

# OKLAHOMA CITY UNIVERSITY
## MEINDERS SCHOOL OF BUSINESS

**ADMISSIONS CONTACT:** LESLIE MCKENZIE, MED, DIRECTOR, GRADUATE ADMISSIONS
**ADDRESS:** 2501 N BLACKWELDER, ANN LACY ADMISSION BUILDING, OKLAHOMA CITY, OK 73106
**PHONE:** 405-208-5351 • **FAX:** 405-208-5356
**E-MAIL:** GADMISSIONS@OKCU.EDU
**WEBSITE:** WWW.YOUATOCU.COM

### GENERAL INFORMATION

**Type of School:** private **Affiliation:** Methodist

### STUDENTS

**Enrollment of parent institution:** 3,695 **Enrollment of business school:** 657 **% male/female:** 90/10 **% out-of-state:** 20 **% part-time:** 60 **% minorities:** 30 **Average age at entry:** 28

### ACADEMICS

**Student/faculty ratio:** 13:1 **% female faculty** 31 **% minority faculty** 33 **Joint Degrees:** MBA/JD, 114 credit hours, (MBA=30 and JD=84); MBA/MSN, 75 credit hours **Prominent Alumni:** Michael J. Maples, Former EVP, Worldwide Products, Microsoft; Dennis Dougherty, Founding Partner, Intersouth; Dr. Richard Ng, Pacific Manager, GE; Martha Burger, VP, HR, Treasurer, Chesapeake Energy

### FINANCIAL FACTS

**Tuition:** $10,872 **Fees:** $774 **Books and supplies:** $1,000 **Room & board (on/off campus):** $3,700/$6,000 **% of students receiving aid:** 51 **% of first-year students receiving aid:** 65 **% of students receiving loans:** 11 **% of students receiving grants:** 43 **Average award package:** $4,610 **Average grant:** $2,557

### ADMISSIONS

**ADMISSIONS SELECTIVITY RATING:** 61

**# of applications received:** 44 **% applicants accepted:** 84 **% acceptees attending:** 68 **Average GMAT:** 350 **Average GPA:** 2.88 **TOEFL required of int'l applicants?** yes **Minimum TOEFL (paper/computer):** 500/173 **Application Fee:** $30 **International Application Fee:** $70 **Regular Application Deadline:** rolling **Regular Notification:** rolling **Deferment Available?** yes **Maximum length of**

deferment: 1 year **Transfer Students Accepted?** yes **Non-fall Admissions?** yes **Need-Blind Admissions?** yes **Applicants also look at:** Oklahoma State University, University of Oklahoma

# OKLAHOMA STATE UNIVERSITY
## SPEARS SCHOOL OF BUSINESS

**ADMISSIONS CONTACT:** JANICE ANALLA, ASSISTANT DIRECTOR, MBA PROGRAM
**ADDRESS:** OKLAHOMA STATE UNIVERSITY, 102 GUNDERSEN HALL, STILLWATER, OK 74078-4022
**PHONE:** 405-744-2951 • **FAX:** 405-744-7474
**E-MAIL:** MBA-OSU@OKSTATE.EDU
**WEBSITE:** HTTP://SPEARS.OKSTATE.EDU/MBA/

### GENERAL INFORMATION
**Type of School:** public **Environment:** town **Academic Calendar:** semester

### STUDENTS
**Enrollment of business school:** 319 **% male/female:** 65/35 **% part-time:** 72 **% minorities:** 1 **% international:** 22 **Average age at entry:** 24 **Average years work experience at entry:** 5

### ACADEMICS
**Student/faculty ratio:** 25:1 **Joint Degrees:** MBA/MSTM, 2.5 years; DO/MBA, 1.5 years. **Prominent Alumni:** Tiffany Sewell Howard, COO, The Charles Machine Works; Dennis Reilley, CEO, Praxaire; Charlie Eitel, Chair & CEO, Simmons Companies; Don Humphries, VP & Treasurer, Exxon Mobile

### FINANCIAL FACTS
**Tuition (in-state/out-of-state):** $3,601/$12,610 **Fees:** $1,754 **Books and supplies:** $4,460 **Room & board:** $6,780 **Average award package:** $4,000 **Average grant:** $1,000 **Average student loan debt:** $8,000

### ADMISSIONS
**ADMISSIONS SELECTIVITY RATING: 79**

**# of applications received:** 95 **% applicants accepted:** 66 **% acceptees attending:** 68 **GMAT Range (25th to 75th percentile):** 510-610 **Average GMAT:** 560 **Average GPA:** 3.47 **TOEFL required of int'l applicants?** yes **Minimum TOEFL (paper/computer):** 575/233 **Application Fee:** $40 **International Application Fee:** $75 **Regular Application Deadline:** 7/1 **Regular Notification:** rolling **Deferment Available?** yes **Maximum length of deferment:** 1 year **Transfer Students Accepted?** yes **Non-fall Admissions?** yes **Need-Blind Admissions?** yes **Applicants also look at:** The University of Tulsa, University of Arkansas—Fayetteville, University of Kansas, University of Oklahoma

### EMPLOYMENT PROFILE
**Primary source of full-time job acceptances**

School-facilitated activities 18 (45%)

Graduate-facilitated activities 23 (55%)

**Average starting salary:** $57,151

**Percent employed:** 15

**Grads employed by field: ..........% avg. salary:**

Accounting ....................................3 $43,000
Finance ..........................................45 $52,257
Marketing ......................................9 $49,619
MIS..................................................9 $66,000
Operations.....................................9 $49,000
Consulting......................................9 $49,000
General Management ....................7 $41,500
Other...............................................9 $53,900

# OREGON STATE UNIVERSITY
## SCHOOL OF BUSINESS ADMINISTRATION

**ADMISSIONS CONTACT:** DIANE JARVI, MBA PROGRAM COORDINATOR
**ADDRESS:** 200 BEXELL HALL, CORVALLIS, OR 97330
**PHONE:** 541-737-3716 • **FAX:** 541-737-4890
**E-MAIL:** JARVI@BUS.OREGONSTATE.EDU
**WEBSITE:** WWW.BUS.OREGONSTATE.EDU

### GENERAL INFORMATION
**Type of School:** public **Environment:** town **Academic Calendar:** quarter

### STUDENTS
**Enrollment of parent institution:** 19,162 **Enrollment of business school:** 65 **% male/female:** 55/45 **% minorities:** 13 **Average age at entry:** 29 **Average years work experience at entry:** 3

### ACADEMICS
**Student/faculty ratio:** 3:1 **% female faculty** 15 **% minority faculty** 18

### FINANCIAL FACTS
**Tuition (in-state/out-of-state):** $9,366/$15,603 **Fees:** $525 **Books and supplies:** $1,350 **Room & board:** $6,336

### ADMISSIONS
**ADMISSIONS SELECTIVITY RATING: 82**

**# of applications received:** 142 **% applicants accepted:** 50 **% acceptees attending:** 65 **Average GMAT:** 554 **Average GPA:** 3.23 **TOEFL required of int'l applicants?** yes **Minimum TOEFL (paper/computer):** 575/233 **Application Fee:** $50 **Regular Application Deadline:** 3/5 **Regular Notification:** rolling **Deferment Available?** yes **Transfer Students Accepted?** yes **Non-fall Admissions?** yes **Need-Blind Admissions?** yes **Applicants also look at:** Portland State University, University of Oregon

# PACE UNIVERSITY
## LUBIN SCHOOL OF BUSINESS

***ADMISSIONS CONTACT:*** *JOANNA BRODA, DIRECTOR OF GRADUATE ADMISSION*
***ADDRESS:*** *ONE PACE PLAZA, NEW YORK, NY 10038*
***PHONE:*** *212-346-1531 • FAX: 212-346-1585*
***E-MAIL:*** *GRADNYC@PACE.EDU*
***WEBSITE:*** *WWW.PACE.EDU/LUBIN*

### GENERAL INFORMATION

**Type of School:** private **Environment:** metropolis **Academic Calendar:** semester

### STUDENTS

**Enrollment of parent institution:** 13,670 **Enrollment of business school:** 1,197 **% male/female:** 53/47 **% out-of-state:** 6 **% part-time:** 81 **% minorities:** 8 **% international:** 47 **Average age at entry:** 24 **Average years work experience at entry:** 2

### ACADEMICS

**Student/faculty ratio:** 23:1 **% female faculty** 12 **% minority faculty** 21 **Joint Degrees:** MBA/JD **Prominent Alumni:** Ivan G. Seidenberg, President and CEO, Verizon Communications; John R. Danieli, President, CEO, Owner, Computer Merchant LTD; Herbert Henkel, Chair, President & CEO, Ingersoll Rand; Mel Karmazin, CEO, Sirius Satellite Radio Inc.; Marie J. Toulantis, CEO, Barnes and Noble

### FINANCIAL FACTS

**Tuition:** $29,232 **Fees:** $480 **Books and supplies:** $3,450 **Room & board (on/off campus):** $10,490/$19,427 **% of students receiving aid:** 54 **% of first-year students receiving aid:** 63 **% of students receiving loans:** 30 **% of students receiving grants:** 33 **Average award package:** $14,710 **Average grant:** $5,443 **Average student loan debt:** $20,963

### ADMISSIONS

**ADMISSIONS SELECTIVITY RATING: 79**

**# of applications received:** 870 **% applicants accepted:** 49 **% acceptees attending:** 43 **GMAT Range (25th to 75th percentile):** 490-640 **Average GMAT:** 544 **Average GPA:** 3.21 **TOEFL required of int'l applicants?** yes **Minimum TOEFL (paper/computer):** 570/228 **Application Fee:** $65 **International Application Fee:** $65 **Regular Application Deadline:** 8/6 **Regular Notification:** rolling **Transfer Students Accepted?** yes **Non-fall Admissions?** yes **Need-Blind Admissions?** yes

### EMPLOYMENT PROFILE

**Average starting salary:** $57,000

**Grads employed by field: ..........% avg. salary:**

Accounting ................................... 32 NR
Finance ......................................... 57 NR
Consulting ..................................... 3 NR
General Management ................... 3 NR
Other ............................................. 5 NR

# PACIFIC LUTHERAN UNIVERSITY
## SCHOOL OF BUSINESS

***ADMISSIONS CONTACT:*** *ABBY WIGSTROM-CARLSON, DIRECTOR OF GRADUATE STUDIES & EXTERNAL RELATIONS*
***ADDRESS:*** *OFFICE OF ADMISSIONS, TACOMA, WA 98447*
***PHONE:*** *253-535-7151 • FAX: 253-536-5136*
***E-MAIL:*** *PLUMBA@PLU.EDU*
***WEBSITE:*** *WWW.PLU.EDU/MBA*

### GENERAL INFORMATION

**Type of School:** private **Affiliation:** Lutheran **Environment:** city **Academic Calendar:** 4-1-4-2-2

### STUDENTS

**Enrollment of parent institution:** 3,680 **Enrollment of business school:** 66 **% male/female:** 83/17 **% out-of-state:** 9 **% part-time:** 36 **% minorities:** 7 **% international:** 21 **Average age at entry:** 31 **Average years work experience at entry:** 9

### ACADEMICS

**Student/faculty ratio:** 12:1 **% female faculty** 30 **% minority faculty** 10

### FINANCIAL FACTS

**Tuition:** $17,862 **Books and supplies:** $850 **Room & board:** $6,765 **Average grant:** $1,219

### ADMISSIONS

**ADMISSIONS SELECTIVITY RATING: 74**

**# of applications received:** 44 **% applicants accepted:** 73 **% acceptees attending:** 66 **Average GPA:** 3.23 **TOEFL required of int'l applicants?** yes **Minimum TOEFL (computer):** 230 **Application Fee:** $45 **International Application Fee:** $45 **Regular Application Deadline:** rolling **Regular Notification:** rolling **Deferment Available?** yes **Maximum length of deferment:** 1 year **Transfer Students Accepted?** yes **Non-fall Admissions?** yes **Need-Blind Admissions?** yes **Applicants also look at:** Seattle Pacific University, Seattle University, University of Washington

### EMPLOYMENT PROFILE

**Average starting salary:** $75,000

# PENNSYLVAMIA STATE UNIVERSITY—EMBA

## THE MARY JEAN AND FRANK P. SMEAL COLLEGE OF BUSINESS

**ADMISSIONS CONTACT:** TIM QUIGLEY, ADMISSIONS DIRECTOR
**ADDRESS:** 220 BUSINESS BUILDING, UNIVERSITY PARK, PA 16802
**PHONE:** 866-999-3622 • **FAX:** 814-863-8072
**E-MAIL:** SMEALEXECMBA@PSU.EDU
**WEBSITE:** WWW.SMEAL.PSU.EDU/EXECMBA

### GENERAL INFORMATION

**Type of School:** public **Academic Calendar:** semester

### STUDENTS

**Enrollment of parent institution:** 41,289 **Enrollment of business school:** 44 **% male/female:** 79/21 **% out-of-state:** 50 **% minorities:** 4 **% international:** 8 **Average age at entry:** 39 **Average years work experience at entry:** 16

### ACADEMICS

**Student/faculty ratio:** 2:1 **% female faculty** 15 **% minority faculty** 20

### FINANCIAL FACTS

**Tuition:** $42,000 **Fees:** $484 **% of students receiving aid:** 90 **% of first-year students receiving aid:** 85 **% of students receiving loans:** 67 **% of students receiving grants:** 30 **Average award package:** $29,728 **Average grant:** $40,500 **Average student loan debt:** $34,729

### ADMISSIONS

**ADMISSIONS SELECTIVITY RATING:** 71

**# of applications received:** 40 **% applicants accepted:** 78 **% acceptees attending:** 77 **Average GMAT:** 572 **TOEFL required of int'l applicants?** yes **Application Fee:** $60 **International Application Fee:** $60 **Application Deadline/Notification Round 1:** 3/1 / 3/15 **Round 2:** 5/1 / 5/15 **Round 3:** 6/15 / 7/1 **Early decision program?** yes **ED deadline /notification:** 3/1 / 3/15 **Deferment Available?** yes **Maximum length of deferment:** 1 year **Need-Blind Admissions?** yes **Applicants also look at:** Columbia University, Cornell University, New York University, EMBA, Rutgers, The State University of New Jersey, Temple University, University of Pennsylvania, Villanova University—EMBA

# PENNSYLVAMIA STATE UNIVERSITY—GREAT VALLEY CAMPUS

## SCHOOL OF GRADUATE PROFESSIONAL STUDIES

**ADMISSIONS CONTACT:** JOANN KELLY, GRADUATE ENROLLMENT COORDINATOR
**ADDRESS:** 30 EAST SWEDESFORD ROAD, MALVERN, PA 19355
**PHONE:** 610-648-3248 • **FAX:** 610-725-5296
**E-MAIL:** GVMBA@PSU.EDU
**WEBSITE:** WWW.GV.PSU.EDU

### GENERAL INFORMATION

**Type of School:** public **Academic Calendar:** semester

### ACADEMICS

**Student/faculty ratio:** 18:1 **% female faculty** 44 **% minority faculty** 5

### FINANCIAL FACTS

**Tuition (in-state/out-of-state):** $23,800/$39,000 **Fees:** $600 **Books and supplies:** $1,200 **Room & board (off campus):** $20,000 **% of students receiving aid:** 50 **% of first-year students receiving aid:** 50 **% of students receiving loans:** 50 **% of students receiving grants:** 1 **Average award package:** $4,500 **Average grant:** $15,000 **Average student loan debt:** $8,000

### ADMISSIONS

**ADMISSIONS SELECTIVITY RATING:** 60*

**TOEFL required of int'l applicants?** yes **Minimum TOEFL (paper/computer):** 550/230 **Application Fee:** $45 **International Application Fee:** $45 **Deferment Available?** yes **Maximum length of deferment:** 1 year **Transfer Students Accepted?** yes **Non-fall Admissions?** yes **Need-Blind Admissions?** yes

### EMPLOYMENT PROFILE

| Grads employed by field: | % | avg. salary: |
| --- | --- | --- |
| Accounting | 10 | NR |
| Finance | 10 | NR |
| Human Resources | 4 | NR |
| Marketing | 6 | NR |
| MIS | 7 | NR |
| Operations | 8 | NR |
| Strategic Planning | 5 | NR |
| Consulting | 5 | NR |
| Communications | 2 | NR |
| Entrepreneurship | 5 | NR |
| General Management | 10 | NR |
| Global Management | 8 | NR |
| Quantitative | 2 | NR |
| Venture Capital | 2 | NR |
| Internet/New Media | 2 | NR |
| Nonprofit | 2 | NR |
| Other | 11 | NR |

# PENNSYLVAMIA STATE UNIVERSITY—HARRISBURG CAMPUS

## SCHOOL OF BUSINESS ADMINISTRATION

**ADMISSIONS CONTACT:** DR. THOMAS STREVELER, DIRECTOR OF ENROLLMENT SERVICES
**ADDRESS:** 777 WEST HARRISBURG PIKE, MIDDLETOWN, PA 17057
**PHONE:** 717-948-6250 • **FAX:** 717-948-6325
**E-MAIL:** HBGADMIT@PSU.EDU
**WEBSITE:** WWW.HBG.PSU.EDU/SBUS

### GENERAL INFORMATION
**Type of School:** public **Environment:** village **Academic Calendar:** semester

### STUDENTS
**Enrollment of parent institution:** 3,239 **Enrollment of business school:** 207 **% male/female:** 64/36 **% out-of-state:** 5 **% part-time:** 88 **% minorities:** 7 **% international:** 5 **Average age at entry:** 27 **Average years work experience at entry:** 3

### ACADEMICS
**Student/faculty ratio:** 12:1

### FINANCIAL FACTS
**Tuition (in-state/out-of-state):** $12,000/$17,592 **Books and supplies:** $4,170 **Average grant:** $4,200

### ADMISSIONS
**ADMISSIONS SELECTIVITY RATING: 67**
**# of applications received:** 76 **% applicants accepted:** 91 **% acceptees attending:** 90 **Average GMAT:** 520 **Average GPA:** 3.0 **TOEFL required of int'l applicants?** yes **Minimum TOEFL (paper/computer):** 550/213 **Application Fee:** $50 **International Application Fee:** $50 **Regular Application Deadline:** 7/18 **Regular Notification:** rolling **Deferment Available?** yes **Maximum length of deferment:** 3 years **Transfer Students Accepted?** yes **Non-fall Admissions?** yes **Need-Blind Admissions?** yes

### EMPLOYMENT PROFILE
**Average starting salary:** $45,000

# PENNSYLVAMIA STATE UNIVERSITY—ONLINE MBA

## PENN STATE UNIVERSITY iMBA

**ADMISSIONS CONTACT:** TERA VAN DOREN, PROGRAM COORDINATOR
**ADDRESS:** 222 OUTREACH BUILDING, UNIVERSITY PARK, PA 16802-3601
**PHONE:** 814-898-6527 • **FAX:** 814-898-6528
**E-MAIL:** IMBA@PSU.EDU
**WEBSITE:** WWW.WORLDCAMPUS.PSU.EDU/IMBA

### GENERAL INFORMATION
**Type of School:** public

### STUDENTS
**Enrollment of parent institution:** 83,177 **Enrollment of business school:** 120 **% out-of-state:** 86 **% part-time:** 100 **% international:** 10 **Average age at entry:** 32 **Average years work experience at entry:** 7.5

### ACADEMICS
**Student/faculty ratio:** 30:1 **% female faculty** 23 **% minority faculty** 25

### FINANCIAL FACTS
**Tuition:** $23,000

### ADMISSIONS
**ADMISSIONS SELECTIVITY RATING: 92**
**# of applications received:** 214 **% applicants accepted:** 38 **% acceptees attending:** 93 **Average GMAT:** 602 **Average GPA:** 3.1 **TOEFL required of int'l applicants?** yes **Minimum TOEFL (paper/computer):** 600/250 **Application Fee:** $75 **International Application Fee:** $75 **Regular Application Deadline:** 5/31 **Regular Notification:** 6/7 **Deferment Available?** yes **Maximum length of deferment:** 1 year **Transfer Students Accepted?** yes **Need-Blind Admissions?** yes

# RIDER UNIVERSITY

## COLLEGE OF BUSINESS ADMINSTRATION

**ADMISSIONS CONTACT:** JAMIE MITCHELL, DIRECTOR, GRADUATE ADMISSIONS
**ADDRESS:** PJ CIAMBELLI HALL, 2083 LAWRENCEVILLE ROAD, LAWRENCEVILLE, NJ 08648-3099
**PHONE:** 609-896-5036 • **FAX:** 609-895-5680
**E-MAIL:** GRADADM@RIDER.EDU
**WEBSITE:** WWW.RIDER.EDU/CBA

### GENERAL INFORMATION
**Type of School:** private **Environment:** village **Academic Calendar:** semester

### STUDENTS
**Enrollment of parent institution:** 5,562 **Enrollment of business school:** 276 **% male/female:** 47/53 **% out-of-state:** 28 **% part-time:** 84 **% minorities:** 37 **% international:** 16 **Average age at entry:** 28

## ACADEMICS

**Student/faculty ratio:** 17:1 **% female faculty** 32 **% minority faculty** 23 **Joint Degrees:** BS/BA/MBA; BS/BA/MAcc; Each are 5 year programs. **Prominent Alumni:** Dennis Longstreet, Company Group Chair, Johnson and Johnson; Robert Christie, President and CEO, Thomson Corp.; Bernard V. Vonderschmitt, Chair of the Board, Xilinx, Inc.; Anne Sweigart, Chair, President and CEO, D & E Communications; Kenneth Burenga, Former President and CEO, Dow Jones & Co.

## FINANCIAL FACTS

**Tuition:** $11,520 **Fees:** $210 **Books and supplies:** $5,320 **Room & board:** $8,840 **% of students receiving aid:** 77 **% of first-year students receiving aid:** 73 **% of students receiving loans:** 63 **% of students receiving grants:** 33 **Average award package:** $14,577 **Average grant:** $6,690 **Average student loan debt:** $12,676

## ADMISSIONS

**# of applications received:** 118 **% applicants accepted:** 70 **% acceptees attending:** 87 **GMAT Range (25th to 75th percentile):** 440-540 **Average GMAT:** 486 **Average GPA:** 3.32 **TOEFL required of int'l applicants?** yes **Minimum TOEFL (paper/computer):** 585/240 **Application Fee:** $45 **International Application Fee:** $45 **Regular Application Deadline:** 8/1 **Deferment Available?** yes **Maximum length of deferment:** 1 year **Transfer Students Accepted?** yes **Non-fall Admissions?** yes **Need-Blind Admissions?** yes **Applicants also look at:** Drexel University, Fairleigh Dickinson University, La Salle University, Monmouth University, Rutgers, The State University of New Jersey, Seton Hall University

# ROCHESTER INSTITUTE OF TECHNOLOGY
## COLLEGE OF BUSINESS

**ADMISSIONS CONTACT:** *NANCY WOEBKENBERG, PROGRAM MANAGER*
**ADDRESS:** *105 LOMB MEMORIAL DRIVE, ROCHESTER, NY 14623*
**PHONE:** *585-475-2229 • FAX: 585-475-5476*
**E-MAIL:** *GRADINFO@RIT.EDU*
**WEBSITE:** *WWW.RITMBA.COM*

## GENERAL INFORMATION

**Type of School:** private **Environment:** city **Academic Calendar:** quarter

## STUDENTS

**Enrollment of parent institution:** 15,200 **Enrollment of business school:** 296 **% male/female:** 80/20 **% out-of-state:** 40 **% part-time:** 40 **% minorities:** 8 **% international:** 35 **Average age at entry:** 27 **Average years work experience at entry:** 4.2

## ACADEMICS

**Student/faculty ratio:** 9:1 **% female faculty** 21 **% minority faculty** 5 **Prominent Alumni:** Daniel Carp, Chair & CEO, Eastman Kodak Company; Thomas Curley, President & CEO, Associated Press

## FINANCIAL FACTS

**Tuition:** $25,392 **Fees:** $453 **Books and supplies:** $1,500 **Room & board:** $8,451 **% of students receiving aid:** 17 **% of first-year students receiving aid:** 35 **% of students receiving grants:** 17 **Average grant:** $8,915

## ADMISSIONS

**# of applications received:** 265 **% applicants accepted:** 82 **% acceptees attending:** 66 **GMAT Range (25th to 75th percentile):** 480-620 **Average GMAT:** 557 **Average GPA:** 3.15 **TOEFL required of int'l applicants?** yes **Minimum TOEFL (paper/computer):** 580/237 **Application Fee:** $50 **International Application Fee:** $50 **Regular Application Deadline:** 8/1 **Regular Notification:** rolling **Deferment Available?** yes **Maximum length of deferment:** 1 year **Transfer Students Accepted?** yes **Non-fall Admissions?** yes **Need-Blind Admissions?** yes

## EMPLOYMENT PROFILE

| Grads employed by field: | .........% | avg. salary: |
|---|---|---|
| Operations | 6 | NR |
| Other | 6 | NR |

# SAINT MARY'S UNIVERSITY OF MINNESOTA
## SCHOOL OF GRADUATE & PROFESSIONAL PROGRAMS

**ADMISSIONS CONTACT:** *SARAH LANG, DIRECTOR OF ADMISSIONS*
**ADDRESS:** *2500 PARK AVENUE, MINNEAPOLIS, MN 55404-4403*
**PHONE:** *612-728-5100 • FAX: 612-728-5121*
**E-MAIL:** *TC-ADMISSION@SMUMN.EDU*
**WEBSITE:** *WWW.SMUMN.EDU/GRADPRO*

## GENERAL INFORMATION

**Type of School:** private **Affiliation:** Roman Catholic **Environment:** rural **Academic Calendar:** 2005-2006

## STUDENTS

**Enrollment of business school:** 134

## ACADEMICS

**Student/faculty ratio:** 12:1

## FINANCIAL FACTS

**Tuition:** $8,520 **Books and supplies:** $500 **Average award package:** $18,090

## ADMISSIONS

**# of applications received:** 50 **% applicants accepted:** 80 **TOEFL required of int'l applicants?** yes **Minimum TOEFL (paper/computer):** 550/213 **Application Fee:** $25 **Regular Application Deadline:**

rolling **Regular Notification:** rolling
**Transfer Students Accepted?** yes **Non-fall Admissions?** yes

# SAINT MARY'S UNIVERSITY— CANADA
## SOBEY SCHOOL OF BUSINESS

**ADMISSIONS CONTACT:** LEAH RAY, MANAGING DIRECTOR, MBA PROGRAM
**ADDRESS:** 923 ROBIE STREET, HALIFAX, NS B3H 3C3 CANADA
**PHONE:** 902-420-5002 • **FAX:** 902-420-5119
**E-MAIL:** MBA@SMU.CA
**WEBSITE:** WWW.SOBEY.SMU.CA

### GENERAL INFORMATION
**Type of School:** private **Academic Calendar:** semester

### STUDENTS
**Enrollment of parent institution:** 8,000 **Enrollment of business school:** 82 **% male/female:** 60/40 **% out-of-state:** 60 **% part-time:** 68 **% international:** 40 **Average age at entry:** 28 **Average years work experience at entry:** 6

### ACADEMICS
**Student/faculty ratio:** 5:1 **Joint Degrees:** MBA-CMA, 28 months.

### FINANCIAL FACTS
**Tuition:** $9,235 **Fees:** $480 **Books and supplies:** $1,000 **% of students receiving aid:** 20 **% of first-year students receiving aid:** 10 **% of students receiving grants:** 20 **Average grant:** $2,500

### ADMISSIONS
**ADMISSIONS SELECTIVITY RATING: 85**
**# of applications received:** 114 **% applicants accepted:** 64 **% acceptees attending:** 78 **GMAT Range (25th to 75th percentile):** 550-720 **Average GMAT:** 610 **Average GPA:** 3.3 **TOEFL required of int'l applicants?** yes **Minimum TOEFL (paper/computer):** 580/237 **Application Fee:** $70 **International Application Fee:** $70 **Regular Application Deadline:** 5/31 **Regular Notification:** rolling **Deferment Available?** yes **Maximum length of deferment:** 1 year **Transfer Students Accepted?** yes **Need-Blind Admissions?** yes

# SALISBURY UNIVERSITY
## FRANKLIN P. PERDUE SCHOOL OF BUSINESS

**ADMISSIONS CONTACT:** JANINE VIENNA, MBA DIRECTOR
**ADDRESS:** 1101 CAMDEN AVENUE, SALISBURY, MD 21801-6837
**PHONE:** 410-548-3983 • **FAX:** 410-548-2908
**E-MAIL:** JMVIENNA@SALISBURY.EDU
**WEBSITE:** HTTP://MBA.SALISBURY.EDU

### GENERAL INFORMATION
**Type of School:** public **Environment:** town **Academic Calendar:**

semester

### STUDENTS
**Enrollment of parent institution:** 7,000 **Enrollment of business school:** 75 **% male/female:** 61/39 **% part-time:** 56 **% minorities:** 1 **% international:** 21 **Average age at entry:** 24 **Average years work experience at entry:** 2

### ACADEMICS
**Student/faculty ratio:** 22:1 **% female faculty** 5

### FINANCIAL FACTS
**Tuition (in-state/out-of-state):** $7,470/$16,050 **Fees:** $1,410 **Books and supplies:** $1,000 **Room & board:** $8,000 **Average grant:** $9,482

### ADMISSIONS
**ADMISSIONS SELECTIVITY RATING: 69**
**# of applications received:** 47 **% applicants accepted:** 79 **% acceptees attending:** 84 **Average GMAT:** 490 **Average GPA:** 3.22 **TOEFL required of int'l applicants?** yes **Minimum TOEFL (paper/computer):** 550/213 **Application Fee:** $45 **International Application Fee:** $45 **Regular Application Deadline:** 3/1 **Regular Notification:** 4/1 **Transfer Students Accepted?** yes **Non-fall Admissions?** yes **Need-Blind Admissions?** yes

# SAM HOUSTON STATE UNIVERSITY
## COLLEGE OF BUSINESS ADMINISTRATION

**ADMISSIONS CONTACT:** DR. LEROY ASHORN, ASSOCIATE DEAN/COORDINATOR OF GRADUATE STUDIES
**ADDRESS:** PO BOX 2056, HUNTSVILLE, TX 77341-2056
**PHONE:** 936-294-1239 • **FAX:** 936-294-3612
**E-MAIL:** BUSGRAD@SHSU.EDU
**WEBSITE:** HTTP://COBA.SHSU.EDU/

### GENERAL INFORMATION
**Type of School:** public **Environment:** town

### STUDENTS
**Enrollment of business school:** 164 **% male/female:** 49/51 **% part-time:** 71 **% minorities:** 7 **% international:** 5

### FINANCIAL FACTS
**Tuition (in-state/out-of-state):** $6,822/$11,466

### ADMISSIONS
**ADMISSIONS SELECTIVITY RATING: 63**
**# of applications received:** 108 **% applicants accepted:** 71 **% acceptees attending:** 53 **GMAT Range (25th to 75th percentile):** 460-550 **Average GMAT:** 504 **TOEFL required of int'l applicants?** yes **Minimum TOEFL (paper/computer):** 550/213 **Application Fee:** $20 **International Application Fee:** $20 **Regular Application Deadline:** 8/1 **Regular Notification:** rolling **Transfer Students Accepted?** yes **Non-fall Admissions?** yes **Need-Blind Admissions?** yes

# SAMFORD UNIVERSITY
## SCHOOL OF BUSINESS

**ADMISSIONS CONTACT:** DR. DOUGLAS L. SMITH, DIRECTOR OF GRADUATE
  STUDIES
**ADDRESS:** DBH 344, SCHOOL OF BUSINESS, 800 LAKESHORE DRIVE,
  BIRMINGHAM, AL 35229
**PHONE:** 205-726-2040 • **FAX:** 205-726-2464
**E-MAIL:** BUSINESS.GRADUATE.STUDIES@SAMFORD.EDU
**WEBSITE:** WWW.SAMFORD.EDU/SCHOOLS/BUSINESS/MBA

### GENERAL INFORMATION

**Type of School:** private **Affiliation:** Baptist **Environment:** town
**Academic Calendar:** 9 weeks

### STUDENTS

**Enrollment of parent institution:** 4,440 **Enrollment of business
school:** 160 **% part-time:** 100 **Average age at entry:** 31 **Average
years work experience at entry:** 7

### ACADEMICS

**Student/faculty ratio:** 12:1 **% female faculty** 20 **% minority faculty**
10 **Joint Degrees:** MBA/MAcc, part-time, 18 months to 7 years to
complete program. Concentrations in management, accounting;
MBA/JD.

### FINANCIAL FACTS

**Tuition:** $5,760 **Books and supplies:** $600

### ADMISSIONS

**ADMISSIONS SELECTIVITY RATING: 73**

**# of applications received:** 80 **% applicants accepted:** 76 **%
acceptees attending:** 93 **GMAT Range (25th to 75th percentile):**
470-570 **Average GMAT:** 515 **Average GPA:** 3.0 **TOEFL required of
int'l applicants?** yes **Minimum TOEFL (paper/computer):** 550/213
**Application Fee:** $25 **International Application Fee:** $25 **Regular
Application Deadline:** rolling **Regular Notification:** rolling
**Deferment Available?** yes **Maximum length of deferment:** 1-year
**Transfer Students Accepted?** yes **Non-fall Admissions?** yes **Need-
Blind Admissions?** yes **Applicants also look at:** University of
Alabama at Birmingham

# SETON HALL UNIVERSITY
## STILLMAN SCHOOL OF BUSINESS

**ADMISSIONS CONTACT:** JOAN LILJEGREN, DIRECTOR OF GRADUATE ADMISSIONS
**ADDRESS:** GRADUATE ADMISSIONS—STILLMAN SCHOOL OF BUSINESS, 400
  SOUTH ORANGE AVENUE, SOUTH ORANGE, NJ 07079-2692
**PHONE:** 973-761-9262 • **FAX:** 973-761-9208
**E-MAIL:** STILLMAN@SHU.EDU
**WEBSITE:** WWW.BUSINESS.SHU.EDU

### GENERAL INFORMATION

**Type of School:** private **Affiliation:** Roman Catholic **Environment:**
village **Academic Calendar:** semester

### STUDENTS

**Enrollment of parent institution:** 8,293 **Enrollment of business
school:** 560 **% male/female:** 66/34 **% part-time:** 83 **Average age at
entry:** 26 **Average years work experience at entry:** 4

### ACADEMICS

**Student/faculty ratio:** 25:1 **% female faculty** 21 **Joint Degrees:**
MBA/MSIB, 3-5 years; MBA/JD, 3.5-4 years; MBA/MSN, 2.5-5 years;
MSIB/MA in Diplomacy & International Relations **Prominent Alumni:**
James O'Brien, Managing Director, Morgan Stanley; Gerald P.
Buccino, Chair and CEO of Buccino & Associates; Michael Wilk,
Partner, Ernst & Young; Stephen Lalor, Partner, Ernst & Young;
Joseph M. LaMotta, Chair Emeritus, Oppenheimer Capital

### FINANCIAL FACTS

**Tuition:** $21,810 **Fees:** $615 **Books and supplies:** $1,458 **Room &
board:** $10,200 **% of students receiving aid:** 28 **% of first-year stu-
dents receiving aid:** 38 **% of students receiving loans:** 25 **% of students receiving grants:** 8 **Average award package:** $15,863
**Average grant:** $11,093 **Average student loan debt:** $26,501

### ADMISSIONS

**ADMISSIONS SELECTIVITY RATING: 82**

**# of applications received:** 421 **% applicants accepted:** 56 **%
acceptees attending:** 56 **GMAT Range (25th to 75th percentile):**
500-700 **Average GMAT:** 565 **Average GPA:** 3.3 **TOEFL required of
int'l applicants?** yes **Minimum TOEFL (paper/computer):** 550/213
**Application Fee:** $75 **International Application Fee:** $100 **Regular
Application Deadline:** 6/1 **Regular Notification:** rolling **Early deci-
sion program?** yes **ED deadline /notification:** 4/1 / 4/15 **Deferment
Available?** yes **Maximum length of deferment:** 1 academic year
**Transfer Students Accepted?** yes **Non-fall Admissions?** yes **Need-
Blind Admissions?** yes **Applicants also look at:** Boston College,
Columbia University, Fairleigh Dickinson University, Montclair State
University, New York University, Pace University, Rutgers, The State
University of New Jersey

# SOUTHEASTERN LOUISIANA UNIVERSITY
## COLLEGE OF BUSINESS

**ADMISSIONS CONTACT:** *SANDRA MEYERS, GRADUATE ADMISSIONS ANALYST*
**ADDRESS:** *SLU 10752, HAMMOND, LA 70402*
**PHONE:** *800-222-7358 • FAX: 985-549-5632*
**E-MAIL:** *SMEYERS@SELU.EDU*
**WEBSITE:** *WWW.SELU.EDU/ACADEMICS/BUSINESS*

### GENERAL INFORMATION

**Type of School:** public **Environment:** village **Academic Calendar:** semester

### STUDENTS

**Enrollment of parent institution:** 16,068 **Enrollment of business school:** 169 **% male/female:** 46/54 **% out-of-state:** 3 **% part-time:** 35 **% minorities:** 25 **% international:** 23 **Average age at entry:** 26

### ACADEMICS

**Student/faculty ratio:** 5:1 **% female faculty** 19 **% minority faculty** 16 **Prominent Alumni:** Robin Roberts, ESPN Sportscaster; Russell Carollo, Pulitzer Prize Winner; Harold Jackson, President (Retired), Sunsweet Products; James J. Brady, Former President, National Democratic Party; Carl Barbier, Federal Judge

### FINANCIAL FACTS

**Tuition (in-state/out-of-state):** $3,131/$7,127 **Books and supplies:** $1,000 **Room & board (on/off campus):** $5,180/$7,366 **% of students receiving aid:** 47 **% of first-year students receiving aid:** 56 **% of students receiving loans:** 22 **Average award package:** $7,676

### ADMISSIONS

**ADMISSIONS SELECTIVITY RATING: 62**
**# of applications received:** 51 **% applicants accepted:** 98 **% acceptees attending:** 80 **GMAT Range (25th to 75th percentile):** 420-515 **Average GMAT:** 467 **Average GPA:** 3.14 **TOEFL required of int'l applicants?** yes **Minimum TOEFL (paper/computer):** 525/195 **Application Fee:** $20 **International Application Fee:** $30 **Regular Application Deadline:** 7/15 **Regular Notification:** rolling **Deferment Available?** yes **Maximum length of deferment:** 1 year **Transfer Students Accepted?** yes **Non-fall Admissions?** yes

# ST. BONAVENTURE UNIVERSITY
## SCHOOL OF BUSINESS

**ADMISSIONS CONTACT:** *CONNIE C. HORAN, SENIOR ASSOCIATE DIRECTOR OF ADMISSIONS*
**ADDRESS:** *OFFICE OF GRADUATE ADMISSIONS, PO BOX D, ST. BONAVENTURE, NY 14778*
**PHONE:** *716-375-2021 • FAX: 716-375-4015*
**E-MAIL:** *GRADSCH@SBU.EDU*
**WEBSITE:** *WWW.GRAD.SBU.EDU*

### GENERAL INFORMATION

**Type of School:** private **Affiliation:** Roman Catholic

### STUDENTS

**Enrollment of business school:** 129 **% international:** 3

### FINANCIAL FACTS

**Books and supplies:** $600 **Room & board (on campus):** $8,000 **Average student loan debt:** $25,738

### ADMISSIONS

**ADMISSIONS SELECTIVITY RATING: 60\***
**# TOEFL required of int'l applicants?** yes **Minimum TOEFL (paper/computer):** 550/213 **Application Fee:** $30 **International Application Fee:** $30 **Deferment Available?** yes **Maximum length of deferment:** 1 year **Transfer Students Accepted?** yes **Non-fall Admissions?** yes **Need-Blind Admissions?** yes

# ST. CLOUD STATE UNIVERSITY
## HERBERGER COLLEGE OF BUSINESS

**ADMISSIONS CONTACT:** *GRADUATE STUDIES OFFICE, GRADUATE ADMISSIONS MANAGER*
**ADDRESS:** *720 4TH AVENUE SOUTH, AS-121, ST. CLOUD, MN 56301-4498*
**PHONE:** *320-308-2112 • FAX: 320-308-3986*
**E-MAIL:** *GRADUATESTUDIES@STCLOUDSTATE.EDU*
**WEBSITE:** *WWW.STCLOUDSTATE.EDU/MBA*

### GENERAL INFORMATION

**Type of School:** public **Academic Calendar:** semester

### STUDENTS

**Enrollment of parent institution:** 15,000 **Enrollment of business school:** 109 **% male/female:** 79/21 **% part-time:** 69 **% minorities:** 38 **Average age at entry:** 28 **Average years work experience at entry:** 5

### ACADEMICS

**Student/faculty ratio:** 25:1 **% female faculty:** 26

### FINANCIAL FACTS

**Tuition:** $12,492 **Fees:** $449 **Books and supplies:** $1,650

## ADMISSIONS

ADMISSIONS SELECTIVITY RATING: 74

**# of applications received:** 129 **% applicants accepted:** 78 **% acceptees attending:** 91 **GMAT Range (25th to 75th percentile):** 470-700 **Average GMAT:** 541 **Average GPA:** 3.0 **TOEFL required of int'l applicants?** yes **Minimum TOEFL (paper/computer):** 550/213 **Application Fee:** $35 **International Application Fee:** $35 **Regular Application Deadline:** rolling **Regular Notification:** rolling **Early decision program?** yes **ED deadline / notification:** 4/15, 6/15 / 1/1 **Deferment Available?** yes **Maximum length of deferment:** 2 years **Non-fall Admissions?** yes

## EMPLOYMENT PROFILE

**Average starting salary:** $38,000

# ST. JOHN FISHER COLLEGE
## RONALD L. BITTNER SCHOOL OF BUSINESS

***ADMISSIONS CONTACT:*** *OFFICE OF GRADUATE ADMISSIONS, DIRECTOR OF GRADUATE ADMISSIONS*
***ADDRESS:*** *3690 EAST AVENUE OFFICE OF GRADUATE ADMISSIONS, ROCHESTER, NY 14618*
***PHONE:*** *585-385-8161 • FAX: 585-385-8344*
***E-MAIL:*** *GRAD@SJFC.EDU*
***WEBSITE:*** *WWW.SJFC.EDU/BITTNER/*

## FINANCIAL FACTS

**Tuition:** $41,500

## ADMISSIONS

ADMISSIONS SELECTIVITY RATING: 60*

**Application Fee:** $30 **Regular Application Deadline:** 7/1

# STEPHEN F. AUSTIN STATE UNIVERSITY
## COLLEGE OF BUSINESS

***ADMISSIONS CONTACT:*** *MICHAEL STROUP, MBA DIRECTOR*
***ADDRESS:*** *PO BOX 13004, SFA STATION, NACOGDOCHES, TX 75962-3004*
***PHONE:*** *936-468-3101 • FAX: 936-468-1560*
***E-MAIL:*** *WWW.MBSMITH@SFASU.EDU*
***WEBSITE:*** *WWW.COB.SFASU.EDU*

## GENERAL INFORMATION

**Type of School:** public **Environment:** town

## STUDENTS

**Enrollment of parent institution:** 10,000 **Enrollment of business school:** 62 **% part-time:** 50 **Average age at entry:** 25 **Average years work experience at entry:** 3

## ACADEMICS

**Student/faculty ratio:** 13:1 **% female faculty** 45 **% minority faculty** 7

## FINANCIAL FACTS

**Tuition (in-state/out-of-state):** $1,692/$5,904 **Fees:** $610 **Books and supplies:** $1,000 **Room & board (on/off campus):** $4,500/$6,000 **% of students receiving aid:** 10 **% of first-year students receiving aid:** 10 **Average award package:** $3,300 **Average grant:** $3,300

## ADMISSIONS

ADMISSIONS SELECTIVITY RATING: 70

**# of applications received:** 32 **% applicants accepted:** 72 **% acceptees attending:** 57 **GMAT Range (25th to 75th percentile):** 410-640 **Average GMAT:** 505 **Average GPA:** 3.0 **TOEFL required of int'l applicants?** yes **Minimum TOEFL (paper/computer):** 550/213 **Application Fee:** $25 **International Application Fee:** $50 **Regular Application Deadline:** 8/15 **Regular Notification:** 8/15 **Deferment Available?** yes **Maximum length of deferment:** 1 year **Transfer Students Accepted?** yes **Non-fall Admissions?** yes **Need-Blind Admissions?** yes **Applicants also look at:** Northwestern University, Sam Houston State University, Texas State Univeristy—San Marcos, University of North Texas

## EMPLOYMENT PROFILE

**Average starting salary:** $52,000

| Grads employed by field: | % | avg. salary: |
|---|---|---|
| Accounting | 35 | $55,000 |
| Finance | 5 | $65,000 |
| Marketing | 30 | $45,000 |
| General Management | 15 | $45,000 |

# STEVENS INSTITUTE OF TECHNOLOGY
## THE WESLEY J. HOWE SCHOOL OF TECHNOLOGY MANAGEMENT

***ADMISSIONS CONTACT:*** *JAMES RUNKLE, ASSISTANT DIRECTOR OF GRADUATE ADMISSIONS*
***ADDRESS:*** *1 CASTLE POINT ON HUDSON, 12TH FLOOR, HOBOKEN, NJ 07030*
***PHONE:*** *201-433-4733 • FAX: 201-216-8044*
***E-MAIL:*** *GRADADMISSIONS@STEVENS.EDU*
***WEBSITE:*** *WWW.STEVENS.EDU/GRADUATE*

## GENERAL INFORMATION

**Type of School:** private

## STUDENTS

**Enrollment of parent institution:** 2,919 **Enrollment of business school:** 54 **% male/female:** 89/11 **% part-time:** 83 **% minorities:** 33 **% international:** 44

## ACADEMICS

**Prominent Alumni:** Henry Gantt, Father of Project Management; Alexander Calder, Sculptor; Alfred W. Fielding, Inventor of Bubble Wrap; Lawrence Babbio, Vice Chair and President, Verizon Communications; Charles Stewart Mott, Co-Founder, General Motors.

## FINANCIAL FACTS

Tuition (in-state/out-of-state): $22,500/$22,500 **Books and supplies:** $500 **Average grant:** $13,500

## ADMISSIONS

**ADMISSIONS SELECTIVITY RATING: 79**

**# of applications received:** 60 **% applicants accepted:** 48 **% acceptees attending:** 66 **Average GMAT:** 520 **Average GPA:** 3.20 **TOEFL required of int'l applicants?** yes **Minimum TOEFL (paper/computer):** 550/213 **Application Fee:** $55 **International Application Fee:** $55 **Regular Application Deadline:** rolling **Regular Notification:** rolling **Deferment Available?** yes **Maximum length of deferment:** 2 years **Transfer Students Accepted?** yes **Non-fall Admissions?** yes **Need-Blind Admissions?** yes **Applicants also look at:** Columbia University, Fordham University, Lehigh University, New York University, Rutgers, The State University of New Jersey

# TENNESSEE STATE UNIVERSITY

**ADMISSIONS CONTACT:** *LISA SMITH, DIRECTOR OF PUBLIC SERVICE*
**ADDRESS:** *330 10TH AVENUE NORTH, SUITE K, NASHVILLE, TN 37203*
**PHONE:** *615-963-7137 • FAX: 615-963-7139*
**E-MAIL:** *LSMITH11@TNSTATE.EDU*
**WEBSITE:** *WWW.COB.TNSTATE.EDU*

## GENERAL INFORMATION

**Type of School:** public **Environment:** city

## STUDENTS

**Enrollment of business school:** 250 **Average age at entry:** 28 **Average years work experience at entry:** 4

## FINANCIAL FACTS

Tuition (in-state/out-of-state): $3,884/$10,356

## ADMISSIONS

**ADMISSIONS SELECTIVITY RATING: 72**

**# of applications received:** 39 **% applicants accepted:** 79 **% acceptees attending:** 100 **Average GMAT:** 510 **Average GPA:** 3.20 **TOEFL required of int'l applicants?** yes **Minimum TOEFL:** 500 **Application Fee:** $25 **Regular Application Deadline:** 1/1 **Regular Notification:** 1/1 **Deferment Available?** yes **Maximum length of deferment:** 1 **Transfer Students Accepted?** yes **Non-fall Admissions?** yes **Need-Blind Admissions?** yes

# TEXAS A & M UNIVERSITY— CORPUS CHRISTI
## COLLEGE OF BUSINESS

**ADMISSIONS CONTACT:** *SHARON POLANSKY, DIRECTOR OF MASTER'S PROGRAMS*
**ADDRESS:** *6300 OCEAN DRIVE, CORPUS CHRISTI, TX 78412*
**PHONE:** *361-825-2655 • FAX: 361-825-2725*
**E-MAIL:** *SPOLANSKY@COB.TAMUCC.EDU*
**WEBSITE:** *WWW.COB.TAMUCC.EDU*

## GENERAL INFORMATION

**Type of School:** public **Environment:** village **Academic Calendar:** semester

## STUDENTS

**Enrollment of parent institution:** 8,365 **Enrollment of business school:** 111 **% male/female:** 62/38 **% part-time:** 78 **% minorities:** 21 **% international:** 12 **Average age at entry:** 29

## ACADEMICS

**% female faculty** 25

## FINANCIAL FACTS

Tuition (in-state/out-of-state): $2,313/$7,281 **Fees:** $815

## ADMISSIONS

**ADMISSIONS SELECTIVITY RATING: 64**

**# of applications received:** 33 **% applicants accepted:** 91 **% acceptees attending:** 97 **GMAT Range (25th to 75th percentile):** 430-550 **Average GMAT:** 481 **Average GPA:** 3.16 **TOEFL required of int'l applicants?** yes **Minimum TOEFL (paper/computer):** 550/213 **Application Fee:** $30 **International Application Fee:** $50 **Regular Application Deadline:** 7/15 **Regular Notification:** rolling **Deferment Available?** yes **Maximum length of deferment:** 1 year **Transfer Students Accepted?** yes **Non-fall Admissions?** yes **Need-Blind Admissions?** yes

# TEXAS SOUTHERN UNIVERSITY
## JESSE H. JONES SCHOOL OF BUSINESS

**ADDRESS:** *GRADUATE SCHOOL, 3100 CLEBURNE STREET, HOUSTON, TX 70044*
**FAX:** *713-313-1876*
**WEBSITE:** *WWW.TSU.EDU/ACADEMICS/GRADUATE/ADMISSIONS/APPLY.ASP*

## GENERAL INFORMATION

**Type of School:** public

## FINANCIAL FACTS

Tuition (in-state/out-of-state): $5,856/$13,266 **Room & board (on/off campus):** $6,056/$6,336

## ADMISSIONS

**Regular Application Deadline:** 7/15

# TEXAS STATE UNIVERISTY— SAN MARCOS
## EMMETT AND MIRIAM McCOY COLLEGE OF BUSINESS

**ADDRESS:** *THE GRADUATE COLLEGE, 601 UNIVERSITY DRIVE, SAN MARCOS, TX 78666*
**E-MAIL:** *GRADCOLLEGE@TXSTATE.EDU*
**WEBSITE:** *WWW.BUSINESS.TXSTATE.EDU/*

### GENERAL INFORMATION
**Type of School:** public

### FINANCIAL FACTS
**Tuition (in-state/out-of-state):** $4,390/$8,980 **Books and supplies:** $770 **Room & board:** $6,800

### ADMISSIONS
**ADMISSIONS SELECTIVITY RATING: 60\***
**Application Fee:** $40 **Regular Application Deadline:** 6/1

# TILBURG UNIVERSITY
## FACULTY OF ECONOMICS AND BUSINESS ADMINISTRATION

**ADMISSIONS CONTACT:** *MRS. NETTIE COOLS*
**ADDRESS:** *B234, WARANDELAAN 2, PO BOX 90153, TILBURG, 5000 LE NETHERLANDS*
**PHONE:** *011-31-13-466-2512 • FAX: 011-31-13-466-3072*
**E-MAIL:** *INFOFEB@UVT.NL*
**WEBSITE:** *WWW.TILBURGUNIVERSITY.NL*

### GENERAL INFORMATION
**Type of School:** public

### ADMISSIONS
**ADMISSIONS SELECTIVITY RATING: 60\***
**TOEFL required of int'l applicants?** yes **Minimum TOEFL (paper/computer):** 575/233 **Application Fee:** $100 **Regular Application Deadline:** 6/1

# TROY UNIVERSITY
## SORRELL COLLEGE OF BUSINESS

**ADMISSIONS CONTACT:** *BRENDA CAMPBELL,*
**ADDRESS:** *111 ADAMS ADMINISTRATION BUILDING, TROY, AL 36082*
**PHONE:** *334-670-3178 • FAX: 334-670-3733*
**E-MAIL:** *BCAMP@TROY.EDU*
**WEBSITE:** *WWW.TROY.EDU*

### GENERAL INFORMATION
**Type of School:** public

### STUDENTS
**Enrollment of business school:** 389 **% male/female:** 48/52 **% part-time:** 57 **% minorities:** 41 **% international:** 17

### ACADEMICS
**Student/faculty ratio:** 5:1

### FINANCIAL FACTS
**Tuition (in-state/out-of-state):** $4,638/$8,736 **Fees:** $100 **Room & board:** $4,812

### ADMISSIONS
**ADMISSIONS SELECTIVITY RATING: 60\***
**Application Fee:** $50

# UNIVERSITE LAVAL
## FACULTÉ DES SCIENCES DE L'ADMINISTRATION

**ADMISSIONS CONTACT:** *BERNARD GARNIER, DIRECTOR, MBA PROGRAMS*
**ADDRESS:** *PAVILLON PALASIS-PRINCE, QUÉBEC, QC G1K 7P4 CANADA*
**PHONE:** *418-656-3080 • FAX: 418-656-5216*
**E-MAIL:** *REG@REG.ULAVAL.CA*
**WEBSITE:** *WWW.FSA.ULAVAL.CA/HTML/FORMATION.HTML*

### GENERAL INFORMATION
**Type of School:** public **Academic Calendar:** semester

### STUDENTS
**Enrollment of parent institution:** 38,226 **Enrollment of business school:** 1,111 **% male/female:** 56/44 **% out-of-state:** 21 **% part-time:** 67 **% international:** 31 **Average age at entry:** 35 **Average years work experience at entry:** 4

### ACADEMICS
**Student/faculty ratio:** 25:1 **% female faculty** 32

### FINANCIAL FACTS
**Tuition (in-state/out-of-state):** $2,118/$12,272 **Books and supplies:** $3,000 **Room & board:** $2,301 **% of students receiving grants:** 4

### ADMISSIONS
**ADMISSIONS SELECTIVITY RATING: 79**
**# of applications received:** 1,351 **% applicants accepted:** 53 %

acceptees attending: 49 **Average GPA:** 3.0 **TOEFL required of int'l applicants?** yes **Minimum TOEFL (paper/computer):** 550/213 **Application Fee:** $30 **International Application Fee:** $30 **Regular Application Deadline:** 2/1 **Regular Notification:** rolling **Deferment Available?** yes **Maximum length of deferment:** 1 year **Non-fall Admissions?** yes

### EMPLOYMENT PROFILE

**Average starting salary:** $54,302

# UNIVERSITY OF ALABAMA— HUNTSVILLE
## COLLEGE OF ADMINISTRATIVE SCIENCE

**ADMISSIONS CONTACT:** Dr. J. Daniel Sherman, Associate Dean
**ADDRESS:** ASB 102, Huntsville, AL 35899
**PHONE:** 256-824-6681 • **FAX:** 256-890-7571
**E-MAIL:** GRADBIZ@UAH.EDU
**WEBSITE:** WWW.UAH.EDU

### GENERAL INFORMATION

**Type of School:** public **Environment:** city **Academic Calendar:** semester

### STUDENTS

**Enrollment of business school:** 120 **% male/female:** 58/42 **% minorities:** 12 **Average age at entry:** 29 **Average years work experience at entry:** 6

### ACADEMICS

**Student/faculty ratio:** 5:1 **% female faculty** 23 **% minority faculty** 10

### FINANCIAL FACTS

**Tuition (in-state/out-of-state):** $5,866/$9,432 **Books and supplies:** $600

### ADMISSIONS

**ADMISSIONS SELECTIVITY RATING:** 76

**# of applications received:** 97 **% applicants accepted:** 76 **% acceptees attending:** 84 **Average GMAT:** 548 **Average GPA:** 3.4 **TOEFL required of int'l applicants?** yes **Minimum TOEFL:** 550 **Application Fee:** $40 **International Application Fee:** $40 **Regular Application Deadline:** 8/1 **Regular Notification:** 1/1

**Transfer Students Accepted?** yes **Non-fall Admissions?** yes **Need-Blind Admissions?** yes

# UNIVERSITY OF ALASKA— ANCHORAGE
## COLLEGE OF BUSINESS AND PUBLIC POLICY

**ADMISSIONS CONTACT:** Al Kastar, Director of Admissions
**ADDRESS:** PO Box 141629, Anchorage, AK 99514-1629
**PHONE:** 907-786-1480 • **FAX:** 907-786-4888
**E-MAIL:** ANMBS1@UAA.ALASKA.EDU
**WEBSITE:** WWW.CBPP.UAA.ALASKA.EDU

### GENERAL INFORMATION

**Type of School:** public **Environment:** city **Academic Calendar:** Sept. - May

### STUDENTS

**Enrollment of business school:** 66 **% male/female:** 35/65 **% part-time:** 74 **% minorities:** 12 **% international:** 24

### ACADEMICS

**Student/faculty ratio:** 20:1 **% minority faculty** 22

### FINANCIAL FACTS

**Tuition (in-state/out-of-state):** $3,636/$7,074 **Fees:** $352 **Books and supplies:** $500 **Room & board:** $6,730 **Average grant:** $6,057

### ADMISSIONS

**ADMISSIONS SELECTIVITY RATING:** 85

**# of applications received:** 50 **% applicants accepted:** 36 **% acceptees attending:** 72 **GMAT Range (25th to 75th percentile):** 450-640 **Average GMAT:** 524 **Average GPA:** 3.3 **TOEFL required of int'l applicants?** yes **Minimum TOEFL:** 550 **Application Fee:** $45 **Regular Application Deadline:** rolling **Regular Notification:** rolling **Deferment Available?** yes **Maximum length of deferment:** 1 semester **Transfer Students Accepted?** yes **Non-fall Admissions?** yes **Need-Blind Admissions?** yes

# UNIVERSITY OF ALASKA— FAIRBANKS
## SCHOOL OF MANAGEMENT

**ADMISSIONS CONTACT:** Nancy Dix, Director
**ADDRESS:** PO Box 757480, Fairbanks, AK 99775
**PHONE:** 907-474-7500 • **FAX:** 907-474-5379
**E-MAIL:** ADMISSIONS@UAF.EDU
**WEBSITE:** WWW.UAFSOM.COM/GPMBA.HTML

### GENERAL INFORMATION

**Type of School:** public **Environment:** city

### STUDENTS

**Enrollment of parent institution:** 5,025 **Enrollment of business school:** 47 **% male/female:** 42/58 **% out-of-state:** 55 **% part-time:**

25 % minorities: 33 % international: 55 Average age at entry: 30 Average years work experience at entry: 7

## ACADEMICS
Student/faculty ratio: 3:1 % female faculty 20 % minority faculty 70

## FINANCIAL FACTS
Tuition (in-state/out-of-state): $4,392/$8,964 Fees: $650 Books and supplies: $700 Room & board (on/off campus): $5,580/$10,413 Average grant: $16,928 Average student loan debt: $12,166

## ADMISSIONS
ADMISSIONS SELECTIVITY RATING: 62

# of applications received: 9 % applicants accepted: 133 % acceptees attending: 100 GMAT Range (25th to 75th percentile): 520-625 Average GMAT: 563 Average GPA: 3.29 TOEFL required of int'l applicants? yes Minimum TOEFL (paper/computer): 550/213 Application Fee: $50 International Application Fee: $50 Regular Application Deadline: 8/1 Regular Notification: 8/1 Deferment Available? yes Maximum length of deferment: 1 year Transfer Students Accepted? yes Non-fall Admissions? yes Need-Blind Admissions? yes Applicants also look at: University of Alaska—Anchorage

# UNIVERSITY OF ANTWERP
## MANAGEMENT SCHOOL

ADMISSIONS CONTACT: WIM VAN DRIESSEN, ADMISSIONS OFFICER
ADDRESS: SINT JACOBSMARKT 9-13, ANTWERPEN, 2000 BELGIUM
PHONE: 32-0-3-220-4942 • FAX: 32-0-3-220-4953
E-MAIL: UAMS-MASTER@UA.AC.BE
WEBSITE: WWW.UAMS.BE/MAIN.ASP?C=*UAMSENG

## GENERAL INFORMATION
Type of School: private

## FINANCIAL FACTS
Tuition: $14,500

## ADMISSIONS
ADMISSIONS SELECTIVITY RATING: 60*

Application Fee: $60 International Application Fee: $60 Regular Application Deadline: 8/1 Deferment Available? yes Maximum length of deferment: 1 year

# UNIVERSITY OF ARKANSAS— LITTLE ROCK
## COLLEGE OF BUSINESS

ADMISSIONS CONTACT: DR. KEN GLACHUS, MBA ADVISOR
ADDRESS: 2801 SOUTH UNIVERSITY AVENUE, LITTLE ROCK, AR 72204
PHONE: 501-569-3356 • FAX: 501-569-8898
WEBSITE: WWW.CBA.UALR.EDU

## GENERAL INFORMATION
Type of School: public Environment: city Academic Calendar: semester

## STUDENTS
Enrollment of parent institution: 9,925 Enrollment of business school: 225 % male/female: 58/42 % out-of-state: 1 % part-time: 87 % minorities: 8 % international: 15 Average age at entry: 29

## FINANCIAL FACTS
Tuition: $30,500

## ADMISSIONS
ADMISSIONS SELECTIVITY RATING: 60*

# of applications received: 87 % applicants accepted: 66 % acceptees attending: 74 TOEFL required of int'l applicants? yes Minimum TOEFL: 550 Regular Application Deadline: rolling Regular Notification: rolling Deferment Available? yes Applicants also look at: Babson College, Indiana University South Bend, Rensselaer Polytechnic Institute

## EMPLOYMENT PROFILE
Average starting salary: $40,000

# UNIVERSITY OF BALTIMORE
## MERRICK SCHOOL OF BUSINESS

ADMISSIONS CONTACT: JEFFREY ZAVRONTY, ASSISTANT DIRECTOR OF ADMISSIONS
ADDRESS: 1420 NORTH CHARLES STREET, BALTIMORE, MD 21201
PHONE: 877-277-5982 • FAX: 410-837-4793
E-MAIL: ADMISSIONS@UBMAIL.UBALT.EDU
WEBSITE: HTTP://BUSINESS.UBALT.EDU/GRADUATEPROGRAMS/MBA.HTML

## GENERAL INFORMATION
Type of School: public Environment: metropolis Academic Calendar: semester

## STUDENTS
Enrollment of parent institution: 4,639 Enrollment of business school: 506 % male/female: 57/43 % out-of-state: 16 % part-time: 54 % minorities: 18 % international: 33 Average age at entry: 29

## ACADEMICS
Student/faculty ratio: 15:1 % female faculty 25 % minority faculty 34 Joint Degrees: MBA/MSN, 2-7 years; MBA/PhD in Nursing, 2-7

years; MBA/PharmD, 2-7 years; MBA/JD, 3-7 years. **Prominent Alumni:** William Donald Schaeffer, Govenor, State of Maryland; Peter Angelos, Owner, Baltimore Orioles; Joseph Curran, Attorney General, State of Maryland; Vernon Wright, Vice Chair, MBNA America Bank

## FINANCIAL FACTS

**Books and supplies:** $900

## ADMISSIONS

**ADMISSIONS SELECTIVITY RATING: 73**

**# of applications received:** 376 **% applicants accepted:** 62 **% acceptees attending:** 63 **GMAT Range (25th to 75th percentile):** 470-520 **Average GMAT:** 500 **Average GPA:** 3.0 **TOEFL required of int'l applicants?** yes **Minimum TOEFL (paper/computer):** 550/213 **Application Fee:** $30 **International Application Fee:** $30 **Regular Application Deadline:** rolling **Regular Notification:** rolling **Deferment Available?** yes **Maximum length of deferment:** 1 year **Transfer Students Accepted?** yes **Non-fall Admissions?** yes **Need-Blind Admissions?** yes **Applicants also look at:** Loyola College in Maryland, University of Maryland—College Park

# THE UNIVERSITY OF CHICAGO (EUROPE CAMPUS)
## GRADUATE SCHOOL OF BUSINESS

**ADMISSIONS CONTACT:** SILVIA RULL, ADMISSIONS COORDINATOR
**ADDRESS:** ARAGO 271, BARCELONA, 08007 SPAIN
**PHONE:** 011-34-93-505-21-54 • **FAX:** 011-34-93-505-21-58
**E-MAIL:** BARCELONA.INQUIRIES@GSB.UCHICAGO.EDU
**WEBSITE:** HTTP://GSB.UCHICAGO.EDU/EXECMBAEUROPE

## GENERAL INFORMATION

**Type of School:** private **Academic Calendar:** quarter

## STUDENTS

**Enrollment of business school:** 3,000 **% male/female:** 76/24 **% minorities:** 7 **% international:** 26 **Average age at entry:** 35 **Average years work experience at entry:** 12

## ACADEMICS

**% female faculty** 14 **Joint Degrees:** MBA/AM Area Studies in Business; MBA/AM International Relations and Business; JD/MBA Law and Business; MD/MBA Medicine and Business; MBA/MPP Public Policy Studies and Business; MBA/AM Social Service Administration and Business **Prominent Alumni:** Philip Purcell, Chair and CEO of Morgan Stanley; James Kilts, Chair and CEO of the Gillette Company; Karen Katen, President of Pfizer Pharmaceuticals

## ADMISSIONS

**ADMISSIONS SELECTIVITY RATING: 60\***

**Average GMAT:** 684 **Average GPA:** 3.4 **Application Fee:** $100 **Regular Application Deadline:** 5/1 **Regular Notification:** rolling **Deferment Available?** yes **Maximum length of deferment:** 1 year **Transfer Students Accepted?** yes **Non-fall Admissions?** yes

## EMPLOYMENT PROFILE

**Grads employed by field: ..........% avg. salary:**

| | | |
|---|---|---|
| Finance | 15 | NR |
| Marketing | 17 | NR |
| Consulting | 15 | NR |
| General Management | 37 | NR |
| Other | 16 | NR |

# UNIVERSITY OF COLORADO AT COLORADO SPRINGS
## GRADUATE SCHOOL OF BUSINESS ADMINISTRATION

**ADMISSIONS CONTACT:** MAUREEN CATHEY, MBA PROGRAM DIRECTOR
**ADDRESS:** 1420 AUSTIN BLUFFS PARKWAY, COLORADO SPRINGS, CO 80918
**PHONE:** 719-262-3408 • **FAX:** 719-262-3100
**E-MAIL:** BUSADVSR@UCCS.EDU
**WEBSITE:** HTTP://WEB.UCCS.EDU/BUSINESS

## GENERAL INFORMATION

**Type of School:** public **Environment:** metropolis **Academic Calendar:** semester

## STUDENTS

**Enrollment of parent institution:** 7,407 **Enrollment of business school:** 273 **% part-time:** 100 **Average age at entry:** 29 **Average years work experience at entry:** 7

## ACADEMICS

**Student/faculty ratio:** 8:1 **% female faculty** 15 **% minority faculty** 3

## FINANCIAL FACTS

**Room & board:** $8,000

## ADMISSIONS

**ADMISSIONS SELECTIVITY RATING: 70**

**# of applications received:** 79 **% applicants accepted:** 90 **% acceptees attending:** 76 **GMAT Range (25th to 75th percentile):** 490-560 **Average GMAT:** 540 **Average GPA:** 3.2 **TOEFL required of int'l applicants?** yes **Minimum TOEFL (paper/computer):** 550/213 **Application Fee:** $60 **International Application Fee:** $75 **Regular Application Deadline:** 6/1 **Regular Notification:** rolling **Deferment Available?** yes **Maximum length of deferment:** 1 year **Transfer Students Accepted?** yes **Non-fall Admissions?** yes **Need-Blind Admissions?** yes

# University of Colorado—Denver

## College of Business and Administration

**Admissions Contact:** Graduate Admissions Coordinator
**Address:** Campus Box 165, PO Box 173364, Denver, CO 80217-3364
**Phone:** 303-556-5900 • **Fax:** 303-556-5904
**E-mail:** grad.business@cudenver.edu.
**Website:** www.business.cudenver.edu

### GENERAL INFORMATION
**Type of School:** public **Environment:** metropolis **Academic Calendar:** semester

### STUDENTS
**Enrollment of parent institution:** 11,050 **Enrollment of business school:** 1,249 **% male/female:** 89/11 **% out-of-state:** 1 **% part-time:** 71 **% minorities:** 10 **% international:** 14 **Average age at entry:** 25

### ACADEMICS
**Student/faculty ratio:** 35:1

### FINANCIAL FACTS
**% of students receiving aid:** 29 **Average grant:** $1,000

### ADMISSIONS
**Admissions Selectivity Rating: 60***
**# of applications received:** 547 **% applicants accepted:** 74 **% acceptees attending:** 64 **TOEFL required of int'l applicants?** yes **Minimum TOEFL (paper/computer):** 525/197 **Application Fee:** $50 **Regular Application Deadline:** 6/1 **Regular Notification:** rolling **Deferment Available?** yes **Maximum length of deferment:** 1 year **Transfer Students Accepted?** yes **Non-fall Admissions?** yes **Need-Blind Admissions?** yes

### EMPLOYMENT PROFILE
**Average starting salary:** $57,903

# University of Delaware
## MBA Programs - College of Business and Economics

**Admissions Contact:** Ronald I. Sibert, Director of MBA Programs
**Address:** 103 MBNA America Hall, Newark, DE 19716
**Phone:** 302-831-2221 • **Fax:** 302-831-3329
**E-mail:** mbaprogram@udel.edu
**Website:** www.mba.udel.edu

### GENERAL INFORMATION
**Type of School:** public **Environment:** town **Academic Calendar:** semester

### STUDENTS
**Enrollment of parent institution:** 20,949 **Enrollment of business school:** 302 **% male/female:** 49/51 **% out-of-state:** 27 **% part-time:** 76 **% minorities:** 5 **% international:** 50 **Average age at entry:** 27 **Average years work experience at entry:** 4.6

### ACADEMICS
**Student/faculty ratio:** 30:1 **% female faculty** 14 **% minority faculty** 3 **Joint Degrees:** MAE/MBA, 57 credits **Prominent Alumni:** Hon. Thomas R. Carper, Governor State of DE, Candidate for U.S. Senate; Leonard Quill, CEO & Chair of the Board, Wilm. Trust Corp.; Howard Cosgrove, Chair & CEO, Conectiv; Dennis Sheehy, Partner, Deloitte and Touche

### FINANCIAL FACTS
**Tuition (in-state/out-of-state):** $3,610/$7,710 **Fees:** $646 **Books and supplies:** $1,400 **Room & board (on/off campus):** $6,200/$7,200 **% of students receiving aid:** 60 **% of first-year students receiving aid:** 26 **% of students receiving grants:** 18 **Average award package:** $7,440 **Average grant:** $3,940

### ADMISSIONS
**Admissions Selectivity Rating: 75**
**# of applications received:** 259 **% applicants accepted:** 75 **% acceptees attending:** 65 **GMAT Range (25th to 75th percentile):** 330-750 **Average GMAT:** 555 **Average GPA:** 3.0 **TOEFL required of int'l applicants?** yes **Minimum TOEFL (paper/computer):** 587/240 **Application Fee:** $50 **Regular Application Deadline:** 5/1 **Regular Notification:** rolling **Deferment Available?** yes **Maximum length of deferment:** 1 academic year **Transfer Students Accepted?** yes **Non-fall Admissions?** yes **Need-Blind Admissions?** yes **Applicants also look at:** Temple University, University of Pennsylvania, Villanova University

### EMPLOYMENT PROFILE
**Average starting salary:** $59,568

| Grads employed by field: | % | avg. salary: |
|---|---|---|
| Finance | 18 | $57,000 |
| Human Resources | 4 | $67,000 |
| Marketing | 18 | $63,250 |
| MIS | 9 | $49,250 |
| Operations | 10 | $74,750 |
| Consulting | 18 | $72,700 |
| General Management | 14 | $65,667 |
| Other | 9 | $68,625 |

# UNIVERSITY OF DETROIT MERCY
## COLLEGE OF BUSINESS ADMINISTRATION

**ADMISSIONS CONTACT:** TYRA ROUNDS, DIRECTOR OF RECRUITING
**ADDRESS:** PO BOX 19900, DETROIT, MI 48219-0900
**PHONE:** 313-993-1245 • **FAX:** 313-993-3326
**E-MAIL:** ADMISSIONS@UDMERCY.EDU
**WEBSITE:** WWW.BUSINESS.UDMERCY.EDU

### GENERAL INFORMATION

**Type of School:** private **Affiliation:** Roman Catholic **Environment:** city **Academic Calendar:** semester

### STUDENTS

**Enrollment of parent institution:** 5,571 **Enrollment of business school:** 146 **% male/female:** 88/12 **% part-time:** 76 **% minorities:** 6 **% international:** 11 **Average age at entry:** 32 **Average years work experience at entry:** 5

### ACADEMICS

**Student/faculty ratio:** 30:1 **% female faculty** 17 **% minority faculty** 13 **Joint Degrees:** JD/MBA 3 years **Prominent Alumni:** Thomas Angott, Chair of the Board, C.F. Burger Co.; Thomas Capo, Dollar Thrifty Automotive Group; Armando Cavazos, President & CEO, Credit Union One; James Padilla, President Ford Motor Co.; Emil Simon, Owner, The Rollick Beverage Co.

### FINANCIAL FACTS

**Tuition:** $14,670 **Fees:** $570 **Books and supplies:** $1,200 **Room & board:** $3,584 **Average grant:** $40,000

### ADMISSIONS

**ADMISSIONS SELECTIVITY RATING: 71**

**# of applications received:** 51 **% applicants accepted:** 82 **% acceptees attending:** 83 **GMAT Range (25th to 75th percentile):** 450-650 **Average GMAT:** 520 **Average GPA:** 3.35 **Application Fee:** $25 **International Application Fee:** $50 **Round 1:** 8/15; **Round 2:** 12/15; **Round 3:** 4/15; **Round 4:** 5/15 **Deferment Available?** yes **Maximum length of deferment:** 2 years **Transfer Students Accepted?** yes **Non-fall Admissions?** yes **Applicants also look at:** Oakland University, Wayne State University

### EMPLOYMENT PROFILE

**Average starting salary:** $57,000

# UNIVERSITY OF HOUSTON—CLEAR LAKE
## SCHOOL OF BUSINESS

**ADMISSIONS CONTACT:** KEVIN MCKISSON, REGISTRAR
**ADDRESS:** 2700 BAY AREA BOULEVARD, HOUSTON, TX 77058-1098
**PHONE:** 281-283-2521 • **FAX:** 281-283-2530
**E-MAIL:** ADMISSIONS@UHCL.EDU
**WEBSITE:** WWW.UHCL.EDU

### GENERAL INFORMATION

**Type of School:** public **Environment:** metropolis **Academic Calendar:** semester

### STUDENTS

**Enrollment of parent institution:** 7,853 **Enrollment of business school:** 430 **% male/female:** 85/15 **% part-time:** 65 **% minorities:** 11 **% international:** 9 **Average age at entry:** 31 **Average years work experience at entry:** 5

### ACADEMICS

**Student/faculty ratio:** 18:1 **% female faculty** 31 **% minority faculty** 19 **Joint Degrees:** MHA/MBA, 3 years.

### FINANCIAL FACTS

**Tuition (in-state/out-of-state):** $3,312/$10,980 **Fees:** $5,004 **Books and supplies:** $1,800 **Room & board:** $12,836 **% of students receiving aid:** 20 **Average award package:** $8,300 **Average grant:** $1,000 **Average student loan debt:** $26,916

### ADMISSIONS

**ADMISSIONS SELECTIVITY RATING: 77**

**# of applications received:** 207 **% applicants accepted:** 50 **% acceptees attending:** 68 **GMAT Range (25th to 75th percentile):** 450-550 **Average GMAT:** 502 **Average GPA:** 3.1 **TOEFL required of int'l applicants?** yes **Minimum TOEFL (paper/computer):** 550/213 **Application Fee:** $35 **International Application Fee:** $75 **Regular Application Deadline:** 8/1 **Regular Notification:** rolling **Deferment Available?** yes **Maximum length of deferment:** 1 year **Transfer Students Accepted?** yes **Non-fall Admissions?** yes **Need-Blind Admissions?** yes **Applicants also look at:** Houston Baptist University, University of Houston, University of St. Thomas

# University of Louisiana at Monroe
## College of Business Adminstration

**Admissions Contact:** Miguel Perez, Coordinator of Assessment and Internal Affairs
**Address:** 700 University Avenue, Monroe, LA 71209-0100
**Phone:** 318-342-1100 • **Fax:** 318-342-1101
**E-mail:** perez@ulm.edu
**Website:** http://ele.ulm.edu/MBA/

### GENERAL INFORMATION
**Type of School:** public **Academic Calendar:** semester

### STUDENTS
Enrollment of parent institution: 10,942 **Enrollment of business school:** 77 **% male/female:** 60/40 **% out-of-state:** 11 **% part-time:** 19 **% minorities:** 5 **% international:** 40 **Average age at entry:** 27

### ACADEMICS
**Student/faculty ratio:** 2:1 **% female faculty** 30 **% minority faculty** 4

### FINANCIAL FACTS
**Tuition (in-state/out-of-state):** $1,900/$7,858 **Fees:** $382 **Books and supplies:** $600 **Room & board:** $2,560 **Average grant:** $5,000

### ADMISSIONS
**ADMISSIONS SELECTIVITY RATING: 73**
**# of applications received:** 77 **% applicants accepted:** 58 **% acceptees attending:** 78 **GMAT Range (25th to 75th percentile):** 390-710 **Average GMAT:** 480 **Average GPA:** 3.0 **TOEFL required of int'l applicants?** yes **Minimum TOEFL (paper/computer):** 480/157 **Application Fee:** $20 **International Application Fee:** $30 **Regular Application Deadline:** 7/1 **Regular Notification:** 7/15 **Deferment Available?** yes **Maximum length of deferment:** 1 year **Transfer Students Accepted?** yes **Non-fall Admissions?** yes

# University of Maine
## Maine Business School

**Admissions Contact:** Chris Hockensmith, Assistant to the Director of Graduate Programs
**Address:** 5723 DP Corbett Business Building, Orono, ME 04469-5723
**Phone:** 207-581-1973 • **Fax:** 207-581-1930
**E-mail:** mba@maine.edu
**Website:** www.umaine.edu/business

### GENERAL INFORMATION
**Type of School:** public **Environment:** village **Academic Calendar:** semester

### STUDENTS
Enrollment of parent institution: 11,135 **Enrollment of business school:** 79 **% male/female:** 66/34 **% out-of-state:** 1 **% part-time:**
58 **% minorities:** 2 **% international:** 17 **Average age at entry:** 34 **Average years work experience at entry:** 5

### ACADEMICS
**Student/faculty ratio:** 4:1 **% female faculty** 50

### FINANCIAL FACTS
**Tuition (in-state/out-of-state):** $4,572/$13,032 **Fees:** $570 **Books and supplies:** $700 **Room & board:** $5,728 **Average grant:** $4,500

### ADMISSIONS
**ADMISSIONS SELECTIVITY RATING: 69**
**# of applications received:** 50 **% applicants accepted:** 92 **% acceptees attending:** 72 **Average GMAT:** 538 **Average GPA:** 3.21 **TOEFL required of int'l applicants?** yes **Minimum TOEFL (paper/computer):** 550/213 **Application Fee:** $50 **Regular Application Deadline:** 6/1 **Regular Notification:** 7/1 **Deferment Available?** yes **Maximum length of deferment:** 1 year **Transfer Students Accepted?** yes **Non-fall Admissions?** yes **Need-Blind Admissions?** yes

# University of Manchester
## Manchester Business School

**Admissions Contact:** Gaer Buchanan, Admissions Administrator
**Address:** MBA Admissions Office, Booth Street West, Manchester, M15 6PB England
**Phone:** 00-44-161-275-6364 • **Fax:** 00-44-161-275-6556
**E-mail:** gaer.buchanan@mbs.ac.uk
**Website:** www.mbs.ac.uk

### GENERAL INFORMATION
**Type of School:** public

### ACADEMICS
**Prominent Alumni:** Rijkman Groenink, DipBA 1973, Chair of the Managing Board, ABN AMRO; Robert H. Herz, BA (Econ) 1974, Chair, US Financial Accounting Standards Board; Sir Terry Leahy, BSc 1977, Chief Executive, Tesco; Paul Skinner, DipBA 1969, Chair, Rio Tinto; David Varney, MBA 1971, Executive Chair, Her Majesty's Revenue and Cust.

### FINANCIAL FACTS
**Tuition:** $53,100

### ADMISSIONS
**ADMISSIONS SELECTIVITY RATING: 60\***
**TOEFL required of int'l applicants?** yes **Minimum TOEFL (paper/computer):** 600/250 **Application Fee:** $100 **Regular Application Deadline:** 6/30 **Regular Notification:** 7/31 **Application Deadline/Notification Round 1:** 12/2 / 1/31 **Round 2:** 1/31 / 3/31 **Round 3:** 3/31 / 5/31 **Round 4:** 6/30 / 7/31 **Deferment Available?** yes **Maximum length of deferment:** 1 year

## EMPLOYMENT PROFILE

**Primary source of full-time job acceptances**

School-facilitated activities 43%

Graduate-facilitated activities 57%

**Average starting salary:** $96,900

**Grads employed by field: ..........% avg. salary:**

Finance ...........................................22 $110,240

Marketing ......................................21 $92,100

Operations.....................................12 $93,900

Strategic Planning.........................5 $106,950

Consulting......................................26 $91,800

General Management ...................14 $73,550

# UNIVERSITY OF MANITOBA
## I.H. ASPER SCHOOL OF BUSINESS

**ADMISSIONS CONTACT:** EWA MORPHY, MBA PROGRAM MANAGER
**ADDRESS:** 324 DRAKE CENTER, WINNIPEG, MB R3T 5V4 CANADA
**PHONE:** 204-474-8448 • **FAX:** 204-474-7544
**E-MAIL:** ASPERMBA@UMANITOBA.CA
**WEBSITE:** WWW.UMANITOBA.CA/ASPER

### GENERAL INFORMATION
**Type of School:** public **Environment:** city

### STUDENTS
**Enrollment of parent institution:** 27,000 **Enrollment of business school:** 140 **% male/female:** 87/13 **% part-time:** 89 **% minorities:** 33 **Average age at entry:** 31 **Average years work experience at entry:** 8

### ACADEMICS
**Student/faculty ratio:** 30:1 **% female faculty** 18 **% minority faculty** 32 **Prominent Alumni:** F. Ross Johnson, Chair/CEO, RJM Group; Robert W. Pollock, Chair, Drake International; Gerald W. Schwartz, Chair, President and CEO, Onyx Corp.; Martin S. Weinberg, President, CEO, Assante Corporation; Bill McCallum, President and CEO, Great-West Life Annuity Insurance

### FINANCIAL FACTS
**Tuition:** $15,964 **Books and supplies:** $2,145 **Room & board:** $5,800 **Average grant:** $4,000

### ADMISSIONS
**ADMISSIONS SELECTIVITY RATING: 82**

**# of applications received:** 79 **% applicants accepted:** 63 **% acceptees attending:** 70 **Average GMAT:** 580 **Average GPA:** 3.35 **TOEFL required of int'l applicants?** yes **Minimum TOEFL (paper/computer):** 550/213 **Application Fee:** $75 **International Application Fee:** $90 **Regular Application Deadline:** 6/1 **Regular Notification:** rolling **Transfer Students Accepted?** yes **Non-fall Admissions?** yes

### EMPLOYMENT PROFILE
**Average starting salary:** $65,000

# UNIVERSITY OF MASSACHUSETTS—BOSTON
## GRADUATE COLLEGE OF MANAGEMENT

**ADMISSIONS CONTACT:** WILLIAM KOEHLER, GRADUATE PROGRAM DIRECTOR
**ADDRESS:** 100 MORRISSEY BOULEVARD, MBA OFFICE, BOSTON, MA 02125-3393
**PHONE:** 617-287-7720 • **FAX:** 617-287-7725
**E-MAIL:** MBA@UMB.EDU
**WEBSITE:** WWW.MANAGEMENT.UMB.EDU

### GENERAL INFORMATION
**Type of School:** public **Environment:** metropolis **Academic Calendar:** semesters

### STUDENTS
**Enrollment of parent institution:** 12,000 **Enrollment of business school:** 274 **% male/female:** 48/52 **% out-of-state:** 30 **% part-time:** 65 **% minorities:** 10 **% international:** 27 **Average age at entry:** 29 **Average years work experience at entry:** 6

### ACADEMICS
**Student/faculty ratio:** 13:1 **% female faculty** 35 **% minority faculty** 38 **Prominent Alumni:** Thomas M. Menino, Mayor, City of Boston; Joseph Abboud, Fashion Designer; James Kantelis, CEO, Sprague Energy Corp.; Mark Atkins, CEO, Invention Machine; Joseph Kennedy, U.S. Congressman

### FINANCIAL FACTS
**Tuition (in-state/out-of-state):** $2,590/$9,758 **Fees (in-state/out-of-state):** $6,322/$9,011 **Books and supplies:** $1,000 **Room & board:** $10,000 **% of students receiving aid:** 45 **% of first-year students receiving aid:** 40 **% of students receiving loans:** 62 **% of students receiving grants:** 22 **Average grant:** $14,000 **Average student loan debt:** $19,500

### ADMISSIONS
**ADMISSIONS SELECTIVITY RATING: 87**

**# of applications received:** 263 **% applicants accepted:** 44 **% acceptees attending:** 66 **GMAT Range (25th to 75th percentile):** 520-640 **Average GMAT:** 570 **Average GPA:** 3.31 **TOEFL required of int'l applicants?** yes **Minimum TOEFL (paper/computer):** 600/250 **Application Fee:** $40 **International Application Fee:** $60 **Regular Application Deadline:** 6/1 **Regular Notification:** 7/1 **Application Deadline/Notification Round 1:** 3/1 / 3/15 **Round 2:** 6/1 / 7/1 **Deferment Available?** yes **Maximum length of deferment:** 1 semester **Transfer Students Accepted?** yes **Non-fall Admissions?** yes **Need-Blind Admissions?** yes **Applicants also look at:** Babson College, Bentley College, Boston College, Boston University, Northeastern University, Suffolk University, University of Massachusetts—Amherst

### EMPLOYMENT PROFILE
**Average starting salary:** $71,000

# UNIVERSITY OF MASSACHUSETTS—LOWELL
## COLLEGE OF MANAGEMENT

**ADMISSIONS CONTACT:** *DUNCAN G. LABAY, PHD, MANAGEMENT GRADUATE PROGRAMS DIRECTOR*
**ADDRESS:** *1 UNIVERSITY AVENUE, LOWELL, MA 01854-2881*
**PHONE:** *978-934-2848 • FAX: 978-934-4017*
**E-MAIL:** *MBA@UML.EDU*
**WEBSITE:** *WWW.UML.EDU/COLLEGE/MANAGEMENT/*

### GENERAL INFORMATION
**Type of School:** public **Environment:** city

### STUDENTS
**Enrollment of parent institution:** 12,350 **Enrollment of business school:** 322 **% male/female:** 68/32 **% part-time:** 91 **% minorities:** 4 **% international:** 6 **Average age at entry:** 28 **Average years work experience at entry:** 5

### ACADEMICS
**Student/faculty ratio:** 25:1

### FINANCIAL FACTS
**Tuition (in-state/out-of-state):** $9,921/$19,619 **Fees (in-state/out-of-state):** $5,400/$8,000 **Books and supplies:** $1,000 **Room & board:** $6,011 **% of students receiving aid:** 4

### ADMISSIONS
**ADMISSIONS SELECTIVITY RATING: 70**
**# of applications received:** 181 **% applicants accepted:** 83 **% acceptees attending:** 84 **GMAT Range (25th to 75th percentile):** 480-560 **Average GMAT:** 525 **Average GPA:** 3.0 **TOEFL required of int'l applicants?** yes **Minimum TOEFL (computer):** 230 **Application Fee:** $20 **Regular Application Deadline:** rolling **Regular Notification:** rolling **Non-fall Admissions?** yes

# UNIVERSITY OF MICHIGAN— DEARBORN
## SCHOOL OF MANAGEMENT

**ADMISSIONS CONTACT:** *CHRISTINE BRZEZINSKI, GRADUATE ADMISSIONS COORDINATOR*
**ADDRESS:** *SCHOOL OF MANAGEMENT, 19000 HUBBARD DRIVE, DEARBORN, MI 48126-2638*
**PHONE:** *313-593-5460 • FAX: 313-271-9838*
**E-MAIL:** *GRADBUSINESS@UMD.UMICH.EDU*
**WEBSITE:** *WWW.SOM.UMD.UMICH.EDU*

### GENERAL INFORMATION
**Type of School:** public **Environment:** city **Academic Calendar:** semester

### STUDENTS
**Enrollment of parent institution:** 8,613 **Enrollment of business school:** 414 **% male/female:** 58/42 **% part-time:** 94 **% minorities:** 15 **Average age at entry:** 30 **Average years work experience at entry:** 5

### ACADEMICS
**Student/faculty ratio:** 30:1 **% female faculty** 38 **% minority faculty** 25 **Joint Degrees:** Dual MBA & MSF, 2-5 years part-time; Dual MBA & MSIE, 4-5 years part-time; Dual MBA & Master of Health Services Administration

### FINANCIAL FACTS
**Books and supplies:** $1,200 **Average grant:** $1,500

### ADMISSIONS
**ADMISSIONS SELECTIVITY RATING: 78**
**# of applications received:** 103 **% applicants accepted:** 70 **% acceptees attending:** 75 **Average GMAT:** 561 **Average GPA:** 3.2 **TOEFL required of int'l applicants?** yes **Minimum TOEFL (paper/computer):** 560/220 **Application Fee:** $60 **International Application Fee:** $75 **Regular Application Deadline:** 8/1 **Regular Notification:** rolling **Deferment Available?** yes **Maximum length of deferment:** 1 year **Transfer Students Accepted?** yes **Non-fall Admissions?** yes **Need-Blind Admissions?** yes **Applicants also look at:** Eastern Michigan University, Michigan State University, Oakland University, University of Detroit Mercy, University of Michigan, Wayne State University

# UNIVERSITY OF MINNESOTA—DULUTH

## LABOVITZ SCHOOL OF BUSINESS AND ECONOMICS

*ADMISSIONS CONTACT:* CANDY FURO, ASSOCIATE ADMINISTRATOR
*ADDRESS:* 21 LSBE, 412 LIBRARY DRIVE, DULUTH, MN 55812
*PHONE:* 218-726-8986 • *FAX:* 218-726-6789
*E-MAIL:* GRAD@D.UMN.EDU
*WEBSITE:* WWW.D.UMN.EDU/SBE/DEGREEPROGS/MBA/

### GENERAL INFORMATION

**Type of School:** public **Environment:** village **Academic Calendar:** semester

### STUDENTS

**Enrollment of parent institution:** 10,000 **Enrollment of business school:** 60 **% male/female:** 80/20 **% part-time:** 86 **% international:** 40 **Average age at entry:** 35 **Average years work experience at entry:** 10

### ACADEMICS

**Student/faculty ratio:** 20:1 **% female faculty** 24 **Prominent Alumni:** Jon Gerlach, CFO; Chris Mahai, President/CEO; Elaine Hansen, Director; Jim Vizanko, CFO

### FINANCIAL FACTS

**Tuition:** $8,400 **Books and supplies:** $1,000 **Room & board:** $6,000 **% of students receiving aid:** 8

### ADMISSIONS

**ADMISSIONS SELECTIVITY RATING: 77**

**# of applications received:** 18 **% applicants accepted:** 89 **% acceptees attending:** 94 **GMAT Range (25th to 75th percentile):** 535-640 **Average GMAT:** 585 **Average GPA:** 3.39 **TOEFL required of int'l applicants?** yes **Minimum TOEFL (paper/computer):** 550/213 **Application Fee:** $55 **International Application Fee:** $75 **Regular Application Deadline:** 7/15 **Regular Notification:** 9/1 **Application Deadline/Notification Round 1:** 7/15 / 08/31 **Round 2:** 11/1 / 12/31 **Round 3:** 5/1 / 6/30 **Deferment Available?** yes **Maximum length of deferment:** 1 year without reapplying **Transfer Students Accepted?** yes **Non-fall Admissions?** yes **Need-Blind Admissions?** yes **Applicants also look at:** St. Cloud State University, University of Minnesota, University of St. Thomas

# THE UNIVERSITY OF MONTANA—MISSOULA

## SCHOOL OF BUSINESS ADMINISTRATION

*ADMISSIONS CONTACT:* KATHLEEN SPRITZER, ADMINISTRATIVE OFFICER
*ADDRESS:* SCHOOL OF BUSINESS ADMINISTRATION, UNIVERSITY OF MONTANA—MISSOULA, MT 59812
*PHONE:* 406-243-4983 • *FAX:* 406-243-2086
*E-MAIL:* KATHLEEN.SPRITZER@BUSINESS.UMT.EDU
*WEBSITE:* WWW.MBA-MACCT.UMT.EDU

### GENERAL INFORMATION

**Type of School:** public **Environment:** city **Academic Calendar:** semester

### STUDENTS

**Enrollment of parent institution:** 13,564 **Enrollment of business school:** 184 **% male/female:** 46/54 **% part-time:** 47 **% minorities:** 5 **% international:** 10 **Average age at entry:** 29 **Average years work experience at entry:** 2.5

### ACADEMICS

**Student/faculty ratio:** 26:1 **% female faculty** 31 **% minority faculty** 1 **Joint Degrees:** JD/MBA, 3 years; MBA/PharmD, 5 years

### FINANCIAL FACTS

**Tuition (in-state/out-of-state):** $6,150/$14,230 **Books and supplies:** $1,800 **Room & board:** $8,750 **% of students receiving aid:** 10 **% of students receiving grants:** 10 **Average grant:** $9,000

### ADMISSIONS

**ADMISSIONS SELECTIVITY RATING: 60\***

**# of applications received:** 146 **% applicants accepted:** 75 **% acceptees attending:** 88 **GMAT Range (25th to 75th percentile):** 460-710 **Average GMAT:** 566 **Average GPA:** 3.2 **TOEFL required of int'l applicants?** yes **Minimum TOEFL (paper/computer):** 580/237 **Application Fee:** $45 **International Application Fee:** $45 **Regular Application Deadline:** 4/15 **Regular Notification:** 5/1 **Deferment Available?** yes **Maximum length of deferment:** 1 year **Transfer Students Accepted?** yes **Non-fall Admissions?** yes **Need-Blind Admissions?** yes **Applicants also look at:** Idaho State University, Montana State University, University of Oregon, University of Washington, Washington State University

### EMPLOYMENT PROFILE

**Average starting salary:** $44,031

# UNIVERSITY OF NEBRASKA— LINCOLN
## COLLEGE OF BUSINESS ADMINISTRATION

*ADMISSIONS CONTACT:* JUDY SHUTTS, GRADUATE ADVISER
*ADDRESS:* CBA 125, LINCOLN, NE 68588-0405
*PHONE:* 402-472-2338 • *FAX:* 402-472-5180
*E-MAIL:* CGRADUATE@UNLNOTES.UNL.EDU
*WEBSITE:* WWW.CBA.UNL.EDU

### GENERAL INFORMATION
**Type of School:** public **Environment:** city **Academic Calendar:** semester

### STUDENTS
**Enrollment of parent institution:** 21,675 **Enrollment of business school:** 129 **% male/female:** 75/25 **% out-of-state:** 15 **% part-time:** 50 **% minorities:** 5 **% international:** 17 **Average age at entry:** 26 **Average years work experience at entry:** 6

### ACADEMICS
**Student/faculty ratio:** 6:1 **% female faculty** 19 **% minority faculty** 12 **Joint Degrees:** MBA/JD, 4 years; MBA/Arch, 3 years. **Prominent Alumni:** Marsha Lommel, Pres/CEO, Madonna Rehabilitation Hospital; Vinod Gupta, Founder/Chair, InfoUSA; David Maurstad, Director, Federal Emergency Mgt. Agency (FEMA); Bernard Reznicek, National Director, Central States Indemnity Co.; William Ruud, Policy Director, State of Idaho

### FINANCIAL FACTS
**Tuition (in-state/out-of-state):** $4,788/$12,900 **Fees (in-state/out-of-state):** $715/$675 **Books and supplies:** $944 **Room & board (on/off campus):** $6,660/$6,800 **% of students receiving aid:** 51 **% of first-year students receiving aid:** 64 **% of students receiving loans:** 17 **% of students receiving grants:** 18 **Average award package:** $15,000 **Average grant:** $4,250

### ADMISSIONS
**ADMISSIONS SELECTIVITY RATING: 83**
**# of applications received:** 74 **% applicants accepted:** 70 **% acceptees attending:** 73 **GMAT Range (25th to 75th percentile):** 560-650 **Average GMAT:** 603 **Average GPA:** 3.58 **TOEFL required of int'l applicants?** yes **Minimum TOEFL (paper/computer):** 550/213 **Application Fee:** $45 **International Application Fee:** $45 **Regular Application Deadline:** 6/15 **Regular Notification:** rolling **Deferment Available?** yes **Maximum length of deferment:** 1 semester **Transfer Students Accepted?** yes **Non-fall Admissions?** yes **Need-Blind Admissions?** yes **Applicants also look at:** Arizona State University, Creighton University, University of Iowa, University of Kansas, University of Nebraska at Omaha

### EMPLOYMENT PROFILE
**Average starting salary:** $49,294

| Grads employed by field: | ..........% | avg. salary: |
|---|---|---|
| Accounting | 3 | $48,000 |
| Finance | 20 | $39,375 |
| Marketing | 18 | $50,691 |
| MIS | 9 | NR |
| Entrepreneurship | 6 | NR |
| General Management | 18 | NR |
| Other | 26 | NR |

# UNIVERSITY OF NEVADA—RENO
## COLLEGE OF BUSINESS ADMINSTRATION

*ADDRESS:* MAILSTOP 326, RENO, NV 89557
*PHONE:* 775-784-6869 • *FAX:* 775-784-6064
*E-MAIL:* GRADADMISSIONS@UNR.EDU
*WEBSITE:* WWW.COBA.UNR.EDU/MBA/

### GENERAL INFORMATION
**Type of School:** public **Environment:** city **Academic Calendar:** semester

### STUDENTS
**Enrollment of parent institution:** 1,128 **Enrollment of business school:** 167 **% part-time:** 74 **Average age at entry:** 29

### ACADEMICS
**Student/faculty ratio:** 30:1

### FINANCIAL FACTS
**Tuition (in-state/out-of-state):** $2,520/$7,094

### ADMISSIONS
**ADMISSIONS SELECTIVITY RATING: 60\***
**# of applications received:** 72 **% applicants accepted:** 93 **% acceptees attending:** 76 **TOEFL required of int'l applicants?** yes **Minimum TOEFL:** 550 **Application Fee:** $60 **Regular Application Deadline:** 3/15 **Regular Notification:** rolling **Deferment Available?** yes **Maximum length of deferment:** 1 year **Non-fall Admissions?** yes

### EMPLOYMENT PROFILE
**Average starting salary:** $50,000

# UNIVERSITY OF NEW ORLEANS
## COLLEGE OF BUSINESS ADMINSTRATION

**ADMISSIONS CONTACT:** *ROSLYN SHELEY, DIRECTOR OF ADMISSIONS*
**ADDRESS:** *ADMINISTRATION BUILDING ROOM 103, NEW ORLEANS, LA 70148*
**PHONE:** *504-280-6595* • **FAX:** *504-280-5522*
**E-MAIL:** *ADMISSIONS@UNO.EDU*
**WEBSITE:** *WWW.UNO.EDU*

### GENERAL INFORMATION
**Type of School:** public **Environment:** metropolis **Academic Calendar:** semester

### STUDENTS
**Enrollment of parent institution:** 17,360 **Enrollment of business school:** 810 **% male/female:** 51/49 **% out-of-state:** 30 **% part-time:** 46 **% minorities:** 25 **% international:** 26 **Average age at entry:** 30

### ACADEMICS
**Student/faculty ratio:** 24:1 **Prominent Alumni:** Dr. James Clark, Chair of the Board, Netscape Communications; Michael Fitzpatrick, CEO, Rohm & Haas; Erving Johnson, Starting Center, Milwaukee Bucks; Mike Kettenring, President & General Manager, Gillett Broadcasting; Dr. Reuben Arminana, President, Sonoma State University

### FINANCIAL FACTS
**Tuition (in-state/out-of-state):** $3,300/$10,800 **Books and supplies:** $1,150 **Room & board:** $4,122 **Average grant:** $2,697

### ADMISSIONS
**ADMISSIONS SELECTIVITY RATING:** 67
**# of applications received:** 575 **% applicants accepted:** 67 **% acceptees attending:** 62 **GMAT Range (25th to 75th percentile):** 400-510 **Average GMAT:** 459 **Average GPA:** 3.0 **TOEFL required of int'l applicants?** yes **Minimum TOEFL (paper/computer):** 550/213 **Application Fee:** $40 **Regular Application Deadline:** 7/1 **Regular Notification:** 9/1 **Deferment Available?** yes **Maximum length of deferment:** 1 semester **Transfer Students Accepted?** yes **Non-fall Admissions?** yes **Need-Blind Admissions?** yes

# UNIVERSITY OF NORTH CAROLINA—WILMINGTON
## CAMERON SCHOOL OF BUSINESS

**ADMISSIONS CONTACT:** *KATHY ERICKSON, GRADUATE PROGRAMS ADMINISTRATOR*
**ADDRESS:** *601 SOUTH COLLEGE ROAD, WILMINGTON, NC 28403-5920*
**PHONE:** *910-962-3903* • **FAX:** *910-962-3815*
**E-MAIL:** *GRADSTUDIES@UNCW.EDU*
**WEBSITE:** *WWW.CSB.UNCW.EDU/MBA/INDEX.STM*

### GENERAL INFORMATION
**Type of School:** public **Environment:** city

### STUDENTS
**Enrollment of parent institution:** 10,300 **Enrollment of business school:** 120 **% male/female:** 61/39 **% part-time:** 100 **% minorities:** 3 **Average age at entry:** 31 **Average years work experience at entry:** 8

### FINANCIAL FACTS
**Tuition (in-state/out-of-state):** $4,696/$9,267

### ADMISSIONS
**ADMISSIONS SELECTIVITY RATING:** 88
**# of applications received:** 147 **% applicants accepted:** 44 **% acceptees attending:** 92 **Average GMAT:** 549 **Average GPA:** 3.5 **TOEFL required of int'l applicants?** yes **Minimum TOEFL (paper/computer):** 500/213 **Application Fee:** $45 **International Application Fee:** $45 **Regular Application Deadline:** 2/1 **Regular Notification:** rolling **Deferment Available?** yes **Maximum length of deferment:** 1 year **Non-fall Admissions?** yes

# UNIVERSITY OF NORTH TEXAS
## COLLEGE OF BUSINESS ADMINISTRATION

**ADMISSIONS CONTACT:** *DENISE GALUBENSKI OR KONNI STUBBLEFIELD, GRADUATE ACADEMIC ADVISORS*
**ADDRESS:** *PO BOX 311160, DENTON, TX 76203*
**PHONE:** *940-369-8977* • **FAX:** *940-369-8978*
**E-MAIL:** *MBA@COBAF.UNT.EDU*
**WEBSITE:** *WWW.COBA.UNT.EDU*

### GENERAL INFORMATION
**Type of School:** public **Environment:** city **Academic Calendar:** semester

### STUDENTS
**Enrollment of parent institution:** 31,155 **Enrollment of business school:** 515 **% part-time:** 63 **Average age at entry:** 32 **Average years work experience at entry:** 5

### ACADEMICS
**Student/faculty ratio:** 45:1 **% female faculty** 22 **% minority faculty** 17 **Joint Degrees:** MBA in Operations Management Science/MS in

Engineering Technology; MBA/MS in Merchandising; MBA/MS in Hospitality Management

### FINANCIAL FACTS

**Tuition (in-state/out-of-state):** $2,126/$4,448

### ADMISSIONS

**Admissions Selectivity Rating: 60***

**# of applications received:** 533 **% applicants accepted:** 55 **% acceptees attending: Average GMAT:** 527 **TOEFL required of int'l applicants?** yes **Minimum TOEFL (paper/computer):** 550/213 **Application Fee:** $50 **International Application Fee:** $75 **Regular Application Deadline:** 7/15 **Deferment Available?** yes **Maximum length of deferment:** Three semesters **Transfer Students Accepted?** yes **Non-fall Admissions?** yes **Need-Blind Admissions?** yes

# UNIVERSITY OF QUEENSLAND
## UQ BUSINESS SCHOOL

**ADMISSIONS CONTACT:** THE MANAGER, STUDENT ADMINISTRATION
**ADDRESS:** UQ BUSINESS SCHOOL, THE UNIVERSITY OF QUEENSLAND, ST. LUCIA, Q 4072 AUSTRALIA
**PHONE:** 011-617-3365 6475 • **FAX:** 011-617-3365 6988
**E-MAIL:** POSTGRAD_ENQUIRIES@BUSINESS.UQ.EDU.AU
**WEBSITE:** WWW.BUSINESS.UQ.EDU.AU

### FINANCIAL FACTS

**Tuition (in-state/out-of-state):** $17,050

### ADMISSIONS

**Admissions Selectivity Rating: 60***
**Regular Application Deadline:** 1/30 **Regular Notification:** 1/30

# UNIVERSITY OF SAN DIEGO
## SCHOOL OF BUSINESS ADMINISTRATION

**ADMISSIONS CONTACT:** STEPHEN PULTZ, DIRECTOR OF ADMISSIONS
**ADDRESS:** 5998 ALCALA PARK, SAN DIEGO, CA 92110-2492
**PHONE:** 619-260-4840 • **FAX:** 619-260-7516
**E-MAIL:** MBA@SANDIEGO.EDU
**WEBSITE:** WWW.SANDIEGO.EDU/BUSINESS

### GENERAL INFORMATION

**Type of School:** private **Affiliation:** Roman Catholic **Environment:** metropolis **Academic Calendar:** Sept.-May

### STUDENTS

**Enrollment of parent institution:** 7,486 **Enrollment of business school:** 188 **% male/female:** 51/49 **% out-of-state:** 27 **% part-time:** 55 **% minorities:** 16 **% international:** 19 **Average age at entry:** 27 **Average years work experience at entry:** 4

### ACADEMICS

**Student/faculty ratio:** 2:1 **% female faculty** 27 **% minority faculty** 11 **Joint Degrees:** MBA/JD, 4 years; MBA/MSN, 3 years; MBA/MSRE 2.5 years; MBA/MSGL, 2.5 years; IMBA/JD, 4 years

### FINANCIAL FACTS

**Tuition:** $26,250 **Fees:** $136 **Books and supplies:** $1,260 **Room & board (on/off campus):** $11,330/$8,476 **% of students receiving aid:** 64 **% of first-year students receiving aid:** 67 **% of students receiving loans:** 44 **% of students receiving grants:** 32 **Average award package:** $19,456 **Average grant:** $4,800 **Average student loan debt:** $32,436

### ADMISSIONS

**Admissions Selectivity Rating: 80**

**# of applications received:** 282 **% applicants accepted:** 53 **% acceptees attending:** 42 **GMAT Range (25th to 75th percentile):** 520-620 **Average GMAT:** 570 **Average GPA:** 3.12 **TOEFL required of int'l applicants?** yes **Minimum TOEFL (paper/computer):** 580/237 **Application Fee:** $45 **International Application Fee:** $45 **Regular Application Deadline:** 5/15 **Regular Notification:** rolling **Deferment Available?** yes **Maximum length of deferment:** 1 year **Transfer Students Accepted?** yes **Non-fall Admissions?** yes **Need-Blind Admissions?** yes **Applicants also look at:** Pepperdine University, San Diego State University, University of California, Irvine, University of California, San Diego, University of Southern California

# UNIVERSITY OF SOUTH ALABAMA
## MITCHELL COLLEGE OF BUSINESS

**ADMISSIONS CONTACT:** ASSOCIATE DEAN
**ADDRESS:** 182 AD, MOBILE, AL 36688-0002
**PHONE:** 251-460-6141 • **FAX:** 251-460-6529
**WEBSITE:** HTTP://MCOB.SOUTHALABAMA.EDU/

### GENERAL INFORMATION

**Type of School:** public

### STUDENTS

**Enrollment of parent institution:** 12,300 **Enrollment of business school:** 162 **% male/female:** 55/45 **% part-time:** 20 **% minorities:** 2 **% international:** 30

### ACADEMICS

**Student/faculty ratio:** 20:1 **% female faculty** 21

### FINANCIAL FACTS

**Tuition (in-state/out-of-state):** $1,192/$2,384 **Fees:** $254 **Books and supplies:** $1,200

### ADMISSIONS

**Admissions Selectivity Rating: 71**

**# of applications received:** 70 **% applicants accepted:** 71 **% acceptees attending:** 84 **Average GMAT:** 488 **Average GPA:** 3.1 **TOEFL required of int'l applicants?** yes **Minimum TOEFL (paper):**

525 **Application Fee:** $25 **International Application Fee:** $25 **Regular Application Deadline:** 8/1 **Regular Notification:** 1/1 **Deferment Available?** yes **Transfer Students Accepted?** yes **Non-fall Admissions?** yes **Need-Blind Admissions?** yes

# UNIVERSITY OF SOUTH FLORIDA
## COLLEGE OF BUSINESS ADMINISTRATION

**ADMISSIONS CONTACT:** WENDY BAKER, ASSISTANT DIRECTOR OF GRADUATE STUDIES
**ADDRESS:** 4202 EAST FOWLER AVENUE BSN 3403, TAMPA, FL 33620
**PHONE:** 813-974-8800 • **FAX:** 813-974-7343
**E-MAIL:** MBA@COBA.USF.EDU
**WEBSITE:** WWW.COBA.USF.EDU

### GENERAL INFORMATION
**Type of School:** public **Environment:** metropolis **Academic Calendar:** semester

### STUDENTS
**Enrollment of parent institution:** 37,361 **Enrollment of business school:** 409 **% male/female:** 63/37 **% part-time:** 64 **% minorities:** 11 **% international:** 19 **Average age at entry:** 27 **Average years work experience at entry:** 2.5

### ACADEMICS
**Student/faculty ratio:** 4:1 **% female faculty** 25 **% minority faculty** 7 **Joint Degrees:** MBA/MSM

### FINANCIAL FACTS
**Tuition (in-state/out-of-state):** $5,864/$21,498 **Fees:** $37 **Books and supplies:** $700 **Room & board:** $12,310 **Average grant:** $6,500

### ADMISSIONS
**ADMISSIONS SELECTIVITY RATING:** 75

**# of applications received:** 241 **% applicants accepted:** 77 **% acceptees attending:** 64 **GMAT Range (25th to 75th percentile):** 510-590 **Average GMAT:** 556 **Average GPA:** 3.3 **TOEFL required of int'l applicants?** yes **Minimum TOEFL (paper/computer):** 550/213 **Application Fee:** $30 **International Application Fee:** $30 **Regular Application Deadline:** 6/1 **Regular Notification:** 6/1 **Deferment Available?** yes **Maximum length of deferment:** 1 year **Transfer Students Accepted?** yes **Non-fall Admissions?** yes **Need-Blind Admissions?** yes **Applicants also look at:** Florida State University, University of Central Florida, University of Florida

# THE UNIVERSITY OF SOUTHERN MISSISSIPPI
## COLLEGE OF BUSINESS

**ADMISSIONS CONTACT:** GABRIEL MCPHEARSON, ASSISTANT TO THE DIRECTOR
**ADDRESS:** 118 COLLEGE DRIVE #5096, HATTIESBURG, MS 39406-5096
**PHONE:** 601-266-4653 • **FAX:** 601-266-5814
**E-MAIL:** MBA@USM.EDU
**WEBSITE:** WWW.USM.EDU/MBA

### GENERAL INFORMATION
**Type of School:** public **Environment:** village **Academic Calendar:** semester

### STUDENTS
**Enrollment of parent institution:** 15,030 **Enrollment of business school:** 93 **% male/female:** 58/42 **% out-of-state:** 24 **% part-time:** 59 **% minorities:** 8 **% international:** 8 **Average age at entry:** 27

### ACADEMICS
**Student/faculty ratio:** 30:1 **% female faculty** 25 **% minority faculty** 15 **Joint Degrees:** MBA/MPH, 2-6 years

### FINANCIAL FACTS
**Tuition:** $4,312 **Fees:** $5,430 **Books and supplies:** $1,600 **Room & board (on/off campus):** $5,800/$7,600 **% of students receiving aid:** 75 **% of students receiving grants:** 25 **Average grant:** $8,690

### ADMISSIONS
**ADMISSIONS SELECTIVITY RATING:** 60*

**# of applications received:** 73 **% applicants accepted:** 56 **% acceptees attending:** 76 **GMAT Range (25th to 75th percentile):** 450-560 **Average GMAT:** 508 **Average GPA:** 3.36 **TOEFL required of int'l applicants?** yes **Minimum TOEFL (paper/computer):** 550/213 **Application Fee:** $25 **International Application Fee:** $25 **Regular Application Deadline:** 7/15 **Regular Notification:** rolling **Deferment Available?** yes **Maximum length of deferment:** 2 semesters **Transfer Students Accepted?** yes **Non-fall Admissions?** yes **Need-Blind Admissions?** yes

### EMPLOYMENT PROFILE
**Primary source of full-time job acceptances**
Unknown.....................................13 (100%)
**Average starting salary:** $43,179
**Grads employed by field: ..........% avg. salary:**
Accounting ....................................7 $35,056
Finance ..........................................15 $35,056
Marketing ......................................15 $35,000
Operations.....................................7 $48,600
General Management ....................23 $37,301
Other...............................................31 $58,375

# UNIVERSITY OF ST. GALLEN (SWITZERLAND)

## MBA-HSG

**ADMISSIONS CONTACT:** MR. PRASAD OSWAL, PROGRAM MANAGER
**ADDRESS:** BLUMENBERGPLATZ 9, ST. GALLEN, 9000 SWITZERLAND
**PHONE:** 0041-71-224-7355 • **FAX:** 0041-71-224-2473
**E-MAIL:** MBA@UNISG.CH
**WEBSITE:** WWW.MBA.UNISG.CH

### GENERAL INFORMATION
**Type of School:** public **Academic Calendar:** Jan.-Dec.

### FINANCIAL FACTS
**Tuition (in-state/out-of-state):** $37,800

### ADMISSIONS
**ADMISSIONS SELECTIVITY RATING: 60\***
**Average GMAT:** 690 **TOEFL required of int'l applicants?** yes

# UNIVERSITY OF STRATHCLYDE— GLASGOW
## UNIVERSITY OF STRATHCLYDE GRADUATE SCHOOL OF BUSINESS

**ADMISSIONS CONTACT:** LUCY REYNOLDS
**ADDRESS:** 199 CATHEDRAL STREET, GLASGOW, G4 0QU SCOTLAND
**PHONE:** 141-553-6118 • **FAX:** 141-553-6162
**E-MAIL:** ADMISSIONS@GSB.STRATH.AC.UK
**WEBSITE:** WWW.GSB.STRATH.AC.UK

### GENERAL INFORMATION
**Type of School:** private **Academic Calendar:** 5/6

### STUDENTS
**Enrollment of business school:** 107 **% male/female:** 86/14 **% part-time:** 37 **% minorities:** 88 **% international:** 84 **Average age at entry:** 32 **Average years work experience at entry:** 9

### ACADEMICS
**Student/faculty ratio:** 4:1 **% female faculty** 11 **Joint Degrees:** MBA with a specialism in Leadership Studies, 2.5 - 3 years

### FINANCIAL FACTS
**Fees:** $31,600 **Books and supplies:** $150 **Room & board (on/off campus):** $13,500/$15,300

### ADMISSIONS
**ADMISSIONS SELECTIVITY RATING: 70**
**# of applications received:** 280 **% applicants accepted:** 90 **% acceptees attending:** 42 **Average GMAT:** 560 **Average GPA:** 3.39
**TOEFL required of int'l applicants?** yes **Minimum TOEFL**

**(paper/computer):** 600/250 **Regular Application Deadline:** rolling
**Regular Notification:** rolling **Deferment Available?** yes **Maximum length of deferment:** 2 years **Non-fall Admissions?** yes

### EMPLOYMENT PROFILE
**Average starting salary:** $124,000
**Grads employed by field: ..........% avg. salary:**
Accounting ....................................2 $130,000
Finance .........................................13 $130,000
Marketing ......................................5 $85,500
Consulting.....................................10 $142,000
Entrepreneurship............................10
Internet/New Media......................15 $114,000
Nonprofit.......................................4 $66,500
Other..............................................41 $95,000

# UNIVERSITY OF TENNESSEE AT MARTIN
## COLLEGE OF BUSINESS AND PUBLIC AFFAIRS

**ADMISSIONS CONTACT:** JAMES GREEN, COLLEGE OF BUSINESS & PUBLIC AFFAIRS GRADUATE PROGRAM
**ADDRESS:** 103 BUSINESS ADMINISTRATION BUILDING, MARTIN, TN 38238-5015
**PHONE:** 731-587-7333 • **FAX:** 731-587-7241
**E-MAIL:** BAGRAD@UTM.EDU
**WEBSITE:** WWW.UTM.EDU/DEPARTMENTS/SOBA/

### GENERAL INFORMATION
**Type of School:** public **Environment:** rural **Academic Calendar:** semester

### STUDENTS
**Enrollment of business school:** 200 **% male/female:** 45/55 **% minorities:** 10

### ACADEMICS
**Student/faculty ratio:** 15:1

### FINANCIAL FACTS
**Tuition (in-state/out-of-state):** $3,768/$7,650 **Books and supplies:** $1,000

### ADMISSIONS
**ADMISSIONS SELECTIVITY RATING: 60\***
**Average GMAT:** 504 **Average GPA:** 3.22 **TOEFL required of int'l applicants?** yes **Minimum TOEFL:** 525 **Application Fee:** $25
**Regular Application Deadline:** rolling **Regular Notification:** rolling
**Deferment Available?** yes **Non-fall Admissions?** yes

# THE UNIVERSITY OF TEXAS AT EL PASO

## COLLEGE OF BUSINESS ADMINISTRATION

*ADMISSIONS CONTACT:* YOLANDA RUIZ, GRADUATE COORDINATOR
*ADDRESS:* ROOM 102, COLLEGE OF BUSINESS, EL PASO, TX 79968
*PHONE:* 915-747-5174 • *FAX:* 915-747-5147
*E-MAIL:* COBA@UTEP.EDU.
*WEBSITE:* WWW.UTEP.EDU/GRADUATE/

### GENERAL INFORMATION

**Type of School:** public **Environment:** metropolis **Academic Calendar:** semester

### STUDENTS

**Enrollment of parent institution:** 19,200 **Enrollment of business school:** 209 **% part-time:** 100 **Average age at entry:** 32 **Average years work experience at entry:** 3.8

### ACADEMICS

**Student/faculty ratio:** 4:1 **% female faculty** 19 **% minority faculty** 29 **Joint Degrees:** MBA/MPA, 60-78 credits, 2-6 years

### FINANCIAL FACTS

**% of students receiving aid:** 30 **% of first-year students receiving aid:** 30 **% of students receiving loans:** 24 **% of students receiving grants:** 3

### ADMISSIONS

**ADMISSIONS SELECTIVITY RATING: 63**

**# of applications received:** 140 **% applicants accepted:** 90 **% acceptees attending:** 71 **Average GMAT:** 538 **TOEFL required of int'l applicants?** yes **Minimum TOEFL:** 600 **Application Fee:** $15 **Regular Application Deadline:** 7/1 **Regular Notification:** rolling **Non-fall Admissions?** yes **Need-Blind Admissions?** yes

# THE UNIVERSITY OF TEXAS AT TYLER

## SCHOOL OF BUSINESS ADMINISTRATION

*ADMISSIONS CONTACT:* DR. MARY FISCHER, DIRECTOR OF GRADUATE PROGRAMS IN BUSINESS
*ADDRESS:* 3900 UNIVERSITY BOULEVARD, TYLER, TX 75799
*PHONE:* 903-566-7363 • *FAX:* 903-566-7372
*E-MAIL:* GSMITH@MAIL.UTTYL.EDU
*WEBSITE:* WWW.UTTYLER.EDU/CBT/MBA.HTM

### GENERAL INFORMATION

**Type of School:** public **Environment:** city **Academic Calendar:** semester

### STUDENTS

**Enrollment of parent institution:** 3,459 **Enrollment of business school:** 101 **% male/female:** 59/41 **% part-time:** 98 **% minorities:** 5 **% international:** 5 **Average age at entry:** 32

### ACADEMICS

**Student/faculty ratio:** 15:1

### FINANCIAL FACTS

**Tuition (in-state/out-of-state):** $3,162/$7,458

### ADMISSIONS

**ADMISSIONS SELECTIVITY RATING: 60\***

**% acceptees attending:** 10 **TOEFL required of int'l applicants?** yes **Minimum TOEFL:** 550 **Regular Application Deadline:** rolling **Regular Notification:** rolling **Deferment Available?** yes

# UNIVERSITY OF TOLEDO

## COLLEGE OF BUSINESS ADMINISTRATION

*ADMISSIONS CONTACT:* DAVID CHATFIELD, DIRECTOR MBA & EMBA PROGRAMS
*ADDRESS:* COLLEGE OF BUSINESS ADMINISTRATION, THE UNIVERSITY OF TOLEDO, TOLEDO, OH 43606-3390
*PHONE:* 419-530-2775 • *FAX:* 419-530-7260
*E-MAIL:* MBA@UTOLEDO.EDU
*WEBSITE:* WWW.BUSINESS.UTOLEDO.EDU/

### GENERAL INFORMATION

**Type of School:** public **Environment:** city **Academic Calendar:** semester

### STUDENTS

**Enrollment of parent institution:** 19,480 **Enrollment of business school:** 342 **% male/female:** 65/35 **% part-time:** 69 **% minorities:** 9 **% international:** 23 **Average age at entry:** 28 **Average years work experience at entry:** 3

### ACADEMICS

**Student/faculty ratio:** 10:1 **% female faculty** 21 **Joint Degrees:** JD/MBA, 3 years. **Prominent Alumni:** Edward Kinsey, Co-Founder, Ariba, Inc.; Ora Alleman, VP, National City Bank; Michael Durik, Executive VP, The Limited Stores, Inc.; Marvin Herb, CEO Coca-Cola Bottling Company; Julie Higgins, Exective VP, The Trust Company of Toledo

### FINANCIAL FACTS

**Tuition (in-state/out-of-state):** $8,619/$17,431 **Fees:** $1,064 **Books and supplies:** $1,200 **Room & board (off campus):** $5,830 **Average grant:** $16,116

### ADMISSIONS

**ADMISSIONS SELECTIVITY RATING: 64**

**# of applications received:** 166 **% applicants accepted:** 89 **% acceptees attending:** 54 **Average GMAT:** 510 **Average GPA:** 3.20 **TOEFL required of int'l applicants?** yes **Minimum TOEFL**

(paper/computer): 550/213 **Application Fee:** $40 **International Application Fee:** $40 **Regular Application Deadline:** rolling **Regular Notification:** rolling **Deferment Available?** yes **Maximum length of deferment:** 1 year **Transfer Students Accepted?** yes **Non-fall Admissions?** yes **Applicants also look at:** Bowling Green State University, The University of Findlay

# UNIVERSITY OF TORONTO
## JOSEPH L. ROTMAN SCHOOL OF MANAGEMENT

**ADMISSIONS CONTACT:** CHERYL MILLINGTON, DIRECTOR OF MBA RECRUITING AND ADMISSIONS
**ADDRESS:** 105 ST. GEORGE STREET, TORONTO, ON M5S 3E6 CANADA
**PHONE:** 416-978-3499 • **FAX:** 416-978-5812
**E-MAIL:** MBA@ROTMAN.UTORONTO.CA
**WEBSITE:** WWW.ROTMAN.UTORONTO.CA

### GENERAL INFORMATION
**Type of School:** public **Environment:** metropolis **Academic Calendar:** Sept.-May

### STUDENTS
**Enrollment of parent institution:** 67,000 **Enrollment of business school:** 330 **% male/female:** 73/27 **% part-time:** 19 **% minorities:** 50 **% international:** 40 **Average age at entry:** 28 **Average years work experience at entry:** 5

### ACADEMICS
**Student/faculty ratio:** 7:1 **% female faculty** 22 **Joint Degrees:** JD/MBA, 4 years; BASC/MBA, 5 years, 8 months; MA in Russian & Eastern European Studies/MBA, 4 years **Prominent Alumni:** Joseph L. Rotman, Founder & Chair, Clairvest Group Inc.; Ian Locke, General Partner, Jefferson Partners, Toronto; Don Morrison, COO, Research In Motion, Waterloo, Ont.; John Cassaday, President & CEO, Corus Entertainment; Richard Nesbitt, CEO, TSX Group

### FINANCIAL FACTS
**Tuition (in-state/out-of-state):** $21,800/$29,800 **Books and supplies:** $5,000 **Room & board:** $10,000 **% of students receiving aid:** 70 **% of first-year students receiving aid:** 70 **% of students receiving loans:** 70 **% of students receiving grants:** 20 **Average grant:** $8,000

### ADMISSIONS
**ADMISSIONS SELECTIVITY RATING: 60***
**# of applications received:** 1010 **GMAT Range (25th to 75th percentile):** 550-770 **Average GMAT:** 642 **Average GPA:** 3.39 **TOEFL required of int'l applicants?** yes **Minimum TOEFL (paper/computer):** 600/250 **Application Fee:** $150 **International Application Fee:** $150 **Regular Application Deadline:** 4/30 **Regular Notification:** 7/1 **Application Deadline/Notification Round 1:** 1/15 / 3/15 **Round 2:** 4/30 / 7/1 **Early decision program?** yes **ED deadline /notification:** 1/15 (domestic students only)/3/15 **Deferment Available?** yes

**Maximum length of deferment:** 1 year **Need-Blind Admissions?** yes **Applicants also look at:** McGill University, Queensland University of Technology, University of Western Ontario, York University

### EMPLOYMENT PROFILE
**Primary source of full-time job acceptances**
School-facilitated activities 53%
Graduate-facilitated activities 47%
**Average starting salary:** $83,300
**Percent employed:** 93

| Grads employed by field: | ..........% | avg. salary: |
|---|---|---|
| Finance | 53 | $80,000 |
| Marketing | 8 | $68,526 |
| Operations | 9 | $78,633 |
| Consulting | 18 | $105,500 |
| General Management | 8 | $89,083 |
| Other | 4 | $82,560 |

# UNIVERSITY OF TULSA

**ADMISSIONS CONTACT:** RON COOPER, DIRECTOR, GRADUATE BUSINESS PROGRAMS
**ADDRESS:** 600 SOUTH COLLEGE AVENUE, BAH 217, TULSA, OK 74104-3189
**PHONE:** 918-631-2242 • **FAX:** 918-631-2142
**E-MAIL:** GRADUATE-BUSINESS@UTULSA.EDU
**WEBSITE:** WWW.CBA.UTULSA.EDU

### GENERAL INFORMATION
**Type of School:** private **Affiliation:** Presbyterian

### STUDENTS
**Enrollment of parent institution:** 4,084 **Enrollment of business school:** 106 **% male/female:** 49/51 **% out-of-state:** 44 **% part-time:** 56 **% minorities:** 8 **% international:** 26 **Average age at entry:** 24

### ACADEMICS
**Student/faculty ratio:** 5:1 **% female faculty** 11 **% minority faculty** 5 **Joint Degrees:** JD/MBA; JD/MTAX; METM

### FINANCIAL FACTS
**Tuition:** $12,132 **Fees:** $54 **Books and supplies:** $1,000 **Room & board:** $9,360 **% of students receiving aid:** 92 **% of students receiving loans:** 36 **% of students receiving grants:** 67 **Average award package:** $27,303

### ADMISSIONS
**ADMISSIONS SELECTIVITY RATING: 80**
**# of applications received:** 93 **% applicants accepted:** 62 **% acceptees attending:** 64 **GMAT Range (25th to 75th percentile):** 510-588 **Average GMAT:** 557 **Average GPA:** 3.52 **TOEFL required of int'l applicants?** yes **Minimum TOEFL (paper/computer):** 575/232 **Application Fee:** $30 **International Application Fee:** $30 **Regular Application Deadline:** rolling **Regular Notification:** rolling

Deferment Available? yes **Maximum length of deferment:** 1 year
**Transfer Students Accepted?** yes **Non-fall Admissions?** yes **Need-Blind Admissions?** yes **Applicants also look at:** Oklahoma State University, University of Oklahoma

## EMPLOYMENT PROFILE

**Average starting salary:** $48,964

# UNIVERSITY OF WARWICK
## WARWICK BUSINESS SCHOOL

**ADMISSIONS CONTACT:** JO MOUND, MBA MARKETING AND RECRUITMENT TEAM
**ADDRESS:** WARWICK BUSINESS SCHOOL, COVENTRY, CV4 7AL ENGLAND
**PHONE:** 011-44-0-24-7652-4100 • **FAX:** 011-44-0-24 -7657-4400
**E-MAIL:** WARWICKMBA@WBS.AC.UK
**WEBSITE:** WWW.WBS.AC.UK

### GENERAL INFORMATION

**Type of School:** public **Academic Calendar:** trimester

### STUDENTS

**Enrollment of parent institution:** 18,000 **Enrollment of business school:** 460 **% male/female:** 79/21 **% part-time:** 85 **% international:** 78 **Average age at entry:** 32 **Average years work experience at entry:** 9

### ACADEMICS

**Student/faculty ratio:** 12:1 **Prominent Alumni:** Svein Stokke, Director, Citigroup; Keith Bedell-Pearce, Chair, Norwich & Peterborough Building Society; Mike O'Driscoll, President, Aston Martin, Jaguar, Land Rover; Steven Falk, Director of Financial Services, Manchester Utd FC; Roger Lovering, Head of Card Services, HSBC Bank PLC

### FINANCIAL FACTS

**Tuition:** $46,665 **Books and supplies:** $2,500 **Room & board:** $11,000 **% of students receiving aid:** 20 **% of students receiving grants:** 20 **Average award package:** $21,000

### ADMISSIONS

**ADMISSIONS SELECTIVITY RATING: 89**
**# of applications received:** 300 **% applicants accepted:** 40 **% acceptees attending:** 47 **GMAT Range (25th to 75th percentile):** 550-680 **Average GMAT:** 620 **Average GPA:** 3.0 **TOEFL required of int'l applicants?** yes **Minimum TOEFL (paper/computer):** 620/260 **Application Fee:** $132 **International Application Fee:** $132 **Regular Application Deadline:** rolling **Regular Notification:** rolling **Deferment Available?** yes **Maximum length of deferment:** 1 year **Applicants also look at:** Cranfield University, University of Cambridge, University of London, University of Manchester, University of Oxford

## EMPLOYMENT PROFILE

**Grads employed by field:** .........% avg. salary:
Finance ..........................................8 NR
Marketing .....................................19 NR
Operations....................................4 NR
Strategic Planning .........................8 NR
Consulting.....................................21 NR
Entrepreneurship...........................4 NR
General Management ...................18 NR
Other.............................................18 NR

# UNIVERSITY OF WASHINGTON—
# GLOBAL MBA
## UNIVERSITY OF WASHINGTON BUSINESS SCHOOL

**ADDRESS:** 110 MACKENZIE HALL, BOX 353200, SEATTLE, WA 98195-3200
**PHONE:** 206-543-4661 • **FAX:** 206-616-7351
**E-MAIL:** GMBA@U.WASHINGTON.EDU
**WEBSITE:** WWW.GLOBALMBA.WASHINGTON.EDU

### GENERAL INFORMATION

**Type of School:** public

### ACADEMICS

**Student/faculty ratio:** 8:1 **% female faculty** 29 **% minority faculty** 7 **Joint Degrees:** MPA, 1 year; JD/MBA, 4 years; MBA/MAIS, 3 years; MBA/MHA, 3 years

### FINANCIAL FACTS

**Tuition:** $48,500 **Books and supplies:** $3,000 **Room & board:** $10,338

### ADMISSIONS

**ADMISSIONS SELECTIVITY RATING: 60\***
**TOEFL required of int'l applicants?** yes **Application Fee:** $85
**International Application Fee:** $85 **Regular Application Deadline:** 12/15

# UNIVERSITY OF WEST FLORIDA
## COLLEGE OF BUSINESS

**ADMISSIONS CONTACT:** GRADUATE ADMISSIONS OFFICE, REGISTRAR OFFICER
**ADDRESS:** 11000 UNIVERSITY PARKWAY, PENSACOLA, FL 32514
**PHONE:** 850-474-2230 • **FAX:** 850-474-3360
**E-MAIL:** ADMISSIONS@UWF.EDU
**WEBSITE:** HTTP://UWF.EDU/MBA

### GENERAL INFORMATION

**Type of School:** public **Environment:** city

## STUDENTS

Enrollment of business school: 188 % male/female: 45/55 % part-time: 85 % minorities: 18 % international: 22 Average age at entry: 29

## ACADEMICS

Student/faculty ratio: 25:1

## FINANCIAL FACTS

Tuition (in-state/out-of-state): $7,292/$26,505 Books and supplies: $650 Average grant: $1,000

## ADMISSIONS

**ADMISSIONS SELECTIVITY RATING: 82**

# of applications received: 88 % applicants accepted: 42 % acceptees attending: 92 GMAT Range (25th to 75th percentile): 450-590 Average GMAT: 500 Average GPA: 3.18 TOEFL required of int'l applicants? yes Minimum TOEFL (paper/computer): 550/213 Application Fee: $30 Regular Application Deadline: 6/1 Regular Notification: rolling Transfer Students Accepted? yes Non-fall Admissions? yes

# UNIVERSITY OF WISCONSIN— EAU CLAIRE
## SCHOOL OF BUSINESS

**ADMISSIONS CONTACT:** MS. JAN STEWART, MBA PROGRAM ASSISTANT
**ADDRESS:** 105 GARFIELD AVENUE, EAU CLAIRE, WI 54702-4004
**PHONE:** 715-836-4733 • **FAX:** 715-836-2409
**E-MAIL:** ADMISSIONS@UWEC.EDU
**WEBSITE:** WWW.UWEC.EDU/COB/ACADEMICS/MBA/INDEX.HTM

## GENERAL INFORMATION

Type of School: public Environment: town Academic Calendar: semester

## STUDENTS

Enrollment of parent institution: 10,500 Enrollment of business school: 130 % male/female: 55/45 % out-of-state: 80 % part-time: 90 % minorities: 5 % international: 80 Average age at entry: 28 Average years work experience at entry: 7

## ACADEMICS

Student/faculty ratio: 5:1 % female faculty 30 Joint Degrees: Partner in the University of Wisconsin Internet Consortium MBA Program. Students may combine online courses with on campus courses.

## FINANCIAL FACTS

Tuition (in-state/out-of-state): $6,223/$16,833 Books and supplies: $1,000 Room & board: $4,266

## ADMISSIONS

**ADMISSIONS SELECTIVITY RATING: 60***

Average GMAT: 530 Average GPA: 3.2 TOEFL required of int'l applicants? yes Minimum TOEFL (paper/computer): 550/213 Application Fee: $45 Regular Application Deadline: rolling Regular Notification: rolling Deferment Available? yes Maximum length of deferment: 1 year Transfer Students Accepted? yes Non-fall Admissions? yes Need-Blind Admissions? yes

## EMPLOYMENT PROFILE

Grads employed by field: ..........% avg. salary:

| | | |
|---|---|---|
| Accounting | 20 | NR |
| Marketing | 20 | NR |
| MIS | 10 | NR |
| Operations | 10 | NR |
| Entrepreneurship | 10 | NR |
| General Management | 30 | NR |

# UNIVERSITY OF WISCONSIN— LA CROSSE
## COLLEGE OF BUSINESS ADMINISTRATION

**ADMISSIONS CONTACT:** KATHY KIEFER, DIRECTOR
**ADDRESS:** 1725 STATE STREET, LA CROSSE, WI 54601
**PHONE:** 608-785-8067 • **FAX:** 608-785-6695
**E-MAIL:** ADMISSIONS@UWLAX.EDU
**WEBSITE:** WWW.UWLAX.EDU

## GENERAL INFORMATION

Type of School: public Academic Calendar: semester

## STUDENTS

Enrollment of parent institution: 8,509 Enrollment of business school: 51 % male/female: 63/37 % part-time: 73 % minorities: 4 % international: 7 Average age at entry: 29 Average years work experience at entry: 3

## ACADEMICS

Student/faculty ratio: 25:1 % female faculty 28 % minority faculty 22

## FINANCIAL FACTS

Tuition (in-state/out-of-state): $6,150/$17,252 Books and supplies: $500 Room & board: $4,500 % of students receiving aid: 15

## ADMISSIONS

**ADMISSIONS SELECTIVITY RATING: 73**

# of applications received: 35 % applicants accepted: 83 % acceptees attending: 62 Average GMAT: 550 Average GPA: 3.39 TOEFL required of int'l applicants? yes Minimum TOEFL (paper/computer): 550/213 Application Fee: $48 Regular Application Deadline: rolling Regular Notification: rolling Deferment Available? yes Maximum length of deferment: rolling

Transfer Students Accepted? yes Non-fall Admissions? yes Need-Blind Admissions? yes

# UNIVERSITY OF WISCONSIN— OSHKOSH
## COLLEGE OF BUSINESS ADMINSTRATION

**ADMISSIONS CONTACT:** LYNN GRANCORBITZ, MBA PROGRAM ASSISTANT DIRECTOR AND ADVISOR
**ADDRESS:** 800 ALGOMA BOULEVARD, OSHKOSH, WI 54901
**PHONE:** 800-633-1430 • **FAX:** 920-424-7413
**E-MAIL:** MBA@UWOSH.EDU
**WEBSITE:** WWW.UWOSH.EDU/COLLEGES/COBA/ASSETS/GRAD/INDEX.PHP

### GENERAL INFORMATION
**Type of School:** public **Environment:** village **Academic Calendar:** semester

### STUDENTS
**Enrollment of parent institution:** 10,528 **Enrollment of business school:** 525 **% male/female:** 55/45 **% out-of-state:** 2 **% part-time:** 95 **% minorities:** 2 **% international:** 3 **Average age at entry:** 32 **Average years work experience at entry:** 5

### ACADEMICS
**Student/faculty ratio:** 11:1 **% female faculty** 15 **% minority faculty** 5

### FINANCIAL FACTS
**Tuition (in-state/out-of-state):** $4,664/$13,622 **% of students receiving aid:** 5 **% of first-year students receiving aid:** 5 **% of students receiving loans:** 5

### ADMISSIONS
**ADMISSIONS SELECTIVITY RATING: 70**
**# of applications received:** 115 **% applicants accepted:** 90 **% acceptees attending:** 93 **GMAT Range (25th to 75th percentile):** 470-610 **Average GMAT:** 540 **Average GPA:** 3.1 **TOEFL required of int'l applicants?** yes **Minimum TOEFL:** 550 **Application Fee:** $45 **International Application Fee:** $45 **Regular Application Deadline:** 7/1 **Regular Notification:** rolling **Deferment Available?** yes **Maximum length of deferment:** 3 years **Transfer Students Accepted?** yes **Non-fall Admissions?** yes **Applicants also look at:** Adolfo Ibañez University (Chile), Marquette University

### EMPLOYMENT PROFILE
**Primary source of full-time job acceptances**
Graduate-facilitated activities 100 (100%)
**Percent employed:** 50

# UNIVERSITY OF WISCONSIN— PARKSIDE
## SCHOOL OF BUSINESS AND TECHNOLOGY

**ADMISSIONS CONTACT:** BRAD PIAZZA, ASSISTANT DEAN
**ADDRESS:** 900 WOOD ROAD, BOX 2000, KENOSHA, WI 53141-2000
**PHONE:** 262-595-2046 • **FAX:** 262-595-2680
**E-MAIL:** PIAZZA@UWP.EDU
**WEBSITE:** WWW.UWP.EDU/DEPARTMENTS/BUSINESS

### GENERAL INFORMATION
**Type of School:** public **Environment:** city **Academic Calendar:** semester

### STUDENTS
**Enrollment of parent institution:** 5,000 **Enrollment of business school:** 71 **% part-time:** 100 **Average age at entry:** 33 **Average years work experience at entry:** 3

### ACADEMICS
**Student/faculty ratio:** 6:1 **% female faculty** 35 **% minority faculty** 30

### FINANCIAL FACTS
**Tuition (in-state/out-of-state):** $6,162/$17,500 **Fees:** $277 **Books and supplies:** $300

### ADMISSIONS
**ADMISSIONS SELECTIVITY RATING: 62**
**# of applications received:** 21 **% applicants accepted:** 100 **% acceptees attending:** 95 **GMAT Range (25th to 75th percentile):** 330-680 **Average GMAT:** 460 **Average GPA:** 3.0 **TOEFL required of int'l applicants?** yes **Minimum TOEFL (paper/computer):** 550/213 **Application Fee:** $45 **International Application Fee:** $45 **Regular Application Deadline:** 8/1 **Regular Notification:** rolling **Deferment Available?** yes **Maximum length of deferment:** 1 year **Transfer Students Accepted?** yes **Non-fall Admissions?** yes **Need-Blind Admissions?** yes

# UNIVERSITY OF WYOMING
## COLLEGE OF BUSINESS

**ADMISSIONS CONTACT:** TERRI L. RITTENBURG, DIRECTOR OF MBA PROGRAM
**ADDRESS:** PO BOX 3275, LARAMIE, WY 82071
**PHONE:** 307-766-2449 • **FAX:** 307-766-4028
**E-MAIL:** MBA@UWYO.EDU
**WEBSITE:** HTTP://BUSINESS.UWYO.EDU/MBA

### GENERAL INFORMATION
**Type of School:** public **Environment:** town **Academic Calendar:** semester, full-time/part-time/evening

## STUDENTS

**Enrollment of parent institution:** 11,904 **Enrollment of business school:** 63 **% male/female:** 64/36 **% part-time:** 48 **% international:** 18 **Average age at entry:** 28

## ACADEMICS

**Student/faculty ratio:** 3:1

## FINANCIAL FACTS

**Tuition (in-state/out-of-state):** $2,988/$8,676 **Fees (in-state/out-of-state):** $246/$298 **Books and supplies:** $300 **Room & board:** $6,212 **% of students receiving loans:** 34

## ADMISSIONS

**ADMISSIONS SELECTIVITY RATING: 60***

**Average GMAT:** 558 **Average GPA:** 3.2 **TOEFL required of int'l applicants?** yes **Minimum TOEFL (paper/computer):** 525/197 **Application Fee:** $40 **Regular Application Deadline:** 2/1 **Regular Notification:** rolling **Deferment Available?** yes **Maximum length of deferment:** 1 year **Transfer Students Accepted?** yes **Need-Blind Admissions?** yes

## EMPLOYMENT PROFILE

**Average starting salary:** $38,878

# UTAH STATE UNIVERSITY
## COLLEGE OF BUSINESS

**ADMISSIONS CONTACT:** SCHOOL OF GRADUATE STUDIES, ADMISSIONS OFFICER
**ADDRESS:** 0900 OLD MAIN HILL, LOGAN, UT 84322-0900
**PHONE:** 435-797-1189 • **FAX:** 435-797-1192
**E-MAIL:** GRADSCH@CC.USU.EDU
**WEBSITE:** WWW.USU.EDU/COB

## GENERAL INFORMATION

**Type of School:** public **Environment:** town **Academic Calendar:** semester

## STUDENTS

**Enrollment of parent institution:** 23,107 **Enrollment of business school:** 189 **% male/female:** 99/1 **% out-of-state:** 2 **% part-time:** 79 **% minorities:** 1 **% international:** 1 **Average age at entry:** 30 **Average years work experience at entry:** 5

## ACADEMICS

**Student/faculty ratio:** 30:1 **% female faculty** 19 **% minority faculty** 7 **Joint Degrees:** International MBA in Food and Agribusiness in cooperation with Royal Agricultural College in Cirencester, England. **Prominent Alumni:** Ron Labrum, President & CEO Cardinal Health; Annette Herman, CEO, United Healthcare Utah; Kay Toolson, CEO, Monaco Coach; Mark James, VP Human Resources Honeywell; Michael Kraupp, VP Finance, SkyWest Airlines

## FINANCIAL FACTS

**Tuition (in-state/out-of-state):** $3,940/$12,031 **Fees:** $544 **Books and supplies:** $1,650 **Room & board:** $3,560/$4,200 **% of students receiving aid:** 20 **% of first-year students receiving aid:** 20 **% of students receiving grants:** 20 **Average award package:** $5,300 **Average grant:** $1,500 **Average student loan debt:** $7,500

## ADMISSIONS

**ADMISSIONS SELECTIVITY RATING: 87**

**# of applications received:** 248 **% applicants accepted:** 42 **% acceptees attending:** 82 **GMAT Range (25th to 75th percentile):** 450-730 **Average GMAT:** 545 **Average GPA:** 3.35 **TOEFL required of int'l applicants?** yes **Minimum TOEFL (paper/computer):** 550/230 **Application Fee:** $55 **International Application Fee:** $55 **Regular Application Deadline:** 2/15 **Regular Notification:** 3/15 **Deferment Available?** yes **Maximum length of deferment:** 1 year **Need-Blind Admissions?** yes **Applicants also look at:** Brigham Young University, University of Utah, Weber State University

## EMPLOYMENT PROFILE

**Average starting salary:** $50,000

| Grads employed by field: | .........% | avg. salary: |
|---|---|---|
| Accounting | 35 | $55,000 |
| Finance | 9 | $50,000 |
| Human Resources | 2 | $40,000 |
| Marketing | 20 | NR |
| MIS | 2 | $60,000 |
| Operations | 2 | NR |
| Entrepreneurship | 5 | NR |
| General Management | 25 | $45,000 |

# VALDOSTA STATE UNIVERSITY
## LANGDALE COLLEGE OF BUSINESS ADMINISTRATION

**ADMISSIONS CONTACT:** JUDY TOMBERLIN, GRADUATE SCHOOL
**ADDRESS:** 903 NORTH PATTERSON STREET, VALDOSTA, GA 31698-0005
**PHONE:** 229-333-5696 • **FAX:** 229-245-3853
**E-MAIL:** MBA@VALDOSTA.EDU
**WEBSITE:** WWW.VALDOSTA.EDU/LCOBA/GRAD/

## GENERAL INFORMATION

**Type of School:** public **Environment:** city **Academic Calendar:** semester

## STUDENTS

**Enrollment of parent institution:** 10,500 **Enrollment of business school:** 31 **% male/female:** 50/50 **% part-time:** 100 **% international:** 8 **Average age at entry:** 30 **Average years work experience at entry:** 8

## ACADEMICS

**Student/faculty ratio:** 3:1 **% female faculty** 20

## FINANCIAL FACTS

Tuition (in-state/out-of-state): $3,766/$12,544 **Fees:** $708 **Books and supplies:** $800 **Room & board:** $2,684 **Average grant:** $1,000

## ADMISSIONS

**ADMISSIONS SELECTIVITY RATING: 82**

**# of applications received:** 21 **% applicants accepted:** 48 **% acceptees attending:** 80 **GMAT Range (25th to 75th percentile):** 500-640 **Average GMAT:** 534 **Average GPA:** 3.3 **TOEFL required of int'l applicants?** yes **Minimum TOEFL (paper/computer):** 550/213 **Application Fee:** $25 **Regular Application Deadline:** rolling **Regular Notification:** rolling **Deferment Available?** yes **Maximum length of deferment:** 1 semester **Transfer Students Accepted?** yes **Non-fall Admissions?** yes **Need-Blind Admissions?** yes

# VANGUARD UNIVERSITY
## SCHOOL OF BUSINESS AND MANAGEMENT

**ADMISSIONS CONTACT:** DRAKE LEVASHEFF, DIRECTOR OF GRADUATE ADMISSIONS
**ADDRESS:** 55 FAIR DRIVE, COSTA MESA, CA 92626-9601
**PHONE:** 714-966-5499 • **FAX:** 714-966-5471
**E-MAIL:** GRADADMISSIONS@VANGUARD.EDU
**WEBSITE:** WWW.VANGUARD.EDU/MBA

## GENERAL INFORMATION

**Type of School:** private **Affiliation:** Assemblies of God

## FINANCIAL FACTS

**Tuition:** $17,850 **Fees:** $50

## ADMISSIONS

**ADMISSIONS SELECTIVITY RATING: 60\***

**TOEFL required of int'l applicants?** yes **Minimum TOEFL (paper/computer):** 550/213 **Application Fee:** $45 **International Application Fee:** $45 **Regular Application Deadline:** 8/1 **Transfer Students Accepted?** yes **Non-fall Admissions?** yes **Need-Blind Admissions?** yes

# VIRGINIA COMMONWEALTH UNIVERSITY
## SCHOOL OF BUSINESS

**ADMISSIONS CONTACT:** JANA P. MCQUAID, DIRECTOR, GRADUATE STUDIES IN BUSINESS
**ADDRESS:** 1015 FLOYD AVENUE, PO BOX 844000, RICHMOND, VA 23284-4000
**PHONE:** 804-828-4622 • **FAX:** 804-828-7174
**E-MAIL:** GSIB@VCU.EDU
**WEBSITE:** WWW.GSIB.BUS.VCU.EDU

## GENERAL INFORMATION

**Type of School:** public **Environment:** metropolis **Academic Calendar:** semester

## STUDENTS

**Enrollment of parent institution:** 27,026 **Enrollment of business school:** 218 **% male/female:** 64/36 **% part-time:** 74 **% international:** 1 **Average age at entry:** 27

## ACADEMICS

**Student/faculty ratio:** 20:1 **% female faculty** 15 **% minority faculty** 5 **Joint Degrees:** BS/MAcc (for entering undergraduate students), 5 years; BS in Engineering/MBA; PharmD/MBA; MBA/MSIS

## FINANCIAL FACTS

**Tuition (in-state/out-of-state):** $6,368/$15,904 **Fees (in-state/out-of-state):** $1,382/$1,502 **Books and supplies:** $800

## ADMISSIONS

**ADMISSIONS SELECTIVITY RATING: 84**

**# of applications received:** 134 **% applicants accepted:** 48 **% acceptees attending:** 69 **GMAT Range (25th to 75th percentile):** 490-640 **Average GMAT:** 557 **Average GPA:** 3.2 **TOEFL required of int'l applicants?** yes **Minimum TOEFL (paper/computer):** 600/250 **Application Fee:** $50 **International Application Fee:** $50 **Regular Application Deadline:** 6/1 **Regular Notification:** 7/1 **Early decision program?** yes **ED deadline /notification:** Fall Term has 4/1 deadline 5/1 **Deferment Available?** yes **Maximum length of deferment:** 1 year **Transfer Students Accepted?** yes **Non-fall Admissions?** yes **Need-Blind Admissions?** yes **Applicants also look at:** College of William and Mary, James Madison University, University of Richmond, Virginia Tech

# Wake Forest University, Evening MBA—Charlotte

## Babcock Graduate School of Management

**ADMISSIONS CONTACT:** LESLYE GERVASI, DIRECTOR, MBA PROGRAMS-CHARLOTTE
**ADDRESS:** ONE MORROCROFT CENTRE, 6805 MORRISON BOULEVARD, SUITE 150, CHARLOTTE, NC 28211
**PHONE:** 704-365-1717 • **FAX:** 704-365-3511
**E-MAIL:** CLT.MBA@MBA.WFU.EDU
**WEBSITE:** WWW.MBA.WFU.EDU

### GENERAL INFORMATION

**Type of School:** private **Academic Calendar:** semester

### STUDENTS

**Enrollment of parent institution:** 6,444 **Enrollment of business school:** 556 **% male/female:** 71/29 **% out-of-state:** 75 **% part-time:** 61 **% minorities:** 13 **% international:** 23 **Average age at entry:** 32 **Average years work experience at entry:** 9

### ACADEMICS

**Student/faculty ratio:** 10:1 **% female faculty** 13 **% minority faculty** 13 **Joint Degrees:** JD/MBA, 4 years; MD/MBA, 5 years; PhD/MBA (Graduate School of Arts & Sciences/MBA), 5 years; MSA/MBA, 6 years.

### FINANCIAL FACTS

**Tuition:** $27,000 **% of students receiving aid:** 74 **% of first-year students receiving aid:** 80 **% of students receiving loans:** 70 **% of students receiving grants:** 1 **Average award package:** $22,680 **Average grant:** $12,250 **Average student loan debt:** $39,277

### ADMISSIONS

**ADMISSIONS SELECTIVITY RATING: 60\***

**# of applications received:** 63 **% applicants accepted:** 79 **% acceptees attending:** 100 **Application Fee:** $75 **International Application Fee:** $75 **Regular Application Deadline:** rolling **Regular Notification:** rolling **Deferment Available?** yes **Maximum length of deferment:** 1 year **Need-Blind Admissions?** yes

# Wake Forest University, Evening MBA—Winston-Salem

## Babcock Graduate School of Management

**ADMISSIONS CONTACT:** JAMIE BARNES, DIRECTOR, EVENING & FAST-TRACK EXECUTIVE PROGRAMS
**ADDRESS:** PO BOX 7368, WINSTON-SALEM, NC 27109-7368
**PHONE:** 336-758-5422 • **FAX:** 336-758-5830
**E-MAIL:** ADMISSIONS@MBA.WFU.EDU
**WEBSITE:** WWW.MBA.WFU.EDU

### GENERAL INFORMATION

**Type of School:** private **Academic Calendar:** semester

### STUDENTS

**Enrollment of parent institution:** 6,444 **Enrollment of business school:** 556 **% male/female:** 71/29 **% out-of-state:** 75 **% part-time:** 61 **% minorities:** 13 **% international:** 23 **Average age at entry:** 32 **Average years work experience at entry:** 9

### ACADEMICS

**Student/faculty ratio:** 10:1 **% female faculty** 13 **% minority faculty** 13 **Joint Degrees:** JD/MBA, 4 years; MD/MBA, 5 years; PhD/MBA (Graduate School of Arts & Sciences/MBA), 5 years; and MSA/MBA, 6 years

### FINANCIAL FACTS

**Tuition:** $27,000 **% of students receiving aid:** 75 **% of first-year students receiving aid:** 77 **% of students receiving loans:** 69 **% of students receiving grants:** 11 **Average award package:** $21,811 **Average grant:** $10,058 **Average student loan debt:** $39,882

### ADMISSIONS

**ADMISSIONS SELECTIVITY RATING: 60\***

**# of applications received:** 63 **% applicants accepted:** 83 **% acceptees attending:** 100 **Application Fee:** $75 **International Application Fee:** $75 **Regular Application Deadline:** rolling **Regular Notification:** rolling **Deferment Available?** yes **Maximum length of deferment:** 1 year **Need-Blind Admissions?** yes **Applicants also look at:** Duke University, University of North Carolina—Chapel Hill, University of North Carolina—Greensboro

# WAKE FOREST UNIVERSITY, FAST-TRACK EXECUTIVE
## BABCOCK GRADUATE SCHOOL OF MANAGEMENT

**ADMISSIONS CONTACT:** JAMIE BARNES, DIRECTOR, EVENING AND FAST-TRACK EXECUTIVE PROGRAMS
**ADDRESS:** PO BOX 7368, WINSTON-SALEM, NC 27109-7368
**PHONE:** 336-758-5422 • **FAX:** 336-758-5830
**E-MAIL:** ADMISSIONS@MBA.WFU.EDU
**WEBSITE:** WWW.MBA.WFU.EDU

### GENERAL INFORMATION

**Type of School:** private **Academic Calendar:** semester

### STUDENTS

**Enrollment of parent institution:** 6,444 **Enrollment of business school:** 556 **% male/female:** 71/29 **% out-of-state:** 75 **% part-time:** 61 **% minorities:** 13 **% international:** 23 **Average age at entry:** 36 **Average years work experience at entry:** 14

### ACADEMICS

**Student/faculty ratio:** 10:1 **% female faculty** 13 **% minority faculty** 13 **Joint Degrees:** JD/MBA, 4 years; MD/MBA, 5 years; PhD/MBA, 5 years; MSA/MBA (Master of Science in Accountancy/MBA), 6 years.

### FINANCIAL FACTS

**Tuition:** $44,625 **% of students receiving aid:** 45 **% of first-year students receiving aid:** 56 **% of students receiving loans:** 44 **% of students receiving grants:** 13 **Average award package:** $24,228 **Average grant:** $10,834 **Average student loan debt:** $40,875

### ADMISSIONS

**ADMISSIONS SELECTIVITY RATING: 60***

**# of applications received:** 66 **% applicants accepted:** 68 **% acceptees attending:** 100 **Application Fee:** $75 **International Application Fee:** $75 **Regular Application Deadline:** rolling **Regular Notification:** rolling **Deferment Available?** yes **Maximum length of deferment:** 1 year **Need-Blind Admissions?** yes **Applicants also look at:** Duke University, University of North Carolina—Chapel Hill, University of North Carolina—Greensboro

# WAKE FOREST UNIVERSITY, SATURDAY MBA—CHARLOTTE
## BABCOCK GRADUATE SCHOOL OF MANAGEMENT

**ADMISSIONS CONTACT:** LESLYE GERVASI, DIRECTOR, MBA PROGRAMS—CHARLOTTE
**ADDRESS:** ONE MORROCROFT CENTRE, 6805 MORRISON BOULEVARD, SUITE 150, CHARLOTTE, NC 28211
**PHONE:** 704-365-1717 • **FAX:** 704-365-3511
**E-MAIL:** CLT.MBA@MBA.WFU.EDU
**WEBSITE:** WWW.MBA.WFU.EDU

### GENERAL INFORMATION

**Type of School:** private **Academic Calendar:** semester

### STUDENTS

**Enrollment of parent institution:** 6,444 **Enrollment of business school:** 556 **% male/female:** 71/29 **% out-of-state:** 75 **% part-time:** 61 **% minorities:** 13 **% international:** 23 **Average age at entry:** 29 **Average years work experience at entry:** 7

### ACADEMICS

**Student/faculty ratio:** 10:1 **% female faculty** 13 **% minority faculty** 13 **Joint Degrees:** JD/MBA, 4 years; MD/MBA, 5 years; PhD/MBA (Graduate School of Arts & Sciences/MBA), 5 years; MSA/MBA, 6 years

### FINANCIAL FACTS

**Tuition:** $27,000 **% of students receiving aid:** 79 **% of first-year students receiving aid:** 83 **% of students receiving loans:** 79 **Average award package:** $18,614

### ADMISSIONS

**ADMISSIONS SELECTIVITY RATING: 60***

**# of applications received:** 45 **% applicants accepted:** 98 **% acceptees attending:** 84 **Application Fee:** $75 **International Application Fee:** $75 **Regular Application Deadline:** rolling **Regular Notification:** rolling **Deferment Available?** yes **Maximum length of deferment:** 1 year **Non-fall Admissions?** yes **Need-Blind Admissions?** yes

# WASHINGTON STATE UNIVERSITY
## COLLEGE OF BUSINESS

**ADMISSIONS CONTACT:** *CHERYL OLIVER*
**ADDRESS:** *PO BOX 644744, PULLMAN, WA 99164-4744*
**PHONE:** *509-335-7617 • FAX: 509-335-4735*
**E-MAIL:** *MBA@WSU.EDU*
**WEBSITE:** *WWW.WSU.EDU/MBA*

### GENERAL INFORMATION
**Type of School:** public **Environment:** town

### STUDENTS
**Enrollment of parent institution:** 18,000 **Enrollment of business school:** 74 **% male/female:** 52/48 **% out-of-state:** 48 **% part-time:** 69 **% minorities:** 8 **% international:** 30 **Average age at entry:** 25

### ACADEMICS
**Student/faculty ratio:** 40:1

### FINANCIAL FACTS
**Tuition (in-state/out-of-state):** $10,000/$19,000 **Fees:** $600 **Books and supplies:** $1,080 **Room & board:** $8,720 **Average grant:** $4,000

### ADMISSIONS
**ADMISSIONS SELECTIVITY RATING: 70**
**# of applications received:** 135 **% applicants accepted:** 79 **% acceptees attending:** 22 **GMAT Range (25th to 75th percentile):** 530-650 **Average GMAT:** 550 **Average GPA:** 3.37 **TOEFL required of int'l applicants?** yes **Minimum TOEFL (paper/computer):** 580/237 **Application Fee:** $35 **Regular Application Deadline:** 3/1 **Regular Notification:** 4/1 **Transfer Students Accepted?** yes **Need-Blind Admissions?** yes

# WAYNE STATE UNIVERSITY
## SCHOOL OF BUSINESS ADMINISTRATION

**ADMISSIONS CONTACT:** *LINDA S. ZADDACH, ASSISTANT DEAN OF STUDENT AFFAIRS*
**ADDRESS:** *OFFICE OF STUDENT SERVICES, 5201 CASS, ROOM 200, DETROIT, MI 48202*
**PHONE:** *313-577-4505 • FAX: 313-577-5299*
**E-MAIL:** *L.S.ZADDACH@WAYNE.EDU*
**WEBSITE:** *WWW.BUSADM.WAYNE.EDU*

### GENERAL INFORMATION
**Type of School:** public **Environment:** metropolis **Academic Calendar:** semester

### STUDENTS
**Enrollment of parent institution:** 33,137 **Enrollment of business school:** 1,248 **% male/female:** 60/40 **% part-time:** 89 **Average age at entry:** 28 **Average years work experience at entry:** 5

### ACADEMICS
**Student/faculty ratio:** 35:1 **% female faculty** 10 **% minority faculty** 15

### FINANCIAL FACTS
**Tuition (in-state/out-of-state):** $7,715/$15,057 **Fees:** $831 **Books and supplies:** $800 **Average grant:** $5,373

### ADMISSIONS
**ADMISSIONS SELECTIVITY RATING: 69**
**# of applications received:** 367 **% applicants accepted:** 80 **% acceptees attending:** 67 **Average GMAT:** 510 **Average GPA:** 3.14 **TOEFL required of int'l applicants?** yes **Minimum TOEFL (paper/computer):** 550/213 **Application Fee:** $50 **International Application Fee:** $50 **Regular Application Deadline:** 8/1 **Regular Notification:** rolling **Transfer Students Accepted?** yes **Non-fall Admissions?** yes

### EMPLOYMENT PROFILE
**Average starting salary:** $70,000

# WEBER STATE UNIVERSITY
## JOHN B. GODDARD SCHOOL OF BUSINESS AND ECONOMICS

**ADMISSIONS CONTACT:** *DR. MARK A. STEVENSON, MBA ENROLLMENT DIRECTOR*
**ADDRESS:** *3806 UNIVERSITY CIRCLE, OGDEN, UT 84408-3806*
**PHONE:** *801-626-7545 • FAX: 801-626-7423*
**E-MAIL:** *MBA@WEBER.EDU*
**WEBSITE:** *HTTP://GODDARD.WEBER.EDU/DP/MBA*

### GENERAL INFORMATION
**Type of School:** public **Environment:** village

### STUDENTS
**Enrollment of parent institution:** 16,800 **Enrollment of business school:** 75 **% male/female:** 68/32 **% minorities:** 4 **% international:** 9 **Average age at entry:** 31 **Average years work experience at entry:** 5

### ACADEMICS
**Student/faculty ratio:** 5:1 **% female faculty** 38

### FINANCIAL FACTS
**Tuition (in-state/out-of-state):** $1,793/$6,276 **Books and supplies:** $2,000 **Average grant:** $3,145

### ADMISSIONS
**ADMISSIONS SELECTIVITY RATING: 79**
**# of applications received:** 63 **% applicants accepted:** 75 **% acceptees attending:** 94 **GMAT Range (25th to 75th percentile):** 530-620 **Average GMAT:** 571 **Average GPA:** 3.39 **TOEFL required of int'l applicants?** yes **Minimum TOEFL (paper/computer):** 550/213 **Application Fee:** $30 **International Application Fee:** $30 **Regular Application Deadline:** 7/15 **Regular Notification:** rolling **Deferment**

Available? yes **Maximum length of deferment:** 1 year **Transfer Students Accepted?** yes **Non-fall Admissions?** yes **Need-Blind Admissions?** yes **Applicants also look at:** University of Utah, Utah State University

# WESTERN ILLINOIS UNIVERSITY
## COLLEGE OF BUSINESS AND TECHNOLOGY

**ADMISSIONS CONTACT:** , DIRECTOR OF MBA PROGRAM
**ADDRESS:** 1 UNIVERSITY CIRCLE, 115 SHERMAN HALL, MACOMB, IL 61455
**PHONE:** 309-298-3157 • **FAX:** 309-298-3111
**E-MAIL:** ADMISSIONS@WIU.EDU
**WEBSITE:** WWW.WIU.EDU/USERS/MICOBTD/

### GENERAL INFORMATION
**Type of School:** public **Environment:** village **Academic Calendar:** semester

### STUDENTS
**Enrollment of parent institution:** 132 **Enrollment of business school:** 132 **% male/female:** 58/42 **% out-of-state:** 1 **% part-time:** 37 **% minorities:** 1 **% international:** 15 **Average age at entry:** 24

### FINANCIAL FACTS
**Tuition (in-state/out-of-state):** $3,287/$6,574 **% of students receiving aid:** 34

### ADMISSIONS
**ADMISSIONS SELECTIVITY RATING: 60\***
**# of applications received:** 250 **% applicants accepted:** 50 **% acceptees attending:** 60 **TOEFL required of int'l applicants?** yes **Minimum TOEFL:** 550 **Application Fee:** $30 **Regular Application Deadline:** rolling **Regular Notification:** rolling **Deferment Available?** yes **Maximum length of deferment:** 1 **Non-fall Admissions?** yes

# WESTERN MICHIGAN UNIVERSITY
## HAWORTH COLLEGE OF BUSINESS

**ADMISSIONS CONTACT:** HAL BATES, HCOB ACADEMIC ADVISING AND ADMISSIONS
**ADDRESS:** 2130 SCHNEIDER HALL, KALAMAZOO, MI 49008
**PHONE:** 269-387-5075 • **FAX:** 269-387-5710
**E-MAIL:** BUS-ADV-OFFICE@WMICH.EDU
**WEBSITE:** WWW.HCOB.WMICH.EDU

### GENERAL INFORMATION
**Type of School:** public **Environment:** city **Academic Calendar:** semester

### STUDENTS
**Enrollment of parent institution:** 26,239 **Enrollment of business school:** 303 **% male/female:** 70/30 **% part-time:** 57 **% minorities:** 1 **% international:** 20 **Average age at entry:** 33 **Average years work experience at entry:** 7

### FINANCIAL FACTS
**Tuition (in-state/out-of-state):** $5,502/$12,400 **Fees:** $652 **Books and supplies:** $5,660 **Room & board:** $6,651 **Average grant:** $4,560

### ADMISSIONS
**ADMISSIONS SELECTIVITY RATING: 75**
**# of applications received:** 136 **% applicants accepted:** 70 **% acceptees attending:** 64 **Average GMAT:** 540 **Average GPA:** 3.1 **TOEFL required of int'l applicants?** yes **Minimum TOEFL:** 550 **Application Fee:** $40 **International Application Fee:** $55 **Regular Application Deadline:** 7/1 **Regular Notification:** 8/1 **Deferment Available?** yes **Maximum length of deferment:** 2 semesters **Transfer Students Accepted?** yes **Non-fall Admissions?** yes **Applicants also look at:** Michigan State University, University of Michigan, Wayne State University

# WESTERN NEW ENGLAND COLLEGE
## COLLEGE OF BUSINESS

**ADDRESS:** 1215 WILBRAHAM ROAD, SPRINGFIELD, MA 01119
**WEBSITE:** WWW1.WNEC.EDU/BUSINESS

### GENERAL INFORMATION
**Type of School:** private

### FINANCIAL FACTS
**Tuition (in-state):** $5,988

### ADMISSIONS
**ADMISSIONS SELECTIVITY RATING: 60\***
**Application Fee:** $30 **Regular Application Deadline:** rolling

# WESTERN WASHINGTON UNIVERSITY
## COLLEGE OF BUSINESS AND ECONOMICS

**ADMISSIONS CONTACT:** *CARRIE J. THURMAN, PROGRAM MANAGER*
**ADDRESS:** *516 HIGH STREET, PARKS HALL 419, BELLINGHAM, WA 98225-9072*
**PHONE:** *360-650-3898* • **FAX:** *360-650-4844*
**E-MAIL:** *MBA@WWU.EDU*
**WEBSITE:** *WWW.CBE.WWU.EDU/MBA*

### GENERAL INFORMATION
**Type of School:** public **Environment:** city

### STUDENTS
**Enrollment of business school:** 59 **% male/female:** 52/48 **% part-time:** 35 **% minorities:** 23 **% international:** 5 **Average age at entry:** 27

### FINANCIAL FACTS
**Tuition (in-state/out-of-state):** $5,628/$16,176 **Fees:** $624

### ADMISSIONS
**ADMISSIONS SELECTIVITY RATING:** 71

**# of applications received:** 44 **% applicants accepted:** 77 **% acceptees attending:** 74 **Average GMAT:** 520 **Average GPA:** 3.1 **TOEFL required of int'l applicants?** yes **Minimum TOEFL (paper/computer):** 567/227 **Application Fee:** $50 **International Application Fee:** $50 **Regular Application Deadline:** 5/1 **Regular Notification:** 6/1 **Deferment Available?** yes **Maximum length of deferment:** 1 year, fee required **Non-fall Admissions?** yes


# WIDENER UNIVERSITY
## SCHOOL OF BUSINESS ADMINISTRATION

**ADMISSIONS CONTACT:** *LISA BUSSOM, ASSISTANT DEAN*
**ADDRESS:** *1 UNIVERSITY PLACE, CHESTER, PA 19013*
**PHONE:** *610-499-4305* • **FAX:** *610-499-4615*
**E-MAIL:** *SBAGRADV@MAIL.WIDENER.EDU*
**WEBSITE:** *WWW.WIDENER.EDU/SBA*

### GENERAL INFORMATION
**Type of School:** private **Environment:** town **Academic Calendar:** semester

### STUDENTS
**Enrollment of parent institution:** 6,569 **Enrollment of business school:** 114 **% male/female:** 75/25 **% part-time:** 83 **% minorities:** 21 **Average age at entry:** 30 **Average years work experience at entry:** 7.5

### ACADEMICS
**Student/faculty ratio:** 6:1 **% female faculty** 33 **% minority faculty** 2 **Joint Degrees:** MBA/JD, 3 years full-time, 4 years part-time; MBA/MEng, 2 years full-time, 5 years part-time; MBA/Doctor of

Clinical Psychology, 5 years full-time; MBA in Health and Medical Services Administration/Doctor of Clinical Psychology **Prominent Alumni:** Leslie C. Quick, founder, Quick & Reilly; H. Edward Hanway, CEO, Cigna Corp.; Paul Biederman, Chair, Mellon Mid-Atlantic; Tiffany Tomasso, VP, Sunrise Assisted Living

### FINANCIAL FACTS
**Tuition:** $12,350 **Fees:** $200 **Books and supplies:** $850 **Room & board:** $7,650 **% of students receiving aid:** 22 **% of first-year students receiving aid:** 11 **% of students receiving loans:** 21 **% of students receiving grants:** 3 **Average award package:** $14,290 **Average grant:** $6,435

### ADMISSIONS
**ADMISSIONS SELECTIVITY RATING:** 76

**# of applications received:** 116 **% applicants accepted:** 48 **% acceptees attending:** 82 **GMAT Range (25th to 75th percentile):** 430-480 **Average GMAT:** 470 **Average GPA:** 3.25 **TOEFL required of int'l applicants?** yes **Minimum TOEFL (paper/computer):** 550/213 **Application Fee:** $25 **Regular Application Deadline:** 8/1 **Regular Notification:** rolling **Deferment Available?** yes **Maximum length of deferment:** 1 year **Transfer Students Accepted?** yes **Non-fall Admissions?** yes **Need-Blind Admissions?** yes **Applicants also look at:** DUPE-Drexel University—Professional MBA, La Salle University, Penn State University—Great Valley Campus, Saint Joseph's University, Temple University, University of Delaware, Villanova University


# WILFRID LAURIER UNIVERSITY (CANADA)
## WILFRID LAURIER UNIVERSITY

**ADMISSIONS CONTACT:** *SUSAN MANNING FABER, MBA MARKETING COORDINATOR*
**ADDRESS:** *75 UNIVERSITY AVENUE WEST, WATERLOO, ON N2L3C5 CANADA*
**PHONE:** *519-884-1970* • **FAX:** *519-886-6978*
**E-MAIL:** *WLUMBA@WLU.CA*
**WEBSITE:** *WWW.WLU.CA/MBA*

### GENERAL INFORMATION
**Type of School:** public

### STUDENTS
**% male/female:** 89/11 **% international:** 2 **Average age at entry:** 30 **Average years work experience at entry:** 7

### FINANCIAL FACTS
**Tuition:** $20,000 **Fees:** $20,000 **Books and supplies:** $7,000

### ADMISSIONS
**ADMISSIONS SELECTIVITY RATING:** 80

**# of applications received:** 474 **% applicants accepted:** 69 **% acceptees attending:** 65 **Average GMAT:** 592 **Average GPA:** 3.3 **TOEFL required of int'l applicants?** yes **Minimum TOEFL**

(paper/computer): 550/213 **Application Fee:** $100 **International Application Fee:** $100 **Deferment Available?** yes **Maximum length of deferment:** 1 year, case by case **Transfer Students Accepted?** yes **Non-fall Admissions?** yes **Need-Blind Admissions?** yes

### EMPLOYMENT PROFILE

Average starting salary: $80,000

# WINSTON-SALEM STATE UNIVERSITY
## SCHOOL OF BUSINESS AND ECONOMICS

**ADMISSIONS CONTACT:** TOMIKIA LEGRANDE, DIRECTOR OF GRADUATE ENROLLMENT MANAGEMENT
**ADDRESS:** GRADUATE SCHOOL, ANDERSON CENTER-WINSTON SALEM STATE UNIVERSITY, WINSTON SALEM, NC 27110
**PHONE:** 336-750-2021 • **FAX:** 336-750-2355
**E-MAIL:** GRADUATE@WSSU.EDU
**WEBSITE:** WWW.WSSU.EDU/WSSU/GRADUATESTUDIES/GRADUATE+PROGRAMS/ EVENING+MBA/

### GENERAL INFORMATION

**Type of School:** public **Academic Calendar:** fall

### STUDENTS

Enrollment of parent institution: 5,700 **Enrollment of business school:** 42 **% male/female:** 50/50 **% part-time:** 100 **% minorities:** 48 **% international:** 2 **Average age at entry:** 38 **Average years work experience at entry:** 9.6

### ACADEMICS

Student/faculty ratio: 15:1 **% female faculty** 22

### ADMISSIONS

**ADMISSIONS SELECTIVITY RATING:** 78
**% acceptees attending:** 93 **Average GMAT:** 480 **Average GPA:** 3.0 **TOEFL required of int'l applicants?** yes **Minimum TOEFL (paper/computer):** 550/213 **Application Fee:** $40 **International Application Fee:** $40 **Regular Application Deadline:** 7/15 **Deferment Available?** yes **Maximum length of deferment:** 2 years **Transfer Students Accepted?** yes **Non-fall Admissions?** yes **Need-Blind Admissions?** yes

# WINTHROP UNIVERSITY
## COLLEGE OF BUSINESS ADMINISTRATION

**ADMISSIONS CONTACT:** PEGGY HAGER, DIRECTOR OF GRADUATE PROGRAMS
**ADDRESS:** 213 THURMOND BUILDING, ROCK HILL, SC 29733
**PHONE:** 803-323-2409 • **FAX:** 803-323-2539
**E-MAIL:** MBAOFFICE@WINTHROP.EDU
**WEBSITE:** HTTP://CBA.WINTHROP.EDU

### GENERAL INFORMATION

**Type of School:** public **Environment:** town **Academic Calendar:** semester

### STUDENTS

Enrollment of parent institution: 7,304 **Enrollment of business school:** 250 **% part-time:** 40 **Average age at entry:** 29 **Average years work experience at entry:** 5

### FINANCIAL FACTS

Tuition (in-state/out-of-state): $4,216/$7,753

### ADMISSIONS

**ADMISSIONS SELECTIVITY RATING:** 64
**# of applications received:** 53 **% applicants accepted:** 92 **% acceptees attending:** 73 **Average GMAT:** 490 **Average GPA:** 3.3 **TOEFL required of int'l applicants?** yes **Minimum TOEFL:** 550 **Application Fee:** $50 **International Application Fee:** $50 **Regular Application Deadline:** 7/15 **Regular Notification:** rolling **Deferment Available?** yes **Maximum length of deferment:** 1 year **Transfer Students Accepted?** yes **Non-fall Admissions?** yes

# WRIGHT STATE UNIVERSITY
## RAJ SOIN COLLEGE OF BUSINESS

**ADMISSIONS CONTACT:** MICHAEL EVANS, DIRECTOR, MBA PROGRAMS
**ADDRESS:** 110 RIKE HALL, DAYTON, OH 45435-0001
**PHONE:** 937-775-2437 • **FAX:** 937-775-3545
**E-MAIL:** MBA_DIRECTOR@WRIGHT.EDU
**WEBSITE:** WWW.WRIGHT.EDU/BUSINESS

### GENERAL INFORMATION

**Type of School:** public **Environment:** city **Academic Calendar:** quarter

### STUDENTS

Enrollment of business school: 470 **% male/female:** 57/43 **% part-time:** 32 **Average age at entry:** 31 **Average years work experience at entry:** 5

### ACADEMICS

Student/faculty ratio: 8:1 **% female faculty** 24 **Joint Degrees:** MBA/MSN, 2-5 years; MBA/MS in Economics, 2-5 years

## FINANCIAL FACTS

**Tuition (in-state/out-of-state):** $10,500/$17,796 **Books and supplies:** $1,300

## ADMISSIONS

ADMISSIONS SELECTIVITY RATING: **69**

**# of applications received:** 416 **% applicants accepted:** 84 **% acceptees attending:** 67 **Average GMAT:** 525 **Average GPA:** 3.1 **TOEFL required of int'l applicants?** yes **Minimum TOEFL (paper/computer):** 550/213 **Application Fee:** $25 **Regular Application Deadline:** 8/1 **Regular Notification:** 8/2 **Deferment Available?** yes **Maximum length of deferment:** 4 quarters **Transfer Students Accepted?** yes **Non-fall Admissions?** yes **Need-Blind Admissions?** yes

# SCHOOL SAYS

In this section you'll find schools with extended listings describing admissions, curriculum, internships, and much more. This is your chance to get in-depth information on programs that interest you. The Princeton Review charges each school a small fee to be listed, and the editorial responsibility is solely that of the university.

# AUBURN UNIVERSITY

## AT A GLANCE

What's in it for you? Education, knowledge, and an MBA degree second to none; financial aid and scholarships; location, academic reputation, and opportunities for networking with career advancement—all combine to present a well-earned reputation of quality, opportunity, and results!

## CAMPUS AND LOCATION

Auburn University is a comprehensive Land-Grant University (chartered in 1856) located in Auburn, Alabama approximately 100 miles from Atlanta's Hartsfield-Jackson International Airport. Auburn is ideally located 200 miles from the famous white sand beaches of the Gulf of Mexico and approximately the same distance from the beautiful Appalachian Mountains of Georgia, Tennessee, and North Carolina. The area boasts a particularly beautiful campus which features many historic buildings, trees, seasonal flowering plants, clean air and water in a thriving university community. The campus offers many opportunities for cultural diversity, arts, entertainment, nationally-ranked collegiate sports teams, and outdoor recreational activities. A student body of 23,500 students blends well with the area population of 45,000 citizens who represent the area's educated, diverse, and skilled work force.

## DEGREES OFFERED

The Auburn MBA program is fully accredited by the AACSB-International (1980) and features an outstanding on-campus full-time MBA degree program which requires completion of 36–39 semester hours over 17 months start-to-finish. Additionally, non-traditional students who need flexibility have access to the Auburn Distance Learning MBA Program (limited to the U.S., Canada, and U.S. Military bases) which mirrors completely the on-campus academic program. The executive MBA program (with separate healthcare and technology tracks) for managers and executives; and a physicians executive MBA program for medical doctors combine limited campus residencies, an international study trip, and distance learning modes.

In addition to the MBA degree, the Auburn College of Business offers an array of other masters and doctoral degrees including: MS in finance; master of human resources; MS in economics; master of management information systems; master of accountancy; and PhD in management.

## PROGRAMS & CURRICULUM

The Auburn MBA degree requires completion of 36–39 semester hours and 17 months start-to-finish. Eight of the 12 MBA curriculum classes are core/required classes; four elective courses may be selected from options across a wide variety of academic areas.

Additionally, Auburn MBA students may choose a dual-degree track and earn a masters degree in engineering or management information systems concurrently with their MBA degree. In two years, students could earn two degrees. Concentrations are available to MBA students who choose electives in areas such as: Economics, finance, health care administration, human resources management, management information systems, management of technology, marketing, production/operations management, sports management, and supply chain management.

The Auburn College of Business is housed in the state-of-the-art Lowder Business Building which offers wireless technologies, dedicated computer labs, video classrooms, and instructional areas optimized for student-instructor interactions with enhanced learning environments.

## EXPENSES & FINANCIAL AID

Financial aid is offered to MBA students in the form of graduate research assistantships and graduate fellowships as well as merit-based scholarship awards. Assistantships are awarded on a competitive basis with GMAT scores, previous academic achievement, and skill set/experience being the key criteria.

**Expenses:**
Alabama resident tuition: $2,500 per semester°
Non-Alabama resident tuition: $7,500 per semester°
Student fees: $400 per semester (approx.)

Books: $450 per semester (approx.)
Room and board: $5,000 per semester (approx.)
°University tuition may be waived for students who are awarded a Graduate Assistantship

## FACULTY

Faculty who teach in the Auburn MBA program are all tenure-track and terminally qualified (PhD) in their academic fields. All are accessible and available to students both in class and outside to ensure a productive learning environment and provide guidance to students. Most faculty have previous industry work experience and/or outside consulting experiences which provide real-world balance between theory and practical applications.

The Auburn MBA program invites up to 50 new students to join each year. The recent diverse group is comprised of students from the U.S., Germany, Egypt, Thailand, Turkey, Honduras, Columbia, Brazil, West Bank, India, China, Taiwan, France, Nigeria, and Korea. Approximately one-third have undergraduate degrees in business, one-third with engineering degrees, and one-third in other academic disciplines.

The competitive admissions process values GMAT score, undergraduate GPA/degree/institution attended, resume/work experience/leadership skills, recommendations, and essays in the overall review process. Each applicant is considered on the strength of their overall application, standardized test scores, previous academic achievements, and resume/leadership skills. March 1 is the priority application deadline for fall semester entry.

**Required application items:**
• 4-year bachelors degree
• E-application to Auburn University Graduate School [www.grad.auburn.edu]
• Payment of graduate school processing fee ($25 U.S. citizens; $50 international students)
• 1-page [paper] MBA application form, www.mba.business.auburn.edu
• Official GMAT score
• Official TOEFL score (minimum 550 pbt; 213 cbt)
• Resume/CV
• 3 recommendations
• 2 essays (questions included with paper MBA application form)
• Official transcripts of all previous college credits

**Mail or deliver all items to:**
MBA Admissions
College of Business
415 West Magnolia Avenue, Suite 503
Auburn University
Auburn, Alabama 36849 USA
Telephone: 334-844-4060
Fax: 334-844-2964
E-mail: mbadmis@auburn.edu
Internet: www.mba.business.auburn.edu [click on 'Application info' to access downloadable application form and directions]

## ADDITIONAL INFORMATION

A "Leadership Certificate" offers students opportunities to gain experience and insight in developing personal leadership skills. These events and programs are provided at no additional cost to MBA students and include:
• The Blue Ridge Conference on Leadership in Ashville, NC
• Frequent leadership seminars and Visiting Executive roundtable events
• Essays and research papers which compete for scholarship awards

## CAREER SERVICES & PLACEMENT

Networking, career services, and placement resources are provided to MBA students as they consider options and connections for MBA internships and full-time career jobs. Several career fairs are conducted on campus and in the Lowder Business Building each year. Additional networking opportunities are offered via the periodic visiting executive program.

# BAYLOR UNIVERSITY

## AT A GLANCE

Baylor University offers MBA students the exceptional resources of a premier institution recognized worldwide for academic quality, superior teaching, and a reputation for graduating persons of both competence and character. Baylor's distinctiveness lies in the university's continual pursuit of intellectual excellence and faithfulness to the Christian tradition which, together, inspire action on behalf of the world.

## CAMPUS AND LOCATION

Chartered in 1845 by the Republic of Texas, Baylor University is the oldest institution of higher learning in continuous operation in the state. Baylor has grown to a 735-acre campus with 14,000 students.

Baylor's wireless data network, AirBear, is available throughout campus. With AirBear, Faculty, staff, and students can connect their laptop computers to the Internet from any location on campus.

## DEGREES OFFERED

The Hankamer School of Business offers 13 graduate programs, including a full-time MBA, two executive MBAs, two joint programs with Baylor Law School, and one joint program with the School of Engineering. A recognized specialization in health care administration is offered within the full-time MBA program.

## ACADEMIC PROGRAMS GENERAL

The fully integrated curriculum incorporates general management theory, multidisciplinary applications, personal development, and practical management skills into three core "lockstep" semesters. The "lockstep" format causes students to move through the core courses as a unit, creating a team approach to learning.

Embedded throughout each MBA class are foundational themes: serving the community, working in teams, respecting global relationships. Chief among them, however, is the thread of ethics and responsible behavior. Students perceive Baylor to be in the forefront of serious consideration of ethics.

### First Year Curriculum

The Integrated Management Seminar (IMS) is provided to students without a business undergraduate degree. This semester is waived for students with a business undergraduate degree. See www.baylor.edu/mba/IMS.

Lockstep 1—Core courses are designed to define the purpose of business. Who are the stakeholders? How do firms manage in today's dynamic environment?

### Second Year Curriculum

Lockstep 2—In the core courses you discover ideas and technologies that lead to a company's competitive advantage. Every day you will be challenged to think deeper, consider a greater range of perspectives, debate alternatives, and seek solutions—discovering how companies operate, improve, and sometimes fail.

Lockstep 3—Core courses focus on delivering results for the company. How does a company evaluate its performance? Did it achieve its objectives? The courses describe metrics, financial statements, strategic market planning, market structure, and corporate governance.

## AREAS OF INTEREST

**Health Care Administration:** www.baylor.edu/mba/healthcare
**Finance:** www.baylor.edu/business/financia_markets
**Entrepreneurship:** www.baylor.edu/mba/entrepreneurship

## EXPENSES AND FINANCIAL AID

See *www.baylor.edu/mba/admissions*

## FACULTY

Baylor MBA students can expect a personalized and integrative educational experience administered by a highly supportive academic and administra-

tive community. The MBA Faculty is accessible, involved, and intent on your success. We believe a strong student-professor relationship can have dynamic, lifelong benefits.

While Baylor is known for its teaching excellence, the Hankamer School of Business's recognized strength as an AACSB-accredited school draws upon the expertise of the Faculty as consultants and noted scholars. All professors teaching in the MBA programs hold doctorate degrees, are active in their professional fields, are business consultants, and are well published.

## STUDENT BODY

**MBA Student Profile Fall 2005**
# of full-time MBA students: 72
% accepted per year: 66%
# enrolled per year: 36
Average GMAT: 605
Average age: 22–32
% male/female: 72/28
Average work experience: 2.8 years
Average class size: 15 students

Baylor offers an environment that will not only challenge you academically, but will nourish you personally. Baylor offers a diverse community of people from around the world, with international students comprising 35 percent of Baylor's MBA enrollment. This culturally diverse learning environment gives students the global perspective necessary to succeed in today's world market.

## ADMISSIONS

Admission to Baylor's MBA program is competitive. We're looking for individuals with professional work experience, outstanding scholarship, a commitment to community service, and a motivation to pursue an intense graduate business program. MBA candidates should have strong analytical capabilities and communication skills. See www.baylor.edu/mba/admissions.

## SPECIAL PROGRAMS

The adage is true: the best way to learn something is through practice. It is the concept behind both the corporate-alliance practicum known as Focus Firm and the "Practicum in Portfolio Management" finance class. In the Focus Firm project students research, critically assess, and recommend viable solutions to an identified business dilemma for an actual business. See *www.baylor.edu/mba/focusfirm*. In the portfolio management class, students manage a live fund valued at more than $6 million. See *www.baylor.edu/business/financial_markets*.

## CAREER SERVICES & PLACEMENT

A pivotal function of Career Services is matching our graduates with the perfect job opportunity. To accomplish this objective, each MBA student meets personally with the assistant director of Career Services to determine a personalized plan of action based on his or her unique qualifications, talent, experience, and vocational leanings.

"Friday Morning Live" sessions provide important tools to help you manage your job search. The seminars address critical areas such as self-assessment, job search strategies, and resume development, as well as provide valuable instruction on appropriate interviewing behavior, negotiating successfully, and accepting a job offer in a professional manner. Topics such as "Strategy-Driven Career Plans," "Cover Letters That Work," and "Pounding The Pavement" are presented by recruiters, alumni, and career professionals who have volunteered to share strategies that will facilitate your professional success.

Baylor's Career Services has established relationships with an impressive list of prominent corporations headquartered worldwide—ensuring significant opportunities for our students in every business function and specialty.

# BOSTON UNIVERSITY
## School of Management

BOSTON UNIVERSITY SCHOOL of Management
Fusing the ART, SCIENCE, and TECHNOLOGY of Business.

## THE COLLEGE AT A GLANCE

The Boston University School of Management offers a diverse portfolio of customizable programs that fuse the *Art, Science, and Technology* of business. BU's outstanding Faculty and cutting-edge curriculum combine a robust theoretical foundation with real-world practice to produce innovative, ethical leaders who are ready to take on the challenges of today's ever-changing business environment. Known especially for their ability to apply current technology for strategic advantage, graduate business students at BU learn to think holistically, and develop an intimate understanding of management systems across all business disciplines. Recent program enhancements have led to a dramatic increase in applications, and current levels represent an 85 percent increase over the past two years.

## LOCATION AND ENVIRONMENT

The BU School of Management's sleek, contemporary facilities are located just steps from the Charles River and historic Fenway Park in the Kenmore Square area of Boston. Its location at the heart of one of the most intellectually and culturally stimulating cities in the world makes it an ideal place for graduate study. Moreover, as a division of the fourth-largest private research university in the United States, the BU School of Management provides its students a tremendous opportunity for cross-functional study through one of the most extensive elective menus of any graduate business program in the world.

## MAJOR AND DEGREES OFFERED, ACADEMIC PROGRAMS

The BU School of Management offers over 17 concentrations and dual-degree options that allow students to meticulously match their individual course of study to their interests and career goals.

**Concentrations include:**
• MBA in Health Sector Management
• MBA in Public & Nonprofit Management
• MBA in Entrepreneurship
• MBA in Finance
• MBA in International Management
• MBA in Marketing
• MBA in Strategy & Business Analysis

**Dual-Degree Programs include:**
• MBA/MA in Economics
• MBA/MA in Medical Science
• MBA/MA in International Relations
• MBA/MS in Television Management
• MBA/MS in Manufacturing
• MBA/MPH in Public Health
• JD/MBA
• MD/MBA

Other degree options include the Doctor of Business Administration and the MS in Investment Management.

In addition to the full-time MBA program, BU offers both evening and executive programs designed to accommodate students who wish to keep their day jobs while concurrently pursuing one of several degree options.

## OFF-CAMPUS OPPORTUNITIES

As one of the oldest cities in the country, Boston offers a unique first-hand experience of the American national heritage. Monuments, museums, and historic attractions are just the start of this city's charms. Art galleries, theaters, restaurants, and concert and sporting venues flourish in the "college capital of the country." Public parks, running and biking trails, and nearby beaches and mountains give the area an easygoing, liveable feel, ideal for individuals and families alike.

This convergence of cultural and academic vibrancy attracts more than just students. Opportunities for both internships and full-time post-graduation employment abound in an area saturated with businesses of every size and industry, making Boston a powerful platform from which to launch one's graduate business career.

## FACILITIES AND EQUIPMENT

The School of Management's state-of-the-art facilities are among the newest and best-equipped on campus. Business students have the latest technologies at their disposal, including wireless computing access, spacious modern amphitheater-style classrooms, and a dedicated business library.

The facilities are designed to maximize cross-functionality and facilitate lateral learning opportunities. As Professor Don Smith puts it, "The design of the school building is a terrific metaphor for our team learning concept. Wherever you are in the building, you'll find groups at work—in the team rooms, in the alcoves, on the landings, in Starbucks. Everywhere you look, you see teams of students collaborating."

## TUITION, ROOM & BOARD, AND FEES

Estimated Full-Time MBA expenses for 2006–2007 are as follows:

| | |
|---|---|
| Tuition | $33,330 |
| Fees & Books | $2,366 |
| Room & Board | $10,782 |
| Personal & Transportation | $3,300 |

Please consult the website for costs associated with various other programs.

## FINANCIAL AID

Financial aid is available in the form of loans, scholarships, and academic employment. Approximately 70 percent of students admitted to the full-time program receive a merit-based award, typically ranging from $5,000–$30,000 annually. Loans covering up to 90 percent of expenses are available to both domestic and international students. Finally, a limited number of graduate assistantships and work-study arrangements are available.

## FULL AND PART-TIME FACULTY

The BU School of Management Faculty is comprised of a diverse array of outstanding researchers and experienced practitioners whose expertise spans the entire gamut of traditional business disciplines and current applications of technology. The BU Faculty is known for excellence in both teaching and research, and the school endeavors to foster an atmosphere of continuous development and service to its students. Full-time Faculty members teach even the school's part-time evening MBA program. Currently, the school employs a total of 109 Faculty members, including 78 tenure-track professors.

## STUDENT ORGANIZATIONS AND ACTIVITIES

A wide variety of student clubs and organizations provide BU students with opportunities for peer-to-peer knowledge sharing, networking with alumni and employers, and the enhancement of classroom studies through real-world experience. Largely through student-led initiatives, new clubs are occasionally added to reflect emerging areas of specialized interest. Please consult the website for a list of current club offerings.

## ADMISSIONS PROCESSES AND REQUIREMENTS

The Admission Committee seeks team-oriented candidates with exceptional analytic and communication skills, as well as a demonstrated capacity for leadership. Quantity and quality of work experience, clearly articulated and feasible career goals, and a keen understanding of what makes Boston University's programs unique are important factors in the admission process, along with solid GMAT and undergraduate GPA performance. Application specifics and deadlines vary by program. Please consult the website for more information.

# CALIFORNIA STATE POLYTECHNIC—SAN LUIS OBISPO
## *Orfalea College of Business*

## AT A GLANCE

California Polytechnic State University—San Luis Obispo (Cal Poly) is a nationally ranked public university. Its emphasis is on a "learn by doing" educational experience for its 18,000-plus undergraduate and 1,000-plus graduate students.

With an up-to-date curriculum, including an opportunity to study international firms abroad and a program size that is intentionally limited to foster a sense of community, the Cal Poly Orfalea College of Business MBA program attracts bright, talented, ambitious, and hardworking students and produces outstanding business leaders.

## LOCATION AND ENVIRONMENT

Cal Poly is located in San Luis Obispo, an idyllic city of 45,000 located on the beautiful Central Coast of California, midway between San Francisco and Los Angeles. San Luis Obispo's small-town casual atmosphere makes it an excellent location in which to study and socialize away from the large metropolitan areas; however, it is close enough for easy interviews and contacts.

During their studies, Cal Poly students can enjoy almost any type of outdoor recreation—at the beaches, along coastal dunes and ridges, in forests, mountains, and nearby lakes, ranging from mountain biking, hiking, horseback riding, golf, sailing, kayaking, camping, or just relaxing in an unspoiled natural setting.

The Cal Poly Orfalea College of Business occupies a modern building that was opened in 1992. Multimedia capabilities and instructional technology are integrated into all classrooms. In addition to the largest computer laboratory on campus, the building offers wireless internet, small meeting rooms, and student lounges.

## ACADEMIC PROGRAMS

The Cal Poly MBA program is a 60–64 unit program that provides students who are willing to commit to a rigorous schedule of prescribed courses the option to complete the program in less than 11 months (Track I). A traditional MBA model (Track II) for those not pursing this accelerated option and/or simultaneously pursuing joint/dual degrees is also offered. Innovative elective courses are available to enhance the curriculum, including a transformational two-and-a-half week international business tour.

## DEGREES OFFERED

The Cal Poly Orfalea College of Business offers a Masters in Business Administration (MBA), MBA & MS in Engineering Management (EMP) dual degree, and a Masters in Industrial & Technical Studies (MS in I & TS). In addition, Cal Poly offers a variety of informal dual degree options including MBA & MS in an Engineering Discipline (Non-EMP) dual degree program, a MBA & MS in I & TS dual degree program and a customizable MBA & MS/MS option where a student can link the MBA degree with certain other graduate degree programs on campus.

## OFF-CAMPUS OPPORTUNITIES

Cal Poly MBA students have a proud tradition of competition and getting involved. They have participated in the International Collegiate Business Strategy Competition for nine consecutive years. This competition requires students to develop a comprehensive business plan and implement strategic business decisions on a global basis. Students also participate in an annual MBA Business Ethics Competition held in southern California. There is also the Bank of America Low Income Housing Challenge competition, comprised of a multidisciplinary team of city planners, architects, construction managers, and business managers. This competition involves partnering with community organizations and developers to identify a viable site and affordable housing development proposal.

The Cal Poly MBA program also offers a course and business tour to the People's Republic of China, the largest manufacturing economy in the world. Participants study American and Asian business practices while visiting large cities as well as the rural areas of China. Participants witness economic development and business practices in China firsthand; tour factories, multinational firms, port facilities, and small family firms; meet with business and government officials; and explore potential business opportunities.

## STUDENT ORGANIZATIONS AND ACTIVITIES

With 300 clubs on campus, MBA students have many venues for participation in activities outside the classroom. Offering the ability to demonstrate leadership and collaboration at the graduate level, the MBA Association is a popular choice. This club hosts a variety of fundraising, professional, and social events throughout the school year. The MBA Association also organizes a Professional Speaker Series which provides students the opportunity to meet and network with industry professionals. Many firms also find the Professional Speaker Series to be a valuable recruitment tool. The MBAA is also committed to preserving and promoting continuing relationships with MBA alumni through such events as its Alumni Golf Tournament.

## ADMISSIONS PROCESSES

The Cal Poly MBA program seeks candidates that demonstrate the ability to successfully complete a rigorous academic program. While admission is primarily based on GPA and GMAT achievement, additional factors such as work experience, leadership qualities, and letters of recommendation are also used to develop an overall assessment of the applicant. Interviews are optional.

## EXPENSES AND FINANCIAL ASSISTANCE

**2006–2007 Tuition and Fees—nine-month academic year:**

| | |
|---|---|
| California Residents | $ 4,827 |
| Nonresidents | $15,675 |
| Optional Intensive Session Courses: | $ 2,720 |
| Optional International Business Tour: | $ 4,000 |

Housing, transportation, books, and personal living costs are approximately $13,000.

Cal Poly students have a variety of financial aid programs available for assistance. Programs vary in eligibility criteria, award amounts, and repayment options.

## CAREER AND PLACEMENT

Cal Poly's Career Services Office offers students assistance with job searches and career planning through workshops, counseling sessions, job fairs, online databases, and résumé books. Hundreds of companies recruit on campus during the year, with many focusing primarily on MBA students.

# CALIFORNIA STATE UNIVERSITY—FULLERTON
## College of Business and Economics

### AT A GLANCE
Since 1963, the College of Business and Economics' nationally recognized Faculty, forward-looking curriculum, and flexible programs have attracted talented and diverse graduate students from across the globe. These students have helped make the college the largest accredited business school in California, and the third largest in the U.S. The ollege is one of two schools in the Los Angeles metropolitan area to have earned a prestigious dual accreditation in business administration and accounting from AACSB International, the worldwide accrediting body for business schools.

The CSUF MBA program is based on the notion that no two students are alike. Through a built-in concentration, students create a customized program by selecting four of their total 15 courses. Additionally, students are empowered to take control of their degree by choosing between full- and part-time study and by choosing campus location.

All courses are held on weekdays in the late afternoon or early evening, accommodating the needs of working professionals.

### CAMPUS AND LOCATION
CSUF is a major regional university based in Orange County, one of the most vibrant business communities in the nation. Through experiences in and out of the classroom, students develop the habit of intellectual inquiry, prepare for challenging professions, strengthen relationships to their communities, and contribute productively to society.

### DEGREES OFFERED
MBA; MS Accountancy; MS Taxation; MS Information Systems; MS Information Technology (online); MA Economics

The MBA and MS in Taxation programs are also offered at CSUF Irvine Institute in an accelerated format, allowing students to take one course every eight weeks. Students are able to maximize their classroom hours by taking two courses per semester, but only concentrating on one course at a time.

### ACADEMIC PROGRAMS GENERAL
Our MBA curriculum challenges students academically and encourages them to examine their existing morals, leadership style, and goals. The curriculum has been designed to give students broad, strategic managerial perspectives, while balancing theory with practical application and strengthening leadership skills. Students discuss current issues, learn from past case studies, forecast future trends, and participate in dynamic group discussions.

The MBA curriculum consists of 10 interdisciplinary required courses, four concentration courses, and a business strategy capstone course.

The business strategy capstone moves students out of the classroom and into the workplace. Students put their knowledge and skills to the test as they become consultants for local businesses. The college's consulting teams have won national awards for 13 of the past 14 years (2005).

Our comprehensive MBA program empowers participants to become innovative, visionary, and ethical leaders by exposing them to real world situations from day one. Detailed curriculum information may be found online at http://mba.fullerton.edu.

### AREAS OF INTEREST
Students choose from 11 concentrations to tailor their degree towards their professional, personal, and educational goals.

Concentration areas: Accounting; Economics; E-commerce; Entrepreneurship; Finance; General; Information Systems; International Business; Management; Management Science; and Marketing.

### FACILITIES
Construction has begun on Steven G. Mihaylo Hall, the new home to the College of Business and Economics. The $87.5 million building boasts nearly 10,000 square feet dedicated to student spaces. Graduate students may look forward to their own space once the building opens in Fall 2008.

Students also have access to all university resources including Pollak Library, various computer labs, and recreational facilities.

### EXPENSES AND FINANCIAL AID
The semester cost for California residents is $1,135 part-time and $1,786 full-time. Tuition for nonresident students is $335 per unit in addition to resident fees.

MBA tuition at CSUF Irvine Institute is $1,295 per course and MST tuition at CSUF Irvine Institute is $1,500 per course.

The Michael A. Reagan scholarship is available to incoming graduate students in the college. This is a merit-based scholarship designated for students with a superior academic record.

Other university scholarships, grants, and loans may be found online at *www.fullerton.edu/financialaid*.

### FACULTY
With over 225 Faculty, the college offers access to quality resources derived from the breadth of the various specialization areas taught throughout the program. All graduate-level courses are taught by our most highly qualified Faculty, professionals who have proven themselves as researchers and instructors—not one or the other alone. Ninety-seven percent of all Faculty have a doctorate degree.

### STUDENT BODY
Each program in the college attracts students from across the globe who bring their experiences in a wide variety of industries, management levels, and undergraduate education. This rich diversity adds to a dynamic classroom experience where students learn from both peers and professors. Challenging curriculum, team projects, and intense field experiences give our students a competitive edge.

All students have access to a wide variety of student organizations. The most common is the MBA Association, which enhances students' academic experience by providing social and professional opportunities to network with peers, Faculty members, and business professionals.

### ADMISSIONS
Qualified master's degree candidates are admitted to on-campus programs during the fall and spring semesters, and are admitted during the fall semester for the MBA program at CSUF Irvine Institute and the online MSIT program.

Prospective students must complete an online graduate application (www.csumentor.com) and pay a $55 application fee to be considered for admission. Once the online application is completed, students must submit the following to the College of Business and Economics: GMAT and TOEFL (if applicable) scores, official transcripts from each university attended, Graduate Admissions Checklist, Statement of Purpose, Background Information Sheet, and letters of recommendation. For a complete list of admissions materials, students should visit http://business.fullerton.edu/admissions.

### CAREER SERVICES & PLACEMENT
The Career Center offers a wide array of services and programs for MBA students including the following: walk-in counseling; career counseling; career resources library; Titan Connection online listings for campus interviews.

# CALIFORNIA STATE UNIVERSITY—NORTHRIDGE

## AT A GLANCE

If you want to take your career to the next level, choose a university that offers a high quality, innovative curriculum taught by experienced and dedicated Faculty. The California State University—Northridge (CSUN) evening MBA, with conveniently scheduled evening classes, is geared to working professionals. The course of study begins with an innovative interdisciplinary course that helps you integrate the fundamentals of business in a context that allows you to get to know your classmates. Our interdisciplinary program emphasizes analytical thinking, communications, teamwork, and ethics in a global context. The optional Field Study Project allows graduate teams to work on a real-world consulting project as the culminating experience. An ongoing Business Speaker Series allows students to meet and converse with high-level business leaders.

CSUN's College of Business and Economics (COBE) is accredited by the International Association to Advance Collegiate Schools of Business. The university is also accredited by the Western Association of Schools and Colleges and awards baccalaureate, master's, and doctoral degrees.

## CAMPUS AND LOCATION

CSUN is a vibrant, diverse university community of nearly 33,000 students and more than 4,000 Faculty and staff, situated on a 356-acre campus located in the heart of Los Angeles' San Fernando Valley, which is a suburb of Los Angeles, California.

## DEGREES OFFERED

COBE offer two graduate programs: Masters of Business Administration and a University Certificate in the Fundamentals of Business Administration. In the near future, CSUN is planning to offer two more graduate programs: a Masters of Science in Taxation and a Masters of Business Administration for Executives.

## ACADEMIC PROGRAMS GENERAL

The MBA program is a part-time, self-paced program that is designed for the working student. The program requires 33 to 48 credit hours to complete, depending upon the student's undergraduate background. Typically, students will complete the program in two to three years, depending on their background and work schedule.

The University Certificate in the Fundamentals of Business Administration is a postgraduate (pre-MBA) program that is available to students with or without a business undergraduate degree. This program offers six business foundation courses in modularized form.

The Masters of Science in Taxation program has a clear niche, and its unique focus builds communications skills. The program will consist of eight courses to provide the students with an in-depth knowledge in key areas in the field of taxation.

The Masters of Business Administration for Executives program is for professionals in middle-level management positions who have six or more years of working experience. This MBAe degree is designed for the working professional. The entire program is designed to be completed in about 18 months.

## FACILITIES

COBE is located in a 67,676 assignable square footage (ASF) building—Juniper Hall. This facility has 2,999 full-time equivalence (FTE) lecture spaces in 20,725 ASF. Also, Juniper Hall has 115 FTE in laboratories with 7,000 ASF. In addition, there are 7,200 ASF self-support stations in the graduate research laboratory. The COBE has 202 stations for self-instruction in the 9,800 ASF computer laboratories.

The University Library (Oviatt) is a 282,798 ASF facility. The Oviatt Library is the largest library in the San Fernando Valley, with approximately 1.25 million books and periodical volumes, and more than 3 million microforms.

## EXPENSES AND FINANCIAL AID

Financial assistance in the form of state or federal grants or loans is available. Teaching and graduate assistantships are available in some departments.

The university resident graduate fee (per semester) for six units or fewer is $900, and for seven units or more is $1,551. There are a number of other fees (e.g., Student Association and Union; instructionally related; facilities; and student health) that bring the total basic registration fees to $1,158 for six units or fewer, and to $1,809 for seven units or more.

## FACULTY

All of the MBA Faculty members have PhDs and/or extensive executive management experience. Our Faculty members are excellent teachers who maintain academic and professional currency. Our college actively partners with business, government, and community organizations to enhance its teaching and research mission.

Also, the college encourages each member of the Faculty to continuously update his or her professional knowledge and skills. In addition, the college expects every member of the Faculty to be engaged in scholarship, with an emphasis on applied, discipline-based research.

## STUDENT BODY

Our students are selected based upon their prior academic and professional achievements as well as their potential for future success. Each of our students has something to offer, whether it is an international perspective from students from abroad, the wisdom of experience from students who are well into their careers, or fresh ideas and enthusiasm from those who may be new to the discipline.

## ADMISSIONS

When making admissions decisions, we identify well-rounded students by reviewing three issues: 1) Education—a bachelor's degree from an accredited four-year college or university and a 3.0 GPA in the last 60 semester units (90 quarter units); 2) Experience—professional work experience of at least one year is sufficient; 3) Test Scores—GMAT scores in the 50th percentile or higher.

## SPECIAL PROGRAMS

Field study projects may involve business and strategic plan development, feasibility studies, evaluations of organizational effectiveness, or analysis and design of financial, accounting, and inventory control systems.

## CAREER SERVICES & PLACEMENT

Students and employers have access to review and post open positions in our Career Center. Also, CSUN hosts networking and other special events where students can connect with business leaders and successful alumni.

# THE CHINESE UNIVERSITY OF HONG KONG

## AT A GLANCE

The Chinese University of Hong Kong (CUHK) is a pioneer in business education in Hong Kong, and the first university to establish a full-time MBA degree program in Hong Kong. The Faculty of Business Administration of CUHK is accredited by AACSB International. We are also the first business school outside North America to establish the CUHK Chapter of Beta Gamma Sigma, the international honor society for business and management programs. In addition, we are a member of PIM (Partnership in International Management), an international consortium of outstanding higher education institutions that delivers graduate-equivalent degrees in management.

The MBA Programs were ranked No. 1 in the region for three years in a row (Asia Inc, 2002–2004). "CUHK has a large and strong student base and a wide Hong Kong and China network," Asia Inc commented. The full-time MBA program of CUHK has been ranked No. 69 worldwide by the *Financial Times* in January 2005. The Executive MBA Program was also ranked among the top 15 programs worldwide by London-based *Financial Times* in 2005.

An uncompromising insistence on quality and innovation continues to strengthen our status as one of the leading business schools in Asia. Our achievement is also reflected in our 3,829 graduates, who are very successful businessmen and entrepreneurs, and who hold prominent management positions in local and overseas corporations.

## MBA DEGREES OFFERED

In Hong Kong, we have established:

- the first full-time MBA program (1966)
- the first part-time MBA program (1977)
- the first EMBA program (1993)
- a landmark MBA Program in Health Care (2002)
- the unprecedented partnership in a global executive MBA program with premier business schools across four continents, the OneMBA, Global Executive MBA Program (2002)

We have always adopted a proactive strategy in building our China network. We are among the first universities in Hong Kong to offer joint programs with mainland institutes:

- an unique MBA Program in Finance in cooperation with Tsinghua University, China: Beijing class (2000) and Shenzhen class (2004)
- an Executive MBA Program with Xi'an Jiaotong University, China (2004)
- an Executive MBA Program with the National Sun Yat-sen University and Chang Gung University, Taiwan (2005)

## EXPENSES AND FINANCIAL AID

**Part-time MBA Program (Evening & Weekend Modes):**

U.S. $536 per unit (2006–2007 academic year)

**Full-time MBA Program:**

Tuition fee for the whole program: U.S. $26,654 (2006–2007 academic year)

Estimated room and board per academic year: U.S. $3,000 (on campus)

Food, Local Transportation, and Personal Expense: U.S. $9,692

Estimated cost of books and other academic expenses per academic year (full-time students only): U.S. $1,282

*Total: U.S. $40,628*

**Admission fee:** U.S. $25

**Financial Aid:** Through the generous support of individuals, alumni, business firms, and organizations in Hong Kong, a number of scholarships and awards are offered to outstanding MBA students.

## FACULTY

Our Faculty is an impressive convergence of intellectual capital. With members from all continents, the Faculty represents a good cultural mix as well as a rich and diverse range of interests, expertise, and backgrounds.

Our Faculty members received their PhDs from prominent universities including Cambridge, Chicago, Columbia, Cornell, Harvard, Northwestern, New York, Oxford, Pennsylvania, Western Ontario, and Wharton.

To complement this standing Faculty, noted industry practitioners are invited to serve as adjunct professors and guest lecturers. Distinguished visiting scholars and seasoned leaders serve as speakers in numerous seminars and forums. They inevitably impart practical and experiential knowledge to students and help to broaden their perspectives.

## STUDENT BODY

**Full-time MBA Program:**
Number of students: 97
Average age: 28
Average years of work experience: 5 years
% Women: 35%
International students: 77%.
Part-time MBA Program:
Number of students: 209
Average age: 31
Average years of work experience: 8 years
% Women: 40%
International students: 8%.

## ADMISSIONS

The MBA Program requires applicants to submit undergraduate transcripts (except in extraordinary circumstances, a minimum B average is required), GMAT scores, personal essays, and letters of recommendation. An interview, which can be conducted by telephone, is required. English proficiency (as demonstrated by TOEFL or IELTS scores for nonnative English speakers) is also required. Applicants to the full-time MBA program are expected to have three years of post-qualification work experience. For the part-time MBA program, they must have at least three years of post-qualification work experience.

## CAREER SERVICES & PLACEMENT

The CUMBA Online Career Centre (*http://mbacareer.baf.cuhk.edu.hk*) serves as a job agent to cater to the needs of the students and potential employers. MBA students can search for current job information from various prominent businesses. Companies can also search for MBA candidates (for internships, full-time, and part-time jobs) by using our online resume system. Each year a resume book is produced, containing information about the full-time MBA graduating class.

Our major employers include ABN AMRO Bank; The Boston Consulting Group; CalTEX Companies (Greater China), Ltd.; Citibank; Credit Suisse First Boston (HK), Ltd.; Dah Sing Bank; DBS Kwong On Bank; Deloitte Consulting; Goldman Sachs; Grey Advertising (HK); HKSAR Government; Hong Kong & China Gas Company, Ltd.; HSBC; JPMorgan Chase; KPMG; Mass Transit Railway Corporation; Merrill Lynch (Asia), Ltd.; Nestle (HK), Ltd.; and UBS Warburg.

# CITY UNIVERSITY OF NEW YORK—BARUCH COLLEGE

## Zicklin School of Business

### AT A GLANCE
Baruch's Zicklin School of Business is the largest collegiate school of business in the United States and one of the most academically prestigious. Zicklin's part-time MBA program is ranked 17th in the nation and its Full-Time Honors MBA program is the top graduate business degree granted by a public institution in New York State (*U.S. News & World Report*, 2007). The undergraduate business program was ranked among the top 30 at public institutions. Baruch was also cited as one of the best colleges in the Northeast in the 2006 edition of the Princeton Review's Guide to the Best Northeastern Colleges.

### LOCATION AND ENVIRONMENT
Situated on Lexington Avenue near the Flatiron/Gramercy Park district of Manhattan, in the midst of one of the world's most dynamic business, financial, and cultural centers, Baruch's proximity to Wall Street, Midtown, and the global headquarters of major companies, firms, and organizations is a distinct advantage that provides students with unparalleled internship, career, and networking opportunities. Some of the nation's top executives are Baruch alumni, and many of them regularly come to campus to share their expertise with current students.

U.S. News & World Report has named Baruch the most diverse college in the nation for seven consecutive years. Baruch students come from more than 140 nations, creating a rich social and academic environment that enhances our students' learning and prepares them for a global marketplace.

### FACILITIES AND EQUIPMENT
The Zicklin School is located in Baruch's 800,000-square-foot, 17-floor William and Anita Newman Vertical Campus, which features more than 100 high-technology classrooms and research facilities, a three-level athletic and recreation complex, and a state-of-the-art theater and recital hall. Baruch's Wasserman Trading Floor, within the Subotnick Financial Services Center, is the only business school resource of its kind in New York. It simulates complete trading floor activities, providing access to real-time market data and 42 high-end networked computer workstations. The 1,450-seat William and Anita Newman Library provides the Baruch community with access to extensive information resources in print and electronic formats. A Web-based reference service is available 24 hours a day, seven days a week. In 2003, the library was named best college library in the nation by the Association of College and Research Libraries. The Baruch Computing and Technology Center, the largest student computing center in New York City, provides computer access to 250 students at a time.

### ACADEMIC PROGRAMS
In addition to the undergraduate BBA degree, the Zicklin School of Business offers graduate business degree programs in a variety of formats: the selective, cohort-style Full-Time Honors MBA Program; the Accelerated Part-Time MBA, which enables students to study part-time at an accelerated pace and complete their degree in 28 months; the Flex-Time MBA and MS Programs, which allow students to study toward the degree at a full- or part-time pace; a strategic management Executive MBA; Executive MS programs in finance and in industrial and labor relations; the Baruch/Mt. Sinai MBA in Health Care Administration; the PhD in business (conferred by CUNY); and a joint JD/MBA with Brooklyn Law School.

### FACULTY
Baruch Faculty are among the most distinguished and widely known in their fields. They combine outstanding academic credentials with significant real-world experience. The recent arrival of 40 new Faculty members in the Zicklin School represents one of the most ambitious hiring programs at any business school in the United States. Noted scholars, researchers, consultants, and practitioners, many Zicklin Faculty are regularly called upon for expert commentary by such top media outlets as The New York Times, The Wall Street Journal, The Washington Post, Crain's New York Business, USA Today, CNBC, and CNN.

### CAREER SERVICES
Baruch's undergraduate Career Development Center and the Zicklin School's Graduate Career Management Center work with students to assist them in their career management and job search activities. At the graduate level, students participate in a Career Management Curriculum that covers topics including self-assessment, market assessment, resume writing, job search strategies, interviewing techniques, networking strategies, and compensation negotiation. Companies recruit on- and off-campus for both internship and full-time positions, which are posted regularly throughout the year.

### TUITION AND FEES
New York State residents: MBA $4,400 per semester (full-time), $400 per credit (part-time); MS $3,200 per semester (full-time), $270 per credit (part-time). Out-of-state and international students: MBA $600 per credit; MS $500 per credit. Tuition and fees are subject to change without notice. The average estimated annual cost for books, supplies, transportation, and personal expenses is $12,000. For information about Executive Programs tuition, call 646-312-3100.

### FINANCIAL AID
Full-Time Honors Tuition Scholarships

Graduate assistantships

Mitsui USA Foundation Scholarships in international business

Carl Spielvogel Scholarship in international marketing

Financial aid through various state, federal, and college programs

### ADMISSIONS PROCEDURES AND REQUIREMENTS
**Graduate admission requirements:**

Graduate Management Admission Test (GMAT)
Application
Essay
Resume
Official transcripts from every college or university attended
Two letters of recommendation
Nonrefundable application fee
Flex-Time students:
Average GMAT score: 590
Undergraduate GPA: 3.2
Full-Time Honors MBA students:
Average GMAT score: 650
Undergraduate GPA: 3.4
International students whose native language is not English must take the Test of English as a Foreign Language (TOEFL) and the Test of Written English (TWE).

**Undergraduate admission requirements:**

Visit *www.baruch.cuny.edu/admissions* or call 646-312-1400

Baruch College
Zicklin School of Business
One Bernard Baruch Way, Box H-820
New York, NY 10010
Phone: 646-312-1300
Email: *ZicklinGradAdmissions@baruch.cuny.edu*
Web: *www.baruch.cuny.edu/zicklin*

# CLAREMONT GRADUATE UNIVERSITY

*Peter F. Drucker and Masatoshi Ito Graduate School of Management*

Claremont
GRADUATE UNIVERSITY

## AT A GLANCE
The Peter F. Drucker and Masatoshi Ito Graduate School of Management, located in beautiful Claremont, California, is a unique management school dedicated to training people to become effective and ethical leaders and managers in whatever industries they serve. This focus stems from our belief that management is a liberal art, a human enterprise encompassing perspectives from the social and behavioral sciences. Named after one of the most prominent management thinkers of the twentieth century, Peter F. Drucker, the Drucker MBA program offers a high quality interactive educational experience: small classes averaging 25 students, and instruction from world-renowned professors. Approximately 70 percent of our classroom instruction is either in discussion or case analysis format, and we incorporate team building in classroom projects and presentations.

## CAMPUS & LOCATION
Nestled in the foothills of the San Gabriel Mountains, this charming community is famous for its tree-lined streets, the Claremont Colleges consortium, and charming old town restaurants and shops. Claremont provides the atmosphere of a New England college town within comfortable driving distance of major Southern California attractions.

## DEGREES OFFERED & CURRICULUM
The Drucker School offers the MBA degree. We attract students who already exhibit strong leadership and achievement skills or who clearly show the potential to develop such skills. These students typically wish to develop themselves both as individuals and as professional executives fully competent in the complex, globally connected economy. Consistent with Peter F. Drucker's philosophy of management, our school's mission is to study strategically important managerial issues and advance the theory and practice of management through teaching and field-based research that contributes to the betterment of society. This mission influences all aspects of the quantitatively and qualitatively balanced curriculum.

The Drucker MBA curriculum allows the student to sequentially build knowledge and develop professional skills. Core courses or foundation level courses provide candidates with an understanding of the fundamental disciplines of management. Advanced core courses are geared to help students integrate key concepts and skills necessary for strategy or general management. Elective courses allow students to specialize in a particular field of interest.

Our flexible curriculum allows both full-time and part-time students to select an area of emphasis in strategic management, risk management/finance, leadership, marketing, information sciences, and human resources. Students are also able to take courses outside of the management program. Other disciplines are available to through the various schools in the Claremont Graduate University and within the Claremont Colleges consortium.

## EXPENSES & FINANCIAL AID
These are all estimated costs and are subject to change.

*Tuition:* $20,018 full-time (16 units)/ $1,292 per unit. *Fees:* $125 per semester. *Books & Supplies:* $510 per semester. *Average Rent:* $600–$700/month (We offer on-campus graduate apartments on a first come, first serve basis, as well as off-campus housing resources/assistance.). *Expenses:* Expected expenses for a full-time student are approximately $15,000 per year. This figure is based on 16 units and includes on-campus housing, personal expenses, books, and student fees.

*Financial Aid:* Merit- and need-based scholarships are available for U.S. and international students alike. Institutional financial aid is based on the applicant's GMAT score, academic qualifications, professional work experience, and let-

ters of recommendation. To be considered, applicants must complete the Application for Institutional Financial Aid, which is included in the admission application, and have all application materials submitted by the appropriate admission and financial aid deadlines. Government loans (FAFSA for U.S. citizens and permanent residents) and international student loans are also available. To be considered for need-based aid—Perkins loan and work-study—applicants must have all their admission application materials and FAFSA application completed by March 2. To be considered for Federal Stafford Loans, these same materials must be completed no later than June 2. Please contact the Office of Student Financing at finaid@cgu.edu or call 909-621-8337.

## STUDENT LIFE
Students can participate in clubs, such as the Drucker School Student Association (DSSA), the Management Consulting Association, the Finance and Investment Association, the Marketing Association, Net Impact, Drucker Entrepreneurship Club, and the Drucker International Club.

## ADMISSIONS
We do not require an undergraduate background in business or economics. Nor do we have minimum cut-offs for the GMAT and GPA as we attempt to individualize each student's application by evaluating the whole person. For an application to be complete, applicants must submit the following:

- Application
- Student profile sheet and application for institutional financial aid (if applicable)
- Three letters of recommendation
- Official transcripts from every college/university attended
- Personal statement
- Current resume
- GMAT score
- TOEFL score (for international students)
- $55 application fee
- Interview (by invitation)

**Application Deadlines:**
- Fall semester: February 15
- Spring semester: October 1

If applying for financial aid, all documents must be in by the above dates. We offer rolling admissions based on space availability.

## CAREER MANAGEMENT
The ultimate objective of any successful career services function within a business school is the successful transition of students out of the classroom and into the working world with job and career opportunities closely aligned with the graduates' interests and capabilities. The career management services provided to students at the Drucker School are designed to provide the tools needed to successfully navigate a course into the working world and beyond. While the department has attracted major U.S. corporations to recruit students—companies such as A.T. Kearney, Accenture, Rain Bird, Deloitte & Touche, Johnson & Johnson, and Mattel—our strength has been in training students to successfully conduct a significant portion of their own job and career search. Students have available to them a ready arsenal of programs, workshops, and company information sessions designed to help them define their short- and long-term objectives and provide significant information about companies, industries, and career paths. We invite you to learn more about our capabilities and programs by visiting our website: http://careers.cgu.edu.

# CLEMSON UNIVERSITY

## AT A GLANCE

Clemson University offers a master of business administration (MBA) degree that consistently ranks in the top 50 public MBA programs nationally and the top 90 among all institutions nationwide. Today's growing global economy presents daily challenges and opportunities for those who seek to become business leaders and managers. The Clemson MBA prepares graduates to successfully participate in this fast-paced international landscape by delivering a solid foundation of basic and advanced-level business concepts upon which to build career-specific expertise. Designated areas of focus include entrepreneurship and innovation, supply chain and information management, real estate finance, and marketing research. Alternately, students may design their own area of specialization based on career objectives and course availability. With coordination and planning, qualified students may also earn a second, dual master's degree, earning both in 2 to 2 years. During the summer between their first and second years, MBAs participate in an internship, attend classes abroad typically in Italy or China, or take classes on campus and graduate early. For more information about the Clemson MBA see: *http://business.clemson.edu/mba*

## CAMPUS AND LOCATION

The university is located on over 1,400 wooded acres next to Lake Hartwell in South Carolina's lake and mountain region. The adjacent college town has 35,000 people with large population centers located within 20 to 60 minutes. Students have access to a rich variety of activities and resources including NCAA Division I sports, Fike Recreation Center, the South Carolina Botanical Gardens, the Brooks Center for Fine Arts, and the Spiro Center for Entrepreneurial Leadership.

Clemson's campus-wide wireless LAN is one of the largest Novell Networks in the world. It provides access to free e-mail, the Internet, laser printers, current software, and course-related technologies and software. The MBA program uses state-of-the-art classrooms and technology to enhance the learning environment. MBA students and Faculty each use personal computers to participate in and deliver class-related material.

## DEGREES OFFERED

The Clemson MBA offers a full-time program on the Clemson campus and an evening program for professionals and managers in Greenville, SC at the University Center. Dual master's degrees are available and often earned by qualified MBA students. The School of Business also offers an MS in Marketing Research, MPACC in Accounting, MA in Economics, MS in Management, and PhD's in Economics and Management.

## ACADEMIC PROGRAMS GENERAL

The Clemson MBA is nationally accredited by AACSB and integrates quality academics with experiential learning and professional development. Internationally recognized Faculty effectively bring applied and creative knowledge to the learning environment; a Friday seminar series gives students insight into different industries and critical issues; and internships, assistantships and project courses enhance hands-on experience and critical thinking abilities.

## EXPENSES AND FINANCIAL AID

The Clemson MBA provides an excellent return on investment.

**Estimated Tuition and Fees (Full-Time MBA Program) are:**

|  | Annual cost | Total 2-year cost |
|---|---|---|
| South Carolina Residents | $9,286 | $18,572 |
| Non-residents | $18,510 | $37,020 |
| Graduate Assistants (financial aid) | $2,158 | $4,316 |

Please see *http://business.clemson.edu/mba/info/FACost.htm* for more details.

## FACULTY

The Clemson MBA Faculty is internationally recognized. They are Fulbright Scholars, top publishers, research center directors, innovative entrepreneurs, and award winning teachers and scholars. They have broad work experience, collaborate with industry and government leaders, and are able to effectively communicate this applied knowledge at the graduate level.

## STUDENT BODY

Clemson's MBAs hail from all over the world. They are bright and motivated with an average GPA of 3.3 and GMAT of 615. The typical evening student is 29 with seven years of work experience. The typical full-time student is 26 with three years of work experience. Overall, about 39 percent have engineering degrees, 24 percent pure sciences, 24 percent social sciences and humanities, and 13 percent business. Almost 30 percent are women. Approximately 50 percent are international, representing more than 15 countries. The domestic students come from the South (60 percent), Northeast (20 percent), Midwest (15 percent), and West (5 percent).

The MBA Student Association is student-run and project-oriented. They conduct contracted projects with local businesses, sponsor speakers, and promote professional, service and social events, such as tutoring local elementary school children and organizing an annual fund-raising golf tournament. There are also more than 275 other recognized organizations on campus, including intramural sports, the Graduate Student Association, and international clubs.

## ADMISSIONS

The Clemson MBA seeks candidates whose communication skills, academic abilities, motivation and leadership indicate strong potential for success in business. A number of factors are considered when reviewing applications: work experience (resume), academic credentials (transcripts), standardized tests (GMAT, TOEFL), written statement of purpose, and letters of recommendation. Calculus is the only prerequisite. For more information on admission requirements please see: *http://business.clemson.edu/mba/info/Applinfo.htm*

## CAREER SERVICES & PLACEMENT

MBA Career Services provides individualized attention to each student by providing resume and interview workshops, individualized resume review, cover letter assistance, notification of career fairs and applicable job opportunities, links to alumni mentors, alumni networking events and access to an extensive career research library. Career Services helps MBAs learn how to hone their interviewing skills, find a good employer match, and move down the path of career success.

On average 50-60 percent of MBAs have jobs around graduation with an additional 20-30 percent within three months. The remaining pursue another degree. Hiring companies typically include Michelin, Bank of America, Blackbaud, Ryobi, KPMG, Wachovia Bank, Newell RubberMaid, and many other well-known companies.

# COLUMBIA UNIVERSITY

COLUMBIA
BUSINESS
SCHOOL

## THE UNIVERSITY AT A GLANCE

A Columbia Business School MBA gives graduates the edge in a world that demands smart, flexible, effective business leaders. Tools for mastering a twenty-first-century skill set, including entrepreneurship, globalism and leadership, are woven throughout our rigorous curriculum. The school's network of more than 33,000 alumni reaches into every industry and power structure around the world, giving students unmatched access to information, mentors, and jobs.

Drawing on its New York City location, Columbia Business School provides numerous resources both inside and outside the classroom that help students to grow their current career paths—and explore new ones. Our talent does not go unnoticed; hundreds of employers actively recruit at Columbia Business School each year, conducting thousands of on-campus interviews and numerous corporate presentations.

## LOCATION AND ENVIRONMENT

Columbia Business School is proud to be part of Columbia University in the City of New York. From this great university, MBA students can draw on expertise and networks in law, engineering, medicine and the social sciences to enhance their studies and careers. Students relish the opportunity to immerse themselves in the university's traditional, academic setting, while also taking full advantage of New York City's wide array of cultural and social outlets_including museums, Broadway shows, professional sports teams, concert halls, and restaurants. As home to thousands of multinational companies, a diverse real estate market and the major stock, bond and commodity exchanges, New York City is truly a living laboratory for Columbia MBAs.

## MAJOR AND DEGREES OFFERED

Hailed as one of the most innovative MBA curricula, Columbia Business School's course offerings prepare students to take leadership roles across sectors, while giving them fundamental skills applicable to all disciplines.

Specialized programs such as entrepreneurship, real estate, and social enterprise provide students with the opportunity to focus on cutting-edge issues that are evolving day by day. Dual-degree programs with 11 other university graduate programs are also an option for students whose interests span several fields.

In addition to the renowned MBA program, The Executive MBA offers successful business managers the opportunity to continue working while pursuing an MBA degree.

## ACADEMIC PROGRAM

By encouraging independent thought, assessment, and learning, the Columbia MBA curriculum provides students with the tools for success in many career paths. It also instills an awareness of ethical issues and sensitivity to the effect that business decisions can have on society.

The Columbia core represents about 45 percent of the degree requirement. Upon completion of the core, students may choose from more than 140 elective courses at Columbia Business School and supplement them with more than 4,000 graduate-level classes at the university's other schools, including the Graduate School of Arts and Sciences, International and Public Affairs, Journalism and Law.

Each entering class is divided into clusters of approximately 60 students who take every course together for the first year of the program and overlap regularly thereafter. Like the larger school community, cluster-mates provide a lifetime of friendship, professional advancement, and inspiration.

## OFF-CAMPUS OPPORTUNITIES

Columbia Business School exchange programs and study trips take place in almost every part of the world. Students have the option of spending a semester at one of 23 leading business schools worldwide through the Chazen MBA exchange program. Study tours have explored business practices and innovation firsthand in more than 25 countries.

## FACILITIES AND EQUIPMENT

Columbia Business School is housed in the recently renovated Uris Hall, on the upper part of campus, and in Warren Hall, a light-filled, eight-story building built in 1999. The facilities feature state-of-the-art connectivity throughout, including Express Web Kiosks.

## TUITION, ROOM AND BOARD, AND FEES

Tuition for the 2005–2006 academic year: $38,290

Additional fees: $1130

Room & board: $18,450

## FULL AND PART-TIME FACULTY

Leaders in their fields, the men and women who make up the Faculty create knowledge that will shape business practices for the next generation. In the classroom, lectures and case studies come alive thanks to professors' extensive real-life experience in the business world. Often, Faculty choose to be in New York because the city is a top laboratory for business study. Students frequently socialize with Faculty members, while alumni call them up years after graduation to touch base and ask for advice.

Columbia Business School's New York location and extensive links to the international business community give students an opportunity to also learn from cutting-edge practitioners. In fact, the curriculum is expressly designed to bring such leading practitioners as Columbia graduate Warren Buffett directly into the classroom.

## STUDENT ORGANIZATIONS AND ACTIVITIES

There are nearly 100 active student organizations at Columbia Business School, ranging from the Asian and Hispanic Business Associations to the Ballroom Dancing and Wine Societies.

Dozens of professional organizations including the Columbia Finance Association, the Media Management Association and the Internet and Technology Business Group host meetings with guest speakers, brown-bag discussions and career-related programs.

## ADMISSIONS PROCESSES AND REQUIREMENTS

Columbia looks for well-rounded people from diverse economic, social, ethnic, geographic, and professional backgrounds. Ideal applicants have demonstrated leadership, have the ability to work as members of a team, and can contribute to the academic experience of their peers. Columbia Business School has a rolling admissions process. Applications are reviewed in the order in which they are received and decisions can be rendered at any point during the review period. Application requirements include 2 references and 4 essays. While interviews are not required, many prospective students are invited to interviews with alumni or current students. Interviews are by invitation only.

# THE GEORGE WASHINGTON UNIVERSITY
## School of Business

## AT A GLANCE

The George Washington University's School of Business offers an excellent education in business and management. Our international business, finance, environmental and social responsibility, and entrepreneurship/small business fields are renowned, and the school prides itself on offering students flexibility in their programs of study.

The school's business and accountancy programs are accredited by AACSB International. Increasingly, GW's Business School is regarded as one of the world's best. The *Financial Times* and the *Wall Street Journal* both rank the GW Full-time MBA as one of the Top 50 U.S. schools. *U.S. News & World Report* ranks the GW MBA International Business program in its Top 20. The GW MBA also has been recognized by the World Resources Institute and the Aspen Institute as a "cutting-edge" Top 10 program for leadership in training students in social and environmental stewardship.

This is an exciting time for the school having recently moved into a new business school facility, a $65 million project that has become the physical foundation for the school's future. Located at the corner of 22nd and G Streets, Ric and Dawn Duques Hall brings all of the school's academic and research units under one roof and will feature state-of-the-art technologies.

## CAMPUS AND LOCATION

One of the school's greatest advantages is its location in downtown Washington, DC. Within blocks of campus are The White House, the World Bank, and the International Monetary Fund, as well as the headquarters and offices of thousands of national and multinational corporations, nonprofits, and nongovernmental organizations. George Washington University is also in close proximity to the Northern Virginia technology corridor and the Maryland biotechnology sector.

## DEGREES OFFERED

The George Washington University School of Business offers the MBA in four delivery modes: Full-Time, Accelerated, Executive, and Professional (part-time). Additionally, three joint degrees are offered; the JD/MBA, an international MBA/MA degree, and a MBA/MSF (Master of Science in Finance). Other specialized degree offerings are: Master of Accountancy, Master of Science in Finance, Master of Science in Information Systems Technology, Master of Science in Project Management, and the Master of Tourism Administration. The degree of Doctor of Philosophy is offered in accountancy, business administration, and management and technology.

## ACADEMIC PROGRAMS GENERAL

The School of Business MBA curriculum stresses team work, communications, analytical skills, and strategic thinking utilizing experiential learning projects. Our students have served as consultants to Cadillac on marketing strategies for the new SRX sport utility vehicle, Kendell-Jackson Wineries on strategic marketing initiatives, and have created strategies for America Online on numerous projects. While some opportunities are grounded on campus, like our financial markets trading lab sponsored by NASDAQ, others are miles away. GWSB students have visited Cuba to analyze strategies for the development of sustainable tourism on the island nation. Another group of students traveled to London to study privatization. Other study abroad opportunities currently include trips to China, India, Argentina, Paris, and Montenegro.

## EXPENSES AND FINANCIAL AID

There are many financial aid options available to our students. Merit-based assistance (teaching assistantships, research assistantships, and fellowships) is awarded thru the School of Business or programs. Close to 45 percent of the students enrolled in the Full-Time MBA program receive merit-based fellowships including international students. There are also need-based loan programs for U.S. citizens or permanent residents.

Tuition is per-credit hour based. The rate for the Fall 2006–2007 academic year is $989.00 per credit hour. Living expenses for full-time students is estimated to be $15,600. Books, supplies, and health insurance can add another $2,500.

## FACULTY

The George Washington University School of Business Faculty is exceptionally active as both scholars and practitioners. Through long-standing connections with national and international government and business organizations, the school's Faculty is involved in today's most important business and public management issues. The Faculty in the school of Business is engaged in a wide variety of research activities at the school's four research centers, covering subjects from international business to real-estate management. There are 125 full-time Faculty and over 70 adjunct practitioners teaching in the School of Business programs.

## ADMISSIONS

Each year, approximately 100 new students are selected from a pool of about 1000 applicants to enroll in the Full-Time MBA Program at GW. The Admissions Committee bases its decision on an applicant's work experience, academic preparation and performance, strength of recommendations, scores on the GMAT, the applicant's statement of purpose, and the admissions interview.

## CAREER SERVICES & PLACEMENT

The goal of the F. David Fowler Graduate Career Center is to prepare students to complete successfully in today's competitive marketplace. Whether providing students with job search skills and information, facilitating contact between students and the job market or arranging for interviews for students with employers, the Graduate Career Center plays an active role in student and alumni career development. And don't forget that there are over 30,000 graduates of the School of Business, a huge network of working professionals located around the world.

A variety of career development workshops, specifically created for MBAs, are offered at the Graduate Career Center. Topics include: resume and cover letter preparation, interviewing skills, networking and self-marketing, job search strategies/identifying employers, and salary and offer negotiations.

Specific services include career skills workshops, ERecruiting.com, individual career counseling, career fairs, cooperative education and internships, career leader (an on-line self-assessment tool), and alumni networking events.

# GEORGETOWN UNIVERSITY
## McDonough School of Business

### AT A GLANCE

Offering unparalleled access to global business, policy and thought leaders, the Robert Emmett McDonough School of Business is seated at one of the nation's most prestigious universities in one of the world's most influential cities. Founded in 1789, Georgetown University is the oldest Catholic and Jesuit university in America.

Georgetown University's McDonough School of Business is a premier business school located in the nation's capital. The Georgetown MBA Program develops leaders capable of making complex business decisions in a global environment and who are dedicated to serving their companies, society and humanity. Students gain solid grounding in all core management disciplines, with an emphasis on the global, ethical and political environment of business. Our commitment to understanding international business is demonstrated by the global curricula, the strong presence of international students (more than one-third), and the opportunities provided to study business and management in other parts of the world.

### CAMPUS AND LOCATION

For more than 200 years, Georgetown University has welcomed aspiring leaders to its campus along the banks of the Potomac River. The campus is an oasis within an exciting and dynamic city, and conveniently located to all of Washington, DC. Georgetown is one of the city's liveliest and most engaging neighborhoods. Known for its distinctive brand of energy and style, the city is home to museums, monuments, world-class culture and big-time sports.

### DEGREES

The McDonough School offers the following programs: MBA Full-Time, MBA Evening Program, and International Executive MBA. Additional offerings include the Executive Master's in Leadership and customized executive programs. Georgetown University has many outstanding graduate-level programs, and MBA Full-Time students may pursue the following joint degrees: JD/MBA, MD/MBA, MBA/Master's in Public Policy, MBA/MS Foreign Service, and MBA/PhD Physics.

### ACADEMIC PROGRAMS GENERAL

Georgetown MBA provides a general management framework in accounting, decision sciences, economics, finance, marketing, and management. The curriculum is organized into intensive team-based experiences, courses that integrate various functional areas, and electives. Students may choose courses according to individual interests and career goals. Students may pursue summer internships or study abroad programs. All students undertake a foreign residency, the Global Integrative Experience, in which teams conduct consulting projects for international companies and present their recommendations to top managers at their places of business abroad.

### FACILITIES

Georgetown MBA is located in the historic Car Barn, a modern facility named for its origin as a streetcar depot. The Car Barn is nestled among row houses in the picturesque Georgetown neighborhood, just two blocks from main campus. Students enjoy dedicated study and meeting spaces, student lounge and a wireless LAN which provides access to a range of instructional and technical services. The school is constructing a new facility on main campus to unite the graduate and undergraduate programs under one roof.

### EXPENSES AND FINANCIAL AID

**Georgetown MBA Full-Time Tuition and Fees for 2005–2006**

| | |
|---|---|
| $33,960 | Tuition |
| $268 | Yates Athletic Facility Fee |
| $554 | Allowance for Loan Fees Paid |
| $1,770 | Health Insurance |
| $12,750 | Average Room and Board |
| $2,088 | Average Books |
| $3,630 | Average Personal Expenses |
| $2,360 | Average Travel |
| *$57,380* | *TOTAL* |

Merit-Based Assistance: All admitted applicants are considered for partial and full tuition scholarships (based primarily on scholastic performance, work experience, and other factors demonstrating leadership potential). Assistantships: Over $1.5 million is invested to provide opportunities for students to work with Faculty and to support administrative offices.
Need-Based Assistance: The Office of Student Financial Services assists applicants with financial eligibility to meet their educational and living costs. All U.S. citizens and permanent residents may be considered for federally funded programs.

### FACULTY

With an emphasis on global business, innovation, and ethical decision-making, Georgetown MBA Faculty prepare students to be leaders of the future. Georgetown's tradition of strong student-faculty interaction is illustrated by the Faculty accessibility and involvement—collaborating on research projects, advising student organizations, and assisting in career decision-making.

### STUDENT BODY

Teamwork, cooperation and friendly competition are emphasized. Because classes are smaller, students develop close relationships with one another, Faculty and administrators. This atmosphere of easy camaraderie extends to an active social life, both on Georgetown's campus and in Washington, DC. Students actively shape the future of the school. Through participation in student organizations, students demonstrate leadership skills by planning special events such as professional development activities (including functional days and career treks to domestic and international locations), networking opportunities, and social events.

We enroll smart, hardworking students with some important traits in common: demonstrated leadership ability and accomplishments, cross-cultural awareness, clear career goals, and desire to make a difference in the world. The typical student has worked five years prior to joining Georgetown MBA.

### ADMISSIONS

Georgetown University seeks a diverse student body and encourages applications from a wide variety of backgrounds. A number of factors are considered, including: **Intellectual Capacity and Academic Achievement** as indicated by transcripts, letters of recommendation, and results of standardized tests (GMAT and, for international students, TOEFL or IELTS); **Professional Accomplishments and Personal Strengths** as demonstrated by distinctive and useful achievements, ideas, talents, and motivation for graduate business education; and the **Admissions Interview**.

### CAREER SERVICES AND PLACEMENT

The Career Management Center is an invaluable resource. The Center has two core functions_career advising/counseling services and recruiting/employer relations_which benefit students in distinct but complimentary ways. Students have access to career counseling services, topical workshops, resume/cover letter critiques, mock interviews, and more. Students also benefit from on-campus employer presentations and interviews for internships and full-time employment as well as 24-hour access to job postings from employers seeking Georgetown MBA applicants.

# INDIAN SCHOOL OF BUSINESS
## *Partner Schools: Kellogg, Wharton, London Business School*

## AT A GLANCE

The ISB vision is "to be an internationally top-ranked, research-driven, independent management institution that grooms future leaders for India and the World". Our One Year Post Graduate Program in Management (PGPM-comparable to an international MBA)) offers extraordinary global business learning opportunities at the one of most growing and challenging economies of the world- India. The ISB has formal affiliations with three of the world's leading business schools: Kellogg School of Management at Northwestern University, The Wharton School at the University of Pennsylvania, and London Business School.

## CAMPUS AND LOCATION
### Ecperiencing India & Hyderabad

AT Kearney ranks India as the 6th most attractive investment destination in the world. Over 100 of the Fortune 500 companies have set up R&D centers in India. Hyderabad is located centrally in India, and has merged as India's Knowledge hub and the preferred destination for new business, both Indian and International. The city has been attracting worldwide attention of global technology companies such as Motorola, Oracle, Citicorp and Microsoft have chosen to establish their offices. The ISB campus is spread over a scenic expanse of 260 acres and is situated on the outskirts of Hyderabad, 45 minutes away from the international airport.

## DEGREES OFFERED

The ISB offers a one year Post Graduate Program in Management (PGPM). The ISB program is unique in that it provides the equivalent of a typical two-year MBA program in one year. The program is ideal for working professional who are seeking to launch a global business career.

## ACADEMIC PROGRAMS GENERAL
### Post Graduate Programme in Management

The Program is divided into eight terms. First four terms are core courses and rest four terms are electives for specialization in analytical finance, entrepreneurship, technology, marketing, or leadership & change management. The ISB has tied-up with over 20 global B-Schools including Kellogg, London Business School, Darden, HEC etc. for international student exchange program for two terms.

## FACILITIES

The student villages form the residential wings of the campus. Each is serviced, air conditioned, and has elegant contemporary furniture and fittings, a fully equipped kitchenette, television with cable connection etc. The ISB provides dining, laundry, housekeeping and banking facilities. The ISB offers excellent recreational facilities—a well-equipped gymnasium, swimming pool, tennis, basketball, badminton and squash courts, a football field and jogging track.

## EXPENSES AND FINANCIAL AID
### Estimate of Expenses for 2007–2008 (USD):

Tuition: $29,000 for the complete program
Accommodation expenses: $2500 shared accommodation & $3900 studio accommodation
Dining facilities are available on the campus on pay per meal basis.

## FINANCIAL AID

Tuition waivers at the time of admissions are based on need & merit-based and separate scholarships are available for international students. Some corporations like Citigroup, HSBC, Anand Group also offer scholarships. The ISB offers academic scholarships based on the performance at the first four terms.

## FACULTY
### World-Class Facility

The ISB has a portfolio Faculty model – it aims to achieve an ideal mix of permanent and visiting Faculty that will give the students the benefit of international exposure as well as a strong research base. Recently, Faculty from Wharton, Kellogg, London Business School, Stanford, Chicago, Duke, and Texas among others, have taught at the ISB. Our location in India and the Asian region provides the setting for a thought-provoking interplay of management thinking and practices from the West and the East.

## STUDENT BODY

The collective profile of 349 students of Class of 2006 at ISB is as follows

**Gender:** Women 19%, Men 81%. **Age:** Average 27 years, Range 22–42 years. **Marital Status:** Married 24%, Single 76%. **Work Experience:** Average 5 years, Range 1–20 years. **International work Experience:** No. of students with international experience 25%, Average 3.8 years, Range 0.5–10 years.

## ADMISSIONS

**Rolling Application Process:** Applicable to all international applicants (non-Indian passport), the rolling application process begins on June 1, 2006. The applicant will be interviewed within one month of the application submission date and will be informed about the decision two weeks from the date of the interview. The Post Graduate Program in Management will begin in April, 2007.

### Admission Criteria

- Graduation Degree (10+2+3 or higher)
- Tests (GMAT / GRE)
- Work experience
- Professional Recommendations
- Essays
- Short listed candidates will be interviewed

The ISB looks for achievers and potential leaders from diverse economic, social, ethnic, and geographic backgrounds, who can add to their classmate's experiences. We seek applicants who have superior academic credentials and who display intellectual curiosity. Excellent written and verbal communication skills are essential.

For further information on admissions, please contact:

The Admissions Office
Indian School of Business
The ISB Campus
Gachibowli
Hyderabad 500 032
INDIA
Tel: +91 (40) 2300 7474
Fax: +91 (40) 2300 7099
Email: admissions@isb.edu
Website: www.isb.edu/pgp

## CAREER SERVICES & PLACEMENT

The mission of the" Career Advancement Services (CAS)" office at the ISB is to help students make the right career choices and assist employers to take the right hiring decisions. The Class of 2005 received 351 offers extending across various industries - Consulting, Finance, Marketing, to name a few. The Indian salary average was INR 1 million, while the highest offer received was INR 2.1 million. Offers for international positions were spread across the US, the Middle East, and Asia, with the highest offer being USD 181,000. Our distinctive focus on lateral placements translated into 97 percent (340 offers) of the class receiving lateral offers.

# INDIANA UNIVERSITY OF PENNSYLVANIA
## *The Eberly College of Business and Information Technology*

### THE COLLEGE AT A GLANCE

The Eberly College of Business and Information Technology MBA program (accredited by AACSB International), with its global strategy focus and highly international student and faculty composition, is designed to sharpen students' managerial, analytical, and decision-making skills so that they can compete in today's global environment. The Eberly MBA program has a long tradition of providing cost-effective preparation for a successful career in business. *Money* magazine in the past has ranked Indiana University of Pennsylvania 22nd among all the nation's public universities in terms of educational value.

### CAMPUS AND LOCATION

Indiana University of Pennsylvania enrolls 14,000 students from across the nation and around the globe. With 30,000 residents in the rolling foothills of the Allegheny Mountains, the community of Indiana has been commended in terms of safety. It is a place of tree-lined streets, pleasant neighborhoods, and friendly shops and restaurants. Pittsburgh is a short drive to the southwest from IUP. Pennsylvania enjoys four distinct seasons, including colorful autumns and temperate summers. A variety of recreational activities are available year-round, such as skiing in the winter and swimming or baseball in the summer.

### DEGREES OFFERED

Eberly College offers a full-time, on-campus MBA program for young professionals and recent college graduates that can be completed in 12 months. In addition, an executive MBA program for experienced working professionals is available at IUP's off-campus sites in the Pittsburgh area. Other graduate programs include a Master of Science in Information Technology (MSIT) and a Master of Education in Business and Workforce Development (MEd). The college also offers undergraduate bachelor's degrees in Accounting, Business Education, Business Technology Support, Entrepreneurship and Small Business Management, Finance, General Management, Human Resource Management, Industrial Management, International Business, Management Information Systems, and Marketing.

### PROGRAMS AND CURRICULUM

The Eberly MBA is a 33-credit integrated general management program with an option to complete concentrations (9 additional credits) in accounting, finance, management information systems, supply chain management, international business, human resource management, and marketing. The MBA courses focus on business applications, current analytical tools and techniques, and a strong emphasis on information technology utilization in managerial problem solving. A wide variety of elective courses are available in the concentration areas, including opportunities for MBA internships with local, national, and international organizations.

### FACILITIES AND EQUIPMENT

A state-of-the-art 12 million-dollar facility houses the MBA classrooms. The Eberly complex is a beautiful, four-story facility that offers spacious atriums for student interaction and studying, wireless access, a café, a 450-seat auditorium, and a 24-hour computing lab operation. Students of the Eberly College study in one of the most technologically advanced business schools in the country. The Eberly complex houses over 600 computer workstations, over 20 file servers, nine computing labs including a digital production studio, wireless technology, and access to comprehensive online business periodicals and journals databases. The college has a partnership with SAP America, the worldwide leader in ERP (Enterprise Resource Planning) software.

A new Financial Trading Room in Eberly offers students databases and related software to conduct financial analysis and learn valuation techniques, arbitrage techniques, and portfolio risk management strategies.

### EXPENSES AND FINANCIAL AID

Tuition for Pennsylvania residents for 2005–2006 was $2,944 a semester. Tuition for non-Pennsylvania residents for 2005–2006 was $4,711 a semester. Miscellaneous fees were approximately $500 a semester, and on-campus housing costs were from $1,514 a semester (double) to $2,153 a semester (single).

More than 30 percent of full-time MBA students receive graduate assistantships on a competitive basis that include a full or partial tuition waiver and stipend. International students are eligible to compete for a partial tuition waiver during the first semester of study.

### FACULTY

Eberly MBA courses are taught by faculty members who have doctoral degrees in their fields of specialization and extensive research and publication track records. They have been selected as members of the graduate faculty on the basis of their teaching excellence, research, and professional accomplishments. Their international backgrounds and/or exposure, experience in industry, and current research projects bring an ideal blend of theory and practice to the MBA courses. Eberly faculty serve as editors to nine national and international journals.

### STUDENTS

Eberly provides students with an opportunity to learn with a diverse group of individuals. More than 35 percent of the students are from 22 countries other than the U.S.; 35 percent have previous business work experiences; and 10 percent are currently working full-time in professional careers. Eberly College takes great pride in the activities and initiatives of its College of Business Student Advisory Council, and the members of its 14 student organizations. In addition to having the opportunity to serve on university-wide committees, students serve on Eberly College committees for strategic planning, technology, curriculum, outcomes assessment, student services, and programming.

### ADMISSIONS PROCESSES AND REQUIREMENTS

Requirements for admission include a completed undergraduate degree in any field with a superior academic track record from an accredited institution, GMAT scores, academic/professional letters of recommendation, and the applicant's career goal statement. The average GMAT score of admitted candidates is 530; the average undergraduate grade point average is 3.1. International applicants must also submit an official TOEFL score report with a minimum score of 200 (computer-based test score) and an affidavit of financial support indicating availability of funds to study in the U.S. For information and a complete application packet

- Visit www.eberly.iup.edu/mba
- Contact Dr. Krish Krishnan, Eberly College MBA Program, 301 Eberly College of Business and Information Technology, IUP, 664 Pratt Drive, Indiana, PA 15705
- E-mail iup-mba@iup.edu or Krishnan@iup.edu

### CAREER SERVICES AND PLACEMENT

IUP assists MBA students with job placement through its recruiting programs, computerized job-search database, resume referrals, individual counseling, workshops, and job fairs. Many major corporations recruit on the IUP campus, and recent MBA graduates have accepted positions with companies such as Accenture, Arthur Anderson, BearingPoint, Citizens Bank, CGI-AMS, Coca-Cola, Deloitte & Touche, Deutsche Bank, Dow Chemical, GE, IBM Global Services, Merrill Lynch, MetLife, Novell, Renault, Rockwell International, Siemens, Singapore Airlines, Symantec, Walt Disney, and World Bank.

# JACKSONVILLE STATE UNIVERSITY

## *College of Commerce and Business Administration*

## AT A GLANCE

Jacksonville State University's College of Commerce and Business Administration offers a Master of Business Administration (MBA) degree that ranks in the top 10 percent of all MBA programs in the world. The program allows for students to obtain either a general MBA or the MBA with a concentration in Accounting.

Students are attracted from around the world to our program; approximately 20 percent of JSU's MBA's are international students. While at JSU, students enhance their knowledge of business fundamentals and further their professional development. The end results are successful graduates that are tomorrow's business leaders.

## CAMPUS AND LOCATION

JSU is located in a diverse community of 10,000 set in the natural scenic beauty of the southern Appalachians. The local community as well as the university's proximity to large cities (75 miles from Birmingham, Alabama and 125 miles from Atlanta, Georgia) provides a rich variety of activities and resources for students.

Business programs are housed in the 69,794 square-foot Merrill Building. Multimedia capabilities and instructional technology are integrated throughout the classrooms and facilities.

## DEGREES OFFERED

The CCBA offers the MBA degree with options for either a general degree or a concentration in Accounting. The MBA is offered as an evening program and serves both part-time and full-time students. Classes are offered in 3-hour blocks, one evening per week. Traditional courses are available on campus and beginning in Fall 2006, an online MBA will be offered.

## ACADEMIC PROGRAMS

The JSU MBA is a program with a broad-based appeal. Students are provided with a quality program and an outstanding educational value. Opportunities exist for students to participate in internships and independent studies in addition to the traditional courses in the basic business disciplines. Exciting, real-world case studies are incorporated throughout many of the courses. Ten courses (30 semester hours), including electives make up the general MBA, while the Accounting Concentration requires an additional 3 semester hours and includes 9 semester hours of accounting courses. With careful planning, the program may be completed in 12 to 18 months.

## FACILITIES

The state-of-the-art facilities of the Merrill Building provide an outstanding arena for learning. The CCBA uses the latest communications and course delivery technology to help students network effectively.

## EXPENSES AND FINANCIAL AID

The CCBA provides one of the best returns on investment available. This nationally accredited program provides a top-notch, affordable education as it prepares students to enhance their careers.

## 2005–2006 Academic Year Tuition and Fees

Tuition:

| | |
|---|---|
| In-State Students | $225 per semester hour |
| Out-of-State Students | $450 per semester hour |

Housing, textbooks, and personal living costs are approximately $10,000 per year.

Merit-based financial aid is offered to outstanding candidates each year. The criteria for these awards mirror requirements for admission-academic record, work history, leadership experience, and test scores. Domestic and international applicants are eligible for graduate assistantships. Graduate assistantships provide a salary of approximately $520 per month and paid tuition for six hours of coursework each semester.

## FACULTY

Engaging. Experienced. World-renowned. CCBA MBA Faculty combine exemplary teaching and academic research, bringing expertise, talent, and dedication to the program. Many are involved with consulting practices that keep them "in-the-know" and on the pulse of innovative practices and emerging business trends. Course content combines the latest trends in business management with traditional theories that have withstood the tests of time. MBA Faculty hold doctoral degrees from leading academic institutions and bring a diverse mix of business experiences into the classroom, assisting students both academically and professionally.

## STUDENT BODY

CCBA MBAs are not passive recipients of education, but active players in determining the type of MBA experience delivered. Due to the large number of part-time students enrolled in the program and the fact that many students work full-time, little time is available for club participation. However, students use the classroom and interactions with other students to demonstrate leadership, involvement, and collaboration.

MBA students average nearly 3 years of work experience, a GPA of approximately 3.15 (4.0 scale), and an average GMAT score of approximately 450.

## ADMISSIONS

The CCBA MBA seeks candidates who have demonstrated the ability to complete a rigorous academic program and who possess the potential for success in a professional environment. The admission review process includes consideration of a number of factors that are all important in the admission decision: academic background; standardized tests (GMAT and TOEFL); references; and the student's reason for desiring an MBA.

## CAREER SERVICES & PLACEMENT

JSU's Career Placement Services staff assists in helping students achieve their career goals. Each fall, they sponsor a Career Fair for all business students and each spring a panel of very successful JSU alumni are brought to campus to interact with graduates in an effort to assist with career preparation. Staff members are advocates, consultants, and marketers, assisting with on-campus interviews and resume preparation. They are coaches that believe that businessmen and women's most important asset is the ability to learn to effectively market themselves.

# LOYOLA UNIVERSITY—NEW ORLEANS
## *College of Business*

## AT A GLANCE

This is an exciting time to get an MBA in New Orleans. Loyola is working closely with government agencies, local businesses, and inspired entrepreneurs to rebuild New Orleans. These relationships will create numerous first-hand experiences for our students to practice newly honed business skills, as well as learn about crisis management, creative strategies, entrepreneurship, consulting, and much more.

At Loyola University New Orleans, we provide a distinctive mix of Faculty excellence and individualized attention to create a superb learning environment in which you can excel. By studying with us, you will enhance your ability to critically analyze business issues, work in a team environment, appropriately apply technology, and effectively communicate your ideas. Equally important is the emphasis we place on providing you the foundation necessary to become socially and ethically responsible business leaders.

## CAMPUS AND LOCATION

Loyola University New Orleans is located in the heart of the old residential section of New Orleans. This gracious southern city is one of the most fascinating in the United States. New Orleans is known for its jazz, cuisine, the French Quarter, café au lait, the architecture, streetcars, riverboats, a bustling seaport, the history, the writers, and Mardi Gras. New Orleans offers world-class events and facilities such as the New Orleans Jazz and Heritage Festival, the Crescent City Classic, the Sugar Bowl, the Audubon Zoo, and the Aquarium of the Americas. Music weaves through every aspect of life in the Crescent City, from one of the oldest opera companies in the nation to jazz bands in street parades.

Our school is located five miles, by streetcar, from the Central Business District on a historic avenue in the heart of one of the most beautiful neighborhoods. Across the street you will find Audubon Park, a perfect place to enjoy jogging and picnicking among ancient oak trees or strolling past tranquil lagoons to the Audubon Zoo and the Mississippi River.

## DEGREES OFFERED

Loyola University New Orleans offers a traditional MBA program that can be taken at a full-time or part-time basis. Beginning in June 2007 we will be offering a daytime, full-time accelerated program designed especially for liberal arts graduates and can be completed in 16 months. Additionally, we offer a JD/MBA program in coordination with the law school.

Most students pursue a traditional MBA, but additionally we offer three concentrations. They are International Business, Marketing, and Finance. Concentrations are earned through electives.

## ACADEMIC PROGRAMS

Evening MBA Program

Accelerated Day Program (starts June 2007)

Juris Doctrate/MBA Joint Degree Program

## EXPENSES AND FINANCIAL AID

Tuition is based on credit hours. The Evening Program is $725 per credit hour; the program is 56 credit hours long, but some courses are open for waiver. The Accelerated Day Program is $775 per credit hour, and the program is 60 credit hours.

Graduate Assistantships are given based on the merits of the student's application (GMAT score, GPA, and work experience), as well as skill sets and interests. These are hourly paid positions, where you are considered a part-time employee of the university. Graduate assistants work closely with one or more business professor on academic research, grant administration, and special event planning. To apply for a graduate assistantship, please fill out the application enclosed in your graduate business admission application. Our assistantships are limited to 20 hours per week at $9 per hour.

We also offer a few tuition remission scholarships to a select group of MBA candidates. The scholarships are based on academic merit, considering the student's GPA and GMAT score. All MBA applicants are considered for scholarships as they submit a completed graduate business admission application.

## FACULTY

Loyola Faculty members bring excellent educational credentials and significant business experience to the classroom. Faculty members are highly motivated to provide the best possible educational experience. A strong teaching focus and impressive student-Faculty ratio allow for personal attention from more than 35 full-time Faculty members. Additionally, our Faculty members maintain rigorous research, publication, and presentation activities. Many MBA and undergraduates have co-authored publications with Faculty members.

## STUDENT BODY

The MBA program at Loyola University New Orleans has a diverse student body. Almost 50 percent are female, 50 percent come from undergraduate programs other than business, and 17 percent come from outside the United States.

Our program is purposefully small, creating a close-knit, family-like environment. Classrooms are very interactive with lots of sharing of diverse experiences and ideas. Professors get to know the students well, and the students get to know the professors well. Relationships are made and fostered. The average class size is 14.

## ADMISSIONS

To be considered for admission, prospective students need to submit an application, application fee, official transcripts from any and all colleges and universities attended, 400-word essay, resume, two recommendations, and an official GMAT score. International students must also submit an official TOEFL score, unless they graduated from an English-speaking university, and an Affidavit of Support.

## CAREER SERVICES & PLACEMENT

Once a student is admitted, we are very invested in his or her success. Working through the Career Center and the program administration, we help devise individual job strategy plans. We host job recruitment events on-campus, and make alumni connections. We also have a very active internship program to help students enhance their resumes.

# MCMASTER UNIVERSITY
## *DeGroote School of Business*

## AT A GLANCE

The DeGroote School of Business has earned a strong reputation as a center for academic excellence and innovation. An integral part of our innovative culture is our focus on experiential learning that enables students to gain hands-on experience through co-op work terms, internships and assignments that stimulate learning. This leads to continued personal development and enhances the student's ability to function more effectively after moving into the chosen career path.

As a pioneer in the creation of the co-op MBA model of learning, the DeGroote School of Business is the premier co-op MBA school in Canada. We also offer full-time and part-time MBA options that meet the complex needs and learning styles of the leaders of tomorrow.

Our Health Services Management MBA specialization is the only program of its kind in Canada. It combines expertise found in McMaster's renowned Faculty of Health Sciences and the School of Business with hands-on training gained through work experience in health care organizations.

## CAMPUS AND LOCATION

McMaster campus, which is restricted to pedestrian traffic, is at the western end of Lake Ontario. Area attractions include Cootes Paradise, the Bruce Trail, the Niagara Escarpment, the Waterfront Trail, and the Royal Botanical Gardens.

## DEGREES OFFERED

We offer a general MBA as well as several specializations that include finance, marketing, the management of innovation and new technology, eBusiness, and health services management among others. Additionally, we offer a joint CMA/MBA program specializing in management accounting. The goal of the MBA Program at DeGroote is to develop innovative leaders in the field of management.

## ACADEMIC PROGRAMS GENERAL

In our first year we emphasize the learning of business fundamentals in a variety of areas. As an introduction to our program, students will learn fundamental skills, which they will use and develop throughout our program and their future careers.

The second year of our program offers several options (specializations) that allow a student to choose a course of study that optimally enhances his/her current skills profile.

## FACILITIES

The McMaster University Library consists of Mills Memorial Library (Humanities and Social Sciences), Innis Library in Kenneth Taylor Hall (Business), the H.G. Thode Library of Science and Engineering, and the Health Sciences Library in the Health Sciences Centre. The University Library is a member of the Association of Research Libraries.

Officially opened to the public in June 1994, the museum contains five exhibition galleries, a paper center and an educational access gallery. The Museum of Art offers a year-round program of exhibitions, ranging from historical displays to present-day artistic investigations either organized by the McMaster Museum or loaned by such institutions as the Art Gallery of Ontario and the National Gallery of Canada.

The McMaster Nuclear Reactor (MNR) began operating in 1959 as the first university-based research reactor in the British Commonwealth. Today, users range from students, academics, and small businesses to international industry leaders. The MNR provides a wide range of irradiation, laboratory and holding facilities.

McMaster can accommodate a variety of meetings, events, shows, exhibitions, and athletic events. Gymnasiums, outdoor space, lecture theaters, classrooms, board-rooms, exhibit space, are all available through Conference Services. The McMaster University Student Center has many different spaces available for use by students, university organizations, and external clients.

## EXPENSES AND FINANCIAL AID

Financial assistance is available to our students in the form of teaching assistantships, scholarships, bursaries and loans.

Scholarships awarded by the School of Business to entering MBA students include the following:

Graduate Scholarships (Value $1,500.00 to $5,000.00)

The Alexandra and Jack Bart Memorial Bursary (Value $1,000.00)

The Avery Award (Value $6,000.00)

City of Hamilton Economic Development Department MBA Scholarships (Value $3,000.00)

The DeGroote School of Business Scholarship (Value $1,000.00)

The DeGroote School of Business eBusiness Scholarships (Value $500.00)

The GE Fund Graduate Bursaries in Electronic Business (Variable)

Lillian Russell Award (Value $1,500.00)

The Otis Canada Bursaries (Value $1,000.00)

## FACULTY

Our Faculty members are selected for their research, teaching skills and their ability to generate new business knowledge. Their connections in the business community help to provide students with the opportunities they need to pursue the practical side of their business education and to facilitate their post-graduate activities.

Our research centers and institutes rank among the world's best, and our students reap the benefits of these first-class facilities while they learn from some of the country's finest researchers and educators.

DeGroote Faculty have studied extensively nationally and internationally, bringing their wide variety of experiences and backgrounds to the DeGroote success story.

## STUDENT BODY

The MBA students come from a variety of undergraduate backgrounds in the sciences, arts and engineering, representing both experienced professionals and new graduates, and have interests in all areas of business.

## ADMISSIONS

The core requirements are based on academic performance in the student's final two years of university work as well as the GMAT score. On the margin, work experience and community leadership are also considered.

Candidates for the MBA Co-op Program are selected through a personal interview with Co-op staff in which communications and interpersonal skills, initiative, leadership and general experience are.

## CAREER SERVICES & PLACEMENT

We are very committed to developing strong relationships with our employer partners by meeting their needs on several levels. In addition, we provide full Business Employment Services, which include on-campus recruiting services, excellent on-site interview facilities, company information sessions, job postings and customized services as required.

# MERCER UNIVERSITY
## Stetson School of Business and Economics

## THE COLLEGE AT A GLANCE

Ranked among the leading universities in the South by *U.S. News & World Report* for 16 consecutive years, Mercer University is committed to the highest standards in education and has upheld its historic principles in ethical leadership and intellectual freedom since its founding in 1833. With ten different schools and colleges, Mercer University is one of the most comprehensive universities of its size in the nation. Mercer has schools in law, medicine, pharmacy, engineering, liberal arts, nursing, theology, education, professional studies, and business. The Stetson School of Business and Economics of Mercer University holds accreditation from the prestigious AACSB International, considered the hallmark of excellence among the nation's top business schools.

## LOCATION AND ENVIRONMENT

The business school offers degree programs on the university's campuses in Macon and Atlanta and at Mercer's regional academic centers in Douglas County, Henry County, Savannah, and Macon.

The Atlanta campus is in northeast Atlanta on I-85 just inside the 2-85 perimeter. The campus is primarily a graduate and professional campus. Seventy miles south of Atlanta, on the university's historic Macon campus, the school offers a traditional undergraduate daytime BBA, as well as an MBA and BBA program in the evening.

## ACADEMIC PROGRAMS

Students pursuing a degree in business distinguish themselves from other business majors by earning their degree from Mercer's Eugene W. Stetson School of Business and Economics. The School offers a unique interdisciplinary undergraduate business curriculum called MAPS—*Managed Academic Path to Success*. Through MAPS, students explore and identify their interests, then work with a Faculty adviser to develop a personalized program of study that incorporates and balances a strong business curriculum with their career interest. MAPS also includes a required internship, or hands-on experience, and a course in career development for students to learn how to market their knowledge and skills in today's business world.

The Macon campus also offers an evening MBA and BBA program, designed for adults wishing to advance their education.

In Atlanta, the Stetson School of Business offers an Executive MBA, a Flexible MBA in the evening, and a BBA for transfer students in the evening. In Atlanta, the Executive MBA program is a 16-month program with classes meeting every three weeks on Friday afternoon and Saturday. The MBA program is flexible with evening class meetings once-a-week in 8-week sessions. The BBA program is designed for non-traditional students with classes meeting in the evening once-a-week, as well.

The Douglas County Regional Academic Center offers a BBA program and the Henry County Regional Academic Center offers an Executive MBA program.

## OFF-CAMPUS OPPORTUNITIES

In Macon, the BBA students are required to participate in internships as part of MAPS. In Atlanta, both BBA and MBA students have the opportunity to participate in internships with corporations in the Atlanta area.

## FACILITIES AND EQUIPMENT

The 130-acre Macon campus is a blend of tradition and innovation. Students walk among 100-year-old trees, yet state-of-the-art learning technology is at their fingertips. The Stetson School of Business building was fully renovated in 2000. Students have access to a fully equipped library, a state-of-the-art University Center, dormitories, apartments, and Greek housing.

In Atlanta, the Stetson School of Business building, newly constructed in 2002, has several classrooms and study areas with internet connections and the library is equipped with wireless internet. The library is also equipped with study group rooms and other amenities. Students also have access to student activity groups, apartment housing, cafeteria, and a wellness center.

## TUITION, ROOM AND BOARD, AND FEES

*Macon*

| | |
|---|---|
| Traditional BBA | $12,628/semester |
| MBA | $1,449/3 hour course |

*Atlanta*

| | |
|---|---|
| Executive MBA | $39,000 |
| MBA | $1,612/3 hour course |
| BBA | $1,567/3 hour course |

## FINANCIAL AID

On the Macon campus, Mercer provides a wealth of financial assistance to every qualified student through scholarships, grants, loans, work-study opportunities, or a combination of these. Federal, state, and local funds are also awarded to students, helping make a Mercer education very affordable. Additionally, student loans are available to graduate and undergraduate students in Atlanta and the Regional Academic Centers.

## FACULTY

Students benefit from Mercer's welcoming atmosphere, small classes, and learning experiences guided by caring Faculty members, not the teaching assistants found at many universities. The superb Faculty, with credentials representing some of the world's greatest academic institutions, is distinguished for both teaching and research activities. More than 90 percent of Faculty members hold doctorates or the highest attainable degree in their fields.

## STUDENT ORGANIZATIONS AND ACTIVITIES

On the Macon campus, national sororities and fraternities, a wide variety of organizations, honorary and professional societies, and religious and special interest groups enhance the quality of campus life.

On the Atlanta campus, business students may participate in Phi Kappa Phi, Beta Gamma Sigma (AACSB honor society), Mercer Business Organization, and Delta Sigma Theta.

## ADMISSIONS PROCESSES AND REQUIREMENTS

**Freshman BBA** – Application, SAT, high school transcripts, and resume of academic honors, extra-curricular activities, and work experience.

**Non-traditional Transfer BBA** – Application, college transcripts, resume

**MBA** – Application, GMAT, college transcripts, and resume

**EMBA** – Application, college transcripts, resume, quantitative test, letters of recommendation, and interview

**Contact Information:**

**Macon Campus Programs:**
John P. Cole
Vice President for University Admissions
Mercer University
1400 Coleman Avenue
Macon, Georgia 31207
478-301-2650 • Toll-free: 800-840-8577

**Atlanta Campus and Regional Academic Center Programs:**
Karen Goss
Associate Vice President for University Admissions
Mercer University
3001 Mercer University Drive
Atlanta, GA 30341
678-547-6206 • Toll-free: 800-837-2905
Web Site: www.mercer.edu or business.mercer.edu

# MISSOURI STATE UNIVERSITY
## *The College of Business Administration*

 Missouri State. UNIVERSITY

## AT A GLANCE
The College of Business Administration (COBA) at Missouri State University is the largest public AACSB accredited College of Business in Missouri and in the Midwest Region, with approximately 4,400 students. Meeting rigorous AACSB International (The Association to Advance Collegiate Schools of Business) accreditation standards means that the college and the university have committed the necessary resources to achieve and maintain a high quality, nationally competitive program. Meeting these criteria also insures that COBA graduate students will be taught by terminally-degreed Faculty, a majority of who are actively publishing in their disciplines. Students can enjoy the benefits of a high-quality program while paying tuition rates that are very attractive.

## CAMPUS AND LOCATION
The Missouri State University campus is located in the heart of Springfield, Missouri.

## DEGREES OFFERED
The College of Business at Missouri State includes the five academic departments of Accounting, Computer Information Systems, Finance and General Business, Management, and Marketing, a total of 112 full-time and 35 part-time Faculty offering 25 undergraduate and graduate majors.

COBA has four graduate study programs, including the Master of Accountancy (MAcc), Master of Business Administration (MBA), Master of Science in Computer Information Systems (MSCIS), and Master of Health Administration (MHA).

## ACADEMIC PROGRAMS
The MAcc program is designed to fulfill the education needs of professional accountants. The program offers graduate students the opportunity to build upon the foundation of their undergraduate program and to enhance their business common body of knowledge and specialized accounting knowledge beyond the undergraduate level. The program is intended to meet the "150-hours" education requirement for membership in The American Institute of Certified Public Accountants, and to meet statutory education requirements for the CPA certificate.

The Missouri State MBA program has an important strength, flexibility. Along with integrating a variety of courses offered by the five departments in COBA, Missouri State's MBA program allows students the opportunity to tailor their degree to meet their career needs. Apart from the 21 hours of required credit (7 classes), and with the approval of the director of the MBA program, students may choose an area of concentration (12 credits) to help focus their MBA degree. Since many students seeking MBA degrees have little or no educational background in business, Missouri State's program provides a solid foundation of graduate-level courses that prepare students for the advanced topics covered in the core MBA program. Students with appropriate prior academic preparation in business and economics may be able to forego taking some or all of the foundation courses, limiting their MBA program to 33 semester hours allowing completion of the degree in one calendar year.

The MS CIS Program is an accelerated course of study leading to a Master of Science in Computer Information Systems degree. Developed exclusively for Information Technology (IT) professionals with three or more years of work experience, the program enables students to earn an accredited MS CIS degree in just 23 months without interrupting their careers. Students spend only two weeks each year on campus (one week in July and one week in January). The remainder of the course work is completed via distance learning. The MS CIS Program gained national recognition for being one of the first accredited graduate programs designed exclusively for IT professionals that combined classroom and distance learning.

The MHA degree is a COBA degree that includes a number of health management and policy courses. The program is designed for students holding undergraduate degrees who wish to further their careers in the administration of health organizations. The program can be completed in as little as two years. Students with little or no undergraduate work in business are welcome, and will normally require additional time for completion.

## AREAS OF INTEREST
The MBA program offers concentrations in several areas of the students choosing. The most popular concentrations include: Accounting, Finance, Management, Marketing, International Management, and Computer Information Systems. Concentrations are not limited to business courses so electives may be brought in from other academic areas in the university.

## FACILITIES
COBA is housed in David D. Glass Hall, an 185,000 square foot state-of-the-art building containing classrooms, four computer classrooms and four computer labs supplied with the latest technological equipment.

## EXPENSES AND FINANCIAL AID
Tuition for the 2006–2007 is $199 per credit hour for in state students. Out of state tuition is $388. Graduate assistantships are available which cover the cost of tuition and also provide a stipend.

## FACULTY
All of the COBA graduate Faculty hold PhD's. Many have won teaching and research awards, have practical business experience and are nationally recognized for their accomplishments.

## STUDENT BODY
Our students come from a wide variety of backgrounds. With our graduate students coming from the ranks of working professionals, traditional students and a significant percentage being international, such diversity offers the opportunity for students to share a broad range of perspectives on global business events.

## ADMISSIONS
For specific admission information for a particular graduate program, you may visit the College of Business website at www.coba.missouristate.edu. Qualified applicants may enter the program at the beginning of any semester.

## CAREER SERVICES & PLACEMENT
Students are assisted in their career search by the Career Center located within Glass Hall. Resume preparation assistance, enhancement of interviewing techniques, and internship placement assistance are some of the services provided by the staff of the Career Center. Each year, over 150 firms visit the College of Business during the annual COBA Career Fair and/or recruit on campus.

# MONMOUTH UNIVERSITY
## *School of Business Administration*

**MONMOUTH UNIVERSITY**
where leaders look forward™

## AT A GLANCE

A comprehensive and scholarly environment. A blend of rich tradition and advanced technologies. A community of individuals—unique in their strengths, united in their goal to succeed—and to lead. These are some of the ingredients driving our dynamic, interactive, personalized approach to education.

We look forward to your arrival at Monmouth University. Here you can develop your strengths, energize your life, define your future. Monmouth University. Where leaders look forward.

## CAMPUS AND LOCATION

The university is located in the safe residential town of West Long Branch, New Jersey—an attractive community near the Atlantic Ocean, about an hour and a half from New York City and Philadelphia. Monmouth enjoys close proximity to many high-technology firms and financial institutions, and a thriving business-industrial sector. The university's 155-acre campus, considered one of the most beautiful in New Jersey, includes among more than 50 buildings a harmonious blend of historic and contemporary architectural styles.

We offer graduate information sessions in the evenings, library visits, and other opportunities to meet with admission representatives. Check the Website for details: www.monmouth.edu/visit.

## DEGREES OFFERED

- Master of Business Administration (MBA), with optional tracks in Accounting, Finance, or Real Estate
- MBA with Concentration in Healthcare Management
- Post-MBA Certificates in Healthcare Management or Accounting

## ACADEMIC PROGRAMS GENERAL

The School of Business Administration is accredited by the AACSB–The Association to Advance Collegiate Schools of Business. Alumni include more than 3,100 successful entrepreneurs, managers, and executives from a broad spectrum of the business world.

Monmouth's MBA program includes courses in the key business disciplines of accounting, finance, economics, marketing, management, and business law. The program is constantly improved to reflect evolving business practices and theories. Strong emphases are placed on international, ethical, and technological perspectives within a broad strategic framework.

Monmouth University's graduate courses are offered in the evening to accommodate working professionals whose demanding careers necessitate part-time study.

## FACILITIES

While always meeting our community's evolving and expanding needs with new facilities and modern technologies, Monmouth also celebrates history. Wilson Hall, Monmouth's administrative center and the location of several classrooms, is designated a National Historic Landmark. The Guggenheim Cottage, a wing of the Monmouth University Library, is on the National Register of Historic Places.

Monmouth features a campus-wide computer network, numerous computer labs and cyber cafes, and wireless technologies. Monmouth offers a technologically advanced academic environment with a growing number of Web-enhanced courses and online tools.

## EXPENSES AND FINANCIAL AID

Students may qualify for federal financial aid by filing the Free Application for Federal Student Aid (FAFSA), available online at www.fafsa.ed.gov. The cost per credit for graduate classes during the 2005–2006 academic year is $636. Additional information about expenses is available online at www.monmouth.edu/admission/financialaid/pay/tuitionfees/gtuitionfees.asp. Academic scholarships are available to graduate students in selected majors.

## FACULTY

Recognized for their scholarly achievements by peers in their fields, the Faculty members of the School of Business Administration provide a challenging classroom environment. They bring insight from their research and real-world professional experience into the classroom. Graduate students are drawn into the ongoing, creative work of the Faculty through classroom demonstration, as research assistants, and through attendance at professional meetings. Faculty members also serve as advisors and mentors to students, in many cases not only during the course of their studies but also after they graduate from the University.

## STUDENT BODY

Approximately 6,000 undergraduate and graduate students are members of the Monmouth University community. Our graduate students are a blend of working professionals, and recent graduates of undergraduate programs who have chosen to move directly into graduate study.

## ADMISSIONS

Graduates of colleges of recognized standing, whose records show evidence of ability to do graduate work, may apply for admission.

Regular admission requirements for graduate degree programs offered through the School of Business Administration include either of the following:
1. Possession of a four-year baccalaureate degree and either:
   - GMAT minimum score of 500, or
   - GMAT minimum score of 450, and a minimum total of 1000 when a GMAT is added to 200 times the GPA, or
   - CPA or CFA licensure
2. Possession of a master's or doctoral degree (MS, MD, JD, PhD, EdD, etc.)

The deadline for application for the fall semester is August 1; for the spring semester is December 1; and for summer sessions is May 1. Qualified applicants are given consideration after the deadline on a space-available basis.

## SPECIAL PROGRAMS

The Master of Business Administration with a Concentration in Healthcare Management combines the generalized management preparation of an MBA with intensive training necessary to successfully manage within the healthcare industry. If you already have your MBA and are interested in the healthcare field, consider the certificate program in Healthcare Management.

Monmouth's Real Estate Institute offers two options: a certificate program, designed for real estate professionals who want to round out their education, and a track in real estate as part of the University's MBA program. The REI is the only academic credit-bearing real estate program in New Jersey. All real estate courses are taught by credentialed practitioners.

## ADDITIONAL INFORMATION

Kevin Roane, Director of Graduate Admission
Monmouth University
400 Cedar Avenue
West Long Branch, NJ 07764-1898
Telephone: 800-320-7754, 732-571-3452
E-mail: kroane@monmouth.edu
www.monmouth.edu

## CAREER SERVICES & PLACEMENT

Many services and resources are available in the Life and Career Advising Center (LCAC) to assist students with career exploration, career planning, part-time employment, internships, and job placement. For more information, please visit *http://www.monmouth.edu/academics/lcac.asp.*

# NORTH CAROLINA STATE UNIVERSITY

## MBA Program

### AT A GLANCE

Our focus on outstanding MBA education is illustrated by a reputation for excellence in technology management, an innovative Faculty with cutting-edge teaching and research, quality students from diverse backgrounds, and unmatched value in management education. The curriculum revolves around the role of technology in business, and the ways technology can improve business processes in industry. The NC State MBA Program will help you develop a keen understanding of general business and management principles that will give you an edge in the global marketplace.

The NC State MBA offers both a full-time program and part-time evening program.

### CAMPUS AND LOCATION

NC State was founded in 1887 as a land-grant institution that is one of the nation's leading research universities. Located in the Research Triangle, a world-renowned center of research, industry, technology, and education, the College of Management is housed on the 2,110-acre main campus of NC State, which lies just west of downtown Raleigh, the state capital. NC State serves a total student population of over 29,000.

### DEGREES OFFERED

**MBA—Master of Business Administration**

Full-time (51 credit hours) and part-time (45 credit hours) programs. Concentrations: Biotech-Pharmaceutical Management, Financial Management, Information Technology Management, Marketing Management, Product Innovation Management, Services Management, Supply Chain Management, and Technology Entrepreneurship & Commercialization

### ACADEMIC PROGRAMS GENERAL

The NC State MBA curriculum was designed to prepare students for management careers and to provide unique offerings of technology-oriented courses and concentrations. In this program, you will develop a clear understanding of the business functions, such as marketing and finance. You will also gain hands-on skills in technology-related fields. This approach will make your skills and knowledge adaptable to a variety of industries, functions, and work environments.

The curriculum is built around core classes in the basics of management, a specialized concentration and open electives. The concentration requirement ensures that our graduates have depth in one area that will distinguish them from MBA graduates with a general management orientation. Most concentrations require students to complete a semester-long team project by working closely with a corporate client to solve a relevant business problem.

### FACILITIES

The College of Management is located in Nelson Hall, which houses classrooms, computer labs, and the offices of Faculty members. Classrooms have been remodeled with tiered seating, laptop connections, and complete multimedia. Much of Nelson Hall is wireless accessible. The College of Management's computer lab houses over 100 computers. Students have access to a wide range of spreadsheet, word processing, statistical, and econometric software.

### EXPENSES AND FINANCIAL AID

The 2006–2007 budget for MBA students depends on the number of credit hours the student takes and the student's residency status.

The estimated annual tuition for the 2006–2007 school year is $11,512 for North Carolina residents in the full-time program and $7,129 for North Carolina residents in the part-time program. For non-residents, the estimated annual tuition for the 2006–2007 school year is $23,435 for students in the full-time program and $16,072 for students in the part-time program.

Graduate assistantships are available to full-time students. They cover tuition, health insurance, and a stipend. Grants and loan programs are available through the University's Financial Aid Office.

### FACULTY

The College of Management has built a Faculty rich in technology-related business expertise, management experience, and practical research. Our professors also have a passion for teaching and a commitment to working closely with industry to solve real-world problems.

Our Faculty excel in both traditional scholarly pursuits and practical, corporate-sponsored research. We are home to a number of extensively published scholars and editorial board members of prestigious research journals in accounting, finance, marketing, strategy and operations management. Corporate partnerships and federal grants have jumpstarted some of the college's most high-profile research programs, many of which include both Faculty and student research projects.

### STUDENT BODY

Almost all MBA students have professional work experience, many in high-technology industries. A technical background is not essential for the MBA, but all students must be willing to learn about technology and the management challenges it creates. More than 50 percent of MBA students have undergraduate degrees in science, computer science, or engineering. Over 30 percent were business majors. The rest come from a variety of fields, including the social sciences and humanities.

The average full-time MBA student has four years of work experience. Women comprise approximately 35 percent of each entering class; members of minority groups, approximately 9 percent; and international students, 40 percent.

### ADMISSIONS

MBA students must have a baccalaureate degree from an accredited college or university and are required to have had a course in calculus. Admissions decisions are based on previous academic performance, GMAT scores (610 average), two essays, letters of reference, and previous work and volunteer experience. Applicants whose native language is other than English, regardless of citizenship, must also submit TOEFL scores of at least 250 (computer-based test). Interviews are required for applicants for both the full-time and part-time MBA programs.

### SPECIAL PROGRAMS

The NC State MBA Program now offers a joint masters of MBA and Microbial Biotechnology. This joint degree can be completed in three years.

### CAREER SERVICES & PLACEMENT

MBA students have access to a wide range of programs and services to enhance their marketability. Professional career counseling is available. The MBA program provides workshops on resume writing and cover letters, interviewing skills, and job search strategies. In addition to on-campus recruiting for permanent jobs and internships, the Career Resource Center maintains a job posting service and hosts job fairs.

# NORTHEASTERN UNIVERSITY

## AT A GLANCE

Northeastern University is a world leader in practice-oriented education, known for excellence in the application and integration of theory and practice.

Through rigorous coursework and a six-month corporate residency, the full-time MBA program combines integration of soft skills, a globalization requirement, and a team-consulting project to produce graduates who are prepared to assume leadership positions in business.

## CAMPUS AND LOCATION

Northeastern is located in the center of Boston, the ultimate college town and hub of cultural, educational, and social activity. More than three hundred thousand college students from around the country and world call Boston home, and the city is alive with their energy.

Northeastern's central location puts students close to all the city has to offer. Within walking distance are the world-renowned Museum of Fine Arts, Symphony Hall, and stylish Newbury Street, with great shopping and dining. Students can hop on the "T," and shop at Quincy Market, eat in the North End, cheer on the Red Sox at historic Fenway Park, the Celtics and Bruins at The Garden, hang out in Cambridge's Harvard Square, or enjoy the nightlife on Lansdowne Street.

## DEGREES OFFERED

Northeastern offers a full-time MBA, MBA/Master of Science in Finance, and Master of Science in Accounting/MBA program. The school's programs for working professionals include the Part-time MBA, Master of Science in Finance, Master of Science in Accounting, Master of Science in Taxation, High Tech MBA and Executive MBA. Students may also pursue a JD/MBA or Master of Science in Nursing/MBA. All programs are offered on campus.

## ACADEMIC PROGRAMS GENERAL

The full-time MBA curriculum at Northeastern University offers an integrated approach to business training. Throughout the first year students work on developing content knowledge in key business disciplines and essential managerial skills such as communications, negotiation and persuasion, project management and teamwork, and ethical decision-making. Students also fulfill a globalization requirement, which may be met by taking a course in global business and economics or by completing an overseas field experience.

A six-month corporate residency provides an opportunity for full-time professional MBA-level employment with a corporate partner and enables students to apply their newly acquired business skills and to clarify, refine, or even redefine, career goals.

In the second year, students specialize in one of three career tracks by completing elective courses in an area of finance, marketing, or supply chain management/operations.

## FACILITIES

Northeastern's campus includes nearly 40 research and education centers. The graduate business programs are housed in Dodge Hall, which offers wireless technology in its classrooms and throughout the building, case-study classrooms, work-study rooms for students and a graduate student lounge.

Snell Library offers a cyber café with 24-hour computer access and wireless Internet. It houses over one million volumes and belongs to the Boston Library Consortium, a cooperative with the libraries of nineteen academic and research institutions.

When students need to wind down, they can access first-class athletic and fitness facilities, including the state-of-the-art Marino Center, the Badger and Rosen SquashBusters, and more.

## EXPENSES AND FINANCIAL AID

The tuition for the Full-time MBA program is $29,770. The tuition for the MS in Accounting/MBA and MS in Finance/MBA programs is $42,587.

**Tuition for part-time graduate programs:**

| | |
|---|---|
| MS in Accounting: | $12,530/term |
| Part-time MBA, MS in Finance, MS in Taxation: | $990/credit |
| High Tech MBA: | $1,105/credit |
| Executive MBA: | $68,250 |

**Fees**

| | |
|---|---|
| Medical insurance: | $1,692 |
| Student Activities Fee: | $11 |
| Student Recreation Fees: | $40 (full-time), $15 (part-time) |

Housing, textbook and personal living costs for full-time students are approximately $18,000 per year.

We offer merit-based scholarships and graduate assistantships to outstanding candidates. The criteria for these awards include a candidate's work history, leadership, test scores and academic achievement. Scholarship awards range from $10,000 to full-tuition. Graduate assistantships award one-half or full tuition with a stipend. Full-time MBA students also earn on average $25,000 during their six-month corporate residency.

## FACULTY

Northeastern's reputation for preparing students to succeed in the business world is due in large part to the knowledge, skills and solid management of its Faculty. Many have held positions as company executives and corporate strategists and continue to serve as consultants, directors, and board members.

As scholars and researchers, Faculty members explore a broad array of management issues, with particular focus on international business, innovation and growth for technology-driven organizations, and entrepreneurship. They publish in the most prestigious academic and practitioner journals, and play an active role in a variety of academic organizations and professional forums.

## STUDENT BODY

Many students develop their leadership skills through active involvement with the MBA clubs. The MBA Connection, an umbrella organization, coordinates clubs focused on key business disciplines. They frequently host social and networking events and bring in high-profile speakers—often Northeastern alumni. Students also participate in business cases and business plan competitions throughout the year.

## ADMISSIONS

Northeastern University seeks candidates who demonstrate academic and professional success. In evaluating applications, the Admissions Committee considers professional work experience, leadership, academic credentials, and standardized tests (GMAT and TOEFL).

## CAREER SERVICES & PLACEMENT

The Career Center offers individual assistance to students as they develop their career strategy. Advising sessions with a seasoned professional staff member provides students with the tools and contacts to expand their professional networks. In addition, the Career Center uses an on-line recruiting system, which provides students access to internship and full-time positions offered by corporate partners.

MBA students complete a career management course designed to help students refine their interviewing and resume-writing skills, further develop their portfolios and career development plans.

# NOVA SOUTHEASTERN UNIVERSITY

## *The H. Wayne Huizenga School of Business and Entrepreneurship*

### AT A GLANCE

The H. Wayne Huizenga School of Business and Entrepreneurship is housed in a five-story, state-of-the-art facility on Nova Southeastern University's main campus in Fort Lauderdale, Florida. Named for entrepreneur Carl De Santis, the 261,000 square foot building provides easy access to NSU's extraordinary technological and academic resources, epitomizing the school's growth and innovation. Home to the Entrepreneur Hall of Fame, the venue features distinctive architectural design concepts and a three-story atrium which is frequently utilized to host numerous campus events, lectures, conferences, executive briefings, and professional development seminars for the business community.

### CAMPUS AND LOCATION

Our mission is to offer academic programs at times convenient to students, employing innovative delivery systems and rich learning resources on campus and at distance sites.

In addition to its 300-acre main campus, eight student education centers are located throughout the state of Florida, Nevada, and the Caribbean; in addition, over 30 locations have been established worldwide where students can participate in unique educational offerings. Programs are also available in an online format.

The Huizenga School has also tailored delivery of its bachelor's and master's programs to the particular needs of corporations, offering custom degree programs on-site for companies, including: American Express, BellSouth, Citibank, Palm Beach County Sheriff's Office, Royal Caribbean Cruise Lines, Tyco, and Verizon.

### EXPENSES AND FINANCIAL AID

Nova Southeastern University offers a comprehensive program of financial aid to assist students in meeting educational expenses. Financial aid is available to help cover direct educational costs such as tuition, fees, and books; as well as indirect educational expenses such as food, clothing, and transportation. To qualify and remain eligible for financial aid, students must be fully admitted into a university program, eligible for continued enrollment, a United States citizen, national or permanent resident, and make satisfactory academic progress toward a stated educational objective in accordance with the university's policy on satisfactory progress for financial aid recipients.

For information on sources of financial aid and for application forms, please contact:

Nova Southeastern University

Office of Student Financial Assistance

3301 College Avenue, Horvitz Administration Building

Fort Lauderdale-Davie, Florida 33314-7796

Broward County: 954-262-3380

Miami-Dade County: 305-940-6447, ext. 7410

Toll Free: 800-806-3680

www.nova.edu/cwis/finaid

### FACULTY

Faculty members of the H. Wayne Huizenga School of Business and Entrepreneurship comprise some of the best minds and most dedicated professionals in the industry. Their extensive experience in both the academic and business realms make them sought after as consultants in industry, government, and the nonprofit sector. They bring dynamic, experiential, global perspectives to the classroom and provide the support and guidance necessary for academic success. All faculty members hold a doctoral degree.

### PROGRAMS

The H. Wayne Huizenga School of Business and Entrepreneurship at Nova Southeastern University (NSU) is committed to fostering within its students the ability to work as a team, the tools to manage change and become innovative thinkers, and the freedom to cultivate their entrepreneurial spirit. Founded in 1971, the business school is known for its entrepreneurial perspective in both the delivery and content of its educational programs. Students encounter some of the most enriching coursework available in education today. Graduates include successful leaders, managers, and entrepreneurs around the world.

The Huizenga School serves more than 4,500 bachelor's, master's, and doctoral students in a variety of degree programs as well as a wide range of optional academic specializations and concentrations tailored for preparation in meeting the demands of today's workforce. Within the Huizenga School, the Hudson Institute of Entrepreneurship and Executive Education delivers enriching seminars, workshops, and customized executive education programs. The International Institute for Franchise Education has been established to round out the Huizenga's school executive education portfolio.

Administrators and faculty members are keenly attuned to the complicated demands placed on today's employees, mangers, and leaders. Courses are continually refined to incorporate current and relevant practices. Students at the Huizenga School experience some of the most exciting, enriching coursework available anywhere in education today.

Nova Southeastern University is accredited by the Commission on Colleges of the Southern Association of Colleges and Schools (1866 Southern Lane, Decatur, Georgia 30033-4097; Telephone: 404-679-4501) to award bachelor's, master's, educational specialist, and doctoral degrees.

### CAREER SERVICES AND PLACEMENT

The Office of Career Services provides career consulting and job search assistance to students and alumni in reaching their chosen goals and career destinations. Services are available to students on an ongoing basis, from the time a student enters the university and throughout their career. Located on the fourth floor of the Alvin Sherman Library at NSU's main campus, the Office of Career Services can be contacted at http://www.nova.edu/career or via telephone at 954-262-7201 or 800-541-6682, ext. 7201 for information on programs, individual counseling with a career consultant, job leads, the Career Track model, e-recruiting, and career selection.

# THE OHIO STATE UNIVERSITY
## *Fisher College of Business*

## AT A GLANCE

Ranked as one of the top 25 MBA programs in the United States, Fisher College is also world-renowned for its individual areas of expertise, including corporate finance, brand management, and supply chain management. Notably, Fisher College was ranked third in the United States for its leadership in supply chain management.

Our deliberately small program with approximately 150 students admitted per intake, allows you to reap the advantages of being in an up-close and personal environment. You will have ample opportunity to learn from fellow classmates in team assignments and benefit from the diversity of your classmates—there is a wealth of variety, be it in terms of country of origin (roughly a third are international students) or prior educational and professional experience. Yet you will equally have access to all the resources of a major research university with over 60,000 students.

## LOCATION AND ENVIRONMENT

Located in the heart of the United States, Columbus, Ohio, has more than 1.5 million inhabitants, represents close to 100 nationalities and is the 15th largest city in the nation—a dynamic center of education, research, the arts and culture, as well as a thriving business community.

## DEGREES OFFERED

- Full time MBA
- Part time MBA
- Executive MBA
- Master of Business Logistics Engineering (MBLE)
- Master of Accounting (MAcc)
- Master of Labor and Human Resources (MLHR)
- PhD in Business Administration;Accounting & MIS; Labor & Human Resources

## ACADEMIC PROGRAMS

Fisher College's MBA curriculum allows you to truly customize your degree. After receiving a solid foundation through core classes, students have the opportunity to select from more than 100 elective courses to build their expertise. Students may choose to major in supply chain management and logistics, corporate finance, investment management, financial accounting and reporting, marketing, strategy or interdisciplinary studies. In addition, students can select a career track: global management, services management, real estate, six sigma, health sciences and biotech, consulting, and entrepreneurship. The "make it your own" (MYO) track option allows you to tailor your course selection even further, tailored to your very specific professional objectives.

Another major element of the curriculum is the Professional Leadership & Development program—consisting of seminars, workshops, and training sessions that prepare MBAs to effectively compete for top jobs and build successful careers. You will have ample opportunities to participate in interview training and networking workshops, join leading business executives and alumni in exclusive luncheon series, or learn the ins and outs of a career in consulting.

Numerous international study opportunities with more than 20 prestigious partner business schools around the world complement the MBA program—including global field studies, internship opportunities, and job placement.

## EXPENSES

**2006-2007 Academic Year Tuition and Fees and Fees (Full-Time MBA Program)**
*Annual Tuition*
Ohio Residents          $17,838 (in-state);
Non-residents           $30,435 (out-of-state)

In addition to having one of the lowest tuitions among top 25 MBA programs, there are also generous scholarships and graduate assistantships available. More than 75 percent of each entering class receives some form of financial package. Packages vary in size, and can range from $1,000 to a fellowship with full tuition waivers as well as a monthly stipend. In addition to merit based funding, there are also financial aid sources available through the university.

## FACILITIES AND EQUIPMENT

Just outside of Columbus down-town area, Fisher College offers a state-of-the art, six-building integrated campus with 100 percent wireless facilities, and a corporate conferencing and lodging complex, which includes a full-service dining facility. In close proximity of the business school you have direct access to all university facilities, including our brand new recreational center which offers excellent workout opportunities, be it an Olympic sized pool, cardio equipment, weight training, tennis, or personal trainer options.

## FACULTY

Fisher's academically rigorous, teamwork-oriented MBA program enables a high level of interaction with world-renowned Faculty, with an industry record low student–Faculty ratio of 3:1. Recognized as thought-leaders, our Faculty introduces you to the latest research results and at the same time ensures that through case studies, simulations and overall in-class applications you will have exposure to the latest developments in business.

## STUDENT ORGANIZATIONS AND ACTIVITIES

Our MBAs have a very active social life outside of class and assignments. In addition to building friendships on a more informal basis, you are encouraged to be active in one or more of our many student organizations. Explore the Finance Club, Real Estate Club, the International Club, the Club for Women in Business, the Marketing Organization, the Partner's Club, or more specialized clubs such as the Golf Club. You will have every opportunity to socialize, network and give back to the community. Our Fisher Serves club is a student run organization that not only engages in community service activities such as charity fund raising activities, but also uses your skills to offer pro-bono consulting to local businesses or serve on the board of non-profit organizations.

## ADMISSIONS

The admissions review process includes consideration of a number of factors that are all important in our decision. Eighty percent of our MBA students have a GMAT score between 600–720. We require a score of 250 or better on the standardized TOEFL test for foreign students.

The program starts the September of each year. We offer a rolling admissions process, however, we strongly encourage you to apply early which will support your chances on securing a space in our competitive MBA program.

## CAREER SERVICES & PLACEMENT

Students have numerous opportunities to meet corporate executives and to network with Fisher College's alumni base of more than 60,000 worldwide, many of whom are renowned business leaders. With more than 300 companies coming to campus to recruit, the Office of Career Services actively partners with students. In fact, you will have your own personalized career advisor and coach, trained and ready to support you in your job search. Over 90 percent of students have accepted a job offer within only three months of graduation.

# PURDUE UNIVERSITY
## *Krannert School of Management*

KRANNERT
SCHOOL OF MANAGEMENT
PURDUE UNIVERSITY

## AT A GLANCE

At the Krannert School of Management, you'll learn to do more than just manage. We'll help you learn the ability to understand the larger issues affecting the world of business. Leadership, social responsibility, teamwork, and entrepreneurial thinking are key components of the Krannert experience—and vital skills in today's changing work environment.

The synergistic programs are stimulating, intense, and develop highly effective business management professionals. The in-class experience includes numerous simulations of management decision-making scenarios, extensive interaction between the Faculty and the students, personal communication and presentation skills enhancement, and team exercises.

## LOCATION

Krannert is located on the campus of Purdue University in West Lafayette, Indiana. Purdue is located in the heart of the Midwestern United States, 126 miles southeast of Chicago, and 65 miles northwest of Indianapolis. Founded in 1869, Purdue is a public university.

## DEGREES OFFERED

Krannert offers three full-time master's degrees, including its highly-ranked MBA program, its Master of Science in Human Resource Management (MSHRM), and its Master of Science in Industrial Administration (MSIA), Krannert's one-year alternative to the MBA. Krannert also offers three part-time executive programs: a two-year EMBA offered in two-week modules on its West Lafayette campus; a two-year International Master's in Management (IMM) offered in two-week modules in West Lafayette and with sister schools in Europe; and a Saturday-only, three-year weekend MBA.

## CURRICULUM

A challenging curriculum provides the foundation for Krannert's status as one of the nation's top-tier schools. Our programs demand hard work and dedication, providing you with the knowledge to build a successful, purposeful career. With an emphasis on the case method, you'll use analytical tools to create models, evaluate alternatives, and make data-driven, real-world decisions.

Krannert offers a strong first-year MBA core, followed by a flexible second year with seven functional option areas including: accounting; finance; management information systems; marketing; operations management; organizational behavior and human resource management; and strategic management.

Krannert also offers six unique interdisciplinary option areas for students looking to customize their degrees a little more. These include: analytical consulting; e-business; global supply chain management; international management; manufacturing and technology management; and technological innovation and entrepreneurship.

With so many options, it is easy for students to add depth to the broad management base provided by the core.

## FACILITIES

Jerry S. Rawls Hall, which has won numerous architectural awards since opening in 2003, is the home of the full-time master's programs. It houses 13 electronically equipped classrooms, a professional career center, a multimedia-based auditorium, 25 team breakout rooms, distance-learning facilities, and sophisticated computer labs.

## EXPENSES AND FINANCIAL AID

Full-time Master's programs (2-years): $28,076 per year
For more information about financial aid, scholarships and graduate assistantships, please visit our website.

## FACULTY

Faculty are the cornerstone of Krannert's programs. In addition to the knowledge they convey, they are dedicated to providing students with a positive educational experience. That means moving beyond typical lectures and exams to experiential learning exercises, computer simulations, and field trips. They also supervise off-site projects with corporate partners.

## STUDENT BODY

When asked to describe the atmosphere at Krannert, students often use words such as "diverse," "welcoming," "family-friendly," and "team oriented." These characteristics give the school a unique personality. With fewer than 400 students enrolled at any given time, we're relatively small compared to other top-ranked institutions. People say hello when you walk through the halls. Faculty and staff members know your name and freely share their time. At Krannert, you're part of the family.

While coursework demands much of a student's time, Krannert also encourages informal interaction through weekly social hours, club events, evening and weekend outings, and other recreational activities. The opportunities extend to the Purdue campus and surrounding community, which provide a safe, clean environment and a variety of cultural offerings. Those who desire the occasional bustle of a big city don't have far to travel, either. Chicago is a two-hour drive to the north, while Indianapolis is only an hour south.

## ADMISSIONS

For more information regarding our student profiles, or to apply online, please visit our website at *http://www.mgmt.purdue.edu/programs/masters*. There you can also register to visit us on campus, as well as request more information.

## CAREER SERVICES AND PLACEMENT

While graduation from a highly ranked school like Krannert is a selling point in itself, students still need help marketing themselves—especially in today's tough job market. That's where Krannert's outstanding array of career services comes into the picture, including:

- Career counseling services
- Online services
- Comprehensive job search services
- Job fairs
- International student Career services
- Internships

# REGENT UNIVERSITY

## AT A GLANCE

At the Regent University School of Business, our mission is "To honor God by developing extraordinarily competent, entrepreneurial people who lead with excellence, integrity, and innovation, guided in all things by Jesus Christ." We graduate students who have the skills expected by the world's leading organizations, who think and act entrepreneurially, and who are empowered by a deep love for God.

## CAMPUS AND LOCATION

Our two campuses are located in Virginia Beach, VA, and Washington, DC. Our online programs are accessible to students who do not live near one of these cities.

The Virginia Beach Campus is located in the "Most Liveable City" (*U.S. News & World Report*, May 2003). The campus is 15 minutes from the ocean and 10 minutes from downtown Norfolk off Interstate 64—two hours south of Richmond and four hours from Washington, DC.

The Washington, DC campus is located across the street from the King Street Metro stop in Alexandria, VA, just a 15-minute ride into the capital, near historic Old Town Alexandria, which offers a nice retreat from the hustle and bustle of the metropolitan life.

## DEGREES OFFERED

MBA (full-time, part-time, online); MA Management (full-time, part-time, online); Certificate of Graduate Studies

## ACADEMIC PROGRAMS

**The School of Business offers nine areas of specialization for MBA and MA in Management students:** E-Business, Entrepreneurship, Finance, Human Resource Management, International Business, Leadership, Marketing, Not-for-Profit Managemen, Organizational Change and Development.

**The Regent University School of Business offers the following certificate programs (complete 9–12 credit hours) to meet students' continuing education and professional development needs:** Business Essentials, E-Business, Entrepreneurship, Financial Planning, Human Resource Management, International Business, Marketing, Not-for-Profit Management, Organizational Change & Development.

## FACILITIES

The Virginia Beach Campus offers housing, dining, library, student lounge, computer labs, Writing Center, bookstore, etc.

## EXPENSES AND FINANCIAL AID

**Tuition rates for academic year 2006–2007:** MBA—$645/credit hour (48 credit hours); MA in Management—$645/credit hour (30 credit hours)
**Program Fees:** Council of Graduate Students (COGS) Fee: $17 per semester
**Academic Service Fee:** $6 per semester
**Technology Fee:** $50 per semester
**Parking Fee:** $50 per year (Virginia Beach campus students only)
**Library Information Research & Resources Course:** $50 (one-time fee only for online course)
**Books and Course Material Costs:** Vary per course
University financial aid is available to degree-seeking students maintaining a minimum of 6–9 credit hours, depending on the specific form of aid the student is seeking. We have a variety of aid programs, including:
University Endowed Scholarships (6 credit-hour minimum)
Virginia Tuition Assistance Grant (VTAG) (9 credit-hour minimum)
Student Loans (6 credit-hour minimum)
Tuition Remission
Other Outside Aid Sources

## FACULTY

Each fall, *Business Reform* magazine ranks Christian colleges and universities across the nation. In 2005, for the second consecutive year, Regent University School of Business was ranked as "#1 Christian Graduate Business Program" and also recognized as "#1 Top Business Faculty" in the nation.

## STUDENT BODY

The fall 2005 School of Business student body for the full-time MBA program was 48% female, 7% international, 33% African American, and 37% married; the median age was 25. For the part-time MBA program, it was 39% female and 79% was married; the median age was 38.

Regent University has a number of student organizations, including the Council of Graduate Students and the International Student Organization. Of particular interest to business students is our award-winning Students in Free Enterprise (SIFE), which offers students the opportunity to develop leadership, teamwork, and communication skills through learning, practicing, and teaching the principles of free enterprise.

## ADMISSIONS

To be considered for admission:
1. Submit Application Form.
2. Pay $40 application fee.
3. Submit resume.
4. Submit Community Life Form.
5. Submit a writing sample.
6. Submit official transcripts.
7. Complete the GMAT.
8. Interview.
Candidates can complete their application requirements entirely online at www.regent.edu/acad/schbus/admissions.
Applications for fall term due July 15.
Applications for spring term due November 15.

## SPECIAL PROGRAMS

Our online MBA and MA in Management programs are accredited and begin with a four-day residency at the Virginia Beach Campus—a residency that gives students the opportunity to build relationships with fellow students, the Faculty, and staff. After that, students may choose to blend on-campus and online courses or to pursue their degrees entirely online.

Regent University offers joint degrees between its various graduate schools and programs. Students may earn two graduate degrees in fewer total credit requirements than if the two degrees were earned separately. A joint degree is available between business and law, government, communication, divinity, communication, education, psychology and counseling, and leadership.

## ADDITIONAL INFORMATION

We developed the Regent Instructional Method (RIM). In this unique approach to education, Faculty members "model the way" of servant leadership, leading as they want their students to lead. Our educational delivery is not instructor-centered, but interactive and experiential. Students learn better from hands-on tasks. Consequently, our curriculum is a practical, dynamic, and fun experience that builds skills and good judgment.

Our hands-on approach integrates three proven educational strategies: case studies, experiential learning, and best practice models.

## CAREER SERVICES & PLACEMENT

The Career Development office seeks to develop students' God-given talents to their fullest potential and to help students network with companies or alumni whose goals coincide with theirs. Career Development organizes many events throughout the year, including distinguished guest speakers; professional development workshops such as resume writing, cover-letter writing, interviewing skills, and job-hunting skills; career and networking fairs; and alumni mentoring/networking programs. They have an online forum for students and alumni to stay aware of the latest job opportunities, career events, and other career development resources.

# RICE UNIVERSITY
## *The Jones Graduate School of Management*

### AT A GLANCE
The small class size provides an intimate, dynamic learning environment in the state-of-the-art facility. Close connections with the Faculty and alumni open a world of opportunities as does the location—Houston—home to the second largest concentration of Fortune 500 headquarters. Whether you are interested in staying in Texas, working elsewhere in the U.S. or relocating internationally, you can achieve your goals with a Rice MBA.

### CAMPUS AND LOCATION
Rice University is located on a beautiful wooded 300-acre campus in central Houston, minutes from the downtown business district and the city's world-class theater district. The campus is located across the street from the renowned Texas Medical Center and within walking distance to the museum district, Houston Zoological Gardens, and Hermann Park. The surrounding neighborhood is one of Houston's most attractive.

### DEGREES OFFERED
The Jones School focuses all of its energy on graduate business education. Available degrees include the MBA, MBA for Professionals, MBA for Executives, MBA/Masters in Engineering with the George R. Brown College of Engineering at Rice, and MBA/MD in conjunction with Baylor College of Medicine.

### ACADEMIC PROGRAMS
In every course, you'll have an unparalleled opportunity to work one-on-one with an accessible, involved, and energetic Faculty. A comprehensive core curriculum focuses on managerial and leadership skills, ethics, and communication skills in addition to the functional areas. An Action Learning Project in the first year gives students the opportunity to learn how to integrate disciplines and turn knowledge into action. Students take 25 credit hours of electives in their second year, which allows them to custom design their curriculum to suit career goals.

### FACILITIES
The Jones School moved into its home in August 2002. The 167,000-square-foot building offers state-of-the-art facilities, including the best, broadest, and most in-depth finance center of any business school. Other features include the Business Information Center (BIC); tiered classrooms; behavior research and observation room for marketing research and interviews; a 450-seat auditorium; and a career planning center. Fully loaded laptops are provided to all students, and the Jones School is equipped to make sophisticated use of electronic access.

### EXPENSES AND FINANCIAL AID
Application fee: $100

Tuition: $32,150 for the 2006–2007 year. Laptop computer, hardware, and software are included in this price.

Total estimated expenses: approximately $51,000 per year

Financial Aid: Approximately 75 percent of students attending the Jones School receive some form of financial aid and/or merit-based scholarships. Rice University's Office of Student Financial Services also administers a variety of loan programs.

### FACULTY
The Jones School's Faculty is consistently recognized for their knowledge, research, teaching ability, and student focus. Each member of the Jones Faculty maintains a balance between teaching and research, ensuring that students receive the most current, leading-edge education.

### STUDENT BODY
The Jones School attracts students both nationally and internationally. In fact, 32 percent of first year students hail from outside the United States and another 23 percent are from outside of Texas. The average Jones Schools student has five years of experience and is 28 years old. Our students have worked in a wide array of industries and functions and bring that diverse knowledge to the classroom and to their teammates.

Our students like to be involved on campus and in the community. Jones School students have formed a number of organizations to learn more about various professions and to improve their skills. These organizations sponsor guest speakers, visit area businesses, and take on special projects. In addition, weekly corporate-sponsored "partios"—parties on the Jones School patio—provide relaxation and opportunities to network and bond with fellow students.

### ADMISSIONS
**Admissions Selection Criteria:**

The Jones School considers each aspect of the application when making admissions decision. The application requirements include: GMAT (GRE or MCAT for join candidates); TOEFL for international applicants; transcripts from educational institutions; resume; confidential evaluations; essays; interview (invitation only); completed application form and application fee.

Academic Background: You must have a four-year undergraduate degree from an accredited college or university. If you are an international applicant, your undergraduate degree must be the equivalent of a U.S. four-year degree. Your undergraduate and graduate GPAs, GMAT scores (GRE or MCAT for joint candidates), choice of major, electives, course load, and grade patterns are all considered.

Leadership Potential: Your demonstrated leadership and management experiences, both on the job and through extracurricular activities, will help us assess your leadership potential.

Confidential Evaluations: Evaluations from employers and/or professors shed perspective on your capabilities, enabling us to assess your qualifications more accurately.

Essays: Three essays that articulate your career goals, work experience, and reasons for choosing the Jones School are a crucial component of your application. Use them to convey intangibles: why you are pursuing an MBA; how you have benefited from your academic, professional and personal opportunities; what qualities you will bring to the Jones School; what you will seek from us; etc.

### CAREER SERVICES & PLACEMENT
The Career Planning Center (CPC) is housed within the Jones School building and works only with Rice MBA students and alumni. The CPC serves to support each student's development of a career plan throughout their two years at the Jones School. From day one of orientation to graduation, the CPC works individually with students to ensure they develop the strategy, job search skills, and networking opportunities that will help them succeed in the MBA job market.

# SAN JOSE STATE UNIVERSITY
## *Lucas Graduate School of Business*

San José State
UNIVERSITY

## THE COLLEGE AT A GLANCE
Located in the heart of Silicon Valley, SJSU is California's oldest institution of public higher education. The SJSU College of Business, with almost 6,000 undergraduate and graduate students, is one of the largest business schools in the country.

In 2006, SJSU alumni Donald & Sally Lucas donated $10 million for business graduate programs at SJSU. The donation exemplifies SJSU's strong linkages to both alumni and the community. The donation will allow further exploration of critical business issues, help the university hire and retain the best Faculty, and develop both innovative courses and an executive education program.

SJSU's Lucas Graduate School of Business is accredited by the prestigious AACSB (Association to Advance Collegiate Schools of Business) International. It offers an accessible, high-value education that empowers people of all ages and backgrounds to transform their lives. Pursuing a business graduate degree is an investment in the future. For the competitive edge, consider San Jose State University's Lucas Graduate School of Business—where serious academic accreditation, innovative programs, and an exceptional Faculty give you the education needed to be successful in today's global business environment.

## LOCATION AND ENVIRONMENT
The main campus is in downtown San Jose. Restaurants, museums, nightclubs, cinema, coffeehouses, concerts, theater, and professional sports are all located within walking distance of the campus. Students can access the entire Bay Area through local mass transit options.

## DEGREES OFFERED/ ACADEMIC PROGRAMS
The Lucas Graduate School of Business integrates theory with practical application. Instruction includes: case studies, lecture, research, team projects, and presentations by members of the business community.

- On-Campus MBA: In a traditional university environment, this program appeals to both full-time students (a two-year MBA program) and working individuals who attend school part-time and need evening classes.

- Off-Campus MBA: Students can complete the MBA in the evening in as few as 18 months, taking courses that meet in 8-week modules. For students who need to tailor the MBA to their lifestyle (work, travel, and family), this is the most flexible MBA program.

- MBA-One: An intense 12-month lock-step program which provides valuable networking opportunities and lifelong business connections. Classes meet three afternoons per week off-campus.

- MBA/MS Engineering: A 32-month double-degree program for engineering professionals who wish to pursue technical and executive management positions. Courses are offered off-campus in 8-week modules.

- Master of Science in Accountancy (MSA): An intense daytime 12-month lock-step program for individuals with non-accounting baccalaureate degrees. Starts in early June, and requires both on-campus courses and a professional, paid 10-week internship.

- Master of Science in Taxation (MST): A flexible evening degree program designed for tax professionals. Classes are offered in 10-week modules off-campus to accommodate both full-time and part-time students.

- Master of Science in Transportation Management (MSTM): a 28-month program that meets the educational needs of working transportation professionals through evening "distance learning" technology.

## FACILITIES AND EQUIPMENT
On-campus classes are held in the 82,000 square foot Boccardo Business Education Center. All rooms offer wireless internet access, and most classrooms are equipped for multimedia instruction. Classes in the Off-campus programs are held at Rose Orchard Technology Center. Both locations have well-equipped computer labs.

## TUITION, ROOM AND BOARD, AND FEES
For California residents, total tuition for On-Campus MBA is about $10,000 (2 classes per semester). Total tuition and fees for non-residents is about $27,000 (3 courses per semester). All students in the Off-Campus MBA and MBA-One pay a tuition/fee total of about $25,000, while the MBA/MSE tuition and fees total about $28,000.

For California residents, MS Accountancy tuition is about $8,000; for non-residents, about $18,000. MS Taxation tuition and fees total about $11,000 (for all students). MS Transportation Management tuition and fees total about $7,500 (for all students).

Built in 2005, SJSU's Campus Village offers graduate students exceptional furnished housing at competitive rates (www.sjsucampusvillage.com). Amenities include: high-speed Internet access, cable TV options, laundry facilities, and a convenience store. The 15-story apartment building is designed for upper-division and international students.

## FINANCIAL AID
Financial aid eligibility for U.S. residents is determined by the Financial Aid office after the student completes the Free Application for Federal Student Aid (FAFSA). Loans, Work-Study programs, fellowships, and scholarships may be available.

## FULL AND PART-TIME FACULTY
The 100 Faculty members in the College of Business have outstanding academic credentials obtained from top-tier national and international universities. They have priceless business skills gained from experience in global business activities, research, and professional travel. In addition, the College of Business takes advantage of its Silicon Valley location by hiring local-area professionals to teach on a part-time basis. All instructors are regularly evaluated on their teaching performance and take pride in teaching. Many assign classroom projects that connect students to Silicon Valley and work one-on-one with interested students on research. Teaching assistants are not used in the Lucas Graduate School of Business.

## STUDENT ORGANIZATIONS AND ACTIVITIES
SJSU has an active MBA Association, which enhances networking among students and strengthens the links between the students and the business community. The group hosts many social and academic events each year, including the new student orientation, Silicon Valley speakers, and career events.

## ADMISSIONS PROCESSES AND REQUIREMENTS
Applicants must have a four-year bachelor's degree. Priority is given to applicants with at least a 3.0 (last 60 semester units or 90 quarter units), a 500 on the GMAT, and a strong statement of purpose. The TOEFL also may be required. Specific admissions criteria is at www.cob.sjsu.edu/graduate, and the application is on-line at www.csumentor.edu

For domestic applicants (includes U.S. residents, H-1, and H-4 holders), the deadline is May 1 for Fall semester and October 1 for Spring semester. International applicants should complete their application by the March 1 deadline for Fall semester and August 31 for Spring semester.

Contact: Deb Geiger 408-924-3427 or geiger_d@cob.sjsu.edu

# SOUTHERN METHODIST UNIVERSITY
## Cox School of Business

### PROGRAMS & CURRICULUM

The two-year MBA curriculum is composed of 61 credit hours that include a global experience and a modular curriculum. The Cox School's program builds a strong portfolio of diverse international perspectives and course offerings. Cox MBA students can select and complete a concentration in one of the following areas: accounting, financial consulting, finance (corporate or investments), information technologies and operations management, e-business/telecommunications, general management, strategic leadership, marketing (marketing consulting or product and brand management), and strategy and entrepreneurship.

The American Airlines Global Leadership Program is a mandatory, all travel expenses paid, two-week, travel-abroad course. All first-year students visit one of three regions of the world—Asia, Europe, or Latin America—to meet with business and government leaders. The goal is to allow students to experience how business is conducted globally. In addition, the school's location at the gateway to NAFTA and Latin America is well positioned for enhancing international perspectives.

Cox's distinguished Business Leadership Center (BLC) complements the classroom curriculum throughout the two-year period. The BLC's innovative program is designed to help students develop effective management skills through seminars that center on interpersonal and communication skills, team building, and negotiation skills. Courses are organized by business leaders and taught by outside consultants from some of today's most progressive corporations.

An international exchange program allows select students to experience their international business education firsthand by studying abroad. Cox has relationships with schools in Australia, Belgium, Brazil, China, Denmark, England, France, Germany, Japan, Mexico, Singapore, Spain, and Venezuela.

### FACILITIES

Facilities at Cox are some of the most technologically advanced, and include wireless internet access for the over 1,500 students are enrolled in the Cox School working toward BBA, MBA, and executive MBAs. The Cox School of Business complex includes the Joseph Wylie Fincher Memorial Building, the Cary M. Maguire Building, the Trammell Crow Building, and the James M. Collins Executive Education Center. The Fincher Building houses administrative and faculty offices while the Maguire and Crow Buildings house classrooms, computer labs, and student study rooms. Included in the Cox School complex is the Business Information Center (BIC), combining traditional features of a university library with the technological advancements of online databases and other resources.

The Collins Center is a state-of-the-art teaching and conference facility designed to meet the evolving needs of business executives, managers, and professionals. The Collins Center houses the Cox School's Executive MBA Program and Executive Education office.

### EXPENSES

The estimated cost of tuition and fees for 2005–2006 is $33,650; books and supplies are approximately $2,000. Off-campus housing generally costs between $600 and $1,200 per month.

Merit scholarships are awarded to students each year based on individual merit and achievement. Recipients are selected on the basis of demonstrated academic achievement, managerial experience, and managerial potential. A variety of named scholarships and awards are available. Scholarships are awarded for the entire two-year period, subject to satisfactory academic performance. Approximately 75 percent of Cox MBA students receive some form of merit scholarship. The Cox Distinguished MBA Scholars program awards up to 10 full-tuition scholarships each year to new students.

### STUDENTS

Cox MBA students come from all regions of the United States and the world. Each fall, Cox enrolls approximately 100 new students into the full-time MBA program and joint degree programs (Juris Doctor and MA of Arts Administration). Students have a wide variety of academic disciplines and professional experiences. Cox's small size not only promotes collaboration among students, it also creates a close and supportive environment for students, the faculty, and the staff. The small size also gives students significant opportunities to assume leadership roles in MBA student organizations and advisory groups.

# TEXAS CHRISTIAN UNIVERSITY (TCU)
## *Neeley School of Business*

## AT A GLANCE
The Neeley MBA program at TCU brings together the right combination of what matters most in graduate business education. The intimate program size, nationally acclaimed Faculty, and highly interactive environment allows students to learn from those around them, some of business's best and brightest. Neeley students are challenged to put what they learn into action through innovative programs including the Integrative Project, corporate consulting projects, case and business plan competitions, and the Educational Investment Fund. The Neeley School invests in each individual student's development with extensive one-on-one coaching, assessments and workshops in communication, leadership, team-building and career development. Located in one of the nation's top business centers, the Neeley School offers meaningful interaction with executives from a wide variety of companies and industries.

## CAMPUS & LOCATION
The Dallas-Fort Worth Metroplex is an ideal setting in which to study business. DFW is consistently cited as one of the best places to conduct business in the nation and serves as home to the corporate headquarters and branch operations of many leading firms. Neeley students have frequent access to this thriving business community through speaker series, mentor programs, corporate consulting projects, and networking events. The area offers students a great quality of life with a pleasant climate, numerous cultural amenities, and abundant sports and recreational activities.

## DEGREES OFFERED
The Neeley Schools offers the following degree options:

- Full-Time MBA—21 months
- Accelerated MBA (full-time)—12 months for applicants with a BBA, at least 3 years of post-graduate work experience, and strong performance on the GMAT
- Professional MBA (part-time, evenings)—24 to 33 months
- Executive MBA (Friday/Saturday on alternating weeks)—21 months

## PROGRAMS & CURRICULUM
The curriculum is designed to help students develop the conceptual framework and analytical tools needed to understand complex business issues from a broader, top-level perspective. The academic program is a well-integrated experience in which projects, cases, and speakers cross disciplinary lines and prepare students to develop creative solutions. Available concentrations include corporate finance and banking, investment management, supply and value chain, entrepreneurship, marketing, consulting and general management.

## FACILITIES
Opened in February 2003, the Steve and Sarah Smith Entrepreneurs Hall provides state-of-the-art classrooms, student lounge, and more than 20 team rooms for MBA students. Additionally, the facility is home to the Ryffel Center for Entrepreneurial Studies and an expanded Neeley Graduate Career Services Center.

## EXPENSES & FINANCIAL AID
The Neeley MBA program is competitively priced for an exceptional, private university. Significant scholarship and financial aid resources are available on a competitive basis to assist students in the transition back to school. More than 75 percent of full-time Neeley MBA students typically receive merit-based awards ranging from $5,000 to $35,000 per year. Also noteworthy is the Martin Luther King/Henry B. Gonzalez Scholarship made available to Neeley MBA students by the PepsiCo Foundation.

## FACULTY
At the Neeley School, students have access to a Faculty made up of talented, caring individuals who are leading experts and respected scholars. Neeley Faculty members are sought-after business consultants, sit on corporate boards, have owned their own businesses, or have held influential positions with leading companies. They maintain close ties with business leaders, many who regularly visit classes to share inside stories about some of business's most exciting moments. Most importantly, Neeley Faculty members are top-notch teachers who are able to help students discover new ways of looking at business issues.

## STUDENTS
Neeley MBA students are in good company, interacting with other highly motivated, rising professionals who have a variety of academic and career successes under their belts. Purposefully selected to create a broad cross-section of industry experience, academic credentials, and geographic backgrounds, Neeley's rich mix of students invariably produces a lively give-and-take in the classroom and the opportunity to evaluate issues from many different perspectives.

## ADMISSIONS
The Neeley School at TCU seeks to bring together highly motivated and academically talented students from a broad range of backgrounds. Admission is competitive and seeks excellence. Candidates should be proactive individuals who can contribute in a highly interactive, team-based learning environment and who have meaningful life and professional experiences from which to draw. Most of all, the Neeley School seeks bright, motivated students who are dedicated to success.

## SPECIAL PROGRAMS
The Professional Development Program provides assessments, one-on-one coaching, and workshops on key managerial "soft skills" valued by employers such as leadership, team building, communication and career development. Students in the Educational Investment Fund manage a portfolio valued in excess of $1.5 million. Through the International Experience Electives, students examine business practices in locations such as Italy, Chile and Germany. The Integrative Project requires first-year students to incorporate all they have learned in business cases or simulations with results presented to Faculty and corporate recruiters from leading area firms. Through the Consulting Projects, teams of students tackle real business issues for corporate clients. Additionally, student teams are sponsored for case and business plan competitions across the country.

## CAREER SERVICES & PLACEMENT
The Neeley School offers everything students need to take their career to the next level: extensive ties to top employers, an international network of alumni, numerous opportunities to meet executives from leading firms, and an interactive MBA mentor program. The Graduate Career Services Center provides individual coaching and frequent workshops—typically led by visiting executives and alumni—to assist in career exploration and expand career management skills. Additionally, MBA Edge matches students with consultants from Stanton Chase, the international executive search firm, for an 8-week program on career development.

# THUNDERBIRD
## *The Garvin School of International Management*

### THE COLLEGE AT A GLANCE

Founded in 1946, Thunderbird, The Garvin School of International Management is the world's first school of global management. Thunderbird is a unique institution, with a curriculum that combines global business courses with international, cross-cultural and language studies, and a Faculty and student body who represents more than 50 different cultures, and a network of more than 33,000 alumni who work in virtually every industry and in every country in the world.

Thunderbird is accredited by the Association to Advance Collegiate Schools of Business (AACSB), the European Quality Improvement System (EQUIS), and the North Central Association of Colleges and Schools (NCA).

Thunderbird has been consistently ranked among the world's leading business schools in both overall business and in the subcategory of international business, and for its executive education program. The School has been ranked by: *BusinessWeek*, The *Wall Street Journal*, *U.S. News & World Report*, *Financial Times*, and *América Economía*.

### LOCATION AND ENVIRONMENT

Thunderbird's campus-based programs are held in North America in Glendale, a suburb of Phoenix, Arizona, U.S.A., the fifth largest U.S. city and a Southwestern business and cultural hub. With a population of more than 3 million, Phoenix is one of America's fastest growing business communities and in 2001, the greater Phoenix area ranked as the 14th largest economy in the nation and the 45th largest in the world.

Thunderbird offers the Global MBA On-Demand program, which is accessible anytime, anywhere. Study abroad options include permanent locations in Prague, Monterrey, Mexico, and between-term locations all around the globe.

### DEGREES OFFERED AND ACADEMIC PROGRAMS

Thunderbird offers a variety of degree programs designed to meet different needs: the MBA in international management for full-time students on campus or online via Thunderbird's Global On-Demand program; Master of International Management (MIM) for full-time students; and Post-MBA degree in international management for full-time students. Executive MBA programs are offered for working professionals, and there are non-degree certificate (both online and offline), language training, and executive training programs.

The MBA in international management program is truly global in every way—from the professors who have lived and worked in all corners of the globe to classmates from more than 60 countries. The curriculum emphasizes three areas: cross-cultural communication, language, and global business skills. Students can further specialize by focusing in global marketing, global finance, or international development.

Students who choose the Global MBA On-Demand option experience a world-class graduate degree program that is accessible anytime, anywhere, through a flexible schedule specifically designed for working professionals. During the twenty-one month program, online learning is complemented by one-week campus experiences in Phoenix, Geneva, and Beijing.

For students who are obtaining their MBA at another select partner university, Thunderbird offers a dual-degree opportunity. Students in this program complement their M.B.A. studies with the tools and knowledge they need to succeed in conducting business in other countries. Upon graduation, students earn both MBA and MIM degrees. Thunderbird also offers a Post-MBA MIM degree program.

The Executive MBA in international management degree program is offered for working professionals. EMBA participants spend five trimesters completing the requirements of the degree. The alternate-weekend format of the EMBA is designed to minimize time away from work and family while maximizing time to interact with fellow students and Faculty members. The format of the program incorporates the traditional international management curriculum as well as more in-depth international studies, including study overseas and language courses.

### OFF-CAMPUS OPPORTUNITIES

Offered in January and May, Winterims/Summerims are two to three-week, intensive, Faculty-led courses conducted on our Glendale campus, at other locations nationwide and in various countries. Designed to expose students to real-world processes such as global team building, government-industry partnering in technology development, consumer marketing, risk management and global business ethics, they give students the opportunity to learn from the world's best business professionals in different parts of the world and to begin building global professional networks long before they graduate.

### FACULTY

You'll learn from multinational, multicultural, multilingual Faculty who are recognized, industry-wide, for their global business expertise. More than half our Faculty have lived and worked extensively in the countries they teach you to do business in. You may also benefit from the expertise of Faculty at our partnering institutions across the world.

### TUITION, ROOM AND BOARD, AND FEES

| | |
|---|---|
| Annual tuition | $32,100 |
| Fees | $1,038 |
| Cost of books | $1,420 |
| Room & board (on/off-campus) | $3,900/$7,200 |

°Figures above pertain to the Full-Time Global MBA Program only and is subject to change. Complete Tuition information can be found on our website at: www.thunderbird.edu

### FINANCIAL AID

Experts with the Thunderbird Financial Aid Office are available to help you to design a financial solution to meet any student's need and to navigate the complex web of federal financial resources, institutional funding programs, scholarships, grants, part-time employment opportunities, loans and other available resources. More than 68 percent of all Thunderbird students regularly receive some form of financial aid—loans and/or awards—to complement their own resources.

### ADMISSIONS PROCESS AND REQUIREMENTS

Admission is offered to those who we believe will succeed within the Thunderbird program, excel in their chosen career, and exhibit the potential to lead effectively. Assessment is based on a qualitative evaluation of the documents an applicant provides. Becoming a Thunderbird is your entry into the global community. It is an investment that yields lifelong profits.

Admissions requirements and application processes vary by program. For complete details, visit: www.Thunderbird.edu.

## AT A GLANCE

The UBC MBA is a rigorous 15-month program built around a challenging and results-focused curriculum that prepares students for business leadership. Students can choose to either enhance the depth of their specialization or to broaden their skill set through a range of more than 80 elective modules in 14 different subject areas. Central to the UBC MBA is an innovative, award-winning three-month core program integrating seven key business disciplines into one foundation course.

## CAMPUS & LOCATION

The University of British Columbia (UBC), located in Vancouver, boasts to be one of Canada's most beautiful university campuses. It was established in 1915 and is the nation's third largest university, with an enrollment of over 38,000 students from around the world. The Sauder School of Business is Canada's premier research business school with internationally renowned Faculty who are at the forefront of management thinking.

## PROGRAMS & CURRICULUM

The Integrated Core provides an intensive foundation in finance, marketing, accounting, human resources, statistics, managerial economics, and information systems. It is team taught as one comprehensive course to mirror the complexity of the global business environment. Individual subject areas are taught separately and from an integrative perspective to help develop students' understanding of the true multidimensional nature of business. Students develop a broad-based, senior-level strategic approach to business decision making, as well as collaborative and leadership skills.

Following the integrated core, students can enhance their marketability by developing expertise in one of seven areas of specialization: entrepreneurship, finance, information technology & management, marketing, organizational behavior & human resources, strategic management, or supply chain management. Sub-specialization is also offered in international business. Each specialization consists of required and elective modules.

Students also have the opportunity to apply their knowledge through either a three-month internship with an organization or an industry project supervised by a Faculty member related to their area of specialization.

The Career Development Program (CDP) is dedicated to enhancing students' personal effectiveness through seminars, workshops, guest speakers, discussion groups, networking events, career coaching, and self-directed activities.

The UBC MBA program offers students a global perspective through specialized international courses, interaction with the multicultural student body and Faculty, and participation in one of the many MBA exchanges. The UBC MBA program exchanges with an impressive list of 24 leading business schools in 21 different countries around the world.

## FACILITIES

The Henry Angus Building is the primary home of the Sauder School of Business, although some executive education seminars take place downtown Vancouver at UBC Robson Square.

The David Lam Management Research Library houses a collection of print and electronic materials covering all facets of business management and acts as a resource for students and academic researchers as well as members of the business community.

## EXPENSES & FINANCIAL AID

Tuition fees for the 15-month MBA program are $36,000 CAD (subject to change—see www.ubc.ca/mba) for both domestic and international students. Participants can expect to spend another $15,000 to $20,000 CAD for books, materials, and living expenses during the program.

All domestic and international students admissible to the program are eligible for merit-based awards up to full tuition. Application to the UBC MBA serves as application to these awards and it is the applicant's advantage to apply early to be considered for scholarships. UBC MBA students also have access to an institutionally negotiated loan package to financially support their studies.

MBA students are not encouraged to work part-time during the program. However, most students earn an average salary of $3,500 CAD per month during their summer internships. Some students are also asked to provide marking or exam invigilation assistance to business school subjects during their program of studies. A number of performance-based scholarships are available to recognize top students in the MBA program.

## FACULTY

The Sauder School of Business has over 100 Faculty members with impressive backgrounds and achievements. For a current list of Faculty and their academic and research profiles, please visit the website at *www.sauder.ubc.ca/Faculty/index.cfm*.

## STUDENTS

Honored by the university's Campus Advisory Board on Student Development for having "a significant positive impact on student life and student development," the UBC MBA program experience fosters a spirit of cooperation and teamwork evident from study groups to social events. Beyond the rich educational experience, the reward is a lifetime network of international friends and business contacts. The business school network links 24,000 alumni in 60 countries around the world.

## ADMISSIONS

Applicants must have a four-year bachelor's degree or recognized equivalent from an accredited institution, with a solid academic record and a competitive GMAT score to be eligible for admission to the UBC MBA. Candidates with diverse academic and professional backgrounds are encouraged to apply. Applicants with less than two years of work experience are admitted to the program only under exceptional circumstances. Successful candidates possess managerial and leadership potential, maturity, ambition, drive and a clear sense of purpose, demonstrated by professional experience, extracurricular activities, personal interests, and written submissions.

## SPECIAL PROGRAMS

UBC offers a joint LLB/MBA degree, which is a four-year program administered jointly by the business school and the law school. A two-year MBA/MAPPS (Master of Arts, Asia Pacific policy studies) joint degree is also offered. Earn your CMA (Certified Management Accountants) designation with your MBA for the combined MBA/CMA.

## CAREER SERVICES & PLACEMENT

The Sauder School of Business Career Centre offers personal consultation and a structured program to assist in identifying, developing, and achieving career goals. Program participants complete a Web-based self-assessment test in the first few weeks of the program to clarify career direction. During the period of study, MBA students receive one-on-one career coaching and skills training in areas such as resume building, cover letter preparation, interviewing, career mapping, and networking.

# UNIVERSITY OF CALIFORNIA—IRVINE
## The Paul Merage School of Business

## AT A GLANCE

Businesses will succeed in today's global environment by driving growth and gaining competitive advantage through a relentless focus on innovation. Innovation is a major engine in the growth of the modern enterprise. Companies must constantly innovate to renew established products, launch new ones, as well as improve customer service levels and business processes. Innovation is frequently enabled by information technology which has emerged as a powerful force in virtually every business function. IT is transforming industries, enabling innovative business models, increasing the efficiency of business processes, creating new ways for companies to market to customers, and changing how work groups and organizations are managed. Today, the use of IT has meant that there is a premium placed on having the ability to manage in the face of an abundance of information. To innovate successfully requires excellent analytic decision making skills and the ability to use IT strategically to enhance the overall performance and growth of the company.

Students in the MBA Program at UC Irvine's Paul Merage School of Business will develop a sophisticated understanding of these new requirements for success in the school's re-designed curriculum that emphasizes the three critical drivers of the Innovation Economy: Strategic Innovation, Information Technology, and Analytical Decision Making.

## CAMPUS AND LOCATION

UC Irvine is located in Orange County, which combines relaxing coastal climate and lifestyle with big-city business centers, entrepreneurial creativity, and cultural attractions. It works and sprawls like Silicon Valley, but looks and lives like Mediterranean Europe.

The area surrounding the campus, Orange County, is a high-tech hub with leading companies in information and communications technology, and in electronics and biotech. Southern California, which is home to the largest concentration of medical manufacturers in the world, produces more biomedical products and research than any other area worldwide, and accounts for 25 percent of all FDA medical product approvals.

But it is not all technology. The diversity of our business region is another key advantage for UC Irvine Paul Merage MBAs. Orange County has become a center for the automotive industry, health care, financial services, and consumer goods and services.

## DEGREES OFFERED

**The following degrees are offered:** MBA (full-time), Md/MBA (full-time), Fully Employed MBA (part-time), Executive MBA (part-time), Health Care Executive MBA (part-time), PhD, Executive degree programs.

## ACADEMIC PROGRAMS GENERAL

The Full-Time MBA curriculum provides you with the knowledge and tools to succeed in the global innovation economy. Each of your courses will build your perspective on the three key themes of strategic innovation, information technology, and analytical decision-making and how they can be leveraged to produce sustainable business growth.

### First Year Curriculum

Year one of the Full-time MBA program consists primarily of the core curriculum which is designed to provide you with a disciplinary knowledge base in areas such as Accounting, Finance, Information Systems, Marketing, Operations Management, and Strategy. Continual emphasis will be placed on the three main themes of the program: Strategic Innovation, Information Technology and Analytical Decision Making and how they can be leveraged for growing your business.

Please visit the following website for more information: http://www.gsm.uci.edu/AcademicPrograms/FullTimeMBA/MBACoreCurriculum

### Second Year Curriculum

After completing the core requirements, you have the opportunity to create a unique focus by selecting a total of eleven elective classes that are multidisciplinary or focus on the application of knowledge. During your second year you are strongly encouraged to take an experiential learning course that is designed as a practicum and will enable you to apply, test, and improve your expertise in your functional area of interest. This practicum will facilitate the application of your academic training from your core and elective classes within real companies, solving real business challenges.

Please visit the following website for more information: http://www.gsm.uci.edu/AcademicPrograms/FullTimeMBA/MBASchedule.aspx

## EXPENSES AND FINANCIAL AID

Please visit the following website for information on costs and financial aid opportunities: http://www.merage.uci.edu/AcademicPrograms/FullTimeMBA/MBACosts.aspx

## FACULTY

What also sets UC Irvine's Paul Merage School of Business apart from other business schools is the caliber of teaching and research conducted by our renowned Faculty. UC Irvine MSB is one of only 11 business schools worldwide where 100 percent of the Faculty have doctorates and is second in percentage of female Faculty members (32 percent). Many opportunities exist to interact closely with our distinguished teacher-scholars and to benefit from their ties to the business community. As consultants to organizations around the globe and leaders in top professional organizations, our Faculty stays at the forefront of current management practices.

Please visit the following website for more information: http://www.merage.uci.edu/FacultyAndCenters/index.aspx

## ADMISSIONS

Admission to UC Irvine's Paul Merage School of Business is competitive with 100–110 seats available each year. The Admissions Review Committee takes a holistic approach when reviewing applications to determine a candidate's ability to successfully participate and contribute to the MBA program.

Please visit the following website for more information: http://www.gsm.uci.edu/AcademicPrograms/FullTimeMBA/MBAFAQs.aspx

## SPECIAL PROGRAMS

Students in the Full-time MBA program have the advantage of being immersed in a learning environment that offers numerous opportunities for involvement outside the classroom. This combination of management education and professional development will enable you to hone skills for future management roles so you will be prepared to meet the changing demands of business.

Please visit the following website for more information: http://www.gsm.uci.edu/AcademicPrograms/FullTimeMBA/MBAAdditionalOpportunities.aspx

## CAREER SERVICES & PLACEMENT

The education, skills and experience you gain as an MBA can open many doors. Determining which of those doors represent opportunities that matter to you can be one of most difficult, important and rewarding things you do as an MBA. Where do you want your MBA to take you? What professional goals have you set for yourself?

As you plan and work toward your next career move, our staff will partner with you to help you make the best use of the resources the school offers. Students in our MBA Programs use the MBA Career Center to explore opportunities, build or polish career management skills and connect with real-world business challenges.

Please visit the following website for more information: http://applicant.merage.uci.edu/StudentLife/CareerServices/index.aspx

# UNIVERSITY OF CINCINNATI

UNIVERSITY OF
Cincinnati

## AT A GLANCE
The University of Cincinnati MBA program provides students a solid foundation in the analytical, functional, teamwork, leadership, and communication skills demanded in today's business world. This practical approach to business education paired with flexible options make the University of Cincinnati MBA program one of the best for students or professionals wishing to build their business skills.

## LOCATION AND ENVIRONMENT
Cincinnati is located on the Ohio River in the southwest corner of the state of Ohio. The University of Cincinnati, founded in 1870, enrolls approximately 35,000 students in nineteen colleges and divisions. The first graduate degrees were awarded in 1888. The university is 10 minutes from downtown Cincinnati, and students have easy access to many cultural and sporting events. These activities range from concerts, ballets, and musicals to intramural and "big time" college sports. UC recently joined the powerhouse Big East conference in 2005. The 200-acre campus is friendly and diverse, reflecting the city's cosmopolitan atmosphere. On campus, students also have access to new Campus Recreation Center, opened in 2006.

## DEGREES OFFERED
Future MBAs are offered multiple options at the UC College of Business, including full and part time programs. Full time MBA options include a full-time 12-month program; a 15-month program that adds a three-month internship; and a 21-month MBA/MS program that, along with a three-month internship, adds an MS degree for those seeking a higher degree of rigorous specialization in addition to an applied general management education.

UC also offers a part-time program on the Clifton campus, in Blue Ash (both evening programs) and on the Wright Patterson Air Force Base (a mid-afternoon program).

## ACADEMIC PROGRAMS
The variety of scheduling options offered make the UC College of Business MBA program attractive to a wide range of students. In both the full-time and part-time programs, students can choose concentrations in construction management, finance, information systems, international business, management, marketing, operations management, quantitative analysis, and commercial real estate.

Students may also choose to pursue one of UC's joint programs with the MBA in Arts Administration, Law, Medicine and Nursing. The UC College of Business also offers masters degrees in accounting, information systems, finance, marketing and quantitative analysis and PhD programs in accounting, finance, information systems, management, marketing, and operations management/quantitative analysis.

## FACILITIES AND EQUIPMENT
All UC M.B.A. classes are held in Lindner Hall, which is located next to the Langsam Library which offers excellent study and research facilities including private graduate study areas and a collection of more than 1.7 million volumes, 20,700 serial subscriptions and 2.1 million microform units. Langsam also has a full-time business librarian on staff to support UC M.B.A. students with corporate research.

## EXPENSES
2005-2006 Academic Year Tuition and Fees (Full-Time MBA)

|  | Ohio Resident | Non-Resident |
|---|---|---|
| Tuition | $4,796.00 | $6,047.00 |
| General Fees | 384.00 | 384.00 |
| ITIE fees | 99.00 | 99.00 |
| Total | $5,279.00/quarter | $6,530.00/quarter |

## FACULTY
The UC MBA Faculty, all on tenure track, bring a wealth of knowledge, research and experience to the classroom. Many have come from the world's leading business schools, with experience in some of the top corporations in the United States. Students learn from award-winning Faculty members, many honored with Fulbright Scholarships and national teaching awards. As a result, students enjoy an excellent classroom experience that is both intellectually stimulating and focused on real-world problem solving.

## STUDENT ORGANIZATIONS AND ACTIVITIES:
UC students have access to many organizations on campus and within the College of Business. Two organizations that keep students involved in the business world are the MBA Association (MBAA) and Net Impact.

Student wishing to provide leadership within the MBA program and the college often choose MBAA as a home for extra-curricular activities. The group organizes community service opportunities, a business speaker's series and many networking events.

The University of Cincinnati boasts the first Net Impact chapter in the surrounding region. This national organization allows students involved to focus their activities around social and economic responsibility in the business world. This group teams student and professional members together to make the most of their MBA experience.

## ADMISSIONS
The University of Cincinnati's MBA program offers an online application process. Applicants are admitted from all under-graduate majors. The only course prerequisite is a course in calculus (preferably business calculus). To apply to the UC MBA program, applicants must submit an official transcript of undergraduate and any graduate work completed, a current resume, two letters of recommendation, responses to two essay questions and official GMAT scores.

All international applicants must also take the TOEFL. The Admissions Committee evaluates applicants based on their entire application package. The average GMAT score is 592 and average undergraduate GPA is 3.2. Prospective students should visit the College of Business Web site for application materials.

## CAREER SERVICES & PLACEMENT
The UC MBA program offers an array of career services. The College of Business is dedicated to helping students develop a comprehensive and effective strategy for finding employment, including defining a career path with career assessment tools and providing employer and Web resources. One of the strengths of the UC MBA program is the individual attention received from Career Services and the variety of services provided, which include career development workshops, videotaped mock interviews, career days, alumni networking databases, alumni networking receptions and on-campus interviewing, both in the College of Business and at the campus wide Career Development Center.

# UNIVERSITY OF HAWAII AT MANOA
## *College of Business*

## A LEADER IN ASIA-PACIFIC BUSINESS

### AT A GLANCE

A leader among U.S. business schools in its focus on the Asia-Pacific region, the College of Business at the University of Hawaii at Manoa provides students with an in-depth understanding of the best business practices, an awareness of languages and cultures, and a solid comprehension of emerging technologies within today's complex global economic environment. Founded in 1949, the college offers students a wide selection of degree, certificate and high-impact executive programs in a unique multicultural learning environment enhanced by collaborative learning, research projects, international speakers, internships, study abroad opportunities and career services. In the past several years, *U.S. News & World Report* has ranked the college among the top 25 U.S. graduate business schools for international business.

The graduate program offers an integrated curriculum in five fields: accounting, finance, marketing, management, and information technology to accentuate the practical application of business theories. The curriculum incorporates the latest technology, offers specific concentration fields such as the recently added Entrepreneurship and Innovation courses and is designed with an Asia-Pacific perspective to respond to the changing economic conditions.

For more information, call 956-8266 or visit www.cba.hawaii.edu.

## CAMPUS AND LOCATION

The College of Business at the University of Hawaii at Manoa is located in Honolulu on the Island of Oahu. Nestled in beautiful Manoa Valley, the college is just minutes away from Waikiki, downtown Honolulu and most major cultural centers.

With the coast of the U.S. mainland to the east and key cities of Asia to the west, Hawaii has established the strongest and most developed business infrastructure in the Pacific. This strategic location sets the university in the center of the world's Pacific commerce.

## DEGREES OFFERED

Bachelor of Business Administration, Master of Business Administration, Master of Accounting, Master of Human Resource Management, Executive MBA, Executive Neighbor Islands MBA, China-International MBA, Japan-focused MBA, Vietnam Executive MBA, Joint JD/MBA, PhD in International Management.

## ACADEMIC PROGRAMS GENERAL

### Real-world curriculum

Experience an advanced curriculum that incorporates core business disciplines and cutting-edge business practices, while focusing on information technology, entrepreneurship, and Asia-Pacific and global strategies. With lectures, case studies and a hands-on practicum, the program fosters a collaborative learning environment for building your network with other future business leaders. Gain valuable real-world experience through an extensive internship program that offers opportunities in a variety of industries to suit your career goals.

## FACILITIES

The university library collections total more than 3 million volumes and more than 25,000 journals and serials. Materials from other libraries in Hawaii and the mainland U.S. are available through interlibrary loan. The Asian Collection in Hamilton Graduate Library has a heavy concentration of materials, including business information related to South and Southeast Asia. The East Asia collections (Chinese, Japanese, and Korean) are ranked among the top fifteen in the United States. The library is also a regional depository for U.S. publications and maintains a large depository of United Nations publications.

## EXPENSES AND FINANCIAL AID

Full-time graduate tuition for the Evening MBA 2005–2006 academic year was $10,896 for state residents and $16,032 for nonresidents. Part-time tuition was $454 per credit hour for residents and $668 for nonresidents. Fees were approximately $85 per semester; books and other materials cost around $300. Tuition for the China International MBA is $30,888. The total cost of the Japan-focused MBA was $29,000, which covered tuition, fees, books, and class materials. The MAcc tuition in 2005–2006 was $338 per credit for residents and $588 for nonresidents.

A variety of scholarships are available. Students from Asia-Pacific countries may qualify to pay Hawaii resident tuition rates.

## FACULTY

All full-time MBA Faculty are a diverse group of internationally accomplished researchers and highly recognized teachers, holding doctoral degrees from Columbia, Carnegie-Mellon, MIT, Stanford, Purdue, Harvard, and other major universities. Our Faculty's international experience and business research in the Asia-Pacific region provide an exceptional learning experience for students.

## STUDENT BODY

The University of Hawaii at Manoa's population of approximately 18,000 students is 24 percent Caucasian, 20 percent Japanese, 8 percent Filipino, 8 percent Hawaiian or part Hawaiian, and 40 percent other ethnicities. Students come to the university from 77 different countries as well as from the U.S. mainland and Hawaii.

## ADMISSIONS

The ideal student entering the program has a solid academic record, high test scores, strong motivation, and well-thought-out career goals.

For further information on admissions, please contact:

Office of Student Academic Services
University of Hawaii at Manoa
College of Business
2404 Maile Way, B-101
Honolulu, HI 96822, U.S.A.
Telephone: 808-956-8266
Fax: 808-956-2657
E-mail: mba@hawaii.edu
Website: www.cba.hawaii.edu

## SPECIAL PROGRAMS

The Pacific Asian Center for Entrepreneurship and E-Business (PACE) provides a focal point for entrepreneurs to interact with students and venture capitalists. A popular annual business plan competition with $80,000 in cash prizes attracts more than forty student teams.

The Pacific Asian Management Institute (PAMI) offers credit courses leading to a certificate in international management or international entrepreneurship. Each summer, 25–30 business students travel on a field study to four Asian countries, visiting factories and boardrooms to study firsthand how business is conducted in Asia.

## CAREER SERVICES & PLACEMENT

The college houses a full-service Internship and Career Development Center continues to place over 500 students in internships and receive more than 700 job opportunities each year and offers the "Business of the Week" program to bring companies on campus for onsite interviews, workshops and presentations.

# UNIVERSITY OF IOWA
## Henry B. Tippie School of Management

### AT A GLANCE

The University of Iowa's Henry B. Tippie School of Management offers a master of business administration (MBA) degree that consistently ranks in the top 50 MBA programs in the world. There are many characteristics that contribute to the quality of the Tippie MBA including a flexible curriculum and great placement results.

We attract the best and brightest students from around the world to our program. While at Tippie, students enhance their knowledge of business fundamentals and further their professional development. The end result is successful graduates that are tomorrow's business leaders.

### LOCATION AND ENVIRONMENT

Iowa City is a diverse, highly cosmopolitan community of 60,000 set in the natural scenic beauty of Iowa's rolling hills and woods. The University of Iowa campus is the heart of Iowa City. The 1,900-acre campus is located along both sides of the Iowa River. The campus community provides a rich variety of activities and resources for students including Big Ten athletics, natural history and art museums, the Center for the Arts, Hancher Auditorium, and the UI hospitals and clinics.

Business programs are housed in the 187,000-square-foot John Pappajohn Business Building and the newly constructed Pomerantz Center. Multimedia capabilities and instructional technology are integrated throughout the classrooms and facilities. In addition to the largest computer laboratory on campus, a wireless LAN provides students access to a full range of technology services. The Pomerantz Center provides additional classrooms for MBA students and a full-service Career Center.

### DEGREES OFFERED

The Tippie School of Management offers a full-time MBA program on campus. The MBA program for professionals and managers is offered during the evening in Cedar Rapids, the Quad Cities, and Des Moines, Iowa. The executive MBA is offered on campus and in Des Moines, Iowa. A dual MBA/masters in engineering program is offered in cooperation with Iowa State University in Cedar Rapids. International MBA programs are offered in Hong Kong and Beijing. The Tippie College of Business also offers a master of accountancy degree and PhD programs in economics and business. Students may also pursue a dual degree program with the MBA in law, nursing, library science, hospital and health administration, and medicine.

### ACADEMIC PROGRAMS

A world-class MBA program improves students' professional and personal lives intellectually, practically, and ethically. The Tippie MBA's integrated program of quality academics, experiential business applications, and professional development does exactly that. Management education at Tippie is characterized by unmatched academic training, guided experience-based learning, and transforming professional development. Five curricular themes challenge you to stretch your intellectual abilities, inspire you to reach new heights of achievement, and elicit your best efforts in every endeavor.

### FACILITIES AND EQUIPMENT

The state-of-the-art facilities of the John Pappajohn Business Building and Pomerantz Center provide an outstanding arena for learning. The Tippie School of Management uses the latest communications and course delivery technology to help your class network effectively.

### EXPENSES

The Tippie MBA provides one of the best returns on investment available. This nationally accredited program provides a top-notch education that can help you take your career to the next level.

**2006–2007 academic Year Tuition and Fees (full-time MBA program)**

**Annual Tuition**

| | |
|---|---|
| Iowa Residents | $12,510 |
| Non-residents | $22,948 |

| | |
|---|---|
| Computer Fees | $225 |
| Health Fees | $190 |
| Student Union, Activities, and Service Fees | $209 |
| Building Fee | $119 |

**Total Tuition and Fees**

| | |
|---|---|
| Iowa Residents | $13,253 |
| Non-residents | $23,691 |

Housing, textbooks, and personal living costs are approximately $12,000 per year.

Merit-based financial aid is offered to outstanding candidates each year. The criteria for these awards mirror those for admission—academic record, work history, leadership experience, test scores—although only those with the highest qualifications receive offers for aid. Domestic and international applicants are eligible for awards. Awards may consist of a scholarship, a graduate assistantship, or both. Most scholarships vary from $3,000 to $6,000. Graduate assistantships provide a salary of approximately $8,000, a contribution toward health insurance costs, and resident tuition status for non-Iowa residents.

### FACULTY

Engaging. Experienced. World-renowned. Tippie MBA faculty combine exemplary teaching and academic research with consulting practices that enhance in-class applications of the latest developments in business. Tippie's faculty realize how critical it is to stay "in-the-know" and on the pulse of emerging business trends and innovative practices. Our teaching combines the latest trends in business management with traditional theories that have withstood the tests of time. It's the best way to send students into the marketplace with a competitive edge.

### STUDENT ORGANIZATIONS AND ACTIVITIES

MBA student organizations provide many venues for participation in activities outside the classroom. These organizations offer the opportunity for students to demonstrate leadership involvement and collaboration. Student clubs organize professional development events, career networking opportunities, social events, and many other activities that enhance the Tippie MBA experience.

Tippie MBAs are not passive recipients of education, but active players in determining the type of MBA experience delivered. Student organizations provide the primary venue for participation in activities outside the classroom. These organizations offer the opportunity for students to demonstrate leadership, involvement, and collaboration. Student clubs organize professional development events, career networking opportunities, social events, and many other activities that enhance the Tippie MBA experience.

The entering class in the full-time MBA program averages nearly 3.5 years of work experience, a GPA of approximately 3.27 (4.0 scale), and a GMAT score of 656.

### ADMISSIONS

The Tippie MBA is seeking candidates who have clearly demonstrated the ability to complete a rigorous academic program and the potential for success in a professional environment. The admission review process includes consideration of a number of factors that are all important in our decision: academic background; standardized tests (GMAT and TOEFL); work experience; leadership; and the admissions interview.

### CAREER SERVICES & PLACEMENT

Tippie MBA Career Services staff are true partners in helping you achieve your career goals. During your first semester, you refine your resume, prepare a portfolio, pair up with an alumni mentor, and complete your personal marketing plan. Staff members are your advocates, consultants, and marketers. They are your coaches as you practice your interviewing skills and learn to market your most important asset—yourself.

# UNIVERSITY OF MASSACHUSETTS—AMHERST
## *Isenberg School of Management*

### AT A GLANCE

As the business school on the University of Massachusetts' flagship campus in Amherst, the Isenberg School shares the institution's commitment to world-class teaching and research. The Isenberg MBA program is housed in the University's new 47,000 square foot Alfond Management Center and offers state-of-the-art learning facilities.

### LOCATIONS AND ENVIRONMENT

Situated between four major East cost cities, the University of Massachusetts Amherst is located in the Pioneer Valley, the beautiful western region of Massachusetts, near the Berkshire Mountains. The University of Massachusetts Amherst, along with four major colleges—Amherst, Hampshire, Mount Holyoke and Smith—constitute the Five College community, which is noted for its extensive educational resources and cooperation.

### DEGREES OFFERED

Full-time MBA; MBA/M.S. Sport Management; MBA/MS Hospitality & Tourism Management; MBA/Masters in Public Policy; Professional MBA; MS in Accounting; PhD in Business Administration (with concentrations in Accounting, or Finance, or Management Science, or Marketing, or Organizational Studies, or Strategic Management); PhD in Sport Management; BBA with majors in Accounting, Finance, Management, Marketing and Operations Management; BS in Sport Management; BS in Hospitality and Tourism Management

MBA PROGRAMS

The Full-time MBA is a two-year, 55-credit program where students complete all core courses in their first year. Additionally, first-year students are required to take a career management course providing structure to their career planning.

Students build their fields of specialization through electives, in the fall of the second year. In the final semester students participate in a team-consulting project for companies and organizations.

Full-time MBA students, as a part of their assistantships, have research and practice opportunities through Isenberg research centers, including the internationally prominent Center for International Securities and Derivatives Markets, Biomedical Innovation Laboratory, the Virtual Center for Supernetworks.

The Professional MBA program is a part-time 37 credit, self-paced program that consists of 11 core courses and 3 elective credits. Students may take up to 4 years to complete their program with many completing in as little as 2-2 years. Professional MBA classes can be taken Online or at one of our three satellite campuses in Massachusetts: Holyoke, Shrewsbury, and Pittsfield. The entire core curriculum is available online every Fall, Spring, and Summer semester.

### EXPENSES & FINANCIAL AID

**Estimate of Expenses for 2006-2007:**

| | |
|---|---|
| Massachusetts resident tuition: | $2,640 |
| Non-Massachusetts resident tuition: | $9,937 |
| Student fees: | $8,000 |
| Room, board, books & misc. expenses: | $8,500 |

Many full-time students receive fellowships and assistantships that offer the opportunity to work alongside Isenberg professors on current research and consulting projects. In exchange for their efforts, each student receives a waiver for tuition, an additional bi-weekly stipend, and comprehensive health insurance. To be considered for an assistantship or university fellowship, students are strongly encouraged to apply by the February 1st deadline.

Additional Financial Aid is available to graduate students through the Financial Aid Office.

### FACULTY

Isenberg School Faculty members have nationally recognized strengths in financial risk analysis, alternative investments, operations and quality management, organization theory, sport marketing, financial and behavioral accounting, hospitality management, entrepreneurship, business leadership, and many other areas.

### ADMISSIONS

Isenberg MBAs bring diverse backgrounds and professional interests to the program. We look for strong academic abilities and meaningful professional experience. Additionally, we strive to build a class of students who demonstrate leadership potential and a commitment to professional growth.

For further information, please contact:

Graduate Programs Office
Isenberg School of Management
121 Presidents Drive
Amherst, MA 01003
Telephone: 413-545-5608
Website: *www.isenberg.umass.edu/mba*

### CAREER SERVICES & PLACEMENT

The MBA Career Management Office plays an essential role in a student's Isenberg MBA experience. This office is a part of the Isenberg School's Chase Career Center and it, offers career advising to both full-time and part-time MBA students and functions as a clearing house for recruiting, job postings, and alumni networking. Graduates have been hired by Deloitte Touche Tohmatsu, EMC, Frito Lay, General Electric, Hamilton Sundstrand, IBM, Liberty Mutual, MassMutual Financial Group, Morgan Stanley, PricewaterhouseCoopers, RSA Security Teradyne, and United Technologies Corporation.

# THE UNIVERSITY OF MIAMI
## School of Business Administration

## THE COLLEGE AT A GLANCE
The University of Miami School of Business Administration is ranked the number one MBA program in Florida by the *Wall Street Journal*. Our business school is one of 506 schools in North America that is fully accredited by AACSB International, The Association to Advance Collegiate Schools of Business, and CAHME, The Commission on Accreditation of Healthcare Management Education.

### LOCATION AND ENVIRONMENT
Coral Gables, home of the University of Miami, infuses old world ambiance with new world technology. Our unique location, in the midst of one of the most dynamic areas of international business growth in the Western Hemisphere, contributes to the classroom environment.

### DEGREES OFFERED
The University of Miami School of Business Administration offers a full time 21-month, 48-credit, MBA Program; and a one year, 32-credit MBA Program, designed for students who graduated within the last five years with an undergraduate degree in business. Executives may earn an MBA degree by attending Saturday classes in one of the following areas: health administration, international business, management, working professional, or MBA/Master of Science in Industrial Engineering (MBA/MSIE).

For more information please visit us at www.bus.miami.edu/grad.

### ACADEMIC PROGRAMS
At the School of Business Administration, the curriculum provides a decidedly flexible framework for learning. A variety of teaching methods are utilized: lecture, discussion, case method, and team projects. Classes are small to encourage exchange between teacher and student, and among students.

### OFF-CAMPUS OPPORTUNITIES
Off-campus MBA programs are offered in Tampa, Orlando, Delray Beach and to residents of Nassau, Bahamas.

### FACILITIES AND EQUIPMENT
The School of Business Administration's $24 million award winning complex, built for the exclusive use of graduate business students, provides the most advanced technology and sophisticated academic environment. This facility is complete with computer access at every seat, a "paperless library," a computer lab exclusive to MBA students and hi-tech classrooms with executive seating. The Ziff Graduate Career Services Center is exclusively dedicated to helping graduate business students find employment opportunities, obtain internships, and prepare to compete for top positions.

### TUITION, ROOM AND BOARD, AND FEES
Graduate tuition for the 2006–2007 academic year is $1280 per credit hour.

### FINANCIAL AID
A limited number of graduate assistantships, offered to outstanding applicants, usually include both a tuition scholarship and a monthly stipend. Graduate students are eligible to apply for student loans and work-study assistance through the university's Office of Financial Assistance Services.

### FACULTY
Educated at some of the world's finest academic institutions, the School of Business Administration Faculty are world-renowned and prestigious. The UM Faculty serve as consultants to *Fortune 500* companies and international corporations across the globe.

### STUDENT ORGANIZATIONS AND ACTIVITIES
The University of Miami values its multicultural community and student organizations. The Graduate Business Student Association is the foremost business organization for MBA students while a variety of student organizations are available within the University of Miami community such as; the Council of International Students and Organizations, Colombian Student Association, Hispanic Heritage Month Association, Latin American Student Association, Latino Greek Council, United Dominicans Association, and Federación de Estudiantes Cubanos to name a few.

### ADMISSIONS PROCESSES AND REQUIREMENTS
The Graduate Business Admissions Committee welcomes applications from individuals whose undergraduate degrees are from accredited colleges or universities. Student applications are reviewed on an individual basis to determine the applicant's potential for success in the MBA Program. A minimum GMAT score and a competitive GPA are essential to be considered for admission. Other factors considered by the Admissions Committee as part of the decision-making process include an essay, letters of recommendation, work experience, and community involvement.

# UNIVERSITY OF NORTH CAROLINA—CHARLOTTE

## AT A GLANCE

The MBA Program at UNC Charlotte offers students the opportunity to invest in themselves and their careers by earning a highly respected MBA. Our program is distinguished by its full and engaging curriculum, taught by our outstanding resident Faculty. It is designed to teach students to think strategically, communicate effectively and work productively as part of a team, giving them the tools to succeed in today's complex, fast-paced business environment.

The MBA is self-paced, allowing students the option of completing the degree in as few as 18 months and as many as six years. The typical student completes the program in 30 months. All courses meet one evening per week, allowing maximum flexibility for students seeking a balance between work, graduate school, family and other commitments.

Students may earn an academic concentration in one of nine defined areas, or one of their own design. These choices allow students to customize their MBA to help them achieve their career goals and develop depth in an area of particular interest.

The MBA program at UNC Charlotte is fully accredited by AACSB International, the premier accrediting agency for programs in business administration and accounting. This prestigious distinction is achieved as a result of the world-class Faculty and highest-caliber students that make up the Belk College of Business.

## CAMPUS AND LOCATION

The UNC Charlotte main campus is located on 1,000 acres on the north side of Charlotte. Students also may attend classes at the UNC Charlotte Uptown in the heart of the center city.

## DEGREES OFFERED

Master of Business Administration (MBA), MBA in Sports Marketing/Management (beginning 2007), Master of Accountancy, Master of Science in Economics, Master of Science in Mathematical Finance, Ph.D. in Business Administration (beginning 2006)

## ACADEMIC PROGRAM

The UNC Charlotte MBA program provides the opportunity for professionals to continue their careers while earning an advanced degree. Students may supplement the general MBA with a concentration in business finance, economics, financial institutions/commercial banking, information and technology management, international business, management, marketing, real estate finance and development, or supply chain management. A self-structured concentration is available. The program is 37 credit hours of core courses and electives. Additional preparation may be required for students not holding an undergraduate degree in a business discipline.

## EXPENSES AND FINANCIAL AID

The UNC Charlotte MBA program offers students a nationally-accredited academic experience with outstanding economic value.

### for Fall 2005—Spring 2006

| Hours Taken | North Carolina resntside (per semester) | Non-Residents of North Carolina (per semester) |
|---|---|---|
| 0-2 | $1,150.15 | $2,426.15 |
| 3-5 | $2,088.15 | $4,639.90 |
| 6-8 | $3,214.50 | $7,042.25 |
| 9+ | $4,464.00 | $9,567.50 |

Graduate Assistantships are available for full-time students on a competitive basis. MBA Enhancement Scholarships are offered on both a merit and need basis.

## STUDENT BODY

MBA students in the Belk College of Business students are bright, motivated and career focused. The majority of our students (80 percent) work full-time while pursuing their MBA part-time. Our average student has more than seven years of professional experience in a wide variety of fields. The diverse industry representation and rich experience of the student body significantly adds to the overall classroom experience.

## ADMISSIONS

Admission to the UNC Charlotte MBA program is highly selective. We seek candidates who are motivated and aim to assume leadership roles in organizations locally and around the world. Candidates must have obtained the equivalent of a U.S. bachelor's degree from a fully accredited university to be eligible for admission to the UNC Charlotte MBA.

Previous study of business is not required, as the program offers a 10 credit preparatory component that provides non-business majors the background they need to be successful in the rest of the program. These preparatory courses are waived for candidates with sufficient undergraduate preparation.

Admissions decisions are based on several criteria, including the applicant's academic achievement, previous work history, and standardized test scores. A completed application form must be accompanied by three letters of recommendation, a current resume, all academic transcripts, a GMAT score, statement of purpose, and a $55 application fee.

Work experience is not required for admission to the MBA program; however, it is strongly recommended. The typical UNC Charlotte MBA student has 5-7 years of professional work experience. Since the admissions decision involves several criteria, there are no set minimums for the GMAT or GPA average. The fall 2005 entering class had an average undergraduate GPA of 3.2 (on a 4.0 scale) and an average GMAT score of 575.

In addition to the above, international students must also submit an official financial statement verifying sufficient resources to cover education and living expenses. International students are also required to provide TOEFL scores (557 on paper-based test or 220 on the computer-based test).

Applications to the MBA are accepted for fall, spring and summer entry on a rolling admissions basis.

## CAREER SERVICES & PLACEMENT

MBA students receive career development and placement assistance from both the MBA program administration and the University's Career Center. The Career Center maintains a list of job postings; oversees on-campus recruiting; and conducts sessions on resume writing, interviewing and employment searches.

To support these efforts, the MBA office also hosts networking events, offers a mentoring program, sponsors job coaching, and presents "Total Professional" seminars to help students market themselves to current and future employers following completion of their MBA.

Top employers of UNC Charlotte MBAs include AG Edwards, Bank of America, BB&T, Belk Stores, Carolina Health Care System, Cisco Systems, Duke Energy, IBM, Ingersoll-Rand, TIAA-CREF, and Wachovia.

# UNIVERSITY OF OREGON
## *Lundquist College of Business*

## AT A GLANCE
The Oregon MBA is a small rigorous program that combines cross-functional training in all the business disciplines with experiential learning and more focused study in nationally prominent areas, such as Entrepreneurship, Sports Business, Securities Analysis, and Sustainable Supply Chain Management. We're proud to be an integral part of the Lundquist College of Business at the University of Oregon, the state's flagship liberal arts institution and a member of the A.A.U., the prestigious association of 62 leading research universities in the U.S. and Canada.

## CAMPUS AND LOCATION
The park-like campus is located in Eugene, the center of Oregon's second largest metropolitan area 100 miles (160 km) south of Portland and 65 miles (100 km) east of the Pacific. Eugene boasts a lively arts scene, thriving natural foods industry, and innumerable opportunities for outdoor activities.

## DEGREES OFFERED
2-year MBA (21 months; fall start only)
Accelerated MBA (15 months; start fall, winter, or spring; BS Business Administration required)
MBA/JD (4 years; separate applications required)
MBA/MA (separate applications required)

## ACADEMIC PROGRAMS GENERAL
1. Small & personal: Entering class maximally 60; electives average below 30 students.
2. Collegial & diverse: Broadly representative of the US and the world, students offer multicultural lessons in diversity, tolerance, and cooperation.
3. Experiential & entrepreneurial: Through consulting, business planning, and competitions students apply classroom learning to the real world and identify and pursue new opportunities.
4. Comprehensive & intense: Because we see the MBA degree as broadly generalist and managerial, we stretch students beyond their comfort zone.
5. Flexible & interdisciplinary: The cross-functional core curriculum provides the broad foundation on which students plan their second year studies in one or several of 7 focus areas.
6. Quintessentially Oregon: The program and its students are the embodiment of Oregon values: concern for community and environment; belief in active, balanced life-styles; commitment to innovation and entrepreneurial initiative.

## FACILITIES
Part of the Lillis Business Complex, brand-new Lillis Hall is an architectural marvel and the 'greenest' public building in Oregon, incorporating the latest in energy-saving technology and environmentally-friendly building design and reflecting our pedagogical values with wireless connectivity, the latest A/V applications, reconfigurable classrooms, learning centers, small group work rooms, study spaces, and a café.

## EXPENSES AND FINANCIAL AID
Tuition at the University of Oregon is one of the most reasonable in the U.S.; our students shoulder the lowest debt load of any ranked program. That's why *Forbes Magazine* has rated us highly for return on investment. We make our admissions decisions without reference to financial status.
**Tuition and UO Fees (per year):**
OR Residents: Full-time - $10,560
Non-OR Residents: Full-time - $15,150
LCB Resource Fee (per year) - $1,650
Warsaw Sports Marketing Center Fee (per year) - $1,500
Matriculation Fee for New Graduate Students (first term only) - $150
University Housing (9 months) - $5,750-9,800
**Miscellaneous:**
Books and supplies - $1,000
Personal expenses - $2,560

Campus parking - $85
Financial assistance comes in the form of merit-based scholar- and fellowships, federal and private-lender loans, and work-study jobs. About 90 percent of Oregon MBA students receive some kind of aid. All applicants are automatically considered for merit-based scholarships.

## FACULTY
Composed of seasoned veterans known nationally for their research, publications, and professional service, newly minted PhDs from leading universities, and successful former business executives, OMBA Faculty members are approachable and helpful. By the end, you will have gotten to know each other well, whether over lunch and coffee or through the give-and-take of class.

## STUDENT BODY
1. The Oregon MBA Association sponsors extracurricular activities and organizes community service events to enrich the overall experience of OMBA students.
2. The UO Investment Group is composed of undergraduate and graduate students who manage investments in excess of $750,000 with returns that routinely beat the S&P 500.
3. Net Impact is a nationwide network of MBAs, graduate students and young professionals who believe that business can both earn a profit and create positive social change. MBA Net Impact works closely with members of the undergraduate Sustainable Business Group.
4. Sustainable Advantage Conference: For almost a decade, OMBA students have played leading organizing roles in the annual Sustainable Business Symposium, hosted by LCB and the UO and recast in 2005 as a conference to acquaint business people with sustainable business practices and help them implement these.

## ADMISSIONS
**Minimum Admissions Requirements:**
GMAT: 600; Quantitative: 60th+ percentile
G.P.A.: 3.0 on 4-point scale
Work Experience: 2 years full-time, post-baccalaureate
TOEFL (computer-based): 250 International applicants only
TOEFL (Internet-based): 93 Writing: 22, Speaking: 26, Listening: 21, Reading 24
**Other factors:** Undergraduate school and major, Application essays, Recommendations, Personal interview
**Deadlines for fall entry:**
Early Admission: November 15
International Admission: February 15
Regular Admission: March 15
Late Admission: May 15
Applicants who have submitted all supporting materials by these deadlines can expect to hear within one month whether they have been admitted, waitlisted, or denied.

## CAREER SERVICES & PLACEMENT
1. Individual counseling and seminars on networking, targeting internships and employers, focusing career goals, self assessment, effective resume writing and interviewing, evaluating and negotiating employment offers.
2. Recruiting and information sessions attract national and regional employers to campus.
3. Through company visits, MBAs have a chance to gather information and to learn more about the management, work environment, products/services, and strategic direction of potential employers.
4. Our web-based Oregon MBA network serves as a communication link between alumni and as a resource for current students to learn about various career paths. We also host regional student-alumni receptions to facilitate mentoring relationships.

# UNIVERSITY OF THE PACIFIC
## *Eberhart School of Business*

### AT A GLANCE
The Pacific MBA prepares graduates to meet the challenges of leadership in a dynamic, technology-driven, global business environment through experiential coursework in a small, supportive environment. Pacific MBA students can expect to benefit from the following:
Personalized Educational Experience
Intense International Experience
Degree Combinations and Options
Expert Career Management
Desirable California Location

### CAMPUS AND LOCATION
Centrally located in the heart of California, Pacific is near Yosemite National Park, Lake Tahoe, Napa Valley, and the California coastline where limitless activities, world-class cuisine, and unparalleled beauty abound. More importantly, the campus is only 80 miles east of San Francisco and 45 miles south of Sacramento, allowing our students direct access to companies and career opportunities in the Silicon Valley and State Capital. The campus is nestled in the midst of a dynamic economy and entrepreneurial culture which creates a unique learning opportunity.

### DEGREES OFFERED
The Eberhardt School of Business (ESB) offers an Accelerated and Traditional MBA Program. In addition, working professionals may complete the coursework on a part-time basis. ESB has developed the following dual-degree and cooperative programs: JD/MBA, Master's International (MBA with a Peace Corps service), and PharmD/MBA.

### ACADEMIC PROGRAMS
The hallmark of the Pacific MBA is a student-centered learning environment that prepares students for success in a collaborative, team-based effort between students, Faculty, and administrators. In addition, our three core program strengths—leadership, innovation, and globalization—are infused throughout the curriculum.
**Students may specialize in the following areas:**
Finance, Marketing, Entrepreneurship, Management Information Systems, and General Management

### FACILITIES
Small classes and excellent instructional facilities reinforce a highly personalized learning environment that encourages one-on-one interactions between students and Faculty. The success of this approach to business and management education is reflected in the excellent job placement record of Eberhardt School of Business graduates.

### EXPENSES AND FINANCIAL ASSISTANCE
The University of the Pacific was recently named by Kaplan/Newsweek as one of the top 10 regional universities with respect to Return on Student Investment.
Annual full-time expenses for the 2005–2006 MBA Program for all students, including international and out-of state students, are as follows:
Tuition: $24,060. Health Center Fee: $240. Student Union Activity and Service Fees: $190. International Travel Expenses: $2,500.
**Total Tuition and Fees**: $26,990
*Housing, textbooks and personal living costs are approximately $14,000 per year
From day one, financial assistance is available in the form of scholarships, graduate assistantships, and loans. We make it a point to make sure our high-achieving MBA students get the assistance they deserve upon entry into the Pacific MBA Program.
The Eberhardt School of Business offers several sources of merit-based assistance. Criteria for these awards include: academic record, test scores, potential contribution, and activities and achievements. Both domestic and international

students are eligible for awards. Assistance awarded may include a scholarship ($1,000 to $6,000), a graduate assistantship (approximately $8,000) or both. Additionally, those students with a minimum 3.25 undergraduate GPA and a 600 GMAT score will be considered for an Eberhardt MBA Scholars Assistantship (approximately $12,000).

### FACULTY
Graduating Pacific MBAs rank the quality and accessibility of the Faculty as one of the top reasons for their satisfaction in attending Pacific. The Eberhardt School of Business is committed to teaching excellence. Faculty research is viewed as a complement to the teaching mission and allows Faculty members to offer instruction that is relevant and current.
The MBA student/Faculty ratio is currently 7:1. This low ratio allows Faculty members to devote considerable time and effort to the personal and professional development of students.

### STUDENTS AND EXPERIENTIAL LEARNING OPPORTUNITIES
The Eberhardt School of Business is AACSB-accredited and is committed to the standards of high quality education and continuous improvement of programs. The school also understands that the classroom is not always the most effective place to learn the skills of successful management.
Students may choose from a wide variety of outside activities, including internships and student clubs and organizations, to further develop their leadership skills. Special opportunities for practical applications of graduate management concepts exist through the Center for Entrepreneurship, Invention Evaluation Service (IES), Institute for Family Business (IFB) and the Business Forecasting Center (BFC).
The Pacific MBA Program annually enrolls approximately 50 students; of this enrollment 42 percent are female and 21 percent are international. The average student is 25 years old with two years of work experience, a 590 GMAT score, and an average undergraduate GPA of 3.60.
About 45 percent of new enrollees possess undergraduate degrees in business, 30 percent in science or technical majors, 17 percent in liberal arts areas, and 7 percent in social sciences.
This diversity of academic, demographic and geographic backgrounds provides for a unique environment to develop teamwork and leadership skills.

### ADMISSIONS
The MBA Admissions Committee completes a personalized review of each application evaluating each individual's potential for a successful professional career. In addition to GPA, GMAT scores and recommendations, factors such as professional, managerial and leadership background are used as indicators of potential for career success.
**Preferred application dates:**
Priority: January 15
On-time: March 1
Applications are reviewed on a rolling basis in the order of receipt and completion. International students and individuals applying to dual-degree programs are encouraged to apply at least 3 months prior to preferred deadlines.

### CAREER SERVICES & PLACEMENT
The Pacific MBA Career Office is dedicated to providing the guidance and tools needed by students in today's economic climate. The ESB Director of Employer Development is committed to securing and developing long-lasting relationships with employers who offer opportunities in a diverse range of industries and business disciplines.
Students begin the process of launching their professional careers during orientation and continue year round with workshops, mock interview, on and off-campus recruiting events and internship opportunities. In addition to career-development workshops, students have an online application and job posting system available. This dedication to our students annually results in an exceptional placement rate for our graduates.

# THE UNIVERSITY OF PITTSBURGH
## *Joseph M. Katz Graduate School of Business*

## AT A GLANCE

The University of Pittsburgh's Joseph M. Katz Graduate School of Business is consistently ranked among the top 50 MBA programs in the United States. A number of factors contribute to this tradition of excellence, including a variety of MBA formats and degree offerings that fit most every need, small class sizes that allow students and Faculty to have substantial and meaningful interaction, a collaborative approach to learning that prepares students for the global workplace, a commitment to the highest standards in educating tomorrow's business leaders, and a staff that shares students' career goals, among many others.

The Katz School has long recognized the importance of globalization and is proud to be home to one of the first federally funded international business centers. Nearly 40 percent of Katz students hail from outside the United States, creating a diverse learning environment.

## CAMPUS AND LOCATION

The Katz School is located in the City of Pittsburgh's Oakland neighborhood. Home to three other institutions of higher education, world-class medical facilities, cultural attractions, eateries, and retail shops, the neighborhood is a lively area for graduate students.

Oakland is just minutes from Downtown Pittsburgh, which features a spectacular skyline, miles of waterfront trails for recreation, and a bustling cultural district. Pittsburgh has experienced a renaissance; the region is the nation's fourth largest corporate center and serves as the headquarters for companies such as H.J. Heinz Co., Mellon Financial Corporation, PPG Industries, Inc., and U.S. Steel, among many others.

## DEGREES OFFERED

The Katz School offers a variety of MBA formats to suit students' needs:

- Katz world-renowned One-Year MBA enables students to refine their management skills and quickly return to the work world. The Competency-Based Coaching Program helps students identify and enhance the skills and attributes necessary for success in their chosen career;

- Katz Two-Year MBA allows students the time to develop their skills in an intended discipline. The program includes a summer internship, the Competency-Based Coaching Program, and a host of electives from which students can design their curriculum;

- The Dual-Degree programs at the Katz School add focused learning in the disciplines of information science, biotechnology, marketing of engineered products, law, or international business to the MBA education. The Competency-Based Coaching Program and internship enhance students' skill development;

- The Katz Part-Time MBA Program allows students the flexibility to build on their undergraduate degree while continuing to pursue their career.

## AREAS OF INTEREST

Concentration areas within our program include: Accounting; Finance; Organizational Behavior & Human Resource Management; Management Information Systems; Marketing; Manufacturing/Operations Management; and Strategy/Environment and Organization.

## FACILITIES

Mervis Hall is home to the Katz School. The cornerstone of extensive renovations to Mervis Hall is the state-of-the-art PNC Team Technology Center—a full-service, self-contained, wired facility designed to educate MBA students in a team-learning environment. The center includes streamlined library facilities, conference rooms, and 18 MBA team meeting rooms.

## EXPENSES AND FINANCIAL AID

2005-2006 Academic Year Tuition and Fees (Full-Time MBA Program)

**Annual Tuition**

| | |
|---|---|
| Pennsylvania Residents | $28,322 |
| Non-residents | $44,419 |
| Professional Fees | $4,000 |
| University Fees | $1,160 |

**Total Tuition and Fees**

| | |
|---|---|
| Pennsylvania Residents | $33,482 |
| Non-residents | $49,579 |

Textbooks and living expenses amount to approximately $12,830 per year.

A number of financial aid options exist for qualified students. For more information about these options, visit www.katz.pitt.edu/mba_adm_aid.html and follow the link to "University Financial Aid office."

## FACULTY

Katz Faculty members are productive professionals who take pride in their scholarly work and use their expertise to enhance students' MBA experience. In 2003, Academic Assessment Services ranked the Katz Faculty first in research productivity in the discipline of management science. Faculty members also rank in the top 30 for research productivity in the disciplines of information systems, economics, organizational behavior, accounting, and strategy. Katz is proud to have among its Faculty the founding editor of the *Journal of Corporate Finance*, the editor of the *Journal of Management Account Research*, and associate editors of the primary accounting and finance journals, including *Accounting Review* and *Review of Financial Economics*.

## ADMISSIONS

Katz offers MBA students personal attention from their first visit to graduation day and beyond. Through the admissions process, officers strive to learn as much as possible about each applicant. To initiate the admissions process, visit www.katz.pitt.edu/apply.html and follow the links to the online application and deadlines. Applications are reviewed in rounds after each of four deadlines. For more information about the admissions process, financial aid, or visiting the facilities, visit the Katz Website, *www.katz.pitt.edu*.

## STUDENT ORGANIZATIONS AND ACTIVITIES

Personal, professional, and leadership development opportunities abound at the Katz School through student organizations and clubs, including the Entrepreneur's Society, the National Association of Women MBAs, and the Toastmasters Club. A complete list of student organizations and clubs is available at www.katz.pitt.edu/studentlife_pro.html.

## CAREER SERVICES & PLACEMENT

The Career Services Center (CSC) is committed to helping Katz students achieve their career goals. Each fall, CSC facilitates a one-credit workshop that helps job-seeking students define a career objective, develop a marketing plan for their career, present a personal portfolio, and sharpen their networking skills. The CSC stresses decisive action in the job search by encouraging participation in the on-campus recruiting process. In addition to coordinating on-campus interviews and job fairs, CSC provides opportunities for students to meet with Katz alumni and corporate contacts in selected major cities across the United States.

# UNIVERSITY OF SOUTH CAROLINA
## Moore School of Business

### AT A GLANCE

Moore School of Business is known for its expertise and experience in international business. Top-ranked in national and international surveys, Moore School's undergraduate and graduate programs offer students opportunities to learn and work in a global business environment.

The 3,100 undergraduate and 700 graduate students are taught by 109 full-time Faculty, including qualified full-time lecturers in specialty areas of business and technology. The school is housed in a modern nine-story building that contains offices, research labs and centers, classrooms, presentation and seminar rooms, television classrooms, computer labs, and a full business library.

### CAMPUS AND LOCATION

Moore School of Business has an urban campus with green space and gardens, historic buildings, and easy access to recreation and cultural events. With its location in the heart of Columbia, South Carolina' capital city, students can take advantage of water sports on the nearby rivers and lakes, hiking and skiing in the mountains, and fishing and sailing on the Atlantic Coast.

### ACADEMIC PROGRAMS

The school is noted for its innovative International Master of Business Administration (IMBA), which offers flexibility in curriculum and length of program. IMBA provides three options: Language Track with its emphasis on intensive language study, overseas internship, and geo-political studies; Global Track with a focus on the political, economic, and business factors affecting the investment climate of various regions throughout the world, and includes the international internship; and the IMBA European Program, an all-English-language, 15-month, partnership with Vienna's leading business school, the Wirtschaftsuniversität Wien.

Specialized master's degree programs provide additional options through the Master of Accountancy, Master of Human Resources, Professional MBA, and Master of Arts in Economics. These offer targeted programs with high placement rates for students with specific career goals. The school offers two doctoral degrees, the PhD in Business Administration and the PhD in Economics.

Moore School's international business specialty has been ranked number one or two for 17 consecutive years in *U.S. News & World Report's* survey of "America's Best Graduate Schools." *Latin Trade* has ranked Moore School number five in its 2005 "Best MBAs for Latin Americans". The school has also been well ranked recently in surveys in *BusinessWeek, Entreprenuer, Forbes*, and *The Economist*.

### EXPENSES AND FINANCIAL AID

A set program fee for each program in lieu of tuition and strong merit-based financial aid packages and work grants make Moore attractive to talented students.

IMBA Language and Global Track program fees are $16,000/year for SC residents, and $23,500/year for non-resident students. IMBA Vienna Program fee is $30,000 for either resident or non-resident.

The Darla Moore Fellowships award $10,000 per year for two years in the IMBA Language and Global Tracks, and $10,000 for the IMBA European Program. Other fellowships awarded range from $5,000 to $12,000 per year and are detailed on the Moore School's Web site.

Fee reductions are offered in conjunction with work grants and range from $5,000 to $20,000. Work grants pay $1,000 per semester for working 10 hours a week in the Moore School of Business.

### STUDENT BODY

Students in the IMBA program tend to be about 26–30 years old (28 years average), with two to seven years of work experience. Twenty-eight percent of the students are women, and 20 percent are foreign nationals. About 30 percent of the students have an undergraduate major of Business, but majors also include Economics, Engineering, International Studies, Political Science, Languages, and Liberal Arts. The diverse student population draws students from South America, Western and Eastern Europe, Asia, Africa, and Australia in addition to the U.S. population. IMBA students have an average GMAT of 630, and an average GPA of 3.35 for undergraduate studies.

### ADMISSIONS

GMAT scores, undergraduate GPA, work experience, and essays are the most important elements of a graduate application portfolio. Depending on the competitiveness of the program to which the student is applying, the GMAT should be between 550 and 680, the TOEFL has a minimum requirement of 600, and the undergraduate GPA should be about 3.0 or higher. Graduate programs prefer students with two or more years work experience. The application deadline for the IMBA is November 15 for best consideration and financial aid, with a second consideration February 15. (October 1 for IMBA Europe). Application may be made online (see http://mooreschool.sc.edu).

### ADMISSIONS CONTACT:

Ms. Reena Lichtenfeld, Director of Graduate Admissions and Enrollment Management

Moore School of Business, University of South Carolina, Columbia, SC 29208
Phone: 803-777-4346
Fax: 803-777-0414
E-mail: gradadmit@moore.sc.edu
Web: mooreschool.sc.edu

### CAREER SERVICES

The Graduate Career Management Office partners with students to achieve their career goals. A highly structured Professional Development Curriculum prepares students for their job search soon after they come to campus. The Birkman Method is used as an assessment instrument to advise students on programs of study, internship opportunities, and job search plans. In addition, Moore School of Business partners with Lee Hecht Harrison, a leading outplacement firm, to provide practical job search help.

More than 150 companies come to USC to recruit students each year. Top recruiters include Citigroup, General Motors, BB&T, BMW, Deloitte Consulting, and BellSouth. Students use online resume services and video conference facilities for contacts and interviews worldwide.

The placement rate of those for whom we have data averages 80 percent within three months of graduation with some programs having a consistent 100 percent placement rate within three months. The mean starting salary is in the $70,000 to $90,000 range depending on field.

# THE UNIVERSITY OF TAMPA
## *The John H. Sykes College of Business*

## AT A GLANCE

By exploring our graduate business program you've recognized that a leading twenty-first century enterprise requires rethinking of yourself and your career. Technological, environmental, demographic, and political changes are transforming the world, creating new demands for performance. Our goal is to provide you with perspective, skills, mentoring, and lots of opportunities for fully expressing your potential and meeting those demands.

The John H. Sykes College of Business is accredited by AACSB International—The Association to Advance Collegiate Schools of Business. The university is also accredited by the Southern Association of Colleges and Schools to award associate, baccalaureate, and master's degrees.

## CAMPUS & LOCATION

The University of Tampa is a medium-sized comprehensive, private university located on approximately 100 acres of prime riverfront land in the heart of downtown Tampa. It is the school of choice for more than 5,100 students from 50 states and U.S. territories and almost 100 countries.

## DEGREES OFFERED

**The John H. Sykes College of Business offers five graduate business programs:**

The MBA program has three formats: Full-Time Day, Part-Time Evening, and Saturday. Each requires between 42.5 and 51.5 credit hours to complete depending upon the applicant's undergraduate background. Full-Time Day MBA students can complete the entire program in as little as 16 months. MBA students in the Part-Time Evening program take approximately three years to complete their degree. The Saturday MBA program offers a convenient schedule for professionals with five years of work experience and can be completed in less than 2 years.

The Master of Science in Accounting (MSA) program prepares students for a professional career in accounting. Offering both full and part-time schedules, the MSA graduate degree program has been designed to satisfy the state of Florida's educational requirements for the Certified Public Accounting examination. The MSA requires 30 credit hours and students can complete the program in 20–30 months part-time and 12–20 months full-time.

The Master of Science in Finance (MS/FIN) program prepares students for careers in the ever-changing financial industry. The MS/FIN program requires completion of 32.5 credit hours and offers tracks in corporate management and investment management. Several courses have integrated the CFA curriculum as provided by CFA Institute and are based upon the Candidate Body of Knowledge (CBOK). Topics in these courses assist students in preparation for the CFA exam. Students can complete the program in 20–24 months part-time and 12–16 months full-time.

The Master of Science in Marketing (MS/MKT) integrates cutting-edge theory and application to prepare students for successful careers in marketing, considered by many to be the foundation of successful business. The MS/MKT program requires 30 credit hours and can be completed 20–24 months part-time and 12–16 months full-time.

The Master of Science in Innovation Management (MS/IM) program focuses on developing managers to lead the process of innovation in all types of business, and takes the global perspective necessary to compete successfully through technology innovation. The MS/IM is offered part-time in the evenings and requires 34 hour hours. Applicants must have five years of relevant work experience with two years in a management position.

## FACILITIES

When it comes to technology, the John H. Sykes College of Business is keeping pace! The 80,000-square-foot facility boasts more than 1,300 data ports for high-speed networking and access to several wireless areas.

The Macdonald-Kelce Library provides complete research and study aids in convenient, comfortable and quiet surroundings. UTOPIA, our online catalog provides Web access to library holdings and links to e-books and databases. Using E-Search, students can remotely access online databases such as Business Source Premier, ABI-INFORM, DISCLOSURE, and Investext.

The Vaughn Center is features a multi-cuisine dining facility, Barnes & Noble Campus Store, cyber café, game rooms, and computer labs.

Limited apartment-style rooms are available for graduate students in Straz Hall.

## EXPENSES & FINANCIAL AID

Tuition for 2006–2007 is $426 per credit hour. Saturday MBA 2006–2007 tuition is $535 per credit hour. The cost of student services fee, books, supplies, health insurance, parking, and personal expenses is additional.

UT graduate assistantships are available each academic year to selected full-time graduate students. Assistantships provide a tuition waiver for up to 9 credit hours per semester, plus a $1,500 stipend. Graduate assistants work 20 hours per week for an academic or administrative office, carry a full course load (at least 8 credit hours), and maintain a 3.0 overall GPA.

## FACULTY

All graduate Faculty members have PhDs. Many of our faculty members have won awards for teaching and professional excellence, owned their own businesses, and have helped lead and build major companies. Faculty members serve on boards and councils throughout the community. They've been quoted in *Fortune, Barron's*, The *Wall Street Journal*, and in dozens of local, national, and international media.

## STUDENTS

Students bring unique cultural practices and perspectives on business, providing an environment in which alternative ideas and ways of thinking are freely exchanged. When international students graduate, they take with them cutting-edge business practices and techniques that make them successful wherever they go. The cultural and educational exchanges that occur at UT provide a perfect training ground for both international and U.S. students.

## ADMISSIONS

Admission to UT's graduate business program is competitive and is based on a number of factors. Individual interviews are recommended but required for MS-IM. All students admitted must have earned four-year undergraduate degrees from a regionally accredited college or university. A specific undergraduate degree is not required. The GMAT is required but may be waived for the Saturday MBA, MS in Finance, MS in Marketing and MS in Innovation Management programs depending upon the applicant's academic background and work experience. International students are required to submit a TOEFL score report.

## CAREER SERVICES & PLACEMENT

Graduate students can expect individualized attention from the professional staff of the Career Services Center. Typical graduate services include resume critique, design and referral, personal career advising, interview skills refreshers, on-campus company interview opportunities, and informational interviews with other professionals from the greater Tampa Bay area.

# THE UNIVERSITY OF TEXAS AT DALLAS
## *School of Management*

### THE COLLEGE AT GLANCE

Founded in 1972, we are a young school that has enjoyed rapid growth and is quickly gaining national and international visibility. With a student body of nearly 4,700—half at the graduate level, our enrollments have more than doubled in the last ten years. We consider this exceptional growth in enrollment to be recognition of the excellence of our faculty and the leading-edge programs we offer. With our sights set on becoming one of the nation's leading public business schools, the high quality, research-focused scholastic environment we have created offers courses and skill sets in line with the hiring needs of today's employers. We often partner with the business community for input that keeps our offerings and research relevant, ensuring that we stay in tune with the needs of employers. Further assuring that our students receive a top-quality business education, we are fully accredited with the AACSB International, The Association to Advance Collegiate Schools of Business.

### LOCATION AND ENVIRONMENT

Dallas is ranked as the nation's second-strongest metropolitan area for high-tech industry and sixth in economic output. The University of Texas at Dallas, which enrolls nearly 15,000 students, is located in the heart of the city's globally connected Telecom Corridor, with nearly 900 companies located within a five-mile radius of our campus. Our freshman class traditionally stands at the forefront of Texas state universities in terms of average SAT scores. The university offers a broad assortment of bachelor's, master's and doctoral degree programs.

### MAJORS AND DEGREES OFFERED

We offer a full complement of bachelor's, master's, and PhD degrees. On the undergraduate level, we offer Bachelor of Science degrees in Accounting and Information Management, Finance, and Business Administration. On the graduate level, we offer the Master of Business Administration (MBA), the Master of Arts in International Management, and the Master of Science in Accounting and Information Management, as well as master of science degrees in various concentration areas.

The 53-credit-hour part-time MBA is our largest program. Our part-time MBA is offered in daytime, evening, and online classes and caters primarily to students who work full-time. We also offer a lockstep day-format Cohort MBA program, which students complete in three semesters. Both the MA and MS programs require 36 hours of study, with classes offered on both a part-time and full-time basis. Classes, primarily at night, allow the student to specialize in accounting and information management, international management, decision sciences, entrepreneurship, finance, managerial economics, marketing, and organization strategies. We also offer a full complement of executive education programs including an executive MBA that is offered both on campus and online and executive master's degree plans concentrating in international management, project management, and medical management.

Our Ph.D. program is distinguished by its emphasis on interdisciplinary research, providing rigorous training in theoretical and empirical skills applied to problems faced by managers. Students work closely with internationally renowned Faculty members to address questions at the leading edge of their field. Research supervision is available in accounting and information management, finance and economics, information systems, marketing, operations research and organizations, and strategy and international management. Students entering the PhD program are provided financial aid in the form of teaching or research assistantships. We offer PhD degrees in international management studies, management science, and accounting and information management.

### FACILITIES AND EQUIPMENT

Our school occupies a 204,000-square-foot state-of-the-art facility, completed in 2003 and designed to offer the latest technologies in the delivery of management education. The UTD School of Management Building contains 29 classrooms with internet access at every desk, as well as the latest audiovisual and online learning support. The building also features two large computer labs, a 350-seat auditorium, conference rooms, break-out rooms, and lounges. There is wireless network access throughout the campus. Classes are designed to equip students with timeless business skills and proficiencies while emphasizing the mastery of managerial concepts, tools and innovations that are born of the newest technologies. The school has been a leader in Internet-based distance learning and in offering flexible alternatives for students to pursue their educational objectives. Certificate, online, part-time, short-course and weekend options are built into many programs.

### FACULTY

Our faculty—one of our greatest assets—is earning an international reputation for its research excellence. *Financial Times* ranks the research productivity of the SOM Faculty thirty-second worldwide, based on publication of research studies in a set of 40 academic journals. Based on publications in the top 24 business journals spanning all areas of business, the school's Faculty ranks thirty-third in research productivity among business school faculties nationwide. Many of the school's full time Faculty of 101, which includes 26 full professors, are internationally renowned in their fields.

### TUITION, FEES, AND HOUSING

Tuition and fees are billed per semester hour depending on course load. A full-time Texas resident undergraduate student carrying 12 hours pays tuition of $3,350; a non-Texas resident undergraduate student carrying 12 hours pays $6,650. For graduate students, a full-time Texas resident carrying 12 hours pays $3,550; a non-Texas resident carrying 12 hours pays $6,850.

UTD has many affordable housing options near its campus in the Dallas suburbs of Richardson and Plano. The Waterview Park Apartments, run by a private company, are available on campus and are approved student residences.

### FINANCIAL AID

The UTD School of Management Committee awards a variety of scholarships and fellowships each fall. Applications are available from the university's office of financial aid, and more information is available at *http://financial-aid.utdallas.edu*. Information on the School of Management's scholarship program is available on our website, *http://som.utdallas.edu/advising*.

### ADMISSIONS PROCESSES AND REQUIREMENTS

Applicants are evaluated based on their personal qualities and academic backgrounds. Personal interviews are not required. Full application information and forms are available at *http://som.utdallas.edu/advising*.

# UNIVERSITY OF WASHINGTON
## Business School, MBA Program, Two-year, Full-time

## AT A GLANCE

More choices. Key connections. A future you define. University of Washington MBA students are immersed in one of the most innovative MBA experiences in the world, built to deliver a personalized education for a career path each student defines for themselves with extensive input. Students begin with first year integrated curriculum that includes tailored development of communication and leadership skills and opportunities for international study and hands-on learning. By doing projects during the school year and internships either with local companies like Microsoft, Amazon.com, and Starbucks, or in places like Thailand or Boston, students connect often with the business community. A unique, individualized approach to career services, a renowned mentor program, and access to 40,000 alumni worldwide provide students with the unparalleled educational flexibility and customized career resources that now distinguish the University of Washington MBA program.

## MBA CURRICULUM

In the first year, the UW MBA program focuses on an integrated study of major business functions — fundamentals in accounting, finance, marketing, ethics, operations management and information systems are woven into modules of varying length. In the spring quarter of year one, students select bridge electives to gain exposure to topics available in year two and develop skills that can be applied in optional summer internships. Year two presents an open-ended opportunity to individualize the program of study. Students can follow a traditional concentration with courses across eleven disciplines or customize a concentration of classes.

## STUDENT BODY

Collaborative learning is enhanced by bringing together people from different backgrounds with experiences and skills who can both teach and learn from each other. The student population at Washington is among the most diverse of all MBA programs in terms of geographic origin, age, background, and career interest. Each MBA class of roughly 100 students is a mix of people with undergraduate degrees in liberal arts, business, engineering, and science. Students range in age from 22 to 45 and have from zero to 15 years of work experience. They come from 30 different industries, from 27 states and from 19 countries. Recent GMAT scores of admitted students ranged from 560 to 780 and GPAs ranged from 2.2 to 4.0.

## FACULTY

The UW Business School philosophy emphasizes a partnership between students and Faculty members. Professors at the UW Business School have achieved recognition for both teaching and research. MBAs praise the Faculty's active involvement in student learning and their integration of research and teaching. Professors take a personal interest in their students and, in return, they demand a high level of student effort and commitment.

## MBA ADMISSIONS

The UW Business School believes that personal connections are essential to business education, just as they are to business. Advance counseling is strongly advised for anyone considering an MBA program. The MBA program encourages campus visits to meet face-to-face with admissions staff or attend a reception held in cities nationwide. If you are unable to visit in person, we encourage you to carefully study our website and make email or telephone connections with our admissions staff and current students.

The UW MBA Program seeks self-motivated men and women who will play a very active role in both their MBA education and in their career search. This is not the school for a passive person hoping an education and job will happen just by being here. The admissions team assesses each candidate's academic record, language capability, work and extra curricular experience, ability to work with others, leadership, professionalism, and the ability to clearly articulate personal career objectives.

**Applicants must:**

- Complete the equivalent of a four-year U.S. bachelor's degree from an accredited college or university

- Meet a general quantitative analysis requirement assessed by looking at each student's academic record, test scores, and work record

- Possess a necessary level of English language skills

- Take the GMAT

- Apply to each school, college, or department of interest if pursuing a dual degree

## MBA APPLICATION DEADLINES

- First deadline: 15 November
- Second deadline: 15 January°
- Third deadline: 15 March
- Start date: mid-September

°Final deadline for international students and all applicants wanting to be considered for Business School scholarships. For current admissions information visit www.mba.washington.edu.

## MBA FEES

The UW Business School MBA program offers a very good value. Out of state tuition is $8,600 per quarter; and Washington residents pay $5,500. Other annual expenses are estimated at about $17,241. Here is a breakdown:

- Room and board: $10,338
- Books, computers, and supplies: $3,000
- Local transportation: $1,260
- Personal expenses: $2,253
- MBA Association dues (for two years): $190
- MBA Club dues: $200

# UNIVERSITY OF WASHINGTON
## Business School, Global MBA Program, One-year, Full-time

### AT A GLANCE
The Global MBA Program offers an accelerated one-year program option for professionals with international business experience and an undergraduate education that includes extensive business and economics coursework. The Global MBA Program draws students from every part of the world who are looking to build on their knowledge and experience to accelerate their careers and to gain a comprehensive view of global business. The compressed structure of the program is especially suited to applicants who already have a clearly focused career goal and a plan for pursuing it when they enter. The program is designed to serve students primarily focused on employment opportunities that will take them outside the United States during their career, though they might begin their post-MBA careers with a position in the United States.

### GMBA CURRICULUM
The four-quarter program begins in June with an accelerated summer MBA core curriculum, followed by a two-week international study tour. The students then complete three academic quarters of coursework, including studies in cross-cultural communication, ethics, and corporate governance, as well as an optional course in US business practice. Ten elective courses, including two in global business, round out the curriculum. Elective courses from departments outside the Business School may be included in the student's program of study.

### GMBA ADMISSIONS
Successful applicants will have earned an undergraduate degree with extensive coursework in business administration or economics and have at least two years of international business experience. By design, the program seeks a diverse mix of students from many regions of the world with work experience in a wide range of industries.

**Applicants must:**

- Complete the equivalent of a four-year US bachelor's degree with extensive coursework in business administration or economics from an accredited college or university

- Meet a general quantitative analysis requirement assessed by looking at each student's academic record, test scores, and work record

- Possess a necessary level of English language skills

- Take the GMAT

- Apply to each school, college, or department of interest if pursuing a dual degree

### GMBA APPLICATION DEADLINES
Deadline to apply for summer 2007 is 15 December 2006. For current admissions information visit www.globalmba.washington.edu.

### GMBA FEES
For admissions fees visit www.globalmba.washington.edu.

### LOCATION
Seattle, WA—where Pacific Rim business opportunities meet Pacific Northwest quality of life. The region's dynamic economy is a hotbed for business development across industrial sectors and an ideal laboratory for real-world practice.

### UNIVERSITY OF WASHINGTON
Since 1975, the university has ranked first among public institutions in the number of federal grants and contracts awarded to its Faculty members. Its sixteen schools and colleges provide education to 34,000 students, who can choose from more than 100 academic disciplines and 5,000 courses. The UW achieves international recognition in both teaching and research.

### DEGREES OFFERED
The UW Business School offers an undergraduate degree and a full range of graduate degrees. Offerings include:

- BA
- MBA
- Evening MBA
- Executive MBA
- Global MBA
- Technology Management MBA
- Master of Professional Accounting
- PhD

### FINANCIAL AID
Financial aid is available from the University of Washington and the UW Business School in the form of loans, work-study, scholarships, and academic employment. All admitted applicants are considered for merit-based scholarships. Once admitted, students may also apply for other business school scholarships. Domestic applicants may obtain federal loan application forms at http://www.fafsa.ed.gov. Visit the UW Office of Student Financial Aid at http://www.washington.edu/students/osfa/ for more information. No scholarship funding is available for the Global MBA Program.

### CONTACT
UW Business School
110 Mackenzie Hall, Box 353200
Seattle, Washington 98195-3200, U.S.A.
Toll-free (in US): 866-778-9622
Tel: 206-543-4661
Fax: 206-616-7351
MBA Program
E-mail: mba@u.washington.edu
www.mba.washington.edu
Global MBA Program
E-mail: gmba@u.washington.edu
www.globalmba.washington.edu

# VANDERBILT UNIVERSITY
## Owen Graduate School of Management

**V VANDERBILT**
Owen Graduate School of Management

## AT A GLANCE

The Vanderbilt Owen Graduate School of Management is dedicated to setting a new standard in business education. Owen stands apart among leading business schools in providing a rigorous, relevant education that fully prepares graduates for their roles as the ethical leaders of tomorrow—persons who will shape their worlds and our future.

The Vanderbilt MBA program offers an intimate, collaborative environment in which individuals are encouraged to fulfill their potential. The Vanderbilt MBA program is world-class, known internationally for its finance program, as well as one of the strongest human and organizational performance programs in the country.

## OUR PROMISE

To students: Here is a place where you'll be challenged to achieve your potential, where you'll find support as you shape your future, discover lifelong friends and mentors, and open doors to new possibilities.

To faculty and staff: Here is a place where you can engage, think, reach, teach, influence people, and transform the world around you.

To business: Here is a place where you will find the men and women who have the skills, the drive, and the determination to move your organization forward.

To alumni: Here is a place that you can call home, where you can build business relationships and inspire those who follow to reach even higher.

## CAMPUS AND LOCATION

Nashville is one of the Southeast's most vibrant and livable cities, featuring excellent restaurants, music venues, sporting events, museums, historic sites, mild weather, and a dynamic business climate.

Vanderbilt University was founded in 1873 and enrolls more than 11,000 undergraduate and graduate students throughout its 10 schools. Vanderbilt is located a mile and a half from downtown Nashville on a park-like campus that was designated a national arboretum in 1988.

Vanderbilt Owen Graduate School of Management opened its doors in 1969 to ten students and ten faculty members. Today, as one of the world's leading business schools, Owen retains one of the nation's best student/faculty ratios of 10:1. Owen is known for a spirit of teamwork, challenging academics, and a stimulating research environment.

## DEGREES OFFERED

Owen offers MBA, executive MBA, MS finance, and PhD degrees, as well as dual degree programs that allow multidisciplinary study in management and another graduate or professional program such as law or medicine.

## ACADEMIC PROGRAMS

All Owen full-time MBA students start with the required courses in "the core"—an intense immersion in the fundamentals of management. Students are required to specify a primary area of concentration in accounting, finance, general management, human and organizational performance, information technology, marketing, operations, or strategy. Students may also pursue an emphasis in brand management, entrepreneurship, environmental management, or international business.

In 2005, Owen launched an MBA degree with a health care specialization, a groundbreaking program that combines the core business education with real-world health care experience. The school also offers a law and business program, which gives students an opportunity to take interdisciplinary courses at Vanderbilt Law School. The executive MBA program meets on alternate weekends over 21 months, and provides the knowledge and the credentials for mid-career managers and executives to succeed in today's dynamic business environment.

The Vanderbilt master of science in finance degree (MSF) is a nine-month intensive program offering an advanced business degree in quantitative financial analysis.

## FACILITIES

The Walker Management Library, ranked by The Princeton Review as the #1 b-school library in the U.S., provides world-class research support for students and faculty.

## EXPENSES AND FINANCIAL AID

**Tuition:**
Full-time MBA (2 years): $33,830 per year (2005–2006)
Executive MBA (2 years): $38,450 per year (all-inclusive: books, fees, etc.)
MS finance (1 year): $33,830 per year (2005–2006)

All admitted applicants are considered for merit-based scholarships. Approximately 51 percent of admitted students are offered scholarships, and the average award is $13,423. U.S. citizens and permanent residents are eligible to apply for Federal Stafford Loans and private loan programs. International students may apply for private loans with a U.S. citizen or permanent resident as a co-signer.

## FACULTY

Owen faculty members have made an impact on NASDAQ, founded the world's first academic research center dedicated to the study of e-commerce and the Internet, and contributed to advances in many other areas of global business. To shape innovative business managers and insightful leaders, professors combine lectures, discussions, case studies, and group projects with experiential learning opportunities in the business community.

## STUDENT BODY

Students come from a wide variety of academic, professional, and personal backgrounds, and from nearly 40 countries. In this tight-knit community, you will find a unique, collegial culture in which students truly flourish, working closely with each other and with faculty, alumni, and the business community to meet and exceed their personal and professional goals. Students share a passion to achieve their goals by working hard, accepting new challenges, and supporting each other through teamwork in the classroom and beyond.

## ADMISSIONS

The Admissions Committee evaluates applicants on the basis of academic ability, professional experience, personal qualities, and leadership potential. Applicants offered admission average a 3.3 GPA, 652 GMAT, and five years of post-baccalaureate work experience. http://admissions.owen.edu.

## SPECIAL PROGRAMS

Owen hosts information sessions, receptions, and on-campus weekend events, and participates in major recruiting events around the world. We encourage visits to campus, especially when classes are in session.

## CAREER SERVICES & PLACEMENT

Owen offers a highly personal approach to career management, ensuring that each student receives individual attention and access to the knowledge, resources, and guidance required to accomplish their career goals. The Career Management Center supports students with counseling, negotiation assistance, industry seminars, on-campus interviews, recruiter feedback, networking trips, and more.

Salaries for Vanderbilt MBAs are highly competitive with other top business schools. The rigorous curriculum, extensive recruiting contacts, global alumni network, and reputation for creating well-rounded managers help propel graduates into successful careers in many different industries, functional areas, and geographic regions. Plus, the relationships built at Owen will support and enhance your career opportunities for years to come.

# VIRGINIA COMMONWEALTH UNIVERSITY
## *Graduate Studies in Business*

## AT A GLANCE

Virginia Commonwealth University (VCU) is a public research institution with an enrollment of approximately 29,000 students on two campuses in the capital city of Richmond, Virginia.

School of Business Highlights

The School of Business is located on VCU's Monroe Park campus in Richmond's historic Fan District. It employs 100 full-time faulty and enrolls more than 2,100 undergraduate and 480 graduate students. Students receive instruction primarily from graduate Faculty, over 95 percent of whom hold a doctorate or equivalent professional degree.

The School of Business is accredited by the AACSB-The International Association for Management Education. This level of accreditation is granted to fewer than 10 percent of institutions that offer business degrees. The VCU School of Business is an integral part of the Richmond business community. Students regularly participate in local internships and workshops, and are heavily recruited by local companies.

## DEGREES OFFERED

Master of Business Administration

Master of Science in Business (concentrations): Finance, Decision Sciences, Global Marketing Management, Real Estate Valuation, Master of Accountancy, Master of Arts in Economics, Master of Science in Information Systems, Master of Taxation

Dual Degrees: MBA/PharmD, MBA/MSIS

Doctor of Philosophy in Business with the following concentrations: Information Systems, Accounting, Management

## ACADEMIC PROGRAMS

The Master of Business Administration (MBA) focuses on the development of functions and techniques of management, as well as an understanding of environmental and economic forces that influence administration and decision making. The program consists of seven foundation courses, eight advanced courses, and three electives.

## FACILITIES

The School of Business is currently housed in the VCU Business Building, a facility that offers state-of-the-art technology classrooms, computer facilities, and team meeting rooms.

A new School of Business building is under construction, due to be completed for the Fall 2007 semester. This new building will include a central atrium/student commons, trading room, career services center, corporate education center, and terraced courtyards.

## EXPENSES AND FINANCIAL AID

For the 2005–2006 academic year, in-state tuition and fees for full-time students were $3875.50 per semester. Out-of-state tuition and fees for full-time students totaled $8,703 per semester. In-state tuition rates for part-time students were set at $405.25 per credit hour. Out-of-state part-time students paid $940.40 per credit hour.

A limited number of master's assistantships are available for full-time master's-level students with exemplary academic credentials.

## FACULTY

Many of the 102 Faculty members have been recognized nationally for their teaching effectiveness, research contributions, and service to professional organizations. Faculty members are best known for their contributions in information systems, financial research, global marketing management, and international business activities.

## STUDENT BODY

Approximately 500 students are currently enrolled in the master's and doctoral programs of VCU's School of Business. Women make up 40 percent of the graduate student population, and students have an average of six years of work experience beyond their undergraduate degrees. Students may pursue the program on a full or part-time basis.

## ADMISSIONS

Application requirements:
- Application for admission
- Two copies of official transcripts from each university or college previously attended
- Three letters of recommendation
- Current resume
- A personal statement
- Current GMAT score (for all programs except MA in Economics which requires the GRE)

Application procedures vary slightly by degree program. Please contact Graduate Studies in Business for more detailed guidelines for your desired program.

## SPECIAL PROGRAMS

The Master of Science in Business curriculum offers much more focused study in a particular area of business.

**Decision Sciences** provides students with quantitative skills and experience in analyzing problems arising in a business environment.

**Finance** provides a comprehensive education in financial management investments and security analysis, international finance funds management, and derivatives.

**Global Marketing Management** offers students the opportunity to concentrate their studies in international marketing and contemporary issues in marketing management.

**Information Systems** offers a distinct focus on enterprise systems and provides students hands-on experience.

**Real Estate Valuation** is one of only eight programs in the United States that satisfies the rigorous educational requirements of the Appraisal Institute's MAI designation.

In addition, the School of Business offers degree programs leading to the Master of Accountancy, Master of Arts in Economics, Master of Taxation, and Doctor of Philosophy in Business. The Master of Arts degree in Economics is designed to provide the necessary applied quantitative background for positions in the private and government sectors.

The Master of Taxation program offers existing tax professionals the opportunity to update and expand existing tax knowledge, while also offering entry-level students training in the field of taxation.

The Master of Accountancy program offers students a specialization in Finance, Information Systems, and Managerial and Systems Controllership. The Doctor of Philosophy (PhD) program prepares individuals for Faculty positions at colleges and universities that stress both research and teaching. PhD students select one area of concentration and one minor area of study. Students can concentrate in Accounting, Information Systems, or Management.

## ADDITIONAL INFORMATION

Relationships developed through the university's Business Council serve as a pathway to business by providing more than 150 internship opportunities annually to students in School of Business programs.

The Alumni Council, the leadership group for the School's 14,000 alumni, provides advice and assistance for various activities throughout the year. The Alumni Council sponsors special events, education series, and recruitment activities for School of Business students annually.

## CAREER SERVICES & PLACEMENT

Students have access to a career counselor throughout their program. The career center maintains an active job bank and assists students in resume and interview preparation.

# WASHINGTON UNIVERSITY IN ST. LOUIS
## *Olin School of Business*

## AT A GLANCE
At Olin, you'll find a supportive community where each person's interests and ideas make a difference. With approximately 130 MBA students in a class, you are assured of receiving individual attention from our Faculty and staff. And it's likely that you'll get to know our dean, Mahendra Gupta.

Olin's curriculum is based on the understanding that no two students are identical; therefore no single, prescribed curriculum is expected to meet everyone's needs. That's what makes the Olin curriculum different: it's flexible, it's based on a relatively small set of required classes and a large number of electives, and it acknowledges students' individual strengths and career aspirations.

Experiential learning is an important element in your learning strategy. We offer a broad and innovative menu of hands-on learning opportunities that enable you to apply your classroom knowledge to real-life business situations. These programs help you develop confidence in your leadership ability, gain consulting experience, and hone your communication and teamwork skills.

For more information on the Olin experience at Washington University in St. Louis, visit our website at: www.olin.wustl.edu

## CAMPUS AND LOCATION
Founded in 1853, Washington University is recognized among the Top 20 universities in the United States, according to *U.S. News & World Report*. The university is located in a picturesque suburban setting and is within walking distance of Forest Park. The Hilltop Campus, where Olin is situated, is seven miles west of the Mississippi Riverfront and the St. Louis Arch. Learning takes place in the supportive, comfortable atmosphere of a small college with the resources and amenities of a larger university. St. Louis is a thriving metropolitan center with notable art galleries, museums, theatre, sporting events, and bustling ethnic neighborhoods. It is home to a dynamic corporate community that fosters projects, internships, and mentoring programs for Olin MBAs.

## ACADEMICS
Olin offers one of the most flexible curriculums among nationally ranked full-time MBA programs. Required courses comprise just one-third of the program. In fact, at the conclusion of the fall semester of your first year, you'll have completed all but two courses of the required core curriculum. You determine the academic content of the remaining two-thirds of the program-choosing concentrations and electives suited to your needs, your interests, and your career goals. Areas of concentration include: Accounting; Entrepreneurship; Finance; General Business; International Business; Marketing; Operations Management and Technology; and Strategy/Consulting.

In cooperation with other Washington University schools, Olin offers MBA students the option of concurrently earning a second graduate degree. This dual degree option is available in the areas of: Architecture; Biomedical Engineering; East Asian Studies; Health Administration; Law; and Social Work.

## STUDENT BODY
The full-time MBA program enrolls approximately 130 new students each year. They have diverse undergraduate backgrounds ranging from business and the humanities to engineering and the sciences. The diversity of the class is further enhanced by the wide range of work experiences our students have had and by the fact that our students come from throughout the country and around the world. Upon arrival, students have the opportunity to participate in one or more of Olin's 24 student organizations. These organizations allow students to further expand their professional network and hone leadership skills.

## ADMISSIONS
Admission to Olin is selective. The Olin Admissions Committee reviews applications based on a series of four deadlines with the earliest falling in mid-November. Qualified full-time MBA students are admitted to start in the fall semester only. The committee reviews all information in the application to determine a candidate's ability to perform in an intensely rigorous academic environment. The committee also seeks to identify students who will add significantly to the academic, cultural, and social character of the School. Prospective students may submit an Olin application in hard copy using the .pdf on our website or online through Embark. Qualified underrepresented minority applicants who apply to Olin through the Consortium for Graduate Study in Management (www.cgsm.org) adhere to those deadlines and material requirements and do not submit a regular application. The committee also requires a current GMAT score (less than five years old), results of the TOEFL exam (if applicable), official transcripts from each university previously attended, work history forms, essays, a résumé, and two letters of recommendation. Interviews are strongly encouraged.

## CAREER SERVICES & PLACEMENT
Through an aggressive program targeting the needs of students and employers, Olin's Weston Career Center (WCC) actively assists all MBA students in developing and sustaining their self-managed career goals. The center boasts a highly successful recruiting record that is attributable to extensive student involvement, a vital alumni network, cutting-edge information systems, and dynamic corporate partnerships. Over 150 companies request interviews and hire Olin students each year. In addition to sponsoring several road shows (student-organized visits to targeted regions and companies), the WCRC also participates in "Managing Your Career Strategy," a required course for first-year MBAs and provides workshops on job search techniques, interviewing, and salary negotiation.

## EXPENSES AND FINANCIAL AID
All applicants are considered for merit-based scholarships; there is no separate application process for these awards. In addition, financial aid in the form of loans is available to all students. For more information on loans and for updated program costs, please visit our website.

## DEGREES OFFERED
BSBA
MSBA
MBA (full-time)
MBA through Professional MBA program (part-time/evening)
MS Finance (full-time, 1yr)
Master's of Accounting (length varies on background)
Executive degree programs
PhD

# WILLAMETTE UNIVERSITY
## Atkinson Graduate School of Management

### THE SCHOOL AT A GLANCE
Willamette University's MBA programs build the knowledge and real-world experience needed for career entry, change, or advancement. The power of a Willamette MBA is personified by the careers of alumni who are achieving success in business, consulting, government and not-for-profit organizations. The Willamette MBA is accredited by AACSB International, and has been profiled as one of the best business schools by *BusinessWeek*, *U.S. News & World Report*, Princeton Review, Vault.com, and *Beyond Grey Pinstripes*.

### CAMPUS AND LOCATION
Willamette University is located in Salem, Oregon. Willamette's Portland Center is located in the Pearl District of Portland, Oregon; one of the fastest growing cities for highly educated people between the ages of 25 and 34.

Salem and Portland offer an excellent quality of life, friendly people, mild climate and quick access to the resources of the wonderful Pacific Northwest. Professionally, the area is home to a multitude of businesses (including Northwest legends Nike, Intel, and Tektronix) and hosts a variety of government and nonprofit organizations. Seventy percent of alumni choose to stay in the Pacific Northwest after graduation.

### DEGREE OFFERED
Willamette offers the Master of Business Administration degree, and is one of only 46 AACSB accredited programs in the world that focuses on the graduate level of education.

### ACADEMIC PROGRAMS
A selection of MBA formats is available.
- Full-time MBA – 21 month Full-Time MBA: builds the knowledge and real-world experience needed for career entry or change, and is dually accredited for business (AACSB International) and public administration (NASPAA). Areas of interest include: Accounting, Finance, General Management, Human Resources, Information Systems, International Management, Marketing, Organizational Analysis, Public Management, and Quantitative Analysis.
- Professional MBA: 24 month program for working professionals with three or more years of experience. Courses are taught in the evening. Students develop an enterprise wide view of management, immediately apply what they learn to their work place, and complete their MBA while employed.
- Accelerated MBA: 12 to 15 month program for students seeking career change or advancement who have strong knowledge of business and professional work experience. Accelerated students focus their studies in their career area of interest.
- MBA/JD: four year joint degree that combines Willamette's MBA and Doctor of Jurisprudence programs.

### FACILITIES
Classrooms are spacious and modern. Students have wireless access to the Internet, email and network software and printing services. A laptop computer with wireless LAN capability and a standard suite of software is required.

The campus in Salem includes two libraries, state-of-the art classrooms, recreational and fitness facilities, dining centers, a student center, a concert hall, an art museum, student apartments, and more. The Portland Center is conveniently located in the Pearl District with easy access to the MAX train, other public transportation and public parking.

### TUITION
Tuition for MBA students for the 2005–2006 academic year is $10,800 per semester, or $21,600 for the two semester academic year. Tuition for Professional MBA students for the 2005–2006 academic year is $6,000 per semester, or $18,000 for the three semester academic year. The cost of textbooks is included in the PMBA tuition rate.

### FINANCIAL AID
Merit-based scholarships, Federal Stafford Loans, and private educational loans and graduate assistantships are available to eligible students.

### FACULTY
Faculty are excellent teachers who are committed to their students and to the educational model of "'learning by doing." They are also leaders of community and professional organizations; authors of books, articles, and software; editors and reviewers of professional journals; entrepreneurs; and consultants. They make Willamette an exciting place to learn.

### STUDENTS
"Dedicated, creative, ethical, exceptional, friendly, hard working, leader, professional, respected, team player," are word references used to describe Willamette MBA students. Our students come from around the world and throughout the U.S. to prepare for the next step in their career, and they represent a diversity of experience and age common in organizations. Some have academic backgrounds in liberal arts and sciences, while others have a background in business or engineering. Some are pursuing careers as managers of large corporations. Others are seeking opportunities in small business, entrepreneurial ventures, government or nonprofit agencies. 40 percent of the students are women; 60 percent are men. 28 percent are international students.

### ADMISSIONS
Applicants are evaluated on an individual basis. All applicants must submit the application for admission, official GMAT score, official copies of all college/university transcripts, two references and essays. International applicants must also submit financial documents required for an I-20, a photocopy of the name page of their passport, and a TOEFL score of 230 or higher.

Work experience is not required for the Full-Time MBA; it is specifically designed to build the knowledge and work experience employers value. Applicants for the Professional MBA and Accelerated programs must meet work experience requirements.

For more information, contact:

Admission Office
Willamette University Atkinson Graduate School of Management
Telephone Toll Free: 1-866-MBA-AGSM
E-mail: *mba-admission@willamette.edu* or pmba
Web: *www.willamette.edu/mba*

### CAREER SERVICES & PLACEMENT
Career services include an organized program of the best practices of career management, workshops, internship programs, on-campus interviews, employment postings, databases, individual counseling, mentoring programs, career/networking fairs, and student professional organizations.

94 percent of 2005 graduates received a job offer within three months of graduation. A sample of employers includes Adidas America, Brighton Jones, Hewlett Packard Company, Intel Corporation, Northwestern Mutual Financial, Providence Health Systems, and United Nations

100 percent of students seeking an internship participated in an internship. A sample of employers includes Columbia Sportswear, Merrill Lynch, Microsoft, Morgan Stanley, Nike, Oregon Zoo, Saber Consulting, Spacekraft, T-Mobile, Tektronix, U.S. State Department, and State of Oregon.

# DECODING DEGREES

Many business programs offer a number of degrees, including joint or combined degree programs with other departments (or with other schools) that you can earn along with your MBA. You'll find the abbreviations for these degrees in the individual school profiles, but we thought we'd give you a little help in figuring out exactly what they are.

| | | | |
|---|---|---|---|
| AGSIM | American Graduate School of International Management | IMBA | International MBA |
| AM | Social Service Administration | IPD | Interdisciplinary Product Development |
| APC | Advanced Professional Certificate | JD | Juris Doctorate |
| BA | Bachelor of Arts | LLB | Bachelor of Law |
| BASC | Bachelor in Engineering | MA | Master of Arts |
| BBA | Bachelor of Business Administration | MAB | Master of Agribusiness |
| BPA | Bachelor of Public Affairs | MAcC | Master of Accountancy (or Accounting) |
| BS | Bachelor of Science | MAAE | Master of Arts in Applied Economics |
| BSB | Bachelor of Science in Business | MAEcON | Master of Arts in Economics |
| BSBA | Bachelor of Science in Business Administration | MAg | Master of Agriculture |
| CIS | Computer Information Systems (or Sciences) | MAIB | Master of Arts in International Business |
| | | MAIS | Master of Accounting and Information Systems |
| DBA | Doctor of Business Administration | MALL | Master of Arts in Language Learning |
| DDS | Doctor of Dental Surgery | MAPS | Master of Asian Pacific Studies |
| DMD | Doctor of Dental Medicine | MAR | Master of Arts in Religion |
| DO | Doctor of Osteopathic Medicine | MArch | Master of Architecture |
| DPS | Doctor of Professional Studies | MAS | Master of Actuarial Science |
| EdD | Doctor of Education | MBA | Master of Business Administration |
| EDM | Executive Doctor of Management | MBE | Master of Business Education |
| EMBA | Executive MBA | MBI | Master of Business Informatics |
| EMIB | Executive Master of International Business | MBS | Master of Business Studies |
| EMPA | Executive Master of Public Administration | MD | Doctor of Medicine |
| EMS | Executive Master of Science | MDIV | Master of Divinity |
| EMSM | Executive Master of Science in Management | ME | Master of Engineering |
| | | MECOM | Master of Electronic Commerce |
| EMSMOT | Executive Master of Science in Management of Technology | MEd | Master of Educational Leadership/ Master of Education |
| EMST | Executive Master of Science in Taxation | MEM | Master of Engineering and Management |
| GDPA | Graduate Diploma in Accounting | MEng | Master of Engineering |
| GEMBA | Global Executive Master of Business Administration | MF | Master of Forestry |
| | | MFA | Master of Fine Arts |
| HRIM | Hotel, Restaurants and Institutional Management | MHA | Master of Health Administration |
| | | MHR | Master of Human Resources |
| IAMBA | Information Age Master of Business Administration | MHRM | Master of Human Resources Management |

| | | | |
|---|---|---|---|
| MIA | Master of International Affairs | MSG | Master of Science in Gerontology |
| MIAS | Master of International and Area Studies | MSGFA | Master of Science in Global Financial Analysis |
| MIB | Master of International Business | MSHA | Master of Science in Health Administration |
| MIE | Master of Industrial Engineering | MSHFID | Master of Science in Human Factors in Information Design |
| MILR | Master of Industrial and Labor Relations | MSIAM | Master of Science in Information Age Marketing |
| MIM | Master of International Management | | |
| MIS | Management Information Systems | MSIB | Master of Science in International Business |
| MISM | Master of Information Systems Management | MSIE | Master of Science in Industrial Engineering |
| MLAS | Master of Liberal Arts and Science | MSIM | Master of Science in Industrial Management |
| MMIS | Master of Management Information Systems | MSIMC | Master of Science in Integrated Marketing Communications |
| MMR | Master of Marketing Research | MSIR | Master of Science in Industrial Relations |
| MMS | Master of Management Science | MSIS | Master of Science in Information Systems |
| MNO | Master of Nonprofit Organizations | MSISE | Master of Science in Industrial and Systems Engineering |
| MOD | Master of Science in Organizational Development | MSISM | Master of Science in Information Systems Management |
| MPA | Master of Public Administration | | |
| MPAcc | Master of Professional Accounting | MSIT | Master of Science in Information Technology |
| MPH | Master of Public Health | MSITM | Master of Science in Information Technology Management |
| MPIA | Master of Public and International Affairs | | |
| MPL | Master of Planning | MSM | Master of Science in Management |
| MPP | Master of Public Policy | MSMIS | Master of Science in Management Information Systems |
| MRED | Master of Real Estate Development | MSMOT | Master of Science in Management of Technology |
| MS | Master of Science | | |
| MSA | Master of Science in Accountancy (or Accounting) | MSN | Master of Science in Nursing |
| MSAIS | Master of Science in Accounting Information Systems | MSOD | Master of Science in Organization Development |
| MSAT | Master of Science in Accountancy, Taxation | MSpAd | Master of Sports Administration |
| MSB | Master of Science in Business | MSRE | Master of Science in Real Estate |
| MSBA | Master of Science in Business Administration | MSS | Master of Social Science |
| MSE | Master of Science in Engineering | MSSA | Master of Science in Social Administration |
| MSEC | Master of Science in Electronic Commerce | MST | Master of Science in Taxation |
| | | MSTM | Master of Science in Telecommunications Management |
| MSF | Master of Science in Finance | MSW | Master of Social Work |
| MSFA | Master of Science in Financial Analysis | MTAX | Master of Taxation |
| MSFS | Master of Science in Foreign Services | | |

| | |
|---|---|
| MTLM | Master of Transportation and Logistics Management |
| NEMBA | National Executive Master of Business Administration |
| PharmD | Doctor of Pharmacy |
| PhD | Doctor of Philosophy |
| SM | Master of Science |
| TSM | Telecommunications Systems Management |
| VMD | Doctor of Veterinary Medicine |

# INDEX

# ALPHABETICAL LIST OF SCHOOLS

# S

# T

## V

# W

# X

# Y

# ABOUT THE AUTHOR

Nedda Gilbert is a graduate of the University of Pennsylvania and holds a master's degree from Columbia University. She has worked for The Princeton Review since 1985. In 1987, she created The Princeton Review corporate test preparation service, which provides Wall Street firms and premier companies tailored educational programs for their employees. She currently resides in New Jersey.

# NOTES

# NOTES

# NOTES

# NOTES

# NOTES

# NOTES